Stages of the Path *and the* Oral Transmission

The Library of Tibetan Classics is a special series being developed by the Institute of Tibetan Classics aimed at making key classical Tibetan texts part of the global literary and intellectual heritage. Eventually comprising thirty-two large volumes, the collection will contain over two hundred distinct texts by more than a hundred of the best-known authors. These texts have been selected in consultation with the preeminent lineage holders of all the schools and other senior Tibetan scholars to represent the Tibetan literary tradition as a whole. The works included in the series span more than a millennium and cover the vast expanse of classical Tibetan knowledge—from the core teachings of the specific schools to such diverse fields as ethics, philosophy, linguistics, medicine, astronomy and astrology, folklore, and historiography.

Stages of the Path and the Oral Transmission: Selected Teachings of the Geluk School

This volume contains works from two of the most important sets of teachings of the Geluk school, the stages of the path (*lam rim*) and the teachings of the oral transmission (*snyan brgyud*), especially the teachings on mahāmudrā. The stages of the path present a systematic, step-by-step cultivation of the Buddhist path to enlightenment using key elements distilled from the scriptures and Indian treatises. Following Tsongkhapa's (1357–1419) composition of his magnum opus, the *Great Treatise of the Stages of the Path to Enlightenment*, the stages of the path became an integral component of the teachings of the Geluk school. The teachings of the oral transmission originate in important oral instructions of Tsongkhapa, especially those that evolved from his visions of Mañjuśrī.

The present volume is divided into four parts. Part 1 contains some of the central texts of the stages of the path instructions, such as the two root verses by Tsongkhapa, Gomchen Ngawang Drakpa's (fifteenth century) extensive stages of the path in verse, Panchen Losang Chökyi Gyaltsen's (1570–1662) *Easy Path*, and the Fifth Dalai Lama's (1617–82) *Words of Mañjuśrī*. Part 2 features the Seventh Dalai Lama's guide to the *Hundreds of Gods of Tuṣita Guru Yoga*, Panchen Losang Chökyi Gyaltsen's *Offering to the Guru*, and Gyalrong Tsultrim Nyima's (nineteenth century) *Letter of Final Testament Sent upon the Wind*. Part 3 contains Panchen Losang Chökyi Gyaltsen's mahāmudrā root text together with its commentary and important texts by Yongzin Yeshé Gyaltsen (1713–93) and Shar Kalden Gyatso (1607–77). The final part presents two concise works of essential oral teaching from Ngulchu Dharmabhadra (1772–1851).

The works in this volume were selected in consultation with the late His Eminence Khensur Lati Rinpoché.

THE LIBRARY OF TIBETAN CLASSICS • VOLUME 6

Thupten Jinpa, General Editor

Stages of the Path *and the* Oral Transmission

Selected Teachings of the Geluk School

Translated by Thupten Jinpa
and Rosemary Patton with Dagpo Rinpoché

Wisdom

in association with the Institute of Tibetan Classics

Wisdom Publications, Inc.
199 Elm Street
Somerville MA 02144 USA
wisdomexperience.org

Library of Congress Cataloging-in-Publication Data
Names: Thupten Jinpa, translator. | Patton, Rosemary, translator. | Dagpo Rimpoché, translator.
Title: Stages of the path and the oral transmission: selected teachings of the Geluk School / translated by Thupten Jinpa, and Rosemary Patton with Dagpo Rinpoche.
Description: Somerville, MA: Wisdom Publications, [2021] | Series: Library of Tibetan classics; volume 6 | Includes bibliographical references and index.
Identifiers: LCCN 2021054611 (print) | LCCN 2021054612 (ebook) | ISBN 9780861714452 (hardcover) | ISBN 9781614297741 (ebook)
Subjects: LCSH: Lam-rim. | Dge-lugs-pa (Sect)—Doctrines. | Mahāmudrā (Tantric rite)
Classification: LCC BQ7645.L35 S84 2022 (print) | LCC BQ7645.L35 (ebook) | DDC 294.3/44—dc23/eng/20220706
LC record available at https://lccn.loc.gov/2021054611
LC ebook record available at https://lccn.loc.gov/2021054612

ISBN 978-0-86171-445-2 ebook ISBN 978-1-61429-774-1

26 25 24 23 22
5 4 3 2 1

Cover and interior design by Gopa & Ted2, Inc.

Printed on acid-free paper that meets the guidelines for permanence and durability of the Production Guidelines for Book Longevity of the Council on Library Resources.

Printed in Canada.

Message from the Dalai Lama

THE LAST TWO MILLENNIA witnessed a tremendous proliferation of cultural and literary development in Tibet, the Land of Snows. Moreover, owing to the inestimable contributions made by Tibet's early spiritual kings, numerous Tibetan translators, and many great Indian paṇḍitas over a period of so many centuries, the teachings of the Buddha and the scholastic tradition of ancient India's Nālandā monastic university became firmly rooted in Tibet. As evidenced from the historical writings, this flowering of Buddhist tradition in the country brought about the fulfillment of the deep spiritual aspirations of countless sentient beings. In particular, it contributed to the inner peace and tranquility of the peoples of Tibet, Outer Mongolia—a country historically suffused with Tibetan Buddhism and its culture—the Tuva and Kalmuk regions in present-day Russia, the outer regions of mainland China, and the entire trans-Himalayan areas on the southern side, including Bhutan, Sikkim, Ladakh, Kinnaur, and Spiti. Today this tradition of Buddhism has the potential to make significant contributions to the welfare of the entire human family. I have no doubt that, when combined with the methods and insights of modern science, the Tibetan Buddhist cultural heritage and knowledge will help foster a more enlightened and compassionate human society, a humanity that is at peace with itself, with fellow sentient beings, and with the natural world at large.

It is for this reason I am delighted that the Institute of Tibetan Classics in Montreal, Canada, is compiling a thirty-two-volume series containing the works of many great Tibetan teachers, philosophers, scholars, and practitioners representing all major Tibetan schools and traditions. These important writings will be critically edited and annotated and will then be published in modern book format in a reference collection called *The Library of Tibetan Classics*, with the translations into other major languages to follow later. While expressing my heartfelt commendation for this noble project, I pray and hope that *The Library of Tibetan Classics* will not only make these important Tibetan treatises accessible to scholars of Tibetan studies but will also create a new opportunity for younger Tibetans to study and take interest in their own rich and profound culture. It is my sincere hope that through the series' translations into other languages, millions of fellow citizens of the wider human family will also be able to share in the joy of engaging with Tibet's classical literary heritage, textual riches that have been such a great source of joy and inspiration to me personally for so long.

The Dalai Lama
The Buddhist monk Tenzin Gyatso

Special Acknowledgments

THE INSTITUTE OF TIBETAN CLASSICS expresses its deep gratitude to the Ing Foundation for its generous support of the entire cost of translating this important volume. The Ing Foundation's long-standing patronage of the Institute of Tibetan Classics has enabled the institute to support the translation of multiple volumes from *The Library of Tibetan Classics*.

The Ing Foundation would like to dedicate this volume to His Holiness the Fourteenth Dalai Lama. May His Holiness's life be long, and may all his noble wishes be fulfilled.

Publisher's Acknowledgment

THE PUBLISHER WISHES TO extend a heartfelt thanks to the following people who have contributed substantially to the publication of *The Library of Tibetan Classics*:

Pat Gruber and the Patricia and Peter Gruber Foundation
The Hershey Family Foundation
The Ing Foundation

We also extend deep appreciation to our other subscribing benefactors:

Anonymous, dedicated to Buddhas within
Anonymous, in honor of Dzongsar Khyentse Rinpoche
Anonymous, in honor of Geshe Tenzin Dorje
Anonymous, in memory of K. J. Manel De Silva—may she realize the truth
Dr. Patrick Bangert
Nilda Venegas Bernal
Serje Samlo Khentul Lhundub Choden and his Dharma friends
Nicholas Cope
Kushok Lobsang Dhamchöe
Diep Thi Thoai
Tenzin Dorjee
Richard Farris
Gaden Samten Ling, Canada
Evgeniy Gavrilov & Tatiana Fotina
Petar Gesovic
Great Vow Zen Monastery
Ginger Gregory
the Grohmann family, Taiwan
Gyaltsen Lobsang Jamyang (WeiJie) and Pema Looi
Rick Meeker Hayman
Steven D. Hearst
Jana & Mahi Hummel
Curt and Alice Jones
Julie LaValle Jones
Heidi Kaiter
Paul, Trisha, Rachel, and Daniel Kane
Land of Medicine Buddha
Dennis Leksander
Diane & Joseph Lucas
Elizabeth Mettling

Russ Miyashiro
Kestrel Montague
the Nalanda Institute, Olympia, WA
Craig T. Neyman
Kristin A. Ohlson
Arnold Possick
Magdalene Camilla Frank Prest
Quek Heng Bee, Ong Siok Ngow, and family
Randall-Gonzales Family Foundation
Erick Rinner
Andrew Rittenour
Dombon Roig Family
Jonathan and Diana Rose
the Sharchitsang family
Nirbhay N. Singh
Wee Kee Tan
Tibetisches Zentrum e.V. Hamburg
Richard Toft
Alissa KieuNgoc Tran
Timothy Trompeter
Tsadra Foundation
the Vahagn Setian Charitable Foundation
Ellyse Adele Vitiello
Jampa (Alicia H.) Vogel
Nicholas C. Weeks II
Mr. and Mrs. Richard and Carol Weingarten
Claudia Wellnitz
Bob White
Kevin Michael White, MD
Eve and Jeff Wild

and the other donors who wish to remain anonymous.

Contents

Foreword *by His Eminence Ganden Tri Rinpoche* xv

Preface xvii

Introduction 1

Technical Note 39

PART 1: THE STAGES OF THE PATH

1. A Song of Spiritual Experience: Essential Points of the Stages of the Path
Tsongkhapa Losang Drakpa 43

2. Three Principal Elements of the Path
Tsongkhapa Losang Drakpa 51

3. Essence of All Excellent Discourses: Well Ascertaining the Way to Practice Taught in the Stages of the Path to Enlightenment
Gomchen Ngawang Drakpa
Translated by Rosemary Patton with Dagpo Rinpoché 55

4. An Easy Path: A Direct Guide to the Stages of the Path to Enlightenment
Panchen Losang Chökyi Gyaltsen 155

5. Words of Mañjuśrī: A Guide to the Stages of the Path
The Fifth Dalai Lama Ngawang Losang Gyatso
Translated by Rosemary Patton with Dagpo Rinpoché 207

PART 2: GURU YOGA

6. Source of All Siddhis: A Guide to the "Hundreds of Gods of Tuṣita" Guru Yoga
The Seventh Dalai Lama Kalsang Gyatso 385

7. Offering to the Guru
Panchen Losang Chökyi Gyaltsen 411

8. A Letter of Final Testament Sent upon the Wind: A Guide to Mahāmudrā Combined with the Uncommon Guru Yoga of the Ensa Oral Transmission Endowed with Pith Instructions and Oral Teachings
Gyalrong Tsultrim Nyima 431

PART 3: GELUK MAHĀMUDRĀ AND GUIDE TO THE VIEW

9. Highway of the Conquerors: Mahāmudrā Root Text According to the Precious Geden Lineage
Panchen Losang Chökyi Gyaltsen 617

10. Prayer to the Lineage Gurus of Geden Mahāmudrā
Panchen Losang Chökyi Gyaltsen 627

11. A Lamp So Bright: An Extensive Explanation of the Root Text of Mahāmudrā of the Tradition of the Precious Geden Lineage
Panchen Losang Chökyi Gyaltsen 637

12. An Experiential Guide to Mahāmudrā of the Sacred Geden Lineage
Shar Kalden Gyatso 691

13. Source of All Higher Attainments: A Very Secret Short Work Revealing Key Points of the View
Yongzin Yeshé Gyaltsen 707

PART 4: THE THREE ESSENTIAL POINTS

14. Sacred Words of the Great Siddha: A Condensed Practice of the Three Essential Points
Ngulchu Dharmabhadra 717

Foreword

His Eminence Ganden Tri Rinpoche

The Library of Tibetan Classics (*Bod kyi tsug lag gces btus*) series is a singular collection featuring unique instructions of all the major Tibetan spiritual traditions and their shared Mahayana heritage, especially the bodhisattva ideal and the Vajrayana. The collection spans the domains of classical Tibetan knowledge—Buddhist philosophy, logic and epistemology, Abhidharma psychology, and ethics, as well as grammar, linguistics, poetics, medicine, astro-sciences, history, and the performing arts. This comprehensive library of thirty-two volumes of key Tibetan texts has been developed by Thupten Jinpa, the longtime principal English translator to His Holiness the Dalai Lama. Many of the original Tibetan volumes feature introductory essays by Dr. Jinpa, who is versed not only in both sutra and tantra but in the full spectrum of Tibetan literature, and these essays have become invaluable resources for students and scholars of classical Tibetan texts.

To date, English translations of sixteen volumes from the series have been published, including Dr. Jinpa's own translations *Mind Training: The Great Collection*, *The Book of Kadam*, and *Illuminating the Intent* by the illustrious Tsongkhapa. By creating this special series, and by widely disseminating the texts featured in the series to an international readership through high-quality translations, Dr. Jinpa has set a clear standard for the preservation and revitalization of classical Tibetan knowledge and traditions, and through this he has made a lasting contribution to the long-term continuity of the Buddha's doctrine, which is a source of benefit and happiness for all beings. So I take this opportunity to express my admiration for Dr. Jinpa and for the practical contributions he has made, and it gives me great pleasure to write a foreword for this volume in particular.

For his translations in the present volume, Dr. Jinpa's rich introduction provides illuminating background for seminal works of the Geluk school. Featured here are instructions on the *lamrim*, or stages of the path, guru yoga, Geluk mahāmudrā, guide to the view, and the three essential points. With respect to stages of the path, the master Dromtönpa said:

> The wondrous sacred words are the three baskets of scripture,
> which are enriched by the instruction on the path of the three capacities.
> This precious Kadam tradition is a golden rosary,
> and whoever tells its beads makes their lives meaningful.

The precious Kadam tradition was initiated by the master Atiśa, established by the precious Dromtönpa, disseminated by the three Kadam brothers, and spread widely by Langri Thangpa, Sharawa, and Jayulwa. Later, Guru Mañjuśrī—the great Tsongkhapa—composed his extensive, intermediate, and short treatises on the stages of the path to enlightenment. Keeping in mind especially those of more modest intellect, Jé Tsongkhapa has said in his *Great Treatise*, "Since those who know how to put everything that is taught into practice seem barely to exist, one should also offer practical instructions in condensed form." Based on this advice texts such as the Fifth Dalai Lama's *Words of Mañjuśrī* and Dakpo Gomchen's *Essence of All Excellent Discourses* came to be composed, both featured in this volume. With respect to the unique features of this instruction on the stages of the path, Jé Tsongkhapa states:

> This concise instruction that distills the essence of all scriptures—
> through reciting it or listening to it for even a single session,
> you will definitely receive powerful waves of merit of
> teaching and hearing the Dharma; so contemplate its meaning.

If, as stated above, reciting or listening to even a single discourse on the stages of the path based on embracing guru yoga as the life force of one's personal practice brings such extensive benefit, what need is there to speak of disseminating this instruction through translation into English, a language spoken across the world today.

This translation has been made possible through the power of past aspirational prayers, and the volume will surely become a vital educational and spiritual resource for many people and regions of the world where the precious Buddhadharma has not historically been part of their spiritual heritage. I express my deep gratitude to everyone whose efforts have made the publication of this volume possible. May it be a source of benefit to the flourishing of the Buddha's doctrine and the welfare of all beings.

Lobsang Tenzin
The 104th Ganden Tripa

Preface

It is a profound source of joy for me to be able to offer in English this special anthology of teachings of the Geluk school of Tibetan Buddhism, founded near Lhasa by the celebrated master Tsongkhapa in the early fifteenth century. This volume, number 6 in *The Library of Tibetan Classics*, contains fifteen texts on four key areas of practice: (1) the *lamrim*, or stages of the path, based on instructions of the masters Atiśa and Tsongkhapa, (2) *guru yoga* based on Tsongkhapa's oral transmissions, (3) *mahāmudra* and *guide to the view*, drawn on and inspired by Tsongkhapa's oral teachings, and (4) the *three essential points*, stemming from a unique instruction of the Indian mystic Mitrayogi.

Beginning with two short works in verse by Tsongkhapa himself, the texts in this volume enjoy deep affection by members of this Tibetan tradition, and some of them are published here for the first time in English translation. These texts serve as important guides for fundamental spiritual transformation, from the initial stage of turning one's mind to the Dharma up to the liberating stage of gaining insight into the ultimate nature of reality. Whether it is cultivating deep appreciation of the transient nature of life, overcoming attachment to objects of senses, experiencing deep devotional fusion of one's mind with that of the guru and meditation deity, developing universal compassion and the altruistic mind intent on enlightenment for the benefit of all beings, cultivating stillness of mind in the form of tranquil abiding, generating insight into no-self and emptiness, or actualizing mind's essential nature in the form of pure luminosity, this volume offers a truly rich resource. Most Geluk practitioners today use the two guru-yoga texts featured in this volume, Dulnakpa's *Hundreds of Gods of Tuṣita* and Panchen Losang Chögyen's *Offering to the Guru*, as essential parts of their daily practice. Panchen's text in particular is used by many, myself included, as an all-encompassing daily meditation manual covering the entire domain of Dharma practice, including even a daily dose of mind training, or *lojong*.

I wish foremost to express my deep personal gratitude to His Holiness the Dalai Lama for consistently being such a profound inspiration and an exemplary embodiment of the best of the Tibetan tradition, including that of Tsongkhapa. It is from His Holiness and his two tutors—Kyabjé Ling Rinpoché and Kyabjé Trijang Rinpoché—that I received the transmissions of Geluk lamrim, the two guru yogas, and Geluk mahāmudra. I also acknowledge Kyabjé Zong Rinpoché, from whom I received the transmission of Ngulchu's manual on Mitrayogi's instruction on the three essential points, and my own personal teacher at Ganden Monastery, Kyabjé Zemey Rinpoché, at whose feet I studied for eleven years, receiving from him also numerous practice transmissions.

I thank Rosemary Patton and her teacher Dagpo Rinpoché for translating for this volume Gomchen Ngawang Drakpa's *Essence of All Excellent Discourses* and the Fifth Dalai Lama's *Words of Mañjuśrī*. The care and devotion that they brought to their engagement with the two texts is evident from the clear and accurate translations they have produced. To the following individuals and organizations, I owe my sincere thanks: to David Kittelstrom at Wisdom for his incisive editing; to my fellow Tibetan editor Geshé Lobsang Choedar for assisting me sourcing all citations; to the Buddhist Digital Resource Center for providing me access to its immense digital library of Tibetan texts, without which I can't imagine how I could have penned my lengthy introduction to this volume; and to my wife Sophie Boyer-Langri for taking on the numerous administrative chores that are part of a collaborative project such as this.

Finally, for its long-term patronage of the Institute of Tibetan Classics, I would like to express my deep gratitude to the Ing Foundation, whose generosity made this volume possible.

May the experience of engaging with these precious Tibetan texts be meaningful and transformational to all readers, as it has been for so many Tibetans over centuries.

Thupten Jinpa
Montreal, 2022

Introduction

THE GELUK SCHOOL of Tibetan Buddhism emerged from the teachings of the great fourteenth-century Tibetan master Jé Tsongkhapa (1357–1419), arguably the most influential figure in the history of Tibetan Buddhism. *Geluk* literally means "the Geden tradition" and derives its name from Geden (or Ganden) Monastery, founded by Tsongkhapa in 1409 on Wangkur Mountain, which lies toward the east of the holy city of Lhasa and offers, from its summit, a spectacular view of the wide Lhasa valley. Ever since the founding of Ganden on the slopes of this mountain, the mountain itself came to be known also as Geden Mountain and Tsongkhapa's followers "those of Geden Mountain" (Riwo Gedenpa).

Tsongkhapa appeared at a watershed moment in the history of Buddhism in Tibet. The long process of translating the canons of Indian Buddhism—the sutras, tantras, and commentarial treatises—was largely complete after several centuries of painstaking labor by generations of Tibetan translators often working in partnership with Indian pandits. By then, the entire Tibetan heritage of Indian Buddhist texts had been compiled into the two canonical collections, the Kangyur (translations of scriptures) and Tengyur (translations of treatises), with Butön Rinchen Drup (1290–1364) having prepared what became the standard classification system for these texts. It was therefore a time when Tibetans could read, digest, and reflect upon these vast canons in their entirety. Tsongkhapa was among the first of the Tibetan masters to do this. Through deep engagement with these Indian texts—which included even a four-year reading retreat at Tsal Gungthang Monastery, where the full sets of the Kangyur finalized by Butön were housed—extensive meditative cultivation, prolonged periods of critical reflection on personal understanding, and profound meditative experience, as well as mystical visionary encounters with the meditation deity Mañjuśrī, Tsongkhapa came to synthesize the vast Indian Buddhist heritage into a unique and remarkable system of Buddhist thought and practice. In a collection of works running into nineteen large volumes, Tsongkhapa shared his vision of this new synthesis.

Briefly, Tsongkhapa's synthesis involved creating a coherent integrated system based on taking the best from existing Tibetan traditions as well as the best from the Indian Buddhist sources themselves. Within this synthesis, fidelity to basic norms of morality, cultivation of the bodhisattva's universal compassion and its altruistic ideals, the profound view of emptiness, and deep nondual meditative experience of the Vajrayāna path of innate bliss are all envisioned to reside seamlessly within the mind of a single practitioner. Before his passing in 1419, and especially after the founding of Ganden Monastery in 1409, Tsongkhapa's students came to identify themselves as members of the master's unique system, referred to as "the sacred tradition of Jé Tsongkhapa,"[1] with Ganden as its "mother monastery." By the time Tsongkhapa passed away, the master had left an indelible legacy, with a vast body of writing on every topic of Buddhist thought and practice, as well as a spectrum of students—from erudite scholars to altruistic bodhisattvas, from prolific authors to hermits and mystics, from ordinary monks to high abbots of monasteries, and from simple nomads to ruling elite, including none other than Miwang himself, the king of central and western Tibet.[2] So deeply revered was Tsongkhapa that he came to be referred to, especially by his devout followers, with such elevated epithets as "Mañjuśrī Lord and Second Buddha Tsongkhapa the Great," "Great Tsongkhapa, the Second Buddha from the East," "Great Tsongkhapa, the Dharma King of the Three Realms," "Supreme Master Tsongkhapa," and simply "Supreme Guru."[3] In fact, after the master's passing in 1419, Tsongkhapa increasingly came to be deified to the point of being turned, as we will see below, into a transhistorical figure that could be an object of devotion, a focus of daily guru-yoga meditation, and a presence in mystical visionary experience.[4]

From a broader Tibetan Buddhist historical perspective, Tsongkhapa is recognized especially for his key contributions in the following areas. First and foremost is his original contribution to Madhyamaka philosophy in Tibet, especially through his extensive writing on the subject. Second, his two great syntheses—one on the Sutra Vehicle and the other on the Tantra Vehicle, known respectively as the *Great Treatise on the Stages of the Path* and the *Great Treatise on Mantra*—are admired for their masterful and structured presentation of the entire Buddhist path. Third, more specifically in relation to tantra, Tsongkhapa is revered for (1) his extensive expositions of the Guhyasamāja tantra, drawing particularly on the lineages of two important Tibetan translators of the tantra, Gö Lotsāwa Khukpa Lhetsé (eleventh century) and Marpa Lotsāwa (1012–1100),[5] (2) his authoritative works on the Cakrasaṃvara tantra, especially of the traditions of Indian mystics Lūipa, Kṛṣṇācārya, and Ghaṇṭāpa, (3) his systematic writings on the Yamāntaka family of tantras, especially Vajrabhairava, and (4) his influential exposition of the uniqueness of the Kālacakra tantra. Fourth, Tsongkhapa is universally accredited with the spread of monastic tradition rooted in strict adherence to Vinaya discipline across the Tibetan cultural sphere. Highlighting some of these key aspects of Tsongkhapa's contribution, the Eighth Karmapa Mikyö Dorjé (1507–54) calls Tsongkhapa "the reformer of Buddha's doctrine," "the great trailblazer of Madhyamaka philosophy in Tibet," "supreme among those who propound emptiness," and "one who helped spread robed monastics across Tibet and from China to Kashmir."[6]

Many of Tsongkhapa's immediate disciples brought the master's new tradition to different parts of the Tibetan plateau. From western Tibetan regions to the eastern and northeastern part of Tibet in Kham and Amdo, from central Tibet to the southern and southeastern regions of Ölkha and Dakpo valleys, Tsongkhapa's disciples founded new monasteries, converted older ones to the new tradition, and established hermitages for those aspiring to dedicate their entire life in hermit-style practice. By the end of the fifteenth century, the new tradition had become widespread across the entire Tibetan plateau. In particular, in Ganden, Drepung, and Sera (the latter two founded, respectively, by Jamyang Chöjé in 1416 and Jamchen Chöjé in 1419), the tradition produced three of the largest monasteries in the history of the world. Collectively known as "the three great centers of learning" (Densa Chenpo Sum), these mega monasteries served as major scholastic universities providing formal advanced study of "five disciplines"—Logic and Epistemology, Perfection of Wisdom studies, Madhyamaka philosophy, Abhidharma, and Vinaya. To this list of great centers of learning would be added Chamdo Jampa Ling in Kham (founded by Sherab Sangpo in 1437), Tashi Lhunpo in Tsang (founded by the First Dalai Lama in 1447), and Labrang Tashi Khyil in Amdo (founded by Jamyang Shepa in 1709).

An important pedagogical method embraced in these monastic universities was the Tibetan tradition of dialectical debate instituted by the famed logician Chapa Chökyi Sengé (1109–69). This emphasis on debate as a key medium gave rise to a vibrant intellectual culture of debate as well as the creation of formal curricula and textbooks (*yig cha*), with those by Jetsun Chökyi Gyaltsen (1469–1544/46), Panchen Sönam Drakpa (1478–1554),

Khedrup Tenpa Dargyé (1493–1568), and Jamyang Shepa (1648–1722) adopted as official textbooks by the main monastic colleges. These great monastic universities attracted students from the entire Tibetan plateau as well as from Mongol regions of Inner Asia and the trans-Himalayan Buddhist regions of Bhutan, Nepal, and India. Over time, the formal mastery of the five disciplines came to be officially recognized with the title of *geshé lharampa,* conferred at the end of a public examination in the form of a series of debates held at the annual Great Prayer Festival in the Jokhang Temple in Lhasa.

With formalization of the reincarnation systems of the Dalai Lamas and Panchen Lamas, the Geluk tradition also produced the two most well-known lama institutions of Tibetan Buddhism, revered across the Tibetan Buddhist cultural sphere. In particular, following the Fifth Dalai Lama's assumption of political leadership in 1642, the Geluk effectively became Tibet's state church, and the Dalai Lama's rule lasted until the historic tragedy that struck the Tibetan nation in the mid-twentieth century.

Beyond the Tibetan plateau, thanks to two of Tsongkhapa's disciples—Jamchen Chöjé and Jang Dharma—the Geluk had already reached mainland China during Tsongkhapa's own life, becoming an important presence at the Chinese imperial court. This connection with the Chinese imperial family was renewed during the life of the Fifth Dalai Lama, following his visit to Beijing in 1652, with the strongest connection emerging during the Qing dynasty with China's Manchu rulers. A key figure in dissemination of the Geluk at the Qing court was the famed master Changkya Rölpai Dorjé (1717–86), who had a close personal relationship with the Qianlong emperor and made Mount Wutai his winter retreat for nearly two decades.

Thanks to the Third Dalai Lama Sönam Gyatso's (1543–88) meeting with the powerful Mongol chieftain Altan Khan in 1578—the latter bestowed the title Dalai Lama on Sönam Gyatso—Tsongkhapa's tradition began to spread widely in the Mongol regions, eventually becoming the dominant Buddhist tradition there, with the emergence of major monasteries, such as Balden Beeyen Monastery (established 1654) and Ganden Monastery (founded in 1838), and great Buddhist scholars, like Khalkha Dzaya Paṇḍita (1642–1715), Ngawang Palden (1797–1864), and Losang Tamdrin (1867–1937).[7]

This volume features a special selection of texts from the Geluk tradition, structured around four important genres: (1) the stages of the path (*lam rim*) teachings, (2) the practice of guru yoga, (3) Geden (or Geluk) mahāmudrā and guide to the view instruction, and (4) the "three essential points" instruction, the latter stemming from the Indian mystic Mitrayogi (twelfth century). Of these, the teachings in the second and third categories belong to what is known as the Geluk oral transmission. The following considerations have guided my choice of these four genres to represent the core teachings of the Geluk school specifically in this volume: (1) All four represent important practice lineages within the Geluk tradition, with the stages of the path considered a defining feature of the tradition's approach, and guru yoga and Geden mahāmudrā representing its tradition of oral transmission. (2) These instructions tend to be among those most widely taught in the tradition. And (3) being practice lineages, the texts belonging to these four genres are designed as practice manuals. Of course, as I am the editor of the volume, the selection also reflects my own personal practice.

The Stages of the Path

The genre of *lamrim*, or stages of the path, traces its origin to the Indian Bengali master Atiśa (980–1054), who spent the final years of his life in Tibet and, more specifically, to a short text he composed at the express wish of the ruler of the Ngari region of western Tibet, Jangchup Ö. The ruler requested a teaching that would be comprehensive, easy to engage, and impactful on the practitioner's mind. In response, Atiśa composed his famed *Lamp on the Path to Enlightenment.*[8] The genius of this text lies in correlating specific elements of the Buddhist teaching as key methods for "three types of persons" to attain three distinct levels of spiritual goals.[9] The levels of the three types of persons relate not to differences of intellect or mental acumen but to the scope of their spiritual goals. The goal of those of "lesser capacity" is to continue to enjoy happiness within cyclic existence, especially by obtaining a favorable rebirth. The primary goal of those of "intermediate capacity" is freedom from cyclic existence. Finally, the goal of the persons of "great capacity" is the cessation of suffering not just of oneself alone but of all sentient beings. These goals in turn propel the specific practices. Atiśa concluded the text with a brief section on tantra, and he later composed a lengthy commentary on his own verses.

Atiśa's *Lamp* gave rise to an extensive literature on the stages of the path, first in the Kadam school and later in the Geluk. Sometimes this genre is divided into two subclasses, with the name *lamrim* reserved for the more "practice-oriented" teachings, while texts that were "more presentation-oriented" were referred to as the *stages of the doctrine* (*bstan rim*).[10] The

Kadam master Potowa's (1027–1105) *Blue Compendium* is a typical example of the first category, while Drolungpa's (eleventh century) *Great Treatise on the Stages of Doctrine* is a well-known example of the second.[11] These subsequent elaborations introduced crucial preliminary components to Atiśa's *Lamp*, aimed at establishing a stable foundation to one's practice. These includes the topics of (1) proper reliance on a spiritual teacher as the foundation to one's practice, (2) contemplation of the preciousness of human existence so that one seizes the rare opportunity it accords to practice Dharma, and (3) contemplation of death and impermanence to bring an urgency to one's spiritual pursuit.

Tsongkhapa was deeply taken by the elegance and comprehensiveness of Atiśa's *Lamp*.[12] Not only did he see in this framework a complete map of the entire path to enlightenment, but he also more importantly found in it a unique way to bring all key elements of the Buddhist teachings into a single integrated path, leading from the initial stage of turning one's mind to the Dharma up to the attainment of full awakening of buddhahood. Thus, instead of viewing the framework primarily as presenting the paths of three different types of persons, Tsongkhapa understood it as presenting a graduated course to enlightenment from the perspective of a single practitioner whose ultimate aim is to attain buddhahood for the sake of all beings. On this understanding, the practices associated with the first two levels essentially become preliminaries for the practitioner whose aim is buddhahood. To underline this point, Tsongkhapa refers to the practices of the first two levels as "training the mind in the stages of the path *shared with* persons of lesser capacity" and "*shared with* persons of intermediate capacity." Tsongkhapa thus uses Atiśa's framework to underline the crucial importance of embracing a path that is nonerroneous, comprehensive in scope, and well structured in its sequence, with instructions on all key elements presented and with buddhahood as the ultimate aim. He invokes the analogy of how, in the context of successful treatment of an illness, simply having the right kind of medicine is not enough. It must also be comprehensive in its efficacy against the given illness, and it must be administered at the right time.[13] In speaking of the significance of the three persons' framework, Tsongkhapa writes:

> There are two great benefits for guiding [trainees] by differentiating [the path] in terms of the three types of persons: it counters the arrogance of thinking one is a person of highest capacity even though the paths shared with the initial and intermediate capac-

> ities have not yet arisen; and it is most helpful to all—those of advanced, intermediate, and lesser mentalities.[14]

Briefly, here is the psychology behind Tsongkhapa's use of Atiśa's framework as a graduated training for a single person. As beings in samsara, our mind is deluded by ignorance at a fundamental level—by our instinctual tendency to grasp at things, including our own existence, based on an assumption of objective intrinsic existence. This very basic tendency manifests in various ways, giving rise to distorted perceptions of our own existence and reality and to habitual attachment, aversion, anger, jealousy, and so on. The imprints of such conditioning are so deep that only a systematic and methodical "deconditioning" could lead us to true freedom. Such a systematic approach begins with turning our mind away from attachment to the world and turning it toward a higher spiritual pursuit. Having turned our mind from the mundane, we need to train our mind through contemplations on, for instance, impermanence, no-self, and emptiness so that our mind can be freed from ignorance and the afflictions it induces. To this end, we need to engage in the threefold training: *morality* to establish a firm foundation in the application of mindfulness and meta-awareness, *concentration* to help refine our attentional capacity so we can focus our mind in a sustained manner, and *wisdom* to deepen our insight into the nature of reality.

In tandem with countering our deeply ingrained grasping, especially at selfhood, we also need to challenge our naïve perceptions and attitudes vis-à-vis self and others. Crucially this entails challenging our assumptions about the boundary between self and other and expanding our empathic concern so that we can genuinely view others' suffering and needs as if they were our own. In other words, as practitioners on the path of enlightenment, we need to cultivate universal compassion—a genuine spontaneous wish to see the suffering of all beings alleviated—to the point that we spontaneously experience *bodhicitta*, a deeply altruistic wish to become a buddha for the sake of all beings. Once such an aspiration has arisen in us, such that it is ever-present and spontaneous, we then enact this intention by engaging in the bodhisattva practices, especially the six perfections. And it is this path of the six perfections, including especially the union of compassion and the wisdom realizing emptiness—the ultimate nature of reality—that leads to full awakening.

Throughout all these stages, especially on the paths of the intermediate and great capacities, the process of engaging in the path entails not just formal sitting meditation but also profound transformation of our very outlook ("mindsets" in contemporary psychology) through insights gained from ascertainment engendered through inquiry. To use scientific language, ascertainment and its continual reinforcement underlie the mechanism by which enduring change takes place in our mind. As such, the Buddhist path to enlightenment, especially as envisioned in Tsongkhapa's lamrim, consists of both a "deconstructive process" of undoing various levels of attachment, grasping, and conditioning and a "constructive process" of cultivating qualities of compassion, altruistic intent, concentration, and wisdom. Even within undoing, the process is not confined to nonengagement, such as stopping certain thoughts; it involves active ascertainment of the truth, which then directly opposes the grasping mind. For example, in the context of selflessness, *we cannot simply suspend grasping at selfhood; we need to actively ascertain the absence of selfhood.*

This said, Tsongkhapa is not saying that everyone must start with the path of the lesser capacity; the point is that the realizations of the advanced levels presuppose that one has gained the realizations of the lower levels. For example, if you have already taken refuge in the Three Jewels and have laid a firm foundation of living a moral life, you can jump straight to the paths shared with the intermediate capacity and focus on such practices as developing genuine renunciation based on contemplation of the general and specific sufferings of cyclic existence. Similarly, if you have already developed genuine renunciation, you can jump directly to the path of the advanced capacity and focus on cultivating universal compassion and the awakening mind. For Tsongkhapa, what is important is that you engage in your practice on the basis of "having an understanding of the overall framework of the Buddha's teaching" and "seeing the entire body of the path."[15] The image here is one of a spiritual traveler embarking on a journey with a clear map of where he is going; Tsongkhapa sees the lamrim framework of the paths of the three types of persons as offering exactly such a map.

Tsongkhapa's most well-known lamrim text is, of course, his *Great Treatise on the Stages of the Path to Enlightenment*.[16] Completed in 1402, the *Great Treatise* is best described as a grand synthesis of the sutra path, written primarily from the perspective of how to bring the essence of the entire path to buddhahood into the practice of a single trainee. Tsongkhapa identifies two key sources for the instructions presented in detail in his *Great Treatise.* He writes, "This instruction [of stages of the path] is, in general, that of the *Ornament of Realizations* composed by the revered Maitreya. In particular, the source text for this work is Atiśa's *Lamp on the Path to Enlightenment*."[17]

The *Great Treatise* is broadly divided into four parts, with a lengthy introductory section that grounds the instruction in Atiśa's *Lamp* and then presents such preliminary topics as the importance of relying on a spiritual teacher and the need to appreciate the rare opportunity afforded by one's human existence. The main part of the work is then divided into the paths of the three types of persons—those of the lesser capacity, intermediate capacity, and advanced capacity. In his *Great Treatise,* Tsongkhapa (1) brings the best of the oral teachings of the Tibetan Kadam tradition founded by Atiśa and his chief Tibetan disciple Dromtönpa, especially in the preliminary section to inspire immersion in Dharma practice, such as through appreciating the value of human existence and contemplation of death; (2) grounds the key practices in the great works of Indian Buddhist masters such as Śāntideva; (3) offers ways to engage with key topics through critical inquiry; and (4) presents clear instructions on how to bring contemplation of the key topics into your personal practice. In essence, Tsongkhapa fused all major transmission lineages of Tibetan lamrim teachings into a single integrated tradition, including composing the official supplication prayers to the lineage masters of the specific transmission strands of lamrim teaching.[18]

In 1415 Tsongkhapa prepared another more practice-oriented version of lamrim that came to be known as the *Middle-Length Treatise on the Stages of the Path.*[19] Later, a short, forty-five verse text he had composed few years earlier, *A Song of Experience* (the first work featured in our volume), came to be referred to as the shortest in a collection of three lamrim texts by Tsongkhapa: the extensive, the middle-length, and the short. In addition, there is his *Three Principal Elements of the Path* (a fourteen-stanza work featured in our volume), which Tsongkhapa composed as a letter to Tsakho Ngawang Drakpa, one of his earliest students. Mention should also be made of three other short lamrim texts by Tsongkhapa: *Foundations of All Excellences* (in thirteen stanzas), *Brief Presentation of the Stages of the Path* (an instruction written at the request of one Könchok Tsultrim), and *A Few Words on the Structure of the Path,* an instruction for one Sherab Sangpo.

Numerous masters within Tsongkhapa's Geluk tradition also composed works on lamrim, including especially producing "guidebooks," structured as step-by-step practical instructions, on how to implement Tsongkhapa's lamrim teachings within the context of a life's practice. The tradition came to revere five such texts in particular, and adding these to Tsongkhapa's extensive, middle-length, and short lamrims, the custom emerged to group these collectively as "the eight great guides on lamrim." Those five are: (1)

Gomchen Ngawang Drakpa's (fifteenth century) *Essence of All Excellent Discourses* (chapter 3 in our volume), (2) Panchen Losang Chökyi Gyaltsen's (1570–1662) *Easy Path* (chapter 4), (3) the Third Dalai Lama's (1543–88) *Essence of Refined Gold,*[20] (4) the Fifth Dalai Lama's (1617–82) *Words of Mañjuśrī* (chapter 5), and (5) Panchen Losang Yeshé's (1663–1737) *Swift Path.*

The first, Gomchen's guide, is composed entirely in verse, and as explicitly stated in its subtitle, a key purpose of the text is to help "ascertain the ways to practice taught in [Tsongkhapa's] *Stages of the Path.*"[21] The text follows the structure of Tsongkhapa's two lengthy lamrim works, especially the *Middle-Length* version, such that the seventeenth-century Geluk master Jamyang Shepa remarked that Gomchen's verse text constitutes a condensed versified version of Tsongkhapa's *Middle-Length Stages of the Path.*[22] Composed in a lucid and fluid verse, the text lends itself to easy memorization, and a custom evolved of serious practitioners memorizing the text so they can chant the specific sections to themselves as they meditate on them. The author is most known as the second abbot of Dakpo Shedrup Ling Monastery, and as his title Gomchen (literally "great meditator") suggests, he came to be revered as a great practitioner who devoted much of his later life to solitary retreat.[23]

The author of our next text, Panchen Losang Chökyi Gyaltsen (known also in its slightly abbreviated form Panchen Losang Chögyen) was a renowned figure in the history of Tibetan Buddhism, well beyond his role as tutor to the Fifth Dalai Lama. A great teacher, practitioner, and author, Panchen had so many remarkable disciples capable of stewarding the vast transmissions of teaching and practice he both inherited as well as engendered, he left a powerful legacy. Recognizing Panchen's enduring contribution, the eighteenth-century author of *Biographies of the Lineage Gurus of Lamrim*, Yongzin Yeshé Gyaltsen writes:

> Therefore, with respect to all aspects of Tsongkhapa's tradition—whether in the domain of sutra or tantra—when it came to upholding and propagating the excellent tradition of precious Jé Tsongkhapa, this master, the most revered Losang Chökyi Gyaltsen, became equivalent to precious Jé Tsongkhapa himself, as if he had appeared once more.[24]

Panchen's *Easy Path* shows how to meditate on specific topics in the lamrim, especially in formal sessions. Its title *Easy Path* (*Bde lam*) is meant to conjure the image of a road that has been engineered to make travel easy.

Written in fluid language, the main substance of the text is the "contents of the specific contemplations"—guided meditations—the author wishes his reader to engage in. To bring out the immediacy of the text's tone and voice, I have cast these contemplations as direct speech. From the text's colophon, it is clear that the work was based on notes taken by a disciple at a teaching Panchen conducted and later edited by the master himself.[25] An important feature of Panchen's *Easy Path* is the explicit tantric elements it brings into lamrim practice. These include viewing the guru as Munīndra Vajradhara and visualizing the descent of nectars and light rays from the guru at specific points of the practice, especially following supplications. According to one source, this unique tantric-flavored lamrim instruction stemmed from an oral teaching Tokden received from Tsongkhapa.[26] Panchen's *Easy Path* gave rise to an entire subgenre of lamrim texts, such as his immediate successor Panchen Losang Yeshé's *Swift Path*, Gungthang Tenpai Drönmé's (1762–1823) *Essence of the Supreme Path: Presentation of All the Meditation Topics of the Easy Path in Verse*, Akhu Sherab Gyatso's (1803–75) *Oral Teachings on the Easy Path*, and Shamar Gendun Tenzin's (1852–1912) *How to Engage in Guided Meditation on the Topics in the Easy Path*.[27]

Our next text is the Fifth Dalai Lama's (1617–82) *Words of Mañjuśrī*. Completed in 1658, the author states that he wrote the text in response to a request from a student, one Jampa Trinlé, who having received guided instruction on the lamrim from the author for a month and half, asked to have the practices written down. The author notes how, apart from a tradition that takes the Third Dalai Lama's *Essence of Refined Gold* as the basis and supplementing it with selected passages from Tsongkhapa's *Great* and the *Middle-Length* treatises, there did not appear to be a step-by-step guidebook on lamrim.[28] This said, he does not appear to view his own *Words* as representing such a step-by-step guide; he sees it rather as a guide that also combines explanations of important sections, especially on the later part, the sections on tranquil abiding and insight. The Fifth Dalai Lama describes his work as "a treatise guiding the reader through the stages of the path to enlightenment."

A notable feature of this text is its distinctive format. The Fifth Dalai Lama opens each topic with a general introduction, then offers a lucid presentation of the topic, followed sometimes with a brief analysis, and ends with a brief conclusion followed by "stanzas between sections" in the style of an interlude, what are called in the Indo-Tibetan tradition *intermediary verses*.[29] These verses summarize the key points of the topic. In addition, the text is powerful in its use of vivid metaphors. The text is also unique in its identification of Jetsun Sherab Sengé, the founder of Segyü and Gyümé, as the source of its particular transmission of Tsongkhapa's lamrim instruction.

I would like to draw special attention to three parts of the text. In the section on generating the awakening mind, the author offers one of the most succinct explanations I have come across of the psychology behind the steps in the traditional Tibetan training in universal compassion and its culmination in the arising of awakening mind. Next, the text's presentation on the six perfections is also a gem on the topic, offering in few pages a clear understanding of each of these perfections. Finally, in the section on the perfection of wisdom, presented within the framework of cultivating insight into emptiness, the author addresses two critical questions: the authenticity or lack thereof of the approach of so-called nonmentation and how to maintain the right balance between discursive analysis and single-pointed resting, or placement, of the mind during formal sitting practice aimed at cultivating insight.[30]

Other notable lamrim texts by Geluk masters include:[31]

1. Chenga Lodrö Gyaltsen's (1402–71) *Summary Outlines of the Stages of the Path* and *Essence of Altruism: A Guide Text on the Stages of the Path*, possibly the two earliest lamrim texts within the Geluk school after Tsongkhapa's own texts
2. Ensa Losang Döndrup's (1505–66) *How to Practice the Essence of the Stages of the Path*
3. Khedrup Sangyé Yeshé's (1525–90) *Source of All Attainments: Guidance on the Paths of the Three Types of Persons on the Basis of a Common Mahayana Guru Yoga*
4. Panchen Losang Chökyi Gyaltsen's *Guide to the Stages of the Path in Verse* and his commentary on Atiśa's *Lamp on the Path to Enlightenment* entitled *A Celebration Unlocking All Excellences*
5. The Fifth Dalai Lama's commentary on the *Three Principal Elements of the Path* entitled *Treasury of Scripture and Reasoning*
6. Changkya Ngawang Chöden's (1642–1714) *Instructions on the Stages of the Path in Verse: An Easy Path to Omniscience*, a lengthy work of over two hundred folios
7. Jamyang Shepa Ngawang Tsöndrü's (1648–1721) *Oral Teachings of the Guru: How to Practice within an Easy Approach the Essence of Words of Mañjuśrī*[32]

8. Panchen Losang Yeshé's commentary on Tsongkhapa's *Three Principal Elements of the Path*
9. Phurchok Ngawang Jampa's (1682–1762) *An Easy Approach to the Stages of the Path Revealing All Key Points*
10. The so-called *Southern Transmission of the Words of Mañjuśrī*, a practical guide to the lamrim compiled by Gendun Jamyang (eighteenth century)[33]
11. Panchen Palden Yeshé's (1738–80) *Ambrosial Vase of Altruism: A Direct Guide to the Stages of the Path*
12. Yeshé Tsöndrü's (1761–1816) *Essence of Dharma Nectar: How to Practice the Profound Instructions of the Stages of the Path by Relying on Verses*
13. Chusang Yeshé Gyatso's (1789–1856) *Lamp Illuminating the Distilled Points of Lamrim Instruction Based on the Topical Outlines of the Great Treatise on the Stages of the Path*
14. Shamar Gendun Tenzin's *How to Engage in Guided Meditation on the Topics in the Easy Path*
15. Kalsang Tenzin Khedrup's (nineteenth century) *Summation of Precious Qualities: A Combined Explanation of the Easy Path, the Swift Path, and Words of Mañjuśrī*
16. Drakar Losang Palden's (1866–1928) *Stages on the Path to Enlightenment: A Stream of Nectar Beneficial to All*
17. Phabongkha Dechen Nyingpo's (1878–1941) *Liberation in the Palm of Your Hand*[34]
18. Jikmé Damchö Gyatso's (1898–1946) *Nectar Essence of Excellent Discourses: Verse Instructions on Key Points of the Stages of the Path*

In addition, three other texts deserve special recognition as important aids to studying Tsongkhapa's *Great Treatise*. They are (1) the voluminous *Four Interwoven Annotations on the Great Treatise on the Stages of the Path*,[35] (2) Yangchen Gawai Lodrö's (1740–1827) *Essential Glossary on Elucidating Key Terms of the Great Treatise on the Stages of the Path*,[36] and (3) Shamar Gendun Tenzin's *Memorandum on the Difficult Points of the Insight Section of the Great Treatise on the Stages of the Path*.[37] Although the practice of reading Tsongkhapa's *Great Treatise* with annotations by later masters may have begun earlier, an established tradition of teaching Tsongkhapa's text on the basis of the *Four Interwoven Annotations* appears to have begun with the great eighteenth-century master Yongzin Yeshé Gyaltsen.[38] The text by

Yangchen Gawai Lodrö is a highly useful aid to help elucidate the meaning of terms, especially the more archaic terms embedded in the sayings of the early Kadam masters that Tsongkhapa cites extensively in the first part of his *Great Treatise*. The third, Shamar's text, is a much-cherished work that came to be embraced as a crucial aid to unlocking the difficult passages from the emptiness section.

The Practice of Guru Yoga

Guru yoga refers to a practice in Tibetan Buddhism that involves viewing one's guru as indivisible in nature from one's meditation deity—an enlightened being—honoring the guru with praises, offerings, and supplications, and seeking their blessings. In general, the topic of the guru, or *lama*, and how a trainee should relate to the guru is not confined to Vajrayāna practice. One finds legendary examples in the Mahayana sutras as well, including those of the bodhisattva Sadāprarudita and the bodhisattva Maṇibhadra, who, in their efforts to first search for their destined guru and then honor them with single-pointed dedication, incur great personal sacrifice. One finds also in works such as Maitreya's *Ornament of Mahayana Sutras* specific qualifications for a teacher on the Mahayana path. This said, guru yoga in the Vajrayāna context entails deep devotion rooted in viewing the guru as a buddha that goes way beyond relating to him or her as the doorway to cultivating the buddhas' enlightened deeds. Guru yoga requires the establishment of a special bond based on initiation in an empowerment ceremony, during which the guru is visualized as inseparable from the meditation deity whose mandala the trainee is being initiated into. The well-known explanatory tantra of Guhyasamāja tantra, *Vajra Garland*, contains an entire chapter on the relationship between the guru and the disciple, while Aśvaghoṣa's *Fifty Verses on the Guru* outlines the key points pertaining to this important relationship.[39] The devotional aspect of this relationship comes into particularly stark relief in the writings and hagiographies of the great adepts, or *mahāsiddhas*, such as Saraha, Lūipa, and Tilopa.

Although the term *guru yoga* does appear in the writings of some later Indian Buddhist authors (just barely),[40] the more established term within the Indian Vajrayāna tradition appears to be *guru cultivation* (*guru sādhana*, or *bla bsgrub* in Tibetan), with specific practices for cultivating the "outer," "inner," and "secret" aspects of the guru.[41] In particular, Nāropa's *Cultivating the Guru* contains most of the key elements one finds in a typical Tibetan guru-yoga practice, including outer, inner, and secret offerings and viewing the guru as indivisible from Vajradhara. Thus there is no doubt that the Tibetan tradition of guru yoga as a self-standing practice does have an Indian origin. However, the practice as an all-encompassing daily meditation, especially inviting the guru to enter one's heart and fusing one's mind with that of the guru, appears to be unique to Tibet. The flavor of this approach is beautifully captured in the following:

> When alive, at the point of death, or in the intermediate state,
> contemplating the guru within one's heart
> and fusing one's mind indivisibly with that of the guru:
> [to practice] this is the pith instruction.[42]

Guru yoga is popular in all Tibetan traditions, and one finds distinct guru yogas focused on deeply revered figures within specific lineages, such as for Jé Tsongkhapa in the Geluk tradition. In such a guru yoga, you as the trainee would view your root guru in the form of Tsongkhapa and as being, in nature, indivisible from the meditation deity. At the conclusion of the practice, you would draw the guru into your heart and request him or her to be constantly present and to grant blessings, as the following stanza succinctly captures:

> O precious root guru, most glorious,
> reside upon a lotus within my heart.
> Sustain me with your great kindness, and grant me
> the siddhis of your body, speech, and mind.[43]

Among the numerous guru yogas that emerged in the Geluk tradition, two acquired special status. They are the *Hundreds of Gods of Tuṣita* (*Ganden Lhagyama*) guru yoga composed by Dulnakpa Palden Sangpo (b. 1402) and Panchen Losang Chögyen's *Offering to the Guru* (*Lama Chöpa*), both featured in our volume. Both guru yogas are recognized as oral transmissions stemming from Jé Tsongkhapa himself. The first comes from the Segyü (*srad rgyud*) tradition, Segyü Monastery being the tantric college founded by Jetsun Sherab Sengé (1382–1445) in Tsang province in 1432 to uphold Tsongkhapa's tantric traditions.[44] The author of the *Hundreds of Gods of Tuṣita* guru yoga, Dulnakpa, was the second abbot of Segyü Monastery. Panchen's *Offering to the Guru* belongs to the Ensa Oral Transmission (Ensa Nyengyü) tradition, closely associated with masters of an important Geluk hermitage called Ensa (also spelled Wensa, literally, "place of solitude") established by Sönam Chokkyi Langpo (1439–1505) in Tsang province in the fifteenth century. Masters associated with this hermitage, especially three—Ensapa Losang Döndrup, Khedrup Sangyé Yeshé (1525–91), and Panchen Losang Chökyi Gyaltsen—played a crucial role in thematizing many of the oral traditions traced to Tsongkhapa through a special lineage that also includes Tokden Jampal Gyatso (1356–1428), Khedrup Jé, and Baso Chökyi Gyaltsen. This key oral transmission is taken up again below.

The Miktsema Prayer

Though distinct, the Segyü and Ensa guru yogas share two key features: (1) they both take Tsongkhapa as their focus of meditation, and (2) they both employ recitation of the Miktsema prayer in the manner of a mantra to evoke blessings from Tsongkhapa. The Miktsema prayer derives its name from two key syllables—*mik* (from *dmigs me*, "objectless") and *tse* (from *rtse ba'i*, "of compassion")—from the first line of the following prayer:

> You are Avalokiteśvara, great treasury of objectless compassion,
> you are Mañjuśrī, embodiment of stainless wisdom,
> you are Vajrapāṇi, destroyer of all dark forces,
> you are the crown jewel among the learned of the Land of Snows.
> I supplicate at your feet, O Tsongkhapa Losang Drakpa.[45]

This original version of Miktsema is known as the "five-lined Miktsema," which is the standard version recited by every member of the Geluk tradition. When "You are Vajradhara, source of all attainments," is added before the first line, it is known as the "six-lined Miktsema." In addition, two more versions, both in nine lines, are known, respectively, as "the nine-lined Miktsema of the Segyü tradition" and "the nine-lined Miktsema of the Ensa tradition." In that order, they are:

> You are the blessed Teacher, the lord of the doctrine,
> you are Vajradhara, lord of the sixth, pervading lord of all buddha families,
> you are Avalokiteśvara, great treasury of objectless compassion,
> you are Mañjuśrī, embodiment of stainless wisdom,
> you are Vajrapāṇi, destroyer of all dark forces,
> you are the crown jewel among the learned of the Land of Snows.

I supplicate at your feet, O Tsongkhapa Losang Drakpa.
May your body, speech, and mind enter into mine, and bless me.
O my guru, may I become just like you.

And:

You are sovereign sage Vajradhara, source of all attainments,
you are Avalokiteśvara, great treasury of objectless compassion,
you are Mañjuśrī, embodiment of stainless wisdom,
you are Vajrapāṇi, destroyer of all dark forces.
Losang Drakpa, you are the crown jewel among the learned of the
Land of Snows.
To you, O guru buddha, embodiment of all refuge,
I respectfully supplicate with my three doors.
Bless me that I and others may become tamed and free,
and grant us attainments, both supreme and ordinary.[46]

These two guru yogas postdate Tsongkhapa, but the core practice of using the Miktsema prayer is found in two short guru-yoga instructions in Tsongkhapa's collected works: one transmitted to Tokden Jampal Gyatso by the master on a one-to-one basis, and a second transmitted similarly to Khedrup Jé. There is also a third compiled by Baso Chökyi Gyaltsen on the basis of an oral teaching from his elder brother Khedrup Jé. The first text does not explicitly focus on Tsongkhapa but presents a visualization of the guru in the form of Mañjuśrī and then guides the practitioner through a detailed instruction on receiving the four empowerments (vase, secret, wisdom-gnosis, and word) in the form of a blessing.[47] The two latter instructions take Tsongkhapa as their focus, viewing him as indivisible from Mañjuśrī, and use the Miktsema recitation as their primary medium for supplicating the master. In the instruction transmitted to Khedrup Jé, following recitation of the Miktsema in the manner of mantra repetition, these supplications are made:

O precious guru, bless me that my mind is turned to Dharma,
bless me that my Dharma practice meets with success,
bless me that no obstacles appear on my path,
bless me that all my distorted states of mind cease, and
bless me that all undistorted states of mind arise in my mind.[48]

The heart of the practice involves four sets of repetition of Miktsema correlated with receiving the four empowerments in the form of a blessing. To conclude this process, you imagine the master joyfully accepts your supplications, and then the guru enters your heart, which is in the shape of an eight-petaled lotus, and its petals close up and are wrapped around by golden letters of the Miktsema.[49] In another text, an instruction on a Mañjuśrī meditation that combines his peaceful and wrathful aspects, Tsongkhapa presents explicit visualization practices aimed at specific objectives, such as enhancing intelligence associated with exposition, debate, and composition, cultivating deeper comprehension of the meaning of the scriptures, cultivating the perfect view of emptiness, cultivating great compassion, generating the awakening mind, and pursuing the practices of the completion stage.[50] It is these instructions of Tsongkhapa that later Geluk masters such as Dulnakpa, Ensapa, and Panchen see as the source of their Miktsema-based guru yogas.

Miktsema can of course be chanted on its own, or in conjunction with chanting the *Hundreds of Gods of Tuṣita* guru yoga—which is what most Geluk practitioners do as part of their daily practice. Repetition of the Miktsema a hundred thousand times on the basis of guru-yoga practice within a retreat is also considered an important preliminary for serious meditators in the Geluk tradition.[51] However, as can be seen in both Seventh Dalai Lama's guide to the *Hundreds of Gods of Tuṣita* (chapter 6) as well as Gyalrong Tsultrim Nyima's *Letter of Final Testament Sent upon the Wind* (chapter 8), a practice developed of correlating repeated recitation of the Miktsema with specific aspects of Mañjuśrī—outer, inner, and secret—as well as with threefold forms of intelligence, such as the triad of clear, swift, and penetrating intelligence and the intelligence associated with teaching, debate, and composition. Over time, Miktsema recitation came to be used also for rites of healing, longevity, dispelling obstacles, and even protecting crops.[52] By the beginning of the eighteenth century, so much Miktsema literature had evolved that a large anthology entitled the *Miktsema Cycle of Teachings* (*Dmigs brtse ma'i chos skor*) was compiled by Jamyang Dewai Dorjé (a.k.a. Drupwang Jampal Gyatso, 1682–1741), a master associated with the famed Gephel Hermitage.[53] This cycle was expanded by the noted Mongolian master Yeshé Döndrup Tenpai Gyaltsen (a.k.a. Thöyön Yeshé Döndrup, 1792–1855).[54] In the second half of the nineteenth century, Yeshé Döndrup's main disciple, Thöyön Jamyang Trinlé, expanded the cycle further, the resulting collection running to three volumes. Since then, the three-volume anthology has come to be known as the *Miktsema Compendium* (*Dmigs brtse ma'i be'u bum*). The standard version, as it stands today, was finalized by the Gomang abbot Khyenrab Tenpa Chöphel (1840–1907) toward the end of the nineteenth century.[55]

The Segyü Transmission Lineage

As noted above, Segyü Monastery and its counterpart in Central Tibet, Gyümé Monastery, were founded by Sherab Sengé to uphold Tsongkhapa's tantric teachings. These monasteries, later joined by Gyütö, established formal studies of tantra, based on Tsongkhapa's expositions of the root tantras of Guhyasamāja, Cakrasaṃvara, and Vajrabhairava and maintained many of the important rites associated with these and other meditation deities and protector deities. With respect to Tsongkhapa's practice lineages, the Segyü tradition of transmission came to be known for its role as the custodian of what are called "the eight great instructional guides of Tsongkhapa."[56] They are the practical guides on:

1. The completion stage of Guhyasamāja (*Five Stages on a Single Cushion*)
2. The completion stage of Cakrasaṃvara according to Lūipa tradition (*Sheaves of Attainments*)
3. The completion stage of Cakrasaṃvara according to Ghaṇṭāpa tradition (*Opening the Eyes to See the Hidden Meaning*)
4. The yoga of Vajrabhairava (*Stages of the Four Yogas*)
5. Great Wheel Vajrapāṇi (*Realization of the Great Wheel*)
6. The completion stage of Kālacakra (*Vajra Verses on the Six Yogas*)
7. The Six Yogas of Nāropa (*Endowed with Three Convictions*)
8. The transference of consciousness (*Opening the Golden Door*)[57]

According to Thuken Chökyi Nyima, the Segyü lineage appears to also contain "many special instructions on the principal mantras on the generation and completion stages of the trio of Guhyasamāja, Cakrasaṃvara, and Vajrabhairava as well as a multitude of very profound sutra and mantra teachings, such as guidelines on the stages of the path to enlightenment."[58] Thuken also reports that three masters—Jamyang Shepa,[59] Changkya Ngawang Chöden, and Thangsakpa Ngödrup Gyatso—made special concerted efforts to seek out the aging master at Segyü Monastery, Gyüchen Könchok Yarphel (b. 1602), and the latter conferred upon them the instructions of the Segyü tradition as if "pouring the entire content of one vase into another."[60] Clearly there are aspects of the Segyü tradition that are oral in nature; however, insofar as the tradition's transmission of Tsongkhapa's advanced tantric teachings is concerned, it appears that almost all the transmissions of the lineage are text based rather than drawn on oral teachings. In any case, thanks to the huge popularity of Dulnakpa's *Hundreds of Gods of Tuṣita*, known also as "the guru yoga of the Segyü tradition," the name Segyü became an indelible part of the Geluk practice lineage.

The Ensa Oral Transmission

Unlike its counterpart, the Segyü, the primary source for the Ensa Oral Transmission is, as indicated by its name, oral tradition. *Oral transmission* (*nyengyü*),[61] as referring to a distinct genre of pith instruction, is not unique to the Geluk tradition. Interestingly, although Baso Chökyi Gyaltsen and Chenga Lodrö Gyaltsen do use the phrase in the sense we understand today, Tsongkhapa and Khedrup's own preferred phrase seems to be *shalshé* (*zhal shes*, literally "learned from the mouth").[62] Also, while the Ensa Oral Transmission is part of the Ganden (or Geluk) Oral Transmission, the two are not identical.

Many of the instructions in the Ensa Oral Transmission trace their source not just to Tsongkhapa himself but to the revelations he received in his visions of Mañjuśrī. One such source is the Mañjuśrī Cycle of Teachings, an anthology of oral instructions Tsongkhapa received from Mañjuśrī with the mystic Umapa Pawo Dorjé acting as the medium.[63] Beyond this anthology are several shorter pieces Tsongkhapa inscribed based on Mañjuśrī's instructions, such as his (1) *Guide to the View Equalizing Samsara and Nirvana*, (2) *Mañjuśrī's Advice on Practice*, an eighteen-line instruction Tsongkhapa received when he experienced a grand vision of Mañjuśrī at Gyasok Phu cave, and (3) a remarkable short teaching from Mañjuśrī on how to bring together all key elements of the path in a format that optimizes the impact on one's practice in this lifetime.[64] A further source of the transmission is the special guru-yoga teachings Tsongkhapa conferred upon Tokden Jampal Gyatso and Khedrup Jé on a one-to-one basis. Finally, there is the mysterious "emanated scripture," which includes, in addition to pith instructions, a prophecy text that Ensapa refers to as the *Secret Mirror of Prophecies*.[65] According to Ensapa, the prophecies contained in this text were revealed by Tsongkhapa and Mañjuśrī at the request of Tokden and "several celestial beings of good fortune" at Ganden.[66]

In any case, the Ensa Oral Transmission, at its core, is an unbroken lineage of mouth-to-ear transmission traced to Mañjuśrī via Tsongkhapa and passed on through a chain of teachers with special destiny: from Tsongkhapa to the mystic Tokden Jampal Gyatso and Tsongkhapa's "singular heart disciple" Khedrup Jé; and from those two, especially the latter, to Baso Chökyi Gyaltsen. A key attribute of all these masters of the lineage is their perceived possession of the mysterious "emanated scripture," with Baso passing it on to Mahāsiddha Dharmavajra (Chökyi Dorjé), and the latter to Ensapa. The last reports that when he received the transmission in its entirety, Dharmavajra instructed him not to share it with just anyone and emphasized the strictly sealed nature of the transmission.[67]

There is no doubt that it was thanks to Ensapa—the most famous master connected with the Ensa Hermitage—that the designation Ensa Oral Transmission, or Ensa Nyengyü, came to be coined.[68] Ensapa is deeply revered in the Geluk tradition as someone who had attained buddhahood in his lifetime and is often referred to as Gyalwa Ensapa, "Conqueror Ensapa."[69] Living mostly at Ensa Hermitage, Ensapa devoted most of his time to meditative practice based on Tsongkhapa's numerous oral teachings. At the heart of Tsongkhapa's teaching, according to Ensapa, is the meditative practice rooted in guru yoga and focused on the threefold great bliss—great bliss of the *ground* (the nature of reality), great bliss of the *path*, and great bliss of the *result*.[70] In addition to numerous guru-yoga texts, Ensapa's writings contain experiential songs,[71] a self-exhortation entitled *Great Bliss Treasury*, and instructional texts covering important themes from Tsongkhapa's oral tradition like cutting off (*gcod*), guide to the view (*lta khri*), fourfold mindfulness guidance on tranquil abiding and insight, as well as a collection of sealed texts (*bka' rgya ma*) containing material of highly esoteric nature, including extensive discourse from a mysterious prophecy text. That the master was self-consciously focused on Tsongkhapa's oral transmission is evident from his own words. He writes:

> Supreme son of Mañjuśrī, guru,
> you who are hailed as Losang Drakpa—
> upholding the heart of your teaching, your oral transmission,
> these days, it seems to be me alone.[72]

From Ensapa, the lineage of the Ensa Oral Transmission passed on in its entirety to Khedrup Sangyé Yeshé (1570–1662), who in turn was succeeded by Panchen Losang Chögyen as the principal custodian of the transmission.

Among the various transmissions of teaching belonging to the Ensa lineage, the following distinct genres of teachings are the most well known:

- Guru yoga as formalized in Panchen's *Offering to the Guru* (chapter 7)
- Guide to the view
- Geden mahāmudrā, formalized in Panchen's *Highway of the Conquerors* (chapter 9) and its autocommentary, *A Lamp So Bright* (chapter 11)
- Cutting Off teaching, especially in the form of the rite of offering one's illusory body
- A transference of consciousness (*'pho ba*) practice based on Amitābha entitled Hero Embarking on a Campaign[73]

Guru Yoga of the Ensa Tradition

Several features of the Ensa tradition of guru yoga command special attention. First, unlike its counterpart, the *Hundreds of Gods of Tuṣita*, the Ensa guru yoga, exemplified by *Offering to the Guru*, involves aspects of practice that belong to highest yoga tantra, especially generating yourself into an enlightened form and evoking, at least at the imaginative level, the gnosis of innate bliss and emptiness. Second, the practice includes a unique deity-yoga wherein three principal meditation deities—Cakrasaṃvara, Guhyasamāja, and Vajrabhairava—are practiced "in an integrated manner and not in isolation from each other." Third, the guru is visualized as indivisible from the meditation deity in an approach known as the *triple being*—the *commitment being*, your guru in the form of Tsongkhapa; the *gnosis being*, Vajradhara at the heart of Guru Tsongkhapa; and the *concentration being*, a *hūṃ* syllable at the heart of that Vajradhara. Fourth, the guru yoga includes receiving the four empowerments in the form of a blessing preceded by fervent single-pointed supplication to the guru declaring him or her to be the embodiment of all refuges. Finally, in the Ensa guru yoga is found the method to practice the entirety of the paths of sutra and tantra on a single cushion by embracing guru yoga as the life force of one's path. The practice of this kind of enhanced guru yoga became so extolled that embracing guru yoga as "the foundation of one's path," as "one's heart practice," and as "the life force of one's path" became catchphrases in the Geluk tradition.[74]

Although several masters in the Ensa lineage composed guru yoga texts, especially Panchen's two immediate predecessors—Ensapa himself and Khedrup Sangyé Yeshé[75]—it is Panchen's *Offering to the Guru* that became the standard guru yoga of the lineage. Part of the popularity of Panchen's text is certainly owing to his gifts as a writer; however, the main reason lies in the text's success at offering a practice manual that is comprehensive yet short, that is profound yet lucid, and that powerfully evokes the devotional spirit essential for guru yoga. For many practitioners in the Geluk tradition, Panchen's text serves as the basic framework—à la *sādhana* (literally "method of cultivation")—for one's daily practice, including even a daily dose of mind training, or *lojong*. Given that the main features of the deity yoga embedded in the text were based on the Guhyasamāja sādhana, Phabongkha Dechen Nyingpo in the early twentieth century composed two adapted versions of Panchen text, relating the guru yoga formally to two other important meditation deities: Cakrasaṃvara and Vajrabhairava.[76]

Among the numerous guides on Panchen's root text, Yongzin Yeshé Gyaltsen's extensive commentary, *A Treasure House of Instructions on the Oral Transmission*—popularly known as the *Great Guidebook on Offering to the Guru*—came to enjoy the status of the standard guidebook.[77] In addition, *A Letter of Final Testament Sent upon the Wind* (chapter 8) by Gyalrong Tsultrim Nyima—a *jadrelwa* (*bya bral ba*), literally a "do-nothing" hermit—came to attract much affection among Geluk practitioners of the Ensa Oral Transmission. The present Dalai Lama, for instance, states that he holds the text very dear to his heart.[78] As will be discussed below, a unique feature of Gyalrong's text is its formal presentation of how to use Panchen's guru yoga as the "uncommon preliminary practice" for the "main practice" of mahāmudrā. Thus Gyalrong's *Letter of Final Testament* is a guide to Geden mahāmudrā as well.

Keeping the Guru at the Heart

From the perspective of the individual practitioner, guru yoga in the Geluk tradition serves several powerful functions. It helps establish and sustain a deeply personal connection to Jé Tsongkhapa, by maintaining daily meditation on him and chanting the Miktsema prayer. By maintaining the awareness of one's guru in the form of Tsongkhapa "ever present" within one's heart, the practice offers a powerful method to sustain mindfulness so that one can bring both awareness and intention into everyday activities.[79] Finally, it offers a structured practice that can transport one, through the force of devotion, to an inspired plane where one's identity becomes fused with one's guru, Jé Tsongkhapa, and the meditation deity. The following selected verses capture the devotional spirit, the personal and intimate nature of the relationship, the practitioner's fervent yearning for connection, and what I have called "identity fusion":

> By the force of conqueror Tsongkhapa
> being my supreme vehicle teacher through all my lives,
> may I never be separated even for an instant
> from the excellent path praised by the conquerors.[80]

And:

> May the gnosis of innate great bliss arise in me,
> may the stain of grasping at things as real be cleared away,
> may the network of doubts in my mind be cut away, and
> swiftly, may I come to be just like you.[81]

And:

> Your divine body and my body, O Father,
> your divine speech and my speech, O father,
> your divine mind and my mind, O Father—
> bless me so they become indivisibly one in truth.[82]

Before I conclude this section on guru yoga, allow me to address briefly what might seem like a strange paradox at the heart of Tibetan guru-yoga practice. There is no denying that guru yoga (as well as lamrim) emphasizes the need to view one's guru as a buddha, a fully enlightened being, and discourages the student from perceiving any faults in the guru. Yet insofar as the guru himself or herself is concerned, if they are just a human like any other, no amount of devotion on the part of the student is going to make the guru an actual buddha. In fact, if he or she starts to believe in the literal truth of the student's perspective, this could lead to a tragic delusion, with potentially harmful consequences on both sides of the relationship. So what is going on here? Is there a way to retain the inspirational power, the intimacy of connection, and the identity fusion the practice offers without the danger of sliding into blind devotion and loss of rationality?

Here, we can take cues from the tradition itself. On the part of the trainee, as the tradition recommends, it would be helpful to be cognizant of at least the essentials of the qualifications recommended for a guru, especially in the Vajrayāna context. A well-known text even recommends a twelve-year period to examine whether the guru and the student are a fit for each other![83] At minimum, the student needs to perceive in the potential guru certain basic qualifications: a degree of *inner peace*, *humility* acquired through Dharma practice, *personal integrity* rooted in sound moral discipline, *loving concern* for the student, and a *good command* of the content to be transmitted. With respect to the first, Tsongkhapa remarks, "It has been said that those with no inner peace themselves have no basis for bringing inner peace to others."[84] As for humility, the Tibetan tradition explicitly adopts specific practices, such as the guru prostrating in front of the throne before he or she sits on it and immediately reciting a verse reminding oneself of the law of impermanence. Furthermore, the teacher is urged to contemplate, when his or her students prostrate to him, that they are paying homage not to his or her person but to what they represent—the teaching. And without loving concern for the student, frankly, someone shouldn't even be in the business of teaching Dharma. The trainee may also want to keep in mind an insight from the tradition on what the definitive guru is that one is supposed to rely on ultimately: "Initially you rely on the human teacher as your guru; as you progress, you rely more on scripture as your guru; and finally, you rely on your own realization as your guru."[85] Even when relying on the human guru at the initial stage, if, as suggested by Tsongkhapa, one is able to do so on the basis of having an overview of the essence of the entire Buddhist teaching, the progressive levels of trust in the guru will come to unfold in an organic manner, leading to a rich relationship that will form the bedrock of one's path. In the end, as the tradition instructs us, the definitive guru is found not outside but within. Thuken Chökyi Nyima captures this point:

> Clear-light vajra mind, indivisible sphere and awareness,
> you, the pervading lord, are my definitive guru.
> With your kindness alone I hope to become free, so do not let
> me down.
> Pray smile upon me and grant the feast of attainments.[86]

Geden Mahāmudrā

We now arrive at part 3 of our volume. Panchen's root text on mahāmudrā, *Highway of the Conquerors*, along with its autocommentary, *A Lamp So Bright*, has been singularly responsible for the wide dissemination of a Geluk version of mahāmudrā practice. Thanks to Panchen being recognized as the main custodian of the Ensa Oral Transmission, Geden mahāmudrā, as formalized in Panchen's text, also came to be embraced from its inception as belonging to the Ensa lineage.

In general, the term *mahāmudrā*, literally "the great seal," is found extensively in Indian Buddhist tantric writings, often listed as one of four seals—the pledge seal (*samayamudrā*), action seal (*karmamudrā*), reality seal (*dharmamudrā*, alternatively listed as gnosis seal, *jñānamudrā*), and great seal (*mahāmudrā*)—with different meanings in varied contexts.[87] This said, it is in the writings of the mahāsiddhas such as Saraha, Padmavajra, and Tilopa that we find special use of the term *mahāmudrā* and its close association with a host of other important terms: "the innate" (*sahaja*), "primordial nature," "innate gnosis of bliss and emptiness," realization of "the unborn, selfless nature of the mind," and "union." In these sources, the attainment of mahāmudrā is encouraged through a nonconceptual approach, through *nonmentation* (*amanasikāra*).

On the surface, the rhetoric in these writings, with their advocacy of abandonment of thought or any form of "contrived" meditation and their embracing of a nondual approach of relaxing into the luminous and blissful nature of the mind, seems dismissive of the "mainstream" Buddhist path, including tantric practices. The question arises of whether the mahāmudrā approach should be viewed as separate from Buddhist tantra. On this point, Sakya Paṇḍita (1182–1251) famously asserted:

> For me, mahāmudrā is the self-arisen gnosis
> that comes about through the gnosis
> ensuing from the empowerments and
> from the concentrations of the two stages.
> Its realization, if one is skilled in tantric method,
> can be attained in this very life.
> Apart from such realization,
> the Buddha taught no other mahāmudrā.
> Those interested in mahāmudrā should cultivate it
> in accord with the treatises on tantra.[88]

The Kagyü tradition, on the other hand, singles out mahāmudrā as a signature practice of the tradition alongside the Six Yogas of Nāropa. In Gampopa's *white panacea* or "single-remedy" teaching, explicit especially in Lama Shang's works,[89] there are indeed passages that could be read as indicating that mahāmudrā alone is a complete path, that a nonconceptual approach alone could give rise to such an attainment, and that mahāmudrā could be taught and practiced outside the context of tantra.[90]

This brief background should suffice here as historical context for the emergence of Geden mahāmudrā. An excellent recent study has traced in depth the complex history of mahāmudrā in Tibet, especially its early history in the Kagyü tradition and Sakya Paṇḍita's critiques, while at the same time providing a magisterial explanation of the place of Geluk mahāmudrā in this historical context.[91] This study also offers a clear account of Geluk mahāmudrā's similarities and differences with the Kagyü version. On the whole, the Geluk tradition resolves the debate by differentiating two kinds of mahāmudrā: sutra mahāmudrā and tantra mahāmudrā. Briefly, the first refers to realization of the nature of mind—its conventional nature in terms of *vacuity, luminosity*, and *awareness* and its ultimate nature, *emptiness*—within the cultivation of tranquil abiding and insight. In contrast, tantra mahāmudrā is *the clear light of innate great-bliss mind that has arisen through the entry, abiding, and absorption of the winds inside the central channel.*[92] With respect to tantra mahāmudrā, Tsongkhapa writes that "the *doha* songs of the Great Brahman [Saraha] also present how, on the advanced levels of the path as described above, one takes to heart innate gnosis alone, shunning all other elaborations and sustaining it."[93]

Once two types of mahāmudrā are distinguished, it then becomes possible to engage in mahāmudrā practice with no formal tantric empowerment. The Geluk tradition introduces an important nuance to the approach of nonmentation and nondiscursiveness in the context of sutra mahāmudrā. Various techniques offered in mahāmudrā instructions to calm our thoughts, our habitual and constant rumination, are deeply appreciated for their efficacy, such as the "six methods of resting the mind" (p. 662). Such techniques are especially germane to the cultivation of tranquil abiding. When cultivating insight into the nature of the mind, however, Gelukpa masters say that even in the context of sutra mahāmudrā, we must rely on inquiry, which is by nature discursive, for it is through analysis that we gain insight into emptiness of the mind. So while the ultimate aim is to arrive at a state totally free of thought—a truly nondual and nonconceptual realization of mind's ultimate nature—disciplined application of thought in the form of analytical meditation remains essential, at least on the beginner's stage. For masters of Geden mahāmudrā, lumping all thoughts together—habitual rumination on the one hand and disciplined applications of the mind on the other—and dismissing them equally belies a coarse understanding. Hence Changkya's reassurance:

> Since the innate nature can dawn through even contrived
> meditation,
> you elder meditators need not be persistent.[94]

According to Geluk masters, what is required when it comes to insight is a balanced approach, where discursive analysis alternates with settled meditation that rests single-pointedly on the conclusion arrived at, namely the emptiness of the mind. In the tantric context, the emphasis on nonmentation and nondiscursivity are for advanced levels of realization, especially the arising of an innate gnosis wherein bliss and emptiness are fused indivisibly in a nondual way such that even the subtlest dualistic appearance has ceased. That state, given the subtle level of the mind employed, has no need for any discursive analysis; the mind's absorption into emptiness itself gives rise to successful attainment of the union of tranquil abiding and insight.

The absence of any text by Tsongkhapa himself that explicitly differentiates sutra and tantra mahāmudrā does not mean there is no basis in his writing for such a distinction. We know from his biography that Tsongkhapa received Kagyü mahāmudrā teachings from Drakpa Jangchup (1356–85), the Phakdru Kagyü master, as well as Drigung Chökyi Gyalpo (1335–1407), the then Drigung Kagyü patriarch. And judging by Khedrup Jé's *Record of Teachings Received*, Tsongkhapa appeared to have also taught what is known as the Fivefold Mahāmudrā to at least some disciples.[95] Gungthang Tenpai Drönmé speaks also of Tsongkhapa teaching Gungru Gyaltsen Sangpo (1384–1450) both mahāmudrā and the standard "guide to the view" approach, leading to the emergence of the phrase "new" and "old" styles of meditation.[96]

One possible missing link in connecting Geden mahāmudrā to Tsongkhapa is the role of Tokden Jampal Gyatso (1356–1428), a senior disciple a year older than Tsongkhapa. Tokden served as an occasional medium for communication between his guru and Mañjuśrī. According to his biography written by Chenga Lodrö Gyaltsen (1402–72), Tokden appeared to have composed "a text on mahāmudrā, the innate union," in which he had presented a guide that harmonizes the lamrim with the approach of all types of mahāmudrā instruction.[97] Tokden maintained that, if one were to take the mind itself as the focus, then the practice of "resting one's mind in the luminous and vivid mind itself and so forth is similar to the intention of the early mahāmudrā masters."[98] Lodrö Gyaltsen reports that Tokden would teach two distinct styles of cultivating tranquil abiding, one focused on the "object aspect" and another focused on the "subject aspect," and had in fact composed an instructional text presenting these two styles of meditation. The second involves primarily the practice of resting one's mind in a nondiscursive state simply aware of the mind's luminous and awareness nature, along the lines typical of many Kagyü mahāmudrā instructions. Lodrö Gyaltsen then goes on to conclude that "this is a way to cultivate tranquil abiding that is easy to understand, easy to maintain, easy to engage with, and easy to practice; it also represents the great way of cultivating concentration taught in all the lineages."[99] Despite Tokden's enthusiasm for and advocacy of this particular style of meditation, he too is clear that this practice of tranquil abiding focused on the subject aspect should not be confused with insight into the mind's ultimate nature, emptiness, although when it is combined with analysis, it could lead to such a realization.

Chenga Lodrö Gyaltsen himself, a student of both Tsongkhapa and Tokden, authored a verse text entitled *Mahāmudrā Illuminating the Essence*. In this work, the author defends nonmentation or nondiscursive meditation on several grounds: (1) It is not that there is no meditative focus; it's that it is defined by its approach of nondiscursive single-pointed resting.[100] (2) Though devoid of discursivity, there is still alert mindfulness. (3) In nondiscursive meditation, there is indeed no exertion nor any form of ritual. (4) The scriptures state that it's from nondiscursive and undistracted states of mind that all higher qualities of the mind flow. The author concludes with the following exhortation:

> As nondiscursive concentration
> has been hailed by all, both sutras and tantras,
> and as it has been praised with a single voice
> and embraced by the teachers of all practice lineages,
> I would appeal to you thus:
> "Pray, strive in this practice."[101]

Two other prominent Geluk teachers prior to Panchen Losang Chögyen who wrote explicitly on mahāmudrā were Khedrup Norsang Gyatso (1423–1513), a famed authority on the Kālacakra tantra and Tibetan astro-science, and Panchen Sönam Drakpa, a student of the Second Dalai Lama and a tutor to the Third Dalai Lama. Panchen Losang Chögyen's contemporary

Khöntön Paljor Lhundrup (1561–1637), a tutor to the Fifth Dalai Lama, also wrote a work with mahāmudrā as an important focus. The works by the first two aim primarily to defend the mahāmudrā of the early Kagyü masters against critiques from Sakya Paṇḍita and others by demonstrating how the teaching accords with both sutra and especially tantra.[102] Khöntön's, on the other hand, seeks to demonstrate the convergence of the essential import of the three distinct Tibetan instructions—Middle Way View, Mahāmudrā, and the Great Perfection.[103] But all three masters share three key points vis-à-vis mahāmudrā: (1) Nonmentation and nondiscursive meditation focused on the nature of mind is an excellent way to cultivate tranquil abiding. (2) Such a nondiscursive approach alone does not lead to the realization of mind's ultimate nature—its emptiness—and attainment of insight; for this, discursive analysis is indispensable. (3) In the completion stage of tantra, when the entry of the winds into the central channel gives rise to innate bliss and the gnosis that is the union of bliss and emptiness has arisen, then the nondiscursive approach alone can lead to the attainment of insight on emptiness.

In tracing the source of Geluk mahāmudrā to Tsongkhapa more directly, Yongzin Yeshé Gyaltsen states that the master gave only indications of the presence of such a teaching. He points to two statements from Tsongkhapa that suggest the time was not right to compose a special instruction.[104] Also, in the eighteen-lined instruction Tsongkhapa scribed after experiencing a vision of Mañjuśrī at Gyasok Phu cave, the key focus of mahāmudrā—meditating on the nature of the mind—is explicit right in its opening verse: "Without abiding anywhere, contemplate your mind as space-like."[105] Whatever the case, there was clearly a recognition by Ensapa's time of a unique Geluk mahāmudrā traceable to Tsongkhapa, especially to his oral teaching. Thus Ensapa declares:

> Not included in the path I have just outlined,
> and not known at present in this Land of Snows,
> there is the definitive instruction on mahāmudrā.
> At this point though, I dare not commit it to writing.[106]

Shar Kalden Gyatso (1607–77), a disciple of Panchen, tells us that Panchen taught his mahāmudrā text liberally to his numerous meditator disciples, and speaks of how once, when the master taught mahāmudrā at Ganden Monastery, several among the attendees attained unique mental abiding and, as a result, later became great yogis.[107] Speaking of the unique approach entailed in Geden mahāmudrā, especially as formalized in Panchen's text, the Geluk master Changkya Rölpai Dorjé writes in the eighteenth century:

> The instruction on mahāmudrā meditation presented in [Panchen's] guide is neither common with the sutra system nor with any of the first three classes of tantra. This can be discerned from the fact that its preliminary is an uncommon guru yoga. In view of this, both the meditating subject and the method for cultivating tranquil abiding and insight diverge on important points from other guides to the Middle Way view.[108]

Thus, even though Geluk tradition accepts a sutra mahāmudrā that does not require tantric empowerment, full-fledged practice of mahāmudrā is understood to require such an empowerment, especially as its preliminary is the practice of guru yoga according to highest yoga tantra. Panchen himself recommends using his own *Offering to the Guru* as an uncommon preliminary.[109] It appears that the tradition to teach Panchen's mahāmudrā text with his guru yoga, *Offering to the Guru*, in a combined way began quite early, possibly during Panchen's own time. Changkya Ngawang Chöden's (1642–1714) short guide on Geden mahāmudrā, based on the instructions of his guru Gyüchen Könchok Gyaltsen (1612–87), presents the formal structure of how to combine the practices of mahāmudrā and Panchen's guru yoga.[110] This tradition was later widely disseminated by Yongzin Yeshé Gyaltsen. Gyalrong Tsultrim Nyima's (nineteenth century) text in our volume presents the combined practice of these two instructions in detail.

Panchen's mahāmudrā attracted an extensive secondary literature within the Geluk tradition in the form of formal expositions, summary points, notes from live teachings, and so on. The most well known among them include, in chronological order: Shar Kalden Gyatso's *Guidebook on Mahāmudrā*, his *Experiential Guide* (chapter 12 in this volume), and his *Quotations from Kalden Gyatso's Ocean of Instructions on the Profound Teaching on Geden Mahāmudrā*; Changkya Ngawang Chöden's *Guidebook on Mahāmudrā*; Yongzin Yeshé Gyaltsen's *Bright Lamp of the Excellent Path of Oral Transmission*; Gugé Yongzin Losang Tenzin's (1748–1813) *Storehouse of Attainments Both Common and Supreme*; Gungthang's *Garland of Nectar Drops*; Keutsang Jamyang Mönlam's (1750–1814) *Excellent and Completely Virtuous Path to Freedom*; Ngulchu Dharmabhadra's (1772–1851) *Clearing Away All Delusion*; Gyalrong's *Letter of Final Testament* (chapter 8 in this volume);

and Akhu Sherab Gyatso's two texts on how to engage in a combined practice of *Offering to the Guru* and mahāmudrā.[111] Of these, Yongzin Yeshé Gyaltsen's extensive *Bright Lamp* guidebook on mahāmudrā came to be the standard exposition of Panchen's mahāmudrā texts, and Yongzin also composed the Geden mahāmudrā dedication prayer.[112]

Guide to the View

As noted above, one of the key teachings from Tsongkhapa's oral transmission is the "guide to the view" (*lta khri*, pronounced "tatri"). The instruction guides the trainee to the view of emptiness via a concise but structured approach. In one way, "guide to the view" can be understood broadly, with Geden mahāmudrā considered a subset within it. Alternately, the guide to the view instruction, especially as presented from the perspective of a beginner seeking an experiential understanding of view, can be considered a distinct approach of "seeking meditation on the basis of the view," with Geden mahāmudrā the approach of "seeking the view on the basis of meditation" (*Highway of the Conquerors*, verse 13). This beginner's approach is sometimes described also as "the way of sustaining the ascertainment" or as "the way to cultivate experience through study and reflection."[113] This beginner's approach needs to be appreciated within the context of five distinct styles of emptiness meditation Tsongkhapa describes in his *Vajra Lines on the View*: (1) when cultivating experiential understanding of the view at the beginner's stage, (2) when cultivating insight on emptiness based on a similitude tranquil abiding, (3) when cultivating insight on the basis of genuine tranquil abiding, (4) when one has gained direct realization of emptiness, and (5) when meditating on emptiness with the unique subject of Vajrayāna completion stage—namely, the gnosis of innate bliss and emptiness.[114]

Although the genre of guide to the view itself predates Tsongkhapa, his Geluk tradition is where it became most widespread. In general, Tsongkhapa's approach to cultivating the view of emptiness is to emphasize study and practice based on the great Madhyamaka treatises—especially those by Nāgārjuna, Āryadeva, Buddhapālita, and Candrakīrti—rather than reliance on a pith practical instruction. That said, his collected works do contain several short guide to the view texts. To represent this aspect of Tsongkhapa's oral transmission, our volume features a short text from Yongzin Yeshé Gyaltsen (chapter 13).[115]

The Geluk guide to the view instruction presupposes the practitioner has developed at least some intellectual understanding of emptiness according to Prāsaṅgika Madhyamaka. Most of the texts on the instruction trace their origin to Tsongkhapa through a unique lineage that includes three key disciples: Tokden, Khedrup, and Baso (as in the case of Ensa oral transmission). They all emphasize the need to engage in formal preliminary practice of guru yoga followed by main meditation framed in terms of the selflessness of the person and that of phenomena, each composed of space-like meditative equipoise and illusion-like post-equipoise. Some texts also recommend, as a preliminary, chanting the *Supplicating the Lineage Gurus of the Near Transmission* composed by Tsongkhapa.[116] An alternative lineage, passing through Sherab Sengé, frames the instruction within a *fourfold mindfulness*—mindfulness of all beings as mothers, mindfulness of one's gurus as buddhas, mindfulness of one's body as a deity body, and mindfulness of appearances as devoid of intrinsic existence.[117] Whichever of the two approaches one adopts, the actual meditation must be preceded by setting one's intention and settling the mind, as instructed in the following: "Next, set a forceful intention that 'I will observe how self appears to my innate sense of self.' After this, relax your mind and rest it for a little while without focusing on anything specific. As you proceed in this way, your mind will come to settle down, allowing it to abide clear and vivid."[118]

Geluk guide to the view is, first and foremost, a practice of self-inquiry where a refined attention allows the main part of your mind to experience the natural arising of a sense of self—even imagining, if necessary, a scenario where the thought "I am" arises in a pronounced manner, such as when you are unjustly accused or afraid—while a small part of your mind incisively observes how that sense of self arises. The crucial point here is that this observation of how you experience the sense of self is simultaneous with the arising of the sense of self itself, not a subsequent reflection after the fact. What is demanded here is a refined *meta-awareness* that, while having the power to observe, does not disturb your attention on the focal object, which is your sense of self.

Tsongkhapa tells us that when we meditate in this way, inquiring ever more deeply into how sense of self arises in us, we will come to appreciate that it is a challenging task indeed. The sense of self arises in us in all sorts of ways. Sometimes it feels as if the self is fused with our body and mind, and at other times the self seems to be distinct from our body and mind, underpinned by an assumption that something enduring has been part of our existence from the start. It takes time to get a good sense of how our innate sense of self appears to us; and even when we initially succeed in catching a glimpse, it is only fleeting. We need to ascertain, in a sustained manner through focused attention, how self appears to our innate sense of self—that is, our ordinary everyday experience of being a sentient creature. "If you have excellently realized the way your innate sense of 'I am' perceives self," writes Tsongkhapa, "you have ascertained the object of negation. Then examine how such self is perceived and conceived in relation to *mine*—your aggregates and so on."[119]

Once we have identified the self as perceived by our innate sense of "I am" and have examined its existence in terms of whether such a self is identical with or distinct from the aggregates, we then need to sustain the force of our ascertainment that no such self exists in reality. At that point, three factors converge: we have recognized the mode of *perception* of our innate sense of self, we have identified its mode of *apprehension*, and we have gained the *ascertainment* that there is no such self at all.[120] Here, the important thing is that we ensure that in our meditation our mind rests single-pointedly on pure absence in the form of a categorical negation—that the self as perceived and conceived does not exist at all—as if the contemplating mind itself has assumed the form of this absence. Stressing this point about meditating on emptiness as if the mind is fused with it, Tsongkhapa on another occasion writes, "If you meditate on emptiness as something external, it would lead to a contemplation of something truly existing; therefore meditate by fusing it inseparably with your mind."[121]

On the beginner's stage, before you have attained stable and sustained attention, you need constant reinforcement to maintain the force of your ascertainment. At that time, your efforts should be focused on constantly renewing the ascertainment of that pure absence. However, as your capacity for sustained attention increases through the practice of tranquil abiding, you will be able to extend the periods of resting in the ascertainment, and thanks to the increased power of your mental stability, you will be able to apply subtle analysis in a sustained way. Finally, when you attain tranquil abiding, analysis itself will lead to stability, and stability will in turn support analysis, such that the two culminate into a union.

An important part of the practice is seizing the occasions offered by everyday life. First observing how your innate sense of self arises, especially in emotionally charged situations, you then view everything as illusion-like through the force of the ascertainment of emptiness you developed during formal meditation. Tsongkhapa speaks of bringing the awareness of this illusion-like character of phenomena through the power of *experience* gained in formal sitting and through the power of *mindfulness* and *meta-awareness*. Together, these reinforce the ascertainment that although self appears to possess intrinsic existence to your naïve sense of "I am," not even an iota of such objective intrinsic status exists.[122]

To sum up, here is the ideal approach to cultivating the view of emptiness as proposed in Geluk "guide to the view" instructions. First, develop a basic intellectual understanding of emptiness according to the Prāsaṅgika Madhyamaka through personal study, teachings received from your guru, or a combination of both. Then, having received a transmission of a chosen text on guide to the view, engage in formal meditation. This meditation has the following elements: (1) preliminary guru yoga, especially supplicating the lineage gurus for blessing, (2) the main practice, and (3) the concluding practice of dedication. The main practice has two parts—space-like emptiness meditation in equipoise and cultivation of the illusion-like perspective in post-equipoise. In the first you ensure your meditation has four key points—identifying the object of negation, ascertaining the entailment, ascertaining the absence of identity, and ascertaining the absence of difference. In the second—the periods between formal sitting sessions—you take that awareness of emptiness and extend the perspective, viewing everything as illusion-like and continuing to reinforce the impact of the formal meditation by, for example, reading or chanting verses from songs on the view, such as these words of Seventh Dalai Lama, which evoke the experience of beginning to taste the view:

> Just as clouds clear in the autumn sky,
> all dualistic perceptions and experiences come to cease
> in the sphere of the union of space and mind.
> I, a yogi of unborn space, see this nature does not exist in any way;
> its deception of appearances and existence—
> I see it all as a spectacle of grand illusion.
> Through the joy of the union of appearance and emptiness,
> I find certainty in the undeceiving truth of dependent arising.[123]

The Three Essential Points

The instruction known as the "three essential points" is, as noted above, associated with the Indian mystic Mitrayogi, who came to Tibet at the invitation of Trophu Lotsāwa Jampa Pal (1173–1236) at the end of the twelfth century. As such, it is neither part of the oral transmission stemming from Tsongkhapa nor unique to his Geluk tradition. This said, its dissemination within the Geluk lineage does pass through Tsongkhapa, with his student Khedrup receiving the transmission directly from the master.[124] Khedrup also composed a lineage prayer tracing the transmission back to its origin in Mitrayogi. Several among Tsongkhapa's immediate students composed texts on this instruction, including Baso Chökyi Gyaltsen and Bodhisattva Kunsang (1366–1444).[125] As can be discerned from the two texts by Ngulchu Dharmabhadra featured in our volume, the instruction, a practice of Avalokiteśvara according to highest yoga tantra, correlates three distinct practices to the three stages of our existence: (1) for the present life, meditation on emptiness based on deity yoga, preceded by contemplating impermanence and suffering and cultivating the awakening mind, (2) for the moment of death, transference of consciousness, and (3) for the intermediate state, the mixings.

The root text of the instruction in five stanzas, though attributed to Mitrayogi, an Indian master, does not appear to have made its way into any of the editions of Tengyur. The Tengyur does contain, however, a short four-verse text possibly by the same Indian master bearing the title *Heart Yoga* (*Yogasāra*), which contains the second stanza with a slightly different fourth line.[126] So, quite possibly, the earliest version of the root text we have is the one scribed by Trophu Lotsāwa and contained in the anthology known as *Cycle of Pith Instructions of Dharma Master Trophu Lotsāwa Jampa Pal.*[127] This anthology contains, in addition to the root text, a summary outline of the text, a prose commentary, and an oral teaching on contemplating one's mind as unborn. There appears to be some divergence of opinion as to whether the five-verse root text is entirely by Mitrayogi or whether some part of it is an addition by Trophu Lotsāwa. Changkya Ngawang Chöden states that Baso considers the entire text to be by the mystic himself, the Second Dalai Lama says the final stanza is by Trophu Lotsāwa, while Changkya's own guru, the Fifth Dalai Lama, considers only the first stanza to be by the Indian mystic with the remainder added by Trophu Lotsāwa.[128] Changkya's text, in fact, offers a highly useful comparison of several key texts on the instruction, providing the reader a rich textured appreciation of it. By and large, Geluk masters, in their wish to ground the instruction within the framework of the overall path, subsume the Indian mystic's instruction—especially the part pertaining to this life—within four main themes: (1) instruction on inspiring motivation, the *condition*; (2) instruction on cultivating the awakening mind, the *cause*; (3) instruction on supplicating the guru and meditation deity, *the method*; and (4) instruction on contemplating one's mind as unborn, the *actual practice*.[129]

Among the texts on this special instruction authored by masters in the Geluk tradition, the most well-known ones are those by Baso Chökyi Gyaltsen, the Second Dalai Lama, the Third Dalai Lama, Panchen Losang Chögyen, the Fifth Dalai Lama, Changkya Ngawang Chöden, Panchen Losang Yeshé, Phurchok Ngawang Jampa, Yongzin Yeshé Gyaltsen, Könchok Jikmé Wangpo (1728–91), Trichen Tenpa Rabgyé (1759–1815), Ngulchu Dharmabhadra, and Kirti Losang Trinlé (1849–1904). As noted earlier, Khedrup Jé composed a prayer to the lineage gurus of this instruction, and this was later supplemented by Phurchok Ngawang Jampa and Yongzin Yeshé Gyaltsen, tracing the transmission lineage up to the mid-eighteenth century.

Undoubtedly, the huge popularity of the instruction in the Geluk tradition has to do with its being cast as a revelation conferred on Mitrayogi by none other than Avalokiteśvara, Tibet's favorite meditation deity. Also the brevity of the root text and the simplicity of its framework offers a comprehensive way to practice the essence of what the Tibetan tradition calls the union of sutra and tantra. In fact, at least two of the well-known texts on the instruction—one by Ngulchu in eighteen verses (chapter 14 in this volume) and the other by Kirti Losang Trinlé—were composed in the style of a daily practice, in that they could be meditated on or chanted on a daily basis. In my introduction to the Tibetan edition of the volume, I observed that this instruction could be particularly appropriate for today's Tibetan Buddhists, who feel that they just don't have enough time for serious Dharma practice.

The eighth-century Indian Buddhist master Śāntarakṣita, who was instrumental in establishing Buddhism in Tibet, speaks of two distinct ways in which trainees might engage with Dharma practice. One is to enter the Dharma primarily by the force of *faith* and devotion, and the other is by way of the *nature of reality* (*dharma*).[130] For the latter, understanding derived from study and critical reflection becomes key. Assuming that many contemporary readers of this volume in English will belong to the second category, I have labored in my introduction to offer extensive background on the four genres of instruction presented in this volume. My hope is that this appetizer of an introduction essay will whet the reader's appetite for the real feast: direct engagement with the texts of the great masters of the tradition.

Technical Note

THE TIBETAN TITLE of the volume translated here is *Dpal dge ldan pa'i lam rim dang snyan brgyud kyi chos skor*, which means *The Glorious Gandenpas' Dharma Teachings on the Stages of the Path and the Oral Transmission*. This edition was prepared specifically for *The Library of Tibetan Classics* and its Tibetan equivalent, the *Bod kyi gtsug lag gces btus*. Bracketed numbers embedded in the text refer to page numbers in the critical and annotated Tibetan edition published in New Delhi in modern book format by the Institute of Tibetan Classics (2005, ISBN 978-81-89165-06-2) as volume 6 of the *Bod kyi gtsug lag gces btus* series. In preparing this translation, the Institute of Tibetan Classics edition served as the primary source, with reference also to other editions. The Tibetan titles of the texts translated in the present volume (followed by their page range in the Tibetan edition) are:

Lam rim gyi chos skor
1. Lam rim nyams mgur (3–7)
2. Lam gyi gtso bo rnam gsum (9–10)
3. Lam rim legs gsungs nying khu (11–74)
4. Lam rim bde lam (75–121)
5. Lam rim 'jam dpal zhal lung (123–273)

Zab lam bla ma'i rnal 'byor
6. Dga' ldan lha brgya ma'i khrid yig (277–300)
7. Bla ma mchod pa'i cho ga (301–13)
8. Bla ma mchod pa'i khrid yig kha chems rlung bskur ma (315–494)

(Note: In the Tibetan volume two texts, the root text of mahāmudrā and the lineage guru prayer, have been listed under a single entry as *Phyag chen rtsa ba dang brgyud 'debs*. Here, however, we have listed the two texts separately as 9 and 10.)

Dge ldan phyag rgya chen po dang dbu ma'i lta khrid

9–10. Phyag chen rtsa ba dang brgyud 'debs (497–503)

11. Dge ldan bka' srol phyag rgya chen po'i rtsa ba rgyas par bshad pa yang gsal sgron me (505–47)

12. Dge ldan bka' brgyud phyag rgya chen po'i nyams 'khrid (549–62)

13. Lta ba'i gnad ston pa'i yig chung shin tu gsang ba dngos grub kun 'byung (563–70)

Snying po don gsum gyi nyams len

14. Snying po don gsum gyi ngag 'don (573–75)

15. Snying po don gsum gyi zin bris grub chen zhal lung gsal ba'i me long (577–94)

The titles of all texts referred to in the translation are rendered in English, regardless of whether translations of those texts have been published in English. Original Tibetan titles can be found in the bibliography. The conventions for phonetic transcription of Tibetan words are those developed by the Institute of Tibetan Classics and Wisdom Publications. These reflect approximately the pronunciation of words by a modern Central Tibetan; Tibetan speakers from Ladakh, Kham, or Amdo, not to mention Mongolians, might pronounce the words quite differently. A table of transliterated spellings of the Tibetan terms and names used in the book can be found after the translations. Sanskrit diacritics are used throughout, except for certain terms that have entered the English language—namely, Mahayana, mandala, sutra, samsara, and nirvana.

Pronunciation of Tibetan phonetics

ph and *th* are aspirated *p* and *t*, as in *pet* and *tip*.
ö is similar to the *eu* in the French *seul*.
ü is similar to the *ü* in the German *füllen*.
ai is similar to the *e* in *bet*.
é is similar to the *e* in *prey*.

Pronunciation of Sanskrit

Palatal *ś* and retroflex *ṣ* are similar to the English unvoiced *sh*.
c is an unaspirated *ch* similar to the *ch* in *chill*.
The vowel *ṛ* is similar to the American *r* in *pretty*.
ñ is somewhat similar to the nasalized *ny* in canyon.
ṅ is similar to the *ng* in *sing* or *anger*.

Part 1
The Stages of the Path

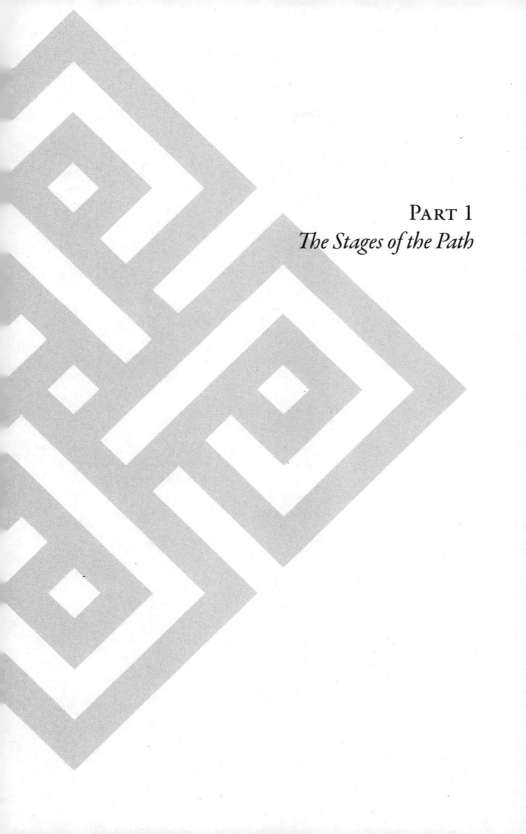

1. A Song of Spiritual Experience

Essential Points of the Stages of the Path

Tsongkhapa Losang Drakpa

1
Your body is created from a billion perfect factors of goodness,
your speech fulfills the yearnings of countless sentient beings,
your mind perceives all objects of knowledge exactly as they are.
O chief of Śākya clan, I bow my head to you.

2
You're the most excellent sons of such a peerless teacher,
you carry the burden of the enlightened activities of all conquerors,
and in countless realms you engage in ecstatic display of emanations.
O Maitreya and Mañjuśrī, I pay homage to you.

3
So difficult to fathom is the Mother of Conquerors;[131]
you who unravel its content as it is are the jewels of the world,
hailed with renown throughout the three realms.
O Nāgārjuna and Asaṅga, I pay homage to you.

4
Excellently stemming from these two great trailblazers
are the two paths of *profound view* and *vast practice.*
The custodian of this treasury of instructions, preserving all key points
of these paths without error, O Dīpaṃkara [Atiśa], I pay homage to you.

5
You are the eyes for seeing the myriad collections of scripture,
you are the supreme gateway for fortunate ones voyaging to liberation,

stirred by compassion you illuminate the most skillful approaches.
O spiritual teachers, respectfully, I pay homage to you.

6
This [instruction on the] stages of the path to enlightenment
flowed excellently in succession from Nāgārjuna and Asaṅga,
crown jewels of all the learned ones of this world.
Your banners of fame flutter vibrantly among sentient beings.

7
Among instructions, it is the most precious of all gems,
fulfilling all the wishes of beings without exception.
It is also the ocean of the most glorious well-uttered insights,
the confluence of a thousand rivers of excellent treatises.

8
It helps you see all teachings as free of contradiction,
it helps all scriptures dawn on you as personal instructions,
it helps you easily discover the enlightened intention of the conquerors,
and it helps protect you from the abyss of grave negative deeds.

9
Therefore this most excellent instruction, relied upon
by countless fortunate ones like the learned ones of India and Tibet,
this teaching on the stages of the path of persons of three capacities: [4]
what intelligent person would not be captivated by it?

10
This concise instruction that distills the essence of all scriptures—
through reciting it or listening to it for even a single session,
you will definitely receive powerful waves of merit of
teaching and hearing the Dharma; so contemplate its meaning.

11–12
The root of creating well the auspicious conditions
for all the good things of this and future lives
is to rely properly, with effort in both thought and action,
on the sublime spiritual teacher who reveals the path.

Seeing this, never forsake him, even at the cost of your life,
and please him with the offering of following his advice.
I, a yogi, practiced in this manner;
you who aspire to liberation should do likewise.[132]

13–14
This life of leisure is far more precious than a wish-granting jewel;
finding such an existence happens just once.
Hard to find, and yet, like a flash of lightning, it easily vanishes.
Contemplating this, you must see all mundane pursuits
like empty grain husks floating on the wind,
and you must extract the essence of your human life.
I, a yogi, practiced in this manner;
you who aspire to liberation should do likewise.

15–16
There is no certainty you will elude birth in the lower realms after death;
protection from such terror lies in the Three Jewels alone.
Make firm therefore the practice of going for refuge,
and ensure that its precepts are never eroded.
This depends in turn on fully contemplating white and black karma
and their effects and on perfectly observing the ethical ideal.
I, a yogi, practiced in this manner;
you who aspire to liberation should do likewise.

17–18
Until you've obtained the form best suited to
the excellent path, you'll fail to make great strides in your journey.
Strive therefore to create all the causes for such a form.
Your three doors, so sullied with negative karma and transgressions—
it is especially vital to purify your karmic obscurations,
so prioritize constant application of the four powers.[133]
I, a yogi, practiced in this manner;
you who aspire to liberation should do likewise. [5]

19–20
Without striving to contemplate the ailment, the truth of suffering,
a genuine aspiration for liberation does not arise;

without contemplating the causal process of suffering's origin,
the way to uproot cyclic existence is not understood.
Thus it's vital to prioritize seeking renunciation through disenchantment
with cyclic existence and to recognize the links that chain you to samsara.
I, a yogi, practiced in this manner;
you who aspire to liberation should do likewise.

21–22
The awakening mind is the central beam of the supreme vehicle;
it's the foundation and the support of all expansive deeds;
for the two accumulations,[134] it is like a philosopher's stone;
it's a treasure mine of merit holding myriad virtues.
Recognizing these truths, heroic bodhisattvas uphold
the precious supreme mind as the heart of their life's commitment.
I, a yogi, practiced in this manner;
you who aspire to liberation should do likewise.

23–24
Generosity is the wish-granting jewel that satisfies the wishes of beings;
it's the best weapon to cut the knots of miserliness;
it's a deed of the bodhisattva dauntless and giving birth to courage
and is the basis to proclaim renown throughout the ten directions.
Knowing this, learned ones seek the excellent path
of giving away entirely their body, wealth, and virtues.
I, a yogi, practiced in this manner;
you who aspire to liberation should do likewise.

25–26
Morality is the water that cleanses the stains of ill deeds,
the cooling moonlight soothing the burning agony of the afflictions.
It dignifies you amid people like the majestic Mount Meru;
it draws all beings to you with no display of power.
Knowing this, sublime ones guard, as they would their own eyes,
the perfect discipline they have adopted.
I, a yogi, practiced in this manner;
you who aspire to liberation should do likewise.

27–28
Forbearance is the supreme adornment of the powerful;
it's the greatest bulwark against the torments of the afflictions.
Against its enemy, the serpent of hatred, it is the sky-cruising garuḍa;
against the weapon of harsh words, it's the mightiest armor.
Knowing this, acquaint yourself with
the armor of excellent forbearance by every possible means.
I, a yogi, practiced in this manner;
you who aspire to liberation should do likewise.

29–30
When you don the armor of dauntless diligence,
knowledge of scripture and realization increases like the waxing moon. [6]
Your conduct comes to be imbued with noble purpose,
and whatever initiative you undertake succeeds.
Knowing this, bodhisattvas expend great waves of effort,
which helps to dispel all forms of laziness.
I, a yogi, practiced in this manner;
you who aspire to liberation should do likewise.

31–32
Meditative absorption is the king that reigns over the mind.
When at rest, it stands unwavering as the king of mountains;
when engaged it takes up all objects of virtue.
It induces the great bliss of a serviceable body and mind.
Knowing this, great accomplished yogis
ceaselessly apply concentrations, destroying the enemy distraction.
I, a yogi, practiced in this manner;
you who aspire to liberation should do likewise.

33–34
Wisdom is the eye that sees profound suchness,
the path destroying cyclic existence at its root.
It's a treasury of higher qualities praised in all scriptures,
hailed as the supreme lamp for dispelling the darkness of delusion.
Knowing this, those who aspire to liberation strive
with myriad endeavors to cultivate this path of the wise.

I, a yogi, practiced in this manner;
you who aspire to liberation should do likewise.

35–37
The power to cut the root of cyclic existence is not found
in one-pointed meditative absorption alone,
and no amount of probing with wisdom divorced
from the path of tranquil abiding will stop the afflictions.
So saddling this wisdom decisively penetrating the true mode of being
astride the horse of unwavering tranquil abiding, and with
the sharp weapon of reasoning of the Middle Way free of extremes,
tear down all sites of objectification of the mind grasping at extremes.
With such expansive wisdom probing with precision,
enhance your intellect so it realizes true suchness.
I, a yogi, practiced in this manner;
you who aspire to liberation should do likewise.

38–39
What need is there to say that concentration is attained
through one-pointedness? But discriminative awareness
probing with precision can engender concentration too,
abiding utterly stable and unwavering in the true mode of being.
Wondrous are those who see this and strive
to unite tranquil abiding and insight.
I, a yogi, practiced in this manner;
you who aspire to liberation should do likewise.

40–41
The space-like emptiness of meditative equipoise
and the illusion-like emptiness of subsequent realization—
praised are those who cultivate method and wisdom
by binding them together, journeying beyond the bodhisattva deeds.
Realizing this and not content with partial paths—
this is indeed the way of the fortunate ones. [7]
I, a yogi, practiced in this manner;
you who aspire to liberation should do likewise.

42–43
Having thus correctly cultivated the shared paths
essential for the supreme paths of causal and resultant vehicles,
enter the great ocean of tantras
by relying on the counsel of learned guides.
Through applying their quintessential instructions,
make this human life you have obtained meaningful.
I, a yogi, practiced in this manner;
you who aspire to liberation should do likewise.

44–45
To cultivate familiarity in my own mind
and to also benefit fortunate others,
I've explained here in words easily understood
the complete path that pleases the conquerors.
Thus I pray: "Through this virtue may all beings
never be parted from the perfectly pure and excellent path."
I, a yogi, prayed in this manner;
you who aspire to liberation should pray likewise.

This brief presentation of the practices of the stages of the path to enlightenment, written in the form of a memorandum, was composed by the well-read monk the renunciant Losang Drakpai Pal at the great mountain retreat of Geden Nampar Gyalwai Ling. [8]

2. Three Principal Elements of the Path

Tsongkhapa Losang Drakpa

Homage to the most venerable gurus!

1
I shall explain here to the best of my ability
the essential points of all the scriptures of the Conqueror,
the path acclaimed by all excellent bodhisattvas,
the gateway for fortunate ones aspiring to liberation.

2
You who are not attached to the joys of cyclic existence,
who strive to make meaningful this life of leisure and opportunity,
and who place your trust in the path that pleases the conquerors—
O fortunate ones, open your hearts and listen.

3
Without perfect renunciation you cannot pacify
your yearning for the pleasures and fruits of samsara's ocean.
And the craving for existence keeps you thoroughly enchained,
so you should first seek true renunciation.

4
By contemplating often that such a human life is rarely found
and that you have no time to spare, preoccupation with this life
will cease.
By contemplating over and over the truth of karma and samsaric suffering,
preoccupation with the next life will cease.

5
Having familiarized yourself in this way, when not even an instant
of admiration arises for the treasures of cyclic existence,
and when the thought that aspires to liberation arises both night
and day,
at this point true renunciation has arisen.

6
Furthermore, if such renunciation is not sustained
by the perfect awakening mind, it will not become a condition
for the perfect bliss of unsurpassed enlightenment.
Therefore, intelligent ones, generate the supreme awakening mind.

7–8
Swept ever away by four powerful rivers,
bound tightly with fetters of karma most secure,
trapped in the iron mesh of self-grasping,
enveloped by the thick mists of ignorance:
they endlessly take birth within cyclic existence,
ceaselessly tormented by the three kinds of suffering.
Contemplating this condition of all your mothers,
you must generate the supreme awakening mind.

9
Without the wisdom realizing the ultimate nature,
though you gain familiarity with renunciation and the awakening mind,
[10]
you will be unable to cut the root of cyclic existence.
So strive in the methods for realizing dependent origination.

10
When, with respect to all phenomena of samsara and nirvana,
you see that the laws of cause and effect never deceive,
and when you have dismantled every basis of objectification,
then you have entered the path that pleases the buddhas.

11
As long as the two understandings—
of *appearance*, undeceiving dependent origination,
and of *emptiness*, the absence of all positions—remain separate,
then you have not realized the intent of the Sage.

12
However, if at some point, not in alternation but at once,
the instant you see that dependent origination is undeceiving,
this dismantles the entirety of the object of grasping at certitude,[135]
then your analysis of the view is complete.

13
Furthermore, when appearance dispels the extreme of existence
and when emptiness dispels the extreme of nonexistence,
and you understand how emptiness arises as cause and effect,
you will never be swayed by views grasping at extremes.

14
Once you have thus understood as they are
the key points of the three principal elements of the path,
O child, seek solitude and, enhancing your power of diligence,
swiftly accomplish your ultimate aim.

This advice was given by the monk Losang Drakpai Pal to Ngawang Drakpa, a member of the ruling family of the Tsakho region.[136] [13]

3. Essence of Excellent Discourses[137]

Well Ascertaining the Way to Practice Taught in the Stages of the Path to Enlightenment

GOMCHEN NGAWANG DRAKPA
Translated by Rosemary Patton with Venerable Dagpo Rinpoché

Homage to the perfect gurus![138]

1 His excellent practice of the three trainings—[the teaching] both as scripture and realization—
has given him the capacity to uphold the Buddha's thought unerringly.
Relying on this great spiritual teacher,
I will practice the stages of the paths of sutra and tantra.

This explanation of the stages of the path to enlightenment has four sections:[139] the greatness of the author, the greatness of the [lamrim] teaching, how to listen to and explain the teaching, and how students are progressively guided by the actual teaching. For the first, refer to other works.

THE GREATNESS OF THE [LAMRIM] TEACHING

This has four parts.

THE GREATNESS OF ALLOWING YOU TO REALIZE THAT ALL THE TEACHINGS ARE FREE OF CONTRADICTIONS

2 Understanding that everything taught in the three vehicles about what is to be rejected and realized
is a method for any given individual to achieve buddhahood,
either as a primary path or an auxiliary one,
is realizing that all the teachings are free of contradictions.

The greatness of allowing you to recognize all discourses as practical instructions

3 By relying on precious personal instructions,
once you have ascertained the content of all the Buddha's discourses
and become skilled in knowing which practices require analytical meditation and which require placement meditation,
you cease to reject the teaching, and the discourses dawn as practical instructions.

The greatness of allowing you to easily master the Buddha's principles

4 Although the great treatises are the finest instructions,
it is difficult for an untrained mind relying on them to master the Buddha's intent,
or doing it requires much time and great effort,
while with this instruction you can easily realize it. [14]

The greatness of automatically avoiding very serious misdeeds

5 Thus, thanks to this instruction, you cease to forsake the excellent discourses—
imagining some of the Buddha's words to be obstacles
to attaining buddhahood and others to be methods conducive to it—
and thereby automatically avoid grave misdeeds.

How to listen to and explain the teaching

This has three parts: how to listen to the teaching, how to explain the teaching, and the way to conclude common to both [teacher and student].

How to listen to the teaching

This has three parts: contemplating the benefits of listening to the teaching, serving and honoring the teaching and spiritual teachers, and how to actually listen.

Contemplating the benefits of listening to the teaching

6 "The mind of all those who hear it is filled with faith.
You delight [in spiritual practice] and are constant in it.
Your wisdom grows and your ignorance ceases.
Thus it is worth buying even with your own flesh."[140]

Serving and honoring the teaching and spiritual teachers

7 "Listen to the teaching with complete faith and reverence,
free of pride and scorn for the teaching and the teachers;
cultivate respect for them—serving and honoring them and so on—
and consider the spiritual teachers as you do the Buddha."[141]

How to actually listen

This has two parts: cultivating the six recognitions and removing three faults like a vessel's.

Cultivating the six recognitions

8 Generate the recognitions: yourself as a patient, the spiritual teachers as physicians,
the Dharma as medicine, its steady practice as a treatment,
the tathāgatas as superior beings,
and [the wish for] the teaching to remain a long time.

Removing three faults like a vessel's

9 Dispel the faults like a vessel that is overturned, pierced, or soiled.
Listen very well, and remember what you hear.
In brief, while mindful of all the causes of buddhahood's attainment
and the benefits of hearing, take delight in listening.

How to explain the teaching

This has four parts: contemplating the benefits of explaining the teaching, serving and honoring the Teacher and the teaching, [15] the attitude and behavior with which to teach, and differentiating whom to teach from whom not to teach.

Contemplating the benefits of explaining the teaching

10 While rejecting consideration for gain, honor, and the like, as well as afflictive thoughts[142]
and incorrect explanations, teach [as the Buddha] taught the sutras and so on,
and you will gain the countless benefits
disclosed in *Invoking the Altruistic Resolve* and *Questions of the Householder Ugra.*[143]

Serving and honoring the Teacher and the teaching

11 When he taught the Mother of Conquerors, the Teacher prepared his own seat,
since for the buddhas the teaching is to be cherished.[144]
Recall therefore the good qualities and the kindness
of the teaching and the Teacher and generate reverence for them.

The attitude and behavior with which to teach

This has two parts: attitude and behavior.

Attitude

12 Abstain from withholding information, bragging, weariness with teaching,
criticizing others, procrastination, and jealousy.
Cultivate love for your followers and maintain the five recognitions.[145]
See the virtue of teaching correctly as the means for your happiness.

Behavior

13 Once you have prepared yourself well, washed, and so on,
sit on a throne and pronounce the profound *dhāraṇī*.
With a friendly demeanor, confident of the meanings and illustrations,
expound the excellent teaching using ample citations and reasoning.

Differentiating whom to teach from whom not to teach

14 Having been so requested, teach those whose behavior, when they listen,
accords with the Vinaya; when you know that they are worthy recipients,
it is taught that exceptionally you may teach when unsolicited.

The way to conclude common to both [teacher and student]

Next, dedicate the virtue of teaching and listening to consummate enlightenment.

15 In this way, every time you teach or listen,
you will gain the innumerable benefits that are taught.
Cherish this important advice that ensures successful teaching and listening,
for it is the foremost instruction on the preliminaries. [16]

Relying on Spiritual Teachers

How students are progressively guided by the actual teaching

This has two parts: how to rely on spiritual teachers, the root of the path, and while relying on them, how to progressively train your mind.

How to rely on spiritual teachers, the root of the path

This has two parts: a detailed explanation to ascertain [the topic] and a brief explanation for meditational purposes.

A Detailed Explanation to Ascertain [the Topic]

This has six parts: the defining characteristics of the spiritual teachers on whom to rely, the defining characteristics of the students who rely on them, the way to rely on them, the benefits of relying on them, the disadvantages of not relying on them, and a summary of the above.

The Defining Characteristics of the Spiritual Teachers on Whom to Rely

16 Next, since practice of the actual teaching
and every single good quality in a student's mind
depend on pleasing the excellent spiritual teachers,
knowing how to rely upon them is crucial from the start.

17 [Rely on those who] have broken in the mount of their mind by
training in ethical discipline;
on those who through meditative concentration have made it
serviceable with the reins of mindfulness and meta-awareness;[146]
on those who perceive profound suchness with the eye of wisdom,
have studied much, and whose good qualities surpass their students'.

18 Understanding suchness by citations and reasonings alone is also
acceptable.
[Rely on those] who are proficient teachers skilled in guiding others
in steps,
on those who have loving natures because their teachings are inspired
by compassion,
and on those who have surmounted discouragement by teaching with
diligence[147] and constant delight.

19 Although the five—the three trainings, understanding suchness, and
compassion—
are key qualities, if they are difficult to find [in others] given the
times,
follow those whose good qualities exceed their bad qualities.
Students are to rely on those possessing all these good qualities.

The defining characteristics of the students who rely on them

20 Rejecting bias, possessing intense aspiration,
having the intelligence to distinguish a path that is spiritual from one that is not,
paying close attention when listening to the teaching—
ensure that you have these, for they are what characterize a [good] student. [17]

The way to rely on them

This has two parts: how to rely on them in thought and how to rely on them in deed.

How to rely on them in thought

This has two parts: cultivating faith, the root; and cultivating reverence for them by recalling their kindness.

Cultivating faith, the root

21 With great faith, focus on the spiritual teachers' good qualities.
Do not consider their faults for even an instant,
for it will hinder your achievement of spiritual realizations.
If, out of carelessness, you do impute faults to them, confess it immediately.

Cultivating reverence for them by recalling their kindness

22 At this point, recall their kindnesses
and contemplate them while reciting them with a melody,
as taught in the *Ten Dharmas* and *Adornment of Trees* sutras.[148]
These are the ways to rely on spiritual teachers in thought.

How to rely on them in deed

23 Please them [by offering them] your life, children, spouse, wealth, and retinue,

by bathing, massaging, wiping, and nursing them,
by never disobeying them, whatever they instruct you to do,
and most importantly by offering them your practice.

The benefits of relying on them

24 The benefits are pleasing the buddhas, being close to spiritual teachers,
not falling into unfortunate realms, becoming immune to karma and afflictions,
and by enhancing your good qualities, achieving your temporary
and ultimate goals, and as such, they surpass those of making offerings to buddhas.

The disadvantages of not relying on them

25 If through ignorance you commit a breach of reliance on your spiritual teacher,
you will roast in the Relentless hell[149] after death.
Good qualities will not arise in you, and those you have will decline.
[Meeting] bad companions and false teachers also incurs these disadvantages.

A summary of the above

26 In sum, if you sincerely wish to practice the Dharma,
rely long on teachers who guide you infallibly.
By understanding the benefits and disadvantages as you do so,
value your commitment to the gurus more than you do your life. [18]

A brief explanation for meditational purposes

This has two parts: how to actually meditate and why it is necessary to meditate using both meditative approaches.

How to actually meditate

This has two parts: what to do in the actual meditation sessions and what to do between meditation sessions.

What to do in the actual meditation sessions

This has three parts: the preliminary practices, the actual meditation, and the concluding practice.

The preliminary practices

27 Next, in a clean place set up symbols of [the buddhas'] body, speech, and mind.
Arrange faultless offerings in an attractive way.
On a seat in the posture with crossed legs and straight back,
take refuge and generate the awakening mind, taking care to be sincere.

28 Visualize the merit field, with the guru as the main figure.
Perform the seven-limb practice that includes the key elements for accumulation and purification.
Of these, by five—homage, offerings, request, supplication, and rejoicing—
you gather the accumulations; confession purifies obscurations; and joy increases [virtue].
29 Dedication ensures that the virtues of accumulation, purification, and increase
are never depleted. To summarize,
there are three—accumulation, purification, and increase—along with rendering [virtue] inexhaustible [by dedication].
Then, after a mandala [offering], make requests for your desired goals:
30 that all kinds of unmistaken thoughts—reverence for the spiritual teachers and so on—
may arise in your mind, that external and internal
obstacles may ease, and so on.[150] With intense aspiration,
be sure to supplicate again and again.

The actual meditation

This has two parts: how to meditate in general and how to meditate in the present context.

How to meditate in general

31 To make your mind receptive to virtue,
be certain of the order and number of meditation topics,
and with neither excess nor want, be intent upon them while applying mindfulness and meta-awareness;
otherwise, the virtuous practices of a lifetime will be flawed.

How to meditate in the present context

32 In this context, reflect on the advantages of relying on spiritual teachers and
on the disadvantages of not relying on them, and refrain from considering faults.
With faith that is conscious only of their good qualities,
generate and sustain heartfelt reverence by reflecting on their kindness.

The concluding practice

33 At the end dedicate the virtue. Following this routine,
divide the day and night into four sessions and expend every effort.
Initially, do many short sessions, ending them on a good note. [19]
Once you have mastered these, you may meditate as you see fit.

[What to do between meditation sessions]

34 Between sessions, do not put the topics you are meditating
out of your mind but recall them again and again.
For their sake accumulate merit and purify your obscurations.[151]
Furthermore, restrain the doors of your senses and eat with moderation.

35 Strive in the yoga of no-sleep,[152] and when you do sleep,
apply proper posture, mindfulness, meta-awareness, and the like.
The practice of the preliminaries, actual meditation, conclusion, and between sessions
is the same up to insight with the exception of the actual meditations.

Why it is necessary to meditate using both meditative approaches

36 Just as gold becomes malleable when heated and washed,
the practice of focusing on disgust and delight [respectively, for example]
for black and white karmas and their effects
with firm apprehension of the object and prolonged analytical meditation,
37 also renders feasible tranquil abiding[153] and insight, whichever you desire.
Accordingly, to realize nonconceptual cognition,[154] analytical meditation is best.
When working to achieve tranquil abiding,
excessive analysis is inappropriate and placement meditation required.

38 Consequently, both scholars and meditators—
to ensure achieving tranquil abiding, faith in teachers, and so on—
should train using both analytical and placement meditations.
Moreover, as laxity and excitation hinder mental stability,
39 vigorous clarity is ideal for dispelling laxity
and vigorous disgust for dispelling excitation,
as taught in numerous excellent and authoritative treatises.
Since they remove adverse conditions, do not think it wrong to apply them.

Human Existence with Leisure and Opportunity

While relying on [spiritual teachers], how to progressively train your mind

This has two parts: urging to take full advantage of a [human] rebirth with leisure and the way to take full advantage of one.

Urging to take full advantage of a [human] rebirth with leisure

This has three parts: identifying leisure and opportunity, contemplating their great potential, and contemplating how difficult they are to attain.

Identifying leisure and opportunity

This has two parts: leisure and opportunity.

Leisure

40 Being born in a remote land, with incomplete senses, wrong views, [20]
and in a place where the Buddha's teaching is not found are the four human non-liberties.
Adding [rebirth as] a long-life god or in the three unfortunate realms, there are eight.
It is taught that averting these constitutes "leisure."

Opportunity

This has two parts: personal opportunities and general opportunities.

Personal opportunities

41 These are being [born] a human, in a central land, with complete senses;
not having committed an act of immediate retribution; and having faith in the three scriptural collections.

General opportunities

These are that a buddha has appeared, he has taught the Dharma, his teaching remains,
there are those who follow it, and there are those with compassion for others.

Contemplating the great potential of leisure and opportunity

42 Once you have attained a life with the ten opportunities,
to strive after this life's concerns is to behave like an animal.
Only a rebirth as a man or woman on three continents
is a suitable basis for taking vows, not one in Uttarakuru.[155]

43 In most rebirths as a god of the higher realms or the desire realm,
it is not possible to achieve an ārya path for the first time.[156]
Having attained a human life with a powerful mind,
if you use it meaninglessly, you are like someone stupefied by magic.

44 Not only is it the basis needed to travel the Tathāgata's path,
it is also the basis for creating the causes of a fortunate rebirth,
and those of wealth and entourage caused by generosity and so forth, and not any other.
For these reasons persistently contemplate its great potential.

Contemplating how difficult they are to attain

45 Tending entirely to nonvirtue is the door to unfortunate realms.
Anger is the thief who plunders your virtue.
You who fail to purify past misdeeds and refrain from future ones
yet take your ease, think what kind of life awaits you!

46 Since achieving happiness depends on the Dharma, you must practice it.
Because you have spiritual teachers as well as leisure and opportunity, you *can* practice it.
If you do not do it now, it will be difficult to find leisure and opportunity in the future.
As your time of death is not set, practice it from this day forward.

47 Compared to an unfortunate birth, a fortunate one is nearly impossible to attain.
If ordinary fortunate rebirths are rare, consider how exceptional leisure and opportunity are.
In brief, identify the nature of leisure and opportunity,
and contemplate the difficulty of attaining them from the perspective of karma and its effects. [21]

The way to take full advantage of leisure and opportunity

This has two parts: ascertaining the system of the spiritual path in general, and actually taking full advantage of them.

Ascertaining the system of the spiritual path in general

This has two parts: the way all discourses are included in the paths of persons of three capacities, and the reason you are guided in steps along the paths of persons of three capacities.

The way all discourses are included in the paths of persons of three capacities

48 Every spiritual path—the topic of all the [Buddha's] discourses—
is without doubt included in the paths of persons of three capacities,
for no discourse was ever given for any reason
other than to ensure the achievement of fortunate rebirths and definite goodness.

49 As the [three] stages lead respectively to the three: excellent fortunate rebirths and definite goodness,
the latter being twofold [and the second of which is] foremost, they are exhaustive.[157]

The reason you are guided in steps along the paths of persons of three capacities

This has two parts: what it means to be guided along the paths of persons of three capacities, and the reasons why you are to be guided like this in that order.

What it means to be guided along the paths of persons of three capacities

As for how to be guided, with some paths shared with persons of lesser and intermediate capacity
as preparations, you are led to the path of persons of great capacity.

The reasons why you are to be guided like this in that order

This has two parts: the actual reasons and the purpose.

THE ACTUAL REASONS

50 "The awakening mind is the central beam of the supreme vehicle.
For completing the two accumulations, it is like a philosopher's stone."[158]
All temporary and ultimate objectives without exception
are undoubtedly achieved by this supreme aspiration.

51 To realize the state of mind that carries such advantages,
you need to take profound delight in its benefits.
Since it is achieved by reflecting on the paths shared with persons of lesser and intermediate capacity,
be sure you contemplate them, and your achievement will be assured.

52 Its prime causes are love and compassion.
If, when you reflect on the way you are personally deprived of happiness
and tormented by suffering, you are not horrified,
how could you possibly find the suffering of others unbearable?

53 Thus you should reflect on how you are subjected to the unfortunate realms' miseries
and deprived of happiness even in fortunate births, relating it to yourself personally
according to the teachings for persons of lesser and intermediate capacity,
and love and compassion will emerge for sentient beings, your friends.

54 Furthermore, as the accumulations and purifications of persons of lesser and intermediate capacity
are the means to prepare your mind for the awakening mind,
contemplate how the topics of persons of lesser and intermediate capacity [22]
are prerequisites to the path of persons of great capacity, and treasure their practice.

55 Having trained in this way, stabilize the awakening mind
by performing the aspirational bodhicitta ceremony and studying the precepts.
Then, when you feel you can bear the load of bodhisattva practice,
take the vow of engaging bodhicitta and guard yourself against root transgressions even at the cost of your life.

56 Refrain from lesser and intermediate transgressions, and restore [your vow] if it declines.
Train in the six perfections in general and in tranquil abiding in particular
to attain clairvoyance and special insight.
Once you have a decisive understanding of suchness, engage in tantra.

57 Furthermore, having understood the profound and vast paths
along with their order, definitive number, and association,
cease contenting yourself with an incomplete path for achieving buddhahood.

THE PURPOSE

58 If you ask, since the paths of persons of lesser and intermediate capacity
are prerequisites for the great, why speak of three,
it is to overcome the pretense of being a bodhisattva without having trained in them
and to benefit those of great, intermediate, and lesser capacities.

59 The need to generate the attitudes of persons of the three capacities in steps
is explained in the sutras and by the great trailblazers.[159]
A person of lesser capacity is not a suitable recipient of the supreme path,
but there is no harm in teaching the shared paths to persons of intermediate and great capacity.

The Path Shared with Persons of Lesser Capacity

Mindfulness of Death

Actually taking full advantage [of a life with] leisure and opportunity

This has three parts: training the mind on the stages of the path shared with persons of lesser capacity, training the mind on the stages of the path shared with persons of intermediate capacity, and training the mind on the stages of the path of persons of great capacity.

Training the mind on the stages of the path shared with persons of lesser capacity

This has three parts: the actual training in a lesser-capacity person's attitude, the measure of having generated that attitude, and the elimination of false ideas regarding it.

The actual training in a lesser-capacity person's attitude

This has two parts: generating concern for future lives and relying on the methods for happiness in future lives.

Generating concern for future lives

This has two parts: while reflecting on life's brevity, cultivating mindfulness of death; and reflecting on how future lives will be: the joys and sufferings of the two kinds of rebirths.

While reflecting on life's brevity, cultivating mindfulness of death

This has four parts: the disadvantages of not cultivating mindfulness of death, the advantages of cultivating it, [23] what kind of mindfulness of death to produce, and the way to cultivate mindfulness of death.

The disadvantages of not cultivating mindfulness of death

60 By telling yourself every single day "I'll not die today"
and thinking about this life alone, the mind's vision declines,
virtue weakens, and the three doors are sullied by sin.
What could be worse than turning your back on the Dharma
this way?
61 Therefore, from deep within your heart, be mindful of death
and see the vanity of attributing great importance to this life.

The advantages of cultivating it

Maintaining that you will not die is the source of all woe.
Mindfulness of death is a treasure trove of all excellence.

62 In brief, now that you have the means to fulfill beings' aims,
understand the drawbacks of postponing Dharma practice, of sleep
and lethargy,
of idle talk, food and drink, distractions, and so forth,
and embed in your heart the uncertainty of your time of death.

What kind of mindfulness of death to produce

63 Then, although you cannot actually halt death,
you should fear a death linked with sin.
The way of the wise is to eradicate the causes of unfortunate
births
and produce those of fortunate births and definite goodness
before dying.

The way to cultivate mindfulness of death

This has three parts: being mindful of death's certainty, contemplating the uncertainty of the time of death, and contemplating that at the time of death nothing but the Dharma is of any use.

Being mindful of death's certainty

This has three parts: thinking that the lord of death is sure to come and that nothing can repel him, thinking that life span cannot be extended and that it shortens unceasingly, and thinking about having to die before finding the time to practice the Dharma in this life.

Thinking that the lord of death is sure to come and that nothing can repel him

64 For now, it is difficult to be fearless in the face of death.
"The three worlds' impermanence is like autumn clouds;
[observing] beings' birth and death is like watching scenes from
a play;
beings' lives pass like flashes of lightning in the sky
65 and are swiftly spent like water down a steep mountainside."[160]
When thoroughly trained in the fact of impermanence,
there is not a single external phenomenon that does not reveal it.

Thinking that life span cannot be extended and that it shortens unceasingly

[24] Although still alive, you draw nearer to death every day:
66 "Heroic being! From the very night
you were first conceived in this world,
you have henceforth, every single day,
raced without pause toward the lord of death."[161]

Thinking about having to die before finding the time to practice the Dharma in this life

67 When very old and very young, you do not think of the Dharma.
In between, given the time spent on food, drink, illness, and such,
even were you to live to a hundred, there would barely be time for
the Dharma.

68 Although it is not certain whether you will live today or die,
the way of the wise is to maintain the latter.

If you assume the former, you will feel remorse when the time to
die comes.
Since you have to die anyway, is it not best to be prepared for it?

Contemplating the uncertainty of the time of death

This has three parts: thinking that your time of death is uncertain as the life span in Jambudvīpa is indeterminate,[162] thinking that your time of death is uncertain as the body is extremely fragile, and thinking about the abundance of factors of death and the scarcity of those of life.

Thinking that your time of death is uncertain as the life span in Jambudvīpa is indeterminate

69 The life span in Jambudvīpa is extremely uncertain.

Thinking that your time of death is uncertain as the body is extremely fragile

This fragile body carries innumerable factors of death.

Thinking about the abundance of causes of death and the scarcity of those of life

Although there are a few life-sustaining conditions, when they
become factors of death,
you are sure to die, so take advantage of the Dharma!

Contemplating that at the time of death nothing but the Dharma is of any use

70 In brief, [think], "As I will have to give up the good things of this life,
and they will also doubtlessly let me down,
I refuse to get caught up with my body, loved ones, and belongings,
and I resolve to practice the Dharma."

71 For these reasons, do not belittle this instruction,
ignoring it and instead reaching up to high teachings beyond
your grasp.

If you feel disheartened, thinking you will achieve nothing even
though you meditate, [25]
make supplications [to the merit field] and bolster your courage.

Reflecting on the Way Future Lives Will Be: The Joys and Sufferings of the Two Kinds of Rebirths

This has three parts: contemplating the sufferings of hell beings and contemplating the sufferings of hungry ghosts and animals.

Contemplating the Sufferings of Hell Beings

72 Thus you will soon die; you have no time to stay.
At the time, you will not cease to exist, but depending on how your
karma
propels you, you will take birth in one of two kinds of lives [fortunate
and unfortunate].
If you fall into an unfortunate birth, the torments of heat and cold,

Contemplating the Sufferings of Hungry Ghosts and Animals [and Their Duration]

73 of emaciation from hunger and thirst, or of stupidity will be countless
and unbearable for [in a hell birth] as long as an intermediate eon.[163]
A human month being equivalent to a single day,
a hungry ghost's long life is ten thousand of its own years.
74 Animals too may be tormented by suffering for as long as an eon.
If you cannot even bear the prick of a thorn,
ask yourself what will happen when you are faced with the
unfortunate realms' torments.

Refuge: The Gateway to the Buddha's Teaching

Relying on the Methods for Happiness in Future Lives

This has two parts: (1) training in taking refuge, the excellent gateway to the teaching, and (2) developing the faith of conviction [in karma and its effects], the root of all happiness and goodness.

Training in taking refuge, the excellent gateway to the teaching

This has four parts: identifying the objects of refuge, what makes them worthy of refuge, what makes a refuge practice effective, and the precepts to observe once you have taken refuge.

Identifying the objects of refuge

75 When relying on methods for securing happiness in future lives,
those who seek liberation take as refuges
those who are entirely free of all faults
and possess all the various good qualities
as well as the Dharma and the ārya Sangha.

What makes them worthy of refuge

76 Worthy of refuge are those who are entirely free of all personal fears,
who are skilled in the methods to free others from their fears,
and who have compassion that embraces all. [26]
The Buddha has already provided the external conditions for refuge;
you must provide the internal ones: trust and firm regard for them as your refuge.

What makes a refuge practice effective

77 If you ask what makes a refuge practice effective:
a beautiful body, splendid with the glory of all the signs and marks,
[speech] that with a single utterance answers all queries at once,
wisdom and compassion that fully encompass the sphere of knowable entities,
78 and activity that is spontaneous and ceaseless—
these are in brief the Buddha's good qualities.
In addition, the Dharma's quality is to generate the above when contemplated.
The Sangha's quality is to practice the teaching well.
79 Those who achieve within themselves all of the following:
in-depth knowledge of the Three Jewels' specific qualities,

the view of the Buddha as the Teacher, the Dharma as the actual refuge, and the Sangha as companions,
and of our Teacher, his Dharma, and his Sangha
80 as faultless while the others are the opposite,
are considered by that to have an effective refuge practice.

THE PRECEPTS TO OBSERVE ONCE YOU HAVE TAKEN REFUGE

The proscriptive precepts are refraining from taking refuge in other deities,
refraining from the intention to harm or kill, and not frequenting tīrthikas.

81 The prescriptive precepts are making offerings, paying homage, cultivating faith, and so on
in relation to any likeness of the Tathāgata, even those made of wood;
feeling the same reverence that you have for the actual teachings and sanghas
for just a single line of the Dharma or an inch's worth of yellow robes;
82 also being your own witness to forsaking irreverence
and cultivating unconditional reverence in relation to the Three Jewels;
knowing the difference between Buddhist and non-Buddhist teachers, teachings, and students;
while recollecting the Jewels' kindness, sincerely endeavoring to make them offerings;
83 guiding sentient beings to the virtue of taking refuge;
and doing whatever activity you undertake only after putting your trust in the Jewels.
This is how to enter the Buddha's teaching
and establish the basis for generating all vows.
84 Previously accumulated karmic obscurations are attenuated and spent.
If the merit of it were to materialize, space could not contain it.
You do not fall into unfortunate realms, and you are invulnerable
to human and nonhuman hindrances; you achieve all your goals

85 and quickly realize buddhahood. Therefore, six times over a day and night,
take refuge while recalling these benefits.
Whatever befalls you, never forsake refuge.
When it is a matter of life or death, if you consider abandoning it [27]
86 or espouse two different refuges, you break your commitment.
With a fear of cyclic existence
and an understanding of the Jewels' ability to protect you from it,
refuge common [to all vehicles] consists in the attitude of putting your trust in them,
without ever abandoning them even in jest.

Karma and Its Effects

Developing the faith of conviction [in karma and its effects], the root of all happiness and goodness

This has three parts: contemplating karma and its effects in general, contemplating them in particular, and having contemplated them, how to turn from [nonvirtue] and to practice [virtue].

Contemplating karma and its effects in general

This has two parts: the actual contemplation of karma and its effects in general and contemplating the different kinds individually.

The actual contemplation of karma and its effects in general

This has four parts: karma is certain, karma increases greatly, karma not accomplished is not experienced, and karma once accomplished does not dissipate.

Karma is certain

87 From general virtuous and nonvirtuous karmas
arise general happiness and suffering; specific instances of happiness and suffering
arise from subtle specific instances of each kind of karma.

Karma increases greatly

88 Minor virtues and sins produce [respectively] great happiness and suffering.

Karma not accomplished is not experienced

Without accomplishing virtue and sin, it is impossible to experience happiness and suffering.

Karma once accomplished does not dissipate

Karma you have accomplished does not dissipate;
you do not experience effects of what you have not accomplished;
and karma is not exchanged like the giving and receiving [of gifts].[164]

Contemplating the different kinds individually

This has two parts: explaining the importance of the ten paths and establishing karma and its effects.

Explaining the importance of the ten paths

89 Although all actions of the three doors are not included in the ten,
classifying them broadly as ten karmic paths has been taught.[165]
If you do not adopt so much as a single virtuous practice such as ethical discipline
and yet portray yourself a Mahayanist,
90 it is taught that in the eyes of the buddhas you are deceiving the whole world.
Thus those who guard their speech, control their minds well,
and abstain from committing physical nonvirtues
are those who are endeavoring to follow the Great Sage's path. [28]

Establishing karma and its effects

This has three parts: black karmic paths, white karmic paths, and an explanation of other categories of karma.

Black karmic paths

This has three parts: actual black karmic paths, their difference in terms of seriousness, and explaining their effects.

Actual black karmic paths

91 Here is the way to analyze all ten nonvirtues, killing and so on,
from the point of view of the basis, attitude, action, and completion.
The basis [of killing] is a sentient being other than yourself; the attitude
consists of identification, an affliction, and a motivation.

92 Identification has four possibilities—recognizing a being to be so-and-so and the rest.[166]
The affliction is any of the three mental poisons; the motivation is the wish to kill.
When the motivation is nonspecific, it is a sin regardless of mistaking the object.[167]
The action is to stab, poison, use black magic, and so forth,

93 either doing it yourself or having it done for you.
For the conclusion, it is taught that owing to your action
the being to be killed must die before you do.[168]
The principle of the nonspecific motivation also applies to the remaining nine paths.

94 The basis of theft is property owned by another.
Within the attitude, identification and the affliction are analogous to killing.
The motivation is the wish to deprive the owner of property not given to you.
The action is accomplished by either force or stealth,

95 by doing it yourself or having it done for you.
Moreover, concerning things left in your care, debts, and so on,
deceiving someone is in most cases equivalent to theft.
It is taught that it is concluded by the component that is the thought of ownership.

96 The bases of sexual misconduct are unsuitable sexual partners such as your mother,

unsuitable orifices such as the mouth, anus, and so forth,
unsuitable locations such as near a stupa, your teacher, and so on,
and unsuitable times—during pregnancy, when one-day vows have been taken, and the like.
97 Within the attitude, while identification must be unmistaken for sexual misconduct,
for sexual relations it is taught that it is the same whether it is mistaken or not.
The *Treasury* however gives a different explanation.[169]
The affliction may be any of the three mental poisons; the motivation
98 is the wish for sexual relations that constitute sexual misconduct.
The action is striving to that end.
It is [most often] concluded by contact between the two [genitals].

The bases for lying are the eight—what you saw and so on[170]—and the interlocutor hearing you.
99 Within the attitude, identification is alteration of what you have seen
into what you have not seen, and so forth; for the affliction, it is as before.
The motivation is the wish to express the altered identification.
The action is speaking or concurring without speech,
100 for it is the same if you express yourself with gestures or other signals.
Whether spoken for your sake or another's, it is still lying. [29]
For all three—lying, divisive speech, and cruel speech—
it is taught that it will also be a karmic path when you have someone do it for you,
101 but the Vinaya states that you must speak yourself.
It is concluded when the other person understands what you say.
The three, lying and the rest, become idle talk when what you say is not understood.

The bases of divisive speech are compatible or incompatible sentient beings.
102 Within the attitude, identification and the affliction are the same as for lying.
The motivation is the wish to divide those who are compatible or to prevent reconciliation of those who are incompatible.

The action can be to speak truthfully or untruthfully, pleasantly or unpleasantly.
You can speak either for your sake or someone else's.
103 It is concluded when the divisive words spoken have been understood.

The basis for cruel speech is a sentient being toward whom
you feel hostile; the first two components of the attitude are as above.
The motivation is the wish to speak cruelly.

104 The action is to speak unpleasantly,
either truthfully or untruthfully, about any shortcomings in
family line, body, ethical discipline, and so on.
It is concluded when your interlocutor has understood what you said.

105 For idle talk the basis is a meaningless topic.
Within the attitude there is identification of the chosen topic,
the affliction can be any of the three mental poisons, and the motivation is
the wish to engage in senseless and futile talk.
106 The action is to begin to speak idly.
It is maintained that it is concluded once you have spoken idly.

The basis of covetousness is another person's wealth or property.
Within the attitude, identification consists of recognizing it as such.
107 The affliction is one of the three poisons, and the motivation is the desire for ownership.
The action is to pursue that thought.
It is concluded when, in relation to whatever it is, the wealth and so on,
the thought "May it be mine!" occurs.
108 The basis of ill will and the first two components of the attitude
are the same as those of cruel speech; the motivation is the wish to strike someone and so on,
the wish that someone's belongings deteriorate, and the like.
The action is to reinforce that thought.
109 It is concluded by the decision to strike someone and so forth.

It is asserted that the basis of wrong views is something that exists.
Identification is recognizing the denial as true.

The affliction is any of the three poisons; the motivation is the wish to deny its existence.

110 The action is to pursue that thought
and undertake denying the existence of the four: causes, effects, agents, and existents.[171]
It is concluded when you are certain of your denial.

Mental karmas,[172] being intentions, are karmas but not karmic paths.

111 The seven physical and verbal karmas are both karmas and karmic paths.
The three, covetousness and so forth, are karmic paths but not karmas. [30]
An action that an intention instigates is necessarily a karmic path.

Their difference in terms of seriousness

This has two parts: the seriousness of the ten karmic paths and, in addition, a brief explanation of powerful karma.

The seriousness of the ten karmic paths

112 For the seven physical and verbal karmas, the preceding ones are more serious than the succeeding.
For the three mental ones, the succeeding ones are more serious than the preceding.
Moreover, it is said that karmas motivated by intense forms of any of the three poisons
or done over a long period of time, habitually, or frequently are more serious.

113 It is taught that five factors: karmas generated continually, intensely,[173] with no antidotes,
or in relation to bases possessing major good qualities—
the latter being twofold: the knowledgeable and the beneficent—
strengthen any virtues or nonvirtues that you do.[174]

In addition, a brief explanation of powerful karma

This has four parts: powerful with respect to the field [of action], powerful with respect to the basis, powerful with respect to the object, and powerful with respect to attitude.

Powerful with respect to the field [of action]

114 In relation to the Three Jewels, gurus, worthy recipients of offerings,
your parents, and so on, whatever good or harm you do,
the [respective] merit or wrongdoing will be more powerful.
Stealing the property of the first two Jewels is redressed by returning it.
115 Taking the Sangha's property is not cleansed until you experience the result.
Robbing the Sangha of its food source leads to rebirth in a great hell.
Stealing anything else from it leads to a rebirth in the darkness surrounding the Relentless hell.
Compared to angrily throwing all sentient beings of the ten directions
116 into a dark prison, it is worse to say of a bodhisattva,
"He's evil. I never want to see him again!" and turn your back on him.
Compared to destroying as many stupas as there are grains of sand[175] in the Ganges River,
it is taught that it is a far greater sin to have angry or malevolent thoughts
117 toward a bodhisattva or to speak unkindly to one.[176]
Compared to lovingly restoring the sight
of all sentient beings in the ten directions who have been blinded,
or releasing all prisoners and establishing them in the joy of the Brahmā realm,
118 it is taught that aspiring to the Great Vehicle, wanting to meet bodhisattvas,
or singing their praises generates far greater merit.
Compared to killing all sentient beings of Jambudvīpa or stealing their belongings,
it is graver to prevent someone from offering a bodhisattva a handful of food.

Powerful with respect to the basis

119 Regret your past sins, guard yourself against future ones, do not conceal them,

and as an antidote to them, accomplish virtue—the sins of the wise are lighter.
Disregarding your sins and priding yourself on your knowledge is particularly serious. [31]
Compared to a lay bodhisattva's offering to the buddhas
120 of butter lamps [with wicks] as tall as Mount Meru and as numerous
as the three realms' beings, an ordained bodhisattva's offering
of a single oil lamp to the buddhas is superior.
Following this logic, the practice of the path by those who possess vows
121 is far more potent than that of those who do not.
Compared to the sinful deeds committed unceasingly
over a hundred years by a householder involved in the ten nonvirtues,
it is more serious for a bhikṣu with faulty morality, wearing the victory banner of yellow robes,
122 to partake of offerings made by the faithful for a single day.
Thus it is taught that sins also become powerful with respect to the basis.
With a basis endowed with vows, depending on whether they are threefold, twofold,
or one-day vows, whatever good or evil done will be [proportionally] greater.
123 It is worse than eating blazing lumps of molten iron
for those of faulty morality not to refrain completely from the above-mentioned sin.
It is taught that compared to sins committed in relation to the Dharma,
the sinfulness of the ten nonvirtues is insignificant.

Powerful with Respect to the Object

124 Among the different kinds of generosity, giving the teaching,
and among the different kinds of offerings, offering your practice of instructions—these are superior.
There are many other kinds of powerful karma with respect to the object.

Powerful with respect to attitude

It is taught that all that is done intensely and over long periods—
125 virtues imbued with the thought to achieve omniscience
and misdeeds akin to angry or malevolent thoughts—
constitute powerful karmas with respect to attitude.
The virtue of the three fundamentals does not counterbalance the sin of ill will.[177]

Explaining the effects of black karmic paths

This has three parts: maturation effects, effects concordant with the causes, and environmental effects.

Maturation effects

126 It is taught that from a very grave act of killing up to very grave wrong views,
the maturation effect is rebirth as a hell being; for the ten of average gravity,
as a hungry ghost; and for the ten of lesser gravity, as an animal.
The *Ten Grounds Sutra* inverts the effects of those of average and lesser gravity.[178]

Effects concordant with the causes

127 It is taught that for killing, the effect concordant with the cause is to have a short life.
For theft, it is to lack resources.
For engaging in sexual misconduct, it is the inability to keep a spouse.
For lying, it is to be subject to much slander; for divisive speech,
128 it is to be separated from loved ones; for speaking cruelly, [32]
it is to be told unpleasant things; for idle talk,
it is to have your words ignored; for the three mental nonvirtues,
it is to be subject to attachment, aversion, and ignorance, respectively.

Environmental effects

129 It is taught that the environmental effect of killing is that in a future life,
food, drink, medicine, and fruits will not be sustaining.
Theft leads to droughts, floods, and poor crops;
sexual misconduct to a swampy, filthy, or repulsive environment;
130 lying to unproductive labor, whether in fields or on boats;
divisive speech to uneven terrain that makes travel difficult;
cruel speech to an abundance of logs, thorns, and stones;
idle talk to inferior tree fruit and to it ripening unseasonably;
131 covetousness to the decline of excellences daily, monthly, and yearly;
ill will to epidemics, obstacles, diseases, conflicts, and wars;
wrong views to a decline of the world's best resources.

White karmic paths

This has two parts: white karma and its effects.

White karma

132 Now I will explain the white karmic paths.
In the present context, of the four—basis, attitude, action, and completion—
the basis [of not killing] is another sentient being; as for the attitude,
it is the wish to refrain from killing owing to seeing its drawbacks.
133 The action is the intention to completely refrain from killing.
The completion is the physical karma of thoroughly accomplished abstention.
This is the virtue of abstaining from killing; apply these to the rest.

Its effects

134 Among the ten virtues, the maturation effects of the three—those of lesser, average, and great [weight]—
are, respectively, rebirth as a human, a desire-realm god, and a higher-realm god.

Their concordant and environmental effects are the opposite of those of the nonvirtues; apply them here.

An explanation of other categories of karma

Although it is certain that virtuous karmas propel you into a happy rebirth
135 and nonvirtuous karmas propel you into a bad rebirth, it is taught that
their completing karmas are not necessarily the same, and that four possibilities exist.[179]
What is both accomplished intentionally and accumulated is karma whose effects must be experienced.
The opposite is karma whose effects are not certain to be experienced.

136 [The former] is karma accomplished intentionally either physically or verbally.
Excepting ten instances—what is done in dreams and so forth—
accumulated karma is identified as most of the rest.[180] [33]
Nonaccumulated karmas are the ten of what is done in dreams and so forth.

137 Karmas whose effects must be experienced are labeled from the perspective of when that occurs:
they are called "visible phenomena" when experienced in the very same life,
"karmas whose effects are experienced after rebirth" when experienced in the next life,
and "karmas experienced at another time" when experienced in the life after that or later.
These are the three categories.

Contemplating karma and its effects in particular

This has three parts: the advantages of full fruitions, their functions, and the causes of full fruitions.

The advantages of full fruitions

138 With the advantages of full fruitions, their functions, and their causes,
you attain an excellent life basis that engenders omniscience.
They concern life span, complexion, lineage, influence,
trusted speech, [renown for] great power, male birth, and strength.

Their functions

139 A long life span ensures the accumulation of virtue; complexion—the ability to attract disciples;
good lineage—the application of your instructions; influence—drawing sentient beings;
trusted speech—gathering them by the four means; [renown for] great power—
having what you do acknowledged and your instructions quickly heeded;
140 male births permit vast wisdom and fewer obstacles;
strength brings great enthusiasm and the quick attainment of supernormal powers.

The causes of full fruitions

The causes of full fruitions are [for long life and so on, respectively,] not harming sentient beings;
giving light—butter lamps and so forth—and new clothes;
141 overcoming pride; giving food, clothing, and so forth when requested;
habitually abstaining from the four verbal nonvirtues;
making aspirational prayers and honoring the gurus and the Three Jewels;
reflecting on the disadvantages of being a female and saving others from castration;
142 and helping in whatever way is suitable and providing food and drink.
If the eight have the three, the full fruitions will be excellent.
The three are pure attitude, pure practice, and pure field.
For pure attitude, there are two in relation to you:

143 dedicating to supreme enlightenment whatever virtuous causes you produce
and producing these causes from the depths of your heart.
On seeing those who comply with the teaching, refraining from rivalry and [instead] rejoicing
and, if you cannot do these, daily making the wish that you can [34]
144 are the two in relation to others.
For [pure] practice, there are also two: those that relate to you and to others.
The first is longstanding, intense, and uninterrupted [practice];
the second is inciting those who have yet to engage [in virtue] to do so,
145 to praise those who do for the purpose of gladdening them,
and to ensure that they continue and do not give up.
As for pure field, since both the attitude and the practice
yield an abundant and excellent harvest, they are called *fields*.

Having contemplated them, how to turn from [nonvirtue] and to practice [virtue]

This has two parts: a general explanation and, in particular, the way to purify yourself by means of the four powers.

A general explanation

146 Having learned about black and white karmas and their effects,
if you do not achieve uncontrived ascertainment of this topic of meditation,
when you meditate on emptiness, you will reject karma and its effects,
and whatever your practice, it is certain it will not please the buddhas.
147 The *King of Meditations Sutra* states:
"The moon and the stars may fall from their places,
mountains, cities, and the rest may crumble,
the space element itself may take on another form,
148 but you [Buddha] will never speak falsely.
Like magical illusions, bubbles, mirages, and lightning,
all phenomena resemble the moon's reflection in water.
Sentient beings, children of Manu,[181]
149 who after death move on to another life, do not exist [truly] either,

yet the karma they accomplish does not vanish.[182]
White or black, it bears fruit accordingly.
This way of reasoning is excellent indeed;
150 though subtle and difficult to comprehend, it is what the Buddha perceives."[183]
Furthermore, the *Satyaka Chapter* says:
"O king, do not kill.
Their life is what all sentient beings hold dearest.
151 Therefore those who wish to live long
should not contemplate killing even in the back of their mind."[184]
According to this instruction, as concerns nonvirtues such as the ten,
forswear even so much as the intention to commit them.
152 As this system is very subtle and hidden,[185]
you need to apply discriminating intelligence to establish it with certainty. [35]
In this regard, do not display bravado as in a contest;[186]
instead, I ask you to examine your three doors daily and strive to be conscientious,
for it is taught that all that befalls us is the consequence of our actions.

In particular, the way to purify yourself by means of the four powers

153 Correct your transgressions with the procedures specific to each of the three vows.
It is taught that the four powers are the best means to purify yourself of sin.
Strong and repeated regret about nonvirtues committed is the power of eradication.
Memorizing sutras, believing in emptiness,
154 reciting profound dhāraṇīs, making images of buddhas,
striving to present offerings to the Three Jewels, and reciting [the buddhas'] names:
these six and others constitute the [power of] engaging the antidotes.
Abstaining from faults and transgressions henceforth is the power of turning away from them.
155 Generating the awakening mind and refuge form the power of the support.

Regarding how sins are purified, it is taught that the suffering to be experienced
is shortened, reduced in intensity, or discontinued definitively,
or what would otherwise have been experienced severely in an unfortunate rebirth
156 occurs instead in the present life as just a minor illness.
The four powers even purify karmas whose effects are certain to be experienced.
Confession [without all four] weakens their capacity to produce maturation effects.
Although restoration is possible, it is best to avoid contamination in the first place.

The measure of having produced the attitude of a person of lesser capacity

157 Turning from concern for this life and feeling concerned mainly about future lives
is the measure of having produced the attitude of a person of lesser capacity.

The elimination of false ideas regarding it

Since with a fortunate rebirth you can achieve the supreme resultant qualities,
aspiring to one does not necessarily produce causes for samsara.[187]

The explanation ascertaining well the way to practice the path shared with persons of lesser capacity is complete.

The Path Shared with Persons of Intermediate Capacity

Training the mind on the stages of the path shared with persons of intermediate capacity

This has four parts: the actual training in this attitude, the measure of having generated the attitude, eliminating false ideas regarding it, and establishing the nature of the path leading to liberation.

The actual training in this attitude

[36] This has two parts: identifying the aspiration to liberation and the method to generate it.

Identifying the aspiration to liberation

158 As humans and gods have not transcended the suffering of conditioned existence
and are certain to fall again into unfortunate rebirths, their end can only be grim.
Given this, you must train in the attitude shared with persons of intermediate capacity.
Liberation is complete freedom from what binds you to cyclic existence.
The desire to attain it is the aspiration to liberation.

The method to generate it

This has two parts: contemplating the truth of suffering—the drawbacks of cyclic existence—and contemplating the origins—the process that propels you into cyclic existence.

Contemplating the truth of suffering—the drawbacks of cyclic existence

This has two parts: demonstrating the need to explain the truth of suffering first among the four truths and the actual meditation on suffering.

The Varieties of Suffering

Demonstrating the need to explain the truth of suffering first among the four truths

159 When reflecting on sufferings—the flaws of the appropriated aggregates—
you will see their faults, and the wish to discard them will arise of its own accord.
Once you have thoroughly understood how you are tormented by misfortune,
you will strive earnestly at the method to overcome its causes.
160 When you see that you *can* overcome them, you will be determined to attain cessation,
in which case, you will accomplish the paths leading to cessation.
For that reason, the sequence of suffering, its origins, its cessation, and the path
is essential for practice and should be highly valued.
161 Regarding the shared topics of meditation explained in the path of persons of lesser capacity
and the specific topics explained in the present context,
once you have properly ascertained which require analytical meditation and which placement meditation,
cultivate them in an intense and prolonged mental state.
162 The good qualities of the three vehicles[188] are accomplished by actual tranquil abiding and insight
or by states resembling them.

The actual meditation on suffering

This has two parts: contemplating the general sufferings of cyclic existence and contemplating the sufferings of specific states.

Contemplating the general sufferings of cyclic existence

This has two parts: contemplating the eight sufferings and contemplating the six sufferings.

Contemplating the eight sufferings [37]

163 The suffering of *birth* has five aspects:
Birth is associated with pain and associated with dysfunctional tendencies.
It is the basis of suffering and the basis of afflictions as well.
It is suffering as it induces unwanted separation [at death].

164 The suffering of *aging* also has five aspects:
A good physique declines, strength wanes, and senses deteriorate.
The ability to enjoy things decreases, and life span degenerates.
Reflect on these sufferings

165 and on the five sufferings of *illness*:
those of physical change, increasing mental anguish and so on,
a lack of desire for attractive things, the obligation to undergo
unpleasant treatments against your wishes, and the loss of your life.

166 The suffering of *death* also has five aspects:
the loss of your body, belongings, dear relatives, and entourage,
and the unmitigated suffering of anxiety. Reflecting well
on how you undergo these, foster disenchantment.

167 Suffering arises from the mere *encounter with people disliked*,
from the apprehension of being harmed by them, the dread of their criticism,
the fear of dying horribly,
and terror at the thought of falling into an unfortunate realm after death.

168 The *loss of what you care for* has five aspects as well:
When separated from your loved ones and so on, sorrow fills your mind.
You lament and inflict bodily harm on yourself.
Missing them and longing for them, you grieve.
No longer able to enjoy their company, you mourn.

169 The suffering of *not getting what you want despite seeking it*
resembles the suffering of the loss of what you care for.

Though you strive after and pursue your goals,
you fail and, filled with despair, are despondent.

170 *Appropriated aggregates lead to future suffering.*
They are also the basis for the sufferings of illness, aging, and so on.
As for manifest suffering and the suffering of change, [38]
both occur in relation to dysfunctional tendencies.
171 As from the very moment [the appropriated aggregates] arise they are in the nature
of the suffering of conditioned existence, they are [by nature] suffering.

Contemplating the six sufferings

The six sufferings are those of lacking certainty, lacking satisfaction,
abandoning your body repeatedly, being conceived repeatedly,
172 repeatedly changing status, and lacking companions.
These are condensed into three: the fact that nothing in samsara is reliable,
that samsaric pleasures indulged in never fully satisfy you,
and that you have been propelled like this since beginningless time.
173 The first, unreliability, has four aspects: of the body attained,
of harms and benefits received, of excellent resources, and of companions.
The second [dissatisfaction] is easy to understand; know that the third means
that there is no beginning to your series of lives.

Contemplating the sufferings of specific states

174 Humans also undergo sufferings like those of the unfortunate realms.
Demigods are plagued by envy for the gods.
Desire-realm gods also suffer at [the prospect of] falling after their death,
from being cowed,[189] torn to pieces, killed, and expelled.
175 As they have obscurations, higher-realm gods enjoy no freedom.
Although their meditative states are good, they will fall in the end.

Thoroughly reflect on these sufferings and others to induce disenchantment.

The Origins of Suffering

Contemplating the origins—the process that propels you into cyclic existence

This has three parts: how afflictions arise, how with them you accumulate karma, and how you die and are reborn.

How afflictions arise

This has three parts: identifying afflictions, the sequence in which they arise, and the drawbacks of the afflictions.

Identifying afflictions

176 If you put an end to the afflictions,
like seeds deprived of moisture, the seedlings of suffering will not grow,
despite your numerous karmas.
So become expert in applying the afflictions' antidotes. [39]

177 *Attachment* clings to attractive things.
Anger is a harsh state of mind, an attitude of hostility toward its objects.
Pride is an inflated state of mind that involves a sense of superiority.
Ignorance is an afflicted unawareness of the truth, and so on.

178 *Doubt* is a state of mind divided between what exists and does not, what a thing is and is not.
The *personal identity view*[190] is an afflicted form of wisdom that observes the self and so on.
Extreme views consider the self as perceived by the personal identity view
and apprehend it as either eternal or subject to annihilation.

179 *Holding to the superiority of views* is an afflicted form of discernment that observes

wrong views and the rest, along with their bases—the view holder's aggregates—
and regards them as superior. The *view of the supremacy of ethics and conduct*
is an afflicted form of discernment that maintains that these are paths to liberation.

180 *Wrong views* are afflicted forms of discernment that fall into denying what exists and affirming what does not.
I have explained these according to the general system of tenets.

The sequence in which they arise

Those who maintain that ignorance and the personal identity view are distinct
say that the personal identity view that mistakes the aggregates for the self
181 arises from ignorance that is unclear regarding the aggregates' mode of existence
and that the other afflictions arise from these.
Those who maintain that the two are one assert that the personal identity view
is the root of the afflictions; there are two schools of thought.[191]

The drawbacks of the afflictions

182 They destroy you, destroy other sentient beings, and destroy your ethical discipline.
You lose confidence and receive fewer offerings; teachers and protectors admonish you.
You quarrel, lose your reputation, and are reborn in states lacking leisure.
As you lose both [the virtue] gained and that which you have yet to gain, you are despondent.
183 Reflect extensively and keenly on these drawbacks,
and whenever any root or secondary affliction arises, be aware of it.
Think, "One has come!" and prize countering it with the antidotes.

How with them you accumulate karma

This has two parts: identifying the karma that is accumulated and the way it is accumulated.

Identifying the karma that is accumulated

184 *Karma as intention*—mental karma—is the mental factor
that moves the mind concomitant to it toward an object.
The physical and verbal karmas that are motivated
by karma as intention are called *intended karmas*.[192]

185 Nonvirtuous karmas are *nonmeritorious karmas*, [40]
Meritorious karmas are virtues of the desire realm.
Immoveable karmas are said to be contaminated virtues
of the form and formless realms.

The way it is accumulated

186 As āryas do not accumulate new karmas for projection into samsara,
all those who do accumulate it are ordinary beings, up to and including
the *supreme dharma* level of the Mahayana path of preparation.

How you die and are reborn

This has five parts: the factors of death, attitudes at death, where heat withdraws from, how after death you reach the intermediate state, and how from there you take birth in a new life.

The factors of death

187 The factors of death are the depletion of life span, the depletion of merit,
and the failure to avoid danger, regarding which the sutra mentions nine factors.[193]

Attitudes at death

At death, either of the two, virtuous or nonvirtuous states of mind,
may arise in your mind while coarse consciousness persists.

188 If you die in an ethically neutral state of mind,
neither of the two states of mind mentioned above occurs.

The virtuous have the impression of moving from darkness toward light,
and their death throes are less intense; for the sinful it is the opposite.
189 When the nonvirtuous die, various unpleasant forms
appear to them, and they are subjected to acute suffering.
Those whose actions were neutral experience neither pain nor joy at death.

It is taught that, except in the case of a rebirth as a god or hell being,
190 death throes are experienced for all birth scenarios.

When you die, between virtuous and nonvirtuous states of mind,
those that are most habitual for you will manifest; if both are equally habitual,
whatever thought occurs first will remain, and you will think of nothing else.

191 However, when the subtle consciousness comes into play,
both kinds of mental states cease and thoughts becomes neutral.
When dying, as long as various appearances remain clear to you,
attachment to self occurs owing to longstanding habit.

192 By the power of attachment to self, you think, "I will cease to exist";
a feeling of attachment to your body emerges that generates the intermediate state.
Stream enterers and once returners do not yield to attachment to self.
No attachment to self occurs in nonreturners.

Where heat withdraws from

193 For the virtuous and the sinful, respectively, heat withdraws first [41]
from the lower and upper body; consciousness leaves from the heart.
Initially, at birth, [consciousness] enters the blood and semen in [what becomes] the heart's center,
from where it also departs in the end at death.

How after death you reach the intermediate state

194 Like the tipping of a scale, you enter the intermediate state the moment you die.
You are born in it with complete senses, your body's shape like that of your future rebirth,
which it is stated both may and may not be redirected.[194]
Fellow intermediate-state beings and those with pure divine sight
195 see intermediate-state beings, who perceive their next place of birth.
The virtuous and the sinful in the intermediate state
see light and darkness respectively.

The *Entry into the Womb Sutra*[195] says that [their color] is like that of
a [burnt] log, smoke, water, and gold, respectively,
196 for [rebirth as a] hell being, animal, hungry ghost, and desire-realm god,[196]
and that the intermediate-state being is white for [future] form-realm beings.
There is no intermediate state in the case of rebirth in the formless realm.

In the intermediate state for a god rebirth you ascend, while for a human one you move forward.
197 In the intermediate state for rebirth as a wrongdoer, you advance with your head lowered.

As for life span, the maximum duration is seven days.
If you find your place of rebirth [in the interim], the duration is not certain; if not found after seven days,
you change bodies; it is possible to remain [in the intermediate state like this] up to seven weeks.

198 As an intermediate-state being's seeds may be altered,
someone in the intermediate state of a god may be born in another state,
as can any other kind of intermediate-state being; the principle is the same.

Some believe that the intermediate state of a god can last seven days
199 of a god life and so on, but here this is not accepted.

How from there you take rebirth

It is said when its [future] parents are coupling, an intermediate-state being
perceives them or does not—two ways are taught.
However, when it is to be born a female, it desires the man and wants to lie with him.
200 When it is to be born a male, it desires the woman and wants to exclude the man.
Then it sees only the male and female genitals,
and feeling angry with them, the intermediate state being dies, it is taught.
Like the tipping of a scale, it is conceived.
201 Once thick semen is generated through the parents' intense desire,
drops of both semen and blood inevitably ensue.
They join in the place of birth and assume a form like skin atop [boiled] milk.
Simultaneously, by the power of the consciousness at conception,
202 two aspects of great elements for the senses [those of blood and semen]
and those other than these[197] combine,
and an assemblage of semen and blood possessing senses ensues.
Then, for those who assert one, the storehouse consciousness enters it.
203 Those who do not assert a storehouse consciousness
maintain that a mental consciousness takes conception; there are two views.

If you do not hasten to the place of birth out of delight in it, [42]
you cannot possibly take birth in that place.
204 Therefore, butchers and such who are to be reborn in a hell
see beings to be slaughtered in that place and, by the force of habit, rush there with delight.
When they feel angry with the appearance of their place of birth,
their intermediate state ceases, and they are reborn in it.
205 When animals, hungry ghosts, humans, desire-realm gods,

and form-realm gods take birth, in their birth place they see
beings of the same kind as them and rush there with delight.
Next, they feel angry with the birth place and so on—the rest is the same as before.

206 Those to be born spontaneously long for a place; those to be born from heat and moisture long for smells;
those to be born in a hot hell long for warmth; and those destined for a cold hell coolness.
According to the *Treasury*,[198] [the process] for egg birth resembles womb birth.

The measure of having generated the attitude

207 Being repulsed by samsara and drawn to a state of peace
with the same will to escape
as those stuck in a burning house or prison
is the measure of having generated the attitude shared with persons of intermediate capacity.
208 Since without it you only pay lip service to the wish to accomplish the path to liberation
and you cannot achieve great compassion either,
do not content yourself with a mere understanding but pursue it earnestly.

Eliminating false ideas regarding it

209 Wandering in samsara under the influence of karma and affliction
is to be greatly feared by bodhisattvas as well,
but they delight in being reborn in it motivated by compassion and prayer.
This is how the sutra is to be understood.[199]

Establishing the nature of the path leading to liberation

This has two parts: the kind of life with which you overcome cyclic existence and the kind of path to meditate on to overcome it.

The kind of life with which you overcome cyclic existence

210 If householders make every effort, they too can overcome samsara.
However, buddhas and their children sing many praises
of the ordained life as the basis for rejecting samsara's faults. [43]
As the vow of ordination is that of individual liberation,
hold on to this root of the Dharma as you do your life.

The kind of path to meditate on to overcome it

211 The excellent path to overcome samsara involves the three trainings.
Moreover, "compared to one who, moved by faith,
for as many eons as there are grains of sand in the Ganges,
serves and honors billions of buddhas with food and drink,
212 parasols, banners, and rows of butter lamps,
one who observes a single precept for a day and night
at a time when the sacred Dharma is utterly disintegrating
and the Sugata's teaching is coming to an end
213 will gain far greater merit."[200]
Keep these words in mind! The *Questions of Subāhu Tantra* states:
"All aspects of the Vinaya—the pure ethical discipline
of individual liberation that I, the Buddha, taught—
214 except for the [external] signs and the rituals [of monasticism]
should be upheld by lay practitioners of mantra."[201]
Accordingly, you who aspire to liberation,
by your practice of sutra and mantra—each one reinforcing the other—
spread and develop the Buddha's teaching!

This completes the explanation ascertaining well the way to practice the path shared with persons of intermediate capacity.

The Path of Persons of Great Capacity

Generating the Aspiration to Buddhahood

Training the mind on the stages of the path of persons of great capacity

This has three parts: showing the awakening mind to be the sole gateway to the Great Vehicle; how to generate that aspiration; and having generated the awakening mind, how to train in bodhisattva practice.

Showing the awakening mind to be the sole gateway to the Great Vehicle

215 Though you attain simple liberation, given that at the buddhas' urging
you must ultimately join the Great Vehicle, [you should from the start],
"Enter the vehicle the Buddha Śākyamuni taught out of compassion;
by nature it consists only of helping others."[202]

216 [The awakening mind] is the source of all goodness, your own and others',
and the sole path traveled by all wise beings.
By working for others' welfare, you naturally accomplish your own.
Ah, entering the sublime path is indeed the sublime achievement!

217 The awakening mind is the gateway to the Great Vehicle. [44]
You may have nothing else, but with it you become a Mahayanist;
by losing it, you fall from the Great Vehicle.

How to generate that aspiration

This has two parts: the steps to training in the awakening mind and the way to sustain it by a ceremony.

The steps to training in the awakening mind

This has two parts: the seven-point causes-and-effect instruction and the training based on the works of the bodhisattva Śāntideva.

The seven-point causes-and-effect instruction

This has two parts: ascertaining the order and the actual steps of the training.

Ascertaining the order

This has two parts: showing that compassion is the root of the Great Vehicle path and the way the other causes and effect are its causes and effect.

Showing that compassion is the root of the Great Vehicle path

218 For complete buddhahood, the awakening mind, the altruistic resolve,[203]
compassion, love, the wish to repay kindness, recalling kindness,
and recognizing your mothers are the seven definitive causes and their effect.
For the harvest that is the state of a buddha,
compassion is like the seed, moisture, fertilizer, and ripe fruit.

The way the other causes and effect are its causes and effect

219 From the three—meditating on recognizing your mothers, recalling their kindness, and wishing to repay it—
arises the attitude of cherishing all sentient beings, who are viewed as congenial.
From this in turn follows the love that holds them dearly to the heart
like one's child;[204] from love issues compassion.

220 Although śrāvakas and pratyekabuddhas with the four immeasurable qualities exist,[205]
they do not adopt the responsibility to end the suffering of all beings,
whereas sublime heroes make the altruistic intention and take that responsibility,
affirming, "I will achieve happiness and the rest for my mothers."
It is inspired by compassion, and in turn it induces the awakening mind.

The actual steps of the training

This has three parts: cultivating the wish to pursue others' welfare, cultivating the wish to pursue enlightenment, and identifying the awakening mind—the training's result.

Cultivating the wish to pursue others' welfare

This has two parts: producing the basis for cultivating that attitude and engendering the actual attitude.

Producing the basis for cultivating that attitude

This has two parts: producing an equanimous state of mind toward sentient beings [45] and producing the view that all of them are dear.

Producing an equanimous state of mind toward sentient beings

221 Cease the bias by which you divide beings,
arguing that they are either your friends or your enemies,
and cultivate equanimity toward them, free of any attachment and aversion,
by following the instruction to visualize those indifferent to you and so on.

Producing the view that all of them are dear

This has three parts: meditating on your mothers, recalling their kindness, and cultivating the wish to repay their kindness

Meditating on your mothers

222 In your wandering through beginningless lives,
there is no type of womb in which you have never been born.
Thus it is established that all sentient beings have been your mothers.

Recalling their kindness

At the time, they cared for you as dearly as has your mother of this life.

Cultivating the wish to repay their kindness

223 What could be worse than not wanting to repay their kindness?

Engendering the actual attitude

This has three parts: cultivating love, compassion, and the altruistic intention.

Cultivating love

Visualizing sentient beings who are deprived of happiness,
cultivate love—the wish that they find happiness and so on.
For its benefits refer to the sutras, *Precious Garland*, and so on.[206]

Compassion

224 Visualizing sentient beings tormented by the three kinds of suffering,
cultivate compassion—the wish that they be free of their suffering and so on.
As for the sequence of the meditation, begin with your loved ones.

The altruistic intention[207]

Then, while reflecting on sentient beings, who are deprived of happiness and afflicted with suffering,
225 train in the altruistic intention, assuming responsibility for freeing them.

Cultivating the wish to pursue enlightenment

Seeing the need to attain enlightenment for others' sake,
reflect well on the buddhas' good qualities and generate the wish to attain them.
226 Induce the ascertainment that omniscience is necessary for your sake as well.

Identifying the awakening mind—the training's result[208]

> Having in this way trained in both objectives of the awakening mind,
> commit yourself to attaining complete enlightenment for others'
> sake. [46]

The training based on the works of the bodhisattva Śāntideva

> 227 Since cherishing yourself is the door to all misfortune
> and cherishing others the source of all excellence,
> invert the two attitudes that are
> cherishing yourself and neglecting others,
> and devote even the movement of your breath to others' welfare
> alone.

The way to sustain it by a ceremony

This has three parts: taking [the vow] you have not yet taken, keeping what you have taken from decline, and restoring the vow if it declines.

Taking [the vow] you have not yet taken

This has three parts: from whom to take it, on what basis to take it, and the ceremony for taking it.

From whom to take it

> 228 You are to take it from someone who has the vow of engagement

On what basis to take it

> once you have trained your mind on both shared paths
> with great enthusiasm for the awakening mind,

The ceremony for taking it

> excellently actualizing it with the three-part ceremony: preliminaries,
> main section, and conclusion.

Keeping what you have taken from decline

This has two parts: training in the causes that sustain the awakening mind in this life and training in the causes that prevent its loss in subsequent lives.

Training in the causes that sustain the awakening mind in this life

229 [With bodhicitta] you become worthy of the homage of gods and men.
You are watched over by twice as many protectors as a universal sovereign.
Mantra [recitation] is effective and confers the two kinds of attainments.[209]
"After deeply pondering the matter for many eons,
230 the buddhas saw its unique benefits."[210]
If the merit of it were to materialize, it would fill the sky and beyond.
Since its decline would mean wandering long in unfortunate realms,
do not abandon it even momentarily and recommit to it six times daily.

Training in the causes that prevent its loss in subsequent lives

This has two parts: training in giving up the four dark deeds that weaken it and practicing the four light deeds that prevent its weakening.

Training in giving up the four dark deeds that weaken it

231 Deceiving preceptors, those helpful to you, and celebrants[211] with lies;
making others regret the virtue they accomplished and did not repent; [47]
speaking unpleasantly of bodhisattvas within their hearing;
and being deceitful and hypocritical for no good reason.
232 Deceit and hypocrisy are explained [respectively] as using tactics to conceal your faults
and affecting possession of good qualities that you lack.

Practicing the four light deeds that prevent its weakening

Contrary to these four are the four light deeds:
abstaining from lies; maintaining honesty;
233 consciously regarding bodhisattvas as your spiritual teachers
and encouraging sentient beings so inclined to develop the aspiration to complete enlightenment.
The eight prevent the loss of the supreme aspiration in future lives.

Restoring the vow if it declines

234 Being able to take it again if it declines is unique to this vehicle.
You might break your vow of engagement, but as long as you maintain aspirational bodhicitta
and neither give up aspirational bodhicitta
nor abandon a sentient being, then transgressing any other bodhisattva precept
is only a fault that damages the virtues to which you have made a commitment.[212]

Working toward Buddhahood

Having generated the awakening mind, how to train in bodhisattva practice

This has three parts: having generated the awakening mind, why it is necessary to train in the [bodhisattva] precepts; showing that by training in method and wisdom separately, you do not achieve buddhahood; and explaining the process of training in the precepts.

Having generated the awakening mind, why it is necessary to train in the precepts

235 Although simply producing aspirational bodhicitta already carries great benefits,
making it your core practice is best.
Its practice consists of taking the vow and observing its precepts.[213]

Showing that by training in method and wisdom separately you do not achieve buddhahood

236 As buddhahood cannot be achieved by either method or wisdom in isolation,
train conjointly in unmistaken and complete method and wisdom.
The *method* in question is the awakening mind explained above;
wisdom is the view that penetrates the ultimate mode of being.[214] [48]
237 When meditating on emptiness, imbuing it with the awakening mind
and, when practicing generosity and the rest, imbuing them with wisdom—
this is what is meant by practicing method and wisdom conjointly.

Some say that by means of discerning wisdom,
238 you are to establish the ultimate mode of being
and then place [the mind] on this view and think of nothing else,
calling this one-pointed mental placement "meditation on the ultimate mode of being."[215]
[Others] when asked, "In what do you believe?" say,
239 "Excellent logical reasoning
cannot determine any reality, so the mind too should conceive nothing;
remaining in a state of suspension is best.[216]
By holding this view, all kinds of wrongdoing
can become causes of buddhahood."
240 [Question] Well then, for you what is wrong with meditating analytically
by means of discriminating wisdom?
[Answer] "All conceptions that think 'this is this' are instances of apprehension
241 of the self of phenomena and conceptions of the three spheres,
owing to which one fails to eliminate the causes of cyclic existence."
[Question] Then since contemplating refuge, spiritual teachers' qualities, and leisure and opportunity,
practicing mindfulness of death and the unfortunate realms' sufferings,
242 cultivating love, compassion, and the awakening mind,
and training in the precepts of engaging bodhicitta

must each be ascertained individually,
you dare assert these are all obstructions to omniscience?
243 If this were the case, then since the more you meditated on the selflessness of phenomena,
the weaker these good qualities of refuge and so forth would become,
would not view and conduct then become as incompatible as hot and cold?
And if these [good qualities] did not serve as causes of buddhahood,
244 it is indeed strange that according to your view
misdeeds like anger can serve as causes of buddhahood!
If you assert that it is like armor practice[217]—
all-inclusive—and that this [meditation] includes all the rest,
245 then why could not [a single practice of] generosity as in statements the likes of "anointing [a mandala] with cow dung and urine"[218]
also be enough on its own?
If, for you, this is just verbiage and not in fact true,
what arguments can you put forth then to justify your assertions?

246 At the initial [learning] stage, if you know how to correctly establish the two truths,
then, [when practicing] the path, method and wisdom will [be correct and] produce their results, the two kāyas.[219]
Even a partial explanation will allow those of vast intelligence to understand this.

Thus I pay homage to those endowed with objectless compassion,
247 who decisively teach existents' lack of inherent nature
without it contradicting cause and effect to the slightest degree.

Explaining the Process of Training in the Precepts

This has two parts: how to train in the Great Vehicle in general and how to train in the Mantrayāna in particular. [49]

How to Train in the Great Vehicle in General

This has three parts: cultivating the desire to train in bodhisattva precepts; having cultivated it, taking the vows of the buddhas' children; and having taken these, how to train in the precepts.

Cultivating the desire to train in bodhisattva precepts

Without having taken the mantra vows or those of individual liberation,
it is not appropriate to train in those precepts.
248 Here, however, you first familiarize yourself with the precepts
and then take the vows, a method that makes them very firm.

Having cultivated it, taking the vows of the buddhas' children

For the way to take them, refer to the explanation found in the *Ethics Chapter*.[220]

Having taken these, how to train in the precepts

This has three parts: the basis of the training, how the precepts are included in these, and the process by which to train in them.

The basis of the training

All the precepts fall within the six perfections.

How the precepts are included in these

This has two parts: certainty with respect to the number of actual topics and, in addition, certainty as to their sequence.

Certainty with respect to the number of actual topics

249 There are six ways to determine the six perfections' number.
The number is certain in terms of: high rebirth, accomplishing the two goals,
fulfilling others' goals, and encompassing the entire Great Vehicle.
It is established in terms of including the different methods.
250 Their number is also certain in terms of the three trainings.
With an excellent life basis, whatever the goal—yours or others—
whatever vehicle you abide in, whatever methods you use,
and whatever trainings you accomplish, they will fall within [the practice of] the six perfections.

In addition, certainty as to their sequence

251 Among the six perfections, a subsequent perfection arises based on
the one that precedes it.
Since each is superior to the one preceding it,
and the preceding one is coarser than the subsequent one, the
sequence is certain.

The process by which to train in them[221]

This has two parts: how to train in [bodhisattva] practice in general and how to train in the last two perfections in particular.

How to train in [bodhisattva] practice in general

This has two parts: training in the perfections that develop into buddha qualities and training in the four means of gathering others to mature their minds.

Training in the perfections that develop into buddha qualities

This has six parts: the way to train in generosity, ethical discipline, forbearance, diligence, meditative absorption, and wisdom.

The way to train in generosity

[50] This has three parts: the nature of generosity, its divisions, and the way to cultivate it in you.

The nature of generosity

252 The virtuous intention to give and what that virtue motivates—
the intention in the mind when engaging in physical or verbal
giving—
constitute generosity's actual nature.

Its divisions

Its divisions are giving Dharma and so on.[222]

The way to cultivate it in you

253 The best is to generate the heartfelt thought
to give all your possessions to others.
The perfection of generosity is not the simple rejection of miserliness.
Understand that generosity is complete when the intention to give has been perfected.
254 When you give your body, possessions, and virtue produced in the three times,
if you infuse it with all six perfections,
you will fulfill all your immediate and long-term needs.

Ethical discipline

255 Referring mainly to the ethic of abstention,
ethical discipline consists of the intention to give up and turn from harming others
along with its bases;[223] it has three divisions.[224]
The vow of individual liberation within a bodhisattva's mind
256 is the vow of ethical discipline, not the bodhisattva vow.[225]
If the bodhisattva vow of abstention degenerates,
it is taught that all vows decline as a consequence.
The precepts to which you have committed yourself,
257 even the subtlest, are to be kept pure without exception.
Among sentient beings, those with pure ethical discipline are as majestic as mountains.
Without duress or coercion, all beings pay them homage.
They are faultless, adorned thereby, and so on—its benefits are numerous.

Forbearance

258 The nature of forbearance is not being affected by another's harm or by suffering
and having belief in the teaching.
Its divisions are threefold—certainty regarding the Dharma and so forth.[226]
Neither virtues destroyed by ill will and wrong views

259 nor nonvirtues neutralized by the four powers
can produce their results, even when the conditions for them are met.
This is what is meant by "destruction of the maturation effect."
It is taught that it is not necessarily the same for effects concordant with the cause.
260 Because holding wrong views, abandoning the sacred teaching,
scorning bodhisattvas or gurus out of pride, and so on
produce very serious maturation effects and destroy virtues
the same way anger does, you are to strive to put an end to them as well. [51]
In brief, with respect to forbearance and non-forbearance,
be mindful of their benefits and drawbacks, and prize adopting the one and rejecting the other.

Diligence

261 Diligence is mainly a mental state
of delight in collecting virtue and helping sentient beings.
For the sake of alleviating a single being's suffering,
abiding exclusively in the hells for billions and billions of countless eons
262 without allowing your zeal for complete enlightenment to wane
is called "armor-like [diligence]."
Adding to this the diligence for collecting virtue and for accomplishing sentient beings' welfare, there are three.
Reject sloth, self-deprecation, and attachment to negative activities.
263 Its conducive conditions are the powers of aspiration, constancy, joy, and suspension.[227]
While associating it with the six perfections and aspiring to virtue,
abide in diligence and nurture it in others as well.

Meditative absorption

264 Meditative absorption is defined mainly as a mental state
that focuses one-pointedly on a virtuous object.
In terms of nature there are two kinds: mundane and supramundane.
In terms of orientation there are three: tranquil abiding, insight, and both combined.

265 In terms of function, the divisions are: generating physical and mental bliss,
achieving good qualities, and helping sentient beings. [The three functions are defined:]
(1) whenever you enter a state of absorption, physical and mental pliancy arise,
(2) you achieve the clairvoyances, liberations, totalities, and masteries,
266 and (3) you practice the eleven ways to assist others as needed.[228]
These are the three divisions according to function.
While aware of the benefits [of engaging] and the drawbacks [of not engaging], engage in it.
As before, train in it while associating it with all six perfections.

Wisdom

267 Wisdom observes an examined object
and is a state of mind that analyzes phenomena thoroughly.
Three divisions are taught: wisdom that realizes the ultimate, the conventional,
and the welfare of sentient beings.
268 Wisdom is the root of visible and invisible good qualities.
It eradicates all the misfortunes of cyclic existence and of [personal] peace.
It reconciles what appears to be incompatible.
Without it, views and ethical discipline will be flawed.
269 Using wisdom to analyze the topics of learning and reflection
quickly leads to sublime wisdom, the fruit of meditation.
Letting yourself forget the teaching and placing all your hopes in meditative absorption
is like letting valuable cattle go and clinging to their hoofprints. [52]
Therefore practice wisdom while associating it with all six perfections.

Training in the four means of gathering others to mature their minds

270 "Giving necessities" [is giving] even your life and the rest without hesitation.

"Pleasant speech" is teaching disciples the perfections.
"Implementation of practice" is prompting them to implement what you have taught.
"Consistency with practice" is doing what you have taught others to do.
271 Strive at these key elements to mature others' minds.
Giving necessities gladdens them, and they then heed you.
Next, pleasant speech dispels their ignorance and doubts.
Encouraging implementation of practice inspires them to accomplish it.
272 Consistency with practice is practicing yourself such that others take you as a model.

Concerning cultivating the six perfections in meditative equipoise and post-equipoise,
you cultivate tranquil abiding, insight, and the forbearance that is certainty regarding the profound Dharma in meditative equipoise
and generosity, ethical discipline, part of forbearance,
273 and parts of meditative absorption and wisdom in post-equipoise.[229]

If, before taking the vows of engagement, you have developed great enthusiasm
for [bodhisattva] practice and become confident [that you can uphold them],
they will be very firm when you take them in a ceremony.

This concludes the explanation of how to ascertain well the way to cultivate aspirational bodhicitta and train in bodhisattva practice in general.

Introduction to Tranquil abiding and Insight

How to train in the last two perfections in particular[230]

This has six parts: the benefits of cultivating tranquil abiding and insight, explaining how all states of concentration are included in the two, the nature of tranquil abiding and insight, why it is necessary to cultivate both, how the order is certain, and how to train in each.

The benefits of cultivating tranquil abiding and insight

274 All mental states of one-pointed focus on virtuous objects
and all states of wisdom of discriminating analysis—be they initial or more—
are included in the categories of tranquil abiding and insight, respectively.
The latent predispositions that generate more and more
275 wrong perceptions in the mind,
and the states of mind that by wrongly conceiving their objects
activate these latent predispositions
are known [respectively] as "dysfunctional tendencies" and "bondage to signs."
They are eliminated by cultivating tranquil abiding and insight.

Explaining how all states of concentration are included in the two

276 Since the good qualities, whatever they are, of the perfections of meditative absorption and wisdom [53]
are qualities of tranquil abiding and insight,
by thoroughly practicing both tranquil abiding and insight,
which include all states of concentration, you accomplish the roots
of the good qualities of the three vehicles that the Buddha taught.

The nature of tranquil abiding and insight

277 Tranquil abiding is a nonanalytical mental state that, having quelled distraction to external objects,
abides one-pointedly on its object
and is induced by the bliss of pliancy.
When analytical meditation, riding the mount of tranquil abiding,
induces pliancy by its own power, special insight is attained.
Since it perceives distinctly, it is called "special insight."

Why it is necessary to cultivate both [tranquil abiding and insight]

278 Some assert that although tranquil abiding has clarity, its clarity lacks vigor,
while insight has it. This is incorrect,
for the difference [between having vigorous clarity or not] is one of the absence or presence of laxity;
tranquil abiding too must be free of laxity,
279 and all states of concentration free of laxity
are guaranteed to have mental clarity.
Whether it is tranquil abiding or insight that is observing emptiness,
in either case emptiness must be understood; however, given that
280 not all nonconceptual states of concentration necessarily realize emptiness,
you should keep in mind that both states of concentration not aimed at emptiness
and states of concentration that understand emptiness
can be blissful, clear, and nondiscursive.
281 With the achievement of tranquil abiding, not only does the wisdom analyzing the ultimate mode of being
surmount the fault of instability,
every topic requiring analytical meditation
avoids the fault of excessive instability,
and this strengthens any virtue that is accomplished.

How the order is certain

282 As regards the present system in which tranquil abiding and insight must be produced in that order,
one might ask, "What is wrong with a person with a preexisting understanding of selflessness
achieving tranquil abiding and the insight into emptiness concurrently?"
283 [Answer:] We do not assert that having a simple understanding and experience of the ultimate mode of being
requires achieving tranquil abiding first.

For a person who does not yet have [a realization of] emptiness arisen-from-meditation,
attaining special insight arisen-from-meditation with emptiness as its object
284 without prior analytical meditation
is possible in highest yoga [tantra],
but in the three lower classes of tantra and in this [sutra] context,
although you may seek an understanding of selflessness
285 and analyze it repeatedly before you achieve tranquil abiding,
that alone will not allow you to achieve tranquil abiding. [54]
If you practice nonanalytical placement meditation,
you may achieve tranquil abiding, but since you lack
286 training in insight, you will achieve tranquil abiding first
and insight only later, and thus the order remains the same.
Insight is achieved by discerning wisdom's
analysis inducing pliancy.
287 Whether it is in relation to the way things are [ultimately] or in their diversity,[231]
the order is certain; if it were otherwise,
it would contradict the sutras and the treatises of numerous scholars and practitioners.
This order concerns an initial attainment.
288 Afterward, you may meditate on insight first.
Thanks to insight included in the preparatory stage [of the first absorption],
some achieve the tranquil abiding that is included in the actual absorption.[232]

How to train in each

This has three parts: how to train in tranquil abiding, how to train in special insight, and how to unite the two.

Tranquil abiding

How to train in tranquil abiding

This has three parts: relying on the prerequisites for tranquil abiding, the way to cultivate tranquil abiding on their basis, and the measure of having achieved tranquil abiding by meditation.

Relying on the prerequisites for tranquil abiding

289 The prerequisites for tranquil abiding are to reside in a harmonious place that has five good qualities,[233]
have few desires, be content, have few activities, have pure ethical discipline,
and reject thoughts of desire.

The way to cultivate tranquil abiding on their basis

This has two parts: the preliminary phase and the central phase.

The preliminary phase

Meditate on the preliminary topics, the awakening mind, and so forth.

The central phase

This has two parts: in what physical posture to meditate and an explanation of the meditative process.

In what physical posture to meditate

290 In the central phase, sustain the physical posture having eight features.[234]

An explanation of the meditative process

This has two parts: how to generate faultless states of concentration and how to produce the mental states on that basis.

How to generate faultless states of concentration

This has three parts: what to do before focusing the mind on the object of meditation, what to do while focusing on the object, and what to do once focused on the object.

What to do before focusing the mind on the object of meditation[235]

Possessing joy and bliss, you are physically satisfied and achieve happiness in this life.

Since you have achieved pliancy, your mind is amenable to virtue.
As uncontrolled distraction toward incorrect objects [55]
291 has been quelled, misbehavior is avoided.
Your virtue is potent, and you soon attain clairvoyance and other supernormal powers.
Realizing insight into the profound, you gain freedom from cyclic existence.
Moreover, regardless of what you meditate on, you are enchanted
292 with the evident advantages of states of concentration and this enhances your faith.
Faith induces aspiration, which in turn inspires diligence.
From it arises pliancy, which completely precludes the laziness
that weakens states of concentration.

What to do while focusing on the object

This has two parts: identifying the object, the basis on which the mind is placed, and how to focus the mind on it.

Identifying the object, the basis upon which the mind is placed

This has two parts: objects of meditation in general and determining the objects relevant to the present context.

Objects of meditation in general

This has two parts: the actual objects and indicating the objects suited to specific persons.

The actual objects

293 Universal objects, objects purifying behavior, objects of skill,
and those purifying afflictions are the four kinds of general objects.[236]

Indicating the objects suited to specific persons

Specifically, the object for those with strong attachment is ugliness;
For those with much distraction, the movements of their breath.
294 Furthermore, to discern the remedies that reject attachment and so forth,

examine how, in relation to objects of attachment and so on,
attachment and the rest arise with great, average, or lesser intensity.

Determining the objects relevant to the present context

295 In the case of great distraction, breathing is the appropriate object.
As taking the body of the Tathāgata and so on[237] as an object
serves many purposes, practice that.
By repeatedly observing an excellent likeness of the Teacher,
296 memorize his physical features.
This will allow an image of the Buddha to appear in your mind.
Next, mentally picture it as the actual Buddha.
To facilitate its appearance, first meditate on the physical features roughly.
297 When these have become stable, meditate on the details.
Having many different objects of meditation precludes achieving tranquil abiding.
You visualize several times sequentially the head,
the two arms, the torso, and the two legs; [56]
298 when you, in the end, have a general mental image
of the entire body together and distinguish the features roughly
from head to foot including the limbs,
it may not be clear and include its radiance,
299 but you should content yourself with it, for you have "found the object."
If you keep repeating the sequential visualization in hopes of making it clearer,
it may become sharper, but it will hinder your state of concentration.
It may not be very well defined, but if you do not err concerning the object,
300 you will soon attain a state of concentration and easily achieve clarity.
At this stage, if the color, shape, size, or number
of the object of meditation changes, do not pursue it;
unerringly maintain the original object—this is of great importance.
301 If it is difficult to get an image of the deity to appear no matter what you do,
place your mind on one of the other objects mentioned above

or on the view ascertaining emptiness and maintain it there,
as achieving tranquil abiding is the priority.

How to focus the mind on it

This has three parts: presenting the flawless method, rejecting flawed methods, and explaining the duration of sessions.

Presenting the flawless method

302 The two attributes that states of concentration require are
the vigorous clarity that is a very clear mind
and the nondiscursive stability
that remains one-pointedly on the chosen object.
303 Some assert four, adding bliss and limpidity.
However, limpidity is already present, and bliss is not needed at this point.
Therefore, as explained above, it definitely requires two features.
Laxity hinders the achievement of vigorous clarity,
304 and excitation thwarts one-pointed nondiscursiveness.
So, having identified the contrary conditions—coarse and subtle laxity and excitation—
prize relying on the conducive conditions—mindfulness and meta-awareness.
Once the previously ascertained object of meditation has appeared,
305 vigorous mindfulness is said to "tie the mind" to it
and prevent the mind from being distracted by other objects.
Thus, in the present context, mindfulness has three features:
a specific object, a mode of apprehension, and a function.[238]
306 Furthermore, as explained above, once the object of meditation is found,
the mind maintains it and thinks
that it is tied to the object. Once a heightened and firm mode of apprehension [57]
is achieved, without thinking of anything else,
307 you unwaveringly sustain the force of that state.
This is the key point of applying mindfulness.
Moreover, cultivating states of concentration consists mainly
of sustaining mindfulness; as for mindfulness,

308 as its mode of apprehension is one of ascertainment [of the object],
if the ascertainment's mode of apprehension is not tight,
clarity may be achieved but not vigorous clarity.
Even those who believe in objectless meditation[239]
309 must admit distraction-free meditation,
in which case, as it is taught, the way to sustain mindfulness, free of distraction,
without losing the focal object does not differ.

Rejecting flawed methods

310 Some think that mindfulness—the key point explained above—
may be free of laxity but that it runs a great risk of excitation,
and I have seen them declare that good relaxation is good meditation;
this is a case of mistaking laxity for meditation.
311 If you think there is no such fault since clarity is present,
in this case the mistake lies in not distinguishing lethargy from laxity.
Therefore, I will explain the right balance between tightness and looseness,
which the wise and the serious should guard as they do their life.
312 When you sense that were you to heighten [your focus on the object], excitation would occur,
you must slacken it a degree.
When you sense that were you to leave it as is, laxity would arise,
you are to heighten it a degree.
313 You will know how to place your mind by observing it intelligently,
without letting mindfulness's focus decline.
Meta-awareness just observes and watches from a corner of the mind,
checking whether the root object is still present
314 and whether laxity or excitation has arisen.
Before the vigor of the initial state of mind is depleted,
from time to time, neither too seldom nor too often,
monitor it and, similarly from time to time,
315 recall the original object of meditation.
Meditating thus with strong mindfulness, you will be aware of laxity and excitation.

If you meditate for long periods without comprehending the key
point of mindfulness,
your mental acuity will decline, and your forgetfulness increase
greatly.
Understand the phrase "the mind expresses the object again and
again"[240]
to mean that mindfulness sustains it and does not forget it.

Explaining the duration of sessions

316 While you still have the fault of weak meta-awareness
that fails to quickly identify the forgetfulness that tends to
distraction
as well as laxity and excitation,
the instruction is to conduct frequent but short meditation sessions.
317 Once you have overcome both faults, you may extend the sessions
slightly.
Setting an hour or two hours as the duration of [58]
a meditation session, continue as long as you are able.
Adapting [the duration] to your personal mental capacity,
without forcing yourself, meditate even as you reject obstacles.

What to do once focused on the object

This has two parts: what to do when laxity and excitation occur and what to do when laxity and excitation are absent.

What to do when laxity and excitation occur

This has two parts: applying the antidote to failing to identify laxity and excitation and applying the antidote to failing to make an effort to reject them once identified.

Applying the antidote to failing to identify laxity and excitation

This has two parts: the definitions of laxity and excitation and the way to produce meta-awareness that is aware of them in meditation.

The definitions of laxity and excitation

318 By nature, excitation springs from attachment.
Its object is pleasant and attractive.
Its mode of apprehension [of its objects] is troubled and scattered.
It attends to its object with the aspect of craving.
319 Its specific function and role is to prevent the mind
from remaining focused on its object.

Since laxity, which is either virtuous or ethically neutral,
does not apprehend the object tightly,
320 limpidity is present, but the clarity lacks vigor.
Lethargy is either nonvirtuous or an ethically neutral obstruction.
It causes laxity and springs from ignorance.
It is physical and mental heaviness and unserviceability.

The way to produce meta-awareness that is aware of them in meditation

321 When you see that either laxity or excitation is on the verge of arising,
if you do not apply strong meta-awareness,
the simple knowledge of what laxity and excitation are will be useless.
There are two ways to sustain meta-awareness:
322 as explained above, by maintaining mindfulness continually
and, within that state, by standing guard from a corner of the mind
and monitoring whether or not the mind
has moved from its object toward another.
323 The latter is the second part of the key point for sustaining
meta-awareness,
for just as strong mindfulness is a cause of meta-awareness,
so is repeated monitoring from a corner of the mind.

Applying the antidote to failing to make an effort to reject them once identified

This has two parts: identifying intention, the way to reject laxity and excitation, [59] and identifying the causes from which laxity and excitation arise.

Identifying intention, the way to reject laxity and excitation

324 Just as the presence of a magnet makes a piece of metal move,
the mental factor of intention turns the mind
toward virtue, nonvirtue, or the ethically neutral.
In this context, direct application—intention—is the antidote
325 to making no effort when laxity and excitation occur.

Since laxity arises when the mind is turned too far inward,
and its apprehension of the object has loosened,
it is by cultivating joy, not sadness, that you overcome it.
326 Hence, by analyzing deities' forms, images of light,
or whatever objects you desire, generate joy and raise your spirits;
elevate and expand your apprehension of the object;
go walking, perform recitations, or contemplate the six topics of recollection;[241]
327 wash your face with water or gaze at the planets and stars;
reflect on the benefits of the awakening mind and of leisure and opportunity;
avert the causes of laxity and meditate on whatever engenders limpidity.

Excitation runs after objects out of attachment.
328 In this case, meditating on impermanence, renunciation, disillusionment, and so forth
will automatically mitigate excitation.
When mental scattering prevails, the instruction is to bring the mind back immediately.
When excitation predominates, it is also appropriate to instantly recall the mind.[242]

Identifying the causes from which laxity and excitation arise

329 Not guarding the senses, not eating the right amount,
[untimely] sleeping, lacking diligence, and not exercising meta-awareness

are causes common to both laxity and excitation; the causes of laxity
are over-sleeping, practicing tranquil abiding excessively,
330 remaining in a fog, and not delighting in maintaining the focal object.
The causes of excitation are a lack of disenchantment,
unfamiliarity with diligence, an excessively tight focus,
and distraction by thoughts of home, loved ones, and so on.
331 When laxity and excitation are about to arise, you must avert them.
Ignoring them because they are minimal will mar your state of
concentration.
When mental scattering and excitation occur, seek stability within.
When stable, if you suspect laxity, generate vigorous clarity
332 and do not content yourself with simple limpidity.
At first it is difficult to find a balance between them,
but through habit it will not fail to become easier.

What to do when laxity and excitation are absent

333 Once you feel confident that laxity and excitation will not occur
for the duration of a session, meditate with the factor of equanimity [60]
and ease your exertion, without reducing the vigor of your focus.

At the preliminary stage, [the main fault] is laziness.
334 When striving to concentrate, it is forgetting the instruction.[243]
When in meditative equipoise, it is laxity and excitation.
When laxity and excitation occur, it is non-exertion. When free of
laxity and excitation, it is application; these are the five faults.
335 The four that are faith, aspiration, exertion, and pliancy
counteract laziness; the four that are mindfulness, meta-awareness,
application, and equanimity, respectively,
counteract forgetfulness, laxity and excitation, non-application, and
application.
336 In this way, the eight applications oppose the five faults.
Be aware that they are needed in highest yoga tantra as well.

How to produce the mental states on that basis

This has three parts: the actual process of generating the mental states, how they are attained by means of the six forces, and how four attentions are involved in this.

The actual process of generating the mental states

337 Placement, continuous placement, renewed placement,
close placement, subjugation, pacification,
complete pacification, one-pointed attention,
and balanced placement are the nine states to be cultivated.

How they are attained by means of the six forces

338 The following is the way the nine mental states are achieved by the six forces:
the first two forces are for the first two mental states, respectively.
Each of the three middle forces produces two states in succession.
The last one generates the ninth, balanced placement.
Hearing, reflection, mindfulness, meta-awareness, diligence, and thorough familiarization
339 are the six forces...

How the four attentions are involved in this

...There is tight focus,
intermittent focus, uninterrupted focus,
and effortless focus; adding "attention" to each gives the four.
The first attention applies to the first two [mental states],
340 the second attention to the next five,
the third attention to the eighth,
and the fourth attention to the ninth.
This is how the four attentions apply to the nine.

The measure of having achieved tranquil abiding by meditation

This has three parts: explaining the line between achieving and not achieving tranquil abiding, explaining how to travel the spiritual path in general based on tranquil abiding, and explaining how to travel the mundane path in particular. [61]

Explaining the line between achieving and not achieving tranquil abiding

This has two parts: the actual meaning and, secondly, the signs of having attention[244] and the elimination of doubts.

The actual meaning

This has two parts: how attaining tranquil abiding depends on attaining complete pliancy and how tranquil abiding is achieved once complete pliancy is attained.

How attaining tranquil abiding depends on attaining complete pliancy

341 Neither laxity nor excitation is present in the eighth mental state,
but since mindfulness and meta-awareness must still be applied continually,
it is called *direct application* or *effort*.
Given that this is not necessary in the ninth state, it is called *effortless*.
Nevertheless, as pliancy has not yet been attained,
it is still part of the desire realm and is not attention.

How tranquil abiding is achieved once complete pliancy is attained

342 The inability to direct the mind and body toward virtue as you wish
is called *mental and physical dysfunction*.
Once freed of it, the body and mind
become as [malleable as] cotton fluff—completely serviceable to virtue.

343 It is stated that when familiarization with serviceability is complete,
it becomes tranquil abiding: a one-pointed [main mind] accompanied by pliancy.
According to the five signs portending pliancy, as soon as the meditator's
brain feels pleasantly heavy and so on,

344 mental and physical pliancy arise in succession.
The former is known as a perception and the latter as a tangible object.

When physical pliancy first occurs,
although it is associated with physical and mental feelings of bliss and well-being,
345 still the easily identifiable signs of complete
pliancy are yet to be attained. Subsequently,
when any coarse bliss and well-being that could unsettle the mind have subsided
and a state of immovable concentration, as subtle as a shadow,
along with its concordant pliancy are achieved, then tranquil abiding and equipoise—
the lowest attention belonging to the [form] realm—are attained.

The signs of having attention and the elimination of doubts

This has two parts: the actual signs of having attention and the elimination of doubts.

The actual signs of having attention

346 The signs of having attained this attention are:
the ability to purify the afflictions; when in a state of equipoise,
the two kinds of pliancy arise more and more quickly;
the five obstructions[245] rarely occur;
347 a measure of pliancy persists post-equipoise; [62]
having reached this level, tranquil abiding and pliancy
each enhance the other's development;
in equipoise all coarse appearances cease,
348 and you feel that your mind has blended with the sky;
when you rise from it, you feel that you suddenly rediscover your body;
afflictions are weakened; mental scattering is unable to continue;
you have strong stability and experience great clarity;
you can combine sleep with a state of concentration; and you have good dreams.

The elimination of doubts

349 Then, as explained above, if the state of concentration that is attention
realizes the view of selflessness by means of a mental image,

it is posited simply as a path to liberation of a non-ārya.
When it is instilled with the awakening mind, it will be a Great Vehicle path.
350 If neither is present, then by nature it will be the state of concentration
that is common to both Buddhists and non-Buddhists.
Thus, among states of concentrations characterized by bliss, clarity, and nondiscursiveness,
a distinction must be made between meditative states
that correctly realize the ways things ultimately are and those that do not.

Explaining how to travel the spiritual path in general based on tranquil abiding

351 Furthermore, both non-Buddhists and Buddhists
and all yogis of the three Buddhist vehicles
must first rely on tranquil abiding to achieve all the various kinds of special insight:
those that eliminate manifest afflictions with the coarse and peaceful aspects[246]
352 and those that eliminate their seeds; or those that have the aspect of the eighteen elements,
the discernment of characteristics, the truths, and so forth.
Consequently, as explained above, tranquil abiding
is called "the enabling preparatory phase of the first absorption."[247]
353 Concerning insight with the coarse and peaceful aspects,
some Buddhists practice it while others do not.
Non-Buddhists do not have insight [with the sixteen aspects of the four] truths and so on.
Practitioners of highest yoga tantra, when at the generation stage,
may also achieve tranquil abiding but not for the purpose
of achieving insight with the coarse and peaceful aspects.

Explaining how to travel the mundane path in particular

354 The attention from the ninth mental state up to attention [tranquil abiding]
is called "novice at attention."

The one from the attainment of attention up to [and including]
discernment of characteristics
is called "novice at purification of afflictions,"

355 as explained in the *Śrāvaka Grounds.* Thus, the first [of the seven
divisions] of the preparatory phase
and the discernment of characteristics are not concurrent. [63]
If the two were considered concurrent,
tranquil abiding without prior placement meditation would be
possible,
as would tranquil abiding prior to the preparatory phase.

This completes the explanation ascertaining well the gateway to tranquil abiding—the nature of the perfection of meditative absorption.

Insight

How to train in special insight

This has four parts: relying on the prerequisites for insight, the divisions of insight, how to cultivate insight, and the measure of having achieved insight through meditating.

Relying on the prerequisites for insight

This has two parts: a general presentation of how to rely on the prerequisites for insight and how to establish the view in particular.

A general presentation of how to rely on the prerequisites for insight

356 Studying the authoritative works of Nāgārjuna and Āryadeva
and the commentaries that expound their intentions
and establishing the excellent view with the intellect
that distinguishes the definitive meaning from the provisional
357 are the vital prerequisites for special insight.
Consequently, rely primarily on the works of Buddhapālita and
Candrakīrti,
and relate to them the deep and distinctive contents
of all other excellent treatises on the profound.

How to establish the view in particular

This has three parts: identifying the affliction ignorance, demonstrating that it is the root of turning in cyclic existence, and seeking the view of selflessness out of a wish to eliminate grasping at self.

Identifying the affliction ignorance

358 The object of negation, true existence, is grasped
not conceptually but as established by way of its own nature,
from the side of the object, since beginningless time.
359 This conceived object is known as "self" or "nature."
In relation to their bases—persons and phenomena—the two absences [of this object]
constitute the two forms of selflessness;
as such, the two thoughts conceiving this mode of existence
360 in relation to the two bases constitute the two kinds of grasping at self.

Some proponents of Madhyamaka and Cittamātra tenets
maintain that the object of grasping at the self of persons is the mere "I,"
yet when asked for the referent of that mere "I," [64]
361 for some it is the storehouse consciousness, for others mental consciousness, and so on.
The answers vary, but according to the present system,[248]
the mere "I" that is the object giving rise to the simple thought "I am"
is asserted to be the object [of grasping at the self of persons],
362 and the aggregates are not considered to be its referents,
even for a second; this is a unique feature of this system.
Similarly, the object of the innate thought "This is mine"
is just "mine" as well,
363 and it is taught that your eyes, ears, and so on are not to be considered "mine."

If something is the object of the innate view of personal identity,
it must spontaneously give rise to the thought "I" or "mine"; therefore Devadatta's
364 perception apprehending Kratu[249] as established by way of his own nature

is not a view of personal identity but a case of innate grasping at a self.
The objects of innate grasping at the self of phenomena
are the form aggregate—eyes, ears, the world as a container, and so on.
The aspect [mode of perception] of grasping at both the self of persons and the self of phenomena
is the apprehension of them as established intrinsically.

Demonstrating that it is the root of turning in cyclic existence

365 For that reason, neither of these is the mere postulation through tenets
of a permanent, unitary, and independent [self]
or of the perceived and the perceiver as having distinct substances.
Because they do not rely on conditioning by faulty tenets—
366 those born as animals over many eons also have them—
they are known as "*innate* grasping at self."
If the root of samsara is the personal identity view,
since grasping at the aggregates' true existence is [also] the root of samsara,
367 you may wonder "does that not make two distinct roots of samsara?"
In fact, the latter is the cause, and the former is its result,
and although their objects are different, they share the same mode of apprehension.
Thus the objection that you raise does not concern me.
368 They are like, for example, two successive similar moments of ignorance
that your system also recognizes as roots of samsara.
Since the personal identity view is considered to be the ignorance
that apprehends true existence, your objection is not relevant.[250]
When, through ignorance, an object is held to exist truly
and the object in question does not match with your way of thinking,
369 anger flares toward it.
When it matches with your way of thinking, attachment ensues; when it is neutral,
neither of these occurs, but another similar moment of ignorance arises.
The way the rest follows is explained in the intermediate person's path.[251]

Seeking the view of selflessness out of a wish to eliminate grasping at self

This has two parts: why seeking the view realizing selflessness is necessary if you want to reject ignorance, and how to generate the view realizing selflessness.

Why seeking the view realizing selflessness is necessary if you want to reject ignorance [65]

370 Since it is stated[252] that perceiving the object's selflessness
neutralizes the seeds of cyclic existence,
by correctly refuting the object as it is perceived by grasping at self,
you avert all faults—the afflictions—
like the branches and leaves of a tree whose root has been cut.
371 Therefore, if you forego the path that opposes the mode of apprehension
of samsara's root, innate grasping at self, you will find no other path
able to eradicate the seed of the view of self.
372 Without a mind engaging the two kinds of selflessness,
realizing selflessness is inconceivable,
as rejecting [grasping at self] is not like extracting a thorn.
In sum, it is identification of and meditation on the lack of true existence that averts grasping at true existence;
373 thoughts that are forms of incorrect attention are then averted;
their elimination averts the attachment and so forth that are rooted in the personal identity view;
next the karmas that these inspire are averted;
and without the karmas there is no risk of further birth in cyclic existence,
in which case you can be certain that liberation will be attained.

How to generate the view realizing selflessness

This has three parts: the order in which the two views of selflessness are cultivated, the actual process of successively cultivating the two views, and a presentation of the conventional and ultimate truths.

The order in which the two views of selflessness are generated

374 Ascertaining the selflessness of objects based on a mirror image
is easy; based on other objects it is not.
Similarly, realizing the lack of intrinsic existence
in relation to the person is easier; in relation to other phenomena it is not.
375 As in the case of similes, it depends on the base.
For this reason, the order is established according to what is easier:
"Just as you have discerned it in relation to your own self,
extend this mentally to all [phenomena]."[253]
As this explains, the order of meditation is certain.

The actual process of successively cultivating the two views

This has two parts: establishing the selflessness of persons and establishing the selflessness of phenomena.

Establishing the selflessness of persons

This has two parts: identifying the person and establishing its lack of intrinsic nature. [66]

Identifying the person

376 Be they ordinary beings or āryas, every being exists solely as a mere "I"
designated on the basis of the aggregates.
For that reason, the aggregates are the bases of designation,
and the person is what is designated, as the sutras clearly explain.
377 As a basis of designation is not the thing designated,
the view of the aggregates is not the view of the self of persons.
When it is stated[254] that the view of the self perceives the aggregates,
this is to refute a self that is a substance distinct from the aggregates.

Establishing its lack of intrinsic nature

This has three parts: establishing the lack of intrinsic nature of the "I," establishing the lack of intrinsic nature of "mine," and explaining how the person appears as an illusion on that basis.

Establishing the Lack of Intrinsic Nature of the "I"

378 The key point of the object of negation is to identify the mode of apprehension of the view of self,
the key point of the entailment is to refute a third possibility regarding true existence,
the key point of the property of the subject is to see the error of each mode of existence,
the key point of what is to be established is that this naturally leads to ascertaining [the lack of true existence],[255]
379 and when all four key points are present, a perfect view will emerge.
Since [an existent] can only be established as either one or distinct [from its parts],
what exists truly must also be established as either [one or distinct].
Since all [phenomena] possess parts and since partless [phenomena] do not exist,
380 the object of negation appears to be self-sufficient and stand on its own.
If things existed in this way, as they appear to, then they would have to exist truly.
Furthermore, if an intrinsically existing self and aggregates
shared the same nature, they would be entirely indistinct.
381 If you agree with this, then the self could not take up and discard aggregates;
there would have to be as many selves as there are aggregates;
when your aggregates disintegrate, the self too would have to disintegrate,
in which case, the karma accumulator and the one experiencing [its results] in the future,
382 being intrinsically other, would be unrelated.
If you agree with this, then you could not recall your past lives and say who you were,
for sharing a single continuum has been refuted.
If you assert the disintegration of a self and aggregates that were intrinsically one,
383 then a single continuum of past and future lives becomes impossible.
Agreeing with this would mean experiencing [results of] karmas you have not accomplished

and the karma you accomplished being depleted.
If an intrinsically established self and aggregates were distinct,
384 valid cognitions should discern it, but none does.
The aggregates are characterized by production, maintenance, disintegration, and so on,
and since the self would have none of these, it would be permanent and so forth.

Establishing the lack of intrinsic nature of "mine" [67]

385 When you analyze the matter in this way, since you cannot find that
the self and the aggregates are intrinsically one nor that they are intrinsically distinct,
the self as well is neither intrinsically one nor distinct,
and as such the self lacks intrinsic existence.
386 Just as the nonexistent child of a barren women cannot develop eyes,
the self's lack of intrinsic existence applies to "mine."
With the reasoning that examines whether the phenomena ascribed
to their bases of designation are intrinsically one or distinct,
anyone analyzing knowable entities
can realize the two truths—how marvelous!

Explaining how the person appears as an illusion on that basis

This has two parts: explaining the meaning of the expression "to be like an illusion" and the method through which illusion-like appearances occur.

Explaining the meaning of the expression "to be like an illusion"

This has two parts: the correct way illusion-like appearances occur and the incorrect way illusion-like appearances occur.

The correct way illusion-like appearances occur

387 Although nirvana exists from the perspective of a direct nondeceptive perception apprehending it,
it is taught that nirvana too is like an illusion
from the perspective of refuting true existence.

Similarly, although [in post-equipoise] things appear to this perception [as truly existent], they do not exist intrinsically
388 as they appear to; that is, in the perception of persons, forms, sounds, and so on,
appearance [as truly existent] is combined with [awareness of] emptiness, and so it is taught that their appearance is like an illusion.
Emptiness is not nihilistic, since agents and actions, although empty, do exist.
As phenomena fundamentally lack intrinsic existence,
389 and this is known, it is not a mental contrivance.[256]
As this [lack of intrinsic existence] applies to all knowable entities, it is not partial.
As it is established by mind, it is not an unsuitable object of perception.
As it is discoverable by a mind understanding emptiness, it is knowable as well.
390 Yet, as true existence has been negated, it is said to be like an illusion.
[Question:] Since ordinary beings' direct perceptions can establish that reflections, dreams, magical illusions,
and so forth do not exist as they appear,
does that fact not make them āryas?
391 [Answer:] Establishing that a face's reflection, magical horses and elephants,
and houses that appear in dreams are not actual houses and so on
does not mean that you have established their emptiness.
Nevertheless, as previously explained, these are used as concordant examples.
392 The subtle emptiness relative to these phenomena is the fact that
they do not exist in the way they appear; these coarse appearances exclude
their being truly established, a fact that can be established by contemplation. [68]
After realizing the lack of intrinsic existence using these familiar examples of falseness,
393 you then realize it in relation to phenomena not known to be false.
Thus the order of realization is certain—first the examples and then the meaning. "The realizer of one thing's

[emptiness] realizes all [things' emptiness];"[257] the meaning of this statement
is that when [the emptiness of the example] is first realized [inferentially], by simply changing the mind's orientation [to the person],
394 it can be realized in relation to it. As for the way a direct realization [occurs],
[the example and the meaning] are realized concurrently; this is the [sutra's] intent.
Simply knowing that reflections, magical horses and elephants,
and houses that appear in dreams are not real
cannot produce even a partial awareness
of their lack of intrinsic existence.

The incorrect way illusion-like appearances occur

395 By failing to identify the limits of the object of negation as explained above,
some affirm that since the objects, once excluded [one by one] by reasoning, are not found,
the same is true of the mind of the analyzer:
the person ascertaining this nonexistence must also not exist in the least;
396 just as [in equipoise, they say,] there is nothing to be ascertained as either existing or not existing,
[in post-equipoise] various hazy appearances arise.
These are nihilistic states of equipoise and post-equipoise that demolish interdependence.
Instead of meditating on the key point of refuting the object of negation,
397 they merely sustain non-mentation for long periods,[258]
following which things appear like smoke or rainbows—
flimsy, insubstantial, and vague—
but these states of equipoise and post-equipoise do no more than negate things' coarse obstructive property.
398. Whoever by valid cognition succeeds in faultlessly establishing
both the utter absence of intrinsic existence and [the reality of] cause and effect,

along with the relationship between them, has discovered the
profound path.

The method through which illusion-like appearances occur

399 Therefore, once you have negated the reference point
of apprehension of signs in meditative equipoise and have
effectively
accomplished space-like meditation on emptiness,
when, having risen from that state, you observe objects' appearance,
400 the illusion-like post-equipoise state naturally emerges.[259]
Similarly, after intense analytical meditation on emptiness
has induced an ascertainment, as stated previously, illusion-like
perception occurs;
there is no specific meditation for illusion-like perception.

401 In brief, once the mental image of the object of negation has
appeared,
conceived by the ignorance within your mind,
[the person and its aggregates] would have to be distinct or one
if intrinsic existence were to exist as such, [69]
402 but you clearly see that each has arguments to disprove it,
and this induces an ascertainment. Then, by the power of the prior
reasoning,
the conclusion dawns
that the person has not the slightest degree of intrinsic existence.

403 Train again and again in meditating on emptiness in this
manner.
Then [post equipoise] let persons and [other] conventional things
appear to your mind
and reflect on how dependent arisings are tenable
despite their lack intrinsic existence until you are certain of it.
404 The concordant example is that a reflection of a face is devoid
of being a face
yet it arises from the conditions mirror and face.
Similarly, although persons are not intrinsically established,

they result from karma, afflictions, and so forth and are the
experiencers [of their results].
Reflect again and again on how this is tenable.

Establishing the selflessness of phenomena

This has two parts: negation by application of the previously explained reasoning and negation by another reasoning not previously explained.

Negation by application of the previously explained reasoning

405 Next, meditation of the selflessness of phenomena
is fully accomplished by applying the reasoning explained above.

Negation by another reasoning not previously explained

This has two parts: the reasoning of dependent origination and the way to establish the lack of intrinsic existence of noncomposite phenomena as well by means of this and the former reasoning.

The reasoning of dependent origination

Additionally, these do not exist: results occurring not in dependence [on their causes]
and things having parts not being dependent on their parts.
406 As such, by analyzing how things that arise dependently and are designated dependently
are either intrinsically one with or distinct
from what they depend on, you are to refute their true existence.

The way to establish the lack of intrinsic existence of noncomposite phenomena as well by means of this and the former reasoning

Therefore cessation, space, nirvana, and such
are posited [respectively] as what is to be attained, known, and taken as a refuge.
If they were established intrinsically, this would not be tenable.

However, conventionally the distinction between definition and definiendum for each is tenable,
408 otherwise all unrelated things could be others' definitions and definienda.
If you assert that they are related, that nullifies their true existence. [70]
With the reasoning called "one with or distinct from" too,
the parts of noncomposite things and the possessors of those parts
are to be analyzed as either intrinsically one or distinct.
This reasoning also easily establishes their lack of intrinsic existence.

A presentation of the conventional and ultimate truths

This has three parts: the bases and number of the two truths, the significance of these divisions, and an explanation of each division.

The bases and number of the two truths

409 Only knowable entities are classified into the two truths.

The significance of these divisions

Although the two truths share the same nature, their conceptual and nominal identities are distinct.[260]

The explanation of each division

This has three parts: conventional truths, ultimate truths, and why it is certain the truths are two in number.

Conventional truths

This has three parts: the literal meanings of "conventional" and "truth," the definition of conventional truth, and the divisions of the conventional.

The literal meaning of "conventional" and "truth"

Persons who have abandoned ignorance
perceive things—forms and so on—as mere conventional phenomena.

410 Since things exist truly from the perspective of the apprehension of true existence
in those who apprehend it, they are called conventional *truths*.[261]
However, conventional truths are not established by the apprehension of true existence.
That is, it is not just because something exists truly from the perspective of the apprehension of true existence
411 that it is established as a conventional truth.
From the perspective of those who have eliminated the apprehension of true existence,
only *conventional* is posited [in the pair *conventional* and *truth*], not true existence.
Nevertheless, conventional truth can be posited from their perspective.

The definition of conventional truth

412 The flawless definition of a conventional truth is this:
any phenomenon that is perceived by a conventional valid cognition
and in relation to which phenomenon such a cognition is valid on the conventional level.

The divisions of the conventional

413 Svātantrikas, who assert a consciousness that exists through its own characteristics,
deny the distinction between true and false for subjects but admit it for objects.
Those who make a distinction between true and false in the present system
on the basis of worldly conventional valid cognition are laughable.
414 For that reason, although a distinction between true and false conventional realities
is made from the perspective of some ordinary perceptions, [71]
in our system that does not justify establishing true and false conventional realities.
Given that it is impossible for there to be conventional realities
wherein the way things appear matches the way they [ultimately] exist, they can only be false.

Ultimate truths

This has three parts: the meaning of "ultimate object" and "truth," the definition of ultimate truth, and the divisions of ultimate truths.

The meaning of "ultimate object" and "truth"

415 Since it is the "object" and also "ultimate," it is *ultimate object*,
and since it is nondeceptive, it is said to be a *truth*.[262]

The definition of ultimate truth

This has two parts: the actual meaning and a refutation of objections.

The actual meaning

The irrefutable definition of an ultimate truth is this:
a phenomenon that is perceived by a valid rational cognition[263]
416 in relation to which phenomenon such a cognition is valid on the ultimate level.
Although anything that exists is posited as existing from the perspective of conventional minds,
not everything posited by conventional minds exists.
In the present system, the truth of cessation and nirvana are asserted to be ultimate truths,
yet their existence is posited from the perspective of conventional minds.

A refutation of objections

417 Within the superior wisdom of a buddha knowing the way things are ultimately,
appearance and perception are distinguished, and in that perception, duality has ceased.[264]
Some assert that nirvana is not a knowable entity
and that in buddhahood there is no consciousness either,
418 in which case all the effort made to attain the equivalent of a state of ignorance would be pointless.
The mention of "the mind's turnings [having ceased]" refers to [the ceasing of] conceptual thoughts.[265]

Truly existing phenomena do not appear to buddhas' own
perceptions,
but what appears to others does appear to them;
419 all these [appear to buddhas] because they possess omniscience.
Although the buddhas' superior wisdom
that knows both how things are ultimately and how they are in
their diversity is of one nature,
the former is known as "rational cognition" and the latter as
"conventional cognition"
420 according to the way the object is perceived.
Therefore, although the two objects of the two kinds of perception
are not mutually exclusive,
it is maintained that the two subjects are entirely mutually exclusive.

The divisions of ultimate truths

421 Ultimate truths can be classed into sixteen varieties;[266] [72]
if condensed, it is certain that there are the two kinds of
selflessness.
As for the terms *actual ultimate* and *concordant ultimate*,
these are asserted by the great proponents of Svātantrika tenets.[267]
422 Tibetans use the terms *approximate* and *non-approximate*
but the intent of former masters in reference to nonconceptual and
conceptual rational cognitions along with their objects
is that the first two [nonconceptual rational cognition and their
objects] are actual ultimates
and the latter two [conceptual rational cognition and their objects]
are concordant ultimates.[268]
423 This appears to be the understanding [of that Svātantrika view].
Furthermore, of the two elaborations—that of true existence and
that of [subject-object] duality—
neither is found in the former perception; duality however is found
in the latter.
Similarly, there are two kinds of emptiness that are objects.[269]
424 From the perspective of the former subject,[270] both kinds of
elaborations are absent.
The latter is posited [as an approximate ultimate] simply in terms
of the lack of true existence.[271]

Why it is certain the truths are two in number[272]

Since something is either deceptive or nondeceptive and there is no third possibility,
there are, for knowable entities, definitely only two truths.

The divisions of insight

425 There is differentiation and complete differentiation,
each dividing into two: inspection and analysis; these are the four from the angle of nature.
Analytical discrimination, thorough searching,
and arising from signs are asserted to be the categories of insight from the angle of three doors.
426 The six [bases] sought by thorough searching are meanings,
things, characteristics, categories, times, and reasonings.
In brief, the four kinds of insight in terms of nature
are attained by the six kinds of searching.
427 It is taught in the *Śrāvaka Grounds* that the four kinds of attention—
tight focus and so on—relate to insight as well.[273]

How to cultivate insight

This has three parts: what it means to cultivate insight based on tranquil abiding; which path in that system belongs to which vehicle, great or lesser; and how to actually cultivate insight based on tranquil abiding.

What it means to cultivate insight based on tranquil abiding

428 Tranquil abiding and insight are not distinguished by their focal objects,
since each of the two truths can be objects of both tranquil abiding and insight.

Which path in that system belongs to which vehicle, great or lesser

When in meditative equipoise at the completion stage of highest yoga tantra,

special insight is not necessarily analytical meditation, as in the other systems.[274]
Instead, one-pointed placement on the view is asserted. [73]

How to actually cultivate insight based on tranquil abiding

429 Regarding the way to sustain both analytical and placement meditations,
the means to achieve a balance between tranquil abiding and insight
is to make analytical meditation ride the mount of tranquil abiding
and occasionally practice placement meditation: you are to alternate the two.
430 Some say that no matter how much you familiarize yourself with conceptual thought,
nonconceptual superior wisdom cannot arise from it.
This would suggest that that the latter cannot result from the former
in the cases of noncontamination from contamination, the supramundane from the mundane,
431 āryas from ordinary beings, and so on
since they too are causes and effects of different categories.
Some maintain that thusness is beyond the realm of cognition
and that no mind, whatever it may be, can meditate on it,
432 but it is explained that the purpose of expressions like "inconceivable" and "beyond the realm of cognition"
is to counteract the conceit of understanding [emptiness] by learning and reflection alone
and to oppose apprehending the profound as truly existent;
otherwise, they would contradict many scriptures and reasonings.

[The measure of having achieved insight through meditation]

433 During the six preliminaries practices, in sessions, and in between,
by recalling the key points for rejecting laxity and excitation
impelled by mindfulness, meta-awareness, and so on and sustaining stability,
you analyze with discerning wisdom.

434 When this induces complete pliancy, as explained before,
insight is achieved and union of the two is attained as well.

[How to unite the two]

The "two" are tranquil abiding and insight;
"union" means that the two mutually bind and imbue one another.
435 When, by the force of analysis, tranquil abiding [pliancy] is attained,
both "full differentiation of phenomena" [insight] and one-pointed tranquil abiding
mix and combine in equal balance.
The process is the same for both [objects]: the way things are ultimately and in their diversity.
436 In this way, as a means to ascertain the sages' practice,
from relying on spiritual teachers up to tranquil abiding and insight,
[I have composed] this sweet nectar in intelligible verse
so that I may have the good fortune to meet this path.

[How to train in the Mantrayāna in particular]

437 Provided they have the intelligence and courage to bear the great responsibility
of joining the festival of the profound Vajrayāṇa,
the wise, who have trained in the common path,
having learned the paths of action, performance, and yoga [tantras],
438 will drink the river of the four initiations that mature them
and joyfully partake of the liberating path's two stages.
May the sunrays of this effort's virtue
completely dispel the darkness in all beings' minds, [74]
and may they be certain to reach the supreme state—the fruit of
completing the good path that delights the buddhas!

This work, entitled the *Essence of all Excellent Discourses Well Ascertaining the Way to Practice Taught in the Stages of the Path to Enlightenment*, was composed by the one known as Master of Altruism Gomchen Ngaki Wangpo at White Sunrise in Sedong. May it ensure the preservation, spread, and growth of the Buddha's teaching for a long, long time! May all that is auspicious prevail! [77]

4. An Easy Path

A Direct Guide to the Stages of the Path to Enlightenment

PANCHEN LOSANG CHÖKYI GYALTSEN

I PAY HOMAGE at all times at your feet, my most holy and sublime guru, who is indivisible from Munīndra Vajradhara.[275] Pray sustain me with your great compassion.

I present here a guide to the stages of the path to enlightenment, a profound way for fortunate ones to travel to buddhahood. This has two parts: the way to rely on a spiritual teacher and the stages of training the mind having thus relied.

Relying on a Teacher

THE WAY TO RELY ON A SPIRITUAL TEACHER

The first has two sections: how to practice during the actual session and how to practice between sessions.

HOW TO PRACTICE DURING THE ACTUAL SESSION

The first is threefold: the preliminaries, the main part of the session, and the concluding practice.

THE PRELIMINARIES

Seat yourself on a comfortable cushion in a space conducive to practice, adopting an eight-featured posture or whatever posture is most amenable.[276] Then, carefully examining your mindstream, cultivate an excellent virtuous state of mind, and while in that state, visualize the following:

In the space in front of you is a high and spacious jeweled throne hoisted by eight great lions. Seated on this throne, on a cushion of multicolored lotus and discs of moon and sun, is your kind root guru in the form of Buddha Śākyamuni. His body is the color of refined gold, and he is adorned with a crown protrusion. He has one face and two arms; with his right hand he performs the gesture of touching the earth, while his left hand, in the gesture of meditation, holds an alms bowl filled with nectar. Perfectly clad in the three robes of saffron color,[277] [78] he is endowed with the major and minor noble marks. His body has the nature of light, clear and radiant. He is seated cross-legged amid the mass of light radiating from his body.

Around him, in circles, are assembled your direct and indirect gurus, meditation deities, buddhas, bodhisattvas, heroes, heroines, and wisdom Dharma protectors.[278] In front of each of them, on a perfect throne, are the scriptural teachings they have given appearing as texts made of light. Imagine that the figures in this merit field are pleased with you. For your part, contemplating their enlightened qualities and their kindness, you generate great devotion toward them all. Having established this, contemplate the following:[279]

> From beginningless time until now, I and all mother sentient beings have been experiencing the suffering of cyclic existence. In particular, we have endured the myriad sufferings of the three lower realms. Still it remains difficult to fathom the depths and extent of our suffering. So today, at this juncture, when I have obtained this excellent human existence that is so hard to find but once found has great value, if I do not ensure the attainment of supreme liberation, the state of a guru buddha—that is, the total elimination of all sufferings—I will once again have to undergo the suffering of cyclic existence in general and all manner of diverse sufferings in the three lower realms in particular. Since the power to save me from these sufferings lies in you, my guru and the Three Jewels seated before me, I pledge, for the sake of all mother sentient beings, to secure the precious state of a perfect and fully awakened buddha. To this end, I go for refuge to you, my guru and the Three Jewels, from the depths of my heart.

In this way, go for refuge and generate the awakening mind and the four immeasurable thoughts. Then recite the following seven, twenty-one, or more times:

> In particular, for the sake of all mother sentient beings, I seek to achieve, swiftly, swiftly, the precious state of a perfect and fully awakened buddha. To this end, I now embark on the profound

> path of meditation on the stages of the path to enlightenment on a basis of guru-deity yoga. [81]

Now visualize in space in front of you a high and spacious jeweled throne hoisted by eight great lions. Seated on this throne, on a cushion of multicolored lotus and discs of moon and sun, is your kind root guru in the form of Buddha Śākyamuni. His body is the color of refined gold, and he is adorned with a crown protrusion. He has one face and two arms; with his right hand he performs the gesture of touching the earth, while his left hand, in the gesture of meditation, holds an alms bowl filled with nectar. Perfectly clad in the three robes of saffron color, he is endowed with the major and minor noble marks. His body has the nature of light, clear and radiant. He is seated cross-legged amid the mass of light that radiates from his body.

Above and behind him, seated on a cushion of multicolored lotus and discs of moon and sun, is the conqueror Vajradhara surrounded by the masters of the lineage of *blessing and practice*.[280] On his right is Maitreya, who is surrounded by the masters of the lineage of *vast practice*, while on the left is Mañjuśrī, who is surrounded by the masters of the lineage of the *profound view*. In front is your own kind root guru surrounded by the masters from whom you have received teachings directly. Around these [four clusters] are meditation deities, buddhas, bodhisattvas, heroes, heroines, and wisdom Dharma protectors. In front of each of them, on a perfect throne, are the scriptural teachings they have given appearing as texts made of light. Beyond all of these assemblies, radiating in all ten directions, is an inconceivable number of enlightened emanations manifesting in all manner of forms in harmony with and appropriate to the needs of spiritual trainees.

All the figures—the principals as well as their retinues—have at their crown a white *oṃ*, at their throat a red *āḥ*, at the heart a blue *hūṃ*, at the navel a yellow *svā*, and at their secret place a green *hā*. From these syllables radiates light of five colors. As beams of light radiate from the syllable *hūṃ* at the heart of Guru Munīndra throughout the ten directions, they invite, from their natural abodes, wisdom beings identical in appearance to those you have visualized. As they dissolve into their corresponding commitment beings, think that they have now transformed into embodiments of all the sources of refuge.

With this backdrop, perform the rite of seven limbs and offer a mandala.[281] Recite the supplicatory prayers too in accord with the oral tradition so that they definitely penetrate your mental continuum. [80]

Then, beams of light emanate from the *hūṃ* syllable at the heart of Guru Munīndra. The light rays touch all the assembled figures, both peaceful and wrathful, and melting into light, they dissolve into the heart of Guru Munīndra. Guru Munīndra then dissolves into your own root guru, who remains seated on your crown.

From this total transformation emerges on your crown your own kind root guru in the form of Buddha Śākyamuni. He is seated on a lion throne with a cushion of lotus, moon, and sun. He has one face and two arms; his right hand performs the gesture of touching the earth, while his left hand, in the gesture of meditation, holds an alms bowl filled with nectar. Perfectly clad in the three robes of saffron color, he is endowed with the major and minor noble marks. His body has the nature of light, clear and radiant. He is seated cross-legged amid the mass of light that radiates from his body.

Visualizing this, briefly perform the rite of seven limbs and offer a mandala. Then imagine yourself and all sentient beings around you chanting, as if in one voice, the following supplications:

> Guru deity, embodiment of four buddha bodies,
> to you, O Munīndra Vajradhara, I supplicate.
> Guru deity, embodiment of dharmakāya, the absence of obscurations,
> to you, Munīndra Vajradhara, I supplicate.
> Guru deity, embodiment of saṃbhogakāya, the great bliss,
> to you, Munīndra Vajradhara, I supplicate.
> Guru deity, embodiment of nirmāṇakāya, the diversity of forms,
> to you, Munīndra Vajradhara, I supplicate.
> Guru deity, embodiment of all the gurus,
> to you, Munīndra Vajradhara, I supplicate.
> Guru deity, embodiment of all meditation deities,
> to you, Munīndra Vajradhara, I supplicate.
> Guru deity, embodiment of all buddhas,
> to you, Munīndra Vajradhara, I supplicate.
> Guru deity, embodiment of all sublime teachings,
> to you, Munīndra Vajradhara, I supplicate.
> Guru deity, embodiment of all spiritual communities,
> to you, Munīndra Vajradhara, I supplicate.
> Guru deity, embodiment of all ḍākinīs,
> to you, Munīndra Vajradhara, I supplicate.
> Guru deity, embodiment of all Dharma protectors,
> to you, Munīndra Vajradhara, I supplicate."

In particular,

> Guru deity, embodiment of all sources of refuge, [81]
> to you, Munīndra Vajradhara, I supplicate.
>
> This present predicament faced by me and all mother sentient beings—reborn in the cycle of existence and enduring such profuse suffering intensely for so long—is owing to our failure to rely properly on spiritual teachers both in thought and in action. So bless me, guru deity, that I and all sentient beings may rely on spiritual teachers properly in both our thoughts and our actions.

As you make these supplications, imagine five-colored streams of nectar and beams of light radiate from the body of the guru at your crown. These enter the bodies and minds of all sentient beings, including yourself. They purify all the negative karma and obscurations accumulated since beginningless time. They purify in particular all the forces—negative karma, obscurations, sickness, malevolent spirits, and so on—that obstruct your ability to properly rely on your spiritual teachers in both thought and action. Your bodies [those of yourself and of all sentient beings] become clear and radiant and take on the nature of light. All beneficial qualities—longevity, merit, and so on—become increased and enhanced. Specifically, you imagine that extraordinary realizations arise in your mind, empowering you to rely properly on your spiritual teachers in both thought and action.

The Main Part of the Session

This has two parts: how to rely on your spiritual teachers in thought and how to rely on your spiritual teachers in action.

How to Rely on Your Spiritual Teachers in Thought

The first is twofold: (1) cultivating faith, the root factor, and (2) cultivating respect through contemplating your spiritual teachers' kindness

Cultivating Faith, the Root Factor

Visualize that Guru Munīndra emits from his heart the gurus from whom you have received teachings directly. Then, focusing on these [gurus] in space in front of you, contemplate the following:

> All these spiritual teachers of mine are enlightened buddhas. The perfect and fully awakened Buddha has stated in the precious tantras that in the degenerate era the conqueror Vajradhara would assume the guise of spiritual teachers and work for the welfare of sentient beings. [82] So, although their physical appearances are diverse, these spiritual teachers of mine are all forms portrayed by Vajradhara for the sake of those who, like me, lack the capacity to directly see buddhas.

Then make the supplication:

> Bless us therefore, O guru deity, that I and all sentient beings may recognize our spiritual teachers as actual Munīndra Vajradharas.

As you make this supplication, imagine five-colored streams of nectar and beams of light radiate from the body of the guru at your crown. As these enter your body and mind and those of all sentient beings, they purify the forces that obstruct the attainment of the specific objective [cultivating faith in the spiritual teacher and so on]. Imagine that you achieve an extraordinary realization of the specific practice.

You might harbor the thought "A buddha is free of all faults and endowed with all enlightened qualities. Since my spiritual teachers possess this or that flaw motivated by the three poisons, they cannot be buddhas." Should such thoughts occur to you, contemplate in the following manner.

> This is solely because of my own imperfect perception. In the past, Sunakṣatra,[282] for example, owing to his own imperfect perception, saw all the activities of the Buddha as entirely spurious; Asaṅga saw the exalted Maitreya in the form of a dog; and Maitripa saw the yogic adept Śavaripa as indulging in unwholesome activities like killing pigs and so on. Like this, with my spiritual teachers, I perceive faults in them not because such faults actually exist but because my own perception is imperfect.

Then make the supplication:

> Bless us therefore, O guru deity, that not a single moment's thought arises in me or in any sentient being that conceives faults

> in our spiritual teachers. May fervent faith arise in us that we may easily perceive all their actions as virtues.

As you make this supplication, imagine that five-colored streams of nectar and beams of light radiate from the body of the guru at your crown. As these enter your body and mind and those of all sentient beings, they purify the forces that obstruct the attainment of the specific objective. Imagine that you achieve an extraordinary level of realization of this specific practice. [83]

Cultivating respect through contemplating your spiritual teachers' kindness

For this, visualize your spiritual teachers in front of you with clarity and vividness and contemplate the following:

> These spiritual mentors are embodiments of great kindness to me indeed. Owing to their great kindness, I have come to understand the profound path that grants with ease the precious state of a perfect and fully awakened buddha—the supreme enlightenment marking the total elimination of all the sufferings of cyclic existence, including that of the lower realms.

Then make the supplication:

> Bless us therefore, O guru deity, that a profound respect toward our spiritual teachers, born from deep appreciation for their kindness, may arise in me and in all sentient beings.

As you make this supplication, imagine streams of five-colored nectar and beams of light radiate from the body of the guru at your crown. As these enter your body and mind and those of all sentient beings, they purify the forces that obstruct the attainment of the specific objective. Imagine that you achieve an extraordinary level of realization of this specific practice.

How to rely on your spiritual teachers in action

Visualize in front of you your spiritual teachers and contemplate the following:

> I shall devote my body, my life, and my resources unconditionally to these spiritual teachers, who are in reality fully awakened buddhas. In particular, I will please them with the offering of pursuing my meditative practice in accord with their advice.

Then make the supplication:

> Bless me, O guru deity, that I may be able to do this.

As you make this supplication, imagine streams of five-colored nectar and beams of light radiate from the body of the guru at your crown. As these enter your body and mind and those of all sentient beings, they purify the forces that obstruct the attainment of the specific objective. Imagine that you achieve an extraordinary level of realization of this specific practice.

The concluding part of the session

While visualizing your spiritual teacher at your crown, make supplications to him, recite the mantras, [84] and with fervent aspirations dedicate the virtues gained from these activities toward the realization of the immediate and ultimate aims of yourself and others.

How to practice between sessions

Between sessions, read scriptures and commentaries on the way to rely on spiritual teachers, guard the doors of your senses with mindfulness and meta-awareness, eat in moderation, strive in the yoga of not oversleeping, conduct yourself properly when you do sleep, and strive in the yogas of washing and eating as well.

The stages of training the mind having thus relied

This has two sections: (1) urging yourself to make human existence of leisure and opportunity meaningful and (2) the way to make human existence meaningful.

The Value and Rarity of Human Existence

Urging yourself to make human existence of leisure and opportunity meaningful

The first has two parts: how to practice during the actual session and how to practice between sessions.

How to practice during the action session

The first is threefold: the preliminaries, the main part of the session, and the concluding part.

The preliminaries

First, as for the preliminaries, up to the lines "Guru deity, embodiment of all sources of refuge, to you Munīndra Vajradhara, I supplicate"[283] is the same as the preceding topic. Then contemplate the following:

> This present predicament faced by me and all mother sentient beings—reborn in the cycle of existence and enduring such profuse suffering intensely for so long—is because we have not had extraordinary realizations of the great value of a human existence endowed with leisure and opportunity and of how hard it is to obtain such an existence. So bless us, O guru deity, that today extraordinary realizations of the great value and the rarity of a human existence endowed with leisure and opportunity may arise in me and all sentient beings.

As you make these supplications, [85] imagine five-colored streams of nectar and beams of light radiate from the body of the guru at your crown. These enter the bodies and minds of all sentient beings, including yourself. They purify all the negative karma and obscurations accumulated since beginningless time. They purify in particular all the forces—negative karma, obscurations, sickness, malevolent spirits, and so on—that obstruct the arising of the extraordinary realizations of the great value and the rarity of a human existence endowed with leisure and opportunity. Your bodies [those of yourself and of all sentient beings] become clear and radiant and take on the nature of light. All beneficial qualities—longevity, merit, and so on—become increased and enhanced. Specifically, you imagine that extraordinary realizations arise in your mind of the great value and the rarity of a human existence endowed with leisure and opportunity.

The main part of the session

This is twofold: contemplating the great value of a human existence of leisure and opportunity and contemplating how hard it is to obtain.

Contemplating the great value of a human existence of leisure and opportunity

Having visualized the guru deity at your crown, contemplate the following:

> My present existence is said to be endowed with "leisure" because it affords me time to engage in the practice of sublime Dharma, and it is said to be endowed with "opportunity" because the external and internal conditions for pursuing Dharma practice are fully present in this existence. In brief, the human existence of leisure and opportunity that I have obtained is most valuable indeed, for it is on this basis that I can cultivate the conditions for the attainment of birth and resources of the higher realms, conditions such as generosity, morality, and so on. In particular, it is in this existence, within the short life span of a degenerate era, that all three vows[284] can arise and I can attain without difficulty the state of buddhahood.

Then make the following supplication:

> Bless me, O guru deity, that I may not waste this human existence endowed with leisure and opportunity—which is so hard to find and which, when found, is so valuable—and may instead make it meaningful. Bless me that I am able to do this.

As you make this supplication, imagine five-colored streams of nectar and beams of light radiate from the body of the guru at your crown. As these enter your body and mind and those of all sentient beings, they purify the forces that obstruct the attainment of the specific objective. Imagine that you achieve an extraordinary level of realization of this specific practice.

Contemplating how hard it is to obtain

Having visualized the guru deity at your crown, contemplate the following:

> Not only is this human life of leisure and opportunity valuable, it is also extremely hard to obtain. [86] The vast majority of sentient beings, including us humans, spend most of our time indulging in the ten nonvirtuous actions. These actions obstruct the obtainment of a human life of leisure and opportunity. To obtain a human existence fully endowed with leisure and opportunity, these conditions in particular must be present: one must establish the basis through pure morality, complement it with the practice of generosity and the rest [of the perfections], and cement it with unsullied aspiration prayer. Very few actually cultivate these conditions. Furthermore, when compared to the number of unfortunate-realm beings such as the animals, a birth in the higher realms is the barest possibility. Even just among those who happen to take birth in a fortunate realm, those who find a human existence endowed with leisure and opportunity are vanishingly rare, as rare as star shining in daylight. Therefore, I shall not squander this human existence of leisure and opportunity—so hard to find and, once found, so valuable—an existence I have obtained this one time. I shall make it meaningful and extract its essence. I will make it meaningful by relying on my guru buddhas without separation and by practicing the essential instructions of the supreme vehicle as taught by my spiritual teachers.

Then make the following supplication:

> Bless me, O guru deity, that I may be able to do this.

As you make this supplication, imagine five-colored streams of nectar and beams of light radiate from the body of the guru at your crown. As these enter your body and mind and those of all sentient beings, they purify the forces that obstruct the attainment of the specific objective. Imagine that you achieve an extraordinary level of realization of this specific practice.

The concluding part

This is exactly the same as before.

How to practice between sessions

Between sessions, read scriptures and their commentaries that present the teaching on the precious human existence endowed with leisure and opportunity, and so forth, like in the previous topic.

Four Initial Meditations

The way to make human existence meaningful

This has three parts: training the mind in the path that is shared with a person of lesser capacity, training the mind in the path that is shared with a person of intermediate capacity, and training the mind in the path of a person of great capacity.

Training the mind in the path that is shared with a person of initial capacity

The first has two parts: how to practice during the actual session [87] and how to practice between sessions.

How to practice during the actual session

The first, in turn, is threefold: the preliminaries, the main part of the session, and the concluding part.

The preliminaries

Up to the lines "Guru deity, embodiment of all sources of refuge, to you Munīndra Vajradhara, I supplicate," this is the same as the previous topics. Then contemplate the following:

> This present predicament faced by me and all mother sentient beings—reborn in the cycle of existence and enduring such profuse suffering intensely for so long—is because we have failed to contemplate death and impermanence, failed to dread the sufferings of the lower realms and seek refuge in the Three Jewels from the depths of our heart, and failed to develop conviction in the law of karma and properly observe the moral discipline of rejecting certain things and adopting others. So bless me, O guru deity, that mindfulness of death and impermanence may arise in me and in all sentient beings, that we may seek refuge in the Three Jewels out of terror at the sufferings of the lower realms, and that

> the faith of conviction in the law of karma may arise in us so that we may observe the moral discipline of discarding nonvirtue and cultivating virtue.

As you make this supplication, imagine five-colored streams of nectar and beams of light radiate from the body of the guru at your crown. As these enter your body and mind and those of all sentient beings, they purify all the negative karma and obscurations accumulated since beginningless time; in particular they purify the forces that obstruct the attainment of the specific objective. Your bodies [those of yourself and of all sentient beings] become clear and radiant and take on the nature of light. All beneficial qualities—longevity, merit, and so on—become increased and enhanced. Imagine that you achieve an extraordinary level of realization of this specific practice.

The main part of the session

This has four parts: contemplating death and impermanence, contemplating the sufferings of the lower realms, training to seek refuge in the Three Jewels, and generating the faith of conviction in the law of karma. [88]

Contemplating death and impermanence

Having visualized the guru deity at your crown, contemplate the following:

> This human existence of leisure and opportunity, so hard to find and when found so valuable, will soon cease to exist. The lord of death will come inescapably; nothing whatsoever can avert this. There is no extension to my life span, and the conditions that chip away at my life emerge continuously, without interruption. Whether or not I have the chance to practice Dharma while alive, I will still definitely die.
>
> Not only will I die, it is unpredictable when that will be. Humans of this Jambudvīpa continent[285] are not guaranteed a definite life span; so many factors can bring about our death while the conditions for sustaining life are few; and our body is as fragile as bubbles in water. For these reasons, the time of my death is uncertain.
>
> Except for my Dharma practice, nothing else can benefit me at the time of death. Though I may be surrounded by family and friends who care for me dearly, I cannot take with me even a single

> companion. Whatever cherished riches I have amassed, not even an atom's measure of it can be brought along. If at that point I must separate from even my very flesh and bones, which have been with me from birth, what sense is there in clinging to the mundane hallmarks of success?
>
> The enemy—death—will come, and there is no telling when it will do so. I may even die this very day. I must therefore prepare for my death. I must do this by ensuring that I am not attached to the mundane hallmarks of success; I must engage in perfect Dharma practice.

Then make the following supplication:

> Bless me, O guru deity, that I may be able to do this.

As you make this supplication, imagine that five-colored streams of nectar and beams of light radiate from the body of the guru at your crown. As these enter your body and mind and those of all sentient beings, they purify the forces that obstruct the attainment of the specific objective. Imagine that you achieve an extraordinary level of realization of this specific practice.

Contemplating the sufferings of lower realms

Having visualized the guru deity at your crown, contemplate the following:

> This human existence of leisure and opportunity, so hard to find and when found so valuable, will soon cease to exist. Upon its cessation, I will not become nothing; I will take a new birth. There are only two types of realms to take birth in: fortunate migratory realms and unfortunate migratory realms. [89] Now, were I to take birth in an unfortunate migratory realm, I would suffer, for example, as a hell being from intense heat and cold; as a hungry ghost from hunger, thirst, and the like; and as an animal from the unimaginable sufferings born of stupidity and delusion, such as being devoured by another animal. There is no way I will be able to tolerate these intense sufferings of the lower realms. So now, when I have obtained a precious human life of leisure and opportunity, I will seek the state of guru buddha, the total elimination of all sufferings of the lower realms.

Then make this supplication:

> Bless me, O guru deity, that I may be able to do this.

As you make this supplication, imagine five-colored streams of nectar and beams of light radiate from the body of the guru at your crown. As these enter your body and mind and those of all sentient beings, they purify the forces that obstruct the attainment of the specific objective. Imagine that you achieve an extraordinary level of realization of this specific practice.

Training to seek refuge in the Three Jewels

For this, imagine the guru deity at your crown emanates from his body a host of gurus, meditation deities, the Three Jewels, heroes, heroines, and Dharma protectors, filling the entirety of space. Visualize magnificently all your objects of refuge surrounding the guru deity in this way. Then bring to mind the enlightened qualities of their body, speech, mind, and activities. And with the aspiration "Please save me and all mother sentient beings right now from the terror of cyclic existence and especially of the lower realms," recite:

> I go for refuge to the gurus, meditation deities, and the Three Jewels.

Repeat this a hundred, a thousand, ten thousand, a hundred thousand, or more times. Then, on the basis of knowing the immediate and long-term benefits of going for refuge to the Three Jewels, properly observe the precepts of refuge. [90]

Generating the faith of conviction in the law of karma

Having visualized the guru deity at your crown, contemplate the following:

> The Buddha's scriptures declare the following: only happiness and not suffering emerges as the result of engaging in virtuous actions, since these are its cause. Similarly, only suffering and not happiness results when the cause is engaging in nonvirtuous actions.
>
> Furthermore, even if a virtuous or nonvirtuous act I have committed is slight, if that cause does not encounter any mitigating factors, it can yield significant consequences. If I have not engaged in the causes—virtue or nonvirtue—I will not experience their effects, happiness and suffering. However, if I do indeed engage

> in the karmas of virtue or nonvirtue, given that karmic deeds once performed never go astray unless they encounter mitigating factors, they will definitely yield their corresponding effects of happiness and suffering. And the scriptures state that such karma can become even more potent because of their object, the intention, the material involved, and the agent.[286]
>
> I shall therefore develop the faith of conviction in these [facts of karma] and strive in the morality of rejecting certain things and adopting others. I will do this by engaging in virtue, however small, such as the ten virtues, and by ensuring that my three doors of body, speech, and mind are not tainted by even the slightest of nonvirtues, such as the ten nonvirtuous actions.

Then make this supplication:

> Bless me, O guru deity, that I may be able to do this.

As you make this supplication, imagine five-colored streams of nectar and beams of light radiate from the body of the guru at your crown. As these enter your body and mind and those of all sentient beings, they purify the forces that obstruct the attainment of the specific objective. Imagine that you achieve an extraordinary level of realization of this specific practice.

If, despite efforts such as these, you become tainted by nonvirtue because of the weakness of your antidotes and the strength of your afflictions, then strive in their purification and resolution by applying the four powers.[287]

The Concluding Part

This is exactly the same as before.

How to Practice Between Sessions

As with the previous topics, you should read scriptures and related commentaries that present the teachings that are shared with a person of lesser capacity.

With this, the explanation of training the mind in the stages of the path shared with a person of lesser capacity is complete. [91]

Seeking True Liberation

Training the mind in the path that is shared with a person of intermediate capacity

This has two sections: (1) generating the mind aspiring for true liberation and (2) establishing the nature of the path leading to true liberation.

Generating the mind aspiring for true liberation

The first has two parts: how to practice during the actual session and how to practice between sessions.

How to practice during the actual session

The first is threefold: the preliminaries, the main part of the session, and the concluding part.

The preliminaries

Up to the lines "Guru deity, embodiment of all sources of refuge, to you Munīndra Vajradhara, I supplicate" is the same as before. Then contemplate the following:

> This present predicament faced by me and all mother sentient beings—reborn in the cycle of existence and enduring such profuse suffering intensely for so long—is because we have failed to generate a mind that fervently aspires to true liberation based on recognizing that the entirety of cyclic existence is characterized by suffering. So bless me, O guru deity, that the recognition of cyclic existence as suffering and a mind that fervently aspires for true liberation from this may arise in me and all mother sentient beings.

As you make this supplication, imagine five-colored streams of nectar and beams of light radiate from the body of the guru at your crown. As these enter your body and mind and those of all sentient beings, they purify all the negative karma and obscurations accumulated since beginningless time; in particular they purify the forces that obstruct the attainment of the specific objective. Your bodies [those of yourself and of all sentient beings] become clear and radiant and take on the nature of light. All beneficial qualities—longevity, merit, and so on—become increased and enhanced. Imagine in particular that you and all mother sentient beings come to recognize the entirety of cyclic existence as suffering, and a mind fervently aspiring for true liberation arises in all of you. [92]

The main part of the session

This has two parts: contemplating the suffering of cyclic existence in general and contemplating the sufferings of the specific realms.

Contemplating the suffering of cyclic existence in general

Having visualized the guru deity at your crown, contemplate the following:

> Even if, from having properly engaged in the moral discipline of refraining from the ten nonvirtuous actions, I were to attain the fortune of rebirth in the higher realms—placing the sufferings of the lower realms far away—as long as I fail to achieve the true liberation that marks the total eradication of suffering, I will not feel content for even an instant. Imagine a person is convicted in court and condemned to execution in a month. Until that time arrives, he must endure daily the intense agony of tortures such as having melted wax poured on him and being beaten with clubs. Then imagine that, say, thanks to some appeal, he is to be spared the immediate pains of beatings and such. That person will experience not even a slight thought of happiness, for he will still be drawing ever closer to the terror of his death with each passing day. Likewise, as long as I fail to attain the true liberation that marks the total eradication of suffering, it does not matter what state of fortunate rebirth I may obtain; once the momentum of the past good karma is depleted, I will once again fall to the three lower realms. I must then endure such profuse sufferings intensely for so long. So long as I keep taking birth in this cycle of existence owing to the power of karma and afflictions, my existence will continue to be defined by suffering.
>
> Enemies turn into friends, and friends turn into enemies. So, I cannot predict who will benefit me and who will harm me. As for the pleasures of cyclic existence, no matter how much I indulge in them, I cannot finally satisfy my discontent. Not only that, since these mundane pleasures increase my attachment, they give rise to incessant myriad sufferings. No matter how many times I may obtain an excellent existence [in the higher realms], I will have

> to discard it again and again. There is thus nothing secure about simply obtaining an excellent existence. As I have been connecting with a new birth over and over since beginningless time, [the cycle of] birth has no conceivable end. As for the triumphs one might enjoy in the cycle of existence, however much I may achieve them, they bring no security, since they all must ultimately be discarded. Since I will have to depart alone to the next world, without any companion, my friends can bring no certain security either. [93]
>
> Therefore, today, at this juncture when I have obtained the precious human existence of leisure and opportunity, so hard to find and when found so valuable, I shall seek the precious state of the guru deity, the elimination of all the sufferings of cyclic existence.

Then make this supplication:

> Bless me, O guru deity, that I may be able to do this.

As you make this supplication, imagine five-colored streams of nectar and beams of light radiate from the body of the guru at your crown. As these enter your body and mind and those of all sentient beings, they purify the forces that obstruct the attainment of the specific objective. Imagine that you achieve an extraordinary level of realization of this specific practice.

Contemplating the sufferings of the specific realms

Having visualized the guru deity at your crown, contemplate the following:

> So long as my psychophysical aggregates appropriated [by karma] exist, I will remain subject to suffering. Leaving aside the suffering of the three lower realms, even with just the aggregates of a human birth, I will have to endure sufferings such as thirst and hunger, chasing after things, separation from loved ones, confrontations with enemies, the frustration of not finding desired objects even when I seek them, unwelcome predicaments, and the experiences of birth, aging, sickness, and death. If I find the appropriated aggregates of a demigod, I must endure sufferings such as the torment of unbearable jealousy at the gods' prosperity and, because of this, afflictions of my body as well. If I find the appropriated aggregates of a desire-realm god, when I enter combat with the

> demigods, I must experience such pains as severed limbs, lacerated flesh, and mortal wounds. Against my will, I will perceive the five portents of death and endure the pain of knowing that I will be sundered from all the heavenly riches. And I will know that the sufferings of the lower realms are nigh. Even if I chance to find the karmically appropriated aggregates of the two higher realms [of form and formlessness], I have not gained the power to remain there, and so once the momentum of past good karma has been exhausted, countless sufferings will greet me, such as descent into the lower realms.
>
> In brief, this [psychophysical complex of] karmically appropriated aggregates serves as the basis for the pains of this life, [94] those of birth, aging, sickness, and death, and it brings forth in both this and future lives the two other types of suffering—manifest suffering and the suffering of change. Furthermore, this [complex of] appropriated aggregates has coexisted by its very nature with the suffering of pervasive conditioning from the moment it came into being. I must therefore seek the state of a guru buddha that is total freedom from cyclic existence characterized by karmically appropriated aggregates.

Then make this supplication:

> Bless me, O guru deity, that I may be able to do this.

As you make this supplication, imagine five-colored streams of nectar and beams of light radiate from the body of the guru at your crown. As these enter your body and mind and those of all sentient beings, they purify the forces that obstruct the attainment of the specific objective. Imagine that you achieve an extraordinary level of realization of this specific practice.

The concluding part

This is exactly the same as before.

How to practice between sessions

As with the previous topics, you should read scriptures and related commentaries that reveal how the entirety of cyclic existence has the character of suffering.

The Nature of the Path Leading to True Liberation

Establishing the nature of the path leading to true liberation

This has two parts: how to practice during the actual session and how to practice between sessions.

How to practice during the actual session

The first is threefold: the preliminaries, the main part of the session, and the concluding part.

The preliminaries

Up to the lines "Guru deity, embodiment of all sources of refuge, to you Munīndra Vajradhara, I supplicate" is the same as before. Then contemplate:

> This current predicament faced by me and all mother sentient beings—reborn in the cycle of existence and enduring such profuse suffering intensely for so long—is owing to our failure to generate the mind aspiring to true liberation and our failure to train perfectly in the path of the threefold training. [94] Bless me today, O guru deity, that I may be able to generate the mind aspiring to true liberation and train perfectly in the path of the threefold training.

As you make this supplication, imagine five-colored streams of nectar and beams of light radiate from the body of the guru at your crown. As these enter your body and mind and those of all sentient beings, they purify all negative karma and obscurations accumulated since beginningless time and the forces in particular that obstruct generation of the mind aspiring to true liberation and the perfect training in the threefold path. Your bodies [those of yourself and of all sentient beings] become clear and radiant and take on the nature of light. All beneficial qualities—longevity, merit, and so on—become increased and enhanced. Imagine in particular that an extraordinary level of realization of the mind aspiring to true liberation and of perfect training in the threefold path arises in you and all mother sentient beings.

The main part of the session

Having visualized the guru deity at your crown, contemplate the following:

> Awareness in itself is neutral. But focusing primarily on "I" and what is "mine" induces thoughts grasping at intrinsic existence. This grasping at selfhood engenders emotions such as attachment to my own group, hostility toward others, and conceitedness rooted in the false view of being superior to others. These cause doubts and wrong views to arise, such as rejecting the true Teacher who has revealed the truth of no-self and rejecting his teachings—the law of karma and its effects, the four noble truths, the Three Jewels, and so on. And because of these [deluded emotions and views], all other afflictions proliferate. Compelled by these afflictions, I accumulate karma and create my present predicament—roaming in the cycle of existence enduring all sorts of sufferings against my wishes. I now recognize that the root of all my suffering lies in ignorance. I must seek by all means the state of a guru buddha that marks the permanent eradication of all the sufferings of cyclic existence. To this end I will train properly in the path of the threefold training.
>
> In particular, I will properly observe the moral discipline of the precepts I have taken, which have great benefits if observed and extremely grave consequences if not. I will observe these and not forsake them even at the cost of my life. [96]. Since *not knowing* is a door to downfalls, to counter this I will study the precepts and know them. Since *lack of respect* is a door to downfalls, to counter this I will be respectful toward the Teacher, toward the precepts he has prescribed, and toward my colleagues who engage in the pure conduct of monastic discipline and follow the precepts faithfully. Since *lack of heedfulness* is a door to downfalls, to counter this I will cultivate a sense of shame and a regard for others, and I will maintain heedfulness. Since *excessive afflictions* is a door to downfalls, I will meditate on impurity [of the body] to counter lustful attachment, I will cultivate loving kindness to counter aversion, and I will contemplate dependent origination to counter ignorance. In this way, I will ensure that I am never sullied by transgressions and train properly in pure ethical discipline.

Then make this supplication:

> Bless me, O guru deity, that I may be able to do this.

As you make this supplication, imagine five-colored streams of nectar and beams of light radiate from the body of the guru at your crown. As these enter your body and mind and those of all sentient beings, they purify the forces that obstruct the attainment of the specific objective. Imagine that you achieve an extraordinary level of realization of this specific practice.

The concluding part of the session

This is exactly the same as before.

How to practice between sessions

As with previous topics, you should do things like reading about the precepts according to the individual liberation vows.

With this, the explanation of training the mind in the stages of the path shared with a person of intermediate capacity is complete.

Training the mind in the path of a person of great capacity

This has two sections: how to generate the awakening mind and how to train in the [bodhisattva] practices after having generated the mind.

The Seven-Point Causes-and-Effect Instruction

How to generate the awakening mind

The first has two parts: the actual generation of the awakening mind and the way to sustain the generated mind through a rite.

The actual generation of the awakening mind

The first is twofold: how to generate the awakening mind through the seven-point causes-and-effect instruction and how to generate the awakening mind through the equalizing and exchanging of self and others. [97]

How to generate the awakening mind through the seven-point causes-and-effect instruction

This involves first establishing even-mindedness[288] toward all sentient beings and then cultivating the recognition of [others as] mothers up to, finally, the awakening mind. This presentation has two parts: how to practice during the actual session and how to practice between sessions.

How to practice during the actual session

This is threefold: the preliminaries, the main part of the session, and the concluding part.

The preliminaries

Up to the lines "Guru deity, embodiment of all sources of refuge, to you Munīndra Vajradhara, I supplicate" is the same as before. Then make this supplication:

> Bless me, O guru deity, that the unique realizations of even-mindedness toward all sentient beings—free from the biases of attachment and aversion based on discriminatory feelings of closeness and distance—and of the recognition of others as mothers, recollection of their kindness, repayment of their kindness, and cultivation of loving kindness, compassion,[289] and the awakening mind may arise in me and all sentient beings.

As you make this supplication, imagine five-colored streams of nectar and beams of light radiate from the body of the guru at your crown. These enter your body and mind and those of all sentient beings, purifying all the negative karma and obscurations accumulated since beginningless time; in particular they purify the forces that obstruct the arising of mind states such as even-mindedness toward all sentient beings free from the biases of attachment and aversion based on discriminatory feelings of closeness and distance. Your bodies [those of yourself and of all sentient beings] become clear and radiant and take on the nature of light. All beneficial qualities—longevity, merit, and so on—become increased and enhanced. Imagine in particular that mindstates such as even-mindedness toward all sentient beings free from the biases of attachment and aversion rooted in discriminatory feelings of closeness and distance have arisen in you and other beings.

The main part of the session

Equanimity

While visualizing the guru deity at your crown, vividly imagine before you a neutral person, someone who has neither helped you nor caused you any harm. Then contemplate the following:

> On their part, this person wishes to be happy and does not wish to suffer. Therefore, on my part, I will not harbor biases toward them—at times viewing them to be close and helping them and other times viewing them to be far and causing them harm. I will cultivate even-mindedness free from the biases of attachment and aversion rooted in discriminatory feelings of closeness and distance.[290] [98]

Then make the supplication "Bless me, O guru deity, that I may be able to do this" and so on.[291]

Once your mind becomes even toward them, vividly imagine before you someone who you know and like, and cultivate even-mindedness toward that person. For this, contemplate the following:

> My attachment is the reason I do not have even-mindedness toward this person. In the past too, I have taken [repeated] births in this cycle of existence because of my craving after what is appealing.

Like this, prevent craving and cultivate this state of mind.

Once your mind becomes even toward this person, then vividly imagine before you someone who you know and dislike and then cultivate even-mindedness by contemplating thus:

> My one-sided perception is the reason that this person appears unappealing and I feel aversion toward them and that I do not have a balanced mind toward them. If I fail to cultivate even-mindedness toward this person, it will simply be impossible for the awakening mind to arise in me.

Thinking thus, prevent aversion and cultivate this state of mind.

Once you develop a mind that is balanced toward this person, then visualize two individuals in front of you—one a loved one, such as your mother, and another, someone you dislike, such as an adversary. Then contemplate the following:

> From their own sides, these two individuals are absolutely equal in wanting to be happy and not wanting to suffer. From my

> perspective too, even the person I cherish as a loved one today, the number of times they have been my enemy in this beginningless cyclic of existence is impossible to count. Similarly, the person who I today view as an adversary, the number of times they have lovingly cared for me in this beginningless cycle of existence is impossible to count. Therefore, for which one should I feel attachment and for which one should I feel aversion? I shall maintain even-mindedness [toward all] and be free from the biases of attachment and aversion rooted in discriminatory feelings of closeness and distance.

Then make the supplication "Bless me, O guru deity, that I may be able to do this" and so on.[292]

Having equalized your mind [toward these two individuals], you then cultivate even-mindedness toward all sentient beings. The way to do this is as follows. Contemplate:

> From their own side, all sentient beings are equal in wanting to be happy and not wanting to suffer. From my own perspective too, all sentient beings are my friends. Therefore I will not divide them into two camps—viewing some as close and helping them while holding others as distant and harming them. Instead I will remain even-minded toward all beings, free from the biases of attachment and aversion rooted in discriminatory feelings of closeness and distance.

Then make the supplication "Bless me, O guru deity, that I may be able to do this" and so on. [99]

Recognizing all beings as your mother

After this, the method for cultivating the subsequent stages—from the recognition of [all beings as] your mother up to the awakening mind—is as follows. While visualizing guru deity at your crown, contemplate:

> Why can it be said that all sentient beings are my kin? Since the cycle of existence has no beginning, my births have no beginning either. In this sequence of life after life, there is not a single direction or place that I can point to and say I have not been born

> there. To count how many times I have taken rebirth would be impossible, and there is not even a single form of life that I can say I have not been born as. Not only that, the number of times I have been born as such life forms is incalculable. Not a single sentient being can I point to and say, "This one has not been my mother." In fact, they have been my mother countless times. For each and every sentient being, not a single one can I say they have not been my mother in my life as a human being. In fact, the number of times each has been my mother in the past is beyond count, and they will continue to be my mother in the future. Therefore, all beings are definitely my mothers and have nurtured me with kindness.

Should the thought occur that since sentient beings are countless, they can't all have been your mother, contemplate the following:

> Just because sentient beings are countless does not mean they cannot all have been my mother. Just as sentient beings are countless, so too have been my births. Therefore all beings certainly have been my mother.

Should the thought occur that since all sentient beings and you do not recognize each other [as mother and child], they cannot have been your mother, contemplate this:

> Just because all sentient beings and I do not recognize each other [as mother and child] does not mean that they have not been my mother. Even in this life, there are numerous instances where parents and children do not recognize each other.

Furthermore, should the thought occur that all sentient beings may have been your mother in the past, but this is ancient history and does not make them your mothers, contemplate:

> In that case, since my mother of yesterday is today no more, it would mean that she was not my mother. When it comes to being my mother, there is no difference between my mother of yesterday and my mother today. There is also no difference at all

> between the two in terms of nurturing me with kindness. In just this way, there is no difference between my mothers of past lives and my mother of this life in being my mother. There is also no difference in their having nurtured me with kindness. Therefore, in every manner, all sentient beings are indeed my mothers.

Contemplate in these ways.

Recollecting their kindness

When you have gained [some] experience with this, cultivate the thought recollecting their kindness as follows. While visualizing the guru deity at your crown, imagine your actual mother, not in her youthful state but as an elderly woman, [100] and then contemplate:

> This person, my mother, is not only my mother in this life; she has also been my mother countless times throughout beginningless lifetimes. In this very life in particular, she first nurtured me when I was in her womb. At the time of my birth, she placed me on a soft mattress, stroked me tenderly with the tips of her ten fingers, held me closely to her warm body, greeted me with affectionate smiles, gazed at me with joyful eyes, cleaned my nose with her mouth, and wiped my excrement with her hand. When I became even slightly ill, she felt anguish greater even than she would for a life-threatening injury to herself. Lovingly, she shared with me all her material possessions, which she accumulated with the greatest physical hardship and without regard to karma, pain, reputation, or even life. She brought, to the best of her ability, incalculable benefit and joy to me, and she protected me from countless dangers and sorrows. She has therefore been most kind to me indeed.

Once you gain experience with this [focus on your mother], extend it to other loved ones such as your father. The way to do this is as follows. While focused on a clear and vivid image of your father and so on, contemplate:

> The number of times this person has been my mother throughout beginningless lifetimes is beyond calculation. And every time he was my mother, just as my mother of this life has nurtured me

> with kindness, this person too nurtured me with kindness. Therefore he too has been most kind to me indeed.

And once you gain experience with this, meditate on neutral sentient beings. The way to do this is as follows. Vividly imagine the neutral sentient beings in front of you and contemplate:

> Right now it appears as if these sentient beings and I are completely unrelated. However, the number of times they have been my mother in the past is beyond calculation. And every time they were my mother, they too nurtured me with kindness just as my mother of this life has done. They too are therefore embodiments of great kindness to me.

Once you gain experience with this, extend the meditation to your enemy. The way to do this is as follows. Vividly imagine your enemy in front of you and contemplate:

> What is the point of considering this person to be my enemy today? The number of times they have been my mother throughout beginningless lifetimes is beyond count. And every time they were my mother, they strove to find immeasurable benefit and happiness for me. They protected me from countless dangers and sorrows. More specifically, we have been related to each other countless times in such a manner that I found it unbearable when they were not around and they felt it unbearable when I was not around. [101] It is owing to the power of our negative karma that we are in this situation [of being enemies] today. Otherwise, he is indeed a dear parent who has nurtured me with kindness.

Once you gain experience with this, then contemplate the kindness of all sentient beings.

Repaying their kindness

Having thus recollected their kindness, the cultivation of the thought to repay their kindness is as follows. While visualizing the guru deity at your crown, contemplate the following:

> All these beings, my mothers who have nurtured me with kindness throughout beginningless time, have minds that are in turmoil owing to the demonic force of their afflictions. They have no control over their own minds and as a result have lost their sanity. As for eyes to see the path to fortunate rebirths and the definite goodness [of liberation], they have none. Nor do they have spiritual teachers who can be guides for the blind. Every single moment, they are tormented by their own indulgence in negative acts. How can I abandon these sentient beings wandering in the cycle of existence and walking along the edge of the terrifying abyss of the lower realms? This would be inconsiderate of me. Therefore, to repay their kindness, I will free them from the sufferings of cyclic existence and lead them to the joy of liberation.

Then make the supplication "Bless me, O guru deity, that I may be able to do this" and so on.

Cultivating loving kindness

Loving kindness is cultivated as follows. Focus on someone you care about deeply, such as your mother, and then contemplate:

> Let alone uncontaminated bliss, she lacks even the contaminated kind of happiness. What she conceives as happiness currently will turn into suffering. Even though she wants to be happy and strives for it in all her endeavors, her efforts become causes for the suffering of the lower realms. Even in this life, her efforts amid hardship and despair lead only to more pain; she has no genuine enduring happiness whatsoever. *How I wish that she finds happiness and all the causes of happiness. May she find happiness and the causes of happiness. I will help her find happiness and its causes.*[293]

Then make the supplication "Bless me, O guru deity, that I may be able to do this" and so on.

Once you gain experience with this, shift your focus to other loved ones such as your father, then to neutral beings, then to your enemies, and finally to all sentient beings.

Cultivating compassion

Next is the cultivation of compassion. While visualizing the guru deity at your crown, first cultivate compassion for those sentient beings who are in desperate distress, such as a sheep this very moment under the butcher's blade. [102] The way to meditate on this is as follows.

Cultivate a vivid image of such a sentient being in front of you and reflect upon its tragic fate—its limbs bound, its chest ripped open, the butcher's arm extending deep inside its chest as the creature is conscious of its imminent death. With eyeballs rolling wildly, it gapes at the butcher's face. While picturing this scene of desperate suffering, make this aspiration:

> How I wish this animal to be free of suffering and all the causes of suffering. May it be free of suffering and all the causes of suffering. I will help it become free of suffering and all the causes of suffering.

Then make the supplication "Bless me, O guru deity, that I may be able to do this" and so on.

Once you gain experience with this, cultivate compassion focused on the following types of sentient beings—those who carelessly consume provisions of the monastic community, those degenerate in their morality, those who forsake the Dharma, those harboring wrong views, and those who harm other sentient beings and are seemingly expert in the commission of all sorts of negative karmic deeds. The way to do this meditation is as follows. Cultivate a vivid image of these beings in front of you and contemplate:

> If such is the conduct and actions of these beings, they will have no happiness at all even in this present life. And the moment they die, they will no doubt be instantly reborn in the lower realms. Once reborn in the lower realms, they will have to endure all manner of harsh suffering for a long, long time. How I wish, therefore, that they can become free of suffering and all the causes of suffering. May they be free of suffering and all the causes of suffering. I will help them become free of suffering and all the causes of suffering.

Then make the supplication "Bless me, O guru deity, that I may be able to do this" and so on.

Once you have gained experience with this, vividly imagine in front of you a loved one such as your mother and contemplate:

> This person, my loved one, constantly strives to care for her loved ones and fend off her adversaries and is tormented by manifest suffering and the suffering of change. Not even a brief moment of [genuine] happiness exists for her. In this life too, she has been wholly preoccupied with unwholesome activities, and the thoughts of virtue have failed to take root in her. Therefore, the moment she dies, she will instantly be reborn in the lower realms, where she will have to endure all manner of harsh sufferings for a long, long time. How I wish, therefore, if she can become free of suffering and all the causes of suffering. [103] May she be free of suffering and all the causes of suffering. I will help her become free of suffering and all the causes of suffering.

Then make the supplication "Bless me, O guru deity, that I may be able to accomplish this" and so on.

Once you gain experience with this, cultivate it similarly in relation to neutral beings, your enemies, and finally all sentient beings.

Cultivating the altruistic intention

Once you have gained experience with loving kindness and compassion capable of rousing your heart, cultivate the altruistic resolve. For this, while visualizing the guru deity at your crown, contemplate the following:

> I will help all sentient beings tormented by suffering and bereft of happiness to become free of suffering and its causes. I will help them find happiness and its causes. I will especially help them achieve the perfect and fully awakened state of buddhahood that represents the total elimination of the two obscurations along with their imprints.[294]

Then make the supplication "Bless me, O guru deity, that I may be able to do this" and so on.

Cultivating the awakening mind

Next, cultivate the awakening mind as follows. While visualizing the guru deity at your crown, contemplate:

> Do I have the ability to lead all sentient beings to the perfect and fully awakened state of buddhahood? Right now, I cannot lead even a single sentient being to the perfect and fully awakened state of buddhahood. Not only that, were I to achieve the state of either of the two kinds of arhats,[295] I would be able to fulfill the needs of only a few sentient beings. I would have no ability to lead all sentient beings to the perfect and fully awakened state of buddhahood. Who then has this ability? It is the perfect and fully awakened buddhas who possesses this.
>
> The enlightened qualities of a buddha's body consists of being adorned perfectly with all the major and minor noble marks. As for his speech, it has the enlightened quality of being effortless and endowed with sixty perfect melodies, such that even a single sound can teach the Dharma to all sentient beings, each in their own tongue. His mind is such that it has the enlightened quality of directly perceiving all phenomena, both the way things really are and things in their diversity. And since his compassion takes in all sentient beings like the love of a mother for her only child and is without any discrimination, without any biases born of discriminatory feelings of closeness and distance, a buddha never fails to seize the moment when someone is ready to be tamed. [104] His enlightened activities are spontaneous. Even with respect to the light radiating from his body, speech, and mind, every single ray of this light has the power to lead countless sentient beings to the state of omniscience.
>
> In brief, it's a buddha alone who possesses all the higher qualities and who is free from every kind of flaw. Therefore, to successfully accomplish the welfare of both myself and others, I must achieve the state of buddhahood. I must therefore ensure by every means the swift attainment of this perfect and fully awakened state of buddhahood for the sake of all sentient beings.

Then make the supplication "Bless me, O guru deity, that I may be able to accomplish this" and so on.

As you make this supplication, just like one candle lit from another, a replica emerges from the guru at your crown and dissolves into you. Imagine that you now arise as Munīndra Buddha. You are seated upon a high and spacious throne hoisted by eight great lions on which is a cushion of multicolored lotus and discs of moon and sun. Your body is the color of refined gold, and you are adorned with a crown protrusion. You have one face and two arms; with your right hand you perform the gesture of touching the earth, while your left hand, in the gesture of meditation, holds an alms bowl filled with nectar. Perfectly clad in the three robes of saffron color, you are endowed with all the major and minor noble marks. Your body has the nature of light, clear and radiant. You are seated cross-legged amid the mass of light radiating from your body.

With this awareness of yourself as Munīndra Buddha, as you send forth to all sentient beings your body, material resources, and your roots of virtue in the form of five-colored nectars and beams of light, imagine that all sentient beings attain the perfect happiness of higher realms and the definite goodness of true liberation.

The concluding part

This is exactly the same as before.

How to practice between sessions

As in the previous topics, you should do things like reading scriptures and related commentaries that present practices of loving kindness, compassion, and the awakening mind. [105]

The Equalizing and Exchanging of Self and Others

How to generate the awakening mind through the equalizing and exchanging of self and others

Having first engaged in the three practices—equanimity of even-mindedness toward all beings, recognition of them as mothers, and reflection on their kindness—imagine with vividness all sentient beings around you. Then examine your mind to see who you care most about and who you are indifferent to—your own self or others? The thoughts cherishing your own self and thoughts disregarding others will arise spontaneously. When they do, at that very instant, contemplate the following:

> It makes no sense to cherish my own self and disregard others because others and I are equal in wanting to be happy and in wanting to avoid suffering. Therefore, just as I cherish my own self, I must also cherish others. For in the same way that I am happy when others care for me, others will be happy if I care for them. Furthermore, I have cherished my own self throughout

> the beginningless cycle of existence out of a wish to enjoy perfect prosperity, but not only have I failed to fulfill my own welfare or that of others, I have had to endure all sorts of suffering as a result. I therefore acknowledge that this self-cherishing is the source of all calamities, the entire cycle of existence, including the sufferings of the lower realms. I therefore resolve that any self-cherishing thoughts yet to arise will not do so and that any that have already arisen will be relinquished. And since the thought cherishing others is the source of all higher qualities, I resolve that the thoughts cherishing others that are not yet arisen will newly arise and that those already arisen will be enhanced.

Then make the supplication "Bless me, O guru deity, that I may be able to do this" and so on.

Again contemplate:

> In brief, because Munīndra forsook his own self, cherished others, and pursued only other's welfare, he became fully enlightened. Had I conducted myself in this same manner, I too would have become fully enlightened long ago. As I failed to do so, I have up to now been wandering in the cycle of existence. If in the future, too, self-cherishing continues to reside in me, no fresh instances of thoughts cherishing others will arise. [106] Even if such new thoughts were to arise in me, they would be unable to establish any sort of continuity. I will therefore not engender thoughts that forsake others and cherish my own self alone, not even for a single moment. I will instead forsake my own self and hold others as most dear. And on this basis, I will take others' sufferings and their negative karma upon myself and offer to others all my happiness and virtuous karma. I resolve to free all sentient beings from suffering and guide them to perfect happiness. This said, of course, I do not have that ability right now. Who does then? The perfect and fully awakened buddhas have such an ability. I will therefore, for the sake of all mother sentient beings, attain the state of perfect and fully awakened buddhahood.

Then make the supplication "Bless me, O guru deity, that I may be able to accomplish this" and so on.

The way to sustain the generated mind through a rite

This has two parts: receiving the vows that have not been received and guarding the vows that have already been received.

Receiving the vows that have not been received

Although [Tsongkhapa's] *Stages of the Path*[296] presents the rites for the aspirational and engaging aspects [of the awakening mind] in a sequence, it seems more convenient to perform the two jointly through a single rite, as is the approach of Śāntideva.[297] The way to do this is as follows.

First make sure that all the general preliminary practices have been performed; specifically, make sure that all the topics from relying on a spiritual teacher up to generating the awakening mind have been practiced to a point where they have become securely integrated into your mental continuum. Then, visualizing the guru deity at your crown, contemplate:

> I will swiftly attain the state of perfect and fully awakened buddha for the sake of all sentient beings. To this end I will uphold, from this very moment until I have reached the heart of enlightenment, the vows of the bodhisattvas and train in their expansive deeds. Until I have attained buddhahood, I will uphold the thought "I will attain buddhahood for the benefit of sentient beings."

Then, imagining that you are repeating after your guru Munīndra, recite the following lines:

> All buddhas and bodhisattvas,
> pray attend to me. [107]
> Just as the sugatas of the past
> generated the mind of awakening
> and, accordingly, abided by
> the bodhisattva vows,
> so too I generate the awakening mind
> for the benefit of all beings;
> I shall train in the bodhisattva vows
> in accord with their sequence.[298]

Once you have repeated these lines three times, imagine you have received the bodhisattva vows. Then recite:

Today my life is made fruitful;
I've obtained well the human birth.
Today I am born in the buddha's family;
I've become a child of the buddhas.

Now, in whatever way I can,
I will act as becomes my lineage.
I will act thus and will not sully
this pure and earnest family.[299]

This is how you should rejoice.

Guarding the vows that have already been received

While visualizing the guru deity at your crown, contemplate the following:

> I will swiftly attain the state of perfect and fully awakened buddha for the sake of all mother sentient beings. To this end I will contemplate the benefits of the awakening mind and affirm this mind three times during the day and three times during the night. Irrespective of the way sentient beings behave, I will not forsake even a single sentient being. I will strive in activities, such as venerating the Three Jewels, to gather the two accumulations to help enhance this mind I have generated. Furthermore, I will renounce the four dark factors that degenerate the awakening mind—(1) deceiving one's teacher and the like with lies, even in jest or to evoke laughter; (2) causing others to regret their performance of virtuous deeds; (3) out of hostility uttering unpleasant words to bodhisattvas who have entered the Mahayana path; and (4) engaging in false pretenses and deceit driven by ulterior motives. I will properly practice the conditions that enhance the awakening mind, such as cultivating the four bright factors.[300] In brief, I will guard, even at the risk of my life, the pure bodhisattva vows unsullied by transgressions of any of the eighteen root precepts and the forty-six secondary precepts. I will observe these until I have reached the heart of enlightenment.

Then make the supplication "Bless me, O guru deity, that I may be able to accomplish this." [108]

The Six Perfections and the Four Means of Gathering

How to train in the bodhisattva practices after having generated the mind

This has two parts: how to train in the bodhisattva practices in general and how to train in the last two perfections in particular.

How to train in the bodhisattva practices is general

This has two parts: how to practice during the actual session and how to practice between sessions.

How to practice during the actual session

This is threefold: the preliminaries, the main part of the session, and the concluding part.

The preliminaries

The preliminary practices up to the lines "Guru deity, embodiment of all sources of refuge, to you Munīndra Vajradhara, I supplicate" is the same as before. Then make this supplication: "Bless me, O guru deity, that I and all mother sentient beings may be able to train properly in the expansive practices of the bodhisattva, which are profound and vast" and so on.[301]

The main session

This has two parts: (1) practicing the six perfections, the factors that help mature your own mind, and (2) practicing the four means of gathering, the factors that help mature others' minds.

Practicing the six perfections, the factors that help mature your own mind

While visualizing the guru deity at your crown, contemplate the following:

> I will swiftly attain the state of perfect and fully awakened buddha for the sake of all mother sentient beings. To this end, I will train earnestly in the practice of the three categories of giving: (1) giving Dharma to those lacking Dharma teachings to the best of my ability and without consideration of material reward, fame, and the like; (2) giving fearlessness to those sentient beings who are being harmed by humans, nonhumans, and the natural elements

> by protecting them from these fears; and (3) giving material requisites to those who are poor and destitute, without miserliness and with no expectation of reward or personal benefit. In brief, I will swiftly attain the state of perfect and fully awakened buddha for the sake of all mother sentient beings. To this end, I will give to all sentient beings, without any sense of loss, my body, my material resources, and my roots of virtue.

Then make the supplication "Bless me, O guru deity, that I may be able to do this" and so on. To magnify your giving intention in this manner is to practice the perfection of generosity. [109]

Next is the practice of morality. While visualizing the guru deity at your crown, contemplate the following:

> I will swiftly attain the state of perfect and fully awakened buddha for the sake of all mother sentient beings. To this end, I will relinquish all the misconduct of transgressing precepts I have taken, such as the vow to renounce the ten nonvirtuous actions. I will ensure that the perfect virtues—the six perfections like giving and so on and [the observance of] morality—not yet arisen will arise in me, and that those that have already arisen will increase ever more. I will also connect all sentient beings to the perfect virtues of morality and the rest and lead them to paths that mature them and [ultimately] free them.

Then make the supplication "Bless me, O guru deity, that I may be able to do this" and so on.

The practice of forbearance is as follows. While visualizing the guru deity at your crown, contemplate the following:

> I will swiftly attain the state of a perfect and fully awakened buddha for the sake of all mother sentient beings. To this end, I will ensure that, even if all beings rise up as my enemies, I will not engender even momentary anger. In return for their harmful actions toward me, I will instead seek their well-being. I will seek to establish the complete manifestation of the buddha's enlightened qualities, such as his perfection of forbearance, in me and in all other beings. Furthermore, when misfortunes such as illness

> or insufficient food, shelter, bed, and so on strike me, I will contemplate the following. "My experience of sufferings such as these is the result of bad karma I accrued in the past. Furthermore, experiencing these [adversities] will cleanse me of many of my past actions, so there is little point in viewing these as unwanted misfortunes. More specifically, since the practice of forbearance in the course of Dharma practice brings me closer to the path to omniscience, I should welcome these sufferings. And in this way, I should cut the continuity of my own and others' cycle of existence. Furthermore, were I to develop faith in the consequences of positive and negative actions, in the blessings of the Three Jewels, in the inconceivable power of the buddhas and the great bodhisattvas, in the unexcelled enlightenment of the buddha, in the twelve branches of scripture,[302] and in the precepts of the bodhisattvas, this would have powerful effects. [110] I will therefore develop conviction in these, and to help achieve the buddha's unexcelled enlightenment, I will train earnestly in the essential points of the bodhisattva practices, the substance of the twelve branches of scripture.

Then make the supplication "Bless me, O guru deity, that I may be able to do this" and so on.

Next is the practice of diligence. While visualizing the guru deity at your crown, contemplate the following:

> I will swiftly attain the state of a perfect and fully awakened buddha for the sake of all mother sentient beings. To this end, even if my quest for buddhahood—seeking the conditions to attain each and every single one of the major and minor noble marks of the buddha, each and every single practice of the bodhisattvas such as giving—entails remaining in the unrelenting hell for a hundred thousand eons, I will not surrender my effort and will instead cultivate joy. I will amass in me all the virtuous practices, the profound as well as the vast, and also lead others to the path of virtue. I will thus attain the unexcelled enlightenment.

Then make the supplication "Bless me, O guru deity, so that I am able to do this" and so on.

Next, practice meditative absorption as follows. While visualizing the guru deity at your crown, contemplate:

> I will swiftly attain the state of a perfect and fully awakened buddha for the sake of all mother sentient beings. To this end, I will train in all aspects of the bodhisattva's practice of meditative absorption—in terms of its nature, the mundane and supramundane levels of absorption; in terms of its category, tranquil abiding and insight as well as the meditative absorption that is the union of the two; and in terms of its function, meditative absorptions that bring about physical and mental well-being in this life, meditative absorptions that serve as the basis for the attainment of higher qualities, and meditative absorptions that support altruistic work for the welfare of other sentient beings.

Then make the supplication "Bless me, O guru deity, that I may be able to do this" and so on.

Next is the practice of wisdom. While visualizing the guru deity at your crown, contemplate the following:

> I will swiftly attain the state of a perfect and fully awakened buddha for the sake of all mother sentient beings. To this end, I will train in the three categories of the bodhisattva's wisdom—wisdom that knows the ultimate truth, the abiding nature of reality; wisdom that knows the conventional truth, the five fields of knowledge; [111] and the wisdom that knows how to accomplish the welfare of sentient beings.[303]

Then make the supplication "Bless me, O guru deity, that I may be able to do this" and so on.

The four means of gathering, the factors that help mature others' minds

While visualizing the guru deity at your crown, contemplate the following:

> I will swiftly attain the state of perfect and fully awakened buddha for the sake of all mother sentient beings. To this end, I will, through giving, draw all sentient beings into my circle of

> connections, engage in eloquent speech teaching the Dharma through the use of forceful as well as nurturing words, work toward the goal by exhorting others to practice the Dharma, and be consistent with the goal by practicing myself what I teach others. By means of these excellent factors for securing others' welfare, I will lead all sentient beings to the paths that mature and [ultimately] free them.

Then make the supplication "Bless me, O guru deity, that I may be able to do this" and so on.

The concluding part

This is the same as before.

How to practice between sessions

As in the preceding topics, do things like reading scriptures and related commentaries that present the bodhisattvas' expansive deeds, which are both profound and vast.

Training in Tranquil Abiding

How to train in the last two perfections in particular

This has two sections: (1) how to train in tranquil abiding, the essence of meditative absorption, and (2) how to train in insight, the essence of wisdom.

How to train in tranquil abiding, the essence of meditative absorption

The first has two parts: [112] how to practice during the actual session and how to practice between sessions.

How to practice during the actual session

This is threefold: the preliminaries, the main part of the session, and the concluding part.

The preliminaries

Having undertaken the preliminaries in general and trained in particular in the attitudes of persons of lesser and intermediate capacities, secure the conditions essential for cultivating tranquil abiding. These include staying with pure ethical discipline in a place conducive to your mind—a good location with good companions; avoiding excessive interaction with many people; discarding coarse thoughts that might lure you to objects of sensual desire; living with the ethos of having few desires, being easily contented; and on the basis of these, seating yourself on a comfortable cushion with your legs crossed and your hands in the gesture of meditation and settling your breathing into a relaxed pace.

The main part of the session

As for the object upon which you cultivate tranquil abiding, numerous alternatives are mentioned, but it is good to focus on a meditation deity. This constitutes an excellent recollection of the buddha (*buddhānusmṛti*) and also helps make you a suitable vessel for meditative practice of tantric deity yoga. Here is how you do this.

Imagine that rays of light emanate from the heart of the guru deity at your crown. At the tips of these rays, which resemble the threads of a spider's web, Śākyamuni Buddha appears in front of you in space, the size of a yellow pea. He is seated on a cushion of a multicolored lotus and a moon disc. His body is the color of refined gold, and he is adorned with a crown protrusion. He has one face and two arms; his right hand performs the gesture of touching the earth, while his left hand, in the gesture of meditation, holds an alms bowl filled with nectar. Perfectly clad in the three robes of saffron color, he is endowed with the major and minor noble marks. His body has the nature of light, clear and radiant. He is seated cross-legged amid the mass of light radiating from his own body. Engage in meditation with single-pointed focus on this image.

Alternatively, you could contemplate the following. An exact replica emerges from the guru deity at your crown, like one lamp being lit from another, and then dissolves into you. Due to this, you emerge as Śākyamuni Buddha, seated on a throne hoisted by eight great lions on a cushion of a multicolored lotus and a moon disc. Your body has the color of refined gold and is adorned with a crown protrusion. You have one face and two arms; [113] your right hand performs the gesture of touching the earth, while your left hand, in the gesture of meditation, holds an alms bowl filled with ambrosia. Perfectly clad in the three robes of saffron color, you are endowed with the major and minor noble marks. Your body has the nature of light, clear and radiant. You are seated cross-legged amid the mass of light radiating from your own body. Engage in meditation with single-pointed focus on this image, which resembles a rainbow in the sky.

When you are meditating, say a red color appears whereas you wish to visualize yellow, a standing position appears though you intend to visualize a seated posture, or multiple forms appear when you intend to visualize only a single form. If these things happen, do not follow these images. Maintain single-pointed focus on your chosen object of meditation. In the initial stage, there might not be a vivid image characterized by lucidity, clarity, and light, so maintain your single-pointed focus on the part of the form that is clear. Undertake this on the basis of a setting a forceful prior intention:

> For at least the duration of this meditation session, I will make sure no mental laxity or excitation arises. And when they do arise, I will recognize it right there and then and relinquish them.

Setting such an intention, constantly refresh your mindfulness of your chosen object of meditation, not letting it to be forgotten, and maintain the continuity of your focused mind. This is an excellent method for someone on the beginner's stage to cultivate mental stability.

Briefly, if you wish to cultivate perfect concentration, you need to engage the eight factors of mental application, which are the antidotes to the five faults. It is stated:

> It arises from the cause, forsaking the five faults
> and engaging the eight factors of mental application.[304]

When you pursue meditative concentration in the preliminary stage, laziness is the fault. There are four antidotes for this: (1) *faith* born of seeing the benefits of concentration, (2) *aspiration* to seek concentration with interest, (3) *diligence* striving for concentration, and (4) *pliancy*, which is the fruit of such a striving. When you are engaged in cultivating concentration with effort, forgetting the instruction is the fault, and its antidote is (5) *mindfulness*. Here too, it is not adequate for such mindfulness to be simply a case of not forgetting the meditation object; it must be endowed with a single-pointed focus on the chosen object and a firm ascertainment that allows your awareness to remain vibrant. [114] When you remain in equipoise in meditative concentration, mental laxity and excitation are the faults, and (6) *meta-awareness* is their antidote. For it is meta-awareness that monitors whether laxity and excitation are occurring. Those with higher mental aptitude will be able to detect when laxity and excitation are about to arise and overcome them. Those of medium ability should detect them immediately after they have arisen and counter them; and even those with the least competency should catch them not too long after their arising and then overcome them.

What, then, is the difference between mental lethargy and mental laxity?[305] Mental lethargy is present when your meditation object becomes blurred and your body and mind feel heavy, dulled. If you feel as if darkness has descended on your mind, and also, even though your mind has not strayed elsewhere, the force of your mindfulness has weakened such that there is no lucidity or clarity of mind, a coarse level of mental laxity has arisen. If, however, there is lucidity and clarity but the force of the cognitive aspect of your mind ascertaining the meditation object has become weakened, even slightly, then subtle mental laxity has occurred. To counter these, reflect on the enlightened qualities of the Three Jewels, bring to mind images that are bright, and apply the instruction of fusing your mind with space.[306]

When the mind does not remain unwaveringly on the meditation object but drifts away slightly, this indicates subtle excitation. To counter this, meditate by applying mindfulness and meta-awareness. However, if your mind still wanders off toward objects of desire despite applying mindfulness and meta-awareness, this indicates coarse excitation. To counter this, meditate on impermanence, the sufferings of the three unfortunate realms and cycle of existence as a whole, and apply the instructions on how to end excitation through a radical approach.[307]

Since failure to apply antidotes when mental laxity and excitation occur is also a fault, ensure that mental laxity and excitation are detected the moment they arise and engage the specific factor of (7) *applying the antidote* to counter them. In this regard, if in order to maintain the mind's quality of vibrancy, you tighten your mind's focus on the object too much, then even though there might be the clarity aspect, the higher level of excitation will make it difficult to attain stability. On the other hand, if you relax your mind too much and lack alertness, there might be stability, but the higher level of laxity will make it difficult to attain clarity. Therefore, evaluating your own personal experience, when you reach a level beyond which excitation arises if your mind is too aroused, relax your mind a little. In contrast, if you let your mind slacken to such a degree that mental laxity arises, [115] when you see that you have reached such a point, you should elevate the level of arousal in your mind. Thus, between these two poles, you need to cultivate mental stability by repeatedly turning your mind away from mental scattering and excitation, and whenever stability does arise, you need be vigilant against mental laxity and cultivate the clarity of a vibrant mind. It's through sustained practice alternating between these two that flawless meditative concentration is attained. Do not be content with a lucid mind that lacks the aspect of clarity capable of ensuring a vibrant force of ascertainment with respect to apprehension [of the meditation object].

[Finally] when even the subtle levels of mental laxity and excitation have ceased and concentration flows with sustained continuity, if you continue to apply the antidotes, this too is a fault. And the antidote against this is to disengage, to not apply any antidotes to laxity or excitation but to let go of your mind and abide in (8) *equanimity*.

As you continue to practice in these ways over a long period of time, you will attain the nine stages of stilling the mind in their gradual order, culminating in the attainment of tranquil abiding endowed with physical and mental pliancy.

The concluding part

This is exactly the same as before.

How to practice between sessions

As in the case of the preceding topics, you should do things such as reading scriptures and the like on the topic of tranquil abiding.

Training in Insight

How to train in insight, the essence of wisdom

This has two sections: how to practice during the actual session and how to practice between sessions.

How to practice during the actual session

The first is threefold: the preliminaries, the main part of the session, and the concluding part.

The preliminaries

This is similar to what was explained in the context of tranquil abiding. In particular, the following preliminaries are indispensable for realizing the view [of emptiness]: (1) listening to the instructions on insight on the basis of relying properly on learned spiritual teachers, (2) making fervent supplications on the basis of viewing your guru as indivisible from the meditation deities, and (3) striving in the gathering of merit and purification of negative karma. These three need to be undertaken in an integrated manner.

The main part of the session

This has two parts: how to establish the selflessness of persons and meditate on it [116] and how to establish the selflessness of phenomena and meditate on it.

How to establish the selflessness of persons and meditate on it

Although the Conqueror's scriptures present numerous types of reasoning to establish selflessness, beginners will understand it more readily if it is established through the following four key points.

The key point of ascertaining the object of negation

In all situations, even during deep sleep, we have, as if in the kernel of our heart, a kind of firm grasping to the notion of "I." This is the innate "I"-grasping. Suppose someone unjustly accuses us of doing a wrong and the thought arises in us, "How dare he accuse me of doing such and such a wrong when I have not done it!" A strong sense of "I" arises grippingly in that moment, as if from the kernel of our heart. It is in such situations that the mode of apprehension by the innate "I"-grasping becomes most evident. At that moment we should examine, from a small part of our mind: *where exactly does the mind grasp at an "I"? In what manner does it do so?*

In general, when a subsequent thought is strong, the preceding thought tends to fade, such that only vacuity remains. Therefore, when the thought "I am" is generated, you need to ensure that the main part of your mind sustains its force, and that only a small part of your mind does the examining. When you examine in this manner, [you will discover that] the locus where the innate "I"-grasping holds on to as an "I" is not something *outside* your five aggregates, from your body and mind. Nor does the mind grasp at it *on* your five aggregates or your body and mind individually. It conceives of such an "I" on the basis of the collection of your five aggregates—your body and mind composite—not as a mere mental construct upon this but with the assumption that there exists an enduring entity "I" right from the beginning. This is the mode of apprehension of your innate "I"-grasping and how it conceives the notion of an "I." The content of this grasping is the object of negation. You need to ascertain this not merely as an understanding derived from another's explanation or as a verbal construct but as a stark fact you have yourself ascertained in relation to your own mental continuum. This then is the first key point, that of ascertaining the object of negation.

The key point of ascertaining the entailment

If this "I" grasped onto by your thought "I am"—so fervently as if from the very kernel of your heart—exists upon the five aggregates, does it exist as identical to them [117] or as something different from them? There is no third possibility for its existence. For in general, whatever the phenomenon, it must exist either as one or as many. For apart from these two modes of existence, there is no third possible way of existing. In this way, conclude decisively.

The key point of ascertaining the absence of identity

Now if one were to conclude, "This 'I' as conceived exists as identical to the five aggregates," the following consequences would ensue. First, just as one single person possesses five aggregates, so too would there be five distinct "I"s with distinct mental continuums. Alternatively, just as the "I" is one, the five aggregates would also be a unitary entity with no parts. Many logical faults such as these would follow. Contemplate therefore that the "I" as conceived cannot be one with the five aggregates.

Furthermore, if the conceived "I" is identical to the five aggregates, then just as the aggregates come into being and cease to be, similarly, the supposedly enduring "I" conceived by the mind would also be subject to birth and disintegration. In that case, do the preceding and subsequent temporal moments of the "I" that undergoes birth exist as identical with or different from each other? If they exist as one, then all three "I"—those of the previous life, of the future life, and of this life—would become an indivisible unitary entity. If, on the other hand, they are distinct from each other, although *mere* distinctness does not entail an absence of any relationship, an *intrinsic* distinctness from each other would entail a separateness that is a total absence of relationship among them. This would imply that the "I" of the previous life, of the next life, and of this life would be three distinct entities with no relationship whatsoever among them, and numerous faults would ensue. For instance, you would experience [the fruits of] karma not committed by yourself, and karma you have created would just wither away. You should thus contemplate that the temporal instances of such an "I" conceived by that grasping mind are neither different from nor one with the five aggregates.

Also, if the "I" as conceived is identical to the five aggregates, it would be a truly existing unitary entity and would then become one thing in all possible senses. In that case the "I" or the self would not be *the appropriator* of five aggregates, and the aggregates would not be *the appropriated* of that "I" or the self.

Since many illogical consequences such as these ensue, you should contemplate that the "I" as conceived does not at all exist as identical to the five aggregates.

The Key Point of Ascertaining the Absence of Difference

If one were to conclude that "Although the 'I' as conceived does not exist upon the five aggregates as identical [to them], [118] it might exist a separate entity." In that case, just as when differentiating the five aggregates and eliminating them one by one, such as form, and so on, you could identify distinctly and say, "This is the aggregate of consciousness," likewise, when you eliminate each of the five aggregates, such as form, one by one, you should be able to identify distinctly and say "This is the 'I.'" This, however, is not the case. Therefore you should contemplate that the "I" as conceived does not exist as separate from the five aggregates.

When, on the basis of applying the analysis of the four key points, you ascertain the absence of "I" as conceived by the innate "I"-grasping, sustain the continuity of this ascertainment single-pointedly, free of mental laxity and excitation. Now when the force of this ascertainment begins to weaken, those on the beginner's level should reinforce their ascertainment of the absence of true existence, as before, on the basis of analysis of the four key points. Those of higher mental faculty, however, could reinforce their ascertainment of the absence of true existence by simply examining whether the self exists as it appears to their innate grasping at self, and the impact would be equal to analysis of the four key points. In this way, sustain with single-pointedness a meditative state characterized by two attributes—a firm ascertainment of the absence of intrinsic existence of "I" on the cognitive level while, on the perceptual level, the total absence that is the simple negation of true existence, which is the object of negation. This, in fact, is the way to cultivate the space-like meditative equipoise.

In the post-equipoise period, contemplate all phenomena such as "I" as displays that resemble illusions. On the basis of experiencing forceful ascertainment of the absence of true existence of all things during meditative equipoise, train so that whatever appears dawns on you as illusion-like manifestations.

How to establish the selflessness of phenomena and meditate on it

This has two parts: (1) how to establish conditioned phenomena as devoid of intrinsic existence and meditate on this and (2) how to establish unconditioned phenomena as devoid of intrinsic existence and meditate on this. [119]

How to establish conditioned phenomena as devoid of intrinsic existence and meditate on this

This is threefold—with respect to matter, to consciousness, and to nonassociated formations. To illustrate the first, take your body as an example. We tend to perceive, as if incontrovertibly, that over and above the mere collection of the five segments of the body[308] composed of flesh and bones, there exists a tangible entity that is our body—not just a designation imputed by our thought but something that possesses an enduring reality. This is in fact the way we perceive [intrinsic existence], namely the object of negation. For if such a body as perceived were to exist upon the body—namely, the mere collection of the five segments made of flesh and bones—the question is, "Does it exist as identical to or as different from the body that is the mere collection of five segments made of flesh and bones?" If it exists as identical to it, since this body that is a mere collection of five segments made of flesh and bones came into being from the parents' semen and ovum, it would mean that the drop of [fused] semen and ovum—the basis into which consciousness enters—would also be your body that is the mere collection of five segments made of flesh and bones. Also, just as there are five parts to your body, your body too would be five bodies, each itself a collection of five parts. If, in contrast, the body exists as different [from the parts that make up your body], then after eliminating each part, the head and so on, it should be possible to point to something and say "This is the body." But this is not the case. Therefore meditate by bringing forth the ascertainment that there is no such body at all.

With respect to the second, [consciousness], take today's consciousness as an example. Is there an intrinsically real consciousness of today over and above today's morning consciousness and today's evening consciousness? If so, does it exist as identical to or different from today's morning consciousness and today's evening consciousness? If it exists as identical to them, then today's evening consciousness should be present in today's morning consciousness. If, on the other hand, it exists as different from them, then after eliminating today's morning consciousness and today's evening consciousness, it should be possible to point to what may be called "today's consciousness." But this is not the case. Therefore meditate by bringing forth the ascertainment that there is no such consciousness at all.

For the third, [nonassociated formations,] take time as an example. If there is an intrinsically real year that is not a mere mental construct overlaid on the twelve months—the basis upon which year is conceived—[120] does it exist as identical to or different from the twelve months? If it exists as one with them, just as there are twelve months, the year too will be twelve. If, on the other hand, it is different from them, then after eliminating each of the twelve months, it should still be possible to point to something and say, "This is the year." But this is not the case. Therefore meditate by bringing forth the ascertainment that there is no such year at all.

How to establish unconditioned phenomena as devoid of intrinsic existence and meditate on this

Take space as an example. As there are numerous parts to the space, those of the cardinal directions and those of the intermediate directions—examine whether they exist as one or as multiple. Through such analysis, bring forth ascertainment of the absence of true existence and meditate as above.

In brief, contemplate that other than being merely imputed by the mind, nothing among all the phenomena of cyclic existence and nirvana, not even an atom, exists with intrinsic reality—be it my "I," my physical and mental aggregates, mountains, fences, houses, and on and on. To maintain such an ascertainment single-pointedly is the space-like meditative equipoise. In the post-equipoise periods, recognize everything you perceive as having a deceptive nature, arising from convergence of causes and conditions yet being devoid of true existence, which is the post-equipoise yoga of illusion. When, on the basis of engaging in these two yogas [the space-like equipoise and the illusion-like post-equipoise period], you attain the meditative equipoise tempered by the bliss of physical and mental pliancy derived through the power of applying analysis, this marks the attainment of authentic insight.

The concluding part

This is the same as before.

How to practice between sessions

As with the preceding topics, you should do things like reading scriptures and commentaries related to the topic of insight.

Having thus trained your mind in the common paths, you should enter the Vajra Vehicle, for when you rely on that vehicle, you will be able to easily perfect the two accumulations without needing to gather them over three innumerable eons. In brief, having been experientially guided on these topics of the stages of the path—from proper reliance on the spiritual teacher up to tranquil abiding and insight—[121] you should engage in their practice on a daily basis, maintaining either four sessions or at least one session, and strive to bring about experience-based effective transformation of your mind. This then is the most excellent way to extract the essence of your human existence of leisure and opportunity.

Colophon

The enlightened intention of peerless Ikṣvāku,[309]
as illuminated by glorious Dīpaṃkara and his sons
and by the second conqueror Losang Drakpa—
I have condensed here in stages of meditation.

As a resource for the fortunate ones journeying to liberation,
someone called Chökyi Gyaltsen has composed this.
Through this virtue may all beings, myself and others,
perfect the practices of the persons of all three capacities.

This direct guide to the stages of the path to enlightenment titled *An Easy Path to Travel to Omniscience* was composed from the notes prepared from a series of guided sessions conducted by the Dharma-utterer Losang Chökyi Gyaltsen. The notes were once again brought before my eyes and have been verified for accuracy. Through this, may I become a victory banner ensuring that the precious teaching of the Buddha never degenerates. May virtue and goodness prevail.

5. Words of Mañjuśrī

A Guide to the Stages of the Path

THE FIFTH DALAI LAMA NGAWANG LOSANG GYATSO

Translated by Rosemary Patton with Dagpo Rinpoché

From the ocean of the two collections, united wisdom and method, [125]
abundant boughs and leaves—the major and minor marks[310] ever pleasing
to behold—gracefully arise.
On their tips are the supreme, delectably ripe fruits—omniscience.
O foremost wish-granting tree, Master of Beings and Friend of the Sun,[311]
please bestow virtue and excellence upon me!

When the continent of vast and profound teachings traditions sank into
the lesser ocean,[312]
the tortoises who by teaching, debate, and composition
skillfully upraised it are known as the two great trailblazers.[313]
I praise those whose pristine renown extends beyond the [three] realms!

In the cool valleys surrounded by snowy mountain ranges,[314]
Atiśa dispelled the darkness of wrong views
with the bright sunshine of the Mahayana Dharma
as he spread the radiance of the Buddha's teaching.

All his discourses are supreme wish-granting gems.
Affixing them to the tips of the victory banners of learning, reflection, and
meditation,
the Kadampas fulfilled our ultimate hopes, goals, and aspirations.
Remarkable is this tradition, which spread in all directions!

Merely by brandishing the hundred-spoked vajra of vast intelligence that
analyzes thoroughly,

he halted the momentum of mountains of false teachings on countless debased and mistaken scriptural systems,
as he aborted the *asurī*[315] overconfidence in false disputations.
I pay homage to the unprecedented Indra[316]—omniscient Tsongkhapa—radiantly renowned for his knowledge, morality, and kindness.

When the sun of the Conqueror's [teachings] was eclipsed by my karma and afflictions,
descending behind the summit of the western mountain,
above the eastern mountain appeared in my imperfect mind the *kumuda*'s friend:[317]
my excellent tutor Khöntön,[318] you [whose feet I wear] as a crown.

The inexhaustible *wealth* of the excellent teaching
is *gloriously* virtuous in the beginning, middle, and end. [126]
Since Mañjuśrī resides in your throat, you have mastered it *spontaneously*.
O spiritual teacher, you are my source of the four *kāyas*![319]

The cool moon rays of your pristine *activity*[320]
swell the moon's nurse,[321] from which appears the powerful king of jewels:
the excellent teaching beneficial for this life and future lives,
which you offer us to end the poverty of samsara and personal peace.[322]

In particular, the great river of instructions of the three, Neusurpa, Potowa, and Chengawa,
whose source is Lake Anavatapta[323]—
Dīpaṃkara [Atiśa], the father and friend in the final era, and his spiritual son [Dromtönpa]—
has flowed into the ocean of my mind.

Weighty is the load of the kindness that I have received in this way.
When I contemplate it, I realize it will be very difficult to repay
until I reach the essence of ultimate enlightenment.
Contemplating it, I can but join my hands at my heart.

Bodhisattva conduct is as vast as space.
The Buddha's view of the ultimate is as subtle as the tiniest particle.

For one like me to shoulder the task of explaining it
is like trying to measure the ocean's waters with half a mango pit.

However, I will not call just holding up a book or reading one aloud an explanation transmission.
This volume shall be a precious vessel
containing the nectar of my lineage-holder master's words
and my authentic spiritual experience.

Herein, to practice according to the explanation of the stages of the path[324] for persons of the three capacities that condenses into one all the key elements of the Tathāgata's entire canon and guides fortunate beings to buddhahood, practitioners must hear it from a spiritual teacher belonging to an unbroken lineage. For this reason [*A Song of Spiritual Experience*] states:

> Transmitted excellently by these two great trailblazers
> are the paths of profound view and vast activity.[325]

and [the *Great Treatise* says]:

> To demonstrate the purity of the teaching's source, explaining the greatness of the author.[326]

also:

> [The author] should possess the instructions that have been transmitted in an unbroken line of great beings originating in the complete and perfect Buddha.[327]

An analysis of these words will reveal their great significance. Furthermore, the order of the lineage issuing from our Teacher, Śuddhodana's son, up to the great Dharma king Tsongkhapa, as presented in the lamrim supplication prayer, is flawless. [127] From that time onward, his followers—scholars and accomplished masters who disseminated Jé Rinpoché's teaching in the ten directions as both scripture and realization—spread and increased like the stars in the sky and the dust on the earth. Accordingly, there must be as many lines of transmission. Nevertheless, these days it has become very common for people to cite only the lineage masters of their own monastery, to teach others while incapable of explaining the more recent lineages, and so on.

I, on the other hand, have made a considerable effort to study and contemplate the detailed explanations that remove doubts concerning the terms of this teaching and their meanings, as well as the practical expositions that indicate how to apply it and so on, each with its specific transmission lineage.

As regards the [practical] expositions, according to the tradition transmitted from Jé Sherab Sengé[328] up to my main guru,[329] which mentions "in a clean and pleasant place," you are to thoroughly clean the place of meditation and so forth, which should be harmonious in terms of time and location. According to the Mother of Conquerors, which states, "Honor the teacher and the teaching,"[330] you are to set up a high seat such as lion throne for the Dharma teacher, and while serving and honoring him, consider him as you do the buddhas. The *Kṣitigarbha Sutra* states:

> Listen to the teaching with complete faith and reverence,
> free of pride and scorn for the teaching and the teachers;
> cultivate respect for them—serving and honoring them and so on—
> and consider the spiritual teachers as you do the Buddha.[331]

As this passage conveys, because it constitutes an auspicious start, it is taught that you must not get it wrong by being disrespectful.

The *Questions of Sāgaramati Sutra*[332] explains that if you begin by reciting the demon-subduing mantra you will become invisible to all demons within a hundred leagues. If you cannot recite the mantra, be sure instead to recite the *Heart Sutra* thrice. Next, without confusing the order, supplicate the complete lineage of lamrim masters from the Buddha up to your main spiritual teacher, and offer a mandala as well.[333] It is taught that novice practitioners will not succeed in their Dharma practice by taking the easy and effortless route, like following a teacher's explanation of a basic text as he points to it with a stick. To avoid the error of personal fabrication, it is very important to use your intelligence and meticulously examine the beginning, middle, and end of the practice in detail. [128]

The source of all goodness and happiness that ends all the misery of samsara and personal peace—for the purpose of achieving complete unsurpassed buddhahood on behalf of sentient beings as vast as the limits of space—is to establish within yourself, through learning, reflection, and meditation, the entire Mahayana teaching: the words of Śrī Dīpaṃkara, who combined into one the two streams of instructions of Ārya Asaṅga and the protector Nāgārjuna, both of whom, through the kindness of the two regents,[334] did not rely on [human] preceptors and thoroughly pioneered the holy collection of vast and profound Dharma taught by the Guide and Sugata.

The "Learning" chapter of the *Collection of Aphorisms* says:

> By learning you understand the teachings,
> by learning you overcome sin,
> by learning you give up what is meaningless,
> by learning you attain the state beyond sorrow.[335]

Accordingly, you must first establish the teaching by learning. The [*Great Final Nirvana*] *Sutra* says, "Listen and learn well and thoroughly."[336] I encourage you to listen, having first overcome the three faults akin to overturned, soiled, and pierced vessels and adopted the six recognitions: seeing yourself as a patient, the teachers as physicians, the teaching that is given as medicine, the careful practice of it as the treatment, the tathāgatas as superior beings, and wishing that the teaching remain for a long time. In brief, listen after establishing within yourself the general and the specific correct motivations, conduct, and so forth required for listening to the Dharma.

Regarding the holy teaching to hear, the *Song of Spiritual Experience* states:

> This [instruction on the] stages of the path to enlightenment
> flowed excellently in succession from Nāgārjuna and Asaṅga,
> crown jewels of all the learned ones of this world.
> Your banners of fame flutter vibrantly among sentient beings.
>
> Among instructions, it is the most precious of all gems,
> fulfilling all the wishes of beings without exception.
> It is also the ocean of the most glorious well-uttered insights,
> the confluence of a thousand rivers of excellent treatises.
>
> It helps you see all teachings as free of contradiction,
> it helps all scriptures dawn on you as personal instructions,
> it helps you easily discover the enlightened intention of the
> conquerors,
> and it helps protect you from the abyss of grave negative deeds.
>
> Therefore, this most excellent instruction, relied upon
> by countless fortunate ones like the learned ones of India and Tibet,

> this teaching on the stages of the path of persons of three capacities:
> what intelligent person would not be captivated by it?[337]

The unsurpassed Teacher, Śuddhodana's son, excellently taught the great and unique way traversed by all sugatas of the three times. The two great trailblazers, independently [of any human teacher], then explained the meaning of all the key elements of his 84,000 sections of scriptures. Their scholar followers established it by their expositions, and the great siddhas practiced it all. The glorious Prince Dīpaṃkara then unerringly condensed it in the form of an instruction for practice called "the stages of the path for persons of the three capacities" and composed *Lamp on the Path to Enlightenment* and other works and thereby disseminated it. The followers of his tradition, known as the eminent Kadampas, upheld and spread this tradition of scholarship, kindness, and ethical discipline throughout the Land of Snows just as the sky covers the earth. Yet again, to eliminate the impurities of mistaken interpretation and incomprehension affecting [the lamrim teachings] owing to changing fortunes, the great Dharma king Tsongkhapa, as if the two trailblazers had returned as the human embodiment of Mañjuśrī, composed the works known as the *Great* and *Middle-Length Treatises on the Stages of the Path to Enlightenment*. Within the Great and Lesser Vehicles, these vital treatises with their excellent, unprecedented explanations are not confined to a partial teaching of scripture and realization, nor do they propound a limited practice.

As the master Dromtönpa said, "My guru knows how to transform all aspects of the teaching into a path."[338] Accordingly, for those who have not developed the wish to be free of the unfortunate realms' sufferings as explained in the path of persons of lesser capacity, genuinely fearing them like a criminal detests prison, it is impossible to develop uncontrived renunciation of cyclic existence. As taught in the path of persons of intermediate capacity, this [renunciation] perceives the samsaric condition as an expanse engulfed in flames and is free of any craving for the happiness of the excellence of a high rebirth as a god or human. [130] Without the slightest taste of the renunciation of samsara, how can you possibly develop genuine uncontrived great compassion that comprehends sentient beings' suffering? Bodhisattvas who generate the aspiration to enlightenment and train in the six perfections without realizing great compassion are like lotuses in the sky.[339] As such, those who wonder about the apparent contradictions in the teachings—for example, between methods to avoid the unfortunate realms on the one hand and methods for rejecting selfish concerns and striving to benefit others on the other—should know that in fact all the scriptures have a cause-and-effect relationship; each, as either a main or auxiliary path, contributes to any individual's achievement of buddhahood and necessarily complements the others. This is [the lamrim's] greatness of allowing you to realize that all the teachings are free of contradiction.

When practicing such topics, as *A Discourse on the Three Gems* states:

> The blame for being destitute of the teaching[340] despite one's great learning lies in not seeing the scriptures as instructions for practice.[341]

Do not fail to understand the key point, which is that from the cause—ascertaining scriptural teachings—you are to produce the effect—the teaching as realization. As Naljorpa Chenpo stated:

> Mastering the instructions does not mean simply learning a short text small enough to fit in your palm; it means understanding all the scriptures as instructions for practice.[342]

Among the Buddha's flawless teachings, there is not one that does not indicate explicitly or implicitly the methods to attain the happiness of fortunate rebirths and definite goodness.[343] Nevertheless, for those who find them difficult to grasp owing to their profound and recondite nature, the great exegetical treatises elucidate their intent. There is not a single separate instruction on how to practice that is not found in the canonical and exegetical works. Ascertaining that the complete significance of their extensive explanations is condensed in the lamrim's three sections—preliminaries, main explanations, and conclusion—is the [lamrim's] greatness of allowing you to see all the scriptures as instructions for practice. Once you have thoroughly understood all the scriptures as instructions for practice, you can assimilate all the aforementioned canonical and exegetical works by learning and reflection.

Why are there separate works such as [Atiśa's] *Lamp on the Path to Enlightenment*, [Drolungpa's] *Stages of the Teaching*, [Tsongkhapa's] lamrims, and so forth? [131] It is because as time passed and their intelligence declined, disciples found it difficult to discern the [scriptures'] meaning and, with very lengthy works, were unable to clear away their doubts. For this reason, based on instructions passed down from the Buddha in an unbroken line of excellent masters, their meaning was condensed in treatises on the stages of the path and so forth. Given this, do not imagine that they do not include the vast meaning of the words of the teaching's 84,000 sections, that parts of it are missing and other parts have been added. There is no need to reprise all their very words as long as the meaning is complete. For example, a single dose of all the medicines included in the large category of twenty-five kinds of camphor can cure a person of fever; it is not necessary to take the complete set of [fever] medicines. For these reasons, [the lamrim] has the greatness of allowing you, by relying on a guru's instructions, to easily discern the Conqueror's intent.

It is inconceivable that there should be the slightest antidote to the two kinds of obscurations[344] to be rejected by each person traveling from the state of an ordinary being to buddhahood that is not taught in the canonical and exegetical works. Since the present treatise condenses the meaning of all the scriptures, practicing it closes the door to all faults. Notably, the *Gathering All Fragments Sutra* says:

> Mañjuśrī, the karmic obscuration of rejecting the sacred teaching is subtle. Mañjuśrī, at times considering the Tathāgata's words favorably and at times considering them unfavorably constitutes abandoning the teaching.[345]

Accordingly, since [the lamrim] puts a halt to all faults of abandoning the teaching, it has the greatness of automatically allowing you to avoid the worst error.

There are three steps to practicing the instruction endowed with these four kinds of greatness: the preliminaries, the main part, and the conclusion.

The preliminaries

Since the lower levels of the stages of the path for persons of the three capacities are preliminaries to the higher levels, there is nothing wrong with viewing the path of persons of great capacity as the main practice and the paths up to and including the path of persons of intermediate capacity as its preliminaries, which coincides with other ways of explaining the path, such as that of mind training. [132] However, according to the outline [of the *Great Treatise*] on how to train in [bodhisattva] practice in general, which reads "How to train in the Mahayana in general and how to train in the Vajrayāna in particular,"[346] the vast path becomes a preliminary in the context of tantra. As such, once you identify the central topic you need to meditate on, you are to distinguish it from its preliminaries, like establishing the mountain that is over there in relation to the mountain over here, and the one here in relation to the one over there. Many people stray onto mistaken paths by failing to identify the role of a topic at hand. Given this, it is important to rely on firsthand practical experience that you gain from the oral traditions of lineage-holder masters. According to this instruction then, each subject, from the difficulty of attaining leisure and opportunity up to special insight, must in turn be taken as a main topic of meditation.

Stanzas between sections

The opportunity to hear the beautiful music of perfect teaching
that issues from my tutor's lips,
objectively and without the faults of flawed vessels—
this I have gained thanks to the store of merit acquired over eons.

In particular, the teaching with the four kinds of greatness—
the lifeblood of all Indian and Tibetan learned and accomplished masters
and the medicine benefiting beings of both great and lesser capacities—
is a path as difficult to find as a second moon.

Those with the good fortune to practice such an excellent path as this
through learning, reflection, and meditation
should banish the vain concerns of this life
and spur themselves on with keen disgust and disenchantment.

They should reside free of diversions on high mountains covered in
 meadows, woods, and flowers,
in small huts or stone shelters just large enough to contain them,
with just their second shadow[347] to accompany them,
in places free of the sound of idle talk that triggers the three mental
 poisons—
a thorn in the side of concentration—
attended only by the gentle echo of babbling brooks
and deer wandering fearlessly to and fro.

They should live with clothes plucked from the trash, by begging for food
untouched by the poisonous waters of improperly acquired goods,
and be able to compel their body, speech, and mind toward pristine virtue.
This is the best way to achieve ultimate happiness. [133]

Relying on Spiritual Teachers, the Root of the Path

Introduction

Thus the first part, the preliminary that is reliance on spiritual teachers, the root of the path, is twofold: the preparation, which consists in [generating] refuge and the awakening mind, and the main topic, the way to practice the path of reliance on spiritual teachers.

Regarding the preparation, some scholars teach that among all the practices, the first is always how to rely on spiritual teachers and that nothing else precedes it. Many appear to take this as true, but if that were the case, it would mean having to admit that there are disciples intended for the stages of the path who train in the topic of reliance on spiritual teachers without having first taken refuge in the Three Jewels. As they have not taken refuge, they have yet to enter the ranks of Buddhists, for both Lord Atiśa and Śāntipa assert that it is refuge that distinguishes a Buddhist from a non-Buddhist. Furthermore, [Tsongkhapa] in his outline of the stages of the path[348] states that refuge is the excellent gateway to the [Buddha's] teaching.

Some suggest that taking refuge is not problematic but that generating the awakening mind is unsuitable because reliance on the spiritual teacher is followed by the topics for persons of lesser capacity. I do not consider this to be a valid argument. There are two kinds of topics of the path of persons of lesser capacity: those of true persons of lesser capacity and the topics shared with them. In our context here, the topics to be practiced are not those of the persons of lesser capacity who aspire to nothing beyond a good rebirth in their next life. They are the topics shared with persons of lesser capacity, constituting the foundation for the paths of persons of the intermediate and great capacities. Hence:

> So that novice beings
> might realize the supreme goal,
> the perfect buddhas taught methods
> in steps like stairs.[349]

[Tsongkhapa] raises the following question: if the topics of persons of lesser and intermediate capacities are preliminaries to the topics of persons of great capacity, why can they not be considered stages of the path of persons of great capacity? Why speak of "the stages of the path shared with persons of lesser and intermediate capacity?"[350] The beneficiaries of the teaching in the present context are disciples who aspire to the path of persons of great capacity. Since the path of persons of lesser capacity is taught to them as a preliminary, not only is there nothing wrong with it being imbued with the awakening mind, it is excellent that it should be. [134] My perfect guru taught based on the *Essence of Refined Gold*,[351] completing it with the two lamrims, and these works clearly name refuge and the awakening mind [as the preparations]. As the great [Indian] treatises do not clearly mention taking refuge and generating the awakening mind at this point, and you have never received experiential explanations or seen or heard oral transmissions and traditions, it makes sense that you, teaching your own personal invention, are surprised by this.

As such, initially for taking refuge, *Praise to the One Beyond All Praise* says:

> What troubles of sentient beings are there
> that you do not remove?
> What worldly beings' excellence is there
> that you do not confer?[352]

Reflect as follows:

> Other than through the Buddha's power, beings cannot possibly escape from samsara's troubles and from personal peace or enjoy temporary and ultimate happiness. Buddhas, who are endowed with exceptional qualities, are in turn the products of the holy Dharma, the truths of cessation and the path. Moreover, correct practice of these depends on the Sangha, those in training and those fully trained. Therefore I entreat the holy objects of refuge, from now until I reach buddhahood, please be my protection and refuge.

Once you have generated ardent faith, think that the refuges and protectors are pleased, and that they have actually come to serve as your protectors and refuges. Thanks to the strength of your heartfelt conviction and the outstanding wisdom, compassion, and strength of the objects of refuge, like birds taking wing in the sky, they come to care for their disciple. Given the nature of causation, it is said:

> Whosoever makes a point of generating faith,
> before such persons, the buddhas dwell.[353]

It is said that this is not merely something you imagine; they are in fact certain to come.

My master did not indicate a detailed meditation [on refuge at this point] like those found in tantric texts. Nevertheless if you fail to practice refuge according to the sutras as taught here, your multiple recitations of refuge formulae will serve only to keep you from idle talk.

On that note, once you have identified the objects of refuge, how do you, as a practitioner of refuge, go for refuge? [135] You reflect on how, owing to your karma and afflictions, you are sunk in the vast ocean of samsaric desolation that is boundless and deep, and how you are tormented by the three kinds of suffering. This should prompt the fear you would feel if you were about to be struck dead by your arch enemy. With faith that is aware of the Three Jewels' ability to protect you from this terror, the aspiration to achieve outstanding qualities like theirs, the overwhelming conviction that makes you think, "No matter what happens to me—fortune or misfortune—I put my trust in you," compassion for sentient beings, and the awareness that although you do not have the ability to free them from suffering now, by supplicating the Three Jewels and relying on them for support, you are certain to gain it, repeat the following in sequence, counting a minimum of twenty-one and a maximum of three hundred times, depending on the length of your session:

> I and all sentient beings as infinite as space, from now until we reach the essence of enlightenment, take refuge in the glorious and holy spiritual teachers, take refuge in the Bhagavān Buddha, take refuge in the holy Dharma, take refuge in the ārya Sangha.

Training in virtue too intensely from the start is a sign of not knowing how to practice. If [your sessions] are too long at the outset, you will easily fall prey to laxity and excitation, and once accustomed to them, it will be difficult to correct them, so it is better to undertake numerous short sessions. By ending your meditation while you still feel like continuing, you will always be happy to start again. Otherwise, the very sight of your meditation cushion will repel you. To avoid becoming impervious to the teaching, it is important to do this properly from the start.

After practicing refuge, repeat the following with great devotion seven or twenty-one times, according to circumstances:

> I take refuge in the spiritual teachers and the precious Three Jewels. Please bless my mindstream. I especially request you to bless me so that the stages of the path for persons of the three capacities may quickly arise in me.

The precise reason you supplicate the Three Jewels, which are superior fields [of action], is to ensure the realization of the topics of meditation that follow. As stated [in the *Great Treatise*]: [136]

> In these times when minds are very weak, when you do not retain the words while memorizing,[354] when you do not understand while contemplating their meaning, and when you do not attain realizations while meditating, the instruction is to rely on the power of a [superior] field.[355]

This is why it is imperative that you start by taking refuge. Having done so, you must train [at least] marginally in the precepts of refuge, in the process you also accomplish the collection [of merit] by making offerings.

Like scattering a hundred birds by firing a slingshot once, since you take refuge and make requests at the outset (thanks to which, by the superior field's power, the paths will arise in you), it is not necessary to recite the words of supplication after each section of meditation topics.

To generate the awakening mind, say the following three, seven, or however many times is suitable, while reflecting on its meaning:

> For the sake of all sentient beings, I will attain complete buddhahood. For that purpose, I will practice the stages of the path for persons of the three capacities.

The express purpose of generating the awakening mind is to transform all the virtues you subsequently produce into causes of your attainment of buddhahood.

How to actually rely on spiritual teachers

Secondly,[356] on the main point of how to actually rely on spiritual teachers, the root of the path, *Ornament of Mahayana Sutras* states:

> Rely on spiritual teachers who are disciplined, pacified, thoroughly
> pacified,

> who have superior qualities and are diligent and rich in scriptural
> knowledge,
> who have an excellent understanding of suchness, skill in teaching,
> and a compassionate nature,
> and who have overcome discouragement.[357]

The spiritual teachers you follow should have tamed their mind well by means of the three higher trainings. They should have studied at length and possess knowledge of the scriptures. They are to have achieved an excellent level of training in the wisdom realizing suchness, and their good qualities should surpass those of their students. With intelligence capable of analyzing the scriptures' meaning by means of reasoning, they should be skilled in guiding disciples along the excellent path in a way that is pleasant to the ear. [137] Without taking into consideration personal gain, honors and so forth, they should have loving compassion for the wretched. They should strive to accomplish others' welfare with diligence and have the forbearance to withstand the hardship involved in teaching repeatedly, without ever becoming discouraged. Excellent gurus endowed with these good qualities are qualified to teach the supreme Dharma.

Regarding disciples, the *Four Hundred Verses* says:

> Those who are unbiased, intelligent, and interested
> are said to be vessels for listening.
> They do not distort the teacher's good qualities
> nor those of their fellow students.[358]

Students should be free of bias—attached to their own views and intolerant of others'. They should have the intelligence necessary to distinguish faulty explanations that are to be rejected from valid ones to be practiced. They should be committed to pursuing the perfect Dharma, revere Dharma teachers, and be very attentive to them. These are the five good qualities that students require. If such students meet with such teachers, just as a bird with two wings can easily fly up in the sky, achieving liberation will not be as difficult as one might imagine.

The way students with such characteristics rely on spiritual teachers has two parts: how to rely on them in thought and how to rely on them in deed. Regarding the former, the *Jewel Torch Dhāraṇī* states:

Faith is the prerequisite of all good qualities. Like a mother,
it generates them, then protects and develops them.
It clears away doubt, frees you from the [four] rivers.[359]
Faith leads you to the city of happiness and goodness.

Faith cuts through the gloom [of non-faith] and clears the mind.
It removes pride and is the root of reverence.
Faith is a jewel, a treasure, and the best pair of feet.[360]
Like hands, it is the means to reap virtue.[361]

Accordingly, it is important to be sure to begin with undivided faith in the spiritual teachers. This requires seeing them as free of all faults and endowed with all good qualities. Nevertheless, "Because of the degenerate times, the gurus appear to be a mixture of faults and good qualities."[362] Since to us, disciples with impure karma, they appear to be a mixture of faults and good qualities, we must begin by ceasing to attribute flaws to them. By doing so, we will naturally come to see them as possessing all good qualities. [138]

A skilled doctor will prescribe potent medicine that will reveal a latent illness and provoke a little pain, which then subsides. Similarly, to overcome the perception of faults in the gurus, you need to consciously make the imperfections that you attribute to their activities apparent to yourself. When you do not make a point of examining the behavior of those you have known for a while, be they friends, enemies, or neither of the two, you will be only vaguely aware of it, and the attitudes that are the three mental poisons will not reveal themselves in relation to it. When you do carefully check how you view their behavior, their good or bad actions will appear to you not as if they were something in the past but as clearly as if they were actively happening now. Spontaneously, you will as a consequence feel either happy or sad. Similarly, you should reflect again and again on your perfect and glorious gurus' physical form, on the sound of their voice, on the extent of their strength of mind and courage—in brief on all their activities, be they good, bad, or indifferent, down to the way they walk, dress, and so forth. You are to bring them to mind naturally and continue until these good, bad, and indifferent impressions appear to you as palpably and clearly as their present actions. Then, when you begin to question whether you see the gurus this way because shortcomings are actually present or despite their absence, think:

> How could excellent gurus have such failings? Having become heavily tainted by obscurations—karma and afflictions—throughout my lives since beginningless time, I have the impression now that they have flaws even though they lack them. How does this differ, for example, from a perfectly white snow mountain appearing blue to a deceptive sense consciousness? Or a visual consciousness afflicted with jaundice seeing a [white] conch as yellow? To act on behalf of beings like us, who are completely conditioned by our mental poisons, it is not impossible that they purposely take imperfect forms, adjusting to our condition.

Contemplate this again and again.

Ignorant meditators' contemplations that involve faith alone are not grounded. Because the matter must be ascertained using examples and reasonings, think:

> The fully accomplished Buddha, free of all faults and endowed with all good qualities, was seen as mass of failings and errors by Sunakṣatra, Devadatta, tīrthikas, and so on. [139] Ārya Asaṅga saw Venerable Maitreya as a female dog, her hindquarters infested with maggots. Master Buddhajñānapāda saw Master Mañjuśrīmitra as an old man, half-householder, half-monk, his head wrapped in a Dharma robe, ploughing fields, and cooking the numerous insects he gathered from their furrows. Nāropa saw Tilopa roasting live fish, and the novice monk Kṛṣṇācārya saw Vajravārāhī as a leper woman. The *Meeting of the Father and Son Sutra* explains that the Tathāgata may also manifest as a demon if it ensures the welfare of sentient beings.[363] There is no difference between these examples and my way of seeing things.

It is taught that conducting such analytical meditations will dissipate the aforementioned dim and distressing view of the gurus' activities just as sunbeams pierce darkness, after which the gurus will appear very clearly as faultless. Even novice practitioners are sure to experience this, provided they meditate on it.

Once you are fully convinced that the gurus are in fact faultless, you can deduce that they have all good qualities. However, it is natural that whatever awareness predominates should override its opposite—the perception of either shortcomings or good qualities. You are to reflect repeatedly and deeply, thinking:

> My spiritual teachers have qualities like knowledge, ethical discipline, practice, kindness, and so on, or at very least such and such minor quality, like being unattached to material things or being able to read aloud well.

In this case, although they exhibit flaws like considerable stinginess or little learning, the perception of these will lessen and be no longer obvious, just as when the moon is shining in a clear sky, sunlight renders it hard to see. It is crucial then that you do your best to stop the view of even the slightest fault and cultivate faith in even the most insignificant good quality, for it will be the source of all goodness and spiritual attainments.

You can generate great unshakeable faith in someone by simply hearing of his or her good reputation, even if the person in question has not been kind or helpful to you. It is nonetheless important to recall [the gurus' personal] kindness toward you to generate deep reverence. Do this by thinking: [140]

> Although there are buddhas as numerous as grains of sand in the Ganges River who are by nature free of all faults and endowed with all good qualities, my feeble fortune prevents my benefiting from their kindness. While my perfect gurus are all tathāgatas of the three times by nature, they have generated an ordinary form and have manifested to guide unruly and hard-to-tame beings. That is why, although they are no different from the buddhas in being free of all faults and possessing all good qualities, from my point of view, they are even greater. Generally buddhas never leave the dharmakāya's state of great bliss, but for the sake of exceptional disciples like ārya bodhisattvas, they will manifest as saṃbhogakāya enjoyment bodies. Since these forms are not visible to śrāvakas and pratyekabuddhas or to ordinary beings in Jambudvīpa, buddhas guide such beings to the path of maturation and liberation with excellent nirmāṇakāya emanation bodies. It is not that the buddhas have purposely abandoned me out of partiality, but just as a north-facing cave is not lit by the sun, my karma and lack of good fortune have prevented me from meeting buddhas in person and savoring the nectar of their words. That is why I have

> been forever turning in samsara and experiencing suffering. Even now, in this human life I have attained, had I not met my excellent teachers, I would not have had the fortune to even hear the words "Three Jewels," and I would have had to keep wandering in an unfree state. Even meeting a buddha in personal could not have benefited me more. My spiritual teachers explain the profound and vast Dharma perfectly, and I hear it. If I manage to put it into practice, I am sure to attain liberation and omniscience. If protecting someone from the fear of sickness and enemies and providing food, clothing, and wealth in this life are considered great kindnesses, what of the kindness of giving protection from the general and specific sufferings of cyclic existence and of providing matchless enduring happiness? Even filling a billion worlds with gold couldn't repay it. For me, the kindness of the holy gurus is without doubt far greater than the kindness of all the buddhas of the three times! [141]

You meditate to generate faith and reverence from the very depths of your heart and the core of your being until your hair stands on end and tears stream from your eyes. If you wish to expand on this, it is taught that you are to recite with a beautiful melody the passage in verse from the *Adornment of Trees Sutra:* "These are my spiritual teachers, my instructors in the Dharma..."[364] and contemplate its meaning.

On the second topic, how to rely [on spiritual teachers] in deed, *Fifty Verses on the Guru* says:

> Here what need is there to say much?
> Do whatever pleases your teachers.
> Give up doing anything that displeases them.
> Examine these and be diligent in each.[365]

It is necessary to do what pleases the perfect teachers and to refrain from what displeases them. In the past, to receive a single line of teaching, our Teacher stuck a thousand butter lamps into his body, drove a thousand nails into it, and offered everything he had: his children, wives, subjects, and possessions. Consider how the bodhisattva Sadāprarudita relied on Dharmodgata, Nāropa on Tilopa; how the great Atiśa for the sake of receiving instructions on the awakening mind from Lama Serlingpa[366] bore adversity on the sea; how Dromtönpa relied on Atiśa, Setsun[367] on Drokmi,[368] Milarepa on Marpa, and so forth. The biographies of these great masters of the past show how, for the sake of the teaching, they endured inconceivable hardships, with no regard for their health or belongings. Although the gurus are not interested in material goods and the like, if for now they behave as though they were, it is to enable their disciples to complete their accumulation of merit. As [*Fifty Verses on the Guru*] states:

> By giving to them, you will be giving
> to all buddhas continuously;
> giving to them constitutes a collection of merit;
> by the collections, you gain the supreme spiritual attainment.[369]

To produce a large collection of merit, you should offer all the cherished belongings you own, and if your teachers tell you to do something difficult or seemingly inappropriate, thinking that it will doubtlessly be useful to you in some way, do not hesitate to do it. Or, if it is something you simply cannot do or you feel is wrong, as [*Fifty Verses on the Guru*] says:

> Upon reflection if you feel incapable of it,
> ask to be excused from doing what you are unable to do.[370]

You must ask to be excused properly, for it is inappropriate to leave it at that without thinking any more of it. [142]

Since it is said that the main way to please your spiritual teachers is to offer them your practice, integrate whatever teachings they have given you through learning, reflection, and meditation.

Once you have determined that not relying on them correctly is the source of all misfortune and that relying on them well is the source of all that is good, then as taught in canonical and exegetical works like the *Adornment of Trees Sutra* and the *Vajrapāṇi Empowerment Tantra*,[371] you need to do more than just pay lip service to it; you must practice accordingly. As new practitioners, you will not be able perform acts of giving and so forth as Sadāprarudita did, without regard for his health and life, but you should pray to be able to do them. Adapt those that you can do to the time, place, and circumstances. When meditating, it is not necessary to imagine that you are doing actual practical service [like serving tea].

In sum, the way to practice the above is found in the "brief explanation on how to meditate" section of the *Great Treatise on the Stages of the Path to Enlightenment*.[372] This preliminary practice [of how to rely on spiritual teachers] is to be identified as a main topic of meditation. Older meditation guides call [relying on spiritual teachers in deed] "the preliminary to reliance on spiritual teachers" and present it initially. This was done with the idea that such an accumulation of merit would prepare one for the realization of the aforementioned analytical meditations, but these days[373] one does not practice in that order.

Furthermore, after cleaning the meditation room as the protector Serlingpa himself did, you should set up representations of the Three Jewels' body, speech, and mind; arrange whatever offerings you have; sit on a comfortable seat, not in a casual manner but in one of the correct postures: cross-legged, half cross-legged, and so on. To practice this, older meditation manuals state that while purifying with the mantra "*Oṃ svabhāva* [*śuddhāḥ sarvadharmāḥ svabhāva śuddho 'haṃ*]" you visualize the commitment beings. According to the oral tradition of Jampalyang Taklung Drakpa Lodrö Gyatso,[374] you are to visualize your main guru as the protector Mañjuśrī and recite *dhīḥ* many times to supplicate him. Some manuals say to visualize your guru in the form of Buddha Śākyamuni and Vajradhara seated on a lotus with many layers of petals. On these you imagine the other gurus seated either like the deities of a mandala or in lateral rows like monks in a monastic assembly, and so on. [143] There are many traditions that are influenced by secret mantra. Here the custom is slightly different from the above.

At this point, following the rite based on the *Medicine Buddha Sutra*,[375] bless the place and religious effects, and then invite, as you would guests,[376] the members of the merit field in relation to whom you will practice this guru yoga. The way to bless the place, throne, and so on is by the power of the Three Jewels' truth, the buddhas' and bodhisattvas' blessings, the two collections' completion, the purity of the ultimate expanse, and by your faith and visualization, saying, "Everywhere the ground is pure, [free of stones and so on, as flat as my palm, made of lapis lazuli, and naturally smooth.]" To bless the place of meditation, you imagine that the ground is made of precious substances and is as smooth as the palm of your hand. On it is a beautiful throne of precious materials, held up by lions, on either side of which are as many precious thrones as there are direct and lineage masters. You picture the entire array as very beautiful and arranged as tiers in height and depth. As found in the *Essence of Refined Gold*, recite:

> Without leaving the purity of the ultimate expanse,
> consider sentient beings in the ten directions with infinite compassion.
> You, who spread the activities of all conquerors,
> O gurus of the three times, come hither with your retinue![377]

And:

> Protector of all sentient beings without exception...[378]

Having invited them with three verses,[379] think that the unequalled Teacher, the King of the Śākyas, indivisible from the kind main guru who has given you this teaching, is surrounded by the gurus of the lineages of vast activity and profound view. They in turn are surrounded by the Sanghas of the three vehicles, both those in training and those fully trained, like heaps of clouds. They come as in the *Story of Sumāgadhā*[380] and settle on the prepared seats.

Visualize the bathhouse saying, "In an exquisitely fragrant bathhouse..."[381] You multiply your body a hundred, a thousand, or ten thousand times—as many times as you are mentally capable—and while holding a precious vase filled with scented water, say, "Immediately after his birth..."[382] and "Although the Conqueror's body, speech, and mind are free of afflictions..." to offer them ablutions as extensively as time allows, using the verses that refer to the six perfections and so on. [144] This is not to suggest that the members of the merit field are sullied by impurities, but since in the eyes of ordinary beings with impure perceptions they are, you offer ablutions to purify that impression.

"As for washing, massage, wiping, sick nursing, extolling their good qualities, and so forth,"[383] when in the presence of your gurus, you should actually perform these. Here [in the preliminary practices, offering ablutions and so on] are their substitute.[384] They constitute the above-mentioned way to please the teachers by making them material offerings.

While reciting, "With the finest perfumes whose scent fills the billion worlds...,"[385] offer fragrance. Saying, "Divine raiment, thin, soft, and light...,"[386] offer garments. Reciting, "Out of compassion for me and all beings...," request them to remain.

Paying homage is the first of the seven parts of the prayer that includes the key elements for purification and accumulation. While sustaining the visualization of the objects of refuge, you pay them homage. You are to recite the well-known verses of supplication to the vast and profound lineages, from "Unparalleled Guide, Teacher, and Conqueror..." up to the Great Lord [Tsongkhapa], as is customary, transforming them into verses of homage [to which you add the following]:

Sherab Sengé, of great knowledge and attainments;
Gendun Drup, truly omniscient;
[Khedrup] Norsang [Gyatso], who has actualized the three kāyas:
O three glorious masters, I supplicate you.

Gendun Gyatso, who delights Sarasvatī;
Gelek Palsang, luminary of eloquence;
Sönam Palsang, prince of knowledge and attainments:
O three excellent masters, I supplicate you.

Sönam Gyatso, whose hand clasps a lotus;
Chöphel Sangpo, lineage holder of the instructions on the
profound;
Nangzé Dorjé, head of all the families:
O three great masters of knowledge and attainment,
I supplicate you.

The one named Śrī Buddha, whose kindness has no equal,[387]
and Lord of Speech Ngawang Losang Gyatso:
you are treasure stores of the vast and profound Dharma.
O assembly of direct and indirect teachers, I supplicate you.

Reciting the passage from, "However many there are [in the ten directions],"[388] pay homage to the conquerors and their spiritual children you have invited. [145]

The mandala is the first offering presented. It should be made of precious materials, but if you cannot afford one, it can be made of something like slate. Barley, for example, can be used to make the heaps. Having prepared these, begin by offering as many thirty-seven-heap mandalas as you like. To offer more, mainly offer the seven-heap version, presenting it twenty-one times or more, with the corresponding recitations and visualizations.

In these times when generating merit is necessary, some people do not offer so much as a single grain of barley by way of material offerings, nor do they make the slightest effort on the physical and verbal level; they claim to make offerings by visualizations and states of concentration alone. Regarding this, Potowa commented:

> Putting a few aromatic herbs in a smelly incense burner and then saying "[I offer] water perfumed by sandalwood and camphor..." is like a blind person trying to fool someone who can see.[389]

While you have resources, offering little or nothing, or things of inferior quality, out of stinginess and laziness is a clear sign of not having developed sincere faith in either the Dharma or in living beings. These days, people who practice the teaching and do it genuinely are as rare as stars visible during the day. Or if there are some, which is highly unlikely, they have no place in society, and are like two-legged people in Tsuta.[390] Many people refuse to do rigorous and regular practice, and are even incapable of enumerating their lineage masters, despite which they boast and show off like some Kāñcī kinglets who have drums beaten to be congratulated for having killed their father.[391] Such arrogant bragging is utterly inappropriate.

For the other offerings, with passages such as "Drinking water mostly arranged as garlands of drinking water...,"[392] offer the two kinds of water, as well as the [other] outer offerings of music and so on. Otherwise you present the five sense objects, the seven emblems of royal power, and so forth with any appropriate verses. When you wish to avoid over-lengthy sessions and facilitate your usual practice slightly, you recite, "With magnificent flowers and beautiful garlands..."[393] and so forth, for the offering part of the practice. You are to think that those to whom you have presented both concrete and visualized offering substances partake of them with great pleasure—not because they long for them but to assist you in completing the collections. [146]

Saying, "[All the ill deeds I have done] out of attachment, aversion, and ignorance...," confess with all four powers all the sins and obscurations you have accumulated with your three doors. With "Be they of the conquerors of the ten directions...," rejoice and delight in all ārya and non-ārya virtues, for in this way you will benefit from merit equal to that generated by their virtue. With "Lights for all worlds in the ten directions...," request them to turn the Dharma wheel. With "You who think to demonstrate passing into nirvana...," supplicate them not to pass into *parinirvāṇa*. In relation to the latter two practices, it is taught that you should be fully convinced that the members of the merit field accept your requests. The passage "[The least of merits that I may have generated] through homage, offering, and confession..." is for dedicating to enlightenment all the virtue you have achieved by the six preceding parts of the practice.

> Just as a drop of water fallen in a great ocean
> is not spent until the ocean is spent,
> so too is virtue dedicated to enlightenment
> not spent until enlightenment is achieved.[394]

This is a crucial point for guarding virtue from destruction and developing it widely.

In old practice manuals, it is taught that the likes of *General Confession*[395] are to be recited at this point, which would enhance this part of the practice considerably, but these days this is not the custom; for ease of exposition, I will expand on confession below.

For the preliminaries just explained and the main part of each topic of meditation, from this point up to special insight, to avoid mistaking the order of the successive meditations, the amount of detail, and so on, you must completely rely on your direct experience of the oral traditions and practices. As such, the *Great* and *Middle-Length* treatises explain that your entire spiritual practice will be flawed if, as some do these days, [you practice] as you do when memorizing philosophical works on your own [selecting certain parts and skipping others]. [147] It is extremely important that intelligent people consider this matter well. Currently, some neglect relying on a guru's empirical explanation and try to practice by taking books as their gurus, which impairs their whole practice, and their efforts amount to nothing.

Furthermore, with constant meta-awareness, while ensuring that no aspect of your behavior lapses, you must devote the main part of the session to meditation of the topic at hand and, between sessions, refer to the extensive explanations concerning it found in the *Great* and *Middle-Length* treatises and elsewhere. It is taught that if you do not restrain your mind, your good qualities will improve very little.

From reliance on spiritual teachers up to the awakening mind, analytical meditation is required foremost, while tranquil abiding and the like mainly require placement meditation. Nevertheless, taking the topic of reliance on spiritual teachers as the example, reflect on the gurus' good qualities using analytical meditation, after which you should put aside other thoughts and do a placement meditation in which you abide one-pointedly on faith. Reflecting repeatedly on the main points concerning how to cultivate tranquil abiding is analytical meditation, and focusing one-pointedly is placement meditation. Without understanding these key points, just claiming "I do not do any analysis—I just meditate!" makes it clear that authentic meditation is wanting. This is explained at length in great treatises like the *Ornament of Mahayana Sutras*, which states:

> Thus, first based on learning, correct contemplation arises; in turn, from correct contemplation issues superior wisdom of the excellent object of meditation.[396]

Stanzas between sections

Ah! If the upstanding who help the wretched suffering from hunger
and thirst
by providing them with food, clothing, and wealth
and who protect those harmed by enemies and adversaries
are thought to be kind and are proclaimed so,
how then can be repaid the kindness of spiritual teachers,
who liberate us completely from all fear of undergoing
the three kinds of suffering in endless samsara
and reveal, as clearly as if it were in the palm of our hand, the gem
of stable happiness?

If achieving just the state of blissful peace is a challenge,
then those who guide us to what is known as "buddhahood free of faults
and endowed with all good qualities,"
which is renowned for being difficult to attain even after many eons,
are true embodiments of the buddhas of the three times! [148]

In our mistaken and deluded minds,
we project all our faults on the gurus' activities—
a sure sign that we are rotten to the core.
Once we see they are ours alone, we are to reject our three mental
poisons.

I have understood that the root of all conceivable benefits and happiness
is the profound method that transforms all we do into spiritual practice:
the pure view that sees only good in all they do
and with faith and reverence the implementation of all they teach.

Leisure and Opportunity

Secondly, the central part—while relying [on spiritual teachers], the way to gradually train the mind—has two parts: the encouragement to take full advantage of a life of leisure and the way to take full advantage of one. The first of these has three parts: identifying leisure and opportunity, contemplating their great potential, and contemplating the difficulty of obtaining them.

Identifying Leisure and Opportunity

The *Friendly Letter* states:

> Holding wrong views, being born an animal,
> a hungry ghost, or a hell being,
> in a place that lacks the Buddha's teaching or is remote,
> as a barbarian, as a mental deficient and mute,
> or as a god of long life—such lives
> are known as the eight non-liberties.
> Once you have attained leisure by avoiding them,
> strive to overcome birth![397]

The eight non-liberties are holding wrong views, the three lower states, a buddha not having appeared, [being born in] a remote land, stupid, or mute, and as a long-life god. By avoiding them, you enjoy the eight kinds of leisure.

[With respect to the ten opportunities,] it is as stated in the following:

> Being born a human, in a central land, with senses complete,
> not having committed any of the five acts of immediate
> retribution,[398] and having faith in the three scriptural
> collections.[399]

The five personal opportunities are being born a human, being born in a central land, having fully functioning senses, not having committed any of the five acts of immediate retribution, and having faith in the three scriptural collections.

> A buddha having appeared and taught the perfect Dharma,
> the teaching remaining, there being those who follow it,
> and the presence of those with compassion for others.[400]

The five general opportunities are: a buddha has appeared and has not passed into *parinirvāṇa*, a buddha or his disciples are teaching the perfect Dharma, [149] the teaching continues without decline in the form of realizations as it existed when the Buddha was alive, others enter it after observing that persons of lesser capacity attain results from the teaching given, and there are some who are compassionate.

Avoid analyzing this superficially and instead relate it to yourself, thinking, "The human life I have now has all eighteen characteristics!" Since you have been born a human, no analysis is required to establish that you are neither a being of one of the three unfortunate realms nor a god. If you have ascertained the existence of past and future lives, karma and its effects, and the Jewels, you do not hold wrong views. As Śākyamuni, the fourth buddha of the fortunate eon, appeared in the world and his teaching continues, you have access to the Conqueror's teaching. Although in the snowy land of Tibet the entire fourfold assembly is not found, the presence of bhikṣus makes it equivalent to a central land. If you understand the words of the scriptures and their meaning to some extent, you are neither stupid nor mute. These are the eight kinds of leisure.

[As we saw above, the five personal opportunities are] in general being a human; in particular being born in what qualifies as a central land according to religious criteria; having five fully functioning senses; not having committed any of the five acts of immediate retribution; and having achieved faith in the three scriptural collections. The first four general opportunities as actually taught are difficult to bring together, but their equivalents exist: a buddha has appeared in the world, he taught the perfect Dharma, the teaching he gave continues without decline, you have committed yourself to that teaching, and benefactors and others provide supportive conditions such as food and clothing. These are the ten opportunities.

Ask yourself whether your present human life has all eighteen kinds of leisure and opportunity. If it does, meditate on it until you are overcome with joy. It is said that if you examine all those who, without verifying the matter, now pride themselves on having a human rebirth complete with leisure and opportunity, the vast majority of them would be found wanting.

Contemplating their great potential

Secondly, although you cultivate a feeling of delight at having a life complete with leisure and opportunity, if you do not ponder the reasons for feeling happy, the joy you have will be no more than the pleasure that greedy people feel when they acquire something that has no real value. Unlike that, be sure to feel delighted for good reason. [150] As *Letter to a Student* says:

> In those who intend to guide sentient beings by relying on the
> path to the sugata state,
> the powerful [awakening] mind that humans attain
> is not achievable by gods, nāgas, or demigods;
> nor by garuḍas, vidyādharas, kinnaras or belly crawlers.[401]

Think as follows:

> As they are mainly experiencing the maturation effect of non-virtuous actions, beings of the three unfortunate realms have very little power to accumulate [virtuous] karma. Gods, though they enjoy the maturation effect of virtue, have but little potential to produce this kind of karma. Humans' aptitude to produce both virtuous and sinful karma is very great. We, the people of Jambudvīpa, have especially powerful karma,[402] which means that by practicing correct adoption and rejection, we can achieve the marvelous results that are high rebirth as a god or human, the nirvana of śrāvakas and pratyekabuddhas, the bodhicitta by which we guide all beings to the sugata state, and buddhahood. The rebirth that I have is many times better than a wish-granting gem!

Through this reflection, you will come to be aware that you have achieved something vital that you have never attained before. Meditate until you experience the kind of profound joy a pauper would feel on finding a treasure.

Contemplating the difficulty of obtaining them

Thirdly, there are three ways to understand the difficulty of attaining them: with reference to similes, their causes, and numbers. Regarding the first, *Guide to the Bodhisattva Way* states:

> Like a turtle poking its neck through the hole
> of a yoke floating on a vast ocean . . .[403]

It is said that when a golden yoke with a single opening drifts on a great ocean, carried by the wind in all directions, and a blind turtle rises to the ocean's surface once every hundred years, it is extremely unlikely that the turtle's neck should pass through the yoke. And here is a simpler simile that you can verify for yourself: if you throw handfuls of dried peas at a wall, the chance that any of them will stick to it is highly improbable. If perchance one or two do stick, think:

> The countless lives I have had in unfree conditions are like the number of peas that have fallen to the ground, and the human lives with leisure and opportunity I have had are like the number of peas that have stuck to the wall.

As you meditate, relate the significance of this simile to yourself until you have truly grasped it, for these are times in which, but for a little luck, you automatically fall, like a rock tumbles down a cliff. In this way you generate both states of mind, fear and joy, in an uncontrived fashion.

Second is the difficulty of attaining them from the perspective of their causes. Generally speaking, to attain a simple fortunate rebirth, you need to observe at least one aspect of ethical discipline. Specifically, to attain a human life with leisure and opportunity—as [Nāgārjuna] said, "From generosity comes wealth, from ethical discipline a fortunate rebirth,"[404]—you must have pure ethical discipline as a base, supplement it with generosity and the rest, and dedicate[405] these [virtues] with stainless prayers. As for the bases for producing these causes, it is very difficult for beings in the three unfortunate realms to generate patently virtuous thoughts. Gods are captivated by the pleasures of states of concentration or of the desire realm. In lands where the teaching has not spread, people may never even hear the word *virtue* spoken. If the number of such places was compared to a heap of barley, those where the teaching has spread would be equivalent to a single grain. To take the example of our country, Tibet, currently within a group of many tens of thousands of people, those committed to observing ethical discipline are very rare, and among them, those who bring together all three of the excellent causes mentioned above are about as common as stars visible during the day.

By redirecting these externally oriented thoughts and looking within yourself instead, you will note that although you may have a vague intention to practice the Dharma, when you add up your virtues, you will find that you have very few of which you can be certain. As for sins and nonvirtues, you amass them [effortlessly] as you go. Think:

> For that reason, if in whatever time I have left in this life I do not achieve a secure position, I will not attain another human rebirth. Expecting one is about as hopeful as planning to harvest barley in the fall after planting mustard seeds in the spring.

Meditate on this until you achieve a genuine experience of it.

For the third, the difficulty of attaining them from the perspective of numbers, imagine you are standing on a small patch of ground that is absolutely swarming with summer insects. Nonetheless hungry ghosts by far outnumber animals, and hell beings are even more numerous than they. As for animals, compared to those that reside in the oceans' depths between the continents, those scattered on land are very rare. While a small patch of earth contains countless small animals, it can only hold roughly ten people. No matter how dense the population of any town or locality, it hardly exceeds a hundred thousand, while the number of tiny organisms it contains is incalculably great. [152] No valid inference is needed to grasp this. Sages and fools alike can understand it directly. Among the various kinds of fortunate rebirths, human lives are scarce; among them, people who meet the Dharma are even rarer. Among those who have met it, most do not remember its words though they study them. When they contemplate them, they do not grasp their meaning, and despite meditating on their meaning, they fail to realize it within. The vast majority of those who have achieved the wisdoms of learning, reflection, and meditation strive after goals that concern this life alone. Given this, you are to meditate persistently until you experience seeing this life complete with all the conditions conducive to religious practice as a greedy person does a unique jewel rarely found in this world.

Stanzas between sections

You have enjoyed the good things of samsara
over many lives, all the while seeing the suffering and misery they cause.
Still, like the idiots that you are, you persist in viewing
as valuable this life's enjoyments: food, wealth, and the rest.

If you continue viewing them as you have in the past till now,
the great demons—white, black, and two-toned worldly concerns[406]—
will enter your heart; you will mistake suffering for happiness
and cast your ultimate goal to the wind.

Having now, for once, attained ship-like leisure and opportunity,
the basis for creating the excellent causes of happiness and goodness,
if you fail to journey to the jewel isle of definite goodness
and instead return to samsara empty-handed, you are indeed rotten
to the core.

Death and Impermanence

The way to take full advantage [of leisure and opportunity]

This has three parts: training the mind on the stages of the path shared with persons of lesser capacity, training the mind on the stages of the path shared with persons of intermediate capacity, and training the mind on the stages of the path of persons of great capacity.

The path shared with persons of lesser capacity

On training the mind on the stages of the path shared with persons of lesser capacity, *Lamp on the Path to Enlightenment* states:

> Those who, by whatever means,
> take personal interest
> in the pleasures of cyclic existence alone
> are known as persons of lesser capacity.[407] [153]

Ordinary persons of lesser capacity, who are interested only in the happiness of this life and strive to overcome its sufferings as do animals, do not qualify as persons of lesser capacity in the present context. According to [Atiśa's] exposition, superior persons of lesser capacity must not be concerned with this life and should instead strive only for happiness in the next. In the present outline, the expression "the path shared [with person of lesser capacity]" implies that prior to renunciation of samsara in its entirety, it is necessary to develop renunciation of the sufferings of three unfortunate realms. For this there are two topics: cultivating concern for future lives and relying on the methods for happiness in future lives. Cultivating concern for future lives has two parts: contemplating impermanence in the form of death and contemplating the suffering of unfortunate rebirths.

Contemplating impermanence in the form of death

Except for some foolish and ignorant people who do not ask whether they will die, most people think that they will die one day but not until they are old. Every year, month, and day they continue to imagine that they will not die, and so even when they are struck with a mortal illness or have reached the age of a hundred, they plainly expect to go on living. As a result, just as, when you have no travel plans and intend to stay home, you do absolutely nothing to prepare for a departure and instead arrange to do things like build a house or plant fields, you are driven only by this life's concerns. To reverse this attitude, think:

> There is no guarantee that I will not die tomorrow. I may gather supplies for next month, but it is not at all sure that by that time I will not have been reborn with a body very different from the one I have now, with horns sticking out!

Once this thought is firmly anchored in you, just as someone who is planning to leave soon for another place makes no arrangements for staying at home but works hard to prepare for the trip, getting packhorses ready and so on, the thought of dying soon naturally prevents you from working hard for this life's goals and automatically prompts you to accomplish what will be useful for your future lives.

It is very important that those of you who are interested in this teaching train your mind in the topic of death and impermanence. It has three parts: contemplating death's certainty, contemplating the uncertainty of the time [of death], and contemplating that at the time of [154] death nothing but the Dharma will be of any use.

Regarding the contemplation of death's certainty, the *Collection of Aphorisms* says:

> If even buddhas, pratyekabuddhas,
> and the buddhas' śrāvakas
> must give up their physical bodies,
> what need be said of ordinary beings?[408]

The *Collection of Aphorisms* further states:

> Wherever you may reside,
> there is no place where death will not find you:
> not in the sky, nor in the depths of the sea,
> not even if you dwell in the heart of a mountain.[409]

We are sure to die because the fully accomplished buddhas who appeared in the past, despite having gained mastery over birth and death, passed into nirvana to prompt those disciples holding the view of eternalism to practice. The same is true of countless superior, average, and lesser people—Indian and Tibetan scholars and saints, kings, ministers, bodhisattvas, and so on, whose lives are narrated in religious histories and annals, in oral traditions, and elsewhere. When you do not think about it, you may have the impression that they are still alive today, but when you examine the matter more closely, except in accounts of past events, none of them remain in any time, place, or circumstance—all have demonstrated passing into nirvana. Think:

> Among the people that I have known personally—preceptors, teachers, parents, friends, relatives, and so on—so many of them have gone on to their next life: friends, enemies, and neutral people alike. Although a large crowd of many thousands of people may gather today, between now and a hundred years from now, everyone in it is sure to die. Given I cannot point out a single person who in the past has not died, who has avoided it somehow, how could I possibly be the sole exception to the rule and escape death? Even if I manage to have an average life span of sixty years, each day is eaten up by twenty-one thousand breaths, each month by thirty days, and each year by twelve months. Twelve of those years constitute a cycle of years, and once five of them have passed, I will have reached the end of my life. The *Play in Full Sutra* says:
>
> > The impermanence of the three worlds is like autumn
> > clouds,
> > [observing] beings' birth and death is like watching
> > scenes in a play,
> > lives pass like flashes of lightning in the sky
> > and are swiftly spent like water down a steep mountainside.[410]

Not for a single moment does a life remain still. [155] Unlike food and wealth, which can be replenished as they are gradually depleted, you cannot add to a spent life span. *Guide to the Bodhisattva Way* states:

> Pausing neither day nor night,
> this life shortens constantly.

If it can never be prolonged,
how could someone like me not die?[411]

Reflecting thoroughly on the question in this way, referring to examples and reasonings, you meditate until you reach the conclusion that you will definitely die.

The second step is the contemplation of the uncertainty of the time of death. With the above meditation, you come to understand that in the end there is no escaping death. You might imagine however that once you have spent some time working on subduing your enemies, caring for your friends, creating conditions conducive to religious practice and so on, you will then be able to practice the Dharma. Although a specific life span for beings in each of the three realms is taught, only the inhabitants of [the northern continent] Kuru are sure to have the long life announced. Specifically, regarding the inhabitants of Jambudvīpa, the *Treasury of Abhidharma* states:

For them [life span] is uncertain; at the end
it is ten years long, to start it is immeasurable.[412]

As such, it is explained that life span is very uncertain, and this is directly verifiable for until now, many people younger than you have died, and many older than you are still alive. Given this there is no guarantee that you will not die before them. The *Collection* says:

Of the two, tomorrow and the next life,
it is unknown which will occur first.
So instead of striving for tomorrow's sake,
it would be better to strive for the sake of future lives.[413]

Of the two, tomorrow or the intermediate state of your next life, you cannot be sure which will occur first. Some people imagine that because of the many available means like diet and medical treatment, factors that sustain life abound. However, as the *Precious Garland* states:

The conditions for death are many,
those sustaining life are few.
As these too may become causes for death,
always practice the Dharma.[414]

Think:

> Food may disagree with me. I may react badly to medicine. As houses may collapse, boats sink, friends deceive me, and so on, the factors sustaining life often become instruments of death. Several elements ensure that a butter lamp continues to burn for a good while—a wick, clarified butter, and so on—but when something like a gust of wind strikes it, it immediately goes out. In the same way, even if my life span is not yet depleted, very many things can affect it—an imbalance of my body's elements, obstructive spirits, spirits who are alternately helpful and harmful, and so forth. As it says in the *Friendly Letter*: [156]
>
> > Many things harm this life, and as it is more
> > impermanent
> > than a water bubble struck by a gust of wind,
> > it is extraordinary that one has the chance to inhale
> > after exhaling
> > and to rise having gone to sleep.[415]

Meditate on this until you truly ascertain that in all cases, your time of death is uncertain. It is crucial that you be on your guard every day, for this terrible enemy is sure to come, and it is uncertain when it will.

The third part is to contemplate that at the time of death, nothing but the Dharma is of any use, regarding which *Guide to the Bodhisattva Way* states:

> When I am seized by Yama's[416] messengers,
> what use are relatives? What use are friends?
> At the time only merit could protect me,
> but that I have failed to acquire.[417]

Think:

> When the time inevitably comes to take the great route known as death and impermanence that comes down like a rockslide on a steep mountainside, then no potions, mantras, states of concentration, or hero's weapons can avert it. The wealth of the affluent cannot bribe it; the words of the eloquent cannot fool it. And it

> goes without saying that I will not have the right to bring with me the many friends and relatives who surround me, nor any power and riches, even if they rivaled a universal sovereign's. I will even have to abandon completely the very body that will have been my constant companion since my mother's womb. Powerless, my consciousness alone will move on, like a hair extracted from a slab of butter. Then the only thing of any use that will follow me is the virtue I will have previously acquired—in other words, the perfect Dharma, nothing else.

Meditate on this persistently until you gain an experience of it.

Some silly people interpret the statement that nothing but the Dharma is of any use when you die to mean that you do not have to die. In our tradition, it is not a matter of not dying but of the way you die. As past Kadam masters used to say, the best practitioners die happily, average ones do not shirk it, and lesser ones die with no regrets.

Stanzas between sections

Once this rebirth impelled by karma and afflictions
has been attained, you proceed toward
death and impermanence without pause.
What fool would prepare to remain indefinitely?

The year, month, and day are uncertain; there is no fixed time
and no precedence between the old and young.
You observe death and yet allot yourself time
and so are like a blind person who only seems to see.

As you neglect pure virtues, your ever-faithful companions,
and continue to imagine that
your unfaithful loved ones, entourage, and wealth will always serve you,
you may have to travel the intermediate state's difficult passage
empty-handed.

The Lower Realms

Unfortunate realm suffering

The second part [of cultivating concern for future lives] is contemplating the suffering of unfortunate rebirths. It has three parts: [157] reflecting on the sufferings of hell beings, animals, and hungry ghosts. The first, reflecting on hell beings' sufferings, has two parts: the hot hells and the cold hells. Regarding the first, the hot hells, [first reflect on] the purpose of meditating on the previous topic, death and impermanence:

> The moment following death, a person does not just cease to exist the way a butter lamp goes out or a pile of straw is consumed by fire. It is certain that there is no choice but to be reborn, and there are only two possible kinds of rebirth, in a fortunate realm or an unfortunate realm. As for the cause of rebirth in a fortunate realm—virtue—I do not recall having produced enough of it in the past to feel completely comfortable. Nor can I know what virtue I may or may not have accomplished in my previous lives. My nonvirtuous karma, on the other hand, is the size of a royal treasury—wherever I look, I have created it. If I have to experience its results, unfortunate realms' sufferings, it would be the same regardless of it happening with my present body or after having moved into another body. When I do not think about it, I have the impression that it is my flesh and bones that feels the pain of a wound for example, but in fact it is my mind that experiences it. Otherwise stabbing a corpse would necessarily cause pain, which it certainly does not. With my present kind of mind, today I enjoy human and divine resources, but when it is suddenly gone, there is no guarantee that I will not be subjected to the agony of the relentless hell.

In this way, to inspire renunciation in you, as the protector Nāgārjuna says, "Every day recall the hells, extremely hot and extremely cold."[418] Accordingly, it is necessary to contemplate hell beings' sufferings. As for the way to do it, these days most often people just rattle off quotations and verses. Broaching the matter externally, they observe others' suffering like a show and fail to relate it to themselves. [158] It is like people watching a court of justice where criminals are punished and tormented in various ways. Although kind people in this situation feel renunciation and compassion, for most it is just a kind of entertainment to be relished. However, if the same people who see it that way were to find themselves in court with their limbs bound in fetters and the rest, their former feeling of pleasure would soon become so painful they could hardly bear it for a moment, and they would be able to think only of how to escape their torment and nothing else. Similarly, when meditating on the sufferings of prison-like samsara, you are in most cases meant to visualize yourself born in one of the six realms and personally experiencing its sufferings. You are to meditate on them subjectively.

It is taught that once you have produced the intermediate state for a hell rebirth as a consequence of a nonvirtue created by hatred, you will have the impression that your body is cold. By longing for warmth, the intermediate state ceases, and you are born in a hot hell.

Generally, in a hot hell environment, the ground below is burning iron, and the periphery burning iron walls. The space above and below is filled with flames. To meditate on the hell called Revival, diligently imagine that you are actually born in a place like the one just described. This should make your hair stand on end and your mind shrink in fear. Once you feel this, think that the vast number of beings born there congregate and, impelled by anger, strike one another with a variety of weapons. As a result, your body is chopped into a hundred or a thousand pieces, you collapse in a faint, and so forth. Continue until you have the impression that you are truly experiencing these. Next, when you hear a voice from the sky cry out, "All of you, revive!" you immediately recover and are once again stabbed with weapons and the like. This is the way to meditate on continuous suffering. Practicing it well will make you lose your appetite and your interest in idle talk and distracting conversations; you will naturally and effortlessly devote all your energy to rejecting sin and accomplishing virtue. If your thoughts and behavior remain unchanged, it means that you are not relating the practice to yourself. [159]

In the Black Lines hell, guardians sear eight lines on your flesh and then chop you to pieces with sharp weapons. Rebirths in the eight hells do not necessarily occur in this order, but when meditating, you follow the sequence found in the commentaries. In Crushing, which comes next, you have the impression of having escaped the former suffering, but when you move on, you find yourself forced between mountains shaped like the faces of goats, sheep, oxen, or lions and are crushed between them until blood streams from all your orifices. In Screams, having escaped once more, you find yourself inside an iron building. The doors slam shut behind you, and as fire blazes from every direction, you are roasted. Conscious that there is no escape, you erupt in piercing screams. For Great Screams, it is taught that you are to meditate that the same iron house is enclosed in a second one. However, according to my guru's explanation, when you leave the [first] iron house and run away, you find yourself forced into a double iron house. As a result, the suffering is twice as great as before. The difference is emotional, for you think, "Although I may escape the inner iron building, I will never manage to escape the outer one!" For example, if you are in a prison with two sets of walls, although you might manage to pierce the first one, doubting your ability to pierce a second one, you agonize.

In Heat, you are impaled straight from your anus to your crown on a blazing iron spear, and flames shoot out from all your orifices, or else your entire body is cooked in a cauldron of molten bronze. In Extreme Heat, you are impaled on tridents; the central point pierces your crown, the lateral ones your shoulders. Your body is wrapped in a sheet of red-hot metal like a roll of woolen cloth. When boiled in molten bronze, your flesh and blood dissolve, and you are reduced to a skeleton. In the Relentless hell, as fire blazes from all cardinal and intermediary directions, your body is indistinguishable from the flames; only your cries are heard.

You don't endure these sufferings for just a short period of time. The *Treasury of Abhidharma* says, "When you calculate fifty human years as a day for desire-realm gods. . ."[419] which is unclear and somewhat difficult to work out. Among the eight hells, Revival has the shortest life span. It lasts 1.62 trillion human years. The life span of each successive hell doubles. When you contemplate this, you cannot help but feel that your heart is about to explode. [160] The *Friendly Letter* says:

> As long as your nonvirtue is not spent,
> your life will not come to an end.[420]

Thinking, "Given this and given my present behavior, what is there to stop my lives in the hells from lasting even longer?" meditate until you are truly shaken.

For the second part, the cold hells, it is taught that while in the intermediate state prior to a rebirth in this kind of hell, you have a sensation of heat and long to be cool. As a result, your intermediate state ends, and you are born in a place surrounded by ranges of frozen peaks. Below are snowy expanses and glaciers with deep crevices; above, snow and sleet storms rage. The place is thick with darkness, and you are struck by piercing winds. Otherwise, the place, the way you are born there, and so on, except for the difference in temperature, are as explained above.

As for the particular hells, in Blisters blizzards blow in from the four directions and strike your body, making you hunch and develop blisters. In Burst Blisters, blood and pus ooze from the blisters. In Achoo, as suffering increases, you cry out loudly. In Kyihoo,[421] as suffering amplifies, your voice cracks, and you emit squeaking sounds from the back of your throat. In Chattering Teeth, suffering intensifies further; you are unable to emit a single sound, and your teeth chatter. In Split Like an Utpala Flower, your body is stung by strong winds; it turns blue and splits into six small cracks. In Split Like a Lotus, your blue skin peels, exposing bright red flesh, which divides into ten cracks. In Greatly Split Like a Lotus, the color is as before, but a hundred cracks or more form. The *Garland of Birth Stories* says:

> By holding nihilistic views, I will find myself
> in my future lives in a place of deep darkness where cold winds blow.
> When I am tormented by the pain of my bones' disintegration,
> who will venture there in the wish to relieve me?[422]

It is taught that the duration of a life in Blisters and its suffering is measured by the time it takes to empty a large storage bin filled with eighty *khal*[423] of sesame seeds—each *khal* being composed of [twenty] large Magadhan *dré*—by removing a single sesame seed every hundred years. The thought of this should make you tremble and induce a strong feeling of revulsion.

If you can generate a feeling of disgust with suffering by understanding the sixteen hells' torments of heat and cold in relation to yourself, an extensive explanation of the adjacent and intermittent hells should naturally prompt a similar experience of renunciation. [161] For this reason, it is taught that it is not strictly necessary to expand on the latter and that the former meditation is sufficient. If you have about two months available, you could extend the meditation topic to include the sufferings of the adjacent and intermittent hells, but for fear of being longwinded, I will not explain them here. You can refer to other works.

For the second part, contemplating the suffering of an animal, the *Friendly Letter* says:

> In an animal rebirth, there are a variety sufferings:
> those of being killed, bound, beaten, and so forth.
> People who forsake virtue, the cause of liberation,
> must eat others and be horribly eaten.[424]

Of the two categories of animals, aquatic and terrestrial, that are explained in [Asaṅga's *Five*] *Sections on Grounds*,[425] those living at the bottom of the sea are found in the depths below the shores of Mount Meru's oceans. Their size and so on are indefinite and diverse. Among those piled up like heaps of grain, the larger swallow the smaller, and the smaller bore into the bodies of the larger. Moreover, it is so dark that they cannot even see their own limbs when they extend and retract them. The habitat, food, drink, and companions of those like crocodiles who live in the ocean are unpredictable. As for the animals scattered on the land, they are pursued by hunters, dogs, and predators against their wishes. Domestic animals are beaten, exploited, and slaughtered. Furthermore, those of the serpent class fear hot sands and [birds of prey like] garuḍas. As for tiny organisms, the slightest change in conditions brings about their death. None of them have the slightest idea of what should be adopted and what should be rejected. Be sure to meditate that you are born as one of the animals just mentioned until you gain a meditative experience of their suffering and so on. Their life span may be as long as an eon or as short as a day; nothing about them is definite.

For the third part, contemplating the suffering of hungry ghosts, the *Friendly Letter* says: [162]

> Hungry ghosts are continuously subjected to the suffering
> of never seeing their desires fulfilled
> and must undergo the unbearable [torments] of
> hunger and thirst, heat and cold, and fatigue and fear.[426]

Among the three categories of hungry ghosts taught, *those with outer obstacles* see fruit trees and rivers, but when they go to help themselves to them, they perceive guards brandishing weapons, or pus and blood, in their stead. *Those with inner obstacles* are found in a town called Kapila that lacks everything desirable—water, fruit trees, and so on—and where they find nothing to eat or drink. If they happen to find a little, given that their mouths are the size of the eye of a needle, their throats as narrow as a horsehair, their stomachs as large as Mount Meru, and their limbs as thin as blades of grass, the food does not fit into their mouths, or if some does, it cannot descend their throats, or when it does, it does not fill their stomach. As a result, they suffer. The food and drink of *those with obstacles regarding food and drink* catches fire and burns their body, or they eat excrement, urine, and their own flesh—such are their hardships. Furthermore, the moonlight in summer feels hot to them, the sunlight in winter, cold; merely glancing at a river is enough to dry it up and make it appear as a deep ravine. In meditation, you are to truly relate these to yourself: you think that you are born with the body of a hungry ghost and experience the various sufferings of hunger and thirst described. These lives do not last just a short time. It is taught that they must be experienced for 15,000 human years. Continue to reflect, getting the measure of it all, until uncontrived renunciation arises in you.

To sum up fully the significance of the above, if we were forced to hold our hand in a flame for the time it takes to drink a cup of tea, to remain naked in the depths of winter for about a day, to go without food and drink for three or four days, or to remain under a pile of stones and earth unable to move, clearly we would find it unbearable. Given that, how could we possibly bear the torments of the three unfortunate realms? The protector Nāgārjuna says:

> A human rebirth in Jambudvīpa is difficult to acquire.
> Having attained one, channel all your efforts
> into ending the causes of the unfortunate realms.[427]

Thinking, "As a human, now is the time to distinguish myself from an animal. I must pluck up my courage," spur yourself on again and again. [163]

Stanzas between sections

In a blazing iron house that is scorching hot,
you are cut, chopped, and squeezed until your blood flows.
From the doors of your senses, flames shoot forth.
The heart of those who do not fear these must be under a demon's sway.

Amid fierce winds, surrounded by dark snowy mountains,
although the sharp weapon of bitter cold has cracked your
feeble body

into thousands of pieces, still you do not die.
It is the foe nonvirtue that causes such constant torment.

When you cannot bear the minor pain
of a small wound, you must be mindless matter
if you do not tremble at the prospect of the endless torment
of being killed to eat your flesh or for your bones and skin.

You are capable of toiling for the sake of the food and drink
of this short life, but to overcome
the horrific torments of hunger and thirst lasting fifteen thousand
human years,
even exertion so intense that you risk your very life will not suffice.

Your fear of the unbearable abyss of the three unfortunate realms
is insufficient even to give you gooseflesh, yet you think yourself
very clever
in adopting this life's eight concerns—overcoming enemies
and caring for friends. Where is there a greater fool than you?

Refuge

The second part, relying on the methods for happiness in future lives, has two parts: taking refuge, the gateway to the Dharma, and contemplating karma and its effects—the source of all goodness and happiness.

The first, [refuge] has two parts: the main topic—taking refuge, the gateway to the Dharma—and its precepts. On the main topic, *Guide to the Bodhisattva Way* states:

> Just as the night, swathed in clouds and darkness,
> is momentarily illuminated by flashes of lightning,
> likewise, by Buddha's power, in beings
> a virtuous thought occasionally dawns.
>
> Thereby comprehend that while virtue remains feeble,
> powerful sins are not in the least depleted.[428]

With the three—fear of misdeeds, faith in good qualities, and compassion for beings like you—first think that dark eons in which one can never hear the words of the perfect Dharma are like nights swathed in darkness and laden with black clouds. The rarity of an eon of light in which you can meet the Dharma is like a flash of lightning in that dark night. [164] Compared to the ocean of your past sins, your virtues are as feeble as the few drops that a blade of *kuśa* grass dipped in water picks up. Moreover, in this life, having become accustomed to the title and appearance of a Dharma practitioner, you have in this way misled others, for when you check your thoughts and behavior against the Buddha's words, almost all of them tend toward nonvirtue. Suppose you suspect a fierce enemy might come, and you hear he will be arriving soon. If you are not aware of how his great strength could kill you, mutilate you, destroy your belongings, and so on, you will neither fear him nor take any precautions. However, if you know that on his arrival, he will destroy you completely, and that he is sure to come within the year, although you do not know exactly when, you cannot possibly feel easy even in passing. To prepare yourself, you might seek out a leader much stronger than the enemy and send for him, perhaps build a sturdy fort or escape to a distant land where he cannot reach you. In the same way, your prior familiarization with impermanence and the unfortunate realms within meditation makes you certain that (1) within the next hundred years you are to meet the enemy, unfortunate realm suffering, and of the two—next month or the Relentless hell—you do not know which will come first, and (2) nothing is more important than for you to seek protection from that suffering.

Concerning the objects of refuge, Master Dignāga states:

> While abiding in the ocean
> that is samsara, both boundless and deep,
> as I am devoured by the countless sea monsters
> of attachment and the rest,
> today in whom am I to take refuge?[429]

While plunged in samsara, which is as deep as the ocean, and maimed by the hideous sea monsters of nonvirtue—attachment and the like—the author asks the question: who should sentient beings seek out for refuge? The *Praise in Hundred and Fifty Verses* provides the answer:

> Whoever is utterly free
> of all faults,
> whoever completely possesses
> all good qualities,
> if you have any sense at all,
> take refuge in such a being.
> It is only fitting to praise this being,
> serve him, and dwell in his teaching.[430] [165]

Someone less powerful and mighty than your enemy cannot protect you from the fear of him. You might count on powerful gods like Brahmā, Viṣṇu, Īśvara and the rest, but as they are not free of samsara themselves and continue to be subject to its torments, they are not definitive objects of refuge. Who are? *Seventy Verses on Going for Refuge* explains:

> The Buddha, Dharma, and Sangha
> are the refuges of those desiring liberation.[431]

The Three Jewels are said to be the definitive objects of refuge. Once you have ascertained that they are infallible, being free of all the aforementioned faults and endowed with all good qualities, you are to take refuge in them.

This can be achieved using many different visualizations. I will explain how to take refuge according to the [lamrim] teaching tradition, which is free of the personal fabrication of making up something similar or taking something from another source. The *Praise with Similes* says:

> Your body adorned with the marks
> is beautiful—ambrosia for the eyes,
> like a cloudless autumn sky
> adorned with clusters of stars.[432]

You should reflect accordingly. You are not to meditate on the Buddha's form as in tantra—doing [an elaborate] visualization in which you picture the commitment beings and so forth before you.[433] It is more like when you visit a large marketplace or festival, and you see all sorts of performances that you enjoy—dances and so on—and the [performers'] beautiful jewelry, trappings, entourage, and so on and all the grand and ordinary people. After leaving and going elsewhere, you can bring them to mind once more through your faculty of recollection. There is no need to make a special point of meditating on them for the jewelry, trappings, performances, and so on to appear to you again as clearly as if you were seeing them with your very own eyes. In the same way, at this point begin by repeatedly examining a painting or statue of the Tathāgata's physical form. Then picture it in your mind, thinking:

> Here is the Tathāgata, his body the color of refined gold. He wears the three monastic garments and is adorned with the marks and signs. One never tires of seeing him.

Thanks to having first perceived this through visual consciousness, it will appear to you distinctly. Then you reflect, thinking, "It is never displeasing to view, and just seeing it has a beneficial effect.[434] The Buddha's body has extraordinary qualities that are lacking in all those who are bodhisattvas and below," until you are filled with intense faith, longing to meet him directly, and great joy at the thought of your good fortune in having the opportunity just to picture the Buddha in your mind. [166]

On his qualities of speech, the *Satyaka Chapter* states:

It is like this: if all sentient beings simultaneously
asked him a great variety of questions,
he would understand them in an instant,
and with a single utterance answer each.
Therefore, know that in the world, the Guide
voices Brahmā's pleasing melody
and turns the wheel of the Dharma
that eradicates the sufferings of gods and humans.[435]

You should reflect in this manner, but since the likelihood of hearing anything resembling the Buddha's speech or finding anything that could qualify as an illustration of it is so small, you are to imagine it by drawing on the sweet sound of, for example, a lute that you find melodious. Think how the pleasing tone of the speech that issues from the throat of the Buddha, with the magnificent physical form described above, has sixty-four harmonious traits, and how if each being of the three realms of existence were to ask him a question simultaneously, the answer he would give in a single language like Sanskrit would be heard in each being's language and would immediately dispel all their doubts. As before, ensure that you gain a meditative experience of this that involves faith, longing, and joy.

As for his mental qualities, *Praise to the One Beyond All Praise* states:

Only your sublime wisdom
comprehends all objects of knowledge.
For everyone other than you,
there remain objects to be known.[436]

His quality of knowledge is such that to him no existents are unknown to it. Thanks to his superior wisdom of omniscience, he is skilled in caring for his followers according to their capacities. The *Praise in One Hundred and Fifty Verses* states:

Afflictions bind all beings indiscriminately.
As for you, wishing to free beings of them,
compassion has bound you for ages.

Should I pay homage first to you
or to your great compassion, which has ensured

> that you remain in cyclic existence for ages till now,
> despite your knowledge of its faults?[437]

As he is bound by great, affectionate compassion for all sentient beings and is equal-minded toward those who anoint him with sandalwood paste on the one hand, and those who would cleave him with an axe on the other, his love for all beings is like a mother's love for her only child. [167] Reflect on these as explained above.

Regarding his activity, the *Praise in One Hundred and Fifty Verses* says:

> You explain how to destroy the afflictions,
> you reveal the demons' deceit,
> you proclaim the endless nature of cyclic existence,
> and you show the way to the fearless state.
>
> O Compassionate One, whose intent is to benefit,
> of the things to be done
> for the sake of sentient beings,
> what is there that you have yet to accomplish?[438]

Although śrāvakas and pratyekabuddhas also have simple love for sentient beings, just having the feeling will not be helpful for them. It is like when an armless woman's child is drowning: the mother is obliged to call upon others to drag her child out of the water. Since the Buddha has fully developed the capacity to help others, he will, if it is useful to beings, enter the flames of hell as eagerly as the greedy enter the pleasure groves of fortunate realms. As explained above, contemplate the ways he works unhindered for sentient beings' welfare.

Such physical, verbal, and mental qualities are not causeless, nor do they arise from incongruous causes. You are to establish that it is by learning and reflecting on the Dharma Jewel as scripture, mainly the topics of the truths of cessation and the path, that one actualizes the Dharma Jewel of realizations: the two truths or the qualities of abandonment and realization. Contemplate this until you achieve uncontrived faith in the Dharma Jewel.

As for the Sangha Jewel, it consists of bodhisattvas such as Maitreya, Mañjughoṣa, and Avalokiteśvara and of śrāvaka sangha members such as Mahākāśyapa and the Excellent Pair.[439] As before, completely mindful of their physical, verbal, and mental activities, contemplate their good qualities, and think, "Although they have not acquired the attributes of actual buddhas, they are practicing the two truths and assist us in realizing refuge."

Emulation is important, as is superior admiring faith. [168] A worldly leader, for example, can prevent enemies from harming you, and a skillful doctor can alleviate the fear of having imbalanced physical elements, but that does not necessarily mean that you want to become like them. Although, when you are very impressed by the power of the one and the medical skill of the other, you may very well aspire to become like them. Actual persons of lesser capacity do not want to achieve the state of the Three Jewels, yet the Three Jewels provide them with partial protection: out of compassion they shield them from temporary suffering and show them the way to worldly happiness. Persons of intermediate capacity must achieve protection by actualizing the realizations of śrāvakas and pratyekabuddhas who are either in training or fully trained. The determination to achieve the bodhisattva path is to be identified as the temporary refuge of persons of great capacity, and the determination to attain complete omniscience is their ultimate refuge. As explained in the *Extensive Commentary on the Chapters on Discipline*:

> You are to take the Buddha as the teacher of refuge, the Dharma as the actual refuge, and the Sangha as the assistants to achieving refuge.[440]

You need to remind yourself of this again and again and think, "I too shall realize such a state."

Since the path of persons of great capacity is preeminent in the present context, if nonabiding nirvana is taken as the actual refuge, you might wonder whether there is any need to consider and take śrāvaka and pratyekabuddha nirvanas and sanghas as refuges. There is indeed one exception: bodhisattvas who have attained the second ground do not need to take refuge in the sanghas and qualities of abandonment and realization of the first ground, which for them are causal refuges, like bridges that protect one from the fear of water. However, we who have yet to enter the path must take refuge in the three vehicles' objects of refuge and must ignore the unsubstantiated talk of those who have not understood the scriptures' key points.

If you lack the kind of wholehearted confident faith and reverence that results from [admiring] faith in the Three Jewels' good qualities and the desire to attain them such that you think, "No matter what the circumstances—joy or sorrow—I entrust myself to you," then you are like someone who cannot be lifted by a hook for lack a ring to catch onto. Despite the Three Jewels' great compassion, in you, wisdom and method remain unconnected. [169] For this reason, the two qualities just mentioned—awareness of their good qualities and the wish to achieve them—must be equally strong. In this frame of mind and motivated by great compassion for sentient beings, think that [the members of the refuge field], under the sway of great compassion for your sake and the sake of all sentient beings, come to you, like birds taking flight. You then repeat the following:

> I take refuge in the Buddha, supreme among bipeds. I pray that he may be my guide to freedom from the fears of samsara and unfortunate rebirths.
>
> I take refuge in the Dharma, the highest degree of freedom from attachment. I pray that it may serve as the actual refuge, freeing me from the fears of samsara and unfortunate rebirths.
>
> I take refuge in the Sangha, supreme among assemblies. I pray that they may serve as assistants in freeing myself from the fears of samsara and unfortunate rebirths.

In each session recite this formula in sequence as many times as possible, a hundred or more. It is also suitable to recite the refuge formula mentioned earlier, but my guru always practiced based on the above words, which are drawn from *Essence of Refined Gold*.

The second part concerns the precepts. It is not enough to take refuge in the main part of a meditation session. It is also necessary to train in its precepts between sessions: having taken refuge in the Buddha, not entrusting yourself to any powerful worldly gods as definitive refuges; having taken refuge in the Dharma, ceasing to harm sentient beings; having taken refuge in the Sangha, not being close friends with those who do not believe in the Three Jewels. These are the three proscriptive precepts. You are to consider as the Buddha Jewel any image of a buddha's physical form, even those of inferior artistry or materials. You are to see as the Dharma Jewel any scripture of four lines or more. You are to see as the Sangha Jewel even those who only show the outward signs of monastic ordination and avoid being disrespectful to them physically, verbally, and mentally. Instead you are to present them offerings and praise and serve them. These are the three prescriptive precepts. Practicing the precepts well eliminates all difficulties and is the excellent source of all benefits, happiness, and goodness in this and future lives. [170]

Stanzas between sections

To achieve this life's happiness, which is as fleeting as a flash of lightning,
people seek powerful leaders and make every effort to flatter them;
seeing this as a great achievement, they are very pleased with themselves.

When I observe those who pursue these goals,
I realize that our encounter with the key points [regarding refuge],
which prompt our protectors, the infallible Three Jewels who shield us
from the unfortunate realms' unbearable terrors,
to show us their smiling countenances unreservedly,
is the consequence of millions of merits acquired in the past.

Enough of experiencing horrific suffering in unfortunate realms
by the power of past nonvirtue!
O wise ones, listen! Now is the time to strive diligently
and achieve an excellent rebirth in a fortunate realm.

Karma and Its Effects

The second part [of relying on the methods for happiness in future lives] is meditating on karma and its effects—the source of all goodness and happiness.

Contemplating leisure and opportunity and the difficulty of attaining them, death and impermanence, and the sufferings of the unfortunate realms may inspire an urgent need to practice the Dharma, but if you have no idea how to practice it, you will have excessive desire for food, clothing, and belongings, deeming them necessary conditions for Dharma practice. For their sake, you will behave badly, spending all your time involved in the eight two-toned worldly concerns.[441] Others may sacrifice the three—food, clothing, and reputation—and mildly suppress the three physical nonvirtues [of killing, stealing, and sexual misconduct], all the while yielding to the remaining seven. Thus they spend all their time entangled in the eight white worldly concerns and sully their three doors with sins and transgressions. As a result, at death white and black karma follow them like their shadow, and as the *Precious Garland* states:

> All suffering stems from nonvirtue,
> as do all the unfortunate realms.
> All fortunate realms stem from virtue,
> as does happiness in all lives.[442]

It is taught that the principle of black and white karmas and their effects is infallible. The one who affirmed it was the Bhagavān Buddha, in relation to whom you previously, in the context of refuge, achieved an experience of genuine faith. The *King of Meditations Sutra* states:

> The moon and the stars may fall from their places, [171]
> mountains, cities, and the rest may crumble,
> the space element itself may take on another form,
> but you would never speak falsely.[443]

Thinking, "It is inconceivable that the Buddha should speak falsely," reflect until unwavering faith in karmic cause and effect arises in you.

You may be in a period free of any manifest physical or mental troubles, not under attack by enemies or spirits, provided with favorable conditions, and so forth, or it may be the opposite, or you may alternate between the two. These are the only three possibilities. Having noted your situation, whatever it is, meditate until you can clearly picture your states of suffering and happiness. As it says in sutra:

> Sentient beings' karma
> is not spent even in a hundred eons.
> When the conditions assemble and the time comes,
> it ripens and bears fruit.[444]

Now, all pleasure, starting with that of a cool breeze refreshing you when you are suffering from the heat, and all pain, from the prick of a small thorn, result solely from virtue and wrongdoing performed in the past. You should contemplate your personal situation, thinking:

> The human life I have now was attained by the power of virtuous karma I produced in the past; in this life, however, I experience this and that suffering as a consequence of nonvirtuous karma I have created.

Similarly, observing the situation of an animal that enjoys a certain degree of comfort, think:

> By its nonvirtuous projecting karma, it attained this kind of rebirth, but by its completing virtue, it benefits in its life from certain [favorable] circumstances.

A single powerful karma can generate many lives, and many weak karmas produce a single life. It is analogous to the way a single wealthy person may serve and make offerings to many celebrants[445] while many poor people may combine to serve and make offerings to a single celebrant. In this way, inferentially, you are to induce a firm conviction [of karmic cause and effect].

Now, even if you could choose to enjoy the pleasures of the gods, those would still not satisfy you, and you cannot bear even the slightest discomfort.

Given this, you must understand that nonvirtue has caused your past experiences of unbearable suffering in the three unfortunate realms and that, if you do not discard it, you will have no choice but to experience the misery it will produce. [172]

To avoid sorrow you must identify its causes, the negative karmas to be rejected, not just vaguely, like saying "the thief was a man," for this will be insufficient. The *Treasury of Abhidharma* says:

> Assembling the most important ones,
> whether virtuous or nonvirtuous,
> karmic paths were taught to number ten.[446]

Accordingly, there are ten [major] sins and nonvirtues: the physical karmas of killing, stealing, and sexual misconduct; the verbal karmas of lying, divisive speech, cruel speech, and idle talk; and the mental karmas of covetousness, ill will, and wrong views.

Among them, it will be a nonvirtue of taking life regardless of the kind of sentient being you kill. For example: in relation to a *basis* [of action] like Devadatta, the specific *attitude* involved consists of identification [of the victim]; an affliction, which can be any of the three mental poisons; and a motivation, the desire to kill. The *action* is, for example, stabbing with a weapon or having someone do it for you. These along with the *conclusion*—death—complete the nonvirtue of killing. Although cases of mistaken identification, unintentional killing (like [insects] dying underfoot), dying before the victim, and so on do not qualify as nonvirtues complete with a basis, attitude, action, and conclusion as just illustrated, they nonetheless constitute nonvirtues of killing.

For stealing, a basis could be gold that you do not own that belongs to someone else. You identify it as such. With any of the afflictions, you are motivated by the desire to take it. The action is to acquire it in any number of ways. It is concluded when the thought "it is mine" occurs to you.

For sexual misconduct, a basis could be an inappropriate sexual object like someone who is involved with another person, a relative, the anus, or mouth; or it could be with a suitable partner, like your wife, but having relations before religious objects or when she is pregnant or has taken the vow of chastity. You identify these and, with any of the afflictions, are motivated by the desire to have sexual intercourse. The action is to pursue that goal. It is concluded by contact between the two genitals and so forth.

For lying, the basis could be, for example, not having clairvoyance. For the person with whom you speak, you portray your lack of clairvoyance as a possession of it. With any of the afflictions, your motivation is the wish to express this. The action is either physical or verbal communication. It is concluded when the meaning is understood.

For divisive speech, the basis involves, for example, two sentient beings whom you identify as such. [173] With any of the afflictions, your motivation is the desire to split them. The action consists of speaking words that have the power to divide them. It is concluded when your words are understood.

For cruel speech, the basis is a sentient being you identify as unappealing. With any of the afflictions, the motivation is the desire to speak cruelly. The action is to utter unpleasant words that pierce the person to the core. It is concluded when your words are understood.

For idle talk, the basis is a topic you identify as meaningless, not included in any of the previous three [verbal nonvirtues]. With any of the afflictions, your motivation is the desire to say pointless things. The action consists, for example, of reciting non-Buddhist treatises or Brahmā's mantra; telling pointless stories about kings, ministers, generals, thieves, and so on; repeating the words of songs and plays out of attachment; and for monastics, flattering others to seek gain. It is concluded as soon as the words are spoken.

For covetousness, the bases are others' belongings, which you identify as such. Any of the afflictions are involved, as well as the following five traits: [great][447] attachment to your own belongings; acquisitiveness; [longing due to] appreciation of other's belongings; the desire to acquire them; being oppressed by the drawbacks [of covetousness from not knowing how to avoid them] and by shamelessness [regarding your covetousness]. With the motivation that is the covetous thought to acquire them, the action is to mentally strive toward that goal. It is concluded by wishing for it.

For ill will, the basis is a being you identify as unappealing. It involves any of the afflictions and the following five traits: anger that clings to the reality of what caused you harm; intolerance of the harm; resentment owing to incorrect attention—ruminating the harm; hostility that makes you want to beat or kill the being [for example]; and being oppressed by the drawbacks [of ill will from not knowing how to avoid them] and by shamelessness [regarding your ill will]. With the motivation that is the desire to kill, bind, and so forth, the action is to mentally strive to that end. It is concluded by your decision to act [on your desire to harm] if you are actually capable of it. It is taught that thoughts like "I would like to achieve the state of Brahmā" and "I wish this person were dead" are concordant [respectively] with covetousness and ill will.

For wrong views, a basis could be, for example, karma and its effects, which you identify as nonexistent. With any of the afflictions, the motivation is the desire to deny the existence of something that exists. The action is to entertain the very thought "It does not exist." It is concluded by your deciding that it is so.[448] [174]

Among the ten, the level of gravity depends on the attitude—on the strength of the affliction that motivates the act. In terms of the object, it is worse to kill one's guru or parent, take their belongings, deceive them, speak to them divisively or cruelly, or be covetous or bear ill will in relation to them. Moreover, in the case of an animal, for example, it is worse to kill animals that have a big body. Likewise, [it is worse] to steal many very valuable things; to have sexual relations with inappropriate partners, like those holding the vow of chastity; to lie and speak divisively in order to create a split in the Sangha; to want to deny the existence of arhats; to fail to confess and decide to refrain from sins and instead delight in committing more and more; and so on. The great seriousness of these can be assessed by deduction. Their opposites are less grave by comparison.

When you plant various seeds, the sprouts that grow will unfailingly match the seeds that were planted. Similarly, the maturation effect of very serious sins is a rebirth as a hell being, for fairly serious ones, as a hungry ghost, and for less serious ones, as an animal. The effect concordant with the cause that is killing is to have a short life, for stealing it is to be poor, for sexual misconduct to be unable to keep a partner, for lying to be criticized, for divisive speech to have few friends, for cruel speech to hear much unpleasant talk, for idle talk to have your words disregarded, for covetousness to be unable to fulfill your hopes, for ill will to be very fearful, and for wrong views to be oblivious to excellent views.

Killing produces the environmental effect of a decline in the potency of food, drink, and medicine; stealing, a decline in harvests; sexual misconduct, foul swamps; lying, a place with deceitful people where one is very afraid; divisive speech, a place where the ground is uneven and travel difficult; cruel speech, an unattractive place with tree stumps, thorns, and the like; idle talk, barren trees; covetousness, the slow decline of all that is excellent; ill will, falling ill and being persecuted by many human and nonhumans; wrong views, the inversion of good and bad. Maturation effects and effects concordant with their causes are experienced by the beings themselves, whereas environmental effects determine the nature of the place or region where they live.

Of the two, definite and indefinite karma, it is taught that the latter produces its results only when certain conditions are met, without which it does not. [175] Most of the karma we now create however is motivated by all three strong mental poisons; we also commit sins regularly, in relation to special objects, and so on. Given this, we are sure to experience the results of many of them. Concerning this the master Vasubandhu states:

> There are three kinds of definite [karmas]:
> those whose results are experienced in this life and so forth.[449]

These three kinds are illustrated in an ancient account. It tells of a person who spoke badly to a fully ordained monk, calling him a woman. As a result, in that life the person's gender changed, which is a result experienced in the very same life. Then for the next hundred lives the person was born a female, which corresponds to both the result experienced in the next life and the result experienced in subsequent lives.

If you have a definite karma to be born in an unfortunate realm, in that same life you cannot attain the forbearance level of the path of preparation. If you have a definite karma to be born in the desire realm, you cannot achieve freedom from attachment.[450] If you have a definite karma to be born in samsara, you cannot free yourself from samsara in that life, and so on.

Once you have ascertained the system of karma and its effects just explained, examine your three mental poisons, as well as the actions they prompt, like killing and stealing. Bring to mind those you enjoy doing, from their bases up to their conclusion. Having elicited hot anger toward your enemies or intense attachment for your homeland, certain people, or things, immediately seize it with mindfulness and meta-awareness and think:

> For lack of meta-awareness, I have committed many sins in the past, but I do not in fact know what I have done. Now that I recognize [my afflictions], whenever one is about to arise, I will make sure to apply its antidote. That is not enough, however. I have to work on practicing the ten virtues. For that, I need to know what they are. The ten virtues are the opposite of the ten nonvirtues. As for their results, abstention from killing that is motivated by powerful virtue will produce the maturation effect of a human

> rebirth. The effect concordant with the cause will be a long life, and the environmental effect [will be the availability of] potent medicines, for example.

Having also reflected well on the way their results are the opposite of the effects of nonvirtues, meditate until you feel intense aspiration and delight.

To analyze in detail some difficult points regarding virtue and nonvirtue, an example of an entirely white karma is an act of generosity that is thoroughly imbued with a virtuous state of mind, from the basis through the attitude and the action up to its conclusion. [176] An example of an entirely negative karma would be an act of killing committed for one's own sake that is completely permeated by a sinful mental state, from the basis to its conclusion. In the case of killing one being to protect the lives of many, the causal act of killing, which is a weak nonvirtuous karma, produces a result concordant with the cause that is painful, but the causal strongly virtuous attitude produces pleasant maturation and environmental effects. Cases of negative karma that have positive maturation effects are to be implemented. Giving things without attachment but with the intention to kill many beings produces maturation and environmental effects of pure suffering due to the very serious nonvirtuous attitude involved. The effects concordant with the cause will be a mixture of positive and negative results: a short life but a profusion of belongings. Since it is a positive action with a negative maturation, it is to be avoided. It is important therefore to reflect thoroughly on karma and its effects and implement rejection and adoption.

It would be a vast improvement on matters if most bearers of meditators' hats, knee straps, net cloth bags, and wands of invisibility[451] and those who stare upward with their eyebrows raised[452] would practice rejection and adoption having even just roughly identified the ten virtues and ten nonvirtues!

To attain a life basis with the eight full fruitions: excellent life span, complexion, lineage, and power along with trustworthy speech, [renown as a great] power, being a male, and strength, you are for example to [respectively] protect others' lives, present light offerings to [holy] images, be as respectful as servants are to others, strive to be generous, speak mindfully, pray to achieve various good qualities, refrain from castrating beings and reflect on the drawbacks of being a female, and be diligent in accomplishing what others cannot. As before, take great care to delight in ensuring that you attain these advantages.

Once you have practiced both analytical and placement meditations on the nature and effects of the ten virtues and nonvirtues, think:

> To attain an excellent rebirth for accomplishing the ten virtues just explained and for achieving enlightenment as well, it is crucial that I am no longer tainted by the aforementioned nonvirtues and that I avoid producing new ones. Nevertheless, it is obvious that I have committed countless sins in the present life and that that is only a fraction of them, for I have done the same in many other lives, not just for my sake but also for the sake of my leaders, children, friends, relatives, spouses, employees, homeland, monasteries, and so forth. [177]
>
> As the *Friendly Letter* says:
>
> > Do not sin for the sake of
> > brahmans, bhikṣus, gods, guests, parents,
> > wives, and entourage, for you will not share with them
> > the maturation effect—rebirth in a hell.[453]
>
> When I undergo the maturation effects of the sins I committed for others' sake, they will not share these with me. I alone will experience them. According to [the *Treasury of Abhidharma*], the karmas whose results are sure to be experienced are irreversible. So, no matter what I do, it seems I will never be able to free myself from samsara.

Once this prospect has deeply troubled you, think:

> Thank goodness our most compassionate and skillful Teacher pronounced a great variety of discourses, some of definitive meaning and others whose meaning is to be interpreted. This is what the Lesser Vehicle explains, but the definitive meaning is that even the worst misdeeds, like the five acts of immediate retribution, can be purified by confession and by abstention from future wrongdoing.
>
> The *Friendly Letter* states:
>
> > A person who, once careless,
> > later becomes conscientious

is as beautiful as a cloudless moon,
like Nanda, Aṅgulimāla, Ajātaśatru, and Udayana.[454]

It is said that Nanda, the Buddha's younger brother, was extremely attached to his wife, that Aṅgulimāla killed a thousand people less one, and Ajātaśatru took the life of his father, Bimbisāra. Nevertheless, they purified themselves of these acts by confession and abstention, and the first two attained arhatship. Although Udayana killed his mother, with profound regret he thoroughly implemented adoption and rejection. As a result, after taking rebirth in hell, like a rebounding ball he attained the fruit of stream entry in the presence of the Bhagavān. Even if I do not get results like these, I must at least close the door to the unfortunate realms.

With intense renunciation spur yourself on. As objects before whom you confess your sins, set up symbols of the Three Jewels' body, speech, and mind. Be fully convinced that they are truly the Three Jewels. First generate the same kind of profound eradicating remorse for your past sins that you would have if you had swallowed poison as well as the intention to abstain from wrongdoing henceforth, thinking, "I will never do this again in the future, even if it costs me my life." Like taking a panacea as an antidote to poison, recite the *Confession by the Four Powers*[455] composed by the Great Lord [Tsongkhapa], or the noble *Three Heaps Sutra*,[456] special dhāraṇīs for purifying sin and rebirth in the unfortunate realms, the names of the tathāgatas, and so forth. [178] Doing prostrations constitutes the actual practice. On the topic of remorse, great treatises suggest reciting the confession chapter of the *Golden Light Sutra*[457] to detail your faults. The activities that constitute the remedies—reading sutras, making holy images, presenting offerings, and so on—are to be accomplished between sessions. Suffusing [whatever is done with the understanding of] suchness can be done either during or between sessions, depending on whether the person's faculties are sharp or dull. It is said that monastics are to do restoration of transgressions practice during the main part of sessions. When practicing, you are to differentiate between [confession] common to all and confession specific [to monastics].

STANZAS BETWEEN SECTIONS

With the cataract of thick ignorance, people are blind
to what is to be adopted and rejected in their lives,
yet they take pride in and attribute great importance to cleaning
their dirty faces, smelly clothes, and the rest.

A little wealth and belongings once acquired are spent,
like birds' flight paths in the sky and drawings on water.
Yet for their sake you spare no pains and, by your three doors,
resort to austerities with endless and intense effort.

As you spend your time being a slave to diversions—
the eight concerns, protecting the friends and deterring the enemies of
this life,
which are as [unreal as] joy and pain in dreams—
I suspect you will become fuel for the Relentless hell.

For the sake of the things of this life, ignorant fools
generate nonvirtuous karma effortlessly.
But for those like me, who have received many teachings,
to cast the ultimate goal to the wind would be a disgrace.

Ah, just as the seeds planted in the spring
produce their particular crops in the fall,
black and white causes produce crops of misery and happiness.
Ponder this, for the key point of adoption and rejection is precious indeed!

With remorse and restraint, in the presence of the Three Jewels,
by the four powers that can purify wrongdoing,
eradicate what has become habitual over time:
all the causes for birth in the bad states of the unfortunate realms.

* * *

With the powerful and skilled oratory of one who bears Mañjuśrī in his
throat, [179]
the form of great compassion, the Lotus Holder,

and the power of the Lord of Secrets,
O Tsongkhapa, you embody the Three Protectors.[458]

I have now set down your teaching—the key points in which to train
from the stages of the path shared with persons of lesser capacity—
faultlessly, accessibly, and concisely but with vast meaning
according to my guru and tutor's explanations.

O intelligent ones, listen to the lute's melody,
the excellent explanations of Indian and Tibetan scholars,
which liberate you from the ocean of samsara's misery and from its origins
and guide you to the excellent treasure isle of cessation and the path.

The Path Shared with Persons of Intermediate Capacity

Regarding the second part, training the mind on the stages of the path shared with persons of intermediate capacity, *Lamp on the Path to Enlightenment* states:

> With the will to turn from samsara's pleasures
> [and the path] whose nature is the rejection of sin,
> those who pursue personal peace alone
> are known as persons of intermediate capacity.[459]

Persons of lesser capacity pursue only fortunate rebirths, the status of a human or god. By comparison, persons of intermediate capacity are not content with this objective. By following the three higher trainings, they aim to achieve the happiness of peace that is freedom from samsara but nothing more. For our purposes, there is no question of seeking just a state of peace. Nonetheless, since achieving omniscience undeniably requires first attaining liberation, you are to practice the stages of the path shared with persons of intermediate capacity.

The sufferings of samsara

Again, since practicing the stages of the path of persons of lesser capacity in the correct order ensures that for the time being you avoid having to be born in the three unfortunate realms and experience manifest suffering, you feel overjoyed, like a person just released from prison. However, just as there is no guarantee that the same person will not return to jail, you may purify yourself of past sins by the four powers, avoid producing more, and accomplish the ten virtues in this life, and by this you may ensure that you attain a fortunate rebirth in your next life, but there is no guarantee whatsoever that you will not produce nonvirtuous karma once more [in the next life], since you have not abandoned the afflictions and you do not sustain the fear of the unfortunate realms' suffering that you had in your previous life. [180] By creating new nonvirtuous karma, you will return to the unfortunate realms, as *Guide to the Bodhisattva Way* explains:

> After returning again and again to fortunate births
> and experiencing many kinds of joy,
> you will die and fall into the protracted and terrifying
> sufferings of the unfortunate realms.[460]

When you are suffering from heat for example, and a cool breeze or waterfall hits you, it is pleasurable for a while, but after some time you begin to feel cold and uncomfortable. As this illustrates, contaminated pleasures are all instances of the suffering of change, which is why such temporary pleasures are unreliable. Inspired by renunciation—the wish to be free of the karma and afflictions that now cause your rebirth in samsara and completely bind you to it—your striving in practice allows you to achieve complete freedom from bondage, the state of personal peace. You pursue it by following two steps: contemplating the sufferings of samsara and practicing the stages of the path that grants liberation from them. Contemplating the sufferings of samsara has two parts: contemplating them from the perspective of suffering and its origins, and contemplating them in relation to the twelve links of dependent origination. Contemplating them from the perspective of suffering and its origins has two parts: suffering—the drawbacks of samsara, and its origins—the process of entering samsara.

In the sutras it says:

> O bhikṣus, this is the ārya truth of suffering,
> this is the ārya truth of its origins.[461]

Presenting the result, the truth of suffering, first and its causes, the truth of the origins, afterward might seem like a reversal of cause and effect, however it was done with a specific intent, regarding which the *Four Hundred Verses* says:

> As the ocean of suffering
> has absolutely no limit,
> O child, you who are submerged in it,
> why do you not fear it?[462] [181]

If you mistake the result, suffering, for happiness, you will neither fear it nor think to reject its causes, karma and the afflictions. The converse is when you stop its causes because you want to avoid experiencing their result. Say, for example, you are seated on a dry patch of ground, and suddenly a flood occurs. Your body, clothes, seat, and so on become drenched, and you feel cold, which is comparable to the truth of suffering. Having sought the water's source, determining its point of origin is like ascertaining the truth of the origin. No longer feeling cold is equivalent to the truth of cessation, and the method to achieve it, like digging drainage ditches, is analogous to the truth of the path. The *Sublime Continuum* says:

> Just as an illness is to be diagnosed and its causes removed,
> and health is to be achieved and medical treatment followed,
> so too are suffering, its causes, cessations, and the path
> to be identified, removed, achieved, and followed.[463]

If you do not identify getting drenched as a form of suffering, you will have no desire to stop the water's flow. If you do not see staying dry as a form of happiness, you will not think to build a dam to stop the water's flow. Having understood that all instances of happiness and suffering are results, it is extremely important to adopt the causes that produce the former and reject those that produce the latter. That is why, to fully comprehend the process, you begin by contemplating suffering.

The lamrim teaches you to reflect on the general sufferings of samsara and on the sufferings of specific states within samsara. Those of birth, aging, and so on, are found in the more lengthy explanations of general suffering.

In sum, earlier, in the context of the path of persons of lesser capacity, you meditated on the unfortunate realms' torments and achieved an authentic experience of them. Once you have had a terrible hangover from drinking beer, there is no need to make a special point of reflecting on beer's particularly bitter taste and other defects, for the very sight of it already makes you sick, and you do not in the least crave it. Similarly, at this stage there is nothing wrong with not making a point of contemplating the sufferings of rebirths in the unfortunate realms, and in fact doing so would be as ill timed as stopping to pick flowers in the middle of a horse race. As such you are to focus primarily on the main topic, the fortunate realms' sufferings, and contemplate three topics: human sufferings; those of the other two kinds of fortunate rebirths; and the attendant topic, those shared by all six categories of life. [182]

Human sufferings

Those who take birth impelled by their karma and afflictions are subject to various kinds of suffering—aging, death, and so forth. As their minds are completely agitated by the three mental poisons, they have no choice in the end but to die in a state of physical and mental distress. Although the Buddha taught four kinds of birth, birth from a womb primarily will be discussed here. *Letter to a Student* says:

> Once you have entered the hellish womb
> packed with terrible foul-smelling filth,
> exceedingly confined, and thick with darkness,
> your body is completely cramped and subjected to great torment.[464]

Imagine finding yourself below the stomach, above the intestines, facing the spine, floating in an unclean and smelly slime. As you develop from the "quivering stage" to the point where your limbs form, whenever your mother eats hot food or drinks hot beverages, you feel like you are being thrust into a fire pit; when she ingests them cold, you feel as though you were encased in ice; when she jumps, runs, and so forth, you feel like you are falling down a cliff, and so on. Your mother's various thoughtless behaviors cause you great discomfort. When 266 days have passed, the karmic wind shifts your head downward. As you pass through the very narrow pelvic bones, you suffer like a cow being skinned alive, its flesh then eaten by flies with [sharp] mandibles. This is how you are born—experiencing great pain. For some time after delivery, although you are placed on a soft bed, you suffer as if you were being thrust into a thorn bush, and even minor inconveniences of heat and cold seem unbearable. You have already experienced these, in the period between your life past and now, but due to defilement by the womb and your very young age at the time, you do not remember any of them, which is why you must contemplate them inferentially.

As in the context of the path of persons of lesser capacity, you are to reflect on the sufferings just described as though you were personally experiencing them. Now, if you were encased for a single day in a container just big enough to fit your body that was then entirely filled with feces and other filthy substances, obviously you could not bear it. That, however, would not constitute even a fraction of the aforementioned suffering. You are supposed to meditate until you feel as much disgust at the thought of taking birth in a fortunate realm as a nauseous person does at the sight of food. [183]

With respect to the suffering of aging, the *Play in Full Sutra* says:

> Age renders your attractive body ugly.
> Age steals your charisma and robs you of your strength.
> Age ravishes your happiness and makes you an object of contempt.
> Age kills you and deprives you of your radiance.[465]

Think:

> My hair has gone white, my body is stooped, and my brow is covered in wrinkles. If I look at the decline of my physical strength, for example, and compare myself to how I was in my prime—with my straight body, black hair, wrinkle-free skin, and so on—although I have not yet changed bodies, I may as well have. This is what I have now become. Many days, months, and years have passed. The time I have left to live is decreasing steadily, like waning of the moon, and I will end up in the jaws of death.

Reflect on this until a feeling of intense distaste arises in you.

In this way, as your strength fails, you cannot rise and sit down properly; you totter as you walk; when you talk, your speech is slurred, and so on. As your senses decline, you cannot see or hear as you did before; your memory fails you, and you become forgetful. As for food and drink, eating the same amounts as before causes various sicknesses. Contemplate how these occur in the way described above. Young practitioners still in their prime will be unable to relate to most of the above-mentioned flaws, like white hair. They should therefore contemplate someone old and think, "When this person was delivered from his mother's womb, he certainly was not old and feeble like this; someone young like me will inevitably end up just like him!" [My guru] said to meditate in this way.

Regarding the suffering of illness, you may have fallen seriously ill at some point. If not, then contemplate illness from others' sicknesses stemming from a protracted unbalanced physical constitution, sudden harm by an evil spirit or a weapon, and so on. Concerning this, the *Play in Full Sutra* states:

> Just as late winter winds and snowstorms
> rob trees, grasses, bushes, and herbs of their luster,

> so does illness rob beings of their bloom
> and drain their senses, vital substance, and strength.[466]

Reflect on how you are debilitated by various torments like the pain occasioned by changes in temperature, and on how as a result your skin dries up, you lose weight, and your movement becomes difficult. [184] Doctors and others refuse to give you rich food and beverages in fear that they will aggravate your illness. Against your will you are forced to take various nasty foods and medicines and undergo bloodletting and moxibustion.

On the suffering of dying, the *Play in Full Sutra* states:

> When the time comes to die, move on, and die again,
> you are definitively separated from those that you cherish.
> Like leaves fallen from trees and water in the current of a stream,
> there is no turning back and no encountering them again.[467]

If you manage to recover from an illness, all the trials endured will have been worthwhile. However, illnesses more frequently grow worse, despite the various medical treatments undertaken. Doctors then give up on you, diviners deceive you, friends and relatives surround you and lament, and preparations are made for postmortem practices of virtue and for the disposal of your corpse. As for you, your complexion pales, your mouth dries up, your upper lip curls, your nostrils become pinched, your eyes recede in their sockets, and your breathing becomes labored. You regret your past sins. You are soon to be separated from everything good you ever had—friends and relatives, entourage and servants, wealth and property. You also have to leave behind you in the bed the very body that you cared for so dearly and move on to the next world under the sway of strong attachment. Reflect on how you are afflicted by these great torments.

As for suffering caused by enemies, it goes without saying that suspecting that a dire enemy will harm you bodily, take your life, or damage your reputation distresses you. Furthermore, just having to be in the same house with a true enemy or adversary oppresses you to the point that you feel as though darkness has enveloped you, and when they leave and go elsewhere, you are delighted and feel as if the sun has just come up. In this manner you are to reflect on the angst caused by suspecting you might encounter a reviled enemy.

As for the suffering entailed by friendships, when friends and relatives depart, especially the dearest of them, think how you ruminate on their good qualities and strengths and deeply suffer physically, verbally, and mentally.

Recall how delighted you are when they return as well. In this way contemplate the sorrow occasioned by fear of separation from your loved ones.

As for the suffering that ambition causes, businessmen, farmers, and so on work hard to achieve their goals only to see their merchandise lost and their crops destroyed by hail. [185] Political leaders and their ministers fail to defeat their foes and protect their friends. Monastics are unsuccessful in observing their ethical discipline due to their weak antidotes. They fail to become proficient in learning and reflection owing to poor intelligence and so forth. Such is the suffering of the unsuccessful pursuit of ambitions.

Furthermore, there are the sufferings of the powerful becoming powerless—for example, the rich being reduced to poverty, the gregarious finding themselves alone—and these are comparable to returning to your homeland to find nothing as it was before.

In brief, meditate until you have gained a deep understanding that owing to various unwelcome situations like hunger and thirst, or heat and cold, the human condition is also characterized by suffering.

Although in general the [*Great* and *Middle-Length Treatises on the*] *Stages of the Path to Enlightenment* prescribe the contemplation of eight sufferings, six sufferings, and so on, to simplify in teachings given to small groups, most often seven sufferings are explained mainly in relation to humankind. Following this you are taught to reflect on the sufferings of the other two kinds of fortunate rebirths as well as on the eight, three, and six kinds.

The sufferings of the gods and demigods

Regarding the sufferings of the other two kinds of fortunate rebirths, the *Friendly Letter* says:

> It is said that your complexion becomes unattractive,
> your seat loses its appeal, your flower garlands wilt,
> and your clothes start to smell;
> as for your body, it perspires for the first time.
> These five signs portending death from the higher states
> appear to gods residing in the divine realms.[468]

Desire-realm gods are not subjected to sufferings like the birth and aging of humans, but when death approaches, their physical splendor suddenly fades, they no longer want to sit on their comfortable seats, their flower garlands wilt, their clothes acquire an unpleasant smell, and they perspire, which they never did before. These are the five signs of death's approach. The signs that death is imminent are that their body's radiance declines, ablution waters stick to their body, their clothing and ornaments make unpleasant sounds, their eyes blink, and they feel attached to specific objects. As they become conscious that the ten portend their death, they grow despondent. In particular, when those called [*knowers of*] *three times*[469] investigate the matter, they see where they will take rebirth. If they are certain to shortly be reborn in a hell, for example, they suffer horribly, exactly as if they had already been born there. [186] Humans can only surmise that they will be born in a hell and can never be absolutely certain of it, but it is different for gods, which is why their suffering is said to be far more devastating.

Gods undergo other sufferings as well: those of lesser merit feel intimidated when they encounter gods of greater merit; more powerful gods banish the weaker; when battling demigods, gods kill others and are themselves killed—their bodies and limbs are cut and chopped to pieces.

Gods of the form and formless realms do not experience manifest sufferings such as these. However, just as a ship's pigeon eventually returns to its vessel, after the karma that projected such gods into a state of meditative concentration is depleted and they die, they must endure manifest suffering once more in the desire realm. Contemplate this well.

Sufferings shared by all six categories of life

As long as you are not free of samsara, you are exposed to future suffering. For example, you may become a universal sovereign or Brahmā by the power of your merit, but [once that is exhausted] you will again become a slave. Then there are present sufferings: those of birth, aging, illness, and death in this life. There is also *manifest suffering*, like pain made more acute when, say, salt water comes into contact with a festering boil. There is the *suffering of change*: when tired from walking, you experience a sense of well-being by resting, but after sitting for some time, your legs and back begin to hurt. *The suffering of pervasive conditioning* is analogous to the experience of being encased in ice—until you are free of it, you never know what it is to feel warm.

To distill the significance of the above, once you have taken rebirth with impure appropriated aggregates, you are helplessly subjected to suffering because of your present aggregates, and they inevitably induce future suffering. *Appropriated* refers to aspiration and attachment. For example, just as a fire that issues from wood is called a *wood fire*, so too are the aggregates named after the causes that produce them: the desire for a future body and attachment to the present body. Similarly, just as a tree that bears fruit is known as a fruit tree, so too are the aggregates named after their results, for once they are produced, they give rise to aspiration and attachment. [187] As one leads to another, you turn in samsara.

In addition to the aforementioned sufferings, there is that of *uncertainty*, regarding which the *Friendly Letter* says:

> As fathers become sons, mothers become wives,
> those who were your enemies become your friends,
> and the contrary occurs as well,
> nothing is certain for beings in cyclic existence.[470]

Relationships with parents, companions, friends, and enemies are often reversed not only over consecutive births but within single lives as well. Beloved ones of the first half of your life may very well become your enemies in the second half. Someone you thought to do away with last year, and who would have killed you as well, may by next year become a very dear friend and the like. This is all plain to see, which means you cannot rely on amiable and inimical relationships with any certainty. In these terms you contemplate the suffering of uncertainty.

Regarding discontent with what you have, the *Friendly Letter* comments:

> A leper infested with maggots,
> despite seeking relief by approaching a fire,
> is not appeased; know that it is the same
> for attachment to sense objects.[471]

Although in the past you drank the choice nectar of the gods, then mother's milk, and finally sewage and molten bronze in volumes far surpassing those of countless great oceans, still you feel dissatisfied. Contemplate your inability to ever feel fulfilled by experiencing objects of desire, like a leper who sits by a fire.

On the impossibility of calculating the number of your bodies, *Dispelling Sorrow* explains:

> If all the heads you had cut off
> in fights and quarrels with others

were placed in a pile, its height
would surpass that of the Brahmā realms.[472]

Putting aside the bodies you lost to various illnesses, and so on, if you were to heap together just the heads you lost each time it was cut off by a blade, the pile would reach higher than the Brahmā realms. Think, "If I do not free myself from cyclic existence, the process of repeatedly giving up my body will never end."

With regard to passing through countless birth canals [the *Friendly Letter*] says:

> If you were to count back to your original mother using pellets
> of earth
> the size of juniper berries, there would never be enough soil.[473]

If you were to try to tally your personal mother, her mother, and again her mother, and so on using small pellets of earth made of this vast planet's soil, it would be impossible [for lack of sufficient soil]. [188] This is the explicit meaning of the expression "original [mother]," but the actual meaning is that you cannot count how many mothers you have had [over past lives]. Based on this, you generate renunciation in relation to your past and future conceptions.

On the uncertainty of high and low status it also says:

> Although as Indra you might become worthy of the world's
> honors,
> by the power of karma, you will fall again to the earth.
> Although you might become a universal sovereign,
> in samsara, you will revert to being the slave of a slave.[474]

Reflect on the fact that though you become Indra, king of the gods, or a universal sovereign, if something occurs to activate a nonvirtuous karma produced in the past and not yet spent, you will later be reborn with inferior status as the slave of a slave, or in an unfortunate realm. Even if you are born as the sun and moon,[475] who illuminate the world with their light, you will later be reborn in dense gloom. Ponder how many people drunk with pride in their own power and wealth are punished by kings or destroyed by their adversaries and end up powerless and wretched.

As for having to leave everything behind, the *Guide to the Bodhisattva Way* states:

> Although a body arises whole,
> if the flesh and bones that come with it
> disintegrate and scatter,
> what is to be said of other companions?[476]

Contemplate this until you shrink in fear at how when you die, you have to go on alone, friendless.

In the past you have already experienced the sufferings just explained, and given your present behavior, it is only fitting that they should befall you again. Potowa says:

> Regarding the sufferings of illness, death and so on, once you have been born in one of the six classes, you fall sick because you must fall sick and die because you must die. It is not as if these events occur unexpectedly and unjustly, for they define and characterize cyclic existence. As long as you remain in samsara, they are unavoidable. If you are fed up with them, the Buddha taught that you must give up taking birth, and for this you must abandon its causes.[477]

This is easy to understand.

Stanzas between sections [189]

In an unclean womb, amid slimy substances,
in the dark where no forms are visible,
you are beset by many kinds of intense suffering.
As for the attractive body of the full bloom of youth,
its dark hair turns as white as snow;
the radiant glow of its complexion grows as dim as the dark;
its upright posture bends like a bow,
and plagued by aging, desirable things lose their appeal.

Medicine, diviners, and rituals are of no avail.
Daily your condition declines.
Friends, loved ones, servants, and entourage grow weary and shun you.
These are the messengers of Death summoning you.

Now is the time to leave behind in your bed
the impure form aggregate you thought inseparable from your mind
and for your mental consciousness alone to cross the long and treacherous defile
of the intermediate state and wander on through cyclic existence:

Though you repel them by every possible means,
bitter enemies and evil spirits rain injury upon you.
Though you do all you can to care for friends and belongings,
they scatter to the ten directions like clouds in a drought.

While physically you enjoy the delights of a god realm,
mentally you are subjected to the actual torments of hell:
the sufferings that the signs portending death inflict
are such that they would cleave a heart of steel.

Just as a bird soaring in the sky
must eventually return to earth,
though you reach the three realms' peak of existence,
'tis sad but you must spin again in the firebrand wheel of samsara.

As excellent and glorious lords of all gods and men
once again become slaves, and the slaves of slaves,
and sun and moon gods are born in the depths of darkness,
it's time to take your leave of samsara!

Suffering's Origins

The second part concerns meditating on the origins [of suffering]—the process of entering samsara.

Having understood that the condition of cyclic existence is suffering as just explained, if you no longer desire it, you must reject its causes. Since rejecting them requires identifying them, what are they? They are the [truth of] the origin. Of its two components, karma and afflictions, afflictions are preeminent. Just as seeds planted in dry farmland fail to grow unless they are watered, fertilized, and so forth, as the *Exposition of Valid Cognition* says: [190]

> Once craving for samsara is overcome,
> karma cannot launch another life,
> for its contributing cause has been expended.[478]

If someone who has accumulated a karma to be born as an animal attains the state of peace before the karma in question has ripened, as it has been rendered sterile, it will not produce a result. *Guide to the Bodhisattva Way* states:

> Even if all gods and demigods
> arose as my enemies,
> they still could not seize me
> and thrust me into the Relentless hell's inferno.
>
> Yet the potent foes that are the afflictions
> can in an instant cast me into flames of the Relentless hell
> so hot that though they met Mount Meru,
> not even ashes would remain.[479]

Even if all beings arose as your enemies, they could not compel you to take rebirth in a state of woe, but the enemies that are the afflictions, once the conditions have been met, cannot but torment you with violent suffering and reduce you to ashes.

Afflictions are defined as states of unrest, like the mental agitation generated by attachment, anger, and so forth. You must determine this empirically by observing a state of mind that creates great inner turmoil.

Potentialities of the afflictions on your mindstream are like oils stains on a piece of paper: very difficult to remove. When apparently healthy people have a dormant illness, eating something may trigger symptoms and induce pain. Likewise, seeing attractive things—young men and women, horses, livestock, clothing, precious metals and stones, and the like—kindles latent attachment so that it reveals itself. *Attachment* is the affliction that is a strong desire to enjoy these, gaze at them, touch them, and so on. In meditation, you are to visualize an object to which you are attached, regardless of whether it is actually present, until your natural mental state transforms into manifest attachment and replaces your current thought. Once you are overwhelmed by attachment, identify it precisely so that whenever it appears in the future, you will be in a position to apply its antidotes immediately. I was taught that it is pointless to practice if you allow your afflictions free rein. It is like having to kill someone called Devadatta. To avoid confusing him with someone else, first you need his precise description; then when he appears, you can strike him with a weapon. [191] When Geshé Ben Gungyal[480] said that he stood guard at the threshold of the afflictions gripping a short spear, their antidotes, I believe this is what he was referring to.

Anger is the affliction of fierce animosity that resembles a red-hot ember inflamed by the wind: it surfaces upon seeing enemies or inimical people and makes you feel intensely hostile and contemplate what you can to do hurt them.

Pride is the affliction that, under the influence of self-grasping, has the aspect of conceit: based on your high birth, wealth, knowledge, physical prowess, and so on, you see yourself as superior to others and think, "So and so does not compare with even a single pore of my body."

Ignorance is the affliction that obscures and obfuscates all conventional and ultimate existents, like karma and its effects, the four truths, suchness, and so forth, just as in a windowless house containing many colorful things of various shapes, the darkness prevents your distinguishing white from black, good from bad, and so on.

Doubt is the affliction that, for example, makes you hesitate about the truth of what is explained in the scriptures—the Three Jewels, karma and its effects, and so on—and hinders your ascertainment of the phenomena in question.

The *personal identity view*[481] is an afflicted discernment that apprehends a self, calling it "I" or "mine," in relation to a basis of designation such as one's five aggregates, which are impermanent, since their present moment of existence ceases the moment after, and are not one, since they are collections of many parts.

Extreme views are afflicted discernments that regard the "I" that is apprehended in relation to the aggregates as both permanent and stable, or subject to annihilation, which precludes being conceived in a future life.

Holding to the superiority of views is an afflicted discernment that has as its object any of the three that are the personal identity view, extreme views, and wrong views, and the aggregates in relation to which these views arise, and apprehends them as superior.

Holding to the superiority of ethics and conduct is the afflicted discernment that views (1) ethical disciplines that reject what are considered bad ethics; (2) modes of conduct like hair cutting, wearing human and animal skins or using skeletons, fasting, using five kinds of fire, standing on one leg and looking at the sun, going naked and applying ashes to your body while observing silence; and (3) the aggregates in relation to which these arise, and wishes to attain liberation by their means. [192] Feeling arrogant about your authentic ethical discipline is not holding to the superiority of ethics. It is taught that the latter must involve a wrong view, as when very ordinary people who have attained clairvoyance see how in a past life they behaved like a dog or pig, and imagining it to be the way to attain another human rebirth, they conclude that they are to behave similarly in this life.

Wrong views are afflicted discernments that deny the existence of karma and its effects and past and future lives or that assert the creation and destruction of the world by Brahmā, Īśvara, Viṣṇu, and the like.

The same principle applies to every other type of affliction as well. Do not content yourself with memorizing them and reciting them by heart. Make a point of generating each of them in you. Then later, the moment one of them emerges, you will be able to identify it effortlessly, without the slightest difficulty, just as in a large gathering you easily recognize a person you know well. Otherwise, you will be like one who blindly shoots an arrow into a crowd before identifying the enemy.

When only one of the ten afflictions is present, it is relatively easy to detect it, but just as it is slightly harder for a doctor to diagnose a patient who is suffering from several diseases, when two or three afflictions occur simultaneously, it is more difficult to distinguish each. Say you have a pressing desire for a certain cart and hope to acquire it; if someone comes along and suddenly makes off with it, you will be angry with that person. The intensity of your anger will be directly proportional to the degree of your attachment to the cart. You view the cart as existing truly, and you apprehend what is merely an assemblage of about seven parts as existing from its own side. You adhere to the superiority of that view, and so on. As about four afflictions occur simultaneously, thorough analysis is required to recognize them.

Although the two, ignorance and the personal identity view, can be considered together as the root of all the afflictions, in a comprehensive analysis you differentiate them. Ignorance is like the darkness that prevents you from clearly distinguishing the nature of a rope, for example, while the personal identity view is like the resulting perception that apprehends the rope as a snake. As such, the two form the root of all afflictions, for in association with attachment and anger, they prompt all faults [afflictions]. The *Exposition of Valid Cognition* says: [193]

> Due to [grasping at] self, there is the concept of "other";
> the [notions of] "self" and "other" give rise to attachment and
> aversion;
> in complete dependence on these,
> all [other] faults occur.[482]

Although you may now act as if to slightly curb the afflictions that cause all faults, when you fail to uproot them, their latent tendencies function to increase them in the same way that a mirror reflects images. When you stand in front of a mirror, immediately the image of your face appears in it. In the same way, encounters with various phenomena like enemies and friends cause the afflictions to reveal themselves: they appear in relation to such observed objects.

Distance from spiritual teachers and Dharma friends and distractions like the behavior and conversations of bad companions with strong afflictions can all kindle afflictions. Explanations given by false teachers—those, for example, who claim to have attained liberation without having discarded their afflictions—also reinforce them. Just as people who have memorized their prayers well will carry on reciting them uninterruptedly despite their thoughts having turned elsewhere, afflictions increase by the force of habit owing to thorough familiarization with them in the past. Triggered by attachment and aversion, exaggeration of the way people harm or help you, for example, intensifies the afflictions, as does improper attention, like imagining that the principle of karma and its effects is untrue because a certain person is happy despite having committed much wrongdoing.

Having identified these six causes, if you fail to practice as though you were lying in wait for an enemy in a narrow and treacherous defile, you will come under the sway of afflictions and in this and future lives commit manifold sins. These in turn will induce samsaric suffering and will delay your attainment of nirvana considerably. The fundamental cause of all your sorrows is having kept company with them in the past. If you find unbearable those who harm you slightly in this life and see them as your foes, then why can you not do the same for your enemies the afflictions, which in all your lives since beginningless time have brought you nothing but misery? [194] By repeatedly applying the antidotes that oppose them, you can eradicate them, and unlike other enemies, they will not return. [*Guide to the Bodhisattva Way*] says:

> Common enemies banished from one land
> can very well take up residence in another and,
> after recovering their strength, from there return.
> It is different with the enemies the afflictions.
>
> The afflictions are rejected by the eye of wisdom.
> Once eliminated from my mind, where can they go?
> Where can they reside whence to return and harm me?
> But due to my weak intellect and absence of effort, this has yet
> to occur.[483]

Once you have taken rebirth under the impetus of your karma and afflictions, you cannot escape dying and being conceived again. Timely death is dying when your life span is depleted. In [the *Great Final Nirvana*] *Sutra*[484] the Buddha taught nine causes of untimely death, such as careless eating habits and behavior.[485] There are many such factors, but what will help and harm you at death and thereafter are virtuous and nonvirtuous karmas, and karmas as intention produced by the afflictions explained above, for they will determine your joy or misery.

People who have accomplished great virtue in their lives sometimes have problems with their property, health, and even their life, and in the end undergo severe death throes. Others who have led very sinful lives may experience great happiness. As a result, some fools mistakenly view the principle of karma and its effects as false. In fact, these [sinful and virtuous] people could very well be experiencing the results of the powerful sin and virtue of a past life.

Moreover, *Guide to the Bodhisattva Way* states:

> Is it not fortunate when the life of a person doomed to be executed
> is spared by having a hand cut off instead?
> Is it not fortunate that a person avoids the hells
> by experiencing human suffering instead?[486]

Like a criminal whose life is at stake getting off by having a hand cut off, suffering experienced as a human can replace the suffering that would otherwise be experienced in a future infernal birth.

King Śikhin of Kurukṣetra sprinkled dust on Ārya Kātyāyana. As a result, first a shower of jewels fell, but later he died buried under a pile of dirt in a dust storm, which can be understood.[487] [195]

On what specifically determines your next rebirth, the *Treasury of Abhidharma* [*Autocommentary*] states:

> The karmas that determine your rebirth in samsara are those that are
> serious,
> those nearest, those to which you are accustomed,
> and those done earlier; among these,
> the former mature prior to the subsequent.[488]

As long as your mind carries various virtuous and nonvirtuous karmas, on your deathbed the sinful or virtuous thoughts to which you have become most accustomed in your life will arise. Those that occur when external breathing is about to cease are the *coarse thoughts at death*. The *subtle mind of death* occurs when external breathing has ceased but internal breathing has not. At the time of the coarse mind of death, you naturally have the kinds of thoughts that over the past have become most familiar to you: nonvirtuous ones like attachment to friends and aversion to enemies, or virtuous ones like mindfulness of the Three Jewels. In some whose minds are unclear due to illness, a friend can help kindle good thoughts by relating an assortment of edifying tales. When, for example, sins [and virtues] carry equal weight, it is uncertain which will ripen at death, but those to which you have become most accustomed will prevail.

Virtuous thoughts may arise in very sinful people at death, allowing them to be reborn in a fortunate realm, and sinful thoughts may occur to people who have done much good, triggering a rebirth in an unfortunate realm. This is an important point. However, since it is possible to know your own mind, you can feel glad or remorseful in relation to what you recall having done in the past. Sinful people who do not know right from wrong will inevitably have the kind of immoral thoughts of which they have made a habit in that life. Despite this, [having someone recite to them] the tathāgatas' names and special dhāraṇīs can help them avoid a rebirth in an unfortunate realm. While the subtle mind of death is manifest, neither virtuous nor nonvirtuous perceptions occur, for thoughts [at that time] are ethically neutral.

The virtuous generally experience few death throes. As if in a dream, they see beautiful forms and have the impression of moving from darkness into light. It is the opposite for the nonvirtuous. When both the virtuous and the nonvirtuous are about to die, the thought occurs that they will die, and they feel very attached to their body. As a result, their consciousness leaves their body, and as the needle of a scale tips, they are immediately born in the intermediate state with a body shaped like that of their future life. [196] The color of an intermediate-state being to be born in a hell is that of a burnt log; for the intermediate state of an animal birth, it is smoke-colored; for the intermediate state of a hungry ghost birth, it is the color of water; for the intermediate state of a god or human birth, it is the color of gold; for the intermediate state of a form-realm birth, it is white. In the intermediate state for a god rebirth you ascend, for a human rebirth you move forward, and in the intermediate state for rebirth in an unfortunate realm you descend. After up to forty-nine days, you see your future parents coupling as if in an illusion. Compelled by attachment and aversion, you then enter and are conceived. A rebirth in a hell can be triggered, for example, by seeing an animal and wanting to slaughter it.

You are to meditate on the way you wander in cyclic existence, which resembles a firebrand wheel, until renunciation appears in you.

Stanzas between sections

From beginningless time your mind
has never for an instant been separated
from its companions, the afflictions, which follow in its wake
and plunge you into samsara's ocean, with no end.

Against your will, the winds of karmas churn it well
into waves of the three kinds of utter misery.
Always reflect on samsara, like a firebrand wheel,
and your afflictions, enemies most dire.

If you pride yourself on being a hero
who has killed an enemy in this life,
now the time has come to tame
the afflictions—your enemies of all time.

Now that you have successfully attained a life with leisure and
opportunity
and understood the key points of the three higher trainings,
if you do not conquer the army of suffering's origins,
I suspect you will continue [trudging] wearily on the plain of birth
and death.

The Twelve Links of Dependent Origination

The second part consists in contemplating suffering in the context of the twelve links of dependent origination.

Ignorance is like darkness that prevents you from seeing external forms. There are two kinds: ignorance of karma and its effects and ignorance of suchness. By either you produce black or white compositional karma, based on which you are projected into rebirths in unfortunate or fortunate realms.

Concerning how you are projected, there are four kinds [of links]: projecting causes and completing causes, projected effects and completed effects. [197] Taking the example of rebirth in a fortunate realm, inspired by a virtuous karma of a past life and motivated by the link of *ignorance* regarding suchness (but not of karma and its effects), you produce a virtuous karma relative to the desire realm. This link of *compositional karma* places an imprint on the link of *consciousness* of the causal period. These constitute the projecting causes. The link of *craving* for either nonseparation from a pleasant feeling or separation from a painful one directly activates the karmic imprint placed therein. This, along with the link of *grasping*, which consists of aspiration and attachment, reinforces the karma that, once potentialized, becomes the link of *existence* that leads to the next rebirth. These three constitute the completing causes. From them, the causal consciousness is conceived in the womb of the mother of that life, within which are found the resultant consciousness as well as the aggregates of feeling, discrimination, and mental formations that constitute the name link. When you add to these the form aggregate—the parents' sperm and ovum, moisture and warmth, and the like—you have the *name-and-form* link. Next the *six sources* link is produced. It consists of the six sources, the eyes and so forth. When these have developed, the three that are an object, a sense, and a consciousness come together, and an object is encountered and noted as pleasant, unpleasant, or neutral. This is the link of *contact*. Due to this encounter, one of the three that are pleasant, unpleasant, or neutral feelings ensues, which is the link of *feeling*. These four constitute the projected effects. Once conception of the consciousness in one of the four ways of taking birth is complete, emerging [from, e.g., the womb] is the link of *birth*. The maturation of the youthful aggregates of birth is aging, and the abandonment of the aggregates is death; they correspond to the link of *aging and death*. These final two links constitute the completed effects.

If you meditate well in this way on how you move from fortunate realms to unfortunate ones through the twelve links of dependent origination, your meditation will cover the key points of the topics of the paths of persons of both lesser and intermediate capacities. The great Geshé Phuchungwa[489] taught mind training in relation to the twelve links of dependent origination in the order of their occurrence as well as in reverse order. [198]

My guru taught me that once the paths of persons of lesser and intermediate capacities have been explained in the above manner, the current norm is to teach those of superior intelligence the steps of the twelve links of dependent origination in a concise manner and to abstain from teaching them to those of average or less than average intelligence, which does not constitute an omission. It is customary to teach those who easily understand the twelve links of dependent origination the topics of the path of persons of lesser capacity from reliance on spiritual teachers up to refuge in the usual way, based on one's personal experience, then to teach [the remainder of] the path of persons of lesser capacity according to the twelve links of dependent origination in relation to a rebirth in an unfortunate realm, in the order of occurrence and in reverse order, and finally to explain the links in relation to a rebirth in a fortunate realm in the order of occurrence and in reverse order in the context of the path of persons of intermediate capacity.

Stanzas between sections

Having placed imprints of karma and afflictions
on your consciousness in a previous life,
both craving and grasping reinforce one imprint
and potentialize it to produce your birth of the next life.

The aggregation of name-and-form is produced
in which the elements and sources are well defined.
These experience contact and feeling in relation to desired objects,
and with birth and aging and death, you turn yet again.

In the past, you have experienced countless times
samsara's twelve links of dependent origination
in the order in which they occur—causes then effects.
Would it not be best to produce them in reverse order?

The Path of Liberation from Samsara

The second part covers the steps to practice the path that grants liberation from the above. Concerning this the *Friendly Letter* says:

> Were your clothes or head to suddenly catch fire,
> still you should defer extinguishing it
> and continue striving to end rebirth,
> for no goal is greater than that.
>
> With pure ethical discipline, wisdom, and absorption,
> you attain nirvana, the state that is peaceful, disciplined,
> stainless, ageless, deathless, and inexhaustible,
> far superior to the sun and moon, and to earth, air, fire, and water.[490]

The three precious trainings are to be mastered, for [199] training in ethical discipline, which turns a distracted mind into an undistracted one, prevents afflictions from taking control [when they arise], thanks to which you enjoy the pleasures of desire-realm gods and humans. Training in states of concentration, which turns an unabsorbed mind into an absorbed one, prevents the afflictions from manifesting, thanks to which you enjoy the pleasures of the form-realm and formless-realm gods. Training in wisdom, which turns an unfree mind into a free one, eradicates the seeds of the afflictions, thanks to which you achieve liberation and nirvana. Before cultivating the training in wisdom, you must first accomplish the training in states of concentration that render your mind serviceable, and prior to that, to overcome distraction, you must accomplish the training in ethical discipline. Because of their cause-and-effect relationship, by practicing them in the correct order, you can realize liberation from samsara. For that reason, the Buddha taught, "Accomplish cessation; meditate on the path," by which he meant that before accomplishing the goal, true cessation, you must practice the path that allows you to achieve it. The relationship between these two truths resembles the relationship between the truths of suffering and its origins.

Disciples practicing the path of persons of intermediate capacity alone, and not the stages of the path of persons of great capacity, should be taught the path just mentioned at length. However, since here it is a question of the stages of the path *shared with* persons of intermediate capacity, only the higher training in ethical discipline is relevant, not the other two, for they are treated in the context of tranquil abiding and special insight [in the path of persons of great capacity]. Since abstention from the ten nonvirtues of the path of persons of lesser capacity and pure ethical discipline in the present framework are both included in the topic of ethical discipline that is part of training in general bodhisattva practice, you might think that there is no need to treat them separately. However, it is indeed necessary, for as the *Song of Spiritual Experience* says:

> Your three doors are so sullied with sins and transgressions,
> it is especially vital to purify your karmic obscurations.[491]

To produce the paths of persons of great and intermediate capacity in you, it is essential that you apply the methods to cleanse yourself of sins and transgressions, such as the ten nonvirtues.

Some bodhisattvas have vows of individual liberation, and others do not. For those who lack them, since the substitute taught is none other than abstention from the ten nonvirtues, it is also suitable for practice in the present context. [200]

On the training in ethical discipline, the *Friendly Letter* says:

> It is taught that ethical discipline is the foundation of all good qualities,
> like the ground is for all things, both animate and inanimate.[492]

According to the strength of your antidotes [to wrongdoing], you are to take one of the seven kinds of vows for personal liberation. However, it is not enough to just take the vows, you must also keep them. As ignorance is one of the doors to transgressions, to close it ensure that you assimilate the minutiae of the precepts. As a remedy to carelessness, with mindfulness make it perfectly clear to yourself what is to be adopted and rejected; guard yourself with meta-awareness that examines what is right and wrong; cultivate a sense of shame and consideration for others and fear of the maturation effects [of your actions]. As a remedy for irreverence, with belief in the Teacher, his words, and the companions to practice, cultivate reverence. As an antidote to your numerous afflictions, quell the strongest and check daily whether you have transgressed any precepts. By means of restoration practice, the four powers, and so on, confess those that you have contravened and promise to refrain from them. The *Questions of Brahmā Sutra* says:

> Rely on your precepts.
> Be genuinely careful of them.
> Do not give them up afterward.
> Do not terminate them even at the cost of your life.
> Always diligently keep them.
> Practice discipline well.[493]

Pure ethical discipline is the very root of all short and long-term happiness and goodness. Its benefits, which are explained in the *King of Meditations Sutra* and elsewhere, are immense, especially in this age when the five degenerations are on the rise.[494] Atiśa and the Kadampas especially emphasized pure ethical discipline. Sharawa explains:

> In general, whatever your situation, good or bad, act according to the Dharma. If, within it, you act according to what the Vinaya teaches, that will suffice, for your acts will be fundamentally pure, withstand analysis, make you happy, and be ultimately rewarding.[495]

As this statement is absolutely true, I ask you to stop looking for branches where there are no roots and make it your core practice.

Stanzas between sections

In the field-like base of pure ethical discipline,
water and fertilizer—a serviceable mind,
ripen the harvest that is the path of special insight,
thereby eradicating poverty of the samsaric condition. [201]

Proudly astride [the elephant] Airavata that is a conscientious attitude,
the One with a Thousand Eyes [Indra]—mind in absorption
with his hundred-spoked vajra-like understanding of selflessness—
halts the progression of samsara's mountains.

Amid the forests of samsara's endless wilderness
grows the wish-granting tree, the three trainings.
As it can never be scorched by the flames of suffering,
it has become a lovely celestial park of stable happiness.

* * *

With the sharp weapon of your pure and fine [intelligence],
you cut the entire web of ignorance.
O Tsongkhapa, you are indeed an emanation of Mañjuvajra!

With the instructions of this guru of the three realms' beings,
the precious shaft of renunciation of the evils of suffering and its origins
raises the parasol of the three trainings,
that is beautifully adorned with its finial, the jewel of nirvana.

Having completely twirled these good explanations up to samsara's peak,
I will now explain how from Lake Anavatapta of great compassion,
the four rivers of vast bodhisattva activity
flow down in a never-ending stream
to finally reach the great ocean of omniscience.

The Path of Persons of Great Capacity

On the third part, the way to train the mind on the stages of the path of persons of great capacity, *Lamp on the Path to Enlightenment* states:

> Based on an understanding of their personal suffering,
> those whose sole desire is to eradicate
> all the suffering borne by others
> are known as superior beings.[496]

With the path of persons of intermediate capacity emerges the fear of samsaric suffering and a genuine wish to be free of it. Those who train exclusively in the path of persons of intermediate capacity pursue personal peace alone. In the present context of training in the path shared with persons of intermediate capacity, persons of great capacity are those who, based on an understanding of their own suffering, come to find others' misery similarly intolerable and, out of a desire to free them of it, accomplish the appropriate methods.

What methods are to be applied to achieve this goal? [202] As the *Condensed Presentation of the Perfections* states,

> The way to accomplish the welfare of the world
> is to definitively give up the two vehicles lacking that potential
> and enter the vehicle that the Conqueror Śākyamuni compassionately taught,
> which by nature is devoted exclusively to helping others.[497]

You may achieve liberation by practicing the four truths in forward and reverse order, but you will neither complete your own goals thereby nor be capable of working extensively to benefit others. Given this, avoid entering the śrāvaka and pratyekabuddha paths, which lack the ability to accomplish others' welfare to a great extent, and instead enter the Great Vehicle. On the need to accomplish sentient beings' goals, *Letter to a Student* states:

> Cattle also eat easily found mouthfuls of grass on their own

and, when tormented by great thirst, find water and drink it happily.
Here, all the efforts of those who accomplish others' welfare
are their glory, their [source of] joy, and their superior capacity.

The horse-drawn chariot of the sun illuminates all,
and the earth supports the world, and neither sees it as a burden.
The nature of disinterested persons of great capacity is similar,
for they are wholly devoted to achieving the world's happiness and
benefit.[498]

Even animals pursue happiness in this life alone. By comparison, the skill and capacity of superior beings resemble that of the sun and moon, which dispel darkness, or this great earth, which supports the world. With great courage, these beings assume responsibility for others' welfare, for which [the awakening mind] is essential.

Guide to the Bodhisattva Way states:

Once they have realized the awakening mind, in an instant
miserable beings who are bound to the prison of cyclic existence
are addressed as "sons of the tathāgatas"
and become objects of homage for the world's gods and men.[499]

It is taught that as soon as someone suffering in samsara realizes bodhicitta, he or she becomes a bodhisattva, whereas if you lack the awakening mind, no matter what other great qualities you may have, such as the three precious higher trainings, you will not have entered the ranks of the Great Vehicle.

The *Sublime Continuum* says:

Faith[500] in the supreme vehicle is the seed.
Wisdom [combined with method] is the mother generating buddha
qualities.
The joy of absorption is her womb; these along with compassion, the
nurses,
together engender the Buddha's children.[501] [203]

Water and fertilizer are common conditions that produce a variety of crops. So too can a mother of the merchant class produce children of different castes. A specific cause, like a barley seed or a father of the brahman caste, can only produce one kind of result: once barley is planted, it will never sprout and grow into a wheat plant, and the son of a brahman father will never belong to the fisherman caste. Similarly, the wisdom understanding selflessness and so on is the mother needed to achieve freedom from cyclic existence by means of either the Great or the Lesser Vehicle. In contrast, the awakening mind, like a father, is the specific cause of buddhahood. It is comparable to a precious diamond that clears away the entire misery of both samsara and personal peace and so surpasses all lesser gems.

The practice of the stages of the path of persons of great capacity has two parts: how to generate the awakening mind and how to train in bodhisattva practice once you have generated it. The first, how to generate the awakening mind, has two parts: the stages of training in the awakening mind and committing to the awakening mind in a ceremony.

The stages of training in the awakening mind

Generally, a condition for generating the awakening mind is the direct observation of buddhas' and bodhisattvas' good qualities. Failing this, it is to learn of them from the collection of scriptures on the bodhisattva path; or for want of learning them in great detail, it is to learn roughly why this spiritual quality is vital to attaining buddhahood and so on, and to not be able to bear the thought of the Mahayana teachings' decline. If they are not declining, then reflect on how, in this very degenerate age, it is difficult [to have the opportunity] to develop the aspiration to even śrāvaka and pratyekabuddha enlightenment, to say nothing of supreme enlightenment. Grounded in these, you can generate the aspiration that is the wish to achieve buddhahood.

Bodhicitta is also cultivated based on four causes: lineage, spiritual teachers, compassion, and tirelessness; and four strengths: personal strength, others' strength, the strength of the cause (familiarization with the Great Vehicle in past lives), and the strength of application (familiarization with virtue in the present life). Thus many causes and conditions for the generation of bodhicitta are taught: four causes, four strengths, and so on.[502] [204] Currently there are two key methods: the sevenfold instruction transmitted by the great lord Atiśa and the instruction transmitted by the bodhisattva Śāntideva.

The sevenfold cause-and-effect instruction

What is the purpose of training the mind in the first, the great lord's sevenfold cause-and-effect instruction? Buddhahood arises from the awakening mind, which in turn arises from altruistic intention. This arises from compassion, which arises from love. The latter arises from [the wish to] repay kindness, which in turn arises from mindfulness of it, and this arises from recognizing that all beings are your mothers. This pivotal sequence starts with recognizing beings as your mothers; however, great compassion does not necessarily come between altruistic intention and love.[503] As *Entering the Middle Way* says:

> For the excellent harvest of buddhahood,
> compassion is said to be the seed, the moisture that nurtures it,
> and the fruit that ensures its perennial function.
> For these reasons, I begin by extolling compassion.[504]

Committing yourself to freeing beings from samsara initially depends on compassion. Moreover, in the middle, not being disheartened by the difficulty involved and not straying into the Lesser Vehicle also depend on compassion. At the end, once buddhahood is attained, not abiding in a state of śrāvaka and pratyekabuddha peace and instead accomplishing the welfare of all sentient beings without difficulty also depend on it. To generate great compassion, the beings who are its objects must appeal to you, which is why you have to see them all as your mothers. When those who have not trained in this path recall and reflect on the kindness of loved ones like their mother, they feel love and compassion for them that is biased, for not only do they lack the same for those they dislike, such as their enemies, they want the opposite for them—that they should suffer and be deprived of happiness. If we do not first achieve equanimity, we may seem to be meditating on the path, but our love and compassion remain limited to a few. To remedy this, we must start by cultivating equanimity.

Since the goal is to achieve sympathetic love for your mothers and so on, you may wonder why you should first curb the feeling of affinity you currently have for them. Within the cause-and-effect instruction, sympathy must be entirely free of attachment, but the love we now have is inspired by attachment. [205] For example, just as a bed laid out on uneven ground with holes and bumps is uncomfortable, the highs and lows of attachment and anger make it impossible to achieve love. Unlike neutral feelings,[505] equanimity is an infinite quality, one that is free of attachment and anger toward sentient beings. To cultivate it, you first clearly visualize someone who is neither a friend nor an enemy and recall the person's appearance, behavior, and so on. While picturing the person, let any feelings of hostility or affection arise. The anger by which you perceive him to be inimical or the attachment by which you see him as appealing may not be very potent, but even if they are only slight, it is taught that you should apply the antidote to whichever is strongest and meditate until you achieve equanimity.

You start by visualizing a neutral person because it is easier to achieve equanimity in relation to a person for whom such a feeling is manifest. Next, you visualize a dire enemy and a dearly loved one of this life and let feelings of anger and attachment surface. By in-depth reflection on the fact that in past lives, your enemy was a friend who helped you often and your friend a dangerous enemy who killed you and so on, you even out your feelings of hostility and attachment for them. I can assure you that this meditation is largely facilitated by having already achieved a spiritual experience of the uncertain nature of relationships in the path of persons of intermediate capacity.

Like driving away a hundred birds by firing a slingshot once, if you can achieve effortless equanimity toward all beings in relation to the three objects of observation, that will be sufficient. When you still find it somewhat difficult to generate equanimity in this manner, the instruction is to meditate taking several examples of people in each category.

When with this method, in relation to all beings—enemies, friends, and neutral beings alike—you manage to even out your great hostility for those of the one category and utter attachment for the other, you then begin to build the foundation for the wish to pursue others' welfare. This involves [first] coming to recognize that all sentient beings are your mothers. To do this, reflect as follows:

> Cyclic existence is unlimited, and so is the number of my past births. How could I possibly not have taken rebirth by being conceived in the womb of every sentient being? [206]

While contemplating this, you may well imagine it, but since you are meditating on beings in general, it will be difficult to be fully convinced of it. That is why you are to picture your mother of this life in front of you with her present age, shape, appearance, and manner. Obviously, she was your mother is this life, but so was she in many other lives. For example, in the sutras the Tathāgata explains that his mother of that life was also his mother in many of his past lives when he was still training on the path. Moreover, he said the same about other beings' past and future lives. In meditating on this, by recalling that the words of infallible beings are incontrovertible and understanding the matter inferentially, you will become deeply and thoroughly convinced of it.

Next [in succession] meditate on your father, other relatives, people you are indifferent toward, and enemies of this life as well as those of other categories like hell beings. In the end, your view of all sentient beings as your mothers will cease to be contrived, and you will come to see them as you do your mother of this life.

Once you have experienced this, to generate the awareness of their kindness, as before, you clearly visualize your mother as she appears to you with all her features. Then think:

> My mother of this life carried me in her womb for almost ten months. She neglected her own happiness, hunger, and thirst. Everything she did, good or bad, was done for the sake of her child. She gave me a life with leisure and opportunity. These were her great kindnesses to me at the beginning. After I was born, she cared for me by placing me on a bed of soft cloth. She nurtured me tenderly, looked at me with loving eyes, greeted me with kind smiles, called out to me with affectionate names, nourished me with her sweet milk, fed me food with her tongue, wiped my nose with her mouth and my stool with her hand, held me to her warm body, protected me from the dangers of fire, water, and heights, and she would have truly chosen to fall sick or die if it meant her child could avoid falling sick or dying. These were her great kindnesses to me in the middle period. Later she educated me or had others educate me, starting with simple things like how to eat, walk, and so on. Disregarding any sin, suffering, and bad reputation it may have entailed, everything she cherished as deeply as her own heart—the land, houses, wealth, and belongings she worked so hard to acquire, laboring until she was exhausted—she gave it all to me.

Pondering her great kindness to you, meditate until your eyes fill with tears, your hairs stand on end, you are deeply moved and overcome with loving concern. [207] Then gradually reflect on how, from your father to your enemies, all other beings of the six categories, when they were your mother countless times in the past, for your sake did the same as your mother of this life has. Although when they were your animal mothers, they did not accomplish all of the above, they are mentioned because when they were your human mothers, there is not one of these kindnesses that they did not show you.

After achieving an experience of the awareness of beings' kindness, next, concerning the thought to repay kindness, *Letter to a Student* says:

> While aware that your loved ones are sunk in samsara's ocean,
> and fallen among its waves,
> it would be utterly shameless to seek personal liberation,
> neglecting those you no longer recognize due to having changed
> lives.[506]

Think:

> The minds of sentient beings, my mothers, are troubled by the demon-like afflictions. Their eyes to see what to adopt and what to reject are blinded by ignorance. They lack the staff of the profound and sacred Dharma, and a guide for the blind: a spiritual teacher to lead them to the city of liberation. Having slipped from the resting place of high rebirth and liberation, and fallen into the abyss of cyclic existence, they wander in the prison of the three kinds of suffering. It is only because of having changed lives that I do not recognize them; in fact, they are the kind fathers and mothers who have helped me over multiple lives. If they cannot count on me, their child, who can they count on? If it is not my responsibility, as their child, to protect them, whose is it? For example, when parents, friends or loved ones are in trouble, have been imprisoned, attacked by bandits in the wilderness, or frightened by wild animals, if I have a way to help them, what would be more shameless and disgraceful than for me to just sit back, relax and do nothing for them? The *Verses on the Nāga King Bherī* [*Sutra*] says:
>
> > The oceans, Mount Meru,
> > and the earth are not my burdens.
> > Not repaying kindness on the other hand
> > is my great responsibility.[507]
>
> While I have the opportunity to protect my kind mothers, were

> I instead to neglect them, enter the lesser path, and pursue peace for just myself, the holy beings would be deeply disappointed in me. So I will give up that idea and accomplish all beings' welfare.

Then, if you wonder how to help them, think: [208]

> I will care for them by removing each of their temporary sufferings—providing the hungry with food, the thirsty with drink, those suffering from illness with medicine, the poor with goods, and so forth. Since this will allow me to acquire merit, it is not inappropriate. However, if I focus mainly on helping them by providing them with samsaric power and wealth, I should keep in mind that they have been born as Brahmā and other worldly gods like Īśvara and as universal sovereigns countless times before, and despite this they still have not achieved any real happiness. These were just more occasions for them to experience sufferings like poverty, heat, and cold. By mainly providing them with contaminated happiness, since pleasure changes into suffering, the greater their power and wealth becomes, the more their grief will increase; it will be like pouring salt on a wound. For this reason, I shall lead all beings to a state of either liberation or omniscience.

Be sure to reflect on this well to inspire yourself.

Just setting the foundation for generating the wish to pursue others' welfare is insufficient. You are to actually produce it by cultivating the three: love, compassion, and the altruistic intention. Although there is no fixed order or causal relationship between love and compassion—respectively, the wish for others' happiness and the wish to end their suffering—generally the custom is to begin with love. *Precious Garland* says:

> Even giving three times each day
> three hundred special dishes of food
> does not match the merit
> of one brief moment of love.
>
> You become loved by gods and men,
> and they protect you.

You know mental joy and much [physical] well-being.
Poison and weapons do not harm you.

You achieve your goals effortlessly
and are born in Brahmā's realm.
Even if you do not achieve liberation,
you will attain these eight benefits of love.[508]

To cultivate love, which has unlimited advantages, contemplate your mother of this life. She may or may not be experiencing manifest suffering, like illness and poverty. Nevertheless, reflect on how [in any event] she lacks happiness from being subject to the suffering of change and the suffering of pervasive conditioning. Once you have generated a strong wish to establish your mother, who is deprived of happiness, in a state of joy, say: [209]

> How marvelous it would be if sentient beings, my mothers of old[509] who are deprived of happiness, could be happy! May they be so. By all means I will ensure that they are happy.

Repeat this many times, reflecting on the meaning. You should meditate similarly in relation to all beings unconditionally, in the same sequence as before—friends, enemies, and so on. You are to adapt your meditation to each circumstance: in the three unfortunate realms beings are undergoing manifest sufferings, and in the fortunate realms they either are or are not experiencing the same.

When you consider refusing to help someone because you deem the person an enemy who has hurt you, remember that it was the harm you did to him in a past life that has circled back to you now. In any case, the person's actions were prompted by his afflictions, against his will. If your present mother or another loved one was crazed by a demon and struck you with a weapon, you would not get angry with her. Instead, you would look for a way to have the demon exorcized. Similarly, your old mothers of the past that you now mistakenly see as enemies are crazed by the demon-like afflictions. For this reason, you should think as before, "How marvelous it would be if they could be free of the demonic afflictions and could find happiness!" and so forth. This practice is of great importance.

Imagining that cultivating love for your enemies will not be problematic because you have already meditated on the fact that they have been your mothers indicates a complete lack of discernment. It is self-evident that some unscrupulous people perceive their mother of this life as an enemy, hurt her in a variety of ways, and may go so far as to kill her.

Once you have cultivated love for sentient beings, next, for compassion, visualize as before your present mother tormented by one of the three kinds of suffering, and think:

> Alas! My mother of this life is affected directly by suffering and indirectly by the origins of suffering. She does not have the slightest chance to be happy. How I wish she could be free of this misery!

Recite:

> How marvelous it would be if sentient beings, my mothers of old who are tormented by suffering, could be free of suffering! May they be free of it. By all means I will ensure that they are free of suffering.

Repeat this many times, thinking about what you are saying. [210] Here as well you should extend your reflections to include all beings: friends, enemies, and neutral people.

The *Great Treatise on the Stages of the Path* explains that these meditations will be facilitated if you have already achieved a pre-experience understanding[510] of the paths of persons of lesser and intermediate capacity and also by generalizing your own experience of suffering to others.[511]

The simple wish for others' happiness and the desire that they may be free of suffering are found in Lesser Vehicle beings as well. For the love and compassion that I have just explained, such wishes are insufficient, however, for the ones here are the love and compassion that can engender a genuine altruistic intention—the thought "I will make this happen!" In other terms, the pure, altruistic intention that these two qualities inspire is more than just the wish that beings be freed of suffering and established in happiness. It is a commitment, the thought "I resolve to accomplish it!" While thinking that you take personal responsibility for establishing in happiness and for freeing from suffering these dear sentient beings, you say:

> I will see to it that these sentient beings, my mothers of old who are deprived of happiness, find happiness. I will see to it that these

> sentient beings, who are tormented by suffering, are freed from suffering.

Repeat this many times and generate a pure, superior, and committed resolve.

Next, while mindful of the buddhas' qualities of body, speech, mind, and activity as explained in the context of refuge, think, "If I were to attain the state endowed with these superior qualities, I too would be capable of guiding sentient beings," and thereby generate a precious aspirational bodhicitta equal to the awakening mind that initiates three countless eons [of accumulations].

If you imagine that the genuine altruistic intention is no different from the intention to lead beings to nirvana that you have already developed in the context of repaying beings' kindness, you should see that the difference between the wish to repay kindness and altruistic intention is like the difference between thinking you would like to buy a certain item and deciding to do it—a fine distinction that must be made.

Exchanging self and others

Since the sevenfold cause-and-effect instruction includes everything that is found in Śāntideva's tradition and only differs in the way the instruction is given, it is not strictly necessary to teach both, provided the former has been trained in well. [211] However, owing to the variety of disciples' mental capacity, the *Great* and *Middle-Length* treatises explain each tradition, for which reason it is customary to teach both.

Regarding exchanging self and others, founded in the works of the bodhisattva Śāntideva, *Guide to the Bodhisattva Way* states:

> Whoever wishes to quickly protect
> himself and others
> should exchange self for others
> and practice the secret instruction.[512]

And:

> Whatever happiness there is in the world
> derives from wanting others' happiness.
> Whatever misery there is in the world
> derives from wanting personal happiness.

What need is there to say much?
The childish pursue their personal goals.
The Sage accomplishes others' goals.
Note the difference between the two!

If I fail to exchange completely
my happiness for others' suffering,
I will not attain buddhahood
nor know any joy in samsara.[513]

Since cherishing yourself is the source of all suffering and cherishing others the source of all goodness and happiness, it is important to contemplate this. Do not imagine that since you are now incapable of tolerating the slightest inconvenience, you can never generate an attitude as lofty as exchanging self and others. [*Guide to the Bodhisattva Way*] continues:

Do not turn away from this difficulty,
for by the power of familiarization,
those whose name alone used to frighten you when heard
become those from whom you cannot bear to be parted.[514]

Your aversion to those you initially see as hostile enemies, whose sight alone repulses and terrifies you, later, after a reconciliation, can become strong attraction. Similarly, through familiarization, you can invert your feelings about yourself and others.

In practice, "exchanging self and others" does not mean that Devadatta, for example, should think he is Yajñadatta but that Devadatta, instead of cherishing himself, should cherish the other person, Yajñadatta, and that instead of neglecting the other person, Yajñadatta, he should neglect himself. That cognitive process is what is called "exchanging self and others."

To actually cultivate the exchange of self and others, think, "Until now I have cherished myself and pursued my own goals, and that has only brought me misery," and train so that you come to see yourself the way you have been viewing others. It is taught that training in transposing your self-cherishing to others, by the force of habit, will allow you to invert the objects of your present cherishing and neglect. [212]

To facilitate this, as explained in the *Seven-Point Mind Training*,[515] the *Precious Garland* says you are to make these wishes:

May I experience the effects of their sins!
May they experience the effects of all my virtue![516]

Giving-and-taking as indicated here has been the main practice of past masters. As before, it involves visualizing your mother in front of you. With intense compassion for her, while you exhale straight from your right nostril, you think that all the imperfect virtue and happiness that you carry within you ride upon your breath and enter your mother through her left nostril. As they permeate her body, she experiences superior joy. You then inhale through your left nostril, thinking that the air brings with it all your mother's sins, obscurations, and suffering. They enter and gather as dark mass in your heart. You think, "My mother is now entirely free of suffering and has found happiness." You are to train in this repeatedly, alternating the two. You then do the same in relation to your father of this life, your loved ones, neutral beings, and enemies as well as the beings of each of the six realms. Although you may as yet lack such great strength of mind, it is said that by the force of habit, you will gradually come to be able to give away more and more from your food, clothing, and bed up to your head and limbs and so on, fearlessly.

Stanzas between sections

Diligently cultivating utter disgust
with samsara's endless great ocean of suffering,
some of you climb the precious staircase of the three trainings
and enter the house of personal peace and happiness.

You see beings, your mothers who helped you in many lives,
inside the terrible prison of samsaric suffering,
where they weep and wail, and yet
you dare abandon them—who could be more unscrupulous
than you?

With the awareness of the kindness of all beings seen as your parents
and fierce gales of love and compassion,
the ship of altruistic intention bearing the great load of others' welfare
will take you straight to the jewel isle of omniscience.

Even bitter enemies, those who are like thorns in your heart,

will come to be seen as your dear friends and loved ones [213]
through the kind thought to equalize and exchange self and others.
Cut the root of the deluded attitude that is bias!

Once the self-cherishing attitude is forsaken,
the key that is repaying harm with kindness
will instantly open the door to happiness and benefit:
the effortless achievement of the two aims. O wondrous good fortune!

Committing to the Awakening Mind in a Ceremony

Once you have trained well in the state of mind explained above that includes both the aspiration to others' welfare and the aspiration to enlightenment, if you do not then rely on a ceremony, you will just generate the nature of the awakening mind [and not formalize it]. An excellent ceremony is important to enter the perfect path. You should refer to the *Great* and *Middle-Length* treatises for the preliminaries to the practice (taking refuge, accumulating merit, and cultivating the awakening mind), its main part (upholding aspirational bodhicitta in a ceremony), and the final phase (the explanation of the precepts that prevent the awakening mind's decline in this and future lives).[517] Since knowing all the details of the practice depends on having participated in its transmission, be sure to avoid personal invention and oversimplification.

Furthermore, the *Life of Maitreya* states:

> Although you may not be able to train in the practices of conquerors' sons, you will draw immense benefits from simply generating the awakening mind.[518]

However, the *Exposition of Valid Cognition* says:

> The Compassionate One directly showed
> the methods for overcoming suffering.
> If the causes of the methods' effects are unclear,
> it will be difficult for you to explain them.[519]

The purpose in generating aspirational bodhicitta by the altruistic intention that is inspired by great compassion is not just to have the kind thought, "I wish all beings were free of suffering." The methods are to be applied. This requires first making the bodhisattva precepts that are the means to attain buddhahood your core practice. *Guide to the Bodhisattva Way* states:

Just as you know the difference
between wanting to travel and traveling,
in the same way, O sages,
learn step by step the difference between these two.[520] [214]

The distinction between aspirational and engaging bodhicittas is established taking the example of wanting to travel to a country versus endeavoring to reach it. When by training thoroughly you have achieved an initial experience of aspirational bodhicitta, you should listen to an explanation of the precepts of bodhisattva vows. Once you have a good understanding of the benefits of training in the six perfections and so on, the drawbacks of not training in them, the primary and secondary transgressions, and the rest, generate very intense and uncontrived diligence for the practices of adoption and rejection relative to them. Then receive the bodhisattva vows in the ceremony that combines the two great trailblazers' traditions. The practices of abstention from the primary and secondary transgressions and of restoration [of damaged vows] are explained in detail in the *Ethics Chapter*.[521] The Great Lord [Tsongkhapa] in his *Great* and *Middle-Length* treatises advises referring to this work, as does *Essence of Refined Gold*.

At this point the current custom is to defer the topic of taking the vows of engaging bodhicitta and instead give an experiential presentation of the six perfections and so on. You may question its validity, as it differs from the sequence in which the great treatises explain aspirational and engaging bodhicittas and the six perfections. In fact, these important works present this order for those who generate the qualities in that manner; it is not certain however that everyone is capable of doing the same. Among those who have yet to enter the path, some take the bodhisattva vows, and later, when they realize aspirational bodhicitta, attain the lower level of the path of accumulation. They generate engaging bodhicitta on reaching the path of accumulation's middle level, when their aspirational bodhicitta evolves into engaging bodhicitta. Then there are those who, by realizing aspirational bodhicitta, enter the path of accumulation without having taken the bodhisattva vows. Their attainment of the middle level of the path of accumulation coincides with their generation of engaging bodhicitta. It is also possible to take bodhisattva vows at the end of the middle level.

Since there is no definitive order, the *Compendium of Training* says, "For this reason, according to your ability, commit yourself well to at least one virtue and sustain it."[522] Having generated aspirational bodhicitta, you might find yourself incapable before long of upholding all its precepts. For this reason, it is advised to train progressively, according to your mental capacity, starting with one virtue, for example; in this way, in the end, you will be able to train in all bodhisattva deeds. [215] It is with this idea in mind that the six perfections are explained following the way to maintain aspirational bodhicitta by a ceremony.

You might wonder if carrying on from this point and completing all the topics of meditation up to tranquil abiding and special insight without taking bodhisattva vows does not contradict the terms of the ceremony. Indeed, all the teachings on the previous topics—the sevenfold cause-and-effect instruction and so on—are *bases* for achieving genuine spiritual experiences; they are for concordant spiritual experiences alone, not genuine ones. Similarly, the explanations of the six perfections are given for the purpose of providing the bases for creating propensities for an inner experience of bodhisattva practice. Past masters gave experiential teachings on the three beings' paths over a period of between one month and a year, but here it is different. Take the example of repeatedly cultivating great compassion, which can induce a genuine altruistic intention, until it truly arises in you. If "experiential teachings" must mean doing the same for all practices, starting with the way to rely on spiritual teachers and up to tranquil abiding and insight, it would mean practicing with great effort for a very long time, and it would be impossible to achieve effortlessly in a short life of the degenerate age. As a result, when I said above that the bodhicitta resulting from the sevenfold cause-and-effect instruction is the aspiration to enlightenment required to initiate a period of three countless eons [of accumulation], I was referring to genuine bodhicitta. Confusing it with [just] having received an explanation of bodhicitta according to the stages of this path and doing the meditations and the ceremony for maintaining bodhicitta, and then proudly imagining yourself a bodhisattva on the path of accumulation, would be the epitome of ignorance. Please understand this! For these reasons, it is explained that when you have yet to enter the path, hastily taking the vows of engaging bodhicitta in these times when afflictions abound, their antidotes are weak, and you cannot guard yourself from primary and secondary transgressions and the rest will entail grave consequences, for you will be deceiving the entire world—buddhas, bodhisattvas, and gods alike. Holy direct and lineage masters have adapted their teachings to the mental capacities of their disciples, as they are aware that the risks can be great for relatively little benefit. [216]

Stanzas between sections

From the shoots of an [initial] experience arisen from learning
that are matured by the heat and moisture of the rigors [of reflection and meditation]
issues the ripe fruit of valid realizations.
This is the sole path traveled by three vehicles' āryas and non-āryas.

When the sharp weapons of adverse circumstances befall them,
their assurance that all beings are their parents dies,
yet with the nectar of compassion, they still attain the immortality of altruistic intention!
Such "bodhisattvas" are [as plausible as] sky lotuses.

The journey on the Mahayana path is as great as the sky,
the teachings of Indian and Tibetan scholars are as deep as the sea,
present-day beings' intelligence is as obscure as the dark,
and the discernment of most proud scholars is as thin as grass.

For these reasons, the magic fingers of these good teachings
unravel the knot of difficulty for the sake of those less intelligent,
and for the intelligent, the treasury of the throat cakra[523]
[provides] an inexhaustible supply of wish-granting objects.[524]

Bodhisattva Practice

Introduction

The second part is on how to train in bodhisattva practice once you have generated the awakening mind, concerning which the *Ornament of Mahayana Sutras* explains:

> A fortunate rebirth with excellent resources and body,
> an excellent entourage, and excellent endeavors,
> never letting these cause afflictions,
> and not erring in one's activities.[525]

Completing the vast activities of a bodhisattva requires a long series of [good] rebirths. Moreover, your practice of the path will be much more effective if your resources, body, entourage, ability to complete what you undertake, and so on are excellent; if you do not let afflictions develop in relation to them; and if you are familiar with the key points regarding what to adopt and reject. Thus, in relation to fortunate rebirths, the number [of perfections] is certain.[526]

Concerning what is to be accomplished in such a rebirth, three perfections are devoted to others' welfare—generosity, ethical discipline, and forbearance—and three to one's personal welfare—wisdom, meditative absorption, and diligence. Thus, in terms of accomplishing the two aims, the number is certain.

It is also certain from the perspective of fully accomplishing others' welfare, relieving poverty with material goods, [practicing] nonviolence by refraining from harming others, not repaying harm with harm, not being discouraged by the hardships involved in accomplishing others' welfare, inspiring others by displaying supernormal powers and so on, and overcoming their doubts and liberating them with sound explanations. [217]

Their number is certain as well with respect to encompassing the entire Mahayana: since you are not attached to material possessions, you observe the precepts; as you are forbearing in the face of suffering induced by others' errors, you delight in virtue; and since thanks to tranquil abiding your mind and body are serviceable, your wisdom of special insight develops.

Relative to all kinds of methods their number is certain: habituating yourself to giving is the method to prevent attachment to belongings; guarding yourself from carelessness is the way to avoid being distracted by acquisitiveness; accepting suffering is how you avoid abandoning sentient beings; joyously persevering without discouragement is the means to increase virtue; mental and physical pliancy are the methods to eliminate the afflictions; and detailed analysis is the way to discard the obstructions to omniscience.

From the point of view of the three trainings the number is certain: ethical discipline that is accompanied by generosity and forbearance is by nature the training in ethical discipline; the last two perfections are by nature the other two trainings; and diligence is needed for all three.

If you have generosity that is indifferent to belongings, from the cause that is nonattachment, ethical discipline arises; if you have ethical discipline, from the cause that is abstention from wrongdoing, forbearance arises; if you have forbearance, from the cause that is non-discouragement in the face of hardship, diligence arises; if you have diligence, from the cause that is striving day and night, meditative absorption arises; if you have absorption, from the cause that is a serviceable mind, wisdom arises.

Among the six perfections, the preceding perfections are inferior to the subsequent, and the subsequent are superior to the preceding; they are respectively coarse and subtle as well. The *Ornament of Mahayana Sutras* states:

> As the subsequent [perfections] arise based on the preceding,
> as they are respectively inferior and superior,
> and as they are [relatively] coarser and more subtle,
> they were taught in that order.[527]

The six perfections

Training in bodhisattva practice—the Mahayana paths whose number is in this way certain—has two parts: training in the six perfections to mature your mindstream and training in the four means of gathering others to mature their mindstream. The first, training in the six perfections to mature your mindstream, has six parts: generosity, ethical discipline, forbearance, diligence, meditative absorption, and wisdom. [218]

The perfection of generosity

The perfection of generosity is by nature a bodhisattva's nonattachment that does not care for body and belongings, any intentions concurrent with it, as well as the physical and verbal karmas of fully giving the things to be given that they motivate. How is the perfection of generosity completed by such giving? As physical and verbal karmas—intentions—are of prime importance, overcoming stinginess regarding belongings and so on is insufficient because that is something that śrāvaka and pratyekabuddha arhats also achieve. Here, by reflecting on the benefits and drawbacks, you must develop the heartfelt intention to give. The *Garland of Birth Stories* says:

> This body has no essence and no self and is easily destroyed;
> it is [by nature] suffering, mean, and always unclean.
> Whoever fails to delight in using such a body
> to help others lacks wisdom.[528]

If you imagine that the perfection of generosity is fully accomplished when, by giving things, sentient beings' poverty is ended, *Guide to the Bodhisattva Way* states:

> Were generosity perfected
> by ending beings' poverty,
> then since beings are still indigent,
> how could past protectors have completed it?[529]

As this suggests, since today countless beings are still poor, the implication would be that past buddhas had not fully accomplished the perfection of generosity. In fact, the perfection of generosity is complete familiarization with the thought to give everything to others—belongings and virtue, along with the results of giving—wholeheartedly and free of stinginess. [*Guide to the Bodhisattva Way* says]:

> The wish to give to all beings
> all belongings along with the results of giving
> is taught to be the perfection of generosity;
> consequently, it is a state of mind.[530] [219]

Regarding the practice of the perfection of generosity just described, Geshé Sharawa says:

> I am not explaining the benefits of giving to you. I am explaining the drawbacks of withholding.[531]

It is unsuitable for ordained bodhisattvas to give only material goods acquired after considerable effort and fatigue, for it interferes with their three activities: learning, reflection, and meditation. They should emphasize giving the Dharma. Free of attachment, they should also give the goods they acquire readily and easily, but mainly lay bodhisattvas are to give these.

Once you have thoroughly determined the ways to practice generosity in general, as well as exceptions depending on the status of the giver, you are to reject all the following attitudes when practicing giving Dharma, protection, and material goods: maintaining the superiority of bad views such as thinking that practicing the three kinds of generosity produces no results, thinking that giving wrongly[532] is a practice, protecting one being while forsaking countless others, and thinking that giving flesh and blood resulting from killing is a spiritual practice. You should avoid scorning the beneficiaries of your generosity; competitiveness; conceit by which you think, "No one conveys the Dharma with such deep meaning and eloquence, protects as many sentient beings, or gives as nice things as I do"; hoping for renown—that people will comment, "He was generous in all three ways"; discouragement that makes you feel unable to give much; regret for having given; partiality that makes you generous in all three ways to your friends but not your enemies and the like; expecting to be thanked for teaching the Dharma and protecting lives; hoping for gold in return for silver; and hoping for maturation effects like being knowledgeable and fearless and having excellent belongings in the future.

The *Condensed Presentation of the Perfections* says:

> When directly approached by a person requesting something,
> bodhisattvas, to increase their collections for complete
>   enlightenment,
> identify their [possessions] as belonging to others
> and regard the person as their spiritual teacher.[533]

The way to view the purpose is to think, "In this way may I complete the perfection of generosity." The way to view your things is to think, "Since from the start I gave all my Dharma, ability to protect others, and belongings to others, now it is like borrowing the things I have entrusted to others [to give them again]." [220] The way to view the recipients is to think, "These people are like spiritual teachers; thanks to them I will complete my perfection of generosity." These are the three specific thoughts to have when being generous.

As to how to give, giving should not be sullied by untoward faults such as concealing profound teachings and giving easier ones; giving only partial protection when you can protect from all fears; giving things of inferior quality, few things, or things you have taken from others by force. Give with an open and friendly expression, speak in a pleasant manner that is free of any hostility toward others, and accept the hardship involved.

Ten kinds of recipients are taught: enemies, friends, neutral beings, those with good qualities, those with shortcomings, superiors, inferiors, equals, the happy, and the wretched. In sum, as the list includes all beings, the point is to identify them individually and to adapt your attitude to each—to love your enemies, admire those with many good qualities, and so on.

Giving the Dharma is teaching, according to your knowledge, the Buddha's sacred words of both the Great and Lesser Vehicles, the commentaries, and the ordinary sciences—grammar, logic, technology, medicine, and so on—with a genuinely altruistic intention. It includes conferring vows and so on consistent with the capacity of those listening. You should also make the wish, "Once they have studied, reflected, and meditated on these, may they accomplish much for the sake of others and for their sake!" After teaching the Dharma, the tradition of authentic spiritual teachers is to dedicate the virtue created. Furthermore, you may not be known as a teacher, but if your friends or others are involved in wrongdoing or nonvirtue, you can point out their errors, explain to them what to adopt and what to reject, and have them stop it and accomplish virtue instead. In this way, with the three specific thoughts,[534] truly strive to give the Dharma.

If you have no one to whom to be generous in this manner, imagine that you are teaching the perfect Dharma to all sentient beings and that they thereby benefit greatly from this gift. You can visualize, for example, that hearing the teaching frees hell beings of suffering and its causes, and you can make excellent prayers on their behalf. [221]

[*Giving protection from fears*:] Similarly, if you have the power to do so directly, you should protect sentient beings from the fears of being sentenced to death by a political leader, the fears of having their body, belongings, and their very life harmed by wild animals or enemies, and from the fears of fire, floods, and the like. If you lack that ability, you can explain to others how to overcome these. Since there are countless beings in other realms undergoing such sufferings, think from the depths of your heart that you provide them with the gift of protection and that thanks to this their terrors cease. Imagine that, empowered by generating the aspiration to enlightenment, you mentally emanate heavy rains that fall on the hot hells and extinguish its fires, or you wish for it to happen.

As for *giving material gifts*, with the three specific thoughts in mind, you give food, beverages, beds, medicine for the sick, fine silks and gems, horses and elephants, land, buildings, domains, fields, your eyes, head, major and secondary limbs—in other words, your entire body—and all your belongings. When you are hungry and poor yourself and cannot manage this, imagine that you emanate large quantities of food, both raw and cooked, and give it to hungry ghosts and other beings suffering from starvation, thanks to which their deprivation ends. You are to adapt what you give to the recipients. Wise bodhisattvas practice generosity by emanating these extensively.

From now on, as much as you are able, try to actually accomplish the three practices of generosity just explained—teaching the Dharma starting from as little as four lines, showing those suffering from the heat where they can find shelter, giving food and clothes to the poor, and the like. It is taught that if you are capable of these but you content yourself with just doing visualizations, you are deceiving yourself.

Having ascertained what I explained above, carefully check whether you are stingy due to attachment to the things to be given, whether you tend to think, "Since I do not have many belongings myself, I cannot give any away," or whether you are particularly attached to beautiful things. To curb these inappropriate attitudes, reflect repeatedly as follows:

> Although in the past I was born countless times in high states as the child of Vaiśravaṇa and the like and in low states as a hungry ghost and so on, this is the state I am in now. [222] While I often acquired things, like wish-granting gems, that were far superior to what I own now, I have lost them all.

If you have a real intention to give but it is most often in the hope of receiving something in return or with expectations regarding the maturation effect, continuously inspire yourself thinking:

> Although in the past I made offerings and was generous countless times and, as a result, attained the states of Īśvara, Brahmā, and so on, it was all in vain. Now when I give so much as a morsel of food, I will dedicate it in such a way that it becomes a cause of supreme enlightenment.

During meditation sessions, be sure to visualize giving in the three ways by emanating gifts mentally. Between sessions endeavor to actually give, and familiarize yourself with the idea of giving.

You may wonder whether you are to practice giving in the three ways to the maximum of your ability, but this is not necessarily the case. *Guide to the Bodhisattva Way* explains:

> Without powerful compassion,
> do not give away your body,
> or if you do, give it to accomplish important goals
> for this and future lives.[535]

From the perspective of time, purpose, and recipient, it is inappropriate to give away your body until your compassion is so great that it defuses the painful austerity of cutting off your flesh; nor is it right to give it for a limited purpose, to demons who intend to cause harm, or when someone like a madman begs you for it. This is how to determine whether to give away your body.

Regarding external factors, it is unfitting from a temporal perspective to teach the Mahayana to those of very inferior capacity and to offer food to monastics in the evening. When it comes to the recipient, it is inappropriate to give meat, alcohol, garlic, onions, leftovers, and unclean food to those observing vows, to give animals to people who are very likely to harm them, to give harmful food to sick people, and to give books to those who see them only for their monetary value or to those who just want to test you. Regarding the objects given, it is not right to give servants away if it would make them unhappy by going against their wishes.

Giving that is unsuitable in terms of purpose is, for example, providing criminals protection from the fear of incarceration by releasing them from prison, as it would make many people suffer, or giving poison, weapons, and so on when those seeking them have malevolent intentions.

Once you have carefully studied the general principles and the particular cases, reflect as follows: "Since I am doomed to die soon, [223] the things I could give away will let me down, and I too will have to give them up; as such they are utterly futile." In this way cultivate a heartfelt intention to give.

Stanzas between sections

By giving body and belongings, with an intense wish to give,
to beings whose kindness cannot be repaid,

I achieve over endless periods of time
a store of inexhaustible wealth—the jewel of stable happiness.

Moreover, the endless suffering of poverty
does not befall me alone.
It is the lot of all mother sentient beings as well.
Upon reflection, the thought of it is unbearable.

Having committed scores of dark deeds in the past,
such is the situation I find myself in now.
Once I have completed the perfection of generosity,
I pray that I may liberate boundless beings.

The Perfection of Ethical Discipline

Guide to the Bodhisattva Way states:

> Where could fish and the like
> be sent to escape being killed?
> It is said that ethical discipline is perfected
> by achieving the intention to abstain.[536]

Ethical discipline is the intention to abstain that is desisting from harming others and from the thought to harm others. The perfection of ethical discipline is gradual and increasing familiarization with this intention until it is complete. It does not depend on all sentient beings having been freed of harm.

On the [bodhisattva] ethical discipline of abstention from wrongdoing, *Lamp on the Path to Enlightenment* states:

> Those who maintain [one of] the seven vows for individual liberation
> other than the [bodhisattva] vows
> have the good fortune to take bodhisattva vows,
> while others do not.[537]

Some misinterpret this and say that it means one must have prātimokṣa vows [before taking the bodhisattva precepts]. However, there are gods [who lack prātimokṣa vows] who have a valid basis for training in bodhisattva precepts. [224] The *Commentary on Lamp on the Path* explains this saying, "Now I would like to describe the *superior* basis for [bodhisattva] vows of ethical discipline."[538] It is therefore incorrect to assert that [the *Lamp*] is referring to a universal basis and not a superior one.

How is this category of ethical discipline to be identified? When those having prātimokṣa vows train in bodhisattva precepts, the vow of abstention concordant with their actual vow for personal liberation[539] in the present context is identified as the bodhisattva ethical discipline of abstention. For those who do not have a prātimokṣa vow, the vow of abstention that is avoidance of the ten nonvirtues and is concordant with the vows for personal liberation is identified as the [bodhisattva] *ethical discipline of abstention from wrongdoing.* The *Condensed Presentation of the Perfections* states:

> Do not let the ten karmic paths decline,
> for they are the easy path to high rebirth and liberation.
> By sustaining them with the superior attitude
> that is the wish to benefit beings, you attain the result [bodhisattva vows].[540]

If you are ordained, you must repeatedly check with mindfulness and meta-awareness whether you have been sullied by the primary and secondary transgressions you promised in the presence of your preceptor to abstain from. When you do not have a prātimokṣa vow, you are to verify whether you have committed any of the ten nonvirtues explained above in the path of persons of lesser capacity.

According to the custom of past Kadam masters, you are to note daily the virtues and sins you accomplish using black and white stones. After calculation, you rejoice when you find more white stones than black and feel great remorse when there are more black than white. In sessions, first you confess the sins that mindfulness and meta-awareness catch, consistent with the number of black stones, and do restoration practice applying all four remedial powers. You are also to think and repeat, "May I complete the perfection of ethical discipline!"

When strong feelings of attachment arise in relation to objects of desire, do not give them free rein but curb them by contemplating their unattractiveness and recalling the drawbacks of wrongdoing. Having reflected on the consequences of whichever affliction is strongest, apply its remedies. By these meditations, you will achieve pure ethical discipline. Although by nature the way to abstain from the ten nonvirtues is similar for each of the three kinds of persons,[541] the motivation specific to each differentiates them.

The *ethical discipline of collecting virtue* consists of any physical or verbal virtue performed by those possessing the bodhisattva vows: cultivating the three trainings,[542] honoring any superior fields of action such as gurus, extolling the Three Jewels, expressing delight in others' virtues, viewing harm done to you as the outcome of your past karma, dedicating virtue and making aspirational prayers, presenting offerings to the Three Jewels, practicing virtue conscientiously and continuously, guarding the doors of the senses from afflictions, eating in moderation, practicing diligently at the beginning and the end of the night, applying antidotes while relying on spiritual teachers or being your own guide if you have not found any, and confessing your transgressions to superior beings. [225] States of concentration are cultivated during meditation sessions, and preparations for making offerings to the Three Jewels and so on are done between sessions. In both contexts you must exercise conscientiousness, meta-awareness, and so on. The time for welcoming gurus, preparing their seats, and so on is indeterminate. According to the present tradition, in relation to all the above-mentioned practices, during sessions you engage in either analytical or placement meditations, whichever is appropriate.

The *ethical discipline of helping sentient beings* consists in bodhisattvas' assistance to sentient beings. Eleven aspects are taught. (1a) In blameless ways, showing others how to prevent thieves stealing their belongings is helping those that need help in their activities. (1b) Providing the sick with medicine and the lame with transport to their destination are examples of helping those who are suffering. (2) Showing people how to reject wrongdoing by teaching the Dharma is an example of helping those who are unaware of the methods. (3) Providing hospitality and so on is helping those who have been helpful. (4) Protecting beings from harm by the likes of lions and tigers is helping those who are frightened. (5) Alleviating the distress of those who have lost their parents, had their belongings stolen by thieves and brigands, and so on by explaining about impermanence is helping those who are grieving. (6) Giving tasty food to those in want of it is an example of helping the poor. (7) Giving clothes adapted to a person's religious status, explaining ugliness to people who have attachment, and so on is helping those wishing to live in a community. (8) When you encounter those who you fail to guide to virtue, refraining from physically or verbally indicating your disapproval and instead benefiting them [by adapting to them] is helping those who wish to befriend you. [226] (9) Praising good qualities such as ethical discipline is helping those who are practicing well. (10) Punishing the sinful, for example, is helping those engaged in wrongdoing. (11) Deterring others from sin by producing visions of hell realms, for example, or creating various magical displays to inspire others is helping disciples by means of supernormal powers.

There are many variables; you may or may not be capable of all eleven, and it may or may not be the appropriate time for them. Nevertheless, you should practice them during sessions using analytical meditations. It is key to not content yourself with just enumerating them. The *Condensed Presentation of the Perfections* states:

> If you cannot achieve personal goals because your ethics have declined,
> how will you ever be able to accomplish others' aims?
> For that reason, while striving well for others' sake,
> value [your ethics] and prevent their transgression.[543]

It is taught that ethical discipline is the very root of achieving the two aims. As such, I ask you to apply the methods to increase your familiarization with the ethical discipline of rejecting ill will and harm toward others.

Stanzas between sections

In the garden of a life with excellent leisure and opportunity
are wish-granting trees, the three kinds of ethical discipline,
bowing under a great load of fruit, nirvana,
that drips with luscious juices of happiness and benefit.

The numerous acts of generosity collected over countless eons
are pure virtues for attaining wealth,
but experiencing their results in a divine or human rebirth or failing to do so
depends entirely on ethical discipline.

So when the cart, a good rebirth attained just this once,
gets stuck through carelessness in the mire of transgressions,
those who fail to drag it by restoration practice onto the broad expanse of happiness
and instead remain idle must indeed be possessed by the devil [of ignorance].

The Perfection of Forbearance

Guide to the Bodhisattva Way states:

> Unruly beings are [as infinite] as space,
> I cannot possibly overcome them all.
> If I could just overcome my anger,
> I will have overcome all my foes.
>
> Where could I ever find enough leather
> to cover the entire surface of the earth?
> With just the leather of the soles of my shoes,
> I will have covered the surface of the earth.
>
> Similarly, I cannot possibly control
> all external [harmful] elements,
> but once I have come to control my mind,
> what need is there to control anything else?[544] [227]

The perfection of forbearance is accomplished once familiarization with the intention to halt anger and so on toward sentient beings is complete. It is not necessary that all beings be free of their unruly states of mind. Śāntideva states:

> All the good deeds accomplished
> and collected over a thousand eons
> by acts of generosity, homage to the sugatas, and the like
> are destroyed by a moment's anger.[545]

Even the Sarvāstivādin texts state that anger toward a superior being destroys virtuous roots. Specifically, *Entering the Middle Way* states:

> Since anger toward a bodhisattva
> destroys in an instant the virtue collected
> by giving and ethical discipline over a hundred eons,
> there is no greater sin than anger.[546]

It is taught that if the anger of a less spiritually advanced bodhisattva toward a more advanced bodhisattva can destroy a hundred eons worth of virtues, then the anger of an ordinary being who is not a bodhisattva toward one is extremely grave: it renders a thousand eons' worth of virtues unfruitful and so on. Anger arises in us at the slightest provocation, without the least effort. As for the objects of anger, bodhisattvas are like coals covered in ash in that we cannot know for sure where they are, which is how we have obliterated our virtue in the past and why anger is definitely the root of all our troubles. Śāntideva continues:

> Whoever strives then defeats anger
> finds happiness now and hereafter.[547]

Renouncing anger not only delivers from short-term mental and physical suffering, it also brings happiness in all lives. Therefore, with determination, think, "I will train in the perfection of forbearance."

First visualize a malevolent person who is hurting you now, or if there isn't one, someone who harmed you in the past. Once this has prompted red-hot anger in you, observe it and reflect:

> *Guide to the Bodhisattva Way* states:
>
> > If, under the sway of the afflictions,
> > I can be led to take my own dear life,
> > under the circumstances
> > how could I avoid physically harming another
> > person?[548] [228]
>
> Clearly a strong affliction like loathing for someone can make you commit suicide by stabbing yourself, jumping off a cliff, and so on. I cherish myself, and you would think that would make me incapable of hurting myself, but under the sway of an affliction, that is exactly what I can be led to do. In this situation, I would not get angry with myself, so when others cannot help but hurt me when they too are swayed by strong afflictions, why should I get angry with them? I may object that these harmful people must be able to control themselves because, for example, they do not hurt their friends, but in fact it is out of attachment that they protect their friends. If beings were free, since they all want

> to avoid suffering, for sure there would be no one left who was tormented by it.

By this reflection, it is said that you will come to see malicious people the same way you do someone impelled by a political leader to go and inflict harm on others.

Moreover, if it is in a person's nature to harm and he does so, it is like faulting fire for being hot and burning. If the harm is adventitious, then getting angry with the person is just as unreasonable as getting angry with the sky when its clouds obscure the sun. In fact, it is the weapon like a club that hurts you directly, and indirectly it is the anger that incites its use. So why blame the person? If you want to direct your anger to the root cause of your injury, then recall that the injury is the outcome of similar harm that you inflicted on others in the past. As *Guide to the Bodhisattva Way* states:

> In the past I have inflicted
> similar injury on sentient beings;
> thus, as an abuser of others,
> it is only right that I am harmed now.[549]

Moreover, think:

> If I cannot put up with even minor wrongs like being criticized or physically injured by harmful people, then since I have created so many causes for rebirth in unfortunate realms, how will I be able to stand the suffering once I am born in a hell?

In this way, feel disgusted again and again with the faults you see in yourself. Reflect:

> When water falls in water, both can only be wet. Likewise, both my body and weapons are sources of suffering, so it is only natural that I feel pain. [229] If even śrāvakas, who pursue their own welfare, do not get angry, how could it be right for me to get angry—I who know that all beings are my parents and who have generated bodhicitta to achieve their welfare?

It is taught that this meditation brings physical and mental comfort.

If you still relish others' praise, implicitly you dislike their criticism. *Guide to the Bodhisattva Way* states:

> Praise and the honors of renown
> will not increase my merit or lengthen my life,
> they will not boost my strength or ensure my good health,
> nor will they secure my physical well-being.[550]

Not only do praise and fame fail to increase happiness in future lives, they do not even do it in this life. They also lead to many problems: they cause pointless distraction and make others jealous. [On the other hand] by the decline of your reputation, others will not harm you in the short run, and in the long run, by avoiding distraction, you will achieve buddhahood. You should think therefore, "This [loss of reputation] will bring great happiness; it is the buddhas' blessing," and feel glad.

Reflect that if you are struck by something like a sharp weapon, it may be painful physically, but it does not affect your mind; as for verbal abuse, it hurts you neither physically nor mentally.

Although with these meditations you may succeed in remaining equanimous in the face of praise and scorn, you might still suddenly feel that you cannot bear the thought of your enemies' advantages. Concerning this, *Guide to the Bodhisattva Way* states:

> Even if an enemy is unhappy,
> why should you be pleased?
> For your simple wishes
> do not suffice to cause him harm.
>
> Even if your wish for his suffering were fulfilled,
> why should that please you?
> If your answer is, "It will gratify me,"
> what could be more despicable?
>
> Once caught on the dreadful, sharp hook
> cast by fishermen—the afflictions—
> infernal guardians are sure to cook you
> in the cauldrons of hell.[551]

Think the following to generate a strong wish to avoid anger:

> It is pointless for me to be annoyed because a person has found happiness, and how would my getting angry with him harm him? If it did, by the karma we both create, we will end up roasting in hell.

Reflect:

> Although I may manage in this way to apply the antidotes to the anger that I feel toward those who harm me, I wonder, could I bear it if misfortune suddenly befell me? [230] In fact, if there is nothing to be done about a problem, getting angry is futile and ineffective. If something can be done about it, then it should be done, and there is no point in getting angry. So now when I am faced with unwanted suffering, I will see it as the result of my nonvirtuous deeds of past lives. In this life, if I did not experience painful feelings like these, I would never adopt and reject what I should, and I would just continue turning in the endless round of cyclic existence. Moreover, since suffering helps to generate disgust with samsara, which in turn is the basis for achieving liberation and nirvana, it is a real blessing. Just as undergoing painful and invasive medical treatments like surgery and cauterization eases a painful illness, experiencing sufferings in this life, like those you endure when you are struck with a sickness, can replace having to take rebirth later in the Relentless hell.

Having ensured that you gain a spiritual experience of the above during meditation sessions, between sessions accept the suffering involved in cultivating pure conduct, like wearing clothes made from rags from the refuse heap. Accept the suffering brought on by worldly concerns—praise and scorn and so on. Accept the suffering that conduct such as not lying down involves. Accept the suffering involved in thoroughly upholding the teaching, like making offerings to the Three Jewels. Accept the suffering involved in living by mendicancy—having an unattractive physical appearance, inferior clothing, and so on and giving up sense pleasures like singing and dancing. Accept the suffering of fatigue from diligently accomplishing virtue. Accept the suffering involved in helping sentient beings by protecting their lives and so on.

Accept the suffering relative to concerns of this life, like giving up business and so on. Be sure to accustom yourself to the idea of accepting those you cannot as yet fully accept. *Guide to the Bodhisattva Way* states:

> There is nothing at all
> that does not become easier through habit.
> Thus, through habituation to minor problems,
> you will come to bear great ones as well.[552]

By progressive habituation, you will in the end be able to put up with anything and complete the perfection of forbearance.

STANZAS BETWEEN SECTIONS [231]

The forest of virtue produced over many lives
is reduced to ashes by a single blaze of anger.
The pile of charred tree trunks of nonvirtue it leaves reaches as high as the peak of existence.
This enemy, anger, is the source of all suffering!

Irresistibly impelled by karma and afflictions, from the peak of a steep mountain,
the results of nonvirtue plummet us downward.
How can you dispute the fact
that those residing in samsara's abyss are overcome [by suffering]?[553]

When facing the aligned troops of suffering's origins in battle,
if you don the sturdy armor of forbearance,
you will not be pierced when struck by the sharp weapons of harsh words.
In this way you will travel to nirvana; its benefits are marvelous indeed!

The Perfection of Diligence

Guide to the Bodhisattva Way states, "What is diligence? It is delight in virtue."[554] The perfection of diligence is the development of authentic delight in collecting virtue and working to benefit sentient beings until it is utterly complete. The *Ornament of Mahayana Sutras* states:

> Among [the ways to] collect virtue, diligence is supreme.
> Based on it, all good qualities are attained.
> With diligence, you achieve excellent happiness in this life,
> and both mundane and supermundane attainments.
>
> With diligence, you gain the enjoyments of this world that you desire.
> With diligence, you are endowed with excellent moral purity.
> With diligence, you transcend [the view of] the personal identity.
> With diligence, you achieve the supreme enlightenment of
> buddhahood.[555]

Diligence is the source of all mundane and supermundane happiness and goodness. To practice it, to start there is *armor-like diligence*. Counting a thousand great eons as one day, thirty of these as a month, and twelve of those as a year, armor-like diligence is the thought "I will not give up diligence even when I realize that attaining buddhahood requires remaining in the hells alone for up to a trillion great eons made up of such years for the purpose of ending a single being's suffering. [232] It goes without saying then that I will not do it for shorter periods." Such is armor-like diligence. Counting the time from beginningless samsara until now as one day, and calculating months and years accordingly, even if it took a hundred thousand of such years to generate the awakening mind once and see a single buddha, and as many of such years as there are grains of sand in the Ganges River to know the mind and behavior of a single being, and you had to do the same for each being, the fact of not feeling that it was too long and delighting in it is said to be sublime [armor-like] diligence. You should think:

> As before in the context of generosity, just as getting used to being generous in thought and in deed, starting by giving single morsels

> of food, eventually enables us to give our head and body without hesitation, in the present context as well, I will start by practicing virtue for just one morning.

Following this intention, with great diligence you then earnestly cultivate virtues like generosity. You commit yourself to exercising diligence progressively over days, months, years, and in the end for your entire life. As a result, although you make every effort, you will not find the time long nor find it difficult. Your delight will grow, and you will succeed in achieving the aforementioned armor-like diligence. You are to initiate meditative sessions by recalling the Three Jewels, deciding to apply the antidotes to the three mental poisons, and being determined not to let anything interfere with your meditation—analytical or placement, whichever is appropriate—until the end of the session. For the first sessions, it might be somewhat difficult to curb your sloth and craving for inferior pleasures and exercise great diligence, but it is said that as you continue meditating, it will gradually become easier, and your delight will increase tremendously.

If laziness in the form of procrastination suddenly occurs, and you find yourself thinking that you still have plenty of time, recall what *Guide to the Bodhisattva Way* says:

> It is owing to craving idleness,
> experiences of pleasure, and sleep
> and to lacking revulsion toward samsaric suffering
> that laziness prevails.[556]

It is taught that attachment to inferior pleasures like sleep, lethargy, and so on results in laziness in the form of procrastination—the postponement of virtue. [233] In this case the physical conduct to adopt is to sit in a well-ventilated place, wear thinner clothing, or get up and move around. Reflect, "As I can see with my own eyes, the time of death has nothing to do with how old or young you are, and I too will die soon. After death, it will be hard for me to find another good rebirth like this one," and meditate until you feel so restless that you have no time even to quench your thirst. If these remedies are insufficient, and you still feel drawn to lesser pleasures like stories about bears, recall what *Guide to the Bodhisattva Way* states:

> Among the many causes of delight, why do you reject the
> boundless [practice of the] excellent Dharma, the supreme joy,

and instead delight in the sources of misery:
distractions, amusements, and the rest?[557]

Think:

> By letting myself be distracted by these small short-lived pleasures, I am closing the door to the perfect teaching and will be reborn in an unfavorable realm.

When meditating in this way, if you feel discouraged and think, "Given that the goal I am pursuing—the condition of a blessed buddha—is endowed with all good qualities and free of all faults, it will be hard to achieve," reflect on the following:

> *Guide to the Bodhisattva Way* states:
>
> > Do not be discouraged, thinking,
> > "How can I attain enlightenment?"
> > For the Tathāgata,
> > who is a truth-speaker, announced this truth:
> >
> > "Even bees, flies, gnats,
> > and worms,
> > by generating powerful diligence,
> > all achieve supreme enlightenment so difficult to attain."
> >
> > Why then should someone like me, who has been born a human
> > and knows what is harmful and beneficial,
> > not attain buddhahood,
> > provided I do not abandon the bodhisattva deeds?[558]
>
> The Blessed One, who has such superior qualities, said that all types of sentient beings attain buddhahood, so why should not I?

Contemplate this to raise your spirits. Although you pluck up your courage and think, "I *shall* attain buddhahood," you might question your ability to give away your body, limbs, and so on, but *Guide to the Bodhisattva Way* states:

Such ordinary medical therapies
the Supreme Physician does not prescribe.
With extremely gentle treatments
he cures countless grave illnesses.

The Teacher first encourages
giving vegetables and the like.
Later, once schooled in these,
slowly you can also give your own flesh.

When you have come to see your body
as you see vegetables and the like,
what difficulty will there be
in giving away your flesh and the rest?[559] [234]

With great delight, reflect that you will give your eyes, head, and so on once it has become as easy as giving dishes of vegetables, in which case it will involve no difficulty.

When training in bodhisattva practice in this manner, if you begin to feel that you can no longer bear being born in samsara, think about what *Guide to the Bodhisattva Way* states:

Since they have rejected sin, [bodhisattvas] do not suffer.
As they are wise, their minds are not troubled.
Thus it is wrong thinking and sin
that harm the mind and body.

As merit brings physical well-being
and wisdom brings mental well-being,
why should remaining in samsara for others' sake
dishearten the compassionate ones?[560]

Contemplate this, and reflect that since bodhisattvas have given up sin, for lack of a cause, they do not experience suffering, its result.

To collect virtue, strive to make offerings to the Three Jewels and so on. To help sentient beings, endeavor to show others how to avoid having their belongings stolen and so forth, as in the context of the ethical discipline [of helping others]. You are to meditate on this once you have identified the particulars of the present topic.

Do not content yourself with achieving only a few of the good qualities just explained; cultivate the power of aspiration by recalling the benefits of training in bodhisattva practice and the drawbacks of not doing so. Develop the power of constancy for not abandoning your practice of diligence, the power of joy in continuity along with great delight, and the power of abandonment—conscious of the instruction to rest when tired.[561] As *Guide to the Bodhisattva Way* states:

> Like seasoned warriors, who battle
> their enemies with swords,
> you must avert the weapons that are the afflictions
> and pulverize your enemies, the afflictions.[562]

Just as skillful people, when fighting an enemy, will strike their foes with weapons and avert their blows, here, in both defeating manifest afflictions and protecting the mind from latent ones, I urge you to cultivate and exercise diligence.

Stanzas between sections [235]

The more you indulge in the pleasures of ignorant sleep, lethargy,
and the rest,
and in the excitation and carelessness of pointless distraction,
the more you feel dissatisfied,
like the thirsty person who drinks salt water.

If, driven by anger, you can summon the courage
to attack a powerful enemy you are incapable of overcoming,
then discouragement regarding buddhahood that *is* attainable
is a poor misguided attitude.

Knowing that there is no time in this life,
do not postpone the perfect Dharma that creates stable happiness.
Goad yourself with the cane of diligence,
and you are sure to travel to the isle of liberation.

The Perfection of Meditative Absorption

Guide to the Bodhisattva Way states:

> Having generated diligence in this way,
> place your mind in meditative concentration.[563]

The perfection of meditative absorption is a fully accomplished meditation in which the mind is one-pointed, as it abides free of distraction toward other objects.

Concerning absorption and wisdom, past masters, in works such as the *Great* and *Middle-Length* treatises, have composed separate sections on tranquil abiding and insight, some of which are brief expositions and others detailed. I will explain the meditation on tranquil abiding in relation to the fifth [perfection] and the meditation on insight in relation to the sixth by summarizing their essential content for the purpose of practice, and I will conclude with a brief explanation of the four means of gathering others.

On the meditation on tranquil abiding (*śamatha*)—the practice of meditative absorption (*dhyāna*) or states of concentration (*samādhi*)—the *Unraveling the Intent Sutra* states:

> When practitioners cultivate
> special insight and tranquil abiding,
> they free themselves of bondage to dysfunctional tendencies
> and bondage to signs.[564]

Wisdom eradicates the experience of bondage to dysfunctional tendencies along with their seeds, and *meditative absorption* inhibits the experience of manifest bondage to signs.[565] They are called [respectively] *special insight* and *tranquil abiding*. Among the three vehicles, states of concentration go by many different names, but all without exception are included in tranquil abiding and insight. [236] Tranquil abiding is a superior state of concentration in which the mind naturally focuses on its object. It is attained once the bliss of mental and physical pliancy has arisen through the continual observation of a single object with mindfulness and meta-awareness. Wisdom cuts the bonds of grasping at signs.[566] The *Moon Lamp Sutra* explains:

> By the power of tranquil abiding, the mind becomes immoveable.
> By special insight, it comes to resemble a mountain.[567]

Just as water requires a container to fulfill its function, for a state of mind to penetrate its object, the awareness penetrating it must be immoveable. When it is obscured by the darkness of ignorance, you are to light the lamp of wisdom to observe each aspect of the complex pattern of existence without confusing any of its parts. If the draft of distraction makes its light flicker, it will shine less brightly, which is why a state of concentration that halts [the mind's] movement is absolutely necessary. If you fail to overcome distraction by relying on tranquil abiding, not only will [your understanding] of the mode of existence be ineffectual, so will all other virtuous practices in relation to karma and its effects, love, compassion, mantra recitation, and so on. *Guide to the Bodhisattva Way* states:

> A person whose mind is distracted
> remains in the jaws of the afflictions.[568]

And:

> All mantra recitations and austerities,
> even practiced over long periods,
> the Knower of Suchness said are pointless,
> when done with a mind turned elsewhere.[569]

Śāntideva also states:

> Knowing that insight fully combined with tranquil abiding
> completely conquers the afflictions,
> first seek tranquil abiding.[570]

To cut the root of grasping at self, you must cultivate the wisdom understanding selflessness. Prior to that you are to develop tranquil abiding, regarding which the *Ornament of Mahayana Sutras* says:

> The place where the intelligent practice
> is one with ready supplies, in a safe
> and healthy location, and with good companions
> and the requirements for a meditator's success.[571]

Supplies like food and clothing needed for spiritual practice should be readily available. The place should be free of harmful elements like dangerous animals, thieves, enemies, and evil spirits. It should be healthy, not one where you fall sick, and include practitioner companions. It should be free of all kinds of diversions that are pointless distractions. Such is the ideal place for applying this instruction. [237] Those who, despite having such a place available to them, create sources of distraction have failed to link method and wisdom.

You should (1) have few desires and (2) not delight in large quantities of good food and clothing; (3) be content with begging for food and with clothes made from rags from the refuse heap; (4) avoid involvement in numerous activities like business, medicine, astrology, and so on; (5) uphold pure ethical discipline; and (6) reflect well on the drawbacks of attachment[572] and on impermanence. Your practice should be grounded in these six conditions.

[Objects of meditation]

As for the way to practice, the Tathāgata taught four kinds of objects of meditation. The *objects for purifying behavior* are ugliness as the antidote to attachment, love as the antidote to aversion, interdependence as the antidote to ignorance, the five elements and the aspects of consciousness visualized individually [as the antidote to pride], and counting the movements of your breath [as the antidote to distraction]. *Objects of expertise* are, for example, the five aggregates—form and so on—the eighteen elements, the eyes and so on, the twelves spheres, the twelve links of dependent origination, and the causes and conditions of virtuous and nonvirtuous karmas and their effects. *Affliction-purifying objects* are, for example, the view of peaceful and coarse aspects—the relative peacefulness of higher realms compared to the coarseness of lower ones—and so on, from the desire realm up to the sphere of nothingness. *Universal objects* include all the above.

Śrāvaka Grounds quotes the following from *Questions of Revata*:

> Revata, if a monk-meditator engaged in meditation is exclusively affected by attachment, he should focus his mind on the object

> ugliness; if he is affected by anger, on love; if he is affected by ignorance, on the links of dependent origination; if he is affected by pride, on the classifications of the elements.[573]

Due to strong habituation to afflictions like attachment over past lives, the three poisons may arise at the slightest pretext and persist a long time. [238] To remedy this, you need to counteract your strongest affliction, such as attachment. If you did not become particularly habituated to afflictions in past lives, and if in this life you are involved in a number of them in equal measure, you may choose whatever object you like; there is no need to favor one. When, for example, you have a fever but no wind illness is associated to it, a treatment for fever alone will be sufficient, but for a combination of fever and wind illnesses, you will need to complement the fever medicine with a wind medicine.

Since the sutras teach four kinds of objects of states of concentration, some people wrongly imagine that all four are to be meditated on, but this will not only fail to further mental stability, it will in fact cause distraction. As Āryaśūra states:

> Maintaining a single focal object,
> stabilize your mental reflections.
> By changing focal objects often,
> your mind will be disturbed by afflictions.[574]

It is as taught. Regarding the most relevant objects, the master Bodhibhadra says:

> There is "inward-turned tranquil abiding," such as meditating on the body as a *khaṭvāṅga* staff and observing drops in relation to the body, and "outward-turned tranquil abiding" that focuses on a [deity's] body and speech.[575]

The latter is the principal tradition, but it is not suitable to place the image of a deity in front of you and just stare at it. Master Yeshé Dé's[576] refutation of this indirectly challenges many "great meditators" who take the likes of pebbles and small fruits as objects of meditation and whose words are as widespread as the wind. According to the present tradition, from the start, states of concentration must be cultivated based on mental consciousness.

[THE FIVE FAULTS AND THE EIGHT APPLICATIONS]

All past masters agree, however, that tranquil abiding is achieved by rejecting the five faults using the eight applications. This is explained at great length in the *Great* and *Middle-Length* treatises. *Differentiation of the Middle and Extremes* states:

> By maintaining [diligence], serviceability is achieved,
> by which all goals are attained;
> it results from reliance on the eight applications
> that reject the five faults.
>
> Laziness, forgetting the instruction,
> laxity and excitation,
> nonapplication, and application
> are viewed as the five faults.[577] [239]

The five faults are laziness that is the absence of delight in meditation and being drawn to its opposing factors; forgetfulness that is the lack of clarity of the chosen object of meditation or the loss of it; being affected by either laxity or excitation, even if the object is not lost; not applying the antidotes that reject these despite you knowing they are affecting you; and excessive application of the antidotes to laxity and excitation when they are absent instead of focusing primarily on the object. These are to be identified promptly.

Regarding their antidotes, *Differentiation of the Middle and Extremes* continues:

> The base [aspiration] and what is based on it [diligence],
> the cause [of aspiration, faith] and its effect [pliancy],
> not forgetting the focal object,
> identifying laxity and excitation,
> application to reject them,
> and remaining serene once they have been quelled.[578]

The ability to diligently persist in cultivating states of concentration is what has a base; what it is based on and arises from is the aspiration that seeks states of concentration; once its benefits have been seen, then it is faith captivated by states of concentration that prompts aspiration; striving diligently results in pliancy. These four exclude laziness.

With regard to the antidote to forgetting, the *Compendium of Abhidharma* says:

> What is mindfulness? In relation to a familiar object, it is mental nonforgetfulness; its function is to prevent distraction completely.[579]

Nonforgetfulness is continual mindfulness that does not abandon any focal object with which you have repeatedly familiarized yourself in the past. Since mindfulness with its three traits prevents the mind from wandering from its object, it quells forgetting.

Regarding the antidotes to laxity and excitation, *Essence of the Middle Way* says:

> Tie this wandering elephant of mind,
> firmly to a sturdy post, its object,
> with the rope of mindfulness,
> and gradually tame it with the hook of meta-awareness.[580]

If laxity or excitation occur while mindfulness is maintaining the mind on its object, just as a wild elephant is tamed with an iron hook, meta-awareness monitors laxity and excitation and prevents them from taking over. *Guide to the Bodhisattva Way* states:

> Examining over and over again
> the state of your mind and body,
> this in brief is all
> that characterizes guarding yourself with meta-awareness.[581]

You eliminate laxity and excitation by focusing the mind on the focal object and maintaining it there continually.

As for rejecting laxity and excitation, nowadays the terms *laxity* and *excitation* are on the lips of all great meditators, who have rendered them as widespread as the wind. [240] Nevertheless most only know the terms and are not capable of identifying them. Those who attempt to detect them fail to distinguish laxity from lethargy and confuse the two. As they take all instances of laxity for genuine states of concentration, the majority spend their entire life in the mountains in vain.

The *Compendium of Abhidharma* says:

> What is excitation? It is mental agitation that derives from attachment and draws one toward attractive objects. Its function is to hinder tranquil abiding.[582]

It is described as a mental state that is agitated by desire for pleasant things. Thoughts influenced by anger that direct the mind toward enemies are not instances of excitation. Nevertheless, all thoughts that turn the mind to other objects and impede concentration must be halted since they hinder tranquil abiding. Moreover, the second *Stages of Meditation* states:

> You should know that when a mind does not perceive its object clearly and resembles a person blind from birth, someone sitting in the dark, or someone with their eyes closed, then laxity is present.[583]

While observing any object, if only the limpidity aspect is present and vigor is lacking in the apprehension of the object, this mental state that lacks clarity and is slack in its mode of apprehension is to be identified as *laxity*. *Lethargy*, on the other hand, is a mental state that derives from ignorance, whose aspect is mental and physical heaviness and unserviceability. As it is either an obstructive indeterminate[584] or nonvirtuous, lethargy is never virtuous, while laxity can be.

Concerning the opposite of not applying the antidotes that counter laxity and excitation when they occur, the *Compendium of Abhidharma* says:

> What is intention? It fully brings together the mind [and its object] and is mental karma. Its function is to cause the mind to engage in virtue, nonvirtue, and the ethically neutral.[585]

Intention is the mental factor that engages the mind in virtue, nonvirtue, or the ethically neutral. In the present context, when with meta-awareness you have identified laxity and excitation, as *Essence of the Middle Way* indicates:

> When slack,[586] lighten [your mind] by meditating
> on vast objects.[587]

Because laxity occurs when the mind is turned too far inward, you combat it by expanding your object slightly.[588] If that is insufficient to eliminate laxity and it persists, check it by abandoning your meditation topic momentarily and reflecting on the six [objects of] mindfulness—the Three Jewels, generosity, ethical discipline, and deities—and on the advantages of attaining a life with leisure and opportunity. Alternatively, you could go for a walk, visualize light, wash your face, sit in a cool place, and so forth. [241]

[On excitation,] *Essence of the Middle Way* says:

> Quell excitation by recalling
> impermanence and so forth.[589]

When excited by objects of attachment, counter it by cultivating intense disenchantment with [reflection on] impermanence, suffering, and so on. Following this example, it is vital to contemplate the antidotes to any factor, like anger, that scatters your thoughts.

In brief, you are to reject the causes common [to both laxity and excitation]: not guarding the doors of the senses, not eating in moderation, sleeping at the beginning and the end of the night, sleep, lethargy, indulging excessively in sense objects, and so on.

Concerning countering excessive application of laxity and excitation's antidotes, the latter two *Stages of Meditation* say: "If you exert yourself when the mind is in equipoise, it will be distracted."[590] At the end of the eighth mental state, as the mind is free of any influence of laxity and distraction, it is balanced. At that point, being overly wary of laxity and excitation and making excessive effort to apply [their antidotes]—heightening the mind, drawing it inward, and so on—will only impair your state of concentration. The application of equanimity, which knows to relax, is the remedy to excessive use of the antidotes to laxity and excitation.

On simply hearing the term "relax," some assert that good relaxation is good meditation. They let their mind come under the sway of laxity and wrongly take this state of simple clarity for true meditation. At this point, knowing to relax means relaxing your effort, not loosening the vigor of your mode of apprehension. As for the timing, most great meditators relax once they have achieved a little experience [of meditation]. In our system it is different: the time for it is when the intensity of laxity and excitation has declined, which is to say at the ninth mental state.

You are to practice once you have properly understood how to adopt the eight applications that reject the five faults. For this, do not imagine that it is enough to have learned the terms just explained. If you do not know how to use what you have learned in your practice, learning will remain a purely intellectual exercise, and like many people, you will fail to relate the teaching to yourself. [242] Some fools imagine that a core instruction is sufficient and that all that comes of the aforementioned explanations by the great treatises is fatigue. But before traveling to a distant land, for example, you certainly need to learn all about the situation on the route, either on your own or from someone else. If you depart uninformed, the undertaking will fail. In the same vein, concerning all those who claim to be great meditators but have no idea how to progress by solving the problems that arise in meditation, just sitting determinedly with their body straight and their eyes closed, [Sakya Paṇḍita] says in his *Clear Differentiation of the Three Vows*:

> It is said that the mahāmudrā meditations of ignorant people
> in most cases lead to animal rebirths.[591]

I believe this passage applies perfectly here. Nowadays, this tendency is increasingly prevalent in us and in others. It is as common as insects in summer, which is why the omniscient Butön stated:

> Were I to speak nonvirtuously, it would contravene the Dharma.
> Were I to speak according to the Dharma, the Tibetan people would
> rise against me.[592]

If I dwell on this too much, I will stick out like a white crow.[593]

How to focus on one object

Having ascertained the above, *Lamp on the Path to Enlightenment* says, "Place your mind in a virtuous state on any one of the given objects."[594] In the present context, concerning the single object on which to focus, generally the Buddha's form is appropriate. Among the reasons for this, the *King of Meditations Sutra* says:

> With a physical form the color of gold,
> the Protector of the World is forever splendid.
> A bodhisattva whose mind is absorbed on such an object
> is said to be a meditator.[595]

As visualizing the Tathāgata's body coincidently produces the great merit that recollecting the Buddha brings, it is analogous to a cornerstone that supports two walls, or a person who, while resolving something like a commercial concern, settles another matter at the same time.

Begin by looking at a two or three-dimensional image of the Buddha's form and then visualize it repeatedly. You are to picture each of the following—the shape of the crown protuberance, the face, eyes, arms, legs, clothes, and so on, and the color of each as well, from the whites of the eyes, pupils, and so on—individually without confusing any of them. [243] Do not succumb to various changes that may occur, like a seated position turning into a standing one or a blue color changing into white. You may not succeed immediately in clearly perceiving the Buddha's actual form with the whites of the eyes, the pupils, and so on, but by consistently meditating on the general shape and appearance of the Buddha's form, you will eventually come to see it as described. Since your meditation will be hindered by persevering in the hope of soon seeing the form as it is, keep your expectations reasonable.

You are to sit in the eightfold posture on a soft and comfortable seat with your legs in full or half-lotus position, your half-closed eyes lowered toward the tip of your nose, your body straight, your hands in the equipoise mudrā, your head straight so that the tip of your nose and your navel are aligned, your teeth and lips in their natural position, the tip of your tongue touching the palate, and your breathing calm. Counting your inhalations and exhalations twenty-one times, for example, is taught as the means to overcome distraction toward the exterior. Then, with intense aspiration induced by faith in the benefits of states of concentration, and diligence that wholeheartedly delights in the practice of virtue, visualize in the space before you, at the level of the point between your eyebrows, the buddha form that you have previously familiarized yourself with in the size that suits you. Without forgetting the object and constantly mindful of it, and combining both vigorous clarity and firm stability that does let the mind scatter elsewhere, meditate in a fully focused manner free of faults like excessive tension.

When you think that you have achieved some mental stability, do not lose the object but sustain it with mindfulness and guard yourself with meta-awareness. When clarity is present but you observe a slight decrease in the level of vigor in the mode of apprehension, note that subtle laxity has arisen and check it. If the clarity suddenly loses its vigor, and only limpidity[596] remains, then be aware that coarse laxity is present. When a pleasant object of desire is on the verge of appearing, recognize it as subtle excitation, and when an object of attachment suddenly emerges, recognize it as coarse excitation. [244] Quell laxity and excitation with their antidotes, and do your best to maintain your mind on the very clear object for an hour.

As too tight a focus leads to an increase in excitation and excessive looseness to an increase in laxity, it is difficult to achieve the right degree of vigor. As the wise Candragomin says:

> When effort is applied excitation arises;
> when it is neglected slackness occurs.
> When between them it is hard to find a proper balance,
> what am I to do with my perturbed mind?[597]

[The nine mental states and four attentions]

A beginner may not perfectly master how to practice all eight applications that reject the five faults. Be that as it may, among the nine mental states, in the [first] one called *mental placement*, the mind may not remain on the object for long, but you meditate with effort that is consistent with your capacity.

In the first mental state, your mind does not remain focused on the object. Other thoughts ensue the way water flows down a steep mountainside, and you have the impression that since you began to practice, your discursive thoughts have increased. What then are you to do? In the past, before you received the instructions for this practice, your situation was comparable to finding yourself on a thoroughfare with a continuous stream of travelers: when you have no interest in watching them, you do not notice how many there are, but when you make an effort to observe them, you can estimate the number of caravans and so on. In the past you were unaware of the constant flow of your underlying thoughts. Now, thanks to the work on your mind that you have undertaken, you begin to be conscious of your thoughts.

In his *Ornament of Mahayana Sutras*, the protector Maitreya explains the four attentions and how to achieve the nine mental states by means of the six forces. Accordingly, among the six, it is with the force of hearing that you achieve the first mental state, *mental placement*. At this point you simply focus your mind on the object following the instructions on how to meditate that you have only heard [and have yet to apply].

Gradually as you meditate, like the irregular rate at which water flows through a gorge, at times your thoughts calm down, at others they suddenly increase, and you have the impression that your thoughts are abating. At this point, through the force of reflection, you achieve the second mental state of *continuous placement*, in which you can maintain the object for a short while. [245] During these two states, laxity and excitation are frequent, a state of concentration infrequent, and among the four attentions, *tight focus* is present.

Next, after further familiarization, like a pool of water fed by three distant sources, you find your mind stable when it is not disturbed by any opposing conditions and unstable when they occur. You have the impression that your discursive thoughts are wearing out. At the time, by the third force, mindfulness, you accomplish the third mental state called *renewed placement*, in which you become quickly aware when you are distracted and refocus your mind on the object.

In the fourth mental state, called *close placement*, you reduce the size of your originally larger object. The fifth mental state called *subjugation* is achieved by the force of meta-awareness; it delights in the virtues of states of concentration. In the sixth mental state called *pacification*, you become aware of the drawbacks of distraction and stop it. Both the seventh and eighth mental states are achieved by the fifth force, diligence. The seventh state, called *complete pacification*, with effort rejects afflictions such as attachment and quells them. As these five mental states, from the third to the seventh, are interrupted by laxity and excitation, among the four attentions, this is the time of the second, *intermittent focus*.

Next, as you gradually pursue meditation, like an ocean with waves, whatever discursive thoughts arise are dispelled on the spot by mild application of the antidotes; given this, the impression you have is called *thought application*.[598] At that point, by the above-mentioned fifth force, you attain the eighth mental state called *one-pointed attention* and achieve a continuous state of concentration. Since the eighth mental state is not interrupted by laxity and excitation, among the four attentions, this is the time of the third, *uninterrupted focus*.

Steadily continuing to meditate, like a waveless ocean, a state of concentration occurs naturally in all circumstances, independent of any effort to sustain it with the antidote, mindfulness. In this way an equipoise arises in which you have the impression [called] *non-thought application*. Through the force of thorough familiarization, you then achieve the ninth mental state called *balanced placement*. [246] As you focus on the object effortlessly, among the four attentions this is the time of the fourth, *spontaneous focus*.

Thinking that it would be wrong at this stage to make an effort to stop laxity and excitation, some past masters have stated that relaxation is excellent, which has been misunderstood and misconstrued to mean that the vigor of the mode of apprehension should be reduced. This important point *must* be understood, for it is not just because a person owns a meditator's special knee strap, hat, and bag that he is successfully meditating!

For the nine mental states, among the four attentions explained above, the attention that corresponds to the first two states is called *tight focus* and the one for the next five is called *intermittent focus*. Perhaps you think this must be an error, that it should be intermittent focus for the first two and tight focus for the following five, but it is not actually a problem. The middle group of five involves both tight and intermittent focus, but the focus for first two cannot be called "intermittent" because both laxity and excitation are prevalent and a state of concentration only occurs from time to time. On the other hand, the middle five for the most part consist of placement meditation that is occasionally (but repeatedly) interrupted by laxity and excitation. It is like the following example: of three people present, the first is given some meat, the second both meat and *tü*,[599] and the third, in addition to these two foods, is given clarified butter. The first person will be called "the one who was given meat." The second, although he was given meat, will not be called "the one who was given meat" but "the one who was given both." The third has both of these, but calling him "the one who got both" would not be right, as he received all three foods.

[Attainment of tranquil abiding]

When the ninth mental state arises in this way, where the state of the concentration is free of subtle laxity and excitation and is effortlessly sustained for long periods, you might wonder whether this is tranquil abiding. *Ornament of Mahayana Sutras* states:

> Through familiarization, no application [is needed];
> then when strong mental
> and physical pliancy are attained,
> it is called *mental contemplation*.[600]

From this point onward, what is known as *mental contemplation* is an approximation of tranquil abiding. To attain actual tranquil abiding, it is necessary to achieve the superior bliss of physical and mental pliancy.

That said, you may wonder whether pliancy is entirely absent when the state of concentration of the ninth mental state first arises. [247] Actually, although subtle pliancy is in fact present, it is difficult to discern because it is faint, which is why the state is qualified as "mental contemplation that is concordant with tranquil abiding." For example, the full moon of the fifteenth day of the month can only be achieved by the gradual increase of portions of moon from the second day onward. Although the small slice of the moon of the second day is a moon, it is not the moon of the fifteenth day. Similarly, mental pliancy arises once subtle pliancy has developed to the point that it quells the dysfunctional tendencies that depend on afflictions and prevent you from generating virtue at will. Thanks to it, serviceable winds circulate in the body, freeing it of all physical dysfunctional tendencies and generating physical pliancy with which the body feels as light as cotton fluff. From it dawns an intense feeling of physical bliss, which in turn generates a feeling of mental pleasure that is the bliss of mental pliancy. When you attain physical pliancy and immediately experience very intense mental bliss, you have yet to achieve tranquil abiding. You realize it as soon as the strong pleasure subsides slightly and you attain immoveable pliancy concordant with the mind's stable concentration on the object. (Given this, when those who now pride themselves on being great meditators are measured against the great treatises, I have the impression that they have in fact achieved nothing.) The decline in the strong pleasure does not, however, imply that pliancy has ceased. It is taught that it is like the case of the agitating delight you feel on hearing good news subsiding after some time, which does not change the fact that you heard good news.

The attainment of tranquil abiding with its superior bliss of physical and mental pliancy coincides with the attainment of the preparatory phase of the first absorption [of the form realm], but it does not enable you to control manifestations of the afflictions. If you wonder whether this conflicts with what was said about the higher training of concentration—that tranquil abiding checks manifestations of the afflictions—in fact that statement referred to insight having the aspect of peacefulness and coarseness and so on, which is included in the category of tranquil abiding. For this reason, further training on the path is required. By following the training that consists in meditating on the mundane path—insight with the aspect of peacefulness and coarseness—most desire-realm afflictions to be abandoned by the path of meditation decline, and you attain the actual first absorption along with joy and bliss, various kinds of clairvoyance, and genuine supernormal powers.

[248] By meditating gradually, you abandon all manifestations of afflictions up to the nothingness level and attain the mind of the peak of existence.

If, after reaching the preparatory phase of the first absorption, you instead meditate on the insight that analyzes the two kinds of selflessness, you can realize the śrāvaka path of seeing, for example, and in the process attain the advantages of the actual first absorption with the aspect of peacefulness and coarseness and above without having to meditate on them. It is however the uninterrupted paths of the path of meditation[601] of any of the three vehicles that serve as the antidote to the afflictions and eradicate them.

Stanzas between sections

Having understood the drawbacks of the faults of laziness and the rest
and seen the advantages of the eight applications, faith and so on,
[you attain] the marvelous state of concentration—conception-free[602]
tranquil abiding
with the clarity and bliss of pliancy that the ninth mental state induces.

Having practiced little meditation in the past,
the three mental poisons—the afflictions—are not reduced, only hidden;
those who then take their ease and profess to be good practitioners
are then destabilized by small obstacles, which exposes their flaw of
mediocrity.

Though their minds are completely unstable,
being untrained in the [nine] mental states shared with tīrthikas,
they boast of having attained buddhahood
beyond samsara and personal peace. They need to think again!

If, as it is said, the various clairvoyances, supernormal powers,
and so on
are attained thanks to the difficult points taught in the sutras and
commentaries,
the signs of attainments of those who proudly sit in the sun on
a full stomach
will be [nonexistent] like water extracted from rock.

Alas, over time with delusions and distractions,
I have wasted my life in meaningless pursuits.

Now in an excellent place free of diversions,
I will delight in practicing in this way.

With bliss that pervades mind and body,
if I understand the important techniques
that ensure the easy transformation of all I do into virtue,
illustrious buddhahood should not be far off!

The Perfection of Wisdom

The perfection of wisdom is fully accomplished once the mind's familiarization with the wisdom realizing the ultimate that understands suchness, the wisdom realizing the conventional—skill in the five sciences—and the wisdom knowing how to faultlessly accomplish sentient beings' present and future welfare is complete. [249] [Nāgārjuna's] *Hundred Verses of Wisdom* says:

> Wisdom is the root of all
> visible and invisible good qualities.
> For this reason, to accomplish both,
> thoroughly train in wisdom.[603]

The purity of the first five perfections, generosity and so on—such as giving away your flesh as if it were no more than an extract from a medicinal plant, free of pride and discouragement—and the way bodhisattva universal sovereigns are not drawn to sense objects depend on wisdom. In brief, wisdom is to be pursued because all good qualities, mundane and supramundane, arise in dependence on it. Among the many possible kinds of wisdom to seek, it is crucial you cultivate the special insight that eradicates both coarse and subtle afflictions. You may wonder whether you should cultivate special insight into the worlds' peacefulness and coarseness, which prevents the afflictions from manifesting. Concerning this, *Praise to the One Beyond All Praise* states:

> Although the people not following your teaching,
> who are blinded by ignorance,
> may go as far as the peak of existence,
> they will fall again into the world and be subjected to
> suffering.[604]

Although tīrthikas and so on reject all manifest afflictions up to nothingness and attain the mental state of the peak of existence, they are not free of samsara. The *King of Meditations Sutra* says:

Although you cultivate mundane concentrations,
as they do not destroy the notion of self,
the afflictions arise again,
as when Udraka cultivated these concentrations.[605]

Because they had not rejected grasping at self, beings like the tīrthika Udraka Rāmaputra were troubled by the afflictions and regressed to lower mental states. Given this, in no case are followers of the Great Vehicle to pursue these states of concentration.

If you then question the purpose of the tranquil abiding that you have striven in the past to meditate on, [*Praise to the One Beyond All Praise*] says: [250]

Although the followers of your teaching
do not attain the actual [first] absorption,
they are able to overcome cyclic existence,
even with the demons glaring at them.[606]

Once you have attained the preparatory stage of the first absorption, put aside pursuing the actual first absorption and the rest and then, by meditating on supramundane insight into selflessness, attain a state of liberation that is freedom from cyclic existence. Since in this case you are not achieving omniscience through the practice of the final perfection, you might doubt that this path is in any way superior to the path of persons of intermediate capacity. Your limited vision, like the way a one-eyed yak eats grass, is to blame for entertaining such a mistaken notion. I have already explained at length the way to train in the awakening mind and bodhisattva deeds, which are quite distinct from the path of persons of intermediate capacity. Furthermore, the Great Lord [Tsongkhapa] says:

Without the wisdom realizing the ultimate nature,
though you gain familiarity with renunciation and the awakening mind,
you will be unable to cut the root of cyclic existence.
So strive in the methods for realizing dependent origination.[607]

[As persons of great capacity] not only have the awakening mind but in conjunction with it meditate on the path that is the higher training in wisdom, their path is complete, unlike the paths of persons of lesser and intermediate capacity.

Since tranquil abiding and insight are included in the practice of training in meditative concentration and wisdom within the path of persons of intermediate capacity, you may wonder what need there is to join them to the bodhisattva deeds. [Nāgārjuna's] *Sixty Verses of Reasoning* states:

> By this virtue, may all beings
> complete the collections of merit and wisdom
> and attain the two excellent [bodies of a buddha]
> that result from merit and wisdom.[608]

To achieve buddhahood you need to attain both a form body and a truth body. On what basis are they achieved? The glorious Candrakīrti explains:

> Conventional truths are the methods;
> ultimate truths result from the methods.
> Whoever does not know how to distinguish the two
> enters the bad path of mistaken conceptions.[609]

This implies the following:

> Whoever knows well how to distinguish the two
> enters the good and unmistaken path.[610] [251]

The view at *base* level is the correct understanding of conventional truths, the appearance aspect—which is that all existents are established conventionally and arise interdependently without error between cause and effect—and the correct understanding of ultimate truths, the emptiness aspect—which is that no existent is even slightly established by way of its own nature. On the *path* you practice a vast accumulation of merit, with bodhisattva deeds such as generosity, and concurrently you practice the profound view of emptiness. In this way you attain the two *results*, a form body and a truth body, which are the ultimate objectives of persons of great capacity.

[The stages of training in wisdom]

As for the methods to attain them, I have already given an experiential explanation on how to achieve the collection of merit. Regarding the stages of practice for accomplishing the collection of wisdom, generally, in the Land of Āryas[611] there were four distinct schools of tenets with varying views. However, two major traditions, Madhyamaka and Cittamātra, are preeminent. Furthermore, *Precious Garland* says:

> As this teaching is profound, he knew
> it would be difficult for beings to understand,
> which is why, after attaining buddhahood,
> the Sage declined to teach the Dharma.[612]

Knowing it would be hard for others to realize the key point of establishing the absence of incompatibility between emptiness and the system of karma and effects, the Buddha acted as if it would be difficult for him to agree to turn the wheel of the Dharma.

The glorious protector Nāgārjuna, whose advent the Buddha prophesized in the *Descent into Laṅkā Sutra,*[613] correctly explained this difficult system. Although many people claim to be his followers, liberation cannot be attained with just the view [held by Svātantrikas, for example] that asserts that all existents are established by way of their own nature. The glorious Candrakīrti states:

> Those outside the path of the worthy teacher Nāgārjuna
> do not possess the means to attain peace.
> They deviate from conventional and ultimate truths
> and, because of this divergence, fail to achieve liberation.[614]

As the protector Nāgārjuna's intent must be correctly established, which of his commentators should be followed? [In *Entering the Two Truths*] the great Atiśa writes:

> If you ask, "Who realized emptiness?"
> Nāgārjuna, whose coming the Tathāgata prophesized,
> and his disciple Candrakīrti, who saw the truth of ultimate nature.
> Only with the instruction stemming from them
> do you realize the truth of ultimate nature.[615] [252]

You should practice according to the commentaries of the glorious Candrakīrti. His *Extensive Commentary on Four Hundred Verses* states:

> Here *self* is any thing's nature, or character of nondependence on others. Its nonexistence is *selflessness*. Know that it is twofold, as it is distinguished in relation to phenomena and persons: the selflessness of phenomena and the selflessness of persons.[616]

What is the order between the two kinds of selflessness? [*Four Hundred Verses* states:]

> First non-merit is to be overcome,
> in the middle the self is to be overcome,
> in the end all views are to be overcome.
> Whoever knows this is wise.[617]

Bad views such as the repudiation of karmic cause and effect have been rejected previously in the context of the paths of persons of lesser and intermediate capacity, as [Nāgārjuna] says:

> First, the source of all faults,
> nihilism, was completely rejected.[618]

In the middle, the self of persons is to be abandoned and, in the end, the self of phenomena. This order is established according to instructions for practice. Although the great treatises present the selflessness of phenomena first, when it comes to practice, the point of crucial importance is that the correct order is different. The view of the selflessness [of persons] will not arise in the mind of a person who does not believe in karma and its effects, and grasping at the self of phenomena cannot be destroyed without having overcome grasping at the self of persons.

As such, although you previously avoided the faults of each affliction like attachment with the specific antidotes that are their direct opposites, you failed to eliminate all faults for lack of destroying their root, ignorance. *Four Hundred Verses* says:

> Just as the body sense [pervades] the body,
> ignorance pervades all [afflictions].
> Thus, by defeating ignorance,
> you defeat all afflictions.

> Once you have perceived dependent origination,
> ignorance cannot arise.
> For this reason, put all your effort into it
> and explain this topic alone.[619]

For example, by cutting a tree at its root, all its branches, flowers, and so on will wilt. Similarly, it is taught that by abandoning grasping at self, all afflictions are quelled. *Entering the Middle Way* says: [253]

> Having mentally perceived that all the faults of the afflictions
> arise from the personal identity view
> and understood that an [inherent] self is its object,
> a yogi rejects this self.[620]

Precious Garland says:

> As long as the aggregates are grasped [as truly existing],
> they will be apprehended as the "I."
> From the apprehension of the "I," [projecting] karma arises,
> and from karma birth ensues.[621]

To ascertain the two kinds of selflessness, the great Dharma king Tsongkhapa supplicated Mañjuśrī. He then generated the view in his mindstream by following the method for realizing the correct view that Mañjuśrī had taught him.

According to the instructions he gave his followers, two different lineages arose: a transmission lineage originating from Khedrup Gelek Palsang,[622] who explained the view from the perspective of preliminaries and a main topic, and the transmission lineage originating from Khedrup Sherab Sengé,[623] who taught it from the perspective of four kinds of mindfulness. In any case, there is no difference between them. In the present context of an experiential exposition of the Perfection of Wisdom Sutras—the stages of the path to enlightenment—since I have already covered the practice of the preliminaries following the order for practice, I will not repeat it here. The main topic has two parts: the practice of the selflessness of persons and the practice of the selflessness of phenomena.

Practicing the selflessness of persons

Various arguments are used for the first—for example, the three key points of the dependent origination argument and the nine key points of the sevenfold argument. Although the Great Lord [Tsongkhapa] explained these at length in his expositions of special insight in works such as the *Great* and *Middle-Length* treatises, he mainly taught based on the four key points.

In the present tradition of an experiential exposition applied and transmitted orally by the great trailblazer, the omniscient Norsang Gyatso,[624] the father, and his spiritual son, the first key point is to ascertain how the innate grasping at "I" apprehends the "I." [254] Buddhapālita states:

> If you fail to correctly identify both the self in the expression "All phenomena are devoid of self" and the nonexistent object of negation, it will be like leading an army into battle without knowing where the enemy lies or like shooting an arrow before locating the target.[625]

Guide to the Bodhisattva Way states:

> Without identifying the designated phenomenon,
> you will not apprehend its noninherent existence.[626]

It is taught that when the mental image of the object to be negated does not clearly appear to your mind, you will not ascertain the selflessness that negates it. "Persons" are beings of the six classes—non-āryas, āryas of the three vehicles, and so on. What is called "self" or "nature" is a mode of existence that is established from its own side, self-sustaining, and not designated by a mind. There are three kinds of innate grasping at an "I" that apprehend a self or "I" on the basis that is a person: a grasping at an "I" in which the "I" appears as a simple designation by mind in relation to the basis of designation; a grasping at an "I" in which it appears as established by way of its own nature; and a grasping at an "I" in which it appears in neither of these ways. The first is the grasping at an "I" of someone in whose mind the Madhyamaka view has arisen; the second is the actual innate grasping at an "I" that in the present context is to be demolished by its antidote; the third is the "I" perceived by the conventional valid cognition of ordinary beings whose minds are not affected by tenets, and who differentiate it neither as nominally designated nor as established by way of its own nature.

Although, whether asleep or awake, we always have the thought "I am" firmly anchored in us, just as an image appears when a face meets a mirror, it is in painful or joyful situations that the thought manifests most strongly; in their absence, it is less apparent. Despite this, most of those who teach the view these days fail to investigate whether such grasping occurs in them. They repeat purely empty words about how innate grasping at the "I" perceives the "I" and attempt to practice thereupon, and so they are about as precise as the person who points to someone and accuses them of having stolen something from him the previous day despite having only gotten a glimpse of them.

First [to identify the object], you may now be experiencing manifest pain or pleasure due to someone's harm or help. If not, repeatedly bring to mind former experiences of this nature. [255] Say, for instance, someone accused you of theft, or say someone helped you achieve a desired objective. [In the first case] you think, "Although the thought to steal never even crossed my mind, this person has accused me of theft!" This will kindle great anger toward your accuser, and the "I" that was the object of the accusation of theft will appear so firmly from the depth of your heart that you can almost see it with your eyes and touch it with your hands. Similarly, when you think, "This person has been a help to me," the "I" that received assistance will appear very plainly in your heart's core. In either situation, manifest grasping will supersede all other coarse thoughts. Having purposely intensified your innate grasping at "I," you then examine how your mind apprehends it. It is very difficult to grasp at the "I" and simultaneously examine how you apprehend it. If you examine the mode of apprehension too forcefully, the vigor of the mode of apprehension [of the "I"] will abate, and it will become unclear. What then is to be done? Thanks to training in tranquil abiding, the mind can sustain any object of analytical or placement meditation. Instead of focusing on an object like the Buddha's physical form, you bring to mind the thought "I am." While the major part of the mind focuses firmly on it, a fraction of the mind will observe the mode of apprehension and what is apprehended. It is said to be like two people walking along a road together: by and large they are watching where they are going, but from the corner of their eye, they are observing their companion.

Up to this point the "I" that thinks "I am" simply appears in your heart's core; you have yet to identify the base on which you have established it. A fraction of the mind is then to examine this thoroughly. It can appear in a variety of ways. At times the "I" may seem to be based on the body, at times on the mind, at others it may seem to be based on one of the other aggregates, and so on. In the end, you will identify the "I" as established on the basis of both your body and mind—the two as inseparable as a mixture of milk and water—from its own side, by way of its own nature, primordially, and in a self-sustaining manner. [256] This is the first key point: ascertaining the object of negation, which is to be explored until it is experienced profoundly.

Once you have generated it in you, and both the "I" apprehended by innate grasping at "I" and your five aggregates, like water poured into water, are together identified to be self-sustaining, then if this is true, the more you analyze it, the firmer your ascertainment should become. If it is false, then [the more you analyze it], the more your perception of it should fade.

Clear Words says:

> Is the object of grasping at self of the nature of the aggregates,
> or is it distinct from them?"[627]

The "I" appears to be established inseparably from all five aggregates without distinction. Although in relation to a single thing like a pot, for example, the terms "distinct" and "inseparable" do not apply, here the "I" and the aggregates appear [respectively] as the aspect of the phenomenon designated and as the basis of designation. Applying the model used to analyze other existents, investigate whether the "I" that is established as naturally self-sustaining and the five aggregates are one, whether they are distinct, and whether there is a third option. In the end you will come to realize that there is no third possibility and conclude that they must be either one or distinct. This is the key point of ascertaining the entailment.

Formerly the "I," a phenomenon designated upon the bases of designation that are the aggregates, appeared as self-sustaining and as indissociable from them. By practicing the second key point, your prior ascertainment cannot last, and you begin to experience doubts about the "I" being either one with the aggregates or distinct from them. However, it is not enough to question whether they are one or distinct; you must draw a conclusion. You investigate the matter, asking yourself whether the "I" perceived by innate grasping at true existence is one with the two, the body and mind. In fact, it can only be one with the body or one with the mind. If it were one with the body, you could not attribute a feature to a base and speak of "my body." You would have to speak of "the I of the I" or "the body's body." It is likewise for the mind, which you are to determine as well.

If, when reflecting on this, all you can do is repeat the words and you cannot manage to truly understand the matter, think as follows:

Fundamental Wisdom says: [257]

> When you affirm that apart from the appropriator,
> there is no self,
> if the appropriator is the self,
> then the self you assert does not exist.[628]

If the "I" and the aggregates are intrinsically one, they must be utterly one without the slightest distinction, which means that they could only be partless. In relation to a single partless "I," you cannot assert two different things: an appropriator of the five aggregates and the five aggregates appropriated by it. Given this, to speak of "my body" and "my aggregates" becomes meaningless.

If that does not allow you to finalize the question, reflect on the fallacies implied: since both the "I" and the body are one, after death when your body is cremated, the "I" too would be cremated; and just as the "I" is conceived in your mother's [womb] of your next life, so too would the [same] body have to be conceived; or just as the body could not be conceived again, neither could the "I." By meditating in this way, you will begin to question whether the "I" is one with the body, in which case you will also doubt that it is one with the mind. [You could also] reflect on the following fallacy: since when it is naked, the "I" suffers from the cold, and when it is deprived of food and drink it suffers from hunger and thirst, after death when the mind is born in the formless realm, since the mind is one with the "I," it would have to use coarse material things like food and clothing. These lines of reasoning are easy to contemplate and suitable for beginners.

For those trained in wisdom, further developments will settle the issue. *Entering the Middle Way* says:

> If the aggregates were the self,
> then since they are multiple, the self too would be multiple.[629]

Just as there are five aggregates, the "I" too would be fivefold, or just as there is but one "I," the aggregates could not be fivefold. With these reasonings you reflect on the fallacies of the self being multiple.

In the same vein, *Fundamental Wisdom* says:

> If the self were the aggregates,
> it would be subject to production and destruction.[630]

Since the five aggregates intrinsically arise and disintegrate, you would have to admit that the "I" also intrinsically arises and disintegrates in the same way. Along similar lines, as the "I" of the past life and the "I" of the present life can only be either the same or distinct, if they were the same, by the power of being intrinsically one, the sufferings of stupidity, dumbness, being exploited, and being put to work of the "I" of a past animal rebirth would have to be experienced by the "I" in the present human rebirth, and the joys of the present human life would also have to have been experienced in the past animal rebirth, which is preposterous. [258]

Accordingly, *Entering the Middle Way* says:

> Whatever is distinct by way of its own characteristics
> cannot be part of the same continuum.[631]

If the "I" of a past life and the "I" of the next life are intrinsically distinct, they are distinct without the slightest relation, making it impossible for people to recall that they were born as so-and-so in a former life, any more than Devadatta could recall having been born Yajñadatta in a past life. Furthermore, your accumulation of karma for a fortunate rebirth would be wasted, for someone other than you would enjoy its result: the maturation effect that is a high rebirth. Why? Because the agent of the karma and the one who experiences its effects would not be included in the same basis, the mere "I," and they would be unrelated. In the case of being harmed or helped in this life by karma produced in a past life, you would be experiencing the results of karma that you did not produce. If you were not harmed or helped by it, there would be no point in rejecting sin and accomplishing virtue in the present life because you would not experience its effects in the future.

Thanks to these reflections, once you have ascertained the third key point, ascertaining the absence of true identity, you might think that the "I" and the five aggregates could only be distinct, but *Entering the Middle Way* states:

> For that reason, there is no self apart from the aggregates,
> because without the aggregates, there is no conception of it.[632]

The distinction [of two things] established by way of their own nature necessarily implies that they are unrelated. Given this, just as among the five aggregates, each is identified individually as the aggregate of form and so on, you should be able, after eliminating the five aggregates, to identify an "I" and state, "This is the I." When you analyze the matter in depth, however, you find no such thing.

As for the manner of not finding it, it is not enough to just repeat the empty words "It is not findable." When someone claims to have lost something like an ox, for example, if the owner simply says, "It is not in such-and-such a place," he will not be believed. Its loss will be acknowledged only after it has been sought high, low, and in between and still not found. Here you are to meditate until you reach a conclusion and establish the matter with certainty. [259]

Entering the Middle Way says:

> As there is no [inherent] agent, there is no [inherent] action,
> nor is there an [inherent] "mine" or an [inherent] "I."
> Thus it is by the view of the emptiness of "I" and "mine"
> that meditators are completely liberated.[633]

Until now you have perceived the "I" as truly existent, as something almost visible and tangible. It is taught that once you no longer find the "I" and it has disappeared completely, you have begun to acquire Madhyamaka views. First you understand the view in a manner issuing from learning, then you practice it with a mental state issuing from reflection. As for the attainment issuing from meditation, initially it is not authentic insight, as explained in the context of tranquil abiding.[634] It is nevertheless a minor attainment of the view, like the moon on the second day of the [lunar] month.

At this point, unless you have imprints of emptiness [meditation] from former lives, you will have the impression that you have suddenly lost something you were holding in your hand, whereas when you have such imprints, you will have the impression that you have suddenly found a precious gem that you had lost.

Having established the view of selflessness, how are you to contemplate it? You meditate on it by practicing the six preliminaries, physical posture, mindfulness, and meta-awareness as explained above in the context of tranquil abiding.

Some people analyze the view once and then remain in a state of non-mentation calling it suchness [meditation]; others simply bring to mind the view previously analyzed and place their mind on it. There have been many such variants, but these are no more than ways to cultivate tranquil abiding;

they lack the specific features of [insight] meditation. Potowa in his *Blue Compendium* explains:

> Some say that when you are learning and reflecting,
> you establish the lack of inherent existence with reasonings,
> and then when you meditate, you are only to meditate
> nonconceptually.[635]
> If this were the case, as your meditation on emptiness is distinct from
> and unrelated [to what you established earlier], it would not serve as
> an antidote [to grasping at self].
> For this reason, even when meditating,
> you are to analyze individually whatever [reasonings] are familiar
> to you—
> the lack of being one or multiple, dependent origination, and so
> forth—
> and remain a little in a nonconceptual[636] state as well.
> Meditating in this way will be the antidote to the afflictions.
> For those who wish to follow the prince [Atiśa]
> and intend to practice the system of the perfections,
> this is the procedure for cultivating wisdom.
> Moreover, once familiarized with the selflessness of persons,
> you undertake [phenomena's selflessness] in the same way.[637] [260]

Many of those who pride themselves on being great meditators establish the view having analyzed it by means of reasoning, but when the time comes to meditate, they meditate only nonconceptually. There is not the slightest difference between this and caring for your horse well when you are at home but going on foot when the time comes to travel. The flaw here lies in not having understood how to cultivate special insight based on tranquil abiding. When it is said in the context of tranquil abiding that nonconceptuality is necessary and conceptions are to be stopped, it means that when focusing on an object like the Buddha's physical form, you are not to let any other thoughts arise. If all conceptions were to be rejected, since the Tathāgata's figure on which you focus is a conception, stopping them would mean losing such an object of meditation. This wrong view based on a misinterpretation of *nonconceptual thought* induces the conclusion that since all discriminating analysis of selflessness is conceptual, it is to be avoided in [insight] meditation. It comes from not understanding [nonconceptuality in relation to] tranquil abiding. In fact, thanks to being imbued with tranquil abiding, you avoid the intrusion of afflictive thoughts like attachment, and thanks to wisdom's discriminating analysis, the analytical meditation you practice is incisive. The firmer your tranquil abiding, the more vigorous is your insightful wisdom.

Before you achieve tranquil abiding, alternating analytical and placement meditations hinders tranquil abiding. Once you attain tranquil abiding, if you have the impression that excessive analysis is slightly reducing your [mind's] stability, favor placement meditation. If emphasis on placement meditation reduces your interest in analysis, alternate it with analytical meditation.

It is not appropriate to focus on selflessness in analytical meditation and then in placement meditation focus on any object you like, such as nonmentation or a deity's form. When engaged in analytical meditation, you reflect on selflessness, and when engaged in placement meditation, you must remain one-pointedly absorbed in the same, avoiding any thoughts other than the nonexistence of a self that is established by way of its own nature. Not just any nonconceptual state is appropriate. The final *Stages of Meditation* says:

> For this reason, as said in the excellent teaching, non-mindfulness and non-contemplation[638] are to be preceded by discriminating wisdom of emptiness. Why is that? Because it is only with discriminating wisdom of emptiness that you can achieve non-mindfulness and non-contemplation, not with anything else.[639] [261]

Given this, once Khedrup Gelek Palsang's followers have clearly ascertained the nonexistence of the "I" by analyzing the four key points, they must maintain the continuity of that ascertainment and [occasionally] recollect the four key points analyzed. [Khedrup Gelek Palsang] said that it is incorrect to [simply] meditate that the "I" does not exist and is not established the way it appears. Some of Khedrup Sherab Sengé's followers assert that once you have ascertained [its lack of true existence], you meditate that the "I" is not established the way it appears. There are various traditions.

To sum up, once you have established [selflessness] through learning and reflection on the above analysis of the four key points, you ascertain clearly in meditation that the "I" as perceived by the mind that conceives "I am" and grips it tightly in the heart's core is not established by way of its own nature based on the aggregates. This is the actual object of meditation, which you are not to forget. Meta-awareness monitors whether a conception apprehending the "I" has intruded. When necessary, by means of a little analysis, you can reaffirm that the "I" is not established by way of its own nature, and then you once more absorb your mind in how it does not exist in this manner. During this process, your considerable prior familiarization with the conception of grasping at a self will mean that, despite practicing with tight focus, as in the framework of the nine mental states of tranquil abiding, the apprehension of the "I" will remain frequent and strong, and the awareness of its lack of true existence will occur only sporadically. But through gradual habituation, [this will be inversed, and] it will be the mind viewing the "I" as lacking true existence that will be interrupted repeatedly by the apprehension of the true existence. Next, with just a little mindfulness, you will be able to reject apprehension of true existence as soon as it arises and achieve uninterrupted [focus]. Subsequently, as in the ninth mental state, you achieve a meditation in which you can relax your efforts and no longer rely on complete application, which is partial union of tranquil abiding and insight and concordant with it.

To illustrate, just as space is established based on a clear white sky as the simple absence of the object of negation—obstructive phenomena—similarly, the veritable way to cultivate space-like absorption at this point is to sustain one-pointed equipoise, uninterrupted by any other phenomena, on the nonimplicative negative: the clear void that is the simple absence of the object of negation—true existence. [262]

When tranquil abiding [pliancy] is engendered by the power of discriminating analysis alone, the result is to be identified as [genuine] noncontemplation or nonconceptual cognition.[640] If you doubt that nonconceptual cognition can result from analysis that involves various conceptual cognitions, then as the *Kāśyapa Chapter Sutra* states:

> Kāśyapa, consider this: when, for example, the wind rubs two branches together, they can catch fire; having done so, the two branches are then consumed. Similarly, Kāśyapa, if you have discriminating conceptual cognition of emptiness, an ārya wisdom understanding will arise. Having arisen, it will consume the discriminating conceptual cognition of emptiness.[641]

It is said that when analysis "rubs together" various branch-like conceptual cognitions, it gives rise to the fire-like view of emptiness that burns all branch-like conceptual cognitions, and just as all the branches of conceptions are burned and consumed, so are conceptual cognitions.

At the stage of complete nonapplication, you attain an approximation of special insight. By sustaining it meditatively, you achieve a pliancy that is induced by analytical meditation, and physical and mental serviceability that is far more intense than the bliss of physical pliancy prompted formerly by absorption in the context of tranquil abiding. Having achieved it, you realize actual special insight and henceforth have a true path of the union of tranquil abiding and insight. I proclaim loud and clear that this is the assertion of scholars who uphold the pure tradition without mixing fish and turnips.[642]

Many fools and scholars of the Sakya and Dakpo [Kagyü schools] and others say, "If there is conceptual thought, there is no view," and that meditation on the view must be free of discursive thought. They refute Gelukpas by saying that it is not right that the small fish of insight should jump in the still waters of tranquil abiding.[643] Many of our followers as well proclaim in loud voices that the above [mistaken] position is a decisive point of the path. However, until a true view of space-like absorption is achieved, failing to engage in an analysis that approximates insight and just remaining under the sway of tranquil abiding often becomes a path of tranquil abiding alone, devoid of insight, and bringing only limited progress. [263] Our system does not maintain that once you have attained the union of tranquil abiding and insight beyond effort, the small fish of insight should jump in the still waters of tranquil abiding. This is a case of the sun of refutations and assertions rising before the dawn of [understanding of] the other's views.

Before understanding the views explained in the *Great* and *Middle-Length* treatises, some [Geluk] followers as well are fooled like the hare frightened by the sound of a branch falling into the water.[644] They fail to clearly differentiate between the way to practice the lamrim in the beginning, middle, and end and the way [what you are contemplating] appears to the mind, and they equate them, which is comparable to saying that from the perspective of physical youth, maturation, and decline there is no difference between a newborn baby and a centenarian. Reflect on this well.

After practicing space-like absorption, what happens in the subsequent state? The *King of Meditations Sutra* states:

> Like mirages, smell-eaters' cities,
> magical illusions, and dreams,

> the objects [appearing in] meditation are empty of inherent nature;[645]
> understand this to be true of all phenomena.[646]

In the state subsequent to meditative equipoise, once the object of negation has been refuted, the merely nominal "I" that remains must appear like an illusion.

In this tradition, the mode of appearance is not that of magical horses and elephants or dreams that are understood to lack true existence. If that were the case, then magicians and wise elders should also understand how the "I" appears. To those who have yet to identify what exists and what does not exist by a former practice of analysis of views, a vague misty aspect appears, but this also is not how illusory appearances occur in the present context. What kind of appearance is needed? Understanding that horses and elephants produced by magic are not horses and elephants does not allow you to understand that the horses and elephants are not established by way of their own nature. For this reason, the glorious Dharmakīrti states:

> Without repudiating its object,
> [the erroneous subject] cannot be eliminated.
> [Likewise] you reject desire, aversion, and so on
> in relation to good qualities and bad
> by seeing that [the qualities of] their objects do not exist,
> not as you remove external objects.[647] [264]

The apprehended object cannot be removed the way a thorn is extracted; it must be refuted.

Because they are affected by a superficial cause of error, eyes directly see magical horses and elephants, but in the world a wise elder knows that these horses and elephants do not exist as seen. Similarly, because they are affected by underlying cause of error [the conception of true existence], conventional perceptions also directly perceive horses and elephants [as existing truly]. Nevertheless, from the perspective of their nature, it must be understood that they are like illusions in that they are empty of inherent existence. Although you know that a lion produced by magic does not exist, you actually see the lion killing the magic elephant and so on and are convinced of having seen it. My guru said that a special feature of this [Prāsaṅgika] teaching is to be profoundly convinced that persons, who are not established by way of their own nature and appear as illusions, produce black and white karma and experience its maturation effect.

In terms of the process by which reasonings are used to refute that horses and elephants are established by way of their own nature, a conventional consciousness's perception of horses and elephants as truly existent is a mistaken consciousness, similar to the perception of magic horses and elephants [as real]. In relation to worldly consciousness, the perception of horses and elephants as actually existing is unmistaken, and the perception apprehending magic horses and elephants [as real] is mistaken. When drawing such an analogy, attention is to be paid to these fine distinctions. If in thinking that horses and elephants are not established by way of their own nature, you affirm that horses and elephants in conventional terms are the same as magic horses and elephants, that would conflict with what *Entering the Middle Way* states:

> Whatever objects worldly consciousnesses perceive
> through the unmistaken six senses
> are true for just the world . . .[648]

It would be a denial of conventional existence.

Conscious that future disciples might fail to understand this key point and fall into the extreme of nihilism, Mañjuśrī encouraged the Great Lord [Tsongkhapa] to stress the appearance aspect.[649] In his *Great* and *Middle-Length* treatises and in his commentaries to *Entering the Middle Way* and *Fundamental Wisdom*, he establishes the appearance aspect from many angles. The lion of speech Taktsang Lotsāwa says:

> After analysis with many reasonings, he asserts
> that imperfect mistaken appearances are validly established.[650]

I believe that the origin of his mistake is the same.

How to meditate on the selflessness of phenomena [265]

The second topic is the way to meditate on the selflessness of phenomena. The key point of *identifying the object of negation* concerns, for example, a body that appears to stand on its own and exist from its own side and not as a designation of "body" to all five limbs, from the crown of the head to the soles of the feet. The key point of *ascertaining the entailment* is the conclusion that a body established in this manner can only be either one or distinct from its upper and lower parts, its limbs, and so on. The key point of *ascertaining the absence of true identity* is that if they were one, the bases of designation—the body's head, legs, arms, flesh, bones, and skin—and the phenomenon designated [the body itself] would certainly be separate and distinct. If the two were distinct, then after mentally putting aside each body part, from the crown to the soles of the feet, there would be nothing left to identify as a body. Therefore, apart from a simple body that is conceptually designated on the basis that is a body complete with the five limbs, there is no self-sufficient body established from its own side: this is the key point of the *ascertaining the absence of true difference*. With this unequivocal ascertainment, you have an initial attainment of the view of selflessness of phenomena. If the body did not depend on a designation by a conceptual cognition and was established by way of its own nature based on a form complete with all five limbs, then [similarly] the piece of wood found in a forest still with its branches and leaves and the piece of wood already shaped by a carpenter into a pillar should in each context appear to a mind as a pillar and be identified as such. Likewise, last month's nameless baby and the following month's baby named Tashi should be identifiable as Tashi when met at either time, which is not the case.

Moreover, consciousness is designated upon a basis of designation that is a collection of many moments of consciousness—yesterday's consciousness, today's consciousness, and so forth. Time is established based on a collection of years, months, days, and so on. For noncomposite space, take for example a thousand hollows: since each has a piece of space, space is established based on the collection of these. [266] The view is to be established in relation to every phenomenon by means of the four key points.

However, following the example used in *Clear Words* of a cart being burned and its parts being burned along with it,[651] by realizing the self's lack of inherent existence, you eliminate the apprehension of inherent existence of its bases of designation, the five aggregates, and thereby subsidiarily realize the selflessness of phenomena. Once you have established the selflessness of the person well and practiced it, it is not difficult to establish the selflessness of phenomena.

Regarding the selflessness of phenomena as well, *Four Hundred Verses* says:

> The viewer of one thing's [emptiness]
> is explained to be the viewer of all [things' emptiness];
> one thing's emptiness
> is the emptiness of all things.[652]

Āryadeva also says:

> Whoever sees the suchness of one thing
> in that way sees the suchness of all things.[653]

If you realize the emptiness of one thing, you can also realize it in relation to other things. By applying what I explained in the context of the selflessness of persons to something like a form, you will come to understand the lack of inherent existence of all phenomena, from form up to omniscience. Past masters gave several examples, but if it were necessary to meditate on it in relation to each and every phenomenon, [it would take so long that] the meditator would have to first master immortality! When you are learning and reflecting, if taking a few examples is insufficient to allow you to gain an understanding, then you may as well give up what for you will be no more than a distraction—counting things with your fingers,[654] questioning and hoping for understanding. You will be better off just remaining in a state of meditative concentration wrapped in your shabby monastic cloak.[655]

Stanzas between sections

Within the gloom of ignorance's deep darkness
the coiled rope, mind-and-body, appears
as the dreadful poisonous snake—the thought "I am"—
due to which we undergo every terror of the three types of suffering.

By adhering to the true existence of the magic horse—grasping at self—
against our will, we journey through every land of interminable samsara
and experience lands of suffering and happiness like those that haunt
 our dreams.
How very foolish it is not to understand our mistake!

The "I" that we cherish dearly as truly existent
is unfindable when sought. That is its emptiness,
as traceless as a bird's path through the sky.
I have understood this key point of all things' primordial emptiness.

Although devoid of [true existence], the sufferings of burning in
 the hells,
the pleasures of enjoying divine and human resources, and the like

are experienced and are thus like illusions. [267]
I have understood this key point of infallible dependent origination.

The knowledge of how to faultlessly establish
conventional existence just by primordial emptiness is the Middle Way.
When you swing the weapon of sharp wisdom [that understands it],
you sever the tight bonds of afflictive grasping at self.

Although this is the sole path
traveled by all āryas of the three vehicles,
these days fools pretending to uphold the teaching
plumb it in the way a fathom is measured in the dark.

Still, reflecting on the kindness of my supreme and incomparable tutor,
I proclaim in a loud voice his unmistaken teachings
on the profound key points that are as deep as the sea
and present him with clouds of superb offerings—these excellent words.

The Four Means of Gathering a Following

On the second part, training in the four means of gathering others to mature their mindstream, the *Ornament of Mahayana Sutras* says:

> For generosity, it is the same; explaining [the perfections], having
> them practiced,
> and applying them personally
> are what is meant by pleasant speech, implementation of the aims,
> and being consistent with the aims.[656]

While bodhisattvas are training in the practice of the sons of conquerors, to accomplish the aims of sentient beings, they are to mature their mindstream by applying the four methods for gathering a following.

This involves [first] assembling followers by giving them material goods, protection, and the Dharma according to each disciple's nature.

You then speak pleasantly to those you have gathered, with a cheerful and smiling countenance, asking after their health and so on according to social norms. You explain the benefits of the teaching to which they aspire, whatever it may be. Expressing yourself agreeably, to guide them along the excellent path, you teach the Dharma especially to those of lesser intellect, those who have committed various sins, those involved exclusively in this life's concerns, careless ordained people, and so on. [268] As the people in whom you have elicited delight for the realm of virtue vary, you are not to force those who cannot conceive of a state of definitive happiness to follow the path to liberation, nor Hīnayānists to follow the Mahayana, for it will not benefit them. It would be like giving a person sick with a fever a preparation including camphor before maturing their fever with a decoction of herbs, which would harm the patient and make the illness spread.

Implementation of the aims consists of ensuring that others gradually train in virtue, starting with the smallest kinds, by, for example, explaining which virtues must be cultivated to assure a long life free of illness and, ultimately, guiding them to the state beyond suffering.

Furthermore, since encouraging others to practice without practicing yourself could elicit comments such as, "For us to tame our minds, first you must tame yours," you practice even more than they do or at a strict minimum to the same degree, which is being consistent with the aims.

The concluding phase

The concluding practices are prayers and dedications.

It is most important to truly engage in the above practices with perseverance [in retreats]. Afterward, how are you to conduct your daily practice, distilling the essentials? When taking refuge and generating the awakening mind, you reflect on suffering in accordance with the paths of persons of lesser and intermediate capacity; next, in the context of guru yoga, you make a special point of confessing your sins and accumulating merit; subsequently, the main practice consists of meditating on the awakening mind, alternating giving and taking, and on tranquil abiding conjoined with insight.

Stanzas between sections

With courageous diligence[657]
And innate intelligence,
by understanding and implementing the key points of the six perfections' profound meaning,
you will reach the summit of your personal goals unhindered.

If you do not stray[658] onto the lesser path of the bliss of peace like śrāvakas and pratyekabuddhas,
you will, by practicing the four means of gathering others to mature them,
generate a constant stream of pure white activities
resembling the current of a river with the eight good qualities.[659]

I have completed this unprecedented work, which, like a garuḍa king,
[allows you to] completely traverse the firmament of samsara and personal peace
by the power of its paired wings, method and wisdom,
and in the end reach Indra's realm—the three kāyas. [269]

* * *

I have completed this [work], which is the essence of the excellent lineage holders' words and the gradual explanation of how to apply the practical exposition that pleases the conquerors: the stages of the path for persons of the three capacities that thoroughly explain the unmistaken methods guiding [disciples] to the state of omniscience. The methods consist of acquiring a large store of merit and wisdom by following the path of the six perfections that mature your own mindstream and allow you to attain buddhahood; and relying on the four means of gathering others that mature their mindstream. When practiced well, this teaching is like the supreme wish-granting gem: it fulfills beings' hopes, which is why [Tsongkhapa, in his *Song of Spiritual Experience*] praised it widely:

> As this instruction fulfills all beings' goals without exception,
> it resembles the most precious of all gems...[660]

* * *

Beings are agitated by wave after wave of desire for this life's ever unstable samsaric resources.
By such craving they are fallen in the boundless ocean of cyclic existence and strangled by its sea monsters—the three fearsome sufferings.
If those swayed by the confusion of ignorance have no prospect of attaining even the trinket of personal peace, their chances are very slim
of even hearing of—much less actually attaining—the supreme wish-granting gem that allows you to fulfill both goals and is so difficult to secure.

As the thick forest of afflictive obscurations and knowledge obscurations has been consumed by the two collections' flames,
[buddhahood] is free of the wasteland—a frightful and rather unbearable place[661]—and unharmed by the wild animals of the lesser path.
It is a pleasure grove of altruistic activity, a garden of medicinal plants, and a place of repose for those who see it or hear of it.

To establish beings in buddhahood—the union of the two kāyas utterly free of all flaws—
in the mouth of your compassion for all without exception, amid heaps of clouds—your white teeth—
are red flashes of lightning—your fine smooth tongue—from which resounds the thunder of the three vehicles' teachings. [270]

[Your peacock-like disciples], having been thereby impregnated[662] with high rebirth and certain goodness,
display the beautiful fan of their feathered tails—the dexterity of the ten powers.
O son of Śuddhodana and guru of all beings, it is thanks to you that they can perform a dance of happiness and benefit!

The savor of the incomparable ambrosia of the twelvefold scriptures,
swirled like an eternal knot in the heart of the two regents, whose instructions completely
intoxicated the great trailblazers, Nāgārjuna and Asaṅga, who in turn intoned eloquent words.
A heavenly sheer mantle of their sweet renown then enveloped the divine realm—the Land of Āryas.

The mirror of emptiness reflects without hindrance
the image of the six perfections' practice; its radiance, like that of a thousand suns,
was blown to the Snowy Land's skies by the breeze of Atiśa's altruistic intention,
where clouds of ignorance had obscured the excellent tradition for years.

[Tsongkhapa,] unable to bear this situation, his fingers of compassion
clasping the sharp weapon of incisive Mañjuvajra wisdom,
cut the net of error and misconception,
prompting the emergence of intelligent, fortunate beings of great renown.

From Brahmā's mouths flowed the waters with eight good qualities—
Buddha's words, both his canon and their explications.
Having drunk them, Tsongkhapa skillfully distinguished the provisional from the definitive.
He was an unprecedented Jahnu,[663] as all will agree.

On this earth, those who wish to uphold his tradition abound;
and although, like waters heavily laden with [gold] dust,
they cover the entire face of the earth,
sages who know it well are as rare as stars seen in the day.

With excellent voices of confidence in teaching, debate, and composition,
my tutors sound the supreme right-turning Dharma conches
for their fortunate disciples to hear.
Without doubt they are omniscient and nothing else!

Incomplete therapeutic [instructions] that claim to be profound can at times be poisonous
and are unequal to the instruction utterly complete with all the teachings' key points,
which is invaluable for guiding
the three kinds of practitioners along the path to the supreme state.

The words and meanings of the two lamrim treatises are as deep as space;
they do not fit the mold of lesser intelligence.
As the waters of well-intentioned new compositions fall to the two extremes,
they either fail to fill the vessel that is the mind or spill over from it.[664]

Works lacking the key points, like dry branches,
do not enable the fruit of excellent meaning to ripen;
those containing an excess of leaf-like empty words
are as lackluster as paintings of lamps. [271]

For that reason, this treatise contains the complete meaning
and is free of excess words, just as there is no hare on the moon.[665]
But how could the unprecedented new moon of this treatise
possibly arise from a pond such as my mind?[666]

Nevertheless, when the fingers of great learning dexterously draw [tight]
the bowstring—the scriptures' difficult key points—with an arrow
that then hits its target of fine detailed explanations,
it deflates the pride of skilled archers who are vain about their knowledge.

There are some far too nearsighted to see the final analysis
of the scriptures' meaning by logical reasoning,
who still delight so much in nonvirtuous talk that the tips of their tongues
reach as far as the peak of existence; they would do better to rest!

It is excellent when the bearers of saffron-colored cloth hats[667]
can uphold the teachings of their tradition,
but many lose their spiritual parents' gems of scriptural knowledge and realizations
to the thief of distraction and, in the end, arrive empty-handed.[668]

Some tarnished like old brass, their dull faculties accustomed to ignorance,
compare excellent upholders of the teaching to refined gold,
but when they display their wares in the great marketplace of numerous scholars,
they reveal the bad color of their own ignorance—the shame of it!

When a bird is very young and still inside its egg,
'tis difficult for its faculty of discernment to be complete;
once it has grown the full wings of adulthood,
'tis strange it cannot fly up in the sky of teaching and practice![669]

Although I lack the distinction of being knowledgeable without having studied
that impresses the many people easily amazed by the like,[670]
I am proud of the little knowledge of the five sciences I have acquired
in the way that a pauper toils to accumulate wealth.

The merit that unravels the knot of difficulty regarding the essence
of Buddha's supreme activity—teaching—is like a thousand-spoked
blazing golden wheel.[671] Thanks to it, may I reach
the palace atop [Meru's] tiers: [a buddha's] fourfold fearlessness.[672]

The deities who protect the traditions of those bearing yellow hats
are Mahākāla and Kālarūpa: may these Īśvaras[673] with their blazing eyes
burn the troops of desire-realm gods [hindrances] and at once
raise the banner of scriptural knowledge and realization as high as samsara's peak!

The warmth of my intelligence having ripened the golden egg, this work I have composed,
may it produce the excellent result like four-faced Brahmā, the four kāyas,

and may sentient beings become creators, omniscient [buddhas],
makers of the inexhaustible ornamental wheel![674]

* * *

There are several lamrim commentaries, by Chenga Lodrö Gyaltsen[675] and others, in which the first part[676] is imprecise and fails to summarize the meaning for meditation, while the latter part is far too concise, which is not useful for beginners. [272] For those of proficient intellect, who have the eyes of intelligence to see the works of the great omniscient Tsongkhapa, referring to other works is like "washing in dirty water at the edge of a lake with the eight characteristics,"[677] as the saying goes. In the tradition of this [Segyü] lineage, up to the time of [the Third Dalai Lama] the omniscient Sönam Gyatso, the only reference works were [Tsongkhapa's] two lamrim treatises and the uncorrupted oral instructions of lineage masters. There is no mention of anyone using teaching notes. From Chenga Rinpoché Shönu Chöphel Sangpo[678] onward, masters taught based on [Sönam Gyatso's] *Essence of Refined Gold*, supplementing it with the two lamrim treatises, but their commentaries were not recorded.

The scholar of sutra and tantra Jampa Rinchen,[679] born in É, the home of many bright people, was the master of Ganden Hermitage next to Palkhor Dechen Monastery at Nyangtö.[680] He requested of me an experiential instruction and with considerable perseverance received it well, in detail, over the period of a month and a half. He persistently entreated me to note the instructions I gave.

Generally, it is useful to neither yourself nor others to practice based on reading transmissions and book learning alone, without having properly received an experiential instruction from a lineage-holder guru. Moreover, some people, presumptuous and bold regarding the Dharma, give [experiential] instructions without having received one themselves.[681] Atiśa's Kadam followers said, "Teaching others when you have no personal practice is like trying to pour from one empty vase into another."[682] On the one hand, I doubted whether in these degenerate times it would help sustain the teaching for someone like me to write a clear explicit exposition for practice. On the other hand, people of inferior intellect in this age of decline fail to understand the gurus' teachings properly and incur the fault of teaching incorrectly, and so I thought that composing one might be useful. [273] I have therefore composed the present exposition of the stages of the path to enlightenment entitled the *Words of Mañjuśrī*, having first correctly received from Jamyang Lama[683] the faultless oral instructions of the Dharma king Khöntön,[684] the great, omniscient, and incomparable master of all the Conqueror's words in the degenerate age, and also received a profound explanation of every single word of the *Great Treatise on the Stages of the Path to Enlightenment* twice from the skilled orator and lord of speech, the venerable guru Könchok Chöphel.[685] Thanks to their kindness, I dared raise my head slightly with enough self-confidence to explain the stages of the path.

I, the fortunate monk of Sahor,[686] Ngawang Losang Gyatso Jikmé Gocha Thupten Langtsödé, otherwise known as Jamyang Gawai Shenyen, completed this work in what in the Land of the Āryas is called *vilamba*, here known as the thirty-second year [of a sixty-year cycle]; in what in the land of the Manchu emperor is called *wuzu*, the earth male-dog year; in what is known as *śrāvaṇa* in Sanskrit, the male-bird month; in what in Chinese is called *tshiyöl*, the seventh Hor month; and according to Kālacakra, in the month Average Joy[687] of dispelling the darkness of darkness, the month of the vowel of *ā* and the consonant *ma*; according to the *yangchar*[688] system of astrology, in the second half of the month Second Joy; the month of the vowel *ā* and the consonant *tsa*;[689] in the juvenile stage of life; the earth element; the desire-realm attribute smell; on Sunday, at the planetary juncture of sun and the fourth fire, in the Tatakāla house of the lion; in the great park where the entire canon and their commentaries have been translated, the great Palden Drepung Monastery. The scribe of Drongmepa,[690] Trinlé Gyatso, recorded it.

May the fortunate and intelligent followers of the teaching realize this [path], and may virtue flourish!

Part 2
Guru Yoga

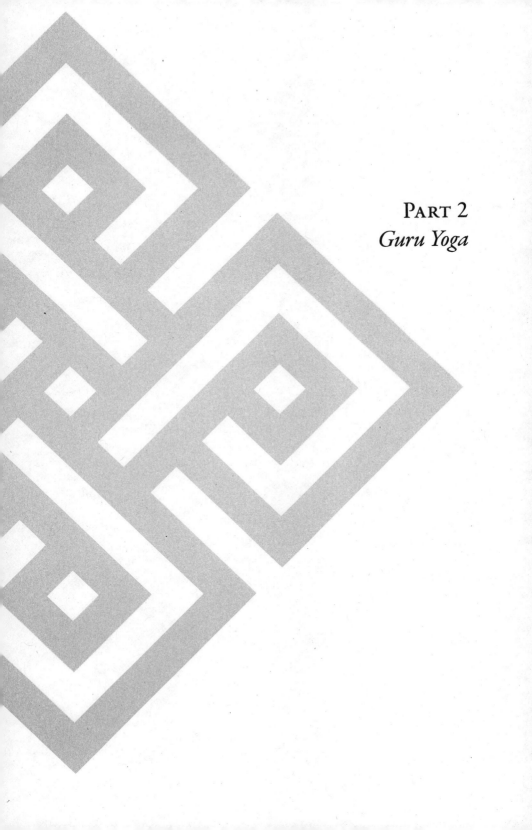

6. Source of All Siddhis

A Guide to the "Hundreds of Gods of Tuṣita" Guru Yoga

The Seventh Dalai Lama Kalsang Gyatso

Herein is a guide to the "Hundreds of Gods of Tuṣita," a guru yoga associated with supplication to the great Tsongkhapa as the embodiment of the wisdom, compassion, and power of all conquerors by way of the Miktsema prayer verse.[691]

Namo Guru Mañjughoṣāya!

With knowledge immersed in the elaboration-free sphere,
though you have cut all fetters that bind to cyclic existence,
you embrace beings wandering in existence like a mother would her only child—
to you, gentle lord, god of gods, I pay homage.[692]

The dawn that shows the way to good fortune for the Land of Snows
brought forth on the horse-like sun, whose rays illuminate the entirety
of the Sage's teaching and dispel misfortune—the darkness of both samsara and nirvana—
O Losang Drakpa, pray nurture me until my enlightenment.

Embracing your intelligence, the youthful Mañjuśrī, with love
is the embodiment of compassion, Avalokiteśvara.
Your mighty power encompasses secrets, wrathful king Vajrapāṇi.
This convergence of all three lineages into one is your unique quality.

On the surface of a mirror that is clean and free of blemishes,
the forms that your kindness takes appear again and again.
When I see this great wonder, O savior,

I feel the cycle of ordinary delusions becoming undone.

Therefore I will present here the stages of the yoga
of fervently supplicating you, exalted guru embodying all refuges,
and the unexcelled words of faultless sublime ones
as a way to create all supreme and common attainments.

The *Mañjuśrī Root Tantra* states:

> When I enter nirvana,
> and when this the earth becomes barren,
> you will assume the form of a youth
> and perform the deeds of a buddha.
> At that time there will be a great monastery,
> most joyful, in the Land of Snows.[693]

It had thus been clearly prophesized how, toward the end of an era, Mañjuśrī would reveal himself in the guise of an ordinary person and perform the deeds of a buddha and how, at that time, his monastery would obtain the name Ganden. So through prophecies and countless perfectly liberating deeds, Jé Tsongkhapa has been conclusively established as indivisible from the lords of the three buddha families of knowledge, compassion, and power.[694] Furthermore, in relation to the entirety of the Buddha's teaching of both sutra and tantra, Jé Tsongkhapa expelled all possible stains arising from lack of understanding, wrong understanding, and doubt, and on this basis, he taught the teaching exactly as it is to all the fortunate ones. Thus, for this teaching of [Buddha Śākyamuni], he is indeed a second Buddha, and hence his kindness remains incomparable. So making supplications to the Dharma king, the great Tsongkhapa, on the basis of viewing him as embodying all objects of refuge, is indeed a source of all *siddhi* attainments. Furthermore, this supplication verse famed as the Miktsema is endowed with blessings more powerful than those of many profound secret tantras. It is also possible, on the basis of this supplication prayer, to engage in rites of various levels associated with enlightened activities.

Numerous guru yogas, both common and uncommon, are associated with this supplication verse. Here, however, I present the extraordinary oral teaching known as the *Hundreds of Gods of Tuṣita*, which was transmitted aurally from the mouths of the past sublime masters of the Segyü lineage, who were all learned and realized. I received [this instruction] excellently from my most kind root guru, Trichen Ngawang Chokden,[695] who was in essence the all-pervading lord Vajrasattva. I present here the stages of meditative visualization in a format wherein their essences are distilled and made easy to practice.

Dulnakpa Palden Sangpo, a senior master of this lineage, subdued the regal spirit Pehar. This spirit was once causing the deaths of many people in a Sé family household, creating harms particularly through possessing a beloved son of the family. In response to Dulnakpa's command, Pehar pledged at that time to never cause obstacles for anyone reciting the Miktsema prayer on the basis of this guru yoga. So we find in the statements of the past masters that for anyone who recites Miktsema prayer associated with this guru yoga, [279] none of the eight classes of beings[696] in general, and no regal spirit or malevolent force like Pehar in particular, will have any power to cause harm. Therefore, among all the methods for averting obstacles and for enhancing one's practice, this guru yoga is the most excellent.

The guru yoga practice has three parts: the preliminaries, the main part of the session, and the concluding activities.

The preliminaries

The first, the preliminaries, is as follows. In a clean and appealing environment, and in front of the representations of the Three Jewels in general and especially an image—a painting or a sculpture—of the exalted guru [Tsongkhapa], lay out in a beautiful way the offerings, including a mandala offering. Then be seated on a comfortable cushion. For any virtuous activity, it is important to examine your motivation thoughts and transform them. Given that, make sure your thoughts are not directed outward and contemplate the following:

> Today I have found this human existence of leisure and opportunity, which is superior even to the wish-granting jewel, for it is on this basis that the aims of both myself and others in this and future lives can easily be realized. Yet, not only do those born in lower realms such as the animal realm spend their entire lives trying to achieve the happiness of this life alone, most beings who have attained a human life do the same. Having spent their lives pursuing nonvirtuous and neutral activities, they will in the end, after they die, have to experience endless births in the lower realms.

> Just like these beings, were I too to concern myself only with the means to achieve happiness in this life alone, there would then be no difference between me and those born in the animal realm. I must therefore not waste this existence and make sure that I extract the essence of Dharma practice, which is certain to bring benefits throughout all time, in both this and future lives. As for Dharma practice, too, if I set it aside with the thought "I will do it tomorrow, or the day after," since both my body and life are unreliable, there is no guarantee I will not die this very day. Were I to die today, alas! what will happen? Owing to my failure to master my mind, I have accumulated so much negative karma. As for virtuous mental states, I recall none that I can feel confident of having gathered. After my death, it appears I have no choice but to depart to the alarming destinations of the lower realms. [280] I will not inflict this suffering upon myself; I will instead practice Dharma, so that even were I to die this very instant, I would have no regrets. Since this yoga of supplicating the exalted master Tsongkhapa as the embodiment of the three buddha families is the root of the path, I will strive in this practice.

Then continue:

> Within my current ability, however, I have no power whatsoever even to free myself from the suffering of cyclic existence in general and that of the lower realms in particular. Therefore I and all desperate sentient beings need to rely on something special, something that possesses the capacity to save us in every situation. Here, the Buddha is a savior free of all faults and endowed with all excellent qualities. His great compassion is free of discriminatory feelings of closeness and distance, and he sees the entire expanse of knowledge. As such he is able to save me without ever letting me down. I will therefore take him as my refuge and as my teacher. Since it is the sublime Dharma alone that is the actual method to free all beings, both myself and others, from suffering and its causes, I will take it as my actual refuge. Since the Sangha community is the undeceiving companion for practicing Dharma, I will take it as my companion for cultivating the path. Thus for the sake of all beings, both myself and others, I will rely upon the Three Jewels as my refuge.

With these contemplations, visualize in front of you—as vividly as if you were seeing it with your eyes—a lotus tree most extensive and vast on whose hub is the Dharma king, the great Tsongkhapa, who is in essence indivisible from your own kind root guru. He is flanked on his two sides by his two principal spiritual sons. Around them are your direct and indirect teachers, meditation deities, buddhas, bodhisattvas, heroes and ḍākinīs, and hosts of guardian Dharma protectors.

Then, contemplating the enlightened qualities of the body, speech, mind, and activities of these objects of refuge, cultivate fervent devotion and respect and the thought of terror over the suffering of cyclic existence in general and of the lower realms in particular. Then, convinced that these objects of refuge can save us from such [suffering], cultivate the thought "*Whatever situation I find myself in, high or low, in this life, in the next, or in the intermediate state, it is you, O gurus and the Three Jewels, who know best.*" Imagine you are surrounded by all beings of the six realms and they too see perfectly the objects of refuge. And, just like yourself, imagine that they too go for refuge on the basis of generating the trust "You know best" combined with feelings of terror [about suffering]. [281] As you recite the words of going for refuge, imagine that they join the recitation. Then recite the following fourfold refuge formula three times:

> From this moment until we reach the heart of enlightenment, I and all sentient beings equal to the expanse of space go for refuge to the glorious and sublime gurus.
> We go for refuge to the blessed ones, fully awakened buddhas.
> We go for refuge to the sublime teachings.
> We go for refuge to the noble Sangha members. (3x)

Next, reflect upon how all sentient beings have been your mother and how, in your numerous past lives, they have performed immeasurable acts of kindness for you, how on countless occasions for your sake they have even given their lives. Then, contemplating their kindness and generating the wish to repay their kindness, contemplate:

> These mothers have been sources of such great kindness for me. How sad it is indeed that today they are tormented by the endless and unbounded sufferings of cyclic existence! The responsibility to dispel their suffering and secure their happiness now falls upon me, and yet I have no capacity whatsoever to save them. Were I to

> attain a state free of all faults and endowed with all enlightened qualities, however, then not only would I achieve for myself the unexcelled bliss of the perfection of relinquishment and realization, I would be able to liberate other sentient beings as well. I must, therefore, by every possible means, attain swiftly, so very swiftly, the state of buddhahood.

Having thus cultivated such fervent aspiration, recite the lines for upholding the altruistic awakening mind three times—the verse "To the Buddha, Dharma, and excellent community."[697]

Next, contemplating how sentient beings are bereft of happiness and tormented by suffering, cultivate the thoughts "How I wish they could find happiness; may they find happiness; I shall help them find happiness," and recite the following:

> May all sentient beings find happiness and its causes.
> May they be free of suffering and its causes.
> May they never be divorced from happiness that is absence of suffering. [282]
> May they abide in equanimity, free from biases of attachment and hostility rooted in discriminatory feelings of closeness and distance.

Reciting these lines three times, cultivate the four immeasurable thoughts.

The main part of the session

The second, the main part of the session, is threefold: inviting the field of merit, gathering the accumulations on its basis, and making supplications and requesting higher attainments.

Inviting the field of merit

Above Mount Meru is the realm of the Trāyastriṃśa (Thirty-Three) gods, in space above this is the Yāma (Conflict-Free) god realm, and above this in space is the god realm Tuṣita. Set apart from the majority of Tuṣita gods, like a monastery situated outside a town, is the palace of the holy Lord Maitreya with its towering victory banners. In front of this is said to be the courtyard Yiga Chözin (Where Joyful Minds Uphold Dharma), where Maitreya confers his teachings.

Imagining yourself facing Mount Meru, visualize Maitreya's buddhafield in the space above. The ground is made of various precious materials, yet it is so soft that it depresses when pressed down and bounces back when released. There are lakes, waterfalls, wish-granting trees that fulfill all needs the instant they are wished for, and forest groves, flower gardens, and so on, all of which induce delight through merely thinking of them. At the center [of all this] is an excellent mansion made of various precious materials with towering banners. It radiates lights so brilliant they can outshine the sun and moon. It is bedecked with garlands of full and half loops made of precious minerals from which hang adornments of bells, yak tails, and the like. In front of this is the Yiga Chözin courtyard, with ground of gold with square patterns inscribed in lapis lazuli. The courtyard is adorned with fruit trees, fragrant and delicious, and varieties of flowering plants of extraordinarily vibrant colors. The beauty of the courtyard is such that one never tires of gazing at it.

At the center of this [courtyard] is a precious throne hoisted by eight lions. On this spacious and vast throne is the holy Lord Maitreya, [283] whose body, the color of a refined gold, radiates light like the brilliance of a hundred thousand suns. Adorned with precious ornaments and wearing silk garments of heavenly material, he is seated in the *bhadra* posture,[698] his face turned toward you. Around him, countless assemblies of perfect retinues converge from all ten directions, figures such as Master Atiśa, Tsongkhapa and his sons, and so forth. Imagine that you too have reached this buddhafield. Cultivate fervently, for a short time but not too short, the thought that you can see with your own eyes the qualities of the buddhafield and hear the murmuring sound of Maitreya teaching. Doing so has enormous benefits; it could constitute the cultivation of perfect buddhafields and plant the seed for taking birth in such buddhafields in the future.

Next, at Maitreya's heart, at the center of a golden disc that resembles a polished mandala base marked with the pattern of an endless knot, visualize above it a cluster of clouds hovering in the sky on which sits the exalted guru Tsongkhapa, his complexion pale with a red tinge. From his hands, which perform the gesture of teaching, emerge on each side the stem of a blue lotus with the flower opened at ear level. On the right flower is a sword of wisdom, while on the left is a Perfection of Wisdom text. On his head, he wears a golden paṇḍita hat, and he is attired in the three robes of a monk. He is seated in the crossed-legged *vajrāsana* posture. On his right is the all-knowing Gyaltsab, whose head is slightly bowed, while on the left is the all-knowing Khedrup, whose body subtly sways. Their complexion, attire, and so forth are similar to the principal figure [Tsongkhapa], their right hands perform the gesture of teaching, and their left hands, in the gesture of meditation, each hold a text. They too are seated in the crossed-legged *vajrāsana* posture. Visualize the trio well in this way. Imagine also that rays of light radiating from Maitreya's heart manifest at their tips countless emanations suited to the specific needs [of sentient beings] that are projected out and then drawn back in.

Then, with fervent devotion and respect induced by contemplating the enlightened qualities of the body, speech, and mind of Tsongkhapa, generate the wish "How I wish he would appear before me here to be my savior, my refuge, and my ally." With ardent yearning, recite: [284]

1. **From the heart of the lord of hundreds of gods of Tuṣita,**
   at the tip of a mass of intensely white curd-like clouds,
   appears Losang Drakpa, the omniscient Dharma king,
   together with his sons; pray come before us here.

As you invite in this way, you imagine atop a white cloud mass that resembles a long silk scarf emerging from Maitreya's heart, great Tsongkhapa sits with his two sons, who appear in front of you spontaneously. This trio is surrounded, like a crowd gathering in a marketplace, by teachers, buddhas, bodhisattvas, heroes and ḍākinīs, and assemblies of guardian Dharma protectors. Alternatively, visualize the exalted guru and his two sons as the embodiment of all refuges. This latter approach is known as the All-Encompassing Jewel tradition.

Furthermore, when the Lord of Secret Karmavajra[699] was instructed by his meditation deity to receive the *Compendium of Training* (the *Śikṣāsamuccaya* of Śāntideva) from Maitreya himself, and accordingly when he received the *Compendium of Training* from exalted Tsongkhapa, Drupchen Rinpoché saw Maitreya on Tsongkhapa's head, Mañjuśrī on his right shoulder, and Sarasvatī on his left. Also, when Tsongkhapa was drawing near, Drupchen received a prophecy that Lord Maitreya was coming.[700] Our exalted guru is thus, in essence, the same as Maitreya. On the ordinary level, too, since he was prophesized to be reborn as Mañjuśrīgarbha in Tuṣita, one emanation [of Tsongkhapa] will manifest as a principal spiritual son of Maitreya. It is with these understandings, the teacher explains, that Tsongkhapa is here invited as emerging from the heart of Maitreya.[701]

Gathering the accumulations on the basis of the merit field

The second, gathering the accumulations on the basis of the merit field, is as follows. Having invited the merit field, you gather the accumulations by means of the seven limbs. Of these, you first appeal to [the gurus] to not enter nirvana.

The limb of appealing to not enter nirvana

For this, visualize before you a spacious and vast lion throne flanked on each side with a smaller throne. On these sit the exalted guru and his two sons on cushions of lotuses and moon discs. [285] Then contemplate:

> You are the guide for me and for sentient beings like me, whose eyes are blind to the norms of what is to be adopted and what is to be rejected; you are the healing physician for those of us tormented by the powerful disease of the mental afflictions; you are the helmsman for us drowning in the great ocean of suffering. There is no one other than you in whom we, bereft of savior and refuge, can place our hope as refuge. I appeal to you, therefore, please remain as our savior unwavering for a hundred eons and help the stainless teachings of sutra and tantra flourish through exposition and meditative practice.

With these thoughts, recite the following verse and make the supplication.

2. **In the sky ahead on a lion throne with lotus and moon,**
the most revered guru smiles brightly with joyful expression.
As the supreme field of merit for my devout mind
and for the flourishing of teaching, pray stay for a hundred eons.

The significance of making the appeal to not enter nirvana first is this. The guru is clearly the supreme field for gathering merit, and in order to gather such merit in relation to him, he must remain firmly as such a field of merit. So, the teacher explains, a supplication is first made for his long life.

The limb of prostration

For the limb of prostration, imagine that you multiply your body by the number of atoms in the buddhafields, and through all these bodies and through the bodies of all sentient beings, you all perform prostrations; with speech you all chant songs of praise; and with your minds you all supplicate with fervent devotion and respect. Then contemplate:

> Your omniscient mind perceives the entirety of knowable things not one by one but simultaneously in a single moment of time. Your speech is such that even a single expression can be heard by each being of fortunate karma in their own language and suited to their own mental faculty, granting them both immediate and ultimate well-being. Your body is endowed with the major and minor noble marks, born of immeasurable merit, such that even the merit causing a single pore of your body is a hundred times greater than that of a universal sovereign, a śrāvaka, a pratyekabuddha, and an ordinary being. [286]

While contemplating these qualities [of mind, speech, and body], recite this verse:

3. **Your wisdom mind perceives the entire expanse of knowledge,**
your eloquent speech adorns the ears of those who are fortunate,
your beauteous body, famed glory shining resplendent—
I bow to you, meaningful to see, hear, and contemplate.

The limb of offering

For this limb visualize incalculable beautiful and captivating offering goddesses who are capable of engendering bliss to both the eyes and the mind of the beholder. They carry in their hands water for drinking and water for washing the feet, for washing the face, and for sprinkling, loose blooms and stemmed flowers with sweet fragrance and attractive colors, clouds of incense, lamps dispelling darkness, perfume for anointment, a variety of food with a hundred flavors, and different musical instruments such as wind instruments, cymbals and bells, drums, and string instruments. Imagine also the five sense objects—beautiful forms, melodious sounds, sweet fragrances, delicious tastes, and soft textures—the seven precious emblems of a royal kingdom, and the symbols and substances of auspiciousness.[702] Also bring to mind such non-owned offerings as rivers and lakes, forests, flowers, mountains of medicinal plants—in brief, all categories of offerings without exception that can please [the merit field]. Also bring to mind the mass of Samantabhadra offering clouds, which have arisen from the play of deep meditative absorption of the conquerors and their children. Then recite the following verse:

4. **Excellent offerings of water, varieties of flowers,**
fragrant incense, bright lights, perfume, and so on—
this ocean of offering clouds actual and envisioned,
I offer these to you, supreme field of merit.

As you recite these lines, imagine that [the figures in the merit field] accept your offerings, engendering in their minds extraordinary bliss, and that they become sated and pleased. [287]

The limb of confession

In the limb of confession you bring to mind the incalculable negative karma and downfalls you have accumulated over beginningless lifetimes wandering in this cycle of existence and whose effects have yet to be projected. Review in particular all the naturally negative deeds and downfalls you can recollect that you have committed through violation of precepts, such as acting contrary to the three vows. Then contemplate, "As a consequence for all these and also the countless others that I cannot recollect, I will have to undergo immeasurable sufferings, such as taking birth in the hells. In this life, too, they will obstruct my development of higher qualities. They are indeed a source of extremely great injury. What do I do now? Alas, I have accumulated so much negative karma." With such a thought, generate such strong remorse it is as if poison has entered your stomach, and resolve to never commit such negative karma from now on. On this basis, and without concealing your negative karma in the presence of the objects of refuge, imagine making a confession with a feeling of deep pain accompanied by lamentation, and then recite the following verse:

5. **Whatever negative karma of body, speech, and mind**
I have accumulated since beginningless time,
the transgressions of the three vows in particular,
each I confess from my heart with intense remorse.

As you recite these lines, imagine that light rays emanate from those in whose presence you have confessed, and these rays touch your body, speech, and mind, instantly purifying all your negative karma and obscurations, like sunlight entering a dark chamber. It is also good to visualize all other sentient beings purifying their negative karma and obscurations; please learn the details of this from oral teachings.

Going for refuge grounded in admiration and respect for the objects of visualization in whose presence you confess, and fervently generating the awakening mind that wishes "How I long to attain the state of buddhahood for the sake of all these destitute beings" based on engendering powerful compassion by reflecting upon the situation of beings who are just like me—engaging in causal and resultant negative karma—these two [going for refuge and generating the awakening mind] constitute the *power of support*. Feeling remorse for past negative karma you have committed constitutes the *power of repudiation*. Making the resolve never to repeat such acts in future [288] constitutes the *power of turning away from faults*. Performing prostrations and making offerings to the guru, on the basis of visualizing him as the merit field, and sealing the three spheres of the act of confession with nonobservation constitute the *power of engaging the antidotes*. When you confess negative karma with full presence of these four powers, this can cleanse even extremely powerful ones.

The limb of rejoicing

The limb of rejoicing is as follows. The enlightened deeds of our exalted guru performed in his past lives and the enlightened deeds of his three secrets lie beyond comprehension of the ordinary mind.[703] Aside from these, even the deeds of his conventional life—those cognizable by the ordinary mind—include the following. From an early age, he engaged in the study of sutra and tantra, not just a few specific texts but comprehensively, such that, with respect to the four classes of tantra and the three baskets of the Perfection Vehicle, he mastered the works of scholar-siddhas who were their authoritative interpreters. Having decisively mastered through study all the finer details and subtle distinctions among the four Buddhist philosophical schools, he became a scholar unmatched by any great teacher of the Land of Snows.

Whatever he learned from study he did not leave at the level of mere learning. Instead he ensured that all treatises dawned upon him as personal instructions. With everything he learned, not even a hair's width was discarded; he saw all the components of his learning as profound methods for maturation and liberation. On this basis, he strove to implement [the content of these treatises] perfectly through contemplation and meditative cultivation. This too he undertook in a manner free of the slightest contamination by the eight mundane concerns and thinking only of the Buddha's teaching and the welfare of others. Thus attaining all higher attainments, both common and supreme, he traversed to the ground of the supremely realized siddhas.

To beings with fortunate karma, he revealed the uncommon dimensions of the four classes of tantra, especially the two stages of highest yoga class, and all key points of the common path of the Perfection Vehicle, especially the profound Middle Way view. He revealed these in a way so clear and comprehensive, through prolific works of excellence and eloquence, that no scholar-siddha in this Land of Snows has ever matched it. That today people everywhere, both in the central region and in the borderlands, can engage in study, reflection, and meditative cultivation of the entire teaching of the Buddha on the basis of even a rough overview is owing to the kindness of this exalted teacher. That this is so will be understood if one views the situation without bias.

Contemplating these liberating deeds, with your heart rejoicing with admiration, [289] generate the thought "May I too be able to live such a life," and then recite the following verse.

6. **In this age of degeneration, you strove in vast learning and practice.**
Shunning the eight mundane concerns, you made your life purposeful.
For your most expansive enlightened deeds, O lord,
I feel admiration from the very depth of my heart.

The limb of requesting to turn the wheel of Dharma

For this limb, contemplate:

> O exalted guru and your spiritual sons—your mind perfectly free of obscurations and their imprints while never wavering from the clear light of bliss and emptiness thanks to the power of your past aspirations and your great compassion—the forms of your body, speech, and mind arise effortlessly in response to the needs of disciples. Therefore, just as clouds form in the expanse of a clear sky and from this rain pours down effortlessly upon the earth, likewise I appeal to you for the clouds of compassion and wisdom

> to form in the expanse of your dharmakāya. From this may the rain of sublime Dharma, both profound and vast, fall without interruption on the earth that is the intelligence of us, your aspiring disciples.

Contemplating thus, recite the following verse:

7. **Revered sublime gurus, from clouds of wisdom and love**
densely amassed in your dharmakāya sky,
pray loose a rain of teachings, profound and vast,
on the fields of your disciples in perfect accord with our needs.

Both here and in the context of appealing to not enter nirvana, imagine that consent has been granted just as you have requested.

THE LIMB OF DEDICATION

For the limb of dedication, contemplate:

> May all my virtues of the three times—what I have gathered in the past, am gathering at present, and will gather in future—such as from engaging in the practice of this profound path of guru yoga, become conditions generally for the flourishing of the Buddha's teaching and become whatever means are of benefit to all beings throughout the farthest reaches of space. In particular, may my virtues become a condition for the flourishing of this flawless Dharma of our exalted guru—his teaching of sutra and tantra as well as scriptural knowledge and realizations [290]—unobstructed by the stain of any discordant factors and shining like sun in all directions and all times.

Contemplating thus, recite the following verse:

8. **May whatever virtues I have gathered**
benefit the teaching and sentient beings.
In particular, may they help illuminate for a long time
the heart teaching of the Dharma king Tsongkhapa.[704]

Not only is dedication a method for enhancing greatly even the smallest virtue, but it is also an unexcelled means for making them inexhaustible until enlightenment. Furthermore, since it has been stated that all aspirations made by the bodhisattvas are encompassed within the aspiration to uphold the sublime Dharma, this aspiration to uphold the Conqueror's teaching condenses all the aspirations into one. As such it is most excellent and unsurpassed.

Making supplications and requesting higher attainments

Make supplications on the basis of whatever version of the Miktsema prayer you choose.[705] Then contemplate:

> When it comes to possessing the great treasure of objectless compassion, the noble Avalokiteśvara is unrivaled among bodhisattvas. And when it comes to his stainless wisdom pertaining to the entire field of knowledge, it is Mañjuśrī who is unrivaled. Likewise, among all the learned masters of the past in this land of Tibet, if one were to carefully examine with an unbiased mind in whatever context, whether sutra or tantra, none can match our exalted master, something that can be discerned from his excellent writings. So I touch with my crown the feet—the lowest part of the body—of the one born in Tsongkha in the east, unrivaled among all the learned masters of the Land of Snows and indeed the crown jewel, and I supplicate. [291] Bless me so that I may obtain, like you, the perfect qualities of a learned person.

This is to *supplicate from the perspective of the outer aspect by drawing the similarities*; it represents the "outer cultivation" of our exalted guru. [In the Tibetan word for "supplication,"] *sölwa* means "to appeal" and *depa* means "to offer";[706] the term thus means "to supplicate."

Again:

> With his possession of the enlightened quality of constantly gazing upon sentient beings with great objectless compassion, he resembles Avalokiteśvara; and in being a lord possessing stainless wisdom of the entire expanse of knowledge of the two truths, he resembles the exalted Mañjuśrī. In brief, I supplicate you, O great Tsongkhapa, you who possesses compassion and wisdom exactly as present in the mindstreams of Avalokiteśvara and Mañjuśrī,

> respectively. Bless me so that I too can, by striving in meditative practice, attain such extraordinary qualities of realization.

This is to *supplicate from the perspective of the inner aspect, his possession of the corresponding qualities*; it represents the "inner cultivation" of our exalted guru.

Again:

> The essence of the convergence of the great compassion of all conquerors arising in the form of a deity is the noble Avalokiteśvara. Because our exalted guru is identical in nature [to him], he is indeed the embodiment of the compassion of all conquerors. The essence of the convergence of the wisdom of all conquerors into a single form is the exalted Mañjuśrī, and since our exalted guru is Mañjuśrī appearing in human form, he is indeed the nature of the wisdom of all conquerors. The essence of the convergence of the might and power of all conquerors arising in the form of deity is the Lord of Secrets [Vajrapāṇi], and since our exalted guru is identical in nature [to him], he is established indeed as the embodiment of the might and power of all the conquerors. I touch your lotus feet, the lowest part of your body, O great Tsongkhapa, you who embody the essence of the buddha families, and make supplications. Bless me so that, like you, I may attain all the higher qualities of wisdom, compassion, and power of the lords of the three buddha families.

Then recite the following verse. [292]

> You are Avalokiteśvara, great treasury of objectless compassion;
> you are Mañjuśrī, embodiment of stainless wisdom;
> you are Vajrapāṇi, destroyer of all dark forces;
> you are the crown jewel among the learned ones of the Land of Snows;
> I supplicate at your feet, O Losang Drakpa.[707]

This is to *supplicate from the perspective of the secret aspect, viewing him in essence as indivisible from the meditation deities*; it is the "secret cultivation" of our exalted guru.

That this great being is the lord Mañjuśrī is clearly established, such as in the citation from the *Mañjuśrī Root Tantra* referred to above. And given that the *Book of Kadam* states how the lords of the three buddha families share a single nature,[708] this confirms that our exalted guru is a manifestation of the lords of the other two buddha families as well. The master's secret biographies also briefly establish, as do other scriptural citations and reasoning, that he has the same nature as Avalokiteśvara and Vajrapāṇi. This constitutes *supplicating our exalted guru as embodying the lords of all three buddha families.*

The teacher, however, offers an alternative approach to the Miktsema prayer whereby our exalted guru is viewed as Mañjuśrī, Gyaltsab as Avalokiteśvara, and Khedrup as Vajrapāṇi.[709]

Of these three ways of supplicating, the first praises [Tsongkhapa] primarily from the perspective of the qualities of learning or scriptural knowledge, while the remaining two praise from the perspective of the qualities of attainment or realization. Thus when you supplicate on the basis of bringing these points to mind, this constitutes supplicating the lords of the three buddha families as well. And you will, without a doubt, obtain benefits equal to reciting the profound mantras of these deities. [293]

While supplicating in these terms, the way you visualize making the request for the higher attainments is described in the following summary:

> Washing away impurities and dispelling ignorance,
> with body the great and with speech the clear,
> with seeds the swift and with hand implements the profound;
> with the scripture, the sword, and scripture and sword together:
> teaching, debate, and composition.[710]

Thus, having prefaced the visualization by washing away impurities, the main practice consists of seven cultivations: (1) great wisdom through the body, (2) clear wisdom through speech, (3) swift wisdom through the seed syllable of mind, (4) profound wisdom through the hand implements, (5) the wisdom of exposition through the scripture, (6) the wisdom of debate through the sword, and (7) the wisdom of composition through both scripture and sword.

Cultivating great wisdom through the body

The first is as follows. Due to the force of having supplicated thus, imagine that our exalted guru and his two sons become pleased. White rays of light radiate from their hearts in the shape of long extended sleeves whose tips merge to form a single beam that pierces your crown aperture. Through this flows immeasurable white nectar like a stream of milk that, though having such an appearance, is in essence their wisdom mind. As this enters through your crown, it fills your entire body and expels, in the form of smoky fluids and charcoal fluids, all your negative karma, obscurations, and ignorance accumulated since beginningless time as well as illnesses and harms caused by malevolent forces in the form of scorpions, frogs and tadpoles, and so on. Just like a mighty flash flood rushing down a mountain washing away haystacks, imagine they are expelled through the pores of your skin. Then imagine that your body becomes filled with the nectar of wisdom and it becomes clear and radiant.

Once again, as you supplicate, imagine streams of orange light now flow through the light sleeves and enter your crown and fill your entire body. In particular, all the minute particles of nectar appear as images of Mañjuśrī, and they fill up every nook and cranny inside you. Light rays emanate from them and draw forth the wisdom of all the conquerors and their children in the form of countless Mañjuśrī images. They enter through your pores and dissolve into the images of Mañjuśrī inside your body, making the entire interior of your body clear and radiant and filled with deity bodies and light rays. This dispels the darkness of ignorance and dispels, in particular, all factors that obscure you from being able to see by yourself all that is to be adopted and all that is to be rejected. [294] With relation to the full spectrum of knowledge, the light of your intelligence becomes enhanced. Imagine that you have attained, in particular, the *great wisdom* that enables you to discriminate, by yourself, all key points of what is to be adopted and what is to be rejected, especially in relation to the meaning of scriptures.

Cultivating clear wisdom through speech

As before, wash away the impurities and supplicate. Imagine streams of red light flow and fill your entire body; now when the minute particles of nectar pervade your entire body, they take the form of the letters *a ra pa ca na*[711] and the letters of the Miktsema prayer verse. Light rays emanate from these and bring forth, in the form of the letters *a ra pa ca na* and of the Miktsema verse, the wisdom, such as clear wisdom, present in the minds of all the conquerors and their children. Those letters dissolve into the letters that are inside your body, and your body becomes replete with letters and light rays, dispelling the darkness of ignorance in both its general and specific forms. Imagine that you have attained the *clear wisdom* capable of discriminating the subtle and minute aspects of the factors of unenlightened and enlightened existence, just as the tips of strands of *kuśa* grass remain distinct.

Cultivating swift wisdom through the seed syllable of the mind

Washing away the impurities and the rest is the same as the previous cultivation. The unique aspect here is that the minute particles of nectar are in the form of the syllable *dhīḥ*, and the wisdom [of the conquerors and their children] brought forth [at the tips of light rays emanating from your heart] are also dissolved in the form of *dhīḥ* syllables. The light rays purify ignorance, both general and specific forms. You imagine having attained the *swift wisdom* that can disrupt instantly, right there and then, when mental states of not understanding, distorted understanding, or wavering through doubt arise.

Cultivating profound wisdom through the hand implements

Washing away the impurities and so on is the same as above. The unique aspect is that here the minute particles of nectar are in the form of swords and scriptures [the hand implements] and the wisdom [of the conquerors and their children] brought forth [at the tips of light rays emanating from your heart] is also dissolved in the form of swords and scriptures, purifying ignorance. Imagine that you have attained, to an immeasurable degree, the *profound wisdom* that can engage with both the words and meaning of scripture without impediment and through limitless avenues of reasoning. [295]

Cultivating the wisdom of teaching through the scripture

Washing away the impurities and so on is the same as above. The unique aspect here is that the minute particles of nectar are in the form of scriptures that are being taught. Also, the *wisdom of exposition* of the conquerors and their children, both general and specific topics and, in particular, the wisdom of the learned paṇḍitas with great expertise in exposition, are drawn forth similarly in the form of scriptures. As they dissolve into you, your entire body is filled with scriptures and light rays, and all the ignorance pertaining to the words and meanings of scripture are purified. Imagine that you have attained the wisdom that can perfectly comprehend the words and meaning of scripture and teach others on that basis.

Cultivating the wisdom of debate through the sword

All the other elements are the same as above; here the minute particles of nectar are in the form of sword wheels. The wheel of swords is formed by a double-edged blade standing vertically from a hub with the handle shaped like an anklet bell, from which extend [sideways] six blades forming a wheel with six spokes. On the handle of the central blade, on a moon disc, is a clear and radiant syllable *dhīḥ*. On the six spokes, on moon discs that barely touch them, are the letters *oṃ a ra pa ca na* or the letters of the Miktsema verse. In the space between [the six blades] are *dhīḥ* syllables, each on a moon disc, and all together the appearance is of a wheel. Imagine that you draw forth the wisdoms pertaining to general and specific topics in the form of such wheels, all of which dissolve into you. As the wheels rotate clockwise, imagine they slice away the entire matrix of ignorance that obstructs you from destroying the distorted views of your adversaries. Imagine that you have attained the extraordinary wisdom that is unimpeded in debate.

Cultivating the wisdom of composition through both scripture and sword

All the other elements are the same as above; here the minute particles of nectar are in the form of scriptures and sword wheels as described above. The knowledge and wisdom pertaining to general and specific topics are drawn forth, similarly, in the forms of scriptures and swords, which dissolve into you. With the swords cutting away, imagine that the entirety of your ignorance pertaining to composition is purified and that you attain the extraordinary wisdom that is unimpeded in composition.

Perform whichever of these seven rounds of visualizations you wish to cultivate. You don't need to do them all in this exact sequence. [296] Furthermore, if you wish to perform this practice for the purpose of overcoming sickness, you could visualize cooling blue nectar for a bile disorder, cooling white nectar for a phlegm disorder, and so forth, adapting the color of the nectar in relation to the specific illness. In the sacred words of Lord Mañjuśrī too it says:

> For peace white, holding a white lotus;
> with gestures of granting boon and refuge;
> there are the vase water, mirror, and so on...[712]

As this states, there are myriad methods for cultivating enlightened activities on the basis of specific color, hand implement, and so forth. So you could undertake this practice by knowing how to adapt it to your specific needs. As for what I have written here so far, many essential points must still be learned from the oral teachings of sublime gurus for whom the content of the tantras has dawned as pith instructions.

Concluding activities

Having thus supplicated however many times on the basis of the Miktsema prayer, if you wish to undertake an additional special supplication praying for the arising within you of the stages of the path, you could proceed as in the following.

You are Mañjuśrī embodying the wisdom of all conquerors,
you are the White Lotus One with compassion for the beings of
the six realms,
you are Vajrapāṇi, lord of might and power—
O Tsongkhapa, you are the vajra, the magical unity of three
buddha families.

Emerging from your body, speech, and mind, O Lord,
I will cultivate the three vajras through the power of this blessing.
So from now on, in all my lives,
please sustain me with joy.

Now that I have found this body with leisure and opportunity
and have met the tradition of the Buddha's perfect teaching,
bless me that I may cease fixation on the eight worldly concerns,
concerns whose aims, even when realized, must be instantly cast
aside.

There is no certainty when the lord of death's penalty—
the attack on my life force—will arrive.
Bless me that I may, with terror, strive with wholehearted diligence
in Dharma practice certain to secure benefit in all situations. [297]

Bless me that I may act in perfect accord with the ethical norms
linked even to subtle aspects of karma, both bright and dark,

including the boundaries prescribed by the three vows and so forth
pledged in the presence of my abbots, preceptors, and meditation deities.

Bless me that I may generate the wish to attain liberation,
born of deep revulsion and disenchantment
for this wretched samsaric state,
where the beings of the six realms experience only suffering.

Bless me that I may see all beings as my parents,
beings who have endured for my sake the torments
of negative karma and pain through countless lives,
and may I train in compassion and the supreme awakening mind.

Bless me that I may practice the union of
the perfect view that excellently perceives
the ultimate expanse primordially free of elaborations
and the vast activities of gathering merit such as consummate giving.

Bless me that, with the wheel weapon of the swift path, I may
shred samsara's web of karmic winds and conceptual elaborations
and attain in this very life [the state of]
all-pervading Vajradhara, lord of four buddha bodies.

You could recite these lines while contemplating their meaning. If you are doing a short session, it is okay also to skip this.

Next, make the following supplication:

O precious root guru, most glorious,
reside upon a lotus within my heart.
Sustain me with your great kindness, and grant me
the siddhis of your body, speech, and mind.

Now, if you have visualized a retinue [around Tsongkhapa and his two disciples], dissolve them into the father and his two sons. The two sons, in turn, dissolve into the principal figure, and their lion thrones dissolve into that of the principal.

Once again, as you supplicate with the verse "O precious root guru, most glorious...," imagine that our exalted guru, together with his lion throne, enters through your central channel, which you have visualized in the center of your body with its upper end at the crown aperture fully open. As he dissolves into your heart, which you have imagined upside down[713] with its tip split into eight parts, imagine your heart assuming the form of an eight-petaled lotus.

As you once again supplicate as above, our exalted guru, facing the same way as you, enters through your crown and descends through your central channel. [298] As he dissolves into the center of your lotus heart, he fuses inseparably with your wind-mind, which then assumes the form of our exalted guru. Imagine the petals [of your lotus heart] fold upward to close, like pulling a thread when closing a sack, its inside softened by lights of five colors. Imagine it to be tied on the outside by strings of the words of the Miktsema verse and the letters of the *oṃ a ra pa ca na* mantra and crowned at its tip by a half five-pronged vajra, pressing down with its weight. It is also okay if you omit this vajra.

The guru yoga transmitted [by Tsongkhapa] through Khedrup Jé on a one-to-one basis also states that one could close the upper end of the central channel and imagine [the interior of the heart] swathed in five-colored lights.[714] There is also the custom of supplicating "O precious root guru, most glorious..." only one time. So you should do whatever feels right to you.

Next, the concluding dedication and aspiration prayer are as follows.

Thus, through the power of honoring and supplicating
my most holy guru, source of all higher attainments,
may I be sustained joyfully
in all my lives by the guru Mañjuśrī.

By meditating thoroughly on Ajitanatha[715]
amid a billion wonders in the Tuṣita realm
made of numerous precious gems, may I cultivate his perfect realm
and take birth there the instant I part from this life.

Having invited the guru and his sons at the tip
of white clouds streaming from Maitreya's heart,
and having gathered merit by means of the seven limbs,
may my mindstream easily reach maturation.

The wisdom, compassion, and power of the conquerors of the three times
arising as a nirmāṇakāya of union: O Savior,
by conclusively viewing you and supplicating you as the embodiment
of three buddha families, may I achieve all attainments, common and supreme.

In particular, through the stream of wisdom's nectar,
may all the negative karma, obscurations, and ignorance of my doors be cleansed;
may my intellect equal that of Mañjuśrī with respect to all fields of knowledge,
such as exposition, debate, and composition.

May I take birth among the first disciples of Savior Lion's Roar[716]
in the northeastern realm Arrayed with Wondrous Excellences
and spend my time always in the study, contemplation,
and meditative cultivation of sutra and tantra.

In brief, in this and in all my future lives,
may I be never separated from the exalted Losang Drakpa, [299]
father and sons, and may I uphold all the teachings of the Conqueror
and immerse myself in the noble purpose of serving the Dharma and beings.

In this way, conclude your session with perfect dedication and aspiration prayers.

The guru's form is retained within your heart without dissolution until your death. So when you invite the merit field for your supplication in subsequent sessions and they appear in front of you in sequence, imagine that the mantra strings binding your heart are loosened, leading the petals of your lotus heart to open, and they dissolve into the guru at the center. You should also regularly contemplate your own mind as being, in essence, the nature of the guru inside your heart and, on this basis, make supplications to him. When eating meals too, imagine offering the food and drinks to the guru at your heart and that he partakes in them. Furthermore, supplicate him on the basis of viewing whatever appears to you as sharing the same nature as the guru's three secrets. All of these should be sealed by the view that they are mere imputations of the mind and that not even an atom exists objectively from its own side. Perceiving all of these activities as resembling dreams and illusions, strive to train in guru yoga, which is supreme among all virtuous activities.

O Tsongkhapa, you are the sole lord bringing a smile
to all beings as a friend without any need for acquaintance;
with your mouth, a hundred-petaled lotus with excellent attributes,
you drink the immortal nectar, the wisdom of the Conqueror and his
children.

The expanse of space is devoid of boundaries and center;
where in all ten directions could it not pervade?
Likewise, there is no living being ever to be seen
not sustained by Guru Mañjuśrī's enlightened deeds.

Nonetheless, for the sake of that new river Ganges,
the stream that contains the unexcelled attainments,
Bhagīratha fervently performed the rite with unwavering faith and
reverence;
such is the power of interdependence.[717]

Therefore, through this virtue of inscribing here
the stages of the yoga of supplication, may I in all lives
lack neither the courage nor the effort to uphold
Losang Drakpa's teaching, both exposition and practice.

In particular, may I be able to illuminate perfectly in this end age[718]
the Buddha's teaching of sutra and tantra through hearing, exposition,
and practice;
may all conditions adverse to this goal be pacified;
may all favorable conditions be spontaneously realized as wished for. [300]

Colophon

Entitled *Source of All Higher Attainments*, this method for performing the visualization practices of the guru yoga known as the *Hundreds of Gods of*

Tuṣita, in connection with supplication to the most holy great Tsongkhapa and on the basis of the Miktsema prayer, was composed by Losang Kalsang Gyatso, a Buddhist monk who has developed faith in the teaching of Jé Tsongkhapa derived from understanding. It was written on the basis of the guide composed by the supreme realized master Jampal Gyatso.[719] My most kind root teacher, the all-pervading lord and supreme vajra being Trichen Ngawang Chokden—whose very name is difficult to utter—instructed me to compose a guide to this guru yoga. The light of doctrine Jaya Paṇḍita Huthokthu made a similar request. As I had the wish to compose such a work, the following three—Ta-Lama Erteni Darhan-shi Rege-thu Losang Sönam, who is a member of the party of Ruthu Sheyé Gung Gyaltsen of Khalkha Yön, with Nangso Losang Tsöndrü and Kachu Losang Chöwang—also made requests expressing a deep interest in seeing a clear and easily practiced [guidance instruction on] the visualization sequence of this guru yoga complete within the three-part framework of preliminaries, main practice, and concluding activities.

7. Offering to the Guru

Panchen Losang Chökyi Gyaltsen

In the language of India it is called *Gurupūjasyakalpa*.
In Tibetan it is called *Bla ma mchod pa'i cho ga* (*A Rite of Offering to the Guru*).[720]

I bow to the feet of my sublime gurus, whose kindness is unrivaled, and go to them for refuge. I appeal to them: Please always sustain me with your great love in all circumstances.

When relied upon, he grants in a single instant
the great bliss of three buddha bodies along with the common siddhis;
he is the wish-granting jewel conferring everything desired.
Having bowed at the feet of Vajradhara,
I present here a beautiful garland of flowers
picked from the lotus grove of sutras, tantras, and sublime instructions—
the supreme method, unrivaled for securing
the benefit and happiness of every fortunate disciple.

> The foundation of all excellence for those aspiring to liberation, the source of the entire collection of good fortune, the root of all the countless yogic attainments both supreme and common, the summarized essence of all the instructions on the practices a yogi of the supreme vehicle needs to pursue—all of these depend upon proper reliance on the spiritual mentor who reveals to you the path without error. The *Blue Compendium* says:[721]
>
> The starting point where all instructions converge
> is not forsaking your sublime spiritual mentor.

From him comes faith, the awakening mind, and so forth;
he is the treasury, the source of all higher qualities.[722]

Also, the Omniscient [Tsongkhapa] says:

The root of creating well the auspicious conditions
for all the good things of this and future lives
is to rely properly, with effort in both thought and action,
on the sublime spiritual teacher who reveals the path.

Seeing this, never forsake him, even at the cost of your life, [302]
and please him with the offering of following his advice.
I, a yogi, have practiced in this manner;
you who aspire to liberation should do likewise.[723]

And he says:

The good fortune of both this world and the world beyond,
the root of all higher qualities, is the kind master.[724]

Fifty Verses on the Guru too states:

"Higher attainments follow after the master,"
Vajradhara himself has declared.
Knowing this, you should thoroughly
please the guru with all that you have.[725]

The *Synthesis of Precious Qualities* states:

Good disciples who are respectful to the guru
should always rely on their learned gurus.
Why? Because the virtues of learning come from them
and they teach the perfection of wisdom.
"Attainment of the attributes of a buddha depend on the spiritual mentor";
so stated the Conqueror who possesses all higher qualities.[726]

Therefore, as a field for gathering merit and purifying obscurations, the vajra master is superior even to all the buddhas. The *Saṃvarodaya Tantra* says:

> Whether it's the self-arisen Blessed One
> or the meditation deity itself,
> the vajra master is superior even to them,
> for it is he who grants the pith instructions.[727]

For these reasons, the cultivation of guru yoga, which encompasses all the essential points of the path, is the most excellent means of extracting the essence of your human existence of leisure and opportunity. Therefore practice this in the following way.

[First] from within an especially virtuous state of mind, proceed with going for refuge, generating the awakening mind, and cultivating the four immeasurable thoughts. Then, with deity yoga and in the form of any of the three meditation deities Guhyasamāja, Cakrasaṃvara, or Vajrabhairava, imagine light radiates from your body and cleanses the entire cosmos and all its denizens of their impurities. Imagine that the entire cosmos has transformed into a celestial mansion and all its denizens into gods and goddesses, a perfectly pure sphere.

Going for Refuge and Generating the Awakening Mind[728]

Here is how you go for refuge and generate the awakening mind based on chanting the words of Khedrup Sangyé Yeshé:

From within great bliss, I arise as the guru deity,
from whose body a mass of light radiates
to the ten directions, blessing the cosmos and all its denizens.
This transforms them into perfectly arrayed forms
with enlightened qualities pure and manifold.

From within a virtuous mind, great and intensely pure,
I and my old mother sentient beings extending through space,
from now until the essence of enlightenment is attained,
we go for refuge to the guru and the Three Jewels.

Namo gurubhyaḥ
Namo buddhāya
Namo dharmāya
Namo saṅghāya (3x)

Having become the guru deity myself,
I shall, for the benefit of all mother sentient beings,
establish all sentient beings
in the supreme state of a guru deity. (3x)

For the sake of all mother sentient beings, I will quickly, quickly, in this very life, actualize the state of a primordial buddha guru deity. I will free all mother sentient beings from suffering, and I will establish them in great bliss, buddhahood. To this end, I will practice the profound path of the guru-deity yoga. (3x)

Inner offering

> Bless the inner offering and the other offering substances through any appropriate highest-yoga tantra rite or, to perform this briefly, recite:

Oṃ āḥ hūṃ (3x)

> Now contemplate:

Their *essence* is gnosis, their *appearance* is the inner offering [303] and the individual offering substances, and their *function* is to produce within the field of the six senses the special gnosis of bliss and emptiness. Through this, the entire face of the earth as well as the expanse of space are filled with clouds of offering substances of inner, outer, and secret offerings, creating an inconceivable spectacle.

Generating the field of merit

> Here in the main practice, presented in verse since that is easier to engage, recite the following lines with your mind undistracted and contemplate their meaning.

In the vast space of indivisible bliss and emptiness, amid thick clouds of Samantabhadra's offerings,
and atop an unimaginable wish-granting tree adorned with leaves, flowers, and fruits,
a lion throne blazes with jewels. On it is a wide lotus with a sun and a moon,
and there sits my triply kind root guru, who in essence is all the buddhas.

He appears as a saffron-clad monk, with one face and two arms and with a radiant smile.
His right hand is in the teaching gesture, and his left, in meditation pose, holds an alms bowl filled with nectar.
He is wearing the three robes of saffron, and his head is adorned with a paṇḍita's golden hat.[729]

At his heart is the pervasive Vajradhara, with one face and two arms, blue in color.
Holding vajra and bell, he is in union with Vajradhātvīśvarī, both ecstatic in the play of innate bliss and emptiness;
they are adorned with myriad jewel ornaments and draped in heavenly silk robes.[730]

Adorned with major and minor noble marks, blazing with thousands of rays of light, encircled in a five-colored rainbow,
he sits in the vajra posture. His five pure aggregates are the five sugatas;
his four elements are the four consorts; his sense bases, veins, sinews, and joints are in fact the bodhisattvas;
his pores are the twenty-one thousand arhats; his limbs are the wrathful deities;
his light rays are directional guardians, while yakṣas and the worldly gods are but cushions for his feet.

Around him, in respective circles, are the actual and lineage gurus, meditation deities, and hosts of mandala gods;
buddhas, bodhisattvas, heroes and ḍākinīs,[731] and a sea of Dharma protectors.
The three doors of each are marked by three vajras, and from the letter *hūṃ* [at their heart] emerge hook-like beams of light

drawing forth the gnosis beings from their natural abodes, [304] whose inseparability [with the commitment beings] becomes firm.

Invocation

Sources of excellence and good fortune, root and lineage gurus
of the three times, meditation deities, and the Three Jewels,
heroes and ḍākinīs, along with hosts of Dharma protectors,
by the force of your compassion, pray come here and firmly remain.

Though phenomena are utterly devoid of intrinsic going and coming,
in accordance with mentalities of a variety of disciples,
your deeds born of wisdom and compassion issue every form.
O sublime refuges and protectors, please come here with your retinue.[732]

Oṃ guru buddha bodhisattva dharmapāla saparivāra ehyahiḥ.
Jaḥ hūṃ baṃ hoḥ.

The gnosis beings and commitment beings become nondual.

> Viewing the guru and Vajradhara as inseparable in this way is the intention of many of the tantras. Accordingly, *Fifty Verses on the Guru* states:
>
> > Your master and Vajradhara
> > should not be viewed as separate.[733]
>
> Meditating on his five aggregates and so forth as the five buddha families and so forth is the meaning of the following from the *Vajra Garland Tantra*:
>
> > In this body of the vajra master reside
> > the bodies of the conquerors in sequence.[734]
>
> So, in accordance with this, visualize the merit field, summon and absorb the gnosis beings, and cultivate fervent devotion and reverence toward your guru as the embodiment of all three refuges. Then, as the guardian Nāgārjuna states in his *Five Stages*:

> Relinquishing all other offerings,
> undertake the perfect offering to the guru.
> By pleasing him you will obtain
> the supreme gnosis of omniscience.[735]
>
> Generate certainty that making offerings to the guru is more important than making offerings to all other buddhas and bodhisattvas.

The seven-limb worship

> To make the offering of seven limbs, the first limb, prostration, is as follows.

1. Prostration

Through your kindness is granted in an instant
even the expanse of great bliss, the supreme state
of three buddha bodies. Guru, your body is like a jewel;
at your lotus feet, O Vajradhara, I bow down.[736]

Gnosis of all the conquerors of the myriad worlds,
manifesting in the dance of a saffron-clad monk,
supreme skillful means appearing as needed for disciples—
at your lotus feet, O sublime refuge and protector, I bow down.

You help eradicate all faults and their propensities;
you're the jewel treasury of immeasurable higher qualities;
you're the sole source from which flow all benefit and happiness—
at your lotus feet, O venerable guru, I bow down.

Teacher of gods and all beings, you are in fact all the buddhas;
you're the source of all eighty-four thousand teachings; [305]
you shine resplendent amid all ārya assemblies—
at your lotus feet, O most kind guru, I bow down.

To the gurus residing in the three times and ten directions,
to the Three Supreme Jewels and to all worthy of homage,
with faith and respect and with a sea of songs of praise
and emanating bodies equal to atoms in the world, I bow down.

2. Offering

> Having prostrated respectfully with your three doors, make offerings. Make the offerings without any conceptual elaboration of the three elements of offering (the one who is offering, the recipient, and the gift) and by sealing them into the nature of indivisible bliss and emptiness.

To you, refuge and protector, venerable guru and your entourage,
I offer a sea of clouds of various offerings.
From perfect jewel vessels vast and glowing with light,
four streams[737] of purifying nectars gently flow.

Flowers on stems, loose petals, and perfect garlands—
flowers utterly beautiful fill the earth and sky.
Smokes of fragrant incense densely permeate
the sky like monsoon clouds the color of lapis lazuli.

Sun, moon, and masses of lamps intensely bright—
lights dispelling the darkness of the trichiliocosm dance about.
Great seas of scented water perfumed by fragrances
of camphor, sandalwood, and saffron swirl out to the horizon.

Delicious food and drink of a hundred flavors,
delicacies of gods and humans, are heaped as high as Meru.
From a limitless variety of musical instruments
issue melodies filling the three worlds.[738]

Bearing the splendors of form, sound, smell, taste, and touch,
goddesses of outer and inner offerings pervade every direction.[739]

The billion worlds with four continents and Meru,
the seven types of jewels, their approximates, and so forth,[740]
the perfect worlds and their denizens, arousing utter delight,
and the great treasuries containing the wealth of gods and humans—
with a devoted mind I offer these to you, supreme merit field,
O my refuge and protector, treasury of compassion.

Across a wish-granting sea of offerings actually arrayed and imagined
are offering substances arisen from virtues of both samsara and nirvana.

Strewn like thousand-petaled lotuses that captivate every heart,
arrayed everywhere are flowers of virtues, mundane and transcendent,
of the three doors of both myself and others.
I offer to you, O most venerable guru, this pleasure garden
emitting a hundred thousand fragrances of Samantabhadra offerings
and adorned with fruits of the threefold training, two stages, and
five paths.

Libation of Chinese tea with saffron hue and a sweet aroma [306]
that conveys a hundred splendid flavors,
the five hooks, the five lamps,[741] and so forth,
I offer seas of nectar purified, transformed, and increased.

I offer as well beautiful, magical consorts,
splendidly lovely with the glory of youth,
slender and skilled in the sixty-four arts of love—
a host of messengers, field-born, mantra-born, and innate-born.

I offer to you the supreme ultimate awakening mind:
great gnosis of innate bliss free of obscuration inseparable
from ultimate expanse devoid of elaborations, the nature of all
phenomena,
spontaneous, beyond speech, thought, and expression.

I offer varieties of excellent medicines that cure
the afflictions and the 404 diseases.[742]
And to please you, as I offer myself as your servant:
pray sustain me as your subject as long as space remains.

> Having performed outer, inner, secret, suchness, medicine, and service offerings, along with their visualizations, continue with the remaining limbs, such as confession, thusly:

3. Confession

Whatever unwholesome acts of nonvirtue I have committed,
made others to commit, or have rejoiced in since beginningless time,
these I confess with a remorseful mind in the presence
of the compassionate ones, and I vow not to repeat them.

4. Rejoicing

Though phenomena lack the signs of intrinsic nature,
in the dream-like virtues of common and ārya beings,
from which arise all forms of bliss and joy,
I rejoice with the purest of intentions.

5. Requesting to teach

Cumulating a hundred thousand clouds of knowledge and love,
pray pour down the rains of Dharma, profound and extensive,
so that they will produce, sustain, and propagate the jasmine garden
of benefit and happiness of the countless sentient beings.

6. Entreating not to enter nirvana

Although your vajra body, this jewel casket of union,
has neither death nor birth, O sovereign of sovereigns,
in accord with our wishes, pray do not enter into nirvana
but remain until the end of samsaric existence.

7. Dedication

The collection of thoroughly white virtues thus created
I dedicate, so that in all my lives I am never separated from
and am sustained by my triply kind guru, most venerable,
and that I may attain the union of sovereign Vajradhara.

In this way, offer the seven limbs. If there is time, then at the point of confession, [307] recite the specific confessions of the three vows and chant "O guru Vajradhara...,"[743] the bodhisattva's confession of downfalls, and so forth.

Then, as stated in the *Vajrapāṇi Empowerment Tantra*:

> Seize on your guru's qualities
> and never seize on his faults.
> If you seize on his qualities, you will obtain siddhis;
> if you seize on his faults, you won't obtain siddhis.[744]

Apply mindfulness and meta-awareness repeatedly with the thought "I will not allow any thoughts seizing on faults to arise." Contemplate well the benefits of relying on the guru and the disadvantages of not thus relying as explained in the sutras, the tantras, and the sayings of the sublime ones. In particular, view your root guru as the embodiment of the infallible refuge, the Three Jewels, the mere hearing of whose name causes the terror of the lower realms to be robbed away, the mere thought of whom dispels the sufferings of samsara, and when it is appealed to, all higher attainments are granted with ease. With total trust, not placing your hope anywhere else, supplicate fervently many times by reciting the Miktsema[745] and other prayers. Afterward, make the following supplications:

Supplications

You're the source of all qualities, a great sea of discipline
replete with a multitude of gems of vast learning;
saffron-clad lord, you are the second Śākyamuni—
to you, elder who upholds the Vinaya, I supplicate.

You possess the ten qualities that when present
qualify one to show the Sugata's path;
you're the lord of Dharma, the regent of all conquerors—
to you, spiritual mentor of the supreme vehicle, I supplicate.

You guard your three doors and are greatly wise, patient, and honest,
you lack pretense or guile, and you know the mantras and the tantras,
an expert in drawing and explaining the two sets of ten principles[746]—
to you, foremost vajra holder, I supplicate.

In these ways supplicate [the guru] as possessing the qualifications of a guru according to the Vinaya, general Mahayana, and Vajrayāna. Then:

Untamed by the countless buddhas who have come before,
unruly and intractable beings of the degenerate era,
to them you show the sugatas' excellent path as it is—
to you, compassionate refuge and protector, I supplicate.

When the Sage's sun has set owing to the passage of time,
you perform the enlightened deeds of the Conqueror
for the many beings without a protector and refuge, [308]—

to you, compassionate refuge and protector, I supplicate.

To all the conquerors of the three times and ten directions,
even a single one of your pores is rightly praised
as a superior field for us to gather merit—
to you, compassionate refuge and protector, I supplicate.[747]

The wheels of adornment of the three sugata bodies,
through a magical matrix of skillful means,
guide beings in the guise of an ordinary person—
to you, compassionate refuge and protector, I supplicate.

Your aggregates, sense fields, elements, and limbs are
by nature, the five sugata families, the male and female deities,
the bodhisattvas, and the wrathful protectors—
to you supreme guru, embodiment of the Three Jewels, I supplicate.

You are the embodiment of ten million mandalas
arising from the play of all-knowing gnosis;
lord of hundred buddha families, foremost vajra holder—
to you, primordial lord of union, I supplicate.

You're inseparable from the play of unobscured innate joy;
pervading everything stationary and moving, you're the lord of all;
with no beginning or end, you are perfect goodness—
to you, the actual ultimate awakening mind, I supplicate.

> Make single-pointed supplications in this way by expressing the outer, inner, secret, and suchness qualities of the guru, and in particular [recite]:

You are the guru, you are the meditation deity, you are the ḍākinī and the Dharma guardian;
from now until enlightenment I will seek no refuge other than you.[748]
In this life, in the bardo, and in future lives, hold me with your hook of compassion,
free me from samsara and nirvana's dangers, grant me all siddhis, be my constant companion, and guard me from hindrances.[749] (3x)

Through the power of having supplicated three times thusly,
from the centers of the guru's body, speech, and mind,[750]
nectar and beams of light—white, red, and dark blue—
radiate sequentially and all at once
and dissolve into my three centers, both individually and all together.
The four obscurations are purified, the four empowerments obtained;
attaining four buddha bodies, a replica of my guru
joyfully absorbs into me, and I am blessed.[751]

Imagine thus.

Reviewing the entire path and invoking blessings

Next, to once again receive blessings and to invoke compassion, here is how you wish for the attainment of your aims and, at the same time, train your mind in the Mahayana path:

Through the force of making offerings and respectful appeals
to my revered guru, the supreme holy field of merit,
may I be blessed so that I am happily cared for by you,
O protector who is the root of all good fortune.

This life of leisure and opportunity I have found once.
Realizing how hard it is to obtain and yet how quickly destroyed,
bless me that I may extract its meaningful essence,
undistracted by the pointless activities of this life.

Terrified by the blazing fires of suffering of the lower realms,
I go for refuge with all my heart to the Three Jewels.
Bless me that I may zealously strive
to relinquish evil and gather all collections of virtue.

Powerful waves of karma and afflictions surge up violently,
countless sea monsters of three sufferings torment constantly;
bless me that I may generate a powerful desire to be free
from this samsaric existence, boundless and most frightful.

This prison-like samsara so hard to endure,
I will abandon the thought that sees it as a pleasure grove

and seize the ārya's treasure trove, the threefold training.
Bless me that I may raise the victory banner of liberation.

All these distressed suffering beings are my mothers.
Thinking how they have kindly nurtured me again and again,
bless me so that, like a loving mother for her precious child,
genuine compassion for them arises within me.

As for suffering, I do not wish even the slightest;
as for happiness, I am never satisfied;
in this there is no difference between me and others.
Bless me that I may rejoice in others' happiness.

Seeing that this chronic disease of cherishing myself
is the cause of every unwanted suffering,
I will place all blames on it and rebuke it.
Bless me that I may destroy this great demon of self-grasping.

The thought cherishing my mothers and leading them to happiness
I will see as the door to infinite higher qualities.
Bless me so that even if all beings rise up as my foes,
I may cherish them more than my own life.

In brief, the childish pursue only their own self-interest,
while the Sage works solely for the welfare of others.
Bless me that with a mind distinguishing the drawbacks and advantages,
I may be able to equalize and exchange myself with others.

Self-cherishing is the doorway to every misfortune,
cherishing mother beings is the basis of every good quality. [310]
Bless me that I may therefore make this yoga of exchanging
myself with others the heart of my practice.

Therefore, O venerable, most compassionate guru,
bless me that every evil karma, obscuration, and suffering
of mother beings may ripen on me right here and now
and, as I offer others my happiness and virtue,
all sentient being become endowed with happiness.[752]

Even if the world and its inhabitants are filled with the fruits of evil
karma
and unwanted miseries befall me like rainfall,
bless me that I may see this as the cause for depleting the fruits
of my own bad karma and I may welcome adversities into the path.

In brief, whatever appearances arise, good or bad,
through the practice of the five powers,[753] heart of all teachings,
bless me that I may transform them into paths that enhance
the two awakening minds and cultivate the joyful mind alone.

Through the skillful means of the fourfold practice,[754]
whatever I encounter right now[755] I will relate to meditation practice.
Bless me that through mind-training pledges and precepts,
I may make this life of leisure and opportunity most meaningful.

With the magical lift[756] mounting giving and taking astride the breath,
through loving kindness, compassion, and altruistic resolve,
bless me that I may become trained in the two awakening minds
to help free all beings from the vast ocean of existence.

The sole path traversed by every conqueror of the three times
is the perfect bodhisattva vows; bless me that I may bind my mind
with them and apply unswerving effort
in the practice of the supreme vehicle's threefold ethics.[757]

Bless me that I may accomplish the perfection of giving
through the instruction of enhancing the mind of giving
without attachment to my body, resources, and virtues of all three times,
by transforming them into things desired by each sentient being.

Bless me that I may accomplish the perfection of morality:
never giving up, even at the cost of my life, the rules
entailed by the vows of individual liberation, bodhisattva, and tantra,
of gathering virtue, and of pursuing the welfare of sentient beings.

Bless me that I may accomplish the perfection of forbearance:
even if beings in all three realms should become angry with me

and revile, slander, threaten, or kill me,
may I, unperturbed, seek to help them in return.

Bless me that I may accomplish the perfection of diligence:
if, even for the sake of a single sentient being, I have to remain
in the fires of the Relentless hell for an ocean of eons,
may I with compassion, undiscouraged, strive for supreme
awakening. [311]

Discarding the faults of laxity, excitation, and distractions
and abiding single-pointedly in meditative equipoise
on the abiding nature, the emptiness of true existence, bless me that
I may,
through this concentration, accomplish the perfection of absorption.

Bless me that I may accomplish the perfection of wisdom
through the space-like yoga of equipoise on the ultimate
conjoined with the pliancy and great bliss induced
by the wisdom realizing suchness through discernment.

Bless me that I may perfect the illusion-like concentration:
perceiving how outer and inner phenomena—like an illusion, a dream,
or the reflection of the moon in a clear lake—
appear but lack true existence.

Bless me that I may realize the point of Nāgārjuna's thought:
that not even an atom of samsara and nirvana exists intrinsically
yet the dependent origination of cause and effect is infallible,
and that these two do not contradict but complement each other.

Bless me that I may then, through the kindness
of the helmsman Vajradhara, cross the ocean of tantras
and guard the commitments and vows, root of all siddhis,
as dearer even than my own life.

Bless me that I may, through the yoga of the first stage
transmuting birth, death, and the bardo into the three buddha bodies,
purify all stains of ordinary perceptions and apprehensions
and see whatever appears arise as the deity's body.

Bless me that the paths of clear light, illusory body, and union—
arising from placing your feet at the center of
my eight-petal lotus heart inside the central channel—
become manifest in this very lifetime, O my guardian.

If I should die before reaching the start of the path,
bless me that I may travel to the pure land
through the guru's transference effecting immediate awakening—
the instruction on how to perfectly apply the five powers.

In short, in each and in all my lives, may we never be separated,
O guardian, and may I be cared for by you.
Bless me that I may become your chief disciple,
upholding every secret of your body, speech, and mind.

O my guardian, confer upon me the good fortune
to be among the first of your retinue wherever you manifest awakening
and to accomplish, effortlessly and spontaneously,
everything needed and wished for, whether temporary or ultimate.

Having supplicated you like this, O supreme guru,
come to the crown of my head to grant your blessings,
and once again, pray set your glowing feet
on the stamen of my lotus heart and there firmly remain. [312]

> In this way, viewing your guru, the meditation deity, and your mind as inseparable, strive in the practices of engaging in the yoga of the generation and completion stages combined—where in all your activities, for instance, you view whatever you perceive as manifestations of male and female deities, all sharing the nature of bliss and emptiness—not divorced from the practices of the stages of path: the key points of Mahayana mind training.

Dedication

> At the end, seal your virtues with aspiration prayers such as the *Vows of Good Conduct.*[758] If you wish to be brief, recite:

Whatever bright virtue I have created from doing thusly
I dedicate to becoming the causes for accomplishing

the deeds and aspirations of all the sugatas of the three times and their children
and to upholding the sublime Dharma of scripture and realization.

Through the power of that merit, may I never be separated
in all lives from the four wheels of the supreme vehicle.[759]
May I complete the journey on the paths of renunciation,
the awakening mind, the perfect view, and the two tantric stages.[760]

> Dedicate and make an aspiration prayer in that way. Some other aspects of the instructions you should learn orally. If you undertake this [guru yoga] as your daily yoga in this way, you will be practicing the essence of all the sutras and tantras, and it will strengthen the root of all the good fortune of this and future lives. I say:
>
> The milk ocean of sublime sutra, tantra, and instructions
> churned by the mountain king of discerning intelligence
> produced the nectar vase of unprecedented excellent explanations
> as a nourishment for those whose good fortune is well inscribed.
>
> This is the lamp dispelling all the darkness
> that may lie in the hearts of all reverent disciples.
> It is also the iron hook swiftly drawing forth
> all good fortune, mundane and transcendent.
>
> The collection of virtues arising from this endeavor,
> whatever I have obtained pure and white as the moon,
> I dedicate these so they become causes for all beings
> to be sustained by sublime guardians, the root of good fortune.

Colophon

This rite of *Offering to the Guru* was composed in response to repeated requests for such a text from the Vinaya upholders Chökyi Drakpa and Losang Phuntsok. It was written by the Buddhist monk Losang Chökyi Gyaltsen, who has seen the *Offering to the Guru* composed by the great siddha Lingrepa, the one written by the great Pang Lotsāwa, *Offering to the Guru* texts authored by numerous Sakya spiritual mentors, [313] the one written by the omniscient Gendun Gyatso, the *Offering to the Guru* composed by the great scholar-adept and my precious teacher Sangyé Yeshé, and numerous other *Offering to the Guru* texts authored by elevated and less elevated teachers of the various traditions. Having seen these, and having fully comprehended their expressed meaning, I have gathered here all the best parts in perfect accordance with sutra, tantra, and instructions of the sublime ones in a format that shuns literary embellishment and is easy to understand. It was written on the rooftop of the chamber called Lofty Victory Banner at the great center of Dharma Tashi Lhunpo.

8. A Letter of Final Testament Sent upon the Wind

A Guide to Mahāmudrā Combined with the Uncommon Guru Yoga of the Ensa Oral Transmission Endowed with Pith Instructions and Oral Teachings

GYALRONG TSULTRIM NYIMA

I BOW DOWN to and go for refuge to the sublime revered guru who possesses the objectless great compassion. Pray care for me with compassion in all times.

By applying the five stages (the expert jeweler-yogi's purifying gem)
to the tainted white beryl (the very subtle life-supporting wind, manifold atoms, and the primordial mind fused with the four elements into a mass),
and with atoms of five-colored light and the four elements of innate clear light serving as substantial and cooperative causes, the learner's union arises—the convergence into a single entity of the perfectly formed pure illusory body together with the actual innate nature, resplendent and luminous.
Once again, as this gem of [the learner's] union becomes cleansed of all stains, vivid reflections arise at once of both *things as they are* and *things in their diversity*. Without [the yogi] ever wavering from this state,
all ten directions become filled with emanations—a matrix of lights—that satisfy the wishes of sentient beings and pour down spontaneously whatever fulfills their every need. May this wish-granting king of gems endowed with the seven aspects of supreme union grant auspiciousness.[761]

You are father to all conquerors, instructing them how first to generate awakening mind, how in the middle
to engage in the expansive bodhisattva deeds, and how at the end to embrace

the enlightened deeds of all buddhas and pervade the countless realms with
their emanations. [318]
Sometimes the father to all conquerors, at others the chief disciple; I bow
to you who assumes such a fluid identity.[762]

When the sun of the teaching of Śuddhodana's son had shunned the Snowy
Land,
O Mañjuśrī, to accomplish the Lion of the Śākyas' deeds, you relinquished
your five topknots and jewel ornaments and assumed the saffron-clad form.
To you, Jamgön Guru, unrivaled in elucidating excellent way of Nāgārjuna,
I bow down.[763]

I appeal to you, chief in hoisting the banner of the oral transmission
of the revered Tsongkhapa, who is Mañjuśrī, the natural embodiment
of the gnosis of all conquerors, displaying a saffron-clad dance.
O my triply kind guru,[764] pray always reside at the center of my heart.

This path is both the animating lifeblood and the dynamic force that speeds
the instructions in all the sutras and tantras.
Thus, in efforts to cultivate this profound path and
to explain it, my mind can never feel sated.

To arouse the perfection of training in my own mind and
to send my final testament upon the wind, I write this.
O ḍākinīs of the three worlds, please grant your permission;
O Kālarūpa,[765] pray always assist me.

Guru yoga has been hailed in numerous sutras and tantras as the excellent path traversed by all the conquerors of the three times; it is the heart practice of all the masters of both India and Tibet; it has been likened to hands scooping up vast collections of merit and wisdom, to the great fire at the end of the world burning away all negative karma and transgression of precepts, and to a strong iron hook swiftly drawing forth all the siddhi attainments, both common and supreme. I therefore present here the way to undertake a unique guru-yoga practice stemming from the lineage of the supreme siddha Dharmavajra and his spiritual heirs and explain how you could, taking this guru yoga as the preliminary practice, engage in meditative practice of mahāmudrā as presented in its manuals.

This instruction has three parts: (1) presenting the transmission lineage of this instruction to show its authoritative origin, (2) explaining the greatness of the instruction to engender confidence in this teaching, [319] and (3) explaining how to engage in the actual practice of the instruction endowed with these two distinctive features.

Presenting the transmission lineage of this instruction to show its authoritative origin

To present this first point, the text says:[766]

> **In Indian language it is called *Gurupūjasyakalpa*.**
> **In Tibetan language it is called *Bla ma mchod pa'i cho ga***
> **(*A Rite of Offering to the Guru*).**

> **I bow to the feet of my sublime gurus, whose kindness is unrivaled, and go to them for refuge. I appeal to them: Please always sustain me with your great love in all circumstances.**

> **When relied upon, he grants in a single instant**
> **the great bliss of three buddha bodies along with the common siddhis;**
> **he is the wish-granting jewel conferring everything desired.**
> **Having bowed at the feet of Vajradhara,**
> **I present here a beautiful garland of flowers**
> **picked from the lotus grove of sutras, tantras, and sublime instructions—**
> **the supreme method, unrivaled for securing**
> **the benefit and happiness of every fortunate disciple.**

Generally speaking, treatises composed in Tibetan don't have to have the phrase "In Indian language" at the beginning and provide the text's title in two languages [Sanskrit and Tibetan]. The reason this text does so is to indicate that this instruction is not something fabricated in Tibet. Rather, it possesses an authoritative origin in the following manner: "It has its origin in the stainless scriptures of the Buddha; it has been practiced by the sublime masters of India and has come through a lineage of mouth-to-ear transmission; it has been realized by the Dharma king Jamgön Tsongkhapa and his spiritual heirs; and from them it has descended through an uninterrupted lineage of great siddhas with the warm breath of their blessings undiminished."

In general, the sovereign of Dharma, the Blessed Buddha, possesses unrivaled wisdom that sees every means for fulfilling the two aims of sentient beings,[767] and his great compassion extends to everyone without any discriminatory feelings of closeness and distance. [320] He is thus such an embodiment of compassion that, when it comes to fulfilling the needs of sentient beings, even waiting one more moment is to too long for him. And it is the stainless scriptures of the Buddha that contain all the key points of the profound and swift means for realizing the two aims of sentient beings in their entirety and free of error. Therefore it is critical that those who seek the two aims of sentient beings must ensure that the teaching they themselves practice is rooted in undisputed sutras and tantras and that it accords with these scriptures. They should not place their confidence in something that may be touted as profound but does not accord with the scriptures. This [guru yoga], on the other hand, is indeed the supreme tradition of the great lord Atiśa and the second Buddha, Losang Drakpa.

Here in the text, too, it says:

I present here a beautiful garland of flowers
picked from the lotus grove of sutras, tantras, and sublime instructions.

In spring, for example, when flowers bloom freshly in a lotus grove, if a cluster of flowers happens to bloom together, it can rob a person's heart with even a single glance and gratify her mind through its fragrance and flavor. Flowers scattered across a site in a haphazard pattern do not conjure a scene of great beauty, but those same flowers, if strung together in a garland, can be worn as a necklace by those who wish to adorn their elegant body. Likewise, when the best of the instructions emerging from the mouth-to-ear transmission of the great masters of India and Tibet are brought together and are put into compositions, then the instant someone sees or hears the excellent words, their mind is captivated spontaneously and feels gratified through deep contemplation of the excellent meanings of those words. If, in contrast, the words remain scattered and jumbled with the sequence of the instructions mixed up, such a teaching would be unappealing and difficult to engage. This [guru yoga] instruction, however, is error free by nature; with respect to enumeration, nothing is missing; [321] and there is no confusion in the sequence. The instruction is presented in a succinct format with concise expression. Therefore those who wish to actualize all excellences, mundane and transcendent, should embrace this instruction without hesitation and engage in its practice.

Thus the above two lines [of the root text] express the promise to compose and exhort others to listen, and they also explain the authoritative origin of the instruction.

How this guru yoga is taught in undisputed sutras and tantras

One might ask: "How does this [guru-yoga] instruction originate from the undisputed sutras and tantras and from the instructions of sublime masters?"

The guru yoga has in fact been presented in the sutra teachings, such as in the Vinaya.[768] For example, the Vinaya texts explain how the receiving of the vows—lay *upāsaka*, monastic novitiate, and full ordination vows—are contingent on taking refuge [in the Three Jewels] to initiate the process. They also speak of how the abbot and the masters conducting the vow ceremonies should possess specific qualifications, such as one of twenty-one sets of fivefold qualities; how the recipient should, on his part, be free of the inner and outer obstacles and enjoy the relevant inner and outer conditions; how, after having received the vows, the monk should seek a resident teacher for instructions on the norms of what is to be rejected and what is to be adopted; how the monk should seek a master to receive instructions pertaining to study, reflection, and meditative cultivation of a renunciant; how to then mentally relate to the abbot and masters through viewing them as enlightened tathāgatas; how to relate to them through one's body, such as by serving them by massaging, oil rub, and offering warm clothes at night and so on; how, even when calling their names, one should prefix their names with honorific titles. When responding to them, one should say, "I will do as you command," and in this way honor them through your speech. The texts explain how, when obtaining fresh alms, one should offer them first to one's teacher. They explain how one should relate to them in action by doing what has been commanded. As for the disadvantages of not relying on the teacher, these are indicated by stating how acting in contrary ways leads to downfalls, which also indicates, conversely, the extensive benefits of relying on the guru. There are thus numerous sources for the benefits of relying on the guru; fearing excessive length, I will not cite them here. [322]

Within the sutras, for example, the *Flower Ornament Sutra* (*Avataṃsakasūtra*) presents the account of how the bodhisattva Maṇibhadra relied on his spiritual teacher in the past and uses it to illustrate how future spiritual aspirants should rely on the spiritual teacher.[769]

In the precious Perfection of Wisdom scriptures, one finds statements about how finding the profound truth of the perfection of wisdom is contingent on the spiritual teacher alone, how one must traverse the grounds and paths on the basis of relying on a spiritual teacher. These sutras explain that one should rely on a spiritual teacher the way the bodhisattva Sadāprarudita relied on Dharmodgata.[770] These sutras speak of how Sadāprarudita, despite experiencing visions of countless buddhas, remained unsatisfied. His mind was tormented with deep longing, "How I wish to meet my spiritual teacher!" He saw his spiritual teacher as more important than all the buddhas and understood that honoring his spiritual teacher was more important than honoring all the buddhas. Thus, to make offerings to his spiritual teacher Dharmodgata, he gave to the god Indra, who appeared in the guise of a brahman, even pieces from his body, including bone marrow, without any sense of loss; he moistened the site where the teaching would be conducted by using his own blood; and with no regard for sleep and food, he maintained for seven years the single-minded thought "How I wish to hear the words of the precious perfection of wisdom scriptures from my spiritual teacher." The sutras speak of how, through such a quest, the bodhisattva traversed the grounds and paths swiftly. To cite the specific sources here I fear would lead to excessive length. So generate firm conviction by immersing yourself in the [Perfection of Wisdom] sutras.

Furthermore, the *Adornment of Trees Sutra*, the *Ten Wheels of Kṣitigarbha Sutra*, the *Questions of the Householder Ugra*, and other scriptures contain extensive statements about the benefits of relying on the spiritual teacher, including the attitude one should have when relating to the spiritual teacher and the way to cultivate reverence for the spiritual teacher by contemplating his kindness.

The point is that we must, in a single motion, bring all the key points of how to rely on one's spiritual teacher presented in the Vinaya and the sutras into our practice of the profound path of this guru yoga. Therefore the body of statements in the sutras about how to rely on the spiritual teacher [323] constitute an authoritative source for this [guru-yoga] instruction. Do not misconstrue those statements to be unrelated to this guru-yoga instruction.

All the presentations in the sutra sources about how to rely on the spiritual teacher can be summarized under these four headings: (1) the benefits of relying on the spiritual teacher, (2) the disadvantages of not relying, (3) the way to rely in thought, and (4) the way to rely in action. So when you engage in this practice of guru yoga, you should first contemplate extensively, through analytical meditation, the benefits of relying on the spiritual teacher and the disadvantages of not doing so. Then cultivate strong joy and delight in relating to your spiritual teacher and honoring him. Similarly, you should generate remorse for any past misdeeds of relating to your spiritual teacher incorrectly, as if poison has penetrated deep inside your body, and then strongly resolve never to engage in such misdeeds from now on. Then, with fervent intention to purify your negative karma, view your spiritual teacher as indivisible from your meditation deity. Contemplating the enlightened qualities of your guru, prostrate to him by [imaginatively] multiplying your body into countless bodies. Honor him with your body and speech by offering yourself as a servant and uttering his praises, and honor him with material gifts, offering actual articles and imagining that all your virtuous karma of three times takes the form of various articles offered. You should please him with your spiritual practice—by pledging to guard, the way you would guard your eyes, all the precepts of the two advanced vows [of a bodhisattva and tantra] you have taken for the benefit of sentient beings; by undertaking various ritual activities based on invoking the spiritual teacher with his name mantra; by training your mind in all the paths of sutra and tantra; and by seeking blessings—in short, by putting the guru's instructions into practice. This includes your cultivation of *faith*, the root factor, on the basis of viewing your triply kind spiritual teacher as having the qualifications of a teacher prescribed in the Vinaya, the sutras, and the tantras and supplicating him, and your cultivation of *respect* on the basis of contemplating his kindness and supplicating him.

Offer all of these employing secret mantra's great magic of skillful means, whereby you generate your body into a meditation deity and establish the offerings as empty of intrinsic existence, [324] your awareness of emptiness sustained by great bliss. An aspect of this union of bliss and emptiness has in fact arisen in the form of the various articles offered. In this way, you make outer, inner, and secret offerings to your guru. The guru too, the object to whom you make these offerings, must be seen as indivisible from the meditation deity, in both his essence and his appearance. This is how you should practice guru yoga.

In contrast, when these key points of reliance on the spiritual teacher as presented in the sutras and tantras are absent, then you might put great effort into a so-called guru-yoga practice, claiming you are seeing your guru as indivisible from the meditation deity and making outer, inner, and secret offerings to him and supplicating him, but your practice would not even be minimally comprehensive and would have no real impact. This is because the impact of guru yoga should entail the following: you enjoy and delight in relating to your guru, through both thought and action; you feel remorse from your heart whenever and wherever you fail to relate to your guru in a proper manner, and you rectify such transgressions; the resolve to never engage in such transgressions arises with ease; no thoughts imputing faults in your guru arise, and faith that allows you to see all your guru's deeds as marvelous grows; and reverence born of recalling your guru's kindness arises from deep within your heart. Clearly when the key points of relying on your guru expressed in the sutras and tantras are absent, there is simply no way to experience these impacts. In light of these, the omniscient Jé Tsongkhapa says:

> Therefore it is along these lines explained above that you should also understand the instruction renowned as *guru yoga*. Training in a meditation topic for only a single session will get you nowhere. To practice Dharma from the heart, you need to rely for a long time on a spiritual teacher who can guide you accurately. Furthermore, as Chekawa says, "When you rely on the guru, you also risk abandoning your guru." If you rely on the guru without knowing how to do it properly, you will experience loss instead of profit. These teachings on how to rely on the spiritual teacher are evidently one of the most important teachings, for they establish the very foundation of your ultimate aspiration.[771]

This instruction [on guru yoga] has been taught in the precious tantras as well. All four classes of tantra uniformly state the following: one should become a suitable vessel of the profound tantric path through a perfect empowerment ceremony conducted by a qualified vajra master, [325] and one should traverse the profound path of tantra (1) by observing the commitments and the vows as the indispensable basis for attaining all the siddhis, (2) by holding, among all the tantric commitments, those pertaining to the guru as paramount, and (3) by seeing the guru, on the basis of a guru yoga, as indivisible from the meditation deity.

The root and explanatory tantras of Guhyasamāja in particular constitute the ultimate authoritative source for this particular guru-yoga instruction. Now, although all the key points of this instruction were indeed taught in the

Guhyasamāja Root Tantra, they remain sealed in the tantra by the knot of six parameters and four modes.[772] So seeing that even a jewel-like trainee would not be able to realize the meaning on their own, the Conqueror undid the knots and taught explanatory tantras such as the *Vajra Garland*. And it is in the explanatory *Vajra Garland Tantra* that all the key points of this unique guru-yoga instruction have been taught in detail. It states, for example, how to first examine the qualifications of both the guru and the disciple; how to view the guru as indivisible from the meditation deity; how to meditate on the guru's body as the mandala; how, on that basis, to make outer, inner, and secret offerings to the guru; and finally, how, on the basis of the practitioner seeing themself as indivisible from the guru, to engage in meditative practice of the path of the two stages. The tantra presents all of these in clear terms, but given the extensive nature of the sources, and fearing excessive length, I will not cite them here. For a brief presentation of these sources, you could refer to the selected citations provided in Guru Yongzin Rinpoché's guidance instruction on *Offering to the Guru*.[773] For more elaborate understanding of these sources, however, you could read the tantra itself and develop firm conviction.

Differences between the Sutras and Tantras on How to View the Guru as a Buddha

Although all the sutras and tantras are of single voice in stating that we need to consider our guru as a buddha, they differ on how this is to be done. The Vinaya, for example, states that the way to do this is to see the guru as equal in status to a buddha with respect to being an object of either honor or harm. In fact, the Vinaya says that we need to have such regard equal to a buddha not just for our ordination abbot and master but even for a layperson who is sick. Beyond this, I have not seen anything in the Vinaya that speaks of seeing the guru as identical in nature with the Buddha or of seeing him in the form of a buddha. [326]

The sutras contain statements about how the Tathāgata performs activities aimed at fulfilling the welfare of sentient beings through assuming such forms as that of a spiritual teacher, an ordinary human, or a mundane god. Such sutras speak of the importance of constantly bringing to mind the guru's physical appearance, his complexion, his tone of voice, and his activities; thus they present the practice of contemplating the guru in his ordinary [human] appearance along the lines we would normally perceive. Furthermore, as a way to avoid actions that might harm sentient beings, the sutras speak of the need to regard all beings as buddhas. Beyond this, I have not seen in the sutras any statements about seeing the guru in the form of a buddha.

The tantras, however, state that Vajradhara himself would take the form of ordinary human spiritual teachers during this era of degeneration and that, through this, he would secure the welfare of sentient beings. The tantras speak of how the buddhas of the ten directions enter the body of the vajra master and fulfill the needs of the spiritual aspirants, and how the guru himself must be visualized in the form of the meditation deity. Furthermore, the tantras speak of how we need to unambiguously perceive the guru as the embodiment of all higher qualities so that we will, with great hope, engage both spontaneously and deliberately in activities to bring forth these higher qualities. Similarly, we need to unambiguously perceive the guru as having eliminated all faults so thoughts imputing faults to him do not arise in us, whether impulsive or deliberate. For both of these, the tantras speak of how it is necessary to see the guru as equal to a tathāgata. The tantras speak of how this is in fact part of the commitments that are essential for achieving the siddhi attainments. So it is statements like these that we need to contemplate with clear discernment, with distinctness akin to strands of *kuśa* grass. We should not content ourselves with the mere words "See your guru as a buddha." The above is a brief summary of the authoritative sources of the instruction.

The long-transmission lineage of this guru-yoga instruction

One might ask, "How has this instruction emerged from the instructions of sublime scholar-siddhas?" The entirety of the instruction on guru yoga as found in the various sutras and tantras taught by the sovereign of Dharma, the Buddha himself, assuming his nirmāṇakāya emanation as Vajradhara in accord with the needs of spiritual trainees, was received by Maitreya, Mañjuśrī, Vajrapāṇi, and the like, who appeared [on Earth] as the Buddha's bodhisattva disciples. From Maitreya it was transmitted to Asaṅga and his brother [Vasubandhu] and so forth, [327] and from Mañjuśrī it was transmitted to Nāgārjuna and his spiritual son [Āryadeva] and so forth. From Vajrapāṇi the transmission passed on to Indrabodhi, Lord Mahāsukha, Saraha, and so forth. Some of these masters actually wrote the instruction down for the benefit of future trainees.

For example, in his *Ornament of Mahayana Sutras*, Maitreya presents in detail how a student with the right qualifications should rely on a spiritual teacher endowed with appropriate qualifications.[774] Similarly Asaṅga, in his *Bodhisattva Grounds*, describes the qualifications of a spiritual teacher and how a student should honor and make offerings to him.[775] In particular, he explains (1) how, based on five recognitions, one needs to view the spiritual teacher in terms of his qualities, (2) how, based on not thinking of five points, one needs to prevent thoughts imputing faults to him, and (3) how one needs to receive the instructions from the guru on such a basis. In his *Five Stages*, Ārya Nāgārjuna explains in detail how to practice the five stages on the basis of taking guru yoga as the life force of the path.[776] Similarly, in his *Attainment of the Secret*, Lord Mahāsukha explains how to integrate one's meditative cultivation with the practice of innate great bliss on the basis of taking guru yoga as the life force of the path.[777] Following his teaching, similar statements could be found in texts such as *Attainment of the Nondual*, which is part of the "attainment and essence texts"[778] and also in the *doha* songs. Therefore, on this point—taking guru yoga as the life force of the path and meditating based on the instructions of sutra and tantra—all the authoritative masters of India agree.

It is these instructions on profound guru yoga—complete, free of dilution, and representing the heart practice of all the great Indian masters—that the great Atiśa, Martön Chökyi Lodrö, Gö Lotsāwa,[779] and others received and brought to this Land of Snows. As for the instructions that came through Atiśa, the omniscient Jé Tsongkhapa received these from two masters: Dragor Khenchen and Lhodrak Drupchen.[780] Tsongkhapa received those that came through the transmissions of Martön and Gö Lotsāwa in their entirety from Khyungpo Lhepa Shönu Sönam, Chenga Drakpa Jangchup, Chöjé Döndrup Rinchen, and Jetsun Rendawa. [328] These then are the authoritative sources of this guru-yoga instruction from the perspective of the long-transmission lineage.

The unique near-transmission lineage of this guru-yoga instruction

The unique near-transmission lineage of this [guru-yoga] instruction is connected to the story of how the omniscient Jé Tsongkhapa consulted Mañjuśrī through the medium of Lama Umapa. He asked, for example, how he should act to serve the Dharma and sentient beings in accord with the perspectives of his students; he asked who [among his students] should accompany him [on his long retreat]; and he asked for clarifications of difficult points of scripture. Later, when he himself experienced the direct vision of

Mañjuśrī, Tsongkhapa asked the meditation deity questions about subtle and difficult points of sutra, about the unique Prāsaṅgika view [of emptiness] whereby *appearance* dispels the extreme of existence and *emptiness* dispels the extreme of nonexistence. He asked the deity about the subtle and difficult points of tantra, such as how the union of the two truths—the conventional truth of the *illusory body* and the ultimate truth of definitive innate nature [*clear light*]—takes place. Tsongkhapa saw how the instructions conferred by Mañjuśrī during these visions accorded perfectly with the treatises of the great trailblazers,[781] as if forming a single straight line. Tsongkhapa embraced these instructions of the deity as authoritative and in fact guided some of his disciples on the basis of these oral instructions. Seeing this inspired Master Rendawa to develop great admiration, and he asked Tsongkhapa to request from Mañjuśrī, on his behalf, a succinct yet complete instruction on how to attain buddhahood within the short life span of a human in this era of degeneration and send it over to him.[782] On his part, Tsongkhapa made extensive outer, inner, and secret offerings to Mañjuśrī and presented the request.

In his instruction conferred in response to this request, Mañjuśrī states:[783] To attain buddhahood within a single life in this era of degeneration, since both the dharmakāya and rūpakāya must be attained simultaneously and not sequentially, one must first cultivate a method that accords [with this resultant state]. Essential, therefore, is that there be an *illusory body*, which is the substantial cause for attaining the rūpakāya, and the *wisdom of innate bliss and emptiness*, which is the substantial cause for attaining the dharmakāya. He then explained (1) how, to attain the illusory body, [329] one must have the completion-stage instructions on the way, through gradual dissolving of the twenty-five coarse factors including the four elements, the four empty stages[784] arise in sequence; (2) how it is from this fourth empty stage, which is *clear light*, that the illusory body arises; and (3) how this illusory body, in turn, needs to once again be brought into clear light, and so forth. He explained how it's essential to possess the unique instructions of these stages of completion to establish the auspicious conditions.

The deity explained how the first stage needs to include ripening methods, such as imagining the specially visualized deities[785] at specific points of the body like the hairline and so forth and dissolving these deities into clear light, thus laying the auspicious basis for the dissolution of the twenty-five coarse factors leading to the dawning of the four empty stages. He then explained how, when it comes to presenting these instructions in a focused way, the Guhyasamāja root and explanatory tantras in general and the Ārya tradition of Guhyasamāja in particular are unrivaled. He explained how, to generate the union of innate bliss and emptiness, which is the ultimate truth, one must understand the instructions on inducing innate great bliss through dissolving the root and branch winds into the indestructible drop at the heart, in a manner similar to the stages of dissolution experienced naturally at the point of death. He explained how it is essential to know about the inner conditions—the yoga of the channels, winds, and drops, and the yoga of blazing and dripping, which consists of the instruction on generating the four joys, in both forward and reverse sequence, through the melting of the bodhicitta moon at the crown by the sun of inner *tumo* heat (*caṇḍālī*) at the navel—and the outer condition of vitality stopping (*prāṇāyāma*) with the [aid of] the *mudrā* consort.

As methods for ripening these practices, the deity explained how on the first generation stage, we need to establish the auspicious conditions for making our channels and winds serviceable. We do this through generating the winds that course through the [five] sense doors, the twenty-four places such as the crown, and the [eight] cardinal and intermediate directions at the heart into the eight door guardians, the twenty-four heroes and heroines, and five great bliss deities.[786] He explained how, in presenting these instructions in a focused way and in detail, there is nothing that rivals the Cakrasaṃvara root and explanatory tantras in general, and the Lūipa tradition of Cakrasaṃvara in particular. He stated how it is necessary, therefore, to practice in a way that Guhyasamāja and Cakrasaṃvara are not divorced from each other. The deity explained also how, in this particular age of degeneration—when the intelligence of sentient beings is weak, when their capacity for accumulating merit is feeble, when they accumulate negative karma effortlessly, and when the effects of collective karma manifest in the form of relentless adversities both for sentient beings and their environment—to ensure that one's practice of the paths taught in Guhyasamāja and Cakrasaṃvara tantras is successful and free of hindrance, [330] one must rely on a meditation deity that is supremely skilled and extremely powerful. The deity explained this point with the analogy of how one must rely on a skilled and fortunate captain if one embarks on a voyage on the great seas in search of precious gems.

The deity then explained how Vajrabhairava possesses five distinctive features that other meditation deities do not—(1) Mañjuśrī's face is present at both the causal and resultant Vajradhara stages; (2) all his hands display the threatening *mudrā* gesture; (3) he holds an intestine and a burning stove; (4) he holds a *khaṭvāṅga* staff; and (5) he displays a live impaled body—and that there is no question one should rely on Vajrabhairava. In brief, the deity thus explained how it is essential to have the three—Guhyasamāja, Cakrasaṃvara, and Vajrabhairava—not divorced from each other.

The deity then explained how practice of such a profound path of tantra must be preceded by first engaging in the common paths of training the mind in the stages of the path of practitioners of three capacities. With respect to the guru too, Mañjuśrī explained how it is not enough to rely on someone with only partial qualifications of a guru. One must rely on someone who has perfectly eliminated all doubts with respect to the scriptures, both sutra and tantra, through study and critical reflection; someone who has, at the very least, acquired initial experience based on single-pointed meditative cultivation of the contents of his study and critical reflection; someone who instructs his students with compassion on the basis how he himself has practiced and is thus capable of guiding the student through the entirety of the path; and someone who knows the boundaries of the precepts of the three vows and observes them with due commitment.

Regarding those we take as our companions, he explained how important it is to associate with those who are enthused by and dedicated to their practice and to not associate with those who have violated their precepts, who are immoral, and who are overcome by evil. In regard to Dharma protectors too, Mañjuśrī stressed how important it is to rely on not just any protector but on those that accord with our personal practice. He explained how, since Kālarūpa is the ideal protector for those contemplating death and impermanence and the sufferings of the lower realms and on that basis observing the law of karma and its effects, we should rely on Kālarūpa, protector of practitioners of lesser capacity. Similarly, since Vaiśravaṇa is the ideal protector for those who, having seen the entirety of samsara as characterized by suffering and have become motivated to seek freedom from samsara, are guarding the precepts of Vinaya discipline—omissions, commissions, and the exceptions—as if protecting their own eyes, we should rely on Vaiśravaṇa, [331] protector of practitioners of intermediate capacity. Finally, given that Mahākāla is the ideal protector for those who, because of their awareness of others' suffering and inability to bear it, are moved by compassion and take upon themselves the task of relieving others' pain and engage in the general and specific bodhisattva deeds motivated by their wish to seek enlightenment for others' sake, we should rely on Mahākāla, protector of practitioners of great capacity. Mañjuśrī also explained how, given that the entirety of the path to enlightenment is encompassed by the two aspects of method and wisdom, Mahākāla is the protector of the method aspect and Kālarūpa is the protector of the wisdom aspect of the path. The deity explained these in detail.

Mañjuśrī then explained how to undertake the practice of all these instructions in a succinct manner within a single sitting; how to view the guru and meditation deity as indivisible and then honor the guru with outer, inner, and secret offerings; how to supplicate and receive the four empowerments through meditative visualization; and how to train the mind by reviewing the entire path of sutra and tantra. Finally he presented a summary of the oral transmission of guru yoga, which encompasses the entire body of sutra and tantra paths. The deity explained how these instructions are totally different from other practices and how they are extremely great in their richness and impact.[787]

With teachings such as this, Mañjuśrī conferred upon the Omniscient Jé Tsongkhapa the magical volume and crowned him the custodian of his oral transmission. At that time, those actually present at the oral transmission included some gods of good fortune and, among humans, the Omniscient Jé Tsongkhapa himself and Tokden Jampal Gyatso, the teacher said.[788] The Omniscient Jé Tsongkhapa conferred these pith oral instructions to Tokden Jampal Gyatso. On his part, to help initiate the sacred meditative practice lineage of Ganden masters, like the source of a stream, Tokden engaged in single-pointed meditative practice at various solitary places by embracing these oral instructions as his heart practices. As a result, Tokden attained advanced levels of realization. Furthermore, for the sake of future disciples, the Omniscient Jé Tsongkhapa included brief presentations of guru yoga in his commentary on the *Fifty Verses on the Guru* and in his *Guide to the Six Yogas of Nāropa Endowed with Three Convictions*, relating its instructions to authoritative sources in the sutras and tantras, [332] and stated that details should be gleaned from the oral teachings of one's own guru.

The Omniscient Jé Tsongkhapa conferred this instruction [on guru yoga] to Khedrup, a sun among orators, and Tokden, a lord among realized adepts. From these two the instruction passed to Baso Chökyi Gyaltsen, who in turn transmitted it to the great siddha Dharmavajra with the advice that he practice these oral instructions comparable to the glorious Śavaripa (Saraha). On his part, the great siddha Dharmavajra adopted the way of a wounded wild animal, moving from one solitary place to another, where no human presence is found. He devoted his life to single-pointed meditative practice and attained in his lifetime the rainbow-like vajra body. One evening, our supreme guru,[789] Jé Tsongkhapa, revealed his face to the great siddha and conferred upon him numerous instructions of sutra and tantra, including this instruction of the guru yoga of the triple-being guru.[790] The great siddha transmitted these instructions to the conqueror Ensapa, as if pouring the entire content of one vase into another. Ensapa too undertook single-pointed practice of the oral teachings of Tsongkhapa and attained the state of buddhahood within his lifetime. And to indicate the presence of these instructions to future trainees, Ensapa put down in writing, using outlines and summary presentations, to indicate to any future trainees that may emerge the oral instructions of our supreme guru Jé Tsongkhapa. It is from the great Ensapa that Khedrup Sangyé Yeshé received the oral transmission of Jé Tsongkhapa and embraced the profound path of guru yoga as his heart practice. As a sign of having attained stable realization, he experienced repeated outpourings of spontaneous vajra songs as if the door to a treasury had been opened in him. Khedrup Sangyé Yeshé transmitted the oral teachings of Tsongkhapa in general, and this triple-being guru yoga in particular, to Panchen Losang Chögyen. On his part, anxious that the instruction of this triple-being guru yoga, a unique oral teaching of Tsongkhapa—rarer than a buddha—could become lost, Panchen Losang Chögyen composed this text, famed as the *Offering to the Guru: Indivisible Union of Bliss and Emptiness*, a rite containing a step-by-step guide to the oral transmission. Thanks to this, today, those from a young child who can read onward, whether monastic or lay, [333] have the opportunity to engage at will with a pith instruction transmitted from mouth to ear by successive masters of India and Tibet, an instruction that had not been the purview even of those scholars famed as masters of the five fields of knowledge. For such reasons Panchen Losang Chögyen's kindness to the Geluk tradition has been renowned as immense. Those who, on the other hand, speak of Panchen's great contributions in terms of his having authored some ritual texts—the Four Sets of a Hundred, the Blazing Mouth,[791] and so on, which are used by monks to perform rituals for the laity—expose their own true nature without anyone else having to unearth it.

Explaining the greatness of the instruction to engender confidence in this teaching

Next *Offering to the Guru* says:

> **The foundation of all excellence for those aspiring to liberation, the source of the entire collection of good fortune, the**

root of all the countless yogic attainments both supreme and common, the summarized essence of all the instructions on the practices a yogi of the supreme vehicle needs to pursue—all of these depend upon proper reliance on the spiritual mentor who reveals to you the path without error. The *Blue Compendium* says:

> The starting point where all instructions converge
> is not forsaking your sublime spiritual mentor.
> From him comes faith, the awakening mind, and so forth;
> he is the treasury, the source of all higher qualities.[792]

Also, the Omniscient [Tsongkhapa] says:

> The root of creating well the auspicious conditions
> for all the good things of this and future lives
> is to rely properly, with effort in both thought and action,
> on the sublime spiritual teacher who reveals the path.
>
> Seeing this, never forsake him, even at the cost of your life,
> and please him with the offering of following his advice.
> I, a yogi, have practiced in this manner;
> you who aspire to liberation should do likewise.

And he says:

> The good fortune of both this world and the world beyond,
> the root of all higher qualities, is the kind master. [334]

Fifty Verses on the Guru too states:

> "Higher attainments follow after the master,"
> Vajradhara himself has declared.
> Knowing this, you should thoroughly
> please the guru with all that you have.

The *Synthesis of Precious Qualities* states:

> **Good disciples who are respectful to the guru**
> **should always rely on their learned gurus.**
> **Why? Because the virtues of learning come from them**
> **and they teach the perfection of wisdom.**
> **"Attainment of the attributes of a buddha depend on the spiritual mentor";**
> **so stated the Conqueror who possesses all higher qualities.**

Therefore, as a field for gathering merit and purifying obscurations, the vajra master is superior even to all the buddhas. The *Saṃvarodaya Tantra* says:

> **Whether it's the self-arisen Blessed One**
> **or the meditation deity itself,**
> **the vajra master is superior even to them,**
> **for it is he who grants the pith instructions.**

For these reasons, the cultivation of guru yoga, which encompasses all the essential points of the path, is the most excellent means of extracting the essence of your human existence of leisure and opportunity. Therefore practice this in the following way.

These passages, cited above, indicate how all the excellences, from minor instances of good fortune within samsara—happiness, joy, and fame—up to the superior levels of goodness—the paths and results of the Lesser and the Great Vehicles—depend on properly relating to the guru in both thought and action. The passages also indicate how, as a field for accumulating merit and purifying obscurations, the guru is superior even to a buddha. And guru yoga is an incomparable method for accumulating merit easily. For the *Root Tantra of Cakrasaṃvara* says:

> Residing well in the vajra master's body,
> the deity will accept offerings from the practitioner.[793]

And:

> Even a practitioner of weak merit,
> by pleasing the guru, will gain realization.[794]

Illumination of All Hidden Meanings interprets these two passages as stating that, even a practitioner whose merit was weak earlier in life, if he meets a qualified master and honors him by making offerings, Heruka [Cakrasaṃvara] will enter the vajra master's body and will enhance the practitioner's merit. In this way, the practitioner's accumulation of merit is perfected quickly, leading to his attainment of the great seal of supreme attainment later in life.[795] [335]

The benefits of meditating on the guru's body mandala is explained in the *Vajra Garland* explanatory tantra:

> In this very body [of the guru]
> reside all the tathāgatas,
> and thus it is thus called the "mandala of the body."
> This is the body of Vajrasattva himself.
> In distinct Vajrasattva forms,
> all the buddhas without exception
> are present in this buddha body.
> So the yogin will attain nirvana
> swiftly, in this very life.[796]

And it says:

> Beyond the virtue of giving away everything,
> if you see that all the conquerors reside
> there in the vajra master's body
> this would have [great] import indeed:
> you will in the future become a great being.
> Therefore, on behalf of all sentient beings,
> and with offerings of divine substances,
> honor the guru in all your efforts.[797]

The above passage states that, compared to the virtue of giving one's body, life, and material resources to others, if one honors the vajra master in all one's efforts, greater stores of merit will be accumulated by generating all the aspects of the guru's being—his aggregates, elements, and sense bases—as the buddhas and bodhisattvas of the ten directions. In particular, the text on the generation stage of Cakrasaṃvara entitled *Milking the Wish-Granting Cow* states how, compared to meditating on the mandala based on external factors such as colored sand or a painting on canvas, merit is accumulated far more swiftly if one meditates on the mandala based on inner bases—namely, the aggregates, elements, and sense bases.[798] *Fifty Verses on the Guru*, too, says that if one offers an article to a single vajra master with a pure intention, this constitutes making offerings to all the buddhas of the ten directions and thus helps perfect the accumulation of merit most swiftly and leads to the supreme attainment [of buddhahood].[799]

When it comes to burning away powerful karmic obscurations, guru yoga is like the fire at the end of the world. For example, *Sacred Words of Mañjuśrī* says:

> For some blessed with this import,
> I will reside in their body
> and accept offerings from other practitioners.
> By pleasing the deity in this way,
> they will purify karmic obscurations.[800]

This says that if one relies properly on a qualified vajra master, both in thought and action, Mañjuśrī himself will enter the vajra master's body [336] and will accept the offerings made by the practitioner, thus helping cleanse karmic obscurations swiftly.

The *Drop of the Great Seal Tantra* too says:

> Just as when fire burns away a log
> and within moments turns it to ash,
> likewise, if someone pleases the glorious guru,
> within moments his evil karma is burned.[801]

The revered Milarepa accumulated grave negative karma in the early part of his life, killing some thirty people and animals like birds, but having met his guru Marpa Lotsāwa and engaging in hardships, he was able, within a few years, to cleanse his karmic obscurations and realize the great-seal attainment. One finds numerous similar stories of how, as a result of undertaking great hardship in connection with their gurus, sublime beings purified their negative karma and attained extraordinary qualities, such as clairvoyance and miraculous powers. So, when it comes to purifying negative karma, nothing is more powerful than the practice of proper reliance on the spiritual teacher.

However one cultivates the path to the full awakening of buddhahood, whether through the sutra path or the tantra path, if one pursues a robust guru yoga, one's path will advance swiftly. Even if one is cultivating the path to buddhahood through the Perfection Vehicle, if one's practice of relying on the spiritual teacher is formidable—such that one is willing to sacrifice one's body, life, and resources—one's path will become extremely quick. The truth of this can be witnessed in the story of the bodhisattva Sadāprarudita, who traversed from the small stage of path of accumulation up to the eighth bodhisattva ground in a matter of a few years.[802] My own teacher, the glorious sublime master, said that bodhisattva Sadāprarudita was able to advance through so many levels of the Mahayana path and bodhisattva grounds within a few years owing to the power of his reliance on the spiritual teacher; such speed cannot be found within the Perfection Vehicle path otherwise.[803] As for seeking buddhahood through the path of Vajrayāna, strong guru yoga brings extraordinarily swift progress along the path, as stated in *Fifty Verses on the Guru*:

> If one must rely on a guru of special bond
> at all times by offering such un-giveable things
> as one's son, one's spouse, and one's life,
> what need is there to speak of resources?
>
> Then buddhahood itself,
> so hard to find even in eons—
> millions or countless eons in fact—
> will be granted in this very life to the effortful.[804] [337]

Thus if one relates to the vajra master properly, without regard for one's body, life, and resources, and if, on this basis, one strives in the tantric path with great effort, one will attain the state of buddhahood, so difficult to attain even over countless eons, in this very life.

In brief, in the path of the Perfection Vehicle, when the two factors converge—(1) the swift sutra path of generating the awakening mind that holds others dearer than oneself and engaging in the difficult bodhisattva deeds motivated by such a mind and (2) the practice of properly relying on the spiritual teacher based on embracing all the hardships entailed in relating to the guru, without regard for one's body, life, and resources—the pace of one's path through the Perfection Vehicle will be most swift. As for the swift path of Vajrayāna, the paths of the three lower classes of tantra include the magical method to accumulate merit most rapidly through the attainment of such siddhis as that of eye potion, underground travel, and mantra retention,[805] all on the basis of deity yoga and emptiness yoga. All of these make repeated statements about the need to cultivate them on the basis of taking guru yoga as the life force of one's practice. Highest yoga tantra contains the magical method of gathering the merit and wisdom of countless eons in a consummately swift manner through the two factors, that of the ultimate truth (the clear-light union of innate bliss and emptiness) and the conventional truth (the illusory body). If the completion stage of these two truths were cultivated on the basis of taking guru yoga as the life force of one's practice, one would accomplish them quickly indeed. Without guru yoga, actually, they cannot be attained at all. This has been stated repeatedly by the lord Mahāsukha, the great siddha Saraha, and the glorious guardian Ārya Nāgārjuna. When such a swift Vajrayāna path and strong guru yoga converge, the pace of the tantric path develops great momentum. Therefore guru yoga is a swift path shared by both sutra and tantra.

It is indeed this very guru yoga encompassing the entire body of the paths of sutra and tantra that represents the ultimate instruction wherein all key points of the swift paths mentioned above are united in a single integrated practice. With this in mind, my teacher, the glorious sublime being, said that in the phrase [338] "I shall quickly, quickly, in this very life, actualize the state of a primordial buddha guru-deity,"[806] we should understand that the first "quickly" refers to the stages of the path where the key points of all the paths of both sutra and tantra are present, while the second "quickly" refers to guru yoga.

That both common and supreme siddhis[807] can be attained swiftly and without difficulty when one relies on guru yoga is stated in the *Vajra Tent Tantra*:

> Vajra being and buddhahood,
> vajra Dharma and majesty,
> the horse king [Indra's fast mount]—such siddhis
> will be attained without difficulty.
> Eye potion and fleet-footedness,
> sword and mastery of underground,
> pills and flying in the skies,
> invisibility and essence extraction—
> one will attain these swiftly
> by pleasing the wisdom vajra.[808]

Guru yoga is also, therefore, the iron hook that swiftly brings forth siddhis.

Furthermore, because this instruction clearly contains the unique oral teachings that unite the key points of all the undisputed sutras and tantras and their authoritative commentaries within the stages of the path of the three capacities and in a format that can be practiced in a single sitting, this teaching naturally possesses the following four qualities of greatness: (1) it allows all teachings to be understood without contradiction, (2) it allows all scriptures to dawn as personal instructions, (3) it makes it easy to discern the enlightened intent of the conquerors, and (4) grave misdeeds cease of their own accord.[809] Also, in the context of [practices for those of] great capacity, there are two distinct approaches to cultivating loving kindness by viewing others as dear, one stemming from Maitreya and the other from Mañjuśrī, but this text contains the unique oral transmission on combining the two approaches and practicing in a single integrated way.[810] Also, since all the key points of the *Seven-Point Mind Training* are clearly present in this instruction, the greatness of the mind-training teaching applies to this instruction as well, as stated in the following:

> Like a diamond, like the sun, and like a medicinal tree:
> understand the meaning of the treatises and so on.
> This distilled essence of pith instructions
> stems from the lineage of Serlingpa.[811] [339]

Similarly, given that all the key points of the two stages, the heart of all the tantras, are present in this instruction, the qualities of greatness ascribed to the two stages apply to this instruction as well. So when it comes to teaching and engaging in the meditative practice of this instruction, the distillation of the essence of the entire 84,000 heaps of Dharma, my mind never becomes complacent.

These, then, are a brief indication of the greatness of this instruction. Fearing length, I have not extensively cited the authoritative sources. In any case, based on what I have explained to be the transmission lineage and the greatness of this instruction [on guru yoga], you can also discern the transmission lineage and the greatness of the instruction on mahāmudrā. So I have not discussed these two for mahāmudrā separately.

Prerequisites for this guru-yoga instruction on the part of the practitioner

The appropriate practitioner for this instruction is someone who, having trained their mind in the practices of the three capacities in a graduated sequence, has attained at least a minimal degree of simulated experience of the awakening mind. On top of this, they must have received tantric empowerment. As regards empowerment, too, since this instruction aligns with the approach that engages in meditative practice of three meditation deities—Guhyasamāja, Cakrasaṃvara, and Vajrabhairava—in an integrated manner and not in isolation from each other, it is not enough to receive an empowerment into the three lower tantras. They must receive the four empowerments[812] according to one of the three meditation deities, in perfect accord with the rites defined in the tantras. Were they to engage in the practice of this guru yoga without having received such an empowerment, there would be little gain but potential for grave harm. Understand that this is so by relying on the authority of the tantras.

As for the place to practice, those who wish from their heart to practice this guru yoga should not choose just any location. They should choose a meditation place endowed with qualities recommended in the sutras and tantras. At the very least, the place should be conducive to virtuous activity. The *Compendium of Training*, citing sutra sources, describes in some detail the following: the qualities appropriate for a place of solitude, the way to behave in such a place, and the kind of attitude one needs to live in such a place.[813] Similarly, although qualities appropriate for the site of meditative practice are also mentioned in texts such as the *Ornament of Mahayana Sutras*, both the root and explanatory tantras of Guhyasamāja, and the *Questions of Subāhu* [*Tantra*], I will not provide specific citations from these here. [340]

How to engage in the actual practice of the instruction endowed with these two distinctive features

The practice of the instruction endowed with two distinctive features[814] has two parts: how to practice during the session and how to practice between the sessions.

How to practice during the session

The first is threefold: the preliminaries, the main part of the session, and concluding activities.

The preliminaries

This is twofold: general preliminary practices and special preliminary practices.

General Preliminaries

Cleaning and preparing the practice space

Within the first, how to set the intention and how, on this basis, to go for refuge and generate the awakening mind is as follows. The person who has received tantric empowerment and become an appropriate practitioner of this instruction should seek a suitable site for practice, one that is free of faults and has the appropriate features. There he could seek a cave, the base of a tree, or a hut where he would be protected from the dangers of storm, snow, and rain. He should prepare his place well and make it clean by sprinkling water on the ground and sweeping it so that it is appealing to everyone, both oneself and others. This is the tradition mentioned in the Jātaka story of the six brahman brothers[815] as well as that of the master Serlingpa. Here is how you do this. Contemplate:

> For the sake of all mother sentient beings, I will seek in all my efforts to attain the precious state of fully enlightened buddhahood. For this I will sweep away the three poisons present in the minds of myself and all other sentient beings, as well as all the negative karma and its effects brought about by these poisons. (I will do this with the twin forces of the precious awakening mind and the profound middle-way view, the two appearing in the form of a broom—a broom made of palm fronds, twigs, or an animal tail.)[816]

Alternatively, set your causal motivation[817] and then contemplate:

> Just as, following the Buddha's instruction, Cūḍapanthaka cleaned the residence of the monks and as a result purified his powerful karmic obscurations, gained the direct realization of selflessness so hard to discern, and actualized the state of arhat,[818] likewise, in accord with the instruction of my guru buddha, I too will sweep this place to which I am inviting the assembly of the ārya sangha. May similar virtues of abandonment and realization arise in the minds of myself and all other sentient beings.

Or you could contemplate in the following manner:

> Together with five hundred daughters of merchants, the bodhisattva Sadāprarudita cleaned the site where the bodhisattva Dharmodgata would conduct his teaching, even piercing his own body to sprinkle his blood and settle the dust on the ground. As a result, Sadāprarudita was able to traverse within a few years the bodhisattva grounds and paths, which would otherwise have required cultivation for countless years, and generate the precious mind of awakening without much difficulty. Likewise, I will clean this site where I am inviting my spiritual teachers, who are in truth guru buddhas. Through the virtue of this, may the awakening mind and the associated realizations of the grounds and paths arise in me and in all sentient beings.

Again, contemplate:

> Our teacher, the Buddha, himself swept and cleaned the sites where the sangha would reside and instructed us monastics that we too should sweep and clean. He explained that the benefits of sweeping and cleaning would be that one's own mind will become clear, others' minds will be clear, the gods supporting the forces of goodness will be delighted and extend their support, one will engage in the good deeds, one will be reborn in the higher realms, and one will cultivate the buddhafields. Thus may all such benefits come about for me and all other sentient beings as a result of sweeping and cleaning in accord with the Buddha's advice.

In this way, set the immediate motivation. While doing the actual sweeping, utter the phrase "Eliminate dust, eliminate stains."

In fact, the phrase "Eliminate dust, eliminate stains" is an instruction of the Buddha [342] that is extremely powerful and thorough in scope with respect to its meaning. "Dust" can be understood as the manifest afflictions of the three poisons and "stains" as their seeds. The word "eliminate" indicates the eradication of the three poisons, both their manifest forms and their seeds. The lines can thus be understood as referring to the actual antidote: the wisdom realizing selflessness, which is the higher training in wisdom. For such a training in wisdom to arise relies on first training in concentration, which in turn requires first training in morality as a foundation. The training in morality, in turn, requires a causal motivation of true renunciation. This, in turn, has two aspects—renunciation that ceases preoccupation with the next life and renunciation that ceases preoccupation with this life.

To cultivate the first aspect of renunciation, you repeatedly contemplate the infallibility of the law of karma and the general and specific sufferings of samsaric existence. To generate the second aspect of renunciation, you contemplate repeatedly the value of human existence, the difficulty of obtaining it, and death and impermanence. You need to appreciate how both the understanding and the realization of the threefold training, with all that it involves, depends on proper reliance on the spiritual teacher. Thus this instruction "Eliminate dust, eliminate stains" indicates the entire path of the Hīnayāna. So, I believe, it is based on this [simple] instruction that the ārya Cūḍapanthaka traversed the five stages of the Hīnayāna path in their proper sequence and actualized the arhat state.

This instruction can also be related to the practices of those of the Mahayana lineage. In that context, "dust" would refer to the twin forces of self-grasping and self-cherishing, while "stains" would refer to the imprints of self-grasping and its effects—namely, the delusory dualistic perceptions. The word "eliminate" would then indicate the wisdom realizing selflessness, which is the actual antidote. For that realization of selflessness to become an antidote to the imprints of self-grasping, one must rely on its complementary factor—completion of the accumulation of merit of the first two innumerable eons by relying on the six perfections and the four means of gathering others to mature their minds. In fact, all the bodhisattva practices, including their supporting foundation [the awakening mind], are complements to wisdom. [343] The bodhisattva Śāntideva says:

> All these branch practices were taught
> by the Buddha for the sake of wisdom.[819]

Now the antidote that eliminates self-cherishing is the awakening mind that cherishes others more than oneself. Generating such a mind requires first finding the situation of sentient beings wandering in samsara to be unbearable and, on that basis, developing great compassion, which means taking personal responsibility for liberating sentient beings from their suffering. The birth of such compassion depends, in turn, on a deep weariness with wandering in samsara, an absence of the slightest attraction to even the glory of the absorptive mental states of the peak of existence,[820] having ceased preoccupation with the next life. This is in fact the imprint of having trained the mind in the path of intermediate capacity. Of course, if one has not ceased preoccupation with this life, one cannot by any means cease preoccupation with the next life. So it is essential to first train one's mind in the path of the lesser capacity, which helps cease preoccupation with this life. Thus I feel this instruction ["eliminate dust, eliminate stains"] implies all the paths of the three capacities in a sequential manner. This said, the sutra itself should be understood as belonging to the Hīnayāna teaching.

Some, saying that this is just an imaginative fabrication, may laugh at what I have just said. But I would counter that such ridicule would belie an ignorance on the speaker's part of how he himself is weighed down by contradiction. For, on the one hand, he accepts the validity of the Vinaya statements that Cūḍapanthaka realized all five paths of the Hīnayāna through this [simple] instruction and then explained the meaning of this instruction in detail to others, leading them to attain such fruits as the state of a stream enterer and so on. At the same time, such a speaker takes this to be a minor instruction of little import, a simple teaching.

Whatever the case, if when tidying and preparing your place of practice, you need to do things like digging the earth, preparing mud [to make the walls of a hut], cutting grass, and so forth, you should also observe such precepts as choosing the appropriate time and mindfully avoiding harm to animals. Proceeding like this is far superior to the way of those with narrow vision.

Laying out the representations of the Buddha's body, speech, and mind and the offerings

Having swept and cleaned the place of practice and laid out excellently the representations of the Buddha's body, speech, and mind, [344] lay out the offerings. When it comes to offerings, if you acquired the substances through wrong livelihood, your giving would not become extraordinary giving, even if you give to both higher and lower recipients. Those who have taken the bodhisattva vows in particular need to remain free from any wrong means of livelihood; hence giving that conflicts with your precepts and non-giving are both proscribed. As the *Verses on the Compendium of Training* states:

> Through training in perfect livelihood,
> ensure the purity of your substances.[821]

The *Guide to the Bodhisattva Way* says specifically that the buddhas and bodhisattvas would not be pleased with your offerings if they were obtained through harming sentient beings:

> Just as no sensory pleasure can gladden the mind
> of one whose body is engulfed in flames,
> likewise, if you harm sentient beings,
> none among those full of compassion will be pleased.[822]

Again:

> To please these creatures is to please the sovereign sages,
> and to offend them is to offend the sages.[823]

In brief, it is essential that you lay out beautifully whatever offerings you can, free of any of the five wrong means of livelihood.[824]

When you make the offering, do so by contemplating the following:

> For the sake of all mother sentient beings, I must attain the state of a fully enlightened buddha. To this end I will offer fragrant nectar and so forth to all the gurus, buddhas, bodhisattvas, heroes and ḍākinīs, and Dharma protectors in all the ten directions.

And contemplate:

> All the representations of the enlightened body, speech, and mind in all the world systems of the ten directions, exemplified by the representations of enlightened body, speech, and mind in front of me, are mere conceptual designations, and not even an atom of it exists in its own right from the side of their bases of designation. Given that when it comes to their ultimate nature, not even an iota of difference exists among [these representations of body, speech, and mind], I will honor them all equally.

Generate your causal motivation in this way. For your immediate motivation, contemplate the emptiness of the three elements of the act of offering.[825] You should also make offerings on the basis of the six special attitudes explained in *Bodhisattva Grounds*: how [the buddhas and so forth] are the source of higher qualities, how they are an unexcelled field of merit, how they are the most excellent among gods and humans, how their appearance [in the world] is exceedingly rare, how they have no self-concern, and how they reveal all mundane and supermundane truths.[826] In brief, make offerings in this way so that the customs of the great masters will continue without decline. [345] At the end, you could chant the verses that begin "All the waters there are for drinking"[827] and visualize Samantabhadra's cloud of offering.

Here too, even when offering ordinary water, if you do so with the intention of offering nectar, the buddhas and bodhisattvas will see actual nectar and partake of them as such. Doing so would not thus constitute a lie; in fact, you will obtain the merit of offering nectar. For example, it is stated in *Summary of the Great Vehicle* as well as in Madhyamaka texts that, in relation to a single bowl of liquid, gods see it as nectar, humans as water, and hungry ghosts as pus and blood.[828] If this is true, what need is there to speak of how even ordinary offering substances will be perceived [in pure vision] by the buddhas and bodhisattvas because of the power of their merit? This is what my teacher, the glorious sublime being, said.

As to what constitutes wrong livelihood, the *Precious Garland* says:

> *Hypocrisy* is to guard the senses
> to procure resources and service;
> *flattery* is to utter pleasing words
> for sake of resources and service.
>
> *Bribery* is to praise other's resources
> with the thought of obtaining for oneself;
> *coercion* is to directly threaten the other
> to obtain what is coveted.
>
> *Hinting* is to speak highly of
> things one received previously.[829]

These verses are easy to understand. However, with respect to the last one in particular, and if we look at what the *Compendium of Training* says in the context of purifying resources[830]—(1) seeking material resources in a way that involves inflicting bodily harm, (2) seeking material resources through mental injury, (3) seeking material resources through immoral deeds, and (4) seeking material resources through corrupt means—engaging in a genuinely perfect act of giving is seemingly impossible today except in the case of few material offerings such as water. It is for reasons such as this, I think, that gurus shower great praise on the offering of bowls of water.

Preparing your seat and adopting the right posture

Next, sit on a comfortable seat, either with a posture endowed with the eight features[831] or in another manner that is convenient. [346] Then, adopting especially a virtuous state of mind, you go for refuge and generate the awakening mind. To make sure your bottom does not ache or cause your cushion to rot when you sit in meditation for extended periods, you could build a wooden frame that improves air circulation. Alternatively, if you choose the lifestyle of a wandering hermit, you could prepare a sitting frame out of thick jute or twigs tightly bound together, the base made of thicker twigs supporting a sitting space large enough in breadth and width. This base supports a layer of thinner sticks that support the cushion, which is raised slightly higher at the back. Some sources say that one should draw a symbol—a vajra or a lotus—beneath the seat; however, if you use a symbol such as a crossed-vajra or a lotus, you will incur the infraction of walking over symbols of the deities. Thus the excellent custom is to draw, with either limestone or white quartz, the immutable *yungdrung*[832] symbol. Such a symbol, my teacher said, represents the precious stone the diamond, indicating that the ground beneath the site of one's meditative practice aimed at actualizing the buddha's omniscient gnosis is as firm as a diamond and not something that crumbles like dust, incapable of supporting the meditator's seat. On this drawing, place strands of *kuśa* grass with the tips facing inward and the ends facing out; they should be arranged well and not mixed up and jumbled. Mixing the grasses up, the teacher said, would be an inauspicious omen for mixing up the sequence of one's meditation practices. When preparing these things, bring to mind how our teacher, Buddha Śākyamuni, accepted *kuśa* grass from the grass vendor Maṅgala and placed it under his seat and made the firm pledge that he would not rise until he had actualized the omniscience of a buddha. With such firm pledge, he conquered the four māras. In the same way, pledge "Until I have conquered the demon king of self-grasping and his acolytes, I will remain unswayed by any conditions." The teacher explained that this is how we should emulate the deeds of the Buddha.

Next is adopting a posture, such as the one with eight features or any posture that is easy and convenient. Here are the eight features:

1) Your *legs* are crossed in *vajrāsana*—the left foot placed upon your right

thigh, the right leg crossing around from outside of the left and placed on your left thigh. [347] Adopting this posture is auspicious for inoculating yourself against harms by demonic forces of darkness, my teacher said.

2) Your *hands* are in the gesture of meditation—your left palm under and the right, about four finger-widths below your navel, with the tips of your two thumbs touching each other to form a triangle. The teacher said that the triangle indicates the blazing of *tumo* (inner heat) while the tips of two thumbs touching symbolizes the generation of heat—with the bodhicitta channels residing there. This makes your channels supple and enables loving kindness and compassion to arise.

3) Your *back* is straight as an arrow, not bending to the front, back, or to either side. For if your back is bent or crooked, the channels won't be straight, and the winds in the channels will not flow naturally. This prevents the mind, which is dependent on the winds, from becoming serviceable, making it challenging to apply your mind to the chosen meditation topic. In contrast, [when everything flows well,] your mind is applied to the practice like a stream of water that flows easily through a smooth and straight canal.

4) Your *shoulders* remain extended like an eagle. If your shoulders are kept too high, this will cause tension in your body, and if they are kept too low, your body will slump. So keeping your shoulders just so has the important benefit of maintaining a balance between excessive tension and slackness in the body.

5) Your *head* is kept in a slight bow, such that your neck is not too upturned or too bent. For keeping your head too upturned leads to greater distraction, whereas if it is excessively bent, this leads to sleepiness and mental sinking. So keeping your head in a precise position keeps your mind free of these two faults.

6) The *eyes* should rest neither wide open nor tightly closed but slightly downcast, as if softly gazing at the tip of your nose. The teacher said keeping the eyes like this distinguishes the meditator from the non-Buddhists, who meditate with their eyes closed, and the Bönpos, who meditate with their eyes wide open, staring fixedly at a focal object.

7) Your *mouth and teeth* are left in their natural position. The teacher said this is to ensure that one's appearance is appealing to others and to prevent ridicule; that this is so is mentioned in a preamble in the Vinaya.[833]

8) The *tip of the tongue* is slightly behind the teeth. This ensures that when your meditative concentration becomes stable, your mouth is not then prone to drooling and dryness.

These, then, are the oral instructions that make it easy to understand the presentations on how to position one's body taught in the *Vajra Garland* explanatory tantra. [348]

Settling your mind through your breath and setting your intention

Having thus ensured the key points of your posture, ensure the key points of the winds as follows. Having first performed either the "nine-round breathing that clears away the impure winds" or "calming the winds,"[834] then simply observe your breath—the movement of the in breath and the out breath. In this way, clear your mind of any obscuration and, on the basis of such a lucid and clear mind, engage in meditation.

To cleanse the impure winds through the nine-round breathing, first inhale through your left nostril and exhale through the right. Next, inhale through the right nostril and exhale through the left, and then inhale simultaneously through both nostrils and exhale through both. Do it three times each way, making nine rounds. When inhaling, imagine breathing in the blessings of all the buddhas of the ten directions, and when exhaling, imagine breathing out all your negative karma and faults.

"Calming the winds" involves carefully observing the flow of your breathing. Here, examine whether your mind has fallen under the power of preoccupations with this life. If you notice that it has done so, then contemplate:

> This uncouth mind has already dragged me into incalculable suffering, and yet it remains unsatisfied and seeks to make me suffer more, inducing me to squander this human existence of leisure and opportunity I have obtained this once. From here on, however, I will not let myself be besieged by this uncouth mind. May all the buddhas and bodhisattvas of the ten directions bless me so that I may succeed in this endeavor.

With these thoughts, breathing out from both nostrils in a deliberate manner, imagine that all thoughts indicating preoccupation with this life, such as the eight worldly concerns, are expelled. And as you breathe in, imagine that the blessings from the buddhas and bodhisattvas enter into you.

If, while contemplating in this manner, you notice a rise of devotion and reverence for your guru, joy in having found this human existence of leisure and opportunity, and enthusiasm to make this human existence meaningful, rejoice and then, instead of exhaling [immediately], take one long and deliberate breath and imagine that the blessings of the buddhas and bodhisattvas enter into you. Imagine that this entry [of blessings] into you has been made stable.

Having engaged in the breath practice of either clearing the impure winds or calming the winds, then settle into a breathing rhythm that is natural and free of all flawed breathing—without making whirring sounds, breathing with deliberate or forced effort, [349] or breathing in a distracting uneven way. Now breathing in a natural pattern, direct your attention to your breath and count up to three, seven, fourteen, or twenty-one rounds. In this way, let your mind gradually settle into a state free of faults—those of sloth, lethargy, distraction, laxity, excitation, and so on—and allow the mind's refined core or primordial state,[835] that morally neutral vivid clarity and luminosity, to arise. Having allowed such a state to arise, and having gained a degree of stability, if you now undertake your meditation, it will be easier for you to bring specific focal objects to mind and easier to fuse your mind with that object of meditation. The teacher compared this to the way a clear crystal, when it comes into contact with any color, instantly assumes that color. That color then appears to be the clear crystal's own natural color.

As to how you generate an especially virtuous mental state from within such a luminous and aware mind, the teacher said you should do as instructed by Gyaltsab Jé. Gyaltsab Jé states that you should not engage in a manner where the meditation topics of the paths of the three capacities are somehow brought as objects of your luminous and aware mind, like observing a material object with your eyes. Instead, the primordial mind that is luminous and aware is itself generated into the nature of the path.[836] To do this, contemplate:

> Alas! The situation of myself and all other sentient beings equal to the expanse of space has until now been unspeakably tragic: we have remained in constant torment by hundreds of sufferings, both the suffering of cyclic existence in general and sufferings specific to each realm of existence. Yet there is no end whatsoever in sight to our samsaric existence, which is bottomless and endless. So there is no escaping our fate as continuing to remain fuel for the fire of suffering in cyclic existence, both in general and in the three lower realms in particular. Today, thanks to the kindness of my father guru, I have obtained once this precious human exis-

tence of leisure and opportunity, I have met the Buddha's teaching so hard to encounter, and I have obtained in particular the opportunity to study, contemplate, and meditate on the instructions of the oral teachings of our supreme guru, Jé Tsongkhapa. [350] So if today I fail to strive in the means to swiftly liberate myself and all other sentient beings from this vast ocean of samsara, if I squander this once-found most excellent human existence of leisure and opportunity and waste whatever remaining life I may have on meaningless pursuits both day and night, allowing thoughts and actions aimed at pointless goals to assail my body and mind, then what would separate me from animals when it comes to the depth of my ignorance? Therefore today, I must not squander this most precious human existence of leisure and opportunity I have found this once; I must make it meaningful and indeed ensure that I spend both day and night with a sense of purpose. I will engage in the practice of this profound guru yoga that encompasses the entire corpus of sutra and tantra paths, practicing that which is the innermost essence of all purposes.

I must also pursue this on the basis of this very human existence, for obtaining a similar human existence in the future may not be possible. For obtaining such a human existence requires many causes and conditions to come together: a foundation laid through pure morality, that morality complemented by the practices of generosity and so on, and these practices motivated by pure aspiration. But no such pure morality can be found anywhere in me, which means that, far from obtaining such a hoped-for human existence, I will likely end up in a locale where even the words "pure morality" are not heard! Therefore, if I fail to begin making my human existence meaningful before it slips from my hands, when I have found it this one time, then my having found such a human existence would be no different from not having found one in the first place.

This too I must begin immediately, right now, for life is indeed most unstable and fragile, the body and mind tied together in a feeble manner like a bubble in water; it is like a dewdrop on a leaf in the middle of a storm, threatened by a host of conditions for death. There is no certainty that, even between breathing in and breathing out, a gap will not enter and cast everything into darkness. There is no guarantee at all that I will not die this very night! So, today when I am at the crossroads of moving upward or downward, [351] when I have this very narrow window of opportunity to choose my future fate—either a good one or a bad one—I must strive my best to make this human existence meaningful. After death, nothing is of benefit except Dharma practice. I may be surrounded by the most loving family and friends, but not a single person can come with me. I may have gathered a great mass of valuable possessions, but not a single atom can be brought along. Even my very body of flesh, blood, and bones, guarded with such care that I dared not be separated for even an instant, will be discarded against my will. Mere consciousness, stripped of its physical support, will depart like a lost wanderer. If and when I wander in this manner, nothing other than my Dharma practice will be loyal and accompany me as my protector, my refuge, and my ally. Thus I will spend day and night in pursuit of sublime Dharma, which will be of benefit in my future life.

After death, I will not become nothing; I will have to take a new birth. As to where I will be reborn, there are only two possibilities—in the higher realms or in the lower realms—but I will have no say where I am reborn; I am at the mercy of my karma, and I will be tossed by the two types of karma, positive and negative. When it comes to karma,[837] however, I find it difficult to prevent negative karma even when I make an effort; I am instead drawn to it instinctively. And when it comes to positive karma, I find it as hard as trying to make a stream flow uphill. This is because my habituation to negative karma in the past was strong while my habituation to positive karma was weak. This clearly demonstrates the kind of causes that preceded. Even in this life, I accumulate new karma and infractions of precepts, both natural and prescribed, like the falling of rain. And the karma I already possess tends to expand on its own, just as the great ocean absorbs the four great rivers.[838] Leaving aside the power of such a great heap of negative karma, even a single moment of negative karma can lead to birth in one of the three lower realms. This is something the great compassionate one, the Blessed Buddha, declared repeatedly for our sake out of his concern for our fate, without holding anything back or engaging in lies or deception. If this breath of mine were to be cut short while I am still fraught with such an immense heap of negative karma, [352] I will no doubt fly to the lower realms with nothing to prevent it.

Now, if I were to be reborn in the three lower realms, the hell realm has the following sufferings of heat and cold—being burned and cooked, being beaten up and tormented, being cut and sliced open, and having my body splintering into a hundred or a thousand pieces. In the hungry ghost realm, there are the pains of hunger and thirst, of hardship and terror. In the animal realm are the pains of ignorance and delusion, one kind eating another, being abused for labor, being slaughtered, being tied up, and being beaten. Let alone actually experiencing sufferings like this with my body and mind, even hearing about them and seeing them in person could bring on a heart attack. How could I bear it if and when I must undergo these sufferings myself with my own body and mind? Yet I have no power to spare myself from such suffering, for I have already gathered the causes to undergo such suffering; in fact, I indulged in gathering their causes with joy and delight! The time when I must experience such suffering is not in a distant future. In fact, the gap between such unbearable suffering and the present is only this current movement of my breath! And there is no guarantee that this flow of air, moving in and out, will not suddenly cease.

At that point, nothing will save me from my fate. Even if I were to seek out a refuge to protect me, I would have already initiated the process of turning myself into fuel for the suffering of the three lower realms, having already cut the thread of life for birth in the higher realms and the attainment of liberation. It would be too late. Therefore, today, when I have in my own hands still the opportunity to move toward or away from the unbearable suffering of the terrifying realms, if I fail to strive in the means to avert such suffering and instead, like a dog attracted to the sight of blood, willfully indulge in negative and nonvirtuous karmic acts, [353] I would be truly insane. So, with all my effort, I will strive in the means to turn away from such a terrifying state of suffering. To this end, I go for refuge to the Three Jewels from the deepest depth of my heart. And I strive to act ethically in accord with the laws of karma, positive and negative, the only way I can be saved from the fate of such terrible suffering.

Now, as a result of seeking refuge in the Three Jewels from my heart and acting ethically in accord with the laws of positive and negative karma, I may well gain freedom from the lower realms and attain birth in a higher realm. However, as long as I continue to take birth in this cycle of existence, I will remain trapped in suffering, caught as if in a nest of poisonous snakes. Whatever enjoyment of resources I may experience will be like consuming food laced with poison. Whoever my companions are, I will always be accompanied by betrayal and deception, duped as if by a deceptive seductress. Whatever temporary pleasures I may experience, they will lead to unbearable suffering both immediately and in the long run; they will be nothing but conditions severing the thread of birth in higher realms and of liberation. So, if I do not avert making myself beholden to and dependent on particular conditions of samsara—whether location, body, resources, or companions—[these conditions] will definitely prevent my happiness both in the immediate and long term.

The causes that automatically create the location, body, and resources of cyclic existence are karma and the afflictions. Of these two, the afflictions are the principal cause of taking birth in the cycle of existence. And the ultimate root of it all—karma, the afflictions, and suffering—is the ignorance grasping at self-existence. As long as the first link of ignorance remains present in me, the second link, volitional karma, will leave its imprints upon the third link, consciousness; [354] and through this imprint being activated by the links of craving and appropriation, the karmic imprint becomes potent, and from this will emerge the remaining seven links—birth and so on.[839] In this way, through the chain of twelve links of dependent origination, I have taken birth uncontrollably in the cycle of existence. This has been my fate since beginningless time, but as long as this self-grasping stays present within me, I have no choice but to wander uncontrollably in this cycle of existence. So I must strive in all my efforts to expel this self-grasping ignorance from the very bones of my heart. It is the prison guard that prevents me and all others from being free from the prison of this cyclic existence of the three realms, the butcher that drags us all to the three lower realms, and the malignant tumor that prevents us from getting better in every situation, even in our dreams.

The only antidote to this ignorance is the view realizing selflessness. No other powerful virtuous states of mind, including loving kindness and compassion, can eliminate it. I will therefore strive my best to gain excellent experience of this view of selflessness. For this, I need to attain perfect concentration, and the sole foundation for these two trainings [of wisdom and concentration] is the training in morality. In brief, whatever spiritual aspirations I have, whether aimed at birth in the higher realms or at the definite goodness of nirvana, whether for common or for supreme siddhis, all of them are contingent on observing moral discipline based on the precepts I have vowed to uphold. Moral precepts, established through the perfect words of the Blessed Buddha, lead to great benefits if one observes them and lead to grave negative consequences if one fails to observe them. So if I do not strive in guarding the precepts I have taken, it makes no difference what other methods I pursue; I will inescapably cut short the life thread of birth in the higher realms and attainment of liberation. Therefore, with all my effort, I will strive to ensure that the precepts I have taken remain unblemished, and when the stains of transgressions do come about, I will strive in the means to purify them. [355]

Now, seeing the entire samsaric world of the three realms as characterized by suffering and thus being motivated by a strong desire for liberation, even if I engage correctly in the path of the threefold training and, as a result, attain permanent freedom from this cycle of existence, even my own aims would not be fulfilled, and as for others' welfare, such attainment can lead to only partial fulfillment. Furthermore, all these sentient beings are not random beings with no connection to me whatsoever. Every last one of them has been my mother in this beginningless cycle of existence. Not only that, each has been my mother countless times beyond measure. And each time they were my mother, they cared for me like I was the most precious thing imaginable, more important than even their own life. There is no counting the times they endured pain and hardship for my sake, sacrificing their own body and life. Countless times they were plunged into the lower realms because of negative acts they committed in their devotion to me. And if one were to gather up all the material resources, food, clothing, and possessions that they had to accumulate with such efforts through committing negative acts, gaining ill repute, and sacrificing their body, life, and resources for my benefit, there wouldn't be enough space on this earth! The milk they have fed me would be greater than an ocean! This is established by authoritative scriptures and logic. So, when I look at the number of times these sentient beings cared for me as if I were more precious than a wish-granting jewel, the number of times they showered me with kindness through loving hearts and actions, heedlessly committing negative acts, enduring pain, attracting ill repute, and sacrificing their body, life, and material resources in the process, how could I ever repay their kindness?

Not only that, but I will also be reborn as their child countless times beyond measure in the future. And every time I am born as their child, they will hold me as more precious than a wish-granting jewel. [356] They will care for me countless times with loving hearts and actions, making sacrifices in negative karma, pain, ill repute, body, life, and material resources for my sake. Were it not for these sentient beings who care so much for me, who else would ensure my well-being? Who else would relieve my harm and suffering? Who else could I depend on for my happiness? Therefore, these sentient beings are all truly my dear mothers, my closest loved ones, who have been and will be crucial to my well-being, who safeguard my welfare. Thus, were I to remain oblivious to their situation, whether they are well or not, and instead attend to my own welfare alone, this would be thoughtless indeed; I would be no different from an animal.

Furthermore, the root of all misfortune is self-cherishing. Whether the harm caused by humans or nonhumans, threats from such inanimate objects as poison or weapons, the menace of predatory animals, and so on—in brief, all the sufferings of samsara in general and of each specific realm—whatever the causes and conditions that underlie them, they come about primarily through the power of self-cherishing alone. From the peak of existence to the depths of the Relentless hell, self-cherishing is the enemy that never fails to prey on me; it is the demon that draws forth negative karma, suffering, and ill repute against my will; it is the butcher that cuts short the life vein of fortunate rebirth and of attainment of liberation; it is the malignant tumor that prevents me from experiencing happiness even in my dreams. So I must never let myself be under the sway of this self-cherishing, even for a moment, but strive instead with all my strength to cultivate the thought that cherishes others' welfare.

Whether it is this life's happiness, joy, and fame or whether it is birth as a god or a human and the prosperity and happiness that they desire, or even the attainment of liberation and a buddha's omniscience, we can only attain them in dependence on the sentient beings. And when we do rely on sentient beings, we can achieve these goals more easily. At the moment of attaining buddhahood too, all the enlightened activities of the buddha [357] are accomplished in dependence on sentient beings. Without depending on sentient beings, not even the words "a buddha's enlightened deeds" could exist. So, on the one hand, these sentient beings are indispensable friends who seek my welfare; on the other hand, they are indispensable during the stages of my path [to enlightenment] and the resultant state [of buddhahood]. So, like a wish-granting jewel securing my welfare and happiness, there is no difference at all between them and my guru and meditation deities. I must therefore hold these sentient beings as dearer than my own life and view them as more precious than a wish-granting jewel. And on this basis, I will undergo whatever hardships I must for their sake to make them happy, including even sacrificing my body and life.

Although sentient beings wish for happiness, even just meeting the ordinary joys of contaminated character is rare, like a star in day light, to say nothing of extraordinary levels of happiness. Even when they do encounter some minor happiness, it immediately acquires the character of suffering; nothing endures as genuine happiness. As for suffering, they do not wish for this even in a dream, and yet they remain tormented constantly by the general and specific sufferings of samsara. They do not wish for suffering, but they instinctively chase the causes of suffering like a dog attracted by the sight of blood. As a result of such negative karma, they face all sorts of adversities in their present lives, illnesses and harms and such that assail the body and mind like rain falling from the sky. In future lives too, they will fall to the lower realms and experience the fruitional effects[840] [of karma] in the sufferings of both heat and cold. Even if they avoid such a fate [of rebirth in a lower realm], they will meet with the concordant experiential effects and environmental effects, such as lives that are short and fraught with numerous illnesses, difficulty digesting food and medicine, and so on. In particular, as the effect concordant with such karma, they will be uncontrollably led to further commit the same type of acts, thus casting them to the three lower realms. Such will be their fate. Under the sway of karma and the afflictions, [358] these sentient beings are doomed, both immediately and long term. This is sad! How tragic, indeed!

All these sentient beings are truly my dear mothers, my closest loved ones, who have cared for me and will care for me with loving hearts and actions without regard to their own negative karma, suffering, ill repute, or costs in body, life, and material resources. When it comes to granting my welfare and happiness, they are no different at all from a wish-granting jewel, my guru, and my meditation deities. So, knowing at this moment how desperate their situation is, how could I abandon them? Therefore I will ensure that they are free from suffering and all its causes and that they find happiness and all its causes.

On their part, given that their minds are possessed by the powerful demon of affliction, they have no control over their mind; they are mad. Their eyes of intellect to see the path to the higher birth and liberation have been blinded. They are bereft of the guidance of a perfect spiritual teacher. They remain beguiled by the pursuit of mundane pleasures and honor, which are seemingly innocent yet so fraught with problems. With every step and stride of their negative actions of body, speech, and mind, they venture toward the cliff of unimaginable suffering of samsara in general and of the three lower realms in particular. Their fate is thus likely to remain nothing but desperate. Now, if these mother sentient beings do not place their hopes in me, their child, who else can they place their hopes in? On my part too, how could I abandon them, especially when I am aware of their desperate situation, both presently and long term, and the way they remain bereft of protector and refuge? Therefore I will strive with diligence from this moment, with no concern for even my body and life, in pursuit of their freedom from all suffering and their perfect happiness.

I take upon my mindstream this very moment, from all these sentient beings, their eighty-four thousand afflictions together with the most grave karmic acts they have created and their effects—[359] their effects in the present lives, such as all the adversities of illness and harm that assail the body and mind, the fruitional effects of being plunged to the lower realms, their concordant experiential effects and environmental effects, and, in particular, the effects concordant with the act. By taking these from them, I shall ensure that I alone experience all the misfortune of sentient beings until samsara comes to an end, such that these sentient beings will not know suffering, not even its name. I will send them, this very moment, my body, resources, and virtues of all the three times and ensure that they never remain divorced of immediate and long-term welfare, even in their dreams. Bless me, O guru deity, that I may be able to do this.

[Again contemplate:] Now, although the responsibility to free these sentient beings from all suffering and grant them perfect happiness falls upon me, my own current state is such that, let alone *all* sentient beings, I cannot remove all the suffering and ensure the happiness of a single sentient being. Not just me, even śrāvakas and pratyekabuddhas cannot accomplish the complete welfare of a single sentient being. Only a fully enlightened buddha can eliminate the suffering of all sentient beings and enable them to achieve all happiness.

The enlightened attributes of the body of a buddha is his adornment with the major and minor noble marks; nothing in his appearance is unappealing to the eyes; he is a source of help and benefit to all beings even through mere sight, hearing, and thought; and each and every light ray and emanation emitted from his body has the ability to lead countless beings to the paths of maturation and freedom.

As for the enlightened attributes of his speech, it is endowed with sixty melodies, and the utterance in even a single language has the ability to reveal at once the teachings, both brief and extensive, pertaining to both the profound and the vast aspects of the path, appropriate to the fortunes of sentient beings in their own languages. And through this, his speech can lead beings to the excellent paths of maturation and freedom.

Regarding the enlightened attributes of his mind, he knows in a direct manner the entire field of knowledge, the way things truly are and things in their diversity, as well as the natural inclinations, mental dispositions, and habitual tendencies of all sentient beings. [360] Given that his great compassion extends to all sentient beings, without any discrimination, holding them most dear as a loving mother holds her only child, he never wavers even a moment from the right time to help beings tame themselves.

As for his enlightened activities aimed at taming beings, these all come about spontaneously, without effort and without interruption. Thus the buddha's enlightened activities have the capacity to engage, in each and every moment, with the welfare of infinite beings without hindrance. Thus buddhas have fully realized the ability to secure the perfect welfare of other beings.

On my part too, until and as long as I have not actualized this state of buddhahood, I will fail to fully realize even my own ultimate welfare. Therefore I will strive my best to attain the precious state of buddhahood, the complete fulfillment of the twin welfare of self and others. To this end, I will engage in the meditative practice of mahāmudrā on the basis of the profound path of guru yoga.

Flawless scripture and logical reasoning have established that self-cherishing is the root of all misfortune and that the thought cherishing others' welfare is the source of all benefit, happiness, and good fortune. It is inappropriate, therefore, even in a dream to desire the attainment of buddhahood for my own sake alone. If it is for the benefit of others, however—even remaining in the hells for eons equal to the number of particles on this great earth to help bring about the welfare of a single sentient being—it would be appropriate to plunge into a task with the joy and zeal of a poor person who has just unearthed a treasure. This said, it should be unbearable if sentient beings have to wait so long to have their suffering removed and their happiness achieved via such an incre-

> mental approach. I shall thus actualize the precious state of complete buddhahood so I can secure the welfare of countless and immeasurable sentient beings in each and every single moment. To this end I will engage in the meditative practice of Master Tsongkhapa's oral teachings, which constitute a profound and swift path that will bring about the realization of rainbow vajra body within a single lifetime of this age of degeneration. [361]

In these ways, you should forcefully generate the two forms of awakening mind, the former and the latter.[841] This is the magical method to ensure that your practices of the main part of the session are transformed into the path to a buddha's omniscience. It is essential that you cultivate them [the two forms of awakening mind] until they make a deep impression in your mind. In particular, the second form of awakening is the gateway to enter the practice of this unique guru yoga. My precious teacher said that Yongzin Yeshé Gyaltsen stated that this important point emerges in the oral teachings of Drupwang Losang Namgyal.[842]

The reason setting your intention is of utmost importance, whatever virtuous activity you are engaged in, is this. Whether or not any practice of the paths of three capacities meets with success depends on whether you have gained genuine experience through training your mind sequentially in the paths of the three capacities. This is what Mañjuśrī told the omniscient Jé Tsongkhapa. The same point emerges also in the sayings of the peerless Atiśa and the spiritual mentor Dromtönpa. As a background support, we also find the following in the Vinaya scripture, where it says:

> The mind precedes phenomena and mind is primary;
> the mind is swift; accordingly, when someone
> has acted or uttered words with a pure mind, their effects follow him,
> just as the shadow of a tree never abandons him [the prince].
>
> The mind precedes phenomena and mind is primary;
> the mind is swift; accordingly, when someone
> has acted or uttered words with a hateful mind, their effects follow him,
> just as the cart driver's head was severed by the cart.[843]

The scripture here explains, on the basis of stories connected with the observable effects of the karma of a prince and a poor person of the *śūdra* caste,[844] how the mind lies at the root of all karmic acts of body and speech. Also, in his *Friendly Letter*, the guardian Nāgārjuna says:

> Be free of hubris; what more is there to say.
> This alone is the most beneficial point:
> Discipline your mind, for the Blessed Buddha said,
> "The mind is the root of Dharma."[845] [362]

Āryadeva says:

> I have not seen merit and so forth
> in sentient beings separate from the mind;
> so I declare that in relation to all deeds,
> the mind is most important.[846]

[In addition] understanding that if all of one's Vinaya practice—the omissions, commissions, and exceptions—are sustained by the attitude of true renunciation, they would then become the cause for attaining liberation, master Guṇaprabha writes, "With morality of true renunciation as the foundation . . ."[847] In light of these statements, if you generate conviction from the depth of your heart on this point [about setting your intention], you will become skilled in the essential points of practice.

Once again, regarding the key points of posture, there is also the tradition of adopting the "six blazing triangles of *tumo*."[848] To do this use a meditation belt known as a "knee wrap." You can make this by folding a long woolen fabric in half, then measuring its length by wrapping it around your head with your two hands formed into fists extended touching each other in front of you. Cut the fabric to this length and sew the two ends to form a looped sash. You wear this just above your waist and wrap it around just below your two knees, thus forming the following sitting posture: your buttocks are on the cushion, with your two knees slightly raised and your legs crossing each other with the outsides of your feet touching the ground and your hands placed around and under the sides of the sash wrapped around from your back, your palms in the gesture of meditative equipoise about four fingerwidths below the navel. On top and below where the two legs are crossed are two triangles;

the belt wrapped around the two knees form one triangle; on both sides of the body is a triangle where each knee is tied to your back with the belt; and below the navel, your hands in the gesture of meditative equipoise form a triangle where the *tumo* inner heat resides. Forming of these six outer triangles lays the auspicious basis for the blazing of the inner *tumo*. This posture, the six blazing triangles of *tumo*, is the posture highly praised by Jetsun Milarepa, the teacher said. [363]

Going for refuge and generating the awakening mind

Thusly, in an especially virtuous state of mind, go for refuge [in the Three Jewels]. When it comes to visualizing the objects you are seeking refuge in, there are two traditions: visualizing the field in the manner of *gathering at a marketplace* and visualizing it in the manner of an *all-embodying jewel*. The first approach is actually two methods—one that is popular today and the following variant. Here, you visualize a tall and spacious lion throne in the space above. On this throne, slightly to the back, visualize a somewhat smaller lion throne on which sits Buddha Śākyamuni inseparable from your root guru. On the two sides of this smaller throne and slightly in front, imagine rows of figures all seated on lotuses in an arc. On the right are the lineage masters of the *vast practice* such as Maitreya, and on the left are the lineage masters of the *profound view* such as Mañjuśrī.

If you visualize the merit-field tree according to Śāntideva's instruction on equalizing and exchanging self and others, then imagine a Mañjuśrī on each side [of the Buddha], followed in the second row of the right side by Śāntideva, then Eladhari, Viravajra, and so on, who form the lineage masters of the expansive practice.[849] On the left, in the second row imagine Nāgārjuna, then Candrakīrti, and so on, who constitute the lineage masters of the profound view.

Facing Buddha Śākyamuni, leaving a small interval space, is another small lion throne. On this, visualize your own root guru from whom you have received transmission of the instruction, with his physical appearance and skin color as in his normal everyday form. To his right and left, as well as behind this lion throne [of your root guru], forming a semicircle, are seated on lotuses the teachers from whom you personally have received teachings, all facing Buddha Śākyamuni.

In the space above and slightly behind Buddha Śākyamuni is a small lion throne on which is seated Vajradhara. Below him, on the right and left, are

Tilopa, Nāropa, Ḍombīpa, Atiśa, Tsongkhapa, and so on, who are the lineage masters of *blessing and practice*.[850]

Behind Buddha Śākyamuni, close to him, are the meditation deities of highest yoga tantra each seated on their appropriate cushions. Outside them are the meditation deities of yoga tantra, outside whom are the deities of performance tantra, outside whom are the deities of action tantra. In this way, the deities of the four classes of tantra are all facing Buddha Śākyamuni. [364] Behind the lineage masters of vast practice and the profound view on the two sides [of Buddha Śākyamuni] are buddhas such as the buddhas of the fortunate eons and the thirty-five buddhas of confession. Behind them are the bodhisattvas like Mañjuśrī, Vajrapāṇi, Avalokiteśvara, and Kṣitigarbha. Behind them are the ārya pratyekabuddhas and the śrāvakas, including the sixteen arhats. Behind them are the heroes and heroines, and behind them are the Dharma protectors. This then is a way of visualizing [the objects of refuge] like a gathering at a marketplace.

Alternatively, there is the approach where everything is as just described with one difference: you visualize rainbow-colored beams emanating from the heart of Buddha Śākyamuni to the right and left. From these emit crescent rainbows, and above the large lion throne [of the Buddha] and on the two sides are, seated on lotuses and moon discs, the lineage masters of vast practice and the profound view. Behind them, touching the large lion throne, are the buddhas, bodhisattvas, and so on, as described above. This is a variant on the marketplace format. The teacher said that there are numerous variations of this gathering at a marketplace format, such as the merit field of *Offering to the Guru*, but these days only one or two formats seem to be known widely.

As for the "all-embodying jewel" format, this is the merit field in the *Hundreds of Gods of Tuṣita* guru yoga[851] and in Cutting Off practice, the teacher said. These then are the oral teachings connected with the practice of going for refuge.

Once you have established the merit field depicting the objects to whom you go for refuge, you cultivate the causes for seeking refuge and engage in the actual practice of going for refuge by contemplating the following:

> Alas! As for the activities of the three doors of myself and most other sentient beings, when it comes to negative karmic deeds, we find it difficult to prevent negative karma even when trying to, and we instinctively gravitate toward them. [365] But when it

comes to positive karma,[852] however, I find it difficult to prevent negative karma even when I make an effort; I am instead drawn to it instinctively. And when it comes to positive karma, I find it as hard as trying to make a stream flow uphill. This is because my habituation to negative karma in the past was strong while my habituation to positive karma was weak. This clearly demonstrates the kind of causes that preceded. Even in this life, I accumulate new karma and infractions of precepts, both natural and prescribed, like the falling of rain. And the karma I already possess tends to expand on its own, just as the great ocean absorbs the four great rivers. Leaving aside the power of such a great heap of negative karma, even a single moment of negative karma can lead to birth in one of the three lower realms. This is something the great compassionate one, the Blessed Buddha, declared repeatedly for our sake out of his concern for our fate, without holding anything back or engaging in lies or deception. If this breath of mine were to be cut short while I am still fraught with such an immense heap of negative karma, I will no doubt fly to the lower realms with nothing to prevent it.

Now, if I were to be reborn in the three lower realms, the hell realm has the following sufferings of heat and cold—being burned and cooked, being beaten up and tormented, being cut and sliced open, and having my body splintering into a hundred or a thousand pieces. In the hungry ghost realm, there are the pains of hunger and thirst, of hardship and terror. In the animal realm are the pains of ignorance and delusion, one kind eating another, being abused for labor, being slaughtered, being tied up, and being beaten. Let alone actually experiencing sufferings like this with my body and mind, even hearing about them and seeing them in person could bring on a heart attack. How could I bear it if and when I must undergo these sufferings myself with my own body and mind? Yet I have no power to spare myself from such suffering, for I have already gathered the causes to undergo such suffering; in fact, I indulged in gathering their causes with joy and delight! The time when I must experience such suffering is not in a distant future. In fact, the gap between such unbearable suffering and the present is only this current movement of my breath! And there is no guarantee that this flow of air, moving in and out, will not suddenly cease. In any case, there is no guarantee that I will stay alive this night and will not die. [366] What if I were to end up in such place of terror, how would I bear this?

At that point, nothing will save me from my fate. Even if I were to seek out a refuge to protect me, I would have already initiated the process of turning myself into fuel for the suffering of the three lower realms, having already cut the thread of life for birth in the higher realms and the attainment of liberation. It would be too late. Therefore, today, when I have in my own hands still the opportunity to move toward or away from the unbearable suffering of the terrifying realms, if I fail to strive in the means to avert such suffering and instead, like a dog attracted to the sight of blood, willfully indulge in negative and nonvirtuous karmic acts, I would be truly insane.

So I must search from now on for the means to help free myself and all other sentient beings equaling the expanse of space from such a place of terror. But as long as I continue to seek those means with ignorance and delusion, my efforts will only create more problems. So I will exclusively seek out wise guides who know the undistorted means to freedom and strive in the means they teach. What we need is a truly authoritative teacher who can reveal to others independently and clearly, on the basis of their own direct vision, what is to be adopted and what is to be rejected. There may be teachers with mundane attainments such as clairvoyance, miraculous powers, and so on, but this alone does not make them infallible as to the means for gaining freedom from all fear.

It is the Blessed Buddha alone who is such a truly authoritative teacher; others like Brahmā and Indra do not possess even a portion of the qualifications necessary [to be a truly authoritative teacher]. Whether one is a human or a deva god, if one wishes to find the method to gain freedom from all fears, it is the Buddha alone who reveals such a method; [367] the Dharma is that revealed method; and the ārya Sangha are the companions for engaging that method. Apart from these three [Buddha, Dharma, and Sangha], no refuge can be found anywhere.

This said, for us to be freed and saved from all fear, both external and internal conditions need to converge. With respect to

> complete external conditions not lacking in anything, there is the presence of our compassionate Teacher, who attained his state through hundredfold endeavors across innumerable eons. He remains our protector, our refuge, and our ally without wavering in his task even for an instant. This is the case, but because we have failed to manifest the inner condition on our part—namely, placing our trust in him and going to him for refuge and, on that basis, conducting ourselves according to what is to be adopted and what is to be rejected—we have wandered uncontrollably in the cyclic existence of the three realms and have remained bereft of a protector and refuge. Therefore, were I to seek refuge in the Three Precious Jewels, the infallible refuge, from the depths of my heart and conduct myself in accord with what is to be adopted and what is to be rejected, they would without doubt free me and save me from the terrifying place [of samsara]. So today, I and all sentient beings equaling the expanse of space go for refuge to you, infallible refuge, the Three Precious Jewels. Pray save us this very minute from the terrors of samsara in general and those of the lower realms in particular.

In this way, cultivate the mind placing your entire trust [in the Three Jewels], and with your speech utter the phrases "I go for refuge to the guru" and so on.[853] Utter these phrases as if uncontrollably, as one would cry aloud when experiencing an acute physical pain. This act, including such verbal expressions, constitutes the common practice of going for refuge. There is, however, the following uncommon [Mahayana] way of going for refuge:

> All these sentient beings caught in a desperate plight with no power remain trapped, owing to their karma and afflictions, in the terrifying abyss of cyclic existence in general and in the three lower realms in particular. They are truly, first of all, [368] my beloved ones indispensable throughout all my lives in securing my welfare. Second, with respect to being indispensable in the ordinary state, along the path, and in resultant state, they remain the source of my benefit and happiness. In this, there is no difference at all between sentient beings, who are wish-granting jewels, on the one hand and my gurus and meditation deities on the other. How tragic it is that sentient beings' current situation should be

> so desperate: their freedom robbed by karma and affliction, their immediate and long-term fates so hopeless, and bereft of protector and refuge. How tragic indeed!
>
> Now although the responsibility to save these sentient beings from such terror rests upon me alone, my present situation is such that, let alone being a protector and refuge to all sentient beings, I cannot even be a protector and refuge for a single sentient being. Who then has such ability? If I were to attain the precious state of buddhahood, I would then have unimpeded ability to serve as a protector and refuge to all sentient beings. So I shall take such a state as the object of my attainment. I will embrace as my heart practice this mahāmudrā meditation taking the profound path of guru yoga as its basis—a path established by authoritative masters through hundredfold efforts and without concern even for their own body and life. In this way, I will follow the example of these authoritative masters, and without concern for even my body and life, I will strive in this practice with fortitude and with expansive waves of joyful perseverance.

Generating such a thought in a fervent manner constitutes the practice of going for refuge according to the Mahayana in that it entails taking your own resultant Three Jewels as the object of attainment and then seeking refuge in them. The teacher said, in fact, that it is extremely difficult to differentiate between this type of going for refuge and the Mahayana generation of the awakening mind.

Then, visualizing the guru and the Three Jewels as residing with compassion and loving kindness for all sentient beings, and imagining both yourself and others generating [369] fervent faith in and reverence for these objects of refuge, inspired by contemplating their qualities and kindness, imagine chanting aloud in unison the words of the refuge practice. When you do, you can relate this to the well-known visualization practice of imagining purifying [your negative karma and obscurations], receiving the blessings, and being accepted [within the fold of care]. And when you purify the negative karma, you could imagine the lord of death takes the form of an ogre lying on its back on the ground and that all your negative karma enters his mouth and that his mouth then closes shut and is sealed by a thousand-spoked golden wheel. The teacher said this is an oral instruction of Machik Labdrön for ensuring that, while you purify negative karma, you are also cultivating longevity.

Next, when chanting the lines "To the Buddha, Dharma, and the Excellent

Assembly. . . ,"[854] contemplate how it is the two obscurations—the afflictive obscuration and the knowledge obscuration—that lead myself and all sentient beings to samsara in general and to the three lower realms in particular. It is these two that prevent us from attaining liberation and the state of omniscience. You appeal [to the objects of refuge] that you and all other sentient beings may be protected and saved from these two great sources of danger this very moment. This is the Mahayana practice of going for refuge. Then cultivate the thought:

> Through the force of virtue I have gathered throughout all three times, such as through the three sources of virtue that include giving,[855] may I and all other sentient beings quickly attain the precious state of buddhahood. May we swiftly attain such a state, and may I never abandon, even in my dreams, this aspiration to attain buddhahood for the benefit of all sentient beings.

In this way, you generate the aspirational awakening mind accompanied by a pledge.

When chanting the lines "I go for refuge to the Three Jewels" and so on,[856] going for refuge is the same as explained above. The purification of negative karma is done through such contemplations as: "Whatever heaps of negative karma I may possess, which prevent me from enhancing qualities in this life and lead me to the lower realms in future lives, O buddhas, bodhisattvas, and the rest, I declare these in your presence and seek your forgiveness." The practice of rejoicing involves contemplating, "How I wish I may accumulate on my own all virtues that have been gathered by all beings in the universe, both ordinary and ārya beings." [370] With these as a preparation, here is how you uphold the engaging awakening mind:

> For the sake of all mother sentient beings, I will by all means seek the attainment of the precious state of buddhahood. To this end, I will strive with fortitude and with expansive waves of joyful perseverance, with no concern even for my body and life, to engage in the general and specific deeds of the bodhisattva. O guru deity, bless me that I may be able to do this.

The teacher then makes the following points: That all the vows of both lower and advanced vehicles need to be received through taking the practice of going for refuge as their foundation; how the bodhisattva vow does not take root within those who possess grave negative karma within their mind stream and those whose store of merit is extremely small; even when it does arise in such individuals, it does not do so in a way that it can [effectively] serve its function. This, the teacher said, is analogous to how it is difficult for seeds to grow, even if planted, when the soil is fraught with problems like excessive salt, grass, and weeds and where there is lack of fertilizer and moisture; even when seeds do grow [in such soil], they are of little use. Therefore, to uphold the awakening mind, you definitely need to preface it with these three practices—going for refuge, [purifying negative karma, and rejoicing].

[Having generated the mind,] cultivate joy at the arising in you of the awakening mind and the bodhisattva vow. And imagine that, from having such a powerful virtuous state of mind arise in you, Guru Śākyamuni is pleased and that, in the fashion of one butter lamp being lit from another, a replica of guru Śākyamuni emerges and dissolves into you. Then imagine that your three doors—body, speech, and mind—transform instantly into the enlightened body, speech, and mind of Guru Śākyamuni. Then remain in equipoise on this thought for a little while.

Then imagine that immeasurable light radiates from your body—hot rays like sunlight or crystal and cool rays cold like snow or a great river stream—and that this cleanses the defects of the hot and cold hell realms and of the beings therein, turning them into perfect buddhafields inhabited by enlightened buddhas. Again, imagine emanating immeasurable light for the hungry ghosts in the form of wish-granting jewels, food, clothing, shelter, and all sorts of articles of everyday need. [371] For the animals, [imagine light] in the form of abilities, such as the intellect to distinguish what is good from what is bad, the capacity for forethought and mindfulness, a sense of shame and of consideration of others, heedfulness, and so forth. For humans, [imagine light] in the form of food, medicine, clothes, and diverse material things; for the demigods, [light] in the form of loving kindness, compassion, sympathetic joy, equanimity, and so forth; and for the deva gods of lower and higher levels, [light] in the form of increased life span and merit and the capacity for disenchantment, renunciation, and heedfulness, and so forth. These help relieve the beings in the individual realms of their specific suffering; and both the environment and the beings within become purified, the environments turning into buddhafields and their inhabitants into enlightened buddhas.

With the thought that it is most fortunate indeed that today I have the opportunity to lead all these beings of the six realms to the state of Guru Buddha Śākyamuni, rejoice. The teacher said that when compared to what others label as "profound" and "beautiful" instructions, such as "stirring up the pit of the lower realms" and "lifting beings out of the six realms,"[857] there is nothing whose purpose is not satisfied by this practice of "generating the awakening mind by way of bringing the result on to the path" according to the sacred lineage of Master Tsongkhapa. So there is no need to find other such teachings tempting,[858] he said.

Next, following this [generation of awakening mind] with the practice of the four immeasurable thoughts, engaging in the actual cultivation of them, visualizing nectar descending and cleansing, and so forth—contemplate as follows:

> Alas! From when I swept and cleaned my place of practice up to now, so many mother sentient beings have already plummeted into the three lower realms. Their fate is nothing but constant torment by hundreds of sufferings. How could I abandon these sentient beings? I will therefore strive to place all mother sentient beings in the precious state of buddhahood.

In this way, generate a strong intention from the depths of your heart. Then with your voice chant the phrase "**For the sake of all mother sentient beings, I will quickly, quickly, in this very life, actualize**" up to the line "**To this end, I will meditate on the guide to mahāmudrā on the basis of the profound path of the guru-deity yoga.**"[859] Chant this several times.

These constitute, among the four great instructions on the preliminary practices,[860] [372] the instruction on taking refuge and generating the awakening mind—the doors to enter, respectively, the Buddha's teaching and the Mahayana—including the attendant practices. Apply yourself to these practices with earnest effort.

Special Preliminary Practices

This is threefold: generating yourself into the meditation deity, blessing the environment and its inhabitants, and blessing the offerings.

Generating yourself into the meditation deity

To engage in the common-level mahāmudrā practice[861] in connection with this unique guru yoga, it is adequate to do the instantaneous generation of yourself into any of the three meditation deities: Cakrasaṃvara, Guhyasamāja, or Vajrabhairava. However, to engage in the uncommon-level mahāmudrā practice, you need to generate yourself into the deity in a way that ensures the completion of the key points of threefold taking [of death, intermediate state, and birth] into the path, the main practice of the generation stage. For this contemplate the following:

> I and all other sentient beings have revolved since beginningless time through unending rounds of birth, death, and the intermediate in this cycle of existence, and because of this, we remain trapped in this situation of being constantly assailed by great terror. In the future too, there seems to be no end or limit to this cycle of birth, death, and the intermediate state. So we will have no choice but to continue revolving repeatedly through the cycle of birth, death, and the intermediate state and thus remain as fuel for the fires of samsara's suffering in general and that of the three lower realms in particular. Therefore, today, having obtained this once an excellent and wonderful human existence of leisure and opportunity, having met the Buddha's teaching so hard to encounter, and more specifically, having obtained the opportunity to engage liberally in the study, reflection, and meditative practice of the instructions of the oral transmission of our exalted guru, I shall, for the sake of all sentient beings, do my very best to attain the precious state of the three buddha bodies, which represents everlasting freedom from the sufferings of birth, death, and the intermediate state. This I must accomplish on the basis of this present human existence, [373] for in the

future, I may not have another chance to obtain such a human existence.

Obtaining such a human existence requires the convergence of the following conditions: a foundation laid through pure morality; that morality complemented by virtuous practices such as generosity and so on; and these practices sustained by pure aspirations. As for pure morality, I am nowhere near such a place or even going in that direction. I must begin cultivating the conditions immediately, for if I do not, there is no guarantee I will even be alive come the end of the day. At death, I will be separated from my body, material possessions, and loved ones against my will, and the force of the sorrow of such imminent separation will turn my face red and bloated, and tears will flow from my eyes. With no hope of remaining united with my lost loved ones, I will be faced with the terrifying visages of the henchmen of Yama, the lord of death. The fire of remorse for the negative deeds I committed in the past will consume me from within. Because of terrifying visions of the lower realms and its denizens flashing before my eyes, all my senses—my eyes, mouth, and so forth—will remain open wide. My limbs will all shake uncontrollably, and incontinent, I will soil my bed with urine and shit. Such unbearable torments will undoubtedly strike me in this very life, for I am ridden with negative karma. Furthermore, I will experience at that point, when the sign of the earth element dissolves into water, a feeling as if being flattened under a heavy mass of earth, sinking into the earth, and I will see the mirage-like vision. As the sign of the water element dissolves into fire, I will experience myself drowning in deep water or being swept away by forceful currents, and I will see the smoke-like vision. When the sign of the fire element dissolves into wind, I will experience the feeling of being trapped in roaring flames or being consumed by fire, and I will see the vision like fireflies. As the wind element begins to dissolve into consciousness, I will experience the vision like the glow of a butter lamp, and once it actually dissolves, I will experience the following signs: the whitish appearance, the reddish increase, the dark near-attainment, and the clear light of everything being empty. I will thus undergo immeasurable suffering from having to experience all sorts of delusory visions.

> Not just me, all sentient beings equal to the expanse of space are alike in having to undergo such suffering at the time of death. So from now on, I must do my best so that I and all sentient beings, equal to the expanse of space, will not have to undergo such suffering at death. [374] Given that one actualizes the resultant dharmakāya of great bliss as the resultant imprints of the illustrative and actual clear light of the path, I will cultivate the path-level and result-level dharmakāya and actualize them.

Setting your intention in this manner, imagine the objects in whom you are seeking refuge dissolve into Guru Śākyamuni, who in turn melts into blue light and enters you between your eyebrows; imagine you become blessed [by the guru]. Then imagine that you rise instantaneously in the form of Vajrabhairava in union with his consort. Immeasurable streams of red light radiate from the point where Vajrabhairava and his consort are conjoined as well as from the syllable *hūṃ* at the deity's heart; they permeate all the worlds and all the beings within them, and all the worlds transform into celestial mansions and all the beings into Vajrabhairavas. Then the worlds melt into light and dissolve into the deities, and the deities too melt into light and dissolve into you, who are in the form of Vajrabhairava. Your Vajrabhairava form also melts into a blue light simultaneously from above and below, dissolving into the syllable *hūṃ* at your heart.[862] Simultaneously, imagine experiencing at this point the *mirage-like* vision and recognize that the sign of the earth element dissolving into water has now arisen. Then the vowel *ū* of letter *hūṃ* dissolves into the body of the letter *ha*, and at that point, imagine experiencing the *smoke-like* vision and recognize that this is the sign of the water element dissolving into fire. When the body of the letter *ha* dissolves into its head [the straight line], imagine that you experience the *fireflies-like* vision and recognize that this is the sign of the fire element dissolving into wind. When the head bar begins to dissolve into the crescent, imagine experiencing the *butter lamp–like* vision and recognize that this is the sign of the wind element beginning to dissolve into consciousness. Then when the head bar actually dissolves into the crescent, imagine experiencing the whitish *appearance*; when the crescent dissolves into the *bindu* drop, imagine experiencing the reddish *increase*; when the *bindu* drop dissolves into *nada* squiggle, imagine experiencing the darkish *near attainment*; and then the *nada* squiggle too diminishes to the thickness of a strand of hair or a thread of spiderweb, dissolving finally into emptiness, becoming imperceptible. At that point imagine experiencing the arising of clear light and rest your mind in equipoise for a while on this vibrant clear light. [375]

Then, recite the following: "*Oṃ svabhāva śuddhāḥ sarvadharmāḥ svabhāva śuddho 'haṃ / oṃ śūnyatā jñāna svabhāva ātmako 'haṃ.* I and the deities of the merit field, as well as all other phenomena, are dependently designated and hence are emptiness, characterized by the absence of self-existence and free from the four extremes such as permanence and annihilation."[863] In this way recite the two mantras as well as the phrase stating what they mean, and without distraction, maintain the state of clear light characterized by the two attributes [of emptiness and vibrant clarity] as described above, just as instructed.

Once you recognize a degree of stability in this meditation, generate your entire mind into this state of clear light. Then skillfully generate with one part of your mind the thought "I am meditating," "I am seeking buddhahood," thus allowing the arising of an innate sense of self. As you examine how such a sense of self perceives and conceives it, see that there is no doubt that it perceives and conceives the self not as something constructed by your mind but as something existing objectively, from the side of the designative bases, as if possessing an autonomous reality capable of standing in its own right. In this way, ensure that the key point of accurately *identifying the object of negation* is established. Then contemplate that if such a self were to exist exactly as perceived and conceived, it would have to do so either as independently identical with the aggregates—its bases of designation—or as independently distinct from the aggregates. There is no third possibility. In this way, you establish the key point of *logical entailment*. Now if the self is independently identical with the aggregates, just as there are five aggregates, the self too would become five; alternately, just as the self is a single independent entity, the aggregates too would be one independent entity. Through these objections establish the key point of *absence of identity*. Through the objection that, if the self is different from the aggregates, the self and the aggregates would become unrelated to each other, establish the key point of *absence of difference*. Thus, through the force of reasoning establishing the four key points, allow the ascertainment to arise that the self, just like the thought of a snake projected onto a coiled rope, is merely a construct of the mind, and that, on the part of the designative bases themselves, not even an atom can exist objectively.

When such ascertainment arises in your mind vividly, direct the momentum of the main part of your mind to the ascertainment while, with another part of your mind, recall how you earlier experienced innate bliss when you were Vajrabhairava in union with your consort. [376] In this way, you ensure the convergence in a single state of mind two things—the ascertainment of emptiness and the experience of innate bliss—and you maintain this state in a single-pointed manner.

Even when you examine how such a dharmakāya, the union of bliss and emptiness, appears to your mind, it too appears as if possessing an autonomous existence not dependent on anything else. So bring to this appearance your awareness of how, if such a dharmakāya were to exist the way it is being perceived, it would exist as such either as identical to its preceding and subsequent instances or as independent and distinct from these instances, and how maintaining either of these possibilities raises logical problems. Bringing awareness to this ascertainment, allow the understanding to arise that not even an atom exists in the manner in which it appears to my mind.

Once this ascertainment arises in a vivid manner, generate the thought from within such awareness, as if from one part of your mind, "I am this dharmakāya of great bliss within the heart of glorious Vajrabhairava, who is free of all obscurations." Adopting the dharmakāya identity in this manner is called "taking death into the path as dharmakāya." This entails bringing the "mother" clear light, which arises on the ordinary ground through the force of karma and afflictions—in a gradual sequence starting from the mirage-like sign up to clear light—into the present as the "son" clear light through transforming it into the path. This practice has been hailed by Marpa Lotsāwa and others as the "instruction on the meeting of the mother and son clear lights,"[864] so we should cherish it, the teacher said. It is critical to examine whether your dharmakāya identity involves a perception of true existence of the object of engagement, and if so, make corrections. It is also important to be cognizant of subtle and difficult questions such as whether your meditative equipoise [on dharmakāya] and the dharmakāya identity [you adopt] share the same perceived object and aspect. Do not be contented with vague notions and imaginings. In any case, what I have written above about how to meditatively practice taking death into the path as dharmakāya is based on my guru's oral teaching as well as my own personal experience of the practice. What I've written is but a rough outline of what I have understood; there are numerous other subtle and difficult points related to this topic.

This way of meditating on taking death into the path as dharmakāya in accordance with the stages of dissolution of the *subsequent dismantling*[865] process, [377] because it is very close to the actual process of dying—the very thing that is being purified—this approach is superior to other [similar practices]. If one were to do the meditation in accord with the *held-as-a-whole dissolution* process, however, then once the bases of purification and the purifying paths have been introduced, instead of rearising in the form of the meditation deity, you would imagine this very [ordinary] body composed of flesh, bones, and blood melting into a blue light—simultaneously from both above and below—and becoming a vertical blue light about an arm's length tall. This light then gradually shrinks, becoming thinner and thinner, eventually becoming imperceptible and nothing. You then imagine the arising of the all-empty clear light. As to how you generate the son clear light and so forth on this basis, this is as already explained above.

Next, you need to undertake the meditation on taking the intermediate state into the path as the saṃbhogakāya. For this, contemplate the following to introduce yourself to the basis of purification and to the purifying path:

> When the process of my death has finished and the near attainment of the reverse sequence [of the process] has arisen,[866] the being of the intermediate state composed of mere wind and consciousness comes into being. And this consciousness, with no basis, wanders about with no particular aim and destination. At that point, I will experience the unbearable suffering of a hallucination of Yama's henchmen shouting the four commands "Kill him! Hit him!" and so on.[867] Just like me, all sentient beings, my previous parents, have no choice but to experience the suffering of intermediate existence. So from now on, I must do my utmost to ensure that I and all other sentient beings equaling the expanse of space no longer have to endure the intermediate state of existence and that we all become free from the pain of the intermediate state. It is through cultivating the illusory body of the path, both impure and pure,[868] that the intermediate states of beings of this Jambudvīpa earth are purified and, as a result, we actualize the state of the resultant saṃbhogakāya. So I will seek to actualize the saṃbhogakāya of the path and of the result in their proper sequence. However, as to what is to be actualized, the act of actualizing it, and myself who is actualizing, nothing—not even an atom—exists in its own right as an independent entity as it appears to my mind.

From within such a state of mind, imagine arising, instantaneously, in the form of glorious Vajrabhairava together with consort, with one face and two arms [378] and in the nature of light, clear and radiant. Imagine that the beams of light radiate from your body and fill the entire universe. Placing your attention on this, maintain your focus in a single-pointed manner.

Then, with one part of your mind, as you monitor your mind and examine how this deity form you perceive actually appears to your mind, you realize that it appears to possess an autonomous existence not dependent on anything else. You then apply the same reasoning as before, how were it to exist as it appears to my mind, the deity body would be intrinsically identical with or different from the aggregates, and conclude that not even an atom exists in the manner it appears to my mind. When this ascertainment arises in you as a natural consequence, the image of yourself as the deity might get lost; so, while maintaining this ascertainment, another part of your mind recalls the deity form you have visualized previously. Then, focusing on this deity form vividly appearing in your mind, reinforce the ascertainment that this deity form does not exist at all in the manner in which it appears to your mind. In this way ensure the convergence within a single state of mind of the two things—this immediate ascertainment [of emptiness] and the appearance of the deity form—and then maintain this state with single-pointedness. This is how beginners like us should understand and undertake the *nondual yoga of profundity and clarity*.[869]

Although what I have presented here is based on the answers my most revered sublime teacher, who is an actual buddha, gave in response to my queries and so is deserving of your confidence, those with clear intelligence who wish to differentiate the subtleties of difficult points may benefit from examining it critically. As for the statement found in the great treatises, where the nondual yoga of profundity and clarity is defined as the vibrant ascertainment, at the level of cognition, of the absence of intrinsic existence of the deity form and, at the level of perception, the clear appearance of the deity form—each complementing the other—this really refers to the practice of someone who has gained stability in deity yoga. There is no way those on the beginner's stage, myself included, could engage in such meditation in an experiential manner.

As to how you adopt a saṃbhogakāya identity on the basis of taking this deity form that appears but lacks intrinsic existence [379] and generating the thought "I am this glorious all-pervading primordial lord existing as mere wind and consciousness," this is the same as explained above in the context of dharmakāya meditation. There are other instructions where, when you arise out of emptiness in the form of just a *nada* squiggle or the syllable *hūṃ*, this is introduced as "taking the intermediate state into the path as saṃbhogakāya." The teacher said that according to the oral teaching of Guru Yongzin Rinpoché,[870] meditation on taking the intermediate state into the path as the saṃbhogakāya takes place at the point where you have arisen into the deity form but you have not yet marked the three points of your body with the three letters.

Next, you need to meditate on taking rebirth into the path as nirmāṇakāya. For this, first contemplate the following to introduce the basis of purification.

As the supportless consciousness, your intermediate-state being drifting about with no aim or destination, wanders around, it sees the composite mixture of your future parents' regenerative fluids as the coupling of a male and a female, and the desire to engage in copulation arises in you as well. On approaching closer with such lust, the consciousness sees nothing but the male and female sexual organs. The result is that the intermediate-state being, in a fit of rage, faints, which leads it to plunge into the center of the composite mixture [of the two fluids]. It then undergoes the five stages of gestation in sequence: *arbuda* embryo, *kalala* embryo, *peśin* embryo, *ghana* embryo, and *praśākhā* embryo.[871] Approaching the point of birth, it remains wrapped in flesh inside the womb, as if enclosed in a fetid, dirty pot, for as many as nine or nearly ten months. During this period, you endure sufferings such as heat, cold, acute pressure, and bumping about. Then the actual birth is fraught with hundredfold suffering. Thus birth is characterized by suffering: it is fraught with negative tendencies, it is the vehicle for the arising of afflictions, it leads to the pain of parting from loved ones even when one does not wish to, and so on. [Then contemplate:]

> In brief, I have no choice but to connect my consciousness to a birth in a realm of existence where birth is the vehicle for and the basis for the arising of all the suffering of samsara. Just like me, all other sentient beings equaling the expanse of space share the same fate of having to undergo the suffering of birth. So from now on, I will do my utmost to ensure that I and all other sentient beings equaling the expanse of space do not have to connect our consciousness to realms of rebirth and so [380] we may therefore be permanently freed from the suffering of birth. Then set the intention that through the gross nirmāṇakāya form assumed by

> the impure and pure illusory bodies of the path, thus purifying the rebirth of this Jambudvīpa world, I will, as its concordant result, actualize the state of the resultant nirmāṇakāya. To this end I will seek to actualize the states of the path and the results, in their proper sequence, that lead to such realization.

Having set your intention in these terms, then, in the form of the saṃbhogakāya Vajrabhairava, mark your crown with the syllable *oṃ*, your throat with *āḥ*, and your heart with *hūṃ*. Imagine that at the tips of incalculable beams of light radiating from your body are incalculable emanations appropriate to the needs of beings. In this way, cultivate deity yoga with a deity form that appears but lacks intrinsic existence, and taking this deity form as the basis, arise into the coarse buddha form that appears but has no intrinsic existence. Then generate the thought "I am this nirmāṇakāya Vajrabhairava." The way you develop such an identity and so on are the same as explained above [in the context of the dharmakāya meditation].

To do this [full arising into nirmāṇakāya through saṃbhogakāya] meditation more elaborately, you could contemplate:

> From within emptiness emerges the vajra ground, a fence, a tent, together with a canopy and a ring of fire, outside which and around are the eight great charnel grounds. Inside all of this is a celestial mansion, with all its features perfectly complete, containing seats [in the appropriate locations]. At its center emerges in its entirety the causal Vajradhara in the form of Mañjuśrī.[872]

This constitutes taking the intermediate state into the path as saṃbhogakāya. Then contemplate:

> Light rays emanate from my body inviting all the tathāgatas, who then dissolve into me. From this I transform and rise as the resultant Vajradhara in the form of the glorious Vajrabhairava, whose body is smoky blue; I have nine faces, thirty-four arms, and sixteen legs. I am standing with my right leg slightly bent and my left leg extended. I arise in the form of a triple being, together and in union with consort. At my two eyes are *kṣim* syllables, at my two ears *riṃ*, and... [up to the phrase] My heart is marked with *hūṃ*.[873]

Guru Yongzin Rinpoché says that this is the meditation on taking rebirth into the path as nirmāṇakāya, described by Panchen Losang Chögyen as the preliminary to the completion-stage practice of Vajrabhairava, and we can follow this here.[874] [381]

These, then, represent profound pith instruction on how to take birth, death, and the intermediate state of the ordinary ground into the path as the three buddha bodies, which is in fact the essence of the entire generation stage. That the three bases of purification are related to the birth, death, and intermediate state of a human being of this Jambudvīpa land accords with the definitive intent of Ārya Nāgārjuna as understood by Nāgabodhi and excellently interpreted by our peerless savior, the great Tsongkhapa from the east.[875] If intelligent ones examine in an excellent manner, they will gain confidence from the depths of their mind. Fearing excessive length given the extensive nature of the sources, I have not cited them here.

Blessing the Environment and Its Inhabitants

Having generated yourself into the deity, blessing the environment and the beings within it as found in *Offering to the Guru*:

> **Imagine light radiates from your body and cleanses the entire cosmos and all its denizens of their impurities. Imagine that the entire cosmos has transformed into a celestial mansion and all its denizens into gods and goddesses, a perfectly pure sphere.**

Reciting these phrases, visualize according to the description, which is easy to understand.

Blessing the Offerings

Now bless the offerings. As you recite the mantra *Oṃ hrīḥ ṣṭrīḥ vikṛtānana hūṃ phaṭ*, imagine at the same time that from the *nada* squiggle at the top of the letter *hūṃ* at your heart—you in deity form—incalculable terrifying wrathful Yamas brandishing all kinds of weapons emanate and emerge through your right nostril. They drive the obstructive forces outside the perimeter [of the mandala], such as those that pollute the inner offering and the drinking water, those that enter the flowers and eat the flower garlands, those that enter the fragrances and consume their scents for food, and those such as Ekacūḍā[876] who enter the butter lamps. The wrathful deities [you emanated] are drawn back in, entering through your left nostril, and you imagine them dissolving into the *nada* squiggle of the letter *hūṃ*. Doing this is important because such obstructive forces could enter the offerings and turn them into waste, [382] causing obstacles to the practitioner such as mental turbulence, distraction, and listlessness. So doing these visualizations forcefully is critical, the teacher said.

As you recite the mantra *Oṃ svabhāva śuddhāḥ sarvadharmāḥ svabhāva śuddho 'haṃ / oṃ śūnyatā jñāna svabhāva ātmako 'haṃ*, generate the forceful ascertainment that the basis for the inner offering, along with the container, as well as the offering substances—the four types of water, substances of everyday enjoyment[877]—only exist interdependently; they do not exist the way they appear to my mind, as possessing independent existence. From within this understanding, and briefly recalling the bliss experienced from the deity entering into union with the consort, recite the phrase "From within emptiness..." and so forth. At the same time, while keeping awareness of the union of bliss and emptiness in the depth of your mind, generate from another part of your mind the inner offering as follows:

> From *yaṃ* arises the wind mandala in the shape of a bow and from *raṃ* the fire mandala in the shape of a triangle. The straight line of the bow shape and one point of the triangle are facing toward me; on the two empty spaces outside the two lines of the triangle inside the bow are two banners. On the three points of the triangle, each arising from a letter *āḥ*, are three freshly severed human heads with eyes wide open, together forming a tripod. Above this, from a letter *āḥ*, emerges a skull cup, white on the outside, symbolizing bliss, and red on the inside, symbolizing emptiness. The cup is spacious and wide, and its front, its eastern side, is the side facing me. Inside the cup, moving clockwise through the four directions and the center, the five meats of bull meat and so on emerge,[878] respectively, from the letters *bhrūṃ*, *aṃ*, *jriṃ*, *khaṃ*, and *hūṃ* and are in nature Vairocana, Ratnasambhava, Amitābha, Amoghasiddhi, and Akṣobhya.

The "bull" here is the kind one sees in India and Nepal, an animal that has a squarish head like a box and sports horns like those of a water buffalo. There are two ways its meat can be visualized. One is to visualize the entire animal with its meat minced inside the carcass; the other way to visualize the meat is as if the body has been entirely ground up and shaped into a lump. The remaining meats should also be visualized in either of these two ways. [Then continue the contemplation:]

> On top of each of these five meats are the letters *go* (of *goga*), *ku* (*kukkura*), *da* (*daha*), *ha* (*haya*), and *na* (*nara*), representing the first syllables of the names of these creatures.[879] On the four corners [inside the skull cup], clockwise starting from the southeast, from the letters *laṃ*, *maṃ*, *baṃ*, and *taṃ*, and from the center, respectively—seed syllables of the consort of the relevant deity, such as *baṃ* for Vajravaitalī, and the natures of Locanā, [383] Māmakī, Pāṇḍaravāsinī, Tārā, and Vaitalī—emerge the five nectars of excrement, blood, semen, marrow, and urine. On top of these five nectars are the five letters *bi* (*biṭa*), *ra* (*rakta*), *śu* (*śukra*), *me* (*merga*),[880] and *mu* (*mūtra*), each being the first syllables of their names. In the space above each of these five meats and five nectars are the three letters—a blue *hūṃ*, red *āḥ*, and white *oṃ*—the latter stacked on top of the former.

Then, as you recite "From my heart beams of light radiate..." and so forth, visualize the outer forms [of the inner offering substances] in accordance with the words of the recitation, which should be easy to understand.[881] As for reflecting on their inner symbolism, as you visualize the outer forms, imagine the following with one part of your mind. The wind at the navel is stirred when you as the deity enter into union with the consort, and this then ignites the inner *tumo* fire at your navel. This heat travels upward and melts the bodhicitta at the crown, giving rise to an experience of bliss. This blissful mind perceives emptiness, thus leading to the union of bliss and emptiness. This then is a brief way of understanding, not just in words but in terms of your own experience, the symbolism of the outer mandalas of wind, fire, and so forth as well as the white exterior and red interior of the skull cup.

Hūṃ is the seed syllable of the gnosis of ultimate expanse, and it purifies the faults of color, taste, and potency; *āḥ*, the seed syllable of the deity of nectar, Amitābha, is that which turns the offering substances into nectar; *oṃ*, the seed syllable of Vairocana, who is the perfected purity of the aggregate of form, is that which multiplies the nectar. When you recite the mantra *oṃ āḥ hūṃ* three times, imagine vividly—with yourself in the form of the deity—that at your heart, on a cushion of lotus and sun disc, sit all sentient beings, including especially your two parents. Imagine that all their negative karma of body, speech, and mind, as well as the illnesses and harms they suffer, including even their nightmares—everything that brings harm—all of these emerge out of them in the form of smoky fluid or charcoal-color fluid. They dissolve into the nectar in front of you [visualized inside the skull cup], where they become one in taste with the nectar. You then offer this [to all the sentient beings]. The teacher said this is an oral teaching of the Segyü lineage on purifying negative karma and pacifying obstacles.

If you undertake, even once or twice, the practice of consecrating the inner offering properly in this manner, not just in words, this practice, because of the magical power of tantra, can become a factor for ripening many aspects of completion-stage realization. [384] So even tasting the inner offering once will bless all your channels, winds, and drops and establish the auspicious condition for them to become serviceable. This is the reason why, whenever Marpa Lotsāwa would meet with a new student, he would say, "Compared to what is gained by those Tibetans who perform hundredfold empowerment ceremonies, tasting my inner offering once will bring greater merit,"[882] and let them taste from the inner offering, the teacher said.

When you generate other offerings and recite the lines "From within emptiness, from *āḥ*, appears a skull cup, spacious and wide, in which are...,"[883] visualize that inside the skull cup, which is white outside and red inside, there are blue *hūṃs*, the seed of the wisdom of indivisible bliss and emptiness. They then transform, as will be described below, into the offering substances, such as the four types of water, the objects of everyday enjoyment, music, and the five sense objects. You also imagine generating all kinds of offerings, such as the seven precious emblems of royalty, the seven approximate precious emblems,[884] Mount Meru, the four continents and the four subcontinents, the eight auspicious symbols,[885] and so on, an inconceivable quantity that fills the entirety of space. These offering substances should be visualized as having three distinctive features: (1) their *essence* is the wisdom of bliss and emptiness, (2) their *appearance* reflects the forms of particular things, and (3) their *function* is to imbue the deities' senses with great bliss.

This visualization should not be done at the level of words alone. Do it by bringing it to the level of your own experience as follows. While cognizant of how these offering substances appear to your mind, recall how they do not exist as you perceive them and generate an ascertainment that there is simply no way that they can exist exactly as they appear. When such an ascertainment has arisen as a natural consequence, then recall the experience of bliss you engendered as the deity upon uniting with the consort. This blissful mind then ascertains emptiness. It is based on such a union of bliss and emptiness, with its bond unbroken, that you visualize the specific forms of offering substances. This then is the way that those on the beginner's level like me can put into practice what the tantric treatises define as the *essence* [of the offerings]—that it is the object aspect of the gnosis of bliss and emptiness that appears as offering substances. The *appearance* [of the offerings] is by and large easy to understand; [385] however, the teacher said, the offering substances should not be visualized as ordinary material objects but as clear and radiant and having the nature of light. As for their *function*, it says in the *Ornament of Mahayana Sutras*:

> When bodhisattvas, firm in perfect diligence,
> work to mature the hosts of sentient beings,
> they will not be discouraged even if it takes ten trillion eons
> to mature a single virtue in the mind of another being![886]

If, as has been stated, bodhisattvas do not feel discouraged even if they have to endure hardships over ten trillion eons for the sake of a single being—they in fact embrace such a task with joy and delight—what need is there to speak of how a single instant of the wisdom of indivisible bliss and emptiness, the innermost essence of eighty-four thousand heaps of Dharma, could give rise to immeasurable uncontaminated bliss in the minds of the buddhas and the bodhisattvas? Therefore, if you ensure that the significance of the *essence* [of the offerings] is present not just as mere words, then [the significance of] the other two features [*appearance* and *function*] will be naturally ensured.

The principal meaning of *offering* can be understood from the Sanskrit term *pūjā*, which connotes "to please" and "to delight." So if the buddhas and the bodhisattvas, the objects to whom you are making the offering, become pleased, then whatever you are doing becomes an act of offering—movements of your body, utterances of your speech, and thoughts in your mind. The teacher made this point by telling the story of how Ben Gungyal, to counter his thoughts revealing the eight worldly concerns, threw a handful of ash across his altar and offerings.[887] Furthermore, that the practitioner needs to have joy, delight, and enthusiasm in the act of offering is also stated in the chapter on offering in *Bodhisattva Grounds*. The text says:

> A bodhisattva of small merit can accumulate a great collection of merit toward enlightenment through making immeasurable

> offerings to the tathāgatas. Thus bodhisattvas should strive in this act with an uninterrupted flow of delight in the mind and joy in the heart.[888]

With respect to these practices pertaining to general and specific preliminaries, *Offering to the Guru* says: "**[First] from within an especially virtuous state of mind, proceed with going for refuge, generating the awakening mind, and cultivating the four immeasurable thoughts,**" [386] up to the point where it reads, "**Through this, the entire face of the earth as well as the expanse of space are filled with clouds of offering substances of inner, outer, and secret offerings, creating an inconceivable spectacle.**" Here, understanding that the details need to be understood on the basis of oral teachings, the root text presents this as a brief summary that could be practiced by someone on the beginner's level. For practitioners who have gained excellent familiarity with emptiness and deity yoga, the approach is as presented by Khedrup Sangyé Yeshé in the lines, "**From within great bliss, I arise as the guru deity,**" and so forth.[889] There are other subtle points to bear in mind, such as how the object of refuge must be understood in terms of the [resultant] continuum of the practitioner's own mind, and how the danger one is seeking refuge from differs depending on the individual yogi of the two [tantric] stages.

If you wish to consecrate the offerings in an abbreviated manner, you could do so as described in *Offering to the Guru*, and the main part of how you do this is easy to follow. With respect to the three syllables, when you recite them, visualize above each of the offering substances the three syllables *hūṃ*, *āḥ*, and *oṃ*, each latter stacked above the former. Then beams of light radiating from *hūṃ* draw forth all the deities of *vajra mind*, who dissolve back into the letter *hūṃ*. The letter *hūṃ*, in turn, dissolves into the individual offering substances, and through the force of this, all the faults pertaining to the color, smell, and taste of the offerings are purified, transforming the offerings into something clear and pure. The light radiating from *āḥ* draws forth all the deities of *vajra speech*, who dissolve back into the letter *āḥ*. As the letter *āḥ* becomes of a single taste with the offering substances, the offerings transform into medicinal nectar granting absence of illness, longevity nectar granting absence of death, and gnosis nectar granting absence of contamination. The light from *oṃ* draws forth all the deities of *vajra body*, who then dissolve back into the letter *oṃ*. As the letter *oṃ* fuses with the offering substances, imagine that the offerings become inexhaustible no matter how much one enjoys them.

These meditations, generating oneself into the deity and consecrating the environment and its inhabitants as well as the offering substances, constitute the practices of the four complete purities—of environment, body, resources, and activities—common to all four classes of tantra. So they deserve to be undertaken seriously. [387]

Guru Yoga

The main part of the session

The main part of the session has four parts: (1) visualizing the assembly of gurus and meditation deities as the merit field, (2) offering the seven limbs to them, (3) making supplications through deep faith and reverence, and (4) reviewing the entire body of the path of sutra and tantra and receiving the blessings.

Visualization

Visualizing the assembly of gurus and meditation deities as the merit field

The first is as follows. *Offering to the Guru*, the root text, reads:

> **In the vast space of indivisible bliss and emptiness, amid thick clouds of Samantabhadra's offerings,**
> **and atop an unimaginable wish-granting tree adorned with leaves, flowers, and fruits,**
> **a lion throne blazes with jewels. On it is a wide lotus with a sun and a moon,**

Here you visualize the following. Earlier, when consecrating the offerings, you generated the object aspect of the indivisible gnosis of bliss and emptiness as varied offering articles—outer, inner, secret substances—visible to the eyes and filling the entirety of space. Now imagine that amid such a dense cloud of unique tantric Samantabhadra offerings arises a vast tree made of seven types of gems[890] and adorned with all kinds of ornaments and all varieties of lotuses radiating beams of light. The tree stands in the middle of a large lake whose water is excellent in eight ways[891] and is surrounded by golden ground adorned with geometric patterns made of lapis lazuli. The base of the lake is composed of seven types of gems, while its shores are filled with sands of gold. In the depths of this lake all sorts of gems glow with light in all directions. At the center of this lake stands a [massive] wish-granting tree, a source of all wishes.

At the base of this tree, on the right and left, are two nāga kings, Nanda and Upananda. Their right hands push up the tree from its branches, while their left hands each hold a jewel at their heart. The tree's roots, trunks,[892] branches, and stems, its leaves, flowers, and fruits—each of these seven features is formed in a sevenfold manner. Of these, the roots are made of gold, the trunks silver, the branches lapis lazuli, and stems crystal, the leaves beryl,[893] the flowers red pearls [388] the size of chariot wheels, and the fruits diamonds the size of a bowl big enough to hold five *dre*[894] of grain. From the main branches as well as the smaller branches hang jewel earrings, gold bracelets, gold anklets, gold girdles or belts, yards of silk, crowns, nets made of webs of gold and pearls lined with silver bells topped with crescents, tail fans, and gold clam bells. These bells emit various sounds teaching the Dharma. The wish-granting tree is so magnificent that the merely seeing it, hearing it, smelling it, or tasting and feeling it can soothe all the pains of body and mind such as the 404 diseases. Furthermore, it can feed sentient beings who desire food, and it can grant clothes, beds, shelter, and medicine for those who desire these, granting beings whatever they desire in the manner of rain falling from the sky.

The main trunk of the tree is composed of seven individual trunks, six trunks formed around a central trunk. Atop this main tree trunk sits a large multicolored lotus with a hundred thousand petals and an expansive and wide center. On this sits a high and wide lapis lazuli throne raised up by eight great lions and adorned with light-radiating gems so brilliant that even the sun and moon appear dim. On top of this throne is another multicolored lotus with a hundred thousand petals whose tips turn downward, extending slightly over the edges of the lion throne. The tips of the petals of the lower multicolored lotus turn upward so that part of the throne's base is covered by the petals. On each side of the four cardinal directions of the throne are two lions, their fur white with orange on their head, paws, mane, and tail. Their mouths, wide open, bare four fangs, their round eyes are red like flame, and their tongues wag and sometimes curl. With such terrifying forms, they stare into the distance, ready to protect the practitioner from the harms of obstructive forces, demonic possession, spirits of the dead, and ghosts.[895] With the claws of their right paws raised upward supporting the throne, [389] they guard the practitioner against harms from demonic forces above, such as those augured by astrological omens. With the claws of their left paws pressing down on the base of the throne, they guard the practitioner against harms from the demonic forces below—those of earth spirits, nāgas, and so on.

Now if it is commonly established that even putting around the neck of a child, a goat kid, or a calf a protection amulet containing dried dog poo, pig excrement, and poison can guard against dead spirits and malevolent ghosts, what need is there then to speak of the power of the eight lions? These lions are, in fact, the four forms of fearlessness and eight perfect masteries[896] present within the heart of the guru. As such they do indeed have the power to guard against the demonic forces from all three directions, whether above, below, or in between.

The tips and the branches of the six surrounding trunks rise upward from outside the lion throne. Atop the lion throne on the central trunk and inside the multicolored lotus sits a large white lotus with white petals tinged red at their tips, a lotus whose width and depth equal that of the lion throne itself. Above this, stacked like a terrace, are ten more layers of lotuses. The lotus on the eleventh layer has four petals, one for each cardinal direction, and sports a center complete with stamen and pistils. Atop this center part sits a cushion of equal size made of sun and moon discs, resembling a two-layered mirror made of white and red crystal.

That the lotuses are white and tinged with red symbolizes the indivisible union of method and wisdom. The lake whose water is excellent in eight ways symbolizes the practitioner's renunciation, awakening mind, and right view appearing in the form of a lake. The wish-granting tree, a source of all wishes, represents the practitioner's six perfections. The flowers symbolize the twenty-two types of awakening mind[897] and the fruits the four means of gathering others. The two nāgas symbolize the wisdom that realizes everything as illusion-like and devoid of true existence and the compassion that cherishes others' welfare as more important than one's own. That we should visualize these [attributes of the practitioner's mind] in such-and-such forms is part of the instruction of our supreme guru Jé Tsongkhapa's oral transmission. The teacher said that although this does not seem to be known to anyone today, [390] as it has become quite neglected, he has explained it here. If someone with powers of discernment were to carefully examine our supreme guru's oral teachings such as this one, he will gain profound understanding of the key points of the Mahayana path.

Next we read in the *Offering to the Guru* root text **"and there sits my triply kind root guru, who in essence is all the buddhas"** up to **"He sits in the vajra posture."** The moment you utter the words or bring to mind the phrase "There sits my triply kind root guru, who in essence is all the buddhas," engage with the words such that, through the force of your devotion and reverence, tears flow from your eyes and your palms instinctively press together. Your guru is triply kind in that (1) he has conferred the empowerments upon you in perfect accord with the tantras, (2) he has explained the treatises of the tantra to you, and (3) he has conferred the instructions that enable you to easily comprehend the tantras' meaning.

Such a guru is, in essence, the embodiment of the wisdom, compassion, and power of all the buddhas; in appearance, he takes the form of a one-faced and two-armed fully ordained monk clad in a saffron robe. His countenance is fair with a red tinge and bears a smiling expression; his eyes are slender, his nose sports generous nostrils and an elevated ridge, his forehead is broad, and his jaws resemble those of a lion. His right hand at his heart performs the gesture of teaching the Dharma, with the tips of his thumb and index finger holding the stem of a blue lotus that blooms at his right shoulder. Atop this blue lotus stands a blue sword with a golden handle, representing the wisdom of all the buddhas of the three times, the tip of the blade blazing with the fire of wisdom, its radiant brilliance dispelling the darkness of ignorance and filling the entire universe. His left hand, in the gesture of meditation, holds an alms bowl filled with nectar. The tips of the thumb and index finger hold the stem of a blue lotus that blooms at his left shoulder, and on this flower sits the magical volume of oral transmission, distilling the essence of all eighty-four thousand heaps of Dharma. The head of the wrapped volume, with its title marker, is facing the guru.[898]

As if the three colors—maroon, orange, and golden—converge in a single flower, [391] he is clad in the three robes, lower garment, upper garment, and the ceremonial yellow robe, exactly as prescribed in the Vinaya texts, in a manner that is free of any flaw and endowed with all the appropriate attributes. Not only these, the guru is also visualized wearing the thin undershirt and what these days is called a *togak* vest, which serves as a protection against sweating. He is wearing a long-tipped paṇḍita hat made of yellow silk or woolen cloth and shaped like an apricot stone but with a long pointy tip. At his heart, on a moon disc, is the *commitment being*, Buddha Śākyamuni, whose body is the color of refined gold. At his heart, on a sun disc, is the *gnosis being*, blue Vajradhara together with his consort. At his heart, on a sun disc, is the *concentration being*, a blue *hūṃ* with a *nada* squiggle and so forth on its top. Beams of blue light radiate from the *nada*, beams of white light from the *bindu* drop, yellow light from the crescent moon, red light from the letter *ha*, and green light from the vowel *ū*.[899] Thus the syllable *hūṃ* radiates light of five colors. The gnosis being Vajradhara and his consort are adorned with various jeweled ornaments and clad in heavenly silk robes. The two commitment beings [your guru in the form of Jé Tsongkhapa and Buddha Śākyamuni] and the gnosis being [Vajradhara] are adorned with the major and minor noble marks and radiate light of great brilliance. They are seated cross-legged in the vajra posture amid an orb of rainbow light on the eleventh-layer lotus on a cushion of sun and moon discs. In such ways you should visualize them.

Next relates to how to engage in the guru's body as mandala. Here, when you recite the line "**His five pure aggregates are the five sugatas**," visualize the five aggregates as the five tathāgatas. At the guru's crown, in the space beneath the skull and just above the brain tissue, is white Vairocana, who is the perfected nature of the aggregate of form. Inside his throat, at level of his Adam's apple, is red Amitābha, who is the perfected nature of the aggregate of discrimination. At his heart between the two breasts, in the empty space inside the body, is blue Akṣobhya, who is the perfected nature of the aggregate of consciousness. At his navel, inside the body, is yellow Ratnasambhava, who is the perfected nature of the aggregate of feeling. And at the base of the secret organ where the pubic hair begins is green Amoghasiddhi, who is the perfected nature of the aggregate of mental formations.

When you recite "**his four elements are the four consorts,**" [392] imagine the four elements as the four consorts. At the guru's navel, in front of Ratnasambhava, is white Locanā, the essence of the earth element. At the heart, in front of Akṣobhya, is blue Māmakī, the essence of the water element. At the throat, in front of Amitābha, is Pāṇḍaravāsinī, the essence of the fire element. And at the crown, in front of Vairocana, is green Tārā, who is the essence of the wind element.

When you utter "**his sense bases**," imagine the six sense bases as the six bodhisattvas. At the two eyes—the eye organ is said to be a subtle physical organ shaped like a sesame flower or the blossom of a banana tree—are two white Kṣitigarbhas; at each entrance of the eyes is a goddess Rūpavajrā. At the ears—the ear organs are shaped like the ends of tightly bound stalks cut clean—are two yellow Vajrapāṇis; at the entrances of each ear is a goddess Śabdavajrā. At the nose—the nose organ is shaped like two copper bowls stuck back to back—is yellow Khagarbha; at the entrance of the nostrils is the goddess Gandhavajrā. At the tip of the tongue—the tongue organ is shaped like a crescent composed of two finely pointed pieces whose tips do not touch each other—is red Lokeśvara; at the root of the tongue is the goddess Rasavajrā. At the heart, in front of Akṣobhya, is Mañjuśrī, who is the essence of the mental sense base, and his consort Dharmadhātuvajrā. And at the midpoint of the jewel of the secret organ, where there is a cakra, is Sarvanīvaraṇaviṣkambhin, the essence of the body sense base, while at the entrance of the vajra is Sparśavajrā.

When you utter "**veins, sinews, and joints are in fact the bodhisattvas,**" visualize that above Vairocana, at the guru's crown, sits white Maitreya, who is the essence of all the veins and sinews. Imagine on each joint of his limbs, fingers, and toes a green Samantabhadra, who is the essence of all the joints. When you utter "**his pores are the twenty-one thousand arhats,**" imagine the twenty-one thousand pores as twenty-one thousand Mahayana arhats. And when you say "**his limbs are the wrathful deities,**" imagine the ten limbs as the ten wrathful deities: on the front part of the two big toes, with heads facing the tip, is Yamāntaka on the right big toe and Aparājita on the left. On the sockets of the two shoulders are [on the right and left, respectively,] Acala and Ṭakkirāja. On the tips of the right and left knees are, respectively, Nīladaṇḍa and Mahābala. At the crown, above Vairocana and Maitreya, is Uṣṇīṣacakravartin, [393] his mouth wide open and fangs bared in a terrifying pose, while his three eyes stare threateningly up into the sky. Visualizing [this wrathful deity] in this form, the teacher said, is an excellent method for guarding against harms by malevolent forces from above. The explanatory tantra's statement[900] that Hayagrīva should be visualized at the entrance of the mouth should be understood to mean that he is visualized at the root of the tongue, the teacher said. On each heel, facing up to the ankle, is a Sumbharāja. And at the secret organ, below Amoghasiddhi, visualize Amṛtakuṇḍalinī. The body colors, hand implements, ornaments, and expressions of these body-mandala deities should accord with the Guhyasamāja [sādhana].

When you recite "**his light rays are directional guardians, while yakṣas and the worldly gods are but cushions for his feet,**" imagine that the guru's body emits light rays, all appearing in the forms of the fifteen directional guardians and the yakṣa Vajrapāṇi—the latter known also as "the lord of secrets"—as bodhisattvas and universal kings constantly stand guard. Some instructional guides explain the phrase "the worldly gods are but cushions for his feet" as saying that the powerful worldly gods such as Brahmā, Indra, and Rudra raise up the [guru's] lion throne. In the tradition of instruction stemming from Drupwang Losang Namgyal, this phrase is understood to indicate that even these powerful worldly gods will only with great difficulty gain the opportunity to simply touch the feet of this guru Vajradhara with the tip of their crown jewels.[901] That they are not worthy to even be a cushion under the guru Vajradhara's feet indicates that there is no one higher than the guru in the entire sphere of existence, the teacher said. Now, if your triply kind guru in relation to whom you are doing the body-mandala meditation is alive, it then becomes an actual body-mandala meditation. If he is not alive, it then becomes a form of body-mandala meditation. Nevertheless, the teacher said there is no difference in merit between the two. These explanations represent the oral transmission on the difficult points on how to undertake the body-mandala meditation in relation to one's guru found in sources such as the *Vajra Garland* explanatory tantra. Treasure them.

Next, as you recite "**Around him, in respective circles, are the actual and lineage gurus,**" visualize that five-colored light rays, narrow at the base and wide at the tip, emerge to his right. At the tips of these light rays are the lineage gurus of vast practice: [394] Maitreya in his bodhisattva form, Asaṅga and his brother [Vasubandhu], the two Vimuktisenas, and so on.[902] From his heart emerge similar light rays to his left. At their tips are the lineage gurus of the profound view: Mañjuśrī in his bodhisattva form, Nāgārjuna, Candrakīrti, Vidyākokila elder and junior, and so on. If you wish to do this [visualization of the lineage gurus] in combination with mind training (*lojong*) practice, then visualize Mañjuśrī on each side, right and left, in his saṃbhogakāya form followed by the individual gurus of the lineages—those of vast practice and of profound view. This is as explained above in the context of visualizing the objects of refuge when going for refuge.[903] Again, as before, the guru's heart emits five-colored light rays, this time pointing upward, at the tips of which are the lineage gurus of the near transmission of blessing unique to this specific [guru-yoga] instruction: Vajradhara, Mañjuśrī, Jé Tsongkhapa, Tokden Jampal Gyatso, Baso Chökyi Gyaltsen, the great siddha Dharmavajra, the conqueror Ensapa, and so on. On their right and left, like a crowd gathering at a marketplace, imagine the lineage gurus of blessing and practice: Lord Mahāsukha, Indrabodhi, Saraha, Nāgārjuna, Tilopa, Nāropa, Ḍombīpa, the peerless great Atiśa, and so on. Once again, the guru's heart emits light rays as before radiating upward into space. At their tips are all the gurus from whom you have received teachings in person, including especially the guru from whom you received the transmission of this particular instruction. Imagine that all the other gurus you have received teachings from are facing the triple-being guru, as if they are there to support you as guarantors. As for the appearance of these gurus [of the various lineages], their hand implements, and their sitting postures, visualize these according to the sizes explained by guru Yongzin Rinpoché.[904]

Next, as you recite "**meditation deities, and hosts of mandala gods,**" visualize on the four petals in the four cardinal directions of the eleventh layer of lotuses the deities of the four great tantras together with their celestial mansions. In the front are the deities of the Guhyasamāja mandala, on the right the deities of Vajrabhairava mandala, on the left the deities of Cakrasaṃvara mandala, and on the back the deities of the Hevajra tantra mandala. The teacher said that we should visualize that the eastern doors of the mandalas of all four great tantras are facing toward the triple-being guru. [395] On the petals on the next layer of the lotus visualize [other] deities of the highest yoga class, like Kālacakra, Kṛṣṇayamāri, Red Yamāntaka, Mahācakra Vajrapāṇi, Mahāmāyā, Buddhakapāla, and so on. On the petals on the next layer down are deities of the yoga class of tantra: Vairocana Adhisambodhi, Jinavararatna, Śākyakulīndra, Saṃkusumita, Vajradhātu, Durgatiśodhanarāja, and so on. Below this, on the petals of the next layer down, are the deities of performance (*caryā*) tantra: Vairocanādhisambodhi, Bhūtaḍāmara Vajrapāṇi, Krodha Trailokyavijaya, Amitāyus of the performance class, Hayagrīva taught in the *Hayagrīva Tantra*, and so on. Below them, on the petals of the next lotus, are the deities of action (*kriyā*) tantra: Trisamayavyūhamuni, Eleven-Headed Avalokiteśvara, Four-Armed Avalokiteśvara, Uṣṇīṣavijayā, Sitātapatrā, Mārīcī, and so on. Visualize these deities together with their celestial mansion residences.

Next, as you recite the words "**buddhas, bodhisattvas, heroes and ḍākinīs, and a sea of Dharma protectors,**" visualize on the next layer down buddhas such as the thirty-five buddhas of confession, the thousand buddhas of the fortunate eon, and so on. Below them visualize bodhisattvas such as the eight bodhisattva disciples of the buddha like Mañjuśrī, Vajrapāṇi, Avalokiteśvara, and so on and Jñānottara, Prabhāketu, Praṇidhānamati, Śāntendra,[905] and so on in their bodhisattva forms. Below them imagine ārya pratyekabuddhas, all seated in the *vajrāsana*, their hands in meditation gesture, each with their heads crowned by a small protrusion, the teacher said. Below them imagine the sixteen arhats together with their sixteen thousandfold retinues. Below them visualize heroes and heroines (ḍākas and ḍākinīs), each holding a cleaver in their right hand and a skull cup in their left while a *khaṭvāṅga* staff rests on the inside of their left elbow. All the heroes are in a dancing posture, their right leg extended and the left slightly bent, and wear a hero's headband; they are adorned with the "six seals"—a garland of fleshly severed heads and so on.[906] The heroines are also in dancing posture with right leg extended and left slightly bent; they are adorned with the "five seals" such as a garland of human skulls. Below these imagine the Dharma protectors of the supermundane level, such as the three protectors of the practitioners of the three capacities—Mahākāla, Vaiśravaṇa, and Kālarūpa. [396] In the space outside the four cardinal directions of the lion throne, visualize the four directional guardians amid dense clouds: In the east Dhṛtarāṣṭra is surrounded by gandharvas; in the south Virūḍhaka is surrounded by yamas; in the west Virūpākṣa is surrounded by nāgas; and in the north Vaiśravaṇa is surrounded by yakṣas. Imagine these guardian kings stand guard ready to protect the practitioners.

Next, as you recite the words "**The three doors of each are marked by three vajras, and from the letter *hūṃ* [at their heart] emerge hook-like beams of light drawing forth the gnosis beings from their natural abodes, whose inseparability [with the commitment beings] becomes firm**," and also the lines of invocation composed by Khedrup Sangyé Yeshé that read, "**Sources of excellence and good fortune**" up to "**The gnosis beings and commitment beings become nondual**,"[907] contemplate the following.

From the syllable *hūṃ* at the heart, which is part of the three syllables representing the three vajras that mark the three points of the body of the deities of the merit field, emerge blue light rays shaped like hooks. This invokes and draws forth the corresponding gnosis beings. As in the *Story of Sumāgadhā*, imagine some of these gnosis beings arrive flying through the air, some, such as Brahmā and Indra, arrive on foot in a majestic procession with their vast entourage, some appear riding elephants, some ride horses, some even appear with their entire natural dwelling such as a forest or a mountain, some appear while performing all sorts of miracles like shooting flames out of the upper part of the body and water out of the lower part of the body.[908]

As you say *jaḥ*, imagine these gnosis beings descend onto the crown of their corresponding commitment beings. When you say *hūṃ*, imagine that these gnosis beings enter their corresponding commitment beings in such a way that the two remain distinct, without one obstructing the other. When you say *baṃ*, imagine that the gnosis beings become fused with the commitment beings like water mixed with milk. And when you say *hoḥ*, imagine that the gnosis beings reside within their corresponding commitment beings [397] with joy, the teacher said.

The text of the invocation [itself] is easy to understand. The phrase "gnosis beings from their natural abodes" has the following meaning. The guru buddha's mind, which is the dharmakāya of great bliss-gnosis, abides in the ultimate expanse that is the natural abode like water poured into water. While immersed in such a state, wherein gnosis and the ultimate expanse are fused indivisibly into a single taste, all kinds of diverse enlightened form bodies emerge, all appropriate to the needs of individual spiritual trainees. Furthermore, all the deities of the merit field are nothing but manifestations of the guru buddha's dharmakāya, hence it is from the *natural abode* that emanations of the guru are invited. This is how I understand the phrase. If we do not develop this kind of understanding, there is the danger of engendering the false notion that there might be some others more excellent than the guru, such as Vajradhara or the meditation deities.

Seven Limbs

Offering the Seven Limbs to the Merit Field

Next, *Offering to the Guru* presents the offering of seven limbs:

> **Then, as the guardian Nāgārjuna states in his *Five Stages*:**
>
> > **Relinquishing all other offerings,**
> > **undertake the perfect offering to the guru.**
> > **By pleasing him you will obtain**
> > **the supreme gnosis of omniscience.**
>
> **Generate certainty that making offerings to the guru is more important than making offerings to all other buddhas and bodhisattvas.**
>
> **To make the offering of seven limbs, the first limb, prostration, is as follows.**

It is said that we need to develop a deeply felt conviction in the benefits of celebrating the guru through flawless scripture and reasoning, and on such basis, engage in acts such as prostration with a strong and ardent delight. This is because if we engage in such acts with joy and delight, our action acquires greater weight. In particular, given that this instruction emphasizes the practice of reliance on the spiritual teacher, contemplating the benefits of honoring the guru from various angles at this point [398] helps leave an imprint so that later on, when relying on the guru through thought and action comes up, we will engage with the practice like a beggar who has just found a treasure. So [contemplating the benefits of honoring the guru] is vitally important.

Honoring the guru has limitless benefits. These include, briefly, that a practitioner purifies even powerful karmic obscurations, great waves of the accumulations are gathered, both supreme and common siddhis are attained swiftly, and the realizations of the grounds and the paths arise sooner. As for authoritative sources on this point [about the benefits], some were already cited in the section on explaining the greatness of this instruction. There are other sources as well. For example, the *Drop of Gnosis Tantra* says:

> He is the master of the ten grounds;
> his kindness is unexcelled.
> So how can there be a greater teacher,
> one superior to the guru?[909]

Similarly, *Five Stages* says:

> He [Guhyasamāja] is the self-arisen buddha;
> he alone is the special deity.
> Yet he who grants the entire instruction,
> the vajra master, is more superior still.[910]

Attainment of the Nondual too says:

> In the three realms of existence,
> none surpasses the master,
> for it is out of his kindness
> that one attains numerous siddhis.
> He is Vajrasattva himself;
> even all the buddhas salute him.
> To honor the guru is unexcelled indeed,
> so honor him in every way you can.[911]

Similarly, *Fifty Verses on the Guru* says:

> The master from whom one has received
> the excellent empowerments, him the tathāgatas
> residing in all the worlds of the ten directions
> salute throughout all three times.[912]

These citations show how the guru's kindness is greater than those of all the buddhas and bodhisattvas, and how, given that he is worthy of honor even by all the conquerors of the ten directions—who are themselves worthy of honor—he remains an object worthy of honor even by all those who are themselves objects of worship. So what need is there to speak of the guru being worthy of the practitioner's honor? So as this declares, you should reflect [on the importance of honoring the guru] based on flawless scripture and reasoning and generate a deep conviction so that later you can engage with delight in the practices of relying on the guru through thought and action, [399] just like a swan king plunging into a clear lake adorned with lotuses.

[The limb of prostration]

About the first limb, prostration, *Offering to the Guru* says: "**Through your kindness is granted in an instant**" up to "**and emanating bodies equal to atoms in the world, I bow down.**" When you recite these lines, bring to mind the figures in the merit field of *Offering to the Guru* together with their seats; they equal the number of atoms in all the buddhafields. Then, in front of each of these merit fields, imagine yourself in the form of Vajrabhairava without consort, your palms pressed together at your heart. In each of the pores of these Vajrabhairavas imagine another Vajrabhairava. Then imagine prostrating with the full length of your body touching the ground; this is the body prostration. Imagine all these Vajrabhairavas chanting in unison "Through whose kindness" and so forth, which is the speech prostration. Also in accord with the words of the offering prostration, imagine that all the Vajrabhairavas (yourself included) contemplate how the guru is the embodiment of the three buddha bodies, how he is the embodiment of all Three Jewels, and how, in brief, all the great beings worthy of honor in the ten directions are manifestations of the guru, and in this way, imagine generating fervent feelings of devotion and reverence; this is the mind prostration. Offer prostrations like this with your three doors [body, speech, and mind].

Right now, you train in these [kinds of prostrations] through imagination. However, when you attain the bodhisattva grounds, you will gather great waves of merit on each of the grounds through actually prostrating to the buddhas and the bodhisattvas by emanating hundreds and thousands of bodies as well as making offerings to them. This practice of the seven limbs is thus not merely a preliminary practice or some simple practice that one performs because one has nothing better to do. We should understand the seven limbs to be a practice worth undertaking by learned ones and simpletons alike. Here too, although emanating countless bodies is explicitly related in *Vows of Good Conduct* to the limb of prostration, I think it can be related to the remaining limbs as well. For example, the chapter on offering in the *Bodhisattva Grounds* states that bodhisattvas who have gained mastery over material resources manifest in countless bodies and [400] offer the various articles with their thousands of hands.[913]

[The limb of offering]

As you recite "**To you, refuge and protector, venerable guru and your entourage, I offer a sea of clouds of various offerings,**" bring to mind all the offering substances you have laid out. And when you say "**four streams of purifying nectars gently flow,**" imagine that countless beautiful offering goddesses emerge from your heart, all holding precious vessels made of gold, silver, lapis lazuli, beryl, red pearl, or diamond, containing the four types of water all endowed with the eight excellent qualities of water. Imagine that they offer the water to the merit-field deities for their mouths, feet, and hands, and imagine that the deities dip the tips of a sheaf of *kuśa* grass in the sprinkling water and sprinkle water around. Imagine that these offering goddesses return to your heart. Imagine that as a result of offering those specific articles, the gnosis of bliss and emptiness arise in the hearts of the merit-field figures. Contemplate too that all these articles of offering are nothing but mental constructs and that they do not exist whatsoever in the way they appear to your mind. Like this, view them as illusion-like manifestations of bliss and emptiness. Keep this point [about viewing everything in terms of illusion-like manifestations] in mind without fail in the later contexts as well. Now, although it is impossible for the deities of the merit field to ever waver from their meditative concentration of bliss and emptiness, the point of imaging the fresh arising of the gnosis of bliss and emptiness in them is to help prepare you, the practitioner, so that it will arise soon in your own mindstream. Emanating the offering goddesses from the heart and withdrawing them back into the heart signifies the step of bringing all the root and branch winds into the heart and thereby inducing the realizations of the completion stage. We should therefore perform these visualizations without fail, the teacher said.

When you recite "**Flowers on stems, loose petals, and perfect garlands**" and so forth, imagine that the offering goddesses who have emerged from your heart all hold vases made of the seven types of gems [of gold, silver, etc.] containing flowers also composed of the seven types of gems. They also carry trays made of the seven types of gems, [401] holding loose flowers also composed of the seven types of gems, from which they toss flowers into the sky. In the sky these flowers transform into canopies, parasols, victory banners, garlands, flower-decked garden houses decorated with jingling bells and clam bells, all hovering aloft, and the offering goddesses honor the merit-field deities by placing garlands of all types of flowers on their crowns and around their necks. Imagine that around these flowers buzz honeybees trilling all sorts of melodious tunes. Imagine also that loose flowers and petals of both the human world and the heavens, rich in fragrance and color, able to steal the heart of anyone who sees, cover the face of the earth.

Next, as you recite "**Smokes of fragrant incense densely permeate the sky like monsoon clouds the color of lapis lazuli**," imagine offering goddesses holding censers made of the seven types of gems that release incense smoke of teak, white and red sandalwoods, nutmeg, and saffron as well as of fragrant flowers and leaves that can be burned for incense. Imagine some of the goddesses also carry incense holders made of the seven types of gems with tall incense sticks—known as "four strands bound together"—emitting smoke that resembles the color of lapis lazuli and conjures patterns such as the eight auspicious symbols, the seven types of jewels,[914] and so on in such density that the clouds of smoke completely obscure the merit-field tree.

Then, as you recite "**Sun, moon, and masses of lamps intensely bright**" and so forth, imagine that the offering goddesses hold up crystal celestial mansions, discs of moonstone, all types of colorful gems emitting brilliant rays of light, and lights of all kinds, such as oil lamps and butter lamps. Imagine the lights permeate even rocks and high mountains, dispelling darkness throughout the trichiliocosm and the worlds between the various continents. Imagine that these lights intersect with lights coming from other directions and then extend to other places in other directions, creating a vast matrix of light rays across space, creating patterns like the eight auspicious symbols, the seven types of gems, [402] and the seven types of jewels, objects of the five senses, and so on. Imagine they fill the entire world and dispel the darkness of ignorance of all sentient beings. The phrase the light rays "dance about,"[915] the teacher said, refers to the way the light rays converge and intersect each other and extend into other directions as if the light rays were playing and dancing.

Then, as you recite the lines "**Great seas of scented water perfumed by fragrances of camphor, sandalwood, and saffron swirl out to the horizon**," imagine offering goddesses carrying, in containers made of the seven types of gems, scented water of camphor, white and red sandalwood, saffron, nutmeg, and teak exuding their perfumes. Imagine the goddesses touch the hearts of the merit-field figures with these perfumes and anoint different points of their bodies as well. You can also imagine making offerings of fragrance in the form of bodies of water such as lakes, pools, and springs adorned with all sorts of fragrant medicinal plants.

Next, when you recite the lines "**Delicious food and drink of a hundred flavors**" and so forth, imagine that offering goddesses carrying in containers—large bowls, trays, and such made of the seven types of gems—filled with food like rice, sweet breads (*khur ba*), *laddu* sweets, and sesame seed buns; snacks like peaches, nuts, grapes, and sugar cane; and drinks like curd, milk, rice beer, grape wine, and tea—in brief, all the best food and drink that exist in both the heavenly realms and this human world. Imagine also that offering goddesses bear beautiful cakes with perfect aroma, taste, and texture and offer these to the merit field figures.

Then, as you recite the lines "**From a limitless variety of musical instruments**" and so forth, imagine offering goddesses playing wind instruments like conches and flutes, ringing instruments like cymbals and bells, and percussive instruments like earthen pots and drums. Imagine that they offer the music produced by all these varieties of instruments. Imagine also that teachings such as the four fundamental axioms[916] and the law of karma are carried along by the notes and melodies, ripening sentient beings and leading them to release. This is how we should imagine, the teacher said. [403]

Next, as you recite the lines "**Bearing the splendors of form, sound, smell, taste, and touch, goddesses of outer and inner offerings pervade every direction**," imagine offering goddesses bearing the glory of sense objects such as mirrors with vivid reflections, lutes, and so on[917] made of the seven types of gems and the four types of consorts—"like a lotus" and so on—who are expert in arts of love.[918] These goddesses are in the prime of youth, with darting eyes and smiling expressions, slim waists with a slight arch at their hips, their alluring breasts generous and full. Glancing slyly, they are graced by postures of elegance. The goddesses bearing the glory of the inner sense object[919] of sound sing all kinds of songs rich in the hexatonic scales of melody. The goddesses bearing the glory of the inner sense object of smell have bodies and breath that exude natural fragrance of blue lotuses, their bodies are anointed with sweet perfumes of sandalwood and saffron, and they wear around their necks garlands of flowers exuding rich and complex perfume. The goddesses bearing the glory of the inner sense object of taste have full lips like red *bimba*[920] fruit smeared with honey, from which a simple kiss or suck excites desire and pleasure. And of the goddesses bearing the glory of the inner sense object of touch, some have a sexual organ shaped like a lotus, others have one shaped like a conch that is deep with the lower end swirled clockwise, and some have one shaped like the center of a musk's navel. The secret organs of these goddesses have the power to ignite the fire of *tumo* (inner heat). Imagine that you offer countless goddesses like these to the merit-field figures, who in turn plunge into desire and experience bliss and emptiness. Those who are easily contented may not need [to imagine] details such as body size, color and shape of the face and nose, natural body scent, tone of voice, and so on; but these details should be known by those who wish to put the entirety of the oral teachings connected with this instruction into practice.

Alternatively, if you wish to chant more extensive lines connected with offering the inner sense objects, you could chant the omniscient Tsongkhapa's [404] composition that begins with the line "Expert in the sixty-four arts of love making." The only difference is that, in place of the line "I offer this to please the deities of Akṣobhyavajra,"[921] as in the original text, you say, "I offer this to please the guru and meditation deities." As for what to visualize [when chanting these lines], this is the same as explained above.

Also, if you wish to offer inner objects of everyday enjoyment, then after having offered the specific articles of everyday enjoyment, holding bell and vajra in your hands, perform the gesture of embrace and do the chant. And when you recite the lines "At my secret cakra sporting the color of sapphire"[922] and so on, bring to mind how, through the joining of the deity and consort's secret places, red bodhicitta fluid flows from the crest of the consort's secret organ, giving rise to bliss and emptiness. And when you recite the lines "At my emanation cakra, igniting the *tumo* fire," bring to mind how, through the movement of the downward voiding winds in both the deity and the consort, the *tumo* at the navel ignites, melting bodhicitta fluid in the 72,000 channels, which then reaches the *tumo* fire, giving rise to the blazing of bliss. And when you recite the lines "At the center of the dharmacakra is, in actuality, bliss," bring to mind how, through the entry, abiding, and absorption of winds into the central channel, the knots of the channels are undone, giving rise to innate bliss and emptiness, which is the lamp dispelling entire darkness of ignorance. And when you recite the line "Abiding excellently at the center of great-bliss wheel," bring to mind how the *tumo* fire at the navel melts the bodhicitta in the crown, which then flows from the crown down through the throat and so forth, and how this gradual descent induces the four joys in forward and reverse sequence.[923] In the post-equipoise periods, after letting go of the meditative equipoise on innate bliss and emptiness, cultivate the thought that sees everything arising to your six senses as manifestations of bliss and emptiness. Also hear all sounds as the melting of the white and red bodhicitta through the 72,000 channels manifesting as the sounds of vowels and consonants. These inner objects of everyday enjoyment share some similarities with the external objects of everyday enjoyment, and so they are also referred to as "objects of everyday enjoyment." To gain a good understanding of these practices, you need a detailed understanding of the key points of the completion stage. However, fearing excessive length, I will not write more here.

Next, you recite the lines that begin "**The billion worlds with four continents and Meru,**" which pertain to the mandala offering. [405] There are three types of mandala offerings: inner, outer, and suchness. With respect to the *outer mandala offering*, although there are numerous versions such as the one with thirty-seven heaps, here [in *Offering to the Guru* instruction] we should do the version with twenty-three heaps: five heaps consisting of Mount Meru together with the four continents; eight heaps consisting of the eight subcontinents; another eight heaps consisting of the seven precious royal emblems plus the great vase of treasure; plus the sun and moon. This version is understood by the great siddha Nāropa and Abhayākaragupta to be the intention of the lines "This field adorned with the seven precious objects" in the *Guhyasamāja Root Tantra* and is the version they themselves practiced.[924] Just like these Indian siddhas, our peerless savior, the great Tsongkhapa from the east, also recited the mandala offering during his intensive retreat at Ölkha Chölung using this version. So this version is rich in blessing, the teacher said. The version with thirty-seven heaps was invented by Drogön Chögyal Phakpa on the basis of this [twenty-three heaps version] with the addition of the "mountain of gems" from the *Treasury of Abhidharma* and the goddesses of beauty and so forth from Vairocana tantra.[925] The teacher said that this [last] version is most prevalent today.

In the line "**The seven types of jewels, their approximates, and so forth,**" the "approximates" refer to the precious garden, mansion, bed, garment, shoes, nāga hide, and sword, and you imagine offering these; but there is no custom of counting this as a separate heap. In any case, in addition to these twenty-three heaps, imagine offering the following: on each of the heaps is a lotus tree with twenty-five branches, at the tip of each branch is a lotus flower, and on each of these lotuses is Samantabhadra with his palms folded and holding a gem inside. Imagine clouds of Samantabhadra offerings filling the entire space. In relation to the line "The billion worlds with four continents and Mount Meru," the teacher explained how one thousand systems of Mount Meru and four continents together with the iron perimeter constitute the first one thousand world systems. Taking this as the unit of counting and multiplying it a thousand times is the second thousand [or million] world systems; and with this as the basis, multiplying it another thousand times is the third thousand [or billion] world systems. Such a trichiliocosm has a billion worlds of Mount Meru and four continents, the teacher said. [406]

For the *inner mandala offering*, imagine that this body of yours made of flesh, bones, and so forth has its skin stripped off and its various parts—head, limbs, and so forth—severed; the eyes are gouged out, and the tongue, ears, and the nose are cut off as well. Internal organs like the heart are removed, the intestines and such eviscerated, and even the feet and hands are broken into parts at their joints. Then imagine placing the torso on the skin, upon which is placed the severed head; atop this the heart is placed upside down, and the two eyeballs hang over the front and back of the torso; the four limbs are placed in the four directions, while the toes and fingers are split into piles on either side of each of the four limbs. The remaining body parts and internal organs are placed in the various directions. Imagine the skin to be the golden ground, the torso Mount Meru, the four limbs the four continents, the eight sets of digits the eight subcontinents, the head the victorious mansion, the heart the jewel crown of the mansion, the two eyes the sun and moon, and the organs and the internal parts the perfect material resources of humans and gods. Imagining in these ways, offer them [as a mandala].

The *suchness mandala offering* is as follows. While at the perceptual level, you sustain the appearance of a mandala offering, you ensure that a vibrant awareness of its absence of intrinsic existence is present at the level of apprehension. Ensure that these two converge within a single state of mind. This is called "the mandala offering of indivisible appearance and emptiness," "the illusion-like mandala offering of bliss and emptiness," or the "the suchness mandala offering." Here is how a beginner like me performs this mandala offering. Bring to mind the fact that all the visualized elements of mandala offering are nothing but constructs of you, the practitioner's, own mind; nothing exists objectively as an independent entity from the side of the designative bases. Generating a vibrant awareness of this fact, you then recall the experience of bliss engendered by yourself as the deity entering into union with consort, and you thus generate the gnosis of bliss and emptiness. It is this gnosis of bliss and emptiness that is imagined in the form of the mandala. Then you offer it.

Next, as you recite the lines "**Across a wish-granting sea of offerings actually arrayed and imagined**," imagine that all the offerings you have actually laid out and those you have mentally conjured [407] turn into clouds of Samantabhadra offerings in the following manner.

A wish-granting lake resting on a base of gold sand emerges with water that is excellent in eight ways and is perfumed by the fragrances of all sorts of medicinal incense. In this lake, all your offerings—actual and mentally conjured—appear in the form of breathtaking lotus trees made of the seven types of gems, each with a thousand petals, thus turning the lake into a lotus grove. From each of these lotuses radiates 36,000 beams of light, and at the tip of each beam are limitless offerings. Imagine too that this lake is adorned with all kinds of flowers—blue lotuses (*utpala*), water lilies (*kumuda*), white lotuses, hibiscus flowers (*mandarava*), and so on—which are in reality the virtues of you and other sentient beings, both ordinary and ārya beings. On the shores of the lake are trees of the seven types of gems with all sorts of gems dangling from them. These trees represent the wisdom acquired in all three times by you and other sentient beings, both ordinary and ārya beings, through extensive study of the great treatises. Imagine that the ascertainments [you and others have] gained on the topics of study through limitless avenues of reasoning appear in the form of branches with dense foliage of hundreds of thousands of leaves. At the tips of these branches are common attainments such as the three precious trainings and uncommon attainments of the yogas of tantra's two stages, all appearing in the form of fruits rich in diverse colors, scents, and tastes hanging from the branches. Imagine that these trees emit clouds of Samantabhadra offerings. This is how you offer your own practice in accord with the words of the text [of *Offering to the Guru*].

There are also numerous other ways to offer your realization, such as transforming your body into a celestial mansion made of the seven types of gems and then imagining within it all kinds of offerings representing all your higher qualities, such as your wisdom of learning, and offering these to your guru, who is residing inside your heart shaped like an eight-petaled lotus. The teacher said that offering your practice and imagining your guru becoming pleased has special significance. Of these various offerings just described, except for some such as the inner objects of everyday enjoyment and the inner sensory objects, [408] most are offerings associated with the vase empowerment.[926]

Next, the offering associated with the secret empowerment is presented in the lines "**Libation of Chinese tea with saffron hue and a sweet aroma**" up to **"I offer seas of nectar purified, transformed, and increased."** When you recite these lines, imagine offering goddesses emerge from your heart, their right hand bearing the individual offering substances of water for drinking and so on and their left hand holding a skull cup white outside and red inside, with which they scoop up nectar and offer it to the merit-field figures. In this way, you make the *inner offering*. The two lines that begin "Libation of Chinese tea with saffron hue and a sweet aroma" indicate that the custom of this sacred Ganden (Geluk) lineage, which accords great importance to the precepts and boundaries of the morality of individual liberation vows that is the root of the Buddha's teaching, black tea is preferred as the substance of the inner offering. So, this particular offering [of black tea] can be seen as belonging to the class of inner offering. Alternatively, it could be considered part of the outer offering with the understanding that this special tea, not found even in the noble land of India, is offered as a separate article.

[Note:] When performing an actual ceremony of feast (*tsok*) offering to the guru or when [*Offering to the Guru*] is chanted as part of a longevity ceremony, then at this point, before reciting "Libation of Chinese tea with saffron hue and a sweet aroma," tea can be offered [to the guru and the congregation] and the tea ceremony prayer known as "My body appearing in the form of a deity"[927] can be chanted. This is a custom I have witnessed.

At this point of having made the inner offering, there is the custom of performing the tsok feast ceremony. To prepare and perform this tsok ritual, the tradition is to first create a large ritual cake made of dough enriched with the three types of sweets,[928] melted butter, and alcohol. The cake is in the shape of a dome like a full breast with its tip slightly elongated. It is colored with dark red melted butter and studded with discs of white butter all around its main body. At the top as well as on the upper part of the body, it is decorated with white butter latticework. The tip of the cake is pierced by the thin end of a flat length of wood on which are sculpted in butter a crescent, a dot in the shape of a jewel adorned on the sides with a wavy pattern symbolizing light rays, at the middle of which is a *nada* squiggle with three bends. [409] Given there is the custom also of creating a separate first-portion tsok cake, make a separate smaller tsok cake whose shape and decorations resemble the large one. If a large-scale tsok ceremony must be performed, you could have many tsok cakes made in the shape of large bricks and smear them with dark red melted butter. These brick cakes can be stacked up, and on top you can place the large dome-shaped tsok cake and the other substances. There are other customs that involve creating round, square, crescent, and triangular dough cakes, placing the actual tsok cake on top of this, and decorating the tip of the tsok cake with a half vajra and its side with butter garlands and half garlands. The teacher said that these are the customs of other [traditions] such as Bönpos and Nyingmapas and should not be mixed here in this tradition of the Ganden lineage.

Consecrate [the tsok cake] the same way the inner offering was consecrated. The only difference is that from the boiling nectar, you imagine limitless offering articles appearing—the eight auspicious symbols, the seven precious royal emblems, and so on—filling the entirety of space, the teacher said. Even though it is tsok offering, if it happens to be the afternoon, it is inappropriate for us monastics to heedlessly consume it on the excuse that it is tsok offering. With this in mind, the teacher said, Nāgārjuna explained that the rite of offering tsok should be made with substances suitable to the time of the day as well.[929]

If you wish to perform the inner tsok offering ritual, imagine that your body of flesh, bones, and so on is white and radiant, and in front of it visualize, from *yaṃ* wind, from *raṃ* fire, and from *aḥ* emerge three human heads the size of mountains, forming a tripod. Imagine then your skull cup, white outside and red inside, is freshly removed and placed on this tripod. Imagine placing inside this your entire body, which is then sliced by a cleaver into small pieces. Wind stirs and ignites the fire, causing what is inside the skull to boil, and the steam emerging from this attracts from the ten directions the blessings of the buddhas and bodhisattvas, which then fuse into a single taste with the nectar inside the skull cup. Then imagine making offerings [to the merit-field figures].

As to the secret-suchness tsok offering, this involves offering the tsok of indivisible bliss and emptiness, [410] and the way to do this is the same as what was explained in the context of the mandala offering.

Next is the offering associated with the wisdom-gnosis empowerment, which is presented in the lines that include "**splendidly lovely with the glory of youth.**" When you recite these lines imagine that emanating from your heart, as described above, are consorts lotus-like, conch-like, elephant-like, and deer-like, all of them bearing the glory five sense objects and expert in the sixty-four arts of love, such as embracing and kissing.[930] They are adorned with various jewel ornaments such as pearl necklaces and are clad in robes of silk. Imagine countless such goddesses, such as the *field-born*, who reside in the twenty-four places of siddhas, the *innate-born*, who have attained the innate nature, and in particular the *mantra-born* of the generation-stage.[931] Imagine offering them to the guru and meditation deities, following which they dissolve into Vajradhātvīśvarī, the consort of the gnosis being at the guru's heart. Visualize [the gnosis being and consort] entering into union, and imagine that the union of innate bliss and emptiness arises within them. Since all the deities of the retinue share the same mental continuum as guru Vajradhara, the teacher said, you should imagine all the deities experiencing the union of bliss and emptiness. Imagine that owing to the great compassion and power of the guru and the deities, you, the practitioner, experience similar innate bliss and emptiness.

Next is the offering associated with the suchness word empowerment, which the text presents in the lines "**great gnosis of innate bliss free of obscuration inseparable**" and so on. When you recite these lines, imagine you offering to the guru the four types of consorts, engendering within him innate great bliss, which is free of all the obscurations and is fused into a single taste with emptiness. Imagine the two things coalescing, the all-empty clear light and the illusory body—namely, the gnosis body of saṃbhogakāya of mere wind and mind in union with a consort that is its own natural reflection. Imagine that the great compassion and power of the guru and the deities cause you to actualize such a union in your own mental continuum.

Although these offerings of outer, outer, secret, and suchness, as described above, can be found in the texts of Guhyasamāja tantra, primarily they represent the method of making offerings according to Cakrasaṃvara tantra. My sublime teacher, the glorious being, [411] said that if you practice this [*Offering to the Guru*] in such a way that the generation stage is done according to Vajrabhairava, the offerings according to Cakrasaṃvara, and the completion stage according to Guhyasamāja, this would ensure that your practice proceeds in a way that the three—Cakrasaṃvara, Guhyasamāja, and Vajrabhairava—are engaged in an integrated way, not in isolation from one another. During the preliminary practice and the later uncommon meditations associated with mahāmudrā, you can generate yourself into a deity based on any of the three principal meditation deities. But even still, if you can generate yourself as a deity in a way where all the key points of the generation stage of Vajrabhairava are present and you can also correlate the later completion-stage elements with Guhyasamāja tantra, this would be the optimal approach.

Next, as you recite the two lines "**I offer varieties of excellent medicines that cure the afflictions and the 404 diseases,**" imagine sending goddesses from your heart who bear, in containers made of all sorts of precious substances, varieties of medicines capable of curing 404 diseases—medicinal powders, pills, distilled syrups, medicinal roots, and plants. As you offer these to the guru and deities, imagine the power [of these medicines] pacifies all the illnesses afflicting the bodies and minds of sentient beings.

By reciting the two lines "**And to please you, as I offer myself as your servant: pray sustain me as your subject as long as space remains,**" you are supplicating the guru by stating the following:

> From today forward, I offer my body, speech, and mind as servants to you, O guru and meditation deities, to help fulfill your plan to secure the welfare of other sentient beings. Pray accept them. Since you will now own and be the master of my body, speech, and mind, I pledge them to you and will not allow them to be damaged. Bless me, guru and deities, that I may be able to do this.

As to the phrase "to please you," if you use your body, speech, and mind to harm sentient beings, clearly the guru and meditation deities will not be pleased. In contrast, if you use them to benefit sentient beings, this will clearly please them. So this phrase is your pledge to do so. The teacher said there is an auspicious significance in training your mind from right now in offering your body, speech, and mind to the guru.

At this point [in chanting the root text], you could affirm your observance of the vows. For this, with lines "I go for refuge to the Three Jewels"[932] and so on, [412] uphold both the aspiring awakening mind accompanied with making a pledge and the engaging awakening mind rooted in a vow to train in the [bodhisattva] deeds of the six perfections. Then, reciting the lines "All buddhas and the bodhisattvas"[933] and so on, uphold, with the thought aspiring to attain the full enlightenment of buddhahood, the fourteen root precepts and the eight heavy ones, the tantric precepts common to all five buddha families, and the nineteen commitments such as those pertaining to eating and interaction without any discrimination and until you arrive at the heart of enlightenment. Some assert that the four lines beginning "Just as for the guardians of the three times"[934] constitute the ceremony of generating the awakening mind prior to taking the tantric vows. The teacher said, however, that such a statement simply underlines the fact that the awakening mind must be part of the motivation for taking the tantric vows; it is not correct to treat this stanza as an actual ceremony for generating the awakening mind. Be that as it may, upholding the vows here does not occasion any new set of vows; nor does it restore damaged precepts. It does, however, enhance the vows you already have, so doing this would be part of your offering of meditative practice, the teacher said. Some who may be masters of mere words understand this ceremony of upholding the vows to be part of the practice of confession and purification.[935]

The limb of confession

To engage in confession practice, you can perform here the hundred-syllable-mantra meditation and recitation.[936] For this contemplate how the nonvirtues and downfalls committed in the past give rise to, as their observable effects, the problems that assail you in this life and, as their fruitional effects, the sufferings of the lower realms. Contemplate how their experience-concordant and act-concordant effects also assail you in this life. In particular, their act-concordant effects lead you to gather further negative karma uncontrollably, and this then leads to further observable and other effects in sequence. In this way, contemplate how the wheel of karma and its effects keeps turning. Based on such contemplation, generate thoughts of remorse, as though you had ingested poison. This then is the *power of thorough repudiation*.

The *power of the support* involves cultivating the conviction that it is Guru Vajrasattva who has the unobstructed power and ability to purify such karma and its effects and, with such thought, placing your trust in him; supplicating him so that your karma and downfalls may be purified; [413] then, based on your experience, contemplating how other sentient beings share the same situation; and on this basis, generating the awakening mind inspired by compassion.

The *power of engaging the antidotes* is to perform fervent visualizations of nectar descending, maintaining the awareness of how the three spheres [of the act of purification] are devoid of intrinsic existence in a way that is not mere imagination but a powerful understanding, and reciting the hundred-syllable mantra.

The *power of turning away from faults* means imagining that by engaging thusly, your negative karma and downfalls are purified and then resolving to never in the future, even at the cost of your life, engage in those acts that can be refrained from permanently, and even with respect to those that are likely to recur because of karma and the afflictions, to guard against them even if that must be maintained moment by moment.

If you repeat the hundred-syllable mantra on the basis of the convergence of these four powers, it has been established through experience that after repeating it for several tens of thousands of times, you will observe certain signs that your negative karma has been purified. Do not become fixated on being able to say, "I have completed a hundred thousand recitations of the hundred-syllable mantra!"

Regarding the final power here, since we pledge to never commit negative karma in the future, those of us with strong afflictions and weak heedfulness risk incurring the misdeed of telling a lie. But if there is not even a semblance of such a resolve of restraint, then a key element of the four powers will be missing. This would make it difficult to purify our negative karma. So in relation to those negative actions that we can refrain from entirely, we should pledge to guard against them even at the cost of our life, and in relation to those likely to recur owing to the force of our karma and afflictions, we should pledge to guard against them at the cost of our life even if it is only on a moment-by-moment basis. Our supreme guru Jé Tsongkhapa stated that this is the instruction according to the noble Kātyāyana, and the teacher said we should follow accordingly.[937]

If you wish to perform the Samayavajra mantra repetition, as for the rest of the elements, they can be done easily by following its *sādhana* rite.[938] Here too, as above, cultivate the power of thorough repudiation, and then visualize that light rays emanate from the heart of the commitment being at the deity's heart. At the tips of these light rays are countless Samayavajras, who accomplish the welfare of sentient beings, and emanating goddesses bearing all kinds of offerings, who honor the buddhas and bodhisattvas. Then imagine drawing forth from them their blessings of body, speech, and mind in the form of nectar, [414] which dissolves into the mantra circle together with its central seed syllable standing atop a crossed vajra at Samayavajra's heart. Streams of nectar descend from the letters of the mantra and fill the circular hub of the crossed vajra, causing the nectar to flow through the four tips of the crossed vajra and then fill Samayavajra's entire body. Nectars then descend from the point where the deity and his consort are joined in sexual union; they flow through your body down to the tip of your toes. As the nectar fills up your body, imagine all your negative karmas along with their potential effects float up in the form of smoky and charcoal-like liquids. Pushed up in this way, these smoky and charcoal-like liquids exit your body visibly through the openings of your sense organs as well as through your pores. Then imagine that your negative karma and infractions of precepts are purified. This [visualization] is part of an oral teaching, the teacher said.

Next, recite the specific stanzas for rectifying the three categories of vows, and then chant the *Confession of Downfalls* preceded by the verse "O Conqueror, protector of the world"[939] and so on. When you chant the *Confession of Downfalls* sutra, ensure the presence of the power of thorough repudiation by contemplating in depth how negative karma and the downfalls prevent the arising of knowledge of the scriptures and realizations and how, in the future, they cast you into the lower realms. Based on this, supplicate the thirty-five buddhas of confession fervently from the depth of your heart to help purify your negative karma and downfalls. The teacher said that as you utter the name of each of the buddhas, visualize the invocation and the descent of nectars. Chant this in conjunction with as many sets of a hundred prostrations you can manage.

These, then, constitute the *instruction on purifying negative karma, such as through the hundred-syllable mantra*. This is one of four great instructions that constitute the preliminary to engaging in guided meditative practice of mahāmudrā.[940] In addition, there is the *instruction on going for refuge and generating the awakening mind*, the door to enter the doctrine, which takes place at the time of going for refuge. The *instruction on guru yoga*, the door that enables swift entry of the blessings, is implemented when visualizing the guru in the merit-field tree, contemplating the benefits of honoring the guru, honoring him through prostrations, offerings, and so on, and supplicating the guru based on contemplating the benefits of relying on the guru and the faults of not doing so. The *instruction on offering the mandala to gather merit* is practiced when performing the mandala offering. Among these, the tradition is to repeat the mandala offering, the hundred-syllable mantra, and full-body prostrations each one hundred thousand times.

Next, in relation to the lines in the text "**Whatever unwholesome acts of nonvirtue . . . since beginningless time**" and so on, I could say a lot about how to ensure the convergence of the four powers and so forth, but I will not elaborate further. [415]

The limb of rejoicing

Next, rejoicing is presented in the lines "**Though phenomena lack the signs of intrinsic nature**" and so on. For this contemplate as follows:

> Even though there is no intrinsically real virtue or nonvirtue, just like virtuous and negative actions in a dream, virtue and negative

> karma do nevertheless arise in specific forms when the designative bases join in an adventitious manner with their designations. So just as other beings, both ordinary and ārya beings, accumulate such virtuous karma, how I wish I too may gather such karma for the benefit of all sentient beings. O guru deity, bless me that I may be able to do this.

In this way supplicate [the guru]. The practice of rejoicing in the above manner was expounded by our supreme guru Jé Tsongkhapa, interpreting the intent of the precious Perfection of Wisdom sutras, as the magical method to skillfully gather great stores of merit with minimal effort.[941] When you rejoice in the virtuous deeds of those at your own level of mental development or below, you will obtain merit equal to theirs. In contrast, when you rejoice in the virtuous deeds of those above your level, the merit obtained will not equal theirs, the teacher said. The phrase "like a dream" refers to the fact that even though no virtuous or nonvirtuous act exists [in actuality] in a dream, by rejoicing in [the dream action], one does accrue meritorious or demeritorious karma. Likewise, even though neither virtue nor nonvirtue exist on the ultimate level, on the conventional level, merit or demerits are enhanced by rejoicing in virtuous and negative karma accumulated. This is attested by the *Ornament of Realization* and its commentaries.[942] Similarly, just as no one can deny that a beautiful woman in a dream does not exist in reality, fools who dream of such a beautiful woman still lust after her. Likewise, even though there is no virtue or negative karma in the ultimate sense and the karmic act committed has already ceased before its effect comes into being, no one can deny that on the conventional level happiness and suffering arise in future lives from virtuous and negative karma. This is attested by *Entering the Middle Way* and its autocommentary.[943] If we understand these points, we will develop conviction from the depth of our mind.

The limb of requesting to turn the wheel of Dharma

Here, when you recite the lines **"Cumulating a hundred thousand clouds of knowledge and love"** and so on, imagine multiplying your body into countless bodies, some carrying white right-swirling conches, others [416] holding golden wheels with a thousand spokes. Imagine offering these to the merit-field figures and supplicating them with the thought that all good things, every benefit and happiness of every being, including me—the arising of what has not yet arisen, the enduring of what has already arisen, and the enhancement of what is enduring—all this depends on the sublime Dharma alone. With such thoughts, imagine making the request "Pray turn the wheel of Dharma" and having your request delightfully accepted. The teacher said doing this is profoundly auspicious.

At this point in the text [of *Offering to the Guru*], I have witnessed that it is the custom, when the context is a long-life prayer ceremony, to chant the supplication prayer "I supplicate the gurus"[944] and so forth that is associated with the longevity prayer invoking the ḍākinīs. Then we recite the prayers requesting the turning of the wheel of Dharma correlated to the five buddha families with the lines "O Losang, primordial buddha Vajradhara," and so forth, followed by performance of the mandala offering and the reading of the mandala offering statement.[945]

The limb of entreating not to enter nirvana

Next, when you recite the lines "**Although your vajra body . . . has neither death nor birth**," and so forth three times (repeating three times is necessary only during a long-life ceremony),[946] imagine multiplying your body into countless bodies bearing jewel thrones, each hoisted by eight embedded lions and adorned with a crossed-vajra. Imagine offering these to the guru and the merit-field figures. Then make the supplication:

> Although your pure illusory vajra body does not change by way of birth and death, that actual [true] body is not perceptible to us beings. So please do not withdraw your commitment being body, the coarse physical body within which resides your vajra body, which resembles a jewel casket. Instead, remain [with us] enduringly and firmly.

Imagine that as you supplicate this way, your appeal is delightfully accepted. This is profoundly auspicious, and it can be a principal ritual for enhancing your own longevity as well, the teacher said.

The limb of dedication

Next, with respect to dedication, the text reads "**The collection of thoroughly white virtues thus created**" and so on. When you recite these lines, contemplate the following:

> For the sake of all mother sentient beings, I will do my very best to attain the state of buddhahood. [417] And all the virtues I have gathered for that purpose, especially through engaging in the preliminary, the main, and concluding practices of guru-yoga meditation—as well as whatever heaps of positive karma that may have been created through all times by others, both ordinary and ārya beings, connected with the three basic sources[947]—it is their very lack of intrinsic existence that makes them capable of all transactions and activity. Therefore may all beings, me included, be sustained throughout all lives by triply kind gurus, and may we all quickly attain the state of Vajradhara, the true union.

In this way, supplicate and make aspirations.

The extent to which the roots of virtue can be enhanced when they are sustained by the awakening mind throughout all three stages—preparation, the actual act, and completion—is the extent that the afflictions are robbed of the power to destroy the roots of virtue. The teacher made this point by citing the sutra's analogy of how a single ounce of mercury that has the appearance of gold can transform a thousand ounces of base metal into a thousand ounces of gold. In contrast, the entire thousand ounces of base metal do not have the power to exhaust that single ounce of mercury. In the same manner, the capacity of all the roots of virtue sustained by the awakening mind and dedicated toward the attainment of unexcelled enlightenment to produce their effects cannot be destroyed. That this is so is stated in the sutras and in *Guide to the Bodhisattva Way*, which give the analogy of how a drop of water cast into an ocean does not cease to exist so long as the ocean does not dry up, and how an excellent and mature tree does not become depleted as a result of bearing fruit.[948] Furthermore, neither *Entering the Middle Way* nor *Guide to the Bodhisattva Way*, when identifying which roots of virtue can be destroyed by anger, mention the roots of virtue sustained by the factor of wisdom. This indicates that this practice of dedicating roots of virtue toward the attainment of enlightenment by sealing them with the awakening mind and the view [of emptiness] is a skillful means to ensure that the roots of virtue do not get squandered.[949]

Here in the text is the phrase "I am never separated from and am sustained"; this indicates that you are praying to make sure [your roots of virtue] become the causes for being sustained by your triply kind guru, from the beginning up to the advanced stages [of the path] he himself has traversed, and for being led to the path that is complete and error free, allowing you to attain the supreme state [of buddhahood]. The power of the words "be sustained" is indeed great.

Next, perform an extensive mandala offering and make the following supplication: [418]

> Bless me: (1) May all false thoughts—from initial disrespect for the spiritual teacher up to delusory dualistic perceptions—come to cease. (2) May all the stages of the path—from strong devotion and reverence for my spiritual teacher up to the union of no-more learning—quickly arise in my mental continuum. (3) And may outer and inner adverse conditions and all obstacles be pacified.

Fervently make this supplication for three important aims three times.

Whatever your aims, the purification of negative karma, which constitutes adverse conditions, and the accumulation of merit, which constitutes favorable conditions, are crucially important. Therefore, in both the sutras and the tantras, the blessed Buddha taught limitless means to purify [nonvirtue] and accumulate virtue. And this seven-limb practice is indeed the most excellent distillation of the essence of all these methods. These seven limbs can be further condensed into three—accumulation [of virtue], purification [of nonvirtue], and enhancement [of the roots of virtue]. These three, in turn, can be subsumed into the two: accumulation and purification. Finally, all seven limbs can be subsumed into the single practice of enhancing the roots of virtue. For example, in his *Verses on the Compendium of Training*, Śāntideva says, "Just as it says in the rite of the *Vows of Good Conduct*, strive in prostrations and so forth,"[950] indicating that the seven limbs are a principal method for enhancing one's roots of virtue.

Not only that, the teacher spoke of how the blessed Buddha, our most compassionate Teacher, himself engaged in the preliminary practice of seven limbs and of how, in the context of the limb of dedication, he brought to mind all the amazing deeds of the bodhisattvas as objects of admiration and engaged in their practices on this basis. He spoke of how Ārya Nāgārjuna and Āryaśūra engaged in the practice of seven limbs as preliminaries and brought, as part of their dedication, the entire Mahayana path and its result as their objects of aspiration, and engaged in practice on that basis; how, in particular, they practiced by choosing the expansive thought and action of exchanging self and others as their objects of aspiration. He also spoke of how Śāntideva, in particular, prefaced by the seven limbs, undertook his practice by subsuming the entire Mahayana path into two topics—generating the awakening mind as the basis of the bodhisattva deeds and engaging in the bodhisattva deeds. This seven-limb practice is thus indeed a most excellent summation of all the key points of Mahayana practice. [419] Therefore, to someone with a feeble intellect like me, it brings deep joy when I can engender understanding of even this seven-limb practice alone.

Supplication

Supplicating with deep devotion and reverence

Offering to the Guru says:

> **Then, as stated in the *Vajrapāṇi Empowerment Tantra*:**
>
> > **Seize on your guru's qualities**
> > **and never seize on his faults.**
> > **If you seize on his qualities, you will obtain siddhis;**
> > **if you seize on his faults, you won't obtain siddhis.**
>
> **Apply mindfulness and meta-awareness repeatedly with the thought "I will not allow any thoughts seizing on faults to arise." Contemplate well the benefits of relying on the guru and the disadvantages of not thus relying as explained in the sutras, the tantras, and the sayings of the sublime ones. In particular, view your root guru as the embodiment of the infallible refuge, the Three Jewels, the mere hearing of whose name causes the terror of the lower realms to be robbed away, the mere thought of whom dispels the sufferings of samsara, and when it is appealed to, all higher attainments are granted with ease. With total trust, not placing your hope anywhere else, supplicate fervently many times by reciting the Miktsema and other prayers.**

As this states, these are the benefits of relying on the spiritual teacher: You become closer to the state of buddhahood; the buddhas are pleased; you do not fall into the lower realms; in all your lives you are not deprived of meeting a spiritual teacher; you are not easily overpowered by afflictions and negative karma; you do not act contrary to the bodhisattva deeds; because of your constant mindfulness of the bodhisattva deeds, your virtuous qualities become ever more enhanced; all your immediate and long-term aims are realized according to your wishes; your increase of virtuous thoughts and actions gives you the ability to accomplish others' welfare; and even the negative karma whose effects are likely to be experienced in the lower realms are cleansed by ripening earlier in the form of minor physical and mental ailments in this life or even in dreams. [420] The teacher said that [the merit of] properly relying on the guru for even one morning can outshine the roots of virtue gathered by making offerings to countless buddhas. Here, contemplate:

> In brief, great waves of merit are gathered, powerful karmic obscurations are naturally cleansed, and both common and uncommon siddhis are attained. Such benefits as these, inconceivable and inexpressible benefits, have been declared in the sutras and tantras, not just once but repeatedly. Accordingly, those authentic scholar-siddhas who relied perfectly on their spiritual teacher, such as the bodhisattva Sadāprarudita, Maṇibhadra, Tilopa, Nāropa, and Milarepa, experienced these benefits in obvious ways. In the same manner, I too will engage in this practice of relying on the spiritual teacher through powerful waves of diligence and striving without regard for even my body and life, which is the profound method hailed in numerous sutras and tantras. It is the excellent path traversed by all the buddhas of the three times, the heart practice of all the masters of both India and Tibet, the hand that gathers vast collections of merit and wisdom, the great fire at the end of the world that burns away all negative karma and downfalls, and the iron hook that swiftly draws forth the siddhis. O guru deity, bless me that I may be able to do this.

As for the faults of not relying [on the spiritual teacher], contemplate:

> Should there be a breach in my reliance on the spiritual teacher, in this birth my life will be taken from me by epidemics, by diseases like leprosy, by poison and weapons, or by malevolent forces and false evil spirits. After my death I will fall into the hells; or if I manage to avoid this, I will be born in a place where even

> the name *guru* is unheard of; or if I manage to meet a guru, my past habitual conduct will cause my relation to the guru to be breached. Such varieties of grave consequences, powerfully producing their fruitional effects and forcefully obstructing the birth of positive qualities, have been declared [in the sutras and the tantras]. So, let alone actually committing such grave negative karma, even if my life is at risk, may I not witness or engage in such acts even in my dreams. As for my past failure to properly rely on the spiritual teacher, O glorious gurus—embodiments of kindness and compassion—[421] I confess these in your presence and express my remorse. In the future, I will not engage in negative action even if it costs me my life. Since positive qualities immediately degenerate and faults increase if I fall under the influence of negative teachers and evil friends, ruining the fate of both this present and the future life, I will make sure I do not fall under their influence even in my dreams. I will strive with all my efforts to be joyfully sustained by qualified sublime gurus.

Then recite the supplication prayers for the gurus of the near-transmission lineage specific to this [guru-yoga] instruction.[951] When doing this guru yoga in combination with mahāmudrā practice, the teacher said that we should visualize that all the gurus of the near-transmission lineage who have appeared in human form—from the omniscient Jé Tsongkhapa up to our own triply kind root guru—are themselves in essence but appear in the form of Mañjuśrī, and make your supplication on this basis. Mañjuśrī advised our exalted guru that, before engaging in analysis of the view, he needed to do three things in combination: (1) make fervent supplication on the basis of viewing the guru and meditation deity as indivisible, (2) strive fervently over a prolonged period in the practices of gathering virtue and purifying negative karma, and (3) carefully examine the great treatises. Of these three, the advice about supplicating the guru and meditation deity needs to be put into practice here in this guru-yoga instruction in the context of supplicating the gurus of the near-transmission lineage. Although, in general, there are numerous meditation deities, the meditation deity referred to in the phrase "viewing the guru and meditation deity as indivisible" must be understood to be Mañjuśrī, the deity of wisdom. This then is the intent [behind visualizing all the gurus in the form of Mañjuśrī].

Next, with regard to supplicating the [guru deity] and opening his heart to you through repeating his name mantra, this needs to be done in this particular guru-yoga instruction on the basis of repeating the prayer known as the "nine-lined Miktsema of the Ensa tradition," which begins "You are the sovereign sage Vajradhara, the source of all siddhis."[952] The teacher said that the regular Miktsema will not be adequate here. As the mahāmudrā root text says, "After performing fervent supplications a hundred times or so, dissolve the guru into you."[953] [422] When doing this guru-yoga practice in the context of mahāmudrā meditation, you should repeat this [Miktsema] supplication prayer at least 108 times.

There are numerous rites based on this [Miktsema] name mantra[954] supplication prayer involving slight modifications in visualization. Whether these various rites, such as pacification [increase, influence, and wrath],[955] based on applying the name mantra and its associated visualization are successful depends primarily on faith. And there are three avenues for cultivating such faith: contemplating the *outer aspect*, drawing similarities; the *inner aspect*, contemplating the possession of enlightened qualities; and the *secret aspect*, viewing the guru as indivisible from the meditation deity.[956] For the first, contemplate:

> Of all the bodhisattvas, Avalokiteśvara is peerless with respect to compassion; of all the bodhisattvas, the revered Mañjuśrī is peerless with respect to wisdom; and of all the bodhisattvas, Vajrapāṇi is peerless with respect to ability, power, and energy. Likewise, in this Land of Snows Tibet, among all the masters accomplished in learning and attainment, the omniscient Tsongkhapa alone is peerless with respect to the trio of wisdom, compassion, and energy and the trio of exposition, debate, and composition, not only in specific domains but in all aspects. So I supplicate you, my glorious and sublime guru who is in the form of the revered Losang Drakpa, most respectfully with my three doors. Pray sustain me at all times with your great compassion.

In this way, make the supplication. For the second, contemplate:

> Whatever qualities of compassion are found in all the conquerors are present in the heart of Avalokiteśvara, and there is not the slightest difference between Ārya Avalokiteśvara and the omniscient Tsongkhapa with respect to the quality of their compassion.

> Whatever qualities of wisdom are found in all the conquerors are present in the mind of Ārya Mañjuśrī, and there is not the slightest difference between Ārya Mañjuśrī and the omniscient Tsongkhapa with respect to the quality of their wisdom. Whatever qualities of ability, power, [423] and energy are found in all the conquerors are present in the mind of the glorious Vajrapāṇi, and there is not the slightest difference between the glorious Vajrapāṇi and the omniscient Tsongkhapa with respect to their qualities of ability, power, and energy. So I supplicate you, my glorious and sublime guru who is in the form of the revered Losang Drakpa, the embodiment of wisdom, compassion, and energy of all the conquerors, most respectfully with my three doors. Pray sustain me at all times with your great compassion.

In this way, make the supplication. For the third, contemplate:

> The revered Avalokiteśvara is the concentration of the compassion of all the conquerors into a single body manifesting as a meditation deity. That my glorious and sublime guru, the revered Losang Drakpa, is identical in nature to Ārya Avalokiteśvara was indicated to his mother with repeated signs.[957] The revered Mañjuśrī is the concentration of the wisdom of all the conquerors into a single body manifesting as a meditation deity. That my glorious and sublime guru, the revered Losang Drakpa, is identical in nature with Ārya Mañjuśrī has been revealed by numerous buddhas and bodhisattvas; in particular, there were clear signs in his mother's dreams and elsewhere connected with this. The revered Vajrapāṇi is the concentration of the ability, power, and energy of all the conquerors into a single entity manifesting as a meditation deity. That my glorious and sublime guru, the revered Losang Drakpa, is identical in nature with the glorious Vajrapāṇi was clearly indicated to his father in a dream with special signs. So, I supplicate you, my glorious and sublime guru in the form of the revered Losang Drakpa, the embodiment of the wisdom, compassion, and energy of all the conquerors, most respectfully with my three doors. [424] Pray sustain me at all times with your great compassion.

In this way, make the supplication. These three forms of supplication are called the "outer cultivation," the "inner cultivation," and the "secret cultivation of the revered Tsongkhapa."

Now to apply this supplication to the activity of pacification, for example, make the following supplication fervently from the bone of your heart:

> In particular, I supplicate you so that all the negative karma, obscurations, illness, malevolent harms which myself and so and so [adding the name of the person(s) for whose sake you are performing the rite] wish to become pacified be pacified and cleansed. Pray perform your enlightened action so that they become pacified.

Also, the third chapter of the *Kṛṣṇayamāri Tantra* says:

> If the mantra spells taught by
> the gods and rishis do not deceive,
> then that the rites of secret mantra
> uttered by one free of attachment deceives—
> this has never happened in the past
> and will not do so in future.[958]

As this states, if it can be observed that the mantra spells created by attachment-laden mundane gods like Brahmā, Indra, and so on as well as by celestial and human rishis who appease these mundane gods can bear results, what need is there to speak of the mantra uttered by the great rishi the blessed Losang Drakpa—who is free of the attachment of the three realms—being undeniably capable of producing its effects. In this way, cultivate faith in the guru and develop powerful faith in the form of conviction in the efficacy of the rites taught by the guru; these two are, in fact, the principal causes for the success of the rites.

Not only that, when you carefully probe how the three factors—the rite itself, the performance of the rite, and you as the rite's performer—appear to your mind, there is no choice but to perceive them as existing independently of each other and in their own right. Once you have correctly identified how this object of negation appears to the mind, contemplate how, if the object, the rite itself, were to exist in its own right, independently of the performance of the rite and the rite's performer, it would be an object of action with no doer. Similarly, if the performance and the performer were to exist independently of the object of action, the person would also become an actor with no object of action. This would mean that everything, those that are and are not agents of action, could become agents of action. So, bringing reasoning such as this to bear into the depths of your mind, engender the ascertainment that nothing in the three spheres of action exists objectively in its own right. Now, it is precisely because nothing in the three spheres of action exists independently of the others [425] that all [cause and effect] functions can be posited purely on the basis of the three spheres being mutually dependent realities and designations. In fact, the blessed Buddha himself frequently states how from such and such [a cause], such and such effect will come about.[959] So you should proclaim the power of truth: "May the effects of my karma soon come to be." And also view all sentient beings, who are the objects of your action, as your cherished loved ones, the source of benefit and happiness for you in all your lives, seeing them as no different from the guru and the meditation deities in being like wish-fulfilling jewels, granting you benefits, happiness, and all perfect factors of goodness in all contexts—ground, path, and result. Forsake yourself and cherish others as dear, do whatever you can to bring about their immediate welfare, and endure hardships with the ultimate aim of leading them to unadulterated benefit and happiness. Consider these contemplations to be the principal conditions for accomplishing your various rites—those of pacification and so forth. Again, the third chapter of *Kṛṣṇayamāri Tantra* says:

> Your mind becomes the two precious things;
> through these two precious things, rites are accomplished.[960]

And:

> For the wise one versed in the inconceivable
> ultimate nature, free of doubt,
> the siddhis are close.[961]

Having supplicated in the above ways, imagine that from the heart of triple-being guru appear countless white goddesses bearing white vases filled with nectar the color of the moon. They perform ablutions on you and on the person(s) for whose sake the rite [of pacification] is being performed, who you imagine are seated on white moon discs. Imagine that this causes all your negative karma, obscurations, illnesses, and spirit harms to be cleansed and purified and that your body becomes clear as a crystal ball.

You can extend this same visualization to the other two more peaceful [rites]. For example, in the rite of *increase*, the goddess, vase, nectar, and the moon are yellow, and what are increased are life span, merit, material resources, and intellect. In the rite of *influence*, the goddesses are red and hold red vases filled with red nectar in their right hand and iron hooks in their left. Imagine, as they confer ablutions on the person for whose sake the rite is being performed, that all the person's thoughts involving a lack of faith in the Buddha's teaching and cynical attitudes are cleansed along with their causes.

Imagine, in particular, that all the bodily and verbal actions that others direct toward you, the practitioner, [426] motivated by distrust, ill will, vanity, and envy are cleansed and purified. Imagine that the red goddesses grab these beings by the heart with the iron hooks held in their left hands. They are set atop red moon discs, which are then propelled by the winds, thus moving them forth without their control. As they arrive in front of you, they become attracted to you, and with attitudes of interest, faith, and respect, their bodies turn red, and they pledge to do whatever you command them to. Imagine they prostrate to you, bowing their heads at your feet.

When performing the rite of *wrath*, imagine that from the heart of the triple-being guru emerge countless wrathful black Yamāntakas. Fierce and terrifying, they hold cleavers in their right hands and skull cups in their left. Imagine that they use the cleaver to cut and carve up the various parts of the body, such as the head and the limbs, of the recipient on whose behalf the rite is being performed, and they pull out his internal organs—his heart and so on. Imagine that every time the cleaver strikes the body of the recipient, instead of pain, he experiences a surge of the gnosis of bliss and emptiness. Splitting the recipient's body and mind, imagine the body parts sliced by the cleaver are then placed inside the skull cup; and by purifying, transforming, and multiplying, imagine the wrathful Yamāntakas consume the parts with blood dripping from their mouths. Imagine that the recipient's mind, now transformed into the nature of bliss and emptiness, departs to the ḍākinī land and connects with a new birth there. This visualization of imagining the recipient's mind, transformed into the nature of bliss and emptiness, departing to the ḍākinī land is not some anomalous fabrication; it is the intent of our supreme guru Jé Tsongkhapa as understood by Tsakho Ngawang Drakpa and articulated in a vajra song with the line "Split into a hundred pieces, *vajra muḥ*, proceed to the ḍākinī realm!"[962] This point needs to be borne in mind in the context of other wrathful rites as well.

With respect to rites of increase in particular, you should practice here the uncommon oral instruction conferred to the great siddha Pawo Dorjé by Mañjuśrī on how to enhance wisdom and intelligence:

> With body the *great*, and with speech the *clear*;
> the seeds the *swift*, and hand implements the *penetrating*;
> with scripture, the sword, and scripture and sword:
> teaching, debate, and composition.[963]

Were you to do this practice, then at the point where you have completed the supplications explained above, [427] contemplate the following: "In particular, grant your enlightened action so that I and all sentient beings generate intelligence that is great, clear, swift, and penetrating as well as the intelligence of exposition, debate, and composition."

As you make this supplication, imagine that from the heart of the triple-being guru emerge countless yellow goddesses holding yellow vases filled with yellow nectar. They confer ablutions on you and all sentient beings, cleansing in general the negative karma and obscurations gathered since beginningless time, especially those that obstruct the arising of vast wisdom. Imagine that your body and sentient beings' bodies become filled with nectar, and that from particles of the nectar in your body and that of all sentient beings appear Mañjuśrī forms of varying sizes—from larger ones the size of the tip of your thumb to smaller ones the sizes of yellow peas or beans, barley seeds, mustard seeds, or sesame seeds. They fill every part of your body and those of all sentient beings: the upper and the lower parts of the body, outer and inner, the flesh, the space between the skin and the flesh, and even the bone marrow and the bones. The lights emitted from these forms fill your entire body, and then you imagine that you have attained *great intelligence* capable of differentiating good and bad that is no different from that of the revered Mañjuśrī.

Imagine, similarly, that from the nectars appear *aḥ* syllables of varying sizes, filling up the interior of the body, and imagine attaining *clear intelligence* capable of differentiating the subtle points of what is to be adopted and what is to be rejected in a manner like separating the finest tips of the strands of *kuśa* grass.

Again, from the nectar appears the syllable *dhīḥ* of varying sizes, as before, filling up the interior of the body, and imagine attaining *swift intelligence* capable of preventing any distorted interpretation of the scriptures, whether from lack of understanding or distorted understanding, the instant it arises.

Again, from the nectar appear the two hand implements—a text and sword—of varying sizes, as before, filling up the interior of the body, and imagine attaining *penetrating intelligence* capable of engaging without obscuration the words and meanings of the scriptures that are subtle and hard to fathom.

Likewise, imagine from the nectars appear the texts on their own; sword wheels [428] with six spokes, their central hubs marked by letter *dhīḥ* and their six spokes by the six letters *oṃ a ra pa ca na*; and sets of text and sword together. All of these in varying sizes fill up every part of the body, and as the lights radiating from them permeate the inside of your body, imagine attaining extraordinary levels of the intelligence of *exposition, debate,* and *composition.*

These days, most people appear to be quite weak in their power of intellect, and even when they happen to develop their intellect to some degree, year by year, month by month, and even day by day, their intellect seems to wane. Especially when they reach advanced age, their intellect declines to the point where they cannot even remember the words and meanings of the scriptures. It is rare to find any who enhance their intellect over the years, months, and days. That is why I have written more extensively [about this practice of enhancing intelligence] here.

Aware that this guru-yoga instruction includes a unique oral teaching on how to enhance one's wisdom and intellect, my sublime and glorious teacher said that those of us who belong to the sacred Ganden lineage, if we repeat the *arapacana* mantra well when we are doing the Vajrabhairava sādhana[964] and repeat the Miktsema well when we are reciting *Offering to the Guru*, will have no difficulty at all in enhancing our intellect. On my part, I can confirm from my own personal experience how, as a result of engaging in my own small way with this [guru-yoga] practice and the instruction pertaining to the combined peaceful and wrathful deities of the Vajrabhairava sādhana, my own intellect has been modestly enhanced. So develop conviction in this instruction and put it into practice, and then see for yourself.

Perhaps you wish to perform the rite for making rain. If so, then after making supplications as described above, add this special supplication:

> In particular, pray perform your enlightened action of bringing down excellent streams of rain, rejuvenating the soil's potency and essence and increasing crop yields to save those beings in this

> world, specifically in this part of the world where people are tormented by the suffering of drought.

As you supplicate in this way, imagine that countless light rays emanate from the concentration being, the syllable *maṃ* marked by *hūṃ*, which is inside the *bindu* drop atop an orange *maṃ* radiating orange beams of light and standing on a sun disc at the heart of the triple-being guru. [429] At the tips of each of these light rays is an image of our exalted guru, all of which enter the bodies of the nāgas that reside in the various bodies of water—the seas, lakes, pools, brooks, ponds, and waterfalls—and nectars descend from the Tsongkhapa images within the bodies of the nāgas. Imagine that as a result, all the conditions that cause them harm—negative karma, obscuration, spells, and uncleanliness—as well as their harmful thoughts and actions performed out of anger, miserliness, and envy and the threats from birds of prey[965] and burning sands, all of these become pacified. Imagine that they enjoy perfect joy and happiness, and with fervent devotion in their hearts for our supreme guru, they say prayers to him, prostrate to him, make offerings to him, and circumambulate him. Again, imagine that our exalted guru resides at the crown of each sentient being and sends nectar down into their bodies, cleansing and purifying their negative karma and obscuration accumulated from beginningless time in general and, in particular, pacifying the negative karma liable to inflict on sentient beings the effect of famine owing to crop disease, drought, frost, and hail. Imagine that the sentient beings become enriched with the merit that allows them to enjoy the good fortune of soil with abundant potency, essence, and crops.

Again, imagine that countless light rays emanate from the letter *maṃ* marked by *hūṃ* at the heart of the triple-being guru and touch the non-human spirits, such as those of the eight categories of beings,[966] the wind gods in particular. Instantly, then and there, this pacifies any harmful thoughts and actions they might have; imagine that they work to create positive conditions. Imagine that light rays touch the non-sentient conditions that create droughts, and like a stack of hay bursting into flames, these are all incinerated without a trace. Once again, light rays touch all the nāgas, drawing their attention, and with great delight, they shoot up into the air and release from the doors of their senses and from their pores a huge mass of dense clouds. With the sounds of thunder but with no threat from lightning, they pour down excellent streams of rain. Imagine that, as a result, everything—the potency and essence of the soil, as well as the crops—flourish.

Again, if one wishes to perform rites using a wheel [image] as the basis,[967] [430] imagine light rays emanate from the letter *dhīḥ* at the heart of the triple-being guru, touching the *dhīḥ* on the hub of the wheel, which in turn emits light rays that touch the *hūṃ*s on the spokes of the wheel, turning them into the ten wrathful deities. Light rays from the bodies of these wrathful deities touch the letters of the Miktsema standing around [on the wheel's rim]. Then perform a visualization like the one above where light rays and images of Jé Tsongkhapa emanate from them and so on. If obstructive forces still prevent rain from falling despite these rites, there are visualizations of a wrathful nature that can be performed. These days, when seemingly engaged in tasks aimed at helping others, many appear to disrupt their personal practice. What I have presented in the above is some advice on how working for other's welfare can complement one's regular meditative practice. So I have presented these in a clear way.

In relation to this point, my own teacher, the sublime and glorious master, said the following. These days many lamrim practitioners, when requested by others to perform longevity or similar rites, seem to disrupt their personal practice to chant rituals and repeat the Amitāyus longevity mantra. Such practitioners fail to understand that acts performed to help others can be pursued on the basis of their own lamrim practice. To demonstrate that one can perform the various rites on the basis of the lamrim, my teacher cited the following two lines from Jé Tsongkhapa's *Song of Spiritual Experience*:

> Among instructions, it is the most precious of all gems,
> fulfilling all the wishes of beings without exception.[968]

Citing this, the teacher then explained in clear terms how, in the context of requesting blessings in a concentrated format in the lines "Bless me that all obstacles, outer as well as inner, may be thoroughly pacified,"[969] visualizations can be adapted to facilitate the rites of pacification, increase, influence, and wrath. Based on this oral teaching, I have myself undertaken these rites, and so I have written about them here accordingly. Now, if you are combining your guru-yoga practice with the performance of such rites, then it is sufficient to simply visualize the nectars emerging and dissolving associated with the topic of relying on the spiritual teacher.

Furthermore, there is the common visualization practice and the uncommon visualization practice associated with the nine-line Miktsema. The first involves visualizing at the crown of the triple-being guru—beneath the skull and above the fleshy part of the brain—a triple-being Mañjuśrī: outer Arapacana Mañjuśrī, at whose heart is inner gnosis-being Mañjuśrī, [431] at whose heart, in turn, is Guhyasiddhi Mañjuśrī. Inside the guru's Adam's apple, you visualize a triple-being Avalokiteśvara: outer Khasarpāṇi Avalokiteśvara, at whose heart is inner four-armed Avalokiteśvara, at whose heart, in turn, is secret Jinasāgara Avalokiteśvara. At the guru's heart you visualize a triple-being Vajrapāṇi: outer Nīlāmbaradhara Vajrapāṇi, at whose heart is inner Bhūtaḍāmara Vajrapāṇi, at whose heart, in turn, is secret Mahācakra Vajrapāṇi. The teacher spoke to me in a concealed way about this nine-being tiered visualization practice.

I asked my teacher, in a discreet way, about the uncommon visualization [associated with the nine-line Miktsema prayer]. In response, he spoke briefly about cultivations of such and such body Mañjuśrī, such and such speech Mañjuśrī, and such and such mind Mañjuśrī in terms not known previously in any texts. He remarked how such a practice is unique, that all nine deities are visualized in the form of Mañjuśrī alone, and that the oral teaching on this practice seems to have been lost in Tibet today. At the time, I was [in my student years] at the monastic university swallowing wind[970] and had hardly any real practice. So even though I was trying to seek out profound oral teachings, fearing that the teacher might get annoyed, I dared not inquire further. Later, while living in the mountain as a hermit, I was initially focused more on addressing the hindrances to, and cultivating the factors that would enhance, my practice of the stages of the path of the three capacities. So even though I did not actually receive the oral teaching of this uncommon visualization, I mention this as an illustration to indicate to those who proclaim to be custodians of the oral transmission that there does exist such an oral teaching. Let alone the instruction on that uncommon visualization, even the common one does not appear to be found these days in just anyone. Fearing that the transmission of this instruction might get lost, I have written about it here without any possessiveness.

Next, to supplicate [the guru] on the basis of contemplating how he is endowed with the qualifications for the abbot and master stated in the Vinaya texts, the *Offering to the Guru* text says, "**You're the source of all qualities, a great sea of discipline**," and so forth. To supplicate on the basis of contemplating how the guru is endowed with the qualifications for the Mahayana teacher stated in the Perfection Vehicle, the text says, "**You possess the ten qualities that when present qualify one to show the Sugata's path**," and so forth. [432] To supplicate on the basis of contemplating how the guru is endowed with the qualifications for the Vajra master stated in the tantras, the text says, "**You guard your three doors and are greatly wise, patient, and honest**," and so forth. These supplications, together with the earlier supplication based on repeating the name mantra, belong to the part of the practices aimed at cultivating faith, which is the root of all excellences.

Next we supplicate on the basis of remembering the guru's kindness, especially how he instructs us with great compassion—beings whose welfare none of the past buddhas and bodhisattvas have been able to secure, beings trapped in an era even more degenerate than the degenerate era and thus coarse and hard to tame; he instructs us perfectly on the stages of the path to enlightenment, which represent the excellent path of the tathāgatas. To indicate this, the text says, "**Untamed by the countless buddhas who have come before**," and so forth.

In general, the Buddha's doctrine, which the great compassionate blessed Teacher himself cultivated for hundreds of eons, is the sole source of benefit and happiness for all sentient beings. After the Teacher withdrew his physical form, his doctrine was upheld and propagated through numerous means by the seven designated custodians,[971] and they led countless sentient beings to paths of maturation and freedom. In particular, the arhat Upagupta led so many to the fruit of arhatship that counting each with a stick four fingerwidths long would fill a pit eighteen armlengths deep. After this, when the merit of sentient beings declined, conditions adverse to the Buddha's teaching in general, and to the Mahayana in particular, greatly proliferated. So numerous great scholar-siddhas, such as the great trailblazers Nāgārjuna and Asaṅga, without regard to costs to their own body and life, revived the teachings that were lost and propagated the surviving ones, ensuring their long-term survival. Through this they granted the life force of liberation to so many sentient beings, allowing them to attain rebirth in the higher realms and liberation.

In this snowy land of Tibet too, the great religious kings and the translators and the paṇḍitas established the new tradition of Dharma, which had not existed previously; and they did so without regard for costs to their body, life, and material resources. Through numerous means ensuring the Dharma's long-term survival, they thus connected the beings [of Tibet] to the glory of benefit and happiness. [433] However, the demerit of the sentient beings produced many who engaged in the Dharma in distorted ways. These ways were rectified, in their respective times, by the supreme scholar Kamalaśīla, the peerless great Atiśa, and our peerless savior Tsongkhapa from the east and his spiritual heirs, restoring the Buddha's doctrine to its purity like a refined gold free of all dilution and pollutants. In this way, they ensured that sublime beings engaged in the study, reflection, and meditation of the stainless doctrine filled the entire face of the earth.

As for us, who are caught in an age that is more degenerate than the degenerate era, none of these great beings have been able to secure our welfare. We have thus remained bereft of protector and devoid of refuge. In particular, today even the Buddha's doctrine itself remains in a state like that of a deva god struck by the portents of death, and as such it remains feeble, with no one taking charge. So at this time, being unable to bear the decline of the doctrine and, especially, feeling great compassion for the beings of this most degenerate era who are bereft of protector and refuge, our guru reveals to us in clear and accessible terms the scriptures of sutra and tantra as well as their commentarial treatises, which represent the Buddha's speech, supreme among all his enlightened activities. It is therefore thanks to my guru that those like me, not so different from animals, have the opportunity to engage at will in the study, reflection, and meditation of the scriptures of sutra and tantra. Thinking, "How could I ever repay such kindness," supplicate your guru with such reverence that tears flow from your eyes and your body hair stands on end. This supplication is presented in the lines "**When the Sage's sun has set owing to the passage of time**" and so forth.

Next, to supplicate on the basis of contemplating how—in helping to naturally cleanse the negative karma of disciples and effectively gather merit, disciples whose mindstreams are dominated by all manner of strong negative karma and whose merit is weak—even a single pore of the guru is more powerful than all the buddhas of all three times in the ten directions, the text says, "**To all the conquerors of the three times and ten directions,**" and so forth.

Then, to supplicate on the basis of contemplating that it is indeed thanks to the guru's great kindness that those like us have the opportunity to engage with him in accordance with our capacities, being able even to directly perceive the wheels of inexhaustible adornment of his three secrets[972]—something that even bodhisattvas on the higher grounds and the great śrāvaka and pratyekabuddha arhats cannot do—[434] the text says, "**The wheels of adornment of the three sugata bodies,**" and so forth. These then belong to the cycle of practices connected with cultivating reverence based on remembering the guru's kindness.

Next, to supplicate on the basis of contemplating how even the guru's aggregates, sense fields, elements, and so forth are in nature the male and female deities and, as such, how the guru is the embodiment of all the Three Jewels, the text says, "**Your aggregates, sense fields, elements, and limbs are**," and so forth.

To supplicate by contemplating the guru as being in nature the lord of the sixth buddha family, Vajradhara himself, who is the primordial lord of union and the lord of all buddha families, the text says, "**You are the embodiment of ten million mandalas arising from the play of all-knowing gnosis**," and so forth.

To supplicate by contemplating the guru as the dharmakāya great bliss, the progenitor of the entire mandala, both the residence and the deities within, the text says, "**You are inseparable from the play of unobscured innate joy**," and so forth. These, together, belong to the cycle of practices connected to cultivating faith, which is the root factor.

Alternatively, you could relate the verse "The wheels of adornment of the three sugata bodies" and so forth and the verse "Your aggregates, sense fields, elements, and limbs are" and so forth to viewing the guru as nirmāṇakāya; the verse "You are the embodiment of ten million mandalas arising from the play of all-knowing gnosis" and so on to viewing the guru as saṃbhogakāya; and the verse "You are inseparable from the play of unobscured innate joy" and so forth to viewing the guru as dharmakāya.

Or, once again, you could read the verse "The wheels of adornment of the three sugata bodies" and so forth as supplicating the guru by contemplating his outer qualities; the verse "Your aggregates, sense fields, elements, and limbs are" and so forth as contemplating his inner qualities; the verse "You are the embodiment of ten million mandalas arising from the play of all-knowing gnosis" and so forth as contemplating his secret qualities; and finally the verse "You are inseparable from the play of unobscured innate joy" and so forth as supplicating the guru by contemplating his suchness quality. There are thus numerous ways of reading these verses. If you wish to gain definitive understanding of these qualities [of the guru], you should rely on a spiritual teacher in a perfect manner and, the basis of his oral instructions, read the sutras and the tantras closely. Do not be content with some partial understanding.

Next, imagine with your two hands firmly grasp at guru's two feet and, placing your bowed head upon them, [435] make the following single-pointed firm supplication:[973]

You are the guru, you are the meditation deity, you are the ḍākinī and the Dharma guardian;
from now until enlightenment I will seek no refuge other than you.
In this life, in the bardo, and in future lives, hold me with your hook of compassion,
free me from samsara and nirvana's dangers, grant me all siddhis, be my constant companion, and guard me from hindrances.[974]

Here is how you make this supplication. Contemplate:

> O glorious guru, you are the embodiment of all the refuges, and so I will seek no other refuge until I arrive at the heart of enlightenment. Grab me with your hook of great compassion, not wavering even a single instant, in this life, at the point of my death, in the intermediate state, and throughout all births in future lives.

Again:

> You are the embodiment of all the gurus, so please liberate me and all sentient beings from the fears of samsara and nirvana. You are the embodiment of all the meditation deities so please grant all the siddhis, supreme and common, to me and all sentient beings. You are the embodiment of all the ḍākinīs, so please support me and all sentient beings in our quest to fulfill our ultimate aspiration. You are the embodiment of all the Dharma guardians, so help me and all sentient beings be free from all adverse conditions and obstacles.

In this way, supplicate from the very bones of your heart.

[Receiving the Empowerments]

Next is receiving the four empowerments in the form of blessing. For this, the text reads "**Through the power of having supplicated three times thusly,**" and so on. If you wish to receive the four empowerments in the form of a blessing in a brief way, then proceed in accordance with the meaning of the words of the text itself. However, if you wish to practice this in an elaborate way, then practice according to what Lama Tokdenpa inscribed in his notes on Jé Tsongkhapa's oral teachings, transmitted from mouth-to-ear through successive spiritual heirs.[975]

Alternatively, you could do this as in the following. First make a mandala offering, and then, as you supplicate "Guru Vajradhara, embodiment of all refuge, confer on me the vase empowerment," imagine that light rays shaped like hooks emanate from the heart of the gnosis-being Vajradhara at the heart of guru Munīndra Vajradhara Losang Drakpa[976] and radiate in all ten directions. The light rays invite the buddhas of all ten directions, together with their retinues, to confer the empowerment upon you. The invited figures remain above in space, while Guru Vajradhara sets the intention of conferring the empowerment. Goddesses such as Locanā in the space above hold parasols, victory banners, and so forth. [436] They sing songs, dance, and play musical instruments.[977] Chant the verses "The auspiciousness that resides" and "This is the great vajra of empowerment"[978] and so on. Imagine that the goddesses, reciting the mantra *Oṃ sarva tathāgata abhiṣekata samaya śriye hūṃ svāhā*, confer the empowerment by pouring water from above your crown. Your body becomes filled with water, and you experience great bliss. Generate the ascertainment that this bliss too possesses not the slightest intrinsic existence, not even at the minute level of an atom. Thus, as you actualize the gnosis of bliss and emptiness, which is the actual nature of the *vase empowerment*, you purify the five pollutants such as anger with the excess water spilling out from your crown and turning into a crown of Akṣobhya. The invited empowerment deities dissolve into you through your pores. As you do these visualizations, recite the words of the empowerment without any omission. Then contemplate and imagine hearing these words:

> You have now received the vase empowerment. Of the common stains, you have cleansed all past stains of the body, those acquired through killing, stealing, sexual misconduct, and so on; resolve never to commit these acts in the future. Of the uncommon stains, you have washed and purified the stain of perceiving and apprehending your body in ordinary terms.

As you recite these words explaining the purity of the empowerment, imagine that these words are uttered by Guru Vajradhara, and ensure that the meaning of the words is clear in your mind.

Above was a reference to imagining your body being filled with water giving rise to the experience of bliss and emptiness. When you do this, hold a vajra and bell in your hands and perform the gesture of embracing. Imagine actualizing the essence of the *vajra master empowerment*[979]—the principal element of vase empowerment—which is the conjoining of the bliss and emptiness induced by uniting with the consort. That we should imagine in this manner is mentioned in Tokdenpa's notes.[980]

Next, make a mandala offering as before and request the *secret empowerment*. Then contemplate in the following: As you supplicate in the same way as before, the sounds of joy coming from Guru Vajradhara and his consort entering into union invite limitless conquerors in union with their consorts. They enter through the crown of the guru and his consort. The white and red streams from melting of the bodhicitta emerge from the point where the deity and his consort are sexually joined, which permeate your entire body, and bliss arises within you as they touch your tongue in particular. This bliss you experience is, in turn, dependent on so many conditions, including requesting the guru to confer the secret empowerment, so generate the ascertainment that it is impossible for any of this to possess intrinsic existence, even at the minute level of an atom. In this way, imagine that you have actualized the essence of secret empowerment—namely, the gnosis of bliss and emptiness. [437] As a result, among the common stains, you have purified past accumulations of lies, harsh speech, frivolous speech, and so on, and you resolve to never engage in such acts in the future. Of the uncommon stains, you have washed away the perception and apprehension of winds and mantras as being separate, for it has been stated that speech is [in essence] wind. You have thus rehearsed for [the attainment of] vajra speech. In this way, contemplate the purity of the empowerment.

Next, make a mandala offering as before and request the *wisdom-gnosis empowerment*. Then contemplate the following: A replica emerges from guru Vajradhara's consort, Vajradhātvīśvarī, dissolving into Vajravaitalī, your consort, with yourself in the form of Vajrabhairava. From this, your secret place dissolves into emptiness.[981] In this way, you consecrate the space and your secret place, and you and your consort enter into union, causing the consort's downward voiding wind to stir up the winds at your secret place. This sets *tumo* fire ablaze, sending its flame upward and melting the bodhicitta drops at your crown. As the fluid descends and reaches from the crown to the throat, *joy* arises; as it reaches the heart from the throat, *supreme joy* arises; as it reaches the navel from the heart, *extraordinary joy* arises; and as it reaches the base of the secret region, the whitish appearance arises; as it reaches the midpoint, the reddish increase arises; as it reaches the base of the jewel, the blackish near attainment arises; and as it reaches the tip of the jewel, the all-empty *innate joy* arises. In this way, the four joys arise in the forward sequence.

Then generate the ascertainment that this innate joy too, which has arisen in dependence on causes and conditions, such as the deity and consort entering into union, does not possess any intrinsic existence, not even at the minute level of an atom. In this way, generate innate bliss and emptiness. Once again, imagine the melted bodhicitta flowing backward, and as it reaches from the secret place to the navel, *joy* of the reverse sequence arises and so on. In this way, invoke the four joys of the reverse sequence. As you join the fourth joy with emptiness, imagine that you actualize the innate gnosis, which is the essence of the third empowerment. As a result, of the common stains, imagine you have purified the mental stains of covetousness, harmful intent, wrong views, and so on; and of the uncommon stains, you have washed away the stain obscuring the appearance of everything you perceive as manifestations of bliss and emptiness. And you have rehearsed for [the attainment of] vajra mind. In this way, contemplate the purity [of the empowerment].

Next, as you offer a mandala and request the *word empowerment*, imagine that Guru Vajradhara intones with the perfect melodies of Brahmā:

> O child of the family, when you received the third empowerment, while your body [438] and that of the consort were appearing in the form of a deity and consort, your mind of innate bliss was ascertaining emptiness. Just as these two were present at one and the same time, then in the same manner, as you cultivate this fact [your appearance as a deity and cognition of emptiness by the mind of innate bliss], there will eventually arise a body made of mere wind and mind—a saṃbhogakāya in union with a consort that is its own natural reflection—and at that very moment will arise the mind of innate great bliss fused in a single taste with the emptiness of intrinsic existence of all phenomena—namely, the luminous clear light of everything empty. You will thus actualize the state of union, which is the nondual gnosis, the indivisible union of the two [illusory body and clear light]. This is the definitive fourth empowerment.

As this is being indicated to you thusly in words, generate the understanding of what is meant by "union" and of how the union of the two takes place.

Then, in accordance with the meaning of the words "**a replica of my guru joyfully absorbs into me, and I am blessed**," imagine a replica emerges from Guru Vajradhara and dissolves joyfully into you, blessing your three doors. Once again, as you melt into light and bliss, imagine actualizing the all-empty state of luminous clear light. From within this clear light, imagine yourself arising as all-pervading lord Vajradhara and that the body, speech, and mind of Guru Vajradhara and your own body, speech, and mind become indivisibly fused. Perform this visualization with firm conviction. Thusly, you have received the word empowerment. This implants a unique potency to cleanse, of the common stains, the subtle stains of your body, speech, and mind and, of the uncommon stains, the subtle dualistic perceptions along with their imprints associated with appearance, increase, near attainment, and so forth. In this way, contemplate the purity [of the fourth empowerment].

Receiving the four empowerments like this involves the following understanding. While abiding [meditatively] in Vajrabhairava yoga, in the context of the third empowerment, you generate the four joys of forward and reverse sequence. In this way, you join the fourth joy with emptiness, giving rise to innate bliss and emptiness, which is in fact the definitive Heruka (Cakrasaṃvara). Similarly, in the context of the fourth empowerment, two things come to converge into a single entity—the ultimate clear light, which is the pure mind, [439] and the illusory body of mere wind and mind, which is the pure body. This union is in fact the definitive Guhyasamāja. To practice with such an understanding is to pursue your practice in a way that accords with the actual situation that arises in the context of the completion stage where the three—Guhyasamāja, Cakrasaṃvara, and Vajrabhairava—can be practiced in a combined manner, not one in isolation from the other, and at one and the same time. In connection with this, my glorious teacher said that, in the context of the completion stage, there does exist the option of practicing Guhyasamāja, Cakrasaṃvara, and Vajrabhairava in combination without isolating one from another. At the level of the generation stage, however, he said it is by ensuring the key points unique to the specific generation-stage practices of the three deities—Guhyasamāja, Cakrasaṃvara, and Vajrabhairava—in distinct ways that one establishes the auspicious factors specific to the individual tantras. So, on the generation stage, there is no way of practicing the three in combination simultaneously, the teacher said. Furthermore, ever since the precious Khedrup Jé received the empowerment of Vajrabhairava from Jé Rinpoché, he never failed to perform the Vajrabhairava self-empowerment on a daily basis, thus adopting the tradition of ensuring that the stream of blessing remained uninterrupted. Even though we may not be able to do this, if we are able to receive the four empowerments in the form of a blessing as part of this guru yoga as a daily practice in an uninterrupted manner, we will be acting to ensure that the stream of blessings remains uninterrupted. This is thus not a small matter. In particular, the teacher said, Guru Yongzin Rinpoché used to repeatedly praise this receiving of the four empowerments by way of meditative concentration as a means to leave imprints for the tantric path.

Next, with yourself in the form of the primordial lord Vajrabhairava in union, visualize at your heart a sun disc on which sits the syllable *maṃ* marked by *hūṃ* and surrounded by *oṃ aḥ hūṃ*. Around this, in a circle [clockwise], is Vajradhara's name mantra *Oṃ aḥ vajradhara siddhi hūṃ hūṃ*; around this is *Oṃ muni muni mahā muniye svāhā*; around this is Jé Tsongkhapa's name mantra *Oṃ aḥ guru vajradhara sumati kīrti siddhi hūṃ hūṃ*; around this is your own teacher's name mantra, which in my own case is *Oṃ guru munīndra jñāna śasanadhika siddhi hūṃ hūṃ*. Visualize these mantras in concentric circles around the central syllable. Do these visualizations and the repetition of the mantras as you would normally. At the end, recite the verse

> Through this virtue
> may I swiftly become guru-buddha
> and lead all beings without exception
> to this guru-buddha state. [440]

Reviewing the Path

Training the Mind by Reviewing the Entire Path of Sutra and Tantra and Receiving the Blessings

[First] relying on the spiritual teacher is presented by the text in the lines "**to my revered guru, the supreme holy field of merit**" and so forth. [Here is the meaning:] To you, a single pore of whom has been hailed as a field of merit for us disciples that is superior to all the buddhas and bodhisattvas of the ten directions, "**Through the force of making offerings and respectful appeals,**" may I be able to accomplish the following. Here, contemplate:

> By contemplating in depth the benefits of relying on the spiritual teacher and the faults of not relying, I will engage in the practice

> of relying on the spiritual teacher in thought and action with the joy and delight of a poor person who has just found a treasure. Fearing the perils of relating in misguided ways, I will cultivate firm heedfulness and set ablaze the fire of remorse for past errors, purifying them from my heart and resolving to never engage in such acts again. By making fervent supplications and recalling his qualities and kindness, I will engender devotion of such depth that tears flow from my eyes and my body hair stands up in my pores. In my actions, I will relate to my spiritual teacher with fervent reverence, without concern even for my life and limb or for my resources.

Then supplicate:

> Bless me, O my glorious guru, that I may please you who are the root of all that is virtuous and good, and that I may be sustained by you joyfully.

Supplicate in this way and perform the visualization of nectar entering and flowing into you.

To review the human existence of leisure and opportunity conjoined with the contemplation of impermanence, the text says, "**This life of leisure and opportunity I have found once**," and so forth. Here, contemplate:

> Through contemplating how a human existence of leisure and opportunity is hard to find and is easily lost, I will not waste this existence of leisure on unimportant matters, even for a moment, and will instead make it meaningful.

Then supplicate, "Bless me, O guru deity, that I may be able to do this."

Next, contemplating the suffering of the lower realms and, on this basis, seeking refuge in the Three Jewels from the heart and observing the law of karma and its effects are presented in the lines [441] "**Terrified by the blazing fires of suffering of the lower realms**," and so forth. Here, contemplate:

> Contemplating the suffering of the lower realms, my mind gripped by fear, I seek refuge from my heart. I do this through deeply ascertaining the general and specific qualities of the Three

> Jewels and, on this basis, developing conviction that the Three Jewels alone have the power to free us from all the fears. With such conviction I place my hope in them from my heart, and having sought refuge in them, I will implement, in particular, the precepts of refuge, especially observing the law of positive and negative karma and its effects.

Then supplicate, "Bless me, O guru deity, that I may be able to cultivate within myself the seeking of refuge."

Generating a genuine aspiration to liberation is presented in the lines **"Powerful waves of karma and afflictions surge up violently,"** and so forth. Here contemplate:

> As long as I have assumed an appropriated aggregate that is contaminated, I remain at the mercy of karma and the afflictions; I will have no autonomy but will remain under the power of karma and the afflictions. Not only that, this aggregate itself is assailed directly or indirectly, and continuously, by the sea monsters that are the three types of suffering.[982] Seeing this, I will contemplate this situation of ours deeply so that I may generate a fervent intention to gain freedom from the great ocean of cyclic existence.

Then supplicate, "Bless me, O guru deity, that I may be able to do this."

One might ask, "Why is it that the sequence presented here is different from the normal sequence of contemplating the faults of suffering and its origin?"[983] What is presented here is not to indicate the proper sequence of contemplating the truth of suffering and the truth of its origin. Rather it is to indicate that, here in the context of engaging in the practice of the path shared with persons of intermediate capacity, it is not adequate to develop a wish to be free from suffering where the understanding of suffering is at the level shared with animals, non-Buddhists, and so on. What is required is a wish for liberation that is comprehensive [in how it understands the nature of suffering]. To make this important point, the text refers in the first line to "waves of karma and afflictions." Now a wish to be free from suffering in the sense of a painful sensation is something even animals can generate. As for the contaminated levels of pleasure and neutral feeling, except for that of the "peak of existence," there are many non-Buddhist practitioners who can develop the wish to gain freedom from these. However, because such non-Buddhist practitioners do not recognize birth in the peak of existence borne of absorption [442] to be a form of conditioned suffering, something that is under the power of karma and afflictions, they define such a state as the state of liberation. Thus the ability to generate the wish to be free from all conditioned existences, which are at the mercy of karma and afflictions, is unique to Buddhism. This said, without our exalted guru Jé Tsongkhapa's oral teaching, this point would remain quite difficult to appreciate. Therefore Panchen Losang Chögyen says:

> Though there are many [flaws in samsara],
> being terrified of the suffering of pain
> and wishing to be free from it is found even among cattle,
> and the renunciation of tainted happiness
> is found among non-Buddhists as well.
> Therefore, seeing this very appropriated aggregate itself
> to be the door to all suffering, both manifest and potential,
> and as the disease, its effects, and the painful symptoms,
> contemplating in such terms will shake us from the core.[984]

I feel it is this oral teaching that is succinctly summarized here in these lines from *Offering to the Guru*. My own father guru said, "If your notion is that what is referred to as 'ocean of existence' or 'ocean of samsara' is something out there, this will not do. So, just as the glorious Dharmakīrti says, 'This aggregate of samsara itself is suffering,'[985] the contaminated appropriated aggregates themselves are what is meant by 'conditioned suffering' and the 'ocean of samsara.' I have made this very clear to you now."[986] These points seem to be hard to appreciate fully, so those with critical acumen should not be content with merely being able to recite the text of *Offering to the Guru*.

Next, establishing the nature of the path to liberation is presented in the lines "**This prison-like samsara so hard to endure,**" and so forth. Here, contemplate:

> Seeing even the absorptions of the peak of existence akin to an unbearable prison, I will never cultivate admiration for them. I will instead generate an urgent yearning to be free from cyclic existence, and with such a mind I will strive in the practice of the threefold training—the means to help uproot cyclic existence—and cultivate the seven riches of an ārya being.[987] In particular, I will observe the morality of the individual liberation vows I have

> taken—morality being the foundation of rebirth in the higher realms and of the definite goodness of liberation. I will do this through securing the five means of guarding the precepts,[988] not lapsing for even a single moment.

Then supplicate, "Bless me, O guru deity, that I may always be able to hoist liberation's victory banner." [443]

Regarding the words "**seize the ārya's treasure trove, the threefold training,**" you might ask, "the threefold training was already mentioned previously, so why is there a specific seeking of blessing focused on morality with the line '**Bless me that I may raise the victory banner of liberation**'?" Let me explain. In the context of establishing the nature of the path to liberation, you must ascertain that the root of cyclic existence is ignorance grasping at self-existence and appreciate that its direct antidote is the wisdom of selflessness. Gaining genuine experience in relation to the wisdom of selflessness, however, is dependent on the training in concentration. And the foundation, or root, of both of those trainings is clearly the training in morality. Developing conviction about this from the depth of your mind with the help of flawless scripture and reasoning allows you to see that, for now, the training in morality needs to be the primary focus of your practice. The text presents these lines in the way it does to indicate this point.

On this point the glorious master, my teacher, said, "Here, in the context of the path of the intermediate capacity, your primary focus should be the practice of observing morality based on the precepts you have taken. Were you to take the other two trainings as the primary focus, you would risk falling into the path of the Hīnayāna. Here, you may have no wish to enter the lower paths, but you might unwittingly come to view samsara's three realms as a massive raging fire and, out of a strong desire to gain freedom from this, engage principally in the training in concentration and the training in the wisdom realizing selflessness, and this could actually become a path of the Hīnayāna." This statement resembles those of the mahāsiddhas.

As for equanimity, the recognition of other sentient beings as mothers, the recollection of their kindness, how these three lead to loving kindness viewing others as dear, and how such loving kindness then leads to compassion are presented in the text in the lines "**All these distressed suffering beings are my mothers,**" and so forth. Here, contemplate:

> I and all other sentient beings are possessed by the powerful demon afflictions, and as such we have no control over our minds,

> and we suffer from insanity. Our eyes for seeing the path that leads to birth in the higher realms and to the definite goodness of liberation remain blinded. Dire is my predicament, shared by all others, for we remain at the terrifying edge of a cliff from which we may plunge into the three lower realms. [444]

Contemplate:

> When it comes to this desperate situation, there is no difference between me and all others, and so I will relate to all others with only the thought to free them from any bias of attachment and aversion. On the part of sentient beings too, not a single one has not been my mother; not only this, each has been my mother countless times. Furthermore, in terms of being my mother, there nothing to differentiate my mothers of past, present, and future. So, employing flawless scripture and reasoning that sees all my mothers as equal, I will develop conviction from the depths of my mind. And through the example of the kindness of my mother of this present life, I will contemplate how all beings extended that same degree of kindness to me, or possibly even more than my present mother. In this way, and understanding too that I will need to be cared for similarly in the future, I will see all these sentient beings as my dear mothers—my most important loved ones who bring about my welfare—and cherish them. In this way, I will develop the loving kindness that cherishes them as most dear.

Then, reflecting on how these dear beings I cherish remain constantly tormented by suffering and bereft of happiness, generate the thought "I will generate compassion rooted in empathic concern and the wish to see them relieved of suffering."[989] Then supplicate, "Bless me, O guru deity, that I may be able to do this."

Contemplating the equalizing of self and others is presented in the lines "**As for suffering, I do not wish even the slightest**" and so forth. Here, contemplate:

> As for suffering, all sentient beings, myself and others, do not wish for it even in a dream. As for happiness, no matter how much we find, no matter the time and situation, we are never content.

> In this, we are not different at all. Contemplating this in depth, I see clearly that it is inappropriate to cherish my own self while forsaking others. So, when it comes to wishing and working to bring about other sentient beings' perfect welfare, I will pursue these the way I would normally do so in both thought and action when pursuing my own welfare and happiness.

Then supplicate, "Bless me, O guru deity, that I may be able to do this." [445]

The way to contemplate the faults of self-cherishing is presented in the lines "**Seeing that this chronic disease of cherishing myself**" and so forth. Here, contemplate:

> Having reflected on the faults of self-cherishing through flawless scripture and reasoning, I see that this self-cherishing is the cause of everything that is undesirable and of all sufferings. Thus I will keep in the depth of my mind how it is this self-cherishing alone that is to blame for every undesirable thing and every misfortune in all my lives.

Then supplicate, "Bless me, O guru deity, that by assailing it from various angles through both thought and action, I may be able to destroy this self-cherishing demon."

The way to contemplate the benefits of cherishing others is presented in the lines "**The thought cherishing my mothers and leading them to happiness**" and so forth. Here, contemplate:

> Having, through flawless scripture and reasoning, reflected on the benefits of the thought cherishing others, this thought cherishing others reveals itself to be the cause of all good qualities, both mundane and supramundane. Let alone appearing as my loved ones or as neutral, even if other sentient beings all rise up as my arch enemies, I will on my part cherish them as dearer than my own life. I will hold them to be as precious as a wish-granting jewel and as no different from my gurus and meditation deities.

Then supplicate, "Bless me, O guru deity, that with the intention of holding them dear and precious, I may always strive in ways that please them and bring them joy."

The reason why self and others can be exchanged is presented in the lines **"In brief, the childish pursue only their own self-interest,"** and so forth. Here, contemplate that there are indeed numerous flawless arguments for why it is possible to exchange self and others. The essence of all these arguments is this. We ordinary beings have not cultivated familiarity with the thought of exchanging self and others, and so we have cherished ourselves and forsaken others. Because of this, we have failed to accomplish our own welfare and have only been led down the road to ruin. In contrast, our Teacher, the compassionate Buddha, cultivated familiarity, in both thought and action, with the exchanging of self and others over countless eons. As such, he forsook his own self and cherished others, and because of this, he actualized a state perfectly realizing the welfare of both self and others. And he has appeared once again at this present time to be the protector, the refuge, and the ally for us sentient beings of this era when the five degenerations are proliferating rapidly. [446] As I contemplate like this in depth, I realize that were it not for our own lack of confidence and fear rooted in false attitudes, it would indeed be possible for us childish beings to exchange self and others. Then supplicate, "Bless me, O guru deity, that I may generate powerful conviction in my ability to exchange self and others."

Contemplating the benefits of exchanging self and others and the faults of not doing so is presented in the lines "**Self-cherishing is the doorway to every misfortune,**" and so forth. Here, contemplate:

> As I contemplate in depth how self-cherishing is the cause of all misfortunes while the thought of cherishing others and forsaking one's own self is the cause of all good qualities, both mundane and supermundane, may I develop the power of joy in embracing, as my heart practice, the exchanging of self and others in both thought and action.

Then supplicate, "Bless me, O guru deity, that I may be able to do this."

The actual exchanging of self and others is presented in the lines "**Therefore, O venerable, most compassionate guru,**" and so forth. Here, contemplate:

> I have now seen the need to exchange self and others; I have realized that such an exchange is possible and that exchanging self and others actually brings great benefits. I must now embrace this exchanging of self and others as the heart of my personal practice.

> Therefore, from this very moment, I take upon myself the misfortunes of all sentient beings so that they befall me alone and so that sentient beings do not even have to hear the word *suffering*. With no possessiveness, I offer all my happiness and virtues to all sentient beings, and I will ensure that they are never divorced, even in their dreams, from all the conditions that bring benefit and happiness.

Then make the following supplication:

> O my father guru, most compassionate one, bless me that mother sentient beings' suffering and negative karma may all without exception, even what is merely the size of a sesame seed, ripen upon me at this very moment. And by the power of my offering them all my happiness and virtues, may all beings become endowed with perfect factors of happiness and virtue.

Supplicating in this manner, join the visualization of giving and taking (*tonglen*) to the movement of your inhalation and exhalation. The custom here is to recite this supplication three times. [447]

The reason there is an extra line in this stanza is the following. When the omniscient Panchen first composed this text, the first line was not part of the text. He added the line later, in response to his heart disciples' request that, because this practice of *tonglen* is the heart of exchanging self and others, it would be wonderful for it to begin by invoking the guru's compassion. This is what my teacher told me.

The transformation of adverse conditions into the path, the presentation of a lifetime's practice in summary, the measure of having trained the mind, and the commitments and precepts of mind training—these practices are presented in the lines "**Even if the world and its inhabitants are filled with the fruits of evil karma**" and so forth and the lines "**Through the skillful means of the fourfold practice,**" and so forth. Here, in their respective order, contemplate the following:

> All these sufferings we do not desire—filling the entire world and the beings within with negative environmental effects, experience-concordant effects, and act-concordant effects—which befall us like rain, I will not blame on anyone or on anything but my own

> self-cherishing alone. And seeing how my practice can consume the effects of the karma I have gathered while driven by this self-cherishing, I will engage in acts such as transforming adverse conditions into the path. In brief, whatever unbearable conditions befall me, good or bad, I will apply the five forces that integrate a lifetime's practice into a concentrated approach—the power of propelling intention, the power of acquaintance, the power of the positive seed, the power of eradication, and the power of aspirational prayer—and on this basis, I will transform them, naturally and without exertion, into the path enhancing the two awakening minds: the conventional awakening mind and the ultimate awakening mind. Through this may I always be able to sustain the joyful mind alone. Also, through applying the fourfold practice—gathering merit, purifying obscurations, offering *tormas* to the obstructive forces, and entrusting the activities to the Dharma protectors[990]—I will transform adverse conditions into the path. I will also relate all my physical movements, all the words I utter, and all the thoughts in my mind to enhancing the practice of the two awakening minds. Furthermore, I align my actions with the eighteen commitments of mind training and [448] the twenty-two precepts of mind training[991] and, through this, make my human existence meaningful.

Then supplicate, "Bless me, O guru deity, that I may be able to do these."

One might ask, "In the great [Indian] treatises, these two approaches—the sevenfold cause-and-effect method and the equalizing and exchanging of self and others—are presented distinctly; there is no explicit presentation on how to combine the two practices. So how is it that this guru-yoga instruction presents a practice where these two are integrated?"

The issue this raises relates to key points of the Mahayana path that are indeed most challenging. Someone like me, not only can I not comprehend these matters with my own capacity, I cannot even formulate critical questions about them. This said, were I to offer some explanation drawn from my own general understanding, based on the oral teachings joyfully conferred upon me by the spiritual teacher who has sustained me—a Mahayana spiritual teacher who is qualified through having mastered this guru-yoga instruction—I would say this. The root of all Mahayana teachings is great compassion. For with respect to the entirety [of the Mahayana practices]—

the general and specific deeds of the bodhisattva as well as the awakening mind and altruistic resolve that are the basis of these practices—whether they are present and to what degree of strength all depends on whether compassion is present and on how strong it is. Compassion, in turn, necessarily arises on the basis of loving kindness in the sense of holding others as dear. As for the way to cultivate such loving kindness holding others dear, the compassionate Buddha taught two distinct approaches in relation to the mental dispositions of the trainees.[992] There is the method of cultivating the loving kindness of endearment through the progression of three factors—recognizing others as mothers, reflecting on their kindness, and wishing to repay their kindness. This approach is known as the seven-point causes-and-effect instruction. Then there is the approach of cultivating the loving kindness of endearment by contemplating the faults of self-cherishing and the benefits of cherishing others; scholar-siddhas of the past called this latter approach the instruction on equalizing and exchanging self and others.

Those possessing a potent Mahayana lineage (*gotra*) can grab the instruction on equalizing and exchanging self and others as if with their bare hands and succeed from the start. Cognizant of this, numerous masters taught the method. However, if you had a weak Mahayana lineage and were to proceed in this manner, not only would you find it difficult to succeed on the path, you could in fact sustain serious harm. So first [449] you need to establish equanimity by contemplating how there is no reason or purpose for discrimination based on feelings of closeness and distance and by contemplating the faults of such discrimination of closeness and distance. Taking this as the basis, you cultivate the recognition of others as mothers and reflect on their kindness, and this then fosters loving kindness that holds all sentient beings dear—you hold them as precious and cannot bear to abandon them. Then, as you contemplate the equality of self and others, such negative thoughts as delight in other sentient beings' suffering and displeasure in other sentient beings' happiness will come to cease. You then ensure that you make no differentiation, neither in thought nor action, between yourself and others when it comes to removing suffering and cultivating happiness. Then, as you reflect on the faults of self-cherishing, you come to see it as your real enemy, and as you reflect on the benefits of cherishing others, you come to see all sentient beings as your most cherished loved ones, as indispensable sources of welfare throughout all phases of the ground, path, and result. And seeing that they are no different in this respect from your guru and meditation deities, you cultivate the loving kindness of endearment that holds others to be a most precious jewel, more precious than your own life.

One might ask, "Earlier we already cultivated equanimity as the foundation for recognizing others as our mothers, reflecting on their kindness, and so forth. So why should we cultivate equanimity once again through equalizing self and others?"

[Answer:] The equanimity you established as the foundation for recognizing others as your mothers and so on is equanimity in the sense of an absence of the bias of attachment and aversion that is rooted in discriminating feelings of closeness and distance. Such equanimity is not adequate here; you need equanimity that makes you engage with everyone equally with the altruistic intention to help without any bias of attachment and aversion rooted in discriminating feelings of closeness and distance.[993] The first type of equanimity is shared by śrāvakas and the like, while the second type is Mahayana equanimity. My teacher said that for Mahayana equanimity, it is not enough to simply be free of the bias of attachment and aversion that is rooted in discriminatory feelings of closeness and distance; you need an equanimity that engages with all sentient beings equally with the altruistic intention to help without any bias of attachment and aversion. My teacher said that the guru Losang Namgyal, a lord among siddhas, would remark: "Let alone the advanced levels of the Mahayana path, this type of equanimity—which is actually a foundation of the path—[450] is something unmatched by those who claim they have attained clairvoyance and the power of miracles." This, my teacher said, he heard from his own guru.[994]

One might then ask, "In that case, if the loving kindness of endearment can be effected through recognizing others as mothers, reflecting on their kindness, and repaying their kindness, why do we need to cultivate the loving kindness of endearment by contemplating the faults of self-cherishing and the benefits of cherishing others?"

[Answer:] These two forms of the sense of endearment—one developed through recognizing others as mothers and so forth and the other developed through contemplating the faults of self-cherishing and the benefits of cherishing others—are equal in being the loving kindness of endearment, but they differ in potency. Because of this, there is a difference in the potency of the loving kindness, compassion, and altruistic resolve brought about by these two forms of endearment. This means there will be a difference in the potency of the awakening mind brought about by their corresponding altruistic resolve. Because of this, there will be difference in their ability to accelerate the training in the bodhisattva deeds as well. Thus, the first approach is referred to as the practice of those of inferior mental faculty within the Mahayana lineage, while the second is referred to as the practice of those of advanced mental faculty. My teacher, the glorious master, said that whichever of the two instructions you choose to practice, they equally lead to the cultivation of the loving kindness of endearment. That said, as there is indeed a difference in their potency, there will also be a difference in the strength of the loving kindness, compassion, and altruistic resolve they give rise to.

Now to engage without reservation in the most challenging bodhisattva deeds, you need more than strong loving kindness and compassion. You need a potent loving kindness of endearment developed through contemplating the faults of self-cherishing and the benefits of cherishing others. This leads to a wish to see others become free from suffering and enjoy happiness that is so powerful that you would shoulder, without hesitation, sole responsibility for relieving others' suffering and bringing about their happiness. Such a wish is possible if there is a powerful altruistic revolve and not possible if that powerful altruistic resolve is absent.

Take, for example, the story about our Teacher, the Buddha, when he was born as a brahman boy and one day ventured into the forest with his friend Ajita. In the forest he came upon a tigress with her small cubs [451] facing potential disaster [from starvation]. At that time, both bodhisattvas possessed equally strong compassion and awakening mind, but because Ajita had not contemplated the faults of self-cherishing in depth, he went in search of fresh meat to help relieve the tigers' hunger. The great brahman boy, on the other hand, declared, "My dear boy, how futile it is, this round of birth and rebirth" up to the lines "How can one allow this scourge to continue unabated—this self-love that prompts such atrocities?"[995] Triggered by the plight of the tigress and her cubs, the bodhisattva contemplated how self-cherishing lets down both oneself and all others. Then, as stated in the lines "Now suppose I fell down this mountainside; my lifeless corpse would serve to prevent this creature from killing her young,"[996] the bodhisattva generated a powerful altruistic resolve and thereby sacrificed his flesh and gave it to the tigers. My teacher related this story to me as an example in a quiet moment. Such oral teachings are so precious that one would not find them even if one were to set out searching with gold, silver, and so on. You must treasure them.

Having thus contemplated from many angles the faults of self-cherishing and the benefits of cherishing others, you will see the need to exchange self and others, but still you might wonder, "Yes, this is indeed critical, but can such an exchange really be done? If not, my efforts will be in vain." If so, then contemplate from numerous angles how this really can be done. But the thought may arise, "Yes, I could do it, but does it serve a great purpose or a small purpose? If the latter, it would then be inappropriate to expend so much effort on something that serves little purpose." In that case, then [once again] contemplate from many angles the faults of self-cherishing and the benefits of cherishing others and, in this way, enhance your enthusiasm and joy in the thought and action of exchanging self and others. Once you see that you must embrace the exchange of self and others as your heart practice, then make fervent supplications to your guru invoking his great compassion. And on this basis, engage in the actual practice of exchanging self and others—namely, *tonglen* (giving and taking).

To summarize the essence of the above points, contemplate:

> Self and others must definitely be exchanged, and such an exchange is possible. [Furthermore] the benefits of such an exchange are vast, and I must embrace this practice of exchanging, both in thought and action, as my heart practice. [452] So, bless me, O father guru, the embodiment of compassion and love, that through the force of taking upon myself all the negative karma and obscurations of all sentient beings of the three realms this very moment, their negative karma, obscurations, and suffering may ripen upon me and they may become free from all suffering and its causes. And through the force of giving away all my happiness and virtues to them from the depths of my heart, may they become endowed with perfect happiness and virtue.

Make the supplication like this. Hence in the text there is the stanza that begins "Therefore, O venerable, most compassionate guru."

Here you might ask, "Suppose I have contemplated the benefits of cherishing others and generated the loving kindness of endearment and then, unable to bear the way these dear and precious sentient beings are tormented by suffering and are bereft of happiness, I generate compassion for them. Following this, suppose I generate the altruistic resolve to shoulder the responsibility myself to satisfy their wish to be relieved of suffering and enjoy happiness. And suppose such an altruistic resolve then leads to the arising of the awakening mind. What then is the point of adding here something called *tonglen*?"

[Answer:] Such a question comes from a false understanding of the key point about *tonglen*, understanding *tonglen* practice merely as imaginatively visualizing giving away one's own happiness and virtue and taking in others' suffering by placing the two astride the breath. So, let me elaborate here a little. What is called *tonglen* entails the following. Having contemplated the benefits of cherishing others, we generate the loving kindness of endearment holding others more precious than our own life and more valuable than a wish-granting jewel. And contemplating the tragic plight of these dear sentient beings—how they are tormented by suffering and bereft of happiness—compassion arises in us such that find the situation unbearable. Because of this sense of unbearableness, loving kindness wishing to see them enjoy happiness and compassion wishing to see them free from suffering arise spontaneously. However, we cannot leave these at the level of merely wishing to see them enjoy happiness and be relieved of suffering; [453] rather, we must contemplate how these sentient beings remain, as in the phrase "drunk with afflictions, blinded by delusion,"[997] bereft of a protector and refuge. Then contemplate:

> Indeed, these dear and precious sentient beings have brought me so much benefit in the past and will continue to do so in the future. So if they cannot place their hopes in me, in whom can they place their hopes? On my part too, as someone who has been, and will be, the recipient of so much benefit and help from these sentient beings, how could I forsake them? Just as I cannot abandon my dear mother, my gurus, and my meditation deities, how can I forsake sentient beings?

With such an intention of repaying their kindness, think:

> With no hesitation or reservation, I will engage right now in the task of helping sentient beings find relief from suffering and helping them meet with happiness. I take upon myself all their misfortune so that, until the end of samsara, I alone experience all their misfortune and for them there will no longer even be the name *misfortune*. By giving away, this very moment, all of my good fortune and happiness—everything that is good—to all sentient beings, I will ensure that they are never divorced from all the factors of well-being, good fortune, and happiness.

Motivated by such an altruistic resolve, in your action, you place the suffering of others astride your inhalation and your happiness and prosperity astride your exhalation, and in this way you do the visualization of taking and giving. Therefore the cultivation of loving kindness, compassion, and altruistic resolve are all encompassed within *tonglen* practice. Furthermore, *tonglen* is foremost a method to enhance both the focus and the cognitive skills essential to the cultivation of loving kindness, compassion, and the altruistic resolve.

In light of the above, there is no need in this instruction of equalizing and exchanging self and others to have separate meditation topics on great loving kindness, great compassion, repaying kindness, and altruistic resolve. That is why [*tonglen* practice] is presented here. It is not that something called *tonglen practice* independent of such states of mind is somehow being conveyed. Furthermore, it is because we need to perform the visualizations of giving and taking, based on progressive cultivation of these states of mind, that the text itself says, [454] "Therefore, O venerable, most compassionate guru," and so forth.

The teacher shared with me that Yongzin Rinpoché told him that, in *Offering to the Guru* here, Drupwang Losang Namgyal observed that this word "therefore" carries an extremely heavy weight. Words such as this carry numerous meanings and support numerous interpretations, which is why one can speak of the power of words. The point is that such a word supports an extensive range of explanations, not that the word has power from repeated recitation, as with a mantra.

Furthermore, to explain how loving kindness, compassion, and the surge of altruistic resolve connected with *tonglen* could give rise to the awakening mind, the text presents the lines "With the magical lift mounting giving and taking astride the breath, through loving kindness, compassion, and altruistic resolve," and so forth. In connection with these lines, my teacher, the glorious master, said that *tonglen* is a method to enhance both the focus and the cognitive skills essential to altruistic resolve, and that loving kindness and compassion emerge through this *tonglen* practice. This is because *giving* is done in relation to the focus and cognitive aspect of loving kindness, while *taking* is done in relation to the focus and cognitive aspect of compassion. Not only this, repaying kindness is also included in *tonglen*, so there is no need to cultivate it separately. What I have shared here is based on what I have understood from my guru's instruction. Without the guru's oral teaching, even those known as learned ones, let alone those like me, seem to have difficulty even being able to entertain questions concerning difficult points of the path like the present one; what need is there then to speak of the ability to fully comprehend.

Next, the way the surge of altruistic resolve brings forth the awakening mind is presented in the lines "**With the magical lift mounting giving and taking astride the breath,**" and so forth. Here, contemplate:

> Thus, on the basis of the sequential cultivation of loving kindness, compassion, and altruistic resolve in conjunction with the magical lift of *tonglen*, I will contemplate how, even though the responsibility to free other sentient beings from all their suffering and bring about their happiness rests upon me, at the moment I have no such capacity. Who does possess such capacity? If I were to attain the state of perfect buddhahood, then the enlightened activities of such a buddha's body, speech, and mind would come about. As I contemplate this deeply, I am convinced that a time will come when I will have the ability to perfectly bring about others' welfare. [455] In fact, if I fail to attain such a state [of buddhahood], to say nothing of bringing about others' welfare, I would not even fully realize my own welfare.

Then with the support of faith in the enlightened qualities [of a buddha], supplicate, "Bless me, O guru deity, that I may be able to generate a fervent wish to attain the state of perfect buddhahood, the perfect realization of the twofold welfare [of self and others]."

You might ask, "Now, when I see that the responsibility for relieving sentient beings of all suffering and bringing about their happiness rests upon me, isn't it sufficient then to simply generate the wish to attain buddhahood with this objective in mind? What is the point of engaging in extensive discursive contemplation like the above?"

[Answer:] One who is content with simply generating the thought [to attain buddhahood] belies their lack of understanding of how to perfectly realize others' welfare. Such a person not only fails to avert the danger of becoming content with the mere peace of nirvana while [supposedly] pursuing others' welfare, but they also fail to understand how their own perfect welfare is realized, and so they fail to avert the potential for becoming content with the mere peace of nirvana in relation to their own welfare as well. Furthermore, the aspiration to attain buddhahood must be cultivated with an admiring faith in the buddha's qualities as its basis, and so such a person would be generating the awakening mind only at the level of imagination; such a state of mind would not constitute the authentic awakening mind. For the awakening mind to be complete with all its characteristics, it must avert the two kinds of contentment referred to above,[998] and seeing the qualities [of buddhahood] must be the basis for the aspiration [to buddhahood] to arise.

I have written about these points here based on what I have heard from my father guru, which is based on the oral teaching of our exalted guru Jé Tsongkhapa. Citing the words of three masters—Phurchok Lama Jampa, Changkya Rölpai Dorjé, and Jikmé Wangpo[999]—my guru spoke of how difficult it is to even fully understand what awakening mind is, let alone to generate a genuine one with all its characteristics complete. In any case, the elements from the equalizing of self and others up to *tonglen* are unique to the method of equalizing and exchanging of self and others. In contrast, the other elements—the initial equanimity, the recognition of others as mothers, and so forth, as well as the way the surge of the final element, altruistic resolve, gives rise to awakening mind—are common to both methods. My revered father guru said [456] that from the altruistic resolve onward, the two methods converge into one.

Next, the way to uphold the bodhisattva vows is presented in the lines "**The sole path traversed by every conqueror of the three times**" and so forth. Here contemplate:

> For the sake of all sentient beings, I will do my very best to ensure that I attain the precious state of buddhahood. To this end I will embark on the excellent path traversed by all the buddhas of three times and make sure that I am never tainted by transgression of any of the bodhisattva vows—the eighteen root precepts, the forty-six secondary precepts, and the partially concordant ones; I will ensure their purity and guard them as I would guard my eyes. I will practice the threefold ethics,[1000] which are the distillation of all the bodhisattva practices, without regard to costs to my body and life. I will never forsake, not even in my dreams, this aspiration to attain perfect buddhahood.

Then supplicate, "Bless me, O guru deity, that I may be able to accomplish this."

Here, whether one performs a single rite—generating the aspiring awakening mind accompanied by a pledge and the engaging awakening mind in a single stretch—or one performs two separate rites in sequence, either way is fine. One might ask, "In that case, do actual bodhisattva vows arise through this single rite for the aspiring and engaging aspects of the awakening mind or not? If they do, wouldn't the aspiring and engaging aspects of the awakening mind arise simultaneously?"

[Answer:] Certainly, in general, the aspiring awakening mind and the engaging awakening mind do arise sequentially. That said, for a bodhisattva in whom a genuine aspiring awakening mind is already present, whether the bodhisattva vows arise or not will be the same regardless of which of the two rites was used to take the vows. So there seems no contradiction in maintaining that aspiring awakening mind accompanied by a pledge and engaging awakening mind could arise simultaneously [for a bodhisattva]. Similarly, once you have generated even simulated experience of the aspiring awakening mind, then by performing the single rite for generating both the aspiring mind accompanied by a pledge and the engaging awakening mind, you may not receive actual bodhisattva vows, but a similitude of the vows will arise. So, there is no contradiction in maintaining that a similitude of engaging awakening mind does arise at the same time a similitude of aspiring awakening mind accompanied by a pledge has arisen. As to the question of whether these two types of people [the person who generated engaging awakening mind the same time they generated the aspiring awakening mind accompanied by a pledge versus the person in whom only similitudes of the two have arisen] will accrue actual root downfalls when they commit infractions, this is something we must seek conviction about on the basis of the Buddha's words alone. [457] It is difficult to draw a clear line. That said, there is, however, the statement "If a person in whom the vows have not taken root or in whom they have become damaged were to commit a downfall, this would constitute a misdeed,"[1001] so we could look to see if there is a way in which we could understand this question by comparing it to the general approach of the Vinaya rules.

Many, myself included, do not even possess a real understanding of the aspiring awakening mind let alone have experienced the birth of one. So however many times we might participate in the single rite for generating the aspiring awakening mind accompanied by a pledge and the engaging awakening mind, it would be difficult to even attain facsimiles of the aspiring and engaging aspects of the awakening mind let alone generate authentic ones. Even then, such trainees definitely need to observe the precepts; for if we do not observe them, we will accrue downfalls from violating the pledge we made when we took the vows, an act that in itself is a form of "interim virtue."[1002] With this point in mind, my teacher, the glorious and sublime master, would advise us emphatically, "Although when we take the bodhisattva vows, the vows may not actually take birth in those like us, still we need to observe the precepts; for if we do not, we will accrue the downfalls."

Here, some might object: "In the stages-of-the-path texts, the rites for generating the two—the aspiring and engaging aspects of awakening mind—have been presented in sequence for those who possess the *uncontrived* aspiring awakening mind, while for those who have generated the *simulated* aspiring awakening mind, the rite for simultaneous generation of the two have been presented. It would be thus incorrect to perform the single rite for the first type of person."

[Answer:] These texts are simply presenting the procedures for performing the two types of rites mentioned by [past] masters for taking the bodhisattva vows. These texts are not presenting the two rites by correlating them to two distinct types of trainees. So there is no contradiction here, I feel. However, those with discerning minds should examine further. Among those who perform this rite of conferring the vows in the context of a tantric blessing or empowerment, most do not appear to give this point any discernible thought.

Training in generosity is presented in the stanza that includes the line "**Without attachment my body, resources, and virtues of all three times.**" Here, contemplate:

> Through the magic of the instruction on enhancing my thought of giving without any sense of attachment, not just external material possessions, but everything—my body, resources, as well as virtue of three times—by transforming them into whatever sentient beings desire, may I be able to swiftly accomplish the perfection of generosity.

Then supplicate, "Bless me, O guru deity, that I may be able to do this." [458]

Morality is presented in the stanza that includes the line "**entailed by the vows of individual liberation, bodhisattva, and tantra.**" Here, contemplate:

> Through the threefold ethics—the *ethic of restraint*, such as, in the context of individual liberation vows, the 253 precepts as well as the precepts associated with the rites; in the context of bodhisattva vows, the eighteen root precepts and the forty-six second-

> ary precepts defined in terms of their degree of contaminants present; and in the context of tantra, the fourteen root precepts, eight gross transgressions, and commitments pertaining to eating, conduct, and so on; the *ethic of gathering virtue*, and the *ethic of working for the welfare of sentient beings*—may I be able to swiftly accomplish the perfection of morality.

Then supplicate, "Bless me, O guru deity, that I may be able to do this."

Forbearance is presented in the stanza that includes the line "**even if beings in all three realms should become angry with me**." Here, contemplate:

> With ascertainment induced by discriminating wisdom analyzing the faults of anger and the benefits of forbearance, even if every sentient being of the three realms, let alone one or two sentient beings, should rise up not as loved ones or neutral beings but as enemies, I will never cause them even the slightest harm. On their part, even if they were to insult me, slander me, threaten me, or even take my life, through the wondrous bodhisattva logic of exchanging self and others, I will not respond to them with anger, not event for a single moment, and will instead seek their well-being.

Then supplicate, "Bless me, O guru deity, that I may swiftly accomplish the perfection of forbearance through the practice of the three types of forbearance—the forbearance of being unperturbed by harms, the forbearance of voluntarily embracing suffering, and the forbearance born of reflecting upon the Dharma."

Diligence is presented in the stanza that includes the line "**if, even for the sake of a single sentient being, I have to remain**." Here, contemplate:

> Even if, for the sake of each and every single sentient being, I have to remain in the fires of the Relentless hell for an interminable period, an ocean of eons, I will not become discouraged even momentarily. Drawing on my own experience of suffering when relating to the suffering of other beings, such as those in the hells, thanks to the force of my compassion borne of finding such situations unbearable, I will not be disheartened even for a moment but will engage and be with them.

Then supplicate, "Bless me, O guru deity, that I may be able to swiftly accomplish the perfection of diligence through practice of the three kinds of diligence."[1003]

Meditative absorption is presented in the stanza that begins "**Discarding the faults of laxity, excitation, and distractions.**" [459] Here, contemplate:

> As I engage in cultivating concentration characterized by nondiscursiveness and vibrant clarity, when mental laxity—the hindrance to vibrant clarity—arises, I will apply the methods that lift up my mind, such as appreciating my human existence of leisure and opportunity. And when distraction—the hindrance to nondiscursiveness—arises, I will apply the methods for ceasing discursive thinking, such as recognizing thoughts as thoughts, severing thoughts directly, and so on. By applying these methods correctly, may I be free from these hindrances.

Then supplicate, "Bless me, O guru deity, that I may swiftly accomplish the perfection of meditative absorption through single-pointed concentration with my mind focused on emptiness, undistracted and never straying beyond the bounds of mindfulness and meta-awareness."

The way to sustain the space-like meditative equipoise is presented in the lines "**Bless me that I may accomplish the perfection of wisdom through the space-like yoga of equipoise on the ultimate**" and so forth. Here, contemplate:

> Not wavering even the tiniest degree from single pointed equipoise on emptiness within a state characterized by bliss, clarity, and nondiscursiveness, the more I analyze suchness from one part of my mind, the more secure my attentional stability becomes, like a minnow swimming in a clear lake. As a result, this gives rise to great bliss.

Then supplicate, "Bless me, O guru deity, that I may, through this space-like meditative equipoise joined with great bliss, swiftly accomplish the perfection of wisdom."

The way to sustain the illusion-like post-equipoise stage is presented in the stanza that includes the line "**perceiving how outer and inner phenomena—like an illusion, a dream.**" Here, contemplate:

> From having meditated during equipoise on all phenomena being empty of intrinsic existence, once I rise from this session, may I spontaneously perceive whatever appears subsequently to my six classes of consciousness—all phenomena of my external and internal worlds—as dreamlike or like reflections in a mirror.

Then supplicate, "Bless me, O guru deity, that I may swiftly perfect the illusion-like concentration."

The way to maintain Nāgārjuna's view, wherein appearance and emptiness become each other's cause and effect, is presented in the stanza that includes the line "**that not even an atom of samsara and nirvana exists intrinsically.**" Here, contemplate:

> As I contemplate the emptiness aspect—that not even an atom exists with intrinsic nature—this naturally gives rise to the ascertainment of the appearance aspect—that the dependent origination of cause and effect is infallible. Similarly, as I contemplate the appearance aspect—that dependent origination of cause and effects is infallible—[460] this gives rise naturally to ascertainment of the emptiness aspect, the emptiness of intrinsic existence.

Then supplicate, "Bless me, O guru deity, that I may be able to realize the ultimate intent of the excellent Ārya Nāgārjuna, whereby the meaning of emptiness emerges in terms of dependent origination and the meaning of dependent origination arises in terms of emptiness."

The lines "**Bless me that I may then, through the kindness of the helmsman Vajradhara,**" and so forth present the way, thanks to vajra master's kindness, you become a vessel receptive to practicing the path, the way you eliminate doubts through study and critical reflection, and the way, having become an appropriate vessel, you maintain the purity of the vows and commitments. Here, contemplate:

> Thus, having trained in the common paths, I will once again please the vajra master in both thought and action without regard to costs to my body, life, and resources. Having been conferred the four empowerments to their highest standard and thus having been prepared to establish the basis for the path of the two stages together with their attendant factors and to effectively plant

> the seeds for the four buddha bodies, I will, on the basis of the instructions that correlate the root tantras with their explanatory tantras, engage in their study and critical reflection. I will also guard, as more precious than my eyes or life itself, the commitments and vows common and specific to the five buddha families, an act that is the root of attaining the siddhis.

Then supplicate, "Bless me, O guru deity, that I may be able to do this."

How to train in the first stage of the path is presented in the lines "**Bless me that I may, through the yoga of the first stage,**" and so forth. Here, contemplate:

> Bless me, O guru deity, that by practicing the path that transforms birth, death, and the intermediate state of the ground into the three buddha bodies of the path, as well as its attendant factors, I may be sustained through all my lives by my meditation deity. May I be able to ripen all the roots of virtue to actualize the three bodies of the path, and by purifying ordinary perception and conception, may I be able to view whatever I perceive as deities.

How to train in the second stage of the path is presented in the stanza that includes the lines "**arising from placing your feet at the center of my eight-petal lotus heart inside the central channel.**" Here, contemplate:

> Bless me, O guru deity, that through the force of visualizing your form as my triply kind guru at the center of my heart cakra, supplicating you, and engaging in the repetition of your mantra to invoke your attention, [461] I may actualize the two levels of clear light (illustrative and actual), the illusory body (pure and impure), and the levels of union (that of the learner's stage and that of no more learning)—the entire essence of the five stages of completion—within this very life.

Having trained well like this in both the common and the uncommon paths, if you do not succeed in attaining a secure ground, then the way to apply the transference of consciousness at the moment of death is presented in the lines "**If I should die before reaching the start of the path,**" and so forth. Here, contemplate:

> Bless me, O guru deity, that if I die before reaching a secure ground, despite having trained in the entire body of the path of sutra and tantra on the basis of this precious existence of leisure and opportunity, I may, through the application of the transference of consciousness based on guru yoga, which is the method taught in tantra for helping someone with heavy negative karma instantly attain buddhahood, or through the mind training instruction to be applied at the point of death[1004]—namely, the combined application of the five powers of positive seed, aspirational prayer, propelling intention, eradication, and acquaintance—depart to the pure lands, be reborn as a knowledge bearer in the land of ḍākinīs, or be reborn as a fully ordained monastic vajra-holder endowed with the three vows.

The way to make aspirational prayers so that you are sustained throughout all lives by your guru and you become a principal heir or first among the guru's retinue is presented in the lines **"In short, in each and in all my lives,"** and so forth. Here, contemplate thus:

> In brief, having embraced this guru yoga as my heart practice—the distilled essence of the entire eighty-four thousand heaps of Dharma, the heart practice of the learned scholars and accomplished siddhas of both India and Tibet, and that which encompasses the complete paths of sutra and tantra—and having engaged in this practice through great hardship and without regard to costs to my body, life, and resources, and with great waves of effort, at best I seek to attain buddhahood in this very life; and if not, then within two or three lives; at very least, not later than sixteen lives. In these future lives as well, O my father guru, pray sustain me and never leave me; grant me the nectar of instruction distilling the essence of your heart. [462] Reveal to me all the qualities of your body, speech, and mind, without keeping anything secret, qualities that are not perceptible to others. Because of this, may I become your chief spiritual heir, upholding all the secrets of your body, speech, and mind. Furthermore, as you perform such enlightened deeds as gaining full enlightenment, turning the wheel of Dharma, and so forth for our sake, wherever you may perform such deeds as a buddha, may I be born

> among the first disciples of the specific buddha forms you assume. In brief, may it be auspicious that all your enlightened intentions for both immediate and ultimate aims may be realized with ease and in accordance with your aspirations.

As you supplicate in these above ways, imagine that [in each instance] the stains that obstruct the specific objectives [related to the various elements of the path] are cleansed and that the specific realizations relevant to that context are attained.

There is a custom to perform the rite of offering a torma at this point. [If you wish to do this,] gather the torma ingredients in accord with what is found in the tantras and the great treatises of the great siddhas. As for shapes and forms, prepare these in accord with the tradition of those of the Ensa oral transmission. Then consecrate the torma in accordance with the rite of inner offering of any of the three main deities—Guhyasamāja, Cakrasaṃvara, or Vajrabhairava. Imagine that the guru and the assembled deities partake in the torma offering by extracting the essence through their tongues in the form of straws of light. Offer the torma by reciting three or seven times the mantra: *Oṃ āḥ guru buddha bodhisattva ḍākinī dharmapāla saparivāra idaṃ baliṃta kha kha khāhi khāhi.* Also honor them with inner and outer offerings. Then offer them praises by reciting such verses as "Guru is the Buddha, Guru is the Dharma. . ."[1005] as well as the verse "Teacher of gods and all beings. . ."[1006] Here, if you wish to recite praises to the Dharma protectors of the paths of the three capacities, this would be fine too.[1007]

Some appear to mix in here the rites of offering a torma to the mundane protectors, offering them praises, and invoking their action. This betrays a grave misunderstanding. Here, my teacher, the glorious guru, said: [463] "When performing the rite of offering a torma, it is not essential to view yourself—the one offering the torma—in the form of the deity to whom you are offering it, but it is essential, however, that what is being offered—the torma, inner offering, and so forth—is consecrated precisely according to how such rites are found in the sādhanas specific to the deities."

Dissolving the merit field

Next, there is a tradition to make a mandala offering, either a long or a short version, and then dissolve the merit field. So, having made the mandala offering, recite the lines "**Having supplicated you like this, O supreme guru,**" and so forth. There are two ways to dissolve the merit field, the common version and the uncommon version.

The first is as follows. As you refresh your visualization of the merit field and make supplications to the merit-field figures from the very bone of your heart, from the *hūṃ* at the heart of triple-being guru radiate beams of light, which touch all the deities in the outer perimeter as well as the merit-field tree and the various offering substances. As a result, they all shine with brilliance, becoming ever more radiant and clear, eventually all melting into light and dissolving into the wish-granting tree. The tree too melts into light and dissolves into the lion throne. The various deities, both peaceful and wrathful, in the space around the tree also melt into light and dissolve in sequence, with the outer circle dissolving into the inner circle. Finally, the deities of the four classes of tantra dissolve into Guru Munīndra Vajradhara Losang Drakpa from the four sides of his body. The lineage gurus of vast practice and the lineage gurus of profound view dissolve, respectively, into Maitreya and Mañjuśrī. All the gurus from whom you have received teachings dissolve into the root guru from whom you have received the transmission of this guru-yoga instruction. The lineage gurus of practice and blessing as well as the lineage gurus of the near transmission of this guru yoga dissolve into Vajradhara.

Then, focusing your attention on the five figures, the principal one plus the four retinue figures,[1008] then imagine Maitreya and Mañjuśrī dissolving from each side of the triple-being guru. If the guru from whom you have received the guidance instruction on this guru yoga is alive, imagine his entire body absorbing [into the principal figure], and if not then imagine that he first melts into a blue light and then dissolves into the heart of the principal figure. Vajradhara enters through the crown of the principal figure and dissolves into the gnosis being [Vajradhara] at his heart. The lion throne, together with its multilayered lotus cushion, dissolves into the sun and moon discs. [464] Then imagine that the triple-being guru, together with the sun and moon disc cushions, descends to your crown, yourself visualized in the form of Vajrabhairava, and sits at the opening of your crown aperture. He gradually shrinks in size until the triple-being guru is about the size of a pea or the first segment of your thumb. The guru then visibly enters through your crown aperture and becomes inseparable from the extremely subtle primordial wind-mind at your heart. Then imagine in a firm way how the three—the guru, the meditation deity, and your own mind—have become an indivisible entity.

The second [uncommon dissolution] is as follows. Earlier, when consecrating the environment and its inhabitants, you viewed all environments as celestial mansions and the beings within as deities. So, at this stage [when dissolving the merit field], imagine limitless beams of red light radiate from the *hūṃ* at your heart and from the point where you in deity form are joined in sexual union with the consort. These beams of light touch all the environments and their inhabitants, making them all become ever more radiant and clear, eventually all of them melting into light and dissolving into you. Now, if you wish to dissolve the figures of the merit field, as you did in the previous version, imagine that the central figure descends to the opening of your crown aperture. Then visualize the three [main] channels [running vertically] inside your body, slightly closer to the back. Visualize cakras—four, five, or six in number—emerging at the appropriate points in the body according to the way they are visualized generally in completion-stage practice.[1009]

Then imagine that the principal figure of the merit field, seated at your crown, progressively shrinks in size—if you are able, visualize him as small as a barley seed or, if not, the size of a pea—and enters through the crown aperture into the central channel. As he arrives at the crown cakra, light rays emanate from his body, filling all the channels at the crown cakra and illuminating them. This blesses the channels to become supple and the winds to become serviceable. Imagine that all the faults associated with the degeneration of commitments in relation to the guru's body are cleansed and purified. The guru then arrives at the throat cakra; here, perform similar visualization as before about light rays emanating and blessing the channels and the winds and purifying degenerated commitments related to the guru's speech. Next, he arrives at the heart cakra, where you imagine him dissolving into the extremely subtle primordial wind-mind, which is inside the indestructible drop, white on the top and red on the bottom, in the manner of a closed jewel casket. [465] Imagine that your primordial wind-mind and the triple-being guru have fused indistinguishably. Considering the red part of the indestructible drop as the guru's cushion and the white part as the guru's robes, maintain the firm thought that the three—your triply kind guru, meditation deity Jé Tsongkhapa, and your own mind—have become fused into a single taste, transcending even the subtlest trace of separateness and dualistic appearance. This is akin to the repeated directives that we must view the drop, our meditation deity, and our own mind in such a manner that they have become fused indistinguishably into a single taste. At this point [when guru arrives at the heart cakra] too, you should perform, as before, the visualization of light rays emanating and blessing the channels and the winds [and purifying degenerated commitments related to the guru's mind].

Mahāmudrā

Mahāmudrā according to the tantric system

Mahāmudrā, the main practice,[1010] is twofold: mahāmudrā according to the sutra system and mahāmudrā according to the tantric system. Of these two, the latter pertains to meditation on emptiness by a subject, innate great bliss, a subject arisen through the threefold process of entry, abiding, and absorption of winds in the central channel brought about by a unique technique of penetrating the vital point of the vajra body. The Guhyasamāja tantra says the heart should be the primary focus for penetrating the body, while other tantras say it should be the navel. As for where one should focus first, the Jñānapāda tradition of Guhyasamāja says that one should begin by focusing on the *indestructible drop* at the heart, then at the *subtle drop* at the tip of the sexual organ, next at the *light drop* at the tip of the nostrils, and then visualize an extraordinary indestructible drop at the heart. This tradition thus instructs us to penetrate the vital point at the heart first. In the Ārya [Nāgārjuna] tradition of Guhyasamāja, however, it states that one first focuses on the *subtle drop* at the tip of the sexual organ, then at the *mantra drop* at the heart, and next at the *light drop* (at the tip of the nostrils). So this tradition states that one penetrates the vital point of the body by first focusing at the tip of the sexual organ.

In general, it is said that those who have accomplished the subtle drop practice of the generation stage [466] are better off penetrating the vital point of the body at the lower door [the tip of the sexual organ]. In contrast, for those who have accomplished the coarse level of the generation stage but not the subtle stage, it makes no difference whether they penetrate the body first at the heart or at the lower door. In any case, if you try to penetrate the body by focusing first at the heart but cannot draw the wind in there, you should just employ the techniques to penetrate the body at another site. It is said that once you become experienced in drawing in the wind through repeated practice of such techniques, you should then penetrate the vital point of the body at the heart. If you wish is to plant the imprints of practicing mahāmudrā without having accomplished either the coarse or the subtle level of the generation stage, then it seems it makes no difference whether you penetrate the body by focusing on the heart first or on the lower door first. If you wish to take the heart as the vital point to penetrate the body first, then do so as follows.

Just as you did earlier when the merit field was dissolved,[1011] imagine at the center of your heart cakra the extremely subtle wind-mind assumes the form of the triple-being guru complete with the *bindu* drop. Imagine that your mind has entered into it. Then, as you imagine drawing in the winds flowing through the left and right channels to enter, abide, and absorb in the central channel, imagine experiencing the stages of dissolution from the mirage-like up to clear light. Imagine that throughout these stages, you experience the four joys in both forward and reverse sequence. At the point of the fourth joy, the *innate joy*, bring to mind the view [of emptiness] you searched for earlier and remain in meditative equipoise on this union of bliss and emptiness. Then, as you begin to conclude this equipoise, imagine that, when the near attainment of the reverse sequence arises, owing to the force of your intention, you arise simultaneously as the illusory body of the saṃbhogakāya. This illusory body assumes a nirmāṇakāya in the form of the gnosis being residing at the heart of the commitment being—namely, your own body visualized as a meditation deity in union with consort. During the post-equipoise periods, perceive whatever appears to you as empty, and then while maintaining this awareness and bringing the innate bliss you experienced earlier to mind, fuse emptiness and bliss. Then imagine this fusion of bliss and emptiness arising in the form of a deity. In this way, undertake the practices in sequence starting from body isolation. My most revered teacher said that although here the lines "arising from placing your feet at the center of my eight-petal lotus heart"[1012] and so forth explicitly present vajra recitation, which is a part of *vitality stopping*,[1013] when it comes to actual practice, it is essential that you do so in sequence starting with body isolation.

Now, if you penetrate the vital point of the body by focusing first on the lower door, bring the indestructible drop at the heart, together with the guru, down either to inside the cakra at the sexual organ or to the point in the central channel just inside the tip of the jewel. [467] And on this basis, engage in single-pointed meditation. Then, bringing the focus back to the heart, meditate on the mantra drop and so on.

Thus, having ascertained in detail the stages of meditative practice, follow the Ārya tradition of Guhyasamāja for how you should actually engage in the practice itself and how you should remove the hindrances and enhance your practice. Detailed understanding of the unique aspects of the meditative practice of this [mahāmudrā] instruction need to be learned from a guru's oral teaching. All these extremely difficult points pertaining to the intent of the precious tantras can be understood with the help of instructions from authoritative masters who are both learned and realized. Even though someone like me cannot speak about these points by himself, not even in partial terms, I have nonetheless explained them here to the degree I do understand them as a basis for examination by those of discerning minds. For this I have drawn on the words of my sublime guru, the commentary of Guru Yongzin Rinpoché,[1014] and the excellent treatises that present the instructions of the completion stage in clear terms.

Mahāmudrā according to the sutra system

Mahāmudrā according to the sutra system, the first of the two systems, is a meditation on emptiness, the explicit subject matter of the Perfection of Wisdom scriptures. Alternatively, this is known as the way to practice according to the Guide to the Middle Way View instruction.

Some might wonder, "Since there is no difference between this and the Guide to the Middle Way View, there is no point in giving it the name *mahāmudrā*. Furthermore, it seems highly inappropriate to undertake all the elements of its preliminary practice as if preparing for the completion stage."

[Answer:] The point raised is indeed an extremely difficult matter. Allow me to offer a brief explanation based on my own understanding, relying on the words of sublime gurus who are realized in the oral teaching of this particular instruction.

Here, one first, on the basis of applying the method for overcoming such faults as mental laxity, excitation, distraction, and mental scattering, as found in the treatises of the great trailblazers and, in particular, in the unique pith instructions of the great siddhas, recognizes the conventional-truth nature of the coarse level of the primordial mind. Seizing this [conventional-truth nature of the coarse level of the primordial mind] with mindfulness, [468] without any distraction, one gains mastery over this coarse level of mind and then applies it to the meditation on emptiness. Through this way of meditating on emptiness applying the magic of the skillful means of penetrating the vital point of the vajra body, the eighty indicative conceptions along with the winds that propel their movements come to be withdrawn. This allows the primordial subtle mind to become manifest, and one gains mastery over it. Such meditation on emptiness is similar in aspect to, and serves as a ripening factor for, emptiness meditation by the subtle primordial mind. Furthermore, the manner in which the subtle primordial mind meditates on emptiness involves joining bliss and emptiness on the basis of bringing to mind the view that was previously sought and found. For if you were to engage in discursive analysis searching for the meditation object while in that subtle mind, that would become a hindrance for drawing the winds [into the central channel]. Therefore you need to search for the meditative object of emptiness beforehand [i.e., before the arising of the subtle mind]. *So to search for emptiness, as stated above, on the basis of the coarse level of the primordial mind is the method of searching for the meditation object unique to mahāmudrā practice.*[1015] And to do so is most appropriate. Similarly, to give such practice the name *mahāmudrā* is also entirely correct. The epithet *mahāmudrā* is used to refer to meditation on emptiness in the sutras too. For instance, the *King of Meditations Sutra* says, "The nature of all phenomena is the great seal."[1016]

Furthermore, meditation on emptiness with the subtle primordial mind must be preceded by the following preliminaries: one has perfectly received the four empowerments, one has maintained pure observance of the commitments and vows pledged at the time of the empowerments, one has gained experience in the first stage, and one has gathered great waves of merit on the basis of the uncommon guru-yoga practice. Since the context here [in this instruction] is the search for the meditative object, it has great relevance for engaging in such preliminary practices. Those who seek the meditative object, emptiness, without having received the four empowerments, however, have no need for such preliminary practices.[1017] In fact, it would be inappropriate for such people to pursue them. But for those who have received the four empowerments, it is part of their own pledged commitments to engage in the meditative practice of the generation stage, to undertake such practices as the means to maintain pure commitments and vows, and to do the uncommon guru yoga. So they are certainly not without purpose. [469]

How to cultivate the concentration of mental stability

With respect to the actual practice, there are two approaches: *one where one first seeks ascertainment of the view and, on that basis, seeks stability*, and a second where *one first seeks stability and, having found stability, seeks ascertainment of the view*. Of these two, the first is from the standpoint of a special category of individuals who are endowed with secure imprints of the view and have predispositions toward tranquil abiding that are certain to be awakened. In contrast, the second approach is from the standpoint of today's persons, including even those who simply aspire to leave an imprint about the view. Here we will proceed according to this second approach.

For this, as before, dissolve the merit field and focus your attention on the triple-being guru at your crown and make the following supplication with fervent faith and reverence:

> O guru deity, bless me that I may be able to identify the subtle object of negation according to the Prāsaṅgika, without error and in a naked manner, just as done by Nāgārjuna father and son, the supreme siddha Buddhapālita, the glorious Candrakīrti, and Jé Tsongkhapa and his spiritual sons. Bless me so the excellent path of Nāgārjuna, which represents the elimination of such an object of negation and in which dependent origination emerges as the meaning of emptiness, arises swiftly in me.

As you make such a fervent supplication, from the very bones of your heart, as it were, imagine that the guru, either in the form of indivisible union with the indestructible wind-mind at your heart or in his normal human form, dissolves into you. This leads to the inseparable fusing of the guru's body, speech, and mind with your own body, speech, and mind, merging as if into a single taste. Then remain in this state for a little while. While in such a state of mind, wherein all appearances have become somewhat indistinct, rest your mind for a little while without distraction, without entertaining any thoughts about mundane events or affairs—hopes for pleasure, joy, and fame or fears of suffering and disgrace. Then set a strong, forceful intention, "I will ensure that my mind is not distracted by anything," and simply rest your mind in that state that is undistracted, clear, and vivid. In this way, maintain your mindfulness in a continuous manner, single-pointedly free of distraction. As you engage in this, also, with one part of your mind, [470] apply meta-awareness that monitors every now and then whether your mind is still abiding on the meditative object as placed.

Here too, with respect to mindfulness, it is not enough to simply retain the object without losing it. You need is a forceful mindfulness capable of maintaining single-pointed focus on the meditation object with a vibrant mode of apprehension. When you are able to apply such genuine mindfulness, given that meta-awareness is an effect of such mindfulness, it will be readily available whenever required. In fact, there is no meta-awareness that is not contingent upon mindfulness. Note that the statement that meta-awareness is an effect of mindfulness should not be understood to be like the statement "The sprout is an effect of the seed." Rather, it should be understood as analogous to the statement "Light rays are effects of the light." If we relate this point to our own experience, meta-awareness is that activity of monitoring whether our mind is still abiding on the meditative object as placed, and it arises as a finer aspect differentiated from the main mindfulness that continues to remain focused single-pointedly on the meditative object without distraction.

Now if while meta-awareness is monitoring, you see that the mind is abiding on the meditative object as placed, then let your mind rest as it is in a relaxed way. If, in contrast, the mind is not abiding and has lost the vibrancy of its mode of apprehension, you then need to revive vibrancy and then continue with your meditation. When [the hindrances of] mental scattering and excitation occur, you should, while ensuring that the meditative object is not lost from the field of your mindfulness, use a small part of your mind to apply any of the following three distinct methods: (1) look, as it were, at the face of the distracting thoughts themselves, (2) trample on the thoughts, or (3) simply observe how the thoughts arise. When the thoughts naturally dissolve as a result, then let your mind rest in that state that is unobscured, empty, clear, and vivid.

You might ask: "With what kind of body and mind should I apply such distinctive mindfulness and meta-awareness?"

[Answer:] What you need is this. On the surface, there should be a relaxed letting go of effort, both of the body and mind; yet underneath, you should maintain an alert mode of apprehension with firmness. My father guru himself says, "On the surface, keep your mind in a relaxed state; at the core, however, maintain alertness in your mind; this is how you should meditate."[1018] This very approach is taught repeatedly by many learned and realized teachers, such as Candragomin, Saraha, Machik Labdrön, and so on.[1019] [471]

You might think: "The context here is a discussion on how to cultivate concentration, so such an extensive explanation of how to apply mindfulness seems irrelevant."

[Response:] This indeed raises an extremely challenging point, so I will explain briefly from my own understanding based on the instruction of my father guru. When one is applying mindfulness continuously, in the manner explained above, with alertness and with single-pointed focus of the mind without any distraction from the meditation object, from the perspective of the mind's maintenance of the meditation object as introduced by the guru's instruction without any distraction, this is called *mindfulness*. From the perspective of the mind's single-pointed abiding on the meditation object as maintained in mindfulness, this is called *concentration* (*samādhi*). It is actually a single state of mind where a differentiation is made in terms of its aspects. This means that, since concentration arises through the function of mindfulness, there is no distinct practice of maintaining concentration separate from the practice of maintaining mindfulness. With these points in mind, my father guru said, "My guru Yongzin Rinpoché would say that the essence of concentration is indeed mindfulness. Now if we take this to be the case, would it be acceptable to those of you who are learned in the great treatises?"[1020] Furthermore, I feel the perspective offered here is consistent with the following two statements. The omniscient Jé Tsongkhapa states:

> Even someone maintaining a purely nondiscursive meditative state needs to set the thought "I will make sure my mind does not engage in discursive thoughts of any objects" and, on this basis, maintain awareness free of movement and distraction. *Nondistraction* here has the same meaning as mindfulness that ensures there is no loss of the meditative object, and this practice is, in essence, nothing but a practice of mindfulness. And the person who is engaged in such meditative practice should maintain a quality of mindfulness powerful enough to give rise to ascertainment.[1021]

Similarly, most revered Panchen Losang Chögyen says:

> The meaning of *distraction* and *nondistraction* is this:
> the mind that is placed on a chosen meditative object,
> not letting it out of the field of mindfulness and awareness
> and abiding unwavering and single-pointed,
> this is referred to here as *nondistraction*.[1022]

Thus, through engaging in the meditative practice of cultivating mental stability for those on the beginner's stage, as outlined above, [472] and through applying the distinctive method of maintaining mindfulness focused on the mind, you will recognize with abiding stability the conventional nature of the mind, experientially and as introduced by the guru's instruction. You will experience your mind as *clear*, for it is not obscured by laxity, excitation, and so on; as space-like *vacuity*, for it does not exist with any physical properties; as *vivid*, for it has the capacity to reveal the appearance of any kind of object. Even if you do not gain such stable recognition [of the conventional nature of the mind], when you have found a relative degree of stability in your recognition, even a partial one, of the nature of mind, it is at that point that you will need to be introduced to the ultimate nature of the mind. The teacher said that for those like me, a beginner who has found not even a small measure of mental stability, no matter how much their current mind of seeking the meaning of the scriptures may engage in analysis of the ultimate nature of things, no experience of the view is likely to emerge.[1023]

Meditation on the selflessness of persons

It is said that [with respect to emptiness] we should first meditate on the selflessness of persons, so here is how you engage the ultimate mode of being of the person, the meditator him or herself.

For instance, when minnows swim about in still water that is undisturbed by things such as wind, whether they swim deep or just below the surface, this in no way obstructs the water's transparency and stillness. In the same manner, when from within the meditative equipoise cultivated earlier you apply a small part of the mind to an analysis involving four key points, you must do so in a way that does not undermine your meditative equipoise, regardless of how much you analyze in terms of the four key points.[1024] This means that while in such meditative equipoise, without wavering in the slightest and applying a small part of your mind, you need to bring awareness to your innate self-grasping—[discerning] how it is the root of our tendency to blame others, our hopes for happiness, our fears of encountering suffering, and so on. With the main part of your mind directed at your "I"-grasping, with a fine distinct part of your mind, observe how the "I" appears to your innate "I"-grasping mind [473] and examine in a subtle and skillful way how this mind grasps at such an "I." In this way, discern accurately how such an "I" appears and how it is grasped at.

As you examine carefully in this manner, you will discover that the two—the way in which the "I" appears and the way in which it is conceived—often get conflated with your perception of other objects. Sometimes you feel you do recognize them [the appearance and conception of "I"], and yet other times you feel you do not. So it is critical you do not rush to any conclusion. Instead, engage in practices of gathering merit and purifying negative karma, and make frequent supplications [to the guru deity] that you may come to identify the object of negation without error. Then, as you continue your analysis, examine what you recognize to be its *mode of appearance* and its *mode of apprehension* to see whether they are consonant with the authentic instructions of the successive lineage masters stemming from our exalted guru Jé Tsongkhapa. On this point, my father guru says:

> This afflicted mind can really fool you. It hides behind other objects, so sometimes you feel as if you are identifying it and sometimes you do not. Thus we should not rely on being able to identify it once or twice. Rather, aided by gathering merit and purifying negative karma, and by making supplication to our gurus from the very bones of our heart that the recognition of the object of negation may arise in us without error, make repeated efforts to identify it.[1025]

This innate "I"-grasping arises in us naturally and powerfully, even in our dreams. However, the opportunity to readily and clearly recognize such grasping, unmixed with perceptions and apprehension of other things, arises only when, for instance, we are unjustly blamed, or when we experience strong fear and anxiety and so on, but not on other occasions. When such situations do come up, however, it is typically very difficult to pursue inquiry at that moment. And if we turn to inquiry but too late, we will recognize nothing at all. My father guru says, "The moment for the arising of such clear awareness of innate "I"-grasping is so short, for it instantly comes to be conflated with other objects. Thus gaining an accurate recognition of it is most difficult indeed."[1026] In fact, the reason why Cutting Off (*chö*) practice can be a booster for the view of emptiness is because practicing Cutting Off transforms disturbing experiences and hallucinations caused by gods and demons into the path of inducing clear recognition of "I"-grasping; and when such clear recognition does arise, then you have an opportunity to realize the view of emptiness quite easily. [474] That this is so emerges in the words of my guru. Most, however, seem to understand the way Cutting Off enhances the view as a function of how in Cutting Off practice one offers one's body and life to the gods and demons and how this reduces the force of one's clinging and attachment. I feel this interpretation misses the key point.

Similarly, Cutting Off practice can be a booster for the awakening mind that values others as more precious than one's own self. When gods and demons create disturbances and hallucinations to the point where self-cherishing arises spontaneously—to a degree where you cannot simply stop it—then you could seize this self-cherishing as your arch enemy and contemplate its faults from all angles. This helps induce the thought to exchange self with others to the point where you want to let go of your body and mind in their entirety. In contrast, when there are no such threats and you are content, this so-called self-cherishing feels like something that exists elsewhere. To enumerate the faults of self-cherishing and undertake the exchange of self and others on this basis will not impact your mind very much. This is something you can discern if you turn your attention inward and observe.

In brief, when as a result of repeated examinations you come to recognize, as if nakedly, the way the innate "I"-grasping perceives and clings [to an "I"], you will notice that within that awareness is no perception of any aggregates, any shape or color, or any indeterminate vacuity. Rather what is discerned is the appearance and apprehension of an "I" that is independent, existing in its own right as if from the side of the aggregates—something seemingly concrete or tangible. There is simply no other way.

Now, when you examine the modes of appearance and apprehension of "I"-grasping, if perceptions of aggregates, shape, and so forth do occur, this would then represent only the acquired mode of apprehension of self, such as the view of some Buddhist schools that assert that the aggregates or the configuration of aggregates constitutes the self, or the non-Buddhist schools that view the self as an eternal, unitary, and autonomous entity. So when the thought "I am" arises in you naturally, and when you focus on the "I" that has suddenly arisen in dependence on the aggregates—which are its designative bases—if such an "I" appears to possess independent existence and is apprehended accordingly, what are referred to the *mode of appearance* and the *mode of apprehension* of the innate "I"-grasping are present. This is how I understand it. Of course, this [nature of self] has been a challenge for the intellect of so many learned minds of both the Buddhist and non-Buddhist schools. So someone like me could not speak about it on my own even to a partial degree. [475] That said, what I have explained here is what I understand to be indicated in the great treatises as the *innate "I"-grasping*[1027] based on the excellent instruction of our exalted guru Jé Tsongkhapa on the following lines of Candrakīrti and based on the oral teachings of my own father guru. Candrakīrti states:

> You assert the aggregates to be the self
> because the Buddha has said the aggregates are the self.

> But this statement rejects a self that is separate from the aggregates, and he also said in other sutras that form is not self and so on.[1028]

So those with unbiased and discerning minds, please analyze.

With respect to the sequence of the stages in which we seek to identify the appearance and apprehension of the object of negation, first we should cultivate, with study and reflection, a meticulous understanding of how to posit all phenomena as dependently originating nominal realities[1029] through study and critical reflection. Later in meditative equipoise, when as a result of analyzing the manner in which the object of negation—namely, the mode of existence contrary to dependently originating nominal reality—is perceived and apprehended, you have gained error-free identification [of the object of negation], you should then apply logical reasons, such as the absence of identity and difference. Understanding how these kinds of logical reasons are rooted in [the reasoning of] dependent origination or in direct perception, generate the ascertainment endowed with two attributes: *awareness* that the given thing appears in such manner and the *determination* that it does not exist as it appears.

Here is how phenomena are posited as dependently originating nominal realities. Say the thought "There is a snake" arises spontaneously upon seeing a coiled striped rope lying on the ground in conditions of low visibility. From the meeting of two things—the rope that is the basis of the cognitive error and the delusory thought—the perception "snake" appeared inescapably in relation to the rope. Yet in no way do we see this delusory perception [of a snake] for what it is; instead, we have the sense that the perceived snake exists in its own right, not contingent on anything else, and independently of the basis, the coiled rope. The person both perceives such a snake and also conceives its existence just as it appears. Now were it to actually exist as it appears, such a snake could not suddenly arise through the convergence of the presence of a rope, which is the basis of cognitive error, and the apprehension of snake on the rope. And when either of these two conditions is no more, [476] such a snake cannot itself maintain its existence. Nor is it logically possible for it to be otherwise,[1030] for it to not be a dependently originated construct. Yet no one can deny that such a snake is indeed a dependently originated construct; any perception to the contrary can be nothing but delusory.

Similarly, by perceiving the collection of your aggregates engaged in the act of eating when the spontaneous thought "I am eating a meal" has arisen, the convergence of two facts—the mere collection of the aggregates eating (the designative basis) and the designating thought "I am eating a meal"—inescapably induces the vivid sense of an "I" eating a meal. Nowhere is there a sense that such a perception has arisen owing to the delusion of ignorance. Rather, the sense is of an "I" not contingent on anything else—neither a designative basis nor a designating subject—instead existing objectively by way of the collection of aggregates performing the act of eating. Not only do we *perceive* such an "I" who is eating, we also *conceive* such an "I" to exist as it appears. Now if such an "I" were to actually exist as perceived, how could it be that such an "I" arises only suddenly when the designative basis and the designating subject referred to above converge? And why, when either of the two becomes no more, does such an "I" also cease right there and then and cannot itself maintain its existence? It is logically not possible for it to be otherwise, for it not to be a dependently originated construct. Yet to admit [it as not being a dependently originating construct] is untenable. In contrast, if it could remain as the "eating I" independently of other factors, even when the collection of aggregates, the designative basis, stopped eating, then the following consequence would ensue. While the *designative basis* is impermanent, the *designated* ["I"] would be permanent, and the two would possess contradictory characteristics. Furthermore, the eating "I" would not be contingent on the activity of eating, leading to the consequence that there could be an agent of an act without any action. This in turn would lead to the consequence that all the instances of an "I," eating and not eating, would become one. Such logical faults would ensue.

Furthermore, if one accepts the independent existence of an eating "I" even when the mind designating such an "I" has ceased, the existence of such an "I" would not be contingent on the designating mind but would be grounded in the designative bases objectively. [477] In which case, such an "I" should exist either as identical to or different from its designative basis. Yet, both alternatives are vulnerable to numerous logical objections. Also accepting the possibility of a continued autonomous existence of the "I" even after the designating subject has ceased would force the contradiction that the designating mind would be impermanent while what is designated, the "I," would be permanent.

Now you might be thinking, "When a potter has long since passed away, we can still see the pot he created." This is not a problem. Here, as an effect of the throwing of the pot—the spinning of the wheel, the axle, and so on—a clay pot has indeed fully emerged. Given that each of the factors involved underwent moment-by-moment cessation, the completed clay pot also ceased the very moment following its emergence. Later, seeing the presence of its continuum, the coarse character of our cognition gives rise to the thought "This is the same clay pot the potter created in the past." Such a thought reflects a grasping at permanence that is based on conflating the pot's earlier and later moments.

Now if it is asserted to be otherwise [that the "eating I" does not exist when the designating mind has ceased], only two choices remain: it [the "I"] would be either permanent or nonexistent. The fact is that such an "I" is nothing but a dependently originated nominal reality. And to perceive and conceive it otherwise can only be to perceive and conceive it in terms of the object of negation [i.e., as truly existent].

Clearly, there is quite a lot of critical analysis on questions such as "Does the understanding of phenomena as mere conceptual imputations require a prior realization of emptiness?" and "Does the ascertainment of grasping at true existence as delusory require a prior realization of emptiness?" That said, as far as the sequence is concerned—first determining phenomena to be dependently originated nominal realities and on this basis identifying their opposite as the object of negation, and second establishing emptiness, which is the elimination of such an object of negation—this indeed is the sequence according to the instruction of the second Buddha himself [Tsongkhapa] based on interpreting the enlightened intention of the Blessed Buddha as excellently understood by Ārya Nāgārjuna, the supreme siddha Buddhapālita, and the glorious Candrakīrti. So when it comes to engaging in meditative practice too, this sequence is the only suitable choice.

The Four Key Points

When you identify the object of negation through such a process, you overcome the problem of over-negation and under-negation and can thus identify what is to be negated in a way that is free of error and does not lead you to fall into either of the two extremes of eternalism and nihilism. Through such an approach, you are able to realize the view that is free from all extremes, such as of permanence and annihilation. As such you experience the benefit of realizing the view [of emptiness] without difficulty. Aware of this benefit, numerous learned ones and siddhas, starting with the most compassionate Blessed Teacher himself, [478] have highly praised this method of establishing the view on the basis of dependently originated nominal reality. Not appreciating such points, many appear to introduce emptiness by lecturing about things being empty and so on and by engaging in analysis. What you need is to develop deep conviction on this matter [of accurately identifying the object of negation]. It is for this reason—the extreme difficulty of accurately identifying the object of negation in a way that guards against the faults of partial emptiness or mentally fabricated emptiness—that many authoritative masters and adepts of both India and Tibet, including the second Buddha, have guided us through progressive levels when introducing the object of negation, from coarser to progressively more subtle levels of identification. Because of this extreme difficulty of identifying the object of negation accurately, it is said those who realize emptiness as it truly is are as rare as the appearance of stars during daylight. On the other hand, once one has accurately identified the object of negation experientially, then the realization of emptiness can take place in mere hours. Many people seem to respond to the statement "It is extremely difficult to realize emptiness" with the idea that emptiness is difficult to realize because it is in some distant place!

Once you have identified the [*key point of the*] *object of negation* well, contemplate:

> If this "I" existed in the manner in which it appears to me, then it would exist by virtue of an essential nature; it cannot be otherwise. Given that, generally speaking, for something to exist, it must exist either as one or as multiple, and no third possibility exists, I will generate from the depths of my mind the ascertainment that such an "I" would have to exist intrinsically either as identical with the aggregates or as different from the aggregates.

In this way, when the ascertainment of the *key point of logical entailment* has arisen, contemplate:

> Now if the "I" were identical with the aggregates by virtue of its essential nature, it would then become identical with the aggregates with respect to place, time, and everything else. And if the "I" is one with the aggregates in all respects, then just as there are five distinct aggregates, there would be five distinct "I." Alternatively, just as the "I" is indivisibly singular, the aggregates would also be singular with no possibility to differentiate among them. And given that the "I" would be identical with the aggregates with no temporal differentiation between the two, then just as this body aggregate composed of flesh, bones, and so forth came

> into being anew from the fusion of the parents' reproductive fluids, the "I" too would have to be accepted as having come into being anew from the parents' fluids.

Also, contemplate:

> When the body falls apart at end of this life, the "I" too would fall apart and cease its continuity. [479] Furthermore, such an "I" would necessarily be identical with the aggregates with respect to both thought and language as well, leading to such consequences as the following: We should experience the sense of "I am" when observing each of the five aggregates and refer to them similarly with the term "I." Similarly, when observing the "I," we should grasp it as "my body," "my mind," and so on and refer to it with in such terms.

Contemplate these above points in depth, and by relating them to your own personal experience and recognizing all these as consequences to be illogical, ascertain how such standpoints are invalidated by the evidence of direct experience. In these ways, bring forth from the depths of your mind the ascertainment that the "I" does not exist by virtue of an essential nature as identical with the aggregates.

Once you have developed the ascertainment of the [*key point of the*] *absence of identity*, contemplate the following:

> If the "I" does not exist by virtue of its essential nature as identical with the aggregates, then it must exist by virtue of its essential nature as different from the aggregates. This is because with respect to one and many in general, when something does not exist as one, it must necessarily be multiple. Now if by virtue of its essential nature, the "I" is different from the aggregates, it would become totally unrelated to the aggregates, just like a horse and a cow. This would mean that when each and every one of the five aggregates is ruled out as the "I," something should be left that one can point to as that "I." Were this possible, such an "I" would become an unconditioned thing possessing neither body nor mind. Furthermore, just as a horse is devoid of the defining characteristics of a cow—a horned animal with a hump and a

> dewlap—the "I" too would become devoid of the attributes that define the aggregates as conditioned phenomena—namely, arising, ceasing, and abiding. Since the aggregates are in fact characterized by arising, ceasing, and abiding, this would mean that the "I" would possess an autonomous substantial reality with characteristics incompatible with the aggregates. Numerous other such undesirable consequences would follow: When pleasure or pain is experienced by the body and mind, it would be illogical to say "I am experiencing pleasure or pain"; it would be untenable for the "I" to experience the consequences of the karmic deed accrued by the body and the mind; and so on.

Contemplate deeply in these ways how so many ill consequences would ensue, revealing how [such a standpoint] is contrary to your own everyday experience and the meaning of the scriptures. Through contemplations such as these, generate from the depths of your mind the ascertainment [of the *key point of the absence of difference*]—that the "I" does not exist by virtue of its essential nature as different from the aggregates.

Through the impact of having integrated into the depths of your mind ascertainment of the above four key points, you now need to develop certainty with regard to the actual view of selflessness. Here is how this can be done.

Now, for something to exist in its own right, it must do so in one of the two ways that are logically possible for objective existence [that is, as single or multiple]. Yet if you accept either of these two possibilities, so many logical objections ensue. There is thus nothing that exists in either of these ways. [480] Yet there is also no denying that the "I" does in fact *appear* to the mind and is accordingly *conceived* as something independent of any designative basis and designating mind, as something existing objectively from the side of the aggregates, and as something concrete and real. So, just like with the example of the snake conceived in relation to a rope, develop from the depths of your mind the ascertainment that, apart from being grasped at through perceptions constructed by the deluded thought "I am," not even a tiny particle of [the "I"] exists in the way it appears to the mind.

If you wish to keep it brief, undertake only this analysis consisting of four key points. If you wish to elaborate further, you could generate ascertainment on the basis of the sevenfold analysis, which involves adding, as a further differentiation of the fourth key point [that of the absence of difference], examining in terms of the relationship between the *support* and the *supported*, the two aspects of *ownership*, the mere *collection*, and the special *configuration* of the collection.[1031] Here too, if you fail to master the key point of accurately identifying the way in which the object of negation appears to the mind, you might become adept at parroting the numerous lines of reasoning presented in the Madhyamaka treatises, but this would be like waging a battle without having identified the enemy. In contrast, if you have identified the object of negation successfully, then even one or two lines of reasoning can effectively hit the mark. As such, I have not elaborated on the sevenfold analysis here.

Space-like emptiness in meditative equipoise

It is not sufficient to cultivate this ascertainment [of selflessness] simply at the level of imagination. Your ascertainment must have two attributes: first, *at the level of apprehension*, you need firm certainty of the absence of intrinsic existence, and second, *at the level of appearance*, you need a perception of pure absence that is the negation of true existence—namely, the object of negation—in the form of an absolute nonimplicative negation.[1032] If, in the wake of negating self-existence, there remains at the level of apprehension a lingering sense of "I"—some kind of basis for scrutinizing of whether "I" exists in its own right—then an affirmation of an entity is surfacing in your mind in the wake of negating true existence. This would mean that the ascertainment you generated has assumed the form of an implicative negation. Insofar as the perspective of this ascertainment [of selflessness] is concerned, both the self that is the object of negation and the conventional "I" should have come to cease. This is not because you deliberately negated the conventional "I"; rather the perception of it should have ceased as a byproduct of having negated the self—the object of negation.

Furthermore, when you are analyzing whether the "I" has intrinsic existence, do not do so as if you are analyzing something external to you. Rather, as you analyze carefully whether you yourself, the person who is doing the inquiry, possess intrinsic existence and you discover it to be unfindable, you might experience a loss of even your sense of "I," the subject of the inquiry. When this happens, some are said to experience terror, [481] while others may experience joy. Here is why terror may arise. In our mind, our perception is so dominated by an intrinsically existing "I" that we cannot even perceive our conventional self. So when this dominant perception of self, the self that is the object of negation, is dismantled, terror arises in us because we are unable to see any other kind of "I"—we *feel* that the entirety of "I" has become nonexistent. Such a fear arises not because we have actually *seen* the nonexistence of our "I."

You might wonder, "If the conventional self has ceased from the perspective of the ascertainment, wouldn't such a rational cognition constitute a form of nihilism?"

[Answer:] When the conventional self is not found, it is not the case that its nonexistence has been found—that it has been ascertained to be nonexistent. So there is no problem [of falling into nihilism]. Furthermore, if the perception of a conventional self has not ceased from the perspective of rational cognition, then the only other alternative is for it to be perceived as an intrinsically existent "I." This would mean that such rational cognition would not be perceiving the absence of intrinsic existence of the "I." This cannot be right. After all, this is a rational cognition realizing the "I" to be devoid of intrinsic existence. Admittedly, there is indeed a perception of intrinsic existence for the rational cognition—namely, that of emptiness itself. The meditator need not stop such a perception; in fact, such a perception can't be stopped; there is just no way to do this.[1033]

In any case, understanding this point about how emptiness is perceived in terms of a nonimplicative negation by relating it to our own experience is indeed most challenging. Furthermore, it is not sufficient to generate such an ascertainment only once; instead, by relying on the magic of skillful means found in the instructions, we must develop such an ascertainment in a prolonged and concerted manner. The way to do this is, when the ascertainment endowed with two attributes characterized above has manifestly arisen, you let the main part of your mind remain firm in that ascertainment while, from a small part, you apply mindfulness, ensuring that your ascertainment remains undistracted and single-pointed. When the force of the ascertainment begins to wane, or the moment it has waned, you need to immediately apply meta-awareness. So when you observe your ascertainment beginning to wane in strength or when it has already done so, once again, resume your analysis by means of the four key points. In this way, generate ascertainment and sustain its continuum. [482] When you attain some stability with respect to maintaining the continuity of your ascertainment even for a little while, you have reached the *starting point* of gaining an experiential understanding of the view.

On this point about the way to maintain this ascertainment [of the view] endowed with two attributes, my father guru says that we need to sustain the continuity of such ascertainment repeatedly because doing so ensures that such ascertainment abides on its object and maintains its mode of apprehension and does not assume some other distorted form. So constantly refreshing the ascertainment's mode of apprehension and sustaining it without change is what he means by the phrase "sustain the continuity of the ascertainment." This in fact represents the unblemished intention of the following from *Guide to the Bodhisattva Way*:

> With nothing to cognize, what could be known?
> On what grounds could it be called *cognition*?
> For if something non-cognizing can be cognition,
> trees too would become cognitions.
> Hence, I would say that there is no cognition
> without the existence of the cognizable.[1034]

Not appreciating key points such as these on how to sustain [ascertainment], some, on experiencing a sudden birth of ascertainment, ignore the crucial importance of its mode of apprehension and take the perceptual aspect—the space-like vacuity—to be emptiness and consider this to be the object of apprehension and undertake meditative practice on that basis. Others on experiencing a sudden birth of ascertainment let go of the mind, both its object and its subject, and simply rest in a kind of wonderment. Some others generate the ascertainment once and then engage in a mental repetition of the word *selflessness*—a word universal—with the thought "There is no intrinsic existence, there is no intrinsic existence." These are major faults when it comes to the meditation on selflessness. For if you do not meditate on selflessness in such a way that the ascertainment of selflessness penetrates the very core of your mind, whatever form of meditation you might engage in—whether nonimplicative negation or implicative negation or affirmation—will not damage your self-grasping whatsoever.

Bearing these in mind, my father guru says that for those on the beginner's stage, the ascertainment possessing the two features is so brief, it can instantly take the form of an implicative negation or an affirmation, and so one needs great skill in meditative practice. He elaborates:

> The meaning of the statement that you should meditate on emptiness in terms of nonimplicative negation is this. Having applied flawless reasoning and analyzed well whether things possess true existence—the object of negation—such an object of negation

> will utterly dissolve for your mind. At that point your task is simply to rest your mind in such a nonimplicative negation, as if your mind has assumed such a nature. Contrary to this, your mind may be drawn to the thought "emptiness is a nonimplicative negation," [483] but this would be quite inappropriate. In such a state [of ascertainment of selflessness], the only nonimplicative negation to be identified is that the mind itself is a nonimplicative negation. Now, when I say such things, are they acceptable to those of you who are experts in the great treatises?

In this way, my father guru instructs us by asking a rhetorical question. In the *Essence of Eloquence* too it says:

> For example, although the nonexistence of a vase both is a nonimplicative negation and shares a common locus with a physical location, this does not violate the fact that something cannot be both a nonimplicative negation and a conditioned thing.[1035]

Negation, when expressed in words, involves an explicit elimination of its object of negation. Therefore, says the *Essence of Eloquence*:

> With respect to negation too, when it is expressed by words, it involves an explicit elimination of something, and when its form appears to the mind, it does so in terms of a negation of what is to be negated and is cognized in this way.[1036]

Thus [when the ascertainment of selflessness takes place], it must do so in terms of a nonimplicative negation—a form of negation that does not imply anything else, be it an affirmation or an implicative negation, in the wake of its explicit elimination of what is to be negated. It would be an error to perceive it in some other terms, such as in terms of permanence and impermanence, or existence and nonexistence. Were this not so, there would simply be no way for emptiness to be perceived in terms of a nonimplicative negation.

That said, generally speaking, the mind must be admitted to be a conditioned thing; it would be contradictory to say that it is a nonimplicative negation. That this is so is stated by the *Essence of Eloquence*, "For example, although the nonexistence of a vase both is a nonimplicative negation and shares a common locus with a physical location, this does not violate the fact that something cannot be both a nonimplicative negation and a conditioned thing."[1037] This, I feel, echoes the insights of the following from the *Guide to the Bodhisattva Way*:

> [Objection:] When things are subjected to analysis
> with a thorough and discerning intellect,
> at that point the analyzer too should be
> analyzed and so on, and there is no end.
>
> [Reply:] When the thing under scrutiny is analyzed,
> the analyzing intellect will have no support,
> and with no support it can arise no more;
> this is what is referred to as *nirvana*.[1038]

Everyone who is confused [about emptiness] seems to be confused on this issue.[1039] These instructions resemble the words of the mahāsiddhas and are thus extremely challenging to understand. Yet when one does comprehend them, many of the knots tightly binding difficult points seem to get undone on their own; so please treasure the instructions.

There seems to be a great deal of misunderstanding of these points on how those on the beginner's stage should engage in meditative equipoise on space-like emptiness. [484] They are indeed difficult and subtle, and without relying on the guru's instructions, even those who have studied the great treatises for many years and are known to be learned are unable to even entertain discerning doubts on these matters [let alone attain realization]. So it would be inappropriate indeed for someone like me to speak on these matters with much confidence. What I have said here has been presented only as an opening for critical inquiry for those with discerning minds. So refrain from rushing to judgment and carefully analyze.

Illusion-like emptiness in post-equipoise

Next, here is how you meditate on the illusion-like emptiness during periods of post-equipoise. When you rise from your meditative equipoise, maintain single-pointed focus on the absence of intrinsic existence of your "I" that you saw during your meditative equipoise, and then observe how the phenomena of both samsara and nirvana appear to your six senses. As phenomena appear to your senses, do not rely on how they appear to you but probe, "Do they appear to me in such terms because that is how they exist? Or do they take the form they appear to even though they do not exist like that?" In this way, cultivate the ascertainment that even though they appear to have such existence, they do not, and maintain this awareness single-pointedly. Should you find it difficult to develop such an ascertainment, contemplate analogies such as the snake in relation to a striped rope, the reflection of a face in the mirror, and the like and engage in careful analysis. When, as a result, you have generated ascertainment of the illusion-like character of things—the fact that despite their nonexistence, their appearances persist—maintain this awareness with single-pointedness.

Thanks to two factors—(1) the conviction one has that conches are white because one has seen them in the past and (2) a present sensory experience of seeing a conch as yellow because one has jaundice—a specific instance of seeing a conch as yellow can be determined as delusory. Similarly, on the basis of two factors—(1) the ascertainment generated from deeply realizing the absence of intrinsic existence of your "I" in meditative equipoise and (2) your present everyday experience wherein you inescapably perceive an "I"—you should determine that your perception of "I" is such that what appears to it does so despite having no such existence. It has been said that sentient beings not in meditative equipoise perceive all objects of all classes of cognition wholly in terms of intrinsic existence; no aspect of the cognition remains unmistaken.[1040] The most revered Losang Chögyen also clearly states that for us ordinary beings, all our immediate perceptions are perceptions of the object of negation [i.e., intrinsic existence].[1041] Changkya Rölpai Dorjé writes:

> There seem to be among today's scholars
> those who, caught in the web of words—
> "thoroughly withstanding," "true existence," and so on—
> seek only something with horns to be negated,
> leaving intact this everyday solid appearance. [485]
>
> But on my mother's unveiled face
> such vivid dualism is not found, I believe.
> Through excessive discussions off the mark,
> my old mother is likely to run away![1042]

Similarly, my father guru says, "There is no other way to perceive the object of negation except the very way we perceive things. We need to learn to recognize the way the object of negation appears through examining it repeatedly."[1043]

In view of these points, other than by relying on words and concluding that this very perception of our [naïve] innate cognition is itself deluded, we would be hard pressed to develop conviction from the depths of our mind that, when examined with an unbiased mind, things appear to our mind despite not existing in the way they appear. The most compassionate Blessed One has presented countless similes to illustrate this [illusion-like character]. In fact, this key point is said to be so challenging that it is beyond the comprehension of the learned ones of any Buddhist school apart from the Prāsaṅgika Madhyamaka. So it would be ill advised to remain content with mere words. Thus it is said that those on the beginner's stage can meditate on illusion-like emptiness in the form of an intellectual understanding, but it is impossible for them to perceive whatever appears to the mind as illusion-like purely through the force of having *realized* emptiness during meditative equipoise, without having to consciously generate the perspective. When it comes to this practice of cultivating illusion-like perception, the particular Buddhist school of thought, higher or lower, is immaterial if there is no integration of the ascertainment of the absence of what is to be negated in the very core of one's mind. Simply experiencing a dissolution of appearances into some indistinct perception through the force of engaging in meditative concentration—whereby perceptions of [material attributes like] obstruction have been dismantled—is not the meaning of illusion-like [emptiness] at all.

Furthermore, the profound teaching our sacred Ganden lineage calls "the union of two truths," "the indivisibility of appearance and emptiness," "the dawning of appearance and emptiness as cause and effect," "appearance dispelling the extreme of existence and emptiness dispelling the extreme of nonexistence," "the dawning of emptiness as dependent origination and dependent origination as emptiness," and so on points to this: There is, in this meditation on illusion-like emptiness, a method that ensures that the two ascertainments—that of emptiness and that of dependent origination—[486] not only do not undermine each other, they actually complement [and reinforce] each other. Here is how this can be understood.

Taking the snake conceived in relation to a rope as an analogy, as you contemplate deeply the way your "I" is a dependently originated construct and how there is not even the slightest possibility it is otherwise—that its perception arises suddenly when the designative basis meets the designating mind and that, when one of the two ceases, [the perception] cannot sustain itself—and the way, when you search on this basis for an "I" that is not contingent on factors like the designative basis and the designating mind, the ascertainment will arise naturally and without deliberate effort that your "I" simply does not possess any objective existence at the locus where it appears. And as you contemplate deeply based on searching for your "I" in its own right—as something independent of any other factors—and you realize that not even a speck the size of an atom can be found at the locus where it appears, the ascertainment will arise in you naturally, without your having to make any deliberate effort, that its character is as a dependently originated nominal reality. This is how the two ascertainments—that of dependent origination and that of emptiness—reinforce one another as if they are cause and effect of each other. The omniscient Jé Tsongkhapa states:

> As long as the two understandings—
> of *appearance*, undeceiving dependent origination,
> and of *emptiness*, the absence of all positions—remain separate,
> then you have not realized the intent of the Sage.
>
> However, if at some point, not in alternation but at once,
> the instant you see that dependent origination is undeceiving,
> this dismantles the entirety of the object of grasping at certitude,
> then your analysis of the view is complete.
>
> Furthermore, when appearance dispels the extreme of existence
> and when emptiness dispels the extreme of nonexistence,
> and you understand how emptiness arises as cause and effect,
> you will never be swayed by views grasping at extremes.[1044]

Similarly, the most revered Chökyi Gyaltsen writes:

> When *appearance* does not obscure emptiness
> and when *emptiness* does not obstruct appearance,
> the excellent path—where emptiness and dependent origination
> share the same meaning—will then manifest.[1045]

Changkya Rölpai Dorjé too writes:

Not finding my father when sought
is, in fact, the finding of my mother,
and my father is found on my mother's lap!
That's how the kind parents save their child, I am told![1046] [487]

And my father guru says, "When you contemplate the meanings of emptiness and dependent origination, the ascertainments of the two should mutually reinforce one another like two horses who take turns grooming each other."[1047]

Thus maintain the two forms of meditation—*analytical meditation* searching for the meditative object and *placement meditation* subsequently resting on the ascertainment arisen from such analysis—and when you have attained such stability that subtle analysis while settled on the ascertainment does not undermine your ascertainment, then continue to engage in analysis while sustaining your ascertainment. Note that if you were to apply here the coarse level of analysis you applied earlier, when you were searching for the meditative object, you would risk dismantling your ascertainment. So your analysis here needs to be similar to the way a minnow swims about in a clear and calm body of water. You do this by maintaining continuous mindfulness with your mind resting single-pointedly on the ascertainment endowed with the two features and, not wavering even slightly from such a state, engaging in analysis with a small part of your mind. Do this either by simply recalling the four key points [of emptiness meditation] or by simply directing a small part of your mind to the four key points. When you proceed in this way, constantly refreshing the mode of apprehension of your ascertainment, then no matter how much you analyze, not only is your ascertainment not undermined, your analysis in fact helps ensure that the mode of apprehension of your ascertainment remains strong and enduring. When this happens, you have gained good experience of the view.

Thanks to the repeated analysis you engaged in previously when you were searching for the object of meditation and thus becoming trained, you are now capable of generating a strong ascertainment, one that is comparable to engaging in full-fledged analysis of the four key points, by simply directing your mind to it or simply recalling it. Of course, for an optimal experience of the view, you need to attain insight (*vipaśyanā*). But now when it comes to engaging in analysis and the intervals you need between earlier and subsequent analyses, the situation is entirely different compared to when you were first seeking the meditative object. Here, subsequent analyses should be brought in when you sense that the force of your ascertainment is beginning to wane, not when its strength has already decreased. Also, when you engage in analysis, you should do so without losing the mode of apprehension [of the ascertainment].

In brief, in the wake of having engaged in meditation on the space-like emptiness during equipoise, you also need to meditate, in ways such as those outlined here, on the illusion-like emptiness of the post-equipoise period. [488]

The selflessness of phenomena: introducing the mind's ultimate nature

What has been presented thus far is how you maintain meditative equipoise and post-equipoise states from the standpoint of the selflessness of persons. To meditate on the selflessness of phenomena, you could simply extend the same analysis—in terms of four key points—to the five aggregates, and this would indeed constitute a meditation on the selflessness of phenomena. In this [mahāmudrā] instruction, however, the primary aim is to introduce the ultimate nature of the mind. So I will briefly explain here such an introduction.

As practiced earlier, once you have attained stability in your focus on the mind, remain unwavering in this meditative equipoise but with a small part of your mind observe the mind's conventional nature—*this space-like vacuity with no material existence whatsoever.* When it is unobscured by mental laxity and excitation, all sorts of diverse objects can naturally appear to it, and it can also easily move to any object whatsoever; *its immediate perceptions are unstoppable, and luminous and aware, its continuity is unceasing.*[1048] As you observe how this mere stream-like consciousness[1049] appears to your mind and examine it with subtle and skillful awareness, it will undeniably appear to exist without depending on such factors as a designative basis, a designating mind, temporal instances, and so on; it will appear to exist in its own right, as something that could be found to exist objectively at the very locus where it is being perceived. Now were the mind to actually exist as it is perceived, it would have to be either intrinsically identical with or different from its temporal instances, yet asserting it to exist in either of these two terms leads to numerous logical objections. In this way, engage in analytical meditation, carefully examining these points, and engage in placement meditation resting on the ascertainment arrived at following such analysis. And when you arise out of such meditative equipoise, maintain the practice of illusion-like emptiness based on the convergence of the two factors—(a) an *awareness* of how, to your everyday cognition, your mind appears to exist in its own right, without being contingent on any other factors, and (b) the *ascertainment* rooted in your realization that your mind lacks such intrinsic existence. Practice all of these as explained above [in the context of the selflessness of persons].

In the above I have scribed in clear terms the indispensable pith instructions, together with oral teachings, on how those on the beginner's stage can bring about an experience of the view [of emptiness]. There are, of course, numerous other important matters, such as [489] how, based on distinctions among the progressive levels of these practices, (1) you engage in the meditative practice of cultivating semblance insight in dependence on semblance tranquil abiding, (2) how you attain semblance insight on the basis of actual tranquil abiding, (3) how you attain actual insight on the basis of attaining actual tranquil abiding, (4) how you cultivate bliss, (5) how you cultivate the nondual yoga of profundity and clarity, and so on.[1050] As for these, other than seeking to develop a correct [conceptual] understanding of them, it does not appear that those like me have the good fortune to attain them through cultivating them exactly as they are at the experiential level. I have therefore not endeavored to write about them here; please seek to understand them on the basis of the great treatises.

When you are first training your mind in these meditation topics, even if you try to cultivate them extensively in each and every session, you are not likely to have much success. You actually risk becoming discouraged. So, in the first session, for example, you may be better off practicing the meditation topics of the common and uncommon preliminary practices more extensively and practicing the subsequent meditation topics more in the manner of a review, scanning through the words. In the second session, you could focus more on the merit-field practice and the offering of the seven limbs to the merit field, approaching the prior and subsequent meditation topics in the manner of a review. In the third session, you could focus extensively on the supplications, such as to the lineage gurus of the near transmission, followed by the meditative concentration of receiving the four empowerments, cultivating the preceding and subsequent meditation topics in the manner of a review. In the fourth session, you would then focus extensively on reviewing the entire path of sutra and tantra and receiving the blessings, cultivating the preceding meditation topics in the form of a review.

If your primary focus is the preliminary guru-yoga practice, then at the end of one of the four sessions, review the meditation topics of mahāmudrā for an appropriate length. In contrast, if your primary focus is mahāmudrā, then at the end of each of the four sessions, engage in substantial meditative practice of the topics pertaining to mahāmudrā. When I first began my life as a hermit in the mountains, I engaged in guru-yoga practice. At that time, regardless of how much effort I made, I found it difficult to complete even one round of *Offering to the Guru*. [490] So I asked my father guru's advice on how best to undertake the practice [pertaining to these meditation topics]. What I have shared here is the advice he gave me.

Concluding activities

As you examine the three spheres of your meditation practice—the path being practiced, the meditating mind of the practitioner, and the meditator yourself—all three undeniably appear as not constructed by your own mind; they appear to exist objectively, findable at the site where they are perceived to be. Contemplate how, if they were to exist in such a manner, then the topic being meditated on would not be contingent on your mind meditating on it; they would be independent. In that case, there would be something being meditated upon without there being a meditator, and the meditator too would become an intrinsically real meditator with no dependence on the meditating mind meditating. For example, *Fundamental Wisdom* states:

> For an agent that is real, there is no activity,
> so the object would be without an agent.
> For an object that is real, there is no activity,
> so the agent too would have no object of action.[1051]

Thus, when these three spheres of activity are searched for objectively, apart from conceptual imputations of them defined through mutual dependence, not even the minutest particle can be found to exist. The same text states:

> The agent exists in dependence on the object,
> and the object in turn depends
> on the agent. Apart from this,
> we find no other cause of their establishment.[1052]

Contemplate the following:

> In light of the above, the fact that all things are dependent originations of mutually dependent conceptual imputations makes presentations of everyday function tenable. So, through dedicating all my roots of virtue here, may the aims of my aspirations be fulfilled just as prayed for.

With this thought, and through prayers of dedication such as those of the Guhyasamāja sādhana or of mahāmudrā,[1053] dedicate with fervent intention all your roots of virtue that they may become conditions for realizing both temporary and ultimate benefit and happiness.

How to practice between sessions

Guide to the Bodhisattva Way says:

> Having initiated an action with the intention
> "I shall conduct with my body in this way,"
> you should periodically observe thereafter
> how your body is positioned.
>
> With your mind, the rutting elephant,
> tied to the great post of Dharma contemplation,
> while ensuring that it does not break loose,
> you should examine it with all your effort.
>
> Never abandon, even for an instant,
> this striving for concentration.
> And thinking, "Where is mine wandering to?"
> observe your mind with discernment.
>
> If you are not able to do so because of danger,
> festivities, and so on, then just follow your inclination.[1054]

Just as stated above, you should understand deeply the faults of the distracted mind and the benefits of the settled mind and repeatedly set your intention to guard your mind against fruitless activities and inappropriate pursuits. Maintain continuous mindfulness of the intentions you have set, and every now and then, applying meta-awareness, monitor if your mind is on course with the intentions you have set. Also, mindful of the pros and cons, cultivate heedfulness that helps you direct your mind toward virtue and vigilantly guard against fruitless activities and inappropriate pursuits. This [application of heedfulness] is like a foundation for all the practices you do in between sessions.

Conducting yourself like this benefits you in these [two] ways: you ensure the purity of all facets of your precepts, and you swiftly attain meditative concentrations on your chosen meditation topics. Here is how these benefits emerge. First, seeing the benefits of meditative concentration, you generate admiration for it, and on this basis, an interest in pursuing meditative concentration arises in you naturally. Then, when you see that [success in] meditative concentration is rooted in morality, you develop respect for the precepts. This in turn gives rise to constant application of mindfulness and meta-awareness, as these help you conduct yourself in accord with your precepts of what is to be engaged in and what is to be avoided. And thanks to the power of resolute heedfulness, which helps prevent any kind of apprehensiveness regarding what is to be engaged in and what is to be shunned, all the distractions of the three doors come to cease. In this way, meditative concentration [492] is quickly attained and all the precepts come to be perfected. Thus, says the great bodhisattva Śāntideva:

> By what means will all of these be attained?
> They are attained through mindfulness
> because it prevents fruitless pursuits.
> They arise too from deep respect,
> which in turn comes from knowing
> the benefits of serenity, giving rise to effort.[1055]

And:

> By ceasing distractions to the external,
> the mind will not sway from serenity.[1056]

As for other activities, such as the yogas of washing and eating, moderation with respect to food, not sleeping at the start and end of the night but striving in practice, the proper way to sleep, and so forth, understand these from elsewhere.[1057]

You should learn how to relate the words and meaning of *Offering to the Guru: Union of Bliss and Emptiness* and the mahāmudrā root text *Highway of the Conquerors* to their sources in the sutras and tantras and understand them on the basis of two unparalleled works of excellence by Guru Yongzin Rinpoché.[1058] Both of these two excellent texts contain, in relation to many key points of instruction, the statement that they need to be learned from the mouth of one's guru. So what I have done here is to put into words what I myself have received from the excellent vase that is my own father guru's mouth, fearing that not even their names will survive after I have been led away by time's messenger. I have also written this work to help make it easier for others to know how to bring into their practice some of the more difficult aspects of the meditation topics buried amid elaborate scriptural citations and reasoning, and also to send upon the wind a testament of how I have myself developed an understanding of the words and meanings of these two instructions on the basis of my guru's pith instructions and of how I have approached the practice of the relevant meditation topics. As to whether what I have done remains just an effort [with no benefit], please do not rush to judge; read carefully and you will come to appreciate.

Thus I say:

Not tamed by conquerors and their children who have appeared in this realm,
sentient beings rife with afflictions and false views, and so hard to tame
owing to a proliferation of the five degenerations, even for such beings bereft of guardian and refuge like us,
your courage in embracing us as yours is most excellent indeed!

Your pith instructions supple and sharp,
on entering the ears of an ignorant beast-like person like me,
can bring the meaning of Dharma to the mind's core;
this enlightened deed is most amazing indeed!

By relying on the eye lotion prepared through
cultivating the instruction of my teacher,
the source of such excellent wonder,
I have searched the subterrains of sutra and tantra
and examined the great treasures of meditative practice

that are found hidden there; the insights gleaned
I have brought into a discourse here.
Yet as my mind is naturally hazy and feeble,
whatever faults there might be of insufficient explanation,
distorted explanation, explaining too much, or self-fabrication,
I seek forgiveness in the presence of those with Dharma eyes.
Just as when a child commits all sorts of errors,
his loving parents strive with effort to rectify them,
likewise, help me so that these faults do not obscure me.

If, thanks to the kindness of my most revered teacher,
there are nuggets of insight here and there,
then just as when a toddler utters meaningful sentences,
it brings wonder and joy to her parents,
likewise, with compassion in your heart, do be pleased with me.

Through the heap of merit arising from this effort,
may all beings be sustained by perfect spiritual mentors
and become their fortunate disciples,
vessels into which instructions are granted.

May I too never be deprived throughout all my lives
of the presence of sublime spiritual mentors,
and with faith and reverence that sees them as actual buddhas,
may I please them with my thoughts and actions
and be willing to sacrifice my body, life, and resources for their sake.
May I thus be sustained by them with joy,
and may they grant me instructions distilling the entire essence
of their heart without concealment or secrecy.
May I become their chief disciple, with whom they share
all the secret and invisible aspects of their liberating life.
Through ascetic practice sacrificing even life and limb,
through diligence concerted and uninterrupted,
and through practicing according to the guru's instructions,
may the stream of scripture and realization surge within me.
May I become like this the reservoir of my guru's heart.

Today, for most people, the eyes of intelligence
that properly distinguish faults from virtue seem blinded.
As such, they develop a reliance on someone
as a teacher based simply on hearing of their renown.
There thus are many faithful aspirants who seem blind. [494]
Yet even among those with eyes of analysis, many seem robbed
of their autonomy by the demon of envy,
and with no discernment as to teachings and teachers,
they reject them impulsively; such crazed people seem to be
everywhere.

Thus, though the fruits of this effort of mine may be small,
for those who have received a guru's instructions,
may this epistle, a testament I have sent upon the wind,
be transmitted through the hands of a few who are wise and unbiased
and help them prove their worth as humans
through study, reflection, and meditation.

At that point may the special protectors of this teaching—
the six-armed Mahākāla, the Dharma king Kālarūpa,
as well as the great kind Vaiśravaṇa—
be their allies at all times.

Also, may even those so hard to tame who have not been
pacified by any conqueror or bodhisattva
become beneficiaries of this work of mine,
and may they become tamed on the basis of it.

If some, owing to their individual faults, come to
experience, in the near term, frustration and disturbance [from this
work],
may this not cause them to abandon the Dharma
but may it ultimately become a source of benefit and joy.

Colophon

This *Letter of Final Testament Sent upon the Wind*, containing pith instructions as well as oral teachings on how to undertake the meditative practice of mahāmudrā and its uncommon preliminary, the practice of guru yoga, was composed by the do-nothing[1059] Tsultrim Nyima, someone blessed with both of these instructions from the glorious and sublime guru, the most revered Yeshé Tenzin. It was composed at Ganden Lophel mountain hermitage. May it help revive from its embers the fire of instructions of Jé Tsongkhapa's oral transmission.

Sarva maṅgalaṃ (May auspiciousness prevail everywhere!)

Part 3
Geluk Mahāmudrā and Guide to the View

9. Highway of the Conquerors

Mahāmudrā Root Text According to the Precious Geden Lineage

PANCHEN LOSANG CHÖKYI GYALTSEN

[497]
Namo mahāmudrāya.

1
I bow at the feet of my peerless guru,
the sovereign lord among siddhas, who reveals naked
mahāmudrā, the all-pervading nature of everything,
indivisible, and the ineffable expanse of the vajra mind.[1060]

2
I will compose here the instructions of the mahāmudrā oral tradition
of the most realized Dharmavajra, father and son,
the upholders of the sacred Geden lineage who distilled the essence
of the sea of sutra, tantra, and pith instructions and transmitted it well.

3
Here, of the three—preparation, main practice, and conclusion—
since it's the doorway and support beam of the teaching and the Mahayana,
strive first in going for refuge and arousing awakening,
not just with your mouth and with words alone.

4
And since seeing the mind's true nature depends on
gathering merit and purifying obscurations,
proceed first by reciting the hundred-syllable mantra a hundred
thousand times
and repeating hundreds of times the *Confession of Downfalls* with
prostrations.

5
To your root guru, who is inseparable from
all the buddhas of the three times,
make heartfelt supplications again and again.

6
With regard to the main practice of mahāmudrā,
though there seem to be numerous perspectives,
it is divisible in terms of two: sutra and tantra.

7
The latter is the clear light of great bliss
that arises from skillful means such as
penetrating the vital points in the vajra body.

8
This is the mahāmudrā of Saraha and Nāgārjuna,
of Nāropa and Maitripa, taught
in the Attainment and Essence texts[1061]
and is the quintessence of unexcelled tantras.

9
As for the former, this refers to the way of meditating on emptiness
taught explicitly in the long, medium, and short [Perfection of Wisdom].
The supreme ārya, Nāgārjuna, has stated
that there is no path to liberation apart from this.

10
Here I will present a guide to mahāmudrā
that accords with his thought [498]
and expound a way to introduce the mind's nature
that accords with the teaching of the lineage gurus.

11–12
The Innate Union, the Amulet Box,
the Fivefold, Equal Taste, and the Four-Lettered,
Pacification, Cutting Off, and the Great Perfection,

the Guide to the Middle Way View, and so on—
though many teachings exist, each with a different name,
when examined by a yogi who is versed in definitive scriptures
and reasoning and who possesses meditative experience,
they come down to a single intention.

13
Thus, of two approaches—seeking meditation
on the basis of the view and seeking the view
on the basis of meditation—
the presentation here is the latter approach.

14
On a platform conducive to meditative absorption,
your body maintaining the seven-point posture,
dispel the stale winds through the nine-round breathing
and distinguish well the fresh and sullied awareness.

15
With a pure virtuous state of mind, proceed first
with going for refuge and arousing the awakening mind,
and then practice the profound path of guru yoga.
After performing fervent supplications
a hundred times or so, dissolve the guru into you.

16
While in that state where appearances are indistinct,
do not alter it or add anything to it
by thoughts of hope, fear, and so on,
but rest unwavering in equipoise for a while.

17
Do not cease mental activity
as in fainting or falling asleep;
post the sentry of undistracted mindfulness
and station meta-awareness to detect any movement.
Hold the clear and aware nature of mind
with a firm focus and starkly look at it.

18
Whatever thoughts arise, any thought,
note it as that and just that.
Alternatively, like a skilled swordsman,
swiftly cut down the thoughts as they arise.

19
When, after cutting down, your mind is stable,
then, without losing mindfulness, loosen and relax:
"Focus with firmness but loosen and relax;
there lies the spot to rest your mind."[1062]

20
So it is stated; and elsewhere it says,
"This mind, bound in its own entanglement,
when relaxed becomes free, no doubt."[1063]
As taught here, relax without distraction.

21
Whatever thoughts arise, when you observe their nature,
they naturally disappear, and a pure vacuity appears.
Likewise, when you examine the settled mind as well,
you see an unobstructed vacuity and vivid clarity.

22
This is called "merging of stillness and movement."
And whatever thoughts may arise,
do not stop them, but recognize their movement
and place your mind upon their nature.

23
This is analogous to the flights
of a bird captive on a ship:
"It's like the raven that takes off from a ship, [499]
flies to every direction, and lands there again."[1064]

24
In this way, as you maintain meditative equipoise,
its essence will dawn as unobscured

by anything, as lucid and clear and,
since it does not exist in any physical way,
as a pure vacuity just like space,
where everything appears vividly.

25
Thus though the mind's true nature
may be seen as if in a direct manner,
it cannot be grasped at or shown as "this."
Whatever appears, without grasping, rest your mind.

26
"This is the special instruction to grab
buddhahood with one's bare hands."
So proclaim most present-day meditators
of the Land of Snows, with a shared understanding.

27
Be that as it may, I, Chökyi Gyaltsen,
would say the following:
"This is an excellent method for the beginner
to cultivate mental stillness and the way
to introduce the mind's conventional nature."

28
Now, as for the way to introduce
the mind's true nature,
I will set this forth following the oral instructions
of my root guru: as a saffron-clad monk,
the embodiment of the *gnoses* of all the *buddhas*,[1065]
dispelling the darkness of ignorance from my mind.

29
While in that foregoing meditative equipoise,
unwavering, and just like a minnow
darting about in clear water,
analyze skillfully with subtle awareness
the nature of that person who is meditating.

30
The savior Ārya Nāgārjuna himself says:
"The person is not earth nor water,
is not fire, wind, nor space,
is not consciousness—nor is it all of them.
Where then, apart from these, is the person?

31
The person is a composite of six elements;
as such it has no real existence.
Likewise, each element too is in turn
a composite and hence has no real existence."[1066]

32
In accordance with this statement, when you search,
not even a minute particle will be found
of the meditative equipoise, the one who is in equipoise, and so forth.
At that point, maintain the space-like equipoise
without distraction and single-pointedly.

33–34
Alternatively, while in meditative equipoise,
observe your mind as thus characterized:
pure *vacuity* because it does not exist as physical;
unobscured as diverse appearances arise to it;
and *unceasing*, a *luminous* and *aware* continuum
that is uninterrupted in its engagement.
Such a mind appears and is conceived
as independent, but with respect to such objects of clinging,
the guardian Śāntideva states:

35
"The so-called continuums and collections,
just like rosaries, armies, and so on, are false."[1067]
So through scripture such as this and reasoning, [500]
establish this truth of how things do not exist as they appear
and rest your mind single-pointedly in this meditative equipoise.

36
In brief, as my spiritual mentor,
the omniscient Sangyé Yeshé,
who is in accord with reality, states:

37
"When you are fully aware that whatever appears is conceived by thoughts,
then the ultimate expanse dawns independently of anything else.
When your awareness enters into what has thus dawned,
you rest in single-pointed meditative equipoise—*E ma ho*!"[1068]

38
In the same vein, Dampa Sangyé says:
"Whirl the spear of awareness within emptiness;
the view, O people of Dingri, is unobstructed."[1069]
These statements and their likes make the same point.

39
At the conclusion, the virtues that have emerged
from meditating on mahāmudrā
together with the ocean of virtues of all three times,
dedicate these all to the great, unexcelled enlightenment.

40
Thus, having gained familiarity [with this practice],
realize precisely the mode of appearance
of any object that appears within the field of your six senses,
and its mode of being will dawn naked and vivid.
Recognizing whatever appears is the key point of the view.[1070]

41
In brief, whatever appears—
be it your own mind or something else—
do not grasp but ascertain its mode of being
and always maintain that awareness.
Knowing this, bring all phenomena
of samsara and nirvana into a single nature.

42
Here, Āryadeva says:
"The viewer of one thing
is stated to be the viewer of all,
and the emptiness of one
is the emptiness of all."[1071]

43
Thus, within the perfect meditative equipoise
on this ultimate nature of reality,
you are free from the elaborated extremes
of existence and nonexistence and of samsara and nirvana.

44
Yet when you arise from that equipoise and examine,
it is undeniable that actions, agents, and dependent originations
of mere labels and mere concepts naturally appear—
like a dream, like a mirage, like the moon in water,
or like a magician's illusion.

45
When appearance does not obscure emptiness
and when emptiness does not obstruct appearance,
the excellent path—where emptiness and dependent origination
share the same meaning—will then manifest.

46
These were uttered by a renunciant who has heard widely,
someone who is called Losang Chökyi Gyaltsen.
From this virtue may all beings swiftly become victorious
through this path, for there is no second path to peace.

Colophon

This method of pointing out mahāmudrā was written in response to long-standing repeated requests from the master of ten topics Rabjampa Gendun Gyatso and the master of ten treatises Hamdong Sherab Sengé, who, having seen the eight worldly concerns of this life as the play of a madman, live in mountains of solitude as wandering mendicants embracing this path as their heart practice. I have also been approached by many students who have the desire to engage in the practice of definitive mahāmudrā.

In one of his experiential songs addressed to both himself and to others, the lord among the siddhas, the omniscient Ensapa the Great himself, gives instructions on the stages of the path according to the Kadam teachings, beginning from the topic of proper reliance on the spiritual mentor up to tranquil abiding and insight. At the end he says:

> Not the path I have just outlined,
> and not known at present in this Land of Snows,
> there is the definitive instruction on mahāmudrā.
> At this point, though, I dare not commit it to writing.[1072]

There are examples of teaching that, on account of present obstacles, may not be committed to writing but are intended for a later time. There is, for example, the following statement in the *Sublime Dharma of the White Lotus*:

> To help [beings] realize the buddha's gnosis,
> the Buddha used this method spontaneously.
> But he will never say to them [at present]:
> "You will be a fully awakened buddha."
> Why is this so? The savior factors in the timing.[1073]

So in order to fulfill Ensapa's aspiration, I, Losang Chökyi Gyaltsen—upholder of the instructions on sutra and tantra, a renunciant who has been born in the lineage in which (1) the continuity of the blessings of direct experience of this path from the Peerless Teacher, the sovereign among Śākyas, up to my root guru, the omniscient Sangyé Yeshé, remains unbroken and (2) no pollution has sullied the precepts—composed this at Geden Nampar Gyalwai Ling [Ganden Monastery]. [501]

10. Prayer to the Lineage Gurus of Geden Mahāmudrā

PANCHEN LOSANG CHÖKYI GYALTSEN

Namo guru mahāmudrāya.

1

In the mansion of three spontaneous buddha-bodies,
you are the glory, the primordial lord and head of all families—
to you the pervasive lord, great Vajradhara, I appeal:
Bless me so that my mind is released from the clutches of self-grasping,
that I become trained in loving kindness, compassion, and bodhicitta,
and that I attain quickly the supreme state,
mahāmudrā, the path of perfect union.[1074]

2

In the world of ten directions, in the myriad realms,
you are the father begetting conquerors of the three times—
to you, Ārya Mañjuśrī wisdom, I appeal:
Bless me so that my mind is released from the clutches of self-grasping,
that I become trained in loving kindness, compassion, and bodhicitta,
and that I attain quickly the supreme state,
mahāmudrā, the path of perfect union.

3

In the northern country, this Land of Snows,
you, Lord, are the second sage for the Sage's teaching—
to you, most revered Losang Drakpa, I appeal:
Bless me so that my mind is released from the clutches of self-grasping,
that I become trained in loving kindness, compassion, and bodhicitta,
and that I attain quickly the supreme state,
mahāmudrā, the path of perfect union.

4
You are the chief upholder of the teaching
of the practice lineage of Tsongkhapa, son of Mañjuśrī—
to you, Tokden Jampal Gyatso, I appeal:
Bless me so that my mind is released from the clutches of self-grasping,
that I become trained in loving kindness, compassion, and bodhicitta,
and that I attain quickly the supreme state,
mahāmudrā, the path of perfect union.

5
Opening the instruction treasury of oral transmission,
you bring fortunate trainees to maturity—
to you, Baso Chökyi Gyaltsen, I appeal:
Bless me so that my mind is released from the clutches of self-grasping,
that I become trained in loving kindness, compassion, and bodhicitta,
and that I attain quickly the supreme state,
mahāmudrā, the path of perfect union. [503]

6
Perfecting the yogas of tantra's two stages,
you've found the immortal body of an awareness holder—
to you, supreme siddha Dharmavajra, I appeal:
Bless me so that my mind is released from the clutches of self-grasping,
that I become trained in loving kindness, compassion, and bodhicitta,
and that I attain quickly the supreme state,
mahāmudrā, the path of perfect union.

7
Unsullied by the fetters of the eight worldly concerns,
you hoist high the banner of the definitive teaching—
to you, Losang Dönyö Drupa,[1075] I appeal:
Bless me so that my mind is released from the clutches of self-grasping,
that I become trained in loving kindness, compassion, and bodhicitta,
and that I attain quickly the supreme state,
mahāmudrā, the path of perfect union.

8
To the joyful palace of three buddha bodies,
sporting in saffron robes, you guide all beings—

to you, Khedrup Sangyé Yeshé, I appeal:
Bless me so that my mind is released from the clutches of self-grasping,
that I become trained in loving kindness, compassion, and bodhicitta,
and that I attain quickly the supreme state,
mahāmudrā, the path of perfect union.[1076]

9
For the tradition of the conqueror Losang,[1077]
you, omniscient one, are inseparable from the lord himself—
to you, revered Losang Chögyen, I appeal:
Bless me so that my mind is released from the clutches of self-grasping,
that I become trained in loving kindness, compassion, and bodhicitta,
and that I attain quickly the supreme state,
mahāmudrā, the path of perfect union.

10
Each sacred word of sutra, tantra, and treatise,
you integrate their meaning into one and perfect their practice—
to you, great siddha Gendun Gyaltsen,[1078] I appeal:
Bless me so that my mind is released from the clutches of self-grasping,
that I become trained in loving kindness, compassion, and bodhicitta,
and that I attain quickly the supreme state,
mahāmudrā, the path of perfect union.

11
Through great effort you tasted the distilled essence
of the conqueror Losang's teaching and found the supreme state—
to you, Drupai Gyaltsen Dzinpa,[1079] I appeal:
Bless me so that my mind is released from the clutches of self-grasping,
that I become trained in loving kindness, compassion, and bodhicitta,
and that I attain quickly the supreme state,
mahāmudrā, the path of perfect union.

12
You're skilled at instructing fortunate trainees
the nectar essence of profound and vast Dharma—
to you, Gyüchen Könchok Gyaltsen, I appeal:
Bless me so that my mind is released from the clutches of self-grasping,
that I become trained in loving kindness, compassion, and bodhicitta,

and that I attain quickly the supreme state,
mahāmudrā, the path of perfect union.

13
You are master Losang Chökyi Gyaltsen himself
appearing once again for the glory of the teachings and beings—
to you, revered Losang Yeshé, I appeal:
Bless me so that my mind is released from the clutches of self-grasping,
that I become trained in loving kindness, compassion, and bodhicitta,
and that I attain quickly the supreme state,
mahāmudrā, the path of perfect union.

14
You are blessed by the Lord Buddha himself
and have mastered the profound oral-transmission path—
to you, Losang Trinlé, I appeal:
Bless me so that my mind is released from the clutches of self-grasping,
that I become trained in loving kindness, compassion, and bodhicitta,
and that I attain quickly the supreme state,
mahāmudrā, the path of perfect union.

15
You've perfected the practice of the heart of the meaning
of the conqueror Losang's oral teachings—
to you, the supreme siddha Losang Namgyal, I appeal:
Bless me so that my mind is released from the clutches of self-grasping,
that I become trained in loving kindness, compassion, and bodhicitta,
and that I attain quickly the supreme state,
mahāmudrā, the path of perfect union.

16
All the instructions of our sovereign teacher
you impart compassionately, with no error—
to you, most kind one bearing the name Yeshé,[1080] I appeal:
Bless me so that my mind is released from the clutches of self-grasping,
that I become trained in loving kindness, compassion, and bodhicitta,
and that I attain quickly the supreme state,
mahāmudrā, the path of perfect union.

17
The complete and inerrant path, the essence of Buddha's teaching,
you spread far and wide, from central to border lands—
to you, Ngawang Jampa, I appeal:
Bless me so that my mind is released from the clutches of self-grasping,
that I become trained in loving kindness, compassion, and bodhicitta,
and that I attain quickly the supreme state,
mahāmudrā, the path of perfect union.

18
Glorious primordial buddha, sporting saffron robes,
through Dharma you ripened every land, China and Tibet—
to you, Panchen Palden Yeshé, I appeal:
Bless me so that my mind is released from the clutches of self-grasping,
that I become trained in loving kindness, compassion, and bodhicitta,
and that I attain quickly the supreme state,
mahāmudrā, the path of perfect union.

19
In all excellent paths of sutra and tantra,
you have reached the ends of their single-pointed practice—
to you, Khedrup Ngawang Dorjé, I appeal:
Bless me so that my mind is released from the clutches of self-grasping,
that I become trained in loving kindness, compassion, and bodhicitta,
and that I attain quickly the supreme state,
mahāmudrā, the path of perfect union.

20
With steadfast wisdom, like a second Sage,
you illuminate through discourse and writing the Buddha's teaching—
to you, revered Dharmabhadra, I appeal:
Bless me so that my mind is released from the clutches of self-grasping,
that I become trained in loving kindness, compassion, and bodhicitta,
and that I attain quickly the supreme state,
mahāmudrā, the path of perfect union.

21
Your eyes of great nonreferential compassion remain never closed,
and your wisdom, profound and vast, is like that of Mañjuśrī—
to you, Yangchen Drupai Dorjé, I appeal.
Bless me so that my mind is released from the clutches of self-grasping,
that I become trained in loving kindness, compassion, and bodhicitta,
and that I attain quickly the supreme state,
mahāmudrā, the path of perfect union.

22
Perfecting the yoga of bliss and emptiness,
you have traveled to the royal seat of union—
to you, Khedrup Tenzin Tsöndrü, I appeal:
Bless me so that my mind is released from the clutches of self-grasping,
that I become trained in loving kindness, compassion, and bodhicitta,
and that I attain quickly the supreme state,
mahāmudrā, the path of perfect union.

And, once more:[1081]

23
Perfecting the realizations of the profound path,
you bear the banner of doctrine, exposition, and practice—
to you, Losang Tsöndrü Gyaltsen, I appeal:
Bless me so that my mind is released from the clutches of self-grasping,
that I become trained in loving kindness, compassion, and bodhicitta,
and that I attain quickly the supreme state,
mahāmudrā, the path of perfect union.

24
Untouched by stains of infractions and downfalls,
you uphold the essence of the threefold training—
to you, Losang Dönyö Drupa, I appeal:
Bless me so that my mind is released from the clutches of self-grasping,
that I become trained in loving kindness, compassion, and bodhicitta,
and that I attain quickly the supreme state,
mahāmudrā, the path of perfect union.

25
The second Buddha, Master Losang Drakpa,
who once more dances as a saffron-clad one—
to you, revered Gelek Gyatso, I appeal:
Bless me so that my mind is released from the clutches of self-grasping,
that I become trained in loving kindness, compassion, and bodhicitta,
and that I attain quickly the supreme state,
mahāmudrā, the path of perfect union.

26
Dharma treasure of paths profound and vast,
to illuminate it to all those with fortunate minds—
to you, most kind Ngawang Jampa, I appeal:
Bless me so that my mind is released from the clutches of self-grasping,
that I become trained in loving kindness, compassion, and bodhicitta,
and that I attain quickly the supreme state,
mahāmudrā, the path of perfect union.

27
With a lion's roar of flawless reasoning,
you expertly show the excellent path free of extremes—
to you, supremely learned Jikmé Wangpo, I appeal:
Bless me so that my mind is released from the clutches of self-grasping,
that I become trained in loving kindness, compassion, and bodhicitta,
and that I attain quickly the supreme state,
mahāmudrā, the path of perfect union.

28
You're matchless in propagating through teaching and practice
the supreme tradition of our lord, the conqueror Losang—
to you, revered Tenpai Drönmé, I appeal:
Bless me so that my mind is released from the clutches of self-grasping,
that I become trained in loving kindness, compassion, and bodhicitta,
and that I attain quickly the supreme state,
mahāmudrā, the path of perfect union.

29
Through the taste of Mañjuśrī's oral-transmission nectar,
your body of experience and realization is greatly nourished—
to you, revered Könchok Gyaltsen, I appeal:
Bless me so that my mind is released from the clutches of self-grasping,
that I become trained in loving kindness, compassion, and bodhicitta,
and that I attain quickly the supreme state,
mahāmudrā, the path of perfect union.

30
In transient dwellings with single-pointed zeal,
you carry the banner of the practice-lineage tradition—
to you, great siddha Ngödrup Rabten, I appeal:
Bless me so that my mind is released from the clutches of self-grasping,
that I become trained in loving kindness, compassion, and bodhicitta,
and that I attain quickly the supreme state,
mahāmudrā, the path of perfect union.

31
Perfecting the qualities of relinquishment and realization,
you send down a Dharma rain of excellent explanation—
to you, tutor Gendun Gyatso, I appeal:
Bless me so that my mind is released from the clutches of self-grasping,
that I become trained in loving kindness, compassion, and bodhicitta,
and that I attain quickly the supreme state,
mahāmudrā, the path of perfect union.

32
In wisdom, you are the wisest among the wise;
in realization, your attainment of the two stages is consummate—
to you, glorious Tenpai Nyima,[1082] I appeal:
Bless me so that my mind is released from the clutches of self-grasping,
that I become trained in loving kindness, compassion, and bodhicitta,
and that I attain quickly the supreme state,
mahāmudrā, the path of perfect union.

33
Swayed by the power of love for all beings,
you carry the banner of Buddha's teaching, sutra and tantra—

to you, Trinlé Gyatso,[1083] I appeal:
Bless me so that my mind is released from the clutches of self-grasping,
that I become trained in loving kindness, compassion, and bodhicitta,
and that I attain quickly the supreme state,
mahāmudrā, the path of perfect union.

34
You are the friend who dispenses to fortunate trainees
the mind-essence of the second Buddha, Lord [Tsongkhapa]—
to you, most kind Losang Yeshé,[1084] I appeal:
Bless me so that my mind is released from the clutches of self-grasping,
that I become trained in loving kindness, compassion, and bodhicitta,
and that I attain quickly the supreme state,
mahāmudrā, the path of perfect union.

35
In accord with Conqueror's intention, you bring out in manifold ways
the Sage's vast teaching, the holy Dharma of scripture and realization—
to you, matchless Trinlé,[1085] I appeal:
Bless me so that my mind is released from the clutches of self-grasping,
that I become trained in loving kindness, compassion, and bodhicitta,
and that I attain quickly the supreme state,
mahāmudrā, the path of perfect union.

36
Refuge, the treasure of the compassion of all conquerors,
appearing as the guardian of all disciples—
to you, revered Tenzin Gyatso,[1086] I appeal:
Bless me so that my mind is released from the clutches of self-grasping,
that I become trained in loving kindness, compassion, and bodhicitta,
and that I attain quickly the supreme state,
mahāmudrā, the path of perfect union.

37
In the great seat of past realized masters,
you, lord, shine as the glory of devout disciples—
to you, my most kind root guru, I appeal:[1087]
Bless me so that my mind is released from the clutches of self-grasping,
that I become trained in loving kindness, compassion, and bodhicitta,

and that I attain quickly the supreme state,
mahāmudrā, the path of perfect union.

38
Bless me that I may see my guru as a buddha,
that I may become disenchanted with my abode, samsara,
and that, by shouldering the burden of freeing all mother beings,
I may swiftly achieve the mahāmudrā union,
the glory of common and uncommon paths.

39
Your holy body and my body, father,
your holy speech and my speech, father,
your holy mind and my mind, father—
bless me that they may become inseparably one.[1088]

This too was uttered by the monk Losang Chökyi Gyaltsen.

11. A Lamp So Bright

An Extensive Explanation of the Root Text of Mahāmudrā of the Tradition of the Precious Geden Lineage[1089]

PANCHEN LOSANG CHÖKYI GYALTSEN

Namo mahāmudrāya.

The gnosis of all the buddhas of the myriad worlds
displaying the ecstatic dance of a saffron-clad monk,
the exalted guru who is triply kind[1090]—
respectfully I bow at your lotus feet.

I present here a lamp to illuminate mahāmudrā:
the distilled essence of the conquerors of the three times,
the essential point of the ocean of sutras and tantras,
and the trail left by all the great siddhas.

Here, the explanation of the instruction on mahāmudrā, the sacred tradition of the sublime beings who were learned and realized, is threefold: the initial task of composing the text, an explanation of the composed text's actual instruction, and dedication of the virtues derived from the composition.

THE INITIAL TASK OF COMPOSING THE TEXT

To show how one is aligned with the conduct of the sublime ones and so on, one pays homage to the objects of special importance, and to ensure successful completion of composition, one pledges to compose the work. To present these in general, the text reads:

1 **I bow at the feet of my peerless guru,**
the sovereign lord among siddhas, who reveals naked

mahāmudrā, the all-pervading nature of everything,
indivisible, and the ineffable expanse of the vajra mind. [506][1091]

2 **I will compose here the instructions of the mahāmudrā oral tradition**
of the most realized Dharmavajra, father and son,
the upholders of the sacred Geden lineage who distilled the essence
of the sea of sutra, tantra, and pith instructions and transmitted it well.

The meaning of these two stanzas is not difficult to comprehend, so I will not expand on them.

An explanation of the composed text's actual instruction

Here, as for the actual presentation of the instruction by means of preliminaries, the main part, and the conclusion, there are three parts: the preparation, the main practice, and the concluding practice.

The preparation

The first is presented in the following lines:

3 **Here, of the three—preparation, main practice, and conclusion—**
since it's the doorway and support beam of the teaching and the Mahayana,
strive first in going for refuge and arousing awakening,
not just with your mouth and with words alone.

4 **And since seeing the mind's true nature depends on**
gathering merit and purifying obscurations,
proceed first by reciting the hundred-syllable mantra a hundred thousand times
and repeating hundreds of times the *Confession of Downfalls* with prostrations.

5 **To your root guru, who is inseparable from**
all the buddhas of the three times,
make heartfelt supplications again and again.

Numerous learned and realized masters of the Land of the Āryas, such as the great master Śāntipa, the guru Serlingpa, and the great Atiśa, the sole lord, have distinguished Buddhists from non-Buddhists based on the perfect practice of going for refuge. Consonant with this, the exalted Sakya Paṇḍita says, "If you do not go for refuge, you are not a Dharma practitioner."[1092] As this states, you need to make sure that going for refuge has indeed become part of your mindstream. Dampa Sangyé says:

> Commit to the Three Jewels with all your three—your lungs, heart, and chest—
> and from the power of this blessings will come, O people of Dingri.[1093] [507]

Likewise, the guardian Śāntideva states:

> When the awakening mind is aroused, at that very instant,
> even the tormented beings chained in the prison of samsara
> will be called children of the sugatas
> and will be revered by the world, both gods and humans.[1094]

And the great Atiśa states:

> Those wishing to enter the gateway to the Mahayana
> should strive, even if takes an eon, to arouse
> the awakening mind, which resembles sun and moon,
> which dispels darkness and relieves the pain.[1095]

Not only is awakening mind, as stated above, the gateway to the Mahayana, it's also the central pillar of the Mahayana, as stated in the *Awakening of Vairocana Tantra*:

> O Lord of Secrets, the gnosis of the omniscient one has compassion as its root and the awakening mind as its cause and is the culmination of skillful means.[1096]

Whatever profound guidance may be presented by the sublime ones who are the sources of the individual doctrinal systems in this Land of Snows, when it comes to the preliminaries to meditative practice, there is no divergence of opinion among them. They all emphasize the practices of (1) going for refuge and generating the awakening mind, (2) offering the mandala, (3) performing Vajrasattva [meditation and mantra repetition], and (4) practicing guru yoga, calling these the "four guidance instructions."

In particular, the supreme trainee of highest yoga tantra, the lord of yoga Milarepa, first practiced loving kindness, compassion, and the awakening mind, true renunciation and karma and its effects, and death and impermanence and gave instructions on them as well. He says:

> Terrified of the eight states deprived of leisure,
> I've meditated on impermanence and samsara's defects.
> I took seriously the teaching on karma and its effects;
> I committed my innermost mind to the Three Jewels of refuge.
> As my mind became trained in the method of the awakening mind,
> I cut the continuum of obscurations and its propensities.
> I recognized whatever appears as an illusion.
> Now I have no fear of the three lower realms.[1097]

And:

> If you fail to contemplate clearly the causes and effects
> of virtuous and nonvirtuous acts,
> you will meet unbearable woes in the lower realms.
> So even regarding minute aspects of their fruits,
> be aware with heedfulness and mindfulness.[1098]

And:

> If you do not see the faults of sensual objects
> and do not feel revulsion for them from within,
> you'll not be free from the prison of samsara.
> So with the mind that recognizes all things as illusions,
> apply the antidotes to the origins of suffering.[1099]

And:

> If you do not repay the kindness done to you
> by all the beings of the six realms,
> you risk straying into the Hīnayāna. [508]
> So with the force of fervent compassion,
> train in the awakening mind.[1100]

Along such lines as these, Milarepa teaches exactly in accord with the teachings on the stages of the path.

Also, Dakpo Rinpoché[1101]—chief disciple of the exalted Milarepa and initiator of the tradition fusing the two streams of Kadam and mahāmudrā—presents extensive explanation of what are known as "the four teachings of Dakpo" in exact accord with Kadam mind training. The four are ensuring (1) that one's mind is turned to Dharma, (2) that one's Dharma practice hits the mark, (3) that one's path clears away confusion, and (4) that one's confusion dawns as gnosis.

Similarly, in his *Parting from the Four Clingings*, the great vajra-holder Drakpa Gyaltsen says:

> If you cling to this life, you are not a practitioner.
> If you cling to the three realms, that is not renunciation.
> If you cling to self-interest, you are not a bodhisattva.
> If grasping arises, it is not the view.[1102]

Having referred to the four opposing forces in negative terms, he is implicitly teaching their four positive counterparts: (1) As the antidote to clinging to this life, he is teaching the need for the practices of the lesser capacity, such as contemplating leisure and opportunity, impermanence, and the suffering of the lower realms. (2) As the antidote to clinging to cyclic existence, he is teaching the need to recognize the entirety of samsara as within the bounds of suffering and the need to engage in the threefold training. (3) As the antidote to clinging to seeking nirvana's peace for one's own sake alone, he is teaching the need to cultivate loving kindness, compassion, and the awakening mind. And (4) as the antidote to self-grasping, the root of samsara, he is teaching the need to meditate on the selflessness of persons and phenomena.

In brief, this path [of preliminary practice] has been hailed as excellent in the sutras, tantras, and authoritative treatises as well as by the learned and realized masters of India and Tibet. So although these practices are being taught in the context of a preliminary, don't think of them as just preliminaries. Instead undertake their practice in conjunction with the main part of the practice. In general, to be able to see the mind's true nature directly requires extensive accumulation of merit and the purification of negative karma and obscuration, so strive in gathering merit and purification throughout all periods in between sessions.

In particular, the *Ornament of the Essence* states:

> Repeat twenty-one times each day
> the hundred-syllable mantra in accord with the rite.
> This would transform the downfalls and so forth
> so that they will not increase and proliferate;
> thus say the supreme siddhas.
> So engage in this between sessions.
> If you repeat the mantra a hundred thousand times,
> you'll attain the state that is perfectly pure.[1103]

It is stated that if one repeats the mantra twenty-one times on a daily basis, it will prevent downfalls from increasing; [509] and if one repeats it a hundred thousand times, even the root downfalls will be purified. So strive in the practice of Vajrasattva meditation and recitation. Furthermore, strive with strong commitment in the purification practice endowed with the full presence of the four powers, such as through performing hundreds of prostrations combined with the recitation of the [Bodhisattva's] *Confession of Downfalls*.[1104]

Next, view your triply kind root guru—who is the source of all the virtue and goodness of this life and beyond, who enacts the enlightened life of all the conquerors and their children as well all the realized masters—and cultivate the profound-path guru yoga known also as "cultivating the guru." On this basis, engage in uninterrupted supplications from the very bone of your heart again and again. This is of paramount importance. When the great Atiśa was approached by someone asking him in a loud voice, "O Atiśa, I would like to receive an instruction," he replied, "Ha, ha! I have good ears, and what is called instruction is really faith; it's faith, faith."[1105]

The Dharma master Sapaṇ too says:

> Thus the blessings will enter
> the one who has received empowerment
> if he sees the Three Jewels as embodied
> in the guru and supplicates on this basis.[1106]

Also, Dampa Sangyé says:

> If the guru takes you, you'll reach your desired destination.
> Offer him admiration and respect as your fare, O people
> of Dingri.[1107]

The exalted Mila says:

> O teacher, when you journey to central Tibet,
> the vision of the guru may occasionally appear.
> When the vision of the guru does appear,
> supplicate him inseparably at your crown;
> not forgetting, contemplate him at the center of your heart.[1108]

The Main Practice

The main practice is as follows:

> 6 **With regard to the main practice of mahāmudrā,**
> **though there seem to be numerous perspectives,**
> **it is divisible in terms of two: sutra and tantra.** [510]

When it comes to the main practice of mahāmudrā, which I will describe below, there are numerous perspectives. Following what he understands to be the position of Drogön Rinpoché,[1109] the conqueror Drigungpa, for instance, presents mahāmudrā within the context of the three vehicles and the four seals, as in the following:

> In explaining the four profound seals,
> the elder Drogön clearly taught
> that the four seals of the path are
> the means to attain three forms of enlightenment.
> He characterized them in terms of the three vows.
>
> The inseparability of a śrāvaka's body, speech,
> and mind is the action seal (*karmamudrā*),
> their realization of selflessness of persons
> is stated to be the reality seal (*dharmamudrā*),
> their freedom from afflictions is the pledge seal (*samayamudrā*),
> and their nirvana without residue
> of aggregates is the great seal (*mahāmudrā*).
>
> The inseparability of the bodhisattva's
> three doors from the six perfections,

> this indeed is the action seal,
> their freedom from illusion and elaboration
> is the reality seal,
> their not being soiled by the stain of self-interest
> is the pledge seal,
> their equal taste of emptiness and compassion
> is indeed the great seal.
>
> In the context of the path of secret mantra,
> reliance on the messenger is the action seal,
> the inseparable conjoining of
> the wind and mind is the reality seal,
> nondegeneration of vows is the pledge seal,
> and actualization of the innate gnosis
> is the great seal.
>
> On the path of freedom, the *tumo* instruction,
> the yogic exercises, the visualizations,
> and the wind yoga are the action seal,
> the arisen gnosis of great bliss
> is called the reality seal,
> the absence of attachment is the pledge seal,
> and spontaneous actualization is the great seal.[1110]

The great translator Gö Shönu Pal holds the nonconceptual gnosis ascertaining emptiness itself to be mahāmudrā. For example, at the beginning of the history of mahāmudrā in his *Blue Annals*, he writes:

> I now tell the story of mahāmudrā, which seals all the attainments and practices, from the individual liberation vows, which is the foundation of the Buddha's teaching, right up to the glorious Guhyasamāja.[1111]

There are thus numerous perspectives. When summarized, however, mahāmudrā is twofold, divided in terms of sutra and tantra. Of these two, I will explain the former perspective in greater detail in this work. As I will explain the latter in fewer words, I will present that first. [511]

Brief presentation of tantric mahāmudrā

7 The latter is the clear light of great bliss
that arises from skillful means such as
penetrating the vital points in the vajra body.

8 This is the mahāmudrā of Saraha and Nāgārjuna,
of Nāropa and Maitripa, taught
in the Attainment and Essence texts[1112]
and is the quintessence of unexcelled tantras.

Why is it called the *great seal*?[1113] On this, the *Drop of the Great Seal* states:

> *Hand* (*phyag*) refers to the gnosis of emptiness,
> *seal* (*rgya*) is the freedom from samsaric phenomena,
> and *great* (*chen*) refers to union,
> so it's called the *great seal*.[1114]

So here in the latter, the system of tantra, *mahāmudrā* refers to the *illustrative clear light*—the gnosis of innate great bliss realizing emptiness via a generic image and induced by the entry, abiding, and absorption of the winds inside the central channel caused by skillful means such as penetrating the vital points of the vajra body—and the *actual clear light*, the direct realization of emptiness within such gnosis. These, in turn, arise on the basis of having received perfectly the four empowerments, having observed correctly the pledges and the vows, and having gained stable familiarity with the generation stage. This mind of clear light is referred to with such epithets as "the short *ah* of definitive meaning," "the indestructible drop," "the uncontrived mind," "the ordinary awareness," "the ever-present innate mind," and so on.

According to the definitive standpoint of the great siddhas of the Land of the Āryas—the glorious protector Mahāsukha or Saroruhavajra, the great siddha Saraha, Nāgārjunapāda, Lord Śavari, Tilopa, Nāropa, Maitripa, and others—as well as the early Kagyü masters Marpa, Milarepa, Gampopa, Phakmo Drupa, and others, *mahāmudrā* refers to the clear light of great bliss that has arisen through the entry, abiding, and dissolution of the winds inside the central channel. This is the principal subject matter of the Seven Attainment Texts and the Essence Trilogy and is the innermost essence of the highest-yoga class of tantras, vast as an ocean. [512]

These are the Seven Attainment Texts: (1) The protector Mahāsukha composed *Secret Attainment* (*Guhyasiddhi*). This primarily elucidates the intention of the *Guhyasamāja Root Tantra*. Extolling the greatness of the Guhyasamāja, "There is no tantra superior to the glorious Guhya. It's a jewel unique in the three worlds,"[1115] the text briefly presents the generation stage of Guhyasamāja but teaches with special focus the definitive meaning of the root tantra, namely the path of indivisible bliss and emptiness of the advanced levels of the completion stage. This work is recognized as the foundational text for all the other Attainment Texts and the Essence Trilogy. (2) Mahāsukha's disciple Anaṅgavajra composed *Attainment of Method and Wisdom* (*Prājñopayavinśacayasiddhi*). (3) Anaṅgavajra's disciple Indrabhūti composed *Attainment of Gnosis* (*Jñānasiddhi*). (4) His wife Lakṣmīṅkarā composed *Attainment of the Nondual* (*Advayasiddhi*). (5) Ḍombī Heruka authored *Attainment of the Connate* (*Sahajasiddhi*). (6) Dārikapa wrote *Attainment of the Principle of the Great Secret* (*Guhyamahātatvosiddhi*). And (7) Yoginī Cintā wrote *Attainment of the Principle that Follows the Illumination of Reality* (*Vyaktabhāvānugatatattvasiddhi*). The Essence Trilogy is the three *Dohā* collections. Some learned masters such as the omniscient Butön maintain that the *People's Dohā* is authentic [a work of Saraha] while the other two collections are falsely attributed.[1116]

Some might argue that it would be untenable to maintain that the standpoint [presented in the above texts] is not different from Nāgārjuna's *Five Stages* and his presentation of completion stage. For example, passages such as the following in the *Dohās*:

> Just like a brahman spinning the sacred thread,
> the yogi should let his mind rest at ease.
> This mind bound in its own entanglement,
> when relaxed becomes free, no doubt.[1117]

And "the fresh, the uncontrived, and carefree,"[1118] and the *Ten Verses on Reality* too says, "Absence of analysis is the excellent guru"[1119] suggesting that it is through resting the mind, right from start, with no analysis and cessation of mental activity that one attains freedom.

It may be true that there can be misreading of citations such as the above from the Seven Attainment Texts and the Essence Trilogy. Nonetheless, what the omniscient Tsongkhapa says in his *Lamp to Illuminate the Five Stages* and elsewhere as to how what is taught in the *Dohās* and so forth represents practices of advanced levels of the tantra path remains immutable.[1120] Let me explain the meaning of the *Dohās* by way of some examples from the *Dohā Treasury of Songs*:

> Whoever enters emptiness divorced of compassion
> will not find the path supreme,
> and if he cultivates compassion alone,
> he'll remain in samsara and not abide in nirvana.
> Whoever can conjoin the two
> will remain neither in samsara nor in nirvana.[1121] [513]

The text thus explains how it is necessary to conjoin the subject, compassion, which is the innate great bliss, with the object, emptiness. Also, the same texts says:

> If you have realization, then all things are just that;
> no one will know anything other than that.
> Reading is that; retention and meditation are also that;
> upholding a treatise in one's heart also is that.
> There is no view not indicated by that,
> but it is dependent on the guru's words alone.
> Having the guru's teaching enter your heart
> is like seeing a treasure in the palm of your hand.
> Because the innate nature goes unnoticed by the childish,
> the childish, deluded, become deceived—so says the archer.[1122]

This states that when the yogi directly experiences and come to realize the innate mind, then all phenomena are seen manifestations of this innate mind. No person will know anything that is not a manifestation of that innate mind. Furthermore, the actualization of that innate mind represents the direct realization of the essence of reading, retention, and meditation, and it is also the principal purpose of upholding treatises in your heart. There is no view superior to the one indicated by such essence. This said, direct experience of the essence through the power of meditative practice is dependent entirely upon instruction coming from the mouth of the guru, who is part of an uninterrupted lineage of sublime beings beginning from Vajradhara. When such quintessential instruction of the guru enters your heart, and when you place your mind single-pointedly on the essence—emptiness—and meditate on it, you will see the meaning of emptiness nakedly as if you are seeing a treasure on the palm of your own hand. Childish ordinary beings fail to see this innate nature directly, and because of their clinging to true existence, the childish are deceived. So says the archer, Saraha.

The *Dohā Treasury of Songs* also says:

> If it is manifest, what need is there for concentration?
> If it is hidden, you will encounter darkness.
> That innate nature is itself
> neither entity nor nonentity.[1123]

This asks, if this nature, ever-present innate mind, has become manifest through meditative practice, what need is there of the concentration of analytical meditation? If, in contrast, it remains hidden, you will then encounter darkness. [514] And this essence is neither a real entity nor a nonentity in the sense of nothingness. It also says:

> Devoid of meditation, what is there to contemplate?
> Inexpressible, how can it be explained?
> The seal of samsaric existence deceives all beings.
> As for the innate nature, no one can take it away.[1124]

The *Dohā Treasury of Songs* says furthermore:

> No tantra, no mantra, nothing to contemplate or meditate:
> all these serve to cause your own confusion.
> The naturally pure mind is not tainted by meditation,
> so abide in bliss and do not make yourself miserable.
> Eat, drink, and enjoy the act of sexual union:
> always, again and again, fill the cakras.
> Through such Dharma you will transcend the world;
> trampling on the head of the ignorant world, march on.
> Where the wind and mind no longer move,
> where the sun and moon do not enter,
> there, O ignorant ones, find relief for your mind.
> The archer has taught all the instructions and moved on.[1125]

Let me now explain the meaning of these lines a little. The primordial innate nature, the mind of clear light, is what is known as the *ground dharma-*

kāya. When, through the power of meditative practice, it is directly experienced, it is free from investigation, analysis, or verbal expression, so what point is there of meditative concentration involving investigation and analysis? What is there to be said as well? Failing to ascertain this through meditative practice, all beings come to be deceived by the seal of samsaric existence. Even though they are thus deceived, no one can take away or rob their essential nature, the innate mind. For all beings of the three realms in general and the womb-born beings endowed with the six constituents[1126] in particular, the appearance, increase, and near attainment as well as clear light dawn at the time of their death. Although these thus come to dawn, ordinary beings are not able to transform them into the path. Furthermore, even though most beings of the desire realm delight in joining the two sex organs and frequently talk about sex, they fail to understand the import of great bliss. This is as the *Dohā Treasury of Songs* puts it:

> Although they talk about it at this and that home,
> none fully understands the import of great bliss.[1127]

As for the yogis, other than resting their mind wherein their primordial mind in the nature of great bliss has taken emptiness as its object, they do not engage in any mental elaboration, whether good or bad. [515] As for the arising of such a realization of mahāmudrā, if the practitioner is accomplished and the winds enter the central channel on the basis of having trained in the preceding stages of the paths either in his past lives or earlier in this life, then even if the person were to rest his mind in a nondiscursive state and meditate on any chosen object, he will directly realize the mahāmudrā clear light. Such person is given the designation of a *subitist* by the early Kagyü masters. There is, for example, the following in the *Epitome*:

> For those trained and with karmic residue,
> the subitist [path] should be taught.[1128]

The point being made here is the same as what the omniscient Jé Tsongkhapa says in his *Lamp to Illuminate the Five Stages*:

> For someone who is trained and has experienced the entry of the winds into the central channel, it is apparent that the vital winds will gather within the central channel no matter where he focuses his mind.[1129]

In order for trainees other than this type to realize mahāmudrā of this path, they must certainly practice *tumo* and so forth. The exalted Milarepa too first practiced primarily the Six Yogas of Nāropa according to the oral tradition of the glorious Nāropa and Marpa and then actualized mahāmudrā. He writes:

> Mahāmudrā is the fortress of the view,
> the Six Yogas of Nāropa are the fortress of meditation,
> the profound-method path is the fortress of conduct,
> spontaneous realization of the three bodies is the fortress of
> fruition.[1130]

Referring to his "short *ah* of *tumo*," Milarepa also sang its elevated praises. In line with this, the Dharma master Sapaṇ also says:

> Guidance known as the Six Yogas of Nāropa
> is none other than that stemming from Milarepa.[1131]

Master Gampopa too first practiced *tumo* and then attained manifest experience of the innate mind. There are thus numerous examples.

Thus to engage in the meditative practice of mahāmudrā referred to in the context here [of tantra], it is necessary indeed to receive the four perfect empowerments, train in the generation and completion stages, and be trained in the common paths as well. The *Epitome* says:

> Beings on the beginner's stage
> should be taught the gradual path.[1132]

Such a person is given the designation of a *gradualist*. Therefore most of the great siddhas of this path are found within the lineage of the empowerment rites of individual classes of tantras as well. The Dharma master Sapaṇ also says:

> Nāropa emphasized as his teaching
> the empowerment rite and the two stages.[1133]

The exalted Milarepa also states:

If you listen to what I will teach, O son,
you'll have the good fortune of divine Dharma. [516]
I'll open the door through empowerment and blessing
and give you profound instruction of the oral transmission.[1134]

Along the same lines, the *Clear Differentiation of the Three Vows* states:

As for our mahāmudrā,
this is the gnosis arisen from the empowerments;
it's the self-arisen gnosis that emerged
from concentrations during the two stages.[1135]

There is thus no disagreement among the authoritative scholars and siddhas on these points.

Mahāmudrā of the sutra system

To present mahāmudrā of the sutra system in particular, there is once again the following promise:

9 **As for the former, this refers to the way of meditating on emptiness**
taught explicitly in the long, medium, and short [Perfection of Wisdom].
The supreme ārya, Nāgārjuna, has stated
that there is no path to liberation apart from this.

10 **Here, I will present a guide to mahāmudrā**
that accords with his thought
and expound a way to point out the mind's nature
that accords with the teaching of the lineage gurus.

Of the two ways of practicing mahāmudrā, the first, the way of practicing according to the sutra system, is *the way of cultivating the wisdom realizing emptiness,* with emptiness being the explicit subject matter of the three Mother [Perfection of Wisdom] sutras—the extensive, the middle-length, and the concise. This practice has been hailed in the Mother sutras as the true life force of the paths of all three vehicles. The supreme ārya, Nāgārjuna, declares that, apart from this, no other path will lead to liberation. He states:

> The buddhas, pratyekabuddhas, and śrāvakas,
> the path they relied on with certainty
> for liberation is this one alone;
> there is no other—be sure of this.[1136]

Not only that, in Vajrayāna too, there is no different view that is distinct or somehow superior to this one. This is as stated by the exalted Sapaṇ in the following:

> With respect to perfection and secret mantra,
> there is no indication of any difference in the view.
> For if there is a view superior to
> that of perfection's absence of elaboration,
> then that view would entail elaboration.
> If it's free of elaboration, there is then no difference.[1137] [517]

Among those who have embarked on the great highway initiated by the protector Nāgārjuna, who the conqueror himself prophesized to elucidate the definitive meaning [of the scriptures], the great Atiśa says the following about Candrakīrti:

> If you ask, "Who realized emptiness?"
> Nāgārjuna, who was prophesized by the Tathāgata
> and saw the truth of ultimate nature,
> and his disciple Candrakīrti.
> In the instruction stemming from them,
> there is buddhahood, not elsewhere.[1138]

I will thus conduct here a guide to mahāmudrā in accordance with the way in which Candrakīrti has interpreted the intention of Ārya Nāgārjuna. I will explain the method of pointing out the nature of mind in perfect accord with the precious speech of the sublime gurus who possess the uninterrupted blessing transmission of the excellent learned and realized masters.

One might ask, "Why is what is presented here called *mahāmudrā* (the great seal)?" It is because, as stated in the *King of Meditation Sutra*, "The nature of all phenomena is the seal."[1139] Emptiness is the nature of all phenomena, the "seal," and it is "great" or "supreme" because when it is realized, one becomes released from all misfortunes. For it says, "*great* refers to something excellent and measureless."[1140]

Different traditions of mahāmudrā

Now, just as within the Sage's teaching, eighteen subschools evolved yet all aimed equally at freedom as the goal, likewise, with respect to the understanding of mahāmudrā, there are numerous and diverse perspectives, but they are all equal in being methods to attain the fruit, the *union* that is mahāmudrā. To indicate this, and to become versed in differentiating the numerous excellent traditions of the sublime ones, the text reads:

11–12 **The Innate Union, the Amulet Box,**
the Fivefold, Equal Taste, and the Four-Lettered,
Pacification, Cutting Off, and the Great Perfection,
the Guide to the Middle Way View, and so on—
though many teachings exist, each with a different name,
when examined by a yogi who is versed in definitive scriptures
and reasoning and who possesses meditative experience,
they come down to a single intention. [518]

Lord Gampopa sustained his students through the Six Dharmas, the Fivefold, and the Innate Union. On the Innate Union, although there seem to be several different versions of the root text, [there is the following reading]:

> The innate mind itself is dharmakāya,
> the innate concepts are waves of dharmakāya,
> the innate appearances are the light of dharmakāya,
> appearances and mind are the innate indivisible.[1141]

The meaning of these lines is that [the guide to the Innate Union] is threefold: (1) the *preliminary* of four preparatory practices, emphasizing developing respectful devotion and [toward one's teacher] and disenchantment [toward samsara]; (2) the *main practice* consisting of two pointing-out instructions, and (3) the *subsequent practice*, relating your experience to whatever appears. The preliminary practices are similar to those that taught generally, while the main practices consist of introducing tranquil abiding and insight.

The Amulet Box is the tradition of the scholar-siddha Khyungpo Naljor.

It is presented by way of the following: (1) the *preliminary*, the three self-descending factors, (2) the *main practice*, the self-freeing of the four defects, and (3) the *result,* the self-dawning of the three buddha bodies. The main practice is also called "recognizing the thief." The principal instruction of the Shangpa Kagyü is the Six Dharmas of Nigumā: (1) *tumo*, the foundation stone of the path, (2) the illusory body, the natural liberation of attachment and aversion, (3) dream yoga, the natural awakening from deep confusion, (4) clear light, the dispeller of the darkness of ignorance, (5) transference, buddhahood without meditation, and (6) intermediate state, the saṃbhogakāya of the conquerors. The main practice of the Amulet Box is, in fact, the meditative practice of the clear light, one of the Six Dharmas.

As for the Fivefold, this is quite widespread in the Dakpo [Kagyü] lineage. When Jikten Gönpo sang the root lines in a song, he wrote:

> As for the stallion of the awakening mind,
> if you do not race it along the course of altruism,
> the loud cheers of the crowd of gods and humans will not rise.
> So apply your mind earnestly to the preliminary practice.
>
> Your body, a king among deities,
> if you do not hold it fast as an unshakeable ground,
> the hosts of ḍākinīs will not gather around.
> So earnestly generate your body as a meditation deity.
>
> The snow mountain of the four buddha bodies, your guru,
> if the sun of your admiration and devotion does not shine on it,
> the river of blessing will not flow.
> So apply yourself earnestly to this mind of devotion.
>
> The expansive sky of mind itself,
> if you do not clear away from it the massed clouds of concepts,
> the planets and stars of the two types of knowledge will not shine.
> So apply your mind earnestly to nonconceptuality.
>
> The wish-granting jewel of two accumulations,
> if you do not polish it with aspiration prayers, [519]
> your needs and wishes will not come about.
> So apply your mind earnestly to this final dedication.[1142]

Those in the lineage of the Dharma master Gyaré[1143] practice and impart the instructions of the Eight Great Guides, the Six Cycles of Equal Taste, and the Mountain Dharma.

The eight guides are: the guide to the guru as the three buddha bodies, the guide to loving kindness and compassion, the guide to the dependent origination of cause and effect, the guide to the ambrosia drop like the Five-fold [mahāmudrā], the guide to Innate Union, the guide to the Six Yogas of Nāropa, the guide to equalizing the eight worldly concerns, and the guide to the reversal of ill fortune through secret practices.

The Six Cycles of Equal Taste are: taking concepts as the path, taking afflictions as the path, taking sicknesses as the path, taking gods and demons as the path, taking sufferings as the path, and taking death as the path.

As for the Mountain Dharma, there are the "four ornaments of profound teaching" and the "three ornaments of the sphere of oral instructions." Of these the first consists of: the Mountain Dharma, the source of all higher qualities; the secret, the great ship of empowerment; the hidden explanation of the vajra body; and guidance on the intermediate state. The second consists of: the ornament of direct guidance clearing away the obstacles, the ornament of the catalogue of a hundred thousand songs, and the ornament of the minor scattered teachings.

As for the Four-Lettered, its explanation is drawn from the etymology of the word *amanasi*, which is Sanskrit for "nonmentation," and its meaning is shown by way of the word's four letters. Thus the first (*a*) is cutting the mind's root basis, the second (*ma*) shows the method for resting the mind, the third (*na*) cuts off the mind's erroneous forces, and the fourth (*si*) shows how to take the mind into the path.

Dampa Sangyé's sublime teaching on Pacification (Shijé) of suffering is as explained in the following, which he taught when he met the exalted Milarepa:

> This sublime teaching, the pacification of suffering:
> When subduing harmful male and female *yakṣas*,
> it's to bind them with the magic wheel of conduct.
> When illnesses arise in your body,
> it's to fuse the expanse and your awareness into one.
> When subtle conceptualization arises,
> it's to level out and destroy the afflictions.
> When sleeping alone in private,

it's to place yourself in bare awareness.
When in the midst of others,
it's to behold the nature of whatever arises.
When becoming lax,
it's to rouse yourself with the sound of *phat*!
When your mind is dispersed,
it's to cut its very root.
When excitation arises,
it's to rest your mind in the expanse.
When the mind is chasing an external object,
it's to behold the real nature of the object.

This sublime teaching, the pacification of suffering:
when bad omens occur, embrace them as lucky charms;
whatever concepts arise, just delight in them;
when sickness occurs, take them as boons; [520]
whatever befalls you, just delight in it;
when death occurs, take it into the path;
whatever pleases the lord of death, just delight in it.

This sublime teaching, the pacification of suffering,
is the intent of the conquerors of the three times.[1144]

As for Cutting Off, it is the profound teaching of Machik representing the instruction of Dampa and is quite widely known. In addition, there are instructions such as the Great Perfection—distilling the heart teachings of Guru Padmasambhava, including his *Garland of Views: A Pith Instruction*—the Guide to the Middle Way View, and so forth. Although all these instructions are given varied and different names, when the wise who are versed in the scriptures and reasoning distinguish the provisional and the definitive meanings exactly as they are, they see that they all come down to a single intention and are not in contradiction, like heat and cold. This is as stated in *Stainless Light*:

The same jewel is called
on the earth by different names
from one region to the next,
yet no difference exists in its preciousness.[1145]

THE ACTUAL MEDITATION

If asked, "What then is the sequence in mahāmudrā meditation?" I say:

13 **Thus, of two approaches—seeking meditation**
on the basis of the view and seeking the view
on the basis of meditation—
the presentation here is the latter approach.

There are thus two approaches, and either of them may be adopted. As the guardian Śāntideva says:

> Knowing that insight endowed with tranquil abiding
> destroys the afflictions completely,
> first seek tranquil abiding.[1146]

And the *Heap of Jewels Sutra* says:

> Abiding in morality, you achieve meditative absorption,
> and having attained absorption, cultivate wisdom.[1147]

As stated in these citations, the approach presented here is to seek the view on the basis of meditation.

CULTIVATING TRANQUIL ABIDING

Since this is the case, what is the way to cultivate tranquil abiding first? This is twofold: the preparation and the main practice. [521]

THE PREPARATION

The exalted Maitreya says:

> In what sort of place do the wise practice meditation?
> It should be easily accessible and have a pleasant environment,
> where the ground is good and companions good
> and where the yogi has the necessities for comfort.[1148]

So in a place thus described, abide with pure morality, with few desires and content with what you have, and seek the conditions or collections relevant to tranquil abiding. Certainly, you should also engage in the six preparatory practices. So I say:

14 **On a platform conducive to meditative absorption,**
your body maintaining the seven-point posture,
dispel the stale winds through the nine-round breathing
and distinguish well the fresh and sullied awareness.

15 **With a pure virtuous state of mind, proceed first**
with going for refuge and arousing the awakening mind,
and then practice the profound path of guru yoga.
After performing fervent supplications
a hundred times or so, dissolve the guru into you.

"A pure virtuous state of mind" refers to the awakening mind, while "the profound path of guru yoga" is a guru yoga that encompasses all aspects of the path, such as the one I have composed separately.[1149] The rest can be understood easily.

The Main Practice

The Method for Cultivating Mental Stillness

Having begun first with the preparatory stages, I will explain the method for cultivating mental stillness:

16 **While in that state where appearances are indistinct,**
do not alter it or add anything to it
by thoughts of hope, fear, and so on,
but rest unwavering in equipoise for a while.

17 **Do not cease mental activity**
as in fainting or falling asleep;
post the sentry of undistracted mindfulness
and station meta-awareness to detect any movement.
Hold the clear and aware nature of mind
with a firm focus and starkly look at it. [522]

18 **Whatever thoughts arise, any thought,**
note it as that and just that.
Alternatively, like a skilled swordsman,
swiftly cut down the thoughts as they arise.

19 **When, after cutting down, your mind is stable,**
then, without losing mindfulness, loosen and relax:
"Focus with firmness but loosen and relax;
there lies the spot to rest your mind."

20 **So it is stated; and elsewhere it says,**
"This mind, bound in its own entanglement,
when relaxed becomes free, no doubt."
As taught here, relax without distraction.

21 **Whatever thoughts arise, when you observe their nature,**
they naturally disappear, and a pure vacuity appears.
Likewise, when you examine the settled mind as well,
you see an unobstructed vacuity and vivid clarity.

22 **This is called "merging of stillness and movement."**
And whatever thoughts may arise,
do not stop them, but recognize their movement
and place your mind upon their nature.

23 **This is analogous to the flights**
of a bird captive on a ship:
"It's like the raven that takes off from a ship,
flies to every direction, and lands there again."

The concentration being cultivated here is a meditative state with two limbs: vibrant clarity and nondiscursive single-pointedness.[1150] Such authentic tranquil abiding arises based on single-pointed concentration of a desire-realm mind, a state of mind that belongs to the non-equipoised class.[1151] Here, Lord Maitreya says:

> It results from reliance on the eight applications
> that reject the five faults.[1152]

Maitreya states how tranquil abiding is attained through nine stages of stilling the mind, which in turn arise through reliance on the eight applications that are the antidotes against the five faults. In his collection on the grounds,

Ārya Asaṅga explains how these nine mental stages are attained through the six powers and are characterized by four types of mental application.

What kind of object does one focus on to cultivate meditative absorption? In general, the Blessed One spoke of countless types of meditation objects in the context of cultivating faultless concentration, such as the universal objects, objects that purify behavior, objects of expertise, objects that purify the afflictions, and so forth. This said, given that most gurus of this particular instruction lineage [of mahāmudrā] uphold the tradition of conducting the introduction [to tranquil abiding] by taking the mind as the focal object, I will do the same here.

With tears in your eyes and the hairs of your body standing up in their pores, and with your mind fervently moved by devotion and reverence, supplicate your guru for a long time from the very core or bone of your heart. At the end, when your guru dissolves into you, imagine that you have been blessed.

Then, within this state where all appearances have become somewhat indistinct, do nothing by way of contrivance of conceptualization, such as entertaining the hopeful thought "If only I could accomplish such and such immediate and ultimate goals" or having anxious thoughts like "What if such and such undesirable events befall me?" Neither chasing the past nor anticipating the future, rest your mind in equipoise in the present, with no movement at all.

At the time of resting your mind in this way, unlike the total cessation of all mental engagement during fainting or falling asleep, post the sentry of mindfulness ensuring the mind that is abiding unwavering remains undistracted—that is to say, it is not lost to even the slightest forgetfulness. Even though you may tie the meditation object with the rope of mindfulness, if your mindfulness weakens, there is great danger that thoughts involving the mind's movement could proliferate. So you need to place your mind [on the focal object] by stationing the watchman of meta-awareness, monitoring whether your mind has wandered elsewhere due to a weakening of the force of mindfulness. This is as stated in the following in *Essence of the Middle Way*:

> This wandering elephant of mind,
> tie it firmly to a sturdy post, its object,
> with the rope of mindfulness and gradually
> tame it with the hook of meta-awareness.[1153] [524]

In brief, the cultivation of flawless meditative absorption constitutes nothing but the maintenance of mindfulness and meta-awareness. Here too, mindfulness the key: when mindfulness is present, meta-awareness arises as a byproduct, for meta-awareness has been described as a result of mindfulness.

At that point, when all other thoughts have ceased and that *aware* and *clear* mind is perceived, fasten your mindfulness with a firm focus on its nature and starkly observe it with single-pointedness. Observing in this manner, note whatever movement or thought arises and recognize it as just this or that. Doing this depends, of course, on meta-awareness. Alternatively, as explained in a Vinaya text, meditate in way in which an archer and a swordsman fight in a duel: applying the force of your mindfulness and meta-awareness, tread on whatever thoughts arise, instantly cutting them down and thus preventing them from gaining momentum. When, in the aftermath of severing the proliferation of thought, you abide free of movement, ensure that you do not lose mindfulness and meta-awareness, maintaining a state that is alert at the core and relaxed on the surface. In this manner, settle your mind relaxed in meditative equipoise. As Machik writes:

> Focus with firmness but loosen and relax;
> there lies the spot to rest your mind.[1154]

Also, the Great Brahman, Saraha, says:

> This mind, bound in its own entanglement,
> when relaxed becomes free, no doubt.[1155]

So, as suggested in the above, inwardly alert, stay relaxed. And when you sense your mind becoming too alert, such that excitation may arise, relax a little; and when you sense your mind becoming too relaxed, such that mental laxity may arise, strengthen your alertness a little. This way you will find just the right balance. So between those two extremes, relax your mind from the movements of thought, and watch out for occurrence of mental laxity every time stability arises. Master Candragomin writes:

> If effort is applied excitation arises;
> if shunned slackness occurs.
> When it is hard to find a proper balance,
> my mind is perturbed, so what should I do?[1156]

During these times when you are trampling on the thoughts or looking at the face of each thought as it arises, right there and then, the thoughts will vanish on their own accord, giving rise to the dawning of a pure vacuity. Similarly, when you examine the mind as it remains without wavering, [525] you will see an unobstructed pure vacuity, a vivid clarity, with no differentiation between the earlier and the latter instances. This is known to the great meditators as "the merging of stillness and movement," and they refer to it by such a phrase.

Alternatively, you could engage in the following method for stilling the mind: Whatever thought arises, do not suppress it but note where it comes from and where it moves to and rest your mind by simply looking at the nature of that thought. As you rest your mind in this way, movement will eventually cease and your mind will become still. This is analogous to the flights of a bird long captive aboard a ship sailing across a vast ocean. The *Dohā Treasury of Songs* says:

> It's like the raven that takes off from a ship,
> flies to every direction, and lands there again.[1157]

Maintain your meditation exactly as described here. So Yangönpa says:

> Not viewing the thoughts as faults,
> not deliberately meditating on nonconceptuality,
> rest your mind in its natural mode and post a sentry,
> and your meditation will reach tranquil abiding.[1158]

Furthermore, if today's trainees maintain their meditation practice by means of the six methods of resting the mind, theirs will be a king among instructions. How are they done? It is said:

> Rest it like the sun free from the clouds.
> Rest it like a great garuḍa soaring in the sky.
> Rest it like a ship on the great ocean.
> Rest it like a small child looking inside a temple.
> Rest it like the tracks of a bird flying in the sky.
> Rest it like fluffed cotton wool.
> By these methods of resting the mind,
> your yoga will be meaningful.[1159]

Just as the sun when free of clouds remains supremely bright and brilliant, in the same manner, rest your mind in the luminous nature of mind unobscured by conceptual apprehension of signs, by mental laxity and excitation, and so forth.

Just as a garuḍa flying across the sky does so naturally, soaring high without needing much exertion of flapping its wings, in the same manner, maintain your meditation without straying outside the seal of mindfulness and meta-awareness—in such a way that your mind is neither too alert nor too relaxed but possesses vibrant clarity due from being alert at the core yet relaxed on the surface.

Just as waves rise a little on the surface when a great ocean is stirred by winds, but the sea is not moved in its depths, [526] in the same manner, rest your mind in such a way that even if some subtle level of thought does elicit movement when you place your mind on the meditation object, it is not swayed even slightly by the coarse levels of thought.

Just as a small child looking inside a temple does not consider the details of the murals but stares undistracted at the large vibrant patterns, in the same manner, when your mind is focused on the meditation object, whatever objects—attractive or unattractive—may appear to your five senses, simply rest your mind single-pointedly on the meditation object without judgment and without emotions of attachment or aversion.

Just as birds cruising across the sky leave no track, in the same manner, whatever feelings you might be experiencing, whether pleasant, unpleasant, or neutral, rest your mind in equipoise without giving in to any of the three poisons of the mind—attachment, aversion, and delusion.

Just as when cotton wool is fluffed it becomes softer and freer, in the same manner, when you rest your mind in equipoise, you do so free of manifest levels of the three poisons and the rough and hard textures of mental laxity and excitation.

Imprints resulting from maintaining meditative equipoise in this way

What imprints will emerge from maintaining meditative equipoise in the way presented above? Here I say:

24 In this way, as you maintain meditative equipoise,
its nature will dawn as unobscured
by anything, as lucid and clear and,

since it does not exist in any physical way,
as a pure vacuity just like space,
where everything appears vividly.

When you maintain meditative equipoise in this way, the following will unfold: You will experience the nature of your meditative equipoise as unobscured by anything, as lucid and utterly clear. As it does not exist in any physical way, it is a pure vacuity like space, yet like reflections appearing in an unblemished mirror, whatever objects it encounters—good or bad—appear clearly and vividly. It is undefinable by any identifications of "it is this" or "it is not that." Now, however stable such a meditative concentration may be, if it is not imbued with physical and mental pliancy, it is said to be a single-pointedness of mind belonging to the desire realm. A meditative concentration imbued with [physical and mental pliancy, on the other hand] is described as tranquil abiding. [527] Tranquil abiding will be the source of numerous higher qualities such as clairvoyance and other supernatural feats. In particular, all the paths of the three vehicles are attained on the basis of tranquil abiding.

Identifying this path in terms of its own nature

How is this path to be identified with respect to its own nature? Here I say:

25 **Thus though the mind's true nature**
may be seen as if in a direct manner,
it cannot be grasped at or shown as "this."
Whatever appears, without grasping, rest your mind.

26 **"This is the special instruction to grab**
buddhahood with one's bare hands."
So proclaim most present-day meditators
of the Land of Snows, with a shared understanding.

27 **Be that as it may, I, Chökyi Gyaltsen,**
would say the following:
"This is an excellent method for the beginner
to cultivate mental stillness and the way
to identify the mind's conventional nature."

This is how I would respond to the question.

Cultivating insight

Now, to state the promise to present the method of how to introduce the mind's true nature, I say:

28 **Now, as for the way to introduce**
the mind's true nature,
I will set this forth following the oral instructions
of my root guru: as a saffron-clad monk,
the embodiment of the gnoses of all the buddhas,[1160]
dispelling the darkness of ignorance from my mind.

The meaning here is easy to comprehend. Since the promise here is of a different nature, there is no fault of redundancy with respect to the earlier ones.[1161] Thus here there is (1) a general presentation of the various ways of introducing [the mind's ultimate nature] and (2) the distilled essence of those ways of introducing. [528]

A general presentation of the various ways of introducing [the mind's ultimate nature]

The Teacher has stated that when the nature of the mind is realized, that is Buddha,[1162] so buddhahood is not to be sought elsewhere. Saraha too says:

> Mind itself is the seed of everything,
> the source of both samsaric existence and nirvana
> and that which grants all desired goals—
> to this wish-granting jewel mind, I pay homage.[1163]

And Lingrepa says:

> When you realize your own mind, buddhahood will arise.
> When you cut reifications from within, fulfillment will arise.[1164]

As stated in these lines, all excellent sutras and tantras converge on the understanding that it is on the basis of whether one has realized the mind's true nature as it is that samsara and nirvana come into being, and that this is a matter of great gain or loss.

As for the way to meditate by cutting the root basis of the mind:[1165] (1) Some maintain that as you examine, from within the state of meditative equipoise, whether the mind exists anywhere—outside, inside, when arising, abiding, ceasing, and so on—and see that it does not exist anywhere, you have then cut the root basis of the mind, recognized the mind, and attained the goal, mahāmudrā. They maintain this to be meaning of the following passage from the *Treasury of Dohās: A Pith Instruction on Mahāmudrā*:

> The mind as well as all appearances, when sought,
> nothing is found; the searcher too is nowhere.
> The nonexistent does not arise nor cease at any time,
> and it cannot turn into something else.
> This is the abiding nature of natural great bliss.
> Thus all appearances are dharmakāya indeed.[1166]

(2) Now some assert that as you search for the mind and find that it does not exist anywhere—in any part of the body, from the top of your crown to the soles of your feet—and see that it exists nowhere as a material entity with color, shape, and so forth, you have seen the mind's true nature. They understand this to be so because Shang Rinpoché says:

> The abiding nature of your own mind, which is the seed of all,
> is not different whatsoever from the mind of the buddhas
> as well as of their children: they appear as dharmakāya.
> It is not material and is self-luminous;
> not existing as a thing, it is devoid of color and dimension.[1167]

(3) Some maintain: Neither chasing the past nor anticipating the future but resting your mind in the present-moment awareness, which is fresh and uncontrived, you will directly perceive the mind's bare nature. At that point you have cut the root basis of mind [529] and have recognized the mind's nature. Saraha says, "Rest naturally in the fresh, uncontrived mind."[1168] The great siddha Lingrepa too says:

> When you rest in the uncontrived, fresh awareness, realization dawns;
> when you maintain realization like a flowing river, fulfillment occurs.
> Shunning utterly all objectifiable loci and signs,
> abide always in meditative equipoise, O yogi.[1169]

(4) In other teachings it says: Whatever sensory objects such as form, sound, and so forth appear to the mind, or whatever thoughts of good or

bad such as of virtue and nonvirtue arise, as you starkly look at their nature without reacting, neither with rejection nor with affirmation, they will vanish on their own. Following this, rest your mind in that pure vacuity, not identifiable in any way, with a sense of wonder. Seeing thus they assert is to realize the ultimate nature and to recognize the nature of mind. [Tilopa's] *Mother Ganges* says:

> If you wish to realize the truth that transcends thought and
> activity,
> cut the root of your mind but leave your awareness naked:
> let the muddied water of thoughts turn clear.
> Neither reject nor affirm appearances, leave them alone:
> when you do not reject or affirm, that is mahāmudrā.[1170]

(5) Again, many others say: Whatever thoughts may arise, rather than letting them vanish on their own, trample on them and then let them rise back up, at which point they will release themselves. There will, in this way, be a simultaneity of arising and release. And the more thoughts, the more dharmakāyas. They instruct thus by understanding it to be the meaning of the following passage from Lama Shang:

> While resting your mind in this way,
> if thoughts happen to arise suddenly,
> think not of them as anything else
> other than the dharmakāya clear light.
>
> Thus the proliferation of thoughts is
> emptiness emanating from emptiness,
> dharmakāya radiating from dharmakāya,
> union springing from union.[1171]

The Distilled Essence of Those Ways of Introducing

In the *Questions of Rāṣṭrapāla* sutra it says:

> This way of emptiness, peace, and no-arising—
> ignorant of it, beings wander samsara's realms.
> The Compassionate One effects their entry into this truth
> through hundreds of methods and reasons.[1172] [530]

The sutra states that beings wander in samsaric existence owing to their ignorance of the way of emptiness, selflessness. To help free them from samsara, the Teacher, who has great compassion for these beings wandering samsara's realms, effects their entry onto the path of realization of selflessness through hundreds of methods and lines of reasoning that directly or indirectly establish the absence self-existence.

Along the same lines, the guardian Śāntideva says:

> All these limbs of practice
> the Sage taught for the sake of wisdom.[1173]

Atiśa too writes:

> All the eighty-four thousand heaps
> of Dharma that have been taught
> are for arriving at this ultimate reality.[1174]

This says that all eighty-four thousand heaps of Dharma taught by the Conqueror were taught as methods whereby spiritual aspirants can, in the end, perfect the realization of ultimate reality—selflessness.

As for the realization of selflessness by direct perception, you first need to establish it through study and reflection and then meditate upon it. With respect to meditation, too, if you have merely tranquil abiding, you will be like those non-Buddhists [who have attained tranquil abiding but are] unable to eliminate the afflictions. The *King of Meditations Sutra* says: [531]

> Although, in the world, they cultivate concentration,
> they will not destroy the notion of selfhood,
> and their afflictions will rise back again,
> as when Udraka cultivated concentration.[1175]

What then is the meditative concentration that directly brings about the attainment of liberation? The same sutra says:

> If you discern selflessness in relation to phenomena
> and meditate on what has been discerned,
> this would be the cause for attaining the fruit, nirvana.
> No other cause will bring about peace.[1176]

This states that one who discerns phenomena to be devoid of selfhood and meditates on the truth thus discerned will attain the fruit of nirvana.

As for selflessness, there is no difference in the subtlety of its nature, but because of the differentiation [of bases] into persons and phenomena, it is twofold. The glorious Candrakīrti writes:

> To help free beings, the Buddha taught no-self
> in twofold terms—that of phenomena and that of persons.[1177]

[The selflessness of persons]

The scriptures and their commentaries present the selflessness of phenomena first, but when it comes to engaging in meditative practice, you should first meditate on the selflessness of persons. The *King of Meditations Sutra* states:

> Just as you have discerned in relation to self,
> extend this with your mind to all.
> This is the nature of all phenomena:
> it is utterly pure like space.
> So by knowing one, you know all;
> by seeing one, you see all.[1178]

Thus, when meditating on the selflessness of persons, you must first identify the object of negation. *Guide to the Bodhisattva Way* says:

> Without touching upon the imputed entity,
> the absence of its reality cannot be grasped.[1179]

If you fail to identify what is to be negated, it will be like shooting an arrow without seeing the target or waging a battle without knowing who the enemy is. Also, when identifying the object of negation, if you identify it too broadly you will fall into the extreme of nihilism, and if you identify it too narrowly you will fall into the extreme of eternalism. So the danger is very great indeed. *Fundamental Wisdom* states:

> If emptiness is viewed wrongly,
> those of small intellect will be destroyed,
> like handling a snake in the wrong way
> or like a spell wrongly executed.

> Therefore, knowing that it would be hard
> for the feeble-minded to fathom this truth,
> the Sage turned his mind away
> [at first] from teaching the Dharma.[1180]

Also, as the *Eight Thousand Lines* states, it is through grasping at "I" and "mine" that sentient beings wander in the cycle of existence, and so the ultimate root of all faults is the innate self-grasping or the innate grasping at "I."

Within the thought "I am" there are, generally speaking, three kinds: (1) one that takes the "I" qualified by true existence, (2) one that takes it qualified by absence of true existence as a mere name or a mere construct of thought, and (3) one that is the simple thought "I am" without qualifying it in either of these two terms. Of these, the last is a veridical conventional cognition that posits the mere "I," the second arises only within the mental continuum of those who have found the Madhyamaka view and not in others, and the first is the grasping at selfhood of persons. Taking another person as your referent object and grasping at his or her true existence is indeed a grasping at a selfhood of persons; it does not, however, constitute the innate grasping at "I." Innate grasping at "I" or identity view is an afflicted intelligence that focuses upon your own "I" [532] and grasps it as existing by virtue of an intrinsic nature. And it is engendered by its cause, a subtle level of grasping at the selfhood of phenomena. The guardian Nāgārjuna states:

> As long as there is grasping at the aggregates,
> there will be grasping at an "I,"
> when there is "I"-grasping, there is also karma,
> and from karma, there will be birth.[1181]

Since it is the root of samsaric existence, you cannot eliminate self-grasping without repudiating its object of apprehension, its object of clinging. The lord of reasoning [Dharmakīrti] states:

> Without repudiating its object,
> it [the erroneous subject] cannot be eliminated.[1182]

The objects of clinging in grasping at the true existence of the individual, grasping at the true existence of "I," and grasping at the true existence of the person are, respectively, the truly existing individual, the truly existing "I," and the truly existing person. It is these that must be eradicated. This eradication is accomplished only through viewing these as lacking true existence. For it is by ascertaining the person as devoid of true existence and cultivating this familiarity that the grasping at the true existence of the person will come to cease.

[SPACE-LIKE MEDITATIVE EQUIPOISE]

For these reasons, to first present the instruction by way of an experiential guidance on how the object of negation appears and how is grasped, the text says:

29 While in that foregoing meditative equipoise,
unwavering, and just like a minnow
darting about in clear water,
analyze skillfully with subtle awareness
the nature of that person who is meditating.

Thus, while in meditative equipoise resting single-pointedly in the concentration of tranquil abiding you have cultivated, without wavering—like a minnow that swims in a pool of clear water without disturbing it—from within that meditative equipoise and with a subtle cognition, analyze what is the true nature of the one who is engaged in meditation—the individual, the "I," or the self—how it appears to your mind and [533] how you apprehend it. Examine all this subtly and astutely—that is to say, with precise and discriminating awareness.

As you examine in this way, you will discern that the true mode of being is this: the "individual," the "I," the "person"—in fact, all phenomena—are mere names, they are mere constructs of thought, merely imputed, like a snake on a striped rope or like a man conceived upon a cairn or a pile of sticks. A sutra says:

> However much a ghost town may appear,
> such a town exists in none of the ten directions;
> in other words, such a town is just a name.
> Likewise the Sugata sees this world.[1183]

Such is the mode of being [of phenomena] seen by tathāgatas.

Thus, were we not deluded, all phenomena would appear to us as merely nominal, with merely imputed existence. But this is not how they appear to us. Instead, possessed by the demon of ignorance, we perceive the mode of being [of phenomena] in a distorted way and cling to it. Through this we create karma, and by the power of that karma we wander in samsara and experience all manner of suffering.

Let me reveal here the essence of the matter in a stark way: this very mode of appearance and mode of apprehension [we experience] are, in fact, "the mode of appearance of true existence" and "the mode of apprehension of clinging to true existence." For us ordinary beings, therefore, apart from the present way in which things appear to us, there is no other different mode in which the object of negation of the reasoning might appear to us. Given that all instances of cognition of ordinary persons are tainted by ignorance, whatever object appears to us we perceive as truly existent. In view of these points, it is on the basis of ascertaining persons and phenomena as nominal existences that one comes to ascertain the exact manner in which the innate "I"-grasping—the root of samsaric existence—grasps an "I." For it is through such realization that one will be able to ascertain all aspects of the manner in which the subtle object of negation is grasped. The omniscient Tsongkhapa too, on numerous occasions, has demonstrated "how all phenomena are nominal existences and how the object of negation, which is the contrary, is identified."[1184]

With regard to these matters, there does not seem to be that much certainty even in the writings of some of those reputed as master scholars who claim to be guides of many beings; it is only sublime masters who have made meditative practice the heart of their life's activity who possess the greatest familiarity. For example, Khedrup Norsang Gyatso says:

> I see within the constellations trailing the Losang sun
> some with pretense of being learned who, parroting the phrases
> "intrinsic characteristics," "intrinsic existence," and "true being,"
> take reasoned negation of something constructed by their own
> mind— [534]
> an object of negation bound up in words—
> to be the great middle way free from extremes.
> Just as with dream objects or illusory horses and elephants,
> apart from the mere appearances perceived by the mind,
> they have no existence even to the slightest degree.
> Likewise, from the peak of samsara all the way to the hells,

however many sentient beings there may be,
if they do not negate the subtle object of negation, the existence
beyond the mere imputations of each and every being's mind,
however much they may analyze, they do not in the slightest
move beyond a superficial view. This is what I think.[1185]

Thus if, under analysis, the individual and so forth do exist the way they appear to the mind as the "individual," the "person," and the "I," there is then no alternative for them but to possess true existence. Yet no such individual as perceived exists. The person's body and mind are each not the person, and the individual's combined body and mind is also not the person. Neither is each of the six elements the person, nor is the combined six elements the person; yet apart from the six elements, there is also no person.

To illustrate this point, the peerless savior Nāgārjuna says:[1186]

30 **"The person is not earth nor water,**
is not fire, wind, nor space,
is not consciousness—nor is it all of them.
Where then, apart from these, is the person?"[1187]

Along the same lines, *Guide to the Bodhisattva Way* says:

Teeth, hair, and nails are not the self;
the self is not the bones or the blood;
it's not mucus, it is not phlegm;
it's not lymph, it is not pus.

Self is not marrow or sweat;
nor are lungs and liver the self;
nor are internal organs the self;
self is neither excrement nor urine.

Heat and breath are not the self;
the orifices are not, and not by any means
are the six classes of consciousness the self.[1188]

This says that the person, the self, or "I" is not the earth element, the solid aspects of your body like bones and so on; nor is self the body's water element, the fluid aspects like blood and so on; [535] the heat aspects of the body from the crown of head down to the soles of the feet too are not the self; nor is the body's wind element, the buoyant aspects that flow within the channels, the person. Hollow spaces within the body such as the orifices are not the person, and classes of consciousness such as visual consciousness are not the self, nor is the self these factors. Their collection too is not the "I," nor is the "I" the collection of these. Yet apart from these there is no such person, the meditator, as it appears to your mind. In the sutras too it says, "Form is not self, feelings are not self, discrimination is not self, mental formations are not self, and consciousness is not self."[1189]

In view of the above, the meditating person's five aggregates, each of the six elements, their collection, and the configuration of the collection—none of these constitutes the meditating person. For if any of these were the person, there would be such consequences as the oneness of the designative base and the designation, the appropriated and the appropriator, and the constituents and the constituted. There would also be the following problem:

> Now if the aggregates are the self,
> then since they are multiple, the self would be multiple.[1190]

In particular, if consciousness were the person, phenomena such as the person being ill, speaking, seeing, and procreating would become untenable. Also, although the person is one, just as there are six classes of consciousness, there would be six persons; conversely, just as the person is one, the six classes of consciousness would also be partless and one. If the shape of the collection [of the aggregates] were the person, since it would be a material entity, there would be no persons in the formless realm.

Yet there can be no person apart from the five aggregates. If there were, it would be intrinsically unconnected with and separate [from the aggregates] and would thus be devoid of the characteristics that define the aggregates as conditioned phenomena. It is said:

> If it were separate from the aggregates,
> it would lack the characteristics of the aggregates.[1191]

There would also be the faults pointed in the *Elephant's Skills Sutra*:

> If things were to possess intrinsic existence,
> the conquerors and śrāvakas would know this;

things would be absolute and there will no nirvana,
and the wise will never be free from conceptual
elaboration.[1192] [536]

Thus, when you examine from within meditative equipoise, with a subtle part of your mind, the individual, the self, the person, or the "I" who is resting in meditative equipoise that appears to your mind, not even an atom of it exists; there will be pure emptiness in its wake. Then, allowing this generic image of pure vacuity to appear clearly in your mind, rest single-pointedly in meditative equipoise without bringing to your mind anything else in the form of conceptual elaboration. When your apprehension of this pure vacuity, a nonimplicative negation, wanes a little, apply analysis as before while abiding within meditative equipoise and continue to meditate single-pointedly.

This is the way to maintain the space-like meditative equipoise. It is stated that when you first ascertain things in this way, if you have no familiarity with the view, fear will arise; if you do have familiarity, joy will arise.

[Illusion-like post-equipoise]

To present the features of the post-equipoise stage, the text says:

31ab "The person is a composite of six elements;
as such it has no real existence."[1193]

When you rise from the meditative equipoise and examine, you will have this realization: although what appears to my mind has no existence—the person that is perceived in a distorted way because of my mind being possessed by the demon of ignorance—there is certainly, nonetheless, the individual, the person, or the mere "I." Its mode of existence is, however, akin to a man imputed onto a cairn or a snake onto a striped rope. Thus the "person" is a mere label designating a mere collection of your own six elements or five aggregates, a mere convention, a mere conceptual imputation, something unreal and illusion-like, emptiness arising as dependent origination. Cultivate such an ascertainment and meditate. You should also contemplate it through chanting the profound scriptures. The *King of Meditations Sutra* says:

The illusionist conjures images
of horses, elephants, and all sorts of chariots,
yet none are real the way they appear to be.
Like this, understand all phenomena.

Just as a young woman, in a dream,
sees her son being born and dying,
and she is happy when he is born and sad when he dies,
so should you understand all phenomena.

Just as at night the moon's reflection appears
in water that is clear and unmuddied, [537]
yet this water-moon is empty and unreal, ungraspable,
so should you understand all phenomena.

Just as at midday in a summer heat,
a traveler who is tormented by thirst
sees mirages as bodies of water,
so should you understand all phenomena.

In a mirage, no water exists at all;
although deluded beings wish to,
there can be no drinking of unreal water;
so should you understand all phenomena.

Just as people chop through the live trunk
of a plantain tree thinking it has a core
yet there is no core anywhere, outside or inside,
so should you understand all phenomena.[1194]

[The selflessness of phenomena]

Now, when you have gained some experience in your familiarity with the selflessness of the person, then, as stated in the following in *Condensed Perfection of Wisdom*, meditate on selflessness of other persons and phenomena:

Just like yourself, understand all sentient beings to be the same;
just like all sentient beings, understand all phenomena to be the same.[1195]

To indicate this, the text says:

31cd "Likewise, each element too is in turn
a composite and hence has no real existence."[1196]

32 **In accordance with this statement, when you search,**
not even a minute particle will be found
of the meditative equipoise, the one who is in equipoise, and so forth.
At that point, maintain the space-like equipoise
without distraction and single-pointedly.

Thus, with respect to all phenomena of samsara and nirvana—all ordinary beings and āryas, both the outer and inner elements of earth, likewise water, fire, wind, and consciousness, individually as well as their collection and so forth—ascertain how they appear to your mind. And just as you examined the mode of appearance and mode of apprehension in relation to the person and rested your mind in meditative equipoise, here too, establish their [abiding nature]. [538] When, as a result, you have not found even the minutest particle that possesses true existence, at that point, as in the statements "Not finding is the supreme finding" and "Not seeing is the supreme seeing,"[1197] you have seen the mind's true nature and have recognized the mind. So, without any distraction, rest single-pointedly in that awareness and maintain meditative equipoise on this pure negation of true existence, the space-like true nature of phenomena.

Alternatively, as the extremely subtle wind and mind are stated to be the subtle basis of the designation of self, and also as the upholders of pith instructions understand establishing the abiding nature of the mind to constitute introducing the mind's nature, I say:

33–34 **Alternatively, while in meditative equipoise,**
observe your mind as thus characterized:
pure vacuity because it does not exist as physical;
unobscured as diverse appearances arise to it;
and unceasing, a luminous and aware continuum
that is uninterrupted in its engagement.
Such a mind appears and is conceived
as independent, but with respect to such objects of clinging,
the guardian Śāntideva states:

35 **"The so-called continuums and collections,**
just like rosaries, armies, and so on, are false."[1198]
So through scripture such as this and reasoning,

establish this truth of how things do not exist as they appear and rest your mind single-pointedly in this meditative equipoise.

Alternatively, Candrakīrti says:

> It is the mind that constructed the vast diversity
> of both the domain of sentient beings and their universe.[1199]

This explains that the mind is the root of all the worlds and their inhabitants, so if you are able to cut the root basis of the mind, the impact would be unlike employing any other technique. For this, you should proceed in the following manner.

If, while maintaining the continuity of your earlier meditative equipoise, you examine your mind, since it does not exist in a material way, it will appear as *pure vacuity*, like a sun that is *unobscured* by, for instance, clouds. Yet all sorts of diverse forms and all sorts of diverse thoughts arise in it and it moves outward as well. Unlike the flickering of a flame, it is *unceasing*; and it operates fluidly with an uninterrupted continuum of that which is *luminous* and *aware*. Now this mind appears to you as if it is totally independent of the subject that apprehends it. [539] With respect to such a mind—the object clung to just as perceived, or this mind as it appears to you—the guardian Śāntideva says:

> The so-called continuums and collections,
> just like rosaries, armies, and so on, are false.[1200]

So on the basis of scriptures and reasoning, ascertain how "rosary" is merely imputed onto a composite where individual beads are strung on a string, and how "army" is just a name merely imputed onto a collection of individual men bearing arms. Apart from this there is nothing truly existent. Rest single-pointedly in meditative equipoise with the ascertainment that your mind does not exist in accord with how it appears to you. Thus the *Perfection of Wisdom in Eight Thousand Lines* says:

> The mind is devoid of mind, for the nature of mind is clear light.[1201]

This states that there is no intrinsically existing mind in the mind, for the nature of the mind is clear-light emptiness. And in the *Heap of Jewels* too it says:

> The mind has never been seen, is not being seen, and will not be seen by all the buddhas of the three times.[1202]

Also Lord Marpa labels ascertaining the mind's true nature as it is and meditating on it as "grabbing the emptiness of mind with one's bare hands." He says:

> I went to the banks of the River Ganges in the east.
> There through the kindness of the great Lord Maitripa,
> I realized the ground, the unborn reality,
> and grabbed with bare hands the emptiness of mind.
> I saw the primordial nature, reality free from elaboration;
> I met face to face with my mother, the three buddha bodies.
> From then on, this man's elaborations were severed.[1203]

Also, Drogön Phakmo Drupa says:

> Mind is the root of both samsara and nirvana;
> mind's primordial purity is true suchness;
> Since it is primordially peaceful and unborn,
> mind is utterly free of elaborated extremes.[1204]

In brief, I present in the following the oral instruction of my spiritual mentor, the omniscient Sangyé Yeshé, who is true to the meaning of his name and not like the case where someone who is not omniscient but is reputed to be. The text says: [540]

36 **In brief, as my spiritual mentor,**
the omniscient Sangyé Yeshé,
who is in accord with reality, states:

37 **"When you are fully aware that whatever appears is conceived by thoughts,**
then the ultimate expanse dawns independently of anything else.
When your awareness enters into what has thus dawned,
you rest in single-pointed meditative equipoise—*E ma ho*!"[1205]

He says that when you recognize whatever you perceive as "conceived by thoughts"—that is to say, viewing whatever arises as conceptual imputations—then the ultimate truth, the true nature, will dawn within the sphere of your awareness without dependence on any other condition. This is as stated in the following in *Entering the Middle Way*:

> The conventional truth is the means,
> while the ultimate truth is its end.[1206]

"When your awareness enters into what has thus dawned," that is say, when you rest your mind in meditative equipoise through single-pointed fusion of the true nature—which has dawned within the sphere of your awareness—with the subject awareness, this is indeed most wonderful.

In the same vein as these last two lines, Dampa Sangyé says:

38 **"Whirl the spear of awareness within emptiness;**
the view, O people of Dingri, is unobstructed."[1207]
These statements and their likes make the same point.

The intention of statements such as these remains the same.

The concluding practice

The third, the concluding practice, is dedicating the virtues of meditative equipoise on mahāmudrā to unexcelled enlightenment. The root text has the line "Here, of the three—preparation, main practice, and conclusion" [in verse 3], explicitly mentioning a concluding practice, yet where exactly it goes was left implicit and unclear. It is to be applied here at this juncture. Thus to delineate the boundary, I present here the root text:

39 **At the conclusion, the virtues that have emerged**
from meditating on mahāmudrā
together with the ocean of virtues of all three times,
dedicate these all to the great, unexcelled enlightenment. [541]

This is how the root text can be correlated [to the outline].

Now to present together in one place (1) how to maintain your practice in the post-equipoise period after you have risen from meditative equipoise on mahāmudrā, (2) how to ascertain inerrantly the generic concept of the object of negation when you return to meditative equipoise, and (3) how to dispel doubts that might arise either in relation to meditative equipoise or the post-equipoise state, the text says:

40 Thus, having gained familiarity [with this practice],
realize precisely the mode of appearance
of any object that appears within the field of your six senses,
and its mode of being will dawn naked and vivid.
Recognizing whatever appears is the key to the view.

41 In brief, whatever appears—
be it your own mind or something else—
do not grasp but ascertain its mode of being
and always maintain that awareness.
Knowing this, bring all phenomena
of samsara and nirvana into a single nature.

Thus, having cultivated familiarity [with emptiness] during meditative equipoise, whatever appearances might arise during the post-equipoise period, such as of form and so on, within the field of your six senses, such as visual perception, examine carefully with discerning intellect as to how they appear to your mind. When you examine in this way, the truth of their dependent origination—how although they appear to you as if they possess true existence, like something hollow, like an effigy, like a dream, or like the moon's reflection in water, they are devoid of independent essence—will dawn upon you starkly and vividly. Through this your ascertainment of the true nature will grow greater. This is as Lord Mitrayogi says:

> Recognizing whatever appears is the key point of the view.[1208]

What need is there to say more?

Let me sum this up in a succinct way. For us near-sighted ordinary beings, [542] it is precisely the way in which this or that subject—our mind and so on—appears to us that is itself the way we perceive the object of negation. So instead of clinging to perceived things and grasping at them, ascertain the ultimate mode of being of this or that phenomenon—namely, the simple negation of their existing in accord with how they appear to the mind. In this way, rest in space-like meditative equipoise. And when you rise from meditative equipoise and observe what remains in the aftermath of negation, what will appear undeniably to you is the world of dependent origination of everyday activity on the nominal level of mere labels and mere conceptual imputations. This is the yoga of post-equipoise, and you constantly maintain these two in alternation: [the yoga of space-like meditative equipoise and the yoga of illusion-like post-equipoise]. Knowing thus how to maintain meditative equipoise and post-equipoise, rest in meditative equipoise wherein the ultimate natures of all phenomena of samsara and nirvana—the simple negation of their true existence—are indivisibly subsumed into a single truth. And during the post-equipoise state, relate to everything as mere conventional realities, as mere appearances, and as illusion-like. In this way, you should meditate.

42 **Here, Āryadeva says:**
"The viewer of one thing
is stated to be the viewer of all,
and the emptiness of one
is the emptiness of all."[1209]

Do the phenomena of dependent origination appear as mere names and conceptual existences within the perspective of meditative equipoise? In response, I say:

43 **Thus, within the perfect meditative equipoise**
on this ultimate nature of reality,
you are free from the elaborated extremes
of existence and nonexistence and of samsara and nirvana.

Lord Milarepa says:

From the standpoint of ultimate truth,
there are no obstacles, no karma, and no buddhahood;
there is no meditation, no object of meditation,
no grounds to traverse, no paths to realize,
no fruition of buddha bodies and no gnosis,
and therefore there is no nirvana.
All are merely imputed by labels and words. [543]
The three worlds, the stationary and the moving,
have primordially no existence or arising;

they have no basis and nothing innately arisen;
there are no karma and no fruitional effects.
Therefore not even the name samsara exists.
This is how they appear within the final reality.[1210]

And there is the line "The perfection of wisdom is beyond speech, thought, and expression,"[1211] and the scholar-siddha Khyungpo Naljor says, "Mundane appearances are self-liberating, like illusions or dreams."[1212]

If that is so, does this mean karma and its effects and so forth are utterly nonexistent? To state that karma and its effects and so forth do very much exist, since the absence of ultimate existence is not the same as absence of existence, the text says:

44 **Yet when you arise from that equipoise and examine,**
it is undeniable that actions, agents, and dependent originations
of mere labels and mere concepts naturally appear—
like a dream, like a mirage, like the moon in water,
or like a magician's illusion.

Along the same lines, Lord Milarepa also says;

Alas! If there were no sentient beings,
whence would come the buddhas of three times?
A result without a cause is impossible,
and so, from the standpoint of conventional truth,
samsara as well as nirvana—
everything—exists, the Sage stated.
Existence, the appearance of entities, and
nonexistence, emptiness, which is their true nature—
the nature of these two is indivisible and of one taste.
Thus there is no [differentiation between] self-cognition and other cognition.
Everything is a vast union.[1213]

As for their mode of existence, this is to be defined on the basis of being satisfied with their existence at the level of mere labels and mere designations. The supreme ārya, Nāgārjuna, for example, states:

> Because physical entities are mere labels,
> space too is a mere label.[1214]

Thus the final import of the mahāmudrā view as upheld by Ārya Nāgārjuna and his spiritual son [Āryadeva] comes to what is described as "imputed existence, just nominal." Let me explain this clearly. To give an example, it must be acknowledged that a pillar does exist in a house with four pillars, because there are four pillars. [544] And "pillar" is a universal that pervades each of the four individual pillars. Now if one were to search for the identity of the substance of this universal "pillar" by inquiring what exactly it is, none of the four pillars individually is a suitable candidate, nor is the four collectively. Yet, apart from the four pillars individually and their collection, there is nothing else that can be identified as a candidate either. Thus the substance of this universal "pillar" is nothing but a name imputed on those individual pillars, and nothing apart from what is posited on the basis of being satisfied with the mere designation by label can be found if one searches [beyond this]. This is what is called "imputed existence, just nominal," and it is true also of every other phenomenon.

Now the following doubt needs to be clarified. Some earlier and later writers connected with this tradition [of Geden mahāmudrā], while saying that all cognitions of ordinary beings are deluded and that, as such, whatever is perceived is perceived as possessing intrinsic nature, they also assert a mode of perceiving the object of negation that is distinct from our everyday mode of perception—some kind of "true existence" springing like horns from its head! This error seems to derive from their inability to state that what is perceived by our ordinary mind does not exist as it appears to us. In view of this, they should ponder well Candrakīrti's refutation of Svātantrika Mādhyamikas' assertions that form and so forth exist by virtue of their appearance to an undefective mind. This said, it is necessary also to understand (1) how [according to Svātantrika] the five sense consciousnesses are mistaken in that they perceive the five sensory objects to exist self-sufficiently although they do not, (2) how the five are veridical with respect to their perception of things as existing by virtue of intrinsic characteristics, and (3) how, because of that, they are accepted as valid cognitions that posit things on the conventional level.

Many others, recalling how it is said that the person is not negated but only the truly existent person, proceed in their meditative equipoise to set aside the whole person, leaving it untouched, and strive hard to negate merely some mentally contrived "truly existing person." This is completely wrong, for it leads to the extreme of eternalism. Although there is much more to discuss, fearing excessive length, this will suffice.

To indicate how, as you practice in this manner, the excellent path free of the extremes of eternalism and nihilism will manifest, the text says: [545]

45 **When appearance does not obscure emptiness**
and when emptiness does not obstruct appearance,
the excellent path—where emptiness and dependent origination
share the same meaning—will then manifest.

Along the same lines, the omniscient Jé Tsongkhapa says:

> As long as the two understandings—
> of *appearance*, undeceiving dependent origination,
> and of *emptiness*, the absence of all positions—remain separate,
> then you have not realized the intent of the Sage.
>
> However, if at some point, not in alternation but at once,
> the instant you see that dependent origination is undeceiving,
> this dismantles the entirety of the object of grasping at certitude,
> at this point your analysis of the view is complete.[1215]

Entering the Middle Way says:

> Likewise although all things are empty,
> they do arise from emptiness in a robust way.
> Since no intrinsic nature exists in either of the two truths,
> phenomena are neither eternal nor annihilated.[1216]

The guardian Nāgārjuna too states:

> Having understood this emptiness of phenomena
> and yet cause and effect remain tenable,
> this is more amazing than amazing!
> This is more wondrous than wondrous![1217]

The meaning here is easily understood.

When, through maintaining the practice of mahāmudrā by saddling it astride the horse of tranquil abiding, you achieve meditative concentration permeated by the bliss of physical and mental pliancy derived through the force of analysis focused on emptiness, you have reached the heat stage of the path of preparation.[1218]

Some past Kagyü masters present the mahāmudrā path within the framework of four yogas: (1) Since you focus single pointedly on the mind, there is *single-pointedness.* (2) Since you realize the mind as free of elaborations, there is *freedom from elaboration.* (3) Since you realize appearance and the mind as being of a single taste, there is *single taste.* And (4) since you cannot meditate on it with signs, there is *nonmeditation*. In terms of correlating these to the grounds and paths, the master Götsangpa holds that the first yoga correlates to the [path of] imaginative engagement,[1219] the second yoga to the path of seeing, the third yoga to the second up to the seventh bodhisattva ground, and the fourth yoga to the pure grounds.[1220] Shang Rinpoché says:

> With respect to all-accomplishing mahāmudrā,
> the ignorant make the error of counting grounds and paths. [546]
> Yet to please the ignorant, I too will delineate here
> the equivalents of the Philosophy Vehicle's grounds and paths.[1221]

As for how this delineates [the grounds and paths], it is similar to that of the master Götsangpa.

For this correlation of *freedom from elaboration* to the first bodhisattva ground, some textual experts object. They say that this is incorrect because the twelve sets of hundredfold higher qualities[1222] do not appear in the post-meditative equipoise state. Shang Rinpoché writes in response:

> A garuḍa's powers are already complete within the egg;
> as soon as it hatches, its flying powers are displayed.
> The qualities of the three buddha bodies are already complete
> within the mind;
> as soon as the illusory body is dismantled, the welfare of others
> unfolds.[1223]

In response, we find the following statement of Jikten Gönpo:

> If you can find a scriptural citation from a treatise to establish your entailment, I will give you a good horse; what is stated in the *Ten Grounds Sutra* is from the point of view of future lives.[1224]

Perhaps because of such critiques, we also find the following statement from the exalted Sakya Paṇḍita in his response to queries from the monk Namkha Bum:

> In the spiritual traditions of the Drigungpa, Taklungpa, and [other] mahāmudrā advocates, one finds things that do not seem to accord with either the tantra or [sutra] basket. I consider this an imperfect path. Please be sure, however, you do not to share my words with others.[1225]

This said, the enlightened activities of ārya beings remain beyond the comprehension of ordinary beings; and furthermore, since there is the danger of creating most grave negative karma in relation to the Dharma and sublime beings, I, Chökyi Gyaltsen, appeal to you: please reject the power of antagonistic sectarianism and spread everywhere the jewel light by which everything is seen as pure.

Dedicating the virtues derived from the composition

This is as follows:

46 **These were uttered by a renunciant who has heard widely,**
someone who is called Losang Chökyi Gyaltsen.
From this virtue may all beings swiftly become victorious
through this path, for there is no second path to peace.

This states how the promise [to compose] has been fulfilled and dedicates the virtues derived from composing the text to all beings gaining victory in their battle against the two obscurations. [547]

Thus I say:

It is the supreme essence churned from the ocean of sutras and tantras,
the essential point of the intention of all masters of India and Tibet,
the path traversed by all sublime supreme siddhas—
may the sun of mahāmudrā teaching shine here today.

With their minds consumed by the intoxicant of ignorant delusion,
beings trapped in the terrifying prison of cyclic existence

and tormented by the three classes of suffering—
for them, mahāmudrā is a pleasure grove, a source of true respite.

This is the eye that sees the excellent path for countless beings.
This is the tradition upheld by the great sublime beings.
That which reflects the beautiful form of such mahāmudrā,
undiluted and clear, is indeed a jewel mirror.

For those many fortunate ones who, having cut the fetters
of the eight worldly concerns, remain immersed freely
in the bliss of meditative concentration in solitude,
this is also a guru who teaches the flawless excellent path.

Through the collection of virtue arisen from this effort,
like jasmine opened by the spoon-like cool rays of the moon,
whatever supremely white karma I may have amassed
I dedicate toward great awakening so I may help free my mothers.

Through the power of this, may the mind vases
of all beings without exception be filled with the celestial ambrosia
of mahāmudrā, which unites sutra and tantra,
and may they enjoy the great bliss of union.

Colophon

This extensive explanation of the root text of mahāmudrā of the tradition of the precious Geden lineage entitled *Lamp So Bright* was composed at the behest of my student Gendun Gyatso, a *rabjampa*[1226] who is learned in the ten texts, one who has found conviction in this path and takes it as the heart of his meditative practice. Making a perfect offering of spiritual practice untainted by the husks of the eight worldly concerns, he asked me: "Please, as the author of the root text, write your own a commentary on this root text—a commentary that is extensive, decisively comprehensive, wherein the key points of the practice are clear and organized, the background support of valid scriptural citations and reasoning are provided, and it is adorned with the oral instructions of the ear-to-ear transmission." Because of his persistent urging, I, Losang Chökyi Gyaltsen, a renunciant who has traveled to the shores of the seas of the individual mahāmudrā traditions, have written this quickly in the scripture hall of the great Dharma seat of Tashi Lhunpo.

Through this, may the precious teaching be a victory banner that is never damaged.

Sarva maṅgalaṃ.[1227]

12. An Experiential Guide to Mahāmudrā of the Sacred Geden Lineage

SHAR KALDEN GYATSO

Namo mahāmudrāya.

Through your play as Conqueror Losang Drakpa's emanation,
you are most skilled in explaining to others, in a direct way,
the ultimate expanse, the pervasive nature of everything.
Omniscient conqueror, treasury of goodness, my guru, pray nurture me.

The experiential guide to mahāmudrā presented here has two parts: the origin of the lineage [of this practice] and the way to undertake the practice.

ORIGIN OF THE LINEAGE OF THIS PRACTICE

The first is as follows. Conqueror Vajradhara taught it to Mañjuśrī, he to precious Jé Tsongkhapa, he to Tokden Jampal Gyatso, he to Basowa, he to the revered Dharmavajra, and he to Conqueror Losang Döndrup. The latter spoke of the sources of this teaching in numerous guidebooks; he, however, taught it in its entirety to Khedrup Sangyé Yeshé. This guru, in turn, expressed elevated praise of this teaching far and wide. He also composed numerous experiential songs relating to the arising of its realization within him. He taught it to the omniscient Panchen, who authored the root text for this teaching, its extensive explanation *Lamp So Bright*, and the prayer to its lineage gurus. Having composed these texts, Panchen transmitted it, concealing nothing and without reservation, to many great meditators, such as Gendun Gyaltsen, a *rabjampa* in the ten topics, Sherab Sengé, one from Hamdong learned in the ten treatises, and Tsultrim Gyatso, the Dharma master from Samlo. On their part too, because they put it into practice, they realized the teaching exactly as it is. Furthermore, when Panchen gave an experiential guidance on this teaching to many monks at Ganden Monastery, extraordinary levels of mental stillness arose in the mindstreams of disciples like Gendun Chöden, Tsal Rabjampa Gendun Chöden, Phara Bodhisattva [550], and others. Because of this, many among those who attended the teaching gave up the concerns of this life and embraced meditative practice as the heart commitment of their life. Today, they have all become accomplished yogis.

The way to undertake the practice

In a place of solitude, adopting the sevenfold posture of meditation,[1228] ensure that your mind is not tainted by distraction and the like. With a joyful mind, contemplate the great value of the life of leisure and opportunity and the difficulty of obtaining it, death and impermanence, karma and its effects, the faults of samsara, the thought of renunciation, loving kindness and compassion, and the awakening mind. Undertake these contemplations as found in the texts on mind training, the stages of the path, or as explained in my own guidebook.[1229] Then undertake the practice of going for refuge, either as found in the guides from the Ensa oral transmission or as found in texts composed specifically on refuge, and Vajrasattva meditation and recitation, the *Confession of Downfalls*, mandala offering, and guru yoga in accord with how they are presented in their respective guides. Then, having made supplications many times, dissolve the guru into yourself and imagine that you receive blessing from this.

Then, within this state where all appearances have become somewhat indistinct, do nothing by way of contrivance of conceptualization, such as entertaining the hopeful thought "If only I could accomplish such and such immediate and ultimate goals" or having anxious thoughts like "What if such and such undesirable events befall me?" Neither chasing the past nor anticipating the future, rest your mind in equipoise in the present, with no movement at all.[1230]

At the time of resting your mind in this way, unlike the total cessation of all mental engagement during fainting or falling asleep, post the sentry of mindfulness ensuring the mind that is abiding unwavering remains undistracted—that is to say, it is not lost to even the slightest forgetfulness. Even though you may tie the meditation object with the rope of mindfulness, if your mindfulness weakens, there is great danger that thoughts involving the mind's movement could proliferate. So you need to place your mind [on the focal object] by stationing the watchman of meta-awareness, monitoring whether your mind has wandered elsewhere due to a weakening of the force of mindfulness. This is as stated in the following in *Essence of the Middle Way*:

> This wandering elephant of mind,
> tie it firmly to a sturdy post, its object,
> with the rope of mindfulness and gradually
> tame it with the hook of meta-awareness.[1231] [551]

In brief, the cultivation of flawless meditative absorption constitutes nothing but the maintenance of mindfulness and meta-awareness. Here too, mindfulness the key: when mindfulness is present, meta-awareness arises as a byproduct, for meta-awareness has been described as a result of mindfulness.

At that point, when all other thoughts have ceased and that *aware* and *clear* mind is perceived, fasten your mindfulness with a firm focus on its nature and starkly observe it with single-pointedness. Observing in this manner, note whatever movement or thought arises and recognize it as just this or that. Doing this depends, of course, on meta-awareness. Alternatively, as explained in a Vinaya text, meditate in way in which an archer and a swordsman fight in a duel: applying the force of your mindfulness and meta-awareness, tread on whatever thoughts arise, instantly cutting them down and thus preventing them from gaining momentum. When, in the aftermath of severing the proliferation of thought, you abide free of movement, ensure that you do not lose mindfulness and meta-awareness, maintaining a state that is alert at the core and relaxed on the surface. In this manner, settle your mind relaxed in meditative equipoise. As Machik writes:

> Focus with firmness but loosen and relax;
> there lies the spot to rest your mind.[1232]

Also, the Great Brahman, Saraha, says:

> This mind, bound in its own entanglement,
> when relaxed becomes free, no doubt.[1233]

So, as suggested in the above, inwardly alert, stay relaxed. And when you sense your mind becoming too alert, such that excitation may arise, relax a little; and when you sense your mind becoming too relaxed, such that mental laxity may arise, strengthen your alertness a little. This way you will find just the right balance. So between those two extremes, relax your mind from the movements of thought, and watch out for occurrence of mental laxity every time stability arises. Master Candragomin writes:

> If effort is applied excitation arises;
> if shunned slackness occurs.
> When it is hard to find a proper balance,
> my mind is perturbed, so what should I do?[1234]

During these times when you are trampling on the thoughts or looking at the face of each thought as it arises, right there and then, the thoughts will vanish on their own accord, giving rise to the dawning of a pure vacuity. Similarly, when you examine the mind as it remains without wavering, you will see an unobstructed pure vacuity, a vivid clarity, with no differentiation between the earlier and the latter instances. This is known to the great meditators as "the merging of stillness and movement," and they refer to it by such a phrase. [552]

Alternatively, you could engage in the following method for stilling the mind: Whatever thought arises, do not suppress it but note where it comes from and where it moves to and rest your mind by simply looking at the nature of that thought. As you rest your mind in this way, movement will eventually cease and your mind will become still. This is analogous to the flights of a bird long captive aboard a ship sailing across a vast ocean. The *Dohā Treasury of Songs* says:

> It's like the raven that takes off from a ship,
> flies to every direction, and lands there again.[1235]

Maintain your meditation exactly as described here. So Yangönpa says:

> Not viewing the thoughts as faults,
> not deliberately meditating on nonconceptuality,
> rest your mind in its natural mode and post a sentry,
> and your meditation will reach tranquil abiding.[1236]

Furthermore, if today's trainees maintain their meditation practice by means of the six methods of resting the mind, theirs will be a king among instructions. How are they done? It is said:

Rest it like the sun free from the clouds.
Rest it like a great garuḍa soaring in the sky.
Rest it like a ship on the great ocean.
Rest it like a small child looking inside a temple.
Rest it like the tracks of a bird flying in the sky.
Rest it like fluffed cotton wool.
By these methods of resting the mind,
your yoga will be meaningful.[1237]

Just as the sun when free of clouds remains supremely bright and brilliant, in the same manner, rest your mind in the luminous nature of mind unobscured by conceptual apprehension of signs, by mental laxity and excitation, and so forth.

Just as a garuḍa flying across the sky does so naturally, soaring high without needing much exertion of flapping its wings, in the same manner, maintain your meditation without straying outside the seal of mindfulness and meta-awareness—in such a way that your mind is neither too alert nor too relaxed but possesses vibrant clarity due from being alert at the core yet relaxed on the surface.

Just as waves rise a little on the surface when a great ocean is stirred by winds, but the sea is not moved in its depths, in the same manner, rest your mind in such a way that even if some subtle level of thought does elicit movement when you place your mind on the meditation object, it is not swayed even slightly by the coarse levels of thought. [553]

Just as a small child looking inside a temple does not consider the details of the murals but stares undistracted at the large vibrant patterns, in the same manner, when your mind is focused on the meditation object, whatever objects—attractive or unattractive—may appear to your five senses, simply rest your mind single-pointedly on the meditation object without judgment and without emotions of attachment or aversion.

Just as birds cruising across the sky leave no track, in the same manner, whatever feelings you might be experiencing, whether pleasant, unpleasant, or neutral, rest your mind in equipoise without giving in to any of the three poisons of the mind—attachment, aversion, and delusion.

Just as when cotton wool is fluffed it becomes softer and freer, in the same manner, when you rest your mind in equipoise, you do so free of manifest levels of the three poisons and the rough and hard textures of mental laxity and excitation.

What imprints will emerge from maintaining meditative equipoise in the way presented above? When you maintain meditative equipoise in this way, the following will unfold: You will experience the nature of your meditative equipoise as unobscured by anything, as lucid and utterly clear. As it does not exist in any physical way, it is a pure vacuity like space, yet like reflections appearing in an unblemished mirror, whatever objects it encounters—good or bad—appear clearly and vividly. It is undefinable by any identifications of "it is this" or "it is not that." Now, however stable such a meditative concentration may be, if it is not imbued with physical and mental pliancy, it is said to be a single-pointedness of mind belonging to the desire realm. A meditative concentration imbued with [physical and mental pliancy, on the other hand] is described as tranquil abiding. Tranquil abiding will be the source of numerous higher qualities such as clairvoyance and other supernatural feats. In particular, all the paths of the three vehicles are attained on the basis of tranquil abiding.[1238] Kagyüpas use the phrase "meditative concentration characterized by clarity, vacuity, and nonapprehension" to describe such a concentration, and they embrace it as a core practice.

Those who seek the view on the basis of meditation do not seek the view until they have experienced a meditative concentration like that just described. They seek the view from the point when they have stilled the mind with respect to concentration. Those who seek meditation on the basis of the view, on the other hand, [554] examine the way we grasp at self the moment the guru dissolves into us. Whichever of these two approaches you adopt, here is how you search for the view.

First set the fervent intention "I will examine carefully the way my self-grasping apprehends the self," and with this intention, generate a pronounced thought of "I am." Carefully observe how such a thought grasps at an "I" or self. This needs to be done the moment the thought "I am" arises and has yet to fade away. That very moment, the force of the intention you set earlier causes you, with a small part of your mind, to heighten your alertness and examine. At this juncture, you need to examine incisively and with a discerning mind. This is not to be done at all like the coarse way of searching for the mind in terms of "Where is this 'I' or self? What is its form, its color, and so on?" Rather, examine the way the self is conceived by your own innate mind that grasps with the sense of "I am" with such a firm grip on the basis of your aggregates.

To elaborate, in general, even arhats who have eliminated self-grasping and our Teacher, the Buddha, have the mere thought "I am." So the mere thought "I am" is not the same as self-grasping. What you are looking for is this: "What is the mode of apprehension of my own innate sense of self—that strong sense of 'I am' present within the core of my heart that, when I turn my attention inward, I see in all my everyday activities, even in deep sleep?" Now, as you look in this way, within such innate grasping, you discern two levels of grasping—(1) a coarser level, wherein you are grasping at your person as a self-sufficient substantial reality, and (2) a subtle level, wherein you are grasping at it as an objective inherent existence. So you begin by being introduced to the coarser level of grasping, and afterward you are introduced to the mode of grasping of the subtle object of negation. A tradition of such a sequential approach stems in fact from the Dharma master Sherab Sengé.[1239] It also seems to be found in some notes from an oral teaching by Gyaltsab Rinpoché. In general, you find statements to the effect that there does exist, within the grasping in terms of self-sufficient substantial reality, an innate version.[1240] This said, when the subtle object of negation is eliminated based on successful identification of how it is grasped, the coarser level will be negated automatically. So in the tradition stemming from the great Khedrup [Gelek Palsang], [555] one does not engage in a separate identification of the coarser level of the object of negation.

What then is the mode of apprehension of this coarser self-grasping? *Differentiating the Provisional and the Definitive* explains the grasping at self and the aggregates in the manner of a master and servant according to the tradition of the Svātantrika and others.[1241] In this form of grasping, the "I" or self is conceived as a controller that is independent of the aggregates, and the aggregates as what are being controlled and as something not dependent on the self. It is as if something has been added over and above the mode of apprehending the subtle object of negation.

In view of the above, examine the mode of the subtle level of grasping. When you examine carefully in a refined manner as explained above, you will realize that this thought "I am" does not apprehend the "I" or self to be a term you designate onto the aggregates; you apprehend it as an "I" existing objectively [on the part of the aggregates] as a real referent of the term "I." For example, when you reach out your arm in the dark and happen to touch a pillar or a wall, you have the sense that the pillar or wall was already there before you came into contact with it. No one would think that what they are touching was not previously existing in that place. Similarly, from the perspective of your thought "I am," the assumption is that what is being grasped at—this "I" or self—was [objectively] existing on the part of the aggregates even before you happened to [subjectively] grasp at it. Such is the mode of apprehension of your self-grasping. Therefore, *such an "I" or self that is not posited through [mere] designation on the aggregates but exists objectively in its own right* is the subtle self that is object of negation.[1242]

Now if the subsequent mind [identifying this putative self] is too strong, the earlier thought [the self-grasping mind that you are observing] will wane, and except for some kind of vague vacuity, you will be unable to ascertain exactly how the self is being grasped. So while your mind by and large remains undeviating from the very thought "I am," you are observing from a corner of your mind how your mind is grasping at self. It is like when you and another person are walking down a path side by side: your overall sight is on the path while, from a corner of your eye, you also glance at the other person, and there is no conflict [between the two].

In general, the thought "I am" arises spontaneously in us throughout everyday life, even when we are in deep sleep. [556] In particular, when someone unjustly accuses us of something we haven't done—"You did this and that"—we tend to speak forcefully in terms of "I" and "me," and the thought "I am" arises forcefully in our mind too. In such situations, the mode of apprehension of our innate self-grasping tends to be quite obvious. So when such [powerful] thoughts arise, you then need to examine.

Now to reveal the heart of the oral teaching, here is the thing. *How each and every phenomenon, whatever it may be—our body, mind, and so forth—appears to us right now, this itself is the mode of appearance of what is to be negated, the mode of appearance, namely, of true existence. To apprehend things in accord with such appearance constitutes, unmistakably, the mode of apprehending the object of negation, the mode, that is, of grasping at true existence.*[1243] You do not need to seek out some other object of negation. Why? Because all cognitions of ordinary beings like us are instances of mistaken cognitions, and as such, whatever appears to our ordinary-being mind does so as if possessing true existence. And its absence, the negation of such a mode of appearance, is given the label *emptiness*. So my gurus say.

Some say that since the person exists on the conventional level, it cannot be negated, and that what should be negated instead is a truly established person, which has no existence whatsoever. In asserting this, they set aside this thing called *person*—something tangible and real—and conjure something called a *truly existing person* and engage in its negation. This is misguided, for it leads to the extreme of eternalism. Many others assert it is misguided to negate the thought "I am" itself, for this will not contribute in any way toward negating true existence. Some, when the thought "I am" spontaneously arises and one observes from one part of the mind how it is being perceived, instead of cultivating the ascertainment of how if the "I" were to exist in the way in which it appears it must necessarily do so as either identical to or different [from the aggregates], take the vacuity that arises naturally as [the conscious sense of "I"] fades away to constitute true emptiness. Such an assertion is most incorrect, and the fault lies in failing to differentiate between subtle impermanence and emptiness. Again, some, instead of taking the sense of "I am" that spontaneously arises in us to be the innate self-grasping, look for something else. This too is most incorrect. For if it is a sense of "I am" that arises anew only when meditating, [557] it cannot be innate. Furthermore, any sense of "I" or "me" freshly constructed by our mind cannot be the innate grasping at self. For the "I" that is the object of such an apprehension is an "I" contrived by the thought; such apprehension of self is a contrived self-grasping, and the absence that arises in the wake of negating what appears to such a thought is a mentally contrived emptiness.

Some learned ones differentiate two aspects of the thought "I am" and maintain that the existence of "I" as conceived by the thought "I am" should not be negated, for such an "I" does exist. It is the aspect of the thought "I am" that grasps at true existence of "I" that must be negated, for that "I" does not exist. Because of this, they assert that the "I" apprehended by the thought "I am" itself should not be negated, and that what should be negated is the "I" that the thought "I" apprehends to exist as truly established. This too is incorrect. For us ordinary beings, the thought "I am" not qualified by true existence arises extremely rarely and not as part of our continual experience. The thought "I am" we experience day in and day out is indeed the very sense of self that we experience continually in terms of the thought "I," "me." If we do not take this to be the innate self-grasping, we would be going against all guide to the view texts. Furthermore, if there are no instances of cognitions apprehending something as true without qualifying in terms of true existence, this would mean that there could be no instances of apprehending something as not true existence without qualifying it in terms of absence of true existence. Admitting such a thing would lead to absurd consequences.[1244]

Also, when the thought "I am" arises in us [as a result of invoking it for the purpose of meditating on it], it can appear to us in various ways: (1) as if the "I" appears before us like something tangible from outside us, (2) as if the "I" arises from inside in a rigid form, (3) as if the "I" has been forced down [our throat] with a stick, (4) as if the "I" is the aggregates that appear to the thought, and (5) as if the thought "I" vanishes upon observation, with nothing appearing to the mind.

Of these, the first sense arises when, in response to the spontaneous arising of the thought "I am," you close and open your eyes in a rapid manner. Some may even experience fear at that moment. The second sense arises as a function of exerting your mind with the intention "I will observe the manner in which 'I' appears to my thought 'I am,'" and then, at the same time, forcing your body as well. The third sense arises because of excessive tightening of awareness while what is needed is to observe while keeping your awareness relaxed on the surface but alert at the core. Some might experience some tightness around the upper back. With the fourth sense, [558] even though "I" is something projected by our thoughts onto the collection of aggregates, and no such "I" exists separately, the innate "I"-grasping nonetheless perceives an autonomous "I," one that is not the appearance of the aggregates. This fourth sense arises when one fails to differentiate between these two [the appearance of aggregates and that of the "I"]. The fifth sense arises from being a little late in our observation. Instead of observing the mode of appearance of the thought "I am" the instant it has spontaneously arisen, one is observing how the "I" appears after that spontaneous thought "I am" has already ceased. I have heard from my learned gurus that this is how Jé Rinpoché would guide his disciples when he was teaching, and I have also seen it written down in numerous texts.[1245] So you can accept it as trustworthy.

In brief, what we understand is the following. The thought we have right now of "I," "me," is the innate "I"-grasping, and the "I" that is grasped is the "I" to be negated. The simple negation of such an "I"—that absence—is emptiness. Those with the most experience on this point seem to be the great meditators who have embraced meditative practice as the heart of their life's activity. So consult those learned and realized gurus who have experience of this practice, and settle your doubts about this [task of accurately identifying the object of negation].

Thus[1246] if, under analysis, the individual and so forth do exist the way they appear to the mind as the "individual," the "person," and the "I," there is then no alternative for them but to possess true existence. Yet no such individual as perceived exists. The person's body and mind are each not the person, and the individual's combined body and mind is also not the person. Neither is each of the six elements the person, nor is the combined six elements the person; yet apart from the six elements, there is also no person.

To illustrate this point, the peerless savior Nāgārjuna says:

> The person is not earth nor water,
> is not fire, wind, nor space,
> is not consciousness—nor is it all of them.
> Where then, apart from these, is the person?[1247]

Along the same lines, *Guide to the Bodhisattva Way* says:

> Teeth, hair, and nails are not the self;
> the self is not the bones or the blood;
> it's not mucus, it is not phlegm;
> it's not lymph, it is not pus.
>
> Self is not marrow or sweat;
> nor are lungs and liver the self;
> nor are internal organs the self;
> self is neither excrement nor urine.
>
> Heat and breath are not the self; [559]
> the orifices are not, and not by any means
> are the six classes of consciousness the self.[1248]

This says that the person, the self, or "I" is not the earth element, the solid aspects of your body like bones and so on; nor is self the body's water element, the fluid aspects like blood and so on; the heat aspects of the body from the crown of head down to the soles of the feet too are not the self; nor is the body's wind element, the buoyant aspects that flow within the channels, the person. Hollow spaces within the body such as the orifices are not the person, and classes of consciousness such as visual consciousness are not the self, nor is the self these factors. Their collection too is not the "I," nor is the "I" the collection of these. Yet apart from these there is no such person, the meditator, as it appears to your mind. In the sutras too it says, "Form is not self, feelings are not self, discrimination is not self, mental formations are not self, and consciousness is not self."[1249]

In view of the above, the meditating person's five aggregates, each of the six elements, their collection, and the configuration of the collection—none of these constitutes the meditating person. For if any of these were the person, there would be such consequences as the oneness of the designative base and the designation, the appropriated and the appropriator, and the constituents and the constituted. There would also be the following problem:

> Now if the aggregates are the self,
> then since they are multiple, the self would be multiple.[1250]

In particular, if consciousness were the person, phenomena such as the person being ill, speaking, seeing, and procreating would become untenable. Also, although the person is one, just as there are six classes of consciousness, there would be six persons; conversely, just as the person is one, the six classes of consciousness would also be partless and one. If the shape of the collection [of the aggregates] were the person, since it would be a material entity, there would be no persons in the formless realm.

Yet there can be no person apart from the five aggregates. If there were, it would be intrinsically unconnected with and separate [from the aggregates] and would thus be devoid of the characteristics that define the aggregates as conditioned phenomena. It is said:

> If it were separate from the aggregates,
> it would lack the characteristics of the aggregates.[1251]

There would also be the faults pointed in the *Elephant's Skills Sutra*:

> If things were to possess intrinsic existence,
> the conquerors and śrāvakas would know this; [560]
> things would be absolute and there will no nirvana,
> and the wise will never be free from conceptual elaboration.[1252]

Thus, when you examine from within meditative equipoise, with a subtle part of your mind, the individual, the self, the person, or the "I" who is resting in meditative equipoise that appears to your mind, not even an atom of it exists; there will be pure emptiness in its wake. Then, allowing this generic image of pure vacuity to appear clearly in your mind, rest single-pointedly in meditative equipoise without bringing to your mind anything else in the form of conceptual elaboration. When your apprehension of this pure vacuity, a nonimplicative negation, wanes a little, apply analysis as before while abiding within meditative equipoise and continue to meditate single-pointedly.[1253]

In this context, when ascertainment of the person's lack of intrinsic existence suddenly emerges, Gungru Gyaltsen Sangpo takes it to be an authentic approach to rest in it single-pointedly through meditative equipoise.[1254] To do this, however, you must be well experienced in the view of emptiness. Were a beginner to follow this approach, he might initially possess the modal apprehension of vividly ascertaining the lack of objective existence by the force of reflecting on the four essential points, but later, when the continuity of that fleeting ascertainment fades, he will lose the emptiness from within that modal apprehension and turn to something distant and separate. When this happens, emptiness, not inconceivably, will appear as truly established. This statement is found in an oral teaching of Jé Rinpoché himself.[1255]

Alternatively,[1256] if, while maintaining the continuity of your earlier meditative equipoise, you examine your mind, since it does not exist in a material way, it will appear as *pure vacuity*, like a sun that is *unobscured* by, for instance, clouds. Yet all sorts of diverse forms and all sorts of diverse thoughts arise in it and it moves outward as well. Unlike the flickering of a flame, it is *unceasing*; and it operates fluidly with an uninterrupted continuum of that which is *luminous* and *aware*. Now this mind appears to you as if it is totally independent of the subject that apprehends it. With respect to such a mind—the object clung to just as perceived, or this mind as it appears to you—the guardian Śāntideva says: [561]

> The so-called continuums and collections,
> just like rosaries, armies, and so on, are false.[1257]

So on the basis of scriptures and reasoning, ascertain how "rosary" is merely imputed onto a composite where individual beads are strung on a string, and how "army" is just a name merely imputed onto a collection of individual men bearing arms. Apart from this there is nothing truly existent. Rest single-pointedly in meditative equipoise with the ascertainment that your mind does not exist in accord with how it appears to you. Thus the *Perfection of Wisdom in Eight Thousand Lines* says:

> The mind is devoid of mind, for the nature of mind is clear light.[1258]

This states that there is no intrinsically existing mind in the mind, for the nature of the mind is clear-light emptiness. And in the *Heap of Jewels* too it says:

> The mind has never been seen, is not being seen, and will not be seen by all the buddhas of the three times.[1259]

Also Lord Marpa labels ascertaining the mind's true nature as it is and meditating on it as "grabbing the emptiness of mind with one's bare hands." He says:

> I went to the banks of the River Ganges in the east.
> There through the kindness of the great Lord Maitripa,
> I realized the ground, the unborn reality,
> and grabbed with bare hands the emptiness of mind.
> I saw the primordial nature, reality free from elaboration;
> I met face to face with my mother, the three buddha bodies.
> From then on, this man's elaborations were severed.[1260]

When, as a result of analyzing "my mind" in the above way, you ascertain that it has no objective existence, if one has no familiarity with the view, fear will arise; if one does have familiarity, joy will arise.

During the post-equipoise stage, having risen from meditative equipoise, view your "I" or mind of mere label and mere word as illusion-like. You could do this too on the basis of chanting the words of profound scriptures. The *King of Meditations Sutra* says:

> The illusionist conjures images
> of horses, elephants, and all sorts of chariots,
> yet none are real the way they appear to be.
> Like this, understand all phenomena.[1261]

In our tradition, there is no method of mahāmudrā meditation that is separate from emptiness meditation. There is no mahāmudrā separate from emptiness because [562] emptiness—the nature of each and every phenomenon—is accepted to be mahāmudrā. The *King of Meditations Sutra* says, "The nature of all phenomena is the great seal (*mahāmudrā*),"[1262] and the etymology of the term itself also says:

> *Hand* (*phyag*): for phenomena are empty;
> *seal* (*rgya*): for they do not lie beyond its bounds.[1263]

For more extensive explanations, consult [Tsongkhapa's] *Stages of the Path*, the mahāmudrā text *Lamp So Bright*, and other works.

The great seal beyond expression and thought appearing suddenly
through letters is this beautiful maiden of excellent explanation
joyfully attracting the eyes of the sublime beings;
it has emerged through churning the sea of profound instructions.

Through the virtue as pristine as a heap of moon rays,
may I view wealth and honor as children's playthings,
and may I discover the glory of enjoying at will
the nectar of mahāmudrā in places of solitude.

Colophon

This *Experiential Guide to Mahāmudrā of the Sacred Geden Lineage* was presented to the hands of the glorious and excellent Losang Tenpai Gyaltsen[1264]—one who is nondual from Vajradhara and whose kindness remains matchless—by his disciple, the mountain hermit Kalden Gyatso. The intelligent Thösam Gyatso served as scribe.

13. Source of All Higher Attainments

A Very Secret Short Work Revealing Key Points of the View

Yongzin Yeshé Gyaltsen

I pay homage to and go for refuge from my heart to the sublime and revered guru, the supreme siddha Ensapa who is endowed with the objectless great compassion, his spiritual heirs, and their successive lineage teachers. Pray sustain me in all times and bless me that my mindstream may be quickly, quickly ripened and I may attain freedom.

At this juncture, when you have obtained this once the diamond-like body of human existence endowed with leisure and opportunity—so difficult to find and when found so valuable—the most excellent way to extract its essence is to strive in the means of achieving the unexcelled enlightenment characterized by the elimination of the afflictions and their propensities from their very root.

To live in this samsara of the three realms is to experience nothing but suffering, just like falling into a burning pit of fire. All that we perceive at present as pleasurable is nothing but perceptions of joy arisen because an earlier instance of suffering has ceased; it is not definitive happiness. Thus it has been taught. If we remain unable to eliminate the afflictions within our own mental continuum and allow the afflictions to reign victorious, whatever we do will fall under the sway of the afflictions. And so long as we remain under the power of karma and the afflictions, we will have no freedom at all. Now the fact is, because of impermanence, things undergo change every moment, so there is no guarantee [of security] in anything. Furthermore, our situation of wandering [in samsara] without any say is the ultimate form of suffering. When we contemplate such a condition, we will be able to realize that this samsara is characterized by suffering.

The root of all sufferings is the afflictions within our own mental continuum, [564] and the root of all afflictions is this grasping at selfhood. This self-grasping is a form of blind clinging to an object that has no existence.

Our mind has been under the power of the delusion of ignorance since beginningless time, the thought "I am" arises based on our consciousness coming into contact with any of the [five] contaminated aggregates. Even when we are sleeping, the thought "I," "me" arises spontaneously in our dreams. It is essential, therefore, to have an effective recognition that because our mind is deluded how, on the basis of this collection of contaminated aggregates, the thought "I," "me" arises as if such an "I" existed objectively with self-sufficient reality on the part of the aggregates.

Let me give an analogy. When at night we see the shadow of a broom cast by a butter lamp, our mind becomes deluded, and thinking that there is a scorpion, we experience fear. If, in that moment, we were to examine the manner in which this perception is occurring, we would certainly not have the impression that it is being conjured by our own mind. Instead, the perception of the terrifying creature would seem to be coming from the side of the object itself. If we fail to dispel that delusion, we may become afraid and distressed because of it. Just like in this example, although the thought "I am" is constructed by our mind based on the collection of the contaminated aggregates, this is not how it appears to us. Instead, because we are deluded, it feels as if there is indeed an "I" with solid reality that exists objectively on the part of the aggregates. Thanks to such a delusion, all the various afflictions arise, such as attachment to our own self and aversion toward others. On this basis, all sorts of karma are created, and owing to this, our present predicament of revolving uncontrollably in samsara undergoing all those sufferings comes about. This is what has been taught.

Dispelling such a delusion of self-grasping is referred to as meditating on the view [of emptiness]. "So," the gurus say, "it is crucial we understand this key point, for without challenging the afflictions within our mindstream, there can be no arising of the perfect view."[1265]

As for the method of dispelling this deluded perception, we can again use the analogy given above, when at night the deluded perception of, say, a scorpion that is not really there arises. Such delusion, when it arises, can be dispelled by looking more closely with our eyes and with the help of a bright lamp, leading to the ascertainment that there is no such scorpion at all. With such ascertainment arises the conviction that there is no such creature and that its previous perception had occurred because our mind was deluded. [565] At that moment, all the fear and distress that was based on such delusion will subside on its own. Like in this analogy, when we examine well with the eyes of wisdom and with the help of the guru's instruction, this delusion of a concrete "I," "me" in relation to the collection of contaminated aggregates, we will ascertain that it does not exist the way it appears to. At that point, there will arise from the depths of our mind the decisive conclusion that such a perception occurs because our own mind is under the sway of ignorance's delusion and that, in actuality, no such "I" exists at all. This kind of decisive view is called "the profound Madhyamaka view." When such a view has arisen decisively, karma and the afflictions—such as the attachment and aversion engendered by the delusion of "I"-grasping—and the sufferings generated by karma and afflictions will come to cease.

For those of sharp mental acumen who possess past propensities, this much in the form of identifying the self-grasping, the root of samsara, could lead to the arising of a conclusive view. [The rest of us require further analysis.][1266]

Engaging in analysis through reasoning—the means to cease self-grasping—is as follows. Here, contemplate: If this "I" does exist on the aggregates as grasped by the thought "I," "me," does such an "I" exist as identical to or as separate from the aggregates? Nothing can exist without being one of these two alternatives. Now were the "I" to exist as identical to the present aggregates, given that this current body aggregate came into being from the parents' semen and ovum and will eventually be discarded when one dies, then the "I" too would cease its continuity. Insofar as the mere "I" is concerned, however, its continuity has never been interrupted since beginningless time. The thought "I am," from beginningless time, has continued through the force of karma by adopting a body every time [there is new birth]. Even after this present body is discarded, the power of karma will cause us to adopt another bodily form. At that time, we will grasp with the thought "I am" in relation to that new body. It is therefore our delusion that causes us to grasp each collection of the contaminated aggregates as "I" and wander in samsara. And thus it is certain that the aggregates are not identical with the "I."

What if, however, the thought arises that this "I" as perceived by the thought "I am" exists *apart* from the aggregates? Contemplate that no such "I" as grasped at exists apart from the aggregates because, if it did, it should be possible to point to it and say "this is that I," but this is not the case. When our body comes into contact with fire, we say "I've been burned," and the same thought occurs to our mind. [566] Now if the "I" and the aggregates existed separately from each other, there would simply be no basis for the body coming into contact [with fire] as constituting the "I" coming into contact. By analogy, the pillar and vase exist separately from each other, and so contact with the pillar does not constitute contact with the vase. Then, generating the ascertainment that this "I" that is perceived by the "I"-grasping does not exist separately from the aggregates, conclude decisively.

Thus, when you have ascertained that this "I" is not the aggregates themselves and that neither does it exist apart from them, then decisively conclude that, apart from perceiving in this manner because my mind is deluded, there is nothing in reality that possesses true and substantial existence. Based on such a decisive conclusion, cultivate forceful ascertainment. Furthermore, in the case of a conch perceived as yellow due to jaundice, one can ascertain that this yellowness is perceived because one's eyes are deluded and that there is no objective yellowness on the part of the conch. Just so, we should bring forth the ascertainment decisively and from the depth of our mind that it is because our own mind is gripped by the illness of ignorance's delusion that the perception of "I" and the "I" on the collection of the aggregates arises while, in reality, nothing possesses such true and substantial existence.

We can extend this to other beings too. Contemplate that each collection of a bodily aggregate—inherited from the collection of parent's semen and ovum—and a consciousness aggregate appears in diverse forms as human beings, donkeys, horses, and so forth. When such perceptions occur, we do not perceive these as constructs of our own mind; rather, each of these beings appears to us to possess concrete existence from the side of the specific aggregates, and we grasp at them as such. This gives rise to all the afflictions of attachment, aversion, and so on. Owing to these afflictions, we accumulate karma and the conditions for our own suffering. We must therefore cut the root of all these deluded perceptions.

So just as a broom's shadow is misperceived as a scorpion and a distant cairn is misperceived as a man, the mind constructs and conceives in terms of "this is a human being," "this is a horse," and so forth on the basis of each collection of aggregates where numerous causes and conditions have come together, and then grasps at their true existence. In reality, however, nothing whatsoever possesses true existence. In this way, conclude decisively and generate ascertainment.

In brief, all that appears to our six senses is like a magician's illusion, appearing to us yet with no reality; they are like effigies confused for the real things; they are like bubbles in water, with no core; [567] and they are echoes, created from various causes and conditions. Generate certainty again and again from the depth of your mind, decisively concluding that all this deluded appearance has, in reality, no existence as perceived.

We can also contemplate in brief as follows. When it comes to all the appearances I perceive right now, each and every one is posited based on being constructed by my own mind. Beyond that, nothing possesses true existence. In this way, conclude decisively and generate the ascertainment. Though devoid of true existence, the diverse perceptions of happiness and suffering, good and evil, and so on do arise, created by their causes and conditions such as karma and the afflictions. Inducing such ascertainment helps develop the conviction "Based on appearance and emptiness complementing each other, as I train in this path uniting method and wisdom, I will achieve the fruit, the union of the two buddha bodies." Stabilizing this kind of ascertainment constitutes the heart of the practice of [cultivating] the view.

Again, [contemplate that] this body of mine, which is part of the collection of the aggregates in relation to which the thought "I am" arises, came about from my parents' semen and ovum and will eventually be discarded. There is thus no real point in cherishing it and grasping at it as "mine." With such decisive conclusion, rest your mind in the view of its abiding nature. Letting go of your attachment to this body composed of flesh and bones without any hesitation, as you offer it to all agents of harm, such as malevolent spirits, [imagine that] these agents of harm relish your flesh and blood. Imagine that the moment they smell the odor of your flesh and blood and taste them, all their anger, hostility, and so forth is pacified without residue; and imagine that, through metamorphosis, they become enlightened. As your body, a mass of flesh, blood, and so on, becomes empty, rest your mind single-pointedly in meditative equipoise on this space-like imperceptible vacuity.

As you rise from this meditative equipoise, bring to mind the awareness that all this appearance is nothing but false and deluded perceptions. To contemplate in this manner even once in the short term, my holy guru said, averts harms caused by demonic and obstructive forces, and it is particularly powerful for cutting [the fetter of] self-grasping.

Also, when harm such as illness befalls your body, recite *phat* and [568] freely release all attachment to your body, as if it were an abandoned corpse.[1267] And with your mind imagining that you are Heruka abiding in the nature of great bliss, as you recite *oṃ aḥ hūṃ*, imagine that your body of flesh, blood, and bones instantly dissolves and transforms into an ocean of nectar. As you offer this to all beings, both ordinary and ārya beings, the ārya beings become sated by the offering of nectar. The beings of the six classes, including even agents of harm such as the malevolent spirits, also become sated with nectar. Imagine that the moment nectar enters their bodies, all their afflictions together with their propensities become purified and that they attain enlightenment in the form of Heruka. Imagine that their environs become pure realms and the entirety of samsara is emptied. Then with the thought "Since both the worlds and their denizens have been transformed into the myriad worlds of perfect purity, all my aims have now been realized," greatly rejoice. Then, bring together all of these appearances into light, which dissolves into you, and you in turn melt into light and dissolve into your heart. Then, bringing awareness of this space-like vacuity where nothing remains perceptible, recall your earlier ascertainment of the view. Then, with your mind generated as the innate gnosis of great bliss that has emptiness as its object of apprehension, rest your mind single-pointedly in this state as much as you can.

When you rise from this meditative equipoise, imagine that this very gnosis of nondual bliss and emptiness—which is your own wind-mind—arises instantaneously as glorious Heruka, lord and consort. With the thought *I am this embodiment of the innate gnosis of great bliss of all the conquerors arising into a form body*, fervently cultivate this identity. Heruka represents the innate gnosis of great bliss, and the consort, Yoginī, represents emptiness. Being sexually conjoined with the consort means that your own mind—the innate gnosis of great bliss—fuses indivisibly into a single taste with emptiness, the abiding nature of reality. Contemplating these meanings, single-pointedly rest your mind within the nature of great bliss fused with the empty abiding nature for as long as you can. When you rise from this, meditate that whatever you perceive is the body of a deity and, in particular, that your mind of indivisible bliss and emptiness is arising in deity forms. [569]

To summarize everything, cultivate the following: *renunciation* with the thought that nothing about samsara is trustworthy; *awakening mind* with the thought "I shall strive to the best of my ability to singlehandedly liberate all mother sentient beings, and to this end, I must definitely attain buddhahood"; and to the best your ability, rest your mind in the *view* with the thought that in reality, nothing possesses true existence, and everything that appears to me is posited merely through my own mind's construction. At this point, imagine your mind transforms into great bliss. Then, as appearances arise [once again in the aftermath of your equipoise], generate your mind in the form of Heruka lord and consort, and constantly bring to mind and maintain the contemplation "Everything, the world and its inhabitants, is purity alone."

I have put into writing here, in few words and in a very explicit way, the ultimate key points of the most secret of secret pith instructions of the supreme siddha Ensapa father and sons, which present the distilled essence of the ocean of highest yoga tantras.

The natural form of the great compassion of all conquerors,
excellently arising as the savior of this humble person,
most venerable teacher whose kindness is unrivaled,
nurture me continuously until my enlightenment.

From time beginningless until now,
I've been fooled by the great demon of self-grasping;
in the guise of help it has brought harms most foul.
Bless me that this enemy within may be exorcized.

Swept constantly by the powerful currents of karma and afflictions,
transient, instable, and out of control,
this great ocean of existence is the source of all suffering—
bless me that I may soon be free of it.

My mothers who have kindly nurtured me for so long,
desperate, they too suffer hundredfold miseries in samsara's ocean.
By contemplating this fate with uncontrived compassion,
bless me that I may become trained in supreme bodhicitta.

All outer and inner phenomena are like echoes;
though appearing they are empty, and though empty they appear.
May I soon complete the journey on the excellent path
where appearance and emptiness unite, the union of method and wisdom.

Whatever deluded perceptions arise, good or bad,
are nothing but imputations of my own mind.
Without falling prey to the power of attachment and aversion,
may my mind abide in the ultimate expanse of reality.

Not falling under the sway of impure deluded perceptions,
and instead experiencing pure visions of myriad deity circles

and the ecstatic play of innate bliss and emptiness,
may I dance amid heroes and ḍākinīs.

By the youthful pristine awareness of innate great bliss
embracing steadfastly, never to be separated,
the beautiful maiden of primordially pure ultimate expanse,
may I swiftly attain the state of perfect union.

By lucidly inscribing, for the benefit of myself and others,
this innermost essence of the nectar of instructions
of the great Losang Vajradhara Ensapa,
O ḍākinīs of the three spheres, please grant your support.

This short composition explicitly revealing the ultimate key points of the view, a very secret work entitled *Source of All Higher Siddhis*, was composed by the Buddhist monk Yeshé Gyaltsen in accordance with the instructions of the supreme siddha Ensapa. It was written at the great Dharma seat of Tashi Lhunpo, fulfilling a request of the treasurer Losang Tsewang, an important medium for the enlightened activities of the lord of teachings Panchen.[1268] Through this, may the teachings of Ensapa's oral transmission remain for a long time.

Part 4
The Three Essential Points

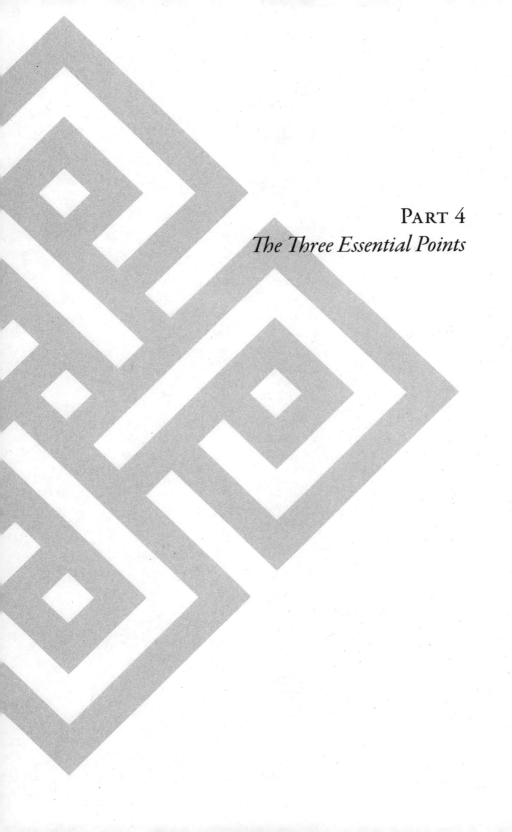

14. Sacred Words of the Great Siddha

A Condensed Practice of the Three Essential Points

NGULCHU DHARMABHADRA

Namo Guru Lokeśvarāya.

Here is a way to practice in a condensed way the three essential points. In a clean place, lay out the sacred representations [of the Three Jewels] and the offerings and be seated well on a cushion. Then recite:

GOING FOR REFUGE AND GENERATING THE AWAKENING MIND

1 To my gurus, who are on a lotus tree in front of me,
and to the Buddha, Dharma, Sangha, and protectors,
with thoughts of impermanence and suffering, I go for refuge.
Pray bless my mindstream and those of all beings.

In this way go for refuge; then generate the awakening mind:

2 To free my kind mothers from samsara's ocean,
I shall generate the awakening mind
and put into practice the instruction that distills
the essence of the sutra and tantra teachings into three points.

Recite the verses on refuge and awakening mind three times.

VISUALIZATION OF THE MERIT FIELD AND SEVEN-LIMB WORSHIP

3 At my crown inside the vase[1269] of a white crystal stupa,
on a lotus and a moon disc, sits Guru Avalokiteśvara;
he is Khasarpāṇi surrounded by a retinue on four levels.
The thousand buddhas are present as lords of the five families.

4 My heart is a thousand-petaled red lotus; at its hub
is Khasarpāṇi and on the petals a thousand white *ah* syllables.
Light rays emitting from the guru deity's three secrets
invite the gnosis beings, making him the embodiment of all refuge.

5 To you, guru deity, I prostrate and make offerings of all kinds,
I confess all my negative karma and rejoice in virtue,
I appeal to turn the wheel of Dharma and to constantly remain,
and I dedicate all my virtues, exemplified by acts such as these.

If you wish, you could make a mandala offering as well.

Practices pertaining to this life

6 O gurus and buddhas, possessors of limitless compassion,
pray help me and beings equal to the reaches of space
purify the two obscurations and perfect the two accumulations,
so that we may soon attain buddhahood. (3x)

7 Having been appealed thusly, the gurus and the buddhas
emit streams of white nectar, which enter my crown
and absorb into the deity and the *ah* syllable at my heart;
nectars flowing from this purify the two obscurations. [574]

8 With these two purities, I become the Great Compassionate
One,[1270]
the guru at my crown dissolves into the deity,
the thousand buddhas dissolve into the thousand *ah* syllables,
and like the vanishing of a rainbow, the stupa dissolves into space.

9 At the heart of the deity, on a moon disc and around letter *hrīḥ*,
are the six syllables, from which light radiates and retracts;
this purifies the world and its denizens and invokes the conquerors'
compassion.
May I be blessed with the three embodiments and the three
perspectives.[1271]

Om maṇi padme hūṃ (*Repeat this mantra*).

10 The lights from his heart draw forth the world, its inhabitants,
my body, the lotus, the *ah* syllable, the mantra, and the seed syllable.
Through reasoning that seeks the nature of my mind and all
phenomena,
their lack of arising as truly existent, I rest in meditative equipoise.

These, then, are the practices pertaining to this life.

Practices pertaining to the time of death

11 My mind as the deity comes out, separating my body and mind;
and inside a skull cup set on a tripod atop fire and wind mandalas,
my old body is purified, transformed, and multiplied,
and its nectar is offered to the guests of both samsara and nirvana.

12 Recalling impermanence, illusion, and emptiness,
I sever the ties with my body, wealth, and loved ones,
and inside my body, at the heart inside the central channel,
appears a Khasarpāṇi the size of a thumbnail.

13 Maitreya, gold in color and seated in the *bhadra* posture,
resides above in Tuṣita, in Yiga Chözin [courtyard].[1272]
As I appeal to this savior, from his heart emerges
a hollow light beam that pierces my crown.

14 With the three thoughts,[1273] I am pulled from my topknot
by a hook and become fused inseparably with Maitreya's mind;
during training I return, and my crown aperture is sealed.
After death, may I be reborn like a new lotus flower in his presence.

This then is the practice pertaining to the time of death.

Practices pertaining to the intermediate state

15 Imagining the perceptions at dying as those of the intermediate state,
through wind, intention, and aspiration, I will recognize the bardo [as
bardo],
and I will view the world as a pure land, beings as deities,
and all as devoid of true existence and illusion-like.

16 Preventing attachment and aversion with emptiness and compassion,
I will with pure perception take birth through my own will.
Endowed with the key points of view, meditation, and action,
this is the flawless instruction of the great siddha Mitrayogi.

This then is the practice pertaining to the intermediate state.

Concluding prayer and dedication

17 Through the virtue of deeds such as these,
may I be cared for in all lives by Guru Padmapāṇi, [575]
and by perfecting the practices of this life, death, and the bardo,
may I become a glory to the teaching and all beings.

Thus I say:

18 This was written for disciples with the open eyes of intellect
by Dharmabhadra, who takes the form of a monk.
Through this virtue, may this instruction, the essence of sutras and tantras,
never degenerate but flourish always in a hundred directions.

Sarva jagagataṃ.

15. A Mirror Reflecting the Mahāsiddha's Sacred Words

Notes on the Three Essential Points

NGULCHU DHARMABHADRA

Respectfully I bow to the kind gurus, who teach
and place atop the banner of exposition and practice
this wish-granting gem condensing into three points
the unadulterated vital essence of all the eighty-four thousand
teachings.

Here, to expound the instruction famed as the "Three Essential Points," which was directly granted to the great siddha Mitrayogi by his meditation deity, the supreme ārya Great Compassion, these are the root verses:[1274]

I bow to great compassion.

In this life, cultivate constantly your meditation deity,
at time of death, practice the instruction of transference,
and in the intermediate state, practice the mixings.
The key point is to practice them constantly.

Recalling impermanence and suffering,
thoroughly generate great compassion,
visualize the guru at your crown and the deity at your heart,
and meditate on your mind as devoid of arising.[1275]

Performing the rite of offering your body
and having discarded all dependencies,
through the medium of a hollow light beam
I'll send my mind to the Tuṣita realm.

Recognizing this as the bardo itself
and transforming the outer, inner, and secret
through the yoga of emptiness and compassion,
the wise connect to the new birth.

Recognizing whatever appears is the key point of the view;
remaining undistracted in this is the key point of meditation;
fusing the tastes of thoughts is the key point of action.
This is the instruction of the great siddha.

Here concludes the instruction on the three essential points.

So it has been taught. Of these, some maintain that the concluding verse, beginning "Recognizing whatever appears is the key point of view," [578] was composed by the translator [Trophu Lotsāwa] while up to that was authored by the great siddha himself. Others hold that the first stanza was written by the great siddha and what comes subsequently is drawn from notes by the translator based on the great siddha's own words. Be that as it may, I will explain the instruction here based on the one-pager[1276] I wrote to facilitate its practice on a regular basis. This has three parts: the salutation, the actual body of the composition, and the concluding activities.

The first, the salutation, is as follows: "*I bow to great compassion.*" Here homage is being paid to the great compassion that is the embodiment of the definitive compassion of all the buddhas. Such great compassion appears in a form with face and arms as Ārya Avalokiteśvara, or Lokeśvara. In the one-pager it reads "**Namo Guru Lokeśvarāya.**" *Namo* means "to bow down to," and *guru* is "teacher." When the words are separated, *loka* means "the world," *īśvara* means "the lord," and *aya* means "to." Thus the phrase means: I bow to the teacher called Lord of the World." The meaning [of the two salutations] remains the same.

The second, the actual body of the composition, has three parts: a brief overview, an extensive explanation, and a concluding summary.

A brief overview

The root text says:

In this life, cultivate constantly your meditation deity,
at time of death, practice the instruction of transference,

> **and in the intermediate state, practice the mixings.**
> **The key point is to practice them constantly.**[1277]

The essential point is this: the person of highest acumen should constantly cultivate the meditation deity in this very life, those of medium acumen should practice the transference instruction at the point of death, and those of the least acumen should practice the mixings during the intermediate state. This said, the practices pertaining to the time of death and the intermediate state should be practiced all the time. And this is the key point of all of your meditative practice.

The extensive explanation

This is threefold: (1) cultivating the meditation deity, the essence of the practice for this life, (2) transference meditation, the essence of the practice for the time of death, and (3) the mixings, the essence of the practice for the intermediate state.

Cultivating the meditation deity, the essence of the practice for this life

The first has four parts: (1) invocation and going for refuge, the condition, (2) generating the awakening mind, the cause, [579] (3) supplicating the gurus and meditation deities, the method, and (4) meditating on your own mind as devoid of arising, the actual reality.

Invocation and going for refuge, the condition

With respect to the first, the one-pager explains in a condensed form the way to engage in the practice of the three essential points in the following manner. "**In the clean place**" explains the need to clean your place of practice; "**lay out representations**" explains that you should lay out, in general, the representations of the Three Jewels and, more particularly, that of Khasarpāṇi, such as his icon; "**the offerings**" explains that you should prepare offerings such as the two waters and other articles of everyday enjoyment of as good a quality as possible and arrange them in a beautiful way; to "**be seated well**" is to sit on a comfortable cushion in the sevenfold or eightfold posture.

Next, to go for refuge, the meaning of "*Recalling impermanence and suffering*" is presented in the lines:

> **To my gurus, who are on a lotus tree in front of me,**
> **and to the Buddha, Dharma, Sangha, and protectors,**

> **with thoughts of impermanence and suffering, I go for refuge.**
> **Pray bless my mindstream and those of all beings.**

"Recalling impermanence" relates to the path of the lesser capacity, while "recalling suffering" relates to the path of the intermediate capacity. Here you recall them by mentally reviewing them. Contemplate, as presented in the *Three Principal Elements of the Path*, the way you turn away from preoccupations with this life and preoccupations with the next life. [Jé Tsongkhapa says]:

> If we know how hard it is to find, we will not remain idle.
> If we see its great value, we will not waste our time.
> If we contemplate death, we will prepare for our next life.
> If we contemplate karma, we will renounce heedless acts.[1278]

As this states, you should contemplate in the following way. This human existence with leisure and opportunity is extremely hard to find and is invaluable. It is also easily destroyed, for this life cannot last long and the reality of death is ever present. In the aftermath of death too, I have no choice but to be reborn in either the fortunate or the unfortunate realms. And let alone the lower realms, even rebirth in the fortunate realms is nothing but suffering. Suffering comes from karma, the causal law, and as for my accumulation of negative karma, the cause of samsara and birth in the lower realms, it is incalculable. Even now I am continually gathering them without any effort. So I have no choice but to experience their fruit, suffering. Only my guru and the Three Jewels can save me from such suffering. So I must go for refuge to the Three Jewels with the thought that I will seek them as objects of my refuge.

Set up your field of refuge as follows. Imagine where you are [580] is a pure realm where the earth is gold and adorned with patterns of strings of lapis lazuli. In front of you is a great sea of milk, and in its center is a large lotus tree whose tip has four large petals that create an opening. At the center of this is a white lotus flower and a moon disc on which sits your kind root guru, the great compassionate Khasarpāṇi. Around him on the hub of the lotus flower are the lineage gurus, starting from Ārya Avalokiteśvara at his front and continuing clockwise up to your own root guru. On the front petal is the sovereign sage Vajradhara, who is surrounded by the deities of the four classes of tantra as well as saṃbhogakāya and nirmāṇakāya buddhas like the thousand buddhas [of the Fortunate Eon]. On the petal to the right [of

Khasarpāṇi], on an excellent throne, is the scriptural Dharma Jewel in the form of texts written on gold leaves with lapis ink, resounding the words of the scriptures, radiating light, and performing the welfare of sentient beings. On the rear petal are the sangha members of the three vehicles—bodhisattvas such as Avalokiteśvara, in either his one-face four-arm form or his one-face two-arm form, pratyekabuddhas, and śrāvakas. On the left petal are ḍākas, ḍākinīs, and Dharma protectors like Six-Arm Mahākāla. Visualize that all the members of your refuge field face you and reside with joy.

Imagine on your right is your father of this life, on your left your mother, in front are your enemies, demons, and harmful spirits, and behind you, in a large mass, are all the sentient beings of the six realms, including those in the intermediate state, all of them in human form and able to speak and understand the meaning of words. Then imagine that you and all other beings, by contemplating the impermanence of death and the sufferings of samsara, both general and specific, experience terror, and from such fear you place your trust and hope in the Three Jewels. In this way, establish the conditions for refuge and fervently go for refuge.

Supplicating that the mindstreams of me and all sentient beings, whose mindstreams have until now been saturated with nonvirtue, may become purified through the arising of loving kindness, compassion, the awakening mind, and the perfect view is the meaning of requesting blessings. Imagine that, as result of such fervent appeals and of going for refuge, white nectar streams from the fields of refuge [581] and dissolves into all of you. Through this all the negative karma of your body, speech, and mind and all your obscurations and their imprints are purified. Imagine that all your bodies transform into the saṃbhogakāya Avalokiteśvara, and all your minds transform into gnosis dharmakāya. Imagine that all the other sentient beings en masse return as if flying to their respective pure lands. The members of the refuge field are gradually absorbed, from the edges to the center, merging eventually into the principal figure. He too dissolves into the point between your eyebrows, and you imagine that you have received the blessing of the Three Jewels.

Generating the Awakening Mind, the Cause

This is presented by the line "*Thoroughly generate great compassion*," which is explained in the following:

> **To free my kind mothers from samsara's ocean,**
> **I shall generate the awakening mind**

> **and put into practice the instruction that distills**
> **the essence of the sutra and tantra teachings into three points.**

Just as the life faculty is fundamental for living beings, great compassion is fundamental to all attributes of the buddha: when it is present all other attributes are present, and when it is absent none of the attributes are present. *Entering the Middle Way* says:

> As compassion alone is accepted to be
> the seed of the perfect harvest of buddhahood,
> the water that nourishes it, and the fruit that is long a source of
> enjoyment,
> I will praise compassion at the start of all.[1279]

In the mundane example of seeking an excellent crop, first the seed is important for producing the crop; in the middle, moisture is important to nurture and enhance the growth; and at the end, for a good harvest, a good ripening of the crop is foremost. In the same way, first engendering the awakening mind relies foremost on compassion; then in the middle, compassion ensures that the awakening mind does not degenerate but is further enhanced; and compassion is vital at the end because it is thanks to compassion that we do not linger in the peace of nirvana but pursue the welfare of the sentient beings.

The way you give birth to such great compassion is by developing a disenchantment with samsara that sees the entirety of samsara as a burning fire and feels terror at the suffering of samsara and the lower realms. You then infer from your own situation that all these old mother sentient beings are also subject to such a terrifying suffering fate. Contemplate as well the incalculable kindness you have received from all sentient beings since beginningless time and how, in the future, they will continue to extend such kindness. Furthermore, even attaining buddhahood [582] depends on sentient beings. In this way, recognize how all sentient beings are dear to you and deserve your concern. Then develop the thought "I alone, through [the wisdom of] profound emptiness, will free all beings from this poisonous ocean of samsara and, through great compassion, will lead them to the peace of nirvana's great ocean that is like a sea of soothing milk." In this way, generate the altruistic revolve. Then contemplate, "Yet at present, I do not have the capacity to accomplish this. So to free sentient beings from the dangers of samsara as well as nirvana, I must somehow attain the precious state of full enlightenment." In this way, generate the aspiring awakening mind. Then generate the thought "Now such buddhahood does not come about without causes and conditions, so I will engage in the practice of this profound instruction renowned as the Three Essential Points, which comprehensively condenses the essence of all the teachings of sutra and tantra into three points." To make such a promise constitutes generating the engaging awakening mind.

Supplicating the Gurus and Meditation Deities, the Method

This is presented by the line "*Visualize the guru at your crown and the deity at your heart*," which is explained in the following:

> **O gurus and buddhas, possessors of limitless compassion,**
> **pray help me and beings equal to the reaches of space**
> **purify the two obscurations and perfect the two accumulations**
> **so that we may soon attain buddhahood.**
>
> **Having been appealed thusly, the gurus and the buddhas**
> **emit streams of white nectar, which enter my crown**
> **and absorb into the deity and the *ah* syllable at my heart;**
> **nectars flowing from this purify the two obscurations.**
>
> **With these two purities, I become the Great Compassionate One,**
> **the guru at my crown dissolves into the deity,**
> **the thousand buddhas dissolve into the thousand *ah* syllables,**
> **and like the vanishing of a rainbow, the stupa dissolves into space.**
>
> **At the heart of the deity, on a moon disc and around letter *hrīḥ*,**
> **are the six syllables, from which light radiates and retracts;**
> **this purifies the world and its denizens and invokes the conquerors' compassion.**
> **May I be blessed with the three embodiments and the three perspectives.**
>
> ***Om maṇi padme hūṃ.***

While remaining in your ordinary form yourself, visualize at your crown a bodhi stupa made of unblemished white crystal radiating lights immeasurably bright. It has all the following features complete: base, three steps, square platform, small lotus, top of the platform, ten virtues, four steps, base of the vase, the vase, base of the canopy, canopy, platform for the parasol, thirteen rings, scripture chamber, parasol, rain cover, moon, sun, and crowning jewel. Inside the vase, at the center of an eight-petaled lotus and on a moon disc, is your kind root guru in the form of Avalokiteśvara Khasarpāṇi. White in color, he has one face and two arms. His right hand is in the gesture of granting wishes, while his left at his heart is in the gesture of teaching. Between his left thumb and index finger, he holds the stem of a white lotus whose petals are open at the level of his left ear. He is in a standing position, with both his legs straight, and he is adorned in silk garments and precious ornaments.

On the four steps are a thousand small doors, [583] and at each entrance is one of the thousand buddhas. The heights of the four steps are, from bottom to top respectively, twenty-four micro-units,[1280] twenty-two, twenty, and eighteen. If, as in the Fifth Dalai Lama's tradition, the buddhas are visualized in the form of the lords of the buddha families, then imagine a buddha resides in the space of two-thirds of a micro-unit, which would mean there would be seventy-two buddhas on each of the four faces of the lowest step, sixty on each face on the next step, another sixty on each face of the next step, and fifty-two on each of the four faces of the last step. On either side of the center line in each of the four directions, in the space of two-thirds a micro-unit, is a buddha slighter larger in size—making eight such buddhas [on each level]. All these buddhas are in the form of the lords of the families, with Vairocana in the east, Ratnasambhava in the south, Amitābha in the west, and Amoghasiddhi in the north. When you dissolve all of them into the *ah* syllable at your heart, do so by visualizing eight large *ah* syllables on the eight petals of the lotus and the buddhas dissolving into them. This system seems excellent.

That said, Panchen Chökyi Gyaltsen says to view the thousand buddhas as the lords of the buddha families in the following manner.[1281] On the steps, on each of the four faces from bottom to top respectively, are seventy-two buddhas, then sixty-four, sixty-two, and fifty. Of these, all two hundred buddhas on the three lower steps of the east are white and display the gesture of supreme enlightenment. All two hundred in the south are yellow and display the gestures of granting wishes and meditative equipoise. All two hundred in the west are red and display the gesture of meditative equipoise. And all two hundred in the north are green and display the gesture of granting refuge. All the buddhas in the four directions on the top step, two hundred in total, are blue and display the gestures of touching the earth and meditative equipoise.

When, upon investigation, I understood this to be Panchen's mature understanding, I recognized that it is strikingly commensurate with the system of visualizing, in the context of the goddess Sitātapatrā (White Umbrella), her central two hundred faces as white, her two hundred right faces as yellow, her two hundred rear faces as red, her two hundred left faces as green, and her two hundred faces on the top as blue. Impressed by this understanding, in the one-pager, I have rendered this as "The thousand buddhas are present as lords of the five families," said the master.[1282] [584] All the buddhas are in nirmāṇakāya form, wearing the three robes and turning their face inward.

With yourself in your ordinary appearance, visualize that inside your body, imagined as an empty shell, your heart is shaped like a lotus with thousand petals on nine levels, with progressively fewer but larger petals from bottom to top. As stated in the lines:

> In shapes of swirling waves and of rising swells,
> shapes of peaking seas and flickering seas,
> shapes of cresting seas and swirling waves,
> and shapes of rising swells and peaking seas—numbering a
> thousand.[1283]

Thus on the lowest level are 194 petals, on the next level are 174, on the next 154, the next 134, the next 114, the next 94, the next 74, the next 54, and on top are 8 petals.

At the center of this eight-petaled lotus, on a moon disc, is your subtle wind-mind in the form of Avalokiteśvara Khasarpāṇi about the size of a thumbnail, while on each petal is a short *a* in standing position facing inward. Generate these like reflections in a mirror, appearing yet devoid of intrinsic existence. On the ground, the lotus represents the red element, *ah* the white element, Khasarpāṇi the winds, the syllable *hrīḥ* at his heart your mind. Thus the master said.

"**The gurus**" refers to the ones residing inside the vase [of the stupa], "**the deity**" indicates the buddha and the meditation deity at your heart. On their body, at their crown is a white *oṃ*, the secret of the exalted body; at their throat is a red *āḥ*, the secret of the exalted speech; at their heart is a blue *hrīḥ* marked by a blue *hūṃ*. Countless beams of red light shaped like hooks radiate, inviting the buddhas and bodhisattvas from their natural abodes, and you imagine that gnosis beings enter into each and every one [of the figures visualized thus far]. If you wish to elaborate, you could visualize the lineage gurus on the thirteen rings [of the stupa].

Next is offering the seven limbs. The fields to which you are offering are those residing at your crown. So focusing on and paying homage to them with your body, speech, and mind is the first limb. The second limb is making offerings, those actually laid out and those imagined, as well as the outer, inner, secret, and suchness offerings. [585] Confessing and purifying the negative karma of naturally reprehensible acts and of the downfalls from transgressing your precepts is the third limb. Rejoicing in the virtues of self and others, as well as those of ordinary and ārya beings, is the fourth limb. Appealing [to the teachers] to turn the wheel of Dharma is the fifth limb. Supplicating them to not enter nirvana and to remain for eons is the sixth limb. For these preceding two limbs, crucially, for the sake of auspiciousness, imagine that the figures in the refuge fields grant their acceptance. For the seventh limb, dedicate the merits such as your present practice with the thought "I dedicate all virtues, my own and others', to the attainment of unexcelled enlightenment for the benefit of all sentient beings."

Then to the object of your supplication, with single-pointed focus, make a twenty-part mandala offering. With your palms folded, make the following supplication:

> O root and lineage gurus and the buddhas residing in the thousand doors, all of you endowed with limitless great compassion: Help me and all sentient beings equal to the extent of space that our two obscurations—afflictive obscuration and knowledge obscuration—may be purified along with their imprints. Likewise, may we, having perfected the two collections of wisdom and merit in the not too distant future—in fact, within this short human life of the degenerate age—attain the state of perfect buddhahood.

Make such a supplication fervently three times or more.

By virtue of supplicating in this way, streams of white nectar glowing with light descend from the bodies of the root and lineage gurus and the buddhas, enter your crown aperture, and absorb into the meditation deity together with the *ah* at your heart. Imagine that any pollution you may have in relation to them because of your wrong deeds is cleansed away and that they become potent in their transformative power and capacity. The streams of luminous white nectar flowing from them purifies the nonvirtue of your three doors and of the two obscurations along with their imprints and exits through your lower openings and through all your pores. Imagine [your impurities] disperse and vanish with no trace. This is a pith instruction on the practice of purifying your negative karma and obscurations containing the essential points of Vajrasattva meditation and recitation.

Next, imagine that you have become the Great Compassionate Jinasāgara, known also as Secret Attainment Avalokiteśvara, lord and consort, endowed with the two purities—your body's pure illusory body and your mind's pure ultimate clear light. [586] If you had earlier visualized the lineage gurus, at this point dissolve the root and lineage gurus into the meditation deity at your heart, and the thousand buddhas into the *ah* syllables on the thousand lotus petals. Imagine that the stupa also becomes no more, as if vanishing into the sky.

Next, as for the main instruction on how to visualize the meditation deity at your heart, visualize yourself as Avalokiteśvara Jinasāgara and visualize at your heart Khasarpāṇi, who is the indivisible nature of your guru and meditation deity. At his heart on a moon disc is a white *hrīḥ* marked by a blue *hūṃ*, which is encircled clockwise by the letters of the six syllables *Oṃ maṇi padme hūṃ*, all white in color. Focused on this mantra, repeat it as many times as you can.

As you recite the mantra, visualize that incalculable light beams radiate from it and that the worlds they touch are purified of all of their stains and faults on contact, turning them into Sukhāvatī pure lands. Again, imagine, at the tips of these beams of light are incalculable Avalokiteśvara bodies touching all sentient beings. Imagine at the crown of each sentient being sits an Avalokiteśvara from whom descends streams of nectar. Imagine that this purifies the two obscurations and their causes for beings in all six realms—hell beings, hungry ghosts, animals, humans, demigods, and gods—and places them in the state of the Great Compassionate One. Again, imagine, at the tips of all these incalculable beams of light are limitless offerings—water for drinking and washing, articles of everyday enjoyment, music, objects of the five senses, the seven royal emblems, and the eight auspicious symbols—which are offered to the buddhas and bodhisattvas residing in the myriad worlds of all ten directions. This invokes their compassion, and the blessing and power of their body, speech, and mind dissolve into the mantra and the syllable at the center of your heart. This gives rise to three embodiments—Khasarpāṇi at your heart, the embodiment of all meditation deities; Guru

Amitābha, the lord of buddha families who is the embodiment of all gurus; and the six-syllable mantra, the embodiment of all mantras. You also become endowed with the three perspectives—viewing whatever appears to your eyes as the body of the Great Compassionate One; whatever sound is heard by your ears as the sound of six-syllable mantra; and [587] whatever thoughts arise, good or bad, as the exalted mind of Guru Compassionate One, emptiness whose essence is compassion.

Meditating on your own mind as devoid of arising, the actual reality

This is presented in the line "*and meditate on your mind as devoid of arising.*" The meaning of this is explained in the following:

> **The lights from his heart draw forth the world, its inhabitants,**
> **my body, the lotus, the *ah* syllable, the mantra, and the seed syllable.**
> **Through reasoning that seeks the nature of my mind and all phenomena,**
> **their lack of arising as truly existent, I rest in meditative equipoise.**

Here, as in the tradition of highest yoga tantra, visualize yourself in the form of a royal prince adorned with ornaments. Inside your body, visualize the central channel stands erect, endowed with its three attributes.[1284] Inside this, at the level of the heart, visualize the meditation deity. Then, akin to the signs that will occur at the time of your death indicating the dissolution of the elements, apply the skillful outer and inner means, such as the process of subsequent dismantling. If you do this, your mind could soon arise as innate wisdom. So imagine your mind has entered the syllable *hūṃ*, and this *hūṃ* emits countless beams of light to the ten directions, touching the worlds and their inhabitants. Then imagine the worlds dissolve into the denizens, and the denizens dissolve into yourself in the form of Jinasāgara. At this point, imagine that the mirage-like sign appears, indicative of the earth dissolving into the water element. Next, as you dissolve into the lotus at your heart, imagine that the smoke-like sign appears, indicative of the water dissolving into the fire element. Next, as the lotus dissolves into the letter *ah*, imagine that the sign like fireflies appears, indicative of the fire dissolving into the wind element. Next, as the letter *ah* dissolves into the meditation deity, imagine that the sign like a glowing oil lamp appears, indicative of the dissolution of wind into the consciousness. Next, as the meditation deity dissolves into the moon disc at his heart, imagine the white appearance arises; when the moon disc dissolves into the mantra circle, the red increase arises; when it dissolves into the letter *hrīḥ*, the darkish near attainment arises; and when even this dissolves and becomes imperceptible, imagine that the all-empty clear light dawns.

At this point, searching via reasoning, such as with the negation of arising from the four possibilities as presented in the lines "Not from itself or from others. . . ,"[1285] establish that everything, including my own mind—from the body aggregate up to omniscience—is nothing but constructs posited by labels and terms, and that not even the tiniest atom exists objectively as truly existent on the part of the things themselves. [588] For if things were to arise from themselves, their arising would be endless and pointless. If, on the other hand, they were to arise from others, darkness could arise from flames and sprouts could arise from pebbles. If things were to arise from both self and others, pillars and vases could arise from things that are both pillars and vases. And if things were to arise from no cause, flowers could arise from the sky. When, after searching in this way, you find that things do not exist as conceived by the mind—that is, as not dependent on their designating thoughts—and you ascertain their nonexistence, rest your mind in equipoise in this very ascertainment, free of laxity and mental excitation.

Transference meditation, the essence of the practice for the time of death

This has four parts: offering your body of illusion as a feast, cutting the rope of mind's attachment, opening the great way to liberation, and shooting your consciousness upward.

Offering your body of illusion as a feast

The first is presented in the line "*Performing the rite of offering your body,*" which is explained in the following:

> **My mind as the deity comes out, separating my body and mind,**
> **and inside a skull cup set on a tripod atop fire and wind mandalas,**
> **my old body is purified, transformed, and multiplied,**
> **and its nectar is offered to the guests of both samsara and nirvana.**

Earlier, at the end of the subsequent dismantling, you meditated on the clear light, and when it was completed, the illustrative clear light of the fourth stage dawned. When you arise from such clear light, you arise as an impure illusory body—a body that occupies a spatial locus separate from your old body. In general, there are two ways in which an illusory body arises: *arising without* and *arising within*. If, in the first instant of clear light, you arise as the meditation deity inside your old body at your heart and then appear outside, this is *arising within*. Consonant with this, the moment you rise from your meditative equipoise, you arise at your heart in the form of Avalokiteśvara Khasarpāṇi about the size of a thumbnail.

Then, the second instant, as you exit your old body and observe it, imagine seeing it as huge, animated, attractive, and gleaming. Visualize in front of it, arising from a *yaṃ* syllable, a blue bow-shaped wind mandala. Atop this, arising from *raṃ*, is a triangular fire mandala, and on this is a tripod made of three human heads, each the size of Mount Meru. Imagine that your mind, as the meditation deity, severs the skull off your old body and places it atop the tripod. Inside this skull cup, which is as vast as the billionfold worlds, your body is placed and cut into pieces. [589] Then the fire is lit, and you imagine that [the pieces of your old body] melt and boil and beams of light radiate from this. They draw forth, in the form of blue light rays, the blessings of the heart of all the buddhas and bodhisattvas of the ten directions, which dissolve into the skull cup, purifying all faults. All the blessings of their speech in the form of red light rays dissolve into the skull cup, transforming the content into nectar. All the blessings of their mind in the form of blue light rays dissolve into the skull cup, enhancing the content such that, no matter how much is consumed, it is never exhausted. Imagine that the contents are transformed into longevity nectar of immortality, medicinal nectar of absence of illness, and gnosis nectar of absence of contamination.

Then visualize Guru Khasarpāṇi in front of you on a lotus and a moon disc atop a lion throne. At the level of his head are your root and lineage gurus, at the level of his heart are the meditation deities and buddhas, and at the level of his navel, in their respective order, are the bodhisattvas, pratyekabuddhas, śrāvakas, heroes and ḍākinīs, and Dharma protectors. They are your guests from the class of nirvana. On the ground below, imagine your samsaric guests, all sentient beings fully present, a teeming multitude. Then imagine that from the heart of the meditation deity, which is your own mind, countless ḍākinīs emanate holding skull cups, which they use to scoop up nectar as an offering to the exalted guests and as gifts to the unexalted guests [sentient beings]. Imagine that every guest is sated and that an extraordinary level of uncontaminated [gnosis of] bliss and emptiness arises in them. With the negative karma and obscurations of the unexalted guests purified, imagine they all transform into the Great Compassionate Avalokiteśvara and depart to their pure lands. Nectar sprinkles around the universe, transforming it into pure land.

Next, the element mandalas—wind, fire, and so forth—dissolve into the throne, the exalted guests dissolve one by one into the guru, and he in turn dissolves into you and thus blesses you. Bring to mind how the object *to whom* you are making the offering, the person *who* is doing the offering, and *what* is being offered all lack intrinsic existence, and in this way, seal all three spheres [of the act of offering] as imperceptible.

Cutting the rope of mind's attachment

This is presented in the line "*and having discarded all dependencies*," which is explained in the following:

> **Recalling impermanence, illusion, and emptiness,**
> **I sever the ties with my body, wealth, and loved ones,**

Recalling death and impermanence, contemplate how, despite your attachment to your body, you will have to discard it with no say on your part, [590] and then cut the rope tying [your mind] to the body. Though you may feel attached to your material resources, they are like the illusory horses and elephants conjured from magical substances and incantations. Thus you may pursue numerous strategies to accumulate wealth, but you do not even have much of a chance to enjoy it when you are living. And if this is true, what power do you have to bring even an atom's worth of your wealth with you when you die? Indeed, the negative consequences from accumulating your wealth through strong attachment and clinging, braving even disrepute—these you will definitely have to experience, for they are inseparable from you, like a body and its shadow. So contemplate, "What is the point of being attached to meaningless wealth, whose import is a conceptual fiction?"

When it comes to your attachment to family and friends, their appeal is also constructed by your mind, for not even an atom exists essentially, in its own right. Thus it's illogical to believe in their certainty. You hold them to be friends at present, but they have been your arch enemies in numerous lives, and the number of times they have attacked and even killed you is incalculable. An enemy can turn into a friend, and a friend can become an enemy. There is no certainty whatsoever. In any case, everyone will forsake everyone in the end, scattering, never to see or hear one other again. This is inevitable.

So contemplate, "What is the point of being attached?" and cut the rope tying [your mind] to all your family and friends. If you do not cut your ties, you will be like the bird trying to fly whose foot is tethered to a rock. This point is critical.

Opening the great way to liberation

This is presented in the line "*through the medium of a hollow light beam*," which is explained in the following:

> **And inside my body, at the heart inside the central channel,**
> **appears a Khasarpāṇi the size of a thumbnail.**
>
> **Maitreya, gold in color and seated in the *bhadra* posture,**
> **resides above in Tuṣita, in Yiga Chözin [courtyard].**
> **As I appeal to this savior, from his heart emerges**
> **a hollow light beam that pierces my crown.**

Visualize that inside your body, toward the center, is the central channel, blue outside, red inside, and endowed with the three attributes: it is (1) bright and translucent, (2) reddish and gleaming, and (3) straight and standing upright. It's about the size of a medium bamboo stick, and its lower part is closed like a snake tail. The channel starts to broaden about four finger-widths below your navel; its upper opening is flush with your crown aperture and wide open. Inside your central channel, at your heart, visualize a Khasarpāṇi the size of a thumbnail; he is the nature of your very subtle wind-mind. Then imagine that to the north, in the space above Mount Meru in the heavenly realm of Tuṣita, is Maitreya's residence, known as the Towering Banner. At this site is the place where Maitreya teaches, called Yiga Chözin (Joyous Mind, Upholding Dharma). [591] Imagine that Maitreya is present there, with his golden body and one face, his two hands in the gesture of turning the wheel of Dharma, and he is teaching his countless disciples. His face turned toward you, supplicate, "Pray bring me to the pure land of Tuṣita." As you make this appeal forcefully with fervent yearning, imagine that a hollow beam of yellow light emerges from Maitreya's heart and visibly pierces your crown.

Shooting your consciousness upward

This is presented in the line "*I'll send my mind to the Tuṣita realm*," which is explained in the following:

With the three thoughts, I am pulled from my topknot
by a hook and become fused inseparably with Maitreya's mind;
during training I return, and my crown aperture is sealed.
After death, may I be reborn like a new lotus flower in his presence.

As your mind, in the form of meditation deity, looks upward through the central channel, it sees clearly Maitreya's heart, resplendent like a gold mandala base wiped until shining. You develop three recognitions: (1) the hollow yellow beam as the path, (2) yourself traveling on that path, and (3) having traveled, your mind inseparably fused with Maitreya's heart. Once again, imagine that a red light shaped like a hook extends from Maitreya's heart through the hollow [yellow] beam and grabs your mind as meditation deity's topknot, pulling the deity upward. As you shout *hik!* you imagine that it becomes fused inseparably with Maitreya's heart. Then rest for a little while in bliss and emptiness.

While training in this, you should imagine bringing your mind as meditation deity back from Maitreya's heart, down to your own heart, and then shoot it back again. You can repeat this process seven or up to twenty-one times during a session. When concluding the session, bring it back to your own heart. Then imagine your central channel is filled with the yellow light from Maitreya's heart, and your crown aperture is sealed by a disc of light formed by swirling lines, enhancing your longevity.

At the time of death, imagine that even the hollow beam dissolves back into Maitreya's heart, and rest in equipoise on bliss and emptiness. This is the dharmakāya aspect of transference. Again, imagine from Maitreya's heart emerges a Khasarpāṇi, who dissolves into the hub of a thousand-petal lotus in front of Maitreya, making the lotus fold all its petals. This is the saṃbhogakāya aspect of transference. Again, beams of light emerge from Maitreya's heart, opening the petals of the lotus. Imagine you are reborn inside in the form of a heavenly child with a discerning intellect [592] who can see Maitreya and hear his Dharma teachings. This is the nirmāṇakāya aspect of transference.

The mixings, essence of the practice for the intermediate state

This is presented in the lines:

Recognizing this as the bardo itself
and transforming the outer, inner, and secret

> **through the yoga of emptiness and compassion,**
> **the wise connect to the new birth.**

These lines are explained in the following:

> **Imagining the perceptions at dying as those of the intermediate state,**
> **through wind, intention, and aspiration, I will recognize the bardo [as bardo],**
> **and I will view the world as a pure land, beings as deities,**
> **and all as devoid of true existence and illusion-like.**
>
> **Preventing attachment and aversion with emptiness and compassion,**
> **I will with pure perception take birth through my own will.**

Although it is not explicitly mentioned in the guide texts, to practice the mixings associated with the intermediate state (*bardo*), one way to measure your present capacity to recognize the bardo as the bardo is to recognize your dreams as dreams. For if you can recognize dreams as dreams [through practicing lucid dreaming], you will be able to recognize the bardo as the bardo and do the mixings. Without such a recognition, no such rounds of mixing can take place. So here is the method to recognize dreams as dreams.

On going to bed, make fervent supplications to your gurus and the Three Jewels to be able to recognize dreams as dreams. Just as you are on the threshold of sleep, set an intention to recognize your dreams as dreams. You could also try visualizing, on the hub of a red lotus at your throat, an *oṃ* syllable encircled by the letters of the mantra *anuttara*, the letters starting at the front and going clockwise. Rest your mind on this mantra and go to sleep. In this way, you could practice mixing the sleeping state with dharmakāya, the dreaming state with saṃbhogakāya, and the waking state with nirmāṇakāya.

The actual practice of the intermediate state is the following. Whatever appearances you have in general, and whatever appearances you experience at death in particular, view them as part of the intermediate state. Furthermore, fervently pray and supplicate that, through the power of wind yoga or through the power of your intention to recognize the bardo as the bardo, you may be able to recognize the intermediate state. By virtue of these, the bardo can be recognized as the bardo. When this occurs, *transformation of the outer* occurs when you meditate on the entire world as a perfect buddha realm; *transformation of the inner* occurs when you meditate on all sentient beings, the denizens, as the meditation deity Great Compassionate One; and *transformation of the secret* occurs when you contemplate that all of these are mere conceptual designations, with not even an atom possessing true existence.

When you can practice such rounds of mixing [593], you will be able to either transport yourself to your desired pure land or take rebirth in a bodily existence conducive to continuing on your path, such as a human existence of this degenerate age that allows you to attain buddhahood in a single lifetime. If you are about to take birth as a human being and gain a body composed of six elements, it is said that as you witness your future parents in copulation, if you are to take birth as a male, you will experience anger toward your father and attachment toward your mother. If, in contrast, you are to take birth as a female, you will experience anger toward your mother and attachment toward your father. At that point, then, you need to prevent the arising of attachment by recalling the emptiness of intrinsic existence and prevent the arising of anger by generating compassion.

Generally speaking, there are three distinct levels of meaning of the word *compassion*—the general meaning, the hidden meaning, and the ultimate meaning. *Compassion* at the level of general meaning refers to what we normally understand by it; at the level of hidden meaning *compassion* refers to the illustrative clear light of mind isolation; and at the level of ultimate meaning *compassion* refers to the actual clear light. Here, you prevent the arising of anger through compassion as understood in terms of the level of general meaning. Also you take rebirth through the perception of pure appearances, such as that of white Avalokiteśvara Jinasāgara and his red consort Guhyajñānā, and with the intention to bring about sentient beings' welfare.

Concluding summary

The concluding summary is presented in these lines:

> **Recognizing whatever appears is the key point of the view;**
> **remaining undistracted in this is the key point of meditation;**
> **fusing the tastes of thoughts is the key point of action.**
> **This is the instruction of the great siddha.**

These lines are explained in the following:

> **Endowed with the key points of view, meditation, and action,**
> **this is the flawless instruction of the great siddha Mitrayogi.**

This is the key point of the view: ensure that all your practices during meditative equipoise are held fast by the glue of the view [of emptiness] and negate the true existence of whatever appears to your mind by recognizing the object of negation. This is the key point of meditation: when ascertainment of the absence of true existence arises, cultivate familiarity with it, maintaining it free of mental laxity and excitation. And this is the key point of action: during post-equipoise, when the force of your ascertainment of emptiness weakens, recall your ascertainment of the absence of true existence and view all phenomena as the equal taste of emptiness. This [teaching] endowed with the key points of view, meditation, and action is an unmistaken instruction of Mitrayogi—a sublime master who has attained the small, medium, and great siddhis—transmitted through an uninterrupted lineage of excellent beings. [594]

The third, concluding activities, is twofold: dedicating the virtue and successfully completing the composition. The first is presented in the following:

> **Through the virtue of deeds such as these,**
> **may I be cared for in all lives by Guru Padmapāṇi,**
> **and by perfecting the practices of this life, death, and the bardo,**
> **may I become a glory to the teaching and all beings.**

The second, successfully completing the composition, is presented in the following:

> **This was written for disciples with the open eyes of intellect**
> **by Dharmabhadra, who takes the form of a monk.**
> **Through this virtue, may this instruction, the essence of sutras and tantras,**
> **never degenerate but flourish always in a hundred directions.**

The meaning of these lines is easy to understand, the teacher said.[1286]

Thus I say:

Son of Śuddhodana, Teacher of this hard-to-tame realm,
just as you emerged from among the saviors of the fortunate eons,
O Dharmabhadra, the lord of today's beings, it is certain
that you emerged from the sphere of buddhas' wisdom and
compassion.

The monsoon thunder of your boundless compassion
has stirred up the clouds of profound and vast teachings,
causing the rainfall of this instruction of the utmost essence
to nourish the shoots of aspirants' liberation—a great wonder.

Therefore this mirror reflecting the sacred words
of the great siddha in the format of a daily practice
I have inscribed with the thought that it may help myself and others.
May all beings be sustained by Ārya Avalokiteśvara.

Colophon

These notes on the Three Essential Points, entitled *A Mirror Reflecting the Mahāsiddha's Sacred Words*, were compiled from the profound guidance on the root text of this instruction as well as on the recitation verse by the most revered Dharmabhadra, the great Ngulchupa, who has attained the status of high learning and meditative realization and who stands out from among the assembly of great learned ones like the sun or moon among the heavenly constellations. The master gave this teaching to a large group of disciples on the third day of the third month (April 29, 1827) and during the waxing moon of the ninth month of the fire-pig year (October 23, 1827), and I, bearing the name Jedrung Tsering, who is counted among the community of his disciples, compiled these notes to help refresh my own memory and thinking it might benefit others whose knowledge is less advanced.

Table of Tibetan Transliteration

Akhu Sherab Gyatso	A khu Shes rab rgya mtsho
Amdo	A mdo
bardo	bar do
Baso Chökyi Gyaltsen	Ba so Chos kyi rgyal mtshan
Basowa	Ba so ba
Ben Gungyal	'Ban gung rgyal
Bönpo	Bon po
Butön Rinchen Drup	Bu ston Rin chen grub
Chamdo Jampa Ling	Chab mdo byams pa gling
Changkya Ngawang Chöden	Ngag dbang blo bzang chos ldan
Changkya Rölpai Dorjé	Can skya Rol pa'i rdo rje
Chapa Chökyi Sengé	Phywa pa Chos kyi seng ge
Chekawa Yeshé Dorjé	'Chad ka ba Ye shes rdo rje
Chenga Drakpa Jangchup	Spyan snga Blo gros rgyal mtshan
Chenga Lodrö Gyaltsen	Spyan snga Blo gros rgyal mtshan
Chenga Rinpoché Shönu Chöphel Sangpo	Spyan snga rin po che Gzhon nu chos 'phel bzang po
Chenga Sönam Gyaltsen	Spyan snga Bsod nams rgyal mtshan
Chenga Tsultrim Bar	Spyan snga Tshul khrim 'bar
Chim Jampaiyang	Mchims 'Jam pa'i dbyangs
Chökyi Drakpa	Chos kyi grags pa
Chökyi Gyaltsen	Chos kyi rgyal mtshan
Chöjé Döndrup Rinchen	Chos rje Don grub rin chen
Chongyé	'Phyongs rgyas
Chöpa Rinpoché Losang Tenpai Gyaltsen	Chos pa rin po che Blo bzang bstan pa'i rgyal mtshan
Chöphel Sangpo	Chos 'phel bzang po
Chusang Yeshé Gyatso	Chu bzang Ye shes rgya mtsho
Dakpo Lhajé	Dwags po Lha rje
Dakpo Rinpoché	Dwags po Rin po che
Dakpo Shedrup Ling	Dwags po bshad sgrub gling
Dakpo Tashi Namgyal	Dwags po Bkra shis rnam rgyal

Damchö Gyaltsen	Dam chos rgyal mtshan
Dampa Sangyé	Dam pa sangs rgyas
Dedruk Khenchen Ngawang Rabten	Sde drug mkhan chen Ngag dbang rab brtan
Densa Chenpo Sum	Gdan sa chen po gsum
Dergé	Sde dge
Desi Sangyé Gyatso	Sde srid Sangs rgya mtsho
Dingri	Ding ri
Döndrup Wangyal	Don grub dbang rgyal
Dragor Khenchen	Grwa gor mkhan chen
Drakar Losang Palden	Brag dkar Blo bzang dpal ldan
Drakpa Gyaltsen	Grags pa rgyal mtshan
Drakpa Jangchup	Grags pa byang chub
Drati Rinchen Döndrup	Bra ti Rin chen don grub
Drepung	'Bras spung
Drepung Parma	'Bras spung par ma
Drigung Chökyi Gyalpo	'Bri gung Chos kyi rgyal po
Drigungpa	'Bri gung pa
Drogön Chögyal Phakpa	'Gro mgon Chos rgyal 'phags pa
Drogön Phakmo Drupa	'Gro mgon Phag mo gru pa
Drogön Rinpoché	'Gro mgon Rin po che
Drokmi Lotsāwa Shākya Yeshé	'Drog mi lo tsā ba Shākya ye shes
Drolungpa	Gro lung pa
Dromtönpa	'Brom ston pa
Drongmepa Trinlé Gyatso	Grong smad pa 'Phrin las rgya mtsho
Drupai Gyaltsen Dzinpa	Sgrub pa'i Rgyal mtshan 'dzin pa
Drupchen Rinpoché	Sgrub chen rin po che
Drupwang Jampal Gyatso	Grub dbang 'Jam dpal rgya mtsho
Drupwang Losang Namgyal	Grub dbang Blo bzang rnam rgyal
Dulnakpa Palden Sangpo	'Dul nag pa Dpal ldan bzang po
É	E
Ensa	Dben sa
Ensa Losang Döndrup	Dben sa Blo bzang don grub
Ensapa	Dben sa pa
Gampopa Sönam Rinchen	Gam po pa Bsod nams rin chen
Ganden	Dga' ldan
Ganden Lophel	Dga' ldan blo 'phel
Ganden Tripa	Dga' ldan khri pa
Geden	Dge ldan
Geden Nampar Gyalwai Ling	Dge ldan rnam par rgyal ba gling
Gelek Gyatso	Dge legs rgya mtsho
Gelek Palsang	Dge legs dpal bzang
Geluk	Dge lugs

Gendun Chöden	Dge 'dun chos ldan
Gendun Chöphel	Dge 'dun chos 'phel
Gendun Drup	Dge 'dun grub
Gendun Gyaltsen	Dge 'dun rgyal mtshan
Gendun Gyatso	Dge 'dun rgya mtsho
Gendun Jamyang	Dge 'dun 'jam dbyangs
Gephel	Dge 'phel
geshé lharampa	dge bshes lha rams pa
Geshé Tsultrim Namgyal	Dge bshes Tshul khrim rnam rgyal
Gö Khukpa Lhetsé	'Gos Khug pa lhas btsas
Gö Lotsāwa Shönu Pal	'Gos lo tsā ba Gzhon nu dpal
Gomchen Ngawang Drakpa	Sgom chen Ngag dbang grags pa
Gomchen Ngaki Wangpo	Sgom chen Ngag gi dbang po
Götsangpa Gönpo Dorjé	Rgod tshang pa Mgon po rdo rje
Gugé Yongzin Losang Tenzin	Gu ge yongs 'dzin Blo bzang bstan 'dzin
Gungru Gyaltsen Sangpo	Gung ru Rgyal mtshan bzang po
Gungthang Tenpai Drönmé	Gung thang Bstan pa'i sgron me
Guru Yongzin Rinpoché	Bla ma yongs 'dzin Rin po che
Gyalrong Tsultrim Nyima	Rgyal rong Tshul khrims nyi ma
Gyaltsab Rinpoché	Rgyal tshab Rin po che
Gyalwa Ensapa	Rgyal ba dben sa pa
Gyasok Phu	Rgya sog phu
Gyüchen Könchok Gyaltsen	Rgyud chen Dkon mchog rgyal mtshan
Gyüchen Könchok Yarphel	Rgyud chen Dkon mchog yar 'phel
Gyüchen Kunga Döndrup	Rgyud chen Kun dga' don grub
Gyümé	Rgyud smad
Gyütö	Rgyud stod
Hamdong Sherab Sengé	Ha gdong Shes rab seng ge
Jadral Tsultrim Nyima	Bya bral Tshul khrims nyi ma
jadrelwa	bya bral ba
Jamchen Chöjé	Byams chen chos rje
Jamgön Guru	'Jam mgon bla ma
Jampa Rinchen	Byams pa rin chen
Jampa Tenzin Trinlé	Byams pa bstan 'dzin 'phrin las
Jampal Ngawang Losang Yeshé	'Jam dpal ngag dbang blo bzang ye shes
Jampalyang	'Jam dpal dbyangs
Jamyang Chöjé Tashi Palden	'Jam dbyangs chos rje Bkra shis dpal ldan
Jamyang Dewai Dorjé	'Jam dbyangs bde ba'i rdo rje
Jamyang Gawai Lodrö	'Jam dbyangs dga' ba'i blo gros
Jamyang Gawai Shenyen	'Jam dbyangs dga' ba'i bshes gnyen
Jamyang Shepa Könchok Jikmé Wangpo	'Jam dbyangs bzhad pa Dkon mchog 'jigs med dbang po

Jamyang Shepa Ngawang Tsöndrü	'Jam dbyangs bzhad pa Ngag dbang brtson 'grus
Jamyang Tenpai Nyima	'Jam dbyangs bstan pa'i nyi ma
Jang Dharma	Byang dar ma
Jangchup Ö	Byang chub 'od
Jangtsé	Byang rtse
Jaya Pandita Huthokthu	Dza ya pandita hu tog thu
Jé Lodrö Tenpa	Rje Blo gros brtan pa
Jé Rinpoché	Rje Rin po che
Jé Sherab Sengé	Rje Shes rab seng ge
Jedrung Tsering	Rje drung tshe ring
Jetsun Chökyi Gyaltsen	Rje btsun Chos kyi rgyal mtshan
Jetsun Milarepa	Rje btsun Mi la ras pa
Jetsun Rendawa	Rje btsun Red mda' ba
Jetsun Sherab Sengé	Rje btsun Shes rab sen ge
Jikmé Damchö Gyatso	'Jigs med dam chos rgya mtsho
Jikmé Wangpo	'Jigs med dbang po
Jikten Gönpo	'Jig rten mgon po
Jokhang	Jo khang
Kachu Losang Chöwang	Bka' bcu Blo bzang chos dbang
Kadampa	Bka' gdams pa
Kagyü	Bka' brgyud
Kalsang Tenzin Khedrup	Skal bzang bstan 'dzin mkhas grub
Kangyur	Bka' 'gyur
Karmapa Mikyö Dorjé	Karma pa Mi bskyod rdo rje
Keutsang Jamyang Mönlam	Ke'u tshang 'Jam dbyangs smon lam
Khalkha Damtsik Dorjé	Khal kha Dam tshigs rdo rje
Khalkha Dzaya Paṇḍita	Khal kha Dza ya Paṇḍita
Khalkha Yön	Khal kha yon
Kham	Khams
Khedrup Jé	Mkhas grub Rje
Khedrup Ngawang Dorjé	Mkhas grub Ngag dbang rdo rje
Khedrup Norsang Gyatso	Mkhas grub Nor bzang rgya mtsho
Khedrup Sangyé Yeshé	Mkhas grub Sangs rgyas ye shes
Khedrup Sherab Sengé	Mkhas grub Shes rab seng ge
Khedrup Tenpa Dargyé	Mkhas grub Bstan pa dar rgyas
Khedrup Tenzin Tsöndrü	Mkhas grub Bstan 'dzin brtson 'grus
Khenchen Khyenrab Tenpa Chöphel	Mkhan chen Mkhyen rab bstan pa chos 'phel
Khöntön Paljor Lhundrup	'Khon ston Dpal 'byor lhun grub
Khyenrab Tenpa Chöphel	Mkyen rab Bstan pa chos 'phel
Khyungpo Lhepa Shönu Sönam	Khyung po lhas pa Gzhon nu bsod nams
Khyungpo Naljor	Khyung po rnal 'byor

Kirti Losang Trinlé	Kirti Blo bzang 'phrin las
Könchok Chöphel	Dkon mchog chos 'phel
Könchok Gyaltsen	Dkon mchog rgyal mtshan
Könchok Jikmé Wangpo	Dkon mchog 'jigs med dbang po
Könchok Tsultrim	Dkon mchog tshul khrims
Könchok Yarphel	Dkon mchog yar 'phel
Kunga Gyaltsen	Kun dga' rgyal mtshan
Kunsang	Kun bzang
Kyabjé Ling Rinpoché	Skyabs rje Gling rin po che
Kyabjé Trijang Rinpoché	Skyabs rje Khri byang rin po che
Kyabjé Zong Rinpoché	Skyabs rje Zong rin po che
Labrang Tashi Khyil	Bla brang bkra shis 'khyil
ladrup	bla sgrub
Lama Shang	Bla ma Zhang
Lama Tokdenpa	Bla ma Rtogs dlan pa
Lama Umapa	Bla ma Dbu ma pa
Lamchung	Lam chung
lamrim	lam rim
Lhasik Repa	Lha gzigs ras pa
Lhatsé Yeshé Tenzin	Lha rtse Ye shes bstan 'dzin
Lhodrak Drupchen Namkha Gyaltsen	Lho brag grub chen Nam mkha' rgyal mtshan
Lhokha	Lho kha
Lingrepa Pema Dorjé	Gling ras pa Pad ma rdo rje
Lodrö Bepa	Blo gros sbas pa
lojong	blo sbyong
Losang Döndrup	Blo bzang don grub
Losang Dönyö Drupa	Blo bzang don yod grub pa
Losang Drakpai Pal	Blo bzang grags pa'i dpal
Losang Lungtok Namgyal Trinlé	Blo bzang lung rtogs rnam rgyal 'phrin las
Losang Namgyal	Blo bzang rnam rgyal
Losang Phuntsok	Blo bzang phun tshogs
Losang Tamdrin	Blo bzang rta mgrin
Losang Tenpai Gyaltsen	Blo bzang bstan pa'i rgyal mtshan
Losang Trinlé	Blo bzang 'phrin las
Losang Tsewang	Blo bzang tshe dbang
Losang Tsöndrü Gyaltsen	Blo bzang brtson 'grus rgyal mtshan
Luphu	Lu phu
Machik Labdrön	Ma gcig lab sgron
Marpa Lotsāwa	Mar pa Lo tsā ba
Martön Chökyi Lodrö	Mar ston Chos kyi blo gros
Miktsema	Dmigs brtse ma
Milarepa	Mi la ras pa

Miruk Phuntsok Ling	Rmi rug phun tshog gling
Miwang Drakpa Gyaltsen	Mi dbang Grags pa rgyal mtshan
Mönlam Palwa	Smon lam dpal ba
Namkha Bum	Nam mkha' 'bum
Namkha Palsang	Nam mkha' dpal bzang
Nangso Losang Tsöndrü	Nang so Blo bzang brtson 'grus
Nangzé Dorjé	Snang mdzad rdo rje
Narthang	Snar thang
Neusurpa	Sne'u zur pa
Ngari	Mnga' ris
Ngawang Chöphel	Ngag dbang chos 'phel
Ngawang Drakpa	Ngag dbang grags pa
Ngawang Jampa	Ngag dbang byams pa
Ngawang Losang Gyatso	Ngag dbang blo bzang rgya mstho
Jikmé Gocha Thupten Langtsödé	'Jigs med go cha thub bstan lang 'tsho'i sde
Ngawang Palden	Ngag dbang dpal ldan
Ngödrup Rabten	Dngos grub rab brtan
Ngulchu Dharmabhadra	Dngul chu Dha rma bha dra
Nyangtö	Myang stod
nyengyü	snyan brgyud
Nyingmapa	Rnying ma pa
Ölkha Chölung	'Ol kha chos lung
Palden Drepung	Dpal ldan 'bras spungs
Paljor Trinlé Rabgyé	Dpal 'byor 'phrin las rab rgyas
Palkhor Dechen	Dpal 'khor bde chen
Palmang Könchok Gyaltsen	Dpal/dbal mang Dkon mchog rgyal mtshan
Panchen Losang Chögyen	Paṇ chen Blo bzang chos rgyan
Panchen Losang Chökyi Gyaltsen	Paṇ chen Blo bzang chos kyi rgyal mtshan
Panchen Losang Yeshé	Pan chen Blo bzang ye shes
Panchen Palden Yeshé	Paṇ chen Dpal ldan ye shes
Panchen Sangpo Tashi	Paṇ chen Bzang po bkra shis
Panchen Sönam Drakpa	Paṇ chen Bsod nams grags pa
Pang Lotsāwa Lodrö Tenpa	Dpang lo tsā ba Blo gros bstan pa
Pawo Dorjé	Dpa' bo rdo rje
Pehar	Pe har
Phabongkha Dechen Nyingpo	Pha bong kha Bde chen snying po
Phabongkha Jampa Tenzin Trinlé Gyatso	Pha bong kha Byams pa bstan 'dzin 'phrin las rgya mtsho
Phabongkha Rinpoché	Pha bong kha Rin po che
Phakdru Dorjé Gyalpo	Phag gru Rdo rje rgyal po

Phakdru Kagyü	Phag gru bka' brgyud
Phakmo Drupa	Phag mo gru pa
Phara Bodhisattva	Pha ra byang chub sems dpa'
Phuchungwa Shönu Gyaltsen	Phu chung ba Gzhon nu rgyal mtshan
Phurchok Lama Jampa	Phur lcog bla ma Byams pa
Phurchok Ngawang Jampa	Phur lcog Ngag dbang byams pa
Potowa Rinchen Sal	Po to ba Rin chen gsal
Rabjampa Gendun Gyatso	Rab 'byams pa Dge 'dun rgya mtsho
Radreng (Reting)	Rwa sgreng
Rendawa	Red mda' ba
Riwo Gedenpa	Ri bo dge ldan pa
Rongpo Chöjé	Rong po chos rje
Ruthu Sheyé Gung Gyaltsen	Ru thu She ye gung rgyal mtshan
Sahor	Za hor
Sakya Paṇḍita Kunga Gyaltsen	Sa skya Paṇḍi ta Kun dga' rgyal mtshan
Samlo	Bsam blo
Sangyé Yeshé	Sangs rgyas ye shes
Sapaṇ	Sa paṇ
Sé	Srad
Sé Chilbu	Se Spyil bu
Sedong	Ze gdong
Segyü	Sras brgyud
Sera	Se rwa
Serlingpa	Gser gling pa
Shalu	Zhwa lu
Shamar Gendun Tenzin	Zha dmar Dge 'dun bstan 'dzin
Shang Rinpoché	Zhang Rin po che
Shangpa Kagyü	Shangs pa bka' brgyud
Shar Kalden Gyatso	Shar Skal ldan rgya mtsho
Sharawa	Sha ra ba
Sherab Sangpo	Shes rab bzang po
Sherab Sengé	Shes rab seng ge
Shok Dönyö Khedrup	Zhog Don yod mkhas grub
Sönam Chokkyi Langpo	Bsod nams phyogs kyi glang po
Sönam Gyatso	Bsod rnam rgya mtsho
Sönam Palsang	Bsod nams dpal bzang
Surchen Chöying Rangdröl	Zur chen Chos dbyings rang grol
Ta-Lama Erteni Darhan-shi Rege-thu Losang Sönam	Tā bla ma erteni dar han shi Rve ge thu blo bzang rnam rgyal
Taklung Drakpa Lodrö Gyatso	Stag lung Grags pa blo gros rgya mtsho
Taklungpa	Stag lung pa
Takphu Tenpai Gyaltsen	Stag phu Bstan pa'i rgyal mtshan
Taktsang Lotsāwa	Stag tshang Lo tsā ba
Taphukpa Damchö Gyaltsen	Rta phug pa Dam chos rgyal mtshan

Tashi Lhunpo	Bkra shis lhun po
Tendar Lharam	Bstan dar lha rams
Tengyur	Bstan 'gyur
Tenpai Drönmé	Bstan pa'i sgron me
Tenpai Nyima	Bstan pa'i nyi ma
tenrim	bstan rim
Tenzin Gyatso	Bstan 'dzin rgya mtsho
Thangsakpa Ngödrup Gyatso	Thag sag pa Dngos grub rgya mtsho
Thösam Gyatso	Thos bsam rgya mtsho
Thöyön Jamyang Trinlé	Tho yon Byams dbyangs 'phrin las
Thöyön Yeshé Döndrup	Tho yon Ye shes don grub
Thuken Chökyi Nyima	Thu'u kwan Chos kyi nyi ma
togak	stod 'gag
Tokden Jampal Gyatso	Rtogs ldan 'Jam dpal rgya mtsho
tonglen	gtong len
torma	gtor ma
Trichen Ngawang Chokden	Khri chen Ngag dbang mchog ldan
Trichen Tenpa Rabgyé	Khri chen Bstan pa rab rgyas
Trinlé Gyatso	'Phrin las rgya mtsho
Trophu Lotsāwa Jampa Pal	Khro phu lo tsā ba Byams pa dpal
Trum	Grum
Tsakho	Tsha kho
Tsal Gungthang	Tshal gung thang
Tsang	Gtsang
Tsangnyön Heruka	Gtsang smyon Heruka
Tsangpa Gyaré Yeshé Dorjé	Gtsang pa rgya ras Ye shes rdo rje
Tsechok Ling	Tshe mchog gling
tsok	tsogs
Tsongkhapa	Tsong kha pa
Tsultrim Gyalwa	Tshul khrims rgyal ba
Tsultrim Gyatso	Tshul khrims rgya mtsho
tumo	tum mo
Umapa Pawo Dorjé	Dbu ma pa Dpa' bo rdo rje
Wangkur	Dbang skur
Wön Gyalsé Jikmé Yeshé Drakpa	'On rgyal sras 'Jigs med ye shes grags pa
Yangchen Drupai Dorjé	Dbyangs can Grub pa'i rdo rje
Yangchen Gawai Lodrö	Dbyangs can Dga' ba'i blo gros
Yangönpa Gyaltsen Pal	Yang dgon pa Rgyal mtshan dpal
Yeshé Döndrup Tenpai Gyaltsen	Ye shes don grub bstan pa'i rgyal mtshan
Yeshé Tenzin	Ye shes bstan 'dzin
Yeshé Tsöndrü	Ye shes brtson 'grus
Yiga Chözin	Yid dga' chos 'dzin

Yongzin Yeshé Gyaltsen	Yongs 'dzin Ye shes rgyal mtshan
yungdrung	gyung drung

Notes

1. *Rje tsong kha pa'i bka' srol.* The first recorded use of this phrase or its variations is found in Khedrup Jé's writings, especially in his *Miscellaneous Writings.*
2. On Tsongkhapa's special relationship with this Tibetan ruler, whose full name is Miwang Drakpa Gyaltsen (r. 1385–1432), see Jinpa, *Tsongkhapa*, 65–67.
3. *'Jam mgon rgyal ba gnyis pa tsong kha pa chen po, Shar rgyal ba tsong kha pa chen po, Khams gsum chos kyi rgyal po tsong kha pa chen po, Rje tsong kha pa chen po*, and *Rje bla ma.*
4. On this deification of Tsongkhapa, see chapter 15 of Jinpa, *Tsongkhapa.*
5. In noting Tsongkhapa's unique role in the flourishing of the Guhyasamāja tantra in Tibet, the author of the influential historical work, the *Blue Annals* (1:44), writes: "The latter [Tsongkhapa] made, in general, great contributions to the Buddha's doctrine, and in particular, it was Tsongkhapa who made Guhyasamāja spread across the entire face of the earth."
6. Jinpa, *Tsongkhapa*, 360.
7. Biographies and translations of selected writings from these three Mongol Buddhist masters can be found in Wallace, *Sources of Mongolian Buddhism.*
8. For a translation of this text, see Dalai Lama, *Lighting the Way.*
9. Tsongkhapa states that the terminology of "three types of persons" predates Atiśa and can be found, for example, in Asaṅga's *Compendium of Ascertainments* (*Viniścayasaṃgraha*) and Vasubandhu's *Treasury of Abhidharma Autocommentary*; see Tsongkhapa, *Great Treatise* (trans.), 1:131.
10. More on this distinction, historical introduction to lamrim literature, and list of key texts, see David Seyfort Ruegg's introduction to Tsongkhapa, *Great Treatise*, and my own introduction in Jinpa, *Book of Kadam.*
11. For an English translation of the former, see Roesler, *Blue Compendium.* The latter has not been published in English translation.
12. For example, in the *Great Treatise* (trans., 1:180), Tsongkhapa introduces the framework of the three types of persons in terms of two important headings: "How all scriptural teachings are included within the paths of the three types of persons" and "Why the trainee is led in a graduated sequence through the paths of the three types of persons."
13. Tsongkhapa, *Brief Presentation on the Stages of the Path*, 238.
14. For an alternate translation, see Tsongkhapa, *Great Treatise* (trans.), 1:139.
15. *Bstan pa spyi'i khog shes pa* and *lam gyi lus yongs su rdzogs pa mthong ba. A Few Words on the Structure of the Path*, 261.

16. For an account of Tsongkhapa's writing of the *Great Treatise* and its scope and structure, see chapter 9 of Jinpa, *Tsongkhapa*, especially 198–206.
17. For a slightly different rendering, see Tsongkhapa, *Great Treatise* (trans.), 1:35.
18. Tsongkhapa, *Opening the Excellent Door to the Path*, 1–4. These prayers consist of making supplications to the lineage masters of (1) vast practice, (2) profound view, (3) the Kadam "textual tradition" (*gzhung pa*), and (4) Kadam "instruction tradition" (*gdams ngag pa*).
19. Variously *Lam rim 'bring* or *Lam rim chung ba*. For a complete English translation by Philip Quarcoo, see Tsongkhapa, *Middle-Length Treatise*.
20. The Third Dalai Lama's text is, in fact, an exposition Tsongkhapa's *Song of Spiritual Experience*, and an English translation of the text by Glenn Mullin is contained in Sonam Gyatso, *Selected Works of Dalai Lama III*.
21. *Byang chub lam gyi rim pa las byung ba'i nyams len gyi sgo rnam par nges pa*.
22. Jamyang Shepa, *Great Treatise on Meditative Absorptions and Formless States*, 100b6.
23. For more detail on Gomchen and his text, see notes 38 and 39.
24. Yongzin, *Biographies*, 556. In English, see Willis, *Enlightened Beings*, 96
25. See page 206 below.
26. "*Dzi na 'jam dpal rgya mtsho la/ lam rim gyi zhal shes sngags dang 'brel ba'i byin rlabs nye brgyud kyi man ngag gnang ba ste bde lam du grags pa de yin/*." Yeshé Döndrup, *Entryway to the Ocean of Pure Faith*, 303.
27. The Tibetan titles of these texts are, respectively, *Lam rim dmar khrid myur lam*, *Byang chub bde lam gyi dmigs skor cha tshang bar tshigs bcad du bsdebs pa lam mchog snying po*, *Bde lam gyi zhal shes*, and *Byang chub bde lam gyi khrid dmigs skyong tshul shin tu gsal bar bkod pa*.
28. This indicates that the Fifth Dalai Lama himself was, at the time of writing, unaware of Panchen's *Easy Path*, which suggests that either Panchen's text appeared after the Fifth's *Sacred Words* or that it was then not yet well known. Interestingly, the Fifth Dalai Lama does not include Panchen, who was in fact one of his teachers, among the masters from whom he received the transmission on the lamrim. In acknowledging the source of his lamrim teachings, the Fifth Dalai Lama writes in his colophon: "having first correctly received through the kindness of Jamyang Lama the faultless oral instructions of the Dharma king Khöntön, the great, omniscient and incomparable master of all the Conqueror's words in the degenerate age, and also received a profound explanation of every single word of the *Great Treatise on the Stages of the Path to Enlightenment* twice from the skilled orator and lord of speech, the venerable guru Könchok Chöphel." My initial assumption was that the phrase "Jamyang Lama" above referred to Khöntön and that the author was acknowledging two masters here: Khöntön and Könchok Chöphel. Rosemary Patton and Dagpo Rinpoché, however, the translators of this work in the present volume, identify "Jamyang Lama" with Paljor Trinlé Rabgyé, a.k.a. Surchen Chöying Rangdröl, and they also find a gloss on this master's name in the opening salutation verses. Judging by the Fifth Dalai Lama's *Stream of the River Ganges: A Record of Teachings Received* (39a1), indeed it was through Paljor Trinlé Rabgyé that the fifth Dalai Lama received the lamrim as well as the Kadam mind-training transmissions that came through Khöntön.

29. Skt. *antaraśloka*; Tib. *bar skabs kyi tshigs bcad.*
30. See pages 355–69.
31. A catalogue of texts at Labrang Monastery published in 1985 entitled *Mirror of Stainless Crystal* (*Dri med shel dkar me long*, pp. 625–30) contains a list of over one hundred individual lamrim texts. Pretty much every generation produced new lamrim texts, the most well known in our present generation being the two-volume work *Illuminating the Conqueror's Intent* (*Rgyal ba'i dgongs gsal*), based on the Fourteenth Dalai Lama's lamrim teachings, the second volume of which contains an extensive annotation on the Fifth Dalai Lama's *Words of Mañjuśrī.* The Tibetan titles of the texts listed here are (1) *Lam rim bsdus don* and *Lam rim khriḍ yig gzhan phan bdud rtsi'i snying po*, (2) *Lam rim snying po nyams su len tshul*, (3) *Skyes bu gsum gyi lam rim gyi khrid dngos grub kun 'byung*, (4) *Byang chub lam gyi rim pa'i khrid tshigs su bcad pa* and *Byang chub lam gyi sgron ma'i rnam bshad phul byung*, (5) *Lam gtso rnam gsum gyi dgongs 'grel lung rigs kyi gter mdzod*, (6) *Byang chub lam gyi rim pa'i gdams pa tshigs su bcad pa kun mkhyen bde lam*, (7) *Byang chub lam gyi rim pa'i dmar khrid 'jam dpal zhal lung gi snying po bsdus pa'i nyams su len tshul khyer bde bla ma'i gsung rgyun*, (8) *Lam gyi gtso bo rnam gsum gyi rnam bshad gsung rab kun gyi gnad bsdus pa legs bshad snying po*, (9) *Byang chub lam gyi rim pa'i khrid nyams su len tshul khyer bde gnad don kun gsal*, (10) *Byang chub lam gyi rim pa'i dmar khrid 'jam dpal zhal lung gi khrid rgyun bsdus pa lho brgyud du grags pa*, (11) *Byang chub lam gyi rim pa'i dmar khrid gzhan phan bdud rtsi'i bum pa*, (12) *Lam rim dam chos bdud rtsi'i snying po*, (13) *Lam rim chen mo'i sa bcad kyi thog nas skyes bu gsum gyi lam gyi rim pa'i man ngag gnad bsdus gsal ba'i sgron me*, (14) *Lam rim bde lam gyi khrid dmigs skyong tshul shin tu gsal bar bkod pa dge legs 'od snang 'byed pa'i nyin byed*, (15) *Lam gyi rim pa'i dmigs rnam skyong tshul bde lam dang myur lam 'jam dpal zhal lung las byung ba'i man nnag zab mo yon tan rin chen bdus don*, (16) *Byang chub lam gyi rim pa kun phan bdud rtsi'i chu rgyun*, (17) *Lam rim rnam grol lag bcangs*, and (18) *Byang chub lam gyi rim pa'i gdams pa'i gnad don tshigs su bcad pa legs gsung bdud rtsi'i snying po.*
32. As its title indicates, this text is a succinct guide on the Fifth Dalai Lama's *Words of Mañjuśrī.* Its transmission came to be known as the "Amdo transmission of *Words of Mañjuśrī*" (*Smad brgyud 'jam dpal zhal lung*).
33. The word "southern" (*lho*) in the epithet "southern transmission" (*lho brgyud*) refers to the Dakpo region, which lies southeast of Lhasa; the transmission being referred to is a unique guide to the lamrim based on the Fifth Dalai Lama's *Words of Mañjuśrī.* Up to the compilation of this text, this guide remained an oral tradition. The account of how this *Southern Transmission Lamrim* relates to the Fifth's *Words* as well as brief biographies of the key masters of this transmission is found in Chökyi Dorjé, *Golden Rosary.*
34. This lengthy lamrim guidebook was scribed by Kyabjé Trijang Rinpoché (1901–81) based on an extensive oral teaching conducted by Phabongkha Rinpoché and is available in two distinct translations in English.
35. *Lam rim mchan bzhi bsgrags.* This work contains the entire text of Tsongkhapa's *Great Treatise* with annotations by four authoritative masters inserted in relevant sections and marked with first letter of the author's name. The four masters are (1) Baso Chökyi Gyaltsen, (2) Taklung Drakpa Lodrö Gyatso (1546–1618) as scribed

by Dedruk Khenchen Ngawang Rabten (seventeenth century), (3) Jamyang Shepa Ngawang Tsöndrü, and (4) Drati Rinchen Döndrup (seventeenth century).
36. *Byang chub lam gyi rim pa chen po las byung ba'i brda dkrol nyer mkho bsdus pa.*
37. *Lhag mthong chen mo'i dka' gnad rnams brjed byang du bkod pa.*
38. According to the catalogue of the *Four Interwoven Annotations* (3b6), the first version of the text was printed at Tsechok Ling Monastery in 1802 "to realize the aspiration of Yongzin Yeshé Gyaltsen." This original edition later underwent careful revision by Minyak Geshé Tsultrim Namgyal (nineteenth century), correcting numerous errors based on comparative study of some eleven texts of various interlinear annotations on Tsongkhapa's *Great Treatise*—single annotation, two annotations, three annotations, and four annotations. This revised edited version was printed at Tsechok Ling Monastery in 1842 and has since formed the basis for all subsequent printings.
39. An English translation of the latter text together with Tsongkhapa's commentary is available under the title *The Fulfillment of All Hopes: Guru Devotion in Tibetan Buddhism*, translated by Gareth Sparham.
40. A global search on Tengyur at https://www.istb.univie.ac.at/kanjur/rktsneu/etanjur/ revealed only three instances of the term *bla ma'i rnal 'byor* (guru yoga) in the entire collection.
41. Though not found in Dergé edition of the canon, the section on tantra in the Narthang Tengyur, vol. *yu*, contains three texts on cultivating the outer, inner, and secret aspects of the guru attributed, respectively, to Tilopa, Nāropa, and Nāgārjuna. All three texts indicate Vibhūticandra as their translator. The Mongolian scholar Losang Tamdrin's (1867–1937) writings (Collected Works, vol. *ka*, 359–87) contain a lucid commentary on Tilopa's text.
42. Yongzin Yeshé Gyaltsen, as quoted in Losang Tamdrin, *Exposition of Mahāsiddha Tilopa's Instruction on Cultivating the Guru*, 385.
43. A well-known verse, embedded in the Seventh Dalai Lama's commentary on page 406 below, chanted at the end of the *Hundreds of Gods of Tuṣita* guru yoga. Most probably, the stanza is adapted from the opening verse of the lineage prayer in Lingrepa's (1128–88) *Offering to the Guru*, 1b4. In Lingrepa's text, the last three lines read: "reside upon the stamen of my lotus heart, / inseparably and constantly, and / grant me blessings of your body, speech, and mind."
44. Handing over Segyü Monastery to Dulnakpa, Sherab Sengé left for Central Tibet, where he founded Gyümé Tantric College in 1433; later, in 1475, Gyüchen Kunga Döndrup (1419–86) founded Gyütö Tantric College.
45. The prayer, minus line 3, was originally composed by Tsongkhapa himself as a praise to his principal teacher, Rendawa. The latter, however, remarked that it was more suited to Tsongkhapa himself and gave it back by addressing the final line to Tsongkhapa instead. Since then, Tsongkhapa's disciples adopted this verse as the key prayer of supplication to their master. The third line was added so that he could be viewed as the embodiment of all three attributes of the enlightened mind: compassion, wisdom, and power.
46. These two versions of nine-lined Miktsema, according to the Segyü and Ensa lineages, are found in various Geluk guide texts on the *Hundreds of Gods of Tuṣita*, such as Phabongkha Dechen Nyingpo's *How to Practice the Profound Path of the*

Hundreds of Gods of Tuṣita Guru Yoga, 13a1. The earliest textual source for these five-lined, six-lined, and nine-lined Miktsema I have found is Drupwang Jampal Gyatso's (1682–1741) *Garland of Wish-Granting Jewels*, where he states (23b1), "Furthermore, there are also oral traditions of the Miktsema in five, six, and nine lines."

47. *A Very Profound Practice Cultivating the Inseparability of the Guru and Meditation Deity*, this text is found in vol. *dza*, the final volume of Tsongkhapa's collected works in nineteen volumes. On receiving the four empowerments in the form of a blessing, see page 548.
48. *Uniquely Profound Guru Yoga Conferred by the Great Dharma King Tsongkhapa to the Omniscient Khedrup in a One-to-One Transmission*, 150.
49. In the instruction compiled by Baso, however, the supplications come after you receive the four empowerments. Furthermore, that text contains an explicit instruction on visualizing your mind in the form of syllable *dhīḥ* on a red eight-petaled lotus inside the central channel and then making supplications to the guru, who is imagined at your crown.
50. Tsongkhapa, *A Unique Practice Cultivating Mañjuśrī That Combines His Peaceful and Wrathful Aspects*, 330.
51. I had the good fortune to be able to do such a retreat at Ganden Monastery when I was a monk.
52. Panchen Palden Yeshé's (1738–80) *Eleven Miktsema Rites* lists eleven rites for: (1) making rain, (2) protecting against crop failure from frost, (3) protecting against weapons via a swallowed mantra, (4) protecting against weapons via an amulet, (5) protecting against stroke, (6) healing stress and tension, (7) protecting from malevolent spirits via a swallowed mantra, (8) binding robbers, (9) extracting blood, (10) granting pith instructions, and (11) guarding against obstacles.
53. The BDRC.io database (W3CN22351) lists the entire three-volume anthology under the name of Jamyang Dewai Dorjé alone. That this master was responsible for only the first, original, volume is evident from the individual volumes' lists of contents. This three-volume anthology enjoyed wide popularity in Tibet and in Mongol areas, the latter thanks to the compilers of the last two volumes being ethnic Mongol lamas.
54. In addition to this anthology on Miktsema, Yeshé Döndrup wrote a lengthy biography of Jé Tsongkhapa and is well known for his *Treasury of Gems: Selected Anthology of Well-Uttered Teachings of Kadam Masters* (*Bka' gdams gces btus legs bshad nor bu'i bang mdzod*). He also compiled the massive anthology known as the Surka Cycle of Empowerments (*Zur ka brgya rtsa*), a supplement to Tāranātha's Rinjung Cycle of Empowerments (*Rin 'byung brgya rtsa*). A scanned copy of an original 1872 print of the *Miktsema Cycle of Teachings* by Ganden Jampa Ling Monastery, Mongolia, of the version compiled by Thöyön Yeshé Döndrup is accessible under BDRC.io number W1NLM1386 bearing the title *Sras rgyud lugs kyi zab lam bla ma'i rnal 'byor dga' ldan lha brgya ma*.
55. A scanned copy of the three-volume anthology printed at Gyabum Lhakhang Printery was reprinted in Delhi by Ngawang Gelek Demo in 1976 and is accessible at BDRC.io, work W22380.

56. On successive masters of the Segyü lineage, see Thuken Chökyi Nyima, *Crystal Mirror* (trans.), 287–89.
57. Several other "branch-like guides" (*yan lag gi khrid*) associated with this lineage include (1) Three Rites of Sixty (three *torma* burning rites associated with Vajrabhairava), (2) Magical Wheel yogic exercises, (3) the rite of burnt offerings, (4) the great *torma* rite of the protector Mahākāla, and (5) the Sitātapatrā (White Umbrella) rite for repelling obstacles. See Thuken, *Crystal Mirror of Philosophical Systems* (trans.), 288–89.
58. Thuken, *Crystal Mirror* (trans.), 288.
59. Jamyang Shepa Ngawang Tsöndrü's biography (58–60), written by Könchok Jikmé Wangpo, provides a long list of teachings the master received from the elderly Könchok Yarphel from the Segyü lineage.
60. Thuken, *Crystal Mirror* (trans.), 289.
61. Spelled *snyan brgyud*, literally "ear-transmitted," the Tibetan word is in fact a translation of the Sanskrit *karṇa tantra*, which in turn appears to be an abbreviation of the longer expression *mukha karṇa paraṃpara*, meaning "mouth-to-ear transmitted tradition."
62. Three anthologies in Tsongkhapa's collected works containing many of his oral teachings (*zhal shes*) were compiled by Khedrup Jé, with some later editing by Baso Chökyi Gyaltsen; their contents overlap. They are (1) the *Doorframe Essential Oral Teachings* (Collected Works, vol. *nya*), containing fifteen instructions; (2) *Twenty-One Short Pieces Pertaining to Guhyasamāja* (Collected Works, vol. *dza*), the final piece being Khedrup Jé's own catalogue of the anthology; and (3) *Short Instructional Pieces Pertaining to Guhyasamāja* (Collected Works, vol. *dza*), a slightly different selection of twenty-one pieces.
63. On Tsongkhapa's relationship to Mañjuśrī, especially through Umapa as the medium, see chapter 5 of Jinpa, *Tsongkhapa*.
64. The third is *An Uncommon Oral Instruction: Lord Mañjuśrī's Teaching Scribed by Revered Tsongkhapa and Sent to Jé Rendawa*. Gyalrong Tsultrim Nyima provides an extensive paraphrase of the entire text of the last work on pages 441–45 below.
65. *Lung bstan gsang ba'i me long*. The earliest explicit mention of to this "emanated scripture" (*sprul pa'i glegs bam*) I have located is in Khedrup Sangyé Yeshé's *Supplicating Conqueror [Ensa] Losang Döndrup by Way of Narrating His Liberating Life Story*, 4a3, where one reads, "Then he enthroned you as his Dharma regent and passed on to your hand the oral transmission's emanated scripture." On this legend of the emanated scripture and how it was handed from one generation to the next, see Roger Jackson, *Mind Seeing Mind*, 145–49.
66. Ensapa, *Source of All Attainments*, 2a3 (2:739). Ensapa goes on to state that the prophecy contains both verse and prose, but because of its strictly sealed status, he cannot present the exact wording and is sharing the essence in a condensed but complete form.
67. Ensapa, *Source of All Attainments*, 16b5 (2:768).
68. The phrase is generally assumed to be coined by Panchen Losang Chögyen, but the actuality is more complex. Panchen speaks of "the sacred lineage of the great conqueror Ensapa" (*rgyal ba dben sa pa chen po'i bka' brgyud*), "the unique oral-transmission instructions of the sacred Ensa lineage" (*dben sa bka' brgyud kyi thun*

mong ma yin pa'i snyan brgyud kyi gdams pa), and "the lineage of the uncommon oral transmission together with the emanated scripture" (*snyan brgyud thun mong ma yin pa sprul pa'i glegs bam dang bcas pa*), but nowhere have I found him to use the now popular moniker Ensa Oral Transmission (*dben sa snyan brgyud*). This name and its meaning as understood today probably stems from Yongzin Yeshé Gyaltsen, but there is no doubt it is Panchen who initiated the special focus on Ensapa and recognized that Ensapa was the first to formally commit key elements of the transmission to writing, especially from the emanated scripture.

69. According to Panchen Losang Chögyen, both Ensapa and his guru, the mystic Dharmavajra, actualized the rainbow body (buddhahood as envisioned in the yoginī tantras). Yongzin (*A Treasure House of Instructions on the Oral Transmission*, 51b2) reports this from his own guru, Drupwang Losang Namgyal, who in turn heard it from Panchen Losang Chögyen.
70. Ensapa, *Guru Yoga in Verse*, 98.
71. In one memorable verse from his *Great Bliss Treasury* (*Miscellaneous Writings*, 58), he writes: "Between Milarepa of ancient times / and Losang Döndrup of our time, / apart from obvious differences in food and clothing, / we alike have no use for grasping at material things."
72. *Miscellaneous Writings*, 26b4 (1:58).
73. A lengthy guide to this tradition of transference of consciousness is found in Akhu Sherab Gyatso's collected works. In addition to these, the Ensa tradition has various rites and deity-yoga practices associated with meditation deities such as Four-Armed Avalokiteśvara and Vajrabhairava, the body-mandala practice of Cakrasaṃvara according to Ghaṇṭāpa, Hayagrīva protector rites, and so on.
74. Tib: *bla ma'i rnal 'byor lam gyi rtsa bar bzung ba, bla ma'i rnal 'byor nyams len gyi snying por bzung ba*, and *bla ma'i rnal 'byor lam gyi srog tu bzung ba*. For example, Yongzin, *Treasure House*, 8a3, 14a5, 14b3, 15a4, and 19a4.
75. Panchen, in fact, mentions Khedrup Sangyé Yeshé's *Offering to the Guru* as one of the sources for his own text; see page 429.
76. Entitled, respectively, as *Dewdrops of Oral Transmission Nectar* and *Sprays of Oral Transmission Nectar* The first became hugely popular among practitioners whose main chosen meditation deity is Cakrasaṃvara and is often used as the basis for the fortnightly ritual feast (*tshog*) ceremonies.
77. The transmission of Panchen's *Offering to the Guru* root text based on Yongzin's extensive guide is highly sought within the Geluk tradition by serious practitioners. Yongzin had earlier authored a shorter guide, *Door Sign to the Treasure House of Orally Transmitted Instructions*, about one-fifth of the length of his extensive guide. His writings contain a yet shorter guide (twenty-six folios): *A Magic Key that Opens the Hundred Treasures of Oral Transmission*. I had the good fortune to receive transmission of Panchen's guru yoga from His Holiness the Dalai Lama as well as his two tutors, Kyabjé Ling Rinpoché and Kyabjé Trijang Rinpoché. From Kyabjé Ling Rinpoché, I also received the transmission of Yongzin's extensive guide. An oral teaching of the present Dalai Lama on Panchen's text, for which I had the honor to be the translator, was published as *The Union of Bliss and Emptiness*.
78. Dalai Lama, *Union of Bliss and Emptiness*, 26.

79. Gungthang Tenpai Drönmé (*Key to Unlock the Secrets of the Oral Transmission*, 22a1) speaks of how, when thoughts contrary to Dharma practice arise, we need to recall the guru's presence in our heart, and how, when virtuous thoughts arise within, we needs to recall the guru's kindness. Gungthang's text is a commentary on a remarkable verse text by Yongzin Yeshé Gyaltsen, *Root Lines on the Heart of Pith Instructions of the Profound Path of Guru Yoga* (*Zab lam bla ma'i rnal 'byor gyi man ngag snying po'i rtsa tshig*), which seems to be missing from Yongzin's own collected works.
80. Khedrup Jé, *Biographical Poem Supplicating the Great Lord Tsongkhapa*, verse 35.
81. Jamyang Chöjé Tashi Palden, *Secret Biography of Lord Master Losang Drakpa: A Poem of Supplication*, 197.
82. Yongzin Yeshé Gyaltsen, *Prayer to the Lineage Gurus of Mahāmudrā*, 410.
83. *Vajra Garland Tantra* (*Vajramālātantra*), chap. 2, Kangyur, rgyud, *ca*, 212a6.
84. For a slightly different translation, see Tsongkhapa, *Great Treatise* (trans.), 1:71.
85. Source: An oral teaching from Kyabjé Zong Rinpoché (1905–84), whose source is possibly "the three gurus" (*bla ma gsum*) referred to in Buddhaśrījñāna's *Sacred Words of Mañjuśrī* (47a2), where the author pays homage to "the three gurus that reveal the ultimate essence through three modalities."
86. Palmang Könchok Gyaltsen, *In Response to a Request*, 126. Palmang's text contains Thuken's entire *Supplications to the Definitive Guru* and a lucid commentary on the verses.
87. In Kālacakra tantra, for example, three of the seals—the action, gnosis, and great seals—are identified as the means, while the pledge seal represents the goal, defined as immutable bliss. In Padmavajra's *Attainment of the Secret* (*Guhyasiddhi*), the first of the Seven Attainment Texts in the Tengyur collection of Indian treatises, we find the following sequence of path: (1) generation stage, (2) action seal, (3) gnosis seal, and (4) great seal. A short tantric work attributed to Nāgārjuna, *Ascertaining the Four Seals* (*Caturmudrāviniścaya*), identifies the four seals sequentially as (1) the action seal, a live consort, (2) the reality seal, wisdom perceiving the sphere of reality, (3) the great seal, the gnosis of union of bliss and emptiness, and (4) the pledge seal, embodied manifestations of the enlightened mind. This last work, as explained by its commentary *Mudrācaturaṭīkā* by Vitakarma, correlates the first with cause, the second with path, the third with result, and the fourth with manifestation or expression of the result. Elsewhere, in the same text (320b7), with the pledge seal differentiated into causal and resultant stages, the *causal* pledge seal is identified as the generation stage, the action seal as the symbol, the reality seal as the path, the great seal as the result, and the fulfilment of others' welfare as the *resultant* pledge seal. See also Jackson, *Mind Seeing Mind*, 38–40.
88. Sakya Paṇḍita, *Clear Differentiation*, 3.164, 33:25b4; Rhoton (trans.), 164–66.
89. For a succinct introduction to Gampopa on mahāmudrā, see Jackson, *Mind Seeing Mind*, 87–92; and on Shang's single remedy, see Roberts, *Mahāmudrā and Related Instructions*, 126–29.
90. I agree with Roger Jackson's conclusions when he observes (*Mind Seeing Mind*, 65) that "Indeed, it can be argued that singling out mahāmudrā as a focus of study

and practice is really a Tibetan idea" and that "mahāmudrā took on an importance for at least some Tibetan traditions that surpassed anything seen in India."

91. Jackson, *Mind Seeing Mind*, especially chapters 4–6 and 15–17.
92. Panchen, *A Lamp So Bright*, 645.
93. For an alternative translation, see Tsongkhapa, *Lamp to Illuminate the Five Stages* (trans.), 122.
94. *Bcos nas bsgom na yang lhan skyes 'char bas/ rtog ldan rgan po rnams u tshugs mi dgos*. Changkya, *Recognizing My Mother*, verse 19. By "elder meditators" Changkya here means the Kagyü masters who insist on a strict nondiscursive approach.
95. Khedrup, *Record of Teachings Received*, 122.
96. Gungthang, *Garland of Nectar Drops*, 9a6. "Old style" possibly refers to the Kagyü mahāmudrā that emphasizes nondiscursivity and "new style" to the guide to the view approach that emphasizes discursive analysis when cultivating the view.
97. Chenga Lodrö Gyaltsen, *Biography of Jetsun Jampal Gyatso*, 39.
98. Ibid., 43. How Tsongkhapa's teaching, especially his instruction on tranquil abiding and insight, relates to Kagyü mahāmudrā appears to have been an important question from the early fifteenth century. The biography of Chenga Sönam Gyaltsen (1386–1434), a senior master of Phakdru Kagyü and the author of possibly the first formal history of Kagyü tradition as well as a student of Tsongkhapa, reports him stating: "Once I came across an instruction summarizing the guru's intention on the topic of tranquil abiding, I wondered whether there were an instruction on cultivating insight based on this exact approach on cultivating mental stillness. When I later saw one, the key points of insight were also in perfect accord with the mahāmudrā tradition." Kunga Gyaltsen, *Meaningful to Behold: The Biography of Dharma Master Chenga Sönam Gyaltsen*, 37a2. Chenga was a younger brother of Tibet's Phakdru ruler Miwang Drakpa Gyaltsen and is known also by his titles the Twenty-Second Chenga and Lhasik Repa, and he is the acknowledged source of inspiration referred to by Panchen Sönam Drakpa in his colophon of *Six Ornaments to Beautify the Holy Dharma of Mahāmudrā*, when he writes, "May I become like the skilled navigator Lhasik Repa (*ded dpon lha gzigs ras pa bzhin gyur cig*)." On the Geluk side, Panchen Losang Chögyen's teacher Khedrup Sangyé Yeshé (*Glory of Bringing into the Light the Essence of Well-Uttered Insights*, 236) also speaks of "establishing the convergence of the intent of Kagyü and Geden" (*'di ni bka' dge dgongs pa gcig tu sgrub pa yin no*).
99. Chenga Lodrö Gyaltsen, *Ultimate and Profound Path*, 39.
100. A major Indian authority associated by the Tibetan tradition with the nonmentation (*amanasikāra*), Maitripa, offers a similar explanation of the meaning of the term. In his *Presenting Nonmentation* (139b5), Maitripa identifies unborn nature (emptiness), selflessness, and clear light as three possible references of the negative particle *non* (*med*, Skt. *a*) and explains the meaning of *nonmentation* not in terms of absence of mentation but as mentation of an absence—namely, any of the three references of *non*.
101. Chenga, *Illuminating the Essence*, 159. Except for a rare mention in relation to Tokden's role, as reported by Chenga, in Yongzin Yeshé Gyaltsen's guide to Geden mahāmudrā, *Bright Lamp of the Excellent Path of the Oral Transmission* (22b1),

most accounts of the origin of Geluk mahāmudrā leave out Chenga Lodrö Gyaltsen and link Tokden to Baso Chökyi Gyaltsen directly.

102. Roger Jackson, in *Mind Seeing Mind*, offers a complete translation of Khedrup Norsang Gyatso's text, *Bright Lamp of Mahāmudrā* (543–66), and a lengthy summary of Panchen Sönam Drakpa's *Six Ornaments to Beautify the Holy Dharma of Mahāmudrā* (187–93).
103. A translation by José Cabezón of this work, *Wish-Fulfilling Jewel of the Oral Tradition* (*Snyan brgyud yid bzhin nor bu*), with a teaching from the present Dalai Lama appears in Dalai Lama et al., *Meditation on the Nature of the Mind*, 63–139.
104. Yongzin, *Bright Lamp of the Excellent Path*, 9b4–10a5. The first passage is from Tsongkhapa's *Queries from a Pure Heart* (119), where Tsongkhapa speaks of there being a unique instruction from his "wise father guru" on the sutra statement "not seeing is the supreme seeing" that is different from the "gross interpretation offered by others." The second passage Yongzin cites is from Tsongkhapa's *Reply to Master Rendawa's Letter* (97), where the master speaks of a unique instruction of Mañjuśrī on renunciation, on the awakening mind, and in particular on how to cultivate experiential understanding of the view.
105. Tsongkhapa, *Mañjuśrī's Advice on Practice*, 73; a complete translation of this short text is found in Jinpa, *Tsongkhapa*, 131.
106. Ensapa, *Treasure House of Great Bliss*, 23b6 (1:52).
107. Shar Kalden, Gyatso, *Experiential Guide to Mahāmudrā of the Sacred Geden Lineage*, 692 of the present volume.
108. Changkya Rölpai Dorjé, *Replies to Questions from Gomang Gungru Rabjampa Jampa Lodrö*, 11a4. A detailed teaching on Panchen's mahāmudrā root text and its commentary by the present Dalai Lama, including his observations on the convergence and divergence between Geluk mahāmudrā and that of Kagyü, is found in Dalai Lama and Berzin, *Gelug/Kagyü Tradition of Mahāmudrā*.
109. Panchen, *Lamp So Bright*, 658 of the present volume.
110. Changkya Ngawang Chöden, *Guidebook on Mahāmudrā*, 3a6–5b3.
111. Roger Jackson's *Mind Seeing the Mind* (241–90) provides excellent summaries of most of the Geluk mahāmudrā texts listed here, except for those of Changkya Ngawang Chöden and Akhu Sherab Gyatso.
112. Yongzin, *Mahāmudrā Prayer Source of All Attainments. Dga' ldan phyag rgya chen po'i smon tshig dngos grub kun 'byung*.
113. *Nges shes kyi rgyun skyong tshul* and *thos bsam gyis myong ba 'don tshul*. For example, Jamyang Gawai Lodrö's (1429–1503) *Guidebook on the View Illuminating Thatness*, 176.
114. This text is number 18 in the anthology *Short Pieces Pertaining to Guhyasamāja* and consists of the root lines and an accompanying exposition on each of the lines for each of the five approaches. That this fivefold list is actually by Tsongkhapa is evidenced from Gyaltsab Jé's reference to it in his *Precious Garland: A Guide to the Profound View*, 189, where he writes, "The view can be maintained in five ways. What is presented here, however, is from the perspective of a beginner who has ascertained the view and has not yet forgotten it."
115. In addition to Tsongkhapa himself, both his senior students, Gyaltsab and Khedrup, composed guide to the view texts of their own, based on Tsongkhapa's

oral teachings. Similarly, two junior students of Tsongkhapa—Baso and Chenga Lodrö Gyaltsen—wrote such texts, with the former's acquiring the title of *Baso's Great Guide to the View* (*Ba so'i lta khrid chen mo*). I hope to find another occasion to explore in more depth the history of the guide to the view instruction and its role in the Geluk tradition.

116. Jamyang Gawai Lodrö, *Guidebook*, 167. An English translation of this prayer can be found in Jinpa, *Tsongkhapa*, 121–23.

117. Panchen Losang Chögyen's writings contain texts representing both of these distinct approaches, respectively: *An Instruction on How to Cultivate the Middle Way View Conferred by Mañjuśrī to Jé Tsongkhapa* and *How to Practice the Essence of the Fourfold Mindfulness, the Nectar of Master Lodrö Bepa's Teaching*. According to the Second Dalai Lama (Gendun Gyatso, *Doorway for Those Aspiring Liberation*, 33a5), the difference between the two approaches is their preliminary practice, with the tradition passing through Khedrup Jé framing the meditation in terms of a "preliminary" and a "main practice," while the second approach frames the preliminary instruction in terms of the fourfold mindfulness. Lodrö Bepa (1400–75), the master in the title of Panchen's text, was a principal disciple of Sherab Sengé.

118. Mönlam Palwa (1414–91), *Dispelling All Extreme Views*, 3b1. Among the numerous guide to the view texts within the Geluk tradition, the most known are those by the First Dalai Lama (1391–74), Panchen Sangpo Tashi (1410–79), Jamyang Gawai Lodrö, the Second Dalai Lama, Panchen Sönam Drakpa, Ensapa, Panchen Losang Chögyen, Fifth Dalai Lama, Shar Kalden Gyatso, Changkya Ngawang Chöden, Jamyang Shepa, Shok Dönyö Khedrup (1671–1737), Changkya Rölpai Dorjé, the Seventh Dalai Lama, Yongzin Yeshé Gyaltsen, Jamyang Tenpai Nyima (1686–1738), Khalkha Damtsik Dorjé (1781–1855), and Akhu Sherab Gyatso.

119. Tsongkhapa, *Guide to the Profound Path of the Middle Way View According to Prāsaṅgika*, 520.

120. Ibid., 522.

121. Tsongkhapa, *Indispensable Oral Teaching on Tranquil Abiding and Insight*, 375.

122. Tsongkhapa, *Guide to the Profound Path*, 524.

123. Kalsang Gyatso, *On Mind Training and Collected Poetic Songs*, 10b1.

124. Khedrup, *Record of Teachings Received*, 120.

125. Changkya refers to these two early Geluk texts on the three essential points in his *Stream of Camphor Juice* (2b3); neither text appears to be extant. I chose Ngulchu's texts to represent this instruction in our volume because I received the instruction based on them.

126. In the colophon of this text, the author's name appears as Śrī Jagatamitrānanda, most probably alternative name for Mitrayogi. That this Jagatamitrānanda is closely associated with Tibetans is evidenced from a letter written by the master to an Indian king named Jayacandra and contained in the Tengyur (Toh 4189), where the translator's colophon lists the author himself as one of the two translators. This name, Jagatamitrānanda, appears also co-translator with Trophu Lotsāwa of the *Cakrasaṃvara Ekajaṭā* sādhana cycle (Toh 2122–26) and as the author of Toh 2129, 2466–69, and 3979. Similarly, the three texts attributed to "Ajita Mitrayogi" at Toh 2130–32 lists "Mitrānanda" also as a translator.

127. *Chos rje khro phu lo tsa ba byams pa dpal gyi man ngag brgya rtsa ma*. An early cursive handwritten version of the anthology discovered at Drepung Monastery is accessible by scan at BDRC.io, item W00KG03569. For more on Trophu Lotsāwa, a key early member of the Trophu Kagyü lineage, see Thuken, *Crystal Mirror* (trans.), 136.
128. Changkya Ngawang Chöden, *Stream of Camphor Juice,* 2a4.
129. Gendun Gyatso, *Staircase to Tuṣita*, 98, and Changkya Ngawang Chöden, *Stream of Camphor Juice*, 2b4.
130. *Commentary on Ornament of the Middle Way* (*Madhyamakālaṃkāravṛtti*), Toh 3885 Tengyur, dbu ma, *sa*, 83a4.
131. The Mother of Conquerors is the Perfection of Wisdom sutras, scriptures key to the Mahayana teaching on emptiness.
132. The last two lines of this pair of verses appear as a refrain at the end of every key topic in the stages of the path instruction. I have rendered this refrain as it appears in Tsongkhapa's original. The tradition among Geluk practitioners, especially when chanting this text, is to modify the refrain as "The exalted lama practiced in this manner; you who aspire to liberation should do likewise."
133. The four powers are (1) the power of reliance on the support, (2) the power of repudiation, (3) the power of the remedy, which is engaging the antidotes, and (4) the power of resolve to turn away from the fault henceforth. Together these four constitute an effective method for purifying negative karma. For a detailed explanation of these powers, see pages 91 and 396.
134. The two accumulations (*saṃbhāradvaya*) are the accumulation of merit (*puṇya*) and the accumulation of wisdom (*prajñā*), both of which must be cultivated in tandem to advance along the path to enlightenment. These are often correlated to the six perfections of a bodhisattva that are outlined in what follows, where the perfections of generosity, ethics, forbearance, diligence, and meditative absorption are said to complete the accumulation of merit, and the perfection of wisdom is said to complete the accumulation of wisdom.
135. This reading is based on Panchen Losang Yeshé's *Essence of Eloquence* (55a4), where he interprets the Tibetan word *nges shes* in this line not as "ascertainment" but as "grasping at certitude." Many other commentators, including the Fifth Dalai Lama and Tendar Lharam, read *nges shes* as "ascertainment," thus making this line read as if this ascertainment dismantles entirely any grasping at the object.
136. As this brief colophon says, this short text in verse was composed as advice to Tsakho Ngawang Drakpa. This figure was one of Tsongkhapa's earliest disciples and served as the master's attendant. The Tibetan word *dbon po*, which I have rendered here as "a member of the ruling family," has multiple meanings. It can refer broadly to male members of a family on the father's side, to a younger brother or nephew of a prominent person such as a local ruler, or to a male member of a ruling family.
137. The work is customarily referred to as the *Gomchen Lamrim*.
138. The author's principal guru was Jé Lodrö Tenpa (1404–78), the founder of Dakpo Shedrup Ling Monastery and the sixth successor to Jé Tsongkhapa on the throne of Ganden.
139. Gomchen's original work is entirely in verse. The outline was added when it

was first printed near the turn of the nineteenth century by Döndrup Wangyal of Dakpo Shedrup Ling, the author's monastery. The outline is drawn from Jé Tsongkhapa's *Middle-Length Treatise on the Stages of the Path.* Verse numbers were added to the 2005 Tibetan edition by the Institute of Tibetan Classics, and the numbering has been revised slightly in this translation.

140. Āryaśūra, *Garland of Birth Stories* (*Jātakamālā*), chap. 32, Toh 4150 Tengyur, skyes rab, *hu*, 121b7.

141. *Ten Wheels of Kṣitigarbha Sutra,* (*Daśacakrakṣitigarbhasūtra*), chap. 7, Toh 239 Kangyur, mdo sde, *zha*, 223a5.

142. This refers to thoughts affected by afflictions (Skt. *kleśa*) such as aversion, attachment, or ignorance.

143. Respectively, *Adhyāśayasañcodana*, Toh 69 Kangyur, dkon brtsegs, *ca*, 135b1, and *Gṛhapati-ugraparipṛcchā*, Toh 63 Kangyur, dkon brtsegs, *ca*, 279a7.

144. Before teaching the Perfection of Wisdom, the Buddha set up a throne and circumambulated it three times to honor not himself but the teaching he was about to give.

145. Tsongkhapa, citing the *Questions of Sāgaramati*, lists these five recognitions in his *Middle-Length Treatise* (trans., 27): viewing yourself as a physician, the Dharma as the medicine, listeners as patients, and tathāgatas as superior beings, along with wishing for the teaching to remain for a long time.

146. A factor that, along with *mindfulness* (*smṛti*), plays an important role in the cultivation of *tranquil abiding* (*śamatha*) by monitoring the mind focusing on its object. Alternate translations commonly found are "vigilance" and "introspection."

147. In the two works I have translated in this volume, I have rendered *brtson 'grus* (Skt. *vīrya*) as "diligence" to match the rest of the book. *Merriam-Webster* defines *diligence* as "steady, earnest, and energetic effort," but this does not capture the connotation that Asaṅga glosses as "mental delight" and Śāntideva as "delighting in virtue." Given these, I elsewhere translate this as "enthusiasm." Another downside to "diligence" is that it makes presenting the "four possible combinations" (*mu bzhi*) between *brtson 'grus* and *rtsol ba* ("effort") problematic, for you can delight in virtue (practice enthusiasm) without making the slightest effort.

148. Respectively, *Daśadharmakasūtra*, chap. 1, Toh 53 Kangyur, dkon brtsegs, *kha*, 170b1. *Gaṇḍavyūhasūtra,* Toh 44 Kangyur, phal chen, *a*, 36b1.

149. Skt. *avīci*, the eighth hot hell.

150. The three main objectives for which supplication is made are the two indicated here as well as the cessation of all mistaken thoughts, from irreverence toward your spiritual teachers up to grasping at the two types of self.

151. Creating merit and purifying wrongdoing is the groundwork that ensures that meditation on whatever topic leads to realization and insight.

152. The instruction is to avoid sleeping at the beginning and end of the night and during the day.

153. *Zhi gnas*, Skt. *śamatha.* Other common translations are "meditative serenity" and "calm abiding." *Zhi* or *zhi ba* ("peace") refers to that fact that all distraction away from the focal object has been "pacified" or quelled; *gnas* refers to the stability aspect. A third important component of *zhi gnas* is mental and physical *pliancy* (*shin sbyang*).

154. In this context "nonconceptual cognition" refers to a direct understanding of selflessness.
155. Uttarakuru (*sgra mi snyan*) is the northern continent in Buddhist cosmology, where, given the excessive hedonism of that existence, beings there are said to be unsuitable vessels for Dharma practice.
156. Here "the higher realms" are the form and formless realms, and "achieving an ārya path" is attaining the path of seeing, which according to Prāsaṅgika tenets, requires realizing emptiness directly, no matter which vehicle one is on.
157. "Definite goodness" is twofold in that it indicates both personal liberation from samsara and buddhahood. Of the two, buddhahood is the ultimate goal sought by those practicing the lamrim. The stages of the persons of the three capacities are exhaustive in that, since all Buddha's discourses were necessarily given as means to achieve either a high rebirth or definite goodness in its two forms, and the three stages of the path produce these results, the lamrim necessarily includes all the essential elements of the Buddha's discourses.
158. These two lines are drawn from Jé Tsongkhapa's *Song of Spiritual Experience*, verse 21. See page 46.
159. As noted above in Tsongkhapa's *Song of Spiritual Experienc*e, the two main trailblazers are Nāgārjuna and Asaṅga.
160. *Play in Full Sutra* (*Lalitavistarasūtra*), chap. 13, Toh 95 Kangyur, mdo sde, *kha*, 88a2.
161. This verse is from Candrakīrti's *Extensive Commentary to Four Hundred Stanzas* (*Catuḥśatakaṭīkā*), Toh 3865 Tengyur, dbu ma, *ya*, 33b4.
162. Our human world. See also note 285 below.
163. In Buddhist cosmology one finds various descriptions of eons (*bskal pa*). One speaks of small, intermediate, and great eons. Two "small" eons (more than five billion years) constitute and intermediate eon, and eighty intermediate eons a great eon.
164. You cannot give the karma you produce to others nor receive others' karma, as you do gifts.
165. Vasubandhu, *Treasury of Abhidharma* (*Abhidharmakośa*), 4.66, Toh 4089 Tengyur, mngon pa, *ku*, 13a7.
166. The four possibilities are (1) identifying the basis, a particular sentient being, as that being, (2) identifying that being as not that being, (3) identifying what is not that being as not that being, and (4) identifying what is not that being as that being. The first and third possibilities are correct identifications, the other two are not.
167. For example, if a man is furious because a cat is stealing food from his kitchen and he decides to take revenge by killing a cat—not a specific one but just any cat—he may kill an innocent cat, but since the man's motivation was unspecific, the karmic path of killing will be complete.
168. Fulfilling these criteria means creating a complete karmic path of killing, which brings graver consequences than an incomplete karmic path.
169. Vasubandhu, *Treasury of Abhidharma Autocommentary* (*Abhidharmakośabhāṣya*) on verse 4.74, Tengyur Toh 4090, mngon pa, *ku*, 204b2.
170. The eight are that which one has (1) seen, (2) heard, (3) discerned (with nose,

tongue, or body), or (4) understood, and the opposites of these—what one has (5) not seen, (6) not heard, (7) not discerned, and (8) not understood.

171. *Causes* are for example good and bad behavior; *effects* are their consequences; *agents* include things like fathers and mothers, those who come from a past life and those who move on to future lives, or those born spontaneously like intermediate state beings; *existents* are exemplified by arhats.

172. Here "mental karmas" (*yid kyi las*) are either the mental factor of intention that occurs prior to a physical or verbal action and motivates it or—in the case of the three mental nonvirtues of covetousness, ill will, and wrong views—the mental factor of intention concomitant with those afflictions.

173. Inspired by a powerful affliction or a powerfully virtuous attitude.

174. Part of this stanza is drawn from verse 42 of Nāgārjuna's *Friendly Letter* (*Suhṛllekha*). Of the two bases, the knowledgeable are those like the Three Jewels or your spiritual teachers, while the beneficent are those like your parents who have cared for you.

175. The literal expression is "grains of sand," but according to the oral tradition is to be understood as referring to the number of water molecules in the Ganges River.

176. These two comparisons come from the *Seal Enhancing the Power of Faith Sutra* (*Śraddhābalādhānāvatāramudrāsūtra*), Toh 201 Kangyur, mdo sde, *tsha*, 61a4.

177. The three fundamentals are the virtues of meditation, ethical discipline, and generosity. This is echoing the final verse of chapter 35 of the *King of Meditations Sutra* (*Samādhirājasūtra*), where it says, "Those with ill will toward others are not protected by ethical discipline or by study, not by meditation or solitude, nor by generosity or offerings to buddhas."

178. *Dasabhūmikasūtra*, Toh 44 Kangyur, phal chen, *kha*, 90a1.

179. The differences account for, e.g., having negative results in a higher birth. For the difference between propelling and completing karmas and the four possibilities, see Tsongkhapa, *Middle-Length Treatise* (trans.), 137.

180. Tsongkhapa enumerates these ten in his *Great Treatise on the Stages of the Path* (trans., 1:241): actions carried out (1) in a dream, (2) unknowingly, (3) unconsciously, (4) without intensity or long duration, (5) mistakenly, (6) forgetfully, and (7) unintentionally, and actions (8) that are naturally neutral, (9) that have been purified through regret, or (10) that have been purified through antidotes.

181. This is an epithet for humans that derives from the Hindu creation story.

182. In the sutra quotation here, "all phenomena resemble the moon's reflection in water" refers to the selflessness of phenomena, and "Sentient beings, children of Manu, who after death move on to another life, do not exist [truly] either" refers to the selflessness of persons. The point it makes is that despite their selfless nature, sentient beings create karma and experience its results.

183. *Samādhirājasūtra*, chaps. 14 and 20, Toh 127 Kangyur, mdo sde, *da*, 47a2 and 70b7.

184. *Satyakaparivarta*, Toh 146 Kangyur, mdo sde, *pa*, 101a2.

185. Only a buddha can fully know the most hidden (*shin tu lkog gyur*) levels of the system of karma and its effect—for example, the time, place, and other circumstances in which a karma was produced in the past. Its slightly hidden facets can, however, be established by inference founded in reasoning.

186. In a contest you may feign qualities that you lack, like strength; in the face of karma and its effects, humility is a more appropriate approach, coming to understand all their workings by examining them in detail, checking your behavior regularly, and adjusting it when necessary.
187. Some assert that it is not right to aspire to a good rebirth in cyclic existence because that creates a cause for rebirth in cyclic existence. However, since the achievement of such a rebirth provides favorable conditions for creating the causes of buddhahood and the resultant qualities of supreme high status (a buddha's body, resources, and entourage), aspiring to one temporarily as a means to that end does not prolong the cycle of rebirth.
188. Here, this refers to the paths of śrāvakas, pratyekabuddhas, and bodhisattvas.
189. They are cowed and distressed at the sight of the far greater splendor and wealth of gods possessing greater merit than theirs.
190. The Tibetan *jig lta* or *'jig tshogs la lta ba* (Skt. *satkāyadṛṣṭi*) is often translated literally as "the view of the transitory" or "the view of the transitory collection," respectively. It is so named to oppose the deceptive perception of the "I" as permanent and one. As its object is one's own self, not another being's, here it is translated as "the personal identity view." The "and so on" here refers to what belongs to the self—the "mine."
191. Among the proponents of the Cittamātra tenets, the Followers of Scripture make a distinction between dark ignorance and the personal identity view, whereas Cittamātra Followers of Reasoning and proponents of Madhyamaka tenets do not.
192. Both karma as intention and intended karma are the omnipresent mental factor of intention. The former occurs prior to a physical or verbal action and motivates it, whereas the latter is the intention present in the mind when a physical or verbal deed is done.
193. *Mahāyānaparinirvāṇasūtra*, chap. 35, Toh 119 Kangyur, mdo sde, *ta*, 71a1. The nine are eating to excess, eating unhealthy food, eating before having digested the previous meal, not expelling undigested food accumulated in the stomach, constipation, not taking medicine correctly, not discriminating familiar activities from unfamiliar ones, untimely outdoor activities (owing to extreme weather conditions), and [certain] sexual relations.
194. This is a reference to the statement in Asaṅga's *Compendium of Abhidharma Abhidharmasamuccaya*, chap. 2, Toh 4049 Tengyur, sems tsam, *ri*, 78a5. that, in certain cases, owing to the force of karma, an intermediate-state being may avert a projected birth in an unfortunate realm and be reborn instead in a fortunate realm.
195. *Āyuṣmannandagarbhāvakrāntinirdeśa*, Toh 58 Kangyur, dkon brtsegs, *ga*, 211a4.
196. The color of intermediate-state beings for a future human rebirth is also gold.
197. This refers to the elements of the consciousness at conception, which are potentialities for the senses.
198. Vasubandhu, *Treasury of Abhidharma* (*Abhidharmakośa*) 3.8, Toh 4089 Tengyur, mngon pa, *ku*, 7a5.
199. The sutra referred to is the *Sutra Teaching the Tathāgata's Inconceivable Secret* (*Tathāgataguhyanirdeśasūtra*), which says that a bodhisattva should not be terrified by samsara.

200. *King of Meditations Sutra* (*Samādhirājasūtra*), chap. 36, Toh 127 Kangyur, mdo sde, *da*, 128a5.
201. *Subāhuparipṛcchātantra*, Toh 805 Kangyur, rgyud, *wa*, 119a7.
202. Āryaśūra, *Condensed Presentation of the Perfections* (*Pāramitāsamāsa*) 6.65, Toh 3944 Tengyur, *khi*, 234b6.
203. *Lhag bsam*, literally "superior resolve" or "higher intention." As explained in verse 220, the attitude consists in personally taking responsibility for liberating all sentient beings from suffering and establishing them in a state of supreme happiness; it prompts the awakening mind, which is the supreme altruistic intention.
204. The attitude described here is loving kindness (or sympathetic love). No specific meditation is required to generate it, as it emerges naturally from meditating on the three previous qualities, those of recognizing all beings as your mothers, recalling their kindness, and wishing to repay it.
205. Śrāvakas and pratyekabuddhas, as Hīnayāna practitioners, also cultivate the four immeasurable qualities: immeasurable equanimity, love, compassion, and joy.
206. Sutras such as *Display of the Qualities of Mañjuśrī's Buddha Realm* (*Mañjuśrībuddhakṣetraguṇavyūhasūtra*), Toh 59 Kangyur, dkon brtsegs, *ga*, 262b5; Nāgārjuna, *Ratnāvalī* 3.83–85, Toh 4158 Tengyur, skyes rab, *ge*, 17b3.
207. The Tibetan edition mistakenly places this section heading after the next line.
208. The Tibetan edition mistakenly places this section heading before the previous line.
209. The two kinds of attainments, or *siddhis*, are the ordinary ones (*thun mong gi dngos grub*), such as long life, great wealth, clairvoyance, and flying, and the supreme attainment (*mchog gi dngos grub*), buddhahood. Excellent realizations such as the awakening mind and the understanding of emptiness are also placed in the latter category.
210. Although Gomchen does not explicitly state it, these two lines are from Śāntideva's *Guide to the Bodhisattva Way*, 1.7ab.
211. "Celebrants" (*mchod gnas*), literally "recipient of offerings," typically means ordained or lay officiants who are requested to perform prayers and rituals in people's homes.
212. The implication is that if you do not transgress your aspirational bodhicitta precepts, you can renew your vow of engaging in the awakening mind by retaking it.
213. The vow is to refrain from eighteen major transgressions and forty-six secondary ones. The precepts are the threefold bodhisattva ethic: the ethics of abstaining from wrongdoing (which includes refraining from eighteen major transgressions and forty-six secondary ones), accomplishing virtue, and fulfilling the welfare of sentient beings.
214. *Yin lugs*, "things as they are," refers to things' ultimate mode of existence, emptiness.
215. Jé Tsongkhapa's *Great Treatise* (trans., 3:331–39) refutes four major philosophical views. Gomchen first mentions the fourth: the confusion between placement or tranquil abiding meditation and analytical or insight meditation on emptiness.
216. This corresponds to one of several views propounded by the Chinese master Heshang, discussed here in verses 239–45 and refuted by Jé Tsongkhapa in his *Great Treatise* (trans.), 2: 87ff. and 3:331–38. The view mentioned in this verse is that logical reasoning cannot determine what is or is not, and that is the way things

exist ultimately. The mind should therefore not apprehend anything and should simply abide in a state of nonmentation (*ci yang yid la mi byed pa*), which constitutes meditation on emptiness. The same view is mentioned in verses 395–97. One implication of this view is that wrongdoing and afflictions can at times become causes of buddhahood and their opposites can hinder its attainment. See *Great Treatise* (trans.), 2:94ff.

217. This is a reference to first of "thirteen practices" (*sgrub ba bcu gsum*) presented in the first chapter of Maitreya's *Ornament of Realizations*. The "all-inclusive" aspect of this "armor practice" (*go cha'i sgrub pa*) is that it ensures that one's practice of each perfection includes the other five perfections as well. The opponent here is claiming that this one practice of nonmentation is a kind of panacea that encompasses all the bodhisattva practices.

218. Gomchen refers here to a passage found in certain rituals, also quoted in the *Middle-Length Treatise on the Stages of the Path*, in which a mandala is offered after anointing the base with cow dung and urine, which in Indian culture is considered to have a cleansing effect. The example is given to illustrate an act of generosity in which the five other perfections are included. See Tsongkhapa, *Middle-Length Treatise* (trans.), 234.

219. These are the two main "bodies" or facets of buddhahood: the truth body (*dharmakāya*) and the form body (*rūpakāya*).

220. Gomchen is referring to the eighth chapter in Asaṅga's *Bodhisattva Grounds* (*Bodhisattvabhūmi*). For an English translation by Art Engle, see Asaṅga, *Bodhisattva Path*, 237–311.

221. The Tibetan edition is in error here. The heading should be corrected to read *gsum pa de la ji ltar bslab pa'i rim pa*.

222. The three divisions of generosity are giving Dharma, giving material things, and giving protection or freedom from fear.

223. The three bases of harming others are the three mental nonvirtues: covetousness, ill will, and wrong views.

224. On the three divisions of ethics, see pages 323–36.

225. This is because their causes differ: when taking the vows of individual liberation, you vow to keep them for the duration of that life, whereas when taking bodhisattva vows, you vow to keep them until you attain buddhahood.

226. The three divisions are the patience dwelling in certainty about the Dharma, the patience of disregarding harm that others inflict on us, and the patience of accepting the suffering we experience.

227. When you are becoming physically and mentally overtired, you are to suspend your practice of diligence and rest for a while before continuing.

228. The details of these second and third functions are drawn from chapter 4 of Maitreya's *Ornament of Realization* (*Abhisamayālaṃkāra*).

229. Although the author has not specified it, diligence is cultivated both in equipoise and post-equipoise.

230. Tranquil abiding (*śamatha*) and insight (*vipaśyanā*) are, respectively, the very essence of the perfections of meditative absorption and wisdom.

231. These terms, "the way things are" (*ji lta ba*) and "things in their diversity" (*ji snyed pa*), refer respectively to the ultimate and conventional truths.

232. The "preparatory" (*nyer bsdogs*) is the culmination of the nine stages of tranquil abiding and the initial stage of absorption of the first of the form realm's four levels of meditative absorption (*dhyāna*) but not yet the "actual" (*dngos gzhi*) stage. When insight belonging to the preparatory stage gives rise to the actual stage of absorption, the sequence can be said to be reversed. See also note 247.
233. The five aspects of a harmonious place are good access to necessities like food, no threat of violence, no conditions conducive to illness, virtuous companionship, and few distractions in the day and little noise at night.
234. See Tsongkhapa, *Middle-Length Treatise* (trans.), 289.
235. This section describes the advantages of tranquil abiding that you are to contemplate before you start to cultivate it.
236. For an explanation of these four objects, see Tsongkhapa, *Middle-Length Treatise* (trans.), 291–92.
237. "And so on" refers to deities' seed syllables, like *hūṃ*, and their attributes, like Mañjuśrī's sword.
238. According to Asaṅga's definition of mindfulness in the *Compendium of Abhidharma* (*Abhidharmasamuccaya*), its specific object is one that is familiar (in that one has previously perceived it), its mode of apprehension is not forgetful, and its function is the complete prevention of distraction.
239. *Objectless meditation* (*dmigs rten med pa'i sgom*) is meditation that does not take an object such as the body of a deity and instead simply sustains the thought "I will conceive no object."
240. Here Gomchen is referring to a passage in Tsongkhapa's *Great Treatise* (trans., 3:54) that explains the phrase "mentally express the instructions on stabilizing your mind" from Sthiramati's commentary on *Differentiation of the Middle and Extremes* (*Madhyāntavibāghaṭīkā*). We find the following: "Hence, nonforgetfulness of the object of meditation—wherein forgetfulness is stopped—is when you 'mentally express' the object of meditation; you bring the object of meditation to mind again and again."
241. The "six recollections" are the Three Jewels, ethical discipline, generosity, and deities.
242. This verse discusses two obstacles to tranquil abiding: excitation, which is first referred to in verse 318, and mental scattering. According to Palmang's *Mirror Reflecting the Mind* (25a2), the latter is not necessarily an affliction and can be virtuous, nonvirtuous, and ethically neutral. An example of virtuous mental scattering is thinking about Avalokiteśvara when you are meditating on Buddha Śākyamuni. Nonvirtuous scattering can be distraction, such as your mind drifting to an object of irritation when you are meditating. Neutral scattering is when the mind moves away from its object into a vague state with no clear object. Excitation derives from attachment and is necessarily drawn to attractive objects. Distraction is broader in that it can derive from any of the three mental poisons—attachment, aversion, and ignorance—and be drawn to any number of objects. When excitation is intense, and strong measures are needed, the instruction is to put aside the initial object of meditation and contemplate topics such as death, the flaws of cyclic existence and so on. When it is mild, simply bringing the mind back to the object will be sufficient.

243. "Forgetting the instruction" means failing to maintain the object in the mind by means of mindfulness.
244. Here and in the following sections, the term *attention* (*yid byed*) is generally used as an equivalent to *tranquil abiding*.
245. The five obstructions are (1) excitation and regret, (2) ill will, (3) lethargy and sleep, (4) attraction to sense objects, and (5) doubt.
246. In insight meditation on the coarse and peaceful aspects, you begin by viewing the desire realm's joys as coarse and those of the first absorption of the form realm as more refined (literally "peaceful") and pursue the latter. The same process is followed for the subsequent levels of the form and formless realms. However as the afflictions are not opposed by the direct antidote to their root cause, grasping at self, these meditations do not culminate in liberation from cyclic existence and as such constitute a mundane path. Supramundane insight meditation views the sixteen aspects—impermanence and so forth—of the four noble truths, for example, in pursuit of the view of selflessness to eliminate the root cause of the afflictions and thereby achieve liberation from cyclic existence.
247. The "enabling" (*mi lcogs med*) preparatory phase, which, as its name implies, is achieved prior to the actual first absorption (*dhyāna*) of the form realm, is so called because its attainment enables the realization of insight. Of its seven divisions, the first two are called "novice at attention" and "novice at purification of afflictions."
248. In the verses on insight, "the present system" is always to be understood as the Prāsaṅgika system of tenets.
249. Or if you prefer, John's perception apprehending George.
250. In verses 367–68 the author refutes the objection that there would be two distinct roots of samsara if both the personal identity view and grasping at the true existence of the aggregates (i.e., phenomena) are considered to be roots of samsara by pointing out that since the personal identity view also grasps at true existence, they share the same mode of apprehension of their objects and as such are not distinct.
251. See verses 176–81 on the origins of suffering.
252. Āryadeva, *Four Hundred Stanzas*, 14.25cd, Toh 3846 Tengyur, dbu ma, *tsha*, 16a5.
253. *King of Meditations Sutra* (*Samādhirājasūtra*), chap. 44, Toh 127 Kangyur, mdo sde, *da*, 44a2.
254. In many sutras and in Candrakīrti's *Entering the Middle Way*.
255. Gomchen's listing of the third and the fourth key points differ from the standard version, as formalized in Tsongkhapa's *Middle-Length Treatise* (trans., 353–54), where the third and the fourth pertain, respectively, to the absence of identity and the absence of difference. Gomchen is using a slightly different listing of the four key points, based on Gyaltsab Jé's *Jewel Garland: A Guide to the Profound View* (190), which is based on Tsongkhapa's guide to the view.
256. This is a reference to the view that since emptiness of intrinsic existence cannot be "found" and is not identifiable, it is artificial to assert it, and it is best is therefore to remain in a state lacking any thought (*tsom 'jog*).
257. Āryadeva, *Four Hundred Stanzas* (*Catuḥśataka*), 8.16, Toh 3846 Tengyur, dbu ma, *tsha*, 9b6.
258. See note 216.

259. It is illusion-like because of the apparent contradiction between the way things appear to you—as existing intrinsically—and the way you know that they exist—free of the slightest intrinsic existence.
260. *Ldog pa tha dad*: the two are mentally conceived and designated differently. In the *Middle-Length Treatise* (Tib., 380), Tsongkhapa explains, "If a sprout, for instance, were a different entity from its own ultimate nature, it would also be a different entity from its emptiness of true existence, so the sprout would be truly established. Since it is not a different entity, it is one entity."
261. What is translated here as "conventional truth" (*kun rdzob bden pa*) could also be rendered "obscuring truth," or "truth for an obscured perception," for the standard etymology of *saṃvṛti*, the Sanskrit for "conventional," is "veil," and conventional truths veil or obscure the perception of ultimate truth.
262. The "object" in question here is one that is perceived by a rational cognition—in other words, a cognition of emptiness. The term usually translated by "ultimate truth" translates literally as "ultimate object truth."
263. See verse 419.
264. "Duality" in the present context refers to true existence.
265. The reference here is to a passage in Candrakīrti's *Entering the Middle Way Autocommentary* (*Madhyamakāvatārabhāṣya*, Toh 3862 Tengyur, dbu ma, *'a*, 255a4), where he writes, "As for the buddhas, given that they have thoroughly comprehended and realized the nature of all phenomena, we maintain that all turnings of mind and mental factors have come to cease permanently." For Jé Tsongkhapa's position on this debate on the presence or absence of mental continuum in buddhahood, which Gomchen is presenting here, see *Illuminating the Intent* (trans.), 245–47 and 541–42.
266. The sixteen types of emptiness, derived from the Perfection of Wisdom literature, are enumerated by Candrakīrti in *Entering the Middle Way* 6.181–218. See Tsongkhapa, *Illuminating the Intent* (trans.), 487–513.
267. Mainly by Bhāviveka in his *Blaze of Reasoning* (*Tarkajvālā*).
268. The first two refer to direct valid cognition of emptiness and the emptiness that is its object, while the latter two refer to inferential valid cognition and the emptiness that is its object.
269. The distinction is made in relation to the subject that perceives emptiness: the object of direct valid cognition is emptiness itself whereas the emptiness that is the object of inference is in fact a mental image of emptiness
270. The direct realization of emptiness.
271. Inferential valid cognition of emptiness is free of the elaboration that is the perception of true existence, but it maintains the second kind of elaboration—perception of subject-object duality—in the sense that although true existence appears to the inferential cognition, it is not grasped by it.
272. This section heading, announced following verse 409, is missing in the Tibetan text but has been added here.
273. Asaṅga, *Śrāvakabhūmi*, Toh 4036 Tengyur, sems tsam, *dzi*, 149a1. These four were given in verse 339.
274. "The other system" refers to sutra and the other three classes of tantra.
275. Munīndra, "the able sovereign," is an epithet of the historical Buddha Śākyamuni.

Vajradhara is the form assumed by the Buddha in the Vajrayāna scriptures, wherein he is depicted as a deity, clad in nonmonastic garments and adorned with jewel ornaments. This compound Munīndra Vajradhara refers to your root guru, a combination of these two aspects of the Buddha. The guru to whom Panchen Lama is paying homage here at the outset of his text is Khedrup Sangyé Yeshé (1525–91).

276. The eight-featured posture for meditation relates to the position of your (1) legs, (2) hands, (3) back, (4) shoulders, (5) head, (6) eyes, (7) mouth and teeth, and (8) tongue. For a description of these eight features, see pages 461–63 below. Often the list includes just the first seven, a posture known as "the sevenfold posture of Vairocana" (*lus rnam snang gi chos bdun*).

277. The "three robes of saffron color" are the upper garment (*bla gos, uttarāsaṃga*), the lower garment (*mthang gos, antarvāṣa*), and the ceremonial shawl (*snam sbyar, saṃghāṭi*).

278. The Dharma protectors visualized in the merit field include supramundane protectors such as Mahākāla and Kālarūpa as opposed to worldly protectors.

279. Although they are not explicitly set off in the original Tibetan text, I have indented the specific meditation instructions when these function as guided meditations, largely rendered here in the first person.

280. *Nyams len byin rlabs brgyud*. I am reading *nyams len byin rlabs* in conjunctive form as "practice" (*nyams len*) and "blessing" (*byin rlabs*). This lineage, beginning with Vajradhara, is essentially a lineage of mahāsiddhas through whom have emerged more esoteric (visionary) and tantric instructions, in which the guru's blessing is an essential element in one's practice.

281. The seven limbs are (1) prostrating, (2) making offerings, (3) confessing negative karma, (4) rejoicing in good deeds, (5) requesting to turn the wheel of Dharma, (6) appealing not to enter nirvana, and (7) dedicating. Two well-known sources for the rite of seven limbs are the *Vows of Good Conduct* (*Bhadracaryāpraṇidhāna*, a part of the *Flower Garland Scripture*) and chapters 2 and 3 of Śāntideva's *Guide to the Bodhisattva Way* (*Bodhicaryāvatāra*). "Offering a mandala" refers to the chanting of a specific prayer while imaginatively offering the entire universe to the objects of worship.

282. *Legs pa'i skar ma*, elsewhere equated with Upadhāna, the Buddha's cousin and disciple.

283. This is a reference to the preliminary practice presented in the context of topic 1—proper reliance on a spiritual teacher—up to where this two-lined supplication appears.

284. "The three vows" are the monastic or nonmonastic prātimokṣa ("individual liberation") vows, the bodhisattva vows, and the tantric vows. A typical Tibetan monastic practitioner would be someone who had taken a monastic vow (of Vinaya discipline), the bodhisattva vows of Mahayana teachings, and tantric vows on the basis of having been initiated into a mandala of the higher tantras.

285. Literally "Black Plum Continent," Jambudvīpa is analogous to the known world in traditional Indian cosmology and is conceived to lie south of Mount Meru.

286. On the power of these four factors—the object (in relation to whom the karmic act is committed), the intention, the material involved (e.g., the value of the

object in the case of stealing), and the agent (the one who committing the act, e.g., whether they have taken a vow)—see pages 83–86.

287. On the four powers associated with purification of negative karma, see page 91.

288. Throughout this section on the preliminary stage of cultivating equanimity, preparing for the practice of the seven-point causes-and-effect instruction, the Panchen Lama uses the word *even-mindedness* (*sems snyoms pa*) to indicate the leveling out of one's feelings and attitudes instead of the more common *equanimity* (*btang snyoms*).

289. Panchen does not explicitly include altruistic resolve (*lhag bsam*) in this list perhaps because he views it as an enhanced form of compassion—endowed with the thought of wanting to alleviate others' suffering by oneself.

290. The Tibetan phrase *nye ring chags sdang* literally means "closeness and distance, attachment and aversion," suggesting a complex psychology of bias that involves discriminatory attitudes rooted in perception of "nearness" and "distance" and emotional responses that manifest in the form of attachment and aversion. For brevity's sake, one could render this phrase simply as "the bias of attachment and aversion."

291. By "and so on," Panchen is referring to the remainder of the instructions that follow after the supplication. These include visualizing the streams of nectar of five colors and beams of light radiate from the guru at your crown, how this flow of nectar and light cleanses all the negative karma and obscurations you have accumulated since beginningless time in cyclic existence, and so on. See page 159 above for the full description.

292. See previous note.

293. These three types of aspiration wishing for another's well-being reflect progressive levels of engagement on the part of the person who is thinking about another's suffering. Three similar levels of aspiration can be identified in relation to compassion—wishing another to be freed from suffering. The third element, a commitment to acting to bring about the desired outcome, constitutes *altruistic resolve*, the sixth and the final cause within the seven-point causes-and-effect nexus connected with generating the awakening mind.

294. The two obscurations are the afflictive obscuration (*kleśāvaraṇa*) and the knowledge obscuration (*jñeyāvaraṇa*). The first has been eliminated by arhats and bodhisattvas on the eighth ground, and the second has been eliminated by buddhas.

295. The two types of arhats are śrāvaka arhats and pratyekabuddha arhats, Hīnayāna practitioners who have attained nirvana, the cessation of their own manifest suffering, but who have not generated the awakening mind (*bodhicitta*) and so cannot attain complete enlightenment or lead others to that state.

296. In his *Great Treatise on the Stages of the Path to Enlightenment*, Tsongkhapa presents the rite for sustaining the awakening mind in two stages, one for the aspirational aspect and the other for the engaging aspect (English translation, 2:61–68 and 2:103, respectively). But Tsongkhapa's presentation of the rites connected with the engaging aspect and the ceremony for taking the bodhisattva vows are actually found in his *Highway to Enlightenment* (*Byang chub gzhung lam*), an exposition

of the "Ethics" chapter of Asaṅga's *Bodhisattva Levels*. In his *Stages of the Path*, Tsongkhapa simply refers the reader to this other work.

297. Panchen is referring here to the approach in chapter 3 of Śāntideva's *Guide to the Bodhisattva Way*. The passages he refers to here are cited below.
298. Śāntideva, *Guide to the Bodhisattva Way* (*Bodhicaryāvatāra*), 3.22–23.
299. Śāntideva, *Guide to the Bodhisattva Way* (*Bodhicaryāvatāra*), 3.25–26.
300. The four bright factors (*dkar po'i chos bzhi*) are the opposites of the four dark factors (*nag po'i chos bzhi*): (1) refraining from lying, (2) maintaining an honest disposition, (3) consciously regarding the bodhisattvas as your teachers, and (4) encouraging sentient beings so inclined to develop the aspiration to full enlightenment. For detailed explanation of these four factors, see Tsongkhapa, *Great Treatise* (trans.), 2:79–80.
301. On this expression "and so on" (*zhes sogs dang*), see note 291.
302. The twelve branches of scripture classify genres of the Buddha's teachings in an elaboration of the standard classification of the three baskets (*tripiṭaka*): (1) discourses (*sūtra*), (2) melodic verses (*geya*), (3) predictions (*vyākaraṇa*), (4) metered verses (*gāthā*), (5) verse sayings (*udāna*), (6) preambles (*nidāna*), (7) stories (*avadāna*), (8) ancient narratives (*itivṛttaka*), (9) birth stories (*jātaka*), (10) vast discourses (*vaipulya*), (11) wondrous accounts (*adbhutadharma*), and (12) decisive explications (*upadeśa*). For a detailed explanation of these twelve branches, see Chim Jampaiyang, *Ornament of Abhidharma* (trans.), 708–13.
303. This threefold division of wisdom, which Panchen adopts from Tsongkhapa's *Great Treatise on the Stages of the Path* (trans., 2:222), is based on Asaṅga's *Bodhisattva Grounds* (trans., 355).
304. Maitreya, *Differentiation of the Middle and Extremes* (*Madhyāntavibhāga*) 4.3, Toh 4021 Tengyur, sems tsam, *phi*, 43a3.
305. The Tibetan original, both the critical edition of this volume as well as the one in the Panchen Lama's collected works, has the erroneous reading "What is the difference between the two, mental lethargy and laxity and excitation?"
306. The Tibetan original has the phrase "fusing your winds and mind with space" (*rlung sems nam mkha' dang bsre ba*), referring to the well-known instruction for countering mental laxity whereby you imagine your mind becoming fused with the vast expanse of space and abiding with such an image in a state of spaciousness.
307. What Panchen has in mind here is the use of abrupt techniques such as the forceful breathing exercise mentioned in texts like Tsongkhapa's *Doorframe Oral Instructions*, 455.
308. The five segments here are, possibly, the head, neck, torso, arms, and legs.
309. The Ikṣvāku refers to a legendary dynasty that ruled the ancient Indian kingdom of Kośala, and the historical Buddha is said to have belonged to this lineage, hence the phrase "peerless Ikṣvāku" for the Buddha.
310. The thirty-two major marks and eighty minor marks that according to scripture characterize the body of a buddha.
311. Epithets for Śākyamuni Buddha.
312. This refers to the Mahayana's decline, the lesser ocean being the Hīnayāna. The analogy is drawn from the Vedic literature, which recounts that when the Vedas

sank into the ocean, Viṣṇu manifested as a tortoise, dove into the ocean to raise them, and then restored them to their former glory.

313. Asaṅga and Nāgārjuna.
314. That is, Tibet, where the Indian master Atiśa spent the final years of his life. Atiśa's Tibetan students were called the Kadampas.
315. The female counterpart of *asura* or demigod.
316. The Hindu god Indra is said to have the power to halt the movement of mountains by simply brandishing his vajra.
317. An epithet for the moon, as the *kumuda* flower blooms in moonlight.
318. The author's guru, Khöntön Paljor Lhundrup (1561–1637), of Dakpo Shedrup Ling Monastery and former abbot of Sera Jé Monastery. The elements that compose his name are italicized in the following verse.
319. The four "bodies" (*kāya*), or aspects, of buddhahood are the two truth bodies (*dharmakāya*)—the *jñānadharmakāya* wisdom truth body and the *svabhāvikadharmakāya* nature truth body—and the two form bodies (*rūpakāya*)—the *saṃbhogakāya* enjoyment body and the *nirmāṇakāya* emanation body.
320. The terms in italics in this verse constitute the name of Khöntön Paljor Lhundrup's close disciple Paljor Trinlé Rabgyé, a.k.a. Surchen Chöying Rangdröl (1604–69), from whom the author received both Geluk and Nyingma teachings, including the instructions on the lamrim according to the Segyü lineage that are the basis for the present work.
321. An epithet for the ocean.
322. In this context, *peace* (*zhi ba*) is the extinction of suffering, or nirvana. In Mahayana Buddhism pursuing liberation from cyclic existence for one's own sake alone is viewed as an inferior objective compared to the bodhisattva ideal of ending suffering for all beings, leading them to the ultimate happiness of buddhahood, and pursuing the enlightenment of a buddha for that purpose.
323. *Ma dros chu bo*, literally "Cool Lake," a site high in the Himalayas that provides the setting for some of the Buddha's discourses.
324. For the author here, this mainly refers to the lamrim works of Tsongkhapa, hence the title *Words of Mañjuśrī*, an allusion to Tsongkhapa as an incarnation of Mañjuśrī.
325. See page 43 above.
326. Tsongkhapa, *Great Treatise* (Tib.), 2.
327. Ibid., 8.
328. Jé Sherab Sengé (1383–1445), the direct disciple of Tsongkhapa who originated the Segyü lineage. Sé is the area of Tsang province where Jé Sherab Sengé had his disciple Dulnakpa Palden Sangpo establish Segyü Monastery for tantric practice. Among the works that belong to the Segyü lineage are Dulnakpa's *Hundreds of Gods of Tuṣita*, the Third Dalai Lama's *Essence of Refined Gold*, the present lamrim, and Gendun Jamyang's *Southern Transmission Lamrim* (*Byang chub lam gyi rim pa'i dmar khrid 'jam dpal zhal lung gi khrid rgyun bsdus pa lho brgyud du grags pa*), which derives from the present text. Jé Sherab Sengé founded Gyümé Tantric College in Lhasa in 1433.
329. Here and elsewhere in the text, "my guru" refers to Surchen Chöying Rangdröl.

330. *Twenty-Five Thousand Lines on the Perfection of Wisdom* (*Pañcaviṃśatisāhasrikāprajñāpāramitā*) Toh 9 Kangyur, nyi khri, *ka*, 3b3.
331. *Ten Wheels of Kṣitigarbha Sutra* (*Daśacakrakṣitigarbhasūtra*), chap. 7, Toh 239 Kangyur, mdo sde, *zha*, 223a5.
332. *Sāgaramatiparipṛcchāsūtra*, Toh 152 Kangyur, mdo sde, *pha*, 111b5.
333. For the rite of the six preliminaries that corresponds to *Words of Mañjuśrī*, see Phabongkha, *Excellent Path of the Conquerors.* Collected Works, *ca*, 3.
334. Maitreya and Mañjuśrī.
335. *Udānavarga*, chap. 22 (Śrutavarga), Toh 157 Kangyur, mdo sde, *sa*, 228b2.
336. *Mahāparinirvāṇasūtra*, chap. 1, Toh 119 Kangyur, mdo sde, *nya*, 33b4.
337. Tsongkhapa, *Song of Spiritual Experience*, vv. 6–9. See full translation in chapter 1 of the present volume.
338. In Tibetan, the expression translates literally as "the four corners of the teaching," which signifies that it includes all the sutras and tantras and all three vehicles. See Tsongkhapa, *Middle-Length Treatise* (trans.), 14 and note 20.
339. In other words, they do not exist.
340. Being destitute of the teaching here signifies not knowing how to practice it.
341. Tsongkhapa, *Discourse*, 86. The "three gems" in this context are teaching, debate, and composition.
342. Naljorpa Chenpo, "the great yogi," Amé Jangchup Rinchen (1015–78). Tsongkhapa quotes this in his lamrim treatises.
343. The expression "definite goodness" (*nges legs*) refers to both the state of liberation from cyclic existence and the ultimate good, buddhahood.
344. The obscurations constituted by the afflictions (*kleśāvaraṇa*) and the obscurations to knowledge (*jñeyāvaraṇa*).
345. *Sarvavaidalyasaṃgraha*, Toh 227 Kangyur, mdo sde, *dza*, 186a6.
346. Tsongkhapa, *Great Treatise* (Tib.), 319.
347. As there is no such thing as a second shadow, this means "with no one."
348. Tsongkhapa, *Middle-Length Treatise* (Tib.), 62.
349. Āryadeva, *Lamp for Integrating the Practices* (*Caryāmelāpakapradīpa*), Toh 1802 Tengyur, rgyud, *ngi*, 60b5.
350. See Tsongkhapa, *Middle-Length Treatise* (trans.), 73–74.
351. The title of this work by the Third Dalai Lama Sönam Gyatso is often properly translated as the *Nectar of Refined Gold*.
352. Mātṛceṭa, *Varṇārhavarṇestotra*, Toh 1138 Tengyur, bstod tshogs, *ka*, 94a7.
353. Source not found.
354. In the present text we find *bzung*, "memorize," whereas the *Great* and *Middle-Length* treatises have *mnyan*, "listen" or "study."
355. Tsongkhapa, *Great Treatise* (Tib.), 135.
356. According to the Fifth Dalai Lama's outline, the entire work is divided into three parts, preliminaries, the main body of the text, and its conclusion. The part on the preliminaries mainly treats the topic of reliance on spiritual teachers, but it is also subdivided into two parts, the preparations and the actual topic. At this point, the former has been covered, and now begins the actual topic of reliance on spiritual teachers.

357. Maitreya, *Mahāyānasūtrālaṃkāra*, 18.10, Toh 4020 Tengyur, sems tsam, *phi*, 24b2.
358. Āryadeva, *Catuḥśataka*, 12.1, Toh 3846 Tengyur, dbu ma, *tsha*, 13a5.
359. The four rivers are ignorance, attachment, craving, and wrong views.
360. Faith constitutes the best pair of feet to take you to liberation and omniscience.
361. *Ratnolkādhāraṇī*, Toh 145 Kangyur, mdo sde, *pa*, 63b7.
362. Puṇḍarīka, *In Service of the Ultimate* (*Paramārthasevā*), Toh 1348 Tengyur, rgyud, *na*, 4b2.
363. *Pitāputrasamāgamanasūtra*, Toh 60 Kangyur, dkon brtsegs, *nga*, 33a7: "I appear as Indra and Brahmā; other times I appear as a demon to accomplish sentient beings' welfare. This worldly beings cannot understand."
364. *Gaṇḍavyūhasūtra*, Toh 44 Kangyur, phal chen, *a*, 299a5.
365. Aśvaghoṣa, *Gurupañcāśikā*, verse 46, Toh 3721 Tengyur, rgyud, *tshu*, 11b5.
366. Lama Serlingpa, "the guru from Golden Isle (Suvarṇadvīpa)," was the eleventh-century master whom Atiśa traveled from India to Sumatra to meet and receive vital instructions on the generation of the awakening mind.
367. This master's complete name is Great Abbot Setsun of Trum (*Grum gyi mkhan po chen po se btsun*). He was a contemporary and a one-time teacher of Dromtönpa.
368. Drokmi Lotsāwa Shākya Yeshé (b. 993), well known for bringing to Tibet the *path and its results* (*lam 'bras*) teachings so central to the Sakya tradition.
369. Aśvaghoṣa, *Gurupañcāśikā*, verse 21, Toh 3721 Tengyur, rgyud, *tshu*, 10b6.
370. Ibid. verse 24, 11a1.
371. *Vajrapāṇyabhiṣekamahātantra*, Toh 496 Kangyur, rgyud, *da*.
372. Tsongkhapa, *Great Treatise*, 48 (Tib.); 1:93 (trans.).
373. "These days" refers to the approach followed in the Segyü Lineage.
374. Taklung Drakpa Lodrö Gyatso (1546–1618) was the thirtieth Ganden Throne-holder and the founder of Jangtsé College of Ganden Monastery. From him, the lamrim teachings passed to Könchok Chöphel, who in turn transmitted them to the Fifth Dalai Lama. The Great Fifth said of Taklung Drakpa Lodrö Gyatso that he was the best Dharma friend he had for exchanging ideas and discussing the Dharma. He added Jampalyang (Sanskrit Mañjuśrī) to his name as an honorific.
375. The Fifth Dalai Lama is probably referring here to the *Account of the Prior Aspirations of the Seven Tathāgatas* (*Saptatathāgatapūrvapraṇidhānaviśeṣavistara*, Toh 503 Kangyur, rgyud, *da*). The Great Fifth composed a lengthy work on this sutra, including a formal Medicine Buddha rite (*sman bla mdo chog*), entitled *King of Gems: A Rite Propitiating the Seven Sugatas*.
376. You visualize empty seats and then invite the members of the merit field to come and sit.
377. Sönam Gyatso, *Essence of Refined Gold*, 5a5.
378. The complete verse reads: "Protector of all sentient beings without exception, / deity who destroys Māra's endless armies, / you who know the ultimate nature of all phenomena, / O Bhagavan, I pray, please come here with your assembly.
379. The third verse reads: How excellent that the Bhagavan has come! / What good fortune and merit we have! / O Bhagavan, for as long as I present offerings, / I pray that you may remain.
380. *Sumāgadhāvadāna*, Toh 346 Kangyur, mdo sde, *aṃ*.

381. Śāntideva, *Bodhicaryāvatāra*, 2.10, Toh 3871 Tengyur, dbu ma, *la*, 8b6.
382. The complete verse reads "Just as gods bathed [the Buddha] immediately after his birth, I too bathe [the merit field] with water divine and pure." It is found in many rites for the six preliminary practices, such as the version of the rite by Kalsang Tenzin Khedrup for the Southern Transmission version of *Words of Mañjuśrī*.
383. Tsongkhapa, *Great Treatise* (Tib.), 42.
384. Some of the ways to rely on your spiritual teachers in deed are to wash and wipe their body and give them a massage. When you don't have the opportunity to do these, offering ablutions according to the practice of the six preliminaries serves as an alternative.
385. Śāntideva, *Bodhicaryāvatāra*, 2.12, Toh 3871 Tengyur, dbu ma, *la*, 4a7.
386. This and the next set of verses referred to are part of a popular liturgy of offering rite, but their exact sources remain unidentified.
387. Śrī Buddha is Surchen Chöying Rangdröl, the author's guru. The next line refers to Ngawang Losang Gyatso, the Fifth Dalai Lama himself.
388. This part of the rite for the six preliminary practices, called the seven-part prayer (*yan lag bdun pa*), is an extract of the *Vows of Good Conduct* (*Bhadracaryāpraṇidhāna*) found in the *Flower Ornament Sutra*.
389. Quoted in Tsongkhapa, *Great Treatise* (Tib.), 135.
390. Tsuta, or Cūta, a land of one-legged inhabitants. See Yangchen Gawai Lodrö, *Rays of Sunlight*, 285.
391. Ibid.
392. According to the oral tradition, bowls of drinking water are to be visualized in rows on top of inverted rainbows in space, hence *garlands*. This passage is found in various rituals.
393. The recitations from here to the end of the next paragraph all come from the *Adornment of Trees Sutra* (*Gaṇḍavyūhasūtra*), Toh 44 Kangyur, phal chen, *a*, 395a–b.
394. *Teachings of Akṣayamati Sutra.* (*Akṣayamatinirdeśasūtra*), Toh 175 Kangyur, mdo sde, *ma*, 107a1: "Venerable Śāriputra, it is thus: just as a drop of water that falls into the great ocean does not disappear, is not in the least spent nor consumed until [the ocean] is burned by the [fires at the end of the] eon, in the same way, a virtue dedicated to complete enlightenment does not disappear, is not in the least spent nor consumed until the essence of enlightenment."
395. *Spyi bshags*, a brief confession rite brought to Tibet by Atiśa.
396. Maitreya, *Mahāyānasūtrālaṃkāra*, 2.10, Toh 4020 Tengyur, sems tsam, *phi*, 2b5.
397. Nāgārjuna, *Suhṛllekha*, verses 63–64, Toh 4182 Tengyur, spring yig, *nge*, 43b4.
398. These are killing your father, mother, or an arhat, shedding a buddha's blood, and creating a schism in the sangha.
399. This and the next verse pertaining to five general opportunities are cited from Tsongkhapa's *Great Treatise*, where they appear to be Tsongkhapa's own summation of these two sets in verse for easy memorization.
400. See previous note.
401. Candragomin, *Śiṣyalekha*, verse 63, Toh 4183 Tengyur, spring yig, *ngi*, 50a2. Garuḍas, vidyādharas, and kinnaras are various nonhuman life forms. Belly crawl-

ers are snakes and other reptiles that crawl on their bellies. Nāgas are usually included in this category.

402. The Tibetan term translates literally as "karma accumulator" and refers to those who have powerful karma that can ripen and produce its results within a single lifetime.

403. Śāntideva, *Bodhicaryāvatāra*, 4.20, Toh 3871 Tengyur, dbu ma, *la*, 8b6.

404. *Precious Garland* (*Ratnāvalī*) 5.38, Toh 4158 Tengyur, skyes rab, *ge*, 123b1.

405. The Tibetan *mtsams sbyor* suggests "to direct to the attainment of the desired result."

406. According to Nāgārjuna, the eight worldly concerns involve gain and the lack of it; happiness and unhappiness; pleasant words and unpleasant words; and praise and blame. The attitudes in relation to them are liking the first in each pair and disliking the second. They are said to be black, white, or two-toned according to various criteria.

407. Atiśa, *Bodhipathapradīpa*, verse 3, Toh 3947 Tengyur, dbu ma, *khi*, 238b1.

408. *Udānavarga*, "Chapter on Impermanence," 1.25, Toh 376 Kangyur, mdo sde, *sa*, 210a1.

409. Ibid. 1.26, 210a1.

410. *Lalitavistarasūtra*, Toh 95 Kangyur, mdo sde, *kha*, 88a2.

411. Śāntideva, *Bodhicaryāvatāra*, 2.39, Toh 3871 Tengyur, dbu ma, *la*, 5b2.

412. Vasubandhu, *Abhidharmakośa*, 3.79, Toh 4089 Tengyur, mngon pa, *ku*, 9b7.

413. This verse was not found in the *Udānavarga*.

414. Nāgārjuna, *Ratnāvalī*, 3.78, Toh 4158 Tengyur, spring yig, *ge*, 9b7.

415. Nāgārjuna, *Suhṛllekha*, verse 55, Toh 4182 Tengyur, spring yig *nge*, 43a6.

416. Yama, the Lord of Death, is death personified.

417. Śāntideva, *Bodhicaryāvatāra*, 2.41, Toh 3871 Tengyur, dbu ma, *la*, 5b3.

418. Nāgārjuna, *A Drop to Rejuvenate the Person* (*Jantupoṣaṇabindu*), Toh 4330 Tengyur, lugs kyi bstan bcos, *ngo*, 115a6.

419. Vasubandhu, *Abhidharmakośabhāṣya*, Toh 4090 Tengyur, mngon pa *ku*, 153a4.

420. Nāgārjuna, *Suhṛllekha*, verse 87, Toh 4182 Tengyur, spring yig, *nge*, 44a5.

421. *Achoo* is a Tibetan interjection used when one feels cold, and *kyihoo* is an interjection equivalent to "Woe is me!"

422. Āryaśūra, *Jātakamālā*, Toh 4150 Tengyur, skyes rab, *hu*, 111b4.

423. A *khal* is a Tibetan unit of both volume and weight, composed of twenty *dré* (*bre*). *Dré* is the name for both a square container and a unit of volume that approximates a quart. Three *khal* make up the load that a yak can carry.

424. Nāgārjuna, *Suhṛllekha*, verse 90, Toh 4182 Tengyur, spring yig, *nge*, 44b6.

425. The *Five Sections on Grounds* (*Sa sde nga*) here refers to the *Yogācāra Grounds* (*Yogācārabhūmi*) Toh 4035.

426. Nāgārjuna, *Suhṛllekha*, verse 91, Toh 4182 Tengyur, spring yig, *nge*, 45a1.

427. Nāgārjuna, *A Drop to Rejuvenate the Person* (*Jantupoṣaṇabindu*), Toh 4330 Tengyur, lugs kyi bstan bcos, *ngo*, 115a7.

428. Śāntideva, *Bodhicaryāvatāra*, 1.5–6, Toh 3871 Tengyur, dbu ma, *la*, 2a1.

429. *Interwoven Praise* (*Miśrakastotra*), Toh 1150 Tengyur, bstod tshogs, *ka*, 181a2.

430. Aśvaghoṣa, *Śatapañcāśatakastotra*, verse 1, Toh 1147 Tengyur, bstod tshogs, *ka*, 110a3.

431. Candrakīrti, *Triśaraṇagamanasaptati*, Toh 3971 Tengyur, dbu ma, *gi*, 251a1.
432. Mātṛceṭa, *Praise to the One Beyond All Praise* (*Varṇārhavarṇestotra*), Toh 1138 Tengyur, bstod tshogs, *ka*, 99b4.
433. In tantra you visualize the objects of refuge or members of the merit field, called *commitment beings*, and then you invite the actual buddhas and so on, called *wisdom beings*, to come from their abodes and dissolve into the beings you have visualized.
434. Just seeing it purifies you of wrongdoing, for example.
435. That is, the *Range of the Bodhisattva Sutra* (*Bodhisattvagocarasūtra*), chap. 9, Toh 146, Kangyur, mdo sde, *pa*, 121a7.
436. Mātṛceṭa, *Varṇārhavarṇestotra*, Toh 1138 Tengyur, bstod tshogs, *ka*, 89b2.
437. Aśvaghoṣa, *Śatapañcāśatakastotra*, verse 6, Toh 1147 Tengyur, bstod tshogs, *ka*, 112a7.
438. Ibid. verse 13, 14b2.
439. Śāriputra and Maudgalyāyana.
440. Kalyāṇamitra, *Vinayavastuṭīkā*, Toh 4113 Tengyur, 'dul ba, *tsu*, 239a5.
441. Here the eight worldly concerns are qualified as two-toned—a combination of white and black—because although afflictions like attachment are present, the motivation is adequate: the intention is to create conditions that favor spiritual practice.
442. Nāgārjuna, *Ratnāvalī*, 4.21, Toh 4158 Tengyur, skyes rab, *ge*, 107b5.
443. *Samādhirājasūtra*, chap. 14, Toh 127 Kangyur, mdo sde, *da*, 47a2.
444. E.g., in the *Hundred on Karma* (*Karmaśataka*), Toh 340 Kangyur, mdo sde, *ha*, 16a3.
445. *Mchod gnas*, which translates literally as "recipient of offerings." The term refers most often to ordained or lay people who perform prayers and ceremonies in people's homes on their request.
446. Vasubandhu, *Abhidharmakośa*, 4.66, Toh 4089 Tengyur, mngon pa, *ku*, 13a7.
447. For the five traits of covetousness and ill will, the passages added in square brackets are drawn from Tsongkhapa's *Great Treatise*, 154 (Tib.), 1:224–26 (trans.), whose source is Asaṅga's *Compendium of Abhidharma*.
448. Wrong views have five additional traits as well. According to Tsongkhapa's *Great Treatise*, 154 (Tib.), 1:226–27 (trans.), they are (1) the ignorance that is not knowing how knowable entities exist, (2) cruelty by which you delight in sin, (3) habitual wrong thinking owing to incorrect reflection, (4) the degenerate thinking of incorrect denial, repudiating generosity, offerings, burnt offerings, ethical conduct, and so forth, and (5) being oppressed by the drawbacks of wrong views from not knowing how to avoid them and by shamelessness regarding your wrong views.
449. *Treasury of Abhidharma* (*Abhidharmakośa*) 4.50, Toh 4089 Tengyur, mngon pa, *ku*, 12b6. The "and so forth" here is karma whose results are experienced in the next life and karma whose results are experienced in a third life or later.
450. "Freedom from attachment" refers the state of an ārya that is attained by realizing emptiness directly. Those with a definite karma to be born in the desire realm can attain it, but only if that karma is first purified.

451. The author is referring to some Kagyü meditators.
452. Here the author is referring to the behavior of some Nyingma meditators.
453. Nāgārjuna, *Suhṛllekha*, verse 30, Toh 4182 Tengyur, spring yig, *nge*, 42a3.
454. Ibid., verse 14, 41a7.
455. Tsongkhapa, *A Rite on the Four Powers as Antidotes Against Negative Karma*, 267–75.
456. *Triskhandhadharmasūtra*, a.k.a. *A Bodhisattva's Confession of Downfalls*, which is an extract from *Ascertaining the Discipline: The Sutra of Upāli's Questions* (*Vinaya-viniścayopāliparipṛcchāsūtra*), Toh 68 Kangyur, dkon brtsegs, *ca*. The extracted confession appears in Śāntideva's *Compendium of Training* (*Śikṣāsamuccaya*).
457. *Suvarṇaprabhāsottamasūtra*, chap. 3, Toh 556 Kangyur, rgyud, *pa*, 6b6–11b3.
458. Lotus Holder is an epithet for Avalokiteśvara, and the Lord of Secrets is Vajrapāṇi.
459. Atiśa, *Bodhipathapradīpa*, Toh 3947 Tengyur, dbu ma, *khi*, 238b1.
460. Śāntideva, *Bodhicaryāvatāra*, 9.157, Toh 3871 Tengyur, dbu ma, *la*, 37a2.
461. For instance, in the *Ascertainment of the Meaning Dharma Discourse* (*Arthaviniś-cayadharmaparyāya*), Toh 317 Kangyur, mdo sde, *sa*, 174a5.
462. Āryadeva, *Catuḥśataka*, 7.1, Toh 3846 Tengyur, dbu ma, *tsha*, 8a4.
463. Maitreya, *Uttaratantra*, 4.52, Toh 4024 Tengyur, sems tsam, *phi*, 69b7.
464. Candragomin, *Śiṣyalekha*, Toh 4183 Tengyur, spring yig, *ngi*, 47b3.
465. *Lalitavistarasūtra*, Toh 95 Kangyur, mdo sde, *kha*, 88b4.
466. Ibid., 88b6.
467. Ibid., 88b7.
468. Nāgārjuna, *Suhṛllekha*, verses 99–100a, Toh 4182 Tengyur, spring yig, *nge*, 45a6.
469. The name given to certain desire-realm gods who are aware of their past life, their future life, and those of others.
470. Nāgārjuna, *Suhṛllekha*, verse 66, Toh 4182 Tengyur, spring yig, *nge*, 43b6.
471. Ibid., verse 26, 42a1.
472. Aśvaghoṣa, *Śokavinodana*, Toh 4177 Tengyur, spring yig, *nge*, 34a5.
473. Nāgārjuna, *Suhṛllekha*, verse 68, Toh 4182 Tengyur, spring yig, *nge*, 43b7.
474. Ibid., verse 69, 43b7.
475. In Indian culture the sun and moon are regarded as sentient beings.
476. Śāntideva, *Bodhicaryāvatāra*, 8.31, Toh 3871 Tengyur, dbu ma, *la*, 24b3.
477. This passage is quoted in Tsongkhapa, *Great Treatise*, 196 (Tib.), 1:280 (trans.).
478. Dharmakīrti, *Pramāṇavārttika*, 2.195, Toh 4210 Tengyur, tshad ma, *ce*, 115a1.
479. Śāntideva, *Bodhicaryāvatāra*, 4.30–31, Toh 3871 Tengyur, dbu ma, *la*, 9a5.
480. Geshé Ben, also known as Geshé Tsultrim Gyalwa, was an eleventh-century Kadam master who began his life as a thief and brigand. After a change of heart, he became Geshé Potowa's disciple and a genuine practitioner.
481. See note 190 above.
482. Dharmakīrti, *Pramāṇavārttika*, 1.221, Toh 4210 Tengyur, tshad ma, *ce*, 116a1.
483. Śāntideva, *Bodhicaryāvatāra*, 4.45–46, Toh 3871 Tengyur, dbu ma *la*, 10a1.
484. *Mahāparinirvāṇasūtra*, section 35, Toh 199 Kangyur, mdo sde, *ta*, 71a1.
485. See note 484 above.
486. Śāntideva, *Bodhicaryāvatāra*, 6.72, Toh 3871 Tengyur, dbu ma, *la*, 12a1.
487. Having become impoverished, the king had nothing but dust to offer Ārya

Kātyāyana. His virtuous intention to make an offering resulted in the rain of jewels falling, while the act of offering dust resulted in his death in a dust storm. The scriptural source of the story was not located.

488. Vasubandhu, *Abhidharmakośabhāṣya*, Toh 4090 Tengyur, mngon pa, *ku*, 94b5.
489. Phuchungwa Shönu Gyaltsen (1031–1106) was one of Dromtönpa's three main disciples known as "the three brothers." The other two are Potowa Rinchen Sal (1027–1105) and Chenga Tsultrim Bar (1038–1103).
490. Nāgārjuna, *Suhṛllekha*, verse 104, Toh 4182 Tengyur, spring yig, *nge*, 43b4. The earth, air, fire, and water mentioned here correspond to paradises in the Hindu belief system.
491. See page 45 above.
492. Nāgārjuna, *Suhṛllekha*, verse 7, Toh 4182 Tengyur, spring yig, *nge*, 41a2.
493. *Brahmāparipṛcchāsūtra*, Toh 158, Kangyur, mdo sde, *ba*. While this sutra does speak of mindfulness of maintaining pure ethical conduct, this passage is not found in the sutra, but it is in Asaṅga's *Yogācāra Grounds* (*Yogācārabhūmi*), Toh 4035 Tengyur, sems tsam, *tshi*, 211b2.
494. Degeneration of fellow sentient beings, era, afflictions, views, and life span.
495. Passage quoted in Tsongkhapa's *Great Treatise* (Tib.), 254.
496. Atiśa, *Bodhipathapradīpa*, Toh 3947 Tengyur, dbu ma, *khi*, 238b2.
497. Āryaśūra, *Pāramitāsamāsa*, Toh 3944 Tengyur, dbu ma, *khi*, 234b6.
498. Candragomin, *Śiṣyalekha*, Toh 4183 Tengyur, spring yig, *ngi*, 52a5.
499. Śāntideva, *Bodhicaryāvatāra*, 1.9, Toh 3871 Tengyur, dbu ma, *la*, 2a5.
500. According to Gyaltsab Jé's *Commentary on the Sublime Continuum*, here *mos pa* (Skt. *adhimukti*) is to be understood as faith and, of its three forms—of clarity or admiration, conviction, and longing or emulation—as faith in the form of conviction.
501. Maitreya, *Uttaratantra*, 1.34, Toh 3846 Tengyur, sems tsam, *phi*, 46a6.
502. See Tsongkhapa, *Great Treatise* (trans.), 2:22–25.
503. Of the two kinds of love, sympathetic love (*yi ong byams pa*) and love that is the wish for others' happiness (*bde ba ster 'dod kyi byams pa*), the former arises naturally from contemplating recognition of all beings as your mothers, being mindful of their kindness, and wishing to repay that kindness. The latter kind of love can be achieved either prior to realizing compassion or after it, before cultivating the superior resolve.
504. Candrakīrti, *Madhyamakāvatāra*, 1.2, Toh 3861 Tengyur, dbu ma, *'a*, 201a2.
505. This is specified because the same term, *gtang snyoms* (Skt. *upekṣā*), applies not only to one of four infinite qualities (the others being love, compassion, and joy) but also to neutral feelings and to a mental factor integral to tranquil abiding.
506. Candragomin, *Śiṣyalekha*, verse 96, Toh 4183 Tengyur, spring yig, *nge*, 52a1.
507. *Nāgarājabherīgāthā*, Toh 325 Kangyur, mdo sde *sa*, 205b3.
508. Nāgārjuna, *Ratnāvalī*, 3.83–85, Toh 4158 Tengyur, spring yig, *ge*, 117b3.
509. This Tibetan expression, literally "old mothers" (*ma rgan*), is to be understood as referring to the fact that sentient beings have been your mother innumerable times over your countless past lives.
510. *Nyams 'og tu tshud pa*, is the stage of mastery of a meditation topic achieved prior

to gaining personal experience with effort, which in turn precedes a spiritual realization qualified as "beyond effort" or "spontaneous."

511. Tsongkhapa, *Great Treatise*, 274–75 (Tib.), 2:44 (trans.).
512. Śāntideva, *Bodhicaryāvatāra*, 8.120, Toh 3871 Tengyur, dbu ma, *la*, 28a5.
513. Ibid. 8.128–30, 25b3.
514. Ibid. 8.119, 28a4.
515. By Chekawa Yeshé Dorjé (1101–75). See Jinpa, *Mind Training*, 83–85.
516. Nāgārjuna, *Ratnāvalī*, 4.85, Toh 4158 Tengyur, spring yig, *ge*, 125a6.
517. Tsongkhapa, *Great Treatise*, 286–304 (Tib.), 2:61–84 (trans.).
518. *Maitreyavimokṣa*, Toh 44 Kangyur, phal chen, *a*, 305a3.
519. Dharmakīrti, *Pramāṇavārttika*, 2.132, Toh 4210 Tengyur, tshad ma, *ce*, 112b2.
520. Śāntideva, *Bodhicaryāvatāra*, 1.16, Toh 3871 Tengyur, dbu ma, *la*, 2b5.
521. See note 220 above.
522. Śāntideva, *Śikṣāsamuccaya*, Toh 3940 Tengyur, dbu ma, *khi*, 10a5.
523. The literal expression is the "belongings cakra," which is the name for the throat cakra that represents the authors' explanations.
524. The wish-granting objects in question are Dharma teachings.
525. Maitreya, *Mahāyānasūtrālaṃkāra*, 17.2, Toh 4020 Tengyur, sems tsam, *phi*, 21a6. This is the first of six verses in which Maitreya indicates the six criteria for establishing that the number of perfections is definitely six, as explained in the following six paragraphs.
526. That is, these six requisite factors are products, respectively, of the six perfections.
527. Maitreya, *Mahāyānasūtrālaṃkāra*, 17.14, Toh 4020 Tengyur, sems tsam, *phi*, 21b7.
528. Āryaśūra, *Jātakamālā*, chap. 1, Toh 4150 Tengyur, skyes rab, *hu*, 3b4.
529. Śāntideva, *Bodhicaryāvatāra*, 5.9, Toh 3871 Tengyur, dbu ma, *la*, 10b2.
530. Ibid. 5.10, 10b3.
531. This passage is quoted in Tsongkhapa's *Great Treatise* (Tib.), 333.
532. Here "wrongly" means with the intention to harm.
533. Āryaśūra, *Pāramitāsamāsa*, Toh 3944, dbu ma, *khi*, 221a7.
534. See above: the view of the purpose of giving, the view of the things to give, and the view of the recipient.
535. Śāntideva, *Bodhicaryāvatāra*, 5.87, Toh 3871 Tengyur, dbu ma, *la*, 13b4.
536. Ibid. 5.11, 10b3.
537. Atiśa, *Bodhipathapradīpa*, Toh 3947 Tengyur, dbu ma, *khi*, 239a4.
538. Atiśa, *Bodhimārgapradīpapañjikā*, Toh 3948 Tengyur, dbu ma, *khi*, 258a5.
539. The vow for individual liberation (*prātimokṣa*) that is the vow to abstain from killing, for example, is *concordant* with the bodhisattva vow of abstention from killing but is not that latter vow because it taken for the duration of one's present life alone while the bodhisattva vows are taken for all one's lives. See Gomchen's lamrim on page 116 above: "The vow of individual liberation within a bodhisattva's mind / is the vow of ethical discipline, not the bodhisattva vow."
540. Āryaśūra, *Pāramitāsamāsa*, Toh 3944 Tengyur, dbu ma, *khi*, 222a2.
541. Here, the three kinds of practitioners are persons of lesser, intermediate, and great capacity.
542. In the present context, "the three trainings" refers to cultivating the wisdoms of learning, reflection, and meditation.

543. Āryaśūra, *Pāramitāsamāsa,* Toh 3944 Tengyur, dbu ma, *khi,* 224a1.
544. Śāntideva, *Bodhicaryāvatāra,* 4.12–14, Toh 3871 Tengyur, dbu ma, *la,* 10b4.
545. Ibid. 6.1, 14b3.
546. Candrakīrti, *Madhyamakāvatāra,* 3.6, Toh 3861 Tengyur, dbu ma, *'a,* 20a5.
547. Śāntideva, *Bodhicaryāvatāra,* 6.6, Toh 3871 Tengyur, dbu ma, *la,* 14b6.
548. Ibid. 6.37, 16a2.
549. Ibid. 6.42, 16a5.
550. Ibid. 6.90, 18a4.
551. Ibid. 6.87–89, 18a2.
552. Ibid. 6.14, 14a3.
553. That is to say, this is the indisputable nature of samsaric existence.
554. Ibid. 7.2, 20a4.
555. Maitreya, *Mahāyānasūtrālaṃkāra,* 17.66–67, Toh 4020 Tengyur, sems tsam, *phi,* 24b1.
556. Śāntideva, *Bodhicaryāvatāra,* 7.3, Toh 3871 Tengyur, dbu ma, *la,* 20a5.
557. Ibid. 7.15, 20b4.
558. Ibid 7.17–19, 20b6.
559. Ibid 7.24–26, 21a2.
560. Ibid. 7.27–28, 21a4.
561. These four powers that enhance diligence are explained in the *Bodhicaryāvatāra,* 7.31–67, and expanded further in Tsongkhapa's *Great Treatise* (trans.), 2:195–201.
562. Śāntideva, *Bodhicaryāvatāra,* 7.67, Toh 3871 Tengyur, dbu ma, *la,* 23a1.
563. Ibid. 8.1, 23a7.
564. *Saṃdhinirmocanasūtra,* chap. 3, Toh 106 Kangyur, mdo sde, *ca,* 9b2.
565. *Dysfunctional tendencies* are defined in Tsongkhapa's *Great Treatise* (Tib.), 422, as a mind's predispositions that can generate more and more afflictions; *signs* are defined as the habitual manifest cravings for wrong objects that activate these predispositions.
566. Here "grasping at signs" is mainly grasping at the wrong object that is intrinsic existence.
567. *Candrapradīpasūtra* (a.k.a. *King of Meditations Sutra, Samādhirājasūtra*), chap. 7, Toh 127, Kangyur, mdo sde, *da,* 20b6.
568. Śāntideva, *Bodhicaryāvatāra,* 8.1 Toh 3871 Tengyur, dbu ma *la,* 23a7.
569. Ibid. 5.16, 10b6. The Knower of Suchness here is the Buddha.
570. Ibid. 8.4, 23b1.
571. Maitreya, *Mahāyānasūtrālaṃkāra,* 14.7, Toh 4020 Tengyur, sems tsam, *phi,* 17b7.
572. In the context of the six favorable conditions for cultivating tranquil abiding, "attachment" refers to eight thoughts of desire to reject, which are enumerated in Asaṅga's *Śrāvaka Grounds*: desire, ill will, physical violence, thoughts concerning your circle of family and friends, thoughts concerning compatriots, thoughts of not dying, scorn for others, and thoughts concerning worldly wealth and so on.
573. Asaṅga, *Śrāvakabhūmi,* chap. 2 Toh 4036 Tengyur, sems tsam, *dzi,* 77a5 ā.
574. *Condensed Presentation of the Perfections* (*Pāramitāsamāsa*), Toh 3944 Tengyur, dbu ma, *khi,* 229a4.
575. *Chapter on the Conditions for Meditative Concentration* (*Samādhisambhāraparivarta*), Toh 3924 Tengyur, dbu ma, *ki,* 90a5.

576. Possibly the late eighth and early ninth-century Tibetan translator of the Shang clan.
577. Maitreya, *Madhyāntavibhāga*, 4.3, Toh 4021 Tengyur, sems tsam, *phi*, 43a3.
578. Ibid. 4.5, 43a4.
579. Asaṅga, *Abhidharmasamuccaya*, Toh 4049 Tengyur, sems tsam, *ri*, 4b3.
580. Bhāviveka, *Madhyamakahṛdaya*, Toh 3855 Tengyur, dbu ma, *dza*, 4a6.
581. Śāntideva, *Bodhicaryāvatāra*, 5.108, Toh 3871 Tengyur, dbu ma, *la*, 14b1.
582. Asaṅga, *Abhidharmasamuccaya*, Toh 4049 Tengyur, sems tsam, *ri*, 8a5.
583. Kamalaśīla, *Bhāvanākrama II*, Toh 3916 Tengyur, dbu ma, *ki*, 47b7.
584. The reference to an "obstructive indeterminate" (*bsgribs lung ma bstan*) is missing in the critical version on which the present translation is based but is found in the blockprint version known as Drepung Parma printed at Miruk Phuntsok Ling Monastery in Lhasa at the request of the seventieth Ganden Throneholder Ngawang Chöphel (1760–1839) and in the version printed by the Sera Jé Library (Bylakuppe) in 2003. The *Great Treatise* (Tib., 463) also describes lethargy as either nonvirtuous or an obstructive indeterminate.
585. Asaṅga, *Abhidharmasamuccaya*, Toh 4049 Tengyur, sems tsam, *ri*, 5a7.
586. The term translated as "slack" (*zhum pa*) here translates literally as "discouraged."
587. Bhāviveka, *Madhyamakahṛdaya*, Toh 3855 Tengyur, dbu ma, *la*, 4a7.
588. When focusing on the Buddha's form, you could increase the size of the figure for example.
589. Ibid., 4a6.
590. Kamalaśīla, *Bhāvanākrama II*, Toh 3916 Tengyur, dbu ma, *ki*, 50b4.
591. Sakya Paṇḍita, *Clear Differentiation*, 24b2.
592. Butön, *Dispelling Bad Views*, 31a2.
593. The literal expression is "turn myself into a white crow" (*bya rog lus dkar sgrub pa*).
594. Atiśa, *Bodhipathapradīpa*, Toh 3947 Tengyur, dbu ma, *khi*, 240a1.
595. *Samādhirājasūtra*, chap. 4, Toh 127 Kangyur, mdo sde, *da*, 13b5.
596. In the case of coarse laxity, the loss of clarity implies that the object is no longer present in the mind. Here *limpidity* refers to one of the mind's fundamental features, the ability to reflect or take on the aspect of the objects it perceives.
597. *Praise in the Form of a Confession* (*Deśanāstava*), Toh 1159 Tengyur, bstod tshogs, *ka*, 205b5.
598. In the context of cultivating tranquil abiding, *thought application* (*rnam rtog 'du byed pa*) and *non-thought application* (*rnam rtog 'du mi byed pa*) refer, respectively, to the seventh and eighth of the eight applications (*'du byed brgyas*) that are antidotes to the five faults. Of the nine mental states covered in the process, in the eighth state, although neither laxity nor excitation are present, mindfulness—which is what "thought" in the expression "thought application" refers to—must still be employed to keep them at bay. In the ninth state, as they are no longer a threat, their antidotes are not needed, and it is a mistake to employ them. As such, the appropriate action is "non-thought application," often called *nonapplication* or *equanimity*.
599. *Thud*, a delicacy made of clarified butter and dried cheese.
600. Maitreya, *Mahāyānasūtrālaṃkāra*, 15.14, Toh 4020 Tengyur, sems tsam, *phi*, 19a7.
601. "Uninterrupted paths of the path of meditation" (*sgom lam bar chad med lam*)

are direct realizations of emptiness in a state of meditative equipoise in which the innate afflictive obscurations and obscurations to knowledge are eliminated in succession.

602. In this context, the conceptions (*rtog pa*) referred to are laxity and excitation.
603. Nāgārjuna, *Prajñāśataka*, Toh 4328 Tengyur, bzo rig pa / thun mong ba, *ngo*, 99b6.
604. Mātṛceṭa, *Varṇārhavarṇestotra*, Toh 1138 Tengyur, bstod tshogs, *ka*, 96a3.
605. *Samādhirājasūtra*, chap. 9, Toh 127 Kangyur, mdo sde, *da*, 27a7.
606. Mātṛceṭa, *Varṇārhavarṇestotra*, Toh 1138 Tengyur, bstod tshogs, *ka*, 96a4.
607. *Three Principal Elements of the Path*, verse 9. See page 52 above.
608. Nāgārjuna, *Yuktiṣaṣṭikā*, verse 60, Toh 3825 Tengyur, dbu ma, *tsa*, 22b4.
609. *Entering the Middle Way* (*Madhyamakāvatāra*) 6.80, Toh 3861 Tengyur, dbu ma, *'a*, 208a2.
610. Here the author is suggesting the conclusion to be drawn based on Candrakīrti's words.
611. An epithet for India.
612. Nāgārjuna, *Ratnāvalī*, 2.18, Toh 4158 Tengyur, spring yig, *ge*, 111a6.
613. *Laṅkāvatārasūtra*, Toh 107 Kangyur, mdo sde, *ca*, 165b5.
614. Candrakīrti, *Madhyamakāvatāra*, 6.79, Toh 3861 Tengyur, dbu ma, *'a*, 208a1.
615. Atiśa, *Satyadvayāvatāra*, Toh 3902 Tengyur, dbu ma, *a*, 72b4.
616. Candrakīrti, *Catuḥśatakaṭīkā*, Toh 3865 Tengyur, dbu ma, *ya*, 190b2.
617. Āryadeva, *Catuḥśataka*, 8.14, Toh 3846 Tengyur, dbu ma, *tsha*, 7b2.
618. *Sixty Verses of Reasoning* (*Yuktiṣaṣṭikā*) verse 3, Toh 3825 Tengyur, dbu ma, *tsa*, 20a2.
619. Āryadeva, *Catuḥśataka*, 6.10–11, Toh 3846 Tengyur, dbu ma, *tsha*, 7b2.
620. Candrakīrti, *Madhyamakāvatāra*, 6.120, Toh 3861 Tengyur, dbu ma, *'a*, 210a4.
621. Nāgārjuna, *Ratnāvalī*, 1.35, Toh 4158 Tengyur, spring yig, *ge*, 108a5.
622. Khedrup Gelek Palsang (1385–1438), otherwise known as Khedrup Jé, one of Tsongkhapa's two foremost disciples.
623. See note 117.
624. Khedrup Norsang Gyatso (1423–1513) of Tashi Lhunpo Monastery was the most prominent disciple of the First Dalai Lama Gendun Drup. His main spiritual son was the Second Dalai Lama, Gendun Gyatso. Khedrup Norsang Gyatso followed Khedrup Sherab Sengé's system.
625. Buddhapālita, *Mūlamadhyamakavṛtti*, chap. 8, Toh 3842 Tengyur, dbu ma, *tsha*, 198a2.
626. Śāntideva, *Bodhicaryāvatāra*, 9.139, Toh 3871 Tengyur, dbu ma, *la*, 36a6.
627. Candrakīrti, *Prasannapadā*, Toh 3860 Tengyur, dbu ma, *'a*, 110b7.
628. Nāgārjuna, *Mūlamadhyamakakārikā*, 27.5, Toh 3824 Tengyur, dbu ma, *tsa*, 18a1.
629. Candrakīrti, *Madhyamakāvatāra*, 6.127, Toh 3861 Tengyur, dbu ma, *'a*, 201b1.
630. Nāgārjuna, *Mūlamadhyamakakārikā*, 18.1, Toh 3824 Tengyur, dbu ma, *tsa*, 10b6.
631. Candrakīrti, *Madhyamakāvatāra*, 6.61, Toh 3861 Tengyur, dbu ma, *'a*, 202a4.
632. Ibid. 6.124, 210a6.
633. Ibid. 6.165, 212a7.
634. When cultivating tranquil abiding and you initially reach the ninth mental state, pliancy is attained, but as it still has to be associated with the bliss of pliancy, you

have not yet realized tranquil abiding. Similarly, in the case of insight, when you achieve an initial understanding issuing from meditation (*sgom byung*), it does not qualify as special insight until it is concurrent with the bliss of pliancy.

635. Here "nonconceptually" (*mi rtog*) refers to a state of nonmentation.
636. Here "nonconceptual" (*mi rtog*) means nonanalytical or placement meditation.
637. Potowa, *Blue Compendium*, 28.4. This is also quoted by Tsongkhapa in his lamrim treatises.
638. "Non-mindfulness" and "non-contemplation" are not to be taken literally, for they refer to placement meditation on the absence of the object of negation, an inherent self.
639. Kamalaśīla, *Bhāvanākrama III*, Toh 3917 Tengyur, dbu ma, *ki*, 62b6.
640. See notes 634–36.
641. *Kāśyapaparivartasūtra*, Toh 87 Kangyur, dkon brtsegs, *cha*, 133a7.
642. This Tibetan idiom means not mixing together things that should be kept separate.
643. Drakpa Gyaltsen, *Parting from the Four Clingings*, 297b2.
644. This verse includes an onomatopoeic term, *chal*, used to describe the sound of something falling into water. It is a reference to a story of a hare who was drinking on the edge of a river when a dead branch fell into the water. Frightened by the sound, it ran off to warn the other animals that there was a fierce creature in the river, so that all the animals fled in fear.
645. The objects, literally "signs," in meditation appear to exist inherently but are devoid of inherent existence.
646. *Samādhirājasūtra*, chap. 9, Toh 127 Kangyur, mdo sde, *da*, 26a6.
647. *Exposition of Valid Cognition* (*Pramāṇavārttika*) 2.222–23, Toh 4210 Tengyur, tshad ma, *ce*, 116a3.
648. Candrakīrti, *Madhyamakāvatāra*, 6.26, Toh 3861 Tengyur, dbu ma, *'a*, 116a3.
649. Khedrup Gelek Palsang, *Secret Biography of Tsongkhapa*, 115.
650. Taktsang Lotsāwa, *Establishing Freedom from Extremes*, 15. Taktsang (1405–77) was an important Sakya scholar who composed a critique of Tsongkhapa's interpretation of Madhyamaka philosophy, sparking a debate that lasted several centuries. Although the Fifth Dalai Lama greatly admired Taktsang, he rejects his critique of Tsongkhapa concerning the possibility of valid cognition perceiving conventional truths, asserting that Taktsang's error was like that of those mentioned above who confuse the mode of existence of illusory creatures such as magic horses with conventional existence.
651. Candrakīrti, *Prasannapadā*, Toh 3860 Tengyur, dbu ma, *'a*, 112a7.
652. Āryadeva, *Catuḥśataka*, 8.16, Toh 3846 Tengyur, dbu ma *tsha*, 9b6.
653. Bodhibhadra, *Explanation of Compendium on the Heart of Wisdom* (*Jñānasāra-samuccayanāmanibandhana*), Toh 3852 Tengyur, dbu ma, *tsha*, 33b3. The root text is a short work attributed to Āryadeva.
654. This refers to the Tibetan custom of counting up to twelve with one hand by touching the thumb to each of the three joints of the other four fingers.
655. What this phrase suggests is, "As your case is hopeless, keep quiet, and 'concentrate'"—in other words, "have a good sleep." The author is most likely scolding Kagyü practitioners, as he does at times.

656. Maitreya, *Mahāyānasūtrālaṃkāra*, 17.73, Toh 4020 Tengyur, sems tsam, *phi*, 24b6.
657. Literally "As if you had a bone in your heart."
658. The Tibetan text has *grol*, "liberated," instead of *gol*, "stray," found in other versions of the work.
659. The eight qualities of water are that it is sweet, cool, smooth, light, clear, clean, soothing to the throat, and calming to the stomach.
660. See page 44 above.
661. This refers to rebirths in fortunate states and underlines their drawbacks, which although less acute than those of lives in unfortunate states, are still considerable.
662. Peacocks are thought to mate in thunderstorms.
663. This is a reference to the Vedic tradition, according to which four great rivers, including the Ganges, flowed from Brahmā's four mouths. The rishi Jahnu, having drunk their waters, then vomited them, after which sixty thousand people drank them in turn, thereby purifying their sins.
664. They are either too concise on some topics or too detailed on others.
665. From the Earth, the moon's face displays the image of a hare, but just as no hare actually exists, the author's work is free of verbosity.
666. This analogy derives from the Vedic view that the moon rises from the ocean.
667. The is a reference to followers of the Geluk school of Tibetan Buddhism, which is sometimes referred to as the Yellow Hat school.
668. This is a reference to merchants who sail the oceans in search of precious gems and are beset by pirates.
669. This and the following verse criticize the tendency to attribute great qualities to young people, notably young reincarnate lamas, and put them on a pedestal before they have achieved anything in relation to the Dharma.
670. Amazed by something that is not what it seems to be. See previous note.
671. The thousand-spoked golden wheel is an attribute of universal sovereigns (Skt. *cakravartin*), literally "wheel turners." It is said to pass before them and take them wherever they wish to go.
672. Here buddhahood is compared to Īśvara's palace on top of the four levels of Mount Meru above ocean level. The four levels represent buddhas' four kinds of fearlessness (*mi 'jig pa bzhi*): fearlessness in terms of their realization of enlightenment, as it is irrefutable; fearlessness with regard to their abandonment of contaminants (afflictions and obscurations), as it is irrefutable; fearlessness in revealing the hindrances to liberation, as they are irrefutable; fearlessness in revealing the path to liberation, as it is irrefutable.
673. The Hindu god Īśvara is said to possess eyes that burn.
674. The god Brahmā, considered the creator of the world, is said to have hatched from a golden egg. The wheel represents a buddha's mental qualities, making the wheel's maker a buddha.
675. Chenga Lodrö Gyaltsen (1402–71) was a disciple of both Tsongkhapa and Khedrup Jé. On his lamrim texts, see introduction, page 12.
676. The "first part" refers to the stages of the path up to the end of the general explanation of the six perfections.
677. A similar expression is found in Sakya Paṇḍita's *Jewel Treasury of Wise Sayings*,

verse 399, where it says that "Being devoted to other teachers while the Buddha, the refuge of beings, is present is like digging a well to get brackish water near a river whose water possesses the eight good qualities."

678. The Third Dalai Lama's main disciple and a lineage master of the Southern Transmission Lamrim.
679. Jampa Rinchen was a geshé from Dakpo Shedrup Ling Monastery. His place of birth, É, is in Lhokha, a southern region of Tibet that includes Chongyé, where the Fifth Dalai Lama was born.
680. Nyangtö is found in Tsang province, southwest of Lhasa.
681. The implication here is that by writing down oral instructions, you run the risk of encouraging this kind of inappropriate behavior in others.
682. See Jinpa, *Wisdom of the Kadam Masters*, 42, where Dromtönpa is credited as saying, "If a beginner without the slightest experience of realization within his or her mental continuum were to help others through teaching, it would have no benefit. It would be like pouring blessings from an empty container: there will be no blessings to pour out."
683. Here Jamyang Lama, an honorific tittle that the author often added to the names of masters he admired, refers to Paljor Trinlé Rabgyé, a.k.a. Surchen Chöying Rangdröl. See note 320.
684. Khöntön Paljor Lhundrup. See note 318.
685. Könchok Chöphel was a contemporary of Khöntön Paljor Lhundrup at Dakpo Shedrup Ling Monastery and the author's tutor at Drepung Monastery. Over his long career, he was abbot of numerous monasteries in central Tibet and served as the Ganden Throneholder for a double term.
686. In relation to Padmasambhava's story, Sahor is often equated with Mandi in the Indian state of Himachal Pradesh, which is most likely the origin of the Fifth Dalai Lama's paternal line as well. The Sahor in the annals of Atiśa is in northeastern India.
687. *'Bring po'i dga' ba*, seventh month.
688. *Dbyang 'char*.
689. Each month has a corresponding vowel and consonant.
690. A place near Sera Monastery. Trinlé Gyatso, uncle of Desi Sangyé Gyatso, served as regent before his nephew.
691. The Miktsema prayer is the famed verse prayer to Jé Tsongkhapa that eventually became tantamount to his name mantra. On this prayer, see page 16 and note 45.
692. "Gentle lord" (*'jam mgon*), referring to Mañjuśrī, the buddha of wisdom; the object of salutation here is Tsongkhapa, widely viewed as an emanation of Mañjuśrī.
693. *Mañjuśrīmūlatantra*, Toh 543 Kangyur, rgyud, *da*, 292b6. These lines are traditionally recognized as representing a prophecy of the coming of Tsongkhapa in Tibet, with the phrase "great monastery, most joyful" (*dgon chen rab dga' ba*) referring to Ganden Monastery, founded by Tsongkhapa in 1409.
694. "Lords of the three buddha families" refers to Avalokiteśvara (compassion), Mañjuśrī (wisdom), and Vajrapāṇi (power). The Miktsema prayer is based on viewing Tsongkhapa as embodying these three.
695. Trichen Ngawang Chokden (1667–1751) was a key teacher to the Seventh Dalai Lama as well as other important Geluk masters of eighteenth century such as

Changkya Rölpai Dorjé. The Seventh Dalai Lama gifted Radreng Monastery to Trichen as his main base, and the lineage of Radreng (or Reting) Rinpoché began from his reincarnation, Trichen Tenpa Rabgyé (1759–1815).

696. They are (1) devas (gods), (2) nāgas, (3) yakṣas, (4) gandharvas ("scent eaters"), (5) asuras (demigods), (6) garuḍas, (7) kinnaras ("half human"), and (8) mahoragas (reptiles).

697. This is the well-known four-line stanza for taking refuge in the Three Jewels and generating the awakening mind:

    To the Buddha, Dharma, and excellent community,
    I go for refuge until I am enlightened.
    Through the merit of virtues such as of generosity,
    may I attain buddhahood for the benefit of all beings.

698. The *bhadra* posture is the posture of sitting on a throne or pedestal with both feet on the ground, a posture typical of most depictions of Maitreya.

699. The Lord of Secret Karmavajra (*gsang bdag las kyi rdo rje*) is the name assumed by Lhodrak Drupchen Namkha Gyaltsen (1327–1401) and indicates his special connection with Vajrapāṇi, who is known as the Lord of Secrets. Tsongkhapa received transmissions of many instructions on the stages of the path (*lam rim*) from this master.

700. The details of Drupchen's meeting with Tsongkhapa were memorialized by Drupchen himself in a text entitled "How I Met Jé Tsongkhapa," a text featured in Tsongkhapa's collected works. See also Jinpa, *Tsongkhapa*, 140–48.

701. The Seventh Dalai Lama is here referring to his principal guru, Trichen Ngawang Chokden.

702. The seven precious emblems of royal kingdom are the (1) royal wheel, (2) royal jewel, (3) queen, (4) minister, (5) royal elephant, (6) royal horse, and (7) military commander; the eight auspicious symbols are the (1) infinite knot, (2) lotus, (3) parasol, (4) conch, (5) wheel of Dharma, (6) victory banner, (7) vase, and (8) golden fish; and, finally, the eight auspicious substances are (1) a mirror, (2) yogurt, (3) *durva* grass, (4) *bilva* fruit (known also stone apple), (5) a right-curling conch, (6) *giwang* (bear's bile), (7) vermillion, and (8) mustard seeds.

703. The three secrets are the enlightened body, speech, and mind.

704. This is the last stanza from Dulnakpa's *Hundreds of Gods of Tuṣita* guru yoga.

705. On different versions of Miktsema prayer, see my introduction. The version used here in the first two forms of supplication is the original four-line one, which reads: "You are Avalokiteśvara, great treasury of objectless compassion; / you are Mañjuśrī, embodiment of stainless wisdom; / you are the crown jewel among the learned ones of the Land of Snows; / I supplicate at your feet, O Losang Drakpa." The five-line version appears on page 16.

706. Spelled *gsol ba 'debs pa*, the word is often used in its abbreviated form *gsol 'debs* (*söldep*).

707. This is the five-line (*lnga skor ma*) version of the Miktsema. In addition to the four-line and five-line versions, there is also a nine-line version (*dgu skor ma*) that is recited in relation to the rite of *Offering to the Guru*; see, page 17.

708. The chapter titled "How the Spiritual Teacher Took Birth as Devarājā in the Land of the River Yamuna," in Atiśa and Dromtönpa, *The Book of Kadam*, 2:518.
709. The Seventh Dalai Lama is here speaking of an oral teaching of his guru Trichen, where Tsongkhapa and his two chief disciples are correlated, respectively, with Mañjuśrī, Avalokiteśvara, and Vajrapāṇi.
710. Umapa, *Mañjuśrī Cycle*, 7a4.
711. The letters *a*, *ra*, *pa*, *ca*, and *na* are the first five letters of the Kharoṣṭhī alphabet, the script of the earliest known texts of the Perfection of Wisdom sutras. *Oṃ a ra pa ca na dhīḥ* is the mantra of Mañjuśrī, here being referred to as the *a ra pa ca na* mantra. When visualizing or chanting, it is always preceded by *oṃ*, thus making the mantra composed of six syllables.
712. Umapa, *Mañjuśrī Cycle*, 45b3.
713. Literally, the text reads "your heart, which you have imagined as standing" (*rang gi snying blos gyen du bslang nas*). However, in the source of this instruction, which is the guru-yoga text transmitted by Jé Tsongkhapa to Khedrup Jé (see next note), the heart is clearly imagined upside down with the pointy part facing upward. With the physical heart visualized upside down, the pointy part is then imagined as splitting into eight equal parts forming eight lotus petals.
714. *Guru Yoga Endowed with Profound Features Conferred through One-to-One Transmission by the Dharma King Tsongkhapa to the Omniscient Khedrup*, Collected Works of Jé Tsongkhapa, vol. *ka*, 151.
715. Another name for Maitreya, literally "the undefeated lord."
716. Lion's Roar (*seng ge'i nga ro*), according to Mañjuśrī's prophecy to Tokden Jampal Gyatso, is the name of the buddha in whose form Tsongkhapa will display the deed of attaining full awakening in the future.
717. The author is here alluding to the well-known myth on the origin of the river Ganges. Briefly, the ancient king Bhagīratha once angered a sage disturbing his deep meditative absorption when the former was on a hunt, resulting in the enraged sage cursing the king and all his descendants. To purify this sin and to help save his descendants, the king prayed to the gods, who in response sent the goddess Ganges to Earth.
718. The "end age" (*dus kyi mtha'*) is the age of degeneration (*kaliyuga*), which is the final and fourth world age marked by strife and discord, according to the ancient Indian system. The three preceding ages are *kṛtayuga*, *tretātyuga*, and *dvāparayuga*.
719. Known also as Jamyang Dewai Dorjé, he was a tutor to two prominent Geluk lamas of the eighteenth century, Takphu Tenpai Gyaltsen (1714–62) and Wön Gyalsé Jikmé Yeshé Drakpa (1696–1750). His guide to the *Hundreds of Gods of Tuṣita* guru yoga is entitled *Garland of Wish-Granting Jewels: A Guide to the Profound Path of the Unique Guru Yoga According to the Segyü Tradition*.
720. In editing my translation of Panchen's root text, I have benefited from Roger Jackson's translation in *Mind Seeing Mind*.
721. Although in Panchen's original, the entire text of *Offering to the Guru* is in a uniform text size, the tradition emerged later to print background explanations in a smaller font, so that the parts meant for meditation or chanting can be more easily identified.

722. Potowa, *Blue Compendium*, 1; see also translation by Ulrike Roesler in *Stages of the Buddha's Teachings*, 39.
723. *A Song of Spiritual Experience*, verses 11–12; the entire text of this song is the first selection in the present volume.
724. Tsongkhapa, *Supplicating the Lineage Gurus of the Near Transmission*, 4.
725. Aśvaghoṣa, *Gurupañcāśikā*, verse 47, Toh 3721 Tengyur, rgyud 'grel, *tshu*, 11b6.
726. *Condensed Perfection of Wisdom in Verse* (*Prajñāpāramitāsañcayagāthā*), Toh 13 Kangyur, sher phyin, *ka*, 9a6. *Synthesis of Precious Qualities* (*Ratnaguṇa*) is an alternate title.
727. Despite efforts, I have not been able to locate this quote in the *Saṃvarodayatantra* (Toh 373) in the Dergé edition of the Kangyur.
728. Panchen's original does not contain any headings for the different sections of the text. These have been added to help the reader see the structure of the text. This section up to the next heading is from Khedrup Sangyé Yeshé's *Source of All Siddhis*, 2a3. It does not appear in Panchen's original work, but its inclusion has become standard, and so it has been included here.
729. In Panchen's original, after this, we read: "Alternatively, from the line 'who in essence is all the buddhas,' you can recite: 'In appearance, he is the pervasive lord Vajradhara . . .'" Thus in the original, these three lines were meant to be an alternative to the immediately preceding three lines offering the option to visualize one's root guru either in human form or as Vajradhara. Later the tradition emerged to visualize Vajradhara not as an alternative but at the heart of the root guru in human form. Since this is how the text is used today, I have adopted this modified version.
730. Following on his suggestion, Panchen states here: "Choose whichever of the two versions that suits your inclination. Having chosen thus, continue as follows:"
731. Tibetan texts often use the phrase "heroes and ḍākinīs" (*dpa' bo mkha' 'gro*), with the male form referred to as *heroes* (*vīra*) and the female form as *ḍākinīs*. Elsewhere, such as in Tsongkhapa's *Song of the Spring Queen*, citing a stanza from the *Abhidhānottara Tantra*, we find references to "heroes and yoginīs, ḍākas and ḍākinīs" (*dpa' bo dang ni rnal 'byor ma/ mkha' 'gro dang ni mkha' 'gro ma*), suggesting that they refer to distinct classes of beings. Because of this ambiguity, I have rendered the phrase "heroes and ḍākinīs."
732. In Panchen's original, this second invocation verse does not exist. Gyalrong Tsultrim Nyima, in his commentary (p. 550) assumes that these two invocation verses as well the subsequent mantra, merging the gnosis beings and the commitment beings, are from Sangyé Yeshé. I have not been able to locate them, however, in the numerous guru-yoga texts of Sangyé Yeshé. In most of Sangyé Yeshé's guru-yoga texts, including especially *Source of All Siddhis*, we find the following well-known invocation: "O root and lineage gurus, embodiments of compassion; meditation deities and the Three Jewels of refuge; ḍākas, ḍākinis, and guardians of the teaching—the entire assembly: as I invite you to honor you, pray come here."
733. Aśvaghoṣa, *Gurupañcāśikā*, verse 22bc, Toh 3721 Tengyur, rgyud, *tshu*, 10b7.
734. *Vajramālātantra*, chap. 64, Toh 445 Kangyur, rgyud, *ca*, 270a2.
735. *Pañcakrama*, Toh 1802 Tengyur, rgyud, *ngi*, 53b4. This exact stanza is found in

Saṃvarodayatantra (Toh 373 Kangyur, rgyud, *kha*, 310b4), the likely source for Nāgārjuna.

736. According to the commentary tradition, with the five verses of prostration in their respective order, one prostrates to the guru as (1) the saṃbhogakāya, (2) the nirmāṇakāya, (3) the dharmakāya, (4) the emanation of the Three Jewels, and (5) all the buddhas.
737. The "four streams" (*chu bzhi*, literally "four waters") refer to water for drinking, washing the feet, rinsing the mouth, and for sprinkling.
738. The three worlds (*sa gsum*, literally "three grounds") are the world underground, on the earth, and up in the heavens—meaning here every conceivable dimension.
739. In the sixteen lines up to here, the first couplet offers the four types of water, followed by couplets for the offerings of flowers, incense, light, food, and music; with final two lines offer the five objects of sensory pleasure.
740. On the seven types of jewels, their approximates, and so forth, see page 514.
741. "Five hooks" refers to the five meats (human, cattle, horse, elephant, and dog) and "five lamps" to the five bodily substances (semen, blood, urine, feces, and marrow). These are imagined and transformed into nectar as part of the "inner offering" rite in the highest-yoga tantra practice.
742. I am following here Yongzin Yeshé Gyaltsen (*A Treasure House of Instructions of the Oral Transmission*, 96a2) who reads this line as speaking of "afflictions and diseases" rather than "the disease of afflictions." The number 404 is calculated by counting the four basic types of disease—disorders of wind, bile, phlegm, and the combination of the three—plus a hundred variations of each.
743. This refers to a short text known as the *General Confession* (*spyi bshags*), which opens with the phrase "O great guru Vajradhara, all the buddhas and bodhisattvas residing in the ten directions, and the venerable monks of the sangha, pray attend to me..." (*Bla ma rdo rje 'dzin pa chen po la sogs pa phyogs bcu na bzhugs pa'i sangs rgyas dang*...). This short confession text appears to be a slightly modified version of Atiśa's *Rite on Confession of Downfalls* (*Āpattideśanaviddhi*), Toh 3974 Tengyur, dbu ma, *gi*.
744. *Vajrapāṇyabhiṣekamahātantra*, Toh 496 Kangyur, rgyud, *da*, 40a1.
745. The famed verse of supplication to Tsongkhapa; see notes 45 and 46. In the Ensa tradition of *Offering to the Guru*, the nine-line version is recited here, as Gyalrong states in his commentary below (p. 535).
746. On the list of two sets of ten principles, see Jackson, *Mind Seeing Mind*, 579n1465.
747. The three preceding verses of supplication focus on recalling the guru's kindness, and as it indicates below, the next four verses, in their respective order, supplicate the guru by expressing his outer, inner, secret, and suchness qualities.
748. Panchen adopts these first two lines from Ensapa's *Guru-Yoga in Verse for Easy Recitation* (46a6), and he modifies the two last lines of that specific verse.
749. This four-lined verse came to be known in the tradition as the Special Single-Pointed Supplication (*phur tshugs gsol 'debs*).
750. Crown, throat, and heart, the three points of the body where one often visualizes the syllables *Oṃ āḥ hūṃ* associated, respectively, with body, speech, and mind.
751. These two verses relate to what is known as "receiving the four empowerments in the form of blessings." As stated in Gyalrong Tsultrim Nyima's commentary

(p. 553), if time permits, you could at this point in the text recite the name mantras of, starting from the inside out, Vajradhara, Śākyamuni Buddha, Tsongkhapa, and your own root guru, followed by the dedication verse: "Through this virtue may I quickly / attain the state of a guru-buddha / and lead all beings / to such a ground." If you wish to perform the "ritual feast" (*tshogs*) on the basis of this guru yoga, the tradition is to insert the rite here. For an excellent translation of this ritual feast, including the chanting of Tsongkhapa's *Song of the Spring Queen*, a celebratory ritual feast song, see Jackson, *Mind Seeing Mind*, 581–88.

752. The tradition is to chant this five-lined verse on *tonglen* (giving and receiving) three times, especially in the context of a group chanting.

753. "The five powers" are (1) the power of propelling intention, (2) the power of acquaintance, (3) the power of the positive seed, (4) the power of eradication, and (5) the power of aspirational prayer. For detailed explanation on these, see Jinpa, *Mind Training*, 377–79.

754. The fourfold practice (*sbyor ba bzhi*), in the context here of mind training, refers to (1) gathering merit, (2) purifying negative karma, (3) offering to spirits, and (4) assigning activities to the Dharma protectors. For a detailed explanation by Sé Chilbu of this fourfold practice in the earliest commentary on the "Seven-Point Mind Training," see Jinpa, *Mind Training*, 110–11.

755. In some versions of the "Seven-Point Mind Training," instead of the phrase "whatever you encounter," it reads "whatever you can (*gang thub*)." Panchen here adopts the first reading.

756. *'Phrul 'degs can*. The imagery here is that of a lift or a lever that could effortlessly place the rider on a horse.

757. The ethics of restraining from negative acts, gathering virtue, and working for sentient beings' welfare.

758. *Bhadracaryāpraṇidhāna* (Toh 1095 Kangyur, gzungs 'dus, *waṃ*). This famed aspirational prayer associated with the bodhisattva Samantabhadra is chanted widely across Tibetan traditions. Though it appears independently in the Tibetan canon, it also appears as the final section of the *Flower Ornament Sutra* (*Avataṃsakasūtra*).

759. These four are mentioned in Nāgārjuna's *Friendly Letter* (*Suhṛllekha* verse 61, Toh 4182 Tengyur, spring yig, *nge* 43b): (1) residing in a place conducive to Dharma practice, (2) relying on a sublime being, (3) making aspiration prayers, and (4) gathering merit.

760. In Panchen's original, the chanting part of *Offering to the Guru* ends here. In practice, however, the tradition has evolved to conclude the rite with five verses of auspiciousness (*shis brjod*), the translations of which can be found in Jackson, *Mind Seeing Mind*, 595–96.

761. This first stanza, composed of four lines each containing twenty-three syllables, pays homage to buddhahood as envisioned according to highest yoga tantra.

762. This second verse, each line composed of nineteen syllables, pays homage to Mañjuśrī. In some contexts, especially in Vajrayāna, he is referred to as "the father of all conquerors." In other contexts, such as in the Mahayana sutras, he has the status of one of the eight principal bodhisattva disciples of the Buddha.

763. In this verse, the author pays homage to Tsongkhapa as an emanation of Mañjuśrī assuming the form of a monk.

764. As will be explained by the author below (p. 505), the "triply kind guru" (*bka' drin gsum ldan gyi bla ma*) is a root guru from whom you have received (1) tantric empowerments (*dbang*), (2) reading transmissions (*lung*), and (3) pith instructions (*man ngag*). The author is paying homage here to his guru Lhatsé Yeshé Tenzin, who was in turn a principal student of Yongzin Yeshé Gyaltsen.

765. Kālarūpa is a supramundane protector with a special connection to Jé Tsongkhapa and hence hugely important within the Geluk tradition.

766. The "text" (*gzung*) here is the preceding work in the present volume, Panchen Losang Chögyen's *Offering to the Guru* (*Guru Pūjā*), which our author considers the root text on guru yoga and for which he offers elaborate explanations on specific parts. Direct citations from Panchen's root text appear in bold.

767. The "two aims of the sentient beings" are their temporary and ultimate aims—namely, the attainment of immediate happiness and the ultimate attainment of liberation.

768. The author is here probably alluding to those statements in the Vinaya scriptures on monastic disciple that pertain to how one should relate to one's guru. One important Vinaya source is the opening portion of the *Chapters on Discipline* (*Vinayavastu*), Toh 1 Kangyur, 'dul ba, *ka*, 1–71.

769. For example, *Adornment of Trees Sutra* (*Gaṇḍavyūhasūtra*), Toh 44 Kangyur, phal chen, *ga* 364a7.

770. One of the most well-known versions of the story of how the bodhisattva Sadāprarudita endured great hardships in seeking his spiritual teacher Dharmodgata and preparing to receiving teaching on the perfection of wisdom is found in the concluding part of the *Eight-Thousand-Verse Perfection of Wisdom* (Toh 12 Kangyur, sher phyin, *ka*, 261a3–276b6.). A poetic retelling of the story is found in Tsongkhapa, *Miscellaneous Writings*, 148–82.

771. Tsongkhapa, *Middle-Length Treatise*, 26–27 (Tib.), 42 (trans.).

772. These hermeneutic principles central to the Ārya tradition of Guhyasamāja are outlined in Āryadeva's *Compendium on the Heart of Wisdom* (*Jñānavajrasamuccaya*). The "six parameters" (*mtha' drug*, *ṣaṭkoṭi*) are hermeneutic aspects of reading the tantra defined in terms of their provisional and definitive meanings: two pertaining to the parameter of meaning (intended [*dgongs pa can*] and not intended [*dgongs min*]), two pertaining to words (provisional [*drang don*] and definitive [*nges don*]), and two pertaining to both word and meaning (literal [*sgra ji bzhin pa*] and nonliteral [*sgra ji bzhin ma yin pa*]). The "four modes" (*tshul bzhi*, *caturnyāya*) refer to four layers of meaning: (1) semantic, (2) general, (3) hidden, and (4) ultimate. For an explanation of these principles in English, see Thurman, "Vajra Hermeneutics."

773. Guru Yongzin Rinpoché is the famed eighteenth-century Geluk master Yongzin (or Kachen) Yeshé Gyaltsen, who was the principal guru of author's root guru, Yeshé Tenzin. Yongzin's guidance instruction on Panchen Losang Chögyen's *Offering to the Guru* remains its most extensive exposition, running into 232 folios and featured in volume *ba* of Yongzin's collected works.

774. *Mahāyānasūtrālaṃkāra*, 18.10; Toh 4020 Tengyur, sems tsam, *phi*, 25b2.
775. *Bodhisattvabhūmi*, Toh 4037 Tengyur, sems tsam, *wi*, 127a1.
776. *Pañcakrama*, chap. 3, Toh 1802 Tengyur, rgyud, *ngi*, 53b4.
777. *Guhyasiddhi*, one of the so-called Seven Attainment Texts. The author's personal name is Padmavajra.
778. On the "attainment and essence texts" (*grub snying skor*), see page 646.
779. Martön Chökyi Lodrö is the famed Tibetan translator Marpa, the root guru of Milarepa, and Gö here is Gö Khukpa Lhetsé. These two translators were instrumental in bringing the tantric texts associated with Guhyasamāja to Tibet.
780. On these two Tibetan masters and Tsongkhapa's relationship with them, see Jinpa, *Tsongkhapa*, 138–42.
781. The "great trailblazers" are the key founding masters of Buddhism in India, especially Nāgārjuna and Asaṅga, the founding masters, respectively, of the Madhyamaka and Cittamātra schools of the Mahayana tradition.
782. The resultant instruction from the meditation deity that Tsongkhapa received on his teacher Rendawa's behalf was inscribed as *An Uncommon Oral Instruction: Lord Mañjuśrī's Teaching Scribed by Revered Tsongkhapa and Sent to Jé Rendawa*.
783. From here up to the end of the sentence ". . . and how they are extremely great in their richness and impact" on page 445, the author provides an extensive paraphrase of Mañjuśrī's instruction conferred to Tsongkhapa at Rendawa's request.
784. "The four empty stages" (*stong pa bzhi*) are the (1) empty, (2) great empty, (3) very empty, and (4) all empty, defined in terms of progressive dissolution of coarse factors, both physical and mental. These four stages are known also as "the four appearances" (*snang bzhi*): (1) appearance, (2) increase, (3) near attainment, and (4) clear light, or luminosity.
785. Specially visualized deities (*lhag mos kyi lha*) is a technical term in the Guhyasamāja sādhana for deities visualized spontaneously and then dissolved into clear light before the visualization of the main deities.
786. The author is referring to what is known as "body mandala" practice, an important element of highest yoga tantra, especially in Guhyasamāja and Cakrasaṃvara tantra, where the yogin meditates that specific parts of their body are deities.
787. Here ends the author's detailed paraphrasing of Mañjuśrī's special instruction conferred to Rendawa via Tsongkhapa.
788. Here I am reading the Tibetan verb *gsungs* ("said" or "taught") as referring to the oral teaching the author himself has received from his own guru.
789. I am rendering the epithet *rje bla ma* (literally "sovereign guru"), used widely within the Geluk tradition to refer to Tsongkhapa, as "our supreme guru" or "our precious guru." The phrase indicates a certain level of intimacy, hence my choice of the word "our" in my rendering.
790. "Triple being" refers to a unique feature of this particular guru-yoga practice, involving three beings in concentric layers—the outer *commitment being* (*samayasattva*, the guru in the form of Tsongkhapa), the inner *gnosis being* (*jñānasattva*, Vajradhara at the heart of Tsongkhapa), and the innermost *concentration being* (*samādhisattva*, the syllable *hūṃ* at the heart of Vajradhara). The Tibetan word *sems dpa' gsum brtsegs* literally means "three beings stacked" or "three beings tiered." For brevity, I have chosen to render the phrase as *triple being*.

791. "Four Sets of a Hundred" (*brgya bzhi*) refers to a healing ritual aimed at "buying off death," often performed for a sick person. The ritual is so called because it involves preparing a hundred lamps, a hundred *shalsé* (oblong dough pieces), a hundred *tsatsa* imprints (bas-relief figures), and a hundred squeezed-palm imprints. "Blazing Mouth" (*kha 'bar ma*) is another healing rite.
792. Since the sources for all the citations in the root text were already provided in chapter 7, I will not repeat them in Gyalrong's text.
793. *Laghusaṃvaratantra*, chap. 33; Toh 368 Kangyur, rgyud, *ka*, 236a2.
794. Ibid., 237b2.
795. Tsongkhapa, *Illumination of All Hidden Meanings*, 165a3. This work is an extensive exposition of the *Root Tantra of Cakrasaṃvara*.
796. *Vajramālā*, Toh 445 Kangyur, rgyud, *ca*, 270b3.
797. Ibid., 270b4.
798. Tsongkhapa, *Milking the Wish-Granting Cow*, 129b2.
799. Aśvaghoṣa, *Gurupañcāśikā*, verses 20–21, Toh 3721 Tengyur, rgyud 'grel, *tshu*, 10b6.
800. Buddhaśrījñāna, *Sacred Words: Meditative Practice of the Second Stage* (*Dvikramatattvabhāvanāna-mukhāgama*), Toh 1853 Tengyur, rgyud, *di*, 15b3.
801. *Mahāmudrātilakatantra*, Toh 420 Kangyur, rgyud, *na*, 67a3.
802. On the story of this bodhisattva, see note 770.
803. The author is here citing an oral teaching from his own root guru, Lhatsé Yeshé Tenzin.
804. Aśvaghoṣa, *Gurupañcāśikā*, verses 17–18, Toh 3721 Tengyur, rgyud, *tshu*, 10b4.
805. The author is probably referring here to what are known as the eight mundane siddhi attainments. See note 807.
806. The text quoted here is from *Offering to the Guru*, in the section on generating the awakening mind. See page 414 above.
807. While *supreme siddhi* is the attainment of buddhahood, eight types of common or mundane siddhis, or powerful attainments, are listed. They are, as presented in the lines that follow: (1) eye potion enhancing the power of sight, (2) fleet-footedness, (3) the sword of invisibility, (4) the power to travel underground, (5) the power to produce medicinal pills, (6) the ability to fly, (7) invisibility, and (8) the power to extract the essences from flowers and so on that one can live on in lieu of eating.
808. *Vajrapañjaratantra*, chap. 15, Toh 419 Kangyur, rgyud, *nga*, 65a7.
809. These are four well-known qualities Tsongkhapa ascribes to the teachings on the stages of the path (*lamrim*). See, for example, page 44, verse 8.
810. In other words, the two principal methods for cultivating bodhicitta—the seven-point causes-and-effect method and equalizing and exchanging self and others.
811. Several later versions of Chekawa's *Seven-Point Mind Training* contain this verse, but it is not found in the earliest version of the text found in Sé Chilbu's commentary. In older mind-training sources, the first two lines are found in *Annotated Root Lines of Mahayana Mind Training* (Jinpa, *Mind Training*, 79), and the last two lines are found in the *Root Lines of Mahayana Mind Training* (Ibid., 73), where the last line reads "stems from the lineage of most sublime masters."
812. Typically, the empowerment ceremony initiating the trainee into a highest yoga tantra practice involve conferring four distinct empowerments—(1) vase

empowerment, (2) secret empowerment, (3) wisdom-gnosis empowerment, and (4) word empowerment—correlating, respectively, to the transformation of one's body, speech, mind, and uniting all three into an indivisible non-dual reality.

813. Śāntideva, *Śikṣāsamuccaya*, chap. 1, Toh 3940 Tengyur, dbu ma, *khi*, 3b2.
814. "Two distinctive features" (*khyad par gnyis ldan*) refers to the authoritative origin and the greatness of the instruction, which were presented in the preceding sections "Presenting the transmission lineage of this instruction to show its authoritative origin" and "Explaining the greatness of the instruction to engender confidence in this teaching." The critical Tibetan edition here mistakenly says *che ba*, "features of greatness," rather than *khyad par*, "distinctive features."
815. This is story 19 in Āryaśūra's *Garland of Birth Stories* (*Jātakamālā*). For translation, see Khoroche, *Once the Buddha Was a Monkey*, 119–25.
816. The parenthetical sentence appears in a smaller font in the original Tibetan, which may indicate a note added by either the author himself or a later editor. This sentence is followed by a note that says, "This step can be added, but there is no fault of omission if you skip it."
817. "Causal motivation" (*rgyu'i kun slong*) is contrasted with "immediate motivation" (*dus kyi kun slong*), the former referring to the basic overall motivation and the latter the state of mind in the moment of the action.
818. This is a well-known story from *Detailed Explanations of the Vinaya* (*Vinayavibhaṅga*, Toh 3 Kangyur, 'dul ba, *ja*, 61a4). It is translated in Rotman, *Divine Stories 2*, 201–12, and retold in Phabongkha, *Liberation* (trans.), 106–12.
819. *Guide to the Bodhisattva Way* (*Bodhicaryāvatāra*) 9.1, Toh 3872 Tengyur, dbu ma, *la*, 30b7.
820. The "peak of existence" (*sris rtse*) is the fourth of the four levels of the formless realm, the highest state of existence within samsara.
821. Śāntideva, *Śikṣāsamuccayakārikā*, verse 31, Toh 3939 Tengyur, dbu ma, *khi*, 2b4.
822. Śāntideva, *Bodhicaryāvatāra*, 6.123, Toh 3872 Tengyur, dbu ma, *la*, 19b2.
823. Ibid., 6.122cd, T 19b2.
824. These five are those that involve weapons, slaves, meat, intoxicants, or poison.
825. These three elements are the act of giving, the article being given, and the recipient. For a classic explanation of this view, see Tsongkhapa, *Illuminating the Intent* (trans.), 112–15.
826. Asaṅga, *Bodhisattvabhūmi*, chap. 16, Toh 4037 Tengyur, sems tsam, *wi*, 126b4.
827. This refers to a four-line stanza from the sutras that is often chanted when offering, for instance, the objects of everyday enjoyment—water for drinking, water for washing, flowers, scents, lights, food, and music. Repeated with modifications for each substance, the first verse reads "Abundant drinking water, water for drinking pervading everywhere, / the light from these waters shines far and wide, / thus disseminating a vast variety of drinking water. / I offer this to the great beings—the conquerors and their children."
828. For a detailed discussion of these contrasting perceptions in relation to a single entity based on Asaṅga's *Summary of the Great Vehicle* and Madhyamaka sources, see Tsongkhapa, *Illuminating the Intent* (trans.), 231–35.
829. Nāgārjuna, *Ratnāvalī*, 5.13–15b, Toh 4158 Tengyur, spring yig, *ge*, 122b2.

830. Śāntideva, *Śikṣāsamuccaya*, Toh 3940 Tengyur, dbu ma, *khi*, 148b2.
831. The posture recommended here is the same as what is commonly known as the "seven-point body posture of Vairocana," with the posture of tongue listed separately, thus making the number eight. Gyalrong explains each of these eight features below.
832. A *yungdrung* is a right-inclining swastika, which is formed by crossing of two z-like patterns. In traditional Tibetan culture, this symbol is associated with immutability, unchanging nature.
833. A "preamble" (*nidāna*) before a specific precept in the Vinaya explains why it was necessary.
834. Tibetan *rlung cham la phab ba*, literally "subduing the winds"; this practice involves taking several deep deliberate breaths to help settle your breath so that it can lead to a settling of your mind.
835. *Sems kyi dvangs ma* and *gnyug sems*. As will become evident later, Gyalrong uses the phrase *gnyug sems* (which I render here as "primordial mind" or "primordial state of mind") frequently to refer to the fundamental and natural state of the mind, which is characterized simply by luminosity and awareness and is, in itself, free of any taints. Intriguingly, Gyalrong differentiates within this primordial mind two levels—a coarse primordial mind (*gnyug sems rags pa*) and a subtle primordial mind (*gnyug sems phra mo*). On this phraseology, see Dalai Lama and Berzin, *Gelug/Kagyü Tradition of Mahamudra*, 226.
836. Despite efforts, I have been unable to identify exactly which of Gyaltsab Jé's works the author's teacher had in mind here. Possibly, he is speaking of *How to Bring the Eight Realizations and Seventy Topics into Meditative Practice*, 114, where the author explains that phrases such as "meditating on compassion" mean that one's mind is itself generated into the very nature of the specific meditation topic.
837. From this point up to the phrase "I would be truly insane" on page 467 is reused verbatim in another context below on page 479.
838. The author is probably referring here to the four great rivers—Brahmaputra, Indus, Ganges, and Sita (no longer extant)—that descend from the Himalayas.
839. That is, birth, name and form, sense powers, contact, feeling, existence, and aging and death, namely the five remaining members of the twelve links of dependent origination. In fact, these five are the results and belong to the category of the truth of suffering, while the five Gyalrong explicitly lists constitute the cause and belong to the category of the truth of origin of suffering.
840. Classical Buddhist texts differentiate three types of karmic effects: (1) the *fruitional effect*, the primary result in the form of a specific rebirth; (2) a *causally concordant effect*, an effect correlated to a specific karma; and (3) *environmental effects*, qualities of the physical environment where one is born and lives. The second is further differentiated further into (a) *concordant experiential effects*—having a short life, for example, for the karma of killing—and *effects concordant with the act*, which manifest as an attraction to pursuing similar behaviors.
841. By "two forms of awakening mind," the author is referring to the two forms of aspiration presented in sequence toward the end of the long series of contemplation. The first one involves aspiring to attain "the state of buddhahood, which

constitutes the perfect fulfillment of the twin aims," buddhahood as defined generally in Mahayana texts, while the second involves aspiring to attain "the vajra rainbow body," buddhahood defined uniquely in highest yoga tantra.

842. Drupwang Losang Namgyal (1671–1741) was a famed Geluk yogi and master who devoted most of his time to solitary meditation as a hermit, hence the epithet *drupwang* (*grub dbang*), literally a "lord among siddhas." His disciples include many noted Geluk teachers of eighteenth century, especially Yongzin Yeshé Gyaltsen, who composed the master's biography.

843. *Vinayavastu*, Toh 1 Kangyur, 'dul ba, *kha*, respectively, 94a7 and 93a5; the same verses are found also in the *Collection of Aphorisms* (31.24–25). A variation on them opens the *Dhammapada*.

844. In the story in the *Chapters on Vinaya*, as well as in Prajñāvarman's commentary on the *Collection of Aphorisms* (*Udānavargavivaraṇa*, Toh 4100, Tengyur, mngon pa, *thu*, 161a1), the story is about a prince and a poor brahman boy, not one of the śūdra caste.

845. *Suhṛllekha*, verse 117, Toh 4182 Tengyur, spring yig, *nge*, 47a4.

846. *Four Hundred Stanzas* (*Catuḥśataka*), 5.4, Toh 3846 Tengyur, dbu ma, *tsha*, 6a5.

847. *Vinayasūtra*, Toh 4117 Tengyur, 'dul ba, *wu*, 1b1.x

848. *Gtum mo gru gsum drug 'bar*. This paragraph, as indicated by its opening phrase "Once again" (*gzan yang*), seems to be an addition from Gyalrong as an afterthought concerning a topic he had already addressed above: the appropriate posture for prolonged meditation, which began on page 461.

849. *Rlabs chen spyod brgyud*. This should not be confused with "vast practice" (*rgya chen spyod brgyud*), the lineage stemming from Maitreya through Asaṅga and so on pertaining primarily to the vast aspect of the path as opposed to the profound aspect, which is represented by the lineage of "profound view" (*zab mo lta brgyud*) stemming from Mañjuśrī through to Nāgārjuna and so on. When the lineage of Śāntideva's unique bodhicitta instruction of equalizing and exchanging of self and others is identified distinctly, it is referred to as "expansive practice."

850. *Nyams len byin rlabs brgyud*. See note 280.

851. On the visualization of the merit field of this specific guru-yoga practice, see 477.

852. From this point on until the phrase "I would be truly insane" appeared verbatim above (pp. 466–67). The only variation is the inclusion of the two new sentences: "In any case, there is no guarantee that I will stay alive this night and will not die. What if I were to end up in such place of terror, how would I bear this?"

853. The author is referring to the refuge formula: "I go for refuge to the guru, I go for refuge to the Buddha, I go for refuge to the Dharma, I go for refuge to the Sangha."

854. This is the well-known verse "To the Buddha, Dharma, and Excellent Assembly, / I go for refuge until enlightenment. / Through my virtue of engaging in giving and so forth, / may I attain buddhahood for the benefit of all beings."

855. The "three sources" here are the virtuous acts of giving, practicing morality, and venerating the buddhas.

856. The full verse reads: "I go for refuge to the Three Jewels, / I confess all my negative karma, / I rejoice in the virtue of all beings, / and I uphold in my mind the buddha's awakening."

857. Respectively, *ngan song dong sprugs* and *rigs drug gnas 'dren*.

858. *'Gram chu ldang ba*, "mouth-watering."
859. In Panchen's root text, this last sentence reads "To this end, I will practice the profound path of the guru-deity yoga."
860. *Sngon 'gro'i khrid chen bzhi*. They are the instructions on (1) taking refuge and generating the awakening mind, (2) making a mandala offering, (3) Vajrasattva meditation and recitation, and (4) guru yoga. The Tibetan word *khrid* in the context of *khrid chen* ("great instruction") literally means "to lead" or "guide" someone, and so I frequently render it as "guide" or "guidance" in this volume. When used as an attribute of a text that explains the meaning of another work, it could be translated as "commentary."
861. Common-level and uncommon-level mahāmudrā here are what are known elsewhere as *sutra mahāmudrā* and *tantra mahāmudrā*.
862. The dissolution sequence that follows relies on being able to distinguish the elements of the syllable *hūṃ*, which looks like ཧཱུྃ. The long vowel *ū* is the letter ཱ with the curved stroke at the bottom. The letter *ha* is the main ཧ element. Above these is the crescent cradling the *bindu* drop, which is ornamented by a *nada* squiggle.
863. The author only gives the two mantras and their glosses in an abbreviated way. For the benefit of the reader, I have provided them here in full.
864. *'Od gsal ma bu phra dpa'i gdams pa*. This practice of taking death on the path as dharmakāya is part of what is called the instruction on *mixings*, which Tsongkhapa identifies as an important instruction of Marpa Lotsāwa based on Guhyasamāja tantra. See Jinpa, *Tsongkhapa*, 269.
865. "Subsequent dismantling" (*rjes gzhig gi sdud rim*) and "held-as-a-whole dissolution" (*ril 'dzin gyi sdud rim*) refer to two distinct methods for dissolution used in a sādhana practice such as of Vajrabhairava. The example of the first is the one described on page 488 and in note 862.
866. "Reverse sequence" here refers to the opposite of the process of dissolution at death described above, wherein the clear light of death becomes the starting point and the process begins with the arising of near-attainment, increase, appearance, and so forth. This reverse process parallels the emergence of a new birth.
867. *Gsod cig rgyob cig sogs sgra bzhi*. The other two commands might be "Cut him!" (*gtub cig*) and "Cook him!" (*tshos shig*).
868. The illusory body is said to be pure if the yogin has attained actual clear light, the fourth of the five completion stages.
869. *Zab gsal gnyis med kyi rnal 'byor*. "Profundity" refers to the emptiness dimension, while "clarity" is the appearance dimension of perceiving oneself as the deity.
870. The author's own root guru, Lhatsé Yeshé Tenzin, was a principal disciple of Yongzin Yeshé Gyaltsen, whose oral teaching is being cited here.
871. For an explanation on these five stages of fetal development according to Buddhist sources, see Jinpa (ed.), *Science and Philosophy, vol. 1*, 355–68.
872. This extract and the next refer to specific sections of the sādhana of Vajrabhairava used in the Geluk tradition, relating the process of generating oneself into a deity together with celestial mansion from emptiness and culminating in the emergence of an entire mandala and deities.
873. At this point in the Vajrabhairava sādhana, specific syllables are visualized at specific points of the deity's body.

874. *A Treasure House of Instructions of the Oral Transmission*, 33b6. I have been unable to identify which Panchen text Yongzin had in mind.
875. The author is referring particularly to Tsongkhapa's *Exposition of the Stages of Presentation*, a detailed commentary on Nāgabodhi's *Samājasādhanavyasthāli* (Toh 1809).
876. *Gtsug phud gcig pa*, literally "with a single topknot."
877. The four types of water are water for drinking, for washing the feet, for rinsing the mouth, and for sprinkling; substances of everyday enjoyment include flowers, incense, lamps, perfume, and food.
878. The five meats (*sha lnga*) are bull meat, dog meat, elephant meat, horse meat, and human meat.
879. These parenthetical notes are in the Tibetan original and may even be by the author himself. Orthographically, the first and the third, for bull and elephant, should perhaps be *goṇa* and *ḍantin*.
880. Possibly, this should be *majja* for marrow instead of *merga*.
881. The author is referring here to the rest of the "inner offering" rite in the Vajrabhairava sādhana.
882. The source of this statement attributed to Marpa has not been located.
883. The reference here is, once again, the self-generation rite of the Vajrabhairava sādhana, specifically the consecration of the outer offering.
884. The seven precious emblems of royal kingship (*rin chen sna bdun*) are (1) royal wheel, (2) jewel, (3) queen, (4) minister, (5) royal elephant, (6) royal horse, and (7) military commander; while the seven secondary precious emblems (*nye ba'i rin chen sna bdun*) are (1) palace, (2) royal bed, (3) royal boots, (4) sword, (5) regal robes, (6) animal skin wear, and (7) royal garden.
885. "Eight auspicious symbols" (*bkra shis rtags brgyad*) are eight auspicious symbols are (1) infinite knot, (2) lotus, (3) parasol, (4) conch, (5) wheel of Dharma, (6) victory banner, (7) vase, and (8) golden fish.
886. Maitreya, *Mahāyānasūtrālaṃkāra*, 9.19; Tengyur, sems tsam, *phi* 8a7.
887. Ben Gungyal Tsultrim Gyalwa (eleventh century) was a famed hermit who was formerly a bandit and later dedicated his life to a single-pointed meditative practice as a student of the Kadam teacher Gönpawa. In the episode mentioned here, he saw that he had made his altar look attractive in anticipation of a visit from a benefactor, and so to undermine his attachment to reputation and material gain, he threw the ash on his altar.
888. Asaṅga, *Bodhisattvabhūmi*, chap. 16, Toh 4037 Tengyur, sems tsam, *wi*, 126a4.
889. For the full text being referred to here, see *Offering to the Guru*, page 413.
890. *Rin chen sna bdun*: ruby, sapphire, lapis lazuli (*vaiḍūrya*), jade, diamond, pearl, and coral.
891. It is sweet, cool, smooth, light, clear, clean, soothing to the throat, and calming to the stomach.
892. As noted below, the tree has seven trunks.
893. My translation of the Tibetan word *spug* as "beryl" is suggestive. In the *Dungkar Great Dictionary* (*Dung dkar tshig mdzod chen mo*, 1295), a *spug* is identified as an extremely rare gem believed to have been formed over a thousand-year crystallization in ice and can be yellowish, green, or multicolored.

894. See note 423 above.
895. *Bar gdon btsan rgyal 'gong.*
896. The "four forms of fearlessness" (*mi 'jigs pa bzhi*) are in asserting his own perfect realization, asserting his perfect abandonment, revealing the path to others, and indicating the obstacles on the path. The "eight perfect masteries" (*dbang phyug brgyad*) are those pertaining to body, speech, mind, miracles, pervasiveness, wishes, activity, and qualities. Together, these attributes generally characterize fully enlightened beings such as buddhas.
897. The progressive levels of awakening mind, such as earth-like and gold-like, are enumerated in Maitreya's *Ornament of Realization* (1.19–20) and *Ornament of Mahayana Sutras*; see Gampopa, *Ornament of Precious Liberation* (trans.), 111–13.
898. A typical loose-leaf Tibetan volume is wrapped in cloth (yellow, orange, red, or even blue) and has a title marker (*gdong tshar*) sticking out from the left end that allows the text to be identified when multiple volumes are arranged with ends facing out, much like a spine for bound books.
899. On the various letters that together form the *hūṃ* syllable and their significances, see page 497 above.
900. *Vajra Garland Tantra* (*Vajramālātantra*), Toh 445 Kangyur, rgyud, *ca*, 270b1.
901. On Drupwang Losang Namgyal, see note 842.
902. They are Ārya Vimuktisena and Bhadanta Vimuktisena, authors of two influential commentaries on Maitreya's *Ornament of Realization*.
903. See page 477.
904. The author is referring here to Yongzin Yeshé Gyaltsen's lengthy guidance on *Offering to the Guru* entitled *Treasure House of Instructions of the Oral Transmission.*
905. Śāntideva cites in his *Compendium of Training* (*Śikṣāsamuccaya*, Toh 3940 Tengyur, dbu ma, *khi*, 99a1) the following verse from *Adornment of the Enlightened Attributes of the Buddha Field of Mañjuśrī*, the probable source for our author: "To Jñānottara and Prabhāketu, / likewise to Praṇidhānamati, / and to Śāntendra and Mañjughoṣa, / I pay homage with respect."
906. These six are ornaments made of human body parts: (1) skull ornaments, (2) bone earrings, (3) a garland of human heads, (4) bone bracelets, (5) a bone sash, and (6) an ornamental chest plate (made of bones). For female figures, there are only five, as the last one is omitted.
907. These passages from Khedrup Sangyé Yeshé, today treated as an integral part of *Offering to the Guru*, are included in our translation of the root text in this volume.
908. *Sumāgadhāvadāna*, Toh 346 Kangyur. The depiction of the emission of two contradictory phenomena—fire and water—is known as *yamaka-prātihārya* and is a popular subject of art, celebrating the Buddha's display of miracles in Śrāvastī.
909. *Jñānatilakatantra*, Toh 422 Kangyur, rgyud, *nga*, 122a4.
910. Nāgārjuna, *Pañcakrama*, Toh 1802 Tengyur, rgyud 'grel, *ngi*, 53b7.
911. Lakṣmīṅkarā, *Advayasiddhisādhana*, Toh 2220 Tengyur, rgyud 'grel, *wi*, 62a3.
912. Aśvaghoṣa, *Gurupañcāśikā*, verse 2, Toh 3721 Tengyur, rgyud 'grel, *tshu*, 10a3.
913. Asaṅga, *Bodhisattvabhūmi*, chap. 16, Toh 4037 Tengyur, sems tsam, *wi*, 125b3.
914. *Nor bu cha bdun*; according to Dungkar, *Great Dictionary* (p. 1212), they are the

king's earring, queen's earring, rhinoceros horn, coral tree, elephant tusk, minister's earring, and three-eyed jewel.

915. This is a reference to the line "lights dispelling the darkness of the trichiliocosm dance about" in *Offering to the Guru.*

916. All conditioned things are impermanent, all contaminated phenomena are in the nature of suffering, all phenomena are without self, and nirvana alone is peace.

917. Offering goddesses bearing offerings of the five sense objects—form, sound, smell, taste, and texture—carry, respectively, a mirror, a lute, a perfume-filled conch, a ritual cake, and a silk scarf.

918. This is a reference to the so-called four types of women, a category well known in classical Indian texts on the art of love. They are (1) like a lotus, (2) like a painting (sometimes listed as "deer-like," as by Gyalrong in the text below), (3) like a conch, and (4) like an animal, listed sometimes as like an elephant. For a detailed description of these four, see Gendun Chopel, *The Passion Book*, verses 30–48.

919. Inner sense objects are distinguished from external sense objects in that, unlike the outer sense objects of a mirror and so on, the objects experienced here are inner sensory experiences.

920. *Bimba* is a Sanskrit word that refers to the fruit of the plant *Momordica monadelpha*, to which the lips of women are often compared in Sanskrit literature.

921. Tsongkhapa, *When Making Offerings to the Deities of the Guhyasamāja Mandala*, 322. The last five stanzas of this short text of sixteen verses relate to offering these goddesses with each verse ending with the line "I offer this to please the deities of Akṣobhyavajra."

922. The first verse of *When Making Offerings to the Deities of the Guhyasamāja Mandala* (321), with the next quote, "At my emanation cakra. . . ," being the second verse, and so on.

923. The four joys of forward sequence are joy, supreme joy, joy of absence (sometimes referred to also as "extraordinary joy"), and innate joy, which occur in sequence when, through ignition of *tumo* fire, bodhicitta melts at the crown and flows down. When, from the tip of the sexual organ, the flow of the bodhicitta is reversed, these four joys are induced in the reverse order.

924. *Guhyasamājatantra*, chap. 8, Toh 442 Kangyur, rgyud, *ca*, 102b3.

925. The fourteen heaps added on the twenty-three to make it thirty-seven are (1) the mountain of precious gems, (2) the wish-granting tree, (3) the wish-granting cow, (4) uncultivated crops, (5) the goddess of beauty, (6) the garland-bearing goddess, (7–12) the goddesses of song, dance, flowers, incense, lamps, and perfume, (13) the precious parasol, and (14) the victory banner.

926. Four empowerments constitute the heart of an initiation into a highest yoga tantra deity practice: the vase, secret, wisdom-gnosis, and word empowerments. Later in *Offering to the Guru* is a rite to receive the four empowerments in the form of a blessing. See page 548.

927. Khedrup Sangyé Yeshé, *Great Bliss and All Goodness*, 156. Gyalrong refers to this nine-stanza prayer by its alternative name, derived from the first line, *Rang lhar gsal bde chen 'khor lo'i steng.*

928. The three types of sweet (*mngar gsum*) are rock sugar, molasses, and honey.

929. The source of Nāgārjuna's statement our author's teacher is citing has not been located.
930. What Gyalrong refers to as the "deer-like" (*ri dwags can*) is generally called the "painting-like" (*ri mo can*). On these four types of consorts and the sixty-four aspects of the art of love, see Gendun Chopel, *Passion Book* (trans.), verses 30–48, and on the calculation of sixty-four for the arts of love, verse 238.
931. Highest yoga tantra texts mention consorts with three levels of realization: field-born (residing in one of the twenty-four power places), mantra-born (consorts who have attained realization of generation stage), and innate-born (consorts who have attained realization of completion stage).
932. The reference here is to a well-known text on generating the awakening mind composed of three stanzas:

    I go for refuge to the Three Jewels,
    I confess all my negative karma,
    I rejoice in the virtues of sentient beings,
    and I uphold in my mind the buddha's awakening.

    To the Buddha, Dharma, and Supreme Assembly,
    I go for refuge until enlightenment.
    To achieve my own and others' aims,
    I generate the awakening mind.

    Having generated the supreme awakening mind,
    I invite all sentient beings as my guests.
    I will engage fully in the wondrous bodhisattva deeds.
    So may I attain buddhahood for the benefit of all beings.

933. This is a reference to a lengthy verse reviewing the main precepts of bodhisattva vows and tantric vows, including pledges specific to the five buddha families. For an English translation of this text, see Dalai Lama, *Kālachakra Tantra*, 186
934. This refers to the second stanza of the text referred to in the previous note:

    Just as for the guardians of the three times,
    what set them on a course to enlightenment
    was the unsurpassed awakening mind,
    I too generate this sublime mind.

935. Our author does not agree. He is making the point that this reviewing of the vows should be treated more as part of the limb of offering—specifically, offering your meditative practice—instead of as part of the limb of confession.
936. The hundred-syllable mantra is the mantra of purification associated with the deity Vajrasattva. It is commonly recited in conjunction with reviewing the four powers described below.
937. Tsongkhapa, *A Rite on the Four Powers*, 272. Tsongkhapa is referring probably to *Chapters on the Finer Points* (*Kṣudrakavastu*, Toh 6 Kangyur, 'dul ba, *tha*, 288a), which tells the story of how the Buddha's disciple Kātyāyana went to a town where the king presented to him performances of music and dance. Rather than allowing

himself to get caught up in the show, Kātyāyana drew his senses within and never wavered from his mindfulness.

938. The practice of Samayavajra is associated especially with purifying negative karma in relation to one's guru. Samayavajra is typically visualized as green with three faces and six arms, sitting on a multicolored lotus in union with consort, and the mantra is *Oṃ āḥ prajñā dhṛk hā hūṃ*. A short Samayavajra sādhana is, in fact, the final text of Tsongkhapa's *Cycle of Short Pieces Pertaining to Guhyasamāja.*

939. The author is referring here to seven stanzas in Śāntideva's *Guide to the Bodhisattva Way* (*Bodhicaryāvatāra*), 2.47–53. These verses are used in the Tibetan tradition as a stand-alone prayer, chanted often as part of everyday confession prayer. For the *Confession of Downfalls* sutra, see note 456 above on the so-called *Three Heaps Sutra.*

940. *Phyag chen gyi khrid dmigs skyong ba'i sngon 'gro khrid chen bzhi.*

941. Tsongkhapa, *Realization Narrative*, verse 2, 72.

942. Chapter 5 of Maitreya's *Ornament of Realization* (*Abhisamayālaṃkāra*) and its associated commentaries examine how karma, both virtuous and nonvirtuous, can be accrued even in dreams.

943. For this discussion in Candrakīrti's *Entering the Middle Way*, see Tsongkhapa, *Illuminating the Intent* (trans.), 278–81.

944. This line and the next, "O Losang, primordial buddha Vajradhara" (*blo bzang dang po'i sangs rgyas rdo rje 'chang*), refer to verses from a prayer composed by Ensapa that is widely used for long-life ceremonies in Geluk monasteries, conducted on the basis of *Offering to the Guru.*

945. "Mandala offering statement" (*maṇḍala bshad pa*) refers to a long formal statement chanted (or read) aloud at the long-life ceremony by a senior disciple of the guru as part of the mandala offering. The text, rendered in poetic prose adorned with extensive literary citations, touches upon various aspects of the life, aspirations, qualities, and contributions of the guru. Typically, once the actual mandala offering rite has been chanted, the mandala offering is picked up from the chant master's desk by two attendants and held before the guru. Then the senior disciple who officiates at the long-life ceremony prostrates to the guru three times and stands in front of the guru touching the mandala offering being held by the two attendants. He then recites the formal statement. These mandala offering statements are often included in the collected works of the senior disciple.

946. This parenthetical note is part of the original Tibetan source text and was probably inserted by the author himself.

947. The three basic sources (*gzhi gsum*) of virtue are giving, practicing morality, and venerating the buddhas.

948. Respectively, *Teachings of Akṣayamati Sutra* (*Akṣayamatinirdeśasūtra*), Kangyur, mdo sde, *ma* 107a1; Śāntideva, *Bodhicaryāvatāra*, 1.12, Toh 3872 Tengyur, dbu ma, *la*, 2b2.

949. For a detailed discussion on this topic of what specific types of virtuous karma are susceptible to being destroyed by anger, based on Candrakīrti's *Entering the Middle Way* and Śāntideva's *Guide to the Bodhisattva Way*, see Tsongkhapa, *Illuminating the Intent*, 135–37.

950. *Śikṣāsamuccayakārikā*, verse 84, Toh 3939 Tengyur, dbu ma, *khi*, 2a7.
951. The reference here is to the lineage guru prayer of mahāmudrā, translated in chapter 10 of this volume.
952. On this special nine-lined Miktsema of the Ensa tradition, see my introduction, page 17.
953. Panchen Losang Chökyi Gyaltsen, *Highway of the Conquerors*, verse 15cd. See page 619 below.
954. Our author refers to the Miktsema prayer as "name mantra" (*mtshan sngags*). Typically, a guru's name mantra consists of the individual guru's name in Sanskrit sandwiched between *Oṃ āḥ guru vajradhara* at the start and *siddhi hūṃ* at the end. Thus Tsongkhapa's name mantra is customarily given as *Oṃ āḥ guru vajradhara sumati kīrti siddhi hūṃ hūṃ*, as Sumati Kīrti is the Sanskrit for Losang Drakpa.
955. The rites for four types of activity are *pacification* (peaceful rite aimed pacification of illness, obstacles, and so on), *increase* (aimed at enhancing longevity, health, merit, and resource), *influence* (aimed at impact and power), and *wrath* (fierce activities of subjugation of malevolent forces).
956. For another explanation of these three aspects, see the Seventh Dalai Lama's guide to the *Hundreds of Gods of Tuṣita* guru yoga translated as chapter 6 in this volume.
957. On the special dreams Tsongkhapa's parents experienced around his birth, see Jinpa, *Tsongkhapa*, 21.
958. *Kṛṣṇayamāritantrarājātrikalpa*, Toh 469 Kangyur, rgyud, *ja*, 167a6.
959. This is a reference to the famed statement on dependent origination in the sutras "This exists, that exists; this has arisen, that will arise; conditioned by ignorance volition occurs" and so on. See, for instance, the *Rice Seedling Sutra* (*Śālistambasūtra*), Toh 210 Kangyur, mdo sde, *tsha*, 116a7.
960. *Kṛṣṇayamāritantrarājātrikalpa*, Toh 469 Kangyur, rgyud, *ja*, 167b2. "The two precious things" (*rin chen rnam gnyis*) are probably gold and silver, which are metaphors for having faith in the inconceivable power of ultimate nature of reality and pleasing the guru through acts of honoring him.
961. Ibid., 167a6.
962. *Brgya phyed mkha' spyod gnas su vajramuḥ*. The author's source for Tsakho Ngawang Drakpa's vajra song not located.
963. Umapa Pawo Dorjé, *Mañjuśrī Cycle of Teachings*, 7a4; see page 401 of the present volume as well.
964. In the mantra recitation section of Vajrabhairava sadhana, the first mantra is that of Mañjuśrī, *Oṃ arapacana dhīḥ*.
965. In Indo-Tibetan tradition, nāga spirits are closely associated with snakes, which are preyed on by carnivorous birds.
966. See note 696.
967. This visualization involves imaging ten wrathful deities of the cardinal and intermediate directions plus the two remaining directions of above and below at the center.
968. *Song of Spiritual Experience*, verse 7ab, 81.
969. Tsongkhapa, *Foundation of All Excellences*, verse 12cd, 3.
970. *Lhag pa 'gam pa*: wasting time and not doing much that is useful.
971. *Gtad rabs bdun*. Mahākāśyapa, Ānanda, Śāṇavāsika, Upagupta, Dhītika, Kṛṣṇa,

and Sudarśana. The Buddha designated Mahākāśyapa to be the principal custodian of his teaching, with others succeeding one after another.

972. *Gsang gsum mi zad rgyan gyi 'khor lo*. "The three secrets" are the body, speech, and mind of the guru, while "the wheels of inexhaustible adornment" indicates how they are like inexhaustible jewel-wheels whose continually spinning activities fulfill perpetually the wishes of sentient beings.
973. This particular form of supplication is known as "single-pointed firm supplication" (*phur tshugs gsol 'debs*), where the literal meaning of the Tibetan phrase invokes the imagery of driving a stake into the ground.
974. Our author provides only the first line of this verse, but I have included the full text here.
975. Lama Tokdenpa, the "realized guru" referred to here, is almost certainly Tokden Jampal Gyatso (1356–1428), a senior student of Tsongkhapa revered for his visions of Mañjuśrī. The final volume of Jé Tsongkhapa's collected works contains a guru-yoga text by Tokden focused on Mañjuśrī entitled *A Very Profound Practice Cultivating the Inseparability of the Guru and the Meditation Deity*. The text's colophon states, "This unique oral teaching of the most revered great Tsongkhapa on supplicating through viewing the guru and meditation deity as inseparable and receiving the four empowerments on a daily basis was inscribed just as it appears in the oral tradition stemming from Tokden Jampal Gyatso."
976. *Thub dbang rdo rje 'chang blo bzang grags pa*: Tsongkhapa with Buddha Śākyamuni at his heart, at whose heart is Vajradhara.
977. This is a reference to a long passage in a typical empowerment rite of the highest yoga tantra class. For an example of a full text, see Dalai Lama, *Kālachakra Tantra*, 265.
978. The two stanzas referred to here are, in their respective order,

    The auspiciousness that resides in the heart of all sentient beings—
    the embodiment of it all is the lord of all sublime lineages;
    it is the great bliss that creates all sentient beings.
    May such auspiciousness confer empowerment to you today.

    This is the great vajra of empowerment;
    all the realms pay homage to this.
    That which originates from the site of all the buddhas,
    I confer upon you [today].

979. Of the four empowerments, the first, vase empowerment, contains several aspects: (1–5) the empowerments of water, diadem, vajra, bell, and name, associated respectively with the five buddha families, which together constitute the "common" vajra disciple empowerment; and (6) the vajra master empowerment, which constitutes the uncommon empowerment.
980. Tsongkhapa, *A Very Profound Practice*, 344.
981. This is an abbreviated reference to the rite of consecrating the sexual organs of the deity ("secret region") and the consort ("space"), as found in liturgical texts on self-generation and self-empowerment according to highest yoga tantra.

982. Evident suffering, the suffering of change, and the suffering of pervasive conditioning.
983. The question being raised is this: Why in the *Offering to the Guru* text does contemplation of suffering's origin (karma and afflictions) precede contemplation of suffering's faults? Doesn't this contradict the normal sequence of contemplation?
984. *Responses to Queries*, verses 6d–8, 328. The line that comes before what is cited here is "As for contemplating the hundredfold flaws of samsara" (*'khor ba'i nyes brgya sems pa'i tshul*), which makes the opening phrase "Though there are many" clearer.
985. *Exposition of Valid Cognition* (*Pramāṇavārttika*), 2.146c, Toh 4210 Tengyur, tshad ma, *ce*, 113a3.
986. This is part of an oral teaching the author is citing from his personal teacher Yeshé Tenzin.
987. *'Phags pa'i nor bdun.* Faith, morality, learning, generosity, a sense of shame, consideration of others, and wisdom.
988. Guarding the precepts by (1) relying on one's spiritual teacher, (2) purifying one's intention, (3) cultivating familiarity with the precepts, (4) being at sites where sugatas reside, and (5) recognizing which acts are contrary to the precepts. See, e.g., Khedrup Jé, *Dusting the Buddha's Doctrine*, 432.
989. *Bral 'dod kyi bsam pas gdung ba'i snying rje.* I am translating the Tibetan word *gdung sems* (literally "sense of distress") as "empathic concern" here.
990. Sometimes, they are enumerated also as (1) making offerings to meditation deities and teachers, (2) purifying negative karma, (3) giving offerings to the harmful forces, and (4) propitiating the Dharma protectors. See Jinpa, *Mind Training*, 76.
991. On the commitments and precepts of mind training (*lojong*), see Jinpa, *Mind Training*, 118–30.
992. That the two instructions—the seven-point causes-and-effect and that of equalizing and exchanging self and others—are essentially two distinct methods for cultivating a sense of endearment (*yid 'ong gi blo*) toward other sentient beings was also noted by Tsongkhapa. See *Illuminating the Intent* (trans.), 50.
993. It is notable that our author makes the point that the type of equanimity (*btang snyoms*) presented in the context of Śāntideva's equalizing and exchanging of self and others is a more active form, not just requiring the absence of bias but entailing an altruistic intention to help others without bias or discrimination.
994. The "teacher's own guru" here is Yongzin Yeshé Gyaltsen, who was in turn a student of Drupwang Losang Namgyal.
995. Āryaśūra, *Garland of Birth Stories* (*Jātakamālā*), Toh 4150 Tengyur, skyes rab, *hu*, 3a7; for full translation of these lines, see Khoroche, *Once the Buddha Was a Monkey*, 7.
996. Khoroche, *Once the Buddha Was a Monkey*, 8.
997. *Nyon mongs kyis smyos gti mug gis ldongs.* It's unclear whether the author is here using two distinct expressions or one composite one. The phrases "drunk with afflictions" and "blinded by delusion" are commonly found in Buddhist texts.
998. As identified above, being content with mere nirvanic peace in relation to securing other's welfare and being content with such peace in relation to realizing one's own welfare.

999. Phurchok Lama Jampa, known more formally as Phurchok Ngawang Jampa (1682–1762), Changkya Rölpai Dorjé (1717–86), and the second Jamyang Shepa Könchok Jikmé Wangpo (1728–91) were deeply revered figures in the Geluk tradition in the eighteenth century.

1000. On the threefold ethics, see below, page 572.

1001. Guṇaprabha, *Vinaya Sutra* (*Vinayasūtra*), Toh 4117 Tengyur, 'dul ba, *wu*, 54b7. "The one in whom the vows have not taken root" refers to someone who has attended an ordination ceremony but with no intention of taking the vows; while one "in whom the vows have become damaged" is, in this specific context of *Vinaya Sutra*, one whose vows have become injured because of having violated it and keeping the act hidden. Our author is suggesting that we can take a cue from this *Vinaya Sutra* passage that states how not a full infraction of the precept but a minor misdeed (*nyes byas*) is said to occur when the person who commits the infraction does not possess full Vinaya vows. Similarly, one could say that a facsimile of a downfall occurs for one who has generated only simulated levels of the bodhisattva vows and then violates the precepts.

1002. "Interim virtue" (*bar ma'i dge ba*) refers to a type of virtue where, as a result of an act, you have accrued virtue that does not constitute the full-blown virtue of that specific act—e.g., taking the bodhisattva vows—but only something approaching it partially.

1003. (1) Armor-like diligence, (2) the diligence of gathering virtue, and (3) the diligence of working for the welfare of sentient beings. For an explanation of these three types, see Tsongkhapa, *Great Treatise* (trans.), 2:184–86.

1004. For an explanation of how to apply the five forces at the point of death, as part of an instruction on transference of consciousness according to mind training (*lojong*), see *Mind Training: The Great Collection*, 379–80.

1005. The full verse reads:

> Guru is the Buddha, Guru is the Dharma,
> Guru is likewise the Sangha.
> Guru is the creator of all.
> I bow down and praise all the gurus.

The first three lines of the stanza are from the *Guhyasamāja Root Tantra*, where the fourth line reads "Guru is the glorious Vajradhara."

1006. This refers to the stanza from *Offering to the Guru* whose first line reads "Teacher of gods and all beings, you are in fact all the buddhas," page 417.

1007. The protectors of the paths of the three capacities are Kālarūpa, Vaiśravaṇa, and Mahākāla; see page 510.

1008. The five figures are (1) the principal figure, Tsongkhapa in his triple-being form, (2) Maitreya (on Tsongkhapa's right), (3) Mañjuśrī (left), (4) Vajradhara (above), and (5) your personal root guru in his ordinary human form (front).

1009. Literally "wheels," the *cakras* indicated here are part of the network of channels formed at crucial points of the yogi's body—crown, throat, heart, and sexual organ; when mid-brows and navel are added, there are six. Typically, cakras are imagined as the junctures where the two side channels (right and left) loop around the central channel to form a knot. From these knots smaller channels branch outward, akin to a diagram of the network of neurons.

1010. The author does not explicitly list this heading, "Mahāmudrā, the Main Practice," as a distinct item in the overall outline of the text. He presents it rather as a stand-alone section focused specifically on mahāmudrā practice. If one were to subsume it within the outline of the text, this section could be treated as part 2 of an additional level of heading added to "How to practice during the main part of the session," within which part 1 would be "Guru Yoga, the Preliminary Practice." Hence my heading here. In presenting the tantra mahāmudrā first and the sutra version second, the author is following the sequence in Panchen Losang Chökyi Gyaltsen's root text on mahāmudrā.

1011. See page 578.

1012. This refers to a specific stanza from *Offering to the Guru* pertaining to the realization of completion stage, explained earlier on page 576.

1013. *Vitality stopping* (*srog rtsol, prāṇāyāma*) is a meditative technique in the completion stage of highest yoga tantra that involves control of winds (*prāṇa*) through advanced breath-based practice. For detailed explanation of this practice, and its connection with "vajra recitation" (*rdor bzlas*), see Tsongkhapa, *Lamp to Illuminate the Five Stages* (trans.), 154.

1014. Most probably, the author is referring here to Yongzin Yeshé Gyaltsen's lengthy commentary on Panchen Losang Chögyen's mahāmudrā root text, *Highway of the Conquerors*.

1015. The emphasis is mine. The author is stating that what is unique about the sutra mahāmudrā meditation on emptiness is that it involves cultivating the meditation object—the emptiness of the mind—by first invoking a state of mind where the meditator is able to experience the conventional-truth aspect of the mind, its natural attributes of vacuity, clarity, and awareness, and take this as the basis for contemplating the mind's emptiness. Tantric mahāmudrā, in contrast, entails meditating on the emptiness of the mind by the subtle primordial mind—engendered through withdrawing the winds into the central channel—and then conjoining that awareness of emptiness with great bliss.

1016. *Samādhirājasūtra*, chap. 17, Toh 127 Kangyur, mdo sde, *da*, 62a2; in the sutra itself, the line reads "The nature of all phenomena is the seal" (*chos rnam kun gyi rang bzhin phyag rgya ste*).

1017. In brief, our author is saying that the reason why this guru yoga, which is practiced as a preliminary to Geluk mahāmudrā meditation, includes many tantric elements is because the ultimate aim is to realize emptiness with the subtle primordial mind as in tantric mahāmudrā. Therefore many elements of this unique guru yoga resemble the generation-stage practice preparing the yogin for completion-stage practice. But to engage in sutra mahāmudrā in itself, which is essentially a meditation on the emptiness of the mind, there is no need for tantric empowerment and generation-stage practices.

1018. This is an oral instruction from the author's personal guru, Lhatsé Yeshé Tenzin.

1019. On these sources, see pages 659–62.

1020. Once again, the author is citing an oral teaching from his guru. The author is rhetorically querying scholars who are experts in differentiating subtle aspects of the mind based on distinct definitions of such constructs as *mindfulness, concentration*, and *meta-awareness*.

1021. Tsongkhapa, *Great Treatise*, 455 (Tib.), 3:50 (trans.).
1022. Panchen Losang Chökyi Gyaltsen, *Responses to Queries*, verse 94, 336.
1023. The author's point is that without some degree of mental stability, analysis can only deepen one's intellectual understanding; it cannot lead to a genuine experience of the view of emptiness.
1024. As explained below, the four key points are (1) the key point of identifying the object of negation, (2) the key point of ascertaining the logical entailment, (3) the key point of the absence of identity, and (4) the key point of the absence of difference. See also pages 201–3, 360–71, and 593–97.
1025. This is cited from a teaching the author received orally from his guru.
1026. As before, the author is citing an oral instruction of his guru.
1027. *Ngar 'dzin lhan skyes.*
1028. *Entering the Middle Way* (*Madhyamakāvatāra*) 6.132, Toh 3861 Tengyur, dbu ma, *'a*, 210b6.
1029. Although the Tibetan compound *rten 'brel btags yod* could be translated in conjunctive terms as "dependent origination and nominal reality," our author appears to be using the term as a single unit, which is better rendered as "dependently originating nominal reality." I also render this Tibetan compound as "dependently originated construct."
1030. The author here uses the unusual phrase *gzhan gshed du 'gro ba*, which I have rendered as a logical alternative in the sense of an otherwise. He uses this phrase several times in this section.
1031. For a detailed explanation on these five points, which are part the "sevenfold analysis" presented in Candrakīrti's *Entering the Middle Way*, see Tsongkhapa's *Illuminating the Intent* (trans.), 456–60.
1032. A *nonimplicative negation* (*med dgag*) is one in which the negating does not imply anything else. This is in contrast to an implicative negation. A typical example of the latter in classical Buddhist texts is "Fat Devadatta does not eat during the day," which implies that he eats at night.
1033. The author is pointing out here that there is not a single instance of cognition for an ordinary person that is not tainted by an appearance of intrinsic existence, at least at the perceptual level, and that even the rational cognition realizing emptiness cannot escape this limitation. And since emptiness is its object, emptiness will inescapably appear to it as possessing intrinsic existence.
1034. Śāntideva, *Bodhicaryāvatāra*, 9.61, Toh 3872 Tengyur, dbu ma, *la*, 33a4.
1035. Tsongkhapa, *Essence of Eloquence*, 456. The point being that a physical place devoid of vase is an instance of the *absence of vase*, which is indeed a nonimplicative negation, but this does not entail that the place itself is that absence.
1036. Tsongkhapa, *Essence of Eloquence*, 344.
1037. This is the same passage from Tsongkhapa cited just above; see note 1035.
1038. Śāntideva, *Bodhicaryāvatāra*, 9.110–11, Toh 3782 Tengyur, dbu ma, *la*, 35a3.
1039. The author is referring here to the crucial point of emptiness being a nonimplicative negation and that it must be perceived and experienced as such in one's emptiness meditation.

1040. The author is referring here to Tsongkhapa's *Illuminating the Intent* (trans.), 64.
1041. *Lamp So Bright*, 681, where Panchen states, "For us near-sighted ordinary beings, it is precisely the way in which this or that subject—our mind and so on—appears to us that is itself the way we perceive the object of negation." The critical Tibetan edition erroneously attributes this to Panchen's *Response to Queries*.
1042. *Recognizing My Mother*, verses 10–11, 2b1. A full translation of this song on the view can be found at tibetanclassics.org.
1043. An oral instruction from the author's personal guru.
1044. *Three Principal Elements of the Path*, verses 11–13, 194b1. See chapter 2 above.
1045. Panchen Losang Chögyen, *Highway of the Conquerors*, verse 45. See below, page 685.
1046. *Recognizing My Mother*, verse 7, 2a2.
1047. An oral teaching from the author's guru.
1048. The italicized emphasis is mine. The author is referring to three key characteristics of the mind that are said to constitute the mind's conventional nature: space-like vacuity (*stong pa*), luminous clarity (*gsal ba*), and awareness (*rig pa*).
1049. *Rnam shes breng tsam de*. The idea here is to settle your mind to a point where what you are perceiving is a kind of bare awareness characterized by *vacuity*, *clarity*, and *awareness* and stripped of any kind of object orientation.
1050. Our author may be thinking here of a famed oral teaching of Jé Tsongkhapa entitled *Vajra Lines on the View*, which mentions five distinct levels of meditative experience of emptiness. See Jinpa, *Tsongkhapa*, 310–11. On Tsongkhapa's list, the last two are meditation on emptiness in an ārya's direct realization of emptiness and meditation on emptiness in the completion stage of tantra, where the meditating subject is the gnosis conjoined with innate bliss.
1051. Nāgārjuna, *Fundamental Verses on the Middle Way* (*Mūlamadhyamakakārikā*), 8.2; Toh 3824 Tengyur, dbu ma, *tsa*, 6a1.
1052. Ibid. 8.12, 6a6.
1053. For the Guhyasamāja prayers referred to here, see Tsongkhapa, *Guhyasamāja Dedication Prayer and Verses of Auspiciousness*. These are the standard dedication prayers recited at the end of Guhyasamāja sādhana practice in the Geluk tradition. The mahāmudrā prayer (*phyag chen smon lam*) referred to here is the one by Yongzin Yeshé Gyaltsen.
1054. Śāntideva, *Bodhicaryāvatāra*, 5.39–42b, Toh 3872 Tengyur, dbu ma, *la*, 11b5.
1055. *Verses on the Compendium of Training* (*Śikṣāsamuccayakārikā*), verse 7, Toh 3939 Tengyur, dbu ma, *khi*, 2a2.
1056. Ibid., verse 9, 2a2.
1057. For a detailed explanation of the practices to be engaged in between the sessions, such as guarding the doors of your senses, engaging in everyday activities with awareness, and disciplines pertaining to habits of diet and sleep, see Tsongkhapa, *Great Treatise* (trans.), 1:100–108.
1058. These are, respectively, Yongzin Yeshé Gyaltsen's *Treasure House of Instructions* and his *Bright Lamp of the Excellent Path*.
1059. The Tibetan word *bya bral*, literally "do-nothing," or "someone with nothing to do," is a common term for a hermit who has chosen the path of single-pointed

meditative practice, often in a place of solitude. Another term, *ri khrod pa*, or "one who is from a mountain hermitage," is the Tibetan equivalent of the term *hermit*.

1060. In the collected works of Panchen Losang Chögyen, the verses of the root text are not numbered. We have introduced verse numbers here in the translation for the benefit of the reader. Please note the numbering here differs slightly from the Tibetan critical edition. In editing my translation, I have benefited from Roger Jackson's eloquent translation in his *Mind Seeing Mind*.

1061. These refer to the Seven Attainment Texts (*grub pa sde bdun*) and the Essence Trilogy (*snying po skor gsum*). On the identification of these texts, see the *Lamp So Bright* autocommentary below, page 686.

1062. In *Lamp So Bright*, Panchen attributes this to Machik Labdrön; see page 661.

1063. Saraha, *Dohā Treasury of Songs* (*Dohākoṣagīti*), Toh 2224 Tengyur, rgyud, *wi*, 73a4.

1064. Ibid., 74b5; a slightly different version appears in Saraha's *Treasury of Dohās* (*Dohākoṣamahāmudropadeśa*, Toh 2273).

1065. "Gnoses of the buddhas" is a gloss on the name of Panchen's root guru, Sangyé (buddha) Yeshé (gnosis).

1066. *Precious Garland* (*Ratnāvalī*), 1.80–81, Toh 4158 Tengyur, spring yig, *ge*, 109b7.

1067. *Guide to the Bodhisattva Way* (*Bodhicaryāvatāra*), 9.101, Toh 3872 Tengyur, dbu ma, *la*, 27b1.

1068. Khedrup Sangyé Yeshé, *Collection of Experiential Songs, Letters, and Replies to Queries*, 67b6.

1069. Dampa Sangyé, *Hundred Verses of Advice*, verse 51, 17a4.

1070. This line is part of a well-known instruction attributed to the Indian mystic Mitrayogi; see page 722.

1071. *Four Hundred Verses* (*Catuḥśataka*), 8.16, Toh 3846 Tengyur, dbu ma, *tsha*, 9b6.

1072. Ensapa Losang Döndrup, *Great Bliss Treasury* (in *Miscellaneous Writings*), 52. I have read the first line according to how it appears in Ensapa's own text, where the first line, in fact, reads: "Not included in the path I have just outlined" (*bshad ma thag pa'i lam 'dir ma gtogs pa*).

1073. *Saddharmapuṇḍarīka*, chap. 2, Toh 113 Kangyur, mdo sde, *ja*, 30a6. The version cited here is slightly different from the one found in the sutra itself.

1074. The last two lines could be read, if we adopt an instrumental case, as in *lam zung 'jug phyag rgya chen po yis/ mchog myur du thob par byin gyis rlobs//* as: "and that I may attain quickly the supreme state / through mahāmudrā, the path of perfect union." However, since all editions of the prayer I have seen render the lines in the genitive case, I have retained this genitive-case reading.

1075. That is, Ensapa Losang Döndrup.

1076. All additional figures from Panchen onward represent the continuing lineage of Geluk mahāmudrā up to the present generation, the last being His Holiness the Fourteenth Dalai Lama. In Panchen's original text, the ninth verse is a generic supplication to the practitioner's own personal root guru (no. 37 in our updated version) followed by a four-line final verse of supplication (no. 38 in our updated version). See the introduction on how the gurus of subsequent generations come to added to the lineage guru prayer.

1077. The verses from here up to verse 37, updating the lineage gurus, are not in the Tibetan edition and hence have no corresponding Tibetan page numbers.
1078. This is one of the senior disciples of Panchen revered as a great adept (*grub pa'i dbang phyug*). In fact, he and the next two in the lineage—Damchö Gyaltsen and Könchok Gyaltsen—are all direct disciples of Panchen and received their transmission directly from Panchen himself.
1079. This is most probably Taphukpa Damchö Gyaltsen, one of the very senior disciples of Panchen.
1080. This is Yongzin Yeshé Gyaltsen.
1081. The phrase "And, once more" (*slar yang*), which must have been added by a later compiler, indicates an alternative transmission lineage of Geluk mahāmudrā from Panchen, starting with his immediate disciple Losang Tsöndrü Gyaltsen.
1082. This is the Fourth Panchen Lama
1083. This is the famed Phabongkha Rinpoché, whose full name is Jampa Tenzin Trinlé, the root guru to many Geluk teachers of the twentieth century, including the Fourteenth Dalai Lama's two tutors. He is also known as Phabongkha Dechen Nyingpo.
1084. This is Kyabjé Trijang Rinpoché, the junior tutor to the Fourteenth Dalai Lama.
1085. This is the senior tutor to the Fourteenth Dalai Lama, Kyabjé Ling Rinpoché, whose full name is Thupten Lungtok Namgyal Trinlé, the last name literally meaning "enlightened deeds."
1086. This is His Holiness the Fourteenth Dalai Lama, whose full name is Jampal Ngawang Losang Yeshé Tenzin Gyatso.
1087. This is the generic supplication to the practitioner's own root guru. From here onward, the concluding verses are all are part of Panchen's original version.
1088. This verse is not found in Panchen's original version, but the tradition to add it here appears to have emerged quite early, since we find it included in Shar Kalden Gyatso's mahāmudrā lineage prayer as well.
1089. In editing my draft translation of the text, I have benefited from consulting Roger Jackson's translation of the entire text in his *Mind Seeing Mind*, 481–538.
1090. For the meaning of the guru being triply kind, see note 764.
1091. As this work is an autocommentary, the Panchen himself has inserted the lines of his root text in the relevant sections here. To help the reader identify these, we have numbered the root verses and bolded them.
1092. Sakya Paṇḍita, *Clear Differentiation*, 3.158d, 32.
1093. Dampa Sangyé, *Hundred Verses of Advice*, verse 3, 16b1. To "entrust all three—one's lungs (*glo*), heart (*snying*), and chest (*brang*)" is a well-known Tibetan expression that implies entrusting oneself fully and without hesitation. The version cited in Panchen's text here reads *glo* (lungs) as *blo* (mind), which is a typographical error.
1094. *Guide to the Bodhisattva Way* (*Bodhicaryāvatāra*) 1.9, Toh 3872 Tengyur, dbu ma, *la*, 2a5.
1095. *Summary of the Methods to Accomplish the Mahayana Path* (*Mahāyānapathasādhanavarṇasaṃgraha*), Toh 3954 Tengyur, dbu ma, *ki*, 300a6.
1096. *Vairocanādhisambodhi*, Kangyur, rgyud, *tha*, 153a6.
1097. Milarepa, *Hundred Thousand Songs*, 477.
1098. Ibid., 477.

1099. Ibid., 478.
1100. Ibid., 477.
1101. Gampopa Sönam Rinchen, a.k.a. Dakpo Lhajé ("the doctor from Dakpo"). In Gampopa's *Great Collection of Dharma Lectures*, 232, the first one is listed as "that one's Dharma practice becomes a Dharma practice" (*chos chos su 'gro ba*).
1102. *Parting from the Four Clingings*, verse 4, 298b2. For full translation of the text, see Jinpa, *Mind Training*, 519–23.
1103. Mañjuśrīkīrti, *Sarvaguhyavidhigarbhālaṃkāra*. Toh 2490 Tengyur, rgyud, *zi*, 238a5.
1104. See note 456 above.
1105. This is part of an oral teaching cited also in Tsongkhapa's *Great Treatise* (Tib.), 37.
1106. Sakya Paṇḍita, *Clear Differentiation*, 3.207, 35.
1107. Dampa Sangyé, *Hundred Verses of Advice*, verse 23, 171a1.
1108. Milarepa, *Hundred Thousand Songs*, 654.
1109. This is a reference to Drigungpa's main guru Phakmo Drupa (1110–70), the founder of Phakdru Kagyü.
1110. Source not located.
1111. Gö Lotsāwa, *Blue Annals*, 983.
1112. The Seven Attainment Texts (*grub pa sde bdun*) and the Essence Trilogy (*snying po skor gsum*) are identified below in the commentary. Each of the Seven Attainment Texts has the word *attainment* (*grub pa*) in its title.
1113. The Tibetan for mahāmudrā, *phyag rgya chen po*, literally means "hand seal great," and the verse Panchen cites glosses the individual syllables of the Tibetan word.
1114. This verse is not found in the *Drop of the Great Seal* (*Mahāmudrātilaka*) text in the Kangyur (Toh 420). As identified in Jackson (*Mind Seeing Mind*, 490n1258), these lines are found in a brief work attributed to Tilopa, *Dharma of the Bodiless Ḍākinī* (*Vajraḍākiniṣkāyadharma*), Toh 1527 Tengyur, rgyud, *za*, 85a6.
1115. Toh 2217 Tengyur, rgyud, *wi*, 5a5. The author is known also as Padmavajra.
1116. Butön, *Catalogue of Tengyur*, 47a3. The other two are the *King's Dohā* (Toh 2263) and the *Queen's Dohā* (Toh 2264). The actual titles of these three *dohās* are, respectively, *Dohākoṣagīti*, *Caryāgīti*, and *Dohākoṣopadeśagīti*.
1117. The last two lines are from Saraha's *Dohā Treasury of Songs*, verse 51ab (73a4), while the source of the first lines in their contiguous form has not been located. Saraha's *Song of Vajra Secrets* (*Mahāmudropadeśavajraguhyagīti*, Toh 2440, rgyud, *zi*, 61a3) contains the line "Look at a brahman spinning the sacred thread" (*bram ze skud 'khal bal ltos shig dang*), and his *Dṛṣṭibhāvanācaryāphaladohāgīti* (Toh 2345, rgyud, *tshi*, 3b4) has the line, "Let it rest like the falling cotton fluff" (*ras bal 'dab mm bzhin du glod la zhog*).
1118. *So ma ma bcos lhug pa*.
1119. This verse is not found in Advayavajra's *Ten Verses on Reality* itself but in Sahajavajra's commentary on it. *Tattvadaśakaṭīkā*, Toh 2254 Tengyur, rgyud *wi*, 172b6.
1120. Tsongkhapa, *Lamp to Illuminate the Five Stages*, 82 (Tib.), 87 (trans.).
1121. Saraha, *Dohākoṣagīti*, verses 16c–17, Toh 2224 Tengyur, rgyud, *wi*, 71b1.
1122. Ibid., verses 18c–20, 71b2.
1123. Ibid., verse 22, 71b4.
1124. Ibid., verse 24, 71b6.

1125. Ibid., verses 25–27, 71b6. These exact lines are cited also in Tsongkhapa's *Lamp to Illuminate the Five Stages* (trans.), 113.
1126. The six constituents (*khams drug*) are bone, marrow, and regenerative fluid (three from the father) and flesh, skin, and blood (three from the mother).
1127. Saraha, *Dohākoṣagīti*, verse 48, Toh 2224 Tengyur, rgyud, *wi*, 73a1. These two lines are cited also in Tsongkhapa's *Lamp to Illuminate the Five Stages* (trans.), 113.
1128. Nāropa, *Ajñāsaṃyakpramāṇa*, verse 2cd, Toh 2331 Tengyur, rgyud, *zhi* 271a4.
1129. Tsongkhapa, *Lamp* (trans.), 362.
1130. Milarepa, *Hundred Thousand Songs*, 523. Where Panchen's version reads "fortress" (*rdzong*) in each of the line, in the source itself, the word reads *bzang*, which means "good" or "excellent." On this reading, the lines should read "Mahāmudrā is the excellent view." Cf. Jackson, *Mind Seeing Mind*, 495n1280.
1131. Sakya Paṇḍita, *Clear Differentiation*, 3.505, 55.
1132. Nāropa, *Ajñāsaṃyakpramāṇa*, verse 3, Toh 2331 Tengyur, rgyud, *zhi*, 271a4.
1133. Sakya Paṇḍita, *Clear Differentiation*, 3.502, 55.
1134. Milarepa, *Hundred Thousand Songs*, 358.
1135. Sakya Paṇḍita, *Clear Differentiation*, 3.164, 33.
1136. *Praise to Mother Perfection of Wisdom* (*Prajñāpāramitāstotra*) verse 16, Toh 1127 Tengyur, bstod tshogs, *ka*, 73b2. In the Tengyur, the second line reads "the mother they relied on with certainty" (*nyan thos rnams kyis nges bsten ma*).
1137. Sakya Paṇḍita, *Clear Differentiation*, 3.254c–255, 39.
1138. *Entering the Two Truths* (*Satyadvayāvatāra*), verse 16; Toh 3902 Tengyur, dbu ma, *a*, 72b4. For translation of the full twenty verses of Atiśa's text, see Apple, *Jewels of the Middle Way*, 117–22.
1139. *Samādhirājasūtra*, chap. 17, Toh 127 Kangyur, mdo sde, *da*, 59a6. On this quote, see also note 1016 above.
1140. Source not located.
1141. Gampopa, *Instruction on the Essential Points*, 296. The version in Gampopa's collected works cited here is slightly different. Advayavajra's *Extensive Explanation of Song Filling Up the Inexhaustible Treasury* (*Dohānidhikoṣaparipūrṇagīti*, Toh 2257 Tengyur, rgyud, *wi*) contains a stanza strikingly similar to the one cited here, with the main difference being the absence of the line "the innate concepts are waves of dharmakāya."
1142. Jikten Gönpo, *A Song on the Realization of the Fivefold*, 87.
1143. Tsangpa Gyaré Yeshé Dorjé (1161–1211), an early master of the Drukpa Kagyü lineage.
1144. Dampa Sangyé, *Vajra Song*, 18b6.
1145. Puṇḍarīka, *Vimalaprabhā*, Toh 845 Kangyur, dus 'khor, *shrī*, 22a3.
1146. *Guide to the Bodhisattva Way* (*Bodhicaryāvatāra*) 8.4, Toh 3872 Tengyur, dbu ma, *la*, 23b1.
1147. *Questions of the Bodhisattva Jñānottara* (*Jñānottarabodhisattvaparipṛcchā*), Toh 82 Kangyur, dkon brtsegs, *cha*, 46b5.
1148. *Ornament of Mahayana Sutras* (*Mahāyānasūtrālaṃkāra*) 14.7, Toh 4020 Tengyur, sems tsam, *phi*, 17b7.
1149. That is, the *Offering to the Guru* (*Guru Pūjā*), chapter 7 in the present volume.
1150. The Tibetan phrase here, *gsal ba'i ngar dang ldan pa dang rtse gcig pa'i mi rtog pa*,

could be more accurately rendered as "*vibrancy* born of clarity and *nondiscursiveness* born of single-pointedness." In any case, Panchen is referring here to two well-known attributes of a meditative mind known more classically as clarity (*gsal cha*) and stability (*gnas cha*).

1151. *Mnyam par ma bzhag pa'i sa pa*. By nature, states of mind in the desire realm are characterized by a lack of focus because of excessive attraction to sense objects. In contrast, states of mind in the form and formless realms are characterized by an absence of such distraction. They are thus said to belong to the equipoised class (*mnyam par bzhag pa'i sa pa*).

1152. *Differentiation of the Middle and Extremes* (*Madhyāntavibhāga*) 4.3, Toh 4021 Tengyur, sems tsam, *phi*, 43a2. See the Fifth Dalai Lama's explanation of these on pages 342–46 above.

1153. Bhāviveka, *Madhyamakahṛdaya*, 3.16, Toh 3855 Tengyur, dbu ma, *dza*, 4a6 (critical edition, 62).

1154. Source of Machik's quote not located.

1155. Saraha, *Dohā Treasury of Songs* (*Dohākoṣagīti*), Toh 2224 Tengyur, rgyud, *wi*, 73a4.

1156. *Praise in the Form of a Confession* (*Deśanāstava*), Toh 1159 Tengyur, bstod tshogs, *ka*, 205b5.

1157. Saraha, *Dohā Treasury of Songs* (*Dohākoṣagīti*), Toh 2224 Tengyur, rgyud, *wi*, 73a4.

1158. Yangönpa, *Parting Teaching on Mahāmudrā Innate Union*, 11a2.

1159. Panchen does not cite his source. A similar citation is found, though with slightly different order of the six, in Dakpo Tashi Namgyal's *Moonbeams of Mahāmudrā*, 329, where he identifies Milarepa as its source.

1160. "Gnoses of the buddhas" is a gloss on the name of Panchen's root guru, Sangyé Yeshé.

1161. Panchen is saying that, even though the reader has encountered two earlier promises for what he intends to present—one at the start of the text and a second one before beginning sutra mahāmudrā—having a new promise here should not be seen as redundant because it relates to the specific topic of introducing the mind's ultimate nature.

1162. The "Teacher" here is the Buddha, and what Panchen has in mind follows texts such as the *Gnosis at the Point of Death Sutra* when it says, "If you realize the mind, this is gnosis, so cultivate the thought of not seeking buddhahood elsewhere." *Ātajñānasūtra*, Toh 122 Kangyur, mdo sde, *tha*, 153a5.

1163. *Dohā Treasury of Songs* (*Dohākoṣagīti*) verse 41, Toh 2224 Tengyur, rgyud, *wi*, 72b5.

1164. Lingrepa, *Experiential Songs* (*nyams mgur gyi rim pa*), 28a6. The full stanza reads: "When you realize your own mind, buddhahood will arise. / When you cut reifications from within, fulfillment will arise. / With stability and no differentiation between equipoise and post-equipoise, / engage extensively in other's welfare, O yogi."

1165. Numbering of these five different explanations has been introduced to assist the reader.

1166. Saraha, *Dohākoṣamahāmudropadeśa*, Toh 2273 Tengyur, rgyud, *zhi*, 122b1.

1167. Lama Shang, *Ultimate Supreme Path of Mahāmudrā*, 2b1. For a translation of Shang's entire text, see Roberts, *Mahāmudrā and Related Instructions*, 83–134.
1168. Exact source not located.
1169. Lingrepa, *Experiential Songs*, 28a6.
1170. *Instruction on Mahāmudrā* (*Mahāmudropadeśa*), Toh 2303 Tengyur, rgyud, *zhi*, 243a3.
1171. Lama Shang, *Ultimate Supreme Path*, 7a3. In the source as featured in *Treasury of Instructions* anthology, there are four intervening stanzas between these two verses.
1172. *Rāṣṭrapālaparipṛcchā*, Toh 62 Kangyur, dkon brtsegs, *nga*, 252b2.
1173. *Guide to the Bodhisattva Way* (*Bodhicaryāvatāra*) 9.1, Toh 3872 Tengyur, dbu ma, *la*, 30b6.
1174. *Entering the Two Truths* (*Satyadvayāvatāra*) verse 16–17, Toh 3902 Tengyur, dbu ma, *a*, 72b5.
1175. *Samādhirājasūtra*, chap. 9, Toh 127 Kangyur, mdo sde, *da*, 27a7.
1176. Ibid.
1177. *Entering the Middle Way* (*Madhyamakāvatāra*), 6.179ab, Toh 3861 Tengyur, dbu ma, *la*, 213a6.
1178. *Samādhirājasūtra*, chap. 12, Toh 127 Kangyur, mdo sde, *da*, 44a2.
1179. Śāntideva, *Bodhicaryāvatāra*, 9.140, Toh 3872 Tengyur, dbu ma, *la*, 36a6.
1180. Nāgārjuna, *Mūlamadhyamakakārikā*, 24.11–12, Toh 3824 Tengyur, dbu ma, *tsa*, 15a2.
1181. *Precious Garland* (*Ratnāvalī*) 1.35, Toh 4158 Tengyur, spring yig, *ge*, 108a5.
1182. *Exposition of Valid Cognition* (*Pramāṇavārttika*) 2.223, Toh 4210 Tengyur, tshad ma, *ce*, 116a3.
1183. *Meeting of Father and Son Sutra* (*Pitāputrasamāgamanasūtra*), Toh 60 Kangyur, dkon brtsegs, *nga*, 43a2.
1184. This is most probably a paraphrase of the following from Tsongkhapa's *Illuminating the Intent* (trans., 181): "(1) how phenomena are posited through conceptualization and (2) presenting grasping at true existence, the contrary apprehension.
1185. Source not located.
1186. This is a gloss on the root-text line "The savior Nāgārjuna himself says."
1187. *Precious Garland* (*Ratnāvalī*) 1.80, Toh 4158 Tengyur, spring yig, *ge*, 109b7.
1188. Śāntideva, *Bodhicaryāvatāra*, 9.58–60, Toh 3872 Tengyur, dbu ma, *la*, 33a2.
1189. For example, *Manifest Renunciation Sutra* (*Abhiniṣkramaṇasūtra*), Toh 301 Kangyur, mdo sde, *sa*, 62a4.
1190. Candrakīrti, *Entering the Middle Way*, (*Madhyamakāvatāra*), 6.129ab, Toh 3861 Tengyur, dbu ma, *'a*, 210b1.
1191. Nāgārjuna, *Fundamental Verses on the Middle Way* (*Mūlamadhyamakakārikā*), 18.1, Toh 3824 Tengyur, dbu ma, *tsa*, 10b6.
1192. The passage is not found in the version of the *Hastikakṣya Sutra* found in the Kangyur (Toh 207). However, an almost identical passage is found in another sutra, the *Concentration of the Gnosis Seal of the Tathāgatas* (*Tathāgatajñānamudrāsamādhi*), Toh 131 Kangyur, mdo sde, *da*, 251b2.
1193. Nāgārjuna, *Precious Garland* (*Ratnāvalī*), 1.81ab, Toh 4158 Tengyur, spring yig, *ge*, 110a1.

1194. *Samādhirājasūtra*, chap. 9, Toh 127 Kangyur, mdo sde, *da*, 26b2.
1195. *Prajñāpāramitāsañcayagāthā*, Toh 13 Kangyur, shes rab sna tshogs, *ka*, 3a6.
1196. Nāgārjuna, *Precious Garland* (*Ratnāvalī*), 1.81cd, Toh 4158 Tengyur, spring yig, *ge*, 109b7.
1197. Kamalaśīla's *Lamp for the Middle Way* (*Madhyamakāloka*, Toh 3887 Tengyur, dbu ma, *sa*, 168b4) cites a passage from *Perfectly Gathering the Teachings Sutra* that reads "Not seeing all phenomena is the perfect seeing"; *Dharmasaṃgītisūtra*, Toh 238 Kangyur, mdo sde, *zha*, 68b6.
1198. *Guide to the Bodhisattva Way* (*Bodhicaryāvatāra*) 9.101, Toh 3872 Tengyur, dbu ma, *la*, 27b1.
1199. *Entering the Middle Way* (*Madhyamakāvatāra*) 6.89 Toh 3861 Tengyur, dbu ma, *'a*, 208b2.
1200. See note 1198 above.
1201. *Aṣṭasāhasrikāprajñāpāramitā*, chap. 1, Toh 12 Kangyur, brgyad stong, *ka*, 3a3.
1202. *Presenting the Thorough Cleansing of Limitless Avenues Sutra* (*Anantamukhapariśodhananirdeśaparivarta*), Toh 46 Kangyur, dkon brtsegs, *ka*, 70b4.
1203. Tsangnyön Heruka, *Meaningful to Behold*, 134.
1204. Phakdru Dorjé Gyalpo, *Like a Precious Ornament*, 2b2.
1205. Khedrup Sangyé Yeshé, *Collection of Experiential Songs, Letters, and Replies to Queries*, 67b6.
1206. Candrakīrti, *Madhyamakāvatāra*, 6.80ab, Toh 3861 Tengyur, dbu ma, *'a*, 207a2.
1207. Dampa Sangyé, *Hundred Verses of Advice*, verse 51, 17a4.
1208. "Root Lines of Instruction on the Three Essential Points" (*Snying po don gsum gyi rtsa tshig*) verse 5a. This is part of a short five-stanza text attributed to the Indian master Mitrayogi (written also as Mitrajvaki), who visited Tibet in the twelfth century at the invitation of Trophu Lotsāwa Jampa Pal. On this root text, see page 36.
1209. *Four Hundred Verses* (*Catuḥśataka*) 8.16, Toh 3846 Tengyur, dbu ma, *tsha*, 9b6.
1210. Milarepa, *Hundred Thousand Songs*, 482.
1211. This is the first line of a well-known praise of the perfection of wisdom attributed to the Buddha's son Rahula and traditionally chanted, in Tibetan Buddhism, before the *Heart Sutra*. The full stanza reads: "The perfection of wisdom is beyond speech, thought, and expression. / Unborn and unceasing, it shares the nature of space. / It is experienced firsthand by the yogi's gnosis. / To this mother of the conquerors of all three times, I pay homage."
1212. Source not located.
1213. Milarepa, *Hundred Thousand Songs*, 483.
1214. *Precious Garland* (*Ratnāvalī*) 1.99, Toh 4158 Tengyur, spring yig, *ge*, 80b3.
1215. *Three Principal Elements of the Path*, verses 11–12. See page 53 above.
1216. Candrakīrti, *Madhyamakāvatāra*, 6.38, Toh 3861 Tengyur, dbu ma, *'a*, 206a2.
1217. *Commentary on the Awakening Mind* (*Bodhicittavivaraṇa*) verse 88, Toh 1801 Tengyur, rgyud, *ngi*, 41b4.
1218. *Heat* is first of the four stages within the path of preparation (within the fivefold paths of accumulation, preparation, seeing, meditation, and no-more training), the remaining three being *peak*, *forbearance*, and *supreme Dharma*.

1219. The "path of imaginative engagement" (*mos spyod kyi lam*) is the first two paths in the five-path schema—the paths of accumulation and preparation. At this level, the practitioner's engagement with emptiness is mediated by imagination and concepts rather than direct. Götsangpa Gönpo Dorjé (1189–1253) was an early master of the Drukpa Kagyü, a student of Tsangpa Gyaré and the guru of Yangönpa.

1220. The "pure grounds" (*dag sa*) are the eighth, ninth, and tenth bodhisattva grounds, so called because by the eighth ground the bodhisattva has eliminated the afflictions together with their roots. Within the five paths schema, the first of the ten bodhisattva grounds is attained when the meditator reaches the third path, the path of seeing, marked by direct realization of emptiness for the first time.

1221. Lama Shang, *Ultimate Supreme Path*, 71. See also translation in Roberts, *Mahāmudrā and Related Instructions*, 122–23.

1222. This is reference to a set of twelve qualities, according to the *Ten Grounds Sutra,* that a bodhisattva obtains on the bodhisattva grounds in an increasing number, with a hundredfold on the first ground, a thousandfold on the second, and so on. For a detailed list of these qualities, see Tsongkhapa, *Illuminating the Intent* (trans.), 527–30.

1223. Lama Shang, *Ultimate Supreme Path*, 66; Roberts (trans.), 211, 114.

1224. Source not located.

1225. *Replies to Kadampa Namkha Bum's Questions*, 511. This comes as part of Sapaṇ's response to a list of fourteen questions from the Kadampa monk. In question number 13, the monk asks, "Is this mahāmudrā teaching of Drigungpa, Taklungpa, and so on, erroneous or not?" There are slight variations in the wording among the different editions of Sakya Paṇḍita's collected works. Some editions read "With respect to the Drigungpa, Taklungpa, and [other] mahāmudrā advocates, there appear to be all sorts, some in accord with the tantras and sutra baskets and others not. Whether or not they are correct paths you should analyze well." The final sentence "Please be sure..." does not appear in all editions—only in the Shalu and the Luphu editions.

1226. Literally, "learned in myriad texts," *rab 'byams pa*, like the more well-known title *geshé,* is an academic title connoting mastery of classical texts.

1227. A Sanskrit phrase meaning "May auspiciousness prevail everywhere!"

1228. On the sevenfold posture, see pages 461–63.

1229. Shar Kalden Gyatso is here referring probably to his *Mahayana Mind Training Dispelling the Darkness of the Mind*.

1230. From the start of this paragraph up to the end of the explanation of the sixth analogy of resting your mind on page 695 was adopted verbatim from Panchen's *Lamp So Bright*, 660–63.

1231. Bhāviveka, *Madhyamakahṛdaya*, 3.16, Toh 3855 Tengyur, dbu ma, *dza*, 4a6 (critical edition, 62).

1232. Source of Machik's quote not located.

1233. Saraha, *Dohā Treasury of Songs* (*Dohākoṣagīti*), Toh 2224 Tengyur, rgyud, *wi*, 73a4.

1234. *Praise in the Form of a Confession* (*Deśanāstava*), Toh 1159 Tengyur, bstod tshogs, *ka*, 205b5.

1235. Saraha, *Dohā Treasury of Songs* (*Dohākoṣagīti*), Toh 2224 Tengyur, rgyud, *wi*, 73a4.
1236. Yangönpa, *Parting Teaching on Mahāmudrā Innate Union*, 11a2.
1237. A similar citation is found in Dakpo Tashi Namgyal's *Moonbeams of Mahāmudrā*, 329, with Milarepa cited as its source.
1238. Here ends the lengthy section Kalden Gyatso brings verbatim (except for verse 24 of the root text, which our author leaves out) from Panchen's *Lamp So Bright*, beginning on page 692.
1239. This is Jetsun Sherab Sengé, a senior student of Tsongkhapa and the founder of Gyümé Tantric College.
1240. The author is here referring to statements such as the one at Tsongkhapa, *Illuminating the Intent* (trans.), 240.
1241. Tsongkhapa, *Essence of Eloquence*, 401.
1242. What is italicized constitutes the hypothetical entity that is to be negated on the subtle level. In other words, if the self were to exist intrinsically, this would be its mode of existence. The emphasis in the sentence is mine.
1243. The emphasis is mine.
1244. The logic behind the consequence presented in these sentences is not clear to me. Perhaps there is an error in the Tibetan text.
1245. Shar Kalden Gyatso is saying that he has heard this oral instruction of Tsongkhapa from his various gurus. Despite efforts, I have not found this list of five senses in any earlier guide to the view texts. In his *Indispensable Oral Teaching on Tranquil Abiding and Insight* (p. 374), Tsongkhapa identifies two basic ways in which we might feel the "I" appears to the thought "I am"—one where you first perceive your aggregates, and another where there is no perception of your aggregates. The first case, again, has two variants: one where you feel the "I" is residing at the core of your aggregates and another where the "I" is indistinguishable from the aggregates. Similarly, in cases where there is no initial perception of aggregates, there could two variants: one where you perceive nothing but a vacuity, and another where you perceive the "I" in physical terms—with, say, color and so on.
1246. From this paragraph up to the end of the sentence "When your apprehension of this pure vacuity, a nonimplicative negation, . . . and continue to meditate single-pointedly" below on page 702 is adopted verbatim from Panchen's *Lamp So Bright*, 673.
1247. *Precious Garland* (*Ratnāvalī*) 1.80, Toh 4158 Tengyur, spring yig, *ge*, 109b7.
1248. Śāntideva, *Bodhicaryāvatāra*, 9.58–60, Toh 3872 Tengyur, dbu ma, *la*, 33a2.
1249. For example, *Manifest Renunciation Sutra* (*Abhiniṣkramaṇasūtra*), Toh 301 Kangyur, mdo sde, *sa*, 62a4.
1250. Candrakīrti, *Entering the Middle Way*, (*Madhyamakāvatāra*), 6.129ab, Toh 3861 Tengyur, dbu ma, *'a*, 210b1.
1251. Nāgārjuna, *Fundamental Verses on the Middle Way* (*Mūlamadhyamakakārikā*), 18.1, Toh 3824 Tengyur, dbu ma, *tsa*, 10b6.
1252. The passage is not found in the version of the *Hastikakṣya Sutra* found in the Kangyur (Toh 207). However, an almost identical passage is found in another

sutra, the *Concentration of the Gnosis Seal of the Tathāgatas* (*Tathāgatajñānamudrāsamādhi*), Toh 131 Kangyur, mdo sde, *da*, 251b2.

1253. Here ends the passage transcribed by our author verbatim from Panchen's *Lamp So Bright*. See note 1246 above.

1254. The author is probably referring here to Gungru's *Stream of Nectar*, 418, where we read the following: "As for the way to cultivate insight, bring to mind the appearance of the person's self-existence and single-pointedly sustain the thought that it does not exist."

1255. Shar Kalden Gyatso is probably referring to the *Indispensable Oral Teaching on Tranquil Abiding and Insight*, 375, where Tsongkhapa is recorded as stating, "If you meditate on an emptiness that is distant and separate, you risk meditating on an eternalist view. So meditate by fusing your mind with it." This text is the final piece in a collection of fifteen oral instructions entitled *Doorframe Oral Instructions on Essential Points* (*Zhal shes gnad kyi them yig*).

1256. Except for the opening word "Alternatively" (*yang na ni*), from here until the end of the quote from Marpa Lotsāwa on page 704 below is adopted verbatim from Panchen's *Lamp So Bright*, 678–79. In Panchen's original, the opening part of this paragraph includes a quote from Candrakīrti's *Entering the Middle Way* followed by the observation about the importance of cutting the root basis of the mind.

1257. *Guide to the Bodhisattva Way* (*Bodhicaryāvatāra*) 9.101, Toh 3872 Tengyur, dbu ma, *la*, 27b1.

1258. *Aṣṭasāhasrikāprajñāpāramitā*, chap. 1, Toh 12 Kangyur, brgyad stong, *ka*, 3a3.

1259. *Presenting the Thorough Cleansing of Limitless Avenues Sutra* (*Anantamukhapariśodhananirdeśaparivarta*), Toh 46 Kangyur, dkon brtsegs, *ka*, 70b4.

1260. Tsangnyön Heruka, *Meaningful to Behold*, 134.

1261. *Samādhirājasūtra*, chap. 9, Toh 127 Kangyur, mdo sde, *da*, 26b2. The advice to chant the words of profound scriptures is found also in Panchen's *Lamp So Bright*, 675, which is clearly our author's source here.

1262. *Samādhirājasūtra*, chap. 17, Toh 127 Kangyur, mdo sde, *da*, 59a6. In the version quoted in Panchen's *Lamp So Bright* (matching the sutra itself), the line reads "The nature of all phenomena is the seal" (*chos rnams kun gyi rang bzhin phyag rgya ste*)—i.e., without the word "great."

1263. Source not located.

1264. Chöpa Rinpoché Losang Tenpai Gyaltsen (1581–1669), also known as Rongpo Chöjé.

1265. The author is citing here an oral teaching and not from a specific text.

1266. This bracketed sentence, not in the original, has been added to make the transition clearer.

1267. Here, the author presents, as part of meditation on cultivating the view, a brief practice of "red offering" (*dmar 'gyed*), a ritual offering of one's body principally associated with Cutting Off (*gcod*) instruction. In the ritual presented here, you generate yourself as the meditation deity Heruka and conclude with a gradual dissolution, culminating in total emptiness, and then rearise from this as you reengage with the world of appearance. Perhaps one reason Yongzin labels his short work as "very secret" (*shin tug gsang ba*) is to underline this advanced tantric dimension. Yongzin's writings contain an independent instructional guide on this rite of offering one's body entitled *Red Offering of Chö* (*Gcod dmar 'byed*).

1268. This is the Third Panchen Lama, Losang Palden Yeshé (1738–80). Losang Tsewang, the person who requested this short instructional text, was Panchen's treasurer, or *chakzö* (*pyag mdzod*), his senior-most attendant, akin to a chief of staff.
1269. This refers to the bulbous vase-like dome of a Tibetan stupa, which sits above a platform composed of a square block with four ascending steps.
1270. Great Compassionate One (*thugs rje chen po*, *mahākaruṇika*) should be understood as an epithet of Avalokiteśvara, specifically in his manifestation as a thousand-arm deity.
1271. As explained in the author's own commentary below (p. 731), the three embodiments (*kun 'dus gsum*) are (1) Khasarpāṇi, who embodies all meditation deities, (2) the guru in the form of Amitābha, who embodies all gurus, and (3) the six-syllable mantra, which embodies all mantras. The three perspectives (*'khyer so gsum*) are (1) viewing whatever you see as the body of Avalokiteśvara, (2) viewing whatever you hear as the sound of the six-syllable mantra, and (3) viewing whatever thoughts arise, good or bad, as the exalted mind of Guru Great Compassion (Avalokiteśvara), endowed with the essence of emptiness and compassion.
1272. On Yiga Chözin, see above page 391.
1273. On the three thoughts, see below page 737.
1274. This commentary is based on two sets of verses—Mitrayogi's root lines below and Ngulchu's own verses translated in the previous chapter. To differentiate the two, I italicize the first and bold the second.
1275. This verse is found in a text in the Tengyur entitled *Heart Yoga* (*Yogasāra*, Toh 2855 Tengyur, rgyud, *ngu*, 196a) by one Śrī Jagatamitrānanda, most probably the same person as the Mitrayogi identified here as the source of this special instruction. In that Tengyur text, however, the last line reads "and meditate on your mind without distraction." On the somewhat complex history of the root text attributed to Mitrayogi, see my introduction, page 36.
1276. This "one-pager" (*shog gcig ma*) is Ngulchu's own verse text. In the format of long Tibetan xylograph, it fits on a single folio.
1277. In the original, although only the first line is cited followed by the phrase "up to," given the brevity of the root text, I have inserted the verses from the root text in their entirety.
1278. "A Reply to Namkha Palsang's Letter," *Miscellaneous Writings*, 265.
1279. Candrakīrti, *Madhyamakāvatāra*, 1.2, Toh 3861 Tengyur, dbu ma, *'a*, 201a2.
1280. Four micro-units (*cha chung*) equal one "door size" (*sgo tshad*), which is the length of full-stretched arms of the principal deity of the mandala, which is in turn equivalent to the height of the deity's body. These two units—*cha chung* and *sgo tshad*—are the two key units of measurement in the drawing and construction of a mandala.
1281. Panchen Losang Chökyi Gyaltsen, *Excellent Guide to the Three Essential Points*, 417.
1282. Here, Jedrung Tsering, the scribe of this text and a senior disciple of Ngulchu, is reporting his guru's words.

1283. Source not located.
1284. The three attributes are, as identified by the author on page 736, (1) bright and translucent, (2) reddish and gleaming, and (3) straight and standing upright.
1285. That is, in the first stanza of Nāgārjuna's *Fundamental Verses* (*Mūlamadhyamaka-kārikā*), Toh 3824 Tengyur, dbu ma, *tsa*, 1a3.
1286. Given that this text was compiled on the basis of notes taken at a live teaching of Ngulchu Dharmabhadra, "the teacher" here refers to this master.

Glossary

action seal (*las kyi phyag rgya, karmamudrā*). In highest yoga tantra, this term refers to a sexual partner whose embrace assists in manipulating energies in the subtle body to hasten enlightenment. The term is often contrasted with the gnosis seal (*jñānamudrā*), which refers to a visualized consort. *See also* mudrā.

affliction(s) (*nyong mongs, kleśa*). Dissonant mental states, both thoughts and emotions, that have their root in ignorance. The term is elsewhere translated as "delusion" or "defilement." Classical Buddhist texts list six root afflictions—attachment, anger, pride, afflicted doubt, ignorance, and afflicted view—out of which attachment, aversion, and ignorance are referred to also as the *three poisons* of the mind. Associated with these root afflictions, especially the three poisons, Abhidharma lists twenty secondary, or derivative, afflictions. They are called *afflictions* because they disturb the individual from deep within.

analytical meditation (*dpyad sgom*). With *placement meditation*, one of the two basic types of meditation practice in Buddhism. Analytical meditation may involve philosophical analysis, review of categories, or observation of mental and physical events. Just as placement meditation is key to attaining tranquil abiding, analytical meditation is essential for the cultivation of insight into the nature of things.

awakening mind (*byang chub kyi sems, bodhicitta*). In the Mahayana, a state of mind cultivated by a bodhisattva. The *conventional* awakening mind is the generation of the aspiration to attain enlightenment for the sake of all beings, and the *ultimate* awakening mind is the direct realization of emptiness of all phenomena, including especially of the enlightened mind. Often, when used on its own, the term *awakening mind* refers to conventional awakening mind, with ultimate awakening mind always referred to with its qualifier "ultimate." Typically, conventional awakening mind is differentiated into *aspiring mind* and *engaging* mind, the latter accompanied by adoption of the bodhisattva vow and expressing it through the practice of the six perfections—generosity, ethics, forbearance, diligence, meditative absorption, and wisdom. The two are compared to someone who has the wish to go and someone who is already going.

cakra (*rtsa 'khor*). In tantric theory, one of a number of "wheels" at the intersection of important channels in the subtle body. The cakras are important for understanding human physiology and meditative praxis and are replete with symbolic significance. The most commonly mentioned are those at the sexual organ, navel, heart, throat, forehead, and crown.

clear light (*'od gsal, prabasvara*). On the completion stage of highest yoga tantra, the luminous, blissful realization of emptiness that is a prelude to the attainment of a buddha's dharmakāya upon enlightenment. In the Guhyasamāja tradition, it is the fourth of the five stages of the completion stage. The term also may refer to the natural clarity of the mind in its subtlest state, which may be manifest at death and on various other occasions.

commitment being. *See* triple being.

completion stage (*rdzogs rim, niṣpannakrama*). In highest yoga tantra, the second and final stage of practice, usually involving manipulation of vital elements in the subtle body and culminating in buddhahood. Completion-stage practices are divided in various ways—for example, the five stages of the Ārya tradition of Guhyasamāja, the six yogas of Kālacakra, and the six yogas of Nāropa.

concentration (*ting nge 'dzin, samādhi*). A meditative state in which one's mind abides in deep equipoise. Often used interchangeably with *meditative absorption* (*bsam gtan, dhyāna*), a key feature of concentration is the heightened quality of focus and absorption and absence of distraction. The term need not always connote a meditative state. In the context of Abhidharma taxonomy of mental factors, for example, concentration is one of the five object-determined factors and is defined as the mind's natural capacity for single-pointedness and focus. *See also* meditative absorption; meditative equipoise; placement meditation; tranquil abiding.

concept/conceptualization (*rnam rtog, vikalpa*). The constructive mental activity that dominates the inner life of sentient beings and obstructs them from seeing things as they really are. For humans in particular, such activity entails processes of interpreting their experience of the world shaped by language-based thought, perspectives, and attitudes. Like conceptual elaboration, it involves a process of superimposition on reality that must be eliminated before enlightenment can be attained.

conceptual elaboration (*spros pa, prapañca*). Conceptual elaborations occur in the domain of thought and language and include all forms of dichotomizing conceptualization, such as subject-object duality as well as grasping at objects and their characteristics. The ultimate truth and its direct realization are marked by total freedom from such conceptual elaborations. The term is sometimes rendered simply as "elaborations."

conventional truth (*kun rdzob bden pa, saṃvṛtisatya*). *See* two truths.

Cutting Off (*gcod*). A meditative practice, probably stemming from India, introduced to Tibet within the Shijé school by Machik Lapdrön. Cutting Off aims to sever attachment to self through a variety of contemplations, the most dramatic of which involves the visualized offering of one's cut-up body to various gods, titans, and animals. Cutting Off practices are found to this day in most Tibetan traditions.

ḍākinī (*mkha' 'gro ma*). In advanced tantric traditions, a female figure who assists a practitioner in deepening meditative realization. As with their male counterparts, ḍākas, there are both worldly and transmundane ḍākinīs. Ḍākinīs may manifest as embodied human beings or in subtler forms, and they may appear alluring or wrathful. In consonance with Buddhist gender symbolism, they signify gnosis, or transcendental wisdom.

dependent origination (*rten 'brel, pratītyasamutpāda*). The general causal law in Buddhist thought that asserts that whatever arises does so in dependence upon causes and conditions. Sometimes taken to be the essential Buddhist teaching, it is given specific instantiation in the twelve links of dependent origination, which explains how it is we continually take birth in cyclic existence. It is also explained by Nāgārjuna as equivalent to, and as a key proof of, emptiness.

dharmakāya (*chos sku*). In earlier traditions, the corpus of the Buddha's teaching; in Mahayana, the aspect of buddhahood that is equivalent to the enlightened mind and is the basis of the enjoyment body and emanation body. Literally "truth body," it is sometimes singular and sometimes divided into a *natural* dharmakāya (*ngo bo nyid sku, svabhāvikakāya*), which is the buddha's emptiness or suchness, and a *gnostic* dharmakāya (*ye shes chos sku, jñānadharmakāya*), which is the buddha's perfect knowledge, compassion, power, and other qualities. When dharmakāya is differentiated into these two dimensions, buddha's embodiment (*kāya*) is explained to be fourfold, the four buddha bodies of (1) natural dharmakāya and (2) gnostic dharmakāya, the two truth bodies, and (3) the saṃbhogakāya enjoyment body and (4) the nirmāṇakāya emanation body, the two form bodies.

drops (*byangs sems, bodhicitta*). When used in the context of Vajrayāna texts, this term refers to the pure essence of the white male and female sexual fluids. These drops are intimately associated with experiences of bliss engendered through deep meditative yogic practices.

emptiness (*stong pa nyid, śūnyatā*). According to the Madhyamaka school, all things and events, including our own existence, are empty or devoid of any independent, substantial, and intrinsic existence. This emptiness of intrinsic existence is the ultimate truth, the ultimate mode of being of all phenomena—the way they actually are—hence referred to also by such epithets as *suchness* or *thatness*. Realization of this truth, emptiness, is said to be indispensable for attaining enlightenment.

form body (*gzugs sku, rūpakāya*). In the most general terms, a buddha's physical body, in contrast to the dharmakāya, the truth body. In Mahayana, the form body is the aspect taken by dharmakāya for the sake of others. It is achieved through the accumulation of merit and is usually subdivided into the saṃbhogakāya enjoyment body and nirmāṇakāya emanation body.

four empty stages (*stong pa bzhi*). These are names given to the arising of the three appearances and the clear light. The empty (*stong pa*), the very empty (*shin tu stong pa*), the greatly empty (*stong pa chen po*), and the all empty (*thams cad stong pa*), or clear light. In some traditions they equate to the four joys.

four joys (*dga' ba bzhi*). These are experienced when the melted drops (*bodhicitta*) pass through the four main cakras. When descending from the crown, the four joys are experienced in the "forward sequence": (1) *joy*, experienced at the cakra of great bliss at the crown, (2) *supreme joy*, experienced at the cakra of enjoyment at the throat, (3) *joy of absence* (sometimes referred to also as "extraordinary joy"), experienced at the dharmacakra at the heart, and (4) *innate joy*, experienced at the emanation cakra at the navel. When the flow ascends from the tip of the sexual organ, these four joys are experienced in the reverse sequence.

generation stage (*bskyed rim, utpattikrama*). In advanced tantric systems (e.g., mahāyoga or highest yoga tantra), the phase of practice preceding the climactic completion stage. In the generation stage one overcomes ordinary appearances by visualizing oneself as a buddha-deity at the center of a complex mandala, identifying one's body, speech, and mind with that of a buddha.

gnosis (*ye shes, jñāna*). In contrast to wisdom (*prajñā, shes rab*), which may be either worldly or transmundane, gnosis usually connotes a realization of the nature of things that is profound and liberating. The "accumulation" of gnosis on the bodhisattva path eventuates in the attainment of a buddha's dharmakāya. *See also* wisdom.

gnosis being (*ye shes pa, jñānasattva*). In tantric meditation practices, the "actual" buddha-deity that is absorbed into the commitment being one has visualized in place of one's ordinary body. The absorption of the gnosis being seals one's identification with the buddha's body, speech, and mind. *See also* triple being.

gnosis seal (*jñānamudrā, ye shes kyi phyag rgya*). *See* action seal; mudrā.

great bliss (*bde chen po, mahāsukha*). Although bliss can occur on the sutra path, and even in the ordinary state before entering the path, this is not *great bliss*, which has to be caused by bringing the winds in the central channel. Great bliss is brought to focus on emptiness to form the "union of bliss and emptiness." *See also* innate gnosis.

held-as-a-whole and subsequent dissolutions (*ril por 'dzin pa, rjes gzhig*). Two dissolution processes beginning from the extremities and proceeding toward the heart; likened to vapor evaporating on a mirror. "Whole" in the first process refers to the body, while "held" means being held by the emptiness, or clear light, into which the body dissolves. Subsequent dissolution is dissolution in which the outer environment dissolves first, followed by the subsequent dissolution of the body.

highest yoga tantra (*bla med rnal 'byor rgyud, niruttarayogatantra*). A Buddhist tantric system recognized as the highest level among four classes of tantra. It often is divided into father tantras (e.g., Guhyasamāja), which stress methods for generating the illusory body, and mother tantras (e.g., Cakrasaṃvara), which emphasize attainment of the clear-light mind. *See also* generation stage; completion stage.

identity view (*'jig tshogs lta ba, satkāyadṛṣṭi*). Literally "view of the transitory collection," our innate sense of self-identity as individuated beings. This identity view can take the form of the thought "I am" when it is based on an underlying assumption of an intrinsically existing self that is the referent of such a "self" or "I." By extension, the identity view can take the form of the thought "mine" in relation to people and things that we appropriate as part of our identity. According to Buddhist thought, the identity view—an important subclass of grasping at self-existence—constitutes a fundamental ignorance and hence a root of all our afflictions. The term is also rendered as *personal identity view*.

illusory body (*sgyu lus, māyākāya*). In completion-stage practice in highest yoga tantra, the simulacrum of the buddha's form body that one will attain at the moment of enlightenment. In the Guhyasamāja tradition, it is the third of the five stages of the completion stage. It is based on the extremely subtle energy that is the basis of our physical being.

innate gnosis (*lhan skyes kyi ye shes, sahajajñāna*). In tantric contexts, the fundamental, luminous awareness that is intrinsic to all beings. Tantric practice aims at the actualization of this gnosis, which is roughly synonymous with buddha nature and clear light. Its synonyms include "primordial gnosis of bliss and emptiness," "gnosis of indivisible bliss and emptiness," "the great bliss gnosis," and "actual clear light."

insight (*lhag mthong, vipaśyanā*). Rendered also as *special insight*, it refers to one of two crucial attainments in Buddhist meditation, the other being tranquil abiding. Insight involves a penetrating realization of the nature of reality, whether articulated in terms of the four noble truths, no-self, or emptiness. Though based on intellectual analysis, insight is only effective in uprooting afflictions if it is conjoined with tranquil abiding.

intermediate state (*bar do, antarābhava*). The state of existence between death and the start of the next rebirth. The being of the intermediate state has a body composed of subtle wind. In advanced completion-stage practice, this state is replaced by the illusory body in the form of a deity.

intrinsic existence (*rang bzhin gyis grub pa, svabhāvasiddhi*). Existence by virtue of some kind of intrinsic nature, something categorically rejected by Nāgārjuna as read through Candrakīrti and Tsongkhapa.

mahāmudrā (*phyag rgya chen po*). Originally part of a system of three or four tantric seals, the "great seal" is synonymous with, *inter alia*, buddhahood, buddha nature, and the emptiness that "seals" all dharmas. Among the Kagyüpa (and Gelukpa) in Tibet, it also refers to a system of meditation, with both sutra and tantra versions, in which one meditates on the nature of the mind.

meditative absorption (*bsam gtan, dhyāna*). A state of mind characterized by a high level of focused attention and one-pointedness. A paradigmatic example of meditative absorption is the state of tranquil abiding (*zhi gnas, śamatha*), where the person has attained a deep state of effortless focus marked by absence of excitation or laxity. When used technically in the context of the "four meditative absorptions," *meditative absorption* refers to four progressively subtler states of mind defined by diminishing levels of feelings and discriminations, with tranquil abiding being only the gateway to such states. *Meditative absorption* is also the term for one of the six perfections in Mahayana Buddhism. The term is often used interchangeably with *concentration* (*ting nge 'dzin, samādhi*). *See also* concentration; meditative equipoise; placement meditation; tranquil abiding.

meditative equipoise (*mnyam gzhag, samāhita*). A single-pointed equipoise of mind on the chosen object of meditation. On the advanced level, meditative equipoise is characterized by direct realization of emptiness in which all forms of duality, subject-object, perception of diversity, and so forth are dissolved, with only single-pointed absorption on emptiness present. Sometimes the term *meditative equipoise* is simply a synonym for formal sitting practice and is contrasted with the post-equipoise practices between sessions.

meta-awareness (*shes bzhin, saṃprajanya*). The mental factor that monitors one's conduct of body, speech, and mind from moment to moment. In meditation practice, it is used in tandem with mindfulness as one of the two crucial faculties. The term is rendered by other translators as "introspection," "clear knowing," or "vigilance."

mixing (*bsre ba*). The completion-stage practice that uses the three states of sleeping, dreaming, and waking as well as death, intermediate state, and rebirth and correlates them with the three buddha bodies of dharmakāya, saṃbhogakāya, and nirmāṇakāya.

mode of being (*gnas lugs*). A synonym for "essential mode of being" (*gshis lugs*), the term refers to the way things are understood to exist from the perspective of their ultimate truth. Often an epithet for *emptiness*. The Tibetan *gnas lugs* is also sometimes rendered more literally as "abiding nature."

mudrā (*phyag rgya*). Literally "seal," a *mudrā* may be (1) a hand gesture made to illustrate a particular state of mind, such as wrathfulness, or an inner activity such as making offerings, or (2) a consort, either visualized as a gnosis seal or an actual live partner, an action seal. These are seals in the sense that they seal the bliss of the yogi by way of meditative union. *See also* action seal; mahāmudrā; reality seal.

nirmāṇakāya (*sprul sku*). A buddha's emanation body, the aspect that appears for the sake of ordinary sentient beings. A single buddha may have multiple emanations, which may be in human, animal, or inanimate forms. The historical Buddha Śākyamuni is generally regarded as a nirmāṇakāya.

obscuration (*sgrib pa, avaraṇa*). Sometimes rendered also as "defilement" or "obstruction," the term refers to factors that obscure and block our attainment of enlightenment. Typically, two classes of obscuration are identified—*afflictive obscurations* (*nyon sgrib, kleśāvaraṇa*), which refers to all the afflictions and their seeds, and *knowledge obscurations* (*shes sgrib, jñeyāvaraṇa*), the subtle residue of dualistic thinking that obstructs perfect wisdom and omniscience and thus is eliminated only by buddhas. The latter is thus sometimes called the *obstructions to omniscience*. Sometimes, two additional classes of obscurations are added: (3) *obscurations to concentration* (*ting nge 'dzin gyi sgrib pa, samādhyāvaraṇa*), referring to the five hindrances to meditation—excitation and regret, ill will, lethargy and sleep, attraction to sense objects, and doubt—and (4) *karmic obscurations* (*las kyi sgrib pa, karmāvaraṇa*).

obstructions. *See* obscuration.

pith instructions (*man ngag, upadeśa*). The Tibetan term *man ngag* has been translated as "pith instruction" (or simply "instruction" at times) and connotes a kind of specialized piece of advice. This Tibetan word and the term *gdams ngag*, which has been translated as "advice," are both equivalents of a single Sanskrit term, *upadeśa*. Although these two Tibetan terms are sometimes used interchangeably, *man ngag* often refers to an ongoing oral lineage.

placement meditation (*'jog sgom*). Rendered in this volume also as "nondiscursive meditation," this is a particular style of meditation practice that engages primarily without discursivity in the manner of resting simply on the chosen object of meditation. Tranquil abiding is attained principally through this kind of resting meditation, where the meditator chooses to remain in equipoise, free of distraction and without any movement of discursiveness, such as analysis, deliberation, or rumination. This style is contrasted with *analytical meditation*, the latter necessarily involving active engagement through discursiveness and analysis.

primordial mind (*gnyug sems, nijacitta*). The fundamental and subtlest level of the mind, which is characterized simply by luminosity and awareness and is, in itself, free of any taints. For ordinary beings, the primordial mind is said to naturally manifest fully only at the moment of death. In this sense, the primordial mind is equivalent to the clear light of death.

primordial nature (*gnyug ma'i rang bzhin*). In mahāmudrā literature, *primordial nature* refers to the fundamental nature of mind as pure luminosity and awareness, which is totally free from any form of conceptual elaboration.

reality seal (*dharmamudrā, chos kyi phya rgya*). The term is used differently in different contexts, as referring to the ultimate nature of reality, wisdom perceiving the sphere of reality, conjoining of subtle wind and mind, among other things.

sādhana (*sgrub thabs*). Literally a "means of attainment," a sādhana is the meditative procedure of a tantric practice, whereby one visualizes oneself as a deity at the center of a mandala and recites specific prayers and mantras. It also may refer to a text that describes those procedures in the mode of a meditation manual.

saṃbhogakāya (*longs sku*). A buddha's enjoyment body, the glorified aspect of a buddha that appears only to select disciples. The saṃbhogakāya is said to possess the major and minor marks of a buddha and to teach Mahayana Dharma in Akaniṣṭha heaven to high-level bodhisattvas for as long as cyclic existence lasts.

self-cherishing (*rang gces 'dzin*). The deeply ingrained thought that cherishes the welfare of one's own self and makes one oblivious to others' well-being. This is one of the "twin demons" (*'gong po gnyis*), according to the Tibetan *lojong* teaching, that lie within our heart and serve as the source of all misfortune and downfall (the other twin demon being grasping at selfhood). These two thoughts—self-cherishing and self-grasping—are the primary target of Mahayana mind training.

self-grasping (*bdag 'dzin, ātmagraha*). Holding on to the self-existence of one's own self, one's physical or mental aggregates, or the external world. *Self* or *self-existence* (*bdag*) here connotes a form of existence whereby one accords substantial, true existence and identity to one's own self and the world. The cultivation of the wisdom of emptiness eliminates this grasping at self-existence.

suchness (*de kho na nyid, tathatā*). The reality of things as they are. Having the same meaning as *thatness* (*de bzhin nyid, tattva*) and *ultimate nature* (*chos nyid, dharmatā*), the term is often a synonym for emptiness.

sutra (*mdo, sūtra*). A discourse of the Buddha contained in the canonical collections. The term is used also as referring to a system of the Buddhist path or a vehicle, in contradistinction to tantra. "Sutra Vehicle" (a synonym to Perfection Vehicle), "sutra path," and "sutra system" are well-known examples of this second usage of the term.

tantra (*rgyud*). A type of text attributed to the Buddha expounding doctrines and practices of a highly esoteric nature, such as deity meditation and yogic practices that employ vital elements of the body, including sexual energy and bliss. As in the case of its contrast, sutra, the term is used also to refer to a system, vehicle, or a path.

tīrthika (*mu stegs pa*). A term used in Buddhist texts to describe adherents of non-Buddhist schools of Indian philosophy and practice.

tranquil abiding (*gzhi gnas, śamatha*). Refers to an advanced meditative state where the meditator has attained physical and mental pliancy derived from the channeling of the mind. It is characterized by the stability of single-pointed attention on a chosen meditation object with the calming of mental distractions. Tranquil abiding is an essential basis for cultivating insight (*vipaśyan*ā), a profound understanding of the subtler aspects of the chosen object, such as its impermanence or emptiness, through refined analysis. *See also* concentration; meditative absorption; placement meditation.

triple being (*sems dpa' gsum brtsegs*). A unique feature of advanced guru-yoga practice involving three beings in concentric layers—the outer *commitment being* (*samayasattva*, the guru in the form of Tsongkhapa), the inner *gnosis being* (*jñānasattva*, Vajradhara at the heart of Tsongkhapa), and the innermost *concentration being* (*samādhisattva*, the syllable *hūṃ* at the heart of Vajradhara). The Tibetan word *sems dpa' gsum brtsegs* literally means "three beings stacked" or "three-tiered being."

true existence (*bden par grub pa, satyasiddhi*). *See* intrinsic existence.

two truths (*bden pa gnyis, dvayasatya*). Conventional truth (*kun rdzob bden pa, saṃvṛtisatya*) and ultimate truth (*don dam bden pa, paramārthasatya*). According to the Madhyamaka school, the *ultimate truth* is emptiness—the absence of intrinsic existence of all phenomena. *Conventional truth*, in contrast, is the empirical aspect of reality characterized by diversity and differentiation and experienced through perception, language, and thought.

ultimate expanse (*chos dbyings, dharmadhātu*). In Madhyamaka writings, this is an epithet for emptiness and used as a synonym for *suchness* and *thatness*. Emptiness is an "expanse" (*dhātu*) in that it is a "field," "sphere," "realm," or "element" in which (metaphorically, at least) all phenomena, of both samsara and nirvana, naturally reside.

ultimate nature (*chos nyid, dharmatā*). A term defined in contrast with *dharma* (phenomena) to refer to the true nature of things, hence *dharma* and *dharmatā*. In Mahayana thought, the term is used invariably as a synonym for other similar terms like *suchness* (*tathatā*) and *thatness* (*tattva*) and, like those terms, refers to emptiness.

ultimate truth (*don dam bden pa, paramārthasatya*). *See* two truths.

vital points of the body (*lus kyi gnad*). Specific points within the body, usually at the very center of the cakras, such as at the crown, mid-brows, throat, heart, navel, and sexual organ. In completion-stage practice these points are concentrated upon in order to bring the winds there for the purposes of withdrawing the mind, loosening the channel knots, and so on.

wind (*rlung, vāyu*). Externally as one of the four elements, wind is mobility and described as "that which is light and moving." Internally it refers to the five root and five secondary winds that move through the channels.

wisdom (*shes rab, prajñā*). The Sanskrit *prajñā* and its Tibetan equivalent *shes rab* have several different applications depending upon their contexts. First, in Abhidharma psychology's taxonomy of mental factors, *prajñā* refers to a specific mental factor that helps evaluate the various properties or qualities of the object of cognition. Second, the term can refer simply to intelligence, as in the context of determining the mental aptitude of different individuals. Third, in the context of the Mahayana path, *prajñā* refers to the wisdom aspect of the path constituted primarily by deep insight into the emptiness of all phenomena. Hence the term *prajñā* and its Tibetan equivalent are translated as "wisdom," "insight," or "intelligence." *See also* gnosis.

yoga (*rnal 'byor*). Literally "union," *yoga* refers to advanced meditative practices, especially in the context of Buddhist tantra. The Tibetan term *rnal 'byor* has the added connotation of "uniting one's mind with the nature of reality."

Bibliography

Canonical Works Cited in the Texts

Canonical Scriptures (Kangyur)

Account of the Prior Aspirations of the Seven Tathāgatas. Saptatathāgatapūrvapraṇidhānaviśeṣavistara. De bzhin gshegs pa bdun gyi sngon gyi smon lam gyi khyad par rgyas pa. Toh 503 Kangyur, rgyud *da.*

Adornment of Trees Sutra. Gaṇḍavyūhasūtra. Sdong pos brgyan pa'i mdo. Toh 44, phal chen *a*: the final (45th) chapter of the *Flower Ornament Sutra* (*Avatataṃsakasūtra*).

Application of Mindfulness Sutra. Saddharmasmṛtyupasthānasūtra. Dam pa'i chos dran pa nye bar gzhag pa. Toh 287, mdo sde *ya–sha.*

Ascertaining the Discipline: The Sutra of Upāli's Questions. Vinayaviniścayopāliparipṛcchāsūtra. 'Dul ba rnam par gtan la dbab pa nye bar 'khor gyis zhus pa'i mdo. Toh 68, dkon brtsegs *ca.*

Ascertainment of the Meaning Dharma Discourse. Arthaviniścayadharmaparyāya. Don dam rnam par nges pa zhes bya ba'i chos kyi rnam grang. Toh 317, mdo sde *sa.*

Awakening of Vairocana Tantra. Vairocanādhisaṃbodhi. Rnam par snang mdzad mgon par rdzogs par byang chub pa. Toh 494, rgyud *tha.*

Chapters on Discipline. Vinayavastu. gzhi. Toh 1, 'dul ba *ka–nga.*

Chapters on the Finer Points of Discipline. Vinayakṣudrakavastu. 'Dul ba phran tshegs kyi gzhi. Toh 6, 'dul ba *tha–da.*

Collection of Aphorisms. Udānavarga. Ched du brjod pa'i tshoms. Toh 326, mdo sde *sa.*

Concentration of the Gnosis Seal of the Tathāgatas. Tathāgatajñānamudrāsamādhi. De bzhin gshegs pa'i ye shes kyi phyag rgya'i ting nge 'dzin. Toh 131, mdo sde *da.*

Condensed Perfection of Wisdom in Verse. Prajñāpāramitāsañcayagāthā. Shes rab kyi pha rol tu phyin pa sdud pa tshigs su bcad pa. Toh 13, shes rab sna tshogs *ka.*

Densely Arrayed Tree Sutra. Ghanavyūhasūtra. Sdong po bkod pa'i mdo. Toh 110, mdo sde *cha.*

Detailed Explanations of Discipline. Vinayavibhaṅga. 'Dul ba rnam par 'byed pa. Toh 3, 'dul ba *ca–nya.*

Discourse on the Tathāgatha's Great Compassion. Tathāgatamahākaruṇanirdeśa. De bzhin gshegs pa'i snying rje chen po nges par bstan pa. Toh 147, mdo sde *pa.*

Display of the Qualities of Mañjuśrī's Buddha Realm. Mañjuśrībuddhakṣetraguṇavyūhasūtra. 'Jam dpal gyi sangs rgyas kyi zhing gi yon tan bkod pa'i mdo. Toh 59, dkon brtsegs *ga.*

Drop of Gnosis Tantra. Jñānatilakatantra. Dpal ye shes kyi kyi thig le rnal 'byor ma'i rgyud kyi rgyal po mchog tur mad du byung ba. Toh 422, rgyud *nga.*

Drop of the Great Seal Tantra. Mahāmudrātilakatantra. Phyag rgya chen po'i thig le zhes bya ba rnal 'byor ma chen mo'i rgyud kyi rgyal po. Toh 420, rgyud *nga.*

Entry into the Womb Sutra. Āyuṣmannandagarbhāvakrāntinirdeśa. Tshe dang ldan pa dga' bo la mngal du 'jug pa bstan pa'i mdo. Toh 58, dkon brtsegs *ga.*

Flower Ornament Sutra. Avataṃsakasūtra. Sangs rgyas phal po che zhes bya ba shin tu rgyas pa chen po'i mdo. Toh 44, phal chen *ka–a.*

Gathering All Fragments Sutra. Sarvavaidalyasaṃgraha. Rnam par 'thag pa thams bcad bsdus pa. Toh 227, mdo sde *dza.*

Golden Light Sutra. Suvarṇaprabhāsottamasūtra. Gser 'od dam pa mdo sde dbang po'i rgyal po. Toh 556, rgyud, *pa.*

Gnosis at the Point of Death Sutra. Ātajñānasūtra. 'Da' ka ye shes mdo. Toh 122 Kangyur, mdo sde *tha.*

Great Final Nirvana Sutra. Mahāparinirvāṇsūtra. Yongs su mya ngan las 'das pa chen po'i mdo. Toh 120, mdo sde *tha.*

Guhyasamāja Root Tantra. Guhyasamājatantra. De bzhin gshegs pa thams cad kyi sku gsung thugs kyi gsang chen gsang ba 'dus pa. Toh 442, rgyud *ca.*

Heart of the Perfection of Wisdom. Prajñāpāramitāhṛdaya. Bcom ldan 'das ma shes rab kyi pha rol tu phyin pa'i snying po. Toh 21, shes rab sna tshogs *ka.*

Hundred on Karma. Karmaśataka. Las brgya tham pa. Toh 340, mdo sde *ha.*

Individual Liberation Sutra. Prātimokṣasūtra. So sor thar pa'i mdo. Toh 2, Kangyur, 'dul ba *ca.*

Invoking the Altruistic Resolve. Adhyāśayasañcodana. Lhag pa'i bsam pa bskul ba'i mdo. Toh 69, dkon brtsegs *ca.*

Jewel Torch Dhāraṇī. Ratnolkādhāraṇī. Dkon mchog ta la la'i gzungs. Toh 145, mdo sde *pa.*

Kāśyapa Chapter Sutra. Kāśyapaparivartasūtra. 'Od srung gi le'u. Toh 87, dkon brtsegs *cha.*

King of Meditations Sutra. Samādhirājasūtra (a.k.a. *Candraprabhasūtra*). *Ting nge 'dzin rgyal po'i mdo.* Toh 127, mdo sde *da.*

Kṛṣṇayamāri Tantra. Kṛṣṇayamāritantrarājātrikalpa. Dpal gshin rje gshed nag po'i rgyud kyi rgyal po rtogs pa gsum pa. Toh 469, rgyud *ja.*

Liberating Life of Maitreya. Maitreyavimokṣa. Part of the *Adornment of Trees Sutra.*

Manifest Renunciation Sutra. Abhiniṣkramaṇasūtra. Mngon par byung ba'i mdo. Toh 301, mdo sde *sa.*

Mañjuśrī Root Tantra. Mañjuśrīmūlatantra. 'Jam dpal gyi rtsa ba'i rgyud. Toh 543, rgyud *na.*

Meeting of Father and Son Sutra. Pitāputrasamāgamanasūtra. Yab sras mjal ba'i mdo. Toh 60, dkon brtsegs *nga.*

Nanda's Abiding in the Womb Sutra. Nandagarbhāvakrāntinirdeśa. Dga' bo mngal na gnas pa bstan pa'i mdo. Toh, 57, dkon brtsegs *ga.*

Perfection of Wisdom in Eight Thousand Lines. Aṣṭasāhasrikāprājñāpāramitā. Shes rab kyi pha rol tu phyin pa brgyad stong pa. Toh 12, brgyad stong *ka.*

Perfectly Gathering the Teachings Sutra. Dharmasaṃgītisūtra. Chos yang dag par sdud pa. Toh 238, mdo sde *zha.*

Play in Full Sutra. Lalitavistarasūtra. Rgya cher rol pa'i mdo. Toh 95, Kangyur, mdo sde *kha.*

Presenting the Thorough Cleansing of Limitless Avenues Sutra. Anantamukhapariśodhanānirdeśaparivarta. Sgo mtha' yas pa rnam par sbyong ba bstan pa. Toh 46, dkon brtsegs *ka.*

Questions of the Bodhisattva Jñānottara. Jñānottarabodhisattvaparipṛcchā. Byang sems ye shes dam pas zhus pa. Toh 82, dkon brtsegs *cha.*

Questions of the Householder Ugra. Gṛhapati-ugraparipṛcchā. Khyim bdag drag shul can gyis zhus pa. Toh 63, dkoṇ brtsegs *nga.*

Questions of Rāṣṭrapāla. Rāṣṭrapālaparipṛcchā. Yul 'khor skyong gis zhus pa. Toh 62, dkon brtsegs, *nga.*

Questions of Sāgaramati. Sāgaramatināgarājaparipṛcchāsūtra. Blo gros rgya mtshos zhus pa'i mdo. Toh 152, mdo sde *pha.*

Questions of Subāhu Tantra. Subāhuparipṛcchātantra. Dpung bzang gis skus pa. Toh 805, rgyud *wa.*

Range of the Bodhisattva Sutra (a.k.a. *Satyaka Chapter*). *Bodhisattvagocaropāyaviṣayavikurvāṇanirdeśasūtra* (*Satyakaparivarta*). *Byang chub sems dpa'i spyod yul gyi thabs kyi yul la rnam par 'phrul pa bstan pa'i mdo* (*Bden pa po'i le'u*). Toh 146, mdo sde *pa.*

Rice Seedling Sutra. Śālistambasūtra. Sa lu ljangs pa'i mdo. Toh 210, mdo sde *tsha.*

Root Tantra of Cakrasaṃvara (*Brief Cakrasaṃvara Tantra*). *Laghusaṃvaratantra. Rgyud kyi rgyal po dpal bde mchog nyung ngu.* Toh 368, rgyud *ka.*

Saṃvarodaya Tantra. Saṃvarodayatantra. Bde mchog 'byung ba. Toh 373, rgyud *kha.*

Satyaka Chapter. Satyakaparivarta. Bden pa po'i le'u. See the *Range of the Bodhisattva Sutra.*

Seal Enhancing the Power of Faith Sutra. Śraddhābalādhānāvatāramudrāsūtra. Dad pa'i stobs bskyed pa la 'jug pa'i phyag rgya'i mdo. Toh 201, mdo sde *tsha.*

Story of Sumāgadha. Sumāgadhāvadāna. Ma ga dhā bzang mo'i rtogs pa brjod pa. Toh 346, mdo sde *aṃ.*

Sublime Dharma of the White Lotus. Saddharmapuṇḍarīka. Dam pa'i chos pad ma dkar po. Toh 113, mdo sde *ja.*

Sutra Teaching the Tathāgata's Inconceivable Secret. Tathāgataguhyanirdeśasūtra. De bzhin gshegs pa'i gsang ba bsam gyis mi khyab pa bstan pa'i mdo. Toh 47, dkon brtsegs *ka.*

Teachings of Akṣayamati Sutra. Akṣayamatinirdeśasūtra. Blo gros mi zad pas bstan pa'i mdo. Toh 175, mdo sde *ma.*

Ten Dharmas Sutra. Daśadharmakasūtra. Chos bcu pa'i mdo. Toh 53, dkon brtsegs *kha.*

Ten Grounds Sutra. Daśabhūmikasūtra. Sa bcu pa'i mdo. Toh 44, phal chen *kha.* Chapter 31 of the *Flower Ornament Sutra* (*Avataṃsakasūtra*).

Ten Wheels of Kṣitigarbha Sutra. Daśacakrakṣitigarbhasūtra. Sa'i snying po'i 'khor lo bcu pa. Toh 239, mdo sde *zha.*

Thorough Ascertainment of Truth Sutra. Arthaviniścaya. Don rnam par nges pa zhes bya ba'i chos kyi rnam grangs. Toh 317, mdo sde *sa.*

Twenty-Five Thousand Lines on the Perfection of Wisdom. Pañcaviṃśatisāhasrikāprajñāpāramitā. Shes rab kyi pha rol tu phyin pa stong phrag nyi shu lnga pa. Toh 9, nyi khri *ka–ga.*

Unraveling the Intent Sutra. Saṃdhinirmocanasūtra. Dgongs pa nges par 'grel pa'i mdo. Toh 106, mdo sde *ca.*

Vajra Garland Tantra. Vajramālātantra. Bshad rgyud rdo rje phreng ba. Toh 445, rgyud *ca.*

Vajra Tent Tantra. Vajrapañjaratantra. Rdo rje gur gyi rgyud. Toh 419, rgyud *nga.*

Vajrapāṇi Empowerment Tantra. Vajrapāṇyabhiṣekamahātantra. Lag na rdo rje dbang bskur ba'i rgyud. Toh 496, rgyud *da.*

Verses on the Nāga King Bherī. Nāgarājabherīgāthā. Klu'i rgyal po rnga sgra'i tshigs su bcad pa. Toh 325, mdo sde *sa.*

Vows of Good Conduct. Bhadracaryāpraṇidhāna. Bzang po spyod pa'i smon lam gyi rgyal po. Toh 1095, gzungs 'dus, *waṃ.*

Canonical Treatises (Tengyur)

Advayavajra. *Extensive Explanation of Song Filling Up the Inexhaustible Treasury. Dohānidhikoṣaparipūrṇagīti. Mi zad ba'i gter mdzod yongs su gang ba'i glu.* Toh 2257, rgyud, *wi.*

Āryadeva. *Four Hundred Stanzas. Catuḥśataka. Bstan bcos bzhi brgya pa.* Toh 3846, dbu ma *tsha.*

———. *Lamp for Integrating the Practices. Caryāmelāpakapradīpa. Spyod pa bsdus pa'i sgron ma.* Toh 1802 Tengyur, rgyud, *ngi.*

Āryaśūra. *Condensed Presentation of the Perfections. Pāramitāsamāsa. Pha rol tu phyin pa bsdus pa.* Toh 3944, dbu ma *khi.*

———. *Garland of Birth Stories. Jātakamālā. Skyes pa rabs kyi rgyud.* Toh 4150, skyes rab *hu.*

Asaṅga. *Bodhisattva Grounds. Bodhisattvabhūmi. Byang chub sems dpa'i sa.* Toh 4037, sems tsam *wi.* See under Western Works for translation, *The Bodhisattva Path to Unsurpassed Enlightenment.*

———. *Compendium of Abhidharma. Abhidharmasamuccaya. Chos mgon pa kun las btu spa.* Toh 4049, sems tsam *ri.*

———. *Summary of the Great Vehicle. Mahāyānasaṃgraha. Theg pa chen po bsdus pa.* Toh 4048, sems tsam *ri.*

———. *Yogācāra Grounds. Yogācārabhūmi. Rnal 'byor spyod pa'i sa.* Toh 4035, sems tsam *tshi.*

Aśvaghoṣa. *Dispelling Sorrow. Śokavinodana. Mya ngan bsal ba.* Toh 4177, spring yig *nge.*

———. *Fifty Verses on the Guru. Gurupañcāśikā. Bla ma lnga bcu pa.* Toh 3721, rgyud *tshu.*

———. *Praise in Hundred and Fifty Verses. Śatapañcāśatakastotra. Bstod pa brgya lnga bcu pa.* Toh 1147, bstod tshogs *ka.*

Atiśa. *Commentary on Lamp on the Path. Bodhimārgapradīpapañjikā. Byang chub lam gyi sgron ma'i dka' 'grel.* Toh 3948, dbu ma *khi.*

———. *Entering the Two Truths. Satyadvayāvatāra. Bden pa gnis la 'jug pa.* Toh 3902, dbu ma *a.*

———. *Lamp on the Path to Enlightenment. Bodhipathapradīpa. Byang chub lam gyi sgron ma.* Toh 3947, dbu ma *khi.*

———. *Rite on Confession of Downfalls. Āpattideśanaviddhi. Ltung ba bshags pa'i cho ga.* Toh 3974, dbu ma, *gi.*

———. *Summary of the Methods to Accomplish the Mahayana Path. Mahāyānapathasādhanavarṇasaṃgraha. Theg pa chen po'i lam gyi sgrub thabs yi ger bsdus pa.* Toh 3954, dbu ma *ki.*

Bhāviveka. *Blaze of Reasoning. Tarkajvālā. Rtog ge 'bar ba.* Toh 3856, dbu ma *dza.* Critical edition in *Dbu ma snying po'i 'grel pa rtog ge 'bar ba* (*Tarkajvālā: An Autocommentary on the Madhyamakahṛdaya*), edited and introduced by Thupten Jinpa. New Delhi: Institute of Tibetan Classics, 2019.

———. *Essence of the Middle Way. Madhyamakahṛdaya. Dbu ma snying po.* Toh 3855, dbu ma *dza.*

Bodhibhadra. *Chapter on the Conditions for Meditative Concentration. Samādhisambāraparivarta. Ting nge 'dzin tshogs kyi le'u.* Toh 3924, dbu ma *ki.*

———. *Explanation of Compendium on the Heart of Wisdom. Jñānasārasamuccayanāmanibandhana. Ye shes snying po kun las btus pa bshad sbyar.* Toh 3852 Tengyur, dbu ma *tsha.*

Buddhapālita. *Buddhapālita: A Commentary on Root Verses of the Middle Way. Buddhapālita-mūlamadhyamakavṛtti. Dbu ma rtsa ba'i 'grel pa buddha pālita.* Toh 3842, dbu ma *tsha.*

Buddhaśrījñāna. *Sacred Words [of Mañjuśrī]: Meditative Practice of the Second Stage. Dvikramatattvabhāvanānāma[mañjuśrī]mukhāgama. Rim pa gnyis pa'i de kho na nyid bsgom pa zhes bya ba'i ['jam dpal] zhal lung.* Toh 1853, rgyud *di.*

Candragomin. *Letter to a Student. Śiṣyalekha. Slob ma la springs pa'i spring yig.* Toh 4183, spring yig *nge.*

———. *Praise in the Form of a Confession. Deśanāstava. Bshags pa'i bstod pa.* Toh 1159, bstod tshogs *ka.*

Candrakīrti. *Clear Words: A Commentary on Root Verses of the Middle Way. Prasannapadā. Dbu ma rtsa ba'i 'grel pa tshig gsal ba.* Toh 3860, dbu ma *'a.*

———. *Entering the Middle Way. Madhyamakāvatāra. Dbu ma la 'jug pa.* Toh 3861, dbu ma *'a.*

———. *Entering the Middle Way Autocommentary. Madhyamakāvatārabhāṣya. Dbu ma la 'jug pa'i bshad pa.* Toh 3862 Tengyur, dbu ma *'a.*

———. *Extensive Commentary on Four Hundred Verses. Catuḥśatakaṭīkā. Byang chub sems dpa'i rnal 'byor spyod pa bzhi brgya pa'i rgya cher 'grel pa.* Toh 3865, dbu ma *ya.*

———. *Seventy Verses on Going for Refuge to the Three Jewels. Triśaraṇagamanasaptati. Gsum la skyabs su 'gro ba bdun cu pa.* Toh 3971, dbu ma *gi.*

Dharmakīrti. *Exposition of Valid Cognition. Pramāṇavārttika. Tshad ma rnam 'grel.* Toh 4210, tshad ma *ce.* Critical edition in *Dpal chos kyi grags pa'i tshad ma sde bdun* (*Seven Pramāṇa Works of Dharmakīrti*), edited and introduced by Thupten Jinpa. New Delhi: Institute of Tibetan Classics, 2015.

Dignāga. *Interwoven Praise. Miśrakastotra. Spel mar bstod pa.* Toh 1150, bstod tshogs *ka.*

Guṇaprabha. *Vinaya Sutra. Vinayasūtra. 'Dul ba mdo rtsa ba.* Toh 4117, 'dul ba *wu.*

Jagatamitrānanda (a.k.a. Mitrayogi). *Heart Yoga. Yogasāraḥ. Rnal 'byor snying po.* Toh 2855, rgyud 'grel *ngu.*

Kalyāṇamitra. *Extensive Commentary on the Chapters on Discipline. Vinayavastuṭīkā. 'Dul ba gzhi rgya cher 'grel pa.* Toh 4113, 'dul ba *tsu.*

Kamalaśīla (ninth century). *Lamp for the Middle Way. Madhyamakāloka. Dbu ma snang ba.* Toh 3887 Tengyur, dbu ma *sa.*

———. *Stages of Meditation II. Bhāvanākrama II. Sgom rim bar pa.* Toh 3916, dbu ma *ki.*

———. *Stages of Meditation III. Bhāvanākrama III. Sgom rim mtha' ma.* Toh 3917, dbu ma *ki.*

Lakṣmīṅkarā. *Attainment of the Nondual. Advayasiddhisādhana. Gnyis med grub pa.* Toh 2220, rgyud 'grel *wi.*

Mahāsukha (a.k.a. Padmavajra). *Attainment of the Secret. Guhyasiddhi. Dpal gsang ba grub pa.* Toh 2217, rgyud *wi.*

Maitreya. *Differentiation of the Middle and Extremes. Madhyāntavibhāga. Dbus dang mtha' rnam par 'byed pa.* Toh 4021, sems tsam *phi.*

———. *Ornament of Mahayana Sutras. Mahāyānasūtrālaṃkāra. Theg pa chen po mdo sde rgyan.* Toh 4020, sems tsam *phi.*

———. *Ornament of Realization. Abhisamayālaṃkāra. Mngon rtogs rgyan.* Toh 3786, shes phyin *ka.*

———. *Sublime Continuum. Uttaratantra* (a.k.a. *Ratnagotravibhāga*). *Theg pa chen po rgyud bla ma.* Toh 4024, sems tsam *phi.*

Maitripa (Advayavajra). *Presenting Non-Mentation. Amanasikāroddeśa. Yid la mi byed pa ston pa.* Toh 2249, rgyud *wi.*

Mañjuśrīkīrti. *Ornament of the Essence. Sarvaguhyavidhigarbhālaṃkāra. Gsang ba thams bcad kyi spyi'i cho ga snying po rgyan.* Toh 2490, rgyud *zi.*

Mātṛceṭa. *Praise to the One Beyond All Praise. Varṇārhavarṇestotra. Bsngags 'os bsngags bstod.* Toh 1138, bstod tshogs *ka.*

Nāgārjuna. *Ascertaining the Four Seals. Caturmudrāviniścaya. Phyag rgya bzhi gtan la dbab pa.* Toh 2225, rgyud *wi.*

———. *Commentary on the Awakening Mind. Bodhicittavivaraṇa. Byang chub sems kyi 'grel pa.* Toh 1801, rgyud 'grel *ngi.*

———. *A Drop to Rejuvenate the Person. Jantupoṣaṇabindhu. Skye bo gso ba'i thigs pa.* Toh 4330, lugs kyi bstan bcos, *ngo.*

———. *Five Stages. Pañcakrama. Rim pa lnga pa.* Toh 1802, rgyud *ngi.*

———. *Friendly Letter. Suhṛllekha. Bshes pa'i spring yig.* Toh 4182, spring yig *nge.*

———. *Fundamental Verses on the Middle Way* (a.k.a. *Fundamental Wisdom, Treatise on the Middle Way*). *Mūlamadhyamakakārikā. Dbu ma rtsa ba'i tshig le'ur byas pa* (*Dbu ma rtsa ba shes rab*). Toh 3824, dbu ma *tsa.*

———. *Hundred Verses of Wisdom. Prajñāśataka. Shes rab brgya pa.* Toh 4328, bzo rig pa / thun mong ba *ngo.*

———. *Praise to Mother Perfection of Wisdom. Prajñāpāramitāstotra. Shes rab kyi pha rol tu phyin ma'i bstod pa.* Toh 1127, bstod tshogs *ka.*

———. *Precious Garland. Ratnāvalī. Rgyal po la gtam bya ba rin po che'i phreng ba.* Toh 4158, spring yig *ge.*

———. *Sixty Verses of Reasoning. Yuktiṣaṣṭikā. Rigs pa drug cu pa.* Toh 3825, dbu ma *tsa.*

Nāropa. *Eiptome. Ajñāsamyakpramāṇa. Bka' yang dag pa'i tshad ma.* Toh 2331, rgyud *zhi.*

Padmavajra. *See* Mahāsukha.

Prajñāvarman. *Exposition of the Collection of Aphorisms. Udānavargavivaraṇa. Ched du brjod pa'i tshoms kyi rnam par 'grel pa.* Toh 4100, mngon pa *thu.*

Puṇḍarīka. *In Service of the Ultimate. Paramārthasevā. Don dam pa'i bsnyen pa.* Toh 1348, rgyud *na.*

———. *Stainless Light. Vimalaprabhā. 'Grel chen dri med 'od.* Toh 845 (Kangyur), dus 'khor *shrī.*

Sahajavajra (a.k.a. Natekara). *Commentary on Ten Verses on Reality. Tattvadaśakaṭīkā. De kho na nyid bcu pa'i rgya cher 'grel pa.* Toh 2254, rgyud *wi.*

Śāntarakṣita. *Commentary on Ornament of the Middle Way. Madhyamakālaṃkāravṛtti. Dbu ma'i rgyan gyi 'grel pa.* Toh 3885 Tengyur, dbu ma *sa.*

Śāntideva. *Compendium of Training. Śikṣāsamuccaya. Bslab pa kun las btus pa.* Toh 3940, dbu ma *khi.*

———. *Guide to the Bodhisattva Way. Bodhicaryāvatāra. Byang chub sems dpa'i spyod pa la 'jug pa.* Toh 3872, dbu ma *la.*

———. *Verses on the Compendium of Training. Śikṣāsamuccayakārikā. Bslab pa kun las btus pa.* Toh 3939, dbu ma *khi.*

Saraha. *Dohā Treasury of Songs* (a.k.a. *People's Dohā*). *Dohākoṣagīti. Do ha mdzod kyi glu.* Toh 2224, rgyud *wi.*

———. *Song of Vajra Secrets: An Instruction on Mahāmudrā. Mahāmudropadeśavajraguhyagīti. Phyag rgya chen po'i man ngag rdo rje gsang ba'i glu.* Toh 2440, rgyud *zi.*

———. *Dohā Song on the Fruits of Meditating on the View. Dṛṣṭibhāvanācaryāphaladohāgīti. Lta bsgom spyod pa 'bras bu'i do ha'i glu.* Toh 2345, rgyud *tshi.*

———. *Treasury of Dohās: A Pith Instruction on Mahāmudrā. Dohākoṣamahāmudropadeśa. Do ha mdzod ces bya ba'i phyag rgya chen po'i man ngag.* Toh 2273, rgyud *zhi.*

Sthiramati. *Commentary on Differentiation of the Middle and Extremes. Madhyāntavibhāgaṭīkā. Dbus dang mtha' rnam par 'byed pa'i 'grel bshad.* Toh 4032, sems tsam *bi.*

Tilopa. *Instruction on Mahāmudrā* (a.k.a. *Ganges Mahāmudrā*). *Mahāmudropadeśa. Phyag rgya chen po'i man ngag.* Toh 2303, rgyud *zhi.*

Tilopa. *Dharma of the Bodiless Ḍākinī. Vajraḍākiniṣkāyadharma. Rdo rje mkha' 'gro lus med pa'i chos.* Toh 1527, rgyud *za.*

Vasubandhu (fourth century). *Treasury of Abhidharma. Abhidharmakośa. Chos mngon pa mdzod kyi tshig le'ur byas pa.* Toh 4089, mngon pa *ku.*

———. *Treasury of Abhidharma Autocommentary. Abhidharmakośabhāṣya. Chos mngon pa mdzod kyi bshad pa.* Toh 4090, mngon pa *ku.*

Vitakarma. *Jewel Heart: A Commentary on the Four Seals. Mudrācaturaṭīkāratnahṛdaya. Phyag rgya bzhi'i rgya cher 'grel pa rin po che'i snying po.* Toh 2259, rgyud *wi.*

Works in Tibetan

This section on Tibetan works includes texts referred to or cited both by the authors and by the translators. Modern book editions of texts are marked "Typeset edition." Numbers of the page range of individual texts, including even those of woodblock editions, are English page numbers.

Akhu Sherab Gyatso (1803–75). *Notes on the Guide to Amitābha Transference of Consciousness "Hero Embarking on a Campaign" from the Ensa Oral Transmission. Dben sa snyan brgyud las byung ba'i 'od dpag med kyi 'pho ba dpa' bo g.yul 'jug ma'i khrid zin*. Collected Works of Akhu Sherab Gyatso, vol. *ga*, 451–544. Lhasa: Zhöl Printery, 1998–99. BDRC W21505.

———. *Nectar Stream Relieving the Pain of Samsara and Nirvana: A Guide Combining "Offering to the Guru" and Mahāmudrā. Bla mchod phyag chen dang sbrags pa'i khrid kyi zin bris srid zhi'i gdung sel bdud rtsi'i chu rgyun*. Collected Works, vol. *ga*, 355–440.

Attributed to Atiśa and Dromtönpa. *The Book of Kadam, Part 2: The Son Teachings. Bka' gdams glegs bam las bu chos*. Typeset edition: Xining Nationalities Press, 1993.

Balmang. *See* Palmang.

Baso Chökyi Gyaltsen (1402–73). *Baso's Great Guide to the View. Ba so'i lta khrid chen mo*. In *Dbu ma'i lta khrid chen mo*. New Delhi: Lha-dkar yongs-'dzin bstan-pa rgyal-mtshan, 1973. BDRC W30180.

Butön Rinchen Drup (1182–1251). *Catalogue of Tengyur. Bka' 'bum dkar chag*. The Collected Works of Butön Rinchen Drup, vol. *zhi*, 405–647. Delhi: Lokesh Chandra, 1971.

———. *Dispelling Bad Views: A Treatise on the Establishment of the Perfection of Wisdom. Shes rab kyi pha rol tu phyin pa'i grub pa'i rab tu byed pa lta ba ngan sel*. The Collected Works of Butön Rinchen Drup, vol. *dza*, 5–65. Delhi: Lokesh Chandra, 1971.

Changkya Ngawang Chöden's (1642–1714). *Guidebook on Mahāmudrā. Phyag chen gyi khrid*. Collected Works of Changkya Ngawang Chöden, vol. *kha*, 307–18. Beijing woodblock print, n.d. BDRC W1KG1321.

———. *Stream of Camphor Juice: A Guidebook on the Three Essential Points. Snying po don gsum gyi khrid yig ga bur chu rgyun*. Collected Works, vol. *nga*.

Changkya Rolpai Dorjé (1717–86). *Recognizing My Mother: A Song on the View. Lta mgur a ma ngos 'dzin*. Collected Works of Changkya Rölpai Dorjé, vol. *nga*, 385–90. Dharamsala: Library of Tibetan Works & Archives, 2000. English translation in Jinpa and Elsner, *Songs of Spiritual Experience*.

———. *Replies to Questions from Gomang Gungru Rabjampa Jampa Lodrö. Sgo mang gung ru rab 'byams pa blo gros kyi dris lan*. Collected Works, vol. *ca*, 109–54.

Chekawa Yeshé Dorjé (1101–75). *Seven-Point Mind Training. Blo sbyong don bdun ma*. In Jinpa, *Mind Training*, 83–85.

Chenga Lodrö Gyaltsen (1402–71). *Biography of Jetsun Jampal Gyatso. Rje btsun 'jam dpal rgya mtsho'i rnam thar*. Collected Works of Chenga Lodrö Gyaltsen, 3:26–52. Typeset edition. Lhasa: Ser gtsug nang bstan dpe rnying 'tshol bsdu phyogs sgrig khang, 2010.

———. *Mahāmudrā Illuminating the Essence. Phyag rgya chen po snying po don gsal*. Collected Works, 3:156–59.

———. *Opening the Door to the Teaching: The Initial Instruction for Training the Mind in the Stages of the Path to Enlightenment. Byang chub lam gyi rim pa la blo sbyong ba la thog mar blo sbyong ba chos kyi sgo 'byed*. Collected Works, 1:1–93.

———. *Ultimate and Profound Path of Oral Transmission: Guide to the View of the Middle Way Free of Extremes. Mtha' bral dbu ma'i lta khrid snyan brgyud zab lam mthar thug*. Collected Works, 5:28–54.

Chökyi Dorjé (nineteenth century). *Golden Rosary: An Old Tale Essential for the Learned and Realized Ones of the Future Who Would Uphold the Southern Trans-*

mission Lamrim. Lam rim gyi khrid rgyun gna' gtam gser gyi phreng ba. Lhasa: Zhöl Printery, 1946. BDRC W00KG03884.

Dalai Lama Tenzin Gyatso with Dagyab Loden Sherap. *Illuminating the Conqueror's Intent*, 2 vols. *Rgyal ba'i dgongs gsal.* Typeset edition. Delhi: The Dalai Lama Trust and Tibethaus Deutschland, 2016. English translation in Dalai Lama Tenzin Gyatso, *The Fourteenth Dalai Lama's Stages of the Path.*

Dampa Sangyé (eleventh century). *Hundred Verses of Advice to the People of Dingri. Gzhal gdams ding ri brgya rtsa.* Gdams ngag mdzod, 13:31–36. Paro: Lama Ngodrup and Sherab Drimey, 1979–81.

———. *Vajra Song Distilling the Essence of Sublime Dharma as the Pacification of Suffering. Dam chos sdug bsngal zhi byed kyi snying por dril ba'i rdo rje'i mgur.* Gdams ngag mdzod, 13:36–38.

Drakpa Gyaltsen (1147–1226). *Parting from the Four Clingings. Zhen pa bzhi bral gyi gdams pa.* The Collected Works of Sakya Masters, vol. 9 (*ta*), 593–97. Tokyo: Tōyō Bunko, 1968.

Drupwang Jampal Gyatso. *See* Jamyang Dewai Dorjé.

Dulnakpa Palden Sangpo (b. 1402). *Hundreds of Gods of Tuṣita. Dga' ldan lha brgya ma.* In Jamyang Dewai Dorjé, *Garland of Wish-Granting Jewels*, <pp.?>.

Dungkar Losang Trinlé (Dung dkar Blo bzang 'phrin las, 1927–97). *Extensive Dictionary* (*Tshig mdzod chen mo*). Beijing: China Tibetology Publishing House, 2002.

Ensapa Losang Döndrup (1505–66). *Guru Yoga in Verse for Easy Recitation. Bla ma'i rnal 'byor tshigs bcad 'du bsgrigs pa.* Collected Works of Gyalwa Ensapa, vol. *ka*, 95–98. Tashi Lhunpo woodblock edition. BDRC W11128

———. *Miscellaneous Writings Including the Great Bliss Treasury of Self-Exhortation. Rang la gdams pa bde chen gter mdzod sogs thor bu'i skor.* Collected Works, vol. *ka*, 46–75.

———. *Source of All Attainments: Prophecies of Spiritual Mentors Who Have and Will Appear at Tashi Lhunpo. Bkra shis lhun por bshes gnyen byon pa dang 'byon par 'gyur ba'i lung bstan dngos grub kun 'byung.* In *Sealed Texts* (*Bka' rgya ma*). Collected Works, vol. *kha*, 737–76.

Gampopa Sönam Rinchen (1079–1153). *Great Collection of Dharma Lectures. Tshogs chos chen mo.* Collected Works of Sgam po pa'i gdan rabs rin byon, 1:228-65. Typeset edition. Beijing: Krung go'i bod rig pa'i dpe skrun khang, 2013. BDRC W3CN8060

———. *Instruction on the Essential Points. Snying po don gyi gdams pa phyag rgya chen po'i 'bum tig.* Collected Works, 2:295–315.

Gendun Gyatso, the Second Dalai Lama (1475–1542). *A Doorway for Those Aspiring Liberation: Establishing the Profound Middle Way View. Zab mo dbu ma'i lta ba gtan la 'bebs pa thar 'dod kyi 'jug ngogs.* Collected Works of Gendun Gyatso, vol. *kha*, 122–59. Dharamsala: The Library of Tibetan Works and Archives, 2006. BDRC W1CZ2857.

———. *Staircase to Tuṣita. Snying po don gsum gyi dmigs rim dga' ldan du bgrod pa'i them skas.* Collected Works, vol. *kha*, 97–115.

Gö Lotsāwa Shönu Pal (1391–1481). *The Blue Annals. Deb ther sngon po*, 2 vols. Typeset edition. Sichuan: Nationalities Press, 1984.

Gugé Yongzin Losang Tenzin (1748–1813). *Storehouse of Attainments Both Common and Supreme: An Explanatory Commentary on the Root Verses and [Auto]commentary of the Mahāmudrā Teaching Tradition of the Precious Ganden Oral Transmission. Dge ldan bka' brgyud rin po che'i bka' srol phyag rgya chen po'i rtsa 'grel rnams kyi 'grel bshad mchog mthun dgnos grub kyi bang mdzod.* Collected Works of Gugé Yongzin Lobsang Tenzin, 5:11–454. Reproduced from the block prints of Tashi Lhunpo. Delhi: Chophel Legdan, 1976. BDRC W23879.

Gungru Gyaltsen Sangpo (1384–1450). *Stream of Nectar: Eloquent Pith Instructions of My Guru. Legs bshad man ngag bdud rtsi'i rgyun.* Collected Works of Gungru Gyaltsen Sangpo, 2:285–421. Typeset edition. Beijing: Dpal brtsegs bod yig dpe rnying zhib 'jug khang, 2007.

Gungthang Tenpai Drönmé (1762–1823). *Essence of the Supreme Path: Presentation of All the Meditation Topics of Easy Path in Verse. Byang chub bde lam gyi dmigs skor cha tshang tshigs bcad du 'debs pa lam mchog snying po.* Collected Works of Gungthang Tenpai Drönmé, vol. *ga*, 491–506. Lhasa: Zhol par khang gsar pa, 2000.

———. *Garland of Nectar Drops: Notes on an Oral Instruction on Geden Mahāmudrā. Phyag chen zin bris bdud rtsi'i thigs phreng.* Collected Works, vol. *ga*, 563–619.

———. *Key to Unlock the Secrets of the Oral Transmission: A Commentary on the Root Verses on the Essential Instruction on the Profound Path of Guru Yoga. Zab lam bla ma'i rnal 'byor gyi man ngag snying po'i rtsa tshig gi 'grel pa snyan brgyud gsang ba'i lde mig.* Collected Works, vol. *ga*, 741–819.

Gyaltsab Darma Rinchen (1364–1432). *Commentary on the Sublime Continuum. Theg pa chen po'i rgyud bla ma'i ṭikka.* Collected Works of Gyaltsab Darma Rinchen, vol. *ga*, 1–322. Typeset comparative edition. Mundgod: Je Yabse Sungbum Project, 2019.

———. *How to Bring the Eight Realizations and Seventy Topics into Meditative Practice. Mngon rtogs brgyad dang don bdun cu dang bcas pa'i 'grel pa nyams su len tshul.* Collected Works, vol. *ca*, 95–128.

———. *Precious Garland: A Guide to the Profound View. Zab mo'i lta khrid rin po che'i phreng ba.* Collected Works, vol. *ka*, 189–97.

Jamyang Chöjé Tashi Palden (1379–1449). *Secret Biography of Lord Master Losang Drakpa: A Poem of Supplication. Rje btsun bla ma Blo bzang grags pa'i dpal gyi gsang ba'i rnam thar gsol 'debs.* In Collected Works of Je Tsongkhapa, vol. *ka*, 137–41. Typeset comparative edition. Mundgod: Je Yabse Sungbum Project, 2019.

Jamyang Dewai Dorjé (a.k.a. Drupwang Jampal Gyatso, 1682–1741). *Garland of Wish-Granting Jewels: A Guide to the Profound Path of the Unique Guru Yoga According to the Segyü Tradition. Srad rgyud lugs kyi zab lam bla ma'i rnal 'byor thun mong ma yin pa'i khrid yig citta ma ṇi'i phreng ba.* The Collected Works of Jamyang Dewai Dorjé, 1:49–78. Lhasa: Zhol bka' 'gyur par khang, 1999. BDRC W7797.

———. *Miktsema Cycle of Teachings. Dmigs brtse ma'i chos skor*, 2.vols. Scan at bdrc.io, W3CN22351.

Jamyang Gawai Lodrö (1429–1503). *Guidebook on the View Illuminating Thatness. Lta ba'i yig de nyid gsal byed.* Collected Works of Jamyang Gawai Lodrö, 2:162–86. Typeset edition. Beijing: Ser gstug nang bstan dpe rnying 'tshol bsdu phyogs sgrig khang, 2009.

Jamyang Shepa (1648–1722). *Great Treatise on Meditative Absorptions and Formless States. Bsam gzugs chen mo.* Collected Works of Jamyang Shepai Dorjé, vol. *na*, 1–525.

Jikten Gönpo (1143–1217). *A Song on the Realization of the Fivefold. Lnga ldan rtogs pa'i mgur.* In *Sgrub thob gong ma rnams kyi zhal gdams phyogs bsgrigs nor bu'i bang mdzod* (*Anthology of Kagyü Masters*). Frederick, MD: Drikung Kagyu Meditation Center, n.d. BDRC W00KG03672

Kalsang Gyatso, Seventh Dalai Lama (1708–57). *On Mind Training and Collected Poetic Songs. Blo sbyong dang 'brel ba'i gdams pa dang snyan mgur gyi rim pa phyogs gzig tu bkod pa.* Collected Works of the Seventh Dalai Lama, vol. *ka,* 397–502. Gangtok: Dondrup Sangye, 1975. BDRC W2623.

Keutsang Jamyang Mönlam's (1750–1814). *Excellent and Completely Virtuous Path to Freedom: Notes on the Mahāmudrā of the Geden Oral Transmission Tradition. Dge ldan snyan brgyud kyi bka' srol phyag rgya chen po'i zin bris rnam grol kun tu dge ba'i lam bzang.* Collected Works of Keutsang Jamyang Mönlam, 2:7–149. Dharamsala: Library of Tibetan Works and Archives, 1984. BDRC W16515.

Khedrup [Jé] Gelek Palsang (1385–1438). *Biographical Poem Supplicating the Great Lord Tsongkhapa. Rje btsun tshong kha pa chen po nyid kyi rnam par thar pa mdo tsam zhig brjod pa'i sgo nas gsol ba 'debs pa.* In *Miscellaneous Writings* (*Gsung thor bu*). Collected Works of Khedrup Gelek Palsang, vol. *ba,* 232–35. Typeset comparative edition, Mundgod: Je Yabse Sungbum Project, 2019.

———. *Dusting the Buddha's Doctrine: A Presentation of the Three Vows. Sdom pa gsum gyi rnam par bzhag pa thub bstan byi dor.* Collected Works, vol. *kha,* 393–565.

———. *Guru Yoga Endowed with Profound Features Conferred by the Dharma King Tsongkhapa to the Omniscient Khedrup Through One-to-One Transmission. Bla ma'i rnal 'byor zab khyad can chos kyi rgyal po tsong kha pa chen pos mkhas grub thams cad mkhyen pa la gcig brgyud kyi tshul du gnang ba.* Collected Works of Jé Tsongkhapa, vol. *ka,* 149–52. Typeset comparative edition. Mundgod: Je Yabse Sungbum Project, 2019.

———. *Prayer to the Lineage Gurus of "The Three Essential Points." Snying po don gsum gyi brgyud 'debs.* Collected Works, vol. *ba,* 249–50.

———. *Record of Teachings Received. Gsan yig.* Collected Works, vol. *ka,* 105–64.

———. *Secret Biography of Tsongkhapa. Rje rin po che'i gsang ba'i rnam thar rgya mtsho lta bu las cha shas nyung ngu zhig yongs su brjod pa'i gtam rin po che snye ma.* Collected Works of Jé Tsongkhapa, vol. *ka,* 113–36.

Khedrup Norsang Gyatso (1423–1513). *Bright Lamp of Mahāmudrā. Phyag rgya chen po gsal ba'i sgron me.* Dharamsala: Library of Tibetan Works and Archives. Accession no. 20379, n.d.

Khedrup Sangyé Yeshé (1525–91). *Collection of Experiential Songs, Letters, and Replies to Queries. Gsung mgur chab shog dris lan phyogs gcig tu bsdebs pa.* Collected Works of Khedrup Sangyé Yeshé, vol. 1, section *ca,* 129–270. Delhi: Dhondup Dorje, 1973, reproduced from personal copy of Dromo Geshé Rinpoché. BDRC W23477.

———. *Glory of Bringing into the Light the Essence of Well-Uttered Insights. Dris lan legs bshad nyin mor byed pa.* In *Collection of Experiential Songs, Letters, and Replies to Queries,* 211–46.

———. *Great Bliss and All Goodness: A Prayer for Offering Tea. Ja mchod bde chen kun bzang.* Collected Works, vol. 2, section *'a,* 149–61.

———. *Source of All Siddhis: A Rite of Offering to the Guru. Bla ma mchod pa'i cho ga dngos grub kun 'byung.* Collected Works, vol. 1, section *nga,* 68–126.

———. *Supplicating Conqueror Losang Döndrup by Way of Narrating His Liberating Life Story. Rgyal ba blo bzang don grub la rnam thar gyi sgo nas gsol ba 'debs pa dngos grub kun 'byung.* Collected Works, 1:1–8.

Könchok Jikmé Wangpo (1728–21). *Biography of the Omniscient Jamyang Shepa. Kun mkhyen 'jam dbyangs bzhad pa'i rnam thar.* Typeset edition. Kansu: Kan su'u mi rigs dpe skrun khang, 1987.

Kunga Gyaltsen (fifteenth century). *Meaningful to Behold: The Biography of Dharma Master Chenga Sönam Gyaltsen. Spyan snga bsod nams rgyal mtshan gyi rnam thar mthong ba don ldan.* Collected Works of Chenga Sönam Gyaltsen, vol. *ka*, 181–342. Lhasa: Reprinted as part of the 'Bri gung chos mdzod chen mo, 2004. BDRC W00JW501203.

Lama Shang (a.k.a. Shang Yudrakpa, 1123–93). *Ultimate Supreme Path of Mahāmudrā. Phyag rgya chen po lam zab man ngag mthar thug.* In *Bka' rnying mkhas grub rnams kyi gdams ngag gnad bsdus*, vol. *ja*, 49–117. Delhi: Bka' brgyud gsung rab nyams gso khang, 1978. BDRC W20749. Translation in Roberts, *Mahāmudrā and Related Instructions*, 83–134.

Lingrepa Pema Dorjé (1128–88). *Experiential Songs Section in the Writings of the Great Siddha. Rje grub thob chen po'i bka' 'bum las mgur gyi rim pa.* Collected Works of Lingrepa Pema Dorjé, vol. 1, 39–26. Palampur: Khams pa sgar gsung rab byams gso khang, 1985. BDRC W23778.

———. *Offering to the Guru: A Source of All Qualities. Bla ma mchod pa yon tan kun 'byung gi dbang chos gcig tu bsgrigs pa.* Thimphu: Chime Namgyal, 1984. BDRC W1KG12538.

Losang Tamdrin (1867–1937). *Exposition of Mahāsiddha Tilopa's Cultivating the Guru. Grub chen te lo pa'i bla ma sgrub thabs kyi rnam bshad.* Collected Works of Lobsang Tamdrin, vol. *ka*, 359–87. New Delhi: Mongolian Lama Gurudeva, 1975. BDRC W13536

Milarepa (1040–1123). *Hundred Thousand Songs of Milarepa. Rje btsun mi la ras pa'i mgur 'bum.* Compiled by Tsangnyön Heruka. Typeset edition. Xinhua: Mtsho sngon mi rigs dpe skrun khang, 1981.

Mitrayogi (twelfth century). *Root Lines of Instruction on the Three Essential Points. Snying po don gsum gyi man ngag gi rtsa ba rdo rje tshig rkang.* In Trophu Lotsāwa's *Cycle of Pith Instructions*, 92a.

Mönlam Palwa (1414–91). *Dispelling All Extreme Views. Lta khrid mthar 'dzin kun sel.* In *Stoṅ thun chen mo of Mkhas-grub dge-legs dpal-bzaṅ and Other Texts on Madhyamika Philosophy*, 525–79. New Delhi: Lha mkhar yongs 'dzin bstan pa rgyal mtshan, 1972. BDRC W00EGS1016265.

Ngulchu Dharmabhadra (1772–1851). *Clearing Away All Delusion: Notes on Mahāmudrā. Zab lam phyag rgya chen po'i zin bris 'khrul ba kun sel.* In Collected Works of Dngul chu Dharmabhadra, vol. *nya*, 3–57. New Delhi: Tibet House, 1981.

Ngawang Losang Gyatso, the Fifth Dalai Lama (1617–82). *King of Gems: A Rite Propitiating the Seven Sugatas. Bde gshegs bdun gyi mchod pa'i chog bsgrigs yid bzhin dbang rgyal.* Collected Works, vol. *na*, 579–688. Gangtok: Sikkim Research Institute, 1991–95. BDRC W294.

———. *Stream of the River Ganges: A Record of Teachings Received. Gsan yig gang ga'i chu rgyun.* Collected Works, vol. *ka*, 11–486. BDRC W294.

———. *Words of Mañjuśrī: Guide to the Stages of the Path. Byang chub lam gyi rim pa'i khrid yig 'jam dpal zhal lung.* Collected Works, vol. *na*, 3–185.

Palmang Könchok Gyaltsen (1764–1853). *Mirror Reflecting the Mind. Sems dang sems 'byung gi rnam bzhag cung zad bshad pa rang rgyud gsal ba'i me long.* Collected Works, vol. *nya*, 376–490. Delhi: Gyalten Gelek Namgyal, 1974. BDRC W2519

———. *In Response to a Request to Write a Commentary on "Supplications to the Definitive Guru" (Nges don gyi bla ma'i gsol 'debs kyi 'grel pa rtsom par bskul ba'i bka' lan).* Collected Works, vol. *ga*, 118–26.

Panchen Losang Chökyi Gyaltsen (1567–1662). *Excellent Guide to the Three Essential Points Based on Ārya Avalokiteśvara. Snying po don gsum gyi khrid yig 'phas pa spyan ras gzigs la brten pa shin tu legs pa.* Collected Works of Panchen Losang Chögyen, 4:417–21. Typeset edition. Beijing: Krung go bod rig pa'i dpe skrun khang, 2009.

———. *Highway of the Conquerors: Root Text on Mahāmudrā. Dge ldan bka' brgyud rin po che'i phyag chen rtsa ba rgyal ba'i gzhung lam.* Collected Works, 4:53–60.

———. *How to Practice the Essence of the Fourfold Mindfulness, the Nectar of Master Lodrö Bepa's Teaching. Rje blo gros sbas pa'i gsung gi bdud rtsi dran pa bzi ldan gyi snying po nyams su len tshul.* Collected Works, 5:308–15.

———. *An Instruction on How to Cultivate the Middle Way View Conferred by Mañjuśrī on Jé Tsongkhapa. Rje btsun 'jam pa'i dbyangs kyis chos kyi rgyal po tsong kha pa chen po la dngos su gnang ba'i zab mo dbu ma'i lta ba nyams su len tshul.* Collected Works, 5:300–307.

———. *Lamp So Bright: Extensive Explanation of the Root Text of Mahāmudrā of the Precious Geden Tradition.* Collected Works, 4:61–104.

———. *Offering to the Guru. Bla ma mchod pa'i cho ga.* Collected Works, 1:553–66.

———. *Responses to Queries: A Musical Tune Bringing Smiles to Losang. Dris lan blo bzang bzhad pa'i sgra dbyangs.* Collected Works, 1:328–42.

———. *Sheaves of Siddhis: On the Generation Stage of Vajrabhairava. 'Jigs byed kyi bskyed rim dngos grub kyi snye ma.* Collected Works, 2:533–73.

Panchen Losang Yeshé (1663–1737). *Essence of Eloquence Containing the Essential Points of All Scripture. Lam gyi gso bo rnam pa gsum gyi rnam bshad gsung rab kun gyi gnad bsdus pa.* Collected Works of Panchen Lobsang Yeshé, vol. *ga*, 289–407. Tashi Lhunpo, n.d. BDRC W1174

Panchen Palden Yeshé (1738–80). *Eleven Miktsema Rites. Dmigs brtse ma'i las tshogs bcu gcig.* Collected Works of Panchen Palden Yeshé, vol. *ca*, 271–319. New Delhi: Mongolian Guru Deva Lama, 1978. BDRC W2046.

Panchen Sönam Drakpa (1478–1554). *Six Ornaments to Beautify the Holy Dharma of Mahāmudrā. Dam pa'i chos phyag rgya chen po la rgyan drug tu mdzad par byed pa'i rgyan drug.* Collected Works of Panchen Sönam Drakpa, 9:432–531. Typeset edition. Lhasa: Bod ljongs mi dmangs dpe skrun khang, 2013.

Phabongkha Dechen Nyingpo (Jampa Tenzin Trinlé Gyatso) (1878–1941). *Dewdrops of Oral Transmission Nectar.* Collected Works of Phabongkha Dechen Nyingpo, vol. *kha*, 245–306. Lhasa: Lobsang Tsöndrü, 1951. BDRC W3834.

———. *Excellent Path of the Conquerors: A Compiled Preparatory Recitation for the Central Tibetan Lineage's Extensive Commentarial Tradition of the Essential Stages of the Path Instructions of* Words of Mañjuśrī. *Byang chub lam gyi rim pa'i dmar khrid 'jam dpal zhal lung gi khrid rgyun rgyas pa dbus brgyud lugs kyi sbyor chos kyi ngag 'don khrigs chags su bkod pa rgyal ba'i lam bzang.* Collected Works, vol. *ca*, 283–304.

———. *How to Practice the Profound Path of the Hundreds of Gods of Tuṣita Guru Yoga: Treasure House of Jewels Marked with a Seal. Zab lam dga' ldan lha brgya ma'i rnal 'byor nyams su len tshul rin chen gter gyi bang mdzod.* Collected Works, vol. *kha*, 465–510.

———. *Liberation in the Palm of Your Hand. Rnam sgrol lag bcang.* See translation under Pabongka Rinpoche.

———. *Sprays of Oral Transmission Nectar. Snyan brgyud bdud rtsi'i gzegs ma.* Collected Works, vol. *kha*, 307–45.

Phakdru Dorjé Gyalpo (1110–70). *Like a Precious Ornament. Rin chen rgyan 'dra zhes bya ba.* Collected Works of Phakdru Dorjé Gyalpo, vol. *ga*, 289–322. Kathmandu: Khenpo Sherap Tenzin and Lama Trinlé Namgyal, 2003. BDRC W23891.

Potowa (1027–1105). *Blue Compendium. Man ngag be'u bum sngon po* (compiled by Dge bshes Dol pa). In *Bstan pa la 'jug pa'i rim pa ston pa'i gzhung bces btus*, 1–41. Bod kyi gtsug lag gces btus pod phreng 10. Delhi: Institute of Tibetan Classics, 2009. English translation in Roesler, *Blue Compendium.*

Sakya Paṇḍita (1182–1251). *Clear Differentiation of the Three Vows. Sdom gsum rab dbye.* In *Sdom pa gsum gyi rnam gzhag ston pa'i gzhung bces btus*, 1–65. Bod kyi gtsug lag gces btus pod phreng 12. Delhi: Institute of Tibetan Classics, 2009. See translation under Western-language works.

———. *Replies to Kadampa Namkha Bum's Questions. Bka' gdams pa nam mkha' 'bum gyis zhus lan.* The Collected Works of Sakya Paṇḍita, 1:507–12. Typeset comparative edition. Beijing: Dpal brtsegs dpe rnying zhib 'jug khang, 2007.

Shar Kalden Gyatso (1607–77). *Experiential Guide to Mahāmudrā of the Sacred Geden Lineage. Dge ldan bka' brgyud phyag rgya chen po'i nyams 'khrid.* Translated in the present volume as chapter 12.

———. *Guidebook on Mahāmudrā. Phyag chen gyi khrid yig.* Collected Works of Shar Kalden Gyatso, 3:254–66. Typeset edition. Lan kru'u: Kansu mi rigs dpe skrun khang, 1999.

———. *Mahayana Mind Training Dispelling the Darkness of the Mind. Theg chen blo sbyong yid kyi mun sel.* Collected Works, 3:421–55.

———. *Quotations from Kalden Gyatso's Ocean of Instructions on the Profound Teaching on Geden Mahāmudrā. Dge ldan phyag chen gdams ngags rgya mtsho las btus pa.* Collected Works, 3:215–36.

Sönam Gyatso, Third Dalai Lama (1543–88). *Essence of Refined Gold. Lam rim gser zhun ma.* Dharamsala: Library of Tibetan Works & Archives, 2000.

Taktsang Lotsāwa (1405–77). *Establishing Freedom from Extremes on the Basis of Knowing All Philosophical Systems. Grub mtha' kun shes nas mtha' bral grub pa.* Typeset edition. Beijing: Nationalities Press, 1999.

Thöyön Jamyang Trinlé (nineteenth century). *Intensifier of the Light of Wisdom: Sādhanas and the Rites of Blessing Empowerment of Meditation Deities of the Mañjuśrī Cycle of Teachings. 'Jam dbyangs chos skor nas bshad pa'i lha tshogs rnams kyi sgrub thabs dang rjes gnang byed tshul gyi cho ga shes rab kyi snang ba 'phel byed.* Delhi: Ngawang Sopa, 1979; reprinted from the personal copy of Kyabjé Yongzin Trijang Rinpoché.

Thöyön Yeshé Döndrup. *See* Yeshé Döndrup Tenpai Gyaltsen.

Thuken Chökyi Nyima (1737–1802). *Supplications to the Definitive Guru. Nges don gyi bla ma'i gsol 'debs.* See Palmang's *In Response to a Request.*

Tokden Jampal Gyatso (1356–1428). *A Very Profound Practice on Cultivating the Inseparability of the Guru and the Meditation Deity.* See below under Tsongkhapa.

Trophu Lotsāwa Jampa Pal (1173–1236). *Cycle of Pith Instructions of Dharma Master Lotsāwa Jampa Pal. Chos rje khro phu lo tsā ba byams pa dpal gyi man ngag brgya rtsa ma.* Cursive hand copy discovered at Drepung Monastery. BDRC W00KG03569.

Tsangnyön Heruka (1452–1507). *Meaningful to Behold: A Biography of Marpa, the Translator. Mar pa lo tsā ba'i rnam thar mthong ba don ldan.* Sichuan: Nationalities Press, 1990.

Tsongkhapa (1357–1419). *Brief Presentation on the Stages of the Path: A Letter Sent in Response to Spiritual Friend Könchok Tsultrim. Bshes gnyen dkon mchog tshul khrims gyis springs pa'i lan du gnang ba lam gyi rim pa mdo tsam du bstan pa.* Collected Works of Jé Tsongkhapa, vol. *kha*, 237–51. Typeset comparative edition. Mundgod: Je Yabse Sungbum Project, 2019.

———. *Cycle of Short Pieces Pertaining to Guhyasamāja.* Collected Works, vol. *dza*, 373–456.

———. *Direct Guide to the Five Stages on a Single Cushion. Rdzogs rim rim lnga gdan rdzogs kyi dmar khrid.* Collected Works, vol. *na*, 533–616.

———. *A Discourse on the Three Gems. Rin po che gsum gyi gtam gyi sbyor ba.* Collected Works, vol. *kha*, 85–87.

———. *Doorframe Oral Instructions on Essential Points. Zhal shes gnad kyi them yig.* Collected Works, vol. *nya*, 425–57.

———. *Endowed with Three Convictions.* See below under *Guide to the Stages of the Profound Path of the Six Yogas of Nāropa.*

———. *Essence of Eloquence: A Treatise on Differentiating the Provisional and the Definitive Meanings of Scriptures. Drang nges legs bshad snying po.* Collected Works, vol. *pha*, 299–464. For English translation, see Thurman, *Central Philosophy.*

———. *Exposition of the Stages of Presentation. Rnam gzhag rim pa'i rnam bshad.* Collected Works, vol. *cha*, 1–122.

———. *A Few Words on the Structure of the Path. Lam gyi rnam gzhag nyung bsdus shig.* Collected Works, vol. *kha*, 257–62.

———. *Five Stages on a Single Cushion.* See *Direct Guide* above.

———. *Foundation of All Excellences. Yon tan gzhi gyur ma.* Collected Works, vol. *kha*, 2–3.

———. *Fulfillment of All Hopes of Disciples: A Commentary on [Aśvaghoṣa's] Fifty Verses on the Guru. Bla ma lnga bcu pa'i rnam bshad slob ma'i re ba kun skong.* Collected Works, vol. *ka*, 213–54. English translation by Gareth Sparham: Wisdom Publications, 1999.

———. *Great Treatise on the Stages of the Path to Enlightenment. Byang chub lam rim chen mo.* The Collected Works of Jé Tsongkhapa, vol. *pa*. English translation by Lamrim Chenmo Translation Committee in three volumes: Snow Lion, 2000–2004.

———. *Guhyasamāja Dedication Prayer and Verses of Auspiciousness. Gsang 'dus smon lam dang shis brjod.* Collected Works, vol. *kha*, 323–28.

———. *Guide to the Profound Path of the Middle Way View According to Prāsaṅgika.*

Dbu ma thal 'gyur ba'i lugs kyi zab lam dbu ma'i lta khrid. Collected Works, vol. *tsha*, 517–25.
———. *Guide to the Stages of the Profound Path of the Six Yogas of Nāropa Endowed with Three Convictions. Zam lam nā ro chos drug gi sgo nas khrid pa'i rim pa yid ches gsum ldan.* Collected Works, vol. *ta*, 277–363.
———. *Guide to the View Equalizing Samsara and Nirvana. Srid zhi mnyam nyid kyi lta khrid.* Collected Works, vol. *ba*, 503–38.
———. *Guru Yoga Endowed with Profound Features Conferred through One-to-One Transmission by the Dharma King Tsongkhapa to the Omniscient Khedrup. Bla ma'i rnal 'byor zab khyad can chos kyi rgyal po tsong kha pa chen pos mkhas grub thams cad mkhyen pa la chig brgyud tu gnang ba.* Collected Works, vol. *ka*, 149–52.
———. *Illuminating the Intent: An Exposition of Entering the Middle Way. Dbu ma la 'jug pa'i rgya cher bshad pa dgongs pa rab gsal.* Collected Works, vol. *ma*, 1–396. English translation by Thupten Jinpa: Wisdom Publications, 2021.
———. *Illumination of All Hidden Meanings: Extensive Commentary on the Laghusaṃvara Tantra. Bde mchog bsdus rgyud rgya cher 'grel pa sbas don kun gsal.* Collected Works, vol. *nya*, 1–340. English translation by David Gray in two volumes: Wisdom Publications, 2017 and 2019.
———. *Indispensable Oral Teaching on Tranquil Abiding and Insight. Zhi lhag gi skor la med mi rung ba'i zhal shes.* Collected Works, vol. *dza*, 373–76.
———. *Lamp to Illuminate the Five Stages. Rdzogs rim rim pa nga gsal ba'i sgron me.* The Collected Works, vol. *ja*, 1–455. English translation by Gavin Kilty: Wisdom Publications, 2013.
———. *Mañjuśrī's Advice on Practice. 'Jam dpal gyis gsungs pa'i nyams len.* Collected Works, vol. *kha*, 73–74.
———. *Middle-Length Treatise on the Stages of the Path. Byang chub lam rim 'bring po.* Collected Works, vol. *pha*, 1–297. English translation by Philip Quarcoo: Wisdom Publications, 2021.
———. *Milking the Wish-Granting Cow. Sgrubs thabs 'dod pa'jo ba.* Collected Works, vol. *ta*, 1–276.
———. *Miscellaneous Writings. Gsung thor bu.* Collected Works, vol. *kha*, 1–392
———. *Opening the Excellent Door to the Path. Lam mchog sgo 'byed.* Collected Works, vol. *kha*, 1–4.
———. *Opening the Eyes to See the Hidden Meaning: An Exposition of the Five Stages According to Cakrasaṃvara. Bde mchog gi rim pa lnga pa'i bshad pa sbas don lta ba'i mig 'byed.* Collected Works, vol. *tha*, 139–86.
———. *Opening the Golden Door: An Extensive Exposition on Transference of Consciousness. 'Pho ba'i rgya cher bshad pa sgo 'byed.* Collected Works, vol. *da*, 383–421.
———. *Queries from a Pure Heart. Dri ba lhag bsam rab dkar.* Collected Works, vol. *kha*, 107–26.
———. *Realization Narrative. Rtogs brjod mdun legs pa.* Collected Works, vol. *kha*, 76–81.
———. *Realization of the Great Wheel. Bcom ldan 'das 'khor lo chen po'i mngon rtogs.* Collected Works, vol. *da*, 423–35.
———. *A Reply to Master Rendawa's Letter. Rje btsun red mda' ba'i gsung lan.* Collected Works, vol. *kha*, 91–101.

———. *A Reply to Namkha Palsang's Letter. Dbon po nam mkha' dpal bzang gis yi ge'i lan du springs pa.* Collected Works, vol. *kha*, 264–66.

———. *A Rite on the Four Powers as Antidotes Against Negative Karma. Sdig pa'i gnyen po stobs bzhi'i cho ga.* Collected Works, vol. *kha*, 267–75.

———. *A Song of Spiritual Experience. Lam rim nyams mgur* (a.k.a. *Lam rim bsdus don*). Collected Works, vol. *kha*, 81–85.

———. *Song of the Spring Queen.* Collected Works, vol. kha, 333–37.

———. *Supplicating the Lineage Gurus of the Near Transmission. Byin rlabs nye brgyud kyi bla ma rnams la gsol ba 'debs pa.* Collected Works, vol. *kha*, 4–5.

———. *Three Principal Elements of the Path. Lam gyi gtso bo rnam pa gsum.* Collected Works, vol. *kha*, 286–87.

———. *An Uncommon Oral Instruction: Lord Mañjuśrī's Teaching Scribed by Revered Tsongkhapa and Sent to Jé Rendawa. Rje btsun 'jam dbyangs kyis gsungs nas rje btsun tsong kha pas yi ger mdzad nas rje red 'da' bar phul ba'i man ngag thung mong ma yin pa gcig.* Collected Works, vol. *na*, 141–49.

———. *A Unique Practice Cultivating Mañjuśrī That Combines His Peaceful and Wrathful Aspects. 'Jam dbyangs zhi khro sbrags sgrub kyi man ngag thun mong ma yin pa.* Collected Works, vol. *dza*, 329–32.

———. *Uniquely Profound Guru Yoga Conferred by the Great Dharma King Tsongkhapa to the Omniscient Khedrup in a One-to-One Transmission.* Collected Works, vol. *ka*, 149–52.

———. *Vajra Lines on the View. Lta ba'i yig chung lta ba rdo rje'i tshig.* In *Short Instructional Pieces Pertaining to Guhyasamāja* (*Dpal gsang ba 'dus pa'i man ngag yig chung skor*). Collected Works, vol. *dza*, 424–27.

———. *Vajra Verses on the Six Yogas [of Kālacakra] and Their Explanation. Sbyor drug gi tshig bcad dang de'i bshad pa.* Collected Works, vol. *da*, 261–63.

———. *A Very Profound Practice Cultivating the Inseparability of the Guru and Meditation Deity. Bla ma dang yi dam dbyer med du sgrub tshul shin tu zab pa.* Collected Works, vol. *dza*, 339–47.

———. *When Making Offerings to the Deities of the Guhyasamāja Mandala. Gsang ba 'dus pa'i dkyil 'khor gyi 'khor lo la mchod pa'i skabs su.* Collected Works, vol. *kha*, 321–23.

Tsultrim Namgyal (nineteenth century), ed. *Four Interwoven Annotations on the Great Treatise on the Stages of the Path; revised edition*, 2 vols. *Lam rim mchan bzhi bsgrags.* Tsechok Ling woodblock edition, 1842. BDRC W636.

Umapa Pawo Dorjé (fourteenth century). *Mañjuśrī Cycle of Teachings. 'Jam dbyang chos skor.* In Thöyön Jamyang Trinlé, *Intensifier of the Light of Wisdom.*<query: page range?>

Yangönpa Gyaltsen Pal (1213–58). *Parting Teaching on Mahāmudrā Innate Union. Phyag rgya chen po lhan cig skyes sbyor gyi thon chos.* Collected Works of Gyalwa Yangönpa, vol. *ka*, 1–18. Thimphu: Kunzang Topgey, 1976.

Yeshé Döndrup Tenpai Gyaltsen, Thöyön (1792–1855). *Entryway to the Ocean of Pure Faith: The Wondrous Life of the Great Lord Tsongkhapa. Rje btsun tsong kha pa chen po'i ngo mtshar rmad du byung ba'i rnam thar pa rnam par dkar ba dad pa rgya mtshor rol pa'i 'jug ngogs.* Rje btsun tsong kha pa chen po'i rnam thar phyogs bsgrigs, vol. 4. Typeset edition. Lhasa: Ser gtsug nang bstan dpe rnying 'tshol bsdu phyogs sgrig khang, 2015.

———. *Miktsema Cycle of Teachings. Dmigs brtse ma'i chos skor.* Featured as *Sras rgyud lugs kyi zab lam bla ma'i rnal 'byor dga' ldan lha brgya ma.* Ganden Jampaling woodblock print, 1982. BDRC W1NLM1386.

Yongzin Yeshé Gyaltsen (1713–93). *Biographies of the Lineage Gurus of Lamrim. Lam rim bla ma brgyud pa'i rnam thar. Lam rim bla ma brgyud pa'i rnam thar.* Typeset edition. Lhasa: Bod ljongs mi rigs dpe skrun khang, 1990.

———. *Bright Lamp of the Excellent Path of the Oral Transmission: A Letter of Instruction on Ganden Mahāmudrā. Dga' ldan phyag rgya chen po'i khrid yig snyan brgyud lam bzang gsal ba'i sgron me.* Collected Works of Yongzin Yeshé Gyaltsen, 22:201–443. New Delhi: Tibet House, 1977.

———. *Door Sign to the Treasure House of Orally Transmitted Instructions: A Guide to Offering to the Guru. Bla ma mchod pa'i khrid yig snyan brgyud man ngag gter gyi kha byang.* Collected Works, 20:79–183.

———. *A Magic Key That Opens the Hundred Treasures of Oral Transmission: Summary of the Guru Yoga Preliminary to Ganden Mahāmudrā. Dga' ldan phyag rgya chen po'i sngon 'gro bla ma'i rnal 'byor gyi bsdus don snyan brgyud mdzod brgya 'byed pa'i 'phrul gyi lde mig.* Collected Works, 22:267–70.

———. *Mahāmudrā Prayer: Source of All Attainments. Dga' ldan phyag rgya chen po'i smon tshig dngos grub kun 'byung.* Collected Works, 14:445–50.

———. *Prayer to the Lineage Gurus of Mahāmudrā.* Collected Works, 23:406–11.

———. *A Treasure House of Instructions on the Oral Transmission: Guidance on Offering to the Guru. Bla ma mchod pa'i khrid yig gsang ba'i gdad rnam par phye ba snyan rgyud man ngag gi gter mdzod.* Collected Works, vol. 15.

Western Language Works

Anonymous. *Annotated Root Lines of Mahayana Mind Training.* In *Mind Training: The Great Collection*, compiled by Shönu Gyalchok and Könchok Gyaltsen; translated by Thupten Jinpa, 75–82. Boston: Wisdom Publications, 2006.

Apple, James B. *Jewels of the Middle Way: The Madhyamaka Legacy of Atiśa and His Early Tibetan Followers.* Studies in Indian and Tibetan Buddhism. Somerville, MA: Wisdom Publications, 2019.

Asaṅga, Ārya. *The Bodhisattva Path to Unsurpassed Enlightenment: A Complete Translation of the Bodhisattvabhūmi.* Translated by Artemus B. Engle. Boulder, CO: Snow Lion, 2016.

Atiśa. *Root Lines of Mahayana Mind Training. Theg pa chen po blo sbyong gi tsa tshig.* In *Mind Training: The Great Collection*, compiled by Shönu Gyalchok and Könchok Gyaltsen; translated by Thupten Jinpa, 71–73. Boston: Wisdom Publications, 2006.

Dakpo Tashi Namgyal. *Moonbeams of Mahāmudrā.* Translated by Elizabeth Callahan. Boulder, CO: Snow Lion, 2019.

Dalai Lama Tenzin Gyatso. *The Fourteenth Dalai Lama's Stages of the Path*, 2 vols. Translated by Gavin Kilty and Sophie McGrath. Somerville, MA: Wisdom Publications, 2022–23.

———. *Kālachakra Tantra: Rite of Initiation.* Edited, translated, and introduced by Jeffrey Hopkins. Boston: Wisdom Publications, 1999.

———. *Lighting the Way.* Translated by Thupten Jinpa. Ithaca, NY: Snow Lion, 2004.

———. *The Path to Bliss*, 2nd ed. Translated by Thupten Jinpa. Ithaca, NY: Snow Lion, 2003.

———. *The Union of Bliss and Emptiness.* Translated by Thupten Jinpa. Ithaca, NY: Snow Lion, 1988.

Dalai Lama, H. H. the, and Alexander Berzin. *The Gelug/Kagyü Tradition of Mahamudra.* Ithaca, NY: Snow Lion, 1997.

Dalai Lama, Khöntön Peljor Lhundrub, and José Cabezón. *Meditation on the Nature of the Mind.* Boston: Wisdom Publications, 2011.

Gampopa. *Ornament of Precious Liberation.* Translated by Ken Holmes. Somerville, MA: Wisdom Publications, 2017.

Gendun Chopel. *The Passion Book: A Tibetan Guide to Love and Sex.* Translated by Donald S. Lopez Jr. and Thupten Jinpa. Chicago: University of Chicago Press, 2018.

Higgins, David, and Martina Draszczyk. *Buddha Nature Reconsidered: The Eighth Karma pa's Middle Path.* Wiener Studien zur Tibetologie und Buddhismuskunde 95.1–2. Vienna: Arbeitskreis für Tibetische und Buddhistische Studien Universität Wien, 2019.

Jackson, Roger. *Mind Seeing Mind: Mahāmudrā and the Geluk Tradition.* Somerville, MA: Wisdom Publications, 2019.

———. *Tantric Treasures: Three Mystical Texts from Buddhist India.* New York: Oxford University Press, 2004.

Jinpa, Thupten, trans. *The Book of Kadam: The Core Texts.* Library of Tibetan Classics 2. Boston: Wisdom Publications, 2008.

———, trans. *Mind Training: The Great Collection.* Compiled by Shönu Gyalchok and Könchok Gyaltsen. The Library of Tibetan Classics 1. Boston: Wisdom Publications, 2006.

———, ed. *Science and Philosophy in Indian Buddhist Classics, vol. 1: The Physical World.* Translated by Ian Coghlan. Somerville, MA: Wisdom Publications, 2017.

———. *Sngon gleng ngo sprod (Introduction). Dpal dge ldan pa'i lam rim dang snyan brgyud kyi chos skor.* Bod kyi gtsug lag gces btus pod phreng 6. New Delhi: Institute of Tibetan Classics, 2005.

———. *Tsongkhapa: A Buddha in the Land of Snows.* Boulder: Shambhala, 2019.

———, trans. *Wisdom of the Kadam Masters.* Boston: Wisdom Publications, 2013.

Jinpa, Thupten, and Jas Elsner. *Songs of Spiritual Experience: Tibetan Poems of Awakening and Enlightenment.* Boston: Shambhala, 2001.

Khoroche, Peter, trans. *Once the Buddha Was a Monkey: Ārya Śūra's Jātakamālā.* Chicago: University of Chicago Press, 2006.

Pabongka Rinpoche. *Liberation in the Palm of Your Hand.* Edited by Trijang Rinpoche. Translated by Michael Richards. Boston: Wisdom Publications, 2006.

Roberts, Peter Alan, trans. *Mahāmudrā and Related Instructions: Core Teachings of the Kagyü Schools.* The Library of Tibetan Classics 5. Boston: Wisdom Publications, 2011.

Rotman, Andy. *Divine Stories: Divyāvadāna, Part 2.* Somerville, MA: Wisdom Publications, 2017.

Roesler, Ulrike, trans. *The Blue Compendium: Teachings on the Graded Path of Potowa Rinchen Sal.* In Dölpa, Gampopa, and Sakya Paṇḍita, *Stages of the Buddha's Teachings.* Library of Tibetan Classics 10. Boston: Wisdom Publications, 2015.

Sakya Paṇḍita. *A Clear Differentiation of the Three Codes: Essential Distinctions Among the Individual Liberation, Great Vehicle, and Tantric Systems*. Translated by Jared Douglas Rhoton. Albany: State University of New York Press, 2002.

———. *A Jewel Treasury of Wise Sayings*. In *Tibetan Book of Everyday Wisdom*, translated by Beth Newman, edited by Thupten Jinpa, 33–96. The Library of Tibetan Classics 27. Somerville, MA: Wisdom Publications, 2018.

Sé Chilbu. *Commentary on Seven-Point Mind Training. Blo sbyong don bdun ma'i 'grel pa*. In *Mind Training: The Great Collection*, translated by Thupten Jinpa, 87–132. The Library of Tibetan Classics 1. Boston: Wisdom Publications, 2006.

Sonam Gyatso, the Third Dalai Lama. *Selected Works of Dalai Lama III: Essence of Refined Gold*. Translated by Glenn Mullin. Ithaca, NY: Snow Lion, 1985.

Thuken Chökyi Nyima. *Crystal Mirror of Philosophical Systems*. Translated by Geshe Lhundub Sopa et al., edited and introduced by Roger Jackson. The Library of Tibetan Classics 25. Boston: Wisdom Publications, 2009.

Thurman, Robert A. F. *The Central Philosophy of Tibet: A Study and Translation of Jey Tsong Khapa's Essence of True Eloquence*. Princeton, NJ: Princeton University Press, 1991.

———. "Vajra Hermeneutics." In *Buddhist Hermeneutics*, edited by Donald S. Lopez Jr., 119–48. Honolulu: Kuroda Institute, 1988.

Tsongkhapa. *The Great Treatise on the Stages of the Path the Enlightenment*, 3 vols. Translated by the Lamrim Chenmo Translation Committee. Ithaca, NY: Snow Lion, 2000–2004.

———. *Illuminating the Intent: An Exposition of Candrakīrti's Entering the Middle Way*. Translated by Thupten Jinpa. The Library of Tibetan Classics 19. Somerville, MA: Wisdom Publications, 2021.

———. *The Middle-Length Treatise on the Stages of the Path to Enlightenment*. Translated by Philip Quarcoo. Somerville, MA: Wisdom Publications, 2021.

Wallace, Vesna A., ed. *Sources of Mongolian Buddhism*. New York: Oxford University Press, 2020.

Willis, Janice D. *Enlightened Beings: Life Stories from the Garden Oral Tradition*. Boston: Wisdom Publications, 1995.

Yangchen Gawai Lodrö. *Rays of Sunlight: A Commentary on "Ganden Wise Sayings."* In *Tibetan Book of Everyday Wisdom*, translated by Beth Newman, 209–356. The Library of Tibetan Classics 27. Somerville, MA: Wisdom Publications, 2018.

Index

Abhayākaragupta, 518
Acala, 507
action, key point of, 722, 739–40
Adornment of Trees Sutra, 61, 224, 225, 436
Advayavajra, *Ten Verses on Reality*, 646
affirmation, 597, 599, 600
afflictions, 134, 423
  antidotes to, 176, 294–95, 352, 787–88n601
  arising of, 708
  cessation of, 709
  coarse and subtle, 354
  defining, 284
  identifying, 97–98, 284–86
  imprints of, 292
  intensifying, 286–87
  karma and, 99
  meditation objects for, specific, 124–25, 339, 340–41
  in origins of suffering, 283, 289–90
  rebirth and, 468
  root of, 286, 707
  selflessness in cutting, 139
  sequence and drawbacks of, 98
  three trainings and, 293, 351
agents, denying existence of, 83, 767n171
aggregates, 202
  as bases of designation, 140
  as deities, 547
  as five buddhas, 416, 506
  grasping, 359
  investigating, 361–65
  name-and-form link and, 291, 292
  Prāsaṅgika view of, 137, 772n250
  as self, refutations of, 34, 98, 141–42, 145, 201, 202–3, 489, 590–96, 670, 674, 697–98, 700, 701–2, 708–10
  suffering of, 94, 96, 173, 278–79, 556
aging, suffering of, 95, 275, 278, 281
aging and death, link of, 291–92
Airavata (elephant), 295
Ajātaśatru, 268
Akhu Sherab Gyatso, 11, 32
Akṣobhya, 496, 506, 549
All-Encompassing Jewel tradition, 392
Altan Khan, 4
altruistic intention, 108, 307, 314
  in aspirational bodhicitta, 311
  awakening mind and, 299–300
  commitment in, 306
  compassion and, 313
  cultivating, 8, 186, 304, 309
  in giving Dharma, 319
altruistic resolve, 106, 563, 565, 568, 569–70, 769n203, 775n289, 775n293
Amdo, 3, 755n32
Amitābha, 22, 496, 497, 506, 728, 732, 826n1271
Amitāyus, 543
Amoghasiddhi, 496, 506, 728
Amṛtakuṇḍalinī, 507
Amulet Box mahāmudrā, 618, 653–54
analogies and examples
  archer and swordsman in duel, 661, 693
  armless woman's drowning child, 256
  bird flying from ship's captivity, 620, 659, 662, 694
  bird's two wings, 220

broom's shadow mistaken as scorpion, 708, 710
butter lamps, 243, 245, 484
captain, skilled, 443
caring for horse, 366
caste, 298–99
cattle and their hoofprints, 118
child of barren women, 142
clear crystal, 464
conches, color perception of, 602, 710
Dharma as medicine, 57
on emptiness of phenomena, 369–70
firebrand wheel, 289, 290
fish and turnips, mixing, 369, 789n642
flower garland, 411, 434
garuḍa, 47
gold, 65
grains of sand in Ganges, 84, 767n175
hare frightened by sound of branch, 369, 789n644
hare on moon, 379, 790n665
harvest, 726
horse and cow, 595–96
illness, treating, 6
on illusion-like phenomena, 90–91, 624, 675–76, 704, 710
lightning flash, 259
magical lift, 425, 796n756
magnet, 130
mercury and gold, 530
Meru, 46
minnows in clear lake, 574, 588, 605, 621, 671
mirror's reflection, 286, 602
moon's reflection, 426, 676, 681
one candle lit from another, 187
peas, throwing dried, 236
person condemned to execution, 172, 212
pillar and vase, 709–10
pillars, 684
plantain tree, 676
potter and pot, 592–93
pouring from empty vase, 381, 791n682
prisoner just released, 271
rope apprehended as snake, 286, 489, 591, 596, 602, 603–4, 671
seed and sprout, 264, 773n260
sky lotuses, 314
star in daylight, 471, 594
Supreme Physician, 336
travel plans, 240, 312, 346
turtle poking neck through yoke, 236
vessel, three faults of, 57, 211, 215
water bubble, 465
water drop in ocean, 530
white crow, 346, 787n593
wish-granting jewels, 45, 46
analytical meditation, 145
ascertaining when required, 56, 94
in Ganden mahāmudrā, 27–28
on gurus, 222
innate mind and, 648, 649
method and, 112–13
and nonconceptual meditation, relationship of, 366–67, 789nn635–36
purpose of, 65, 605
and stability, relationship between, 34, 588, 606, 814n1023
sustaining, 152
on ten virtues and nonvirtues, 265–67, 325
tranquil abiding and, 120, 121, 122, 230–31, 361
Anaṅgavajra, 646
Anavatapta, Lake, 208, 296, 777n323
anger, 7, 329
attachment and, 286, 300–301
destructive power of, 327–28, 332, 530
identifying, 97, 284
rebirth and, 67
in tranquil abiding, 344
wish to avoid, generating, 331
Aṅgulimāla, 268
animals, 298, 484
compassion for, 185
harming, avoiding, 458
in intermediate state, 102–3
karma of, 261
killing, 264
numbers of, 237
rebirth as, 86, 101, 264, 289, 346
suffering of, 75, 168, 249, 467, 479

two categories of, 249
antidotes, 98
applying, 199, 342
applying excessively, 200, 342, 345
mild application, 349
not applying, 344
Aparājita, 507
appearance
as dharmakāya, 666
and emptiness, relationship between, 35, 53, 143, 685, 711
illusory, 370–71, 374
letting be, 667
and mind, indivisibility of, 653
and perception, distinguishing, 149
pure, 739
recognizing, 623, 681, 722, 739
as self-liberating, 683
stressing aspect of, 371
subtle, cessation of, 28
arhats, 187, 509, 775n295
armor practice, 113, 720n217
Arrayed with Wondrous Excellences realm, 408
ārya paths, 67, 766n156
Āryadeva, 32, 136, 440, 684. See also *Four Hundred Verses*
āryas
karma and, 99
seven riches of, 556, 811n987
Āryaśūra. See *Condensed Presentation of the Perfections*; *Garland of Birth Stories*
Asaṅga, 378, 660, 766n159
Bodhisattva Grounds, 441, 459–60, 499–500, 514, 770n220
Compendium of Abhidharma, 343, 771n238
Five Sections on Grounds (*Yogācāra Grounds*), 249
homage to, 43
lineages of, 440
Maitreya and, 160, 222
on mental delight, 765n147
Śrāvaka Grounds, 136, 340–41, 786n571
Summary of the Great Vehicle, 460
Ten Grounds Sutra, 86, 686
visualization, 508
aspirations
application of, 131, 198, 347
for buddhahood, 108, 474–75, 569–70, 577–78
condensing all into one, 399
cultivating, 337
in degenerate age, 299
faith and, 124
karma fruition of, 89
for liberation, 45, 93, 104, 171–74, 555–56, 764n132
to meet guru in all lifetimes, 577–78, 612
moral discipline and, 469
supreme, 69
aspiring awakening mind
ceremony, 70, 311–13
generating, 307, 483, 570–71
maintaining, 111, 524, 769n212
uncontrived and simulated, 572
asurī, 208, 777n315
Aśvaghoṣa
Dispelling Sorrow, 279–80
Praise in Hundred and Fifty Verses, 253, 255–56
See also *Fifty Verses on the Guru*
Atiśa, 206, 295, 546, 777n314
on awakening mind, 639
on Candrakīrti, 652
Commentary on Lamp on the Path to Enlightenment, 323
Entering the Two Truths, 357
on faith, 642
homage to, 43, 207–8
intent of, 378
lineage of, 44, 210–11, 366, 434, 441, 475
on refuge, 216
Serlingpa and, 224–25, 779n366
visualizations, 391, 478, 508
See also *Lamp on the Path to Enlightenment*
attachment, 7, 8
antidote to, 340, 345

bias of, 178, 179–80, 564, 775n290
curbing, 324, 349
engendering, 176
excitation from, 129, 130
freedom from, 782n450
identifying, 97, 284
to inferior pleasure, 334, 337
in intermediate state, 289
meditation object for, 124–25
to negative activities, 117
preventing, 720, 738, 739
at time of death, 100, 735–36
attainment and essence texts, 441. *See also* Essence Trilogy; Seven Attainment Texts
Attainment of the Nondual (Lakṣmīṅkarā), 441, 512, 646
Attainment of the Secret (Padmavajra), 441, 760n87
attainments, two kinds, 110, 769n209
Avalokiteśvara, 256, 735, 741
epithets for, 269, 718, 783n458, 826n1270
homage and supplication, 535, 721, 722
as Jinasāgara, 731, 732, 739
in Miktsema, 16, 17
self-visualization, 727
in three essential points instruction, 36
Tibetan popularity of, 37
triple-being, 544
Tsongkhapa as embodying, 385, 399–400, 401, 791n694
visualizations of, 478, 724–25
See also Khasarpāṇi
aversion, 7
antidote to, 176, 340
bias of, 178, 179–80, 564, 775n290
in intermediate state, 289
preventing, 720, 738, 739
See also anger; hatred/hostility
Avīci. *See* Relentless (Avīci) hell
awakening mind, 8, 12, 712
authentic and facsimiles, 571
benefits of, 191, 311
compassion and, 563
in confession, 396
forcefully generating, 464–75, 801n841
four causes and four strengths, 299
four dark and four bright factors, 191, 776n300
as gateway to Mahayana, 105
generating, instructions on, 186–87, 219, 413–23, 717, 725–27, 807n932
generating, purpose of, 219
higher wisdom and, 355–56
identifying, 109
importance of, 46, 52, 69, 298–99
in paths of three types of persons, 216–17
in power of support, 91
in preliminaries, 63, 156, 617, 619, 638–39, 658
preventing loss in future lives, 110–11
spontaneous experience of, 7
stabilizing, 70
sustaining in this life, 110
symbols of, 504
tantric vows and, 524–25
tonglen and, 568
two types, sequential arising of, 571
uncommon Mahayana refuge and, 482
See also aspiring awakening mind; engaging awakening mind; equalizing and exchanging self and other; seven-point causes-and-effect instruction
Awakening of Vairocana Tantra, 639

Balden Beeyen Monastery, 4
bases of designation, 140, 142, 362, 371–72, 459, 489, 592, 603–4, 674
Baso Chökyi Gyaltsen, 20, 508, 755n35, 757n49
lineages, 21, 33, 36, 445, 691
mahāmudrā and, 761–62n101
oral teachings received, 16, 17
supplication, 628
works, 37, 762–63n115
Ben Gungyal Tsultrim Gyalwa, 284, 499, 783n480, 804n887
Bhagīratha, 409, 793n717
Bhāviveka, *Essence of the Middle Way*, 343, 344, 345, 660, 693

Bimbisāra, 268
birth
consciousness at, 100
four types, 103, 274, 291
in generation stage, 493–94
link of, 291, 292
suffering of, 95, 274, 278
womb, 274, 281
Blazing Mouth, 446, 799n791
bliss
and emptiness, union of, 30, 397, 415, 418, 437, 490, 496, 497, 498–99, 514, 550, 632
innate, 2, 419, 443, 490, 517–18, 523, 551, 552, 582. *See also under* gnosis
meditation experience of, 135
physical and mental, generating, 118
in tranquil abiding, 126
See also great bliss
Blue Annals (Gö Lotsāwa), 644, 753n5
Blue Compendium (Potowa), 6, 366
bodhicitta. *See* awakening mind
bodhicitta fluid, 517, 551
bodhisattva grounds, 513, 686–87, 823n1220, 823n1222
Bodhisattva Kunsang, 36
bodhisattva vows, 114, 425, 769n213
actual and similitude, distinguishing, 571
arising of, 484
ceremony, 109, 190–91
contemplating, 570
difficulty in arising, 483–84
guarding, 191
and personal liberation vow, distinction between, 116, 770n225
restoring, 111, 769n212
bodhisattvas, 7, 299
anger and negativity toward, 110, 117, 327–28
becoming, 298, 313
false, 314
lay and ordained, distinctions between, 85, 318
pretense of, 70
rebirth of, 103
refuge of, 257
six, as sense bases, 506–7
as spiritual teachers, 111
turning one's back on, 84
Bodhisattva's Confession of Downfalls, 268, 642. See also *Confession of Downfalls*
body, 709
attachment to, 100
cultivating wisdom through, 401–2
fragility of, 74
gift of, 116, 317, 321, 335, 336, 436. *See also under* rites
great bliss of, 47
impurity of, meditation on, 176
investigating, 361–63, 371
in mahāmudrā, 586
and mind, separating, 719
in selflessness of persons, 361–63, 595, 673–74
in selflessness of phenomena, 204, 371
body isolation, 582
body mandala practice, 443, 798n786
actual and form of, 508
guru's, 449–50, 506–8
Bönpo tradition, 462, 522
Book of Kadam, 401
Brahmā, 253, 380, 480, 507, 537, 790n674
as creator, 285
melody of, 255, 551
mouths of, 378, 790n663
rebirth as, 278
Brahmā realm, 84, 280
breath
as antidote, 340
calming the winds, 463, 464, 801n834
counting, 464
nine-round breathing, 463, 464, 619, 658
in tranquil abiding, 347
vitality stopping (*prāṇāyāma*), 443, 582, 813n1013
Buddha Śākyamuni
appearance in world, 234
on cause and effect, 538, 809n959

as commitment being, 505–6
compassion of, 105
epithets for, 155, 206, 207, 773n275, 776n309, 776n311
exchanging himself with others, 560
as external refuge, 76
homage and praise to, 43, 378
kuśa grass offering, 461
lineages of, 434, 440
as meditation object, 125, 346–47, 366
miracles of, 805n908
mother of, 301
past lives of, 224, 565
qualities of, 58, 76, 77
reverence for, 294
self-visualizations, 197
seven limbs practiced by, 531
visualizations, 155–56, 157, 158, 197, 227, 254–56, 477–78, 488
ways of seeing, 222, 779n363
buddhahood, 6
aspiration for, 108, 474–75, 569–70, 577–78
awakening mind and, 52
consciousness in, 149
as definite goodness, 766n157
as dependent on sentient beings, 471, 726
Mahayana and tantric views of, 801–2n841
method and wisdom needed for, 112
not seeking elsewhere, 665, 820n1162
in single life, 442, 451
Buddhajñānapāda, 222
Buddhapālita, 32, 136, 360, 585, 593
buddhas, 299
coarse form of, 494
enlightened body, speech, mind of, 473–74
knowledge of karma, 767n185
names of, reciting, 91
offerings to, 85, 104
perceptions of, 671–72
recollection of, 197
superior wisdom of, 149–50, 773n265
thousand, visualizations of, 717–18
See also lords of five families
Butön Rinchen Drup, 1, 346, 646
butter lamps, 487, 515, 708
in analogies, 243, 245, 484
offering, 85, 89, 104, 224, 495

cakras, 314, 517, 576, 580, 582, 648, 785n523, 812n1009
Cakrasaṃvara (meditation deity), 413, 449, 486, 552
Cakrasaṃvara cycle
body mandala in, 798n786
in Ensa tradition, 22
guru yoga and, 23, 759n76
Lūipa tradition, 443
root tantra of, 448
mandala deities of, 509
on offerings, 523
Tsongkhapa contributions to, 3, 19
Candragomin, 586
Letter to a Student, 235, 274, 297–98, 303
Praise in the Form of a Confession, 348, 661, 694
Candrakīrti, 32, 136, 585, 593, 652
Clear Words, 362, 372
Entering the Middle Way Autocommentary, 773n265
Extensive Commentary on Four Hundred Verses, 357–58
Seventy Verses on Going for Refuge, 253
visualizations, 477, 508
See also *Entering the Middle Way*
causes, denying existence of, 83, 767n171
central channel, 407, 427, 517, 576
three attributes of, 732, 827n1284
at time of death, 719
in transference, 736–37
winds in, 27, 30, 581, 583, 649, 813n1015
certitude, grasping at, 53, 764n135
Chamdo Jampa Ling, 3
Changkya Ngawang Chöden, 19, 28, 31, 36, 761n94
Guidebook on Mahāmudrā, 31
Instructions on the Stages of the Path in Verse, 12

Changkya Rölpai Dorjé, 4, 31, 570, 602, 604–5, 791–92n695, 812n999
channels, 462. *See also* central channel
Chapa Chökyi Sengé, 3
Chekawa, 438. See also *Seven-Point Mind Training*
Chenga Drakpa Jangchup, 441
Chenga Lodrö Gyaltsen, 20, 28, 29, 381, 790n675
 Essence of Altruism, 12
 guides to view by, 762–63n115
 mahāmudrā and, 761–62n101
 Mahāmudrā Illuminating the Essence, 29
 Summary Outline of the Stages of the Path, 12
Chenga Shönu Chöphel Sangpo, 381, 791n678
Chenga(wa) Tsultrim Bar, 208, 784n489
cherishing others, 109, 189, 308, 474, 538, 559, 565
Chöjé Döndrup Rinchen, 441
Chökyi Drakpa, 428
Chökyi Gyaltsen, Jetsun, 3–4
Chöpa Rinpoché Losang Tenpai Gyaltsen, 705, 825n1264
Chöphel Sangpo, 228
Chusang Yeshé Gyatso, 13
Cittamātra, 137, 357, 768n191
clairvoyance, 70, 118, 124, 263, 285, 351, 352, 450, 480, 564, 664, 696, 769n209
clarity, 134
 in concentration, 121, 125, 126, 200
 laxity and, 129
 meditation experience of, 135
 vigorous, generating, 131
 in visualization, 198
clear light, 27, 442, 576, 618
 all-empty, 523
 illustrative, 733–34
 illustrative and actual, 645, 739
 meeting of mother and son, 490
 as nature of mind, 678, 703–4, 731
cognition
 nonconceptual, 65, 368, 766n154
 rational, 149, 150
 See also valid cognition
Collection of Aphorisms, 211, 240–42
commitment beings, 226, 416, 505–6, 510–11, 526–27
compassion, 252
 arising of, 299–300, 424
 as cause of awakening mind, 69
 cultivating, 8, 108, 185–86, 304, 306, 309
 and emptiness, conjoined, 647
 of objects of refuge, 76
 renunciation and, 103
 as root of Mahayana, 106, 562–64
 of spiritual teachers, 60
 three levels of meaning, 739
 within *tonglen*, 568
 universal, 7, 8, 12
 See also great compassion
completion stage, 442, 650
 four seals in, 644
 Guhyasamāja, 523
 guru yoga and, 452
 meditative equipoise in, 151–52
 nondiscursive approach to, 30
 preliminaries, 495, 583
 ripening, 498
 texts on, 646
 triple being in, 552
concentration (*samādhi*), 8, 48
 attaining, 610
 common to Buddhists and non-Buddhists, 135
 forgetting instruction, 131, 198, 772n243
 higher training in, 7, 293, 351, 456–57, 469
 illusion-like, 426
 and mindfulness, differentiation between, 587
 of spiritual teachers, 60
 sustained, 200
 tranquil abiding and, 338, 339
concentration being, 505
conception (biological), 102. *See also* gestation, five stages of

conceptual imputations, 593, 608–9, 675, 679–80, 682
Condensed Perfection of Wisdom in Verse, 412, 447–48, 676, 794n726
Condensed Presentation of the Perfections (Āryaśūra)
 on bodhisattva vows, 324
 on ethical discipline, 325–26
 on focal objects for afflictions, 341
 on generosity, 318
 on Mahayana, 297
conduct
 diligence in, 47
 pure, 331
 and view, relationship between, 113, 208–9
confession, 92, 229, 267, 268, 295. *See also under* seven limbs
Confession of Downfalls, 527, 617, 638, 692. See also *Bodhisattva's Confession of Downfalls*
consciousness, 710
 at conception, 102, 768n197
 at death, 289
 link of, 291
 mistaken, 371
 moments of, 372
 selflessness of, 204–5, 674, 702, 708
 six classes of, 674, 701
 stream-like, 606, 815n1049
 worldly, 371
 See also storehouse consciousness
consorts, 443
 four elements as, 506
 four types, 516, 517, 522–23, 806n918, 807n931
contact, link of, 291, 292
conventional truth
 correct understanding of, 356
 definition, 148
 as diversity, 122, 770n231
 meanings of terms, 147–48, 773n261
 Prāsaṅgika view of, 148
covetousness, 82, 83, 767n172
 five traits of, 263
 karmic effects of, 86, 87, 264
craving, 129, 291, 292
crown aperture, 402, 407, 579–80, 719, 730, 736, 737
Cūḍapanthaka, 455, 457, 458
Cutting Off (*chö*), 22, 478, 589–90, 618, 653, 656, 825n1267
Cycle of Pith Instructions of Dharma Master Trophu Lotsāwa Jampa Pal, 36
cyclic existence. *See* samsara (cyclic existence)

daily meditation practices, 15, 18, 23, 376, 428, 552–53
ḍākinī lands, 539–40, 577
ḍākinīs
 guru as embodying, 158, 422, 548
 invoking, 416, 529, 794n732
 See also heroes and ḍākinīs
Dakpo Kagyü, 369, 654
Dakpo region, 3, 755n33
Dakpo Shedrup Ling Monastery, 10, 764n138, 765n139, 777n318, 791n679, 791n685
Dalai Lama lineage, 4
 Gendun Drup, First, 3, 228, 788n624
 Gendun Gyatso, Second, 36, 37, 228, 428, 788n624
 Kalsang Gyatso, Seventh, 18, 35, 791n695
 Sönam Gyatso, Third, 4, 37, 228, 381. See also *Essence of Refined Gold*
 See also Ngawang Lobsang Gyatso, Fifth Dalai Lama; Tenzin Gyatso, Fourteenth Dalai Lama
Dampa Sangyé, 623, 639, 642, 655–56, 680, 817n1093
danger, nine factors in failing to avoid, 99, 768n193
Dārikapa, 646
death
 abundance of causes, 74
 certainty of, 73, 240–42
 clear light at, 649
 coarse and subtle minds of, 288–89
 contemplating, 6, 167–68, 239–44, 245, 466–68, 487, 724
 Dharma practice and, 73, 74–75

diligence and, 334
factors of, 99
fallacies of self and, 363
heat withdrawal at, 100
karma at, 260
manner of, 244
mindfulness of, 71–72
recalling, 735
suffering of, 95, 276, 278, 281, 282
taking into path as dharmakāya, 490–91, 803n864
time of, attitudes at, 99–100
time of, uncertain, 67, 72, 74, 242–43, 244
timely, 287
transference at, 737
visions and signs at, 487–88, 732–33
debate tradition, 3, 404
dedication, 59, 553, 687, 720
in concluding practices, 64, 162, 624, 680, 687
importance of, 63, 230, 780m394
See also under seven limbs
Dedruk Khenchen Ngawang Rabten, 755–56n35
definite goodness, 68, 72, 184, 188, 213, 238, 469, 557, 558, 766n157, 778n343
definition and definiendum, 147
definitive meaning, 136, 267, 378, 619, 645, 656
degenerate age, 299, 313, 381, 409, 793n718
buddhahood in, 442
gurus in, 221, 546
practices for, 443
Vajradhara in, 160, 440
See also five degenerations
deities, meditation, 721
appearance as, 426
cause and condition for, 723–27
and guru, viewing as inseparable, 200, 427, 437, 440, 534–37, 810n975
lack of intrinsic existence of, 494
as meditation objects, 125–26, 130, 197
specially visualized (*lhag mos kyi lha*), 442, 798n785
supplication and visualization, 727–32
in two stages, distinctions in visualizing, 552
viewing all beings as, 719, 738
See also under dissolution
deity yoga, 22, 413, 451, 492
demigods, 96, 173, 174
Densa Chenpo Sum ("three great centers of learning"), 3
dependent origination, 35
as antidote to ignorance, 176, 340, 359
as appearance, 53
infallibility of, 374, 426
in post-equipoise, 144, 145, 675, 681, 682
realizing, 52, 355
reasoning of, 146, 360, 591
verse, 538, 809n959
dependently originating nominal realities/constructs, 591, 592, 593, 603–4, 814n1029
Descent into Laṅkā Sutra, 357
Desi Sangyé Gyatso, 791n690
designating subject, 592, 603–4
desire, eight thoughts to reject, 340, 786n571
desire realm, 67, 99, 133, 265, 649, 659, 782n450, 820n1151
desire-realm gods, 101, 293
death of, 277–78
in intermediate state, 102–3
as knowers of three times, 278, 783n469
rebirth as, 87
suffering of, 96, 173–74, 768n189
See also Brahmā realm; Trāyastriṃśa god realm; Tuṣita god realm
Devadatta, 222
devotion
blind, 24
for entering Dharma, 37
generating, 156, 218–19, 660
in guru yoga, 14, 23–24, 389, 392, 394, 416, 505, 513, 532, 554
in preliminaries, 463–64, 653
to Tsongkhapa, 2, 389, 392

Dharma
abandoning, 214
acting in accord with, 295
disintegration of, 104
giving, 192, 318, 319, 320
mind as root of, 476
quality of, 76, 77
rarity of meeting, 252
reflecting on Jewel, 256
seven designated custodians of, 545, 809n971
sins related to, 85
See also Three Jewels
Dharma practice
conditions for, 260
receptivity to, 575–76
as sole source of benefit, 545
time for, 37, 73–74, 388
at time of death, 74–75, 167–68, 243–44, 466
Dharma protectors
guru as embodying, 548
for method and wisdom, 444–45
for three capacities, 444, 510, 578, 812n1007
visualization of, 156, 157, 774n278
dharmadhātu. *See* ultimate expanse
Dharmadhātuvajrā, 507
dharmakāya, 653, 738, 770n219
basis of, 356
and form body, simultaneous attainment of, 442
ground, 648–49
thoughts as, 667
Dharmakīrti, *Exposition of Valid Cognition*, 286, 311, 370, 556, 670
Dharmavajra (Chökyi Dorjé), 21, 508
homage and supplication, 617, 628, 638
lineages of, 432, 445, 691
rainbow body actualization, 759n69
Dharmodgata, 224, 436, 456
Dhṛtarāṣṭra, 510
Differentiating the Provisional and the Definitive, 697
Dignāga, 253
diligence, 124, 198, 426, 765n147, 770n227, 770n229
armor-like, 47, 117, 333–34
benefits of, 333
contemplating, 194, 573
courageous, 376
force of, 132
four powers that balance, 337
of spiritual teachers, 60
three types, 574, 812n1003
in tranquil abiding, 347, 349
unfamiliarity with, 131
disciples. *See* students and disciples
discursive analysis, 12, 28, 30
dissolution, 488, 582, 803n862, 803n865
held-as-a-whole, 491
of meditational deities, 157–58, 406–7, 442–43, 732–33
of merit field, two methods, 578–80
reverse sequence, 491, 803n866
of subsequent dismantling, 487–91
distraction, 339, 426
antidotes, 47, 340, 574
antidotes, excessive effort in, 345
causes of, 341
meditation object for, 124, 125–26
posture and, 462
divine sight, 101
doha songs, 27, 441
Ḍombī Heruka, 478, 508, 646
Döndrup Wangyal, 764–65n139
doubt, 97, 134–35, 176, 284, 684
downfalls, 571–72, 812n1001
Dragor Khenchen, 441
Drakar Losang Palden, *Stages on the Path to Enlightenment*, 13
Drakpa Gyaltsen, *Parting from the Four Clingings*, 641
Drakpa Jangchup, 28
Drati Rinchen Döndrup, 755–56n35
dreams
as analogy, 426, 676, 681
karma and, 528
recognizing (lucid dreaming), 738
self-grasping in, 589, 708
as sign of attention, 134
Drepung Monastery, 3, 382, 791n685
Drigung Chökyi Gyalpo (Drigungpa), 28, 643

Drogön Chögyal Phakpa, 518
Drokmi Lotsāwa Shākya Yeshé, 225, 779n368
Drolungpa, 6, 213
Dromtönpa, 9, 208, 212, 225, 475, 784n489, 791n682
Drongmepa, 382, 791n690
Drop of Gnosis Tantra, 512
Drop of the Great Seal Tantra, 450, 645, 818n1114
drops, 581. *See also* indestructible drop
Drukpa Kagyü, 819n1143, 823n1219
Drupwang Losang Namgyal, 475, 507, 568, 759n69, 802n842, 811n994
Dulnakpa Palden Sangpo, 387, 756n44
dysfunctional tendencies, 95, 96, 120, 338, 351, 786n565

É, 381, 791n679
eight applications. *See* five faults and eight applications
eight auspicious substances, 394, 792n702
eight auspicious symbols, 394, 498, 515, 522, 731, 792n702, 804n885
eight classes of beings, 387, 542, 792n696
eight perfect masteries, 504, 805n896
eight worldly concerns, 251, 269, 463
  countering, 405, 463, 499
  equalizing, 655
  two-toned, 238, 260, 781n406, 782n441
Ekacūda, 495
Eladhari, 477
elements, five, 340, 487, 488
elements, six, 622, 673, 675–76, 700–701
Elephant's Skills Sutra, 674–75, 702
"Eliminate dust, eliminate stains," 456–57
emanated scripture, 20, 21
empowerments
  for guru yoga, 14
  in mahāmudrā, 27, 31
  vajra master empowerment, 550, 810n979
  See also four empowerments
emptiness, 7, 372–73, 490
  beginner's experience with, 607
  concentration aimed and not aimed at, 121
  conceptual cognition of, 368–69
  concordant examples, 143
  contrived, 699
  and dependent origination, as complementary, 426, 575, 603–5, 624, 685
  fourth joy joined with, 551, 552, 582
  of "I" and "mine," 365
  and impermanence, difference between, 699
  intellectual understanding of, 33, 35
  and karma, compatibility of, 357, 370
  meditation on. *See* emptiness meditation
  as mental contrivance, refutation of, 143, 772n256
  as mind's ultimate nature, 30
  misapprehension of, 599, 603, 669–70
  as nonimplicative negation, 599–600, 601, 698, 814n1039
  of one thing and all things, 624, 682
  order for realizing examples of and meaning, 143–44
  purification by, 91
  as rational cognition, 598, 814n1033
  realization, methods for, 150, 200, 773nn269–71
  realization, rarity of, 594
  recalling, 719, 735
  and selflessness, sequence of, 593
  six perfections and, 378
  as truly existent, counteracting, 152
  See also under bliss
emptiness meditation, 35, 708–11
  brief contemplation, 711
  conventional-truth aspect in, 583–84, 606, 813n1015, 815nn1048–49
  five styles of, 32, 607, 762n114, 815n1050
  karma and, 90
  and mahāmudrā, relationship of, 704
  method and wisdom in, 112
  and mind, inseparability of, 34
  space-like, 145

subtle primordial mind aspect, 584
See also meditative equipoise, space-like
emptiness yoga, 451
endearment, 564–65. *See also* loving kindness
engaging awakening mind
and aspirational, distinction and order of cultivation, 312–13
training in, 112–13
upholding, 483–85
vow, 70, 119, 313, 524
enlightened activities, 187, 256, 474
enlightened qualities, 115–18, 187
enlightenment. *See* buddhahood
Ensa Hermitage, 16, 21
Ensa Oral Transmission (Ensa Nyengyü), 15–16, 17, 20–22, 26, 33, 712, 758n68, 759n73
Ensa tradition guru yoga, 22–23
dissolution in, 578–80
empowerment in, 548–53
endearment, two integrated methods for cultivating, 562–68, 811n992
long-transmission lineage of, 440–41
merit field visualization (main session), 502–11
near-transmission lineage, 441–46, 508, 534
path review and invoking blessings, 423–27, 553–78
place, qualities of, 454
preliminaries, general, 413–21, 455–85, 500
preliminaries, special, 486–501
as preliminary for mahāmudrā, 31, 534, 535, 584, 813n1017
suitability for, 453–54
supplications, 532–48
triple being in, 22, 446, 494, 509, 523, 534–40, 542–44, 579, 798n790
Ensapa Losang Döndrup, 16, 508, 625, 816n1072
on emanated scripture, 20, 21, 758n66
homage and supplication, 628, 707
How to Practice the Essence of the Stages of the Path, 12
rainbow body actualization, 759n69
works of, 21
Entering the Middle Way (Candrakīrti), 528
on aggregates as self, 363, 590–91
on anger toward bodhisattvas, 327
on compassion, 300, 726
on conventional existence, 371
on mind, 678
on paths, deviant, 357
on personal identity view, 359
on roots of virtue, 530
on selflessness, twofold, 669
on selflessness of persons, 363, 364, 365
on two truths, 356, 680, 685
Entry into the Womb Sutra, 101
eons, 75, 766n163
Equal Taste, 618, 653, 655
equalizing and exchanging self and other, 424, 562, 799n810, 811n992
guided instructions on, 188–89, 307–9, 558–61
merit-field visualization and, 477–78
Śāntideva's lineage of, 802n849
equanimity, 107, 775n288
contemplating, 178–80, 557–58
order of cultivating, 300–301, 563
in tranquil abiding, 131, 200, 345, 787n598
two types, 564, 811n993
See also even-mindedness
Essence of Refined Gold (Sönam Gyatso, Third Dalai Lama), 10, 11, 217, 226–27, 258, 312, 381, 754n20, 777n328, 778n351, 779nn378–79
Essence Trilogy (three *Dohā* collections), 645, 646–47, 816n1061, 818n1112, 818n1116
eternalism, 241, 593, 669, 684
ethical discipline, 46, 116, 425
contemplating, 193, 572–73
destruction of, 98
as fundamental virtue, 767n177
of helping others, 336–37
higher training of, 177, 293, 294–95, 457

in lamrim, 8
perfection of wisdom and, 118
in post-equipoise, 119
results of, 236
of spiritual teachers, 60
threefold, 7, 425, 570, 572–73, 796n757
tranquil abiding and, 196, 340
types of, 323–25, 326
vows and, 323–24
ethical ideal, 45
Ethics Chapter, 312
even-mindedness, 177, 178, 179, 775n288
Excellent Pair, 256, 782n439
exchanging self and others. *See* equalizing and exchanging self and other
excitation, 199, 426
absence of, 131, 133, 200
antidotes, 65, 130, 342, 343–45, 574, 771n242
causes, 130–31
coarse, 348
definition, 129
identifying, 344
in insight, 203
in mahāmudrā, methods for, 586, 661, 663, 693–94, 695
mindfulness and, 127
in nine mental states, 349
in tranquil abiding, 126, 128, 198–99, 350
exertion, application of, 131
existence, three stages of, 36
existents, 83, 356, 767n171
Experiential Guide (Shar Kalden Gyatso), 31
experiential instructions, importance of, 381, 791nn681–82
Extensive Commentary on the Chapters on Discipline (Kalyāṇamitra), 257

faith, 252, 547
application of, 131, 198, 347, 352
conviction form of, 298, 784n500
cultivating, 159–61, 223, 399–400, 535–37
Dharma practice and, 37
enhancing, 124
importance of, 642–43
lack of, signs, 229
from listening to teachings, 57
and reasoning, relationship between, 222
in refuge, 255
in spiritual teachers, 61, 64, 221, 437, 438, 779n360
superior admiring, 257
symbols of, 809n960
in three scriptural collections, 66
fear, 72, 78, 251, 252, 297, 560, 597–98
fearlessness
four kinds, 380, 504, 790n672, 805n896
gift of, 192–93
feelings
link of, 291, 292
neutral, 300–301, 784n505
female birth, 89, 102
Fifty Verses on the Guru (Aśvaghoṣa), 14, 445
on buddhahood, 451
on empowerment masters, 512
on offerings to guru, 225, 450
on pleasing guru, 224, 412, 447
on Vajradhara and guru, viewed as inseparable, 416
fire and water, emission of (*yamaka-prātihārya*), 510, 805n908
five acts of immediate retribution, 66, 233, 267, 780n398
five bodily substances (a.k.a. five lamps), 419, 795n741
five degenerations, 295, 560, 784n494
five faults and eight applications, 131, 198–200, 342–46, 659
five meats (a.k.a. five hooks), 419, 496–97, 795n741, 804n878
five obstructions, 134, 772n245
five paths, 822n1218, 823nn1219–20
five powers, 425, 796n753
five recognitions, 58, 765n145
Five Stages (Nāgārjuna), 646
on guru yoga, 441

on gurus, offering to, 416–17
on seven limbs, 511
on vajra masters, 512
Fivefold Mahāmudrā, 28, 618, 653, 654, 655
Flower Ornament Sutra, 435–36
food, 64, 89, 610
forbearance, 116–17, 119, 327, 425–26
armor of, 47, 332
contemplating, 193–94, 328–31, 573
three types, 573, 770n226
forgetfulness, 131, 342, 343
form body (*rūpakāya*), 356, 442, 770n219
form realm, 67, 99, 101, 134, 174, 766n156, 820n1151. *See also* four levels of meditative absorption (*dhyāna*)
formless realm, 820n1151
in contemplations, 174
immoveable karmas of, 99
meditative absorptions of, 352. *See also* peak of existence
rebirth in, 67, 101, 766n156
Foundations of All Excellences (Tsongkhapa), 9
four attentions, 132
four classes of tantra, 122, 396, 397, 438, 478, 494, 501
four complete purities, 501
four continents, 66, 418, 498, 518, 519, 766n155
four empowerments, 552, 757n49
as blessing, 17, 18, 22, 423, 548, 553, 795n751
in guru yoga, 454
in highest yoga tantra, 799n812, 806n926, 810n977
for mahāmudrā, 584, 650
maturing, 153
secret, 520–21, 550–51
vase, 520, 549–50, 810nn978–79
wisdom-gnosis, 522–23, 550–51, 810n981
word, 523, 551–52
four empty stages (also four appearances), 442, 798n784
four fundamental axioms, 516, 806n916
Four Hundred Verses (Āryadeva), 220, 272, 358–59, 372–73, 400, 682
four immeasurables, 106, 156, 390, 485, 769n205
four infinite qualities, 300–301, 784n505
four initial meditations
death and impermanence, 167–68
karma, 169–70
preliminaries, 166–67
suffering of lower realms, 168–69
Four Interwoven Annotations on the Great Treatise on the Stages of the Path, 13, 755n35, 756n38
four joys, 443, 517, 550–51, 552, 582, 806n923
four levels of meditative absorption (*dhyāna*), 122, 135–36, 351, 355, 771n232, 772n247
four māras, 461
four means of gathering others, 118–19
guided contemplation, 195–96
merit of, 457
symbols of, 504
training in, 375–76
four noble truths, 94, 272–73, 293, 297, 772n246
four possibilities of arising, 733
four powers, 45, 91–92, 117, 170, 229, 269, 271, 324, 642, 764n133
engaging antidotes, 525
names, 396
of support, 525
of thorough repudiation, 525, 527
turning away from faults, 525–26
four qualities of greatness, 44, 453, 799n809
four rivers (ignorance, attachment, craving, wrong views), 221, 779n359
four seals (*mudrās*), 26, 643–44, 760n87
Four Sets of a Hundred, 446, 779n791
four streams, 418, 795n737
four teachings of Dakpo, 641
Four-Lettered (mahāmudrā), 618, 653, 655
Friendly Letter (Nāgārjuna), 233, 279
on animal rebirth, 249

on countless rebirths, 280
death and impermanence, 243
on eight non-liberties, 233
on ethical discipline, 294
on gods, suffering of, 277
on life spans, 247
on mind as root of Dharma, 476
on sin, 267
on three trainings, 293
on wrongdoing, abstention from in future, 267–68

Gampopa Sönam Rinchen, 26, 641, 645, 650, 653, 818n1101
Ganden Hermitage, 381
Ganden lineage, 20, 521, 522, 541, 603. *See also* Geluk tradition
Ganden Lophel mountain hermitage, 614
Ganden mahāmudrā, 22
balanced approach of, 27–28
concluding activities, 608–9, 623, 680
dedication prayer, 32, 762n112
emergence of, 27
guide to view in, 32
guru yoga for, 23, 31
initial training in, 607–8
and Kagyü, comparison to, 29
lineage of, 627–36, 691–92
oral transmission of, 5
preparation, 617–18, 619, 638–43, 658, 692
secondary literature on, 31–32
between sessions, 609–11, 815n1057
texts on, 25–26, 761n101
Tsongkhapa's connection to, 28–29, 30, 761n98, 762n104
view, final import of, 684
See also sutra mahāmudrā; tantra mahāmudrā
Ganden Monastery, 3, 625
emanated scripture revealed at, 21
founding of, 1, 2, 4
mahāmudrā taught at, 30–31, 691–92
prophecy on, 386, 791n693
Ganden throneholders
Könchok Chöphel, 791n685
Lodrö Tenpa (sixth), 764n138
Ngawang Chöphel (seventieth), 787n584
Taklung Drakpa Lodrö Gyatso (thirtieth), 226, 779n374
Gandhavajrā, 506
Ganges, origin story, 409, 793n717
Garland of Birth Stories (Āryaśūra), 248, 317
Gathering All Fragments Sutra, 214
Geden Nampar Gyalwai Ling, 49
Gelek Gyatso, 633
Geluk tradition, 380, 790n667
guide to the view genre in, 32–33
guru yoga in, 15–16, 446
important genres in, 4–5
lama institutions of, 4
lamrim texts of, 8–14, 755n31
mahāmudrā in, 27
Miktsema in, 16
name, meaning of, 1
political leadership by, 4
protectors connected to, 797n765
spread of, 3, 4
union of tranquil abiding and insight in, 369
Gendun Chöden, 692
Gendun Gyaltsen, 629, 691, 817n1078
Gendun Gyatso, Rabjampa, 624–25, 634, 688
Gendun Jamyang. See *Southern Transmission of the Words of Mañjuśrī*
General Confession, 230, 780m395, 795n743
generation stage, 443, 449
deity visualization in, 552
mahāmudrā and, 581, 650, 813n1017
threefold taking in, 486, 495
tranquil abiding and, 135
Vajrabhairava lineage, 523
generosity, 46, 115–16, 266, 316, 425
contemplating, 572
and ethical discipline, relationship of, 326
fully accomplishing, 317, 322
as fundamental virtue, 767n177

in gathering others, 375
in post-equipoise, 119
ten kinds of recipients, 319
three categories of, 85, 192–93, 318, 319–20, 770n222
three specific thoughts in, 318, 321
Gephel Hermitage, 18
geshé lharampa title, 4
gestation, five stages of, 493
Ghaṇṭāpa, 3, 19
giving and taking (*tonglen*), 309, 424, 561, 796n752
motivation in, 567–68
purpose of, 566–67, 569
gnosis
of innate bliss and emptiness, 22, 28, 30, 32, 414, 442, 452, 519, 539, 549, 645, 712, 737, 815n1050
nonconceptual ascertaining emptiness, 644
self-arisen, 26
See also innate gnosis; wisdom
gnosis beings
and commitment beings, nonduality of, 416, 510–11
and consorts, union of, 523
in heart of commitment being, 582
Vajradhara as, 505, 506
Gö Lotsāwa Khukpa Lhetsé, 3, 441, 798n779
Gö Lotsāwa Shönu Pal. See *Blue Annals*
gods
formless-realm, 278, 293
form-realm, 103, 278, 293
higher-realm, 87, 96
in intermediate state, 102
purifying, 484
rebirth as, 67, 100, 282, 289
sufferings of, 277–78
See also desire-realm gods
Golden Light Sutra, 268
Gomchen Ngawang Drakpa, *Essence of All Excellent Discourses*, 10, 764n139
Gönpawa, 804n887
Götsangpa, 686
gradualist path, 650
grasping, 8
countering, 7
at extremes, 53
to "I," 201–3
innate, 360–61
link of, 291, 292
at selfhood, 176
at true existence, 772n250
two kinds, 138, 697–98
See also self-grasping
great bliss, 411, 433
of body and mind, 47
of deities, 498
dharmakāya, 223, 488, 490, 510–11, 547
in empowerment, 549
expanse of, 413, 417, 500
importance of, 649
innate, 441, 443, 523, 551, 581, 647
from meditative wisdom, 426, 574
natural, 666
of saṃbhogakāya, 158
threefold, 21
from vajra body, 618, 645
Great Bliss Treasury (Ensapa), 21
great capacity path, 294, 297–99
aspiration, 105–11, 177–91, 217
awakening mind training on, 299–314
bodhisattva practices, 111–19, 315–16. *See also* insight/special insight; six perfections; tranquil abiding
Dharma protector for, 444
loving kindness in, 453
refuge of, temporary and ultimate, 257
ultimate objectives of, 356
great compassion
altruistic attitude and, 103, 311
Avalokiteśvara's, 269
of buddhas, 474
Buddha's, 255–56
cultivating, 18, 313, 457, 721
as fundamental, 726
importance of, 212–13
objectless, 399, 707
in refuge, 258
as root of Mahayana, 562–64

Great Final Nirvana Sutra, 211, 287
Great Perfection, 30, 618, 653, 656
Great Prayer Festival, 4
great trailblazers, 70, 207, 209, 312, 378, 442, 766n159, 777n313, 798n781
Great Treatise on the Stages of the Path to Enlightenment (Tsongkhapa), 2, 11, 209, 226, 338, 369, 371, 771n240
  awakening mind in, two traditions of, 301
  on bodhicitta rite, 190, 775n296
  divisions of, 9
  on lethargy, 787n584
  on nondistraction, 587
  on pre-experience understanding, 306, 784n510
  on relying on superior fields, 219
  sources, 8
  on special insight, 360
  on spiritual practice, 230
  study aids, 10, 13–14, 755n35, 756n38
  on suffering, contemplation of, 277
  teachings and transmissions, 382, 754n28
  when to consult, 311, 312, 342
Great Vehicle. *See* Mahayana
Gugé Yongzin Losang Tenzin, *Storehouse of Attainments Both Common and Supreme*, 31
Guhyajñānā, 739
Guhyasamāja (meditation deity), 413, 444, 454, 486, 552
Guhyasamāja cycle, 523, 798n779
  Ārya tradition, 442–43, 581, 582
  body mandala in, 798n786
  completion stage, 523
  in Ensa tradition, 22
  guru yoga in, 438–39
  Jñānapāda tradition, 22
  mandala deities of, 509
  practices of, 803n864
  sādhana of, 23
  Tsongkhapa's role in, 2–3, 19, 753n5
  on vajra body, 581
Guhyasamāja Tantra, 439, 518, 646, 791n772, 812n1005
Guide to the Bodhisattva Way (Śāntideva)
  on afflictions, 283, 287, 337
  on analysis, 601
  on anger, 327, 328
  on awakening mind, 639
  on bodhicitta, two types, 311–12
  on bodhisattvas, 298, 336
  on cognition and cognizable, 599
  on confession, 808n939
  on death, certainty of, 241–42
  on diligence, 333, 335
  on distractions and amusements, 334–35
  on enemies, 330
  on exchanging self for others, 307–8
  on false collections, 622, 677, 678, 703
  on generosity, 317, 321, 335–36
  on habituation, 332
  on harm, 329
  on human birth, difficulty of, 235–36
  on insight and tranquil abiding, 657
  on karma, 288
  on laziness, 334
  on limbs of practice, 668
  on meditative concentration, 338, 339
  on merit at time of death, 243
  on meta-awareness, 343
  on object of negation, 669
  on offering substances, obtaining, 459
  on practice between sessions, 609
  on praise and fame, 330
  on rebirth, two types, 271–72
  on refuge, 252
  on selflessness of persons, 673, 701
  on suffering at death, 281
  water drop in ocean analogy in, 530
  on wisdom, 457
Guide to the Middle Way View, 583, 619, 653, 656
guide to the view (*lta khri*), 32, 33, 35, 583, 763n118
Gungru Gyaltsen Sangpo, 28, 703, 825n1254
Gungthang Tenpai Drönmé, 28, 760n79
  Essence of the Supreme Path, 11
  Garland of Nectar Drops, 31

guru yoga, 157
  benefits of, 511–13
  as essence of Dharma, 577
  excellence of, 413, 432, 446–53, 524
  functions of, 23
  in guide to the view, 33
  guru viewed as buddha in, 24–25, 439–40
  identity fusion in, 24
  importance of, 437–38, 642–43
  Khedrup Jé's transmission from Tsongkhapa, 407, 793n713
  rites and, 543
  Segyü lineage, 19–20
  in sutra and tantra, 435–37, 438–39, 452
  in Tibetan tradition, 14–15
  Tsongkhapa as focus of, 2, 16, 23–24
  Tsongkhapa lineage of, 15
  See also Ensa tradition guru yoga; *Hundreds of Gods of Tuṣita* (Dulnakpa Palden Sangpo); Miktsema prayer
gurus (*lama*)
  and buddhas, power of, 546
  definitive, 25
  and disciples as single taste, 585
  as embodying Three Jewels, 416, 532, 547–48
  honoring, karmic fruition of, 89
  importance of, 647–48
  karma's power and, 84
  in Mahayana, 14
  and meditation deities, viewing as inseparable, 200, 427, 437, 440, 534–37, 810n975
  name mantras of, 809n954
  qualifications of, 24–25, 421, 435, 444
  as superior to buddhas, 413, 448, 512
  as three kāyas, 547
  three secrets of, 396, 409, 546, 718, 792n703, 810n972
  as triple-being, 585
  triply kind, 432, 437, 504–5, 508, 637, 642, 797n764
  viewing as buddhas, 24–25, 439–40
  visualizations, 504–6, 534–37, 721
  See also guru yoga; spiritual teachers
Ĝyalrong Tsultrim Nyima, *Letter of Final Testament Sent upon the Wind*, 18, 23, 31
Gyaltsab Jé
  as Avalokiteśvara, alternative visualization, 401, 793n709
  guides to view by, 762nn114–15
  on meditation generated into path's nature, 464–75
  Precious Garland, 762n114
  visualizations, 391–92, 401–2
Gyasok Phu cave, 20, 30
Gyüchen Könchok Gyaltsen, 31, 629–30, 817n1078
Gyüchen Könchok Yarphel, 19
Gyüchen Kunga Döndrup, 756n44
Gyümé Tantric College, 12, 19, 756n44, 777n328, 824n1239
Gyütö Tantric College, 19, 756n44

happiness
  Dharma practice and, 67
  in future lives, 75, 76
  karma and, 78
  of others, 471, 472
  root of, 295
  suffering mistaken as, 272–73
  tainted, renouncing, 556
  in this life, 259
harm, 77, 89, 116, 310, 323, 470–71
harsh words, antidote for, 47
hatred/hostility, 47, 176, 246. *See also* anger; aversion; ill will
Hayagrīva, 507
Hayagrīva Tantra, 494
Heap of Jewels Sutra, 657, 678–79, 703–4
Heart Sutra, 210, 822n1211
Heart Yoga, 36, 763n126, 826n1275
hell beings
  life span of, 247, 248
  numbers of, 237
  rebirth as, 84, 86, 100, 101, 102, 264, 267, 268, 282, 289
  suffering of, 75, 168, 467, 479
hells
  adjacent and intermittent, 248

cold, 103, 247–48, 250–51
hot, 103, 245–47, 250
purifying, 484
sequence of rebirth in, 246
hermit lifestyle, 461, 625, 815n1059
Hero Embarking on a Campaign, 22
heroes and ḍākinīs, 389, 392, 415, 416, 459, 509, 734, 794n731, 805n906
Heshang, 769n216
Hevajra tantra, 509
highest yoga tantra, 31, 36, 712, 732
body mandala in, 798n786
buddhahood in, 796n761, 801–2n841
consorts in, 807n931
eight applications in, 131
empowerment in, 549, 799n812, 806n926, 810n977
in Ensa guru yoga, 22
inner offerings in, 414, 795n741
innermost essence of, 645
mandala deities of, 494
special insight in, 122, 151–52
tranquil abiding in, 135
two accumulations in, 452
Highway of the Conquerors (Losang Chögyen), 22, 25–26, 813n1014
on appearance and emptiness, 604
colophon, 624–25
guides on, 611, 815n1058
homage, 617, 637–38
promise to compose, 617, 637–38
Hīnayāna, 300, 306, 375, 457, 458, 557
Hindu paradises, 784n490
holding to the superiority of views, 97–98
human existence contemplations
difficulty of obtaining, 165, 235–37
leisure and opportunity, 66–67, 164, 233–37, 387–88, 423, 425, 464–66, 554, 641, 724
preliminaries, 163–64
between sessions, 166
sufferings of, 96, 173–74, 274–77
human existence/rebirth, 250, 293
conditions for, 487
eight full fruitions, 266
intermediate-state being for, 101, 102–3, 289, 768n196
as maturation effect, 87
preciousness of, 6, 45, 51
taking advantage of, 65–68
Hundreds of Gods of Tuṣita (Dulnakpa Palden Sangpo), 18, 20, 22, 385–86
dedication and aspiration prayers, 407–8
embedded verse, 15, 406, 756n43
field of merit, inviting, 390–92, 478
gathering accumulations, 393–99
preliminaries, 387–90
request for higher attainments, 401
seven cultivations, 401–5
supplications, 399–401, 405–8
transmission of, 386–87
hungry ghosts
in intermediate state, 102–3
numbers of, 237
purifying, 484
rebirth as, 86, 101, 264, 289
suffering of, 75, 168, 249–50, 467, 479
three categories of, 249–50

identity view (*satkāyadṛṣṭi*), 98, 138, 139, 670, 768n191
identifying, 97, 285, 286, 768n190
object of, 137–38, 772n250
rejecting, 359
ignorance, 7, 52, 145, 269, 373, 377, 672, 708
antidote to, 176, 340
identifying, 97, 137–38, 284, 286
personal identity view and, 98, 768n191
as root of afflictions, 358–59
as root of suffering, 176
two kinds, 291
two successive moments of, 138
vows and, 294
Ikṣvāku dynasty, 206, 776n309
ill deeds, antidote to, 46
ill will, 82, 86, 87, 116–17, 263–64, 767n172, 767n177
illness
five sufferings of, 95

404 diseases, 419, 503, 523–24, 795n742
guru yoga for, 404
practices for, 711, 825n1267
suffering of, 275–76, 278, 282
illusory body, 427, 431, 442, 452, 576
arising as, 582
and clear light, union of, 523, 551, 552
dismantling, 686
impure and pure, 491, 494, 803n868
pure, 731
two ways of arising, 734
impermanence, 73, 707
as antidote, 199, 345
contemplating, 6, 7, 167–68, 245, 554, 641
of every phenomenon, 73
of gurus, 25
recalling, 719, 721, 723–24, 735
implicative negation, 597, 599, 600, 814n1032
imprints
of emptiness meditation, 365
of guru yoga, 511
karmic, 292
for mahāmudrā, 581
from meditative equipoise, 663–64, 696
of self-grasping, 457
for tantra, 553
of training, 458
of view, 584
See also propensities
"imputed existence, just nominal," 684
indestructible drop, 443, 580, 581
Indian Buddhism, 1, 2, 14, 26, 756nn40–41
individual liberation (*prātimokṣa*) vows. *See* vows, individual liberation
Indra, 208, 280, 295, 436, 480, 507, 537, 777n316
Indrabhūti, 646
Indrabodhi, 440, 508
inference, 237, 767n185, 773n269
innate gnosis, 26, 27, 28, 551, 644, 712
Innate Union, 618, 653, 655
inner heat (*tumo*), 443, 461, 476–77, 517, 550, 650
insight/special insight (*vipaśyanā*), 65, 94, 117, 120, 295, 338, 772n246
achieving, 70, 152–53, 205
approximation of, 369
arisen-from-meditation, 122
benefits of, 120
divisions, 151
establishing view, 137–51
importance of cultivating, 354
initial understanding of, 365, 788–89n634
kinds of, 135, 772n246
preliminaries, 200
prerequisites for, 136
in selflessness of persons, establishing, 201–3, 605
in selflessness of phenomena, establishing, 204–5
supramundane, 772n246
two truths and, 151
wisdom pāramitā in, 119, 120, 770n230
See also under tranquil abiding (*śamatha*)
Instructions on Mahāmudrā (Tilopa), 667, 821n1170
intellect/intelligence
discriminating, 91
enhancing, 48
increasing rite for, 539, 540–41
threefold, 18
intention, 485
in diligence, 334
in ethical discipline, 116
in generosity, 115, 116
in guide to the view, 33
importance of, 475–76
karma as, 99, 768n192
karmic paths and, 83, 767n172
in lucid dreaming, 738
in mental stability, 585
in post-equipoise, 609–10
in selflessness of persons meditation, 696, 700
in special preliminaries, 486–88
in tranquil abiding, 130, 198, 344
See also motivation

interdependence. *See* dependent origination
intermediate capacity path, 138, 257, 297, 355–56, 358, 724
  aspiration to liberation, 93, 171–74
  attitude, measure of, 103
  Dharma protector for, 444
  focus of, 557
  imprints of, 458
  origins of suffering, contemplating, 97–103, 283–89
  path leading to liberation, establishing, 103–4, 175–77, 293–95
  preliminaries for, 171–72, 175
  as preliminary practice, 214
  suffering, contemplating, 93–97, 271–73
intermediate state (*bardo*), 242, 244
  beings in, 101, 102–3, 289, 493, 768n194
  entering, 101
  generating, 100
  for hell rebirth, 246, 247–48
  mixings in, 36, 721, 723, 737–39, 803n864
  recognizing, 719–20, 722, 737–39
  suffering of, 282
  taking into path as saṃbhogakāya, 491–93, 494
  time in, 101, 102
interpretive meaning. *See* provisional meaning
introductions
  essence of, 667–71
  to mind's ultimate nature, 588, 606–7, 621–23, 652, 665–67, 677–79
Invoking the Altruistic Resolve, 58
Īśvara, 253, 285, 304, 320, 380, 790n673

Jagatamitrānanda, 763n126
Jahnu, 378, 790n663
Jambudvīpa, 84, 250, 766n162, 774n285
  karma in, 235, 781n402
  life span in, 74, 167, 242
Jamchen Chöje, 3, 4
Jampa Rinchen, 381, 791n679
Jampa Trinlé, 11
Jampal Gyatso (a.k.a. Jamyang Dewai Dorjé), 410, 793n719
Jamyang Chöje, 3
Jamyang Dewai Dorjé (a.k.a. Drupwang Jampal Gyatso). See *Miktsema Cycle of Teachings*
Jamyang Lama, identity of, 754n28
Jamyang Shepa Ngawang Tsöndrü, 3, 4, 10, 12, 19, 755–56n35, 758n59
Jang Dharma, 4
Jangchup Ö, 5
Jangtsé College, 779n374
Jayacandra, 763n126
Jedrung Tsering, 741, 826n1282
Jewel Torch Dhāraṇī, 220–21
Jikmé Damchö Gyatso, *Nectar Essence of Excellent Discourses*, 13
Jikmé Wangpo, 633
Jikten Gönpo, 654, 686
Jñānottara, 509, 805n905
Jokhang Temple, 4

Kachen Yeshé Gyaltsen. *See* Yongzin Yeshé Gyaltsen
Kadam school, 9, 14, 777n314
  daily practices of, 324
  on death, 244
  ethical discipline in, 295
  on experiential instruction, importance of, 381, 791nn681–82
  homage to, 207–8
  lamrim in, 5, 212, 625
  mahāmudrā in, 641
  mind-training transmissions in, 754n28
Kagyü tradition
  critiques of, 789n655
  mahāmudrā in, 26–27, 28, 29, 30, 645, 686, 696, 761n94, 761n98
  subitist designation in, 649
  See also Dakpo Kagyü; Drukpa Kagyü; Shangpa Kagyü
Kālacakra (meditation deity), 509
Kālacakra teachings, 3, 19, 29, 382, 760n87
Kālarūpa, 380, 432, 444, 445, 510, 774n278, 797n765
Kalsang Tenzin Khedrup, *Summation of Precious Qualities*, 13

Kamalaśīla, 545–46
Stages of Meditation II, 344, 345
Stages of Meditation III, 345, 367
Kangyur, 1
karma, 52, 290, 423, 516, 554
absence of identity and, 202
averting, 139
black and white, 65, 80–88, 260–61
cessation of, 709
complete act, 262
contemplating, general, 45, 51, 78–79, 261–62, 265–66, 267, 466–68, 724
contemplating, specific, 88–90
conviction in, 169–70
creating, 672, 708
definite and indefinite, 265
emptiness and, 357, 370
exchanging, 79, 766n164
factors that strengthen, 83–86, 170, 767nn173–74
generosity and, 317
identifying, 99, 768n192
imprints of, 292
in leisure and opportunity, attaining, 67
mental, 83, 767n172
mind at root of, 476
nonaccumulated, ten instances of, 88, 767n180
object, powerful with respect to, 85
in origins of suffering, 283, 287–88
power of, 707
projecting, 261, 359
purifying, 45, 200, 294, 450, 483–84, 498, 525–27, 531, 764n133
rebirth and, 75, 291, 468
refuge and, 77, 478–79
rejecting, 90
selflessness of persons and, 141–42, 364
subtle, 91, 767n185
timing of effects, 88
See also karmic effects; ten nonvirtues/black karmic paths; ten virtues/white karmic paths
Karmavajra. *See* Lhodrak Drupchen Namkha Gyaltsen
karmic effects, 801n840
effect concordant with cause, 86, 264–65
environmental effect, 264–65
maturation effect, 117, 264–65, 267
mixed, 266
timing of, 88
Kāśyapa Chapter Sutra, 368
Kātyāyana, 288, 526, 784n487, 807n937
kāyas
four, 208, 777n319
two, 113, 377, 770n219
See also three buddha bodies
Keutsang Jamyang Mönlam, *Excellent and Completely Virtuous Path to Freedom*, 31
Khagarbha, 506
Khalkha Dzaya Paṇḍita, 4
Kham, 3
Kharoṣṭhī alphabet, 402, 793n711
Khasarpāṇi, 723, 826n1271
in transference, 736, 737
visualizations, 717–19, 724–25, 728–30, 731, 734
Khedrup [Jé] Gelek Palsang, 697, 788n622
guides to view by, 762nn114–15
lineage prayer by, 37
lineages of, 21, 33, 36, 359, 367, 445, 763n117
practices of, 552–53
Record of Teachings Received, 28
on *shalshé*, 20
teachings received from Tsongkhapa, 16, 17, 20
as Vajrapāṇi, alternative visualization, 401, 793n709
visualizations, 392, 401–2
Khedrup Ngawang Dorjé, 631
Khedrup Norsang Gyatso. *See* Norsang Gyatso
Khedrup Sangyé Yeshé, 16, 500, 510, 625
guru yoga of, 22, 429
homage and supplication, 155, 629, 773–74n275
lineages of, 446, 691
mahāmudrā instructions of, 623, 679–80

name of, 621, 816n1065
Source of All Attainments, 12, 413–14, 794n728
Khedrup Tenpa Dargyé, 4
Khedrup Tenzin Tsöndrü, 632
Khöntön Paljor Lhundrup, 30, 208, 382, 754n28, 777n318
Khyenrab Tenpa Chöphel, 19
Khyungpo Lhepa Shönu Sönam, 441
Khyungpo Naljor, 653–54, 683
killing, 84, 91, 268
karma and, 80, 86, 262, 264, 766nn166–68
refraining from, 77, 87
kindness
recalling, 106, 182–83, 302–3
repaying, 106, 108, 183–84, 303–4, 567
of spiritual teachers, 161, 223–24, 231, 545–46
of spiritual teaching, 61, 64
King of Meditations Sutra, 260, 295
analogies on phenomena in, 369–70, 675–76, 704
on karma, 90–91
on meditation objects, 346
on mundane concentrations, 354–55, 668
on seal of phenomena, 584, 652, 704, 813n1016
on selflessness of persons, 669
on three fundamentals, 767n177
Kirti Losang Trinlé, 37
knowable entities, 76, 147, 149
Könchok Chöphel, 382, 754n28, 779n374, 791n685
Könchok Gyaltsen, 634
Könchok Jikmé Wangpo, Second Jamyang Shepa, 37, 570, 812n999
Könchok Tsultrim, 9
Kṛṣṇācārya, 3, 222
Kṛṣṇayamāri Tantra, 537, 538, 809n960
Kṣitigarbha, 478, 506
Kuru, 242
Kurukṣetra, 288

Labrang Monastery, 3, 755n31
Lakṣmīṅkarā. See *Attainment of the Nondual*
Lamp on the Path to Enlightenment (Atiśa), 5, 12, 212
influence on Tsongkhapa, 6, 8, 9
on meditation objects, 346
on persons of great capacity, 297
on persons of intermediate capacity, 271
on persons of lesser capacity, 239
purpose of, 213
on vows, 323
Lamp So Bright (Losang Chögyen), 22, 25–26, 602, 691, 705, 815n1041
colophon, 688–89
concluding verses, 687–88
homage, 637
laxity, 121, 426
absence of, 131, 133, 200
antidotes, 65, 130, 342, 343–45, 574
antidotes, excessive effort in, 345
causes, 130–31
definition, 129
identifying, 344
in insight, 203
and lethargy, distinguishing, 127, 199, 343, 344, 787n584
in mahāmudrā, methods for, 661, 663, 693–94, 695
in nine mental states, 349
subtle and coarse, 347
in tranquil abiding, 126, 128, 198–99, 350
laziness, 352
antidotes for, 47, 198, 342
in offerings, 229
overcoming, 334
pliancy and, 124
in tranquil abiding, 131
learning stage, 113
lesser capacity path, 94, 166, 270, 356, 358, 641, 724
attitude of, 92, 768n187
death, contemplating, 71–75, 167–68, 239–44
Dharma protector for, 444

four powers, 90–92
and intermediate path, comparison of, 273
karma, contemplating, 78–90, 169–70, 260–66
as preliminary practice, 214, 216–17, 458
refuge, 75–78, 169, 252–58
suffering of lower realms, contemplating, 168–69, 245–50
Lesser Vehicle. *See* Hīnayāna
Letter of Final Testament Sent upon the Wind (Gyalrong), 18, 23, 31
colophon, 613–14
concluding verses, 611–13
homage, 431–32, 796nn761–62, 797n763
mahāmudrā sequence in, 813n1010
Lhatsé Yeshé Tenzin. *See* Yeshé Tenzin, Lhatsé
Lhodrak Drupchen Namkha Gyaltsen, 392, 441, 792n699
liberation, 271, 766n157
aspiration for, 45, 93, 104, 171–74, 555–56, 764n132
certainty of, 139
nature of path to, 556–57
Liberation in the Palm of Your Hand (Phabongkha), 13, 755n34
Life of Maitreya, 311
life span
animal, 75, 249
degeneration of, 95
depletion of, 99, 241, 287
hungry ghost, 75, 250
increasing, 539
in intermediate state, 101
in Jambudvīpa, 74, 167, 242
karma and, 89
in mindfulness of death, 73
limpidity, 126, 129, 130, 131, 344, 347–48, 787n596
lineages, 89
of blessing and practice, 157, 478, 508, 579, 774n280
expansive practice, 477, 802n849
of Ganden mahāmudrā, 627–36
of Mahayana (*gotra*), 563
near-transmission, 534, 579
of profound view, 157, 477, 508, 579
of vast practice, 157, 477, 508, 579
Ling Rinpoché, 635, 759n77, 817n1085
Lingrepa, 428, 665, 666, 756n43, 820n1164
lions, eight great, 503–4
Lion's Roar, 408, 793n716
Locanā, 497, 506, 549
Lodrö Bepa, 763n117
Lodrö Tenpa, 764n138
logical reasoning, 112
Lokeśvara, 506
longevity, 482, 521, 529, 543, 737, 808nn944–45
lord of death, 73
lords of five families
aggregates as, 416, 506
in three essential points practice, 717–18, 728–29
Losang Chökyi Gyaltsen, 206
Losang Dönyö Drupa, 632, 691
Losang Drakpa. *See* Tsongkhapa
Losang Namgyal, 630
Losang Phuntsok, 428
Losang Tamdrin, 4, 756n41
Losang Trinlé, 630
Losang Tsewang, 714, 826n1268
Losang Tsöndrü Gyaltsen, 632
lotuses, symbolism of, 504
love
as antidote, 340
arising of, 300
as cause of awakening mind, 69
cultivating, 106, 108, 304–5, 306, 309
two kinds, 784n503
loving kindness, 557
compassion and, 563
countering, 176
cultivating, 184, 775n293
naturally emerging, 769n204
within *tonglen*, 568
two approaches to, 453, 564–65, 799n810

Lūipa, 3, 14, 19
lying, 81, 110, 263, 264, 766n170

Machik Labdrön, 482, 586, 656, 661, 693
Madhyamaka, 357, 709
  on emptiness, 32
  on ignorance and personal identity view, 768n191
  on object of negation, 137
  on self as mere name, 670
  Tsongkhapa's contributions to, 2
  view, stages of acquiring, 365
  See also Middle Way; Prāsaṅgika Madhyamaka; Svātantrika Madhyamaka
Mahābala, 507
Mahākāla, 380, 444, 445, 510, 774n278
Mahākāśyapa, 256, 809n971
mahāmudrā
  common and uncommon, 803n861
  meanings and uses of term, 26, 645, 652–53, 704, 818n1113
  perspectives on, 643–44, 686
  as sutra or tantra, variant views on, 26–27, 28, 30, 31, 760n90
  types of, 618–19, 653–55
  See also Ganden mahāmudrā; Kagyü tradition; sutra mahāmudrā; tantra mahāmudrā
Mahāsukha, Lord (Padamavajra), 440, 441, 452, 508, 645, 646, 760n87
Mahayana, 79, 105
  aspiring to, 84
  buddhahood in, 801–2n841
  compassion as root of, 106, 562–64
  decline of, 207, 299, 776n312
  entering, 297–99, 314, 375
  foundations of, 617, 638–39
  four seals in, 643–44
  four wheels of, 428, 796n759
  gurus in, 14
  liberation in, 777n322
  Mañjuśrī in, 796n762
  mundane concentrations and, 355
  reviewing path of, 423–25, 553–78
  seven limbs as summation of, 532
  six perfections as, 315
  teaching to unsuitable students, 321
Maitreya, 256, 453
  buddhafield. *See* Tuṣita god realm
  Differentiation of the Middle and Extremes, 342, 771n240
  in dog's form, 160, 222
  Drupchen's visions of, 392
  epithets for, 407, 793n715
  homage to, 43
  lineages of, 440
  Ornament of Realization, 8, 528, 720n217
  Sublime Continuum, 273
  visualizations, 157, 391, 477, 507, 508, 719, 736, 737
  See also *Ornament of Mahayana Sutras*
Maitripa, 679, 704
  mahāmudrā of, 618, 645
  Presenting Nonmentation, 761n100
  Śavaripa and, 160
major and minor noble marks, 156, 207, 776n310
male birth, 89, 102
Māmakī, 506
mandala offerings, 63, 549, 578
  anointing, 113, 720n218
  extensive, 531
  inner, 519
  outer, 518–19, 806n925
  in preliminaries, 63, 157, 158, 228–29, 640, 774n281
  statement, 529, 808n945
  suchness, 519
  twenty-part, 730
Maṇibhadra, 14, 435–36, 533
Mañjuśrī (a.k.a. Mañjughoṣa), 214, 256, 450
  Drupchen's visions of, 392
  homage and supplication, 43, 385, 431–32, 535, 627, 791n692, 796n762
  in increasing rites, 540–41
  lineage of, 691
  mantra of, 402, 541, 793n711, 809n964
  as mental sense base, 507
  in Miktsema, 16, 17

teachings and transmissions from, 20, 21, 359, 371, 440, 442–45, 453, 475, 534, 540, 798nn782–83
triple-being, 544
Tsongkhapa as embodying, 296, 386, 399–400, 401, 432, 791n692, 791n694, 797n763
Tsongkhapa's visions of, 1, 20, 30, 441–42
visualizations, 157, 402, 477, 478, 508
Mañjuśrī Cycle of Teachings, 20–21, 758n64
Mañjuśrī Root Tantra, 385, 401
Mañjuśrīkīrti, *Ornament of the Essence*, 641–42
Mañjuśrīmitra, 222
Mañjuśrī's Advice on Practice (Tsongkhapa), 20
Mantra tradition. *See* Vajrayāna
mantras
arapacana, 402, 541, 793n711, 809n964
guru's name, 809n954
hundred-syllable, 525–26, 527, 617, 638, 642, 807n936
purifying, 226
Samayavajra, 526–27, 808n938
six-syllable, 718, 727, 731, 732, 826n1271
three-syllable, 497–98, 500–501, 510
Manu, children of, 90, 767n181
Marpa Lotsāwa (Martön Chökyi Lodrö), 3, 441, 490, 798n779, 803n864
on inner offerings, 498
mahāmudrā of, 645, 650
Milarepa and, 225, 450
realization of, 679, 704
Mātṛceṭa. See *Praise to the One Beyond All Praise*
matter, 204
Medicine Buddha Sutra, 226, 779n375
meditation, 314
as fundamental virtue, 767n177
key point of, 722, 739–40
laxity mistaken for, 127
objectless, 127, 771n239
pre-experience understanding and, 306, 784n510
two approaches, necessity of, 65
on ultimate mode of being, 112, 769nn214–15
meditation sessions
daily, number of, 206
duration of, 128, 218
instructions, 64
practicing between, 64, 162, 166, 170, 174, 177, 188, 196, 200, 206, 230, 258, 268, 325, 331, 609–10, 642
meditative absorption, 47, 117–18, 338, 426
contemplating, 195, 574
in post-equipoise, 119
space-like, 368, 369
wisdom and, 48, 338
See also insight/special insight; tranquil abiding
meditative equipoise
nihilistic, 144–45
single-pointed, 623, 679–80
six perfections in, 119, 770n229
space-like, 33, 35, 48, 203, 205, 426, 574, 597–601, 603, 606, 621–22, 671–75, 677, 681–82
Meeting of the Father and Son Sutra, 222
mental consciousness, 137, 341
mental formations, 291, 506, 674, 701
mental scattering, 130, 131, 134, 199, 586, 771n242
mental stability, 198, 584–85, 587–88
"merging of stillness and movement," 620, 659, 662, 694
merit, 380
accumulating, 64, 200, 531, 765n151
from Buddha's visualization, 347
completion of accumulating, 457
depletion of, 99
from guru yoga, 448–50, 451–52
from offerings, 219, 225, 499–500
of refuge, 77
from rejoicing, 528
rite for increasing, 539
from spiritual teachers, 533
at time of death, 243

merit field
  generating, 156, 414–16, 717–18, 724–25
  in preliminaries, 63
  two traditions of, 477–78
Meru, Mount, 46, 85, 390
  in offerings, 418, 498, 518, 519
  symbolism of, 380, 790n672
meta-awareness, 33, 35, 64, 230, 598, 765n146
  application of, 131, 133, 198, 199, 343
  force of, 132
  in karma contemplations, 265–66
  of laxity or excitation, 129
  in mental stability, 585–86
  not exercising, 130
  ordination vows and, 324
  in post-equipoise, 610
  in selflessness of persons, 368
  of spiritual teachers, 60
  in tranquil abiding, 126, 127, 128, 339, 344, 347, 349
  vows and, 294
  while sleeping, 64
method
  wisdom combined with, 48, 298, 340, 711
  without wisdom, limits of, 112–13
Middle Way, 30, 31, 48, 374, 397. *See also* Guide to the Middle Way View; Madhyamaka
Middle-Length Treatise on the Stages of the Path to Enlightenment (Tsongkhapa), 9, 212, 338, 369, 772n255
  on appearance aspect, 371
  awakening mind in, two traditions of, 307
  guides to, 10, 11
  on guru yoga, 438
  on special insight, 360
  on spiritual practice, 230
  on suffering, contemplation of, 277
  on two truths, 773n260
  when to consult, 311, 312, 342
Miktsema Compendium, 19
Miktsema Cycle of Teachings (Jamyang Dewai Dorjé), 18, 757n53
Miktsema prayer, 421, 532, 791n691
  alternative approaches to, 401, 793n709
  blessings of, 387
  composition of, 756n45
  cycles of, 18–19
  in guru yoga, 17–18, 23–24, 410, 757n49
  as name mantra, 535, 809n954
  nine-being tiered visualization, 544
  nine-lined, 16–17, 535, 543–44, 756n46
  number of repetitions, 535
  recitation of, 541
  rites using, 18, 757n52
  versions of, 16–17, 400, 792n707, 795n745
  visualizing, 402–3, 404, 543
Mikyö Dorjé, Eighth Karmapa, 3
Milarepa, 477, 655
  on existence and nonexistence, union of, 683
  on gurus, 643
  mahāmudrā of, 645, 650–51
  Marpa and, 225, 450, 533, 798n779
  on stages of path, 640–41
  on ultimate truth, 682–83
mind
  attachment of, cutting, 735–36
  Buddha's, 255
  as conditioned phenomena, 600–601
  conventional, 621, 664, 703
  conventional, three characteristics, 27, 588–89, 606, 678, 815nn1048–49
  cutting root of, 665–67, 678
  as devoid of arising, meditating on, 732–33
  great bliss of, 47
  innate, 647–49, 653
  investigating, 362, 363
  in mahāmudrā, 586
  nature of, 27, 677
  as primary, 475–76
  as self, mistaking, 592, 673
  settling, 33
  and space, union of, 35, 199, 776n306
  and winds, relationship between, 462, 463

"mind expresses the object again and again," 128, 771n240
mind isolation, 739
mind training (*lojong*), 23, 425, 508, 561, 562, 796n754, 811n990
mindfulness, 64, 598, 605, 765n146
  application of, 131, 133, 198, 199, 343
  forceful, 132, 585–87
  fourfold, 33, 359, 763n117
  in guru yoga, 23–24, 760n79
  in karma contemplations, 265–66
  and meta-awareness, relationship between, 129, 619, 660–61, 692–93
  ordination vows and, 324
  in post-equipoise, 609–10
  power of, 35
  in selflessness of persons, 368
  of spiritual teachers, 60
  in tranquil abiding, 126, 127, 198, 339, 347, 349, 771n238
  vows and, 294
  weakened, 199
  while sleeping, 64
Minyak Geshé Tsultrim Namgyal, 756n38
miserliness, antidote to, 46
Mitrayogi, 5, 35–36, 37, 681, 720, 740, 763n126, 816n1070, 822n1208, 826n1275
Miwang Drakpa Gyaltsen, 2, 753n2
mixing (*bsre ba*), 36, 721, 723, 737–39, 803n864
monastic tradition
  Geluk curriculum in, 3–4
  restoration of transgressions in, 268–69
  suffering of, 277
  tantra in, 19
  Tsongkhapa's contributions to, 3
Moon Lamp Sutra, 339. See also *King of Meditations Sutra*
moral discipline. *See* ethical discipline
Mother of the Conquerors, 43, 58, 210, 764n131
mother sentient beings, 156, 159, 309, 712
  kindness of, 182–83, 302–4, 469–70
  meditations on, 107–8, 389–90
  recognizing, 106, 180–82, 300, 301–2
  suffering of, 52, 424, 472–73, 557–58, 725, 726
motivation
  in black karmic paths, 80, 81, 82, 83
  causal and immediate, contrast between, 800n817
  of great compassion, 258
  in guru yoga, 455, 459–60
  in listening to Dharma, 211
  nonspecific, 80, 766n167
  in virtuous activity, 387
  See also intention
Mountain Dharma, 655
mudrās. *See* four seals (*mudrās*)
mundane path, 135–36, 351, 772n246
Munīndra Vajradhara, 155, 773–74n275
  enlightenment of, 189
  self-visualization, 187–88
  supplicating, 158–59, 166, 171, 178
  viewing guru as, 11
  visualization of, 157, 158, 159–61, 774n280

Nāgabodhi, 495, 804n875
Nāgārjuna, 32, 136, 378, 452, 531, 585, 766n159
  Ascertaining the Four Seals, 760n87
  on eight worldly concerns, 781n406
  on emptiness and cause and effect, 685
  on fortunate rebirth, 236
  Fundamental Wisdom, 363, 608, 669–70, 827n1285
  guru yoga texts of, 756n41
  on hells, recalling, 245
  homage to, 43
  on human rebirth, 250
  Hundred Verses of Wisdom, 354
  intent of, 357, 426, 495, 575, 593
  lineages of, 44, 440
  mahāmudrā of, 618, 645, 651–52, 684
  Sixty Verses of Reasoning, 356, 358
  tradition of, 210–11
  on tsok offerings, 521, 522
  visualizations, 477, 508
  See also *Five Stages*; *Friendly Letter*; *Precious Garland*

nāgas, 235, 780–81n401, 809n965
  in rain-making rite, 542
  symbolism of, 504
Naljorpa Chenpo Amé Jangchup Rinchen, 213, 778n342
Nanda, 268
Nanda (nāga king), 503
Nangzé Dorjé, 228
Nāropa, 222, 224, 518, 533, 756n41
  Cultivating the Guru, 14–15
  Epitome, 649, 650
  mahāmudrā of, 618, 645
  visualizations of, 478, 508
natural abodes, 157, 416, 510–11, 729–30
nectar
  five types, 497
  gnosis, 500, 734
  longevity, 734
  medicinal, 500, 734
Neusurpa, 208
Ngawang Chöphel, 787n584
Ngawang Jampa, 631, 633
Ngawang Lobsang Gyatso, Fifth Dalai Lama, 4, 36, 210, 791n686
  on ascertainment, 764n135
  homage to, 228
  instructions received, 777n320
  Sacred Words, 754n28
  on Taklung Drakpo Lodrö Gyatso, 779n374
  texts of, 37
  on thousand buddhas, visualizing, 728
  Treasury of Scripture and Reasoning, 12
  tutors of, 10, 30
  See also *Words of Mañjuśrī*
Ngawang Palden, 4
Ngödrup Rabten, 634
Ngulchu Dharmabhadra, 31, 36, 37, 631, 720, 740, 741
nihilism, 143, 248, 358, 371, 593, 598, 669
Nīladaṇḍa, 507
nine mental states (tranquil abiding), 132, 133, 200, 348–50, 352, 368, 660, 771n232, 787n598
nirmāṇakāya, 158, 223, 408, 440, 582, 737, 738. *See also under* rebirth
nirvana, 296, 601, 641
  and buddhahood, distinctions between, 777n322
  contentment with, 569–70, 811n998
  delaying, 287
  as illusory, 142
  lacking intrinsic existence, 146–47, 575
  nonabiding, 257
  as peace, 208
  and samsara, single nature of, 623, 681
  as ultimate truth, 149
nonassociated formations, 204, 205
non-Buddhist traditions, 135, 462, 555–56, 639, 668
nonconceptual thought/cognition, 65, 150, 366–67, 368, 766n154
nonconceptuality, 654, 662, 694
nondiscursive meditation, 27–28, 29, 30, 121, 126, 587, 649, 659, 761n94. *See also* nonmentation; placement meditation
nondiscursiveness, meditation experience of, 135, 574
nonhuman life forms, 235, 780n401
nonimplicative negations, 368, 597, 598, 599, 600–601, 675, 702, 814n1032, 814n1035
nonmentation, 26, 144–45, 367, 769–70n216
  Chenga's defense of, 29
  cultivating tranquil abiding through, 30
  in Four-Lettered, 655
  in Geluk tradition, 27, 28
  Maitripa on, 761n100
  remaining in, 365–66, 789n635
  Words of Mañjuśrī on, 12
  See also nondiscursive meditation
nonreturners, 100
nonvirtue, 67, 100, 169–70, 260, 332. *See also* ten nonvirtues / black karmic paths; wrongdoing
Norsang Gyatso, 29, 228, 360, 672–73, 788n624
no-self, 7, 126, 699. *See also* selflessness
Nyangtö, 381, 791n680
Nyingma tradition, 522, 777n320

object of negation, 34
appearance of, 145
erroneous views on, 684–85
identifying correctly, importance of, 597
in identifying ignorance, 137
identifying incorrectly, 360, 669
in post-equipoise, 370, 602, 681–82, 815n1041
in rites, 537–38
in selflessness of persons, 35, 141, 144, 201, 203, 361–62, 367, 368, 489, 588–93, 594, 669, 671, 672, 700, 789n638
in selflessness of phenomena, 204, 371
subtle, 585, 672, 697, 698, 824n1242
offering substances
of everyday enjoyment, 496, 498, 517–18, 804n877
as mental constructs, 514
obtaining, means of, 458–59
tea, 521
three features of, 498–99
See also water
Offering to the Guru (Losang Chögyen), 15–16, 22, 433, 658, 793n721, 794n728, 797n766, 819n1149, 796n760
colophon, 428–29
composition of, 446
dedication, 427–28, 795–96n751
excellence of, 446–53
guides on, 23, 611, 815n1058
as highest yoga tantra, 22–23
homage, 411, 433
invocation, 416, 794n732
preliminaries, 413–23, 500
as preliminary for mahāmudrā, 31
promise to compose, 435
recitation of, 541
sutra origins of, 435–37
tantra origins of, 438–39
transmission of, 759n77
See also Ensa tradition guru yoga
offerings
abbreviated, 500–501
blessing, 495–501
four empowerments and, 520–23
inner, 414, 496–98, 521, 795n741
material, 229
meaning of term, 499
outer, 498, 804n883
perception of, 460
preventing, 84
of realization, 520
six special attitudes in, 459–60
sources on, 523
to spiritual teachers, 61–62, 417
three elements of, 418, 459, 800n825
verses for, 418–19, 795n739
visualization, 394–95
See also mandala offerings; offering substances
Ölkha Chölung, 3, 518
omniscience, 108, 150, 255, 271, 296
once returners, 100
oral traditions (Geluk), 20, 381, 758n61
genres included in, 5
importance of, 215
relying on, 230
Tsongkhapa's, 15, 16, 20, 21, 30, 32, 445, 758n62
origins of suffering, 46, 97–103, 283–90
Ornament of Mahayana Sutras (Maitreya), 14, 454
on diligence, 333
on four means of gathering others, 375
on learning and contemplation, 231
on mental contemplation, 350
on nine mental states, 348
on offerings, function of, 499
on six perfections, 315, 316, 785n525
on spiritual teachers, relying on, 219–20, 440–41
on tranquil abiding, conditions for, 339–40, 657

Pacification (Shijé), 618, 653, 655–56
Padmapāṇi, 720
Padmasambhava, *Garland of View*, 656
Padmavajra, 26, 441, 760n87
Paljor Trinlé Rabgyé (a.k.a. Surchen

Chöying Rangdröl), 210, 228, 382, 754n28, 777n320, 777n329, 780n387, 791n683
Palkhor Dechen Monastery, 381
Palmang, *Mirror Reflecting the Mind*, 771n242
Panchen Lama lineage, 4
 Lobsang Palden Tenapi Nyima, Fourth, 634, 817n1082
 Losang Palden Yeshé, Third, 13, 631, 714, 757n52, 826n1268
 Panchen Losang Yeshé, Second, 10, 11, 13, 37, 630
 See also Panchen Losang Chökyi Gyaltsen
Panchen Losang Chökyi Gyaltsen (a.k.a. Losang Chögyen), 495, 587
 Celebration Unlocking All Excellences, 12
 Easy Path, 10–11, 754n28
 on Ensapa lineage, 758n68
 Guide to the Stages of the Path in Verse, 12
 Lamp So Bright, 22, 25–26, 602, 815n1041
 lineage of, 21, 691
 mahāmudrā teachings of, 30–31
 on rainbow body actualizations, 759n69
 role in Tsongkhapa's oral tradition, 16
 on suffering, 556
 supplication to, 629
 texts of, 37
 on thousand buddhas, visualizing, 728–29
 See also *Highway of the Conquerors*; *Offering to the Guru*
Panchen Sönam Drakpa, Fifteenth Ganden Tripa, 3–4, 29, 761n98
Pāṇḍaravāsinī, 497, 506
Pang Lotsāwa, 428
partless phenomena, 141
path integration, 425, 561
path of accumulation, 312
path of imaginative engagement, 686, 823n1219
path of meditation, 351, 352, 787n601
path of preparation, 99, 265, 685–86, 822n1218
path of seeing, 352, 686, 766n156, 782n450
peak of existence, 282, 354, 458, 555–56, 800n820
Pehar, 387
perceptions
 challenging, 7
 deluded, 708–9, 710, 711
 direct nondeceptive, 142
 illusion-like, 145
 imperfect, 160–61
 ordinary beings' direct, 143–44
 in post-equipoise, 602–3
 pure, 720, 738
 purifying, 426
Perfection of Wisdom. *See* Mother of the Conquerors
Perfection of Wisdom in Eight Thousand Lines, 670, 678, 703
Perfection of Wisdom Sutras, 359, 683, 822n1211
 intent of, 528
 mahāmudrā in, 583, 618, 651
 on relying on spiritual teachers, 436
 script of, 793n711
Perfection Vehicle, 396, 397, 451, 544
personal identity view. *See* identity view (*satkāyadṛṣṭi*)
Phabongkha Dechen Nyingpo, 13, 23, 635, 755n34, 817n1083
Phakmo Drupa (Drogön Rinpoche), 643, 645, 679, 818n1109
Phara Bodhisattva, 692
phenomena
 emptiness of, 370
 equal taste of, 740
 full differentiation of, 153
 illusion-like, 33, 34–35, 48, 145, 203, 205, 426, 574–75, 704, 773n259
 as innate minds, 647
 as one or many, 202
 selflessness of, 90–91, 204–5, 767n182
 space-like nature of, 677
Phuchungwa Shönu Gyaltsen, 292, 784n489

Phurchok Ngawang Jampa, 13, 37, 570, 812n999
pith instructions, 15, 20, 32, 405, 413, 446, 453, 495, 583, 607, 713, 731, 758n61
placement meditation, 230
  and analytical, alternating, 367
  ascertaining when required, 56, 94
  on faith, 231
  purpose of, 65, 605, 606
  on selflessness, 367, 789n638
  sustaining, 152
  on ten virtues and nonvirtues, 265–67, 325
  tranquil abiding and, 122, 136, 361
  See also nondiscursive meditation; tranquil abiding
places, harmonious, 123, 196–97, 771n233
Play in Full Sutra, 241, 275–76
pliancy, 118, 352, 426, 765n153
  from analytical meditation, 369
  application of, 131, 198
  benefits of, 124, 353
  five signs of, 133–34
  in insight, 205
  in tranquil abiding, 664, 696
  in tranquil abiding and insight, 120, 122, 153, 338–39, 350–51, 788n634
pollutants, five, 549
post-equipoise, 711
  bliss and emptiness in, 582
  dependent origination in, 145, 675, 681, 682
  equal taste of phenomena in, 740
  guru yoga in, 408–9
  illusion-like, 33, 35, 48, 145, 203, 205, 574–75, 704, 773n259
  illusion-like emptiness in, 601–6, 607, 623, 675–76, 681–82
  nihilistic, 144–45
  nondual bliss and emptiness in, 712
  perceptions in, 143
  pliancy in, 134
  sense objects in, 517–18
  six perfections in, 119, 770n229
  six senses in, 601–2, 623, 681, 710
  and space-like equipoise, alternating, 682
  three spheres in, 624, 683
postures, 226
  bhadra, 391, 792n698
  eight-featured, 155, 347, 461–62, 723, 774n276, 801n831
  seven-point, 619, 658, 692, 723
  six blazing triangles (*tumo*), 476–77
  sleeping, 64
  for tranquil abiding, 123
  vajrāsana, 391, 392, 415
Potowa Rinchen Sal, 6, 208, 229, 281, 366, 411–12, 447, 784n489
Prabhāketu, 509, 805n905
Praise to the One Beyond All Praise (a.k.a. *Praise with Similes*, Mātṛceṭa), 217, 254, 255, 354, 355
Praṇidhānamati, 509, 805n905
Prāsaṅgika Madhyamaka, 33, 35, 370, 442, 585, 603, 766n156, 772n248
prātimokṣa. *See* vows, individual liberation
pratyekabuddhas, 106, 256, 257, 297, 376, 473, 769n205
precepts
  bodhicitta/bodhisattva, 70, 111, 114, 311–13, 769n213
  bodhisattva and prātimokṣa, relationship between, 323–24, 785n539
  eighteen root, 191
  forty-six secondary, 191
  guarding, 469, 557, 811n988
  of mind training, 561–62
  need for, 571–72
  purity of, 610
  refuge, 77–78, 258
  relying on, 294–95
  within six perfections, 114–18
  See also vows
Precious Garland (Nāgārjuna), 108
  on death, causes for, 242
  on Dharma, difficulty of understanding, 357
  on exchanging self for others, 308
  on karma and "I," 359

on love, 304–5
on mere labels, 683–84
on selflessness of persons, 622, 670, 673, 675, 676, 701
on virtue and nonvirtue, 260
on wrong livelihood, 460
preliminary practices, 59, 63, 500
breath in, 463–64
four great instructions on, 485, 527, 640, 803n860
in guide to the view, 763n117
importance of, 190
and main practices, integrating, 641
offerings, laying out, 458–61, 514
practice space preparation, 454, 455–58
seat and posture, 461–62
special, 486, 488–95, 490–91, 495–501, 803n864
See also awakening mind; refuge
pride, 89, 97, 117, 284, 340
primordial mind (also primordial state), 464, 583–84, 801n835
primordial nature, 26, 679, 704
propensities, 313, 417, 640, 707, 709, 712. *See also* imprints
prophecies, 20, 21, 758n66
on Maitreya, 392
on Tsongkhapa, 386, 791n693, 793n716
prostrations, 268, 393–94, 527
of body, speech, mind, 513
in confession, 617, 638, 642
verses for, 417, 795n736
protection
generosity of, 318, 319–20, 321
from Three Jewels, 45, 217, 224, 253, 257
provisional meaning, 136, 267, 378, 656
pure lands, 427, 719, 731, 738, 739
pure visions, 712–14
purification
basis of, 491, 493, 495
four powers in, 170

Qianlong emperor, 4
Questions of Brahmā Sutra, 295, 784n493
Questions of Rāṣṭrapāla, 667–68
Questions of Revata, 340–41
Questions of Sāgaramati Sutra, 210
Questions of Subāhu Tantra, 104, 454
Questions of the Householder Ugra, 58, 436

Radreng Monastery, 791–92n695
rainbow body, 445, 475, 759n69, 801–2n841
Rasavajrā, 506–7
Ratnasambhava, 496, 506, 728
reasoning, 48, 619, 709
of dependent origination, 146, 360, 591
four possibilities of arising, 733
identity and difference, 147, 591
in karma, understanding, 767n185
in presenting teachings, 59
in understanding suchness, 60
rebirth, 69, 75, 244, 245, 287
afflictions and, 98
death mindfulness and, 72
fortunate, 45, 66, 67, 75, 468
fortunate, drawbacks of, 377–78, 790n661
karma and, 261–62, 288–89, 359
in lower realms, 168–69, 245–50, 423, 467–68, 479–80, 554–55, 641
numbers of, 279–80
process of, 102–3
in samsara, aspiring for, 92, 768n187
selflessness of persons and, 141–42, 364
taking into path as nirmāṇakāya, 493, 494–95
from ten nonvirtuous actions, 264
twelve links and, 291
white karmic paths and, 87
at will, 720, 738, 739
refuge, 8, 45, 259, 423, 554, 717, 802n856
in confession, 396
daily practice, 78
efficacy of, 76–77
fourfold formula recitation, 389
as gateway to Dharma, 252–53
guided meditations, 156–59, 169, 254–57, 388, 413–14, 478–81, 723–25
objects of, 76, 217–18, 253–54, 257, 389
in power of support, 91

in preliminaries, 63, 619, 638–39, 658
and relying on teachers, relationship of, 216
uncommon Mahayana, 481–83
vow/formula, 218–19, 258, 481, 792n697, 802n853
See also merit field
rejoicing, 483–84, 527–28
relative truth. *See* conventional truth
relaxation/resting
instructions on, 620–21, 659, 661, 666–67
misunderstandings of, 345, 350
and total cessation, distinction between, 660, 692
Relentless (Avīci) hell, 62, 84, 253, 269, 283, 331, 426, 765n149
relying on spiritual teachers, 64, 200, 420–21
in action/deed, 61–62, 161–62, 224–25, 437, 780n384
benefits of, 62, 436, 511–12, 532–33
concluding, 162
contemplations, 161, 553–54
faith and, 159–61
faults of not, 62, 435, 533–34
as foundation of path, 6, 44–45, 59
guided meditation, 226–30
importance of, 411–13
preliminaries, 155–59, 216–19
between sessions, 162
in thought, 61, 220–24, 437
three trainings and, 456–57
See also guru yoga
remorse, 269, 438, 487
Rendawa, 441, 442, 756n45, 798n782
renunciation, 46, 268, 296, 712
as inspiration, 272
in lamrim, 8
need for, 51–52
symbols of, 504
two aspects, 457
restoration practice, 324, 326
retreats, 1, 376, 518
Revata, 340–41
rites
body offering, 711–12, 721, 733–35, 825n1267
four activity, 535, 543, 809n955
increase, 539, 540–41
influence, 539
meditation practice and, 543
pacification, 537–39
rain-making, 541–43, 809n967
success in, causes for, 537
three spheres in, 537–38
torma offering, 578, 812n1005
wrath, 539–40
ritual feasts (*tshogs*), 521–22, 795–96n751
robes, three saffron, 156, 774n277
Root Tantra of Cakrasaṃvara, 448, 799n795
Rudra, 507
rūpakāya. *See* form body
Rūpavajrā, 506

Śabdavajrā, 506
Sacred Words of Mañjuśrī (Buddhaśrījñāna), 450
Sadāprarudita, 14, 224, 225, 436, 451, 456, 533
Sahor, 791n686
Sakya Paṇḍita (Sapaṇ), 639
Clear Differentiation of the Three Vows, 346, 642, 650, 651, 652
on mahāmudrā, 26, 27, 30, 687, 823n1225
Sakya tradition, 369, 779n368
samādhi. *See* concentration
Samantabhadra
offering clouds of, 394–95, 415, 419, 460, 502, 518, 520
visualization, 507
Samayavajra mantra repetition, 526–27, 808n938
saṃbhogakāya, 158, 523, 551, 654, 738. *See also under* intermediate state (*bardo*)
Samlo Tsultrim Gyatso, 691
samsara (cyclic existence), 575
disenchantment with, 46, 423–24, 726

eight sufferings of, 95–96
entering, 283–89
fear of, 78
freedom from, 124
grasping at, two kinds, 138
of householders and monastics, distinctions in, 104
measure of repulsion to, 103
neutralizing seeds of, 139
and nirvana, single nature of, 623, 681
rebirth and, 468
root of, destroying, 47, 48
suffering of, general, 172–73, 332, 555–56, 707, 786n553
See also six realms
Saṃvarodaya Tantra, 413, 448
Sangha, 76, 77, 84, 256–57, 264. *See also* Three Jewels
Śāntarakṣita, 37
Śāntendra, 509, 805n905
Śāntideva, 9
bodhisattva vow rite approach of, 109, 190–91
Compendium of Training, 312, 392, 454, 460–61
on delighting in virtue, 765n147
lineage of, 802n849
practice of, 531–32
Verses on the Compendium of Training, 458, 531, 610
visualization, 477
See also *Guide to the Bodhisattva Way*
Śāntipa, 216, 639
Saraha (a.k.a. Śavaripa), 14, 452, 586
Dohā Treasury of Songs, 647, 648, 649, 661, 662, 665, 693, 694
lineages of, 440, 445
mahāmudrā of, 26, 27, 618, 645
People's Dohā, 646
Treasury of Dohās, 666
visualization, 508
Sarasvatī, 392
Saroruhavajra, 645
Sarvanīvaraṇaviṣkambhin, 507
Sarvāstivāda school, 327
Satyaka Chapter, 91, 254–55
Śavari, Lord, 645
Śavaripa. *See* Saraha (a.k.a. Śavaripa)
Sé clan, 387
Secret Mirror of Prophecies (emanated scripture), 20, 21, 758nn65–66
sectarianism, 687
Segyü Monastery, 15, 19, 756n44
Segyü tradition, 15, 16–17, 381, 777n328, 779n373
guru yoga in, 19–20, 386–87
on karma and obstacles, 498
self of persons
appearance and apprehension, distinctions between, 589, 590, 596, 597, 672
five ways of appearing, 699–700, 824n1245
four reasonings on, 489
grasping at, 7, 137–38, 139, 670–71
identifying person, 140
illusion-like appearances, arising of, 145–46
illusion-like appearances, correct, 142–44
illusion-like appearances, incorrect, 144–45
observing arising of, 33–34
self of phenomena, 112, 670
self-cherishing, 189, 308, 310, 424
antidote to, 457
contemplating faults of, 559, 565
in Cutting Off approach, 589–90
harm and, 470–71
as root of all misfortune, 470–71, 474, 560
self-grasping, 52, 373, 424, 599
antidote to, 641
contrived, 699
cutting root of, 339–40, 707–8, 711
eliminating, 457
identifying, 709
ignorance, 468–69, 557
innate, 588, 590, 670, 672, 698, 699, 700
and mere thought "I am," distinctions between, 696–97
pride and, 284
prior familiarization with, 368

of tīrthikas, 355
selflessness, 33, 295, 352
ascertaining, 8, 359
direct perception of, 668–69
meditation on, 355, 599
preexisting understanding of, 121
realizing, 134–35, 137–38, 139, 469, 668
two forms, order of generating, 140, 358–59
two forms, relationship between, 372–73
as ultimate truth, 150
wisdom realizing, 299, 339, 456, 457, 557
selflessness of persons, 33, 360, 594, 767n181
certainty in, 365, 596, 710
continuity in, maintaining, 367–69, 605–6
four key points in establishing, 141–46, 201–3, 361–65, 489, 593–96, 772n255
meditation on, 365–67, 489, 641, 669, 673–75, 696–98, 700–703
misunderstandings about, 698–99
See also under object of negation
selflessness of phenomena, 33
dependent origination reasoning, 146
establishing, 146–47
four key points, 371–72
initial attainment of, 372
meditation on, 113, 622, 641, 676–80
sense consciousness, 222, 684
sense objects
five, 229, 394, 498, 516, 806n917
inner, 516–17, 806n919
sense organs/bases, 291, 506–7
sentient beings
blessing, 495
cherishing, 106
as countless, 181
delight in helping, 117
equanimity toward, 107
ethical discipline of helping, 325
even-mindedness toward, 180
harming, 459
karma of, 90–91
not abandoning, 111
and phenomena, sameness of, 676
purifying, 484
relying on, 471–72
responsibility to free, 473
Sera Jé Monastery, 777n318
Sera Monastery, 3, 791n690
Serlingpa, 224–25, 226, 453, 639, 779n366
Setsun of Trum, Great Abbot, 225, 779n367
Seven Attainment Texts, 645, 646, 816n1061, 818n1112
seven limbs, 730, 774n281
appeal to not enter nirvana, 393, 420, 529
confession, 395–96, 419, 525–27
dedication, 398–99, 420, 529–31
delight in, 511
excellence of, 531–32
offering, 394–95, 418–19, 514–25
in preliminaries, 63, 157, 158, 227–30
prostrations, 393–94, 417, 513–14
rejoicing, 396–97, 420, 527–28
request to turn Dharma wheel, 397–98, 420, 528–29
verses on, 718
worth of, 513–14
seven precious royal emblems, 394, 498, 518, 522, 792n702, 804n844
seven secondary precious emblems, 498, 804n844
seven types of gems, 502, 514, 515, 516, 520, 804n890
seven types of jewels, 418, 514, 515, 518, 804n914
sevenfold analysis, 360, 596–97
seven-point causes-and-effect instruction, 107–9, 177–78, 563, 799n810, 811n992
altruistic intention cultivation, 186
as aspiration, 313
awakening mind cultivation, 186–88
compassion cultivation, 185–86
equanimity, 178–80, 300, 301
loving kindness cultivation, 184
on mother sentient beings, 180–84,

301–4
order of, 106
preliminaries, 178
purpose of, 299–300
Seven-Point Mind Training (Chekawa), 308, 453
sexual misconduct, 80–81, 86, 87, 262, 264
sexual union, 262, 526, 550, 580, 648, 649, 712
Shamar Gendun Tenzin
How to Engage in Guided Meditation on the Topics in the Easy Path, 11, 13
Memorandum on the Difficult Points of the Insight Section of the Great Treatise on the Stages of the Path, 13, 14
shame, cultivating, 176, 294
Shang Rinpoché (a.k.a. Lama Shang), 26–27, 666, 667, 686
Shangpa Kagyü, 654
Shar Kalden Gyatso, 30, 31, 817n1088
Sharawa, 295, 317
Sherab Sangpo, 3, 9
Sherab Sengé, 624–25, 697, 763n117, 777n328, 824n1239
homage to, 228
lineages, 33, 210, 359, 367, 691, 788n624
tantric colleges founded by, 15, 19, 756n44
in Tsongkhapa's lamrim tradition, 12
siddhis, 451, 532
eight mundane, 799n805, 799n807
guru yoga for, 452
supreme, 799n807
signs, 120, 338, 339, 786nn565–66
Śikhin, 288, 784n487
single cushion, 22
single sitting, 445, 453
single taste, 511, 580, 585, 644, 655, 683, 686, 712, 740
Sitātapatrā, 729
six constituents, 649, 819n1126
Six Cycles of Equal Taste, 655
Six Dharmas of Nigumā, 654
six methods of resting the mind, 27, 662–63, 694–95
six perfections, 7, 46–48, 165, 192–95, 312, 376, 764n134
creating bodhisattva propensities from, 313
emptiness of, 378
infused with generosity, 116
meditative sessions on, 334, 335
merit of, 457
number and sequence of, 114–15, 315–16, 785nn525–26
perfection of wisdom in all, 354
preliminaries, 192
between sessions on, 321
symbols of, 504
training in, need for, 70
wisdom in, 112
in *Words of Mañjuśrī*, 12
See also individual perfections
six realms
purifying, 484–85
suffering of, 96, 173–74, 246, 278–81
six recognitions, 57, 211
six recollections, 130, 771n241
Six Yogas of Nāropa, 19, 26, 650, 653, 655
Six-Arm Mahākāla, 725
skillful means, 437, 561–62, 639. *See also* method
sleep, 64, 162, 345, 610, 655–56
concentration combined with, 134
"I"-grasping, innate, 201, 361, 697, 698, 708
mixing with dharmakāya, 738
as obstruction, 72, 130–31, 334, 337, 658, 765n152, 772n245
posture and, 462
solitude, 53, 215, 454, 625, 688, 692, 767n177
Sönam Chokkyi Langpo, 16
Sönam Palsang, 228
Song of Spiritual Experience (Tsongkhapa), 9, 209, 754n20
on fulfilling beings' wishes, 543
on karma, purifying, 294
on lamrim, excellence of, 44, 211–12
on relying on spiritual teachers, 412

in *Words of Mañjuśrī*, 377
Southern Transmission of the Words of Mañjuśrī (Gendun Jamyang), 13, 755n33, 777n328, 780n382
space, 146–47, 372
space-like meditative equipoise. *See under* meditative equipoise, space-like
Sparśavajrā, 507
speech
  Buddha's, 254–55, 260–61
  cruel, 81, 82, 263
  cultivating wisdom through, 402–3
  divisive, 81–82, 263, 264
  idle talk, 81, 82, 263, 264
  karmic effects of nonvirtuous, 86, 87
  nonvirtuous, refraining from, 89
  pleasant, in gathering others, 375
  trusted, 89
spiritual teachers, 67
  as Buddha, viewing, 57, 160
  characteristics of, 60, 220, 222–23
  ethical discipline and, 325
  false, 62, 286
  perceiving faults in, 61, 221–23, 231–32
  scorning, 117
  as truly authoritative, 480
  See also gurus (*lama*); relying on spiritual teachers
śrāvaka tradition, 473
  anger in, 329
  four seals in, 643
  love in, 256
  not straying into, 297, 376
  practices of, 106, 769n205
  realizations of, 257
  See also Hīnayāna
Śrāvastī, 805n908
stages of the doctrine (*bstan rim*), 5
stages of the path (*lamrim*), 209, 369, 379, 777n324
  comprehensiveness of, 68, 766n157
  greatness of, four kinds, 211–14, 215
  homage to instruction on, 44
  lineage of, 209, 212, 779n374, 792n699
  and mahāmudrā, harmonizing, 28–29
  origins of, 5–6
  psychology behind, 7–8
  purpose of, 213–14
  refrain in instructions on, 764n132
  rites based on, 543
  sections of, 213
  subclasses of, 5–6, 11
  tantric elements in, 11
  texts on, 8–14, 381–82
  Tsongkhapa's integrated tradition, 9
Stainless Light (Puṇḍarīka), 656
stealing, 80, 84, 86, 87, 262, 264
Sthiramati, *Commentary on Differentiation of the Middle and Extremes*, 771n240
stinginess, 229, 317, 320
storehouse consciousness, 102, 137
Story of Sumāgadhā, 227, 510
stream enterer, 100, 268
students and disciples, 59, 61, 220, 435. *See also* four means of gathering others
subitist path, 649
subject-object duality, 150, 773n271
Sublime Dharma of the White Lotus, 625
subsequent realization, 48, 369–71. *See also* post-equipoise
suchness, 47, 48, 60, 70, 152, 268, 365, 373, 426
suffering
  accepting, 331–32
  aspiration for liberation and, 45
  causes, identifying, 262
  contemplating, 51, 93, 172–73, 272–73, 464, 724
  contemplating, sequence of, 555, 811n983
  four powers and, 92
  karma and, 78
  of lower realms, 168–69, 245–50, 423, 467–68, 479–80, 554–55, 641
  of others, empathy for, 7, 69, 471–73
  recalling, 721
  varieties of, 94
  See also origins of suffering; three kinds of suffering
suicide, 328
Sukhāvatī, 731

Sumbharāja, 507
Sunakṣatra, 160, 222, 774n282
supernormal powers, 89, 124, 315, 325, 351, 352. *See also* clairvoyance
supplications, 9, 200
  benefits of, 386
  to Ganden Mahāmudrā lineage, 627–36
  to gurus, 544–48
  inner aspect, 400
  in mahāmudrā, 585
  to Munīndra Vajradhara, 158–59, 160–61, 162
  for near-transmission lineage, 534
  Opening the Excellent Door to the Path, 754n18
  outer, inner, secret aspects, 399–400, 422, 535–37
  for pacification, 537–39
  for rain, 541–43, 809n967
  single-pointed firm, 547–48, 810n973
  special additional, 405–6
  Special Single-Pointed Supplication, 422, 795n749
  Supplicating the Lineage Gurus of the Near Transmission, 33
  three main objectives for, 63, 765n150
  See also Miktsema prayer
Surchen Chöying Rangdröl. *See* Paljor Trinlé Rabgyé (a.k.a. Surchen Chöying Rangdröl)
suspension, state of, 112, 769n216
sutra mahāmudrā, 583–84
  insight in, 621, 665–71
  meditation object unique to, 584, 813n1015
  meditative equipoise in, 597–601, 618, 620–21, 622, 651, 663–64
  mental stillness cultivation, 584–88, 619–20, 621, 658–63, 692–95
  nature of path, 621, 664
  post-equipoise of, 622, 675–76
  preliminaries for, 584, 619, 657–58, 813n1017
  selflessness of persons meditation, 588–96, 621–22, 669–76, 696–703
  selflessness of phenomena meditation, 606–7, 622, 676–80
  two approaches to, 619, 657, 696
sutra tradition, 2, 122, 435–37, 439–40. *See also* Perfection Vehicle
Svātantrika Madhyamaka, 148, 150, 357, 684, 697
Swift Path (Panchen Losang Yeshé), 10, 11
sword wheels, 404
sympathetic love, 300, 784n503
Synthesis of Precious Qualities. See *Condensed Perfection of Wisdom in Verse*

Ṭakkirāja, 507
Taklung Drakpo Lodrö Gyatso, 226, 755n35, 779n374
Takphu Tenpai Gyaltsen, 793n719
Taktsang Lotsāwa, 371, 789n650
tantra. *See* Vajrayāna
tantra mahāmudrā, 27, 28, 618, 645, 813n1017
  innate mind in, 647–49
  sources for, 645–47
  training in, 581–84, 650–51, 813n1015
Taphukpa Damchö Gyaltsen, 629, 817nn1078–79
Tārā, 497, 506
Tashi Lhunpo Monastery, 3, 429, 688, 714, 788n624
tea ceremony prayer, 521, 806n927
Teachings of Akṣayamati Sutra, 230, 780m394
Ten Dharmas Sutra, 61
ten nonvirtues / black karmic paths, 79
  abstention from, 294, 323–24
  actual, 80–83
  in contemplations, 165, 172
  effects of, 86, 87, 264–65
  gravity, levels of, 264
  by householders and bhikṣus, distinctions between, 85
  identifying, 262–64
  intention to commit, 91
  purifying, 91
ten virtues / white karmic paths, 87–88, 265–66, 271

Ten Wheels of Kṣitigarbha Sutra, 210, 436
Tenpai Drönmé, 633
Tendar Lharam, 764n135
Tengyur, 1, 36
Tenzin Gyatso, Fourteenth Dalai Lama
  Illuminating the Conqueror's Intent, 755n31
  on *Letter of Final Testament Sent upon the Wind*, 23
  supplication to, 635, 817n1086
  transmissions given by, 759n77
Thangsakpa Ngödrup Gyatso, 19
Thösam Gyatso, 705
thoughts
  afflictive, 58, 765n142
  cessation of, 149, 773n265
  fusing tastes of, 722, 739–40
  as incorrect attention, 139
  in mahāmudrā, methods for, 620, 658, 661, 662, 667, 693, 694
  nonconceptual wisdom from, impossibility of, 152
  at time of death, 100
thousand-spoked golden wheel, 380, 482, 790n671
Thöyön Jamyang Trinlé, 18
three buddha bodies, 704
  complete in mind, 686
  spontaneous realization of, 650
  in transference, 737, 738
  See also form body (*rūpakāya*); dharmakāya; nirmāṇakāya; saṃbhogakāya
"Three Essential Points" instruction, 721–22
  conclusion, 720, 740
  for death, 719, 733–37
  four main themes of, 36–37
  for intermediated state, 719–20, 737–39
  overview, 35–37
  preparation, 717–18
  texts on, 37
  for this life, 718–19, 723–33
  three embodiments, 718, 731–32, 826n1271
  three perspectives, 718, 732, 826n1271
  three thoughts, 719, 737
Three Heaps Sutra. See *Bodhisattva's Confession of Downfalls*
three higher trainings, 7, 55, 271, 290, 296, 309, 641
  in guided contemplations, 175–77
  mastering, 293
  order of, 293
  purpose of, 104, 469, 556, 557
  and relying on spiritual teachers, 456–57
  six perfections and, 114, 316
  spiritual teacher's understanding of, 60, 220
  symbols of, 520
Three Jewels, 8, 226, 268
  admiring faith in, 257–58
  confession and, 269
  honoring, karmic fruition of, 89
  karma's power and, 84
  precepts involving, 258
  protection of, 45
  reflecting on to counter laxity, 199
  resultant, 482
  specific qualities of, 76–77
  supplicating, reason for, 219
  visualization, 169, 482
  See also refuge
three kinds of suffering, 52, 108, 278, 290, 306, 373, 377, 555, 811n982
  of change/uncertainty, 96, 174, 272, 279–81, 282, 305
  manifest, 96, 174, 271, 278, 305, 775n295
  of pervasive conditioning, 174, 278, 305
three mental poisons, 221, 352, 663, 695
  black karmic paths and, 80, 81, 82, 83, 262, 265–66
  counteracting strongest first, 341
  distraction from, 771n242
  objects of, 138
  "sweeping away," 455, 456
Three Principal Elements of the Path (Tsongkhapa), 9, 724

commentaries on, 12, 13
on dependent origination, wisdom of, 355
on emptiness and dependent origination, relationship of, 604, 685
three scriptural collections, 66, 233
three secrets, 396, 546, 792n703, 810n972
three spheres
conceptions of, 112
in meditation, 608
in offerings, 418, 459, 800n825
in post-equipoise, 624, 683
in rites, 537–38
three sweets, 521, 806n928
three types of persons, 44, 212–13, 324, 785n541
all discourses included in, 68
in *Lamp*, 5
reasons for, 68–70
shared paths of, 69, 70, 71, 93, 94, 214–15, 293–94, 297, 555
three essential points and, 723
Tsongkhapa's understanding of, 6–7, 8, 753n12
twelve links meditation for, 292
use of term, 753n9
See also great capacity path; intermediate capacity path; lesser capacity path
three vehicles, 55, 94, 135, 643–44, 664, 768n188
three worlds, 418, 795n738
thickness. *See* suchness
Thuken Chökyi Nyima, 19, 25
Tibetan Buddhism
common emphasis in, 639–40
establishment of, 545–46
fourfold assembly in, 234
mahāmudrā in, 26–27
Tsongkhapa's contributions to, 1, 2–3, 753n5
Tilopa, 14, 222, 224, 533, 756n41
mahāmudrā of, 26, 645
Mother Ganges. See *Instructions on Mahāmudrā* (Tilopa)
visualizations of, 478, 508
time, selflessness of, 205
tīrthikas, 77, 222, 352, 354–55
Tokden Jampal Gyatso, 508, 793n716
Ganden mahāmudrā and, 28
lineages of, 21, 33, 445, 691
mahāmudrā and, 761–62n101
supplication, 628
teachings from Tsongkhapa, 11, 16, 17, 20, 548–49, 550, 810n975
tonglen. *See* giving and taking (*tonglen*)
tormas, 521–22, 562, 578
tranquil abiding (*śamatha*), 27, 94, 117, 120, 668
analysis and, 671
approximation of, 350–51, 365, 788n634
attaining, 133–35, 338–39, 351–52
balancing tightness and looseness in, 127, 199, 348, 620, 661, 693–94
benefits of, 120, 123–24, 361
conditions for, 340, 786n571
factors of, 765n146
four attentions, 348–50
guided contemplation, 197–200
inward- and outward-turned, 341
meditative stabilization pāramitā in, 119, 120, 770n230
methods, 29, 30, 65, 126–28
objects, determining appropriate, 125–26
objects, focusing on, 126–28, 346–48, 771n240
objects, four general, 124, 340
objects for specific afflictions, 124–25, 339, 340–41, 660
obstacles to, 129–31, 771n242
predisposition toward, 584
preliminaries, 196–97, 657–58
prerequisites for, 123
purpose of, 34, 355
sessions' duration, 128
and special insight, relationships between, 28, 48, 121–22, 135, 152–53, 339, 366–67, 368, 369
training in, need for, 70
translations of term, 765n153
two limbs in, 659, 819–20n1150

See also nine mental states (tranquil abiding); placement meditation; six methods of resting the mind
transference of consciousness, 721
in Ensa lineage, 22, 576–77, 759n73
instructions, 733–37
in Segyü lineage, 19
Trāyastriṃśa god realm, 390
Treasure House of Instructions on the Oral Transmission (a.k.a. *Great Guidebook on Offering to the Guru*, Yongzin Yeshé Gyaltsen), 23, 508, 611, 759n77, 805n904, 815n1058
Treasury of Abhidharma (Vasubandhu)
on egg birth, 103
on karma, irreversibility of, 267
on karma, three kinds, 265, 782n449
on life spans, 242, 247
on mandala offering, 518
on sexual misconduct, 81
on ten karmic paths, 262
Trichen Ngawang Chokden, 387, 392, 410, 791n695, 792n701, 793n709
Trichen Tenpa Rabgyé, 37, 791–92n695
Trijang Rinpoché, 635, 755n34, 759n77, 817n1084
Trinlé Gyatso, 382, 791n690
triple being
in completion stage, 552
in Ensa guru yoga, 22, 446, 494, 509, 523, 534–40, 542–44, 579, 798n790
gurus as, 585
and wind-mind, fusion of, 580, 582
Trophu Lotsāwa Jampa Pal, 35–36, 722
truth body. *See* dharmakāya
truth of cessation, 149, 273, 293
truth of path, 273, 293
Tsakho Ngawang Drakpa, 9, 53, 539–40, 764n136
Tsal Gungthang Monastery, 1
Tsal Rabjampa Gendun Chöden, 692
Tsang, 3, 15, 16
Tsangpa Gyaré Yeshé Dorjé, 655, 819n1143
Tsechok Ling Monastery, 756n38
tsok cakes. *See* tormas
Tsongkhapa, 206, 378
Atiśa's framework and, 6–7
Brief Presentation of the Stages of the Path, 9
Confession by the Four Powers (*Rite on the Four Powers as Antidotes Against Negative Karma*), 268, 526, 807n937
Dharmavajra and, 446
Discourse on the Three Gems, 213
as embodiment of Three Protectors/ lords of three buddha families, 270, 385–86, 399–401, 534–37, 791n694
epithets of, 2
Essence of Eloquence, 600
Essence of Refined Gold, 312
A Few Words on the Structure of the Path, (Tsongkhapa), 9
on generation stage, 495, 804n875
Great Treatise on Mantra (Tsongkhapa), 2
Guide to the Six Yogas of Nāropa Endowed with Three Convictions, 445
Guide to the View Equalizing Samsara and Nirvana (Tsongkhapa), 20
on gurus, qualifications for, 25
homage to, 208
Illumination of All Hidden Meanings, 449
Indispensable Oral Teaching on Tranquil Abiding and Insight, 34, 824n1245, 825n1255
Lamp to Illuminate the Five Stages, 646–47, 649
lamrim works of, 8–9, 209, 212
legacy of, 2–3, 546
liberating deeds of, 396–97
lineages of, 19, 433–34, 441, 691
mahāmudrā transmissions received and given, 28
mandala offering of, 518
as Mañjuśrī's emanation, 296, 386, 399–400, 401, 432, 791n692, 791n694, 797n763
Milking the Wish-Granting Cow, 449–50
Munīndra Vajradhara Losang Drakpa visualization, 549, 579, 810n976

name mantra of, 553, 809n954
on object of negation, 672, 821n1184
on preliminaries, 216–17
on refuge, 216
"sacred traditions" of, 2, 753n1
on sense of self, 34
on *shalshé*, 20
Supplicating the Lineage Gurus of the Near Transmission, 33
synthesis by, 1–2
on tantra mahāmudrā, 27
tantric teachings of, 11, 19
Uncommon Oral Instruction, 442–45, 798nn782–83
Vajra Lines on the View, 32
visualizations, 391–92, 401–2, 478, 508
works of, superiority, 381
on wrathful rites, 539–40
See also *Great Treatise on the Stages of the Path to Enlightenment*; *Middle-Length Treatise on the Stages of the Path to Enlightenment*; *Song of Spiritual Experience*; *Three Principal Elements of the Path*
Tsuta, 229, 780n390
tulkus, 380, 790n669
tumo. *See* inner heat (*tumo*)
Tuṣita god realm, 390–92, 719, 721, 736
twelve branches of scripture, 194, 776n302
twelve links of dependent origination, 801n839
four kinds of links in, 291–92
meditation on, 292, 468
two accumulations/collections, 46, 764n134
awakening mind and, 69, 191
in highest yoga tantra, 452
perfecting, 206, 718, 727, 730–31
in sevenfold practice, 63
two buddha bodies and, 356
two obscurations and, 377
two aims of sentient beings, 310, 315, 326, 377, 434, 469, 569–70, 797n767, 811n998
two obscurations, 778n344
contemplating, 483
eliminating, 186, 775n294
lamrim and, 214
purifying, 718, 727, 730–31
six perfections and, 316
two regents, 210–11, 778n334
two sets of ten principles, 421
two stages, 19, 427, 453, 520. *See also* completion stage; generation stage
two truths, 142, 452
distinction between, 147, 773n260
establishing, 113
karma and, 528
number of, 151
as objects of meditation, 151
union of, 442

Udayana, 268
Udraka Rāmaputra, 355, 668
ultimate expanse, 226, 227, 497, 623, 679–80
ultimate truth, 682–83
correct understanding of, 356
definition, 149–50
divisions of, 150, 773n268
meanings of terms, 149, 773n262
as "way things are," 122, 770n231
Umapa Pawo Dorjé, 20, 441, 540
universal sovereigns (*cakravartin*), 280, 354, 380, 482, 790n671
Unraveling the Intent Sutra, 338
Upagupta, 545, 809n971
Upananda (nāga king), 503
Uṣṇīṣacakravartin, 507
Uttarakuru, 66, 766n155

Vairocana, 496, 497, 506, 728, 774n276
Vairocana tantra, 518
Vaiśravaṇa, 444, 510
Vaitalī, 497
vajra body, penetrating vital point, 581–82, 583, 618, 645
Vajra Empowerment Tantra, 532
vajra masters. *See* gurus (*lama*)
vajra recitation, 582
vajra songs, 539–40
Vajra Tent Tantra, 452

Vajrabhairava (meditation deity), 413
dissolving, 579
in Ensa tradition, 22
five distinctive features, 443–44
in generation stage, 523
guru yoga and, 23
self-empowerment as, 552–53
self-generation as, 486, 488, 490, 492, 494, 513, 803n872
triple being form of, 494
visualization options, 552
Vajrabhairava cycle, 3, 19, 509, 541, 809n964
Vajradhara
aspiration for attaining, 420
causal, 494
in degenerate era, 160
in empowerments, 550, 551, 552
as gnosis being, 505, 506, 549
and guru, viewing as inseparable, 15, 416, 547
homage, 411, 433
kindness of, 426, 575
lineages of, 440, 691, 774n280
in Miktsema, 16, 17
name mantra of, 553
as spiritual teacher, 440
supplication to, 627
in Vajrayāna, 773–74n275
visualizations, 415, 477–78, 507–8, 579, 724–25, 794n729
See also Munīndra Vajradhara
Vajradhātvīśvarī, 415, 523, 550
Vajrapāṇi, 792n699
epithet for, 270, 783n458
instructional guide on, 19
lineages of, 440
in Miktsema, 16, 17
supplications, 535
triple-being, 544
Tsongkhapa as embodying, 385, 400, 401, 791n694
visualizations of, 478, 506, 507
Vajrapāṇi Empowerment Tantra, 225, 420
Vajrasattva
body of, 449
meditation and recitation, 525–26, 527, 640, 642, 731, 807n936
Vajravaitalī, 497, 550
Vajravārāhī, 222
Vajrayāna, 110, 153
Buddha in, 773–74n275
common paths and, 444
entering, 49, 206
four seals in, 644
guru yoga in, 14, 451–53
gurus in, 24–25
Mañjuśrī in, 796n762
Perfection of Wisdom and, 652
prerequisites for, 70
refuge visualization in, 782n433
and sutra, union of, 37
in Tsongkhapa's synthesis, 2
vast path as preliminary to, 214–15
valid cognition, 142, 144–45, 684
conventional, 360
conventional truth and, 148
of emptiness, direct, 150, 773nn268–69
inferential, 150, 773n269, 773n271
Vasubandhu
lineages of, 440
Treasury of Abhidharma Autocommentary, 288
visualization, 508
See also *Treasury of Abhidharma*
Verses on the Nāga King Bherī, 303
Vibhūticandra, 756n41
Vidyākokila, elder and junior, 508
views
analysis of, 53, 534
and conduct, relationship between, 113, 208–9
extreme, 97, 285
holding to superiority of, 285
key point of, 722, 739–40
penetrating ultimate mode of being, 112, 769n214
perfection of wisdom and, 118
resting in, 712
right, symbols of, 504
of the supremacy of ethics and conduct, 98, 285

See also guide to the view; identity view; Middle Way; wrong views
Vimuktisena, Ārya, 508, 805n902
Vimuktisena, Bhadanta, 508, 805n902
Vinaya, 295, 444
  on mind, 475
  on nonvirtues of speech, 81
  on spiritual teachers, 435, 439, 797n768
  students according with, 59
  upholding in tantra, 104
Vinaya Sutra (Guṇaprabha), 571–72, 812n1001
Viravajra, 477
virtue
  accumulating, 89, 336
  delight in, 117
  ethical discipline of collecting, 324–25
  gradual training in, 375
  guarding, 64
  interim, 572, 812n1002
  loss of, 98
  of others, causing regret toward, 110
  postponing, 334
  results of, 169–70
  roots, enhancing, 530–31
  three fundamental types, 86, 767n177
  three sources of, 483, 530, 802n855, 808n947
  at time of death, 100
  training too intensely in, 218
  tranquil abiding and, 339
Virūḍhaka, 510
Virūpākṣa, 510
visionary experiences
  Drupchen's, 392
  Tokden's, 810n975
  Tsongkhapa in, 2
  Tsongkhapa's, 1, 20, 30, 441–42
Viṣṇu, 253, 285
Vitakarma, *Mudrācaturaṭīkā*, 760n87
vows, 85
  affirming, 524–25, 807n932, 807n935
  bodhisattva and personal liberation, distinction between, 116, 323–24, 770n225, 785n539
  guarding, 426
  individual liberation, 104, 177, 294, 323–24, 521, 556–57, 785n539
  not taking root, 571–72, 812n1001
  ordination, 324
  refuge and, 435, 483
  restoring, 70
  three, 91, 164, 420, 425, 527, 774n284, 795n743
  See also bodhisattva vows
Vows of Good Conduct, 427–28, 513, 531, 796n758

Wangkur Mountain, 1
water
  eight qualities of, 376, 378, 502, 504, 514, 520, 790n659, 804n891
  four types, 496, 498, 514, 804n877
  offering, 460, 461
wheels of adornment, 381, 546, 547, 790n674, 810n972
White Sunrise (Sedong), 153
wind-mind, 407, 580, 582, 648, 677
winds, 738
  in pliancy, 351
  root and branch, 443, 514
  threefold process of, 581
  vitality stopping (*prāṇāyāma*), 443, 582, 813n1013
  withdrawing, 583–85, 813n1015
wisdom, 7
  bodhisattva's three categories, 195
  Buddha's, 76
  collection of, 357
  and compassion, union of, 7
  cultivating, 8
  higher training in, 293, 456–57, 469
  increasing rite for, 540
  innate, 732
  and method, combined, 48, 298, 340, 711
  nonconceptual, 152, 644
  understanding selflessness, 299, 339
wisdom, perfection of, 12, 47, 118
  contemplating, 195
  as fully accomplished, 354
  in post-equipoise, 119
  See also selflessness

wisdom of innate bliss and emptiness. *See* gnosis
wish-granting lake/sea, 418–19, 502, 504, 520
wish-granting objects, 314, 785n524
wish-granting tree, 502–4, 579
Wön Gyalsé Jikmé Yeshé Drakpa, 793n719
Words of Mañjuśrī (Ngawang Losang Gyatso, Fifth Dalai Lama), 10, 11–12, 755n31
  composition of, 382
  concluding verses, 376–81
  homage, 207–9
  six preliminaries' rite, 210, 227–30
  structure of, 778n356
  title, 777n324
  transmissions of, 13, 755nn32–33, 780n382
wrathful deities, 415, 495–96, 507, 541, 543, 809n967
wrong livelihood, 459, 460, 800n824
wrong views, 116–17, 264, 767n172
  causes of, 176
  five traits of, 782n448
  identifying, 98, 285
  karmic effects of, 86, 87
  nonvirtuous karma of, 82–83
wrongdoing, 267–68, 269, 323–24. *See also* nonvirtue
Wutai, Mount, 4

Yama, 243, 487, 781n416
  four henchmen's commands, 491, 803n867
  god realm, 390
Yamāntaka, 507, 539
Yamāntaka family of tantras, 3
Yangchen Drupai Dorjé, 632
Yangchen Gawai Lodrö, 13, 14
Yangönpa, 662, 694
Yellow Hat school. *See* Geluk tradition
Yeshé Dé, 341, 787n576
Yeshé Döndrup Tenpai Gyaltsen (a.k.a. Thöyön Yeshé Döndrup), 18, 757n54
Yeshé Tenzin, Lhatsé, 556, 797n773, 797n764, 799n803, 803n870, 811n986
Yeshé Tsöndrü, *Essence of Dharma Nectar*, 13
Yiga Chözin courtyard, 390, 391, 719, 736
yoga of blazing and dripping, 443
yoga of channels, winds, and drops, 443
yoga of illusion, 205
yoga of no-sleep, 64, 162, 765n152
yoga of profundity and clarity, nondual, 492, 803n869
yoga tantra, 153
Yoginī Cintā, 646
Yongzin Yeshé Gyaltsen, 475, 493, 802n842
  Bright Lamp of the Excellent Path of Oral Transmission, 31, 32, 762n104, 815n1058
  on Ensa Oral Transmission, 10, 758–59n68
  on Geluk mahāmudrā, 30, 762n104
  guides to *Offering to the Guru*, 23, 439, 759n77, 797n773
  mahāmudrā dissemination by, 31
  oral instructions of, 493, 495, 553, 564, 568, 587, 811n994
  Source of All Higher Attainments, 32
  students of, 797n764, 803n870
  supplication to, 630, 817n1080
  texts of, 37, 583, 813n1014
  See also *Treasure House of Instructions on the Oral Transmission*
yungdrung symbol, 461, 801n832

About the Contributors

THUPTEN JINPA LANGRI was educated in the Tibetan monastic system, where he received the highest degree of *geshé lharam*. Jinpa also holds a BA in philosophy and a PhD in religious studies, both from the University of Cambridge, England. Since 1985, he has been the principal translator to the Dalai Lama, accompanying him on tours throughout the world and translating and editing many books. Jinpa's own works include *Self, Reality and Reason in Tibetan Thought*, several volumes of translations in *The Library of Tibetan Classics*, and the modern biography *Tsongkhapa: A Buddha in the Land of Snows*. He is currently the president and the editor-in-chief of the Institute of Tibetan Classics, based in Montreal, and he also chairs the Mind and Life Institute and the Compassion Institute.

ROSEMARY PATTON began studying Tibetan Buddhism and language in France with Dagpo Rinpoché in 1975 after earning a first degree in English literature and drama at Queen's University in Canada and a second degree in anthropology at the Sorbonne. After attaining a further degree at the Institut national des langues et civilisations orientales (INaLCO) in Paris, she pursued her studies at Drepung Gomang in South India. She has been Dagpo Rinpoché's English-language translator since the late 1980s.

DAGPO RINPOCHÉ (1932–) was born in Kongpo in southeastern Tibet, was recognized as an incarnate lama at age one by the Thirteenth Dalai Lama, and trained as a monk at Dakpo Shedrup Ling and later at Drepung Monastery's Gomang College in Lhasa. After the Communist takeover of Tibet in 1959, he crossed the Himalayas on foot, and the next year he emigrated to Paris, where he worked with scholars and taught at INaLCO until 1993. In 1978 he founded his first Dharma center, which in 1994 became the Ganden Ling Institute. While based in France, he has traveled extensively around the world, guiding students and creating numerous centers for the study and practice of Buddhism.

Institute of Tibetan Classics

The Institute of Tibetan Classics is a nonproit, charitable educational organization based in Montreal, Canada. It is dedicated to two primary objectives: (1) to preserve and promote the study and deep appreciation of Tibet's rich intellectual, spiritual, and artistic heritage, especially among the Tibetan-speaking communities worldwide; and (2) to make the classical Tibetan knowledge and literature a truly global heritage, its spiritual and intellectual resources open to all.

To learn more about the Institute of Tibetan Classics and its various projects, please visit www.tibetanclassics.org or write to this address:

Institute of Tibetan Classics
304 Aberdare Road
Montreal (Quebec) H3P 3K3
Canada

The Library of Tibetan Classics

"This new series edited by Thupten Jinpa and published by Wisdom Publications is a landmark in the study of Tibetan culture in general and Tibetan Buddhism in particular. Each volume contains a lucid introduction and outstanding translations that, while aimed at the general public, will benefit those in the field of Tibetan Studies immensely as well."

—Leonard van der Kuijp, Harvard University

"This is an invaluable set of translations by highly competent scholar-practitioners. The series spans the breadth of the history of Tibetan religion, providing entry to a vast culture of spiritual cultivation."

—Jeffrey Hopkins, University of Virginia

"Erudite in all respects, this series is at the same time accessible and engagingly translated. As such, it belongs in all college and university libraries as well as in good public libraries. *The Library of Tibetan Classics* is on its way to becoming a truly extraordinary spiritual and literary accomplishment."

—Jan Willis, Wesleyan University

Following is a list of the thirty-two proposed volumes in *The Library of Tibetan Classics*. Some volumes are translations of single texts, while others are compilations of multiple texts, and each volume will be roughly the same length. Except for those volumes already published, the renderings of titles below are tentative and liable to change. The Institute of Tibetan Classics has contracted numerous established translators in its efforts, and work is progressing on all the volumes concurrently.

1. *Mind Training: The Great Collection*, compiled by Shönu Gyalchok and Könchok Gyaltsen (fifteenth century). NOW AVAILABLE
2. *The Book of Kadam: The Core Texts*, attributed to Atiśa and Dromtönpa (eleventh century). NOW AVAILABLE
3. *The Great Chariot: A Treatise on the Great Perfection*, Longchen Rapjampa (1308–63)
4. *Taking the Result As the Path: Core Teachings of the Sakya Lamdré Tradition*, Jamyang Khyentsé Wangchuk (1524–68) et al. NOW AVAILABLE
5. *Mahāmudrā and Related Instructions: Core Teachings of the Kagyü Schools*. NOW AVAILABLE
6. *Stages of the Path and the Oral Transmission: Selected Teachings of the Geluk School* NOW AVAILABLE
7. *Ocean of Definitive Meaning: A Teaching for the Mountain Hermit*, Dölpopa Sherap Gyaltsen (1292–1361)
8. *Four Tibetan Lineages: Core Teachings of Pacification, Severance, Shangpa Kagyü, and Bodong*, Jamgön Kongtrül (1813–90). NOW AVAILABLE
9. *Sutra, Tantra, and the Mind Cycle: Core Teachings of the Bön School*
10. *Stages of the Buddha's Teachings: Three Key Texts*. NOW AVAILABLE
11. *The Bodhisattva's Altruistic Ideal: Selected Key Texts*
12. *The Ethics of the Three Codes*
13. *Sādhanas: Vajrayana Buddhist Meditation Manuals*
14. *Ornament of Stainless Light: An Exposition of the Kālacakra Tantra*, Khedrup Norsang Gyatso (1423–1513). NOW AVAILABLE
15. *A Lamp to Illuminate the Five Stages: Teachings on the Guhyasamāja Tantra*, Tsongkhapa (1357–1419). NOW AVAILABLE
16. *Studies in the Perfection of Wisdom*
17. *Treatises on Buddha Nature*
18. *Differentiations of the Profound View: Interpretations of Emptiness in Tibet*
19. *Illuminating the Intent: An Exposition of Candrakīrti's Entering the Middle Way*, Tsongkhapa (1357–1419). NOW AVAILABLE
20. *Tibetan Buddhist Epistemology I: The Sakya School*
21. *Tibetan Buddhist Epistemology II: The Geluk School*
22. *Tibetan Buddhist Psychology and Phenomenology: Selected Texts*
23. *Ornament of Abhidharma: A Commentary on the "Abhidharmakośa,"* Chim Jampaiyang (thirteenth century). NOW AVAILABLE

24. *Beautiful Adornment of Mount Meru: A Presentation of Classical Indian Philosophies*, Changkya Rölpai Dorjé (1717–86). NOW AVAILABLE
25. *The Crystal Mirror of Philosophical Systems: A Tibetan Study of Asian Religious Thought*, Thuken Losang Chökyi Nyima (1737–1802). NOW AVAILABLE
26. *Gateway for Being Learned and Realized: Selected Texts*
27. *The Tibetan Book of Everyday Wisdom: A Thousand Years of Sage Advice.* NOW AVAILABLE
28. *Mirror of Beryl: A Historical Introduction to Tibetan Medicine*, Desi Sangyé Gyatso (1653–1705). NOW AVAILABLE
29. *Selected Texts on Tibetan Astronomy and Astrology*
30. *Art and Literature: An Anthology*
31. *Tales from the Tibetan Operas.* NOW AVAILABLE
32. *A History of Buddhism in India and Tibet*, Khepa Deu (thirteenth century). NOW AVAILABLE

To receive a brochure describing all the volumes or to stay informed about *The Library of Tibetan Classics*, please write to:

support@wisdompubs.org

or send a request to:

Wisdom Publications
Attn: Library of Tibetan Classics
199 Elm Street
Somerville, MA 02144 USA

The complete catalog containing descriptions of each volume can also be found online at wisdomexperience.org.

Become a Benefactor of the Library of Tibetan Classics

The Library of Tibetan Classics' scope, importance, and commitment to the finest quality make it a tremendous financial undertaking. We invite you to become a benefactor, joining us in creating this profoundly important human resource. Contributors of two thousand dollars or more will receive a copy of each future volume as it becomes available, and will have their names listed in all subsequent volumes. Larger donations will go even further in supporting *The Library of Tibetan Classics*, preserving the creativity, wisdom, and scholarship of centuries past, so that it may help illuminate the world for future generations.

To contribute, please either visit our website at wisdomexperience.org, call us at (617) 776-7416, or send a check made out to Wisdom Publications or credit card information to the address below.

Library of Tibetan Classics Fund
Wisdom Publications
199 Elm Street
Somerville, MA 02144
USA

Please note that contributions of lesser amounts are also welcome and are invaluable to the development of the series. Wisdom is a 501(c)3 nonprofit corporation, and all contributions are tax-deductible to the extent allowed by law.

If you have any questions, please do not hesitate to call us or email us at support@wisdompubs.org.

To keep up to date on the status of *The Library of Tibetan Classics*, visit the series page on our website, and subscribe to our newsletter while you are there.

About Wisdom Publications

Wisdom Publications is the leading publisher of classic and contemporary Buddhist books and practical works on mindfulness. To learn more about us or to explore our other books, please visit our website at wisdomexperience.org or contact us at the address below.

Wisdom Publications
199 Elm Street
Somerville, MA 02144 USA

We are a 501(c)(3) organization, and donations in support of our mission are tax deductible.

Wisdom Publications is affiliated with the Foundation for the Preservation of the Mahayana Tradition (FPMT).